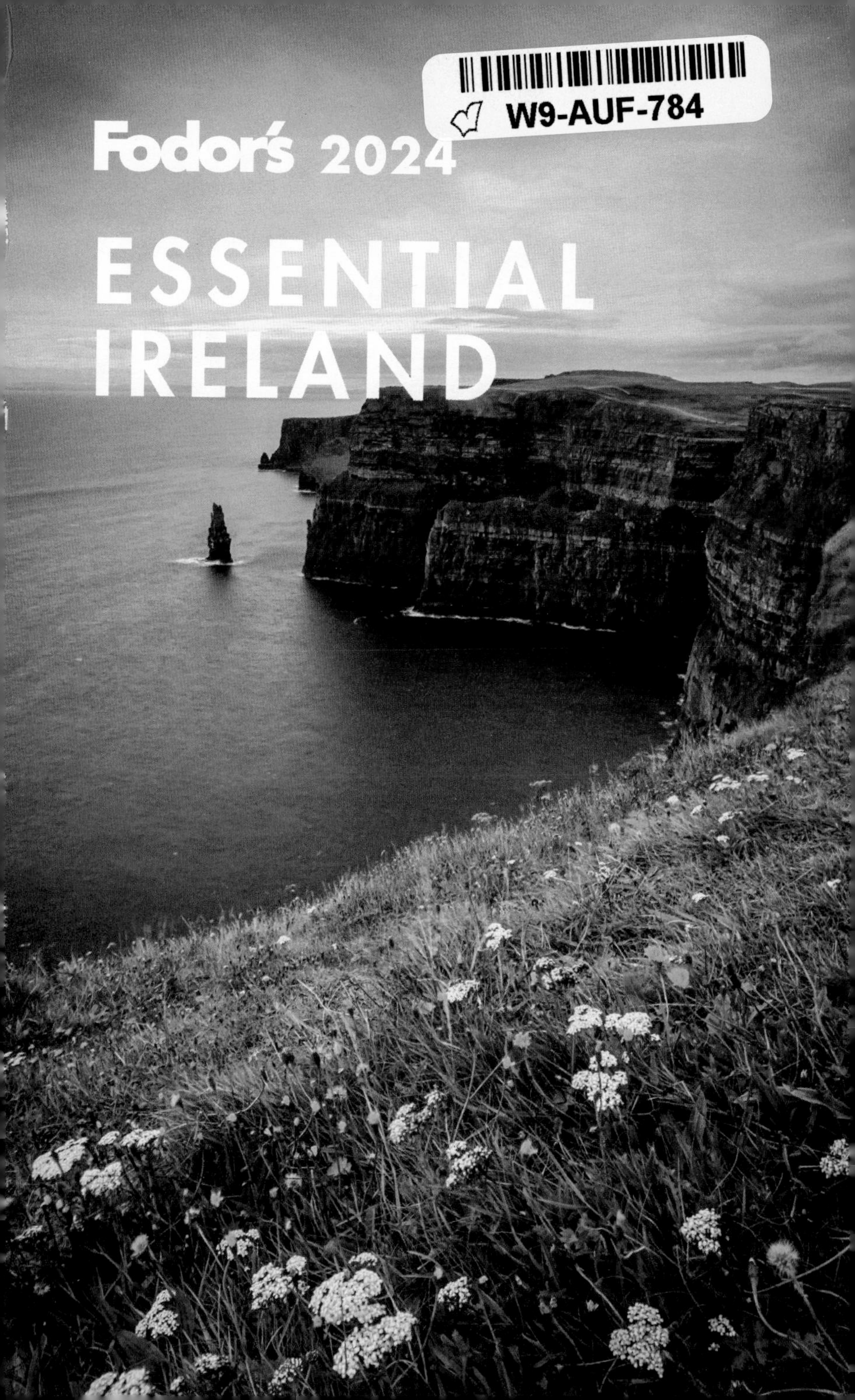
Fodor's 2024
ESSENTIAL IRELAND

Welcome to Ireland

It's a Celtic mystery: how can such a small country be packed with so much history, natural beauty, vibrant culture, and, of course, fun? Norman castles overlook wild, empty beaches, Georgian country houses host impromptu traditional music sessions, excited theatergoers spill out into bustling Dublin pubs. But the real secret is the people: their unique blend of warmth, humor, and irreverence will ensure your trip to the Emerald Isle is a true adventure. As you plan your upcoming travels, please confirm that places are still open and let us know when we need to make updates by writing to us at editors@fodors.com.

TOP REASONS TO GO

★ **Untamed Nature:** From rugged marshlands to glacial lakes, wild Ireland blows the mind.

★ **Living History:** Neolithic Knowth, Celtic Cashel, Christian Glendalough, and more.

★ **Perfect Pubs:** A fire, some chowder, and a pint of stout—the Irish pub is a slow, sacred space.

★ **Festivals:** Oysters in Galway, jazz in Cork, St. Paddy in Dublin; celebrate year-round.

★ **Cracking Culture:** Every second native's a poet or a fiddle player—it's in the air.

★ **Hidden Treasures:** Empty islands, silent forests, untouched beaches: serenity abounds.

Contents

Fodor's Feature

MAPS

COLEMAN
Ulster Bank

Chapter 1

EXPERIENCE IRELAND

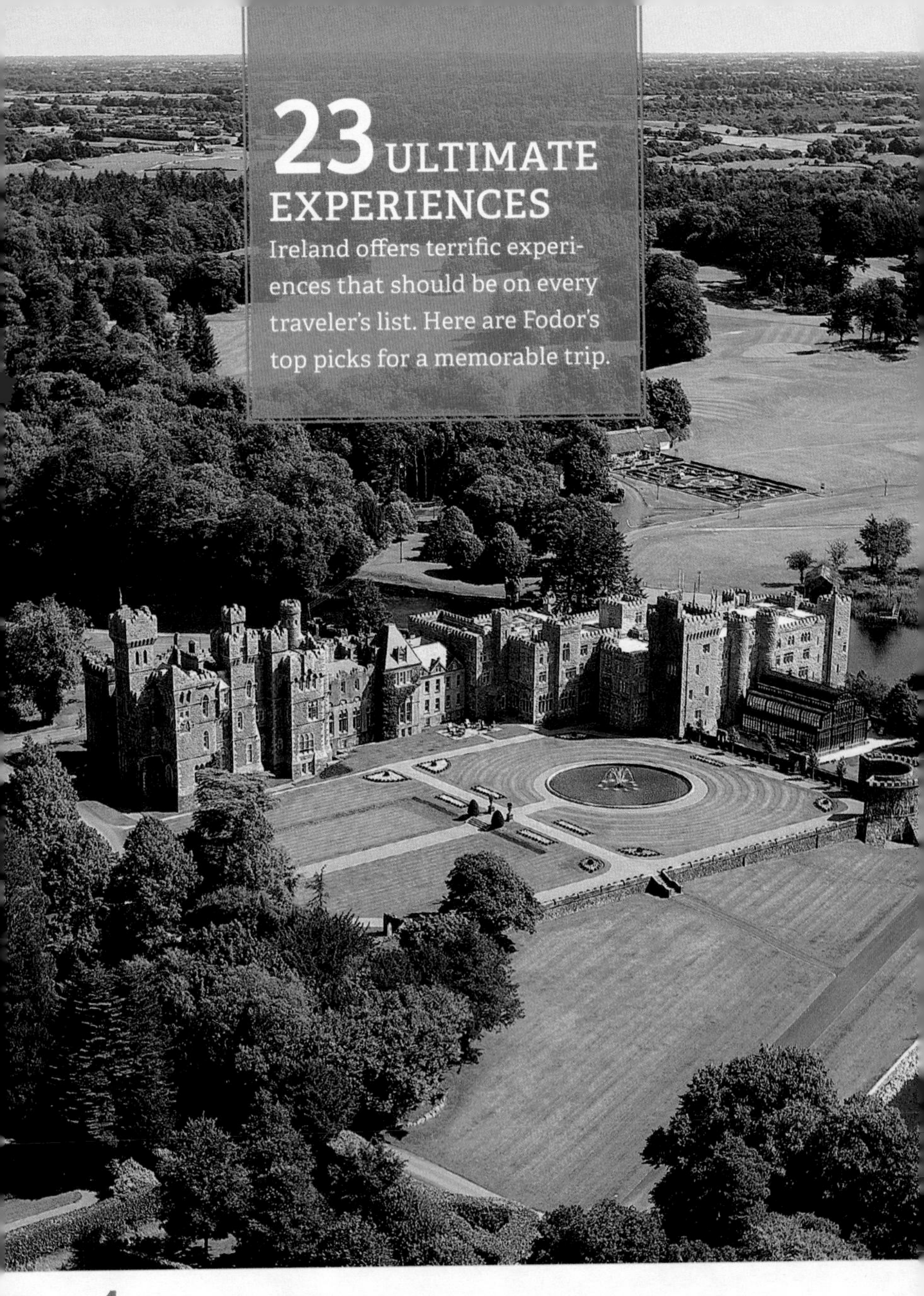

1 A Castle Stay

Enjoy the royal treatment and get your fill of history, luxury, adventure, and charm with a stay in an Irish castle-hotel. Ashford Castle, set on 350 stunning acres and hugging Lake Corrib, offers a fairy-tale feel. *(Ch. 10)*

2 The Giant's Causeway

A UNESCO World Heritage site, the Giant's Causeway was created either by erupting lava 60 million years ago or a mighty Irish giant in love. Decide for yourself! *(Ch. 14)*

3 James Joyce

Visit the James Joyce Centre or join the Bloomsday celebrations in June for readings, performances, and pub crawls as you follow Joyce's footsteps. *(Ch. 3)*

4 A Connemara Hike

With some of the finest rugged scenery and dramatic coastline in all of Ireland, a hike or guided walk in Connemara National Park is a must for lovers of the outdoors. *(Ch. 10)*

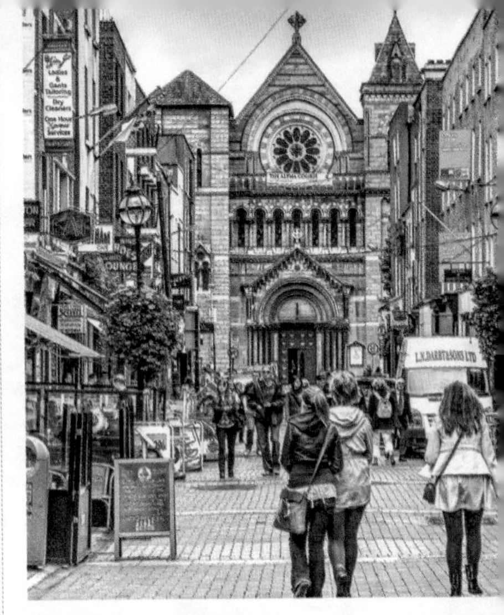

5 Grafton Street

Dublin's pedestrian-only street bustles with shoppers, world-famous buskers, and flower vendors. Smaller side streets offer boutiques with Irish crafts and fashion. *(Ch. 3)*

6 The East Coast

There's much to discover along Waterford's coast, including seaside towns like Tramore, Ardmore, and the unspoiled Gaeltacht area, An Rinn (Ring). *(Ch. 6)*

7 Guinness

The Guinness Brewery and Storehouse tells the history, and the brewing process, of Guinness—Dublin's black blood. The top-floor bar offers city views and a free pint. *(Ch. 3)*

8 Monastic Sites

The Round Tower of St. Kevin's monastic settlement at Glendalough ("Glen of Two Lakes") deep in the Wicklow Mountains, is an iconic feature of Ireland's monastic ruins. *(Ch. 4)*

9 Belfast/*Titanic* Experience

The impressive *Titanic* Belfast presents the tragic story of the biggest ocean liner ever built at the time and commemorates Belfast's connection and industrial heritage. *(Ch. 13)*

10 Derry/Londonderry

Take in Derry's long history, its murals, and the 17th-century town as you stroll its ramparts and then cross the modern Peace Bridge, a symbol of unity. *(Ch. 14)*

11 Trad Music

Ennis is a great place to hear music at any time, but especially during the Fleadh in late August. Singers, musicians, and dancers compete, and much of the music is free. *(Ch. 9)*

12 Killarney National Park

Hike, bike, or hire a car to explore Killarney National Park with its blue lakes, purple mountains, and red deer. Highlights include Muckross Friary and Torc Waterfall. *(Ch. 8)*

13 Skellig Ring

The drive from Waterville to Portmagee is a popular extension to the Ring of Kerry; the narrow road cannot handle tour buses and the coastal scenery is glorious. *(Ch. 8)*

14 National Gallery

The National Gallery is one of Europe's finest smaller art museums with a collection of paintings by Irish artists. *(Ch. 3)*

15 Wild Atlantic Way

Whether you tour it from end to end or just enjoy sections, the Wild Atlantic Way is an epic driving, biking, or hiking journey along Ireland's stunning west coast. *(Ch. 11)*

16 Golfing

From renowned courses designed by celebrated golf architects to welcoming local clubs in every corner of the country, Ireland is a golfer's paradise.

17 Artisanal Cheeses

The revival of Irish farmhouse cheeses was pioneered in Cork: look for pungent Milleens, milder Durrus and Coolea, Gouda-like Gubbeen, and Fermoy Natural Cheese. *(Ch. 7)*

18 Galway

Enjoy the buskers, bookshops, boutiques, festivals, and lively pub culture of Ireland's liveliest city, a university town and favorite weekend getaway for the Irish. *(Ch. 9)*

19 Irish Design

Home to the Crafts Council of Ireland, the Kilkenny Design Centre, and a craft trail that includes Nicholas Mosse pottery, Kilkenny stuns with contemporary Irish design. *(Ch. 6)*

20 Dingle

Sample seafood and music in Dingle Town before heading out on the peninsula to Slea Head. Stop along the coast to investigate the ancient stone beehive huts. *(Ch. 8)*

21 Trinity College

Founded in 1592 to "civilize Ireland," Trinity is best known for its noted alumni and its Old Library, which houses the exquisite illuminated manuscript, the *Book of Kells*. *(Ch. 3)*

22 Croagh Patrick

Join the 30,000 pilgrims, some barefoot, who climb Croagh Patrick on the last Sunday in July, or walk it solo for serene views of Clew Bay and its 365 islands. *(Ch. 10)*

23 The Cliffs of Moher

Rising dramatically out of the Atlantic Ocean, these cliffs are one of Ireland's most breathtaking natural sights, best viewed from a cruise or on a trail from Doolin. *(Ch. 9)*

WHAT'S WHERE

1 Dublin. Get spirited at the Guinness Brewery, stroll through teeming Temple Bar, and be illuminated by the *Book of Kells* at Trinity College's great library.

2 Dublin Environs. The counties outside the Pale are a treasure trove of history, monastic settlements, ancient tombs, battle-fields, and peaceful valleys only an hour from the hubbub of the capital's center. From the lush greenery of Kildare and Wicklow, to the mythology and traditions of Meath and Louth, the historic time line encompasses many of the pivotal pre-Christian and early church locales of Ireland's past. Listen for ancient echoes at the Hill of Tara, hike into prehistory at Newgrange, and opt for opulence at Castletown House.

3 The Midlands. This verdant oasis of bog and lake harks back to the simpler, and slower, life of Ireland 40 years ago. Friendly, almost shy natives, old-style pubs, unspoiled vistas, and walks make for a relaxing adventure into the way we were. Tree-hug one of the great

yews at Tullynally Gardens, lift your spirits at Clonmacnoise, and take a river cruise down the Shannon.

4 The Southeast. Ireland's sunniest corner, the coastal counties have long been the favored hideaway of Dublin folk on vacation. Inland, counties like Kilkenny and Tipperary offer a lion's share of history and important monuments in the main towns, Wexford and Waterford. Follow in the footsteps of St. Patrick at the Rock of Cashel and dig the ducal lifestyle at Lismore.

5 County Cork. After exploring the delights of Cork City—museums, lively pubs, quirky cafés, and lots of good music, trad and otherwise—use it as a base to explore Ireland's largest county, as nearly everyone heads to get the gift of gab by kissing the famous Blarney Stone.

6 The Southwest. The counties of Kerry and Limerick have sights that top every tourist's must-see list—from the Ring of Kerry to the wet-and-wonderful ride out to the Skellig Islands, to Killarney's purple mountains and glittering blue lake, and Ireland's prettiest village, Adare.

WHAT'S WHERE

7 County Clare, Galway, and the Aran Islands. Set with postcard-perfect villages like Doolin, the lunar landscape of the Burren, and the towering Cliffs of Moher—they'll give you a new understanding of the word *awesome*—County Clare is pure tourist gold. As is nearby Galway City: one of Ireland's liveliest, it has a compact historic center bursting with artistic energy. For a complete change of pace, head to the three Aran Islands.

8 Connemara and County Mayo. Connemara is an almost uninhabited landscape of misty bogland, studded with deep blue lakes under huge Atlantic skies and distant purple hills. Nearby is the delightful village of Cong, where fetching ivy-covered thatched cottages contrast with the splendor of Ashford Castle. Clifden and Westport are lively small towns of great charm.

9 The Northwest. Sligo, Leitrim, and Donegal are homelands of rugged, self-sufficient people and roads where wandering sheep and cows are still the norm. Take a poetry

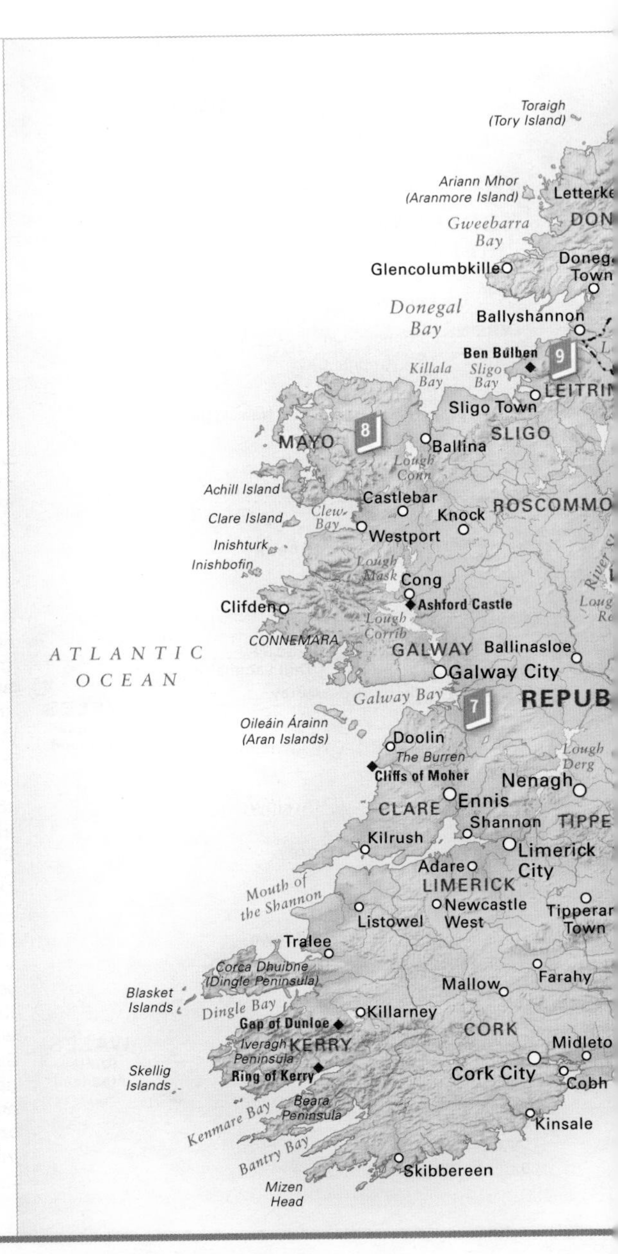

break beside W.B. Yeats's grave near Ben Bulben, discover hidden Glencolumbkille, and immerse yourself in all things Irish in Sligo Town.

10 The Northeast. Despite this region's location, within an hour or two from the Capital, it's often missed by visitors who speed through it on their way to more popular destinations. Yet, veer off the motorway onto the narrow roads that weave their way through the lush countryside to discover a different, authentic Ireland that marches to a slower beat.

11 Belfast. The birthplace of the *Titanic* and the gateway to the rest of Northern Ireland, Belfast is a lively and welcoming modern city. Northern Ireland's capital and largest city has been coming into its own for a few years or so, along with its top attraction, *Titanic* Belfast.

12 Northern Ireland. From the beauty of Antrim's coastline to the vibrant cultural renaissance of Derry, Northern Ireland is full of promise and possibility. Cross the Giant's Causeway and trail after the island's ancient Celtic mysteries in the shimmery Glens of Antrim.

Best Stops on the Wild Atlantic Way

SLIEVE LEAGUE CLIFFS, COUNTY DONEGAL
The cliffs of Slieve League are some of the highest in Ireland and have sculpted the coastline into one of Europe's most stunning panoramas. Watch the spiraling seabirds to see why the area is nicknamed the Lair of the Whirlwinds.

ROUNDSTONE, CONNEMARA, COUNTY GALWAY
Shimmering lakes, mirroring mountains, miles of bogland, islands surrounded by a supernatural fog, and irregular drystone walls that defy gravity are part of the classic Connemara landscape. The sinuous roads skirting the coastal fringe lead to Roundstone, an attractive village in the southwest of the region with a parade of cafés, bars, and shops permeated with the smell of the sea. Spend a few hours here on a sunny day and you will appreciate why painters such as Paul Henry and Frank Egginton were drawn here.

MALIN HEAD, COUNTY DONEGAL
The northernmost point of Ireland, Malin Head, is a windswept corner where the sea hurls foam against rocks and the start of the Wild Atlantic Way. Little wonder that the Star Wars filmmakers chose this location for *The Force Awakens*. The waters here are noted for basking sharks in summer that feed on the plankton-rich waters; keep your eyes peeled and you may also see leaping dolphins or pods of orcas.

CLADDAGH, GALWAY, COUNTY GALWAY
On the west bank of the fast-flowing Corrib River, the small Irish-speaking fishing village of Claddagh was once a distinct community with its own king and a place where fishermen sailed boats known as "hookers" and sold their catches at the market beside the Spanish Arch. The area is also home to a 400-year-old symbol of everlasting love, friendship, and loyalty: the Claddagh Ring.

LISSADELL HOUSE, COUNTY SLIGO
Tap into the spirit of the Nobel Prize–winning poet W.B. Yeats at this magnificent house which was a holiday retreat inextricably linked with the writer. Built in 1834 by the Gore-Booth family, Lissadell was the childhood home of Constance Gore-Booth, who later became Countess Markievicz and fought in the 1916 Easter Rising. She was a close friend of Yeats, and the mansion, along with this part of coastal Sligo, inspired some of his most lyrical poetry.

THE BURREN WAY, COUNTY CLARE
A magical area of limestone karst, the Burren is covered with rare Arctic-Alpine wildflowers, some hidden among the foliage on the clints (flat slabs of pavement). One of the best ways of experiencing its mysterious alchemy is on a ride through traffic-free roads on a bike or on horseback. Join a guided tour of the Burren Way on a quiet gypsy cob, an easygoing

Kinsale

horse that will lead you at an unhurried pace through a lush green valley with the far-crying call of the cuckoo piercing the pockets of stillness.

ACHILL ISLAND, COUNTY MAYO

A seductive place of natural beauty, Achill's bounty of five sandy Blue Flag beaches is a measure of its excellence, and because of its mix of rain and sunshine it is nicknamed "the rainbow island." Achill Island is the starting point for walking or cycling the Great Western Greenway, a delightfully flat 42-km (26-mile) path on a former railway line that snakes alongside the gorgeous sands of Clew Bay.

DINGLE PENINSULA, COUNTY KERRY

Walk, drive, surf, or simply relax on the longest beach on the Wild Atlantic Way in the northern part of the peninsula, now known as Dingle North. The Maharees is a narrow, self-contained 8-km (5-mile) stretch of land known as a tombolo with seven islands and is joined to the land by sand. Head down the dizzying descent of the Conor Pass, the highest road in Ireland, to Dingle town where Fungie, the famed dolphin, makes regular appearances.

LAKES OF KILLARNEY, COUNTY KERRY

Of the three main lakes—Lough Leane (lower), Muckross (middle), and the Upper Lake—the largest is Lough Leane, set in a mountain-ringed valley. From here join a scenic cruise on a water bus or pack a picnic and rent a rowboat to one of the wooded islands. Stop off at Innisfallen, a center of scholarship in the Middle Ages. The island's romantic ruins, including a Celtic cross, date from the 6th or 7th century, and you can still see the weathered ruins of a 13th-century oratory and Augustinian priory. Take a trip west to the Gap of Dunloe and call at the celebrated Kate Kearney's Cottage, founded in 1849, now a bar, café, and craft shop.

KINSALE, COUNTY CORK

Depending on your direction of travel, Kinsale is either the starting point or journey's end of the Wild Atlantic Way. Lying at the head of a sheltered harbor around the mouth of the Bandon River, its setting showcases an appealing port of twisting alleyways filled with boutiques, time-burnished bars, and upmarket restaurants. The town's most compelling sight is the formidable star-shape Charles Fort, built by the British on the east side of the harbor at Summer Cove and one of Europe's best-preserved military sites.

The Best Historical Sights to Visit in Ireland

CÉIDE FIELDS, COUNTY MAYO
Located in a remote coastal region of north Mayo on the Wild Atlantic Way, Céide (pronounced kay-jeh) is a historical bogland and unique ecosystem on which barley was once grown in its cultivation ridges. The fields are among the most extensive Stone Age monuments in the world.

SKELLIG MICHAEL, COUNTY KERRY
Two stark and bare islands of old red sandstone lie 13 km (8 miles) off the southwest Irish coast. An early Christian hermitage, Skellig is on the UNESCO World Heritage list.

CLONMACNOISE, COUNTY OFFALY
Clonmacnoise, which translates from the Irish as "Meadow of the Sons of Nóis," is a monastic site, founded by St. Ciarán in the 6th century.

KILMAINHAM GAOL, COUNTY DUBLIN
With its tiers of cells, overhead catwalks, and grim corridors, Kilmainham prison—where the leaders of the 1916 Easter Rising and Irish revolutionaries were executed by the British—evokes a chilling period in the past.

GLENDALOUGH, COUNTY WICKLOW
In the heart of the Wicklow mountains, Glendalough is a captivating valley carved by Ice Age glaciers. It lays claim to some of the best-preserved monastic sites in Ireland's heritage. It was here that St. Kevin founded his 6th-century settlement, a peaceful place where he retreated to pray.

HILLSBOROUGH CASTLE, COUNTY DOWN
Dating from the 1770s, Hillsborough Castle is the only royal palace in Ireland and it is still used by the British royal family on state visits to Northern Ireland. This Georgian beauty sits 19 km (12 miles) south of Belfast, and was given new life as part of a £16 million renovation completed in 2018.

BRÚ NA BÓINNE, NEWGRANGE, COUNTY MEATH
The Newgrange passage grave known as Brú na Bóinne is one of the most celebrated prehistoric sites in Ireland. Dating to about 3200 BC, Newgrange, a UNESCO World Heritage site, is an enormous mound made of layers of earth and stone.

Rock of Cashel

ROCK OF CASHEL, COUNTY TIPPERARY
Perched high on a solitary lump of gray limestone, the Rock was originally a ceremonial center and home to the kings of Munster, known as the Eóganacht. This spectacular group of medieval buildings includes a 12th-century Round Tower, High Cross, and Romanesque chapel.

KILKENNY MEDIEVAL MILE, COUNTY KILKENNY
Labeled by tourism gurus as the Medieval Mile, this trail runs through Kilkenny's city center, linking a 13th-century cathedral with a hulking, 800-year-old, creeper-clad castle alongside a potpourri of other ancient buildings. Watch a silversmith crafting a Celtic brooch in Kilkenny Design Centre and toast the craft of ale making, mastered by 13th-century local monks, at the Smithwick's Experience.

DÚN AENGUS, INISHMORE, ARAN ISLANDS, COUNTY GALWAY
Far and away the most thrilling ancient site on the three sea-battered Aran Islands, Dún Aengus is a dramatic semicircular fort perched against sheer, 90-meter-high cliffs on the edge of the Western world. The island of Inishmore (meaning "big island") can be reached by ferry from Rossaveal in Galway and Doolin in Clare. Rent a bike on the island to explore its many sights.

Ireland's Top Natural Wonders

BEN BULBEN, COUNTY SLIGO
Seen from a distance, the striking, flat-topped profile of Ben Bulben resembles the capsized hull of a ship. This is the best-known Irish mountain because it is inextricably linked to W.B. Yeats, the country's most illustrious poet.

KILLARNEY LAKES, COUNTY KERRY
They say that the best things come in threes, and aside from seeing the last remnants of ancient Irish trees, the chief reason to visit this area is for the stunning trio of Killarney's famed lakes: Lough Leane (lower), Muckross (middle), and the Upper Lake.

THE BURREN, COUNTY CLARE
Catch a clear spring evening and you will be enchanted by one of the strangest of all effects that the Burren affords: a delicate, pale-pink hue creeping imperceptibly across the rocks, rouging them with sunset.

GIANT'S CAUSEWAY, COUNTY ANTRIM
In the eyes of the 18th-century writer Dr. Samuel Johnson, the Giant's Causeway was "worth seeing ... but not worth going to see." Despite the dis, hundreds of thousands of visitors make the trek each year to the north Antrim coast to explore the phenomenon of a UNESCO World Heritage site where history and folklore coalesce.

SLIEVE LEAGUE CLIFFS, COUNTY DONEGAL
Imagine a remote hilltop where you humble yourself before the ocean and sky. Such a place is Slieve League, home to the highest cliffs in Ireland and one of the west coast's most spectacular sights.

HILL OF TARA, COUNTY MEATH
Long, undulating lines of earthworks, grassy banks, and ditches make up the fascinating Hill of Tara. It's unspectacular at first sight, but you will soon discover a landscape of myth and legend overlapping with history and archaeology. Tara is a many-sided place scrutinized by antiquarians, with monuments, including a passage tomb, a henge, and standing stones, ranging in date from 3500 BC to AD 400.

CLEW BAY, COUNTY MAYO
The island-studded Clew Bay, sitting hard by the Atlantic coastline, is made up of scores of tiny dots, which from a distance look like sleeping whales,

Slieve League cliffs, Donegal

snakes, dragons, or an upturned *curragh* (a traditional boat with a wooden frame). The best place to get a feel for the scale of the bay and its reputed 365 islands is from the Great Western Greenway walking and cycling route along the line of an old railway track.

MACGILLYCUDDY'S REEKS, COUNTY KERRY
At the heart of the ancient yet newly christened Reeks district of Kerry is Carrauntoohil, the highest point in Ireland and part of the oldest red sandstone mountains in Europe. It is a truly magical experience to get up close to these jagged peaks, glacial lakes, babbling streams, and fields ablaze with yellow gorse and wildflowers. The best way to tackle the Reeks is to hire a guide or join a walking tour from Killarney.

DÚN BRISTE SEA STACK, DOWNPATRICK HEAD, BALLYCASTLE, COUNTY MAYO
The squabbling of thousands of seabirds who make their nest on Dún Briste's ragged limestone sea stack, which separated from the mainland in 1393, is reminiscent of children in a playground.

POWERSCOURT WATERFALL, COUNTY WICKLOW
Awe-inspiring Powerscourt, the biggest waterfall in Ireland (England, too), is a dazzling sight, leaping and splashing in a frenzy across the rock face. At nearly 398 feet, it stands in a valley on the River Dargle near the foot of the Wicklow Mountains, and through the centuries has inspired writers and painters. Pack a picnic and keep an eye out for finches, warblers, red squirrels, and sika deer.

Ireland's Top Castles and Manor Houses

ADARE MANOR, COUNTY LIMERICK
Dating to the 1830s and set on an immaculate 842-acre estate shaded by some 19,000 trees, this Limerick property was home to the earls of Dunraven and one of the finest private homes in Ireland.

ASHFORD CASTLE, CONG, COUNTY MAYO
From the moment you enter the stone gates, this stately castle is the stuff of fairy tales, oozing luxury and contemporary cool after a €25 million restoration. Originally built in the 13th century, it was the former hunting lodge of the Guinness family during the 1800s.

HAYFIELD MANOR, CORK CITY
A redbrick charmer, this family-run period house is a hidden bolt-hole within a leafy, 5-meter-high walled garden, a 20-minute stroll from the center of Cork City. White-sash windows and quirky dormers bring radiance to the exterior of this neo-Georgian building that was originally owned by the Musgrave family, a dynasty of Cork merchants.

DROMOLAND CASTLE, NEWMARKET-ON-FERGUS, COUNTY CLARE
For more than 400 years Dromoland Castle, the ancestral home of the O'Briens, barons of Inchiquin and descendants of Brian Boru, the High King of Ireland, has played host to guests who wish to savor its mix of supreme luxury and history.

LOUGH ESKE CASTLE, DONEGAL TOWN, COUNTY DONEGAL

In a remote setting close to the shores of Lough Eske, this eponymous Tudor-style baronial castle is approached by a drive through ancient woodland. The clans of Donegal, the O'Donnells, had their seat on the lake here in the 1470s.

BALLYNAHINCH CASTLE, CONNEMARA, COUNTY GALWAY

A venerable house with impeccable historical cachet, Ballynahinch Castle is set on 700 acres of private woodlands and stands harmoniously in a landscape overlooking a salmon fishery.

BELLINGHAM CASTLE, CASTLEBELLINGHAM, COUNTY LOUTH

At the end of a tree-lined drive and on the banks of a crystal river, Bellingham Castle is exactly what you imagine when you think "gloriously romantic Irish castle."

Parknasilla Resort, Sneem

CABRA CASTLE, KINGSCOURT, COUNTY CAVAN

If you are more drawn to the evil witch than the princess in fairy tales, you can get castle feels of the goose-bumps-inducing variety at Cavan's Cabra Castle, which dates to 1820.

WATERFORD CASTLE, COUNTY WATERFORD

Few, if any, other Irish castles can point to such seclusion as 16th-century Waterford Castle, magnificently secreted away on its own 310-acre wooded island and accessible only via a three-minute private ferry ride.

PARKNASILLA RESORT, COUNTY KERRY

Built in 1897 and set on the Ring of Kerry, Parknasilla has hosted artists and royalty who enjoy the unhurried hospitality for which the "Kingdom" is famed.

CASHEL PALACE HOTEL, CO. TIPPERARY

New billionaire owners and a sumptuous renovation have turned this former Bishop's palace into one of the most luxurious manor house stays in the country.

What to Eat and Drink in Ireland

Soda Bread

BOXTY
Boxty is a blend of mashed potatoes and raw grated potato bulked up with the addition of ingredients like flour, eggs, and milk.

CHIPS
Humble "chipper" vans roam the villages of Ireland plying a bounty of fresh, crispy chips (which Americans know as French fries).

SMOKED SALMON
You'll find smoked salmon all over Ireland, but a visit to Burren Smokehouse gives you a chance to learn about how the products are made.

OYSTERS
You'll find oysters all over the country, but County Galway is renowned for its bivalves, with the native oysters being a particular specialty.

PERIWINKLES AND SEAWEED
Periwinkles are traditionally boiled in seawater and then eaten out of paper bags using a pin to fish out the meat, while seaweed appears in numerous dishes.

IRISH BREAKFAST
Specific items in a full breakfast may vary, but core cast members include

Oysters

black and white pudding, browned mushrooms, sausages, eggs, at least one tomato, and either soda bread or a potato farl.

SODA BREAD

It's hard to say why soda bread in Ireland is so dramatically different from its sad American iteration. Whatever the case, soda bread, with its tender crumb, crusty exterior, and slightly sweet flavor, is better in Ireland.

TEA AND SCONES

You'll find that teatime can come with different food options, governed in part by the time of day you're taking your tea.

POITÍN

In Tunisia, it's called boukha. In Italy, grappa. In the United States, moonshine. In Ireland, this beast is called poitín and—once illegal—it's making a comeback.

WHISKEY

Jameson and Bushmills are fine examples of Irish whiskey, but Ireland has a number of newer craft distillers. Look for Dingle, the Connacht Whiskey Company, Knappogue Castle, and Pearse.

CIDER

While you can find cider in a variety of styles, and with varying levels of sweetness and fermented funk, it's said that the apples of County Armagh are of particularly high quality.

CRAFT BEERS

Craft beer is finding fans across the globe, and Ireland is no exception. Ireland's craft-beer scene is small, but growing interest helps provide a counterpoint to the behemoth that is Guinness.

GUINNESS

Guinness is ubiquitous, omnipresent, and an easy choice for those disinclined to roll the dice on the undulating flavor wheel that modern craft beer represents.

COLCANNON

Colcannon is a traditional dish of mashed potatoes mixed with kale or cabbage. It's simple, hearty, and a good match for Ireland's frequently blustery weather.

What to Buy in Ireland

MOURNE TEXTILES
Using traditional weaving techniques and custom-made handlooms, Irish heritage brand Mourne Textiles is based in a workshop at the foot of the Mourne mountains in Co. Down. Look for wide scarves in earthy tones.

IRISH POTTERY
A visit to one of Ireland's ceramics studios will have you wondering why people focus on Waterford Crystal when there are so many incredible Irish potters and ceramicists producing cool, contemporary designs. Look for work by Nicholas Mosse, Mary Lincoln, and Shanagarry Potters who produce handmade and hand-decorated pottery that follows a 250-year-old tradition of handcrafted pottery in East Cork.

FRAGRANCE
Located in the heart of Co. Clare's Burren, the Burren Perfumery creates small-batch perfumes and cosmetics inspired by the beautiful surrounding landscape. Visit the store to check out the herb garden and tearoom, and to test fragrances, creams, and other products.

KNITWEAR
Specializing in detailed graphic knitwear with contemporary illustrations and bold patterns, Irish knitwear label Electronic Sheep's quirky, unisex sweaters and scarves are everything Grandma's isn't.

JEWELRY
Designed and handcrafted in a seaside village in West Cork, Enibas Jewellery's single or interlocked infinite circles are inscribed "Croí álainn," Irish for "beautiful heart," which makes for a simple but still sentimental alternative to the ubiquitous claddagh ring gift. Also, look for Liwu Jewellery by designer Áine Breen whose work is inspired by the ancient meaning and beauty of Celtic symbols. Delicate necklaces with Celtic symbols for growth, serenity, eternity, and progress make lovely gifts.

CANDLES
Candle making is a traditional craft and for many hundreds of years, candles were the primary means of providing light after darkness fell. Rathbornes candles—which traces its origins back to Dublin, circa 1488—lays claim to the title of "world's oldest candle company" and continues to make a wide range of fine products with captivating scents.

BLANKETS
Originally founded by an Irish Sister of Charity in 1892, Foxford Woollen Mill in County Mayo sources its wool from local sheep, its power from the River Moy, and its talent from local weavers. The high-quality woven rugs, blankets, and tweeds that have been made here for more than 100 years, in the timeless designs of plaid, herringbone, and houndstooth, are available in shades that reflect the earthy colors of the surrounding landscape.

WHISKEY
You don't have to spend much time in Ireland to discover there's a range of craft distilleries as

Whiskey

well as distillery-only special blends such as the Glendalough Distillery Triple Barrel, which uses bourbon, Oloroso sherry, and canteiro-aged Madeira barrels to finish the whiskey. For some of these blends, such as the Triple Barrel, you'll need to buy them on premises, but keep an eye open in the duty-free airport shops as well for Ireland-only selections.

TWEED CAPS

County Donegal's traditional craft of tweed goes back centuries, and is both iconically Irish and easy to find. While we highly endorse head-to-toe Donegal tweed, a Donegal tweed cap from Hanna Hats is definitely easier on the wallet (and, perhaps, the eye). Designed and made in Donegal since 1924, this third-generation company's hats are local, made from the finest Donegal tweed (pure new wool), and stylish, too. PS: they're also waterproof, which comes in handy in Ireland.

AVOCA THROWS

Known for its signature colorful woolen throws, which are woven at one of the oldest mills in Ireland, Avoca throws are every bit as comfortable as they are cheerful. Visit their flagship store to see the mill in action in the hills of Wicklow.

A BODHRÁN

Among the rocky isles and bays of western Ireland in a Franciscan monastery in the village of Roundstone, Malachy Kearns, known as "Malachy Bodhrán," has been building and stretching traditional goatskin drums known as a bodhráns (bow-rawns) for 35 years. Widely used by Irish folk musicians, bodhráns are beautiful and historically significant musical instruments, and Kearns makes some of the best available. These make a great gift for a musician but also a unique souvenir, especially if you have yours personalized with a family crest or other artwork.

SMOKED SALMON

Chances are you ate smoked salmon on your visit to Ireland, and chances are you'll want to continue eating it when you return home. Fortunately, there are a number of award-winning smokehouses located around the country offering vacuum-packed salmon. Notables include Frank Hederman, the Burren Smokehouse, Ballyhack Smokehouse, and Shanagarry, all of which use Irish salmon (mostly organic, farmed salmon). Also, while U.S. Customs is notoriously persnickety about travelers bringing food back to the States, fish is generally exempt.

Top Festivals and Events in Ireland

MIDSUMMER FESTIVAL
Every June, Cork City struts its artistic stuff with the Midsummer Festival, a mix of music, film, and theater. It runs on consecutive weekends in June leading up to the 21st.

ALL-IRELAND HURLING FESTIVAL
Usually the first Sunday in September, the All-Ireland Hurling Final, at Dublin's Croke Park, features the country's two top teams who chase down a heavy leather ball, or *sliothar*, with their ash hurleys at warp speeds.

PUCK FAIR
Puck Fair in Kerry is the oldest festival in Ireland, dating back to pagan times, where a goat is made king for three days of drinking, dancing, and general abandon. Held on the second weekend in August, it's truly one of Ireland's most unusual festivals.

KINVARA CUCKOO FLEADH
Happening on the May bank-holiday weekend, the Kinvara Cuckoo Fleadh is perfectly timed to welcome in the warmer evenings of early summer. A well-established and richly deserved reputation has ensured that the *fleadh* has become a showcase for the best in traditional music.

LISTOWEL WRITER'S WEEK
Listowel Writer's Week (🌐 *writersweek.ie*) is a chaotic and seriously democratic gathering devoted to all things literary. It takes place all over the town of Listowel on the first weekend in June.

TULLAMORE SHOW
Ireland's biggest agricultural gathering, Tullamore Show (🌐 *www.tullamoreshow.com*), attracts 60,000 people annually in mid-August for cattle contests, sheep-shearing competitions, Irish Axe Men demonstrations, exhibits of local artisanal produce, fashion shows, displays of vintage farm machinery, and more.

BLOOMSDAY
Even though it is now reckoned that more Americans and Japanese attend the events surrounding Bloomsday (🌐 *jamesjoyce.ie*) than Irish people, it hasn't taken away a jot from an event that continues to grow regardless. Bloomsday is June 16.

Cork Jazz Fest

THE OULD LAMMAS FAIR
Running for nearly 400 years on the last Monday and Tuesday of August, this harvest fair in the seaside town of Ballycastle in County Antrim features traditional snacks, entertainers, and stalls selling local crafts and specialties.

CROAGH PATRICK
On the last Sunday in July, join the thousands of pilgrims and adventurers who climb Mayo's Croagh Patrick—in your bare feet, for the full purging of your misdeeds.

CRUÍNNIU NA MBÁD
August's Cruínniu na mBád, or the Gathering of the Boats, is basically a big booze-up and regatta to celebrate the unique and beautiful boat that is the Galway hooker.

SIX NATIONS RUGBY TOURNAMENT
Every spring rugby fever grips the country as the Six Nations Tournament begins. The beloved Irish team takes on the might of Wales, France, Scotland, Italy, and its old enemy England in a series of bone-crunching encounters.

KINSALE GOURMET FESTIVAL
Long noted for its cuisine innovations, the Kinsale Gourmet Festival is all about the happy pursuit of great food and wine plus the excitable bravado of this infectious coastal town. It takes place on the second weekend in October.

CORK JAZZ FEST
For jazz lovers, the Cork Jazz Festival on the second-to-last weekend in October is a perfect antidote to the approaching winter.

Ireland Today

Navigating a good conversation in Ireland can be as tricky as driving its winding coastal lanes, but armed with these pointers it can be equally as rewarding.

CRIME

The U.S. Overseas Security Advisory Council cites Ireland as a low-risk country when it comes to crime. Violent crime is rare and it is largely confined to rival drug gangs in the capital and other metropolitan areas. Sensible precautions mitigate any risk. Dial ☎ *999* or ☎ *112* for emergency.

■ TIP→ Ireland's police force, the Garda Síochána, employ a predictably good-humored approach to their Twitter feed (🌐 *https://twitter.com/gardainfo*).

CULTURE

Despite the fact that Ireland is now a major European technology hub, the nation's fondness for the written word is as powerful as ever. Few may match the talent of Shaw, Wilde, Joyce, and W.B. Yeats, but the popularity of best-selling writers such as Anne Enright, Edna O'Brien, Sally Rooney, Roddy Doyle, Colum McCann, Colm Tóibín, John Banville, and Martin McDonagh, is testament to the continuation of a rich literary tradition. A new youthful charge of novelists includes Lisa McInerney, Claire Keegan, Kevin Barry, and Donal Ryan, while playwrights such as Conor McPherson and Enda Walsh tell Irish stories to a world audience.

In the movie world, writer-directors Lenny Abrahamson and Martin McDonagh portray the warts-and-all visions of modern Ireland.

■ TIP→ For the latest in all things Irish culture, follow Hugh Linehan, the arts and culture editor for the *Irish Times*, on Twitter @hlinehan.

ECONOMICS

Until a very recent slowdown, Ireland's economy was expanding rapidly despite continuing uncertainty about the long-term consequences of Brexit. The country has a vibrant entrepreneurial spirit with a newfound business confidence, and commentators wax lyrical about it being of the modern success stories of Europe. As a favorite English-speaking destination for foreign direct investment, Ireland is home to the European HQ of flagship companies, including Meta, Apple, and Google.

While the economy is typically no laughing matter, true to Irish form an annual festival combines stand-up comedy with the serious topic of economics, to create the successful Kilkenomics (🌐 *www.kilkenomics.com*) event.

■ TIP→ David McWilliam, an economist of legendary status in Ireland and founding member of Kilkenomics, has an excellent Twitter feed (@davidmcw) with a unique and independent take on the nation's finances.

HUMOR

When the Nobel Prize–winning German author Heinrich Böll came to Ireland in the 1950s, he detected that the most common saying used to describe any alarming situation was: "Sure it could be worse." Seventy years on, this mantra still holds true, and Ireland is filled with tongue-in-cheek banter and self-deprecating humor. A large dose of cynicism, accompanied by dark comedy, is a coping mechanism for dealing with events over which there is no control.

■ TIP→ Waterford Whispers Twitter account (@WhispersNewsLTD) offers a snapshot of that humor with its cynical take on national and international news.

MEDIA

The three bastions of Irish daily news are the *Irish Times*, the *Irish Independent*, and the *Irish Examiner*. Raidió Teilifís Éireann (RTE) is the high-quality, state-controlled, and publicly subsidized national broadcaster. Newstalk is a populist, 24-hour current affairs and opinion radio station.

■ TIP→ **Online media such as the Journal.ie, national newspapers' social media feeds, and gender-targeted Joe.ie and Her.ie are very influential.**

POLITICS

The staid duopoly of Fianna Fáil and Fine Gael was smashed apart when the Irish republican party Sinn Féin achieved the largest share of first-preference votes in the country's 2020 general election to become a force in the Irish Dáil (Parliament). For many years, the center-right coalition government had success with its liberal social agenda, but the face of Irish politics is changing dramatically, reflected also in the rising support for the progressive Green Party's focus on social justice and the environment. Vital issues relating to housing, homelessness, health, and the slow decline of small towns crying out for regeneration are a major concern. The Irish are fascinated by American politics, so expect to hear as much about U.S. goings-on as Irish.

■ TIP→ **Harry McGee from the *Irish Times* has a Twitter account (@harrymcgee) that provides an impartial news feed on Irish politics.**

RELIGION

Radical changes—part of a rapid shift in social attitudes unimaginable a generation ago—have taken place since Ireland became the first country in the world to vote overwhelmingly in favor of legalizing same-sex marriage. While it remains a predominantly Catholic country, the church's domination and influence has declined. A combination of sex scandals, the historic referendum that overturned the strict abortion laws, and the appointment of an openly gay Taoiseach, Leo Varadkar, have reconfigured the social landscape, resulting in a more outward-looking pluralist democracy. In Northern Ireland, too, the criminal ban on abortion fell and the remaining legal impediments to same-sex marriage were cleared to allow the first civil partnerships to take place.

SPORTS

Depending on what county you are in, and the time of year, soccer, rugby, Gaelic football, or hurling talk can dominate any social gathering. Shane Lowry, who plays his golf at the small Esker Hills club in Offaly, lifted the country's spirits when he won the British Open in 2019, and Rory McIroy ended the 2022 golf season as world number one. At the local level, Gaelic football and hurling are widely played throughout the country and are part of the sporting fabric of every parish. County is pitted against county, passions run deep, and it culminates each September at the All-Ireland championship finals in Croke Park, Dublin, the largest stadium in the country.

■ TIP→ **Follow Irish sports journalist Vincent Hogan's colorful commentary on Twitter (@vincent_hogan).**

If You Like

CHARMING VILLAGES

Adare, Co. Limerick. Right out of a storybook, this celebrated village of low-slung Tudor cottages is adorned with ivied churches and a moated castle from the days when knighthood was in flower.

Birr, Co. Offaly. The epitome of Georgian perfection, with a layout that curls along the contours of its famous castle to the west and enough asymmetrical quirks to make it interesting.

Cong, Co. Mayo. John Ford's *The Quiet Man* introduced this charmer to the world and the singular beauty of its whitewashed single-story cottages with tied-on thatched roofs.

Dunmore East, Co. Waterford. With a streetscape that snakes along its cove, Dunmore East has a mishmash of traditional architecture from thatched cottages to slated town houses that nestle together in a crimson cliff-side setting.

Glengarriff, Co. Cork. Set in a lush valley where the Caha Mountains vanish into the ocean, this comely village has lured visitors for centuries.

Inistioge, Co. Kilkenny. If you think Inistioge, with its perfect Irish village square and meandering pathways along the River Nore, looks like it was peeled straight from a movie set, you'd be right. Its streetscape was filmed in major movies, including *Circle of Friends* and *Widow's Peak.*

Kinvara, Co. Galway. This village is picture-perfect, thanks to its gorgeous bayside locale, great walks, and numerous pubs. North of the town is spectacularly sited Dunguaire Castle, noted for its medieval-banquet evenings.

Lismore, Co. Waterford. Set within some of Ireland's lushest pasturelands and lorded over by the Duke of Devonshire's castle, dreamy Lismore is popular with both romantic folk and anglers (the sparkling Blackwater here teems with salmon).

Roundstone, Co. Galway. Framed by the Twelve Bens mountains, with a pastel-color streetscape that faces the Atlantic Ocean, Roundstone is the most alluring village in Connemara.

Westport, Co. Mayo. On an inlet of Clew Bay, this lively little town's scenic setting includes a charming main street complete with cute painted pubs, Georgian buildings, and a triple-arched stone bridge in the middle of town all festooned with flowers and plants. Add Croagh Patrick Mountain in the background and Clew Bay with its hundreds of islands and you can see why this was once a vacation destination for the 18th-century gentry.

MOVIE LOCATIONS

The Cliffs of Moher. In *Harry Potter and the Half-Blood Prince,* Harry and Dumbledore are perched on County Clare's famous cliffs, facing giant waves and an impenetrable coastline.

Connemara. Brendan Gleeson's portrayal of flawed Sergeant Gerry Boyle unleashing his caustic manner against the beautifully brooding backdrop of Connemara earned him a Golden Globe nomination for *The Guard.*

Co. Antrim. Strictly speaking, not a movie, but HBO's *Game of Thrones* has plucked out as many scene locations from Northern Ireland as it has characters, from the King's Road (the Dark Hedges) to Winterfell (Castle Ward and Shane's Castle).

Curracloe Beach. This County Wexford strand took on a French role as the scene for the U.S. arrival to World War II on D-Day in Steven Spielberg's epic war movie, *Saving Private Ryan.*

Dublin. Neil Jordan's biopic *Michael Collins* stages Dublin beautifully, earning it a cinematography Oscar nomination, with backdrops of Trinity College, the Ha'apenny Bridge and, of course, Kilmainhain Gaol, which also appeared in the original *Italian Job,* starring Michael Caine.

Grafton Street, Dublin. One of Dublin's main shopping streets, Grafton Street has served as a backdrop for several music videos, but it is best known for its supporting role in indie film *Once*, with Irish musician Glen Hansard.

Skellig Michael. Ahch-To (to *Star Wars* fans), Skellig Michael in County Kerry features throughout *Star Wars: The Force Awakens,* and its stubbornly present puffins inspired the entire species of Porgs.

Trim Castle. County Meath's castle doubled as York in *Braveheart,* the biopic of Scottish freedom fighter William Wallace, starring Mel Gibson.

Trinity College. Dublin became Liverpool in multi-award-winning movie, *Educating Rita,* where Ireland's most famous college took center stage.

Yeats Tower (Thoor Ballylee), Connemara, and Cong. Galway's and Mayo's appearances in John Ford's classic, *The Quiet Man,* turned the town of Cong into a tourist attraction (still visited by fans today) and, no doubt, helped the movie earn an Oscar for cinematography in 1953.

LITERARY HAUNTS

Aran Islands, Co. Galway. See what inspired the dark genius of Synge's *The Playboy of the Western World* and the black comedy of Martin McDonagh's *The Cripple of Inishmaan.*

Bellaghy, Co. Derry. Located in the heart of the landscape that shaped his life and work, HomePlace visitor and arts center celebrates the life, inspiration, literature, and legacy of one of Ireland's greatest writers, the late Seamus Heaney.

The Burren, Co. Clare. Walk the actual road through the Burren that is the setting, and title, of Man Booker Prize–winning author Anne Enright's 2015 novel, *The Green Road.* J.R.R. Tolkien visited the West of Ireland on many occasions and spent considerable time in the Burren's fantastical landscapes. An underground lake called Pol na Gollum (or Cave of Gollum) is often held up by fans as evidence that Middle-Earth, at least partly, is descended from here.

Enniscorthy, Co. Wexford. Acclaimed Irish author, Colm Tóibín, was born and raised in this small town in the east of Ireland that would come to form the backdrop to many of Tóibín's novels, among them *Nora Webster* and *Brooklyn.*

Limerick City, Co. Limerick. Frank McCourt's *Angela's Ashes* had thousands heading here to tour Angela's city and partake of the tearfulness of it all.

Sligo Town, Co. Sligo. Take in the town where William Butler Yeats grew up, then visit his grave in Drumcliff to view his beloved mountain, Ben Bulben.

Thoor Ballylee, Co. Galway. This restored 16th-century Norman tower house in Gort, just south of Galway City, was the summer home of W.B. Yeats. Yeats described the house as "a tower set by a stream's edge," and it served as the inspiration for his poems "The Winding Stair" and "The Tower."

Trinity College, Co. Dublin. Founded by Queen Elizabeth I, this university provided the greats—Beckett, Wilde, Stoker—with 30 acres of stomping grounds.

Great Outdoors in Ireland

Top Boating Trips

Imagine the scene: gentle waves lap at the edges of your boat as it heads for open water, drawing a perfect silver line across the tranquil, mirror-flat surface. Every sound is crystal clear—a dog barks, a kingfisher whirs past flying low across the water, and fellow sailors shout a hearty welcome. This magical moment can easily be yours in Ireland, thanks to the wealth of possibilities for either guided tours or private hires.

COAST OR INLAND

Ireland's indented western seaboard from Donegal to Cork has many first-class sailing opportunities. The main towns have sailing clubs in scenic areas. The best option is to choose an area such as West Cork and spend a week sailing from port to port. If you want to enjoy the very heart of Ireland, the River Shannon offers an unequaled choice of boating trips from the Northern Midlands down to Killaloe in County Clare. Cruisers can be hired at Carrick-on-Shannon, Banagher, and Portumna. Crossing the Irish border, the Shannon–Erne Waterway has opened up a little-known area of untamed beauty, and the renaissance of Ireland's canals is a regeneration success.

THE FIVE BEST BOATING TRIPS

Fermanagh Lakes: With 700 km (430 miles) of rivers, lakes, and canals, Fermanagh is tops. Upper and Lower Lough Erne are dotted with islands topped with castles or Round Towers ideal for exploring.

River Barrow: Hire a traditional steel canal boat at Rathangan in County Kildare for a 120-km (75-mile) trip along the idyllic Barrow—Ireland's oldest navigation—passing through a Chaucerian landscape and dropping anchor at Graiguenamanagh (pronounced *grayg-na-mana* and known as Graig); en route, sign up for a canalways pub crawl.

River Shannon Cruising: One of the best places to hire from is the delightful boating town of Carrick-on-Shannon—putter your leisurely way down to Lough Ree or as far as the Lower Shannon.

Royal Canal: With its reconstructed locks and bridges, the 145-km (90-mile) canal is perfect for those on narrow boats, and in 2010 it became fully navigable from Dublin to Richmond Harbor in County Longford. Towpaths run from the Liffey all the way to the Shannon.

West Cork Sailing: The harbors of the ports of call along this coast, such as Kinsale, Glandore, Baltimore, and Bantry, offer delightful overnight stays.

GUIDED TOURS OR PRIVATE HIRE

A first-time boater? Get some courses under your belt by contacting the International Sailing Schools Association. If you want to sit back and have it all done for you, book half-day or full-day guided pleasure cruises. ⇨ *For more info, see "Cruising on the Shannon" in the Midlands chapter.*

INFORMATION

The best resources about boating in Ireland include: International Sailing Schools Association (🌐 *www.issa-schools.org)*; Canalways Ireland; Cruise Ireland (🌐 *www.cruiseireland.com*); Emerald Star Cruisers; and Riversdale Barge Holidays.

Best Walks and Hikes

Catch the right day and an Irish hilltop can seem like a slice of heaven. The country is laced with 33 well-marked walking trails. If you're not feeling adventurous, strolls through a forest park or a lakeside wander are wonderful options. If you're going for bragging rights, consider walking the extension to the world-renowned International Appalachian Trail. The two best websites for hiking information are 🌐 *www.discoverireland.ie/walking*and 🌐 *www.walkni.com*.

THE TOP FIVE HIKING REGIONS

Ballyhoura Country: Whether it's mountain biking or hiking through a lesser-known portal of Irish countryside, Ballyhoura's Mesolithic past comes alive across lakelands, parks, and the ancient Lough Gur in Counties Limerick and Cork.

The Reeks of Kerry: Munster, in the southwest of the country, has Ireland's biggest mountains with MacGillycuddy's Reeks in Kerry (3,414 feet) leading the way in the hierarchy of height. They attract serious hill walkers and serious gongoozlers (those who like to gaze up at the peaks).

Ulster Way: Relaunched in 2009, the 1,000-km (625-mile) circular Ulster Way crosses the most stunning upland areas of Northern Ireland including the impressive Mountains of Mourne.

West Is Best: Many of Ireland's west-coast walking routes are framed by spectacular Atlantic scenery: Connemara, Sligo, and Donegal are renowned for the allure of their hills with thrilling views.

The Wicklow Way: Starting in the suburbs of Dublin, 137 km (85 miles) of trails take you through the heart of the spectacular Wicklow Mountains. Check out some of the gorgeous villages along the way.

THE TOP FIVE WALKS

The Barrow Way, Co. Carlow. Follow the Barrow River on a 113-km (70-mile) meander through the forgotten Midlands, where countless historical sights pepper the pastoral landscape. It's a feast for wildlife lovers as well.

Burren, Co. Clare. An unforgettable trip into an otherworldly place, this lunar landscape is threaded with looped walks, rare flowers, and ancient ruins, many with a backdrop of unbeatable views across Galway Bay. The entire Burren Way is a 123-km (76-mile) pleasure-filled walk.

Glendalough, Co. Wicklow. The gentle, three-hour circular Spink Walk takes you across a wooden bridge, along a boardwalk, through conifer woodland, and alongside the Upper Lake, with sweeping views over the valley.

Silent Valley, Co. Down. Catch a bus from Newcastle and, after a two-hour (undemanding) walk around this idyllic place, you will realize why it was so named.

Slievenamon, Co. Tipperary. An unmistakable landmark famed in song, there is an easy track to the top where a burial cairn reputedly contains the entrance to the Celtic underworld.

WEATHER OR NOT

Irish weather is fickle, mist comes down quickly, and it's easy to get lost. Check the forecast and leave word with someone at your hotel about where you are going. Layers of waterproof gear and fleeces are a good bet so you can strip off when the sun comes out. Even though signposting is generally good in hill areas, bring a map: free walking guides are available from regional tourism offices, but invest in Ordnance Survey Discovery Maps, available at newsagents for €8.

Best Irish Greens

The wonderfully alive, challenging natural terrain is one of the things that makes Irish golf so remarkable. In a country where mountains and sea so often meet, scraggly coastline and rolling hills of heather dominate the courses here, not the other way around. Real golfers are challenged, rather than deterred, by the vagaries of the elements.

THE PERFECT LINKS

Ballybunion Golf Club, Co. Kerry. On the Old Course, one of the country's classics, each and every hole is a pleasure to play. Set on the shore of the Atlantic at the southern entrance to the River Shannon, Ballybunion is famed for tough but pleasant golf, epitomized by the huge dunes—great for a stroll but hellish to play out of.

Ballyliffin Golf Club, Co. Donegal. Designed around imposing dunes and often described as "the Ballybunion of the North," the Glashedy Links at the world-famous Ballyliffin Golf Club has earned notoriety for its devilish bunkers. Running high above both the sea and the club's Old Links, the views from Ballyliffin's Glashedy Links are spectacular, especially from the par-3 7th tee. Designed by Ireland's own Pat Ruddy, Glashedy Links is one of the finest courses in all of Ireland.

Donegal Golf Club, Co. Donegal. This wild and wonderful course sits between the shores of beautiful Donegal Bay and the shadow of the majestic Blue Stack Mountains. From the 5th to the 9th you enter the "Valley of Tears," a fearsome challenge of four perilous holes made all the more challenging by feisty winds.

The K Club, Co. Kildare. You'd have to be a nongolfer and a hermit not to have heard of this course, one of the country's most prestigious and demanding. Arnold Palmer designed the main course, famed for its water obstacles and inland-links feel. The on-site facilities are the best in Ireland.

Lahinch, Co. Clare. Lahinch's old golf course constantly ranks in the world's top 100 because of its spectacular setting and its master architects over the last 126 years, Old Tom Morris and Alister MacKenzie. Goats have full right of access.

Old Head, Co. Cork. Set on a spectacular peninsula jutting out into the wild Atlantic below, the Old Head is the romantic favorite of Irish golf lovers. Often compared to the Pacific sections of Pebble Beach, expect your pulse to race at the stunning views and wildlife.

Portmarnock Golf Club, Co. Dublin. One of the nation's "Big Four" golf clubs (along with Ballybunion, Royal County Down, and Royal Portrush), Portmarnock is a links course near Dublin. Located on a sandy peninsula, it has hosted regular Irish Opens with its 100-plus bunkers ready to trap amateur and pro alike.

Royal County Down, Co. Down. A lunar landscape makes this course as beautiful as it is difficult. It has recently ousted St. Andrews as *Golf Digest*'s best course outside the United States. The sea of craterlike bunkers and the long rough reward the straight and punish the proud.

Royal Portrush, Co. Antrim. This grand old course has made it into *Golf Digest*'s top-10 courses outside the United States. It's a sea of sand hills and curving fairways, with the White Rocks par-5 5th set on the edge of a cliff. Word has it (okay, Royal Portrush recommends) that a long carry over the mounds to the right of the white stone will be rewarded with a much shorter approach to the green.

Ancestor-Hunting in Ireland

More than 39 million Americans claim Irish ancestry, and the desire to trace those long-lost roots back to the "auld sod" can run deep. Here are some pointers for how you can make your trip to Ireland a journey into your past.

The first port of call is a visit to Ireland's online national archives (🌐 www.nationalarchives.ie), which has volumes of information and is constantly releasing genealogy records with an extensive search function through the censuses of 1901, 1911, and 1921, which may help you trace your relations before you leave home.

BEFORE YOU GO

The more you can learn about your ancestors, the more fruitful your search is going to be once you're on Irish soil. Crucial facts include:

- The name of your ancestor
- Names of that ancestor's parents and spouse
- His or her date of birth, marriage, or death
- County, parish, and townland of origin in Ireland
- Religious denomination

The first place to seek information is directly from members of your family. A grandparent or a great-aunt with a story to tell can be the source of important clues. And relatives may have documents stored away that can help with your sleuthing—old letters, wills, diaries, birth certificates, and photos.

ON THE GROUND IN IRELAND

General Register Office. Civil records—dating back to 1865—are available at the General Register Office. Records for Anglican marriages date from 1845. ✉ *Werburg St., Dublin* ☎ *01/863–8200* 🌐 *www.gov.ie/gro.*

The Mellon Centre for Migration Studies. For Northern Ireland, you can find information at the Mellon Centre for Migration Studies at the Ulster American Folk Park. ✉ *Ulster American Folk Park, 2 Mellon Rd., Omagh* ☎ *028/8225–6315* 🌐 *www.mellonmigrationcentre.com.*

National Archives. These extensive archives include census records and, like the National Library, they provide free genealogy consultations on weekdays from 10 am to 1:30 pm. A lot of the archives are now online. ✉ *Bishop St., Dublin* ☎ *01/407–2300* 🌐 *www.nationalarchives.ie.*

National Library of Ireland. Ancestor hunters have long traveled throughout Ireland to comb parish church records, but most of these records are now available on microfilm in Dublin at the National Library of Ireland and increasingly through its online service. The library is a great place to begin your hunting; you can consult a research adviser there free of charge. ✉ *Kildare St., Dublin* ☎ *01/661–2523* 🌐 *www.nli.ie.*

Public Record Office. ✉ *2 Titanic Blvd., Queen's Island, Belfast* ☎ *028/9053–4800* 🌐 *www.nidirect.gov.uk/proni.*

If you'd rather not spend your vacation in a records hall, you can hire a professional to do your spadework. The **Association of Professional Genealogists** in Ireland (🌐 *www.irishgenealogy.ie*) will present you with a "package of discovery" upon your arrival.

The *Irish Times* newspaper also has ancestor-hunting resources (🌐 *www.johngrenham.com*), and the National Library provides references for professionals.

Irish Family Names

Antrim
Lynch
McDonnell
McNeill
O'Hara
O'Neill
Quinn

Armagh
Hanlon
McCann

Carlow
Kinsella
Nolan
O'Neill

Cavan
Boylan
Lynch
McCabe
McGovern
McGowan
McNally
O'Reilly
Sheridan

Clare
Aherne
Boland
Clancy
Daly
Lynch
McGrath
McInerney
McMahon
McNamara
Molon(e)y
O'Brien
O'Dea
O'Grady
O'Halloran
O'Loughlin

Cork
Barry
Callaghan
Cullinane
Donovan
Driscoll
Flynn
Hennessey
Hogan
Lynch
McCarthy
McSweeney
Murphy
Nugent
O'Casey
O'Cullane
(Collins)
O'Keefe
O'Leary
O'Mahony
O'Riordan
Roche
Scanlon
Sheridan

Derry
Cahan
Hegarty
Kelly
McLaughlin

Donegal
Boyle
Clery
Doherty
Friel
Gallagher
Gormley
McGrath
McLoughlin
McSweeney
Mooney
O'Donnell

Down
Lynch
McGuinness
O'Neil
White

Dublin
Hennessey
O'Casey
Plunkett

Fermanagh
Cassidy
Connolly
Corrigan
Flanagan
Maguire
McManus

Galway
Blake
Burke
Clery
Fah(e)y
French
Jennings
Joyce
Kelly
Kenny
Kirwan
Lynch
Madden
Moran
O'Flaherty
O'Halloran

Kerry
Connor
Fitzgerald
Galvin
McCarthy
Moriarty
O'Connell
O'Donoghue
O'Shea
O'Sullivan

Kildare
Cullen
Fitzgerald
O'Byrne
White

Kilkenny
Butler
Fitzpatrick
O'Carroll
Tobin

Laois
Dempsey
Doran
Dunn(e)
Kelly
Moore

Leitrim
Clancy
O'Rourke

Limerick
Fitzgerald
Fitzgibbon
McKeough
O'Brien
O'Cullane
(Collins)
O'Grady
Woulfe

Longford
O'Farrell
Quinn

Louth
O'Carroll
Plunkett

Mayo
Burke
Costello
Dugan
Gormley
Horan
Jennings
Jordan
Kelly
Madden
O'Malley

Meath
Coffey
Connolly
Cusack
Dillon
Hayes
Hennessey
Plunkett
Quinlan

Monaghan
Boylan
Connolly
Hanratty
McKenna
McMahon
McNally

Offaly
Coghlan
Dempsey
Fallon
Malone
Meagher
(Maher)
Molloy
O'Carroll
Sheridan

Roscommon
Fallon
Flanagan
Flynn
Hanley
McDermot
McKeogh
McManus
Molloy
Murphy

Sligo
Boland
Higgins
McDonagh
O'Dowd
O'Hara
Rafferty

Tipperary
Butler
Fogarty
Kennedy
Lynch
Meagher
(Maher)
O'Carroll
O'Dwyer
O'Meara
Purcell
Ryan

Tyrone
Cahan
Donnelly
Gormley
Hagan
Murphy
O'Neill
Quinn

Waterford
Keane
McGrath
O'Brien
Phelan
Power

Westmeath
Coffey
Dalton
Daly
Dillon
Sheridan

Wexford
Doran
Doyle
Hartley
Kavanagh
Keating
Kinsella
McKeogh
Redmond
Walsh

Wicklow
Cullen
Kelly
McKeogh
O'Byrne
O'Toole

What to Read Before Your Trip

***Angela's Ashes*, Frank McCourt.** Frank McCourt's memoir, which begins in Brooklyn and progresses to Limerick, is a tale driven by familial loss, tragedy, and the challenges of intense poverty. Throughout this book McCourt recounts his experiences being a member of a large family and touches on subjects such as illness, hunger, religion, and the impact his alcoholic father had on both himself and his family. Despite having been written in the relatively recent mid-1990s, *Angela's Ashes* is considered a classic and is a good choice for those looking for insight into what it meant to be an Irish immigrant in the early 1900s.

***Are You Somebody? The Accidental Memoir of a Dublin Woman*, Nuala O'Faolain.** Nuala O'Faolain's reputation as a powerful, respected writer who never minces words is clearly on display in this memoir about her own life. The second of nine children, O'Faolain writes about her family (and particularly her hard-drinking, neglectful mother), her time at a convent school, and her university studies, relationships, and work in compelling, beautiful, and painfully honest stories.

***Conversations with Friends*, Sally Rooney.** Irish author Sally Rooney's debut novel, *Conversations with Friends* (2017), examines the tumultuous relationship between four friends. Frances is a coolheaded and darkly observant young woman, vaguely pursuing a career in writing while studying in Dublin. Her best friend is the beautiful and endlessly self-possessed Bobbi. At a local poetry performance one night, they meet a well-known photographer, and as the girls are then gradually drawn into her world, Frances is reluctantly impressed by the older woman's sophisticated home and handsome husband, Nick. But however amusing Frances and Nick's flirtation seems at first, it begins to give way to a strange—and then painful—intimacy.

***The Country Girls*, Edna O'Brien.** The fact that this trilogy was banned after publication tells you a bit about how leery Ireland was of material that questioned the status quo. While these books are about the relationship of two young female friends who decide to move to the city together, it was the focus on sensitive issues such as gender inequality and sexual taboos—and the fact that they were at times sexually explicit and critical of Irish culture—which led to them being banned and the subject of book burnings. Today this trilogy is an example of the barriers female Irish authors faced, but also is a vital story about personal exploration and fulfillment.

***Death of a Naturalist*, Seamus Heaney.** The 34 poems that make up Heaney's first major volume of poetry are largely autobiographical but speak volumes about what life was like on farms across rural Ireland. The Nobel Prize–winning Irish author, poet, and translator recalls a boyhood spent searching for tadpoles in a muddy pond, digging for potatoes, and the death of his younger brother. Life as portrayed by Heaney is beautiful but hard, and this collection of poems draws you into those experiences.

***Dubliners*, James Joyce.** By telling stories about what everyday life was like in the early 1900s for middle-class residents of Dublin, James Joyce spoke both directly and indirectly about class and national identity, topics that were roiling Ireland. Even today, just more than a century later, these issues remain far from settled, particularly as Ireland and Northern Ireland grapple with the potential ramifications of Brexit.

***Foster,* Claire Keegan.** Set in Wexford, a village on the coast of southeast Ireland, *Foster* tells the story of a young girl sent to temporarily live with a foster family while her mother prepares to give birth. Not only is this novella brilliantly written (and available to read for free via the *New Yorker*, where it was published), its importance has been cemented in Ireland, where it is now a part of the curriculum for the Irish Leaving Certificate (the test that determines whether a student can progress to university).

***The Gathering,* Anne Enright.** It's only after her brother Liam Hegarty drowns himself that Veronica, Liam's dearest sibling, begins to consider whether events that unfolded earlier in their life might have contributed to his alcoholism and eventual suicide. While *The Gathering*'s focal point is Liam's death and his wake in Dublin, the Man Booker Prize–winning novel is truly about the cost of untold secrets and hidden trauma, the pain of absent parents, and what it's like to grow up in a large family.

***The Green Road,* Anne Enright.** Anne Enright has shown a proclivity toward examining the more challenging side of family life, and *The Green Road* is no exception. Devoted to telling the story of the Madigan family from each member's viewpoint, the novel deftly weaves together individual narratives while also portraying a whole, fractured family unit. This is one of Enright's most beloved novels, a story that's comedic while being largely dark and which shows how familial obligation can be a heavy weight to bear.

***The Heart's Invisible Furies,* John Boyne.** Set between 1945 and 2015, Irish author John Boyne's 2017 novel tracks a half century of social change in the Republic of Ireland through the life of Cyril Avery, the adopted child of a "fallen woman" who, having to hide his homosexuality in Ireland, moves abroad in order to live openly as a gay man.

***How the Irish Saved Civilization,* Thomas Cahill.** Stereotypes about the Irish erode one of history's great truths: that Ireland is not just a great center of culture, learning, and the arts, but that it was also instrumental in keeping civilization from falling completely apart during the Middle Ages. Thomas Cahill's historical text focuses on how Irish monks helped to preserve knowledge and promote learning during a bleak time in human history. The next time you're thinking about the fact that it's a miracle we're still here at all, pick up this book and give thanks to the Irish.

***The Immortal Irishman: The Irish Revolutionary Who Became an American Hero,* Timothy Egan.** The term "badass" gets thrown around with impunity these days, but Thomas Francis Meagher deserves the title. During Ireland's Great Famine, he planned an uprising against the British and—when that didn't work out—was sentenced to death but ultimately was exiled to the penal colony on Tasmania, an island off the coast of Australia. From there he escaped to the United States, married, worked as a journalist, joined the army, and generally lived a life of drama, adventure, and derring-do. Irish history, while important, is typically a bit of a bummer, but this volume definitely is not.

***Irish Fairy and Folk Tales,* William Butler Yeats.** It might seem a bit clichéd to say that Ireland is a mystical country, but the idea that there's a fairy around every corner truly is something many people embrace, and particularly in the countryside. W.B. Yeats's collection of Irish stories, songs, and poems taps into the island's substantial history of folklore and provides a glimpse of the magical, untamed side of Ireland. Plus, if we're being honest, Ireland's cliffs, deep forests, and fog-shrouded bogs might have you looking over your shoulder for fairies anyway, so at the very least this collection will have you better prepared for the magic that is to come.

***Milkman,* Anna Burns.** Set during the Troubles of the 1970s, Burns's book *Milkman* follows an unnamed young woman who attracts the eye of a paramilitary officer named only as "Milkman," who in short order begins following her and interrupting her life. It's a challenging read noteworthy not only for the tension present within the storyline but also its rambling, stream-of-consciousness style. If you traverse the tangled lanes of this Man Booker Prize–winning novel, you'll find it lives not only in the period of Ireland's most challenging modern-day struggle, but also in the commonplace terror experienced by any person who finds themselves in the crosshairs of unwelcome advances.

***Normal People,* Sally Rooney.** Lavished with praise by critics, long-listed for the Man Booker Prize in 2018, Sally Rooney's *Normal People* is a modern love story that follows the lives of teenage lovers Marianne and Connell for four years as they move from school in a rural Irish town to Trinity College in Dublin, breaking each other's hearts over and over again. The TV adaptation was a worldwide hit for the BBC.

***Say Nothing: A True Story of Murder and Memory in Northern Ireland,* Patrick Radden Keefe.** A great many lives were damaged or destroyed during the period known as the Troubles, but few stories are as shocking as that of Jean McConville, a 38-year-old widowed mother of 10 who on a frigid December night was abducted from her Belfast apartment by masked assailants, never to be seen alive again. McConville's death serves as the centerpiece of this book, which in itself is part detective story, part historical period piece.

***Small Things Like These,* Claire Keegan.** This Booker Prize short-listed novel set in a 1980s rural town captures the dying days of the Catholic Church's stranglehold on the nation's morals, seen through the eyes of one good man and his encounter with a girl trying to escape from an awful "Magdalen Laundry."

***The Sea,* John Banville.** When Max, a recently widowed art historian, returns to the seaside house he knew as a child, he finds himself caught up in a rush of tangled memories, reliving the loves and losses he experienced across his life. This novel, which tells Max's story in the form of a journal, won the Man Booker Prize in 2005, a decision that proved to be controversial both because it beat out Kazuo Ishiguro's stellar *Never Let Me Go* and because of the author's lack of decorum after accepting the award. Said Banville: "The kind of novels that I write very rarely win the Man Booker Prize, which in general promotes good, middlebrow fiction."

***The Wonder,* Emma Donoghue.** When the story gets out that an 11-year-old girl named Anna appears to be living solely on "manna from heaven," a nurse named Lib travels to rural Ireland from England to aid a nun in determining whether Anna is a genuine manifestation of the divine or part of an elaborate con. This novel from the acclaimed writer of *Room* speaks about both Irish faith and a belief in miracles, but also uses Lib's deep yet casual hatred of the Irish to discuss the prejudice the Irish have faced for far too long.

What to Watch Before Your Trip

***The Crying Game* directed by Neil Jordan.** Set in Northern Ireland during the Troubles, this film centers on a member of the IRA who becomes close with a captured British soldier and develops a friendship that causes him to question his loyalty. This film earned fans in both the United Kingdom and the United States, and won a BAFTA Award for Best British Film and an Academy Award for Best Original Screenplay.

***Derry Girls* directed by Lisa McGee**. *Derry Girls* straddles kind of a funny line, in the sense that it's both an ensemble sitcom about a group of adolescent schoolgirls and a period piece about Northern Ireland during the Troubles. That unusual combination helps to keep it lively, though, as it gives you an idea of what it was like to lead a normal life in Northern Ireland, without getting hung up on the legitimately grim details that define so many stories from the era. It also helps that it's both funny and ridiculous, making it a lighter choice and suitable for bingeing.

***The Field* directed by Jim Sheridan.** When a curmudgeonly Irish farmer unceremoniously dumps a murdered donkey in a lake, it sets off a complicated feud centered on land rights, encroaching commercial development, and unresolved family trauma. Incredibly, none of these issues were particularly unusual during the 1930s in Ireland, when questions about the country's future, and who was entitled to its land and heritage, were very much in flux. While the subject matter is vital, the film's all-star cast (including John Hurt, Sean Bean, Richard Harris, Brenda Fricker, and Tom Berenger) has also helped to cement it as a classic.

***The Guard* directed by John Michael McDonagh.** *The Guard* is as Irish as a police buddy comedy can be: funny, but also decidedly grim. In this film, an unhappy, irresponsible sergeant (Brendan Gleeson) partners with a straight-man FBI investigator (Don Cheadle) to try to get to the bottom of a murder potentially connected to several wanted Irish drug runners. Gleeson and Cheadle play off each other marvelously, and the performances and twisting plot helped it become the single most commercially successful independent Irish film in history.

***The Irish Pub* directed by Alex Fegan.** This friendly documentary from director Alex Fegan centers on that most famous of Irish institutions: the humble pub. Watching this film impresses upon the viewer that one of the great treats of visiting Ireland isn't just a chance to drink in an honest-to-goodness Irish pub, but is really about spending some time in a friendly place where you'll be treated well. If you're looking for a movie to get you ready for a trip to Ireland, this is the perfect choice.

***Michael Collins* directed by Neil Jordan.** Michael Collins's role in Irish history, both as a politician and as a violent revolutionary, cannot be overstated. This film, which stars Liam Neeson in the title role, delves into the violence and intrigue that defined the final years of England's rule over Ireland. It's a top-notch action-oriented drama and, while it takes some liberties with the actual history of the time, it's still well worth watching.

***My Left Foot* directed by Jim Sheridan.** Daniel Day-Lewis built his reputation by being a committed character actor, and nowhere is this more evident than in *My Left Foot*. In a truly remarkable, award-winning performance, Day-Lewis portrays a young man from a poor, working-class Irish family with severe cerebral palsy. While his condition greatly limits his ability to move, he learns to express himself creatively using only his left foot, an act which helps him more

What to Watch Before Your Trip

deeply integrate with his family, and later, his community.

***Philomena* directed by Stephen Frears.** When an Irish teenager named Philomena Lee becomes pregnant, her father forces her to move to a convent in Roscrea. There, after being forced to work as an indentured servant for several years, the nuns abruptly give her son up for adoption without her consent. Nearly 50 years later, British journalist Martin Sixsmith embarks on a journey with Philomena to find her son and discover why things unfurled the way they did. This extremely well-received movie is billed as a comedic drama, but it's also heartwarming and blood-curdling, and the fact that it's based on a true story only enhances how you'll feel about the secrets it uncovers.

***The Banshees of Inisherin* directed by Martin McDonagh.** A black comedy about two old friends living in an isolated island community. When one suddenly calls an end to their friendship it unleashes unforeseen results.

***The Quiet Man* directed by John Ford.** John Ford is a legendary director, and this film, a romantic comedy from the 1950s, is one of his lesser-known gems. Filmed in a village by Ashford Castle, *The Quiet Man* sees John Wayne play an Irish-American man from Pittsburgh who returns to purchase the farm that is his family's ancestral home. The pastoral setting and the performances of both Wayne and Maureen O'Hara helped Ford earn his fourth Academy Award for Best Director.

***Rebellion* directed by Colin Teevan**. This miniseries is a lush period piece set around the Easter Rising in 1916, which saw Irish Republicans stage an armed insurrection during the height of World War I in order to break away from British rule. It's a gorgeously shot, meticulously crafted show that portrays the uncertainty and chaos that ruled during this time in Ireland's history. The second season is set during the Irish War of Independence.

***The Secret of Kells* directed by Tomm Moore and Nora Twomey.** While the real *Book of Kells*—a highly ornate illuminated manuscript—is on display at Trinity College Library in Dublin, this animated film is about its creation and importance to the monks who kept it safe. The telling of the story might not be *entirely* historically accurate (there are bloodthirsty Vikings and fairies in equal supply), but it is a spectacular and beautiful movie about a real piece of art that, if you find yourself in Dublin, you absolutely should see in person.

***The Wind That Shakes the Barley* directed by Ken Loach.** Set during the Irish Civil War in the early 1920s, this film centers on two brothers from County Cork who have joined the Irish Republican Army in order to repel British forces. For many years it was the highest-grossing independent film in Ireland's history (*The Guard* now holds that honor), a testament to its popularity. Cillian Murphy's performance is particularly noteworthy, and this film was made during the height of his acting career in the mid-2000s.

***The Young Offenders* directed by Peter Foott.** Shot in Cork, *The Young Offenders* follows two thickheaded youths who—after hearing about a cocaine-filled ship that has capsized off the coast—decide to try earn their fortune by recovering a bale that has reportedly not yet been found. While the main characters are as dense as they are unlucky, this comedy has developed a bit of a cult following both because the characters are remarkably likeable and the story is as funny as it is lively.

Chapter 2

TRAVEL SMART

Updated by
Anto Howard

★ CAPITAL:
Dublin

POPULATION:
4,995,000

LANGUAGE:
Irish and English

$ CURRENCY:
Euro

COUNTRY CODE:
353

⚠ EMERGENCIES:
999

DRIVING:
On the left

ELECTRICITY:
230 volts/50 cycles; electrical plugs have three prongs

TIME:
5 hours ahead of New York

WEB RESOURCES:
www.discoverireland.ie; www.tourismni.com; www.irelands-blue-book.ie

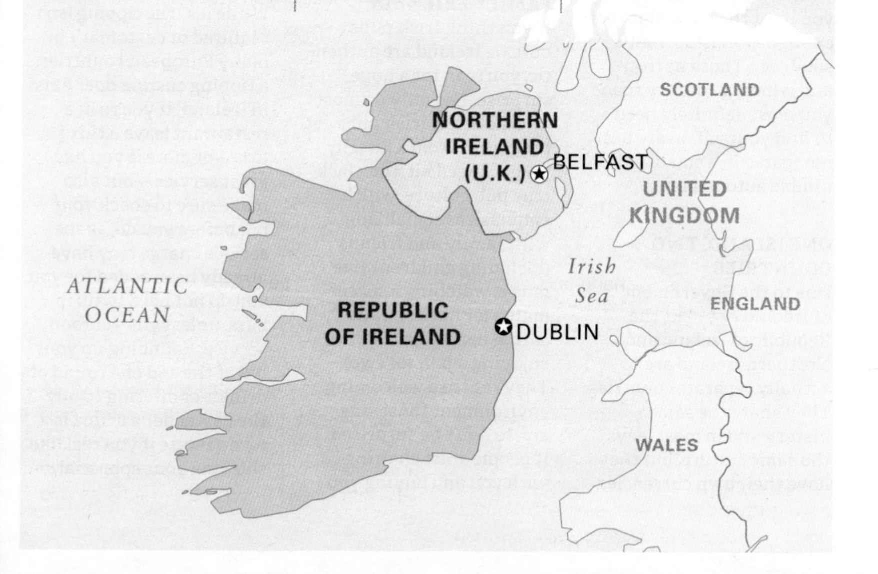

Know Before You Go

YOU'LL BE GRAND

Much of the fun in Ireland—and some of your best memories—will involve just winging it, wandering off the beaten path, getting stuck in traffic behind a herd of cows or sheep, and interacting with locals.

PEOPLE DRIVE ON THE LEFT SIDE OF THE ROAD

This is a simple one, but essential to remember—in Ireland, as in England, people drive on the left-hand side of the road, which any local will tell you is the "right" side of the road. This means that when you rent a car, yes, the driver's seat will be on the right-hand side, and the clutch will be on the driver's left. You may have to do a few rounds of the first roundabout as you leave the airport while your brain adjusts, but you'll get the hang of it soon enough. Bonus tip: rent a small car. Those narrow and winding country roads you most definitely need to find yourself on are best navigated in a small and nimble automobile.

ONE ISLAND, TWO COUNTRIES

Due to the Government of Ireland Act 1920, the Republic of Ireland and Northern Ireland are actually separate countries. They share the same history and in most ways the same culture, but they have their own currencies and differences in language. There's also a border between the two countries, but border crossings are inconspicuously labeled and you won't be stopped at a checkpoint or asked for a passport. This ease of travel was one of the most contentious parts of Brexit, but there is no hard border and fortunately, little has changed for the visitor to Ireland and Northern Ireland.

PUBS ARE FAMILY-FRIENDLY

If you think Irish pubs outside Ireland are authentic, you're in for a huge surprise. Not only do most international Irish pubs get their stuff from a kitschy prepackaged kit, they lack true pub culture, which emphasizes socializing with family and friends (including children), live music, watching a soccer match (or hurling), and eating hearty grub while enjoying a pint (or two). They're also a welcoming environment for strangers, so don't be surprised if people start chatting with you and buying you drinks—just keep in mind you're expected to return the favor.

YOU DON'T NEED TO BE A LORD OR LADY TO STAY IN A CASTLE

While Ireland has its share of trendy new hotels with slick lobbies and amenities, this country's incredible history, and care in preserving it, means that there are a number of castles and estates all over the country that offer lodging. For at least one or two special nights on your trip, splurge to stay in a historic mansion or castle where you can enjoy a prim and proper afternoon tea with hot scones in the wood-paneled salon of a storied estate, or gaze over the ramparts of an honest-to-goodness 15th-century castle. If you've ever had *Downton Abbey*–esque daydreams, this is the way to go.

DON'T TIP THE BARMAN

While it's true tipping isn't required or customary in many European countries, a tipping custom does exist in Ireland. If you're in a restaurant leave a tip of 10%—or more if you had great service—but also make sure to check your bill before you do, as the service charge may have already been added for you. You do not need to tip in bars, unless you get food service. Rounding up your bill at the end of a round of drinks, or offering to buy the bartender a drink, is a nice gesture if you feel like showing your appreciation.

A HERITAGE CARD IS A MUST

Ireland's National Monuments and National Historic Properties are run by the government and many charge an entry fee. By purchasing a flat-rate Heritage Card you gain access to all of these sites (minus one, Muckross Traditional Farms in Killarney). This includes more than 75 heritage sites all over the country, some of which are among the most popular places to visit in Ireland, like Kilmainham Jail, the Rock of Cashel, Muckross House, Kilkenny Castle, Glendalough, Brú na Bóinne, and Clonmacnoise. Plus you can get a discounted rate on the card if you're a senior, a child, a student (make sure to bring a valid student ID), or if you buy a family card. If you plan to visit a number of historic sites this is a great option, but do bear in mind that not every site charges admission, so you should plan your visits in advance to make sure this represents a good savings. Heritage Cards can be purchased at many historic sites, or you can order one by mail, fax, or phone.

IT'S JUST RAIN AND IT WILL PASS

It's not exactly news that it rains in Ireland—hence the lush green valleys and meadows—but it may be a surprise that the weather can be so changeable. Ireland's weather is generally temperate, but stormy weather can roll in and out without warning, and foggy, chilly conditions are common year-round. Watch the morning weather forecast and you will be none the wiser. In fact, you may laugh to see every weather possibility proposed for your day, from hail, a "chance of showers," and treacherous roads due to frost, to "sunny spells" and sun showers. You can get four seasons in one day, sometimes in one hour. All you need to know is that you should not let the weather interfere with your plans, because it will pass. Pack accordingly

DON'T SAY "TOP OF THE MORNIN'" TO ANYONE

Unless you want to be rude, off-putting, or just ignored, you might want to avoid dropping the cheesy Irish sayings when speaking to actual Irish people. Contrary to Hollywood's version of Ireland, people do not greet each other with "Top o' the Mornin' to ye," or depart with a blessing about the road rising up. Lucky Charms and Irish Spring soap might also be questionable to invoke. Plain English is fine until you pick up some more authentic local lingo.

SUMMER DAYS ARE 18 HOURS LONG

Ireland's location in the northern hemisphere means that at the height of the summer the sun sets after 11 pm, providing a total of about 18 hours of daylight. Conversely, during the winter the sun sets in the early afternoon, around 4 pm. Obviously, it is more expensive to visit Ireland in summer, but you really do get bang for your buck with long, leisurely evenings to enjoy the bounty of summer festivals, prolonged sightseeing, and long walks in the beautiful countryside. If you visit in winter, plan your schedule so that your walks and outdoor sightseeing happen in the earlier part of the day, and fill the darker evenings with museums, cultural events, and pubs.

THERE'S MORE TO IRISH FOOD THAN MEAT AND POTATOES

Stereotypes that Irish food is largely centered on potatoes, beef, and lamb are actually pretty fair, but keep in mind that Ireland is an island surrounded by cold Atlantic waters, which means it's a wonderland for certain types of seafood. Smoked fish such as salmon, trout, and mackerel are delicious and easy to find, as is bread made with seaweed (laver), and beautiful oysters. There are 22 Michelin-starred restaurants in Ireland: 18 are one-star restaurants and Dublin's Restaurant Patrick Guilbaud, Chapter One, Liath and Kildare's Aimsir are the only ones with two-star status.

SUNDAYS ARE SLOW DAYS

Ireland doesn't exactly shut down on Sunday as it did in days of old, but it is a day when many businesses (including restaurants) are either closed or have shortened hours, especially outside major cities. Sunday is a great day for sports, and you can always stop by a pub.

Getting Here

Air

Flying time to Ireland is 6½ hours from New York, 7½ hours from Chicago, 10 hours from Los Angeles, and one hour from London.

Flying into Ireland involves few hassles, although an increase in traffic in the last decade has caused a slight increase in flight delays and time spent waiting for baggage to clear customs. There are limited domestic flights within Ireland, including Dublin-Donegal and Dublin-Kerry, plus short flights to the Aran Islands. Checking in and boarding an outbound plane tends to be civilized. Security is professional but not overbearing, and airport staffers are usually helpful and patient. In the busy summer season the lines can get long, and you should play it safe by arriving a couple of hours before your flight.

AIRPORTS

The major gateways to Ireland are Dublin Airport (DUB) on the east coast, 10 km (6 miles) north of the city center, and Shannon Airport (SNN) on the west coast, 25 km (16 miles) west of Limerick. Cork Airport (ORK) also has regular flights to U.K. cities and around the EU. Two airports serve Belfast: Belfast International Airport (BFS) at Aldergrove, 24 km (15 miles) from the city, handles local and U.K. flights, as well as international traffic; George Best Belfast City Airport (BHD), 6½ km (4 miles) from the city, handles local and U.K. flights only. In addition, the City of Derry Airport (LDY) receives flights from Liverpool, London Stansted, and Glasgow in the United Kingdom. If you plan to visit mainly the Southwest of Ireland, use Cork Airport (ORK), which handles flights from the United Kingdom, as well as from Boston, Paris, Mlaga, and Rome.

FLIGHTS

From North America and the United Kingdom, Aer Lingus, the national flag carrier, has the greatest number of direct flights to Ireland.

Aer Lingus flies to Shannon and Dublin from New York's JFK (John F. Kennedy Airport), Chicago's O'Hare, Washington Dulles, Boston, Philadelphia, San Francisco, Seattle, Los Angeles, Miami, and Orlando. Delta has a daily departure from New York's JFK to Dublin, and American Airlines flies to Dublin from New York's JFK and Chicago. United flies direct to Dublin, Shannon, and Belfast, departing daily from Newark Liberty International Airport in New Jersey. Except for special offers, prices for the airlines tend to be similar. London to Dublin is one of the world's busiest international routes. Aer Lingus, British Airways, and CityJet all have several daily flights. Ryanair—famous for its cheap, no-frills service—runs several daily flights from London Gatwick, Luton, and Stansted airports to Dublin, Kerry, Shannon, Cork, and Ireland West Airport Knock. Though the era of dirt cheap flights is over, with such healthy competition, bargains can still be found. British Airways, Flybe, and EasyJet run regularly scheduled flights to Belfast from Birmingham, Manchester, London Gatwick, Luton, and Stansted airports.

Within Ireland, there are services from Dublin to Kerry and Donegal.

Boat

TO AND FROM IRELAND

Ferries are a convenient way to travel between Ireland and elsewhere in Europe, particularly the United Kingdom. There are four main ferry ports in Ireland—two in the republic at Dublin Port and Rosslare, and two in Northern Ireland at Belfast and Larne. The cost of your trip can vary substantially, so compare prices carefully. Bear in mind, too, that flying can be cheaper, so look into all types of transportation before booking.

Irish Ferries operates the *Ulysses,* the world's largest car ferry, between Dublin and Holyhead, Wales (three hours, 15 minutes); there's also a swift service (one hour, 50 minutes) between these two ports. There are several trips daily. The company also runs between Rosslare and Pembroke, Wales (four hours), and has service to France. Stena Line sails several times a day between Dublin and Holyhead (three hours, 15 minutes). The company also runs a fast craft (two hours) and a superferry (three hours) between Belfast and Stranraer, Scotland, as well as a fast craft (two hours) between Rosslare and Fishguard, Wales. There are several trips daily on both routes.

P&O Irish Sea vessels run between Larne and Troon, Scotland (two hours), a couple of times a day. The company also sails from Dublin to Liverpool twice daily (eight hours), with a choice of daytime or overnight sailings.

Brittany Ferries offers an overnight service from Cork to Roscoff in France and Bilbao in northern Spain.

WITHIN IRELAND

There is regular service to the Aran Islands from Ros an Mhíl (Rossaveal) in County Galway and Doolin in County Clare. Ferries also sail to Inishbofin (off the Galway coast) and Arranmore (off the Donegal coast), and to Bere, Whiddy, Sherkin, and the Cape Clear Islands off the coast of County Cork. Bere and Whiddy have a car ferry, but the other islands are all small enough to explore on foot, so the ferries are for foot passengers and bicycles only. Other islands—the Blaskets and the Skelligs in Kerry, Rathlin in Antrim, and Tory, off the Donegal coast—have seasonal ferry services between May and September, less frequently the rest of the year. Fáilte Ireland publishes a free guide and map with ferry details.

Bus

In the Republic of Ireland, long-distance bus service is operated by Bus Éireann, which also provides local service in Cork, Galway, Limerick, and Waterford. There's only one class, and prices are similar for all seats. Note, though, that outside of the peak season, service is limited; some routes (e.g., to the Ring of Kerry) disappear altogether.

Bus Éireann's Expressway buses go directly, in the straightest available line, from one biggish town to another, stopping at a limited number of designated places. There's sometimes only one trip a day on express routes.

A round-trip from Dublin to Cork costs around €25, and a Dublin-to-Galway City round-trip is around €23.

TIP→ Prepaid tickets don't apply to a particular bus time, just a route, so show up at least 30 minutes early to get a seat.

Getting Here

Rural bus service, which rambles around the countryside passing through as many villages as possible, shuts down at around 7 or 8 pm. To ensure that a bus journey is feasible, check online or ask at the nearest bus station. Many of the destination indicators are in Irish (Gaelic), so make sure you get on the right bus.

Citylink, a Galway-based company, has service between Galway, Limerick, Cork, Clifden, and Dublin, as well as Cork and Dublin airports. Prices are competitive, with the two-hour, 45-minute journey from Dublin Airport to Galway costing no more than €18 one-way. This can be cut to two hours, 30 minutes by using the Citylink's Eireagle service, which travels direct to the airport, bypassing the city center. All buses have complimentary Wi-Fi.

Aircoach operates a similar service, with Wi-Fi on most buses, between Dublin, Cork, and Belfast and their respective airports. The three-hour journey from Cork to Dublin costs €20 one-way. Online fares can be cheaper, and booking online guarantees you a seat and priority boarding, ahead of those paying in cash.

IN NORTHERN IRELAND

All buses in Northern Ireland are operated by the state-owned Translink. Goldline is the long-distance bus division, while Ulsterbus runs local services. Service is generally good, with particularly useful links to towns not served by train. Ulsterbus also runs tours. Eurolines buses run from London and from Birmingham, making the Stranraer–Port of Belfast crossing.

FARES AND PASSES

You can buy tickets online, at tourist offices, at bus stations, or on buses (though it's cash-only for the latter option).

You can save money with multiday passes, some of which can be combined with rail service. Consider the Irish Explorer Rail and Bus Pass, which gives you five days out of 15 of bus and rail travel for €160. An iLink Card costs £60 for seven days of unlimited bus and rail travel in Northern Ireland—a great deal when you consider that a one-day ticket costs £16.50.

Some cost-cutting passes include both Northern Ireland and the Republic of Ireland. An Irish Rover bus ticket for travel on Ulsterbus and Bus Éireann covers Ireland, north and south. It also includes city-center bus travel in Cork, Waterford, Limerick, Galway, and on the Metro services in Belfast—but not Dublin.

 Car

U.S. driver's licenses are recognized in Ireland.

Roads in the Irish Republic are generally good, with four-lane highways, or motorways, connecting Dublin with Waterford, Cork, Limerick, Shannon Airport, Galway, and Newry on the border with Northern Ireland. Service areas with restrooms and food are gradually being added; meanwhile, you may have to leave the motorway for comfort stops, usually located in gas stations. National routes and minor roads are slower, but much more scenic. On rural roads, watch out for cattle and sheep.

ROAD SIGNS

Road signs in the republic are generally posted in both Irish and English; destinations in which Irish is the spoken language are signposted only in Irish. The most important one to know is "An Daingean," which is now the official name of Dingle Town.

■ TIP→ If you get lost at any stage feel free to ask a local for directions—they love nothing more than a chat with a stranger plus a chance to show off their knowledge of the "best" way to get from A to B.

Traffic signs are the same as in the rest of Europe. On the newer green signposts, distances are in kilometers; on some of the old white signposts they're still miles. Most important, speed limits are posted in the republic (but not in Northern Ireland) in kilometers.

There are no border checkpoints between the Irish Republic and Northern Ireland, where the road network is excellent and, outside Belfast, uncrowded. Road signs and traffic regulations conform to the British system.

CAR FERRIES

All ferries on both principal routes to the Irish Republic welcome cars. Fishguard and Pembroke are relatively easy to reach by road. The car trip to Holyhead, on the other hand, is sometimes difficult: delays on the A55 North Wales coastal road aren't unusual.

ROAD CONDITIONS

Most roads are paved and make for easy travel. Roads designated with an *M* for "motorway" are double-lane divided highways with paved shoulders; *N*, or "national," routes are generally undivided highways with shoulders; and *R*, or "regional," roads tend to be narrow and twisty.

Rush-hour traffic in Dublin, Cork, Limerick, Belfast, and Galway can be intense. Rush hours in Dublin run 7 to 9:30 am and 5 to 7 pm; special events such as soccer matches also tie up traffic in and around the city, as does heavy rain.

Train

Irish Rail trains are generally reliable, reasonably priced, and comfortable. You can easily reach all the principal towns from Dublin, though service between provincial cities can be roundabout. To get to Cork City from Wexford, for example, you have to go via Limerick Junction. It's often quicker, though perhaps less comfortable, to take a bus. Most mainline trains have one standard class. Round-trip tickets are usually cheapest. The best deals are available online, booking at least one week in advance.

Northern Ireland Railways has three main rail routes, all operating out of Belfast's Central Station: north to Derry via Ballymena and Coleraine, east to Bangor along the shores of Belfast Lough, and south to Dublin and the Irish Republic. Note that Eurail Passes aren't valid in Northern Ireland.

There's only one class of train travel in Ireland (with the exception of the express trains between Dublin and Belfast, which have first-class and standard-class tickets). Seat reservations are part of the package if you book online on Dublin–Cork and Dublin–Belfast routes, but otherwise it's first-come, first-served.

■ TIP→ Get to the station at least 30 minutes ahead to ensure a seat. It's not uncommon on busier routes to find all the seats are occupied.

Essentials

Dining

MEALS AND MEALTIMES

Breakfast is served from 7 to 10 am, lunch runs from 12:30 to 2:30 pm, and dinners are usually mid-evening occasions with last orders at 9 pm. Unless otherwise noted, the restaurants listed are open daily for lunch and dinner.

Pubs are generally open Monday through Thursday 10:30 am–11:30 pm and Friday and Saturday 10:30 am–12:30 am. On Sunday, pubs are open 12:30 pm–11 pm or later on certain Sundays. These hours are due to be extended at time of publication. All pubs close on Christmas Day, but hotel bars are open for guests. Legislation being debated at the time of publishing intends to further liberalize these opening hours.

Pubs in Northern Ireland are open 11:30 am–11 pm Monday–Saturday and 12:30–2:30 pm and 7–10 pm on Sunday (note that Sunday hours are at the owner's or manager's discretion).

Children under the age of 18 cannot enter a pub after 9 pm (or 10 pm May to September).

Smoking is banned in all restaurants and pubs, although it is allowed in outside beer gardens.

PRICES

⇨ *Prices in the reviews are the average cost of a main course at dinner or, if dinner is not served, at lunch. Restaurant reviews have been shortened. For full information, visit Fodors.com.*

What It Costs in Euros and Pounds

$	$$	$$$	$$$$
AT DINNER (IRELAND)			
under €19	€19–€24	€25–€32	over €32
AT DINNER (NORTHERN IRELAND)			
under £20	£20–£30	£31–£35	over £35

Health

COVID-19

COVID-19 has disrupted travel since March 2020, and travelers should expect sporadic ongoing issues. Always travel with a mask in case it's required, and keep up-to-date on the most recent testing and vaccination guidelines for Ireland.

Lodging

In Dublin and other cities, boutique hotels blend luxury with contemporary (and often truly Irish) design. Manors and castles boast a unique combination of luxury and history. Less impressive, but equally charming, are the provincial inns and country hotels with simple but adequate facilities.

You'll meet a cross section of Irish people by hopping from one bed-and-breakfast to the next, or you can keep to yourself for a week or two in a thatched cottage. B&Bs approved by Tourism Ireland display a green shamrock outside. Hotels and other accommodations in Northern Ireland are similar to those in the Republic of Ireland.

Fáilte Ireland has a grading system and maintains a list of registered hotels, guesthouses, B&Bs, farmhouses, hostels, and campgrounds. For each accommodation, the list gives a maximum charge that can't be exceeded without special authorization. Prices must be displayed in every room; if the hotel oversteps its limit, don't hesitate to complain.

■ TIP→ Don't depend on the address used on your accommodation provider's website. Request an Eircode (🌐 *www.eircode.ie*), which gives the exact location of every property in Ireland.

CASTLES AND MANORS

In line with the overall recovery in the hotel industry, Ireland's luxury heritage hotels like Adare Manor (County Limerick), Dromoland Castle (County Clare), and Ashford Castle (County Mayo) have undergone significant restorations recently. Smaller manor houses set on private estates still retain the essence of their original purpose and can be booked through Ireland's Blue Book of Country Houses & Restaurants or Hidden Ireland.

COTTAGES

Vacation cottages, which are usually in clusters, are rented by the week. Although often built in the traditional style, most have central heating and other modern conveniences. It's essential to reserve in advance.

PRICES

⇨ *Prices are the average cost of a double room during high season, not including especially expensive holiday or special-event rates. Hotel reviews have been shortened. For full information, visit Fodors.com.*

What It Costs in Euros and Pounds

$	$$	$$$	$$$$
FOR TWO PEOPLE (IRELAND)			
under €170	€170–€230	€231–€300	over €300
FOR TWO PEOPLE (NORTHERN IRELAND)			
under £82	£82–£115	£116–£160	over £160

Taxes

When leaving the Irish Republic, U.S. and Canadian visitors can apply for and get a refund of the value-added tax (V.A.T.), which currently accounts for a hefty 23% of the purchase price of many goods and 13.5% of some others. Not all stores take part in this tax back scheme, so you need to inquire before you buy. Accommodations and restaurants charge 9% V.A.T., while most items of interest to visitors, right down to ordinary toilet soap, are rated at 23%. Value-added tax is not refundable on accommodations, car rental, meals, or any other form of personal services received on vacation.

Tipping

In some hotels and restaurants, a service charge of around 10%—rising to 15% in plush spots—is added to the bill. If in doubt, ask whether service is included. If there's no service charge, add a minimum of 10% to the total. Taxi drivers or hackney cab drivers, who make the trip for a prearranged sum, don't expect tips. Tip hotel porters at least €1 per suitcase. You don't tip in pubs, but for table service in a bar, a hotel lounge, or a Dublin lounge bar, leave about €2.

Essentials

Tipping Guidelines for Ireland	
Bellhop	€2–€3, depending on the level of the hotel
Hotel Concierge	€5 or more if he or she performs a special service for you
Hotel Doorman	€2–€3 if he helps you get a cab
Hotel Maid	€1–€3 per day (either daily or at the end of your stay, in cash)
Hotel Room-Service Waiter	€2–€3 per delivery, even if a service charge has been added
Restroom Attendant	Restroom attendants in more expensive restaurants expect some small change or €1
Taxi Driver	10%, or just round up the fare to the next euro amount
Tour Guide	10% of the cost of the tour
Valet Parking Attendant	€2–€3, but only when you get your car
Waiter	Just small change (up to a euro or two) to round out your bill if service is already included; otherwise, add 10%

Tours

Guided tours are a good option when either you don't have time to figure it all out for yourself or you're looking for some local perspective and the ease of someone else handling the details. The companies here all run tours to Ireland on a "land-only" basis. A land-only tour includes all your travel (by bus, in most cases) once you arrive in the destination country, but not necessarily your flights. Remember that you'll be expected to tip your guide (in cash) at the end of the tour.

GENERAL TOURS

CIE Tours International is one of the biggest and longest-established tour operators in the Irish market. It runs a selection of fully inclusive, escorted bus tours, or independent fly-drive vacations. An eight-day itinerary with car rental and confirmed hotel bookings starts at €1,745 per person. Starting in Dublin, the Heritage Tour is a seven-day bus tour that takes in Blarney Castle, the Cliffs of Moher, the Skellig Experience, and the Giant's Causeway, among other attractions, with accommodations in superior hotels.

Discovering Ireland Vacations, a young company set up by three friends, aims to create the best holiday experience by using enthusiastic local guides. A customized, eight-day self-driven "Highlight of Ireland" tour starts at €818 per person. The price includes seven nights at a B&B, car rental, and toll-free calls to your vacation specialist. Escorted bus tours include the Irish Spirit 8 Days, which includes one day in Dublin, a drive to Blarney Castle via the Rock of Cashel, Killarney, the Ring of Kerry, and the Cliffs of Moher. Rates start at €2,689 per person.

Vagabond Small-Group Tours of Ireland specializes in off-the-beaten-track tours of Ireland, with small group sizes that allow for a more personal experience, smaller buses, and smaller hotel and guesthouse options. Tours visit the essential, iconic sites such as Blarney Castle, the Cliffs of Moher, and the Ring of Kerry, along with less-trafficked gems like the Beara Peninsula and wild Donegal. Vagabond

Adventure tours offer a more active experience (with hiking, horse riding, cycling, and kayaking) while the Driftwood tours are geared to visitors looking for a more relaxed, less active experience. Rates start at €1,777 per person.

SPECIAL-INTEREST TOURS

Irish Cycling Safaris pioneered cycling holidays in Ireland and offers easygoing to moderate cycling trips along rural back roads with luggage transfer and accommodations in small family-run hotels and guesthouses. A weeklong off-peak tour of West Cork and Kerry, including Killarney, costs €885 per person. Tour groups are accompanied by a local guide who drives the support van. Alternatively, you can opt for a self-guided tour that includes bike rental, itinerary, luggage transfer, and prebooked accommodations for the same price.

Iron Donkey guided group tours have something for all levels here, from novices to hammerheads. The 10-day West of Ireland itinerary sets out from Ennis and passes through Kilkee, the Cliffs of Moher, the Burren coastline, Connemara, Clifden, and Westport (cost is about €2,250 per person). Super thorough and well-run custom tours will meet you at the first lodging (all great options, incidentally), size your bike, review the route, and prep you for the ride.

Golfbreaks.com can customize a golf getaway for you and also has tours of different regions of Ireland. Its Northern Ireland and the Northwest package include rounds at the legendary Royal County Down and Royal Portrush courses.

A long-established company with self-drive holidays and escorted tours, Isle Inn Tours also has an interesting range of activity holidays and escorted hiking holidays averaging 16–19 km (10–12 miles) a day. You stay in family-run guesthouses and characterful small hotels while walking through scenic areas, including the Donegal coast, the Glens of Antrim, Achill Island, and Mayo. Escorted hiking holiday options (prices vary) include a chauffeur-driven itinerary of the Wild Atlantic Way, combining culture and cuisine with seven nights at four- and five-star hotels, gourmet dinners, and a driver to escort you.

Great Itineraries

The Best of Ireland in a Week

Ireland might be a small island, but it's packed with things to do and see, so a bit of planning goes a long way. If this is your first trip to the Emerald Isle, then Dublin, Galway, and Kerry have to be top of the list. But what else? You can use Dublin as a base for all of the east coast and the Midlands. And from Galway you can take in all the wilds of the West and even some of the Atlantic islands. This weeklong itinerary should help make sure you don't miss out on any of the must-sees. If it's not your first trip, you might find some more unusual options in the extension itineraries that follow.

Dublin, Galway City, and Killarney (County Kerry) are three of the most vibrant, fun places for any visitor, but they also make great base camps for exploring the wild, ancient, and stunning parts of this rugged and beautiful island. From these hubs, you can opt for day trips into the countryside or choose to overnight in a more rural country house or B&B. Either way, the days are very long in summer, and driving times should be comfortable.

DAY 1: DUBLIN

Fly into Dublin and use one of its elegant Georgian hotels as your luxurious base, with **Number 31** a great option. Start the day with a trip to **Trinity College,** Beckett's old stomping ground, and its legendary *Book of Kells.* Take in the elegant architecture of Georgian Dublin with a visit to beautiful **Merrion Square,** with the **National Museum** a definite highlight. After lunch at **Fallon & Byrne,** pay your respects to Dublin's favorite tipple by taking a tour of the impressive **Guinness Storehouse.** As evening falls, head to cobblestoned **Temple Bar,** Dublin's party zone, and join locals in this city-of-1,000-pubs for a foamy pint with traditional dinner at **Gallagher's Boxty House.** For your first night in the city, catch a show at W.B. Yeats's old haunt, the **Abbey Theatre,** or listen to a traditional music session at the wild and wonderful **Cobblestone** pub.

DAY 2: EXCURSIONS FROM DUBLIN

First drive to the Boyne Valley, a short trip north of the capital. Spend the morning walking among the Iron Age ruins of the rolling **Hill of Tara.** After a picnic lunch on top of the hill, drive through ancient **Kells**—one of the centers of early Christianity in Ireland—and then to **Newgrange,** famous for its ancient passage graves. One thousand years older than Stonehenge, the great white-quartz structure merits an hour or two at least. Next take the M50 ring road south around Dublin for a spectacular drive through the County Wicklow mountains. You might want to stop in one of the small, quiet towns along the **Wicklow Way** hiking trail and go for a short hike. Drive on to stately **Powerscourt House,** whose gardens epitomize the glory and grandeur of the Anglo-Irish aristocracy. From the profane to the sacred, head next to the "monastic city" of **Glendalough** and the medieval monastery of the hermit St. Kevin. Repair to Ireland's highest village, Roundwood, for dinner at the town's 17th-century inn. Head back to Dublin for the night.

DAYS 3 AND 4: WEST CORK AND KERRY

An early-morning departure from Dublin and a 3½-hour drive southwest takes you to **Killarney,** at the heart of glorious Kerry and West Cork. The **Cahernane House Hotel** is the ideal refuge from the touristy buzz. Although it has been almost transformed into a Celtic theme park by a flood of visitors, Killarney is a good base for exploring your pick of two great Atlantic-pounded peninsulas: the strikingly

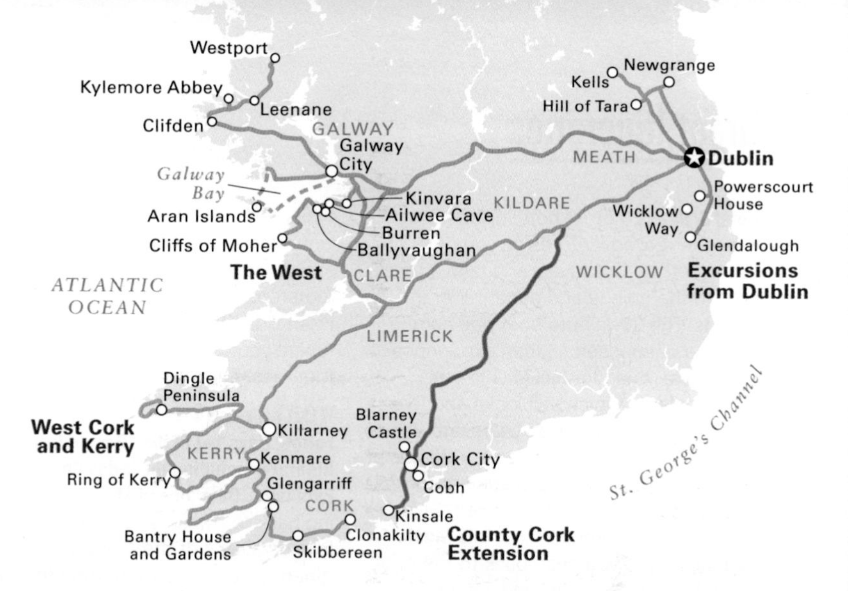

scenic **Ring of Kerry** and the beloved **Dingle Peninsula.** Both offer stunning ocean views, hilly landscapes (like the Macgillycuddy's Reeks mountains), and welcoming towns with great B&Bs. Both drives can be done in a day, or you might choose to focus on one and stop off in the villages along the way or go for a hike. To avoid the crowds in Killarney you could head to serene **Kenmare** for a spot of dinner and some toe-tapping music and dancing, before an overnight in the magnificent **Park Hotel.** The next morning, a beautiful hour-long drive through the mountains and along the coast takes you to the small towns of **West Cork** and the kind of landscape that inspired Ireland's nickname, the Emerald Isle. **Skibbereen, Clonakilty,** and **Glengarriff** are all magical places to spend a few hours and maybe do a little crafts shopping. Finish your drive at picture-perfect **Bantry House and Gardens** where you can splurge on an authentic 18th-century room with stunning views of the bay. Alternatively, head back to Killarney for the night.

DAYS 5–7: THE WEST

An almost three-hour drive north from Killarney will take you straight to **Galway City,** the urban center of the wild and ancient West. But don't make the mistake of rushing through the wonders of County Clare. Take a detour straight for the jaw-dropping 710-foot-high **Cliffs of Moher,** perhaps the single most impressive sight in Ireland. After lunch in the waterside village of **Ballyvaughan** spend a couple of hours exploring the lunar landscape of the harsh, limestone **Burren.** In spring, it becomes a mighty rock garden of exotic colors. If you still have time you could take in the 2-million-year-old **Ailwee Cave** and the picture-perfect village of **Kinvara** before you hit Galway. An evening out in that city is a must, as it's always brim full of music, theater, and truly great seafood. Next morning head northwest to the tiny village of **Clifden,** with some of the country's best Atlantic views. From here, head east through one of the most beautiful stretches of road in Connemara—through Kylemore Valley, home of **Kylemore Abbey,** a huge Gothic Revival castle. After seeing the castle and its grounds, head north through tiny **Leenane** (the setting of the hit Broadway play, *The Beauty Queen of Leenane*) and on to the most attractive town in County Mayo, **Westport.** It's the perfect spot to spend the night: the 18th-century planned town is on an inlet of Clew Bay, and some of the west coast's finest beaches are nearby. The cozy and spectacularly located **Knockranny House**

Great Itineraries

Hotel & Spa is a great hotel option. Day 7 is one of real adventures as you drive an hour south to Rossaveal and take a small boat to the unique and beautiful Aran Islands. The 20-minute boat ride carries you to a quintessential Irish experience. If possible, head for **Inis Meáin,** the middle island, which still looks and feels much as it did a hundred years ago. It's perfect for walking (there's no traffic) and you'll most likely have the ancient tombs and Christian ruins all to yourself. Enjoy a bit of sweater shopping at **Inis Meáin Knitting** before you head back to the boat. Once back on the mainland it's time for the drive back to Dublin. The Georgian luxury and comfort of the **Merrion Hotel** should make your last night in Ireland memorable.

Ireland In Depth

If you have more than a week, these easy add-ons will help you prioritize your time.

COUNTY CORK EXTENSION, 2 DAYS

Follow Day 1 of the "Best of Ireland" Itinerary. Days 2 and 3. On your way from Dublin to West Cork, detour for **Cork City,** a great walking city of bridges and winding hilly streets. A visit to the colorful **English Market** can be combined with a hearty Irish lunch. A few miles outside Cork sits the 15th-century **Blarney Castle,** where you can kiss the famous stone. After your visit, drive to the foodie paradise that is **Kinsale.** Try to take in a serene harbor cruise to help build an appetite. Spend the night at the Georgian **Friar's Lodge.** In the morning on your way out of town, stop off at the unique **Charles Fort,** one of Europe's best-preserved star forts situated atop a sheer cliff face. *Titanic* history buffs will want to stop off at **The Queenstown Story of Cobh Heritage Centre,** which tells the story of the great transatlantic liners. The nearby ***Titanic* Experience** allows visitors to literally follow in the footsteps of embarking passengers. From Cobh, it's only 1½ hours to Killarney where you can pick up Days 2 and 3 of the "Best Of Ireland" Itinerary.

NORTHWEST EXTENSION, 2 DAYS

Follow Days 1–7 of the "Best of Ireland" Itinerary, including the 2-day County Cork Extension. Days 10 and 11. Instead of heading back to Dublin after visiting the Aran Islands (Day 7 of the "Best Of Ireland" Itinerary), drive north through the heart of **Yeats Country** in Sligo. Just north of cozy **Sligo Town** is the stark outline of a great hill, **Ben Bulben,** in whose shadow poet W.B. Yeats wanted to be buried. South of town, follow the signposted Yeats Trail around woody, gorgeously scenic **Lough Gill.** Continuing north, you pass W.B.'s simple grave in unassuming **Drumcliff,** a 3000 BC tomb in **Creevykeel,** and small but vibrant **Donegal Town.** Eat some local seafood then spend the night at the **Central Hotel,** and the next morning head north along the tight, meandering roads of the stunning Donegal coastline. Two wild, breathtaking natural wonders are must-sees on this stretch of coastline. First, the tiny hamlet of **Glencolumbkille** clings dramatically to the rock-bound harbor of Glen Bay. The cliffs surrounding the tiny village rise up to 700 feet and are awash with prehistoric cairns. Keep driving north through the Gaeltacht (Irish-speaking) region and head inland for the mountains, lakes, and moorlands of glorious **Glenveagh National Park.** A beautiful drive through the mountains and past serene **Gartan Lough** will take you to Derry and a night at the Victorian **Merchant's House.** This is ideal for the start of the Northern Ireland Extension below.

NORTHERN IRELAND EXTENSION

Days 12 and 13. Begin exploring the province in historic, divided **Derry City** (called Londonderry by unionists), Northern Ireland's second city. A few hours are sufficient to take in the views from the old city walls and the fascinating murals of the Catholic Bogside district. Continue on to two of the region's main attractions, the 13th-century Norman fortress of **Dunluce Castle** and the **Giant's Causeway,** shaped from volcanic rock some 60 million years ago. Heading south, sticking to coastal roads for the best scenery, you'll soon pass through the **Glens of Antrim,** whose green hills roll down into the sea. Tucked in the glens are a number of small, unpretentious towns with great hotels. Spend the night in the traditional inn that is the **Londonderry Arms Hotel** in serene Carnlough. Early in the morning, head straight to Northern Ireland's capital, **Belfast.** The old port city, gray and often wet, is a fascinating place, recovering from years of strife. A **Black Taxi Tour** is a brilliant way to get to the heart of this old city. Follow this with a visit to the hugely impressive ***Titanic* Belfast** before you start heading back to Dublin. If you're ahead of schedule, take the longer route that passes through the glorious **Mountains of Mourne** and around icy-blue **Carlingford Lough.** Arrive back in Dublin for a final night at the luxurious **Merrion Hotel** before flying home in the morning.

By Car: Some Tips

Road signs are generally posted in both Irish and English, although in Gaeltacht areas new laws mandate signs in Irish only (most such regions are located in the counties along the western coast of the country—Donegal and Connemara, in particular). If traveling in these areas, invest in a detailed map with both Irish and English names.

Another new law has mandated that all speed-limit signs be posted in kilometers—not miles—per hour. Slow down on smaller, countryside lanes and roads: traffic jams can sometimes be caused by flocks of sheep and herds of cattle, not cars.

New divided highways are the fastest way to get from one point to another, but use caution: highways sometimes end as abruptly as they begin.

Contacts

Air

Belfast International Airport. 028/9448–4848 *www.belfastairport.com.* **City of Derry Airport.** 028/7181–0784 *www.cityofderryairport.com.* **Cork Airport.** 021/431–3131 *www.corkairport.com.* **Dublin Airport.** (DUB). 01/814–1111 *www.dublinairport.com.* **George Best Belfast City Airport.** 028/9093–9093 *www.belfastcityairport.com.* **Shannon Airport.** (SNN). 061/712–000 *www.shannonairport.ie.*

Boat/Ferry

Brittany Ferries. *Cork City* 021/427–7801 *in Ireland* *brittanyferries.ie.* **Irish Ferries.** 0818/300–400 *www.irishferries.com.* **Norfolkline.** (44) 208/127–8303 *in U.K.* *www.dfds.com.* **P&O Ferries.** 01/686–9467 *in Ireland,* 01/30444–8888 *in U.K.* *poferries.com.* **Stena Line.** 01/907–5555 *in Ireland,* 028/9074–7747 *in Northern Ireland,* 0844/770–7070 *in U.K.* *www.stenaline.ie.*

Bus

Aircoach. 01/844–7118 *www.aircoach.ie.* **Bus Éireann.** 1850/836–6111 *in Republic of Ireland* *www.buseireann.ie.* **Citylink.** 091/564–164 *within Ireland* *www.citylink.ie.* **Dublin Coach.** 353/465–9972 *www.dublincoach.ie.* **Translink Goldline.** 028/9033–7002 *in Northern Ireland* *www.translink.co.uk.* **Ulsterbus.** 028/9066–6630 *in Northern Ireland* *www.translink.co.uk.*

Train

TRAIN STATIONS Belfast Central Station. *East Bridge St., Belfast* 028/9089–9400 *www.translink.co.uk.* **Connolly Station.** *Amiens St., Dublin* 01/703–2358 *www.irishrail.ie.* **Galway Station.** *Station Rd., Galway City* 091/564–222 *www.irishrail.ie.* **Heuston Station.** *St. John's Rd. W (N4), Dublin* 01/703–2132 *www.irishrail.ie.* **Kent Station.** *Lower Glanmire Rd., City Center North* 021/450–4777 *www.irishrail.ie.*

RAIL COMPANIES Irish Rail. (Iarnrod Éireann). 01/836–6222 *www.irishrail.ie.* **Northern Ireland Railways.** 028/9066–6630 *www.translink.co.uk/services/ni-railways.*

Tours

GENERAL TOURS CIE Tours International. 888/996–0017 *from U.S.* *www.cietours.com.* **Discovering Ireland Vacations.** 800/963–9260 *www.discoveringireland.com.* **Vagabond Small-Group Tours of Ireland.** 1/563–4358 *in Ireland,* 833/230–0288 *toll-free from U.S.* *www.vagabondtoursofireland.com.*

SPECIAL INTEREST TOURS Irish Cycling Safaris. *Belfield Bike Shop, UCD, Dublin* 01/260–0749 *www.cyclingsafaris.com.* **Iron Donkey.** 029/2089–1650 *www.irondonkey.com.* **Isle Inn Hiking Tours.** 800/237–9376 *www.isleinntours.com.*

Visitor Information

Discover Ireland. 800/242–473 *www.discoverireland.ie.* **Discover Northern Ireland.** *59 North St., Belfast* 028/9024–6609 *www.discovernorthernireland.com.* **Irish Landmark Trust.** *Top fl., 11 Parnell Sq., Dublin 1, Georgian Dublin* 01/670–4733 *www.irishlandmark.com.* **Tourism Ireland.** *www.ireland.com.* **Tourism NI.** (NITB). *59 North St., Belfast* 028/9023–1221 *www.discovernorthernireland.com.*

Chapter 3

DUBLIN

Updated by
Anto Howard

Sights ★★★★★ | Restaurants ★★★★★ | Hotels ★★★★★ | Shopping ★★★★★ | Nightlife ★★★★★

WELCOME TO DUBLIN

TOP REASONS TO GO

★ **Georgian Elegance:** Dublin's signature architectural style makes its most triumphant showing in Merrion, Fitzwilliam, Mountjoy, and Parnell squares.

★ **The Guinness Brewery and Storehouse:** A high-tech museum tells the story of Guinness, Dublin's black blood. At the top, the newly extended Gravity Bar has the city's best views.

★ **Destination Dining:** An explosion of inventive new restaurants, alongside an array of classy old favorites, has made Dublin the place to be for dinner.

★ **Magnificent Museums:** From the Renoirs at the Hugh Lane to the Tara Brooch at the National Museum and the first editions of Joyce at the Museum of Literature, Dublin is one big treasure chest.

★ **Trinity College:** An oasis of books, granite, and grass sits at the heart of the city. Highlights are the exquisitely illustrated *Book of Kells* and the ornate Long Room.

1 St. Stephen's Green and Around. From elegant St. Stephen's Green to the stylish shopping stretch of Grafton Street and west to bustling Georges Street, this is the heart of Dublin. Majestic Trinity College and the always inventive Little Museum of Dublin also lie in this key area. South of the canal it stretches into the hip urban village that is Ranelagh.

2 Merrion Square and Around. The streets around Merrion Square and southeast of Trinity form the city's most important Georgian district; to the west of the square four major museums sit side by side. Farther south lie the Grand Canal and more Georgian splendor in upmarket Ballsbridge.

3 Grand Canal Dock and Around. No area of Dublin has undergone more exciting changes in recent years than this old industrial neighborhood east of the city center. "Silicon Docks," as some wags now call it, is now home to HQs for all the tech giants plus a plethora of new hotels, music venues, and activities. The grand Custom House and the Famine Memorial sculptures are must-sees here.

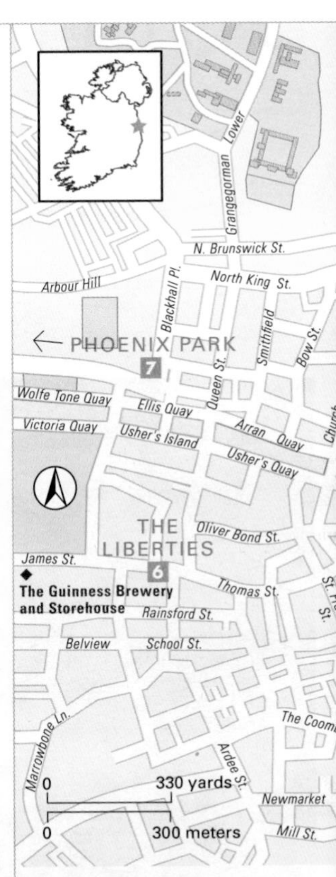

4 Temple Bar and Around. The cobblestone streets and small lanes bounded by Wellington Quay and Dame Street make up Dublin's trendiest—and liveliest—neighborhood. On weekends, the streets are packed with young Europeans, and locals tend to steer clear, favoring hipper spots like Ranelagh and Smithfield.

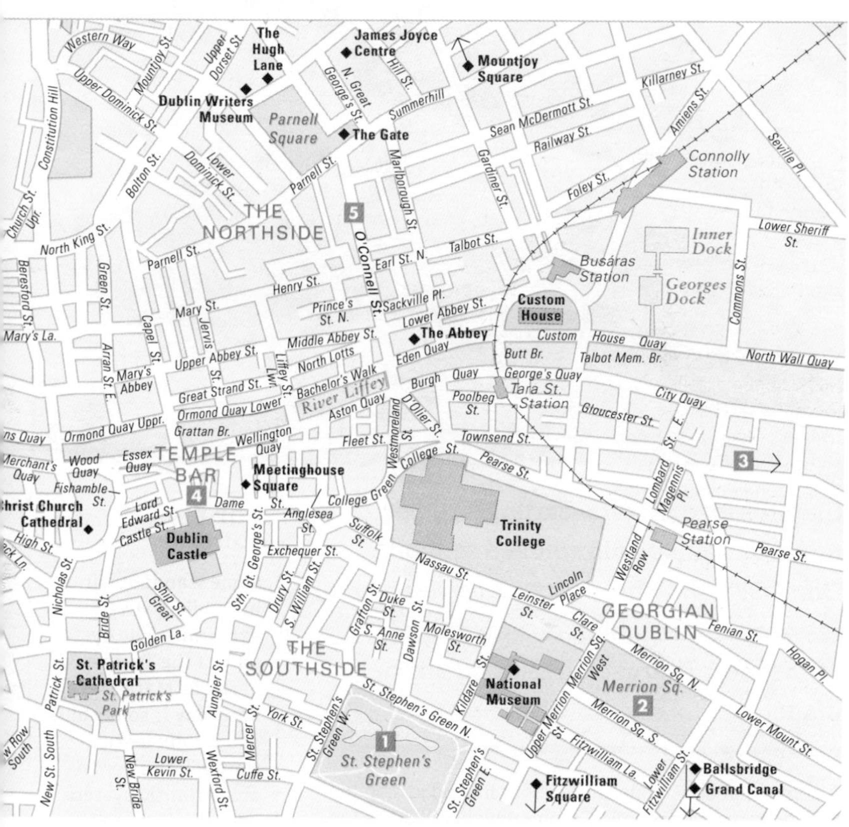

5 O'Connell Street and Around. Less affluent but more eloquent than the Southside, this neighborhood was once home to James Joyce; today it's the site of the James Joyce Centre. Other highlights are historic O'Connell Street and Dublin's two great theaters—the Abbey and the Gate. The artsy, urban suburb of Stoneybatter also falls into this area.

6 Liberties and Around. This former industrial district stretches from Christ Church west to that other Dublin shrine, the Guinness Storehouse. Imposing Dublin Castle houses the Chester Beatty Library—arguably the most impressive museum in Ireland.

7 Phoenix Park and Around. Only a 20-minute walk from the city center, Phoenix Park, Europe's largest public city park, hugs the north bank of the Liffey.

DUBLIN'S SEAFOOD BOUNTY

The Irish treasure of the deep—smoked salmon

Clarenbridge oysters, Carlingford Lough mussels, Ballina wild smoked salmon, Donegal crab—the menus of the top restaurants in Dublin are now full of some of the most flavorsome seafood on the planet.

A somewhat apocryphal story about Ireland joining the EEC (European Economic Community) in 1973 has the government being given a stark choice: you can farm or you can fish, but you can't do both. They chose to protect farming, and the result was the massive overfishing by giant Spanish factory ships off Irish waters. This fact may, in part, explain why Ireland—a relatively pollution-free, sea-surrounded nation—is not one of the first places gourmands think of for great seafood. Historically, there was also a certain snobbery about eating fish, as it was seen as peasant food only suitable for fasting Fridays. Well, things have certainly changed in recent times.

TOP FISHY JOINTS

Some standout joints in Dublin go that extra mile. The oyster stall at the Temple Bar Farmers' Market every Saturday is something of a Dublin institution, where affordable Atlantic oysters and white wine are downed alfresco. The West Pier in Howth has become a hive of buzzing, quality seafood eateries. Fish Shop has taken the traditional Dublin chipper to a whole new culinary level.

SMOKED SALMON

From all corners of Ireland, small producers are now making some of Europe's finest smoked salmon. Obviously, and perhaps unfortunately, the wild Atlantic salmon still has a richer, more piquant taste than its farmed cousin. The word "wild" in the description will tell you the fish isn't farmed. The traditional smoking method uses only Irish oak, which gives it a very distinctive, subtle flavor and deep orange color. The best way to enjoy smoked salmon is over some toasted Dublin brown bread with a simple squeeze of lemon and some coarse black pepper to add that little extra tang.

IRISH CHOWDER

It's the pint of heavy cream and density of mussels tossed into the mix that makes Irish seafood chowder such a great snack on the run. It's also a dish that even the most humble of eateries doesn't usually mess up, although the general rule still applies: the nearer to the coast the eatery is located, the better its chowder. Regular fish stock is often used but clam juice—an Irish specialty—also adds to the unique flavor. Outside of the capital, enjoy chowders at Ireland's great seafood festivals: the Galway Oyster Festival, the event in Baltimore in West Cork, and the Killybegs festival.

Seaweed is a chic new condiment.

When it comes to fish-and-chips, some say the greasier the better.

FISH-AND-CHIPS

Every Dubliner will argue about the best place to get their favorite fast-food dish of fish-and-chips, but few will quarrel with the fact that cod, ray, and haddock are the top three battered delights to go for. Interestingly, the descendants of 1950s Italian immigrants—with names like Macari and Borza—are the recognized masters of the battering art, and you'll find one of their eponymously named shops in almost every neighborhood. Tip: a single portion is usually enough to feed two!

SEAWEED

Yes, the Irish are slowly discovering the delights of farming native seaweed for use in the kitchen and elsewhere. Irish seaweed is usually gathered along the western seaboard, dried, and then sold in small packets, a bit like herbs. Look closely at restaurant menus and you'll find dulse, carrageen moss, and various kelps and wracks all turning up to add spice to risottos, salads, soups, breads, and even ice cream. The local spa industry has cottoned on, developing "algotherapies," including wraps, anti-aging creams, and even full-on seaweed baths.

Having weathered the worst of the pandemic with great solidarity and composure, Dublin continues to blossom as very much a modern European city, with a thriving economy built on an influx of tech giants and large financial institutions. It boasts quality restaurants and hotels to match much larger cities, along with soaring house prices and traffic gridlock to match them, too. But behind the shining glass and steel of this new city, the old Dublin still flourishes in the Victorian parks, Georgian squares, and history-soaked streets. Whether you're out to enjoy the old or new Dublin, you'll find it a colossally entertaining city, all the more astonishing considering its intimate size.

It is ironic and telling that James Joyce chose Dublin as the setting for his famous *Ulysses, Dubliners,* and *A Portrait of the Artist as a Young Man* because it was a "center of paralysis" where nothing much ever changed. Which only proves that even the greats get it wrong sometimes. Indeed, if Joyce were to return to his once-genteel hometown today—disappointed with the city's provincial outlook, he left it in 1902 at the age of 20—and take a quasi-Homeric odyssey through the city (as he so famously does in *Ulysses*), would he even recognize Dublin as his "Dear Dirty Dumpling, foostherfather of fingalls and dotthergills"?

For instance, what would he make of Temple Bar—the city's erstwhile down-at-the-heels neighborhood, now crammed with cafés and trendy hotels and suffused with a nonstop international-party atmosphere? Or the simple sophistication of the open-air restaurants of the tiny

Italian Quarter (named Quartier Bloom after his own creation), complete with sultry tango lessons? Today, Ireland's capital is packed with elegant shops and hotels, theaters, galleries, coffeehouses, and a stunning variety of new, creative little restaurants can be found on almost every street in Dublin, transforming the provincial city that suffocated Joyce into a place almost as cosmopolitan as the Paris to which he fled.

The "Google Effect," large tech companies setting up their headquarters in the Grand Canal Dock area, has brought a flood of cash, youth, and ambition into the city. This has helped ignite a renaissance in some old neighborhoods like Stoneybatter and Ranelagh. But this new money has also highlighted inequalities in the city, pushing rents beyond breaking point and threatening to gentrify some areas beyond recognition. Yet, the fundamentals—the Georgian elegance of Merrion Square, the Norman drama of Christ Church Cathedral, the foamy pint at an atmospheric pub—are still on hand to gratify. And most of all, there are the locals themselves: the nod and grin when you catch their eye on the street, the eagerness to hear half your life story before they tell you all of theirs, and their paradoxically dark but warm sense of humor.

Planning

When to Go

When is it best—and worst—to pay a call on the Irish capital? The summer offers a real lift, as the natives spill out of the pubs into the slew of sidewalk cafés and open-air restaurants. The week around St. Patrick's Day (March 17) is, naturally, a nonstop festival of parades, cultural happenings, and "hooleys" (long nights of partying) throughout the city. Christmas in Dublin seems to last a month, and the city's old-style illuminations match the genteel, warm mood of the locals. The New Year's Festival Dublin (NYF) is an organized three days of music and spectacle to ring in the first day of the new year. January and February are damp hangover months, but there are plenty of hotel and restaurant bargains to be found. A warm sweater is a must year-round, as even summer nights can occasionally get chilly. Dublin gets its share of rain (though a lot less than other parts of Ireland), so an umbrella is a good investment—and best to make it a strong one, as the winds show no mercy to cheaper models.

Planning Your Time

IF YOU HAVE ONE DAY

Begin with Trinity College—the oldest seat of Irish learning and home to the Old Library, the staggering Long Room, and Ireland's greatest art treasure, the *Book of Kells,* one of the world's most famous illuminated manuscripts. Leave the campus and take a stroll along Grafton Street, Dublin's busiest shopping street and the pedestrian spine of the Southside. Take in a few shops and entertaining buskers on the street; at the end of Grafton you will find yourself at the northwest corner of St. Stephen's Green, Dublin's favorite relaxation spot. Head over to the northeast corner of the park to find ground zero for the city's cultural institutions. Here, surrounding the four points of Leinster House (built by the earl of Kildare, Ireland's first patron of Palladianism), are the National Museum, replete with artifacts and exhibits dating from prehistoric times; the National Gallery of Ireland (don't miss the Irish collection and Caravaggio's *The Taking of Christ*); the National Library; and the Natural History Museum.

For a lovely lunch, head back to St. Stephen's Green and the Victorian-era Shelbourne—the lobby salons glow with

Dublin Past and Present

Early Days

Until AD 500, Dublin was little more than a crossroads for four of the main thoroughfares that traversed the country. It had two names: Baile Átha Cliath, meaning Town of the Hurdled Ford, bestowed by Celtic traders in the 2nd century AD; and Dubhlinn, or "dark pool," after a body of water believed to have been where Dublin Castle now stands.

In 837, Norsemen carried out the first invasion of Dublin, to be followed by new waves of warriors staking their claim to the city—from the 12th-century Anglo-Normans to Oliver Cromwell in 1651.

Not until the 18th century did Dublin reach a golden age, when the patronage of wealthy nobles turned the city into one of Europe's most prepossessing capitals. But the era of "the glorious eighteenth" was short-lived; in 1800, the Act of Union brought Ireland and Britain together into the United Kingdom, and power moved to London.

Political Turmoil

The 19th century proved to be a time of political turmoil, although Daniel O'Connell, the first Catholic lord mayor of Dublin, won early success with the introduction of Catholic Emancipation in 1829.

The city entered another period of upheaval in the first decades of the 20th century, marked by the Easter Rising of 1916. A war for independence from Britain began in 1919, followed by establishment of the Irish Free State in December 1921 and subsequent civil war. In its aftermath Dublin entered an era of political and cultural conservatism, which continued until the late 1970s. A major turning point occurred in 1973, when Ireland joined the European Economic Community.

Boom and Bust

The 1990s and first years of the 21st century were truly Ireland's boom time, set in motion to a great extent by the country's participation in the European Union. When Ireland approved the new EU treaty in 1992, it was one of the poorest member nations, qualifying it for grants of all kinds.

Ireland quickly transformed itself into the economic envy of the world, propelled by massive investment from multinational corporations, and gained the nickname the "Celtic Tiger." In 2000 the government announced that Ireland was the world's largest exporter of software. But the later years of the Tiger were fueled by a monumental property bubble, and Dublin, like most of the world, suddenly woke up with one doozy of an economic hangover.

Dublin Today

After the uncertainty of the pandemic years, Ireland is again Europe's fastest-growing economy, and the natives hope they have learned their lesson from the excesses of the earlier Celtic Tiger era. More than a third of the Irish Republic's 5 million people live in Dublin and its suburbs. It's a city of young people, astonishingly so: students from all over Ireland—and the world—attend Trinity College and the city's dozen other third-level institutions.

Waterford chandeliers and blazing fireplaces. From St. Stephen's Green walk west for 10 minutes to pay your respects to "St. Paddy" (St. Patrick's Cathedral). If, instead, the Dublin of artists and poets is more your speed, hop a double-decker bus and head north of the Liffey to the Dublin City Gallery, The Hugh Lane. End the day with a performance at the nearby Gate Theatre, another Georgian stunner, or spend the evening exploring the leafy, urban "village" of Ranelagh with its buzzy streets of trendy restaurants and bars.

IF YOU HAVE THREE DAYS

Dedicate your second day to the areas north and west of the city center. In the morning, cross the Liffey via O'Connell Bridge and walk up O'Connell Street, the city's widest thoroughfare, stopping to visit the General Post Office—the besieged headquarters of the 1916 rebels—on your way to the the Dublin City Gallery, the Hugh Lane (if you didn't have time to visit on the first day). Be sure to join the thousands of Dubliners strolling down Henry, Moore, and Mary Streets, the Northside's pedestrian shopping area. In the afternoon, head back to the Liffey for a quayside walk by Dublin's most imposing structure, the Custom House; then head west to the Guinness Storehouse. Hop a bus or catch a cab back into the city for a blowout dinner at Restaurant Patrick Guilbaud at the Merrion Hotel. Spend the evening on a literary pub crawl to see where the likes of Beckett and Behan held court, perhaps joining a special guided tour. On the third day tour the northern and western outskirts of Dublin from Glasnevin Cemetery and the National Botanic Gardens across to the majestic Phoenix Park and the quaint fishing village of Howth. Back in the city, have tea at Bewley's and catch a musical performance at the Olympia Theatre or a play at the Abbey Theatre.

IF YOU HAVE FIVE DAYS

Follow the two itineraries above and then head west to start your fourth day at Dublin's dawn—a living history of Dublin can be seen at medieval Dublinia, across the street from ancient Christ Church Cathedral, whose underground crypt is Dublin's oldest structure. Head north, jumping across the Liffey to the Four Courts, James Gandon's Georgian masterpiece and until recently the home of the Irish judiciary. Recross the river to the Southside and go west again to visit the Royal Hospital Kilmainham, which houses the Irish Museum of Modern Art, and Kilmainham Gaol, where the leaders of the Easter Rising were executed following their capture. Return via Dublin Castle—residence of British power in Ireland for nearly 800 years, and star of Neil Jordan's film *Michael Collins*—and then move on to the Chester Beatty Library, which connoisseurs prize because of its Chinese and Turkish treasures. On your fifth and final day, you could explore the "new" Dublin of modernist architecture and city waterways in the redeveloped Grand Canal Dock area, including a night at the Daniel Libeskind–designed Bord Gáis Energy Theatre. Alternatively, head to the northern suburbs of Dublin, home to two architectural jewels: picturesque Malahide Castle and Newbridge House, famed for its gorgeous 18th-century salons. The beautiful, buzzing coastal town of Howth is also worth a visit. Back in Dublin, have a final farewell dinner, hopefully at your "local": your favorite neighborhood pub.

Getting Here and Around

AIR

Dublin Airport, 10 km (6 miles) north of the city center, serves international and domestic flights.

AIRPORT CONTACTS Aircoach. ☎ *01/844–7118* 🌐 *www.aircoach.ie.* **Dublin Airport.** ☎ *01/814–1111* 🌐 *dublinairport.com.*

AIRPORT TRANSFERS: BUSES AND TAXIS

Aircoach operates an express shuttle service between Dublin Airport and the city center, with departures outside the arrivals gateway. Journey time from the airport to the city center is normally 30 minutes, but it may be longer in heavy traffic. The single fare is €8 and round-trip is 12. If you have time, you can save money by taking a regular bus for €3.90.

TIP→ Book airport buses in advance for discounts.

The service stops at major hotels. A taxi is a quicker alternative than the bus to get from the airport to Dublin center. A line of taxis waits by the arrivals gateway; the fare for the 30-minute journey to any of the main city-center hotels is about €23 to €26 plus tip (tips don't have to be large). Ask about the fare before leaving the airport.

BOAT AND FERRY

Irish Ferries runs a regular high-speed car and passenger service into Dublin port from Holyhead in Wales. The crossing takes one hour and 50 minutes on the faster *Dublin Swift* and three hours and 15 minutes on the bigger cruise ships. It also has a service from Cherbourg in France, a 20-hour trip. Stena Line has services to Dublin port from Holyhead (3½ hours). P&O ferries also offers a route to Dublin from Liverpool (8 hours). Prices and departure times vary according to season, so call to confirm. In summer, reservations are strongly recommended; book online or through a travel agent. Dozens of taxis wait to take you into town or you can take a bus to the city center.

CONTACTS Irish Ferries. ☎ *0818/300–400, 01/855—2292* 🌐 *irishferries.com.* **P&O Ferries.** ☎ *01/686–9467 in Ireland, 01/30444–8888 in U.K.* 🌐 *poferries.com.* **Stena Line.** ✉ *Dublin Port, Southside* ☎ *01/907–5555* 🌐 *www.stenaline.ie.*

BUS

Busáras, just behind the Custom House on the Northside, is Dublin's main station for buses to and from the city. Dublin Bus runs the city's regular buses. Bus Éireann is the main intercity bus company, with service throughout the country. Aircoach has direct bus connections to Cork and Belfast, and is usually a bit cheaper than Bus Éireann.

In town, there's an extensive network of buses, most of which are yellow and blue double-deckers.

Some bus services run on cross-city routes but most buses start in the city center.

Buses to the north of the city begin in the Lower Abbey Street–Parnell Street area, while those to the west begin in Middle Abbey Street and in the Aston Quay area. Routes to the southern suburbs begin at Eden Quay and in the College Street area. Several buses link to the DART and LUAS stations, and another regular bus route connects the two main provincial railway stations, Connolly and Heuston. If the destination board indicates "an lár," that means that the bus is going to the city center.

BUS FARES AND SCHEDULES

In the city, fares begin at €1.30 and are paid to the driver, who will accept cash but can't give any change. Ticket buying and the city's heavy traffic can slow service considerably. Most bus lines run until 11:30 at night, but some run 24 hours and Nitelink buses run Friday to Saturday until 4:30 am on other major routes; the fare is €3. You can save a lot of money by buying a Leap Card, which works for the bus, DART, and LUAS (trams). You can even order your Leap Card online (🌐 *www.leapcard.ie*) before coming to Ireland. Otherwise, you can get a card at shops throughout the city.

CONTACTS Aircoach. ☎ *01/844–7118* 🌐 *aircoach.ie.* **Bus Éireann.** ☎ *01/836–6111* 🌐 *buseireann.ie.* **Busáras.** ✉ *Store St.,*

Dublin North ☎ *01/836–6111.* **Dublin Bus.** ✉ *59 Upper O'Connell St., Dublin North* ☎ *01/873–4222* 🌐 *dublinbus.ie.*

CAR

Renting a car in Dublin is very expensive, with high rates and a 13.5% local tax. Gasoline is also expensive by U.S. standards, at around €1.70 a liter. Peak-period car-rental rates begin at around €300 a week for the smallest stick models, like a VW Polo. Dublin has many car-rental companies, and it pays to shop around. A dozen car-rental companies have desks at Dublin Airport; all the main national and international firms also have branches in the city center.

Traffic in Ireland has increased exponentially in the last few years, and nowhere has the impact been felt more than in Dublin, where the city's complicated one-way streets are congested not only during the morning and evening rush hours but also often during much of the day. If possible, avoid driving a car except to get in and out of the city (and be sure to ask your hotel or guesthouse for clear directions to get you out of town).

TAXI

There are taxi stands beside the central bus station and at train stations, O'Connell Bridge, St. Stephen's Green, College Green, and near major hotels; the Dublin telephone directory has a complete list. The initial charge is €4.20 (€4.80 after 8 pm and on Sunday), with an additional charge of about €1.30 (€1.70 after 8 pm and on Sunday) per kilometer thereafter. The fare is displayed on a meter (make sure it's on). You may, instead, want to phone a taxi company and ask for a cab to meet you at your hotel, but this may cost up to €2 extra. There is no charge for luggage. Uber is not widely available in Dublin, but Free Now (🌐 *www.free-now.com*) and Lynx (🌐 *www.lynx.ie*) are two online services used by a lot of licensed Dublin taxi drivers and hackney cabs.

Hackney cabs, which also operate in the city, have neither roof signs nor meters and will sometimes respond to hotels' requests for a cab.

Although the taxi fleet in Dublin is large, the cabs are nonstandard, and some cars are neither spacious nor in pristine condition. NXT Taxis is one of the city's biggest but also the busiest. SCR Cabs has some of the friendliest drivers.

CONTACTS NXT Taxis. ☎ *01/888–8888* 🌐 *nxt.ie.* **SCR Cabs.** ☎ *01/473–1166.*

TRAIN AND TRAM

As a delightfully compact city, Dublin does not have—or need—a subway system. But its LUAS trams and DART electric railway are great ways to get around the city center and beyond. The DART (Dublin Area Rapid Transit) connects Dublin with the fishing village of Howth to the north and the seaside resort of Bray to the south on a fast, efficient, super-scenic train line that hugs the coastline, providing one spectacular view after another. But this line also runs through the center city with three convenient stations and then continues to such seaside destinations as Dun Laoghaire, Dalkey, and Bray.

Except for overcrowded rush hours, the LUAS tram service is a fun, efficient way to navigate Dublin and enjoy its sights from your window. Its two lines are connected and run right through the heart of the city, facilitating easy access to sights like the Guinness Storehouse (James Street stop), O'Connell Street (Northside Abbey Street stop), and St. Stephen's Green. Trams are very frequent and run from around 5:30 am until 12:30 am.

Tickets can be bought at stations, and prices have recently reduced to encourage post-covid use. It's also possible to buy weekly rail tickets, as well as weekly or monthly rail-and-bus tickets, from the Irish Rail Travel Centre. Leap Cards work on the buses, DART, and LUAS and can be purchased online (🌐 *leapcard.ie*) or at newsagents throughout the city.

CONTACTS Connolly Station. ✉ *Amiens St., Dublin North.* **DART.** ☎ *01/836–6222* 🌐 *irishrail.ie/about-us/iarnrod-eireann-services/dart-commuter.* **Heuston Station.** ✉ *End of Victoria Quay, Dublin West.* **Irish Rail–Iarnod Éireann.** ☎ *01/836–6222* 🌐 *irishrail.ie.* **LUAS.** ☎ *800/300–604* 🌐 *luas.ie.* **Pearse Station.** ✉ *Westland Row, Southside.*

TRAIN AND TRAM FARES AND SCHEDULES

DART service starts at 6:10 am and runs until 11:55 pm; at peak periods—8 to 9:30 am and 5 to 7 pm—trains arrive every five minutes. At other times of the day, the intervals between trains are 15 to 25 minutes. Individual fares begin at €2.15 and range up to €4.95 one-way. You'll pay a heavy penalty for traveling the DART without a ticket. LUAS trams run from 5:30 am until 12:43 am Monday to Saturday and 7 am until 11:30 pm on Sunday. They come every 7 to 10 minutes at peak times and every 15 to 20 minutes after that. Fares range from €1.70 to €2.60 according to the number of zones traveled. Using a Leap card will save you a lot of money.

TRAINS TO AND FROM DUBLIN

Irish Rail (Iarnród Éireann) runs intercity trains connecting Dublin with the rest of Ireland. Connolly Station provides train service to and from the east coast, Belfast, the north (with stops in Malahide, Skerries, and Drogheda), the northwest, and some destinations to the south, such as Wicklow. Heuston Station is the place for trains to and from the south and west including Galway, Limerick, and Cork. Trains also run from here to Kildare Town, Newbridge, and other west-of-Dublin stops.

Hotels

Despite a flurry of new construction, Dublin hotel prices remain in line with the best hotels of any major European or North American city. Service charges range from 15% in expensive hotels to zero in moderate and inexpensive ones. Be sure to inquire when you make reservations.

As a general rule of thumb, lodgings on the north side of the River Liffey tend to be more affordable than those on the south. Bed-and-breakfasts charge as little as €80 a night per person, but they tend to be in suburban areas—generally a 15-minute bus ride from the center of the city. This is not in itself a great drawback, and savings can be significant. Many hotels have a weekend, or "B&B," rate that's often 15% to 25% cheaper than the ordinary rate; some hotels also have a midweek special that provides discounts of up to 25%.

Restaurants

With the Irish food revolution long over and won, Dublin now has a city full of fabulous, hip, and suavely sophisticated restaurants. While some old favorites closed during the pandemic, the rapidly recovering economy has seen a new cohort of upstart, adventurous eateries crop up alongside award-winning Eurotoques and their sous chefs, who continue to come up with new and glorious ways to abuse your waistline. Instead of just spuds-glorious-spuds, you'll find delicious new entries to New Irish cuisine like roast scallops with spiced pork belly and cauliflower au gratin topped with a daring caper-and-raisin sauce or sautéed rabbit loin with Clonakilty black pudding. Okay, there's still a good chance spuds will appear on your menu—and most likely offered in several different ways. Another postpandemic benefit has been an explosion in outdoor options, with locations like Capel Street now buzzing with alfresco diners and drinkers.

As for lunches or munchies on the run, there are scores of independent cafés serving excellent coffee, and often good sandwiches. Other eateries, borrowing trends from all around the world, serve inexpensive pizzas, focaccia, pitas, tacos, and wraps (which are fast gaining in popularity over the sandwich).

Dubliners dine later than the rest of Ireland. They stay up later, too, and reservations are usually not booked before 6:30 or 7 pm and up to around 10 pm. Lunch is generally served from 12:30 to 2:30 pm. Pubs often serve food through the day—until 8:30 or 9 pm. Most pubs are family-friendly and welcome children until 7 pm, and while the quality of the cuisine they offer varies, it is generally in a different world from what it was even five years ago. The Irish are an informal bunch, so smart-casual dress is typical.

RESTAURANT AND HOTEL PRICES

⇨ *Restaurant prices are the average cost of a main course at dinner or, if dinner is not served, at lunch. Hotel prices are the lowest cost of a standard double room in high season, including V.A.T. and a service charge (often applied in larger hotels). Restaurant and hotel reviews have been shortened. For full information, visit Fodors.com.*

What It Costs in Euros

	$	$$	$$$	$$$$
RESTAURANTS				
	under €19	€19–€24	€25–€32	over €32
HOTELS				
	under €170	€170–€230	€231–€300	over €300

Tours

Dublin is a walker's city, and it's a city full of storytellers. Put two and two together, and it's little surprise that Dublin is a particularly good place for guided walking tours.

PUB AND MUSICAL TOURS

Dublin Discover Ireland Centre (⇨ *see Visitor Information below*) has a booklet on its self-guided Rock 'n' Stroll trail, which covers 16 sights with associations to such performers as Bob Geldof, Christy Moore, Sinéad O'Connor, and U2. Most of the sights are in the city center and Temple Bar.

Dublin Literary Pub Crawl

SPECIAL-INTEREST TOURS | Loveable rogue Colm Quilligan arranges a highly enjoyable evening Dublin Literary Pub Crawl, where "brain cells are replaced as quickly as they are drowned." ☎ *087/263–0270* 🌐 *www.dublinpubcrawl.com* 🎫 *From €15.*

Traditional Musical Pub Crawl

SPECIAL-INTEREST TOURS | Led by two professional musicians who perform songs and tell the story of Irish music, the tour is given April through October, daily at 7:30 pm, and from Thursday to Saturday, at 7:30 pm, the rest of the year. It begins at the Oliver St. John Gogarty and moves on to other famous Temple Bar pubs. ✉ *20 Lower Stephens St., Southside* ☎ *01/478–0191* 🌐 *www.musicalpubcrawl.com* 🎫 *From €19.*

WALKING TOURS

Historical Walking Tours of Dublin

WALKING TOURS | Run by Trinity College history graduate students, these are excellent two-hour introductions to the city. The Tourism Ireland–approved tours take place from May to September, starting at the front gate of Trinity College, daily at 11 am and 3 pm, with an extra tour on weekends at noon. These tours are also available October and April daily at 11 am and November to

March, Friday through Sunday at 11 am. ☎ *087/688–9412* 🌐 *www.historicaltours.ie* 🎫 *From €14.*

1916 Rebellion Walking Tour

WALKING TOURS | This exciting walk outlines the key areas and events of the violent Dublin rebellion that began Ireland's march to independence. The guides are passionately political and the two-hour tour never flags. They meet at the International Bar on Wicklow Street and operate March through October, Monday to Saturday at 11:30 am and Sunday at 1 pm. In February and November tours run Friday to Sunday. ☎ *086/858–3847* 🌐 *www.1916rising.com* 🎫 *From €15.*

Trinity Tours

WALKING TOURS | This company organizes walks of the Trinity College campus daily from February to early December. The half-hour tour includes the *Book of Kells* exhibit; tours start at the college's main gate every 40 minutes from 10:15 am. There are generally nine tours a day. 🌐 *www.tcd.ie/visitors* 🎫 *From €15.*

Visitor Information

The main Fáilte Ireland tourism center (known as Visit Dublin) is on Suffolk Street and is open July and August, Monday–Saturday 9–7, Sunday 10:30–3, and September to June, Monday–Saturday 9–5:30, Sunday 10:30–3. There is a smaller Northside branch on O'Connell Street that is open Monday–Saturday 9–5.

CONTACTS Dublin Discover Ireland Centre O'Connell Street. ✉ *14 Upper O'Connell St., Dublin North* ☎ *01/605–7700, 1850/230–330* 🌐 *visitdublin.com.* **Visit Dublin.** ✉ *25 Suffolk St. off Grafton St., Southside* ☎ *1850/230–330* 🌐 *visitdublin.com.*

DUBLIN PASS

Like many tourist capitals around the world, Dublin now features a special pass to help travelers save on admission prices. In conjunction with Fáilte Ireland (Suffolk Street office and at many other Irish tourist offices throughout Ireland), the Dublin Pass is issued for one, two, three, or five days, and allows free—or, rather, reduced (the cards do cost something)—admission to 30 sights, including the Guinness Brewery, the Dublin Zoo, the Museum of Literature, and Christ Church Cathedral. It also includes an airport transfer. Prices are €69 for one day, €89 for two days, €99 for three days, and €115 for five days; children's prices are much lower (only €49 for one day). You can buy your card online and have it waiting for you at one of Dublin's tourist information offices when you arrive. Another plus: you can jump to the head of any line at participating museums and sights. Get your passes online at (🌐 *www.dublinpass.com*).

St. Stephen's Green and Around

The River Liffey provides useful orientation, flowing as it does through the direct middle of Dublin. If you ask a native Dubliner for directions—from under an umbrella, as it will probably be raining in the approved Irish manner—they will most likely reply in terms of "up" or "down," meaning up and away from the river, or down and toward it. In the past, Dublin's center of gravity was O'Connell Bridge, a diplomatic landmark in that it avoided locating the center either north or south of the river—strong local loyalties still prevailed among "Northsiders" and "Southsiders," and neither group would ever accept that the city's center lay elsewhere than on their own side. The 20th century, however, saw diplomacy fall by the wayside—Dublin's heart now beats loudest southward across the Liffey, due in part to a large-scale refurbishment and pedestrianization of Grafton Street, which made this already upscale shopping address the main street on which to shop, stop, and be seen. At the top of Grafton Street is the city's most famous and recognizable landmark, Trinity College; at the foot of it is Dublin's most popular strolling retreat, St. Stephen's Green, a 22-acre landscaped park with flowers, lakes, bridges, and Dubliners enjoying their leisure time. Finally, south of the canal, there's the ubercool Ranelagh neighborhood, where a new, must-see restaurant or bar seems to open every week.

Sights

Bank of Ireland

BANK | Across the street from the west facade of Trinity College stands one of Dublin's most striking buildings, formerly the original home of Irish Parliament. A pedimented portico fronted by six massive Corinthian columns dominates the grand facade, which follows the curve of Westmoreland Street as it meets College Green, once a Viking meeting place and burial ground. Inside, stucco rosettes adorn the coffered ceiling in the pastel-hue, colonnaded, clerestoried main banking hall, at one time the Court of Requests, where citizens' petitions were heard. Just down the hall is the original House of Lords, with an oak-panel nave, a 1,233-drop Waterford glass chandelier, and tapestries depicting the Battle of the Boyne and the Siege of Derry; ask a guard to show you in. Visitors are welcome during normal banking hours. A recently opened culture and heritage center houses changing exhibitions on Irish artists, writers, and history. ✉ *2 College Green, Southside* ☎ *01/677–6801* 🌐 *visitdublin.com* 🎟 *Free* 🕒 *Closed weekends.*

The Douglas Hyde Gallery of Modern Art

ART GALLERY | Trinity College's starkly modern Arts and Social Sciences Building, with an entrance on Nassau Street, houses the Douglas Hyde Gallery, which concentrates on contemporary art exhibitions and has its own bookstore. Also in the building, down some steps from the gallery, is a snack bar serving coffee, tea, and sandwiches, where students willing to chat about life in the old college frequently gather. ✉ *Nassau St., Southside* ☎ *01/896–1116* 🌐 *douglashydegallery.com* 🎟 *Free* 🕒 *Closed Sun.*

George's Street Arcade

MARKET | This Victorian covered market fills the block between Drury Street and South Great George's Street. Around two dozen stalls sell books, prints, clothing (new and secondhand), local foodstuffs, and trinkets. ✉ *S. Great George's St., Southside* 🌐 *georgesstreetarcade.com.*

Grafton Street

STREET | It's no more than 200 yards long and about 20 feet wide, but Grafton Street, open only to pedestrians, can claim to be the most humming street in the city, if not in all of Ireland. It's one of Dublin's vital spines: the most direct route between the front door of Trinity College and St. Stephen's Green, and the city's premier shopping street, with Dublin's most distinguished department store, Brown Thomas, as well as tried and trusted Marks & Spencer. Grafton Street and the smaller alleyways that radiate off it offer independent stores, a dozen or so colorful flower sellers, and some of the Southside's most popular watering holes. In summer, buskers from all over the world line both sides of the street, pouring out the sounds of drum, whistle, pipe, and string. ✉ *Southside.*

★ Iveagh Gardens

CITY PARK | FAMILY | Dublin's best-kept secret has to be this 1865 Ninian Niven–designed English Landscape walled garden that shockingly few natives seem to even know about. The architect showed off his dramatic flair in the rustic grotto and cascade, the sunken panels of lawn with their fountains, the blooming rosarium, and wonderful little wooded areas. This public park has no playground, but kids really love the "secret garden" feel to the place and the fact that the

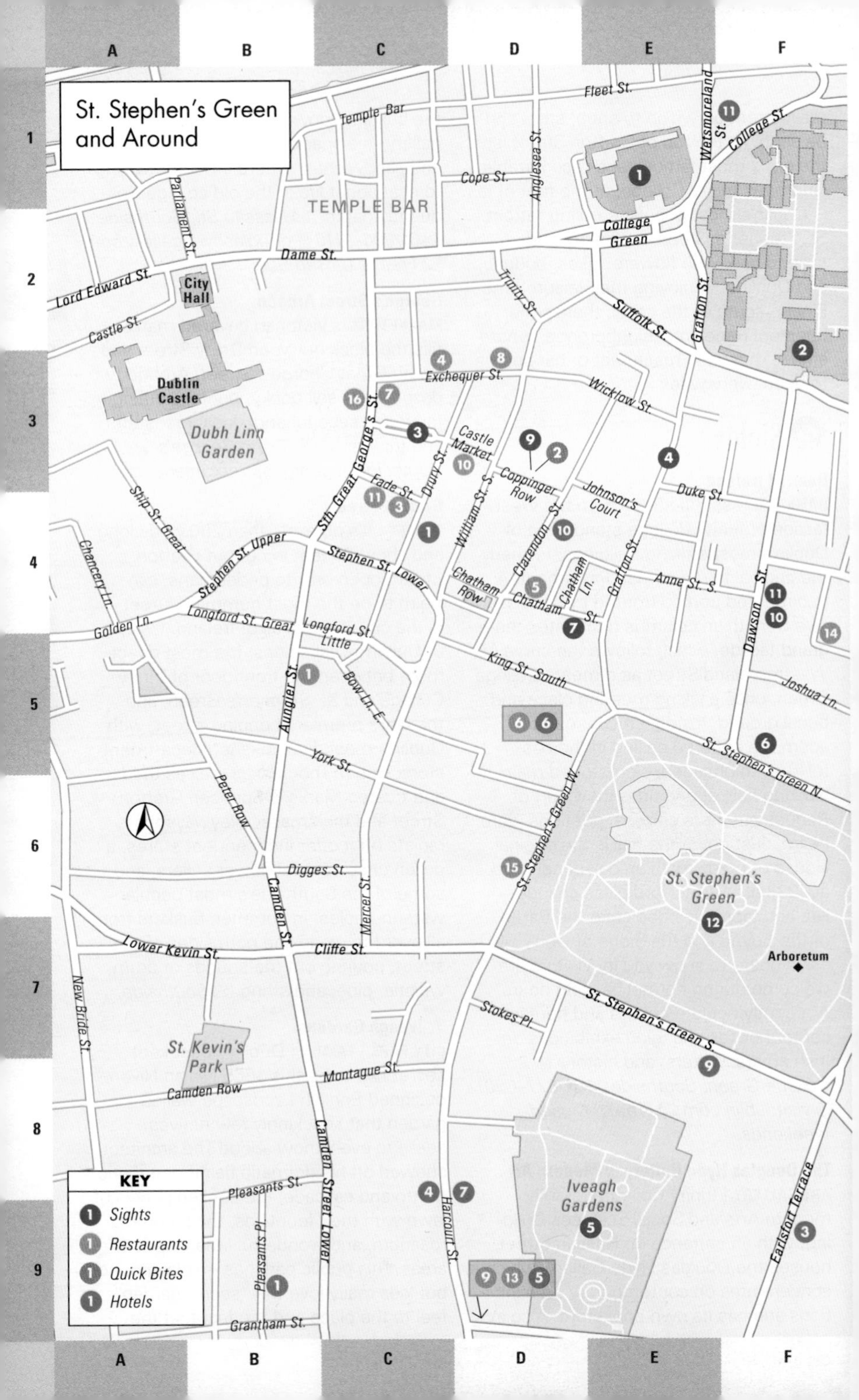
St. Stephen's Green and Around
A
B
C
D
E
F
1
2
3
4
5
6
7
8
9
Fleet St.
Temple Bar
Westmoreland St.
College St.
Anglesea St.
Cope St.
Parliament St.
TEMPLE BAR
College Green
Dame St.
Lord Edward St.
City Hall
Castle St.
Trinity St.
Suffolk St.
Grafton St.
Dublin Castle
Exchequer St.
Wicklow St.
Dubh Linn Garden
Sth. Great George's St.
Castle Market
Drury St.
William St. S.
Coppinger Row
Johnson's Court
Duke St.
Fade St.
Ship St. Great
Clarendon St.
Chancery Ln.
Stephen St. Upper
Stephen St. Lower
Chatham Row
Chatham Ln.
Grafton St.
Anne St. S.
Dawson St.
Chatham St.
Golden Ln.
Longford St. Great
Longford St. Little
King St. South
Aungier St.
Bow Ln. E.
Joshua Ln.
St. Stephen's Green N.
York St.
Peter Row
St. Stephen's Green W.
Digges St.
St. Stephen's Green
Camden St.
Mercer St.
Arboretum
Lower Kevin St.
Cliffe St.
New Bride St.
Stokes Pl.
St. Stephen's Green S.
St. Kevin's Park
Montague St.
Camden Row
Camden Street Lower
Iveagh Gardens
Earlsfort Terrace
Pleasants St.
Harcourt St.
Pleasants Pl.
Grantham St.
KEY
Sights
Restaurants
Quick Bites
Hotels

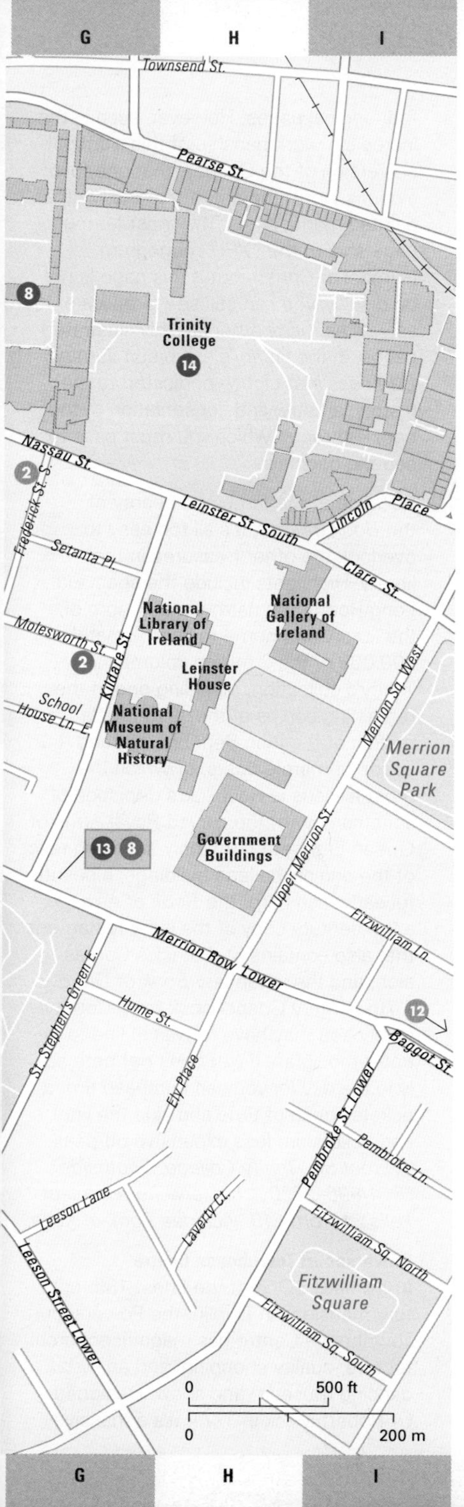

Sights

1 Bank of Ireland........... E1
2 The Douglas Hyde Gallery of Modern Art............... F3
3 George's Street Arcade.................... C3
4 Grafton Street........... E3
5 Iveagh Gardens.......... E9
6 Little Museum of Dublin................. F5
7 Neary's Pub D4
8 The Old Library and the Book of Kells........ G2
9 Powerscourt Townhouse Centre D3
10 Royal Irish Academy F4
11 St. Ann's Church F4
12 St. Stephen's Green E7
13 The Shelbourne Hotel..................... G6
14 Trinity College Dublin... H2

Restaurants

1 Big Fan.................. B5
2 Dunne and Crescenzi................ G3
3 Fade Street Social....... C4
4 Fallon & Byrne C3
5 Glas...................... D4
6 Glover's Alley............ D5
7 The Good World C3
8 The Green Hen.......... D3
9 Host D9
10 La Maison D3
11 L'Gueuleton............... C4
12 Mae I7
13 Nightmarket............ D9
14 One Pico.................. F5
15 Shanahan's on the Green D6
16 Yamamori Noodles C3

Quick Bites

1 Cake Café................ B9
2 The Pepper Pot D3

Hotels

1 Brooks Hotel C4
2 Buswells................. G4
3 Conrad Dublin............ F9
4 The Dean C8
5 The Devlin D9
6 The Fitzwilliam Hotel ... D5
7 Iveagh Garden Hotel ... D8
8 The Shelbourne......... G6
9 Stauntons On The Green E8
10 Westbury Hotel Dublin D4
11 The Westin Dublin....... F1

waterfall has rocks from every one of Ireland's 32 counties. Restoration of the gardens began in 1995 and has left the city with a Victorian treasure complete with a perfect box hedge and a working sundial. Access is from Hatch Street. ✉ *Clonmel St., Southside* ☎ *01/475–7816* 🌐 *iveaghgardens.ie* 🎫 *Free.*

★ Little Museum of Dublin

HISTORY MUSEUM | This clever, eclectic little museum, one of Dublin's best, sets out to tell the history of Dublin in the last hundred years through changing exhibitions of the objects and stories of its citizens. The collection includes art, photography, ads, letters, objects, and ephemera relating to life in the capital since 1900. Housed in the first floor of a Georgian building, it even has an interesting section on U2 and how the city shaped them. There's a slightly informal, hodgepodge feel to the place, but that just adds to the pleasure of strolling around and taking it all in. They even organize a family treasure hunt in St. Stephen's Green. Entrance is by guided tour only and the museum also holds fascinating talks. ✉ *15 Stephen's Green, Southside* ☎ *01/661–0000* 🌐 *littlemuseum.ie* 🎫 *€10.*

Neary's Pub

RESTAURANT | The exotic, Victorian-style interiors here were once haunted by Dublin's literary set, most notably the master bar raconteur Brendan Behan. ✉ *1 Chatham St., Southside* ☎ *01/677–7371* 🌐 *nearys.ie.*

★ The Old Library and the Book of Kells

COLLEGE | Home to Ireland's largest collection of books and manuscripts, the Old Library's principal treasure is the *Book of Kells,* generally considered to be the most striking manuscript ever produced in the Anglo-Saxon world and one of the great masterpieces of early Christian art. The book, which dates to the 9th century, was re-bound in four volumes in 1953, two of which are usually displayed at a time, so you typically see no more than four original pages. However, such is the incredible workmanship of this illuminated version of the Gospels that one folio alone is worth the entirety of many other painted manuscripts. The most famous page shows the "XPI" monogram (symbol of Christ), but if this page is not on display, you can still see a replica of it, as well as many other lavishly illustrated pages, in the library's exhibition *Turning Darkness into Light*—dedicated to the history, artistry, and conservation of the book—through which you must pass to see the originals.

Because of the fame and beauty of the *Book of Kells,* it's all too easy to overlook the other treasures in the library. Highlights include the spectacular Long Room, the narrow main room of the library and home to approximately 200,000 of the 3 million volumes in Trinity's collection, including one of the remaining copies of the 1916 Proclamation of the Irish Republic; a grand series of marble busts, of which the most famous is Roubiliac's depiction of Jonathan Swift; the carved Royal Arms of Queen Elizabeth I, the only surviving relic of the original college buildings; a beautiful early Irish harp; the *Book of Armagh,* a 9th-century copy of the New Testament that also contains St. Patrick's Confession; and the legendary *Book of Durrow,* a 7th-century Gospel book from County Offaly. You may have to wait in line to enter the library if you don't get here early in the day (or you can purchase timed tickets ahead of time and skip the line), and tickets are less expensive off-peak. ✉ *Front Sq., Trinity College, Southside* ☎ *01/896–2320* 🌐 *tcd.ie/visitors/book-of-kells* 🎫 *From €19, includes Book of Kells.*

Powerscourt Townhouse Centre

STORE/MALL | One of the finest 18th-century mansions in Dublin, the Powerscourt Townhouse Centre has magnificent architecture, quality shopping, and an Irish dancing museum and show. Designed by Robert Mack in 1771, it's a massive edifice that towers over the little street it sits on (note the top story, framed by large volutes, which was intended as an observatory). Inside, there are rococo salons designed by James McCullagh, splendid examples of plasterwork in the Adamesque style, and a shopping atrium filled with high-quality Irish crafts shops, installed in and around the covered courtyard. The mall exit leads to St. Teresa's Carmelite Church and Johnson's Court. Beside the church, a pedestrian lane leads onto Grafton Street. ✉ *59 S. William St., Southside* ☎ *01/611–1060* 🌐 *powerscourtcentre.ie.*

Royal Irish Academy

LIBRARY | The country's leading learned society houses important documents in its 18th-century library, including a large collection of ancient Irish manuscripts, such as the 11th- to 12th-century *Book of the Dun Cow,* and the library of the 18th-century poet Thomas Moore. ✉ *19 Dawson St., Southside* ☎ *01/676–2570* 🌐 *ria.ie* 🎫 *Free* ⏲ *Closed weekends.*

St. Ann's Church

CHURCH | A plain, neo-Romanesque granite exterior, built in 1868, belies the rich Georgian interior of this church, which Isaac Wills designed in 1720. Highlights of the interior include polished-wood balconies, ornate plasterwork, and shelving in the chancel dating from 1723—and still in use for organizing the distribution of food to the parish's poor. ✉ *Dawson St., Southside* ☎ *01/676–7727* 🌐 *stann.dublin.anglican.org* 🎫 *Free* ⏲ *Closed Mon., Fri., and Sat.*

★ St. Stephen's Green

CITY PARK | **FAMILY** | Dubliners call it simply Stephen's Green, and green it is (year-round), a verdant, 27-acre Southside square that was used for the public punishment of criminals until 1664. After a long period of decline, it became a private park in 1814—the first time in its history that it was closed to the public. Its fortunes changed again in 1880, when Sir Arthur Guinness paid for it to be laid out anew. Flower gardens, formal lawns, a Victorian bandstand, and an ornamental lake with lots of waterfowl are all within the park's borders, connected by paths guaranteeing that strolling here or just passing through will offer up unexpected delights (such as palm trees). Among the park's many statues are a memorial to William Butler Yeats and another to Joyce by Henry Moore. In the 18th century the walk on the north side of the green was referred to as the Beaux Walk because most of Dublin's gentlemen's clubs were in town houses here. Today it's dominated by the legendary Shelbourne hotel. On the south side is the alluring Georgian Newman House. A large outdoor market springs up around the park at Christmastime. **TIP→ If you have littles in tow, there's a well-maintained playground at the center of the green.** ✉ *Southside* 🎫 *Free.*

The Shelbourne Hotel

HOTEL | The iconic, redbrick, white-wood-trim Shelbourne hotel commands "the best address in Dublin" from the north side of St. Stephen's Green, where it has stood since 1865. You don't have to stay to take advantage of the gorgeous location; stop in for afternoon tea in the very opulent Lord Mayor's Lounge, a true Dublin treat, and bask in the history, grandeur, and other tasty dining options available at Dublin's most iconic hotel. In 1921 the Irish Free State's constitution was drafted here, in a first-floor suite. Elizabeth Bowen wrote her novel *The Hotel* about this very place. ✉ *27 St. Stephen's Green, Southside* ☎ *01/676–6471* 🌐 *theshelbourne.com.*

★ Trinity College Dublin

COLLEGE | Founded in 1592 by Queen Elizabeth I to "civilize" (Her Majesty's word) Dublin, Trinity is Ireland's oldest and most famous college. The memorably atmospheric campus is a must; here you can track the shadows of some of the noted alumni, such as Jonathan Swift (1667–1745), Oscar Wilde (1854–1900), Bram Stoker (1847–1912), and Samuel Beckett

Dublin's Gorgeous Georgians

"Extraordinary Dublin!" sigh art lovers and connoisseurs of the 18th century. It was during the glorious 18th century that this duckling of a city was transformed into a preening swan, largely by the Georgian style of art and architecture that flowered between 1714 and 1820 during the reigns of the four English Georges.

Today Dublin remains in good part a sublimely Georgian city, thanks to enduring grace notes: the commodious and uniformly laid-out streets, the genteel town squares, the redbrick mansions accented with demilune (half-moon) fan windows. The great 18th-century showpieces are **Merrion, Fitzwilliam, Mountjoy,** and **Parnell Squares. Merrion Square East,** the longest Georgian street in town, reveals scenes of decorum, elegance, polish, and charm, all woven into a "tapestry of rosy brick and white enamel," to quote the 18th-century connoisseur Horace Walpole.

Setting off the facades are fanlighted doors (often lacquered in black, green, yellow, or red) and the celebrated "patent reveal" window trims—thin plaster linings painted white to catch the light. These half-moon fanlights—as iconic of the city as clock towers are of Zurich—are often in the Neoclassical style known as Adamesque (which was inspired by the designs of the great English architect Robert Adam).

Many facades appear severely plain, but don't be fooled: just behind their stately front doors are entry rooms and stairways aswirl with tinted rococo plasterwork, often the work of *stuccadores* (plasterers) from Italy (including the talented Lafranchini brothers). Magnificent **Newman House** (✉ *85–86 St. Stephen's Green, Southside* ☎ *01/477–9810*), one of the finest of Georgian houses, is now home to the brand-new Museum of Literature Ireland.

The Palladian style—as the Georgian style was then called—began to reign supreme in domestic architecture in 1745, when the Croesus-rich Earl of Kildare returned from an Italian grand tour and built a gigantic Palladian palace called **Leinster House** in the seedy section of town.

"Where I go, fashion will follow," he declared, and indeed it did. By then, the Anglo-Irish elite had given the city London airs by building the **Parliament House** (now the Bank of Ireland), the **Royal Exchange** (now City Hall), the **Custom House,** and the **Four Courts** in the new style.

But this phase of high fashion came to an end with the Act of Union: according to historian Maurice Craig, "On the last stroke of midnight, December 31, 1800, the gaily caparisoned horses turned into mice, the coaches into pumpkins, the silks and brocades into rags, and Ireland was once again the Cinderella among the nations."

It was nearly 150 years before the spotlight shone once again on 18th-century Dublin. In recent decades, the conservation efforts of the **Irish Georgian Society** (✉ *74 Merrion Sq., Southside* ☎ *01/676–7053*) have done much to restore Dublin to its Georgian splendor. Thanks to its founders, the Hon. Desmond Guinness and his late wife, Mariga, many historic houses have been saved and preserved.

(1906–89). Trinity College, Dublin (familiarly known as Trinity or TCD), was founded on the site of the confiscated Priory of All Hallows. For centuries Trinity was the preserve of the Protestant Church; a free education was offered to Catholics—provided that they accepted the Protestant faith. As a legacy of this condition, until 1966 Catholics who wished to study at Trinity had to obtain a dispensation from their bishop or face excommunication.

Trinity's grounds cover 40 acres. Most of its buildings were constructed in the 18th and early 19th centuries. The extensive West Front, with a classical pedimented portico in the Corinthian style, faces College Green and is directly across from the Bank of Ireland; it was built between 1755 and 1759, and is possibly the work of Theodore Jacobsen, architect of London's Foundling Hospital. The design is repeated on the interior, so the view is the same from outside the gates and from the quadrangle inside. On the lawn in front of the inner facade stand statues of two alumni, orator Edmund Burke (1729–97) and dramatist Oliver Goldsmith (1730–74). On the right side of the cobblestone quadrangle of Parliament Square (commonly known as Front Square) is Sir William Chambers's theater, or Examination Hall, dating from the mid-1780s, which contains the college's most splendid Adamesque interior, designed by Michael Stapleton. The hall houses an impressive organ retrieved from an 18th-century Spanish ship and a gilded oak chandelier from the old House of Commons; concerts are sometimes held here. The chapel, left of the quadrangle, has stucco ceilings and fine woodwork. The looming campanile, or bell tower, is the symbolic heart of the college; erected in 1853, it dominates the center of the square. Guided campus tours are offered, some of which combine entry to the *Book of Kells*, or you can take a self-guided tour via the Visit Trinity app (*tcd.ie/visitors/book-of-kell*). *Trinity College, Southside 01/896–1000 tcd.ie Free, €15 campus tour, €5 self-guided tour.*

Restaurants

Big Fan

$ | CHINESE | Head chef Alex Zhang has brought his own brand of daring Northern Chinese cuisine to this cool, new, city-center spot. The menu changes regularly, but the deep-fried duck wings tossed in secret seasoning and the fresh Irish lobster with tofu egg custard are typically thrilling dishes. **Known for:** buzzing atmosphere; innovative Chinese food; regular new dishes. *Average main: €18 16 Aungier St., Dublin South 01/538–8886 bigfan.ie Closed Tues. No lunch Mon., Wed., and Thurs.*

★ Dunne and Crescenzi

$ | ITALIAN | The unpretentious brilliance of this husband-and-wife restaurant and deli just off Nassau Street is what makes the classy little Italian joint so popular. The menu is extensive but simple: panini, antipasti, a few choice pasta specials, and some evening meat dishes and desserts. **Known for:** Italian wine cellar; killer antipasti; great for large groups. *Average main: €18 14 S. Fredrick St., Southside 01/677–3815 dunneandcrescenzi.com.*

Fade Street Social

$$$ | MODERN IRISH | Former Michelin-star celebrity chef Dylan McGrath has another hit on his hands with Fade Street Social, a cavernous tapas bar, restaurant, and pub all rolled into one. At 8,000 square feet, the place can seem a bit overwhelming, but if you want a busy, fun, all-in-one dining-and-drinking experience, this place is ideal. **Known for:** amazing staff who go above and beyond; great selection of vegan dishes; inventive cocktails. *Average main: €29 4 Fade St., Southside 01/604–0066 fadestreetsocial.com.*

Trinity College's Front Square is paved with cobblestones and dotted with statues of its famous alumni, including Oliver Goldsmith and Samuel Beckett.

★ Fallon & Byrne

$$$ | **FRENCH** | This fresh, one-stop shop for everything organic and delicious in Dublin combines a huge deli with a cozy cellar wine bar and expansive second-floor French brasserie. Located on the top floor of a beautiful old telephone exchange building, the high-ceiling, light-filled dining room is always bustling. **Known for:** hearty brasserie menu; bustling city-center vibe; elegant dining room. *Average main: €28 ✉ 11–17 Exchequer St., Southside ☎ 01/472–1010 🌐 fallonandbyrne.com.*

Glas

$$$$ | **VEGETARIAN** | Its name is the Gaelic word for green, and vegetables sing on the two- or three-course prix-fixe menus (€40–49) at Dublin's first high-end vegetarian restaurant. The brash, luxurious interior matches the daring menu, which includes barbecue celeriac with roast potato puree, cucumber, mint, and potato paper. **Known for:** lush interior; high-end vegetarian dishes; prix-fixe menu. *Average main: €40 ✉ 15/16 Chatham St., Dublin South ☎ 01/672–4534 🌐 glasrestaurant.ie ⏲ No lunch Mon.–Thurs.*

★ Glover's Alley

$$$$ | **CONTEMPORARY** | Named after a nearby street of former glove makers, this new, Michelin-starred eatery's stylish interior has a 1920s retro feel, but chef Andy McFadden's menu is all modern. To start try the scallop ceviche, with foie gras, basil, and radish. **Known for:** hot-shot young chef; great view overlooking Stephen's Green; stylish interior. *Average main: €40 ✉ The Fitzwilliam Hotel, 127–128 St. Stephen's Green, Southside ☎ 01/478–7000 🌐 gloversalley.ie ⏲ Closed Sun. and Mon. No lunch Tues. and Wed.*

The Good World

$ | **CHINESE** | When Dublin's growing Chinese population wants a big, uptown night out, they come here where the food is authentic and inspired—ask for the black-cover Chinese menu. The surroundings are modest, with large round tables (ideal for groups) in a somewhat dark but comfortable room. **Known**

for: tasty fried squid starter; still-warm fresh-baked egg tarts; excellent dim sum. *Average main: €16 18 S. Great George's St., Southside 01/677–5373 www.goodworld.ie.*

The Green Hen

$$$ | **BISTRO** | It can be hard to re-create that classic bistro feel outside France, but this intimate spot in the heart of busy Dublin has managed to get the mix of bustle and tranquility just right. A quick glance at the gilt-framed, mirrored menu reveals that this kitchen is all about rich, evocative French fare—two winners are the rib eye and the panfried bass. **Known for:** best confit in town; adventurous plats du jour; informal bistro vibe. *Average main: €25 33 Exchequer St., Southside 01/670–7238 thegreenhen.ie.*

Host

$$$ | **MEDITERRANEAN** | Foodie and fashionista couple Chloe Kearney and Niall McDermott returned from London to open this standout addition to the flourishing Ranelagh dining scene. Behind the minimalist white exterior lies a small but buzzing ambience and some inventive food with a Mediterranean twist. **Known for:** warm, attentive staff; every dish perfectly executed; can be hard to get a reservation. *Average main: €26 13 Ranelagh, Southside 01/561–2617 www.hostrestaurant.ie Closed Mon. No lunch Sun.–Fri.*

La Maison

$$$ | **FRENCH** | This Breton-inspired, unpretentious eatery has one of the most inviting and good-value menus in the city. The look is very much casual bistro, a satisfying backdrop for starters like the beet risotto with winter truffles, and such mouthwatering mains as the loin of venison with red cabbage and celeriac paste. **Known for:** quality wine list; intimate atmosphere; irresistible chocolate fondant. *Average main: €27 15 Castle Market, Southside 01/672–7258 lamaisondublin.com Closed Mon.*

L'Gueuleton

$$$ | **FRENCH** | This exceptional eatery just off George's Street lost a little of its intimacy when it expanded, but the crowds still come for authentic French food at a fair price. Start with 12 snails, fresh herbs, garlic, and pastis butter. **Known for:** decadent desserts; great people-watching; tip-top service. *Average main: €27 1 Fade St., Southside 01/675–3708 lgueuleton.com.*

★ Mae

$$$$ | **MODERN IRISH** | Located upstairs at the wonderful French Paradox wine shop, this cozy restaurant sees celebrated local chef Grainne O'Keefe work her magic on the best of Irish produce. The fixed-price tasting menu changes with the seasons, moving from starters like aubergine tart with goat cheese and pickled walnut to meat courses like Iberico pork, with anchovy, dates, and confit potato. **Known for:** great wine selection, so opt for the wine pairing; seasonal prix-fixe menu; celebrated chef. *Average main: €70 53 Shelbourne Rd., Dublin South 01/231–3903 maerestaurant.ie Closed Sun. and Mon. No lunch.*

★ Nightmarket

$$ | **THAI** | "Street food" is a painfully abused term in the dining world, but this downstairs Thai joint in the heart of Ranelagh has the authentic flavors and spice of a Bangkok noodle stall. The narrow dining area is beautifully tiled in simple colors and packs out quickly with locals and visitors. **Known for:** best Thai in the city; inventive street food; fills up quickly. *Average main: €24 120 Ranelagh, Southside 01/538–5200 nightmarket.ie Closed Mon. No lunch.*

★ One Pico

$$$$ | **MODERN IRISH** | Chef-owner Eamonn O'Reilly cuts quite a dash, but it's his sophisticated, daring, contemporary cuisine that tends to seduce visitors to his little restaurant tucked away in a quiet lane only a few minutes from

Stephen's Green. As is usual with Dublin's luxe eateries, the fixed-price lunch and pretheater menus offer great value. **Known for:** gregarious chef-host; daring ingredient combinations; prix-fixe menu. *Average main: €89 5–6 Molesworth Pl., off Schoolhouse La., Southside 01/676–0300 onepico.com Closed Sun. and Mon.*

Shanahan's on the Green

$$$$ | **STEAKHOUSE** | Glowing with gilded chandeliers and graced with a few marble fireplaces, this American-style steak house in a restored Georgian town house offers a sleekly elegant setting in which to dine on some of the most tender Irish Angus beef this side of the Atlantic (they cook it in a special high-temperature oven, searing the outside to keep the inside juicy). If steak doesn't float your boat, they also do a mean baked turbot with mussels, clams, and creamed fennel and leek. **Known for:** amazing cheesecake; sumptuous surroundings; deep wine list. *Average main: €62 119 St. Stephen's Green, Southside 01/407–0939 www.shanahans.ie Closed Sun. and Mon. No lunch Tues.–Thurs. and Sat.*

Yamamori Noodles

$$ | **JAPANESE** | The open plan and family-style tables have kept Yamamori popular with noodle addicts and the younger hipster crowd. The meals-in-a-bowl are a splendid slurping experience, and although you'll be supplied with a small Chinese-style soup spoon, the best approach is with chopsticks. **Known for:** bento boxes; hip crowd; efficient service. *Average main: €21 72 S. Great George's St., Southside 01/475–5001 yamamori.ie.*

Coffee and Quick Bites

★ Cake Café

$ | **CAFÉ** | At this dreamy little café, local, organic, and seasonal are the words to live by, where you can chow down on simple savory and sweet delights, all made with a loving, homey touch. The plant-filled courtyard is also the perfect summer spot for a daytime glass of prosecco and small bites. **Known for:** pitch-perfect cakes; personal touches; slow-food philosophy. *Average main: €13 The Daintree Bldg., Pleasants Pl., Southside 01/478–9394 thecakecafe.ie Closed Sun. No dinner.*

The Pepper Pot

$ | **CAFÉ** | The hodgepodge collection of old tablecloths, cutlery, and cups creates a warm, family atmosphere in this sweet little café on the balcony level of the Powerscourt Town House Centre. Weary shoppers resuscitate with the simple menu, fresh-baked goods, TLC, and wonderful people-watching. **Known for:** homey vibe; best salads in the city; divine sponge cake. *Average main: €9 Powerscourt Town Centre, 1st fl. balcony, S. William St., Southside 01/707–1610 thepepperpot.ie Closed Sun. No dinner.*

Hotels

Brooks Hotel

$$$ | **HOTEL** | It has nearly 100 rooms, but this hotel—minutes from Grafton Street—likes to describe itself as a boutique property, and it does manage to convey the personal touch of a much smaller establishment. **Pros:** warm, friendly staff; live piano music in bar; delicious breakfasts at hotel restaurant. **Cons:** office-block exterior; business clientele makes for slightly flat atmosphere; standard rooms on small side. *Rooms from: €290 Drury St., Southside 01/670–4000 brookshotel.ie 98 rooms No Meals.*

Buswells

$$ | **HOTEL** | Situated in the heart of Dublin's museum district, the restrained Georgian facade of Buswells hides a low-key, intimate hotel right at the heart of the city. **Pros:** period interiors; quality

value option; great central location. **Cons:** can book up quickly; busy public areas; light on amenities. *Rooms from: €225* *23–27 Molesworth St., Dublin South* *01/614–6500* *buswells.ie* *69 rooms* *No Meals.*

Conrad Dublin

$$$$ | **HOTEL** | The best thing about the ugly-on-the-outside, seven-story, redbrick, and smoked-glass Conrad are the spectacular views out over the city, so ask for—no, insist on—a room on one of the top three floors. **Pros:** offers concierge-curated experiences; top-notch service; pet-friendly rooms available. **Cons:** drab 1970s-style exterior; slightly cramped standard rooms; poor views on lower floors. *Rooms from: €340* *Earlsfort Terr., Southside* *01/602–8900* *conradhotels.com* *192 rooms* *No Meals.*

The Dean

$$$ | **HOTEL** | This urbane and boldly designed hotel a few minutes from Grafton Street is truly boutique with a unique mix of Georgian and modern architecture and an unusual selection of room sizes and shapes. **Pros:** stunning views from rooftop bar; new gym; great restaurant and bar. **Cons:** very compact lobby; rooms aren't huge; noisy nightlife on the same street. *Rooms from: €299* *33 Harcourt St., Southside* *01/607–8110* *deandublin.ie* *52 rooms* *No Meals.*

★ **The Devlin**

$$$ | **HOTEL** | Located in trendy Ranelagh village, just outside the city center, this boutique property refers to its compact rooms as "pods," and offers a rooftop restaurant and terrace, ground-floor bar and coffee shop, and subterranean 42-seat cinema and bar, making it one of the coolest places to stay in Dublin right now. **Pros:** cool, contemporary design; rooftop restaurant has great city views; lively bar filled with locals. **Cons:** a little outside city center; no parking; some rooms are compact. *Rooms from: €265* *119 Ranelagh Rd., Southside* *01/406–6550* *thedevlin.ie* *40 rooms* *No Meals.*

The Fitzwilliam Hotel

$$$$ | **HOTEL** | Definitely hustle for an upper floor room overlooking iconic St. Stephen's Green at this luxury staple of the central Dublin hotel scene. **Pros:** Michelin-starred restaurant; killer views from some rooms; top-class staff. **Cons:** restaurant can book out; quality of view varies; gets very pricey in peak seasons. *Rooms from: €450* *St. Stephen's Green, Southside* *01/478–7000* *www.fitzwilliamhoteldublin.com* *138 rooms.*

Iveagh Garden Hotel

$$$ | **HOTEL** | Housed in an elegant four-story Georgian terrace just a five-minute walk from St. Stephen's Green, this contemporary-luxe hotel is decorated with rich wallpapers, touches of brass, gleaming mirrors, stylish tiled floors, lots of Navan-manufactured furniture—and it is fully powered by an underground river. **Pros:** Ireland's first sustainable hotel; accessible rooms available for wheelchair users; excellent location. **Cons:** no gym, pool, or spa; nightlife on the same street can be noisy; parking is limited. *Rooms from: €280* *72–74 Harcourt St., Southside* *01/568–5500* *iveaghgardenhotel.ie* *145 rooms* *No Meals.*

★ **The Shelbourne**

$$$$ | **HOTEL** | Paris has the Ritz, New York has the St. Regis, and Dublin has the Shelbourne—resplendent in its broad, ornamented, pink-and-white mid-Victorian facade right off Grafton Street. **Pros:** rooms in front overlook Stephen's Green; history at every turn; spa and wellness center. **Cons:** some noise in front rooms; feels a little stuffy at times; pricey. *Rooms from: €460* *27 St. Stephen's Green, Southside* *01/663–4500, 800/543–4300 in U.S.* *theshelbourne.com* *265 rooms* *No Meals.*

Stauntons On The Green

$$$ | **HOTEL** | Cardinals, politicians, and poets have lived and worked in this gorgeous, original Georgian house on Stephen's Green. **Pros:** Irish art collection; historic building; elegance at a good price. **Cons:** amenities limited; room sizes vary; can book up quickly in summer. *Rooms from: €290 ✉ 83 St. Stephen's Green S, Dublin South ☎ 01/478–2300 🌐 stauntonsonthegreen.ie 50 rooms No Meals.*

★ **Westbury Hotel Dublin**

$$$$ | **HOTEL** | This luxurious, chandelier-filled, modern hotel just off Grafton Street is a favorite with elegantly dressed Dubliners who stop for afternoon tea in the Gallery, the spacious mezzanine-level main lobby, furnished with a grand piano and a grand view out onto the bustling streets. **Pros:** prime people-watching; convenient location; the Art Deco glamour of the Marble bar. **Cons:** tries a little too hard to be posh; books up quickly in summer; pricey. *Rooms from: €480 ✉ Grafton St., Southside ☎ 01/679–1122 🌐 doylecollection.com 205 rooms No Meals.*

The Westin Dublin

$$$$ | **HOTEL** | Reconstructed from three 19th-century landmark buildings opposite Trinity College, the Westin is all about location, but the marble pillars, tall mahogany doorways, blazing fireplaces, Palladian marble busts, and period details also set it apart. **Pros:** beside Temple Bar but not in Temple Bar; in-room spa treatments; some rooms overlook Trinity College. **Cons:** on a busy traffic corner; windowless bar; not cheap. *Rooms from: €490 ✉ College Green, Southside ☎ 01/645–1000 🌐 thewestindublin.com 163 rooms No Meals.*

Nightlife

LIVE MUSIC

The Sugar Club

LIVE MUSIC | There's a touch of Vegas about this landmark venue with the tables and chairs on tiered levels that look down on the stage. The Sugar Club has regular music and performance (some touted as burlesque) nights. *✉ 8 Lower Leeson St., Southside ☎ 01/678–7188 🌐 thesugarclub.com.*

JAZZ

Ha'penny Bridge Inn

LIVE MUSIC | In its tiny but buzzing upstairs room, the Ha'penny Bridge regularly hosts blues and jazz nights and has good comedy on Thursday. *✉ 42 Wellington Quay, Southside ☎ 01/677–0616 🌐 hapennybridgeinn.com.*

PUBS

Against The Grain

BARS | Ireland has gone through a craft-beer revolution and this busy spot is the place to sample a huge variety of them. The classy red pool table and selection of board games are perfect for a rainy afternoon. *✉ 11 Wexford St., Dublin South ☎ 01/470–5100 🌐 galwaybaybrewery.com/againstthegrain.*

★ **Cafe en Seine**

BARS | Dublin's first superpub received a €4 million face-lift just before the pandemic with three floors of opulent Art Nouveau style à la grand Parisian brasserie, an extensive food menu, and a spectacular enclosed garden terrace with a retractable glass roof. This is one of Dublin's more elegant places to socialize. *✉ 40 Dawson St., Southside ☎ 01/677–4567 🌐 cafeenseine.ie.*

Cassidy's

PUBS | Once a quality neighborhood pub with a tasty pint of stout, Cassidy's has morphed into an often overcrowded but very popular spot with a young clientele. *✉ 42 Lower Camden St., Southside ☎ 01/475–6540.*

Davy Byrnes

PUBS | A noted pilgrimage stop for Joyceans, Davy Byrnes is where Leopold Bloom stops in for a glass of Burgundy and a Gorgonzola-cheese sandwich in *Ulysses* (and ruminates before helping a blind man cross the road). The decor—with leather seats and dramatic art on the walls—is more decadent than in Joyce's day ("He entered Davy Byrnes. Moral pub."), but it still serves some fine pub grub. ✉ *21 Duke St., Southside* ☎ *01/677–5217* 🌐 *davybyrnes.com.*

Doheny & Nesbitt

PUBS | A traditional spot with snugs, dark wooden furnishings, and smoke-darkened ceilings, Doheny & Nesbitt has hardly changed over the decades. ✉ *4–5 Lower Baggot St., Southside* ☎ *01/676–2945* 🌐 *dohenyandnesbitts.ie.*

Doyle's In Town

PUBS | A cozy pub, Doyle's is a favorite with journalists from the *Irish Times* and Trinity students. ✉ *9 College St., Southside* ☎ *01/671–0616* 🌐 *doylesintown.com.*

The George

BARS | Dublin's two-floor main gay pub, the George draws an almost entirely male crowd; its nightclub stays open until 2:30 am nightly except Tuesday. The "alternative bingo night," with star drag act Miss Shirley Temple Bar, is a riot of risqué fun. Saturdays are always packed. ✉ *89 S. Great George's St., Southside* ☎ *01/478–2983* 🌐 *thegeorge.ie.*

★ **Grogan's**

PUBS | Also known as the Castle Lounge, Grogan's is a small place packed with creative folk. The old owner was known as a patron of local artists, and his walls are still covered with their work. There's no music or TV, so you can have a proper chat with your pint and toastie. ✉ *15 S. William St., Southside* ☎ *01/677–9320* 🌐 *grogansppub.ie.*

Hogan's

PUBS | A huge space on two levels, Hogan's gets jammed most nights with a cool college crowd. But in the afternoon it's a quieter spot and perfect for people-watching out the large windows. ✉ *35 S. Great George's St., Southside* ☎ *01/677–5904* 🌐 *hogansbar.com.*

★ **Horseshoe Bar**

BARS | The who's who of city society have always been drawn to the elegance of this glorious Dublin institution at the Shelbourne hotel. There's comparatively little space for drinkers around the famous semicircular bar—but this does wonders for making friends quickly. ✉ *Shelbourne, 27 St. Stephen's Green, Southside* ☎ *01/676–6471* 🌐 *theshelbourne.com.*

Kehoe's

PUBS | Popular with Trinity students and local hipsters, Kehoe's has a tiny back room that is nice and cozy, while the upstairs is basically the owner's old living room, open to the public. ✉ *9 S. Anne St., Southside* ☎ *01/677–8312* 🌐 *kehoesdublin.ie.*

The Little Pig

COCKTAIL LOUNGES | This hidden speakeasy is a fabulous spot for a late-night cocktail with its luxurious red velvet walls, polished bronze ceiling, dark velvet seating, and dimmed tassled lamps. The martinis are said to be the best in town, and the sublime Italian dishes (some served in porcelain teacups) are a delightful surprise. ✉ *Wicklow St., Southside* ☎ *01/565–4398* 🌐 *thelittlepig.ie.*

The Long Hall

PUBS | One of Dublin's most ornate traditional taverns, the Long Hall has Victorian lamps, a mahogany bar, mirrors, chandeliers, and plasterwork ceilings, all more than 100 years old. The pub serves sandwiches and an excellent pint of Guinness. ✉ *51 S. Great George's St., Southside* ☎ *01/475–1590.*

McDaid's
PUBS | A landmark that once attracted boisterous Brendan Behan and other leading writers in the 1950s, McDaid's wild literary reputation still lingers, although the bar has been discreetly modernized and is altogether quieter. ✉ *3 Harry St., Southside* ☎ *01/679–4395.*

The Mint Bar
BARS | In the basement of the Westin Hotel and set in a former bank vault, the Mint Bar is a classic cocktail bar with a touch of romance. ✉ *Westin Hotel, College Green, Southside* ☎ *01/645–1000* 🌐 *themintbar.ie.*

Neary's
PUBS | With an exotic, Victorian-style interior, Neary's was once the haunt of music-hall artists and a certain literary set, including Brendan Behan. Join the actors from the adjacent Gaiety Theatre for a good pub lunch. ✉ *1 Chatham St., Southside* ☎ *01/677–7371* 🌐 *nearys.ie.*

The Odeon
BARS | The converted main building of Harcourt Street's old railway station houses this large, modern cocktail bar. Both the lunch and dinner menus include fish-and-chips, burgers, and good salads. Sunday brunch is served between noon and 5. ✉ *57 Harcourt St., Southside* ☎ *01/478–2088* 🌐 *odeon.ie.*

O'Donoghue's
PUBS | A cheerful, tourist-friendly hangout, O'Donoghue's has impromptu musical performances that often spill out onto the street. ✉ *15 Merrion Row, Southside* ☎ *01/676–2807* 🌐 *odonoghues.ie.*

The Old Stand
PUBS | One of the oldest pubs in the city, the Old Stand is named after the now demolished Old Stand at Lansdowne Road stadium, home to Irish rugby and football. The pub is renowned for great pints and fine steaks. ✉ *37 Exchequer St., Southside* ☎ *01/677–7220* 🌐 *theoldstandpub.com.*

★ P Mac's
BARS | Old meets new in this award-winning, cozy spot adjacent to the Drury Court hotel. The dark-wood and bar-mirror interior is classic Dublin, but the craft beer selection and chilled-out, board-gaming atmosphere has a more millennial vibe. ✉ *Drury Court Hotel, 30 Stephen St. Lower, Dublin South* ☎ *01/475–8578* 🌐 *drurycourthotel.ie/home/p-macs-bar-dining.*

★ Peruke & Periwig
COCKTAIL LOUNGES | This stylish, three-floor cocktail bar, named for the wigmakers once located here, has cutting-edge cocktails, plush velvet banquettes, wood panels, and baroque portraits and wigs on the walls. The food is decent, too. ✉ *31 Dawson St., Southside* ☎ *01/672–7190* 🌐 *peruke.ie.*

★ Stag's Head
PUBS | A Victorian beaut, the Stag's Head dates from 1770 and was rebuilt in 1895. Theater people from the nearby Olympia and Trinity students gather around the unusual Connemara red-marble bar, study their reflections in the many mirrors, and drink in all the oak carvings. They host live music and comedy downstairs most nights. ✉ *1 Dame Ct., Southside* ☎ *01/679–3701* 🌐 *stagshead.ie.*

Performing Arts

CLASSICAL MUSIC AND OPERA

St. Stephen's Church
MUSIC | Under its glorious "pepper canister" cupola, St. Stephen's Church stages a tempting program of choral and orchestral events. ✉ *Upper Mount St., Southside* ☎ *01/288–0663* 🌐 *stann.dublin.anglican.org.*

ROCK AND CONTEMPORARY MUSIC

International Bar
MUSIC | A long-established, tiny, get-close-to-the-band venue upstairs, the International also hosts theater in the afternoon and comedy on weekends.

✉ *Wicklow St., Southside* ☎ *01/677–9250* 🌐 *theinternationalcomedyclub.com.*

Opium

MUSIC | Set in a striking, glass-front building, Opium hosts regular rock gigs or bass-thumping international DJ sets. There's a Pan-Asian restaurant out front if you get peckish. ✉ *26 Wexford St., Southside* ☎ *01/475–8555* 🌐 *opium.ie.*

Whelan's

MUSIC | It might look a bit shabby around the edges, but Whelan's is one of the city's best—and most popular—music venues. Well-known performers play everything from rock to folk to traditional music. ✉ *25 Wexford St., Southside* ☎ *01/478–0766* 🌐 *whelanslive.com.*

FILM

★ The Stella

FILM | This gorgeous Art Deco cinema has been restored to all its 1920s glory. Enjoy a cocktail while watching old classics or new releases in the sumptuous leather seats. ✉ *207–209 Rathmines Rd. Lower, Southside* ☎ *01/496–7014* 🌐 *stellacinemas.ie.*

THEATER

★ Gaiety Theatre

THEATER | When this shimmering red-and-gold 19th-century theater is not showing musical comedy, drama, and revues, the sumptuous Gaiety is taken over by Opera Ireland for one of its big shows. ✉ *S. King St., Southside* ☎ *01/677–1717* 🌐 *gaietytheatre.ie.*

Samuel Beckett Centre

THEATER | Home to Trinity College's drama department and the student Players group, as well as visiting European companies, the Samuel Beckett Centre also hosts dance performances by visiting troupes; the theater was built in 1992 and stands near the center of Trinity's campus. ✉ *Trinity College, Southside* ☎ *01/608–2266* 🌐 *tcd.ie/beckett-theatre.*

Shopping

BOOKS

Books Upstairs

BOOKS | An excellent selection of special-interest books is available here, including Irish literature, gay and feminist literature, psychology, and self-help books. There's a cool café upstairs. ✉ *17 D'Olier St., Southside* ☎ *01/679–6687* 🌐 *booksupstairs.ie.*

★ Hodges Figgis

BOOKS | Dublin's leading independent bookstore, Hodges Figgis stocks 1½ million books on three floors. Once considered Ireland's oldest, its independent claim is a bit bogus, as a giant chain bought it some years ago. That noted, it has the stock, staff, look, and even aroma of an independent bookstore, and might even still please James Joyce (who alludes to it in his *Ulysses*). ✉ *56–58 Dawson St., Southside* ☎ *01/677–4754* 🌐 *waterstones.com/bookshops/hodges-figgis.*

★ Stokes Books

BOOKS | A gem of an antique bookstore, Stokes has a great used-book section and specializes in Irish history and literature. While on the small side, Stokes is a treasure trove for book lovers. ✉ *George's Street Arcade, Southside* ☎ *01/671–3584* 🌐 *georgesstreetarcade.ie.*

★ Ulysses Rare Books

BOOKS | Head here for a fine array of first editions of Irish literature and many other books of Irish interest, plus old maps of Dublin and Ireland. ✉ *10 Duke St., Southside* ☎ *01/671–8676* 🌐 *rarebooks.ie.*

CLOTHING

★ Costume

WOMEN'S CLOTHING | A classy boutique for Dubliners with fashion sense and money, Costume showcases local designers such as Helen Steele. Vivetta and Preen are among the international designers featured among the rails of

Dublin Shopping Streets

Southside

Dawson Street. Just east of Grafton Street between Nassau Street to the north and St. Stephen's Green to the south, Dawson Street is full of lively cafés and bars. It's also the address of Hodges Figgis, the best bookstore in the country.

Drury Street. A few streets over from Grafton Street, you'll find one of Dublin's coolest indie streets, home to independent coffee bars, gems like the Irish Design Shop dedicated to top quality Irish design, and interiors and gift stores like Industry and The Printmakers Gallery.

Francis Street. Part of the Liberties, the oldest part of the city and the hub of Dublin's antiques trade, Francis Street and surrounding areas, such as the Coombe, have plenty of shops where you can browse. If you're looking for something in particular, dealers will gladly recommend the appropriate store to you. It's also home to a couple of hot new galleries.

Grafton Street. Dublin's bustling pedestrian-only main shopping street, Grafton Street has two department stores: down-to-earth Marks & Spencer and très chic Brown Thomas. The rest of the street is taken up by shops, many of them branches of international chains, such as the Body Shop and a Disney Store, and a few British chains. This is also the spot to buy fresh flowers, available at reasonable prices from outdoor stands. On the smaller streets off Grafton Street—especially Duke Street, South Anne Street, and Chatham Street—are worthwhile crafts, clothing, and designer housewares shops.

Nassau Street. Dublin's main tourist-oriented thoroughfare, Nassau has some of the best-known stores selling Irish goods, but you won't find many locals shopping here. Still, if you're looking for classic Irish gifts to take home, you should be sure at least to browse along here.

Temple Bar

Cow's Lane. Technically a short lane and not a street, Cow's Lane offers cute cafés, tattoo parlors, the Gutter Bookshop, and an arts and crafts market on Saturday.

Temple Bar. Once dubbed Dublin's hippest neighborhood, Temple Bar is still dotted with small, precious boutiques—mainly intimate, quirky shops that traffic in a small selection of trendy goods, from vintage clothes to some of the most avant-garde Irish garb anywhere in the city.

Northside

Henry Street. Running westward from O'Connell Street, Henry Street is where cash-conscious Dubliners shop. Arnotts department store is the anchor here. Henry Street's continuation, Mary Street, has a branch of Marks & Spencer and the Jervis Shopping Centre.

O'Connell Street. The city's main thoroughfare, O'Connell Street is more downscale than Southside city streets (such as Grafton Street), but it is still worth a walk. Eason's, a very large book, magazine, and stationery store is the flagship shop, and there are a few Irish gift shops plus a much-loved doughnut stand.

colorful, stylish clothes. ✉ *10 Castel Market, Southside* ☎ *01/679–4188* 🌐 *costumedublin.ie.*

★ OM DIVA

WOMEN'S CLOTHING | Owner Ruth Ní Lionsigh has developed a hive of style and fashion creativity in her ever-expanding city-center shop. From hot young Irish designers, to contemporary worldwide fashion and even the best of vintage, OM Diva has it all covered. ✉ *27 Drury St., Southside* ☎ *01/679–1211* 🌐 *omdivaboutique.com.*

DEPARTMENT STORES

★ Brown Thomas

DEPARTMENT STORE | Dublin's most exclusive department store, Brown Thomas stocks the leading designer names (including top Irish designers) in clothing and cosmetics, plus lots of stylish accessories. There's also a good selection of crystal. Their January sales are a big draw. ✉ *Grafton St., Southside* ☎ *01/605–6666* 🌐 *brownthomas.com.*

Dunnes Stores

DEPARTMENT STORE | Ireland's largest chain of department stores, all Dunnes branches stock fashion (including the exciting Savida range), household (try the classy Considered line), and grocery items, and have a reputation for value and variety. Other branches can be found on Henry Street and in the Ilac Centre on Mary Street. ✉ *St. Stephen's Green Centre, Southside* ☎ *01/478–0188* 🌐 *dunnesstores.com.*

Marks & Spencer

DEPARTMENT STORE | More affordable than high-end Grafton Street competitor Brown Thomas, Marks & Spencer stocks everything from fashion (including lingerie) to tasty, unusual groceries. ✉ *Grafton St., Southside* ☎ *01/679–7855* 🌐 *marksandspencer.com.*

HOME AND DESIGN

★ Industry & Co

HOUSEWARES | An intimate space curating and showcasing the very best of Irish furniture, jewelry, and ceramic design—this is a one-stop shop to support Irish makers. Be sure to leave time to visit the popular on-site café. ✉ *41 Drury St., Southside* ☎ *01/613–9111* 🌐 *industryandco.com.*

Irish Design Shop

HOUSEWARES | Two young jewelers got together to open this exciting shop dedicated to the best in Irish design and designers. They sell the work of some of Ireland's best makers with everything from bird feeders, Aran hats and other woolens, and Irish cookbooks to pottery, prints, their own jewelry line, and assorted other treasures. ✉ *41 Drury St., Southside* ☎ *01/679–8871* 🌐 *irishdesignshop.com.*

Kilkenny Shop

CRAFTS | Specializing in contemporary Irish-made ceramics, pottery, and silver jewelry, Kilkenny Shop regularly holds exhibits of exciting new work by Irish craftspeople and has a wide array of gifts fashioned by Orla Kiely and other top Irish designers. ✉ *6–15 Nassau St., Southside* ☎ *01/677–7066* 🌐 *kilkennyshop.com.*

Sweater Shop

SOUVENIRS | They might sell sweaters and scarves but Trinity Woollen Mills is also your one-stop shop for everything kitschy Irish, such as trashy treasures like "the leprechauns made me do it" mugs and Guinness-logo underwear. ✉ *30 Nassau St., Southside* ☎ *01/672–5663* 🌐 *sweatershop.com.*

JEWELRY

Appleby Jewellers

JEWELRY & WATCHES | This is the best known of the several classy, old-style jewelry shops that line tiny Johnson's Court, a delightful little lane off busy Grafton Street. ✉ *5/6 Johnson's Ct., Grafton St., Southside* ☎ *01/679–9572* 🌐 *appleby.ie.*

Dublin à la Mode

The success of shops such as Costume has given young Irish designers the confidence to produce more original and impressive work. One of Dublin's most popular designers, **Helen James** graduated from the National College of Art and Design in textile design. She went straight to New York, where she worked for Donna Karan, among others. She returned to Ireland and developed her line of unique, hand-printed textile accessories. She now specializes in housewares design; her Considered line is carried by Dunnes Department stores throughout Ireland.

A rising star of Irish fashion, **Simone Rocha** gained international acclaim for her elegant, classic eveningwear with some daring twists. She has already expanded into furniture and recently opened stores in London, New York, and Hong Kong.

Another young Irish designer, **Richard Malone,** got rave reviews for his shows at London Fashion Week, with Selfridge's offering up its windows for an installation of his work. His swirling, architectural creations stress fine tailoring and unusual combinations of materials, much of it recycled. New York's MoMA added a piece of his work to its permanent collection.

★ Barry Doyle Design
JEWELRY & WATCHES | A true original with his Celtic modern jewelry, Barry Doyle is a master who allows you to watch him at work in his adjoining studio as he fashions beautiful wedding rings and his lovely Lilac Collection baubles. The store was chosen as one of the top 50 shops in Ireland by *Irish Times* readers. ✉ *George's Street Arcade, Upstairs, Southside* ☎ *01/671–2838* 🌐 *barry-doyledesign.com.*

★ Momuse
JEWELRY & WATCHES | Bespoke jewelry maker Margaret O'Rourke fills this wonderful little shop with her own contemporary, subtle pieces, plus select work from other up-and-coming Irish designers. ✉ *Powerscourt Townhouse Centre, ground fl., Southside* ☎ *01/707–1763* 🌐 *momuse.ie.*

MUSIC

Gael Linn
MUSIC | A specialist in traditional Irish music and Irish-language recordings, Gael Linn is where the aficionados go. ✉ *35 Dame St., Southside* ☎ *01/675–1200* 🌐 *gael-linn.ie.*

McCullogh Piggott
MUSIC | This is the best place in town to buy instruments, sheet music, scores, and books about music. ✉ *11 S. William St., Southside* ☎ *01/670–6702* 🌐 *mc-culloughpigott.com.*

OUTDOOR MARKETS

George's Street Arcade
MARKET | Opened in 1881 as South City Markets, this classic Victorian market right in the heart of town is home to a small but eclectic collection of clothes, books, food, and jewelry stalls. It's covered but feels outdoors, and open every day. ✉ *S. Great George's St., Southside* 🌐 *georgesstreetarcade.ie.*

SHOPPING CENTERS

Powerscourt Centre
SHOPPING CENTER | The regal former town home of Lord Powerscourt (built in 1771) was largely gutted two decades ago to make room for an interior roofed-over courtyard and a space shared by a mix of restaurants, cafés, antiques stores,

and boutiques of original Irish fashions by young designers. A pianist often plays on the dais at ground-floor level. ✉ *59 S. William St., Southside* ☎ *01/679–4144* 🌐 *powerscourtcentre.ie.*

Royal Hibernian Way

SHOPPING CENTER | On the former site of the two-centuries-old Royal Hibernian Hotel, a coaching inn that was demolished in 1983, this complex is home to pricey, stylish shops—about 20 or 30, many selling fashionable clothes and accessories—including Carol Clarke's Irish Jewel. ✉ *Off Dawson St., between S. Anne and Duke Sts., Southside* ☎ *01/679–5919.*

St. Stephen's Green Centre

SHOPPING CENTER | Dublin's city center's largest and most ambitious shopping complex, St. Stephen's Green Centre resembles a giant greenhouse, with Victorian-style ironwork. On three floors overlooked by a giant clock, the 100 mostly small shops sell crafts, fashions, and household goods. ✉ *Northwest corner of St. Stephen's Green, Southside* ☎ *01/478–0888* 🌐 *stephensgreen.com.*

Westbury Mall

SHOPPING CENTER | An upmarket shopping mall, the Westbury is where you can buy a stylish range of designer jewelry, antique rugs, and decorative goods. ✉ *Westbury Hotel, off Grafton St., Southside.*

SWEATERS AND TWEEDS

Avoca

MIXED CLOTHING | A beautiful store with an eclectic collection of knitwear, jewelry, ceramics, and housewares from contemporary Irish designers. There's an artisanal food market in the basement and a fantastic café on the top floor with unmissable cakes. ✉ *11–13 Suffolk St., Southside* ☎ *01/274–6900* 🌐 *avoca.ie.*

★ **Kevin and Howlin**

MIXED CLOTHING | A quintessential Irish store, Kevin and Howlin stocks spiffy fashions, with lots of stylish handwoven tweed men's jackets, suits, and hats, along with an array of treasures woven from tweedy fabrics. All in all, a fabulous, one-stop shop for traditional clothes with flair. Wait until you see the whole wall devoted to headgear—eat your heart out, Ralph Lauren! ✉ *31 Nassau St., Southside* ☎ *01/677–0257.*

Monaghan's

MIXED CLOTHING | If you're into cashmere, you should get yourself into Monaghan's. ✉ *21 S. Anne St., Southside* ☎ *01/677–0823* 🌐 *monaghanscashmere.ie.*

Merrion Square and Around

If there's one travel poster that signifies "Dublin" more than any other, it's the one that depicts 50 or so Georgian doorways—door after colorful door, all graced with lovely fanlights upheld by columns. Today, heading south from Merrion Square all the way to Ballsbridge, visitors can enjoy perfectly planned, tree-lined Georgian streets with some of the most elegant 18th-century buildings in Europe. Included in these are four of the most fascinating and glamorous museums in Ireland, sitting cheek by jowl: the National Gallery, National Library, National Museum of Natural History, and best of all, keeper of the Celtic treasures of ancient Ireland, the National Museum of Archaeology. No part of the city is more uniquely and gloriously Dublin. For convenience we have included the areas slightly farther south, around the Grand Canal and in the heart of the leafy suburb of Ballsbridge, in this section, as they have their own Georgian delights.

Sights

Government Buildings

GOVERNMENT BUILDING | The swan song of British architecture in the capital, this enormous complex, a landmark

Where the Locals Live and Play

Dublin's Coolest Neighborhoods

Get off the tourist trail and check out the cooler, upcoming neighborhoods where Dublin locals live and play.

Ranelagh. Once the home of dingy student bedsits, this "village" just south of the Grand Canal is now the epicenter of chic Dublin life. Young families with cash bought up the gorgeous Victorian redbricks, bringing a slew of inventive eateries and bars in their wake. Ideal for people-watching but also a convenient place to stay (the Devlin hotel is great), stroll down the main drag before wandering back into the city center.

Stoneybatter. On the more down-to-earth (and affordable) Northside, this buzzing city suburb brims with charm amid rows of old terraced houses. A ton of artists and creative types have moved in, and quirky shops and cafés have opened on every corner. The serene and welcoming Sitric Community Garden is typical of the warm vibe.

Smithfield. Even runaway developers and their ugly apartment buildings couldn't ruin the authentically cool look of this converted warehouse neighborhood. The elegant, 19th-century covered fruit market still dominates, but great traditional-music bars like the Cobblestone share the gorgeous cobbled square with an art-house cinema.

Portobello. Bounded by the canal to the south and St. Patrick's Cathedral to the north, these streets of substantial terraced houses offer the convenience of city living with the charm of a quiet suburban life. Only 10 minutes from Stephen's Green, the area is ripe for a morning walk, with Bibi's café the perfect watering hole.

Phibsborough. Since the LUAS tram arrived, this Northside Victorian village has become the latest hot place to live and hang out in Dublin. New art and community organizations offer regular intimate theater, literature, and comedy events in the local pubs, bookstores, and cafés. Nearby Blessington Basin Park is an undiscovered treasure of tranquility.

Dun Laoghaire. Only a vista-filled, half-hour DART ride south around Dublin Bay from the city center, this seaside town has become popular with city dwellers seeking a better quality of life. The ocean is their playground, with a yacht club and marina, water sports, the Forty Foot bathing spot, and some white sandy beaches all within walking distance. George's Street offers chilled-out shopping and dining options.

of Edwardian Baroque, was the last Neoclassical edifice to be erected by the British government. It was designed by Sir Aston Webb, who did many of the similarly grand buildings in London's Piccadilly Circus, to serve as the College of Science in the early 1900s. Following a major restoration, these buildings became the offices of the Department of the *taoiseach* (the prime minister, pronounced *tea*-shuck) and the *tánaiste* (the deputy prime minister, pronounced *tawn*-ish-ta). Fine examples of contemporary Irish furniture and carpets populate the offices. A stained-glass window, known as "My Four Green Fields," was made by Evie Hone for the 1939 New York World's Fair. It depicts the four ancient provinces

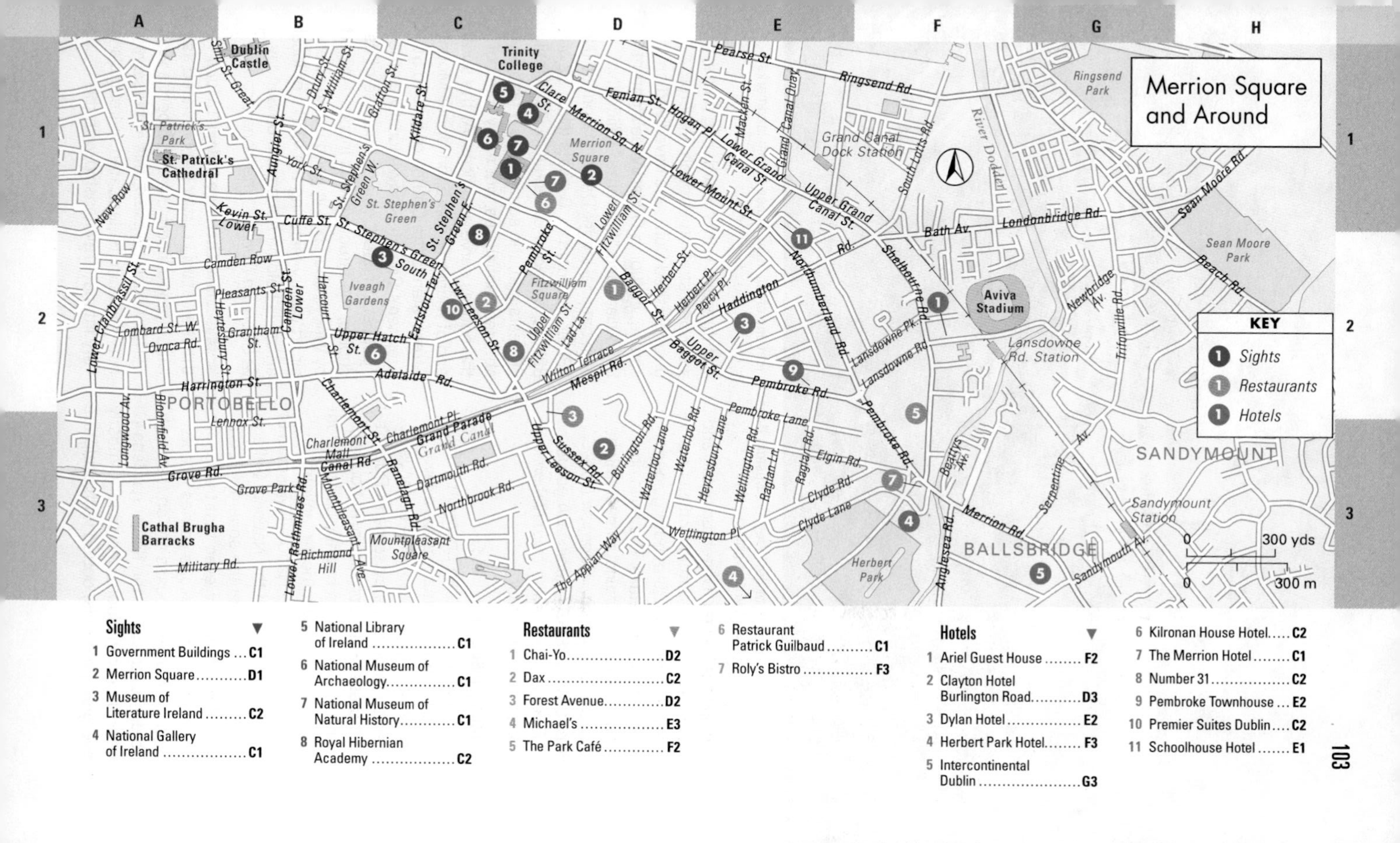

Merrion Square and Around
KEY
Sights
Restaurants
Hotels
A
B
C
D
E
F
G
H
1
2
3
Dublin Castle
Trinity College
St. Patrick's Park
St. Patrick's Cathedral
Merrion Square
St. Stephen's Green
Iveagh Gardens
Fitzwilliam Square
Grand Canal Dock Station
Aviva Stadium
Lansdowne Rd. Station
Ringsend Park
Sean Moore Park
Herbert Park
Sandymount Station
SANDYMOUNT
BALLSBRIDGE
PORTOBELLO
Cathal Brugha Barracks
Mountpleasant Square
Richmond Hill
River Dodder
Grand Canal
Pearse St.
Ringsend Rd.
Fenian St.
Hogan Pl.
Lower Grand Canal St.
Lower Mount St.
Upper Grand Canal St.
Merrion Sq. N.
Clare St.
Kildare St.
Grafton St.
Drury St.
S. William St.
Ship St. Great
Aungier St.
York St.
Kevin St. Lower
Cuffe St.
St. Stephen's Green W.
St. Stephen's Green South
St. Stephen's Green E.
Camden Row
Camden St. Lower
Pleasants St.
Heytesbury St.
Grantham St.
Harcourt St.
Upper Hatch St.
Earlsfort Ter.
Lwr Leeson St.
Pembroke St.
Lower Fitzwilliam St.
Upper Fitzwilliam St.
Lad La.
Baggot St.
Upper Baggot St.
Herbert St.
Herbert Pl.
Percy Pl.
Haddington Rd.
Northumberland Rd.
Shelbourne Rd.
Bath Av.
Londonbridge Rd.
South Lotts Rd.
Sean Moore Rd.
Beach Rd.
Newbridge Av.
Tritonville Rd.
Lansdowne Pk.
Lansdowne Rd.
Pembroke Rd.
Pembroke Lane
Wilton Terrace
Mespil Rd.
Adelaide Rd.
Harrington St.
Lombard St. W.
Ovoca Rd.
Lower Clanbrassil St.
New Row
Longwood Av.
Bloomfield Av.
Lenbox St.
Charlemont St.
Charlemont Pl.
Charlemont Mall
Grand Parade
Canal Rd.
Grove Rd.
Grove Park
Lower Rathmines Rd.
Mountpleasant Ave.
Ranelagh Rd.
Dartmouth Rd.
Northbrook Rd.
Military Rd.
Upper Leeson St.
Sussex Rd.
Burlington Rd.
Waterloo Lane
Waterloo Rd.
Heytesbury Lane
Wellington Rd.
Raglan Ln.
Raglan Rd.
Elgin Rd.
Clyde Rd.
Clyde Lane
Wellington Pl.
The Appian Way
Anglesea Rd.
Merrion Rd.
Beatty's Av.
Serpentine Av.
Sandymouth Av.
0
300 yds
0
300 m
Sights
1 Government Buildings ... C1
2 Merrion Square ... D1
3 Museum of Literature Ireland ... C2
4 National Gallery of Ireland ... C1
5 National Library of Ireland ... C1
6 National Museum of Archaeology ... C1
7 National Museum of Natural History ... C1
8 Royal Hibernian Academy ... C2
Restaurants
1 Chai-Yo ... D2
2 Dax ... C2
3 Forest Avenue ... D2
4 Michael's ... E3
5 The Park Café ... F2
6 Restaurant Patrick Guilbaud ... C1
7 Roly's Bistro ... F3
Hotels
1 Ariel Guest House ... F2
2 Clayton Hotel Burlington Road ... D3
3 Dylan Hotel ... E2
4 Herbert Park Hotel ... F3
5 Intercontinental Dublin ... G3
6 Kilronan House Hotel ... C2
7 The Merrion Hotel ... C1
8 Number 31 ... C2
9 Pembroke Townhouse ... E2
10 Premier Suites Dublin ... C2
11 Schoolhouse Hotel ... E1

Reflected in the waters of the Liffey, the Custom House is just one of the many famed Dublin landmarks spectacularly illuminated at night.

of Ireland: Munster, Ulster, Leinster, and Connacht. The government offices are accessible only via 35-minute guided tours; phone for details. The buildings are dramatically illuminated every night. ✉ *Upper Merrion St., Georgian Dublin* ☎ *01/619–4249* 🌐 *taoiseach.gov.ie* 🎟 *Free; pick up tickets from National Gallery on day of tour.*

★ Merrion Square

PLAZA/SQUARE | Created between 1762 and 1764, this tranquil square a few blocks east of St. Stephen's Green is lined on three sides by some of Dublin's best-preserved Georgian town houses, many of which have brightly painted front doors crowned by intricate fanlights. Leinster House, the National Museum of Natural History, and the National Gallery line the west side of the square. It's on the other sides, however, that the Georgian terrace streetscape comes into its own—the finest houses are on the north border. Even when the flower gardens here are not in bloom, the vibrant, mostly evergreen grounds, dotted with sculpture and threaded with meandering paths, are worth strolling through. Several distinguished Dubliners have lived on the square, including Oscar Wilde's parents, Sir William and "Speranza" Wilde (No. 1); Irish national leader Daniel O'Connell (No. 58); and authors W. B. Yeats (Nos. 52 and 82) and Sheridan LeFanu (No. 70). Until 50 years ago, the square was a fashionable residential area, but today most of the houses serve as offices. At the south end of Merrion Square, on Upper Mount Street, stands the Church of Ireland St. Stephen's Church. Known locally as the "pepper canister" church because of its cupola, the structure was inspired in part by Wren's churches in London. An open-air art gallery featuring the works of local artists is held on the square on Sunday. ✉ *Georgian Dublin* 🌐 *merrionart.com.*

★ Museum of Literature Ireland (*MoLI*)

OTHER MUSEUM | **FAMILY** | Abbreviated as MoLI (pronounced "Molly," Bloom's wonderful wife in *Ulysses*), this impressive new museum is dedicated to Ireland's very intimate relationship with the written word. Located in the elegant Georgian Newman House, exhibits tell the history of Irish literature from the earliest oral storytellers right through to contemporary writers. The star artifact is "copy number one" of *Ulysses*, which was handed to Joyce himself hot from the printing press. The Joyce collection, including the Dedalus Library, is at the heart of the museum, but all the great Irish writers, past and present, are represented. There are lectures, multimedia shows, children's educational programs, and a very tranquil "secret" garden out back. The Commons Cafe is a small eatery with an already big reputation. ✉ *UCD Naughton Joyce Centre, 86 St. Stephen's Green, Georgian Dublin* ☎ *01/477–9811* 🌐 *moli.ie* 🎫 *€12.*

★ **National Gallery of Ireland**
ART MUSEUM | Caravaggio's *The Taking of Christ* (1602), Van Gogh's *Rooftops of Paris* (1886), Vermeer's *Lady Writing a Letter with Her Maid* (circa 1670) ... you get the picture, or rather, you'll *find* the picture here. Established in 1864, and designed by Francis Fowke (who also designed London's Victoria & Albert Museum), the National Gallery of Ireland is one of Europe's finest smaller art museums, with "smaller" being a relative term: the collection holds more than 2,500 paintings and some 10,000 other works. But unlike Europe's largest art museums, the National Gallery can be thoroughly covered in a morning or afternoon without inducing exhaustion.

A highlight of the museum is the major collection of paintings by Irish artists from the 17th through 20th centuries, including works by Roderic O'Conor (1860–1940), Sir William Orpen (1878–1931), and William Leech (1881–1968). The Yeats Museum section contains works by members of the Yeats family, including Jack B. Yeats (1871–1957), the brother of writer W.B. Yeats and by far the best-known Irish painter of the 20th century.

The collection also claims exceptional paintings from the 17th-century French, Dutch, Italian, and Spanish schools, and works by French Impressionists Monet, Sisley, and Renoir. If you are in Dublin in January, catch the sumptuous annual Turner exhibition, with paintings only displayed in the winter light that best enhances their wonders. The amply stocked gift shop is a good place to pick up books on Irish artists. Free guided tours are available on Saturday at 12:30 and on Sunday at 12:30 and 1:30. ✉ *Merrion Sq. W, Georgian Dublin* ☎ *01/661–5133* 🌐 *nationalgallery.ie* 🎫 *Free; special exhibits €15.*

National Library of Ireland
LIBRARY | Along with works by W.B. Yeats (1923), George Bernard Shaw (1925), Samuel Beckett (1969), and Seamus Heaney (1995), the National Library contains first editions of every major Irish writer, including books by Jonathan Swift, Oliver Goldsmith, and James Joyce (who used the library as the scene of the great literary debate in *Ulysses*). In addition, almost every book ever published in Ireland is kept here, along with an unequaled selection of old maps and an extensive collection of Irish newspapers and magazines—more than 5 million items in all.

The library is housed in a rather stiff Neoclassical building with colonnaded porticoes and an excess of ornamentation—it's not one of Dublin's architectural showpieces. But inside, the main Reading Room, opened in 1890 to house the collections of the Royal Dublin Society, has a dramatic dome ceiling, beneath which countless authors have researched and written. The personal papers of greats such as W.B. Yeats are also on display. The library also has a free genealogical consultancy service that can advise you on how to trace your Irish ancestors. ✉ *Kildare St., Georgian Dublin* ☎ *01/603–0200* 🌐 *www.nli.ie* 🎫 *Free* 🕐 *Closed Sun.*

Continued on page 114

LITERARY DUBLIN

A PLAYWRIGHT ON EVERY CORNER

As any visit to the Dublin Writers Museum will prove, this city packs more literary punch per square foot than practically any other spot on the planet. While the Irish capital may be relatively small in geographic terms, it looms huge as a country of the imagination. Dubliners wrote some of the greatest works of Western literature, including these immortal titles: *Ulysses, Gulliver's Travels, Dracula, The Importance of Being Earnest,* and *Waiting for Godot.* Today Dublin is a veritable literary theme park: within a few minutes' walk you can visit the James Joyce Centre, visit the Abbey Theatre, and pop into the pub where Brendan Behan loved to get marinated.

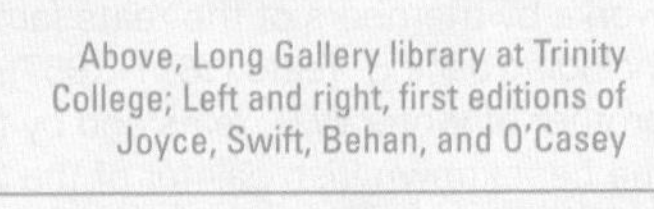

Above, Long Gallery library at Trinity College; Left and right, first editions of Joyce, Swift, Behan, and O'Casey

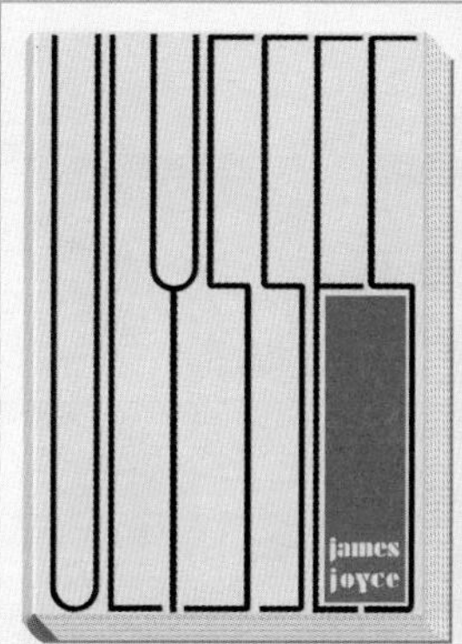

Ulysses, First American Edition

St. Stephen's Green

A WAY WITH WORDS

As tellers of the tallest tales, speakers of Gaelic (reputedly the world's most perfect medium for prayers, curses, and seduction), and the finest practitioners of the art of blarney, it's little surprise that the Hibernian race produced no fewer than four Nobel prize winners: Shaw, W. B. Yeats, Samuel Beckett, and Seamus Heaney. But what is surprising is that this tiny, long-colonized island on the outskirts of Europe somehow managed to maneuver itself to the very heart of literature in the language of the invader itself, English. And at that heart's core lies Dublin.

A ramble through literary Dublin is a crash course in Irish soul.

FOR BETTER OR VERSE

By the 18th century, the Gaelic tradition was trumped by the boom of literature written in English, often by second- or third-generation descendants of English settlers, such as William Congreve, Richard Brinsley Sheridan, and Oliver Goldsmith. With the establishment of the Irish Free State in 1922, so many Irish writers found themselves censored that "being banned" became a matter of prestige (it also did wonders for book sales abroad, with a smuggled copy of *Ulysses* becoming the ultimate status symbol). Sadly, many writers became exiles; most famously, Joyce was joined in Paris by Beckett in 1932.

DUBLIN B(U)Y THE BOOK

Book lovers know that a guidebook to this city is an anthology of Irish literature in itself. Dublin's Northside is studded with landmarks immortalized in James Joyce's novels. A stone's throw from the Liffey is the Abbey Theater, a potent symbol of Ireland's great playwrights. To the south lies Trinity College, alma mater of Jonathan Swift, Bram Stoker, Oscar Wilde, and Samuel Beckett. And scattered around the city are hundreds of pubs where storytelling evolved as the incurable Irish "disease." They are the perfect places to take a time-out while touring Dublin's leading literary shrines and sites.

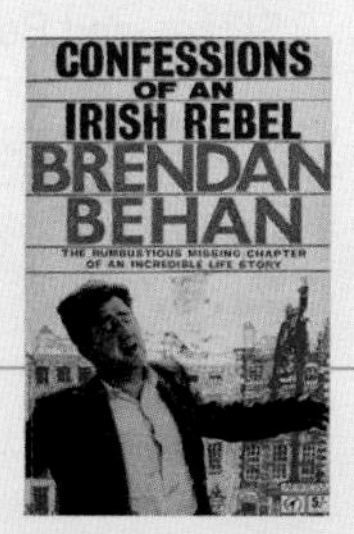

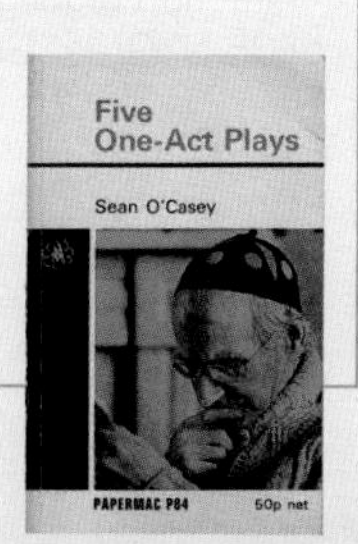

THE TRAIL OF TALES

Allowing you to turn the pages of the city, as it were, with your feet, a literary ramble through Dublin is a magical mystery tour through more than 400 years of Irish history.

The view from Front Square, Trinity College

GATE THEATRE. Landmarked by its noble Palladian portico, this magnificent Georgian theater (built 1784) today sees the premieres of some of Ireland's most talked-about plays. Orson Welles and James Mason got their starts here. ✉ Cavendish Row.

JAMES JOYCE CENTRE. Now an extensive library dedicated to arguably the greatest novelist of the 20th century, this sumptuously decorated 18th-century town house was featured in *Ulysses* as a dancing academy. Letters from Beckett, Joyce's guitar and cane, and a Joyce edition illustrated by Matisse are collection highlights. ✉ 35 N. Great George's St.

ABBEY THEATRE. Hard to believe this 1950s modernist eyesore is the fabled home of Ireland's national theater company, established on a wave of nationalist passion by Yeats and his patron, Lady Gregory, in 1904. Here premiered J. M. Synge's scandalous *Playboy of the Western World* and the working-class plays of Sean O'Casey. The foyer and bar display mementos of the theater's fabled "Abbeyists." ✉ Lower Abbey St.

TRINITY COLLEGE DUBLIN. This 400-year-old college has an incredible record for turning out literary giants like Swift, Goldsmith, Wilde, Synge, Stoker, and Beckett. Majestically presiding over its famous library is the 9th-century Book of Kells, mother of all Irish tomes.

NATIONAL LIBRARY. Joyce used the 1890 Main Reading Room, with its dramatic domed ceiling, as the scene of the great literary debate in *Ulysses*. At No. 30 Kildare Street a plaque marks a former residence of *Dracula's* creator, Bram Stoker. ✉ Kildare St.

National Library of Ireland

Neary's Pub

MERRION SQUARE. An elegant mansion, which can be toured, No. 1 Merrion Square is the former Oscar Wilde family residence. A statue of Oscar reclines in the park opposite. Around the square, note the plaques that indicate former residents, including W. B. Yeats and Sheridan le Fanu, Dublin's most famous ghost-story teller.

ST. STEPHEN'S GREEN. This pretty, flower-filled park is home to a wonderful statue of Joyce.

NEARY'S PUB. The Victorian-style interiors here were once haunted by Dublin's literary set, most notably the raconteur Brendan Behan. E1 Chatham St.

THE WINDING STAIR. Long known as a meeting place for generations of Dublin writers, this bookstore and restaurant makes a perfect pitstop on your literary ramble. E40 Ormond Quay Lower.

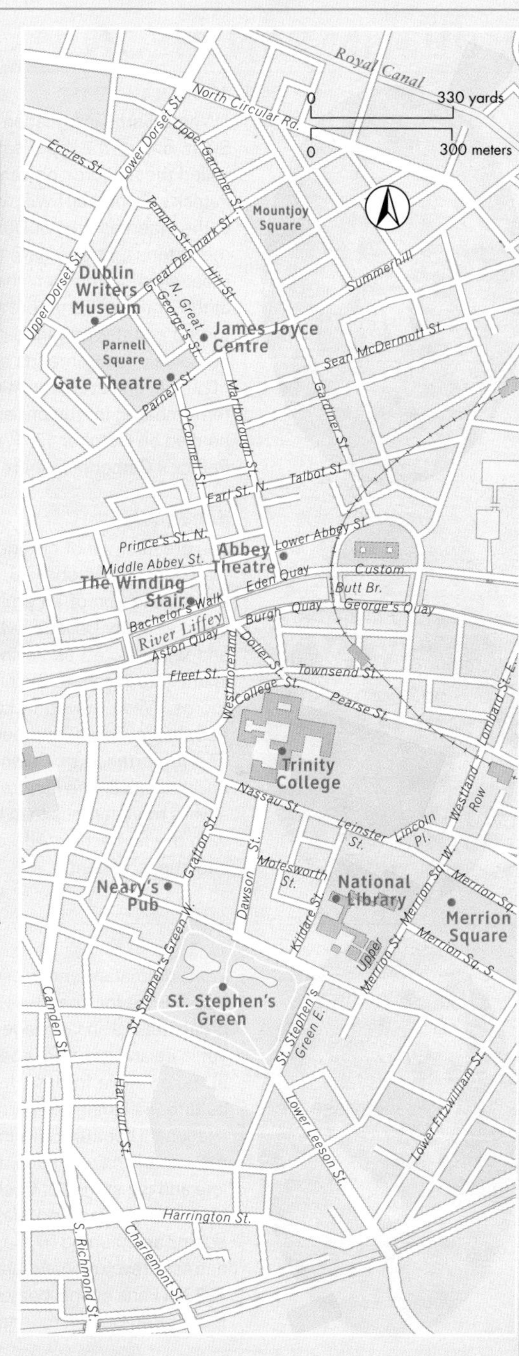

A DUBLIN PANTHEON

JONATHAN SWIFT

"Where fierce indignation can no longer tear his heart": Swift, one of the great satirists in the English language, willed these words be carved on his tomb at Dublin's St. Patrick's Cathedral. Swift was born on November 30, 1667, in the Liberties area of Dublin. Life would deal him many misfortunes, but he gave as good as he got, venting his great anger with a pen sharper than any sword. His rage at the British government's mistreatment of the Irish was turned into the brilliant satire *A Modest Proposal* where he politely recommends a solution to the dual problems of hunger and overpopulation: breed babies for meat. Best remembered for the brilliant moral fable *Gulliver's Travels*, he died on October 19, 1745, and is buried in Dublin's St. Patrick's Cathedral, where he was dean.

OSCAR WILDE

The greatest wit of his age and arguably any other, Wilde was born on October 16, 1834, at 21 Westland Row in Dublin, the son of an eminent eye doctor. He was educated at Trinity College, where he was a promising boxer and was quoted as saying his greatest challenge was learning to live up to the blue china he had installed in his rooms. Wilde moved to London in 1879, where he married, had children, and became celebrated for the plays *The Importance of Being Earnest* and *Salome* and his titillating novel *The Picture of Dorian Gray*. But his life was always more famous than his work and a scandalous affair with the aristocratic Alfred Douglas finally led to his ruin and imprisonment.

W. B. YEATS

Poet, dramatist, and prose writer, Yeats—winner of the Nobel Prize for Literature in 1923—stands as one of the greatest English-language poets of the 20th century. And yet in Ireland itself he is best remembered for his key role in the struggle for Irish freedom and the revival of Irish culture, including his part in forming the Abbey Theatre (National Theatre). Born in the seaside suburb of Sandymount in Dublin in 1865, his fascination with Celtic folklore and the stories of Cuchulainn can be seen throughout his early poems and plays. But many of his greatest poems are haunted by the dashing figure of Maud Gonne, actress, revolutionary, and unrequited love. He died in 1939 in Paris but his body was buried in Drumcliffe, at the foot of Ben Bulben mountain in his beloved County Sligo.

GEORGE BERNARD SHAW

G. Bernard Shaw—he hated George, and never used it either personally or professionally—was born in Dublin in 1856. His father was a boozing corn merchant and his mother a professional singer. When Shaw was a boy his mother ran away with her voice coach, and it may be no coincidence that his plays are dotted with problem child/parent relationships. In 1886 he went to London where plays such as *Pygmalion* and *Saint Joan* helped propel him to international stardom. Pacifist, socialist, and feminist, Shaw was a true original; a radical in the real sense of the word, his work always challenged the norms of his day. He lived to the ripe old age of 94 and died in 1950 after falling off a ladder while trimming trees outside his house.

SEAN O'CASEY

The first working-class Irish literary great, dramatist O'Casey was born at 85 Upper Dorset Street in the inner-city Dublin slums in 1880. Problems with his eyes as a child kept him indoors where he gleaned a love of reading. An early advocate of Yeats's Celtic Revival, he later found his true faith in the socialism of union leader Jim Larkin. His trilogy of great tragicomedies—*Shadow of a Gunman, Juno and the Paycock,* and *The Plough and the Stars*—all deal with ordinary families caught up in the maelstrom of Irish politics and were performed at Yeats's Abbey in the 1920s. Their playful language and riotous action have made them classics ever since. He spent his later life in England and died in Devon in 1964.

BRENDAN BEHAN

Writer, fighter, drinker, and wit, Brendan Francis Behan was born in Dublin's Holles Street Hospital in 1923 into an educated, political working-class family. Urged on by his fiercely patriotic grandmother, he joined Fíanna Eireann, the youth wing of the IRA and in 1939 was jailed for three years for possessing explosives. In prison he began to write but it wasn't until the 1950s that he hit it big with *The Quare Fellow,* a play based on his prison experiences, and later works *The Hostage* and *Borstal Boy*. But it was in the bars of Dublin that the "demon drinker" Behan delivered many of his greatest lines—alas, lost now forever. A self-proclaimed "drinker with a writing problem," he died in 1964 at the age of only 41.

REJOICE!: The Darlin' Dublin of James Joyce

If Joyce fans make one pilgrimage in their lives, let it be to Dublin on June 16th for Bloomsday. June 16th, of course, is the day Leopold Bloom toured Dublin in *Ulysses*, and commemorative events take place all week long leading up to the big day (and night).

Grown men and women stroll the streets attired in black suits and carrying fresh bars of lemon soap in their pockets, imitating the unassuming hero of what is arguably the 20th century's greatest novel. Denounced as obscene, blasphemous, and unreadable when it was first published in 1922 (and then banned in the U.S. until 1933), this 1,000-page riff on Homer's *Odyssey* portrays three characters—Leopold Bloom, a Jewish ad salesman, his wife, Molly, and friend Stephen Dedalus—as they wander through Dublin during the span of one day, June 16th, 1904. Dedicated Joyceans flock to the weeklong event, now called "Bloomstime," for Bloomsday breakfasts (where they can enjoy, like Bloom himself, "grilled mutton kidneys . . . which gave to his palate a fine tang of faintly scented urine"), readings, performances, and general merriment.

But don't despair if you miss Bloomsday, because you can experience the Dublin that inspired the author's novels year-round. James Joyce (1882–1941) set all his major works—*Dubliners, A Portrait of the Artist as a Young Man, Ulysses,* and *Finnegans Wake*—in the city where he was born and spent the first 22 years of his life. Joyce knew and remembered Dublin in such detail that he bragged (and that's the word) that, if the city were destroyed, it could be rebuilt in its entirety from his written works.

Left, Joyce Statue, Earl Street;
Top left, a portrait of James Joyce, 1915
Top right, Bloomsday celebrations

IN THE FOOTSTEPS OF A POET: A James Joyce Walk

Begin in the heart of the Northside, on Prince's Street, next to the GPO (General Post Office), where the office of the old and popular *Freeman's Journal* newspaper (published 1763–1924) was once located and where Bloom once worked.

Head north up O'Connell Street down Parnell Square before turning right onto Dorset Street and then left onto Eccles Street. Leopold and Molly Bloom's fictional home stood at 7 Eccles Street, north of Parnell Square.

Head back to Dorset Street and go east. Take a right onto Gardiner Street and then a left onto Great Denmark Street and Belvedere College. Between 1893 and 1898, Joyce studied at Belvedere College under the Jesuits; it's housed in a splendid 18th-century mansion. The **James Joyce Centre**, a few steps from Belvedere College on North Great George's Street, is the hub of Bloomsday celebrations.

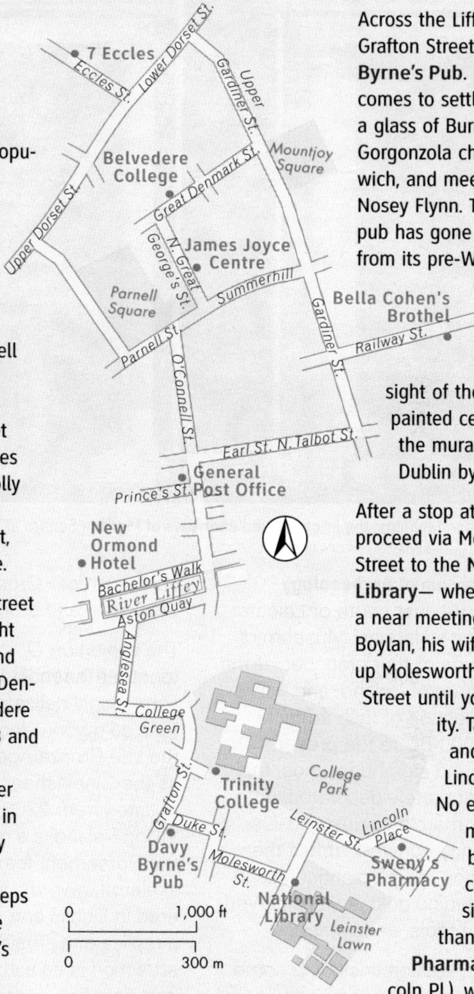

Go back to Gardiner Street and then south until you come to Railway Street on your left. The site of **Bella Cohen's Brothel** (✉ 82 Railway St.) is in an area that in Joyce's day contained many houses of ill repute. A long walk back down O'Connell Street to the bridge and then a right will take you to Ormond Quay. On the western edge of the Northside, the (now closed) **Ormond Quay Hotel,** under threat by developers, was an afternoon rendezvous spot for Bloom.

Across the Liffey, walk up Grafton Street to **Davy Byrne's Pub**. Here, Bloom comes to settle down for a glass of Burgundy and a Gorgonzola cheese sandwich, and meets his friend Nosey Flynn. Today, the pub has gone very upscale from its pre-World War II days, but even Joyce would have cracked a smile at the sight of the shamrock-painted ceiling and the murals of Joycean Dublin by Liam Proud.

After a stop at Davy Byrne's, proceed via Molesworth Street to the **National Library**— where Bloom has a near meeting with Blazes Boylan, his wife's lover. Walk up Molesworth Street until you hit Trinity. Take a right and walk to Lincoln Place. No establishment mentioned by Joyce has changed less since his time than **Sweny's Pharmacy** (✉ Lincoln Pl.), which though no longer a functioning pharmacy, still has its black-and-white exterior and an interior crammed with potions and vials. Today volunteers maintain the shop as it was in Joyce's time.

Topped by half-moon fanlights, the brightly hued doorways of Merrion Square are icons of Dublin's 18th-century Georgian style.

★ National Museum of Archaeology

HISTORY MUSEUM | Just south of Leinster House is Ireland's National Museum of Archaeology, one of four branches of the National Museum of Ireland, and home to a fabled collection of Irish artifacts dating from 7000 BC to the present. Organized around a grand rotunda, the museum is elaborately decorated, with mosaic floors, marble columns, balustrades, and fancy ironwork. It has the largest collection of Celtic antiquities in the world, including gold jewelry, carved stones, bronze tools, and weapons.

The Treasury collection, including some of the museum's most renowned pieces, is open on a permanent basis. Among the priceless relics on display are the 8th-century Ardagh Chalice, a two-handled silver cup with gold filigree ornamentation; the bronze-coated iron St. Patrick's Bell, the oldest surviving example (5th–8th century) of Irish metalwork; the 8th-century Tara Brooch, an intricately decorated piece made of white bronze, amber, and glass; and the 12th-century bejeweled oak Cross of Cong, covered with silver and bronze panels.

The exhibition *Ór - Ireland's Gold* gathers together the most impressive pieces of surprisingly delicate and intricate prehistoric goldwork—including sun disks and the late Bronze Age gold collar known as the Gleninsheen Gorget—that range in dates from 2200 to 500 BC. Upstairs, Viking Ireland is a permanent exhibit on the Norsemen, featuring a full-size Viking skeleton, swords, leatherworks recovered in Dublin and surrounding areas, and a replica of a small Viking boat. A newer attraction is an exhibition entitled *Kinship and Sacrifice,* centering on a number of Iron Age "bog bodies" found along with other objects in Ireland's peat bogs.

The 18th-century Collins Barracks, near Phoenix Park, houses the National Museum of Decorative Arts and History, a collection of glass, silver, furniture, and other decorative arts, as well as a military history section. ⊠ *Kildare St. Annex, 7–9 Merrion Row, Georgian Dublin*

☎ *01/677–7444* 🌐 *museum.ie* 🎫 *Free*
🕑 *Closed Mon.*

National Museum of Natural History
HISTORY MUSEUM | FAMILY | One of four branches of the National Museum of Ireland, this museum is little changed from Victorian times and remains a fascinating repository of mounted mammals, birds, and other flora and fauna. Locals still affectionately refer to the place as the "Dead Zoo." The Irish Room houses the most famous exhibits: skeletons of the extinct, prehistoric, giant Irish elk. The International Animals Collection includes a 65-foot whale skeleton suspended from the roof. Another highlight is the very beautiful Blaschka Collection, finely detailed glass models of marine creatures, the zoological accuracy of which has never been achieved again in glass. Exhibitions include *Mating Game* and *Taxonomy Trail*. Built in 1856 to hold the Royal Dublin Society's rapidly expanding collection, it was designed by Frederick Clarendon to sit in harmony with the National Gallery on the other side of Leinster Lawn. When it was completed, it formed an annex to Leinster House and was connected to it by a curved, closed Corinthian colonnade. In 1909 a new entrance was constructed at the east end of the building on Merrion Street. ✉ *Merrion St., Georgian Dublin* ☎ *01/677–7444* 🌐 *museum.ie* 🎫 *Free* 🕑 *Closed Mon.*

Royal Hibernian Academy (*RHA Gallery*)
ART GALLERY | The Royal Hibernian Academy, an old Dublin institution, is housed in a well-lighted building, one of the largest exhibition spaces in the city. The gallery holds adventurous exhibitions of the best in contemporary art, both from Ireland and abroad. ✉ *15 Ely Pl., off St. Stephen's Green, Georgian Dublin* ☎ *01/661–2558* 🌐 *rhagallery.ie* 🎫 *Free.*

What a Coote!

Check out one of the National Gallery's most eye-catching paintings, Sir Joshua Reynolds's *First Earl of Bellomont* (1773). Depicted in pink silks and ostrich plumes, Charles Coote was a notorious womanizer and was shot in the groin for his troubles by rival Lord Townshend. Famously, Coote gave his inaugural speech as quartermaster general of Ireland in French, continually referred to his County Cavan neighbors as "Hottentots," and wound up marrying the daughter of the super-rich Duke of Leinster.

Restaurants

Chai-Yo
$$ | JAPANESE | FAMILY | The Japanese teppanyaki area at this classy Pan-Asian restaurant on bustling Baggot Street, where the chef cooks your food right on your tabletop, is a feast for the eye as well as the palate. The simplicity of the white walls and dark lacquered furnishings are enhanced by the delicate glassware and fine green-washed porcelain. **Known for:** great fun with kids; live music some evenings; bustling atmosphere. 💲 *Average main: €22* ✉ *100 Lower Baggot St., Georgian Dublin* ☎ *01/676–7652* 🌐 *chaiyo.ie* 🕑 *No lunch Mon.–Wed. and weekends.*

Dax
$$$ | WINE BAR | One of the city's most talked-about wine bars, you can choose to drink or dine (tapas-style) at the bar, in the lush armchairs of the open-plan lounge, or in the more formal, restrained-modern dining room. The Roscoff onion tart is an adventurous starter, while the cold meat platter is a finger-lickin' little bar dish. **Known for:** impressive by-the-glass wines; relaxed

atmosphere; great bar-food options. *Average main: €29 23 Pembroke St. Upper, Georgian Dublin 01/676–1494 dax.ie Closed Sun.–Tues.*

★ Forest Avenue

$$$$ | **CONTEMPORARY** | Named after the street in Queens where chef-owner Sandy Wyer grew up, Forest Avenue is a star on the Dublin food stage. The menu is a five-course taster, and while choice is limited, quality and value are off the charts. **Known for:** warm, friendly vibe; daring tasting menu; pairing wine with food. *Average main: €78 8 Sussex Terr., Georgian Dublin 01/667–8337 forestavenuerestaurant.ie Closed Sun.–Tues.*

Michael's

$$$ | **SEAFOOD** | **FAMILY** | It's all about the seafood at this small family restaurant a little way outside the Southside city center. The atmosphere is warm and ubercasual, and the fish is fresh off the boat from nearby Dublin Bay. **Known for:** menu tied to local catch; beautiful desserts; family-owned vibe. *Average main: €31 57 Deerpark Rd., Mount Merrion, Georgian Dublin 01/278–0377 www.michaels.ie Closed Mon. and Tues. No lunch Wed.*

★ The Park Café

$$$ | **FRENCH** | In this elegant, South Dublin eatery, celebrity chef Richard Corrigan uses his French-inspired genius on the freshest produce from his own Gooseberry Garden farm. The small plates options are some of the most inventive, with Peter's Omelette (with Inis escargot bordelaise, smoked pancetta, Parmesan, and chives) and poached Ballysadare hens egg and caviar as two of the standouts. **Known for:** small plates such as Peter's Omelette; celebrity chef; inventive twist on French classics. *Average main: €30 1 Ballsbridge, Shelbourne Rd., Ballsbridge 01/964–3040 www.parkcafe.ie Closed Sun. and Mon.*

★ Restaurant Patrick Guilbaud

$$$$ | **FRENCH** | Also known as "Dublin's finest restaurant," this Michelin-starred place on the ground floor of the Merrion Hotel boasts a menu described as French, but chef Guillaume Lebrun's genius lies in his occasional daring use of traditional Irish ingredients—so often taken for granted—to create the unexpected. The ambience is just as delicious, if you're into lofty, minimalist dining rooms and Irish modern art (the Roderic O'Conors and Louis le Brocquys are all from the owner's private collection). **Known for:** award-winning chef; Annagassan blue lobster; Irish modern art collection. *Average main: €64 Merrion Hotel, 21 Upper Merrion St., Georgian Dublin 01/676–4192 restaurantpatrickguilbaud.ie Closed Sun. and Mon.*

Roly's Bistro

$$$ | **BISTRO** | While the bistro food at this Ballsbridge stalwart is always top-class, it's the jovial atmosphere and superb service that keep locals coming back. It's famed for the wine list, with great options by the glass, and that certainly helps to explain the wonderful buzz that always seems to be about this popular neighborhood place. **Known for:** separate vegan and vegetarian menu; traditional Sunday lunch offering; heated terrace. *Average main: €30 7 Ballsbridge Terr., Georgian Dublin 01/668–2611 rolysbistro.ie No credit cards.*

Hotels

Ariel Guest House

$$ | **B&B/INN** | The homemade preserves and oven-warm scones are reason enough to stay at this redbrick 1850 Victorian guesthouse, in one of Dublin's poshest tree-lined suburbs a 15-minute walk from St. Stephen's Green. **Pros:** four-poster beds in larger rooms; fantastic collection of Victoriana throughout the house; good price for smaller rooms. **Cons:** no elevator; limited amenities; a good walk to the city center. *Rooms*

from: €224 ✉ 52 Lansdowne Rd., Georgian Dublin ☎ 01/668–5512 🌐 www.ariel-house.net ⇒ 37 rooms 🍽 No Meals.

Clayton Hotel Burlington Road

$$$ | **HOTEL** | The days when Irish and international celebrities partied the nights away at the Burlington hotel might be gone, but this Dublin institution is convenient to St. Stephen's Green and Grafton Street and home to a lively bar and restaurant so it's still a focal point for social events and gatherings. **Pros:** a Dublin institution; large, light-filled rooms; happening cocktail bar. **Cons:** looks a little bit like a parking garage; popular with conferences; rooms are a little basic and bland. $ *Rooms from: €239 ✉ Upper Leeson St., Georgian Dublin ☎ 01/618–5600 🌐 claytonhotelburlingtonroad.com ⇒ 501 rooms 🍽 No Meals.*

Dylan Hotel

$$$$ | **HOTEL** | Formerly a Victorian-era nurses' boardinghouse, then the dreary Hibernian Hotel, the Dylan, with a recent refurbishment of its previous vampy Victorian decor, has sharpened its style with a focus on contemporary Irish design rich in tones and textures that make this boutique property a more refined, opulent option. **Pros:** a quiet side street but still close to bars and restaurants; great bar and restaurant on-site; modern rooms and amenities. **Cons:** business-heavy area; breakfast is extra; no gym or spa. $ *Rooms from: €360 ✉ Eastmoreland Pl., Georgian Dublin ☎ 01/660–3000 🌐 dylan.ie ⇒ 72 rooms 🍽 No Meals.*

Herbert Park Hotel

$$$ | **HOTEL** | Only a short distance from the city, this hotel nestled next to leafy Herbert Park and the doddering Dodder River feels pleasantly secluded—to maximize enjoyment, you'll want to secure a room overlooking the park, or go for one of the two suites with balconies. **Pros:** independently owned hotel; terrace dining in summer; secluded city setting. **Cons:** looks a little like an office block; rooms not too exciting; outside the city center. $ *Rooms from: €295 ✉ Merrion Rd., Georgian Dublin ☎ 01/667–2200 🌐 herbertparkhotel.ie ⇒ 153 rooms 🍽 No Meals.*

★ **Intercontinental Dublin**

$$$$ | **HOTEL** | Set within the show grounds of the Royal Dublin Society, this Victorian-Georgian hybrid—topped by gigantic eaves and a lovely cupola—has an impressive 4 acres of gardens; a big effort has been made to ensure that a bit of greenery can be seen from most rooms. **Pros:** one of the country's top spas; full range of facilities; lobby lounge great for afternoon tea. **Cons:** a bit of an architectural mishmash; not in city center; room design not the most inventive. $ *Rooms from: €420 ✉ Simmonscourt Rd., Georgian Dublin ☎ 01/665–4000 🌐 intercontinental.com/dublin ⇒ 197 rooms 🍽 No Meals.*

Kilronan House Hotel

$$$ | **B&B/INN** | Just a five-minute walk from St. Stephen's Green, this mid-19th-century terraced guesthouse, with its elegant white facade and cozy sitting-room fire, will welcome you home at the end of a long day's sightseeing. **Pros:** great price for location; beautiful, calming facade; cozy sitting room. **Cons:** public areas a bit worn; uncreative room furnishings; no elevator. $ *Rooms from: €299 ✉ 70 Adelaide Rd., Georgian Dublin ☎ 01/475–5266 🌐 kilronanhouse.com ⇒ 14 rooms 🍽 Free Breakfast.*

★ **The Merrion Hotel**

$$$$ | **HOTEL** | Stately and spiffy, and splendidly situated directly across from the Government Buildings between St. Stephen's Green and Merrion Square, this luxurious hotel actually comprises four exactingly restored Georgian town houses. **Pros:** Michelin-starred restaurant; impressive art collection; city-center location. **Cons:** you'll pay extra for a room in the original house; some rooms are overdecorated; some may find the atmosphere a bit formal. $ *Rooms from: €440 ✉ Upper Merrion St., Georgian*

Dublin ☎ 01/603–0600 🌐 merrionhotel.com 🛏 142 rooms 🍽 No Meals.

★ Number 31

$$$ | **B&B/INN** | Whether your lodging style is sublime Georgian elegance or cool modern, this one-in-a-million guesthouse, a short walk from St. Stephen's Green, serves up both—as well as the best made-to-order breakfast in town. **Pros:** the king and queen of guesthouse hosts; serene decor and art; fantastic breakfasts. **Cons:** a few rooms can be a little noisy; no elevator; minimum two-night stay on summer weekends. *$ Rooms from: €250 ✉ 31 Leeson Close, Georgian Dublin ☎ 01/676–5011 🌐 number31.ie 🛏 21 rooms 🍽 Free Breakfast.*

★ Pembroke Townhouse

$$ | **B&B/INN** | "Townhouse" does not do justice to the splendor of the place, but it does hint at the cozy, relaxed atmosphere of the Pembroke, a superb example of classic 18th-century grandeur. **Pros:** a Georgian wonderland; big, airy rooms; privately owned. **Cons:** 15-minute trip to the city center; often books up early; no a/c. *$ Rooms from: €225 ✉ 90 Pembroke Rd., Georgian Dublin ☎ 01/660–0277 🌐 www.pembroketownhouse.ie 🛏 48 rooms 🍽 No Meals.*

Premier Suites Dublin

$$ | **HOTEL** | **FAMILY** | Get a top-floor suite at this modernized Georgian town house just off St. Stephen's Green and lord it over the whole Southside. **Pros:** spectacular city views; ground-floor suites have private entrances; home-away-from-home atmosphere. **Cons:** decor is "motel functional"; lacks facilities; rooms vary in quality. *$ Rooms from: €225 ✉ 14–17 Lower Leeson St., Georgian Dublin ☎ 01/638–1111 🌐 premiersuitesdublinleesonstreet.com 🛏 37 rooms 🍽 No Meals.*

★ Schoolhouse Hotel

$$ | **HOTEL** | Pardon the pun, but this converted Victorian parochial school just off the Grand Canal really is A-plus—set in a gorgeous example of 19th-century architecture complete with turrets and soaring nave (now the setting for the restaurant), this may be the most uniquely upcycled hotel in Ireland. **Pros:** warm, friendly staff; top-class Irish restaurant; in-room spa treatments. **Cons:** a trip to the city center; fills up quickly; no elevator. *$ Rooms from: €229 ✉ 2–8 Northumberland Rd., Georgian Dublin ☎ 01/667–5014 🌐 schoolhousehotel.com 🛏 31 rooms 🍽 No Meals.*

Nightlife

PUBS

Cellar Bar

BARS | An 18th-century wine vault with bare brick walls and vaulted ceilings, this spot at the superstylish Merrion Hotel tends to draw a well-heeled crowd. *✉ The Merrion Hotel, 24 Upper Merrion St., Georgian Dublin ☎ 01/603–0600 🌐 www.merrionhotel.com/dine/the-cellar-bar.*

The 51 Bar

PUBS | Famous for its collection of whiskeys from around the world, the 51 is also a quality sports bar with a beer garden that is always buzzing with activity in fine weather. *✉ 51 Haddington Rd., Ballsbridge ☎ 01/660–0150 🌐 the51bar.com.*

The Horse Show House

PUBS | A Ballsbridge institution, the Horse Show House is a favorite of the boisterous but welcoming rugby and show-jumping set and a great spot to watch sports of any kind. They have a full à la carte menu. *✉ 32 Merrion Rd., Georgian Dublin ☎ 01/668–9424 🌐 horseshowhouse.ie.*

Toner's

PUBS | Though billed as a Victorian bar, Toner's actually goes back 200 years, with an original flagstone floor to prove its antiquity, as well as wooden drawers running up to the ceiling—a relic of the days when bars doubled as grocery shops. Oliver St. John Gogarty, who was the model for Buck Mulligan in James Joyce's *Ulysses,* accompanied W.B. Yeats here, in what was purportedly the latter's only visit to a pub. ✉ *139 Lower Baggot St., Georgian Dublin* ☎ *01/676–3090* 🌐 *tonerspub.ie.*

CLASSICAL MUSIC AND OPERA

The National Concert Hall

MUSIC | Just off St. Stephen's Green, the National Concert Hall is Dublin's main theater for classical music of all kinds, from symphonies to chamber groups. The slightly austere Neoclassical building was transformed in 1981 into one of Europe's finest medium-size concert halls. It houses the cream of Irish classical musicians, the National Symphony Orchestra of Ireland. A host of guest international conductors and performers—Maxim Vengerov, Radu Lupu, and Pinchas Zukerman are just a few of the soloists who have appeared—keep the standard very high, and performances continue throughout the year. The concert year picks up speed in mid-September and sails through to June; July and August also get many dazzling troupes. The smaller, more intimate John Field and Carolan rooms are perfect for chamber music, and also host some interesting talks with musicians, writers, and artists. ✉ *Earlsfort Terr., Georgian Dublin* ☎ *01/417–0000* 🌐 *nch.ie.*

CLOTHING

Cleo

MIXED CLOTHING | Hand-knit sweaters and accessories made from natural fibers are a specialty at Cleo. ✉ *18 Kildare St., Georgian Dublin* ☎ *01/676–1421* 🌐 *cleo-ltd.com.*

Blackrock Market

Held every weekend just off the Main Street in Blackrock Village (take the DART to Blackrock), the mostly covered Blackrock Market is one of the oldest markets in the country and offers a classic, eclectic assortment of bric-a-brac with rare objects, furniture, books, crystals, herbs, and just about everything else. With more than 50 vendors in attendance, this market has a vibrant European-flea-market feel and is a great spot for bargain hunting, souvenir shopping, or just wandering (🌐 *theblackrockmarket.com*).

Activities

HORSE RACING

Leopardstown Racecourse

HORSE RACING | The hub of horse racing in Dublin is Leopardstown, an ultramodern course that in February hosts the Hennessey Gold Cup, one of Ireland's most prestigious steeplechases. Summer and fall are devoted to flat racing, and the rest of the year to racing over fences. You can also nip in for a quick meal at the restaurant. ✉ *Leopardstown Rd., Georgian Dublin* ☎ *01/289–3600* 🌐 *leopardstown.com.*

RUGBY

For many years rugby was a "garrison sport" in Ireland, the preserve of "West Brits" and private-school boys. The success of the Irish team internationally, and Ulster, Leinster, and Munster in European club competitions, has changed that somewhat, and you might see an oval ball being tossed around by kids in any area of the country.

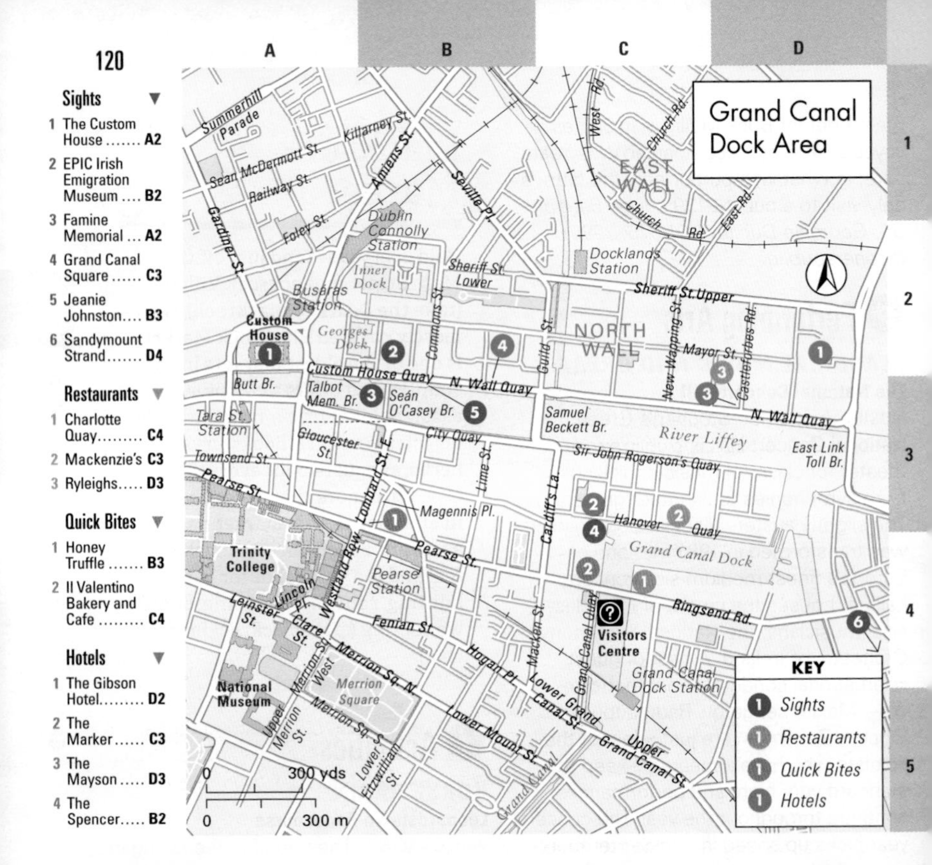

Aviva Stadium

SOCCER | The home ground of Irish rugby and soccer, Aviva's state-of-the-art arena opened in 2010 (on the site of the old Lansdowne Stadium) and can accommodate 50,000 fans. ✉ *62 Lansdowne Rd., Georgian Dublin* ☎ *01/238–2300* 🌐 *www.avivastadium.ie*.

Grand Canal Dock Area

No part of Dublin has seen such seismic change over the last few decades as this once crumbling, industrial area near the port. Opened in 1796 as a terminal where the canal finally meets the Liffey, Grand Canal Dock is now surrounded by shining cathedrals of glass and steel, monuments to the rise of "Silicon Docks," where tech giants like Google, Facebook, and Twitter have set up shop. Across the river, on the north side, the high-rises of the IFSC (International Financial Services Centre) are home to some equally big hitters of the banking world. For visitors, the interest lies in the contrasting elements that make up this glimmering new neighborhood in an old city of stone: the frantic daytime buzz of work and invention versus the weekend chill-out vibe of water sports and rooftop bars; the sleek, hypermodern Daniel Libeskind–designed theater versus the haunting simplicity of the bronze Famine memorial; the hum of activity versus the stillness of the water. Note that while there are some stunning new hotels, top-quality restaurants are still a bit thin on the ground.

The Custom House

GOVERNMENT BUILDING | Seen at its best when reflected in the waters of the Liffey during the short interval when the high tide is on the turn, the Custom House is the city's most spectacular Georgian building. Extending 375 feet on the north side of the river, this is the work of James Gandon, an English architect who arrived in Ireland in 1781, when the building's construction commenced (it continued for 10 years). Crafted from gleaming Portland stone, the central portico is linked by arcades to pavilions at either end. A statue of Commerce tops the copper dome, whose puny circumference, unfortunately, is out of proportion to the rest of the building. Statues on the main facade are based on allegorical themes. Note the exquisitely carved lions and unicorns supporting the arms of Ireland at the far ends of the facade. After the Irish Republican Army set fire to the building during the Irish War of Independence in 1921, it was completely restored and reconstructed to house government offices. A visitor center traces the building's history and significance as well as the life of Gandon. ✉ *Custom House Quay, Dublin North* ☎ *01/888–2000* 🌐 *heritageireland.ie* 🎫 *€6 self-guided tour, €8 guided tour.*

EPIC Irish Emigration Museum

HISTORY MUSEUM | It's fitting that Ireland's emigration museum should be housed near the Dublin docks where so many said goodbye to their island home forever. Deep in the redbrick vaults of the CHQ building, each visitor gets a symbolic "passport" before touring the 20 educational and interactive galleries. The focus is on digitally retelling the moving, human stories of the people who were forced to leave, the adventures and struggles they had, and the huge diaspora they left all over the world. There's a gallery dedicated to famous folk who claim Irish heritage, including numerous U.S. presidents such as Barack Obama, and outlaws like Billy the Kid. The attached Irish Family History Centre can help you trace your own Irish ancestors. If you reserve your tickets online in advance you can save €1–€3 per ticket. ✉ *Customs House Quay (CHQ), Dublin North* ☎ *01/531–3688* 🌐 *epicirelandchq.com* 🎫 *€21.*

Famine Memorial

MONUMENT | These shocking but beautiful bronze sculptures by artist Rowan Gillespie portray a few wasted victims of the Great Famine stumbling desperately along a road in search of salvation. The location, on Custom House Quay, is particularly appropriate as many of the ships carrying survivors to the New World left from here. A matching set of sculptures can be found on the other side of the Atlantic in Toronto. The nearby World Poverty Stone is another monument to the many people still suffering desperate deprivation throughout the world. ✉ *Custom House Quay, Dublin North* 🌐 *dublindocklands.ie* 🎫 *Free.*

Grand Canal Square

PLAZA/SQUARE | At the heart of the whole docklands development, this 10,000-square-meter, modernist square was designed by American landscape architect Martha Schwartz. Situated just to the west of the dock, with one side facing out onto the water, the sloping glass of the Daniel Libeskind–designed theater dominates the square's east side, while the black-and-white checkerboard Marker Hotel is to the north. The unusual red, resin glass–paved surface is supposed to reflect a "carpet" spilling out of the theater and into the public square. ✉ *Grand Canal Sq., Southside* 🌐 *dublindocklands.ie* 🎫 *Free.*

Jeanie Johnston

HISTORIC SIGHT | **FAMILY** | This is a remarkable replica of a 19th-century tall ship that carried poor souls caught in the potato famine to a new life in America. On board, a 50-minute guided tour takes you in the footsteps of passengers and crew, including the impressive craftsmanship on deck, and the shockingly cramped quarters below. Personal stories make it a moving experience. ✉ *Custom House Quay, Dublin North* ☎ *01/473–0111* 🌐 *jeaniejohnston.ie* 🎫 *€13.*

Sandymount Strand

BEACH | South of the docklands, a few blocks west of the Sydney Parade DART station, Sandymount Strand stretches for 5 km (3 miles) from Ringsend to Booterstown. It was cherished by James Joyce and his beloved Nora Barnacle from Galway, and it figures as one of the settings in *Ulysses*; it's also a popular spot with strolling Dubliners today. (The beach is "at the lacefringe of the tide," as Joyce put it.) When the tide recedes, the beach extends for 1½ km (1 mile) from the foreshore, but the tide sweeps in again very quickly. A sliver of a park lies between Strand Road and the beach, the water of which is not suitable for swimming. At the end of the strand there's a wonderful walk out along the south harbor wall to the Poolbeg Lighthouse, which has eye-popping views of Dublin Bay. ✉ *Sandymount, Southside.*

Restaurants

Charlotte Quay

$$$ | **MODERN IRISH** | With a stunning location right on the Grand Canal Dock, this elegant new eatery has a great view over the water to the impressive Bord Gáis Energy Theatre on the other side. The pretheater menu is a great option, with heirloom beetroot with Wicklow blue cheese and candied walnuts as a gorgeous, light starter. **Known for:** attentive and friendly staff; great for larger groups; tempting desserts such as buttermilk and vanilla. $ *Average main: €29* ✉ *Millennium Tower, Charlotte Quay Dock, Dublin South* ☎ *01/908–9490* 🌐 *charlottequay.ie* ⏲ *Closed Mon. No lunch Tues. and Wed.*

★ **Mackenzie's**

$ | **AMERICAN** | The fare is classic American, with generous pancake platters, cheeseburgers, pizzas, sundaes, and giant cookies all designed to encourage lively, casual gatherings and sharing. An open kitchen lines the back wall of the restaurant, and features a copper wood-fired pizza oven. **Known for:** bright and stylish dining room; delicious waffles with buttermilk-fried chicken; close to Bord Gáis Energy Theatre, so great for pretheater drinks and dinner. $ *Average main: €18* ✉ *Opus Bldg., 6 Hanover Quay, Dublin* ☎ *01/533–7566* 🌐 *mackenziesdublin.ie.*

Ryleighs

$$$ | **STEAKHOUSE** | Sitting atop the stylish Mayson Hotel, this rooftop steak house is all about the views, with walls of floor-to-ceiling windows offering vistas of Dublin Bay and the mountains beyond. Decked out in dark wood and leather booths, the sleek interior is contemporary-cool meets 1930s saloon. **Known for:** excellent breakfasts; superb cocktails; warm and friendly staff. $ *Average main: €30* ✉ *The Mayson, 81/82 North Wall Quay, Dublin North* ☎ *01/245–7911* 🌐 *themayson.ie.*

Coffee and Quick Bites

Honey Truffle

$ | **CAFÉ** | Recently voted the best café in the city, this busy little breakfast and lunch spot is the brainchild of former Avoca head chef Eimer Rainsford. Salads dominate the menu, with wonderful combinations to choose from for your salad box. **Known for:** interesting salads; great coffee; genuine service. $ *Average main: €13* ✉ *45 Pearse St., Dublin North* ☎ *01/537–7766* 🌐 *honeytruffle.ie* ⏲ *Closed weekends. No dinner.*

Il Valentino Bakery and Cafe

$ | **BAKERY** | **FAMILY** | Located in a nondescript building in Grand Canal Harbour, this stylish café is gaining a reputation

Grand Canal Dock, also known as Silicon Docks, is a hub of modern condos and office towers on the redeveloped Liffey Waterfront.

for its impressive baked goods. Nearby tech workers flock here in hordes for the inventive salads, sandwiches, handmade pasta, and focaccia *romana*, but it's the stunning array of cakes, tarts, and buns that really entice. **Known for:** decadent cakes; value lunch offerings; bustling atmosphere. *Average main: €14* *5 Gallery Quay, Grand Canal Harbour, Dublin South* *01/633–1100* *ilvalentino.ie* *No dinner.*

Hotels

★ The Gibson Hotel

$$$ | **HOTEL** | The terrace bar at the tastefully modern Gibson Hotel has to be the dream spot to view the impressive skyline and shimmering waterways of Dublin's trendy docklands area. **Pros:** fitness center with sauna; restaurant serves fantastic breakfasts; LUAS right outside for easy transit to Dublin center. **Cons:** slightly off the beaten track; can get busy and loud on concert nights; extra fee for parking. *Rooms from: €289* *Point Village, Dublin North* *01/681–5000* *thegibsonhotel.ie* *252 rooms* *No Meals.*

The Marker

$$$$ | **HOTEL** | The checkerboard facade and sloping, honeycomb ceilings of the Marker make a bold architectural statement, while the view of the docklands from the stunning rooftop bar has quickly become a top Dublin delight. **Pros:** friendly and welcoming staff; lovely pool and spa; attracts the in-crowd. **Cons:** can be loud; not all rooms have views; a little outside the city center. *Rooms from: €345* *Grand Canal Sq., Docklands, Southside* *01/687–5100* *themarkerhoteldublin.com* *187 rooms* *No Meals.*

★ The Mayson

$$$ | **HOTEL** | Dublin's newest boutique hotel combines a 19th-century town house and a former warehouse with an impressive steel-and-glass box. **Pros:** discount if you stay three nights; great views; stylish design. **Cons:** bigger rooms cost more; room size varies; a lot of business travelers. *Rooms from: €290*

✉ *81/82 North Wall Quay, Dublin North* ☎ *01/245–7900* 🌐 *themayson.ie* 🛏 *94 rooms* 🍽 *Free Breakfast.*

The Spencer
$$$ | HOTEL | Built with business guests in mind, this high-rise hotel in the middle of the International Financial Services Centre has been a surprise hit with all travelers interested in the business of good value and clean, quiet rooms with good amenities. **Pros:** weekend bargains available; front rooms have River Liffey views; little nocturnal street noise. **Cons:** room design pretty functional; business clientele; no buzz at night. [$] *Rooms from: €276* ✉ *IFSC, Dublin North* ☎ *01/433–8800* 🌐 *thespencerhotel.com* 🛏 *187 rooms* 🍽 *No Meals.*

Nightlife

The Boat Bar and Restaurant
BARS | The MV *Cill Airne* is a restored, 1960s passenger ship originally built right here in the Dublin docklands. Now located on North Wall Quay, you can sit on the the deck in summer and sip a cocktail from the gorgeous, wood-floor bar. ✉ *Quay 16, North Wall Quay, Dublin North* ☎ *01/817–8670* 🌐 *mvcillairne.com.*

The Marker Rooftop Bar
BARS | On a clear day in summer this classy rooftop bar has stunning, wraparound views across Grand Canal Dock and the whole city beyond. They specialize in cocktails and it's a great spot for a pretheater drink. ✉ *The Marker Hotel, Grand Canal Sq., Southside* ☎ *01/687–5100* 🌐 *themarkerhoteldublin.com.*

The Mayson Bar
BARS | This ground floor bar in a trendy new hotel keeps the exposed brickwork and open feel of the warehouse it used to be. The elegant island bar is an impressive centerpiece, and the outside terrace is a great option in the summer. ✉ *The Mayson, 81/82 North Wall Quay, Dublin North* ☎ *01/245–7900* 🌐 *themayson.ie.*

Mulligan's
PUBS | Synonymous in Dublin with a truly perfect pint of Guinness, Mulligan's started life as a *shebeen* (unlicensed drinking venue) and then, pub lore tells us, was listed as "legal" in 1782. Today, locals and students flock here for a good pint. ✉ *8 Poolbeg St., Southside* ☎ *01/677–5582.*

Performing Arts

VENUES

Bord Gáis Energy Theatre
THEATER | Housed in a brash, Daniel Libeskind–designed building in the growing docklands area of the city, this theater has a 2,000-plus capacity, making it Ireland's biggest theater space. Its calendar includes the best of international ballet, classical music, pop gigs, and even Broadway musicals. ✉ *Grand Canal Sq., Southside* ☎ *01/677–7999* 🌐 *bordgaisenergytheatre.ie.*

3Arena
MUSIC | Home to the grandest, big-gig concerts by rock stars and dance luminaries, the 3Arena is a high-tech, 14,500-capacity venue. ✉ *Northwall Quay, Dublin North* ☎ *01/819–8888* 🌐 *3arena.ie.*

Activities

City Kayaking
KAYAKING | Located right next to the *Jeanie Johnston* tall ship, this experienced outfit offers unique tours of Dublin by kayak along the Liffey. ✉ *Custom House Quay, North Dock, Dublin North* ☎ *085/866–7787* 🌐 *citykayaking.com* 🎟 *Tours from €38, rentals €32.*

Surfdock
WATER SPORTS | FAMILY | Kids and adults are welcome at these water-sports classes right on Grand Canal Dock. Surfing, windsurfing, wakeboarding, paddleboarding, and waterskiing are included, and there's a large shop attached where you can pick up the latest gear. ✉ *Grand*

The hip Mayson Hotel stitches together two historic buildings for a stylish industrial aesthetic.

Canal Dockyard, Southside ☎ 01/668–3945 🌐 surfdock.ie 🎫 €45 for surf lesson.

Temple Bar and Around

Locals complain about the late-night noise, and visitors sometimes say the place has the feel of a Dublin theme park, but a visit to Dublin wouldn't be complete without spending some time in the city's most famously vibrant area. More than any other neighborhood in the city, Temple Bar represents the dramatic changes (good and bad) and ascending fortunes of Dublin that came about in the last few decades. The area, which takes its name from one of the streets of its central spine, was targeted for redevelopment in 1991–92 after a long period of neglect, having survived widely rumored plans to turn it into a massive bus depot or a giant parking lot. Temple Bar took off as Dublin's version of New York's SoHo, Paris's Bastille, or London's Notting Hill—a thriving mix of high and alternative culture distinct from what you'll find in any other part of the city. Things have not gone totally to plan, as the area is blighted with its share of fast food joints, chain restaurants, and postage-stamp-size boutiques selling overpriced trinkets. But the narrow cobblestone streets and pedestrian alleyways are also home to vintage clothing stores, art galleries, roaring traditional-music bars aimed at tourists, a stylish hotel resuscitated by U2, hip restaurants, pubs, clubs, European-style cafés, and a smattering of cultural venues.

Temple Bar's regeneration was no doubt abetted by that one surefire real-estate asset that appealed to the Viking founders of the area: location. The area is bordered by Dame Street to the south, the Liffey to the north, Fishamble Street to the west, and Westmoreland Street to the east. In fact, Temple Bar is situated so perfectly between everywhere else in Dublin that it's difficult to believe this neighborhood was once largely forsaken. It's now sometimes called the "playing ground of young Dublin," and for good reason: on weekend evenings and daily in summer it teems with young people—not only from Dublin but from all over Europe—drawn by its pubs, clubs, and lively scene.

Sights

The Ark

CHILDREN'S MUSEUM | FAMILY | A self-described cultural center for children, The Ark engages and inspires young imaginations through a variety of creative endeavors and activities like music, poetry readings, film, dance, painting, interactive exhibitions, and more. Its theater opens onto Meeting House Square for outdoor performances in summer. A gallery and workshop space host ongoing activities. ✉ *11a Eustace St., Temple Bar* ☎ *01/670–7788* 🌐 *ark.ie* 🎟 *Free.*

Ha'penny Bridge

BRIDGE | Every Dubliner has a story about meeting someone on this cast-iron Victorian bridge, a heavily trafficked footbridge that crosses the Liffey at a prime spot—Temple Bar is on the south side, and the bridge provides the fastest route to the thriving Mary and Henry Streets shopping areas to the north. Until early in the 20th century, a halfpenny toll was charged to cross it. Congestion on the Ha'penny was relieved with the opening of the Millennium Footbridge a few hundred yards up the river. A refurbishment, including new railings, a return to the original white color, and tasteful lighting at night, has given the bridge a new lease on life.

Irish Film Institute (IFI)

ARTS CENTER | The opening of the IFI in a former Quaker meetinghouse helped to launch the revitalization of Temple Bar. It has three comfortable art-house cinemas showing revivals and new independent films, the Irish Film Archive, a bookstore for cineastes, and a popular bar and restaurant-café, all of which make this one of the neighborhood's most vital cultural institutions and *the* place to be seen. On Saturday nights in summer, films screen outdoors on Meeting House Square. ✉ *6 Eustace St., Temple Bar* ☎ *01/679–5744* 🌐 *ifi.ie* 🎟 *Event ticket prices vary.*

Meeting House Square

PLAZA/SQUARE | A spectacular retractable canopy of four 70-foot "umbrellas" has turned this already vibrant square into a year-round playground for Dubliners. The square, which is behind the Ark children's center and accessed via Curved Street, takes its name from a nearby Quaker meetinghouse. Today it's something of a gathering place for Dublin's youth and artists. Numerous cultural events—classic movies, theater, games, and family programs—take place here. (Thankfully, seats can be installed for screenings.) The square is also a favorite site for the continuously changing street sculpture that pops up all over Temple Bar (artists commissioned by the city sometimes create oddball pieces, such as half of a Volkswagen protruding from a wall). The square is also a great spot to sit, people-watch, and take in the sounds of the performing buskers who swarm to the place. There's an organic food market here every Saturday all day. ✉ *Meeting House Sq.* 🌐 *visitdublin.ie.*

National Library Photographic Archive

ART GALLERY | This important photographic resource holds regular exhibitions in its stylish modern building in Temple Bar. The collection comprises approximately 600,000 photographs, most of which are Irish, making up a priceless visual history of the nation. Although most of the photographs are historical, dating as far back as the mid-19th century, there are also a large number of contemporary pictures. Subject matter ranges from topographical views to studio portraits, from political events to early tourist photographs. You can also buy a print of your favorite photo. ✉ *Meeting House Sq., Temple Bar* ☎ *01/603–0200* 🌐 *www.*

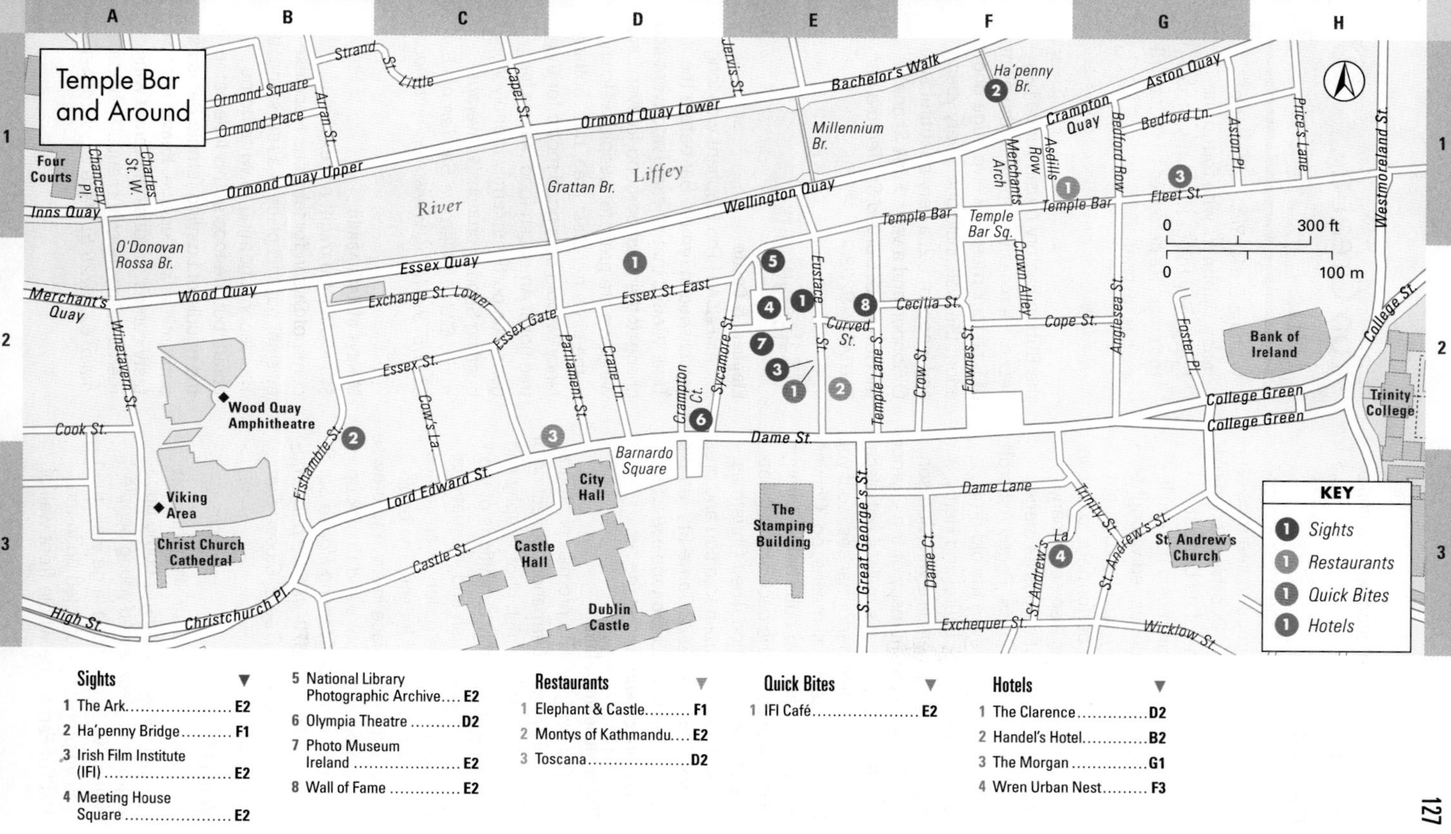

Sights

1 The Ark E2
2 Ha'penny Bridge F1
3 Irish Film Institute (IFI) E2
4 Meeting House Square E2
5 National Library Photographic Archive E2
6 Olympia Theatre D2
7 Photo Museum Ireland E2
8 Wall of Fame E2

Restaurants

1 Elephant & Castle F1
2 Montys of Kathmandu E2
3 Toscana D2

Quick Bites

1 IFI Café E2

Hotels

1 The Clarence D2
2 Handel's Hotel B2
3 The Morgan G1
4 Wren Urban Nest F3

nli.ie/en/national-photographic-archive.aspx 🎫 *Free.*

Olympia Theatre

ARTS CENTER | One of the most atmospheric places in Europe to see musical acts, the Olympia is Dublin's second-oldest theater, and one of its busiest. This classic Victorian music hall, built in 1879, has a gorgeous red wrought-iron facade. The Olympia has brought numerous musical performers to Dublin, and the theater has also seen many notable actors strut across its stage, including Alec Guinness, Peggy Ashcroft, Noël Coward, and even the old-time Hollywood team of Laurel and Hardy. Big-name performers like Van Morrison often choose the intimacy of the Olympia over larger venues. It's really a hot place to see some fine performances, so if you have a chance, by all means, go. Conveniently, there are two pubs here—through doors directly off the back of the theater's orchestra section. Their Christmas Pantomime is a Dublin tradition and great for younger kids. ✉ *72 Dame St., Temple Bar* ☎ *01/679–3323* 🌐 *olympia.ie* 🎫 *Event ticket prices vary.*

Photo Museum Ireland

ART GALLERY | Dublin's premier photography gallery has a permanent collection of early-20th-century Irish photography and also puts on monthly exhibitions of work by contemporary Irish and international photographers. The gallery is an invaluable social record of Ireland. The bookstore is the best place in town to browse for photography books and to pick up arty postcards. ✉ *Meeting House Sq. S, Temple Bar* ☎ *01/671–4654* 🌐 *photomuseumireland.ie* 🎫 *Free* ⏲ *Closed Sun. and Mon.*

Wall of Fame

PUBLIC ART | If you're strolling through Temple Bar and suddenly come upon a group of slack-jawed young people staring wide-eyed at a large wall, then you've probably stumbled upon the Wall of Fame. The whole front wall of the Button Factory music venue has become a massive tribute to the giants of Irish rock music. Twelve huge photos adorn the wall, including a very young and innocent U2, a very beautiful Sinead O'Connor, and a very drunk Shane McGowan. ✉ *Curved St., Temple Bar* ☎ *01/607–9202.*

Too Great a Toll

William Butler Yeats was one of many Dubliners who found the halfpenny toll of Ha'penny Bridge too steep. He detoured to O'Connell Bridge instead.

Restaurants

Elephant & Castle

$$ | **AMERICAN** | The Elephant was long established in Temple Bar before the Tiger (Celtic, that is) came and went and changed the neighborhood forever. Large windows are great for people-watching in the city's trendiest area, but "nothing fancy" would be a good motto for the traditional American food. **Known for:** generous portions; family-friendly vibes; bustling Sunday brunch. 💲 *Average main: €23* ✉ *18 Temple Bar, Temple Bar* ☎ *01/679–3121* 🌐 *www.elephantandcastle.ie.*

Montys of Kathmandu

$$ | **ASIAN** | You might not expect to come to Dublin for fabulous Nepalese cuisine, but this place is a real standout. The decor is nothing to write home about, but the food at this little eatery in the middle of bustling Temple Bar is as authentic as it is unique. **Known for:** spicy, tasty curries; surprisingly varied wine menu; celiac-friendly menu. 💲 *Average main: €22* ✉ *28 Eustace St., Temple Bar*

☎ 01/670–4911 ⊕ www.montys.ie ⊙ No lunch Sun.

Toscana

$ | **ITALIAN** | A genuine trattoria in the heart of crazy Temple Bar, Toscana buzzes with chatter all evening long and offers a popular pretheater menu. A Mediterranean slant to the simple dining room includes plenty of Italian landscapes, cream tones, and wood. **Known for:** quality pizza; seafood; Bailey's cheesecake. *$ Average main: €18 ✉ 3 Cork Hill, Dame St., Temple Bar ☎ 01/670–9785 ⊕ toscanarestaurant.ie.*

Coffee and Quick Bites

IFI Café

$ | **INTERNATIONAL** | This buzzing café bar is a pleasant place for a lunchtime break. Sandwiches are large and delicious, with plenty of vegetarian choices, and the people-watching is unmatched. **Known for:** popular bar and café; glass-roofed courtyard; great refueling spot in the heart of Temple Bar. *$ Average main: €15 ✉ 6 Eustace St., Temple Bar ☎ 01/679–5744 ⊕ ifi.ie/cafebar.*

Hotels

The Clarence

$$$ | **HOTEL** | Temple Bar's most prestigious hotel, and occasional home to your potential new best friends/elevator buddies, co-owners Bono and the Edge of U2, this renovated 1852 grand old hotel is the place to sample Temple Bar's nightlife, even if your pals are too busy rocking to hang. **Pros:** fantastic traditional breakfast at restaurant; the owners might be on premises; friendly staff. **Cons:** rooms a bit small; some rooms suffer from street noise; paying a premium for "cool". *$ Rooms from: €290 ✉ 6–8 Wellington Quay, Temple Bar ☎ 01/407–0800 ⊕ www.theclarence.ie ⇐ 50 rooms 🍴 No Meals.*

Handel's Hotel

$$ | **HOTEL** | Right in the heart of Temple Bar, this basic but well-run hotel somehow manages to feel like something of an oasis from the hustle of this lively neighborhood. **Pros:** offers noon checkout; cleverly designed rooms; option of interconnecting rooms great for families. **Cons:** rooms are small; noisy neighborhood; a little short on amenities. *$ Rooms from: €220 ✉ 16–18 Fishamble St., Temple Bar ☎ 01/670–9404 ⊕ handelshotel.ie ⇐ 40 rooms 🍴 No Meals.*

The Morgan

$$$ | **HOTEL** | A sparkling gem among a lot of very drab hotels in Temple Bar, the Morgan boasts about its chic design and decor, and the excitingly designed bedrooms and luxurious bathrooms are indeed pleasing to the many fashionistas and photographers who love this place. **Pros:** guests have access to nearby pool, gym, and steam rooms; great cocktail bar; extended-stay apartments are a good value. **Cons:** a little overdesigned in places; no parking; no restaurant. *$ Rooms from: €280 ✉ 10 Fleet St., Temple Bar ☎ 01/643–7000 ⊕ themorgan.com ⇐ 121 rooms 🍴 No Meals.*

★ Wren Urban Nest

$$ | **HOTEL** | Meeting a bold claim to be "Ireland's most sustainable hotel" wasn't easy, but the cool, clever Wren managed to pull it off. **Pros:** ultramodern panel-controlled lights and curtains; cheap for the location; cool, relaxed vibe. **Cons:** limited public spaces; some consider rooms too small; may not suit families. *$ Rooms from: €229 ✉ St. Andrew's La., Temple Bar ⊕ wrenhotel.ie ⇐ 137 rooms 🍴 No Meals.*

Nightlife

NIGHTCLUBS

Button Factory

DANCE CLUBS | A happening music venue, the Button mixes top DJs and up-and-coming live acts. The place tends to be on the cutting edge of the Irish dance-music scene. ✉ *Curved St., Temple Bar* ☎ *01/670–9202* 🌐 *buttonfactory.ie.*

The Workman's Club

LIVE MUSIC | Housed in a former workingman's club, this no-frills, hip spot specializes in indie club nights and attracts an artistic and hipster crowd. It has three floors of music and live gigs. Check the website for upcoming nights. ✉ *10 Wellington Quay, Temple Bar* ☎ *01/670–6692* 🌐 *theworkmansclub.com.*

PUBS

Oliver St. John Gogarty

PUBS | A lively bar that attracts all ages and nationalities, the Oliver St. John Gogarty overflows with patrons in summer. On most nights there's traditional Irish music upstairs. ✉ *57 Fleet St., Temple Bar* ☎ *01/671–1822* 🌐 *gogartys.ie.*

★ **Palace Bar**

BARS | Established in 1823, and scarcely changed since the 1940s, the wonderful Palace Bar is still all tiles and brass. Popular with journalists and writers (the *Irish Times* used to be nearby), the walls are lined with cartoons drawn by newspaper illustrators. ✉ *21 Fleet St., Temple Bar* ☎ *01/677–9290* 🌐 *thepalacebardublin.com.*

The Porterhouse

BREWPUBS | One of the few bars in Ireland to brew its own beer, their Plain Porter has won the best stout in the world award at the Brewing Industry International Awards (often referred to as the "Brewing Oscars") beating out the mighty Guinness. The tasteful interior is all dark woods and soft lighting. ✉ *16–18 Parliament St., Temple Bar* ☎ *01/679–8847* 🌐 *porterhousebrewco.ie.*

The Wild Duck

LIVE MUSIC | Filled to the brim with the owner's wonderful collection of art and retro furniture, this eclectic bar hosts jazz, drama, and pretty much anything else you fancy in its small theater space. The piano player in the corner keeps the place hopping at night. ✉ *17/22 Sycamore St., Temple Bar* ☎ *01/535–6849* 🌐 *thewildduck.ie.*

Performing Arts

CLASSICAL MUSIC AND OPERA

Opera Theatre Company

OPERA | Ireland's only touring opera company, the Opera Theatre company performs at venues in Dublin and throughout the country. ✉ *Temple Bar Music Centre, Curved St., Temple Bar* ☎ *01/679–4962* 🌐 *opera.ie.*

THEATER

The New Theatre

THEATER | A troupe with a political agenda, the New Theatre often favors productions by Irish working-class writers like Sean O'Casey and Brendan Behan in its renovated Temple Bar space. ✉ *43 E. Essex St., Temple Bar* ☎ *01/670–3361* 🌐 *thenewtheatre.com.*

Olympia Theatre

THEATER | Dublin's oldest and premier multipurpose theatrical venue, the Olympia hosts drama, pantomime, and live comedy in addition to its high-profile musical performances. ✉ *72 Dame St., Temple Bar* ☎ *01/677–7744* 🌐 *olympia.ie.*

Project Arts Centre

THEATER | A theater and performance space in an ugly modern building at the center of Temple Bar, the Project Arts Center premiers a lot of new Irish theater talent as well as contemporary music and experimental art events. ✉ *39 E. Essex St., Temple Bar* ☎ *01/881–9613* 🌐 *projectartscentre.ie.*

Smock Alley Theatre

THEATER | Smock Alley is a wonderfully atmospheric theater space tucked down a little lane. Now housed in a lovely 19th-century Irish neo-Gothic structure, it stands on the site of a famous 17th-century Dublin theater. ✉ *6/7 Lower*

Some Dubliners now give the overtouristed Temple Bar district the brush-off; others still find it the heart of the city's nightlife.

Exchange St., Temple Bar ☏ 01/677–0014 ⊕ smockalley.com.

Shopping

CLOTHING

Indigo and Cloth

MEN'S CLOTHING | This has become the place where Irish men with a bit of taste come for quality, slightly edgy clothing. Designers like Oliver Spencer and Velour dominate, and they also have a small, but classy, women's section. *✉ 9 Essex St. E, Temple Bar ☏ 01/670–6403 ⊕ indigoandcloth.com.*

MUSIC

Claddagh Records

MUSIC | Head here for a good selection of traditional and folk music. They have another shop on Westmoreland Street. *✉ 2 Cecilia St., Temple Bar ☏ 01/677–0262 ⊕ claddaghrecords.com.*

OUTDOOR MARKETS

Meeting House Square Market

MARKET | Held Saturday from 10 am to 4:30 pm in the heart of Temple Bar, this is a good place to buy homemade foodstuffs: cheeses, breads, chocolate, and organic veggies. *✉ Temple Bar ⊕ visitdublin.ie.*

O'Connell Street and Around

If you stand on O'Connell Bridge or the pedestrian-only Ha'penny span, you'll get excellent views up and down the River Liffey, known in Gaelic as the *abha na life,* transcribed phonetically as Anna Livia by James Joyce in *Finnegans Wake*. Here, framed with embankments like those along Paris's Seine, the river nears the end of its 128-km (80-mile) journey from the Wicklow Mountains to the Irish Sea. And near the bridges, you begin a pilgrimage into James Joyce country—north of the Liffey, in the center of town—and the captivating sights of Dublin's Northside, a mix of densely thronged shopping streets and genteelly refurbished homes.

For much of the 18th century, the upper echelons of Dublin society lived in the Georgian houses in the Northside—around Mountjoy Square—and shopped along Capel Street, which was lined with stores selling fine furniture and silver. But development of the Southside—the Georgian Leinster House in 1745, Merrion Square in 1764, and Fitzwilliam Square in 1825—changed the Northside's fortunes. The city's fashionable social center crossed the Liffey, and although some of the Northside's illustrious inhabitants stuck it out, the area gradually became run-down. The Northside's fortunes have now changed back, however. Once-derelict swaths of buildings, especially on and near the Liffey, have been rehabilitated, and large shopping centers bring the crowds to Mary and Jervis Streets and the "Italian Quarter." The LUAS Red Line links the Northside inner city, including the artsy but down-to-earth, urban suburb of Stoneybatter and the bustling, ethnic dining of Capel Street to the east of the city and Grand Canal Dock. In addition, a little Chinatown has formed on Parnell Street, while a swing bridge has been added between City Quay and the Northside. O'Connell Street itself has been partially pedestrianized, and most impressive of all is the Spire, the street's 395-foot-high stainless-steel monument.

Sights

Abbey Presbyterian Church

CHURCH | Built on the profits of sin—well, by a generous wine merchant actually—and topped with a soaring Gothic spire, this church anchors the northeast corner of Parnell Square, an area that was the city's most fashionable address during the gilded days of the 18th-century Ascendancy. Popularly known as Findlater's Church, after the merchant Alex Findlater, the church was completed in 1864 with an interior that has a stark Presbyterian mood despite stained-glass windows and ornate pews. For a bird's-eye view of the area, climb the small staircase that leads to the balcony. ✉ *Parnell Sq., Dublin North* ☎ *01/837–8600* 🌐 *abbeychurch.ie* 🎫 *Free.*

Dublin City Gallery The Hugh Lane

ART MUSEUM | **FAMILY** | The Francis Bacon studio, reconstructed here exactly as the artist left it on his death (including his diary, books, walls, floors, ceiling, and even dust!), makes this already impressive gallery a must-see for art lovers and fans of the renowned British artist. Built as a town house for the Earl of Charlemont in 1762, this residence was so grand that the Parnell Square street on which it sits was nicknamed "Palace Row" in its honor. Sir William Chambers, who also built the Marino Casino for Charlemont, designed the structure in the best Palladian manner. Its delicate and rigidly correct facade, extended by two demilune (half-moon) arcades, was fashioned from the "new" white Ardmulcan stone (now seasoned to gray). Charlemont was one of the cultural locomotives of 18th-century Dublin—his walls were hung with Titians and Hogarths, and he frequently dined with Oliver Goldsmith and Sir Joshua Reynolds—so he would undoubtedly be delighted that his home is now a gallery, named after Sir Hugh Lane, a nephew of Lady Gregory (W.B. Yeats's aristocratic patron). Lane collected both Impressionist paintings and 19th-century Irish and Anglo-Irish works. A complicated agreement with the National Gallery in London (reached after heated diplomatic dispute) stipulates that a portion of the 39 French paintings amassed by Lane shuttle between London and here. Time it right and you'll be able to see Pissarro's *Printemps,* Manet's *Eva Gonzales,* Morisot's *Jour d'Été,* and the jewel of the collection, Renoir's *Les Parapluies.*

Irish artists represented include Roderic O'Conor, well-known for his views of the west of Ireland; William Leech, including his *Girl with a Tinsel Scarf* and *The Cigarette*; and the most famous of the group, Jack B. Yeats (W.B.'s brother). The museum has a dozen of his paintings, including *Ball Alley* and *There Is No Night*. The mystically serene Sean Scully Gallery displays seven giant canvasses by Ireland's renowned abstract Modernist. They also have a great kids club with workshops and host classical concerts every Sunday (€2). ✉ *Parnell Sq. N, Dublin North* ☎ *01/222–5550* 🌐 *hughlane.ie* 🎫 *Free* ⏲ *Closed Mon.*

GAA Museum

SPORTS VENUE | FAMILY | The Irish are sports crazy and reserve their fiercest pride for their native games. In the bowels of Croke Park, the main stadium and headquarters of the GAA (Gaelic Athletic Association), this museum gives you a great introduction to native Irish sport. The four Gaelic games (football, hurling, camogie, and handball) are explained in detail, and if you're brave enough you can have a go yourself. High-tech displays take you through the history and highlights of the games. *National Awakening* is a really smart, interesting short film reflecting the key impact of the GAA on the emergence of the Irish nation and the forging of a new Irish identity. The exhilarating *A Day in September* captures the thrill and passion of All Ireland finals day—the annual denouement of the intercounty hurling and Gaelic football seasons—which is every bit as important to the locals as the Super Bowl is to sports fans in the United States. Tours of the stadium, one of the largest in Europe, are available. ✉ *St. Joseph's Ave., Croke Park Stadium, Dublin North* ☎ *01/819–2300* 🌐 *crokepark.ie/gaa-museum* 🎫 *Museum €9, museum and stadium tour €16.*

Garden of Remembrance

GARDEN | Opened 50 years after the Easter Rising of 1916, the garden in Parnell Square commemorates those who died fighting for Ireland's freedom. At the garden's entrance is a large plaza; steps lead down to the fountain area, graced with a sculpture by contemporary Irish artist Oisín Kelly, based on the mythological Children of Lír, who were turned into swans. The garden serves as an oasis of tranquility in the middle of the busy city. ✉ *Parnell Sq., Dublin North* ☎ *01/821–3021* 🌐 *heritageireland.ie/visit/places-to-visit/garden-of-remembrance* 🎫 *Free.*

Gate Theatre

ARTS CENTER | The show begins here as soon as you walk into the auditorium, a gorgeously Georgian masterwork designed by Richard Johnston in 1784 as an assembly room for the Rotunda Hospital complex. The Gate has been one of Dublin's most important theaters since its founding in 1929 by Micheál MacLiammóir and Hilton Edwards, who also founded Galway City's An Taibhdhearc as the national Irish-language theater. The Gate stages many established productions by Irish as well as foreign playwrights—and plenty of foreign actors have performed here, including Orson Welles (his first paid performance) and James Mason (early in his career). ✉ *Cavendish Row, Dublin North* ☎ *01/874–4045* 🌐 *gatetheatre.ie* ⏲ *Closed Sun.*

General Post Office (GPO)

HISTORIC SIGHT | The GPO's fame is based on the role it played in the fateful 1916 Easter Rising. The building, with its impressive Neoclassical facade, was designed by Francis Johnston and built by the British between 1814 and 1818 as a center of communications. This gave it great strategic importance—and was one of the reasons it was chosen by the insurgent forces in 1916 as a headquarters. Here, on Easter Monday, 1916, the Republican forces, about 2,000 in number and under the guidance of Pádraig Pearse and James Connolly, stormed the building and issued the Proclamation of the Irish Republic. After a week of shelling, the GPO lay in ruins; 13 rebels were ultimately executed, including Connolly,

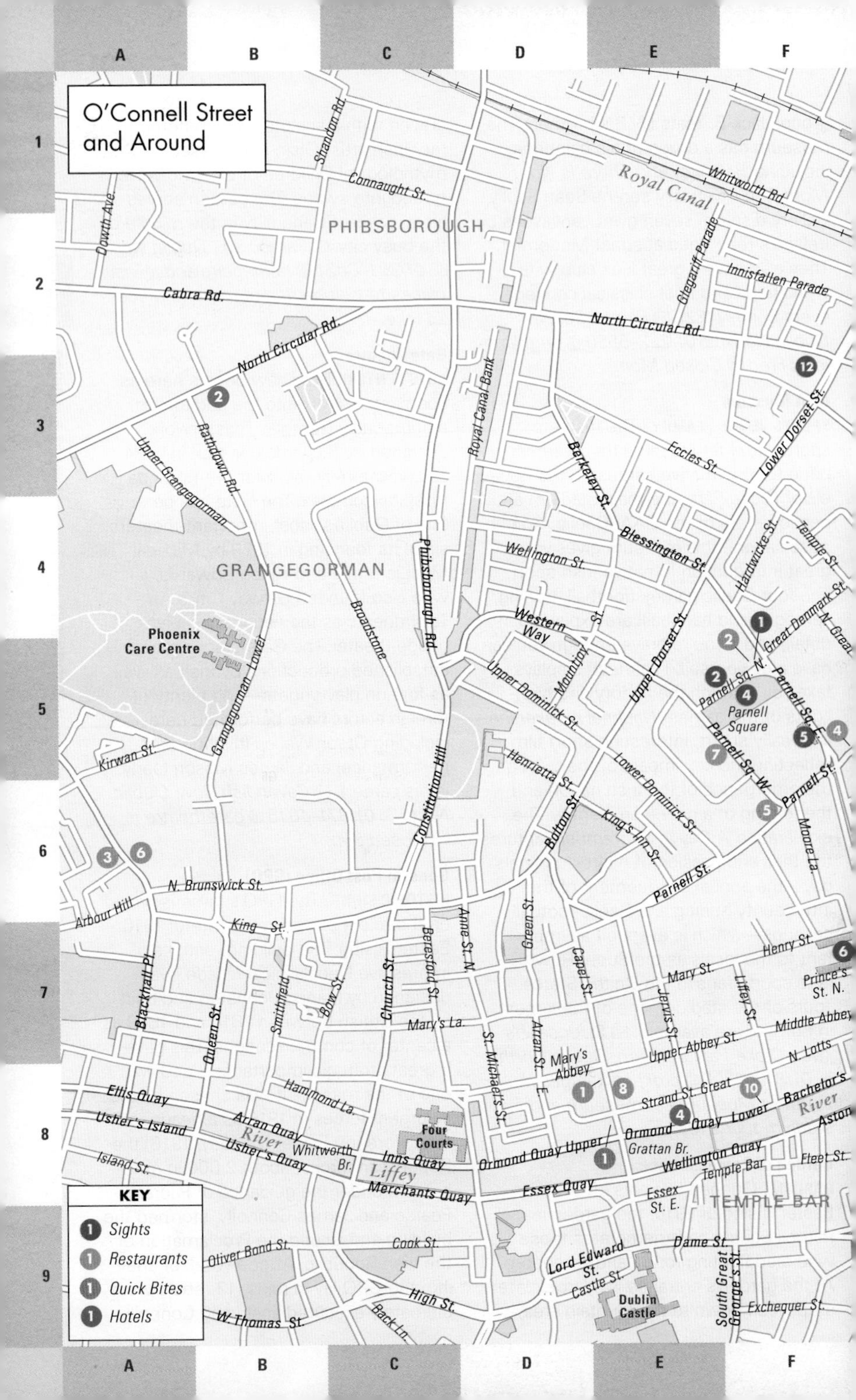
O'Connell Street and Around
KEY
Sights
Restaurants
Quick Bites
Hotels
PHIBSBOROUGH
GRANGEGORMAN
TEMPLE BAR
Phoenix Care Centre
Four Courts
Dublin Castle
Parnell Square
Mary's Abbey
Royal Canal
River Liffey
Shandon Rd.
Connaught St.
Dowth Ave.
Cabra Rd.
North Circular Rd.
Whitworth Rd.
Glengariff Parade
Innisfallen Parade
Royal Canal Bank
Rathdown Rd.
Upper Grangegorman
Berkeley St.
Eccles St.
Lower Dorset St.
Blessington St.
Wellington St.
Hardwicke St.
Temple St.
Phibsborough Rd.
Broadstone
Western Way
Mountjoy St.
Upper Dorset St.
Great Denmark St.
N. Great
Parnell Sq. N.
Parnell Sq. E.
Parnell Sq. W.
Parnell St.
Upper Dominick St.
Lower Dominick St.
Henrietta St.
King's Inn St.
Bolton St.
Moore La.
Grangegorman Lower
Kirwan St.
Constitution Hill
N. Brunswick St.
Arbour Hill
King St.
Blackhall Pl.
Queen St.
Smithfield
Bow St.
Church St.
Beresford St.
Anne St. N.
Green St.
Capel St.
Henry St.
Mary St.
Prince's St. N.
Jervis St.
Liffey St.
Middle Abbey
Mary's La.
St. Michael's St.
Arran St. E.
Upper Abbey St.
N. Lotts
Strand St. Great
Bachelor's
Ellis Quay
Hammond La.
Usher's Island
Arran Quay
Usher's Quay
Whitworth Br.
Inns Quay
Ormond Quay Upper
Ormond Quay Lower
Grattan Br.
Aston
Island St.
Wellington Quay
Temple Bar
Fleet St.
Merchants Quay
Essex Quay
Essex St. E.
Cook St.
Oliver Bond St.
Lord Edward St.
Dame St.
Castle St.
High St.
South Great George's St.
Exchequer St.
Back Ln.
W. Thomas St.

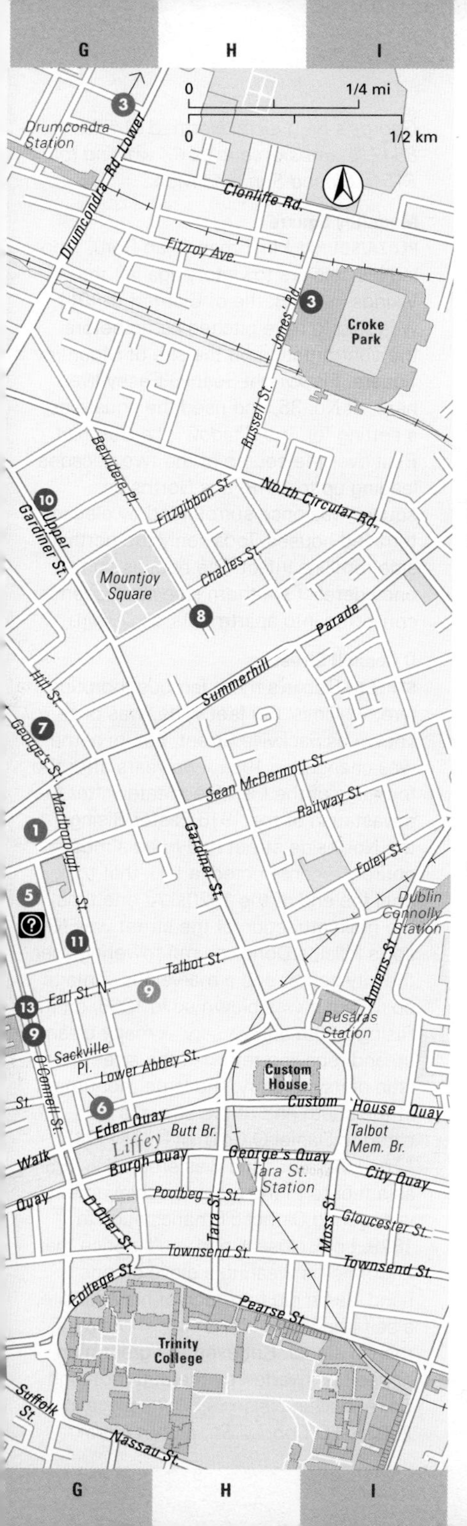

Sights

1 Abbey Presbyterian Church F5
2 Dublin City Gallery The Hugh Lane E5
3 GAA Museum I2
4 Garden of Remembrance F5
5 Gate Theatre F5
6 General Post Office (GPO) F7
7 James Joyce Centre ... G5
8 Mountjoy Square H4
9 O'Connell Street G7
10 St. Francis Xavier Church G3
11 St. Mary's Pro-Cathedral G6
12 Sean O'Casey House F3
13 The Spire G7

Restaurants

1 Brother Hubbard E8
2 Chapter One by Mickael Viljanen F5
3 Grano A6
4 Kimchi Hop House F5
5 Kingfisher F6
6 L. Mulligan Grocer A6
7 Mr Fox E5
8 Musashi Noodles and Sushi Bar E8
9 101 Talbot G6
10 The Winding Stair F8

Quick Bites

1 Soup Dragon E8

Hotels

1 Academy Plaza Hotel G5
2 Charleville Lodge B3
3 Dublin Skylon Hotel G1
4 The Morrison, a DoubleTree by Hilton Hotel E8
5 Riu Plaza The Gresham Dublin G6
6 Wynn's Hotel G7

who was dying of gangrene from a wound in a leg shattered in the fighting and had to be propped up in a chair in front of the firing squad. Most of the original building was destroyed, though the facade survived, albeit with the scars of bullets on its pillars. Rebuilt and reopened in 1929, it is now home to **GPO Witness History,** an impressive interactive museum that brings to life the glory and horror of that violent uprising and the part this famous building played in it. It includes an original copy of the Proclamation of Independence. There's also a café. ✉ *O'Connell St., Dublin North* ☎ *01/872–1916* 🌐 *anpost.com/witness-history* 🎫 *€15* 🕒 *Closed Sun. and Mon.*

James Joyce Centre

OTHER MUSEUM | Few may have read him, but everyone in Ireland has at least heard of James Joyce (1882–1941)—especially since owning a copy of his censored and suppressed *Ulysses* was one of the top status symbols of the early 20th century. Joyce is, of course, now acknowledged as one of the greatest modern authors, and *Dubliners, Finnegans Wake,* and *A Portrait of the Artist as a Young Man* can even be read as quirky "travel guides" to Dublin. Open to the public, this restored 18th-century Georgian town house, once the dancing academy of Professor Denis J. Maginni (which many will recognize from a reading of *Ulysses*), is a center for Joycean studies and events related to the author. It has an extensive library and archives, exhibition rooms, a bookstore, and a café. The collection includes letters from Beckett, Joyce's guitar and cane, and a celebrated edition of *Ulysses* illustrated by Matisse. The interactive exhibition *James Joyce and Ulysses* allows you to delve into the mysteries and controversies of the novel. The center is the main organizer of "Bloomstime," which marks the week leading up to the Bloomsday celebrations. (Bloomsday, June 16, is the single day *Ulysses* chronicles, as Leopold Bloom winds his way around Dublin in 1904.) ✉ *35 N. Great George's St., Dublin North* ☎ *01/878–8547* 🌐 *jamesjoyce.ie* 🎫 *€7, walking tour €15* 🕒 *Closed Sun. and Mon.*

Mountjoy Square

PLAZA/SQUARE | Irishman Brian Boru, who led his soldiers to victory against the Vikings in the Battle of Clontarf in 1014, was said to have pitched camp before the confrontation on the site of Mountjoy Square. Playwright Sean O'Casey lived here, at No. 35, and used the square as a setting for *The Shadow of a Gunman.* Built over the course of the two decades leading up to 1818, this Northside square was once surrounded by elegant terraced houses. Today only the northern side remains intact. The houses on the once-derelict southern side have been converted into apartments. ✉ *Dublin.*

O'Connell Street

STREET | Dublin's most famous thoroughfare, which is 150 feet wide, was once known as Sackville Street, but its name was changed in 1924, two years after the founding of the Irish Free State. After the devastation of the 1916 Easter Rising, the Northside street had to be almost entirely reconstructed, a task that took until the end of the 1920s. At one time, the main attraction of the street was Nelson's Pillar, a Doric column towering over the city center and a marvelous vantage point, but it was blown up in 1966, on the Rising's 50th anniversary. A major cleanup and repaving returned the street to a little of its old glory. The large monument at the south end of the street is dedicated to Daniel O'Connell (1775–1847), "The Liberator," and was erected in 1854 as a tribute to the orator's achievement in securing Catholic Emancipation in 1829. Look closely, and you'll notice that O'Connell is wearing a glove on one hand, as he did for much of his adult life, a self-imposed penance for shooting a man in a duel. But even the great man himself is dwarfed by the 395-foot-high Spire, built in Nelson's Pillar's place in 2003. ✉ *O'Connell St., Dublin North.*

St. Francis Xavier Church

CHURCH | One of the city's finest churches in the classical style, the Jesuit St. Francis Xavier's was begun in 1829, the year of Catholic Emancipation, and was completed three years later. The building is designed in the shape of a Latin cross, with a distinctive Ionic portico and an unusual coffered ceiling. The striking, faux-marble high altarpiece, decorated with lapis lazuli, came from Italy. The church appears in James Joyce's story "Grace." ✉ *Upper Gardiner St., Dublin North* ☎ *01/836–3411* 🌐 *gardinerstparish.ie* 🎟 *Free.*

St. Mary's Pro-Cathedral

CHURCH | Dublin's principal Catholic cathedral (also known as St. Mary's) is a great place to hear the best Irish male voices: a Palestrina choir, in which the great Irish tenor John McCormack began his career, sings in Latin here every Sunday morning at 11 am. The cathedral, built between 1816 and 1825, has a classical church design—on a suitably epic scale. The church's facade, with a six-Doric-pillared portico, is based on the Temple of Theseus in Athens; the interior is modeled after the Grecian-Doric style of St. Philippe du Roule in Paris. But the building was never granted full cathedral status, nor has the identity of its architect ever been discovered; the only clue to its creation is in the church ledger, which lists a "Mr. P." as the builder. ✉ *83 Marlborough St., Dublin North* ☎ *01/874–5441* 🌐 *procathedral.ie* 🎟 *Free.*

Sean O'Casey House

HISTORIC HOME | A onetime construction laborer, O'Casey became Ireland's greatest modern playwright, and this is the house where he wrote all his famous Abbey plays, including *Juno and the Paycock* and *The Plough and the Stars*. You can't go inside but it's worth a look. ✉ *422 N. Circular Rd., Dublin North.*

The Spire

MONUMENT | Christened the "Stiletto in the Ghetto" by local smart alecks, this needle-like monument is the most exciting thing to happen to Dublin's skyline in decades. The Spire, also known as the Monument of Light, was originally planned as part of the city's millennium celebrations. But Ian Ritchie's spectacular 395-foot-high monument wasn't erected until the beginning of 2003. Seven times taller than the nearby General Post Office, the stainless-steel structure rises from the spot where Nelson's Pillar once stood. Approximately 10 feet in diameter at its base, the softly lighted monument narrows to only 1 foot at its apex—the upper part of the Spire sways gently when the wind blows. The monument's creators envisioned it serving as a beacon for the whole of the city, and it will certainly be the first thing you see as you drive into Dublin from the airport. ✉ *O'Connell St., Dublin North.*

The Scars of History

Look for the bullet marks on the pillars of the General Post Office—they're remnants of the 1916 Easter Rising.

Restaurants

Brother Hubbard

$ | **MIDDLE EASTERN** | A delightful slow-food sanctuary within the Dublin dining scene, Brother Hubbard is a cozy, elegantly designed Northside café with a stripped-down but standout menu. The healthy emphasis is on fresh salads and soups with delicious twists; dishes tend to have a Middle Eastern feel, with an Irish touch here and there. **Known for:** meze; guilty-pleasure cakes; great coffee. $ *Average main: €17* ✉ *153 Capel St., Dublin North* ☎ *01/441–1112* 🌐 *brotherhubbard.ie* 🕒 *No dinner Sun.–Wed.*

Dubliners flock to the hip Stoneybatter for its laid-back cafes, global cuisine, and lively nightlife.

★ Chapter One by Mickael Viljanen
$$$$ | MODERN IRISH | When Michelin-starred chef Mickael Viljanen partnered up with this venerable Dublin dining institution, great things were expected. We weren't disappointed. **Known for:** polite and attentive staff; offers chef's table experience; flawless food and service. *Average main: €47* *18–19 Parnell Sq., Dublin North* *01/873–2266* *chapteronerestaurant.com* *Closed Sun. and Mon. No lunch Sat.*

★ Grano
$ | ITALIAN | FAMILY | Owner Roberto Mungo brings his brand of simple Calabrian cooking to this classy little Italian, family-run joint in hip Stoneybatter. There are touches of other Italian regions on the menu, but standouts are Calabrian classics like deep-fried aubergine with tomato, mozzarella, and green pesto and baked mackerel with potatoes, herbs, red pepper cream, and asparagus. **Known for:** great value; delicious small bites; genuine Italian cooking. *Average main: €18* *5 Norseman Ct., Manor St., Dublin North* *01/538–2003* *grano.ie.*

★ Kimchi Hop House
$ | KOREAN FUSION | A unique Korean-Japanese standout in the slew of cheap and cheerful Chinese eateries on Parnell Street (the closest Dublin comes to a Chinatown), Hop House is a restaurant and pub in one. Part of the old Shakespeare pub has been transformed into one of the friendliest, best-value restaurants in the city. **Known for:** superb bulgogi bokkumbap; can get busy; option to eat in beer garden. *Average main: €15* *160 Parnell St., Dublin North* *01/872–8318* *kimchihophouse.ie.*

Kingfisher
$ | IRISH | Don't let the down-at-heels canteen decor put you off—this place has been around for a long time and is a master of the art of fish-and-chips. Their menu is full of seafood surprises like such Dublin favorites as cod and ray (or more unusual choices like mackerel) and you can even order a whole sea bass and rainbow trout. **Known for:** homemade

tartar sauce; friendly, warm atmosphere; great-value menu. *Average main: €17 166–168 Parnell St., Dublin North 01/872–8732 kingfisherdublin.com.*

★ L. Mulligan Grocer

$$ | **IRISH** | This gem of an old Dublin boozer—which was once also the local grocer—has been turned into a gastropub and world-beer emporium, without losing too much of its real Dublin feel. It's the perfect spot for a quick pint of ale and a plate of black pudding (with pear relish and red chard) if you don't feel like a full sit-down meal. **Known for:** huge beer selection; popularity with hipsters; welcoming, friendly staff. *Average main: €21 18 Stoneybatter, Dublin North 01/670–9889 lmulligangrocer.com No lunch weekdays.*

Mr Fox

$$$ | **FRENCH** | The stuffed fox on the wall with the pistol in his hand inspired the name of this warm, gamy, stylish new eatery in a Georgian basement conveniently located near the Gate Theatre. The chef-owner graduated from a Michelin-star kitchen and he brings that elevated standard to the seasonal, fixed-price menu, with dishes like venison with parsnip, black pudding, chestnut, and blackberries. **Known for:** classical French-Irish food with modern touches; sister restaurant of the Pig's Ear; pig's head croquettes. *Average main: €30 38 Parnell Sq. W, Dublin North 01/874–7778 mrfox.ie Closed Sun. and Mon.*

★ Musashi Noodles and Sushi Bar

$ | **SUSHI** | This hot sushi bar on suddenly hip Capel Street has given birth to sister restaurants around the city because it finally made the Japanese staple affordable. Japanese-owned and-run, the restaurant serves fresh and flavorful dishes—all the sushi standards you'd expect but better than anything else in the city. The interior is simple and unfussy: a long, narrow room with dark wood floors and rows of pinewood tables and seats dotted with red cushions. **Known for:** attentive and friendly staff; excellent ramen; BYOB with a very fair €6 corkage charge. *Average main: €17 15 Capel St., Dublin North 01/532–8068 musashidublin.com.*

101 Talbot

$$ | **MEDITERRANEAN** | Close to the Abbey and Gate theaters, so there's no danger of missing a curtain call, this creative eatery focusing on contemporary food—with eclectic Mediterranean and Eastern influences—uses fresh local ingredients. It's very popular with the artistic and literary set. **Known for:** artsy clientele; pretheater option; strong vegetarian choices. *Average main: €24 101 Talbot St., Dublin North 01/874–5011 101talbot.ie Closed Sun. and Mon. No lunch.*

The Winding Stair

$$$ | **IRISH** | Once Dublin's favorite secondhand bookshop–café, the Winding Stair now houses an atmospheric, buzzing little restaurant, with old wooden floors, simple decor, a downstairs bookshop, and grand views of the Ha'penny Bridge and the river Liffey. Hearty portions of upscale traditional Irish food rely on Irish-only ingredients; the pork chop with crispy pigs' ears and hispi cabbage is a standout. **Known for:** views of the River Liffey; historic location; Irish produce–inspired cooking. *Average main: €27 40 Ormond Quay, Dublin North 01/872–7320 winding-stair.com.*

Coffee and Quick Bites

Soup Dragon

$ | **IRISH** | This tiny café and takeout shop serves an astonishing array of fresh soups daily. They come in three sizes, and you can get vegetarian soup or soups with meat- or fish-based broth; best bets include pumpkin chili and coconut; fragrant Thai chicken; beef chili; and hearty mussel, potato, and leek. **Known for:** can have long lines at lunchtime; excellent curries; many gluten- and dairy-free menu items. *Average main: €8 168*

Capel St., Dublin North ☎ *01/872–3277* 🌐 *soupdragon.com* ⏲ *Closed weekends. No dinner.*

Hotels

Academy Plaza Hotel

$$ | **HOTEL** | This modern, architecturally uninspired hotel is centrally located just off O'Connell Street and offers lots of comfort at an affordable, slightly unfashionable–neighborhood price. **Pros:** soundproof windows; triple and quad rooms great value; choice of restaurants. **Cons:** unfashionable location; rooms are not huge; popular with bachelorette parties. *Rooms from: €185* ✉ *10–14 Findlater Pl., Dublin North* ☎ *01/878–0666* 🌐 *academyplazahotel.ie* *304 rooms* *No Meals.*

Charleville Lodge

$ | **B&B/INN** | There's a slightly funky feel to this Georgian wonder. **Pros:** Victorian elegance; near Phoenix Park; public transport nearby. **Cons:** outside the city center; two-night minimum on some rooms on summer weekends; no elevator. *Rooms from: €150* ✉ *268–272 N. Circular Rd., Phibsborough, Dublin North* ☎ *01/838–6633* 🌐 *charlevillelodge.ie* *30 rooms* *Free Breakfast.*

Dublin Skylon Hotel

$ | **HOTEL** | Location, location, and spacious rooms: the three reasons for choosing the Skylon. **Pros:** located between the airport and city center; big rooms suitable for families; prices stable year-round. **Cons:** basic room furnishings; mediocre restaurant; mainly business clientele. *Rooms from: €169* ✉ *Upper Drumcondra Rd., Drumcondra, Dublin North* ☎ *01/884–3900* 🌐 *dublinskylonhotel.com* *126 rooms* *No Meals.*

The Morrison, A DoubleTree by Hilton Hotel

$$$ | **HOTEL** | Showcasing new Irish talent in everything from the textiles to the art on the walls and the sculptures in public spaces—there are even famous Irish song lyrics on the walls in some bedrooms—this sleek, trendy spot remains top of the Northside lodging charts. **Pros:** people-watching in cocktail bar; intensely designed rooms; high-end value option. **Cons:** tries a little too hard to be cool; located on busy road; some may find design over-the-top. *Rooms from: €280* ✉ *Ormond Quay, Dublin North* ☎ *01/887–2400* 🌐 *morrisonhotel.ie* *145 rooms* *No Meals.*

Riu Plaza The Gresham Dublin

$$$ | **HOTEL** | Opened in 1817, it's been a while since this was *the* place to stay for visiting dignitaries and local celebs, but the now-chain-owned Gresham remains a solid city-center option without the astronomical expense. **Pros:** good price for city center; warm, friendly staff; ample facilities. **Cons:** bar and public areas can get busy; room design unexciting; it can bump prices on busy weekends. *Rooms from: €240* ✉ *23 Upper O'Connell St., Dublin North* ☎ *01/874–6881* 🌐 *riu.com/en/hotel/ireland/dublin/hotel-riu-plaza-the-gresham-dublin* *323 rooms* *No Meals.*

Wynn's Hotel

$$ | **HOTEL** | A few doors down from the Abbey Theatre, Wynn's began its life as a Dublin boardinghouse in 1845, and its beautiful stained-glass awning has become something of a landmark as a romantic meeting spot for locals. **Pros:** great location for theater fans; feels like a genuine full-service hotel; a touch of history about the place. **Cons:** decor can feel a bit hodgepodge; rooms are on the small side; can be some noise from ballroom downstairs. *Rooms from: €229* ✉ *35–39 Lower Abbey St., Dublin North* ☎ *01/874–5131* 🌐 *wynnshotel.ie* *65 rooms* *No Meals.*

Nightlife

NIGHTCLUBS

The Academy

DANCE CLUBS | A music hub with four floors of entertainment of every kind, the

Academy is anchored by big-name local and international DJs and gigs. It attracts a young, dance-crazy crowd who like to party until the wee hours. ✉ *57 Middle Abbey St., Dublin North* ☎ *01/877–9999* 🌐 *theacademydublin.com.*

PUBS

The Big Romance

BARS | This cool bar for lovers of electronic music is based around a custom-made sound system and an enviable vinyl collection … oh, and they specialize in craft beers and daring cocktails, too. ✉ *98 Parnell St., Dublin North* ☎ *01/598–4117* 🌐 *thebigromance.ie.*

The Celt

BARS | A hop and skip from O'Connell Street, the Celt offers traditional Irish music seven nights a week and draws a nice mix of locals and tourists. On busy weekends, to quote the natives, the place is "heaving."✉ *81 Talbot St., Dublin North* ☎ *01/878–8655* 🌐 *thecelt.ie.*

The Flowing Tide

PUBS | Directly across from the Abbey Theatre, the Flowing Tide draws a lively pre- and posttheater crowd. No TVs, quality pub talk, and a great pint of Guinness make it a worthwhile visit (although the decor won't win any prizes). ✉ *9 Lower Middle Abbey St., Dublin North* ☎ *01/874–4108.*

Pantibar

BARS | Originally fronted by the infamous Dublin drag queen Panti and a cultural hot spot for the local LGBTQ+ community, this amusingly named gay bar has loud music at night but is pretty chilled-out during the day. ✉ *7–8 Capel St., Dublin North* ☎ *01/874–0710* 🌐 *pantibar.com.*

Quay 14

COCKTAIL LOUNGES | This latest incarnation of the bar at the Morrison Hotel is an uberhip cocktail joint that is trying (perhaps a little too hard) to attract the cool crowd. Still, the bar staff are inventive with their cocktails, and aficionados of Irish whiskeys will be thrilled with the selection. ✉ *Morrison Hotel, Lower Ormond Quay, Dublin North* ☎ *01/887–2400* 🌐 *www.morrisonhotel.ie.*

LIVE MUSIC

Dublin City Gallery The Hugh Lane

CONCERTS | One of the city's most distinctive art museums, the Dublin City Gallery The Hugh Lane is a serene home to Sundays@Noon, a series of free Sunday concerts featuring some top Irish and international talent. Concerts attract a full house, so reserve a spot online and get there early. ✉ *Parnell Sq. N, Dublin North* ☎ *01/222–5550* 🌐 *hughlane.ie.*

Performing Arts

THEATER

★ Abbey Theatre

THEATER | One of the most fabled theaters in the world, the Abbey is the home of Ireland's national theater company. In 1904 W. B. Yeats and his patron, Lady Gregory, opened the theater, which became a major center for the Irish literary renaissance—the place that first staged works by J.M. Synge and Sean O'Casey, among many others. Plays by recent Irish drama heavyweights like Brian Friel, Tom Murphy, Hugh Leonard, and John B. Keane have all premiered here, and memorable productions of international greats like Mamet, Ibsen, and Shakespeare have also been performed. You should not, however, arrive expecting 19th-century grandeur: the original structure burned down in 1951. A starkly modernist auditorium was built in its place—but what it may lack in aesthetics it makes up for in space and acoustics. Criticisms of a reverential, male, and mainstream approach are being addressed, with more female writers, a new spin on old Irish classics, and a second stage offering more experimental drama. But the Abbey will always be relevant since much of the theatergoing public still looks to it as a barometer of

Irish culture. ✉ *Lower Abbey St., Dublin North* ☎ *01/878–7222* 🌐 *abbeytheatre.ie.*

Gate Theatre

THEATER | An intimate 371-seat theater in a jewel-like Georgian assembly hall, the Gate produces the classics and contemporary plays by leading Irish writers, including Beckett, Wilde (the production of *Salome* was a worldwide hit), Shaw, and the younger generation of dramatists, such as Conor McPherson. ✉ *Cavendish Row, Parnell Sq., Dublin North* ☎ *01/874–4045* 🌐 *gatetheatre.ie.*

Shopping

BOOKS

Eason

BOOKS | Known primarily for its large selection of books, magazines, and stationery, Eason also sells an array of toys and audiovisual goodies at its main O'Connell Street branch; all in all, it has about 50 bookstores throughout Ireland. ✉ *O'Connell St., Dublin North* ☎ *01/873–3811* 🌐 *easons.com.*

DEPARTMENT STORES

Arnotts

DEPARTMENT STORE | Fully filling three floors, Arnotts stocks a wide selection of clothing, household accessories, and sporting goods. It is known for matching quality with value. There is a Gap section downstairs. ✉ *Henry St., Dublin North* ☎ *01/805–0400* 🌐 *arnotts.ie.*

JEWELRY

McDowells

JEWELRY & WATCHES | Popular with Dubliners, this jewelry shop has been in business for more than 100 years. ✉ *3 Upper O'Connell St., Dublin North* ☎ *01/874–4961* 🌐 *mcdowellsjewellers.com.*

Activities

FOOTBALL

Soccer—called football in Europe—is very popular in Ireland, largely due to the euphoria resulting from the national team's underdog successes since the late 1980s.

Football Association of Ireland

SOCCER | League of Ireland matches take place throughout the city on Friday evening or Sunday afternoon from March to November. For details, contact the Football Association of Ireland. ✉ *National Sports Campus, Snugborough Rd., Dublin North* ☎ *01/899–8500* 🌐 *fai.ie.*

GAELIC GAMES

Gaelic Athletic Association (*GAA*)

LOCAL SPORTS | The traditional games of Ireland, Gaelic football and hurling, attract a huge following, with roaring crowds cheering on their county teams. Games are held at Croke Park, the stunning, high-tech national stadium for Gaelic games, just north of the city center. For details of matches, contact the Gaelic Athletic Association. ✉ *Croke Park, Dublin North* ☎ *01/836–3222* 🌐 *gaa.ie.*

Antiques

Dublin is one of Europe's best cities in which to buy antiques, largely due to a long and proud tradition of restoration and high-quality craftsmanship. The Liberties, Dublin's oldest district, is, fittingly, the hub of the antiques trade, and is chockablock with shops and traders. Bachelor's Walk, along the quays, also has some decent shops with regular small auctions. It's quite a seller's market, but bargains are still possible.

The Liberties and Around

A cornucopia of things quintessentially Dublin, this area is studded with treasures ranging from the opulent 18th-century salons of Dublin Castle to time-burnished St. Patrick's Cathedral, and from the Liberties neighborhood—containing some of the city's best antiques stores—to the Irish Museum of Modern Art (housed at the strikingly renovated Royal Hospital Kilmainham). You can time-travel from the 10th-century crypt at Christ Church Cathedral—the city's oldest surviving structure—to the modern plant of the Guinness Brewery and its storehouse museum. You can also cross the Liffey for a visit to Smithfield, Dublin's old (but recently modernized) market area where flowers, fruit, vegetables, and even horses have been sold for generations. Traditional-music bars sit side by side here with new hotels and the newly refurbished Old Jameson Distillery museum.

Keep in mind that Dublin is compact. The following sights aren't far from those in the other city-center neighborhoods. In fact, City Hall is just across the street from Temple Bar, and Christ Church Cathedral is a short walk farther west. The westernmost sights covered here—notably the Royal Hospital and Kilmainham Gaol—are, however, at some distance, so if you're not an enthusiastic walker, you may want to drive or catch a cab, bus, or LUAS tram to them.

Sights

★ Chester Beatty Library

LIBRARY | A connoisseur's delight, this "library" is considered one of the overlooked treasures of Ireland. After Sir Alfred Chester Beatty (1875–1968), an American mining millionaire and a collector with a flawless eye, assembled one of the most significant collections of Islamic, early Christian, and Far Eastern art in the Western world, he donated it to Ireland. Housed in the gorgeous clock-tower building of Dublin Castle, exhibits include clay tablets from Babylon dating from 2700 BC, Japanese woodblock prints, Chinese jade books, early papyrus bibles, and Turkish and Persian paintings. The second floor, dedicated to the major religions, houses 250 manuscripts of the Koran from across the Muslim world, as well as one of the earliest Gospels. The first-floor *Arts of the Book* exhibition looks at the different origins and finest examples of books throughout the world. Guided tours of the library are available on Wednesday at 1 pm and Sunday at 3 pm and 4 pm. The gift shop is a real treasure trove and on sunny days the garden is one of the most tranquil places in central Dublin. ✉ *Castle St., Dublin West* ☎ *01/407–0750* 🌐 *chesterbeatty.ie* 🎫 *Free* ⏲ *Closed Mon. Nov.–Feb.*

★ Christ Church Cathedral

CHURCH | From its exterior, you'd never guess that the first Christianized Danish king built a wooden church at this site in 1038; because of the extensive 19th-century renovation of its stonework and trim, the cathedral looks more Victorian than Anglo-Norman. Construction on the present Christ Church—the flagship of the Church of Ireland and one of two Protestant cathedrals in Dublin (the other is St. Patrick's just to the south)—was begun in 1172 by Strongbow, a Norman baron and conqueror of Dublin for the English Crown, and continued for 50 years. By 1875 the cathedral had deteriorated badly; a major renovation gave it much of the look it has today, including the addition of one of Dublin's most charming structures: a Bridge of Sighs–like affair that connects the cathedral to the old Synod Hall, which now holds the Viking multimedia exhibition, Dublinia. Strongbow himself is buried in the cathedral, beneath an impressive effigy. The vast, sturdy crypt, with its 12th- and 13th-century vaults, is Dublin's oldest surviving structure and the building's most notable feature. The exhibition *Treasures of Christ Church* includes manuscripts, various historic artifacts, and the tabernacle used when James II worshipped here. But the real marvels are the mummified bodies of a cat and rat—they were trapped in an organ pipe in the 1860s—who seem

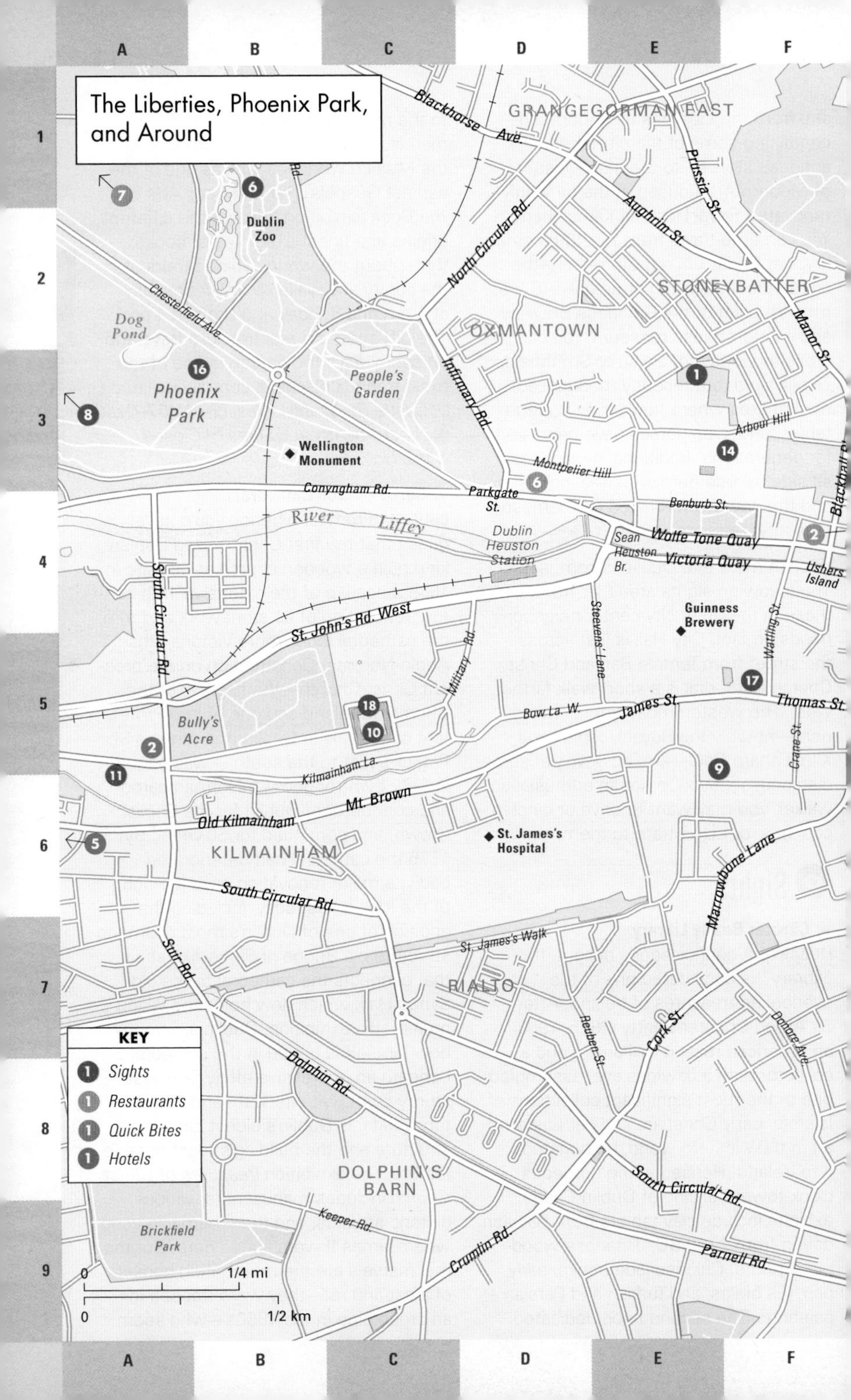
The Liberties, Phoenix Park, and Around
A
B
C
D
E
F
1
2
3
4
5
6
7
8
9
GRANGEGORMAN EAST
Blackhorse Ave.
Prussia St.
Aughrim St.
North Circular Rd.
Dublin Zoo
Chesterfield Ave.
Dog Pond
STONEYBATTER
Manor St.
OXMANTOWN
People's Garden
Infirmary Rd.
Phoenix Park
Arbour Hill
Wellington Monument
Montpelier Hill
Conyngham Rd.
Parkgate St.
Benburb St.
Blackhall Pl.
River Liffey
Dublin Heuston Station
Sean Heuston Br.
Wolfe Tone Quay
Victoria Quay
Ushers Island
South Circular Rd.
Steevens' Lane
Guinness Brewery
St. John's Rd. West
Military Rd.
Watling St.
Bow La. W.
James St.
Thomas St.
Bully's Acre
Kilmainham La.
Crane St.
Mt. Brown
Old Kilmainham
St. James's Hospital
KILMAINHAM
Marrowbone Lane
South Circular Rd.
Suir Rd.
St. James's Walk
RIALTO
Reuben St.
Cork St.
Donore Ave.
Dolphin Rd.
KEY
Sights
Restaurants
Quick Bites
Hotels
DOLPHIN'S BARN
South Circular Rd.
Keeper Rd.
Brickfield Park
Crumlin Rd.
Parnell Rd.
0
1/4 mi
0
1/2 km

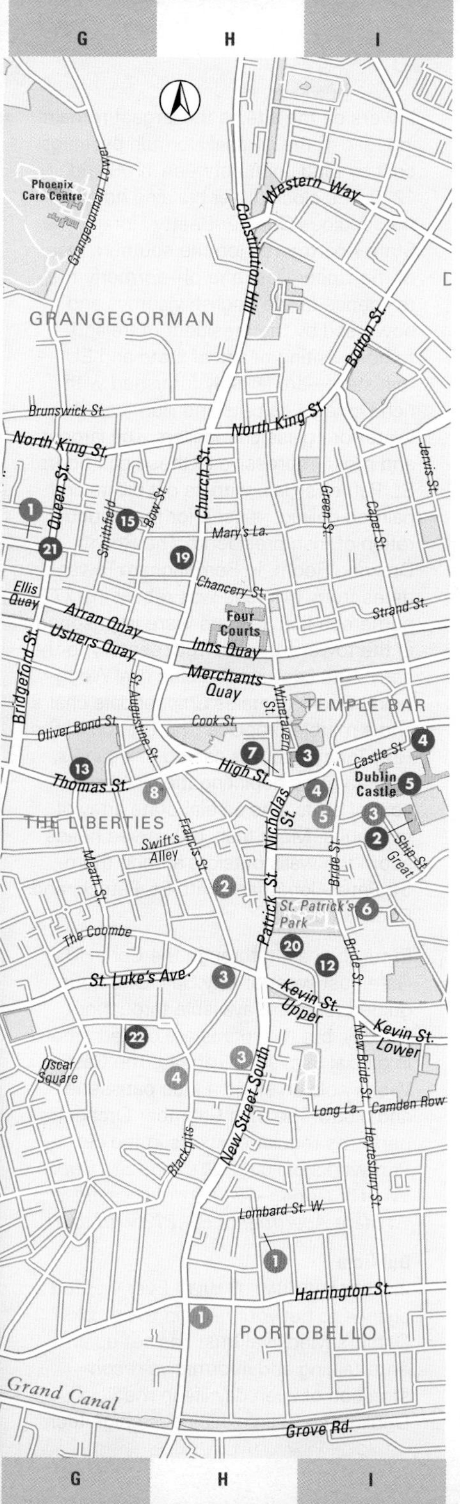

Sights

1. Arbour Hill Cemetery **E3**
2. Chester Beatty Library **I5**
3. Christ Church Cathedral **I5**
4. City Hall **I5**
5. Dublin Castle **I5**
6. Dublin Zoo **B1**
7. Dublinia **H5**
8. Farmleigh **A3**
9. Guinness Storehouse **E5**
10. Irish Museum of Modern Art **C5**
11. Kilmainham Gaol **A6**
12. Marsh's Library **I6**
13. The National College of Art & Design **G5**
14. National Museum of Decorative Arts and History **F3**
15. Old Jameson Distillery **G3**
16. Phoenix Park **B3**
17. Roe & Co. Distillery **F5**
18. Royal Hospital Kilmainham **C5**
19. St. Michan's Church **H4**
20. St. Patrick's Cathedral **H6**
21. Smithfield **G4**
22. Teeling Whiskey Distillery **G7**

Restaurants

1. Bastible **H9**
2. Fish Shop **F4**
3. The Fumbally **H7**
4. Hen's Teeth **H7**
5. Leo Burdock **I5**
6. Nancy Hands Bar & Restaurant **D3**
7. Phoenix Cafe **A1**
8. Variety Jones **H5**

Quick Bites

1. Bibi's **H8**
2. Lovin Catering **H6**
3. The Silk Road Café **I5**

Hotels

1. The Hendrick **G4**
2. Hilton Dublin Kilmainham **A5**
3. Hyatt Centric the Liberties Dublin **H6**
4. Jurys Inn Christchurch **I5**
5. Maldron Hotel Newlands Cross **A6**
6. Radisson Blu Royal Hotel, Dublin **I6**

caught in a cartoon chase for all eternity. At 6 pm on Wednesday and Thursday and 3:30 pm on Sunday, you can enjoy the glories of a choral evensong, and the bell ringers usually practice on Friday at 7 pm. ✉ *Christ Church Pl. and Winetavern St., Dublin West* ☎ *01/677–8099* 🌐 *christchurchcathedral.ie* 🎫 *€11.*

City Hall

GOVERNMENT BUILDING | Facing the Liffey from Cork Hill at the top of Parliament Street, this grand Georgian municipal building (1769–79), once the Royal Exchange, marks the southwest corner of Temple Bar. Today it's the seat of Dublin Corporation, the elected body that governs the city. Thomas Cooley designed the building with 12 columns that encircle the domed central rotunda, which has a fine mosaic floor and 12 frescoes depicting Dublin legends and ancient Irish historical scenes. The 20-foot-high sculpture to the right is of Daniel O'Connell, "The Liberator." He looks like he's about to begin the famous speech he gave here in 1800. The building houses a multimedia exhibition—with artifacts, kiosks, graphics, and audiovisual presentations—tracing the evolution of Ireland's 1,000-year-old capital. ✉ *Dame St., Dublin West* ☎ *01/222–2204* 🌐 *www.dublincity.ie/residential/arts-and-events/city-hall* 🎫 *Free* 🕒 *Closed Sun.*

Dublin Castle

CASTLE/PALACE | 2022 is the centenary of the British handing over power to the fledgling Irish government and it all happened right here, on the grounds of Dublin Castle. As seat and symbol of the British rule of Ireland for more than seven centuries, the castle figured largely in Ireland's turbulent history early in the 20th century. It's now mainly used for Irish and EU governmental purposes. The sprawling Great Courtyard is the reputed site of the Black Pool (Dubh Linn, pronounced "*dove*-lin") from which Dublin got its name. In the Lower Castle Yard, the Record Tower, the earliest of several towers on the site, is the largest remaining relic of the original Norman buildings, built by King John between 1208 and 1220. The clock-tower building houses the fabulous Chester Beatty Library. The State Apartments (on the southern side of the Upper Castle Yard)—formerly the residence of the English viceroys and now used by the president of Ireland to host visiting heads of state and EU ministers—are lavishly furnished with rich Donegal carpets and illuminated by Waterford glass chandeliers. The largest and most impressive of these chambers, St. Patrick's Hall, with its gilt pillars and painted ceiling, is used for the inauguration of Irish presidents. The Round Drawing Room, in Bermingham Tower, dates from 1411 and was rebuilt in 1777; numerous Irish leaders were imprisoned in the tower from the 16th century to the early 20th century. The blue oval Wedgwood Room contains Chippendale chairs and a marble fireplace. The Church of the Holy Trinity features carved oak panels, stained glass depicting the viceroy's coat of arms, and an elaborate array of fan vaults. More than 100 carved heads adorn the walls outside; among them, St. Peter, Jonathan Swift, St. Patrick, and Brian Boru.

Enter the castle through the Cork Hill Gate, just west of City Hall. One-hour guided tours are available throughout the day, but the rooms are closed when in official use, so call ahead. The Castle Vaults hold an elegant little patisserie and bistro. The Irish Chamber Orchestra performs regular concerts in the old Printworks building. ✉ *Castle St., Dublin West* ☎ *01/645–8813* 🌐 *dublincastle.ie* 🎫 *State Apartments €8 (€12 with tour).*

Dublinia

HISTORY MUSEUM | **FAMILY** | Ever wanted a chance to put your head in the stocks? Dublin's Medieval Trust has set up an entertaining and informative reconstruction of everyday life in medieval Dublin. The main exhibits use high-tech audiovisual and computer displays; you can also see a scale model of what Dublin was like around 1500, a medieval maze, a life-size reconstruction based on the 13th-century dockside at Wood Quay, and a fine view from the tower. Dublinia is in the old Synod Hall (formerly a meeting place for bishops of the Church of Ireland), joined via a covered stonework Victorian bridge to Christ Church Cathedral. An exhibition on "Viking Dublin" consists of a similar reconstruction of life in even earlier Viking Dublin, including a Viking burial. There's a guided tour at 2:30 pm every day. ✉ *St. Michael's Hill, Dublin West* ☎ *01/679–4611* 🌐 *dublinia.ie* 🎫 *€15.*

★ Guinness Storehouse

BREWERY | Ireland's all-dominating brewery—founded by Arthur Guinness in 1759 and at one time the largest stout-producing brewery in the world—spans a 60-acre spread west of Christ Church Cathedral. Not surprisingly, it's the most popular tourist destination in town—after all, the Irish national drink is Guinness stout, a dark brew made with roasted malt. The brewery itself is closed to the public, but the Guinness Storehouse is a spectacular attraction, designed to woo—some might say brainwash—you with the wonders of the "dark stuff." In a 1904 cast-iron-and-brick warehouse, the museum display covers six floors built around a huge, central glass atrium, which is shaped like a giant pint glass. Beneath the glass floor of the lobby you can see Arthur Guinness's original lease on the site, for a whopping 9,000 years. The exhibition elucidates the brewing process and its history, with antique presses and vats, a look at bottle and can design through the ages, a history of the Guinness family, a fascinating archive of Guinness advertisements, and the Guinness Academy teaching you how to pull your own perfect pint or how to become a connoisseur taster. You can even get your own selfie on the head of a pint before you drink it, called the "STOUT *ie*" a 3D printer uses malt extract to create a picture. The star attraction is undoubtedly the top-floor Gravity Bar, with 360-degree floor-to-ceiling glass walls that offer a nonpareil view out over the city at sunset while you sip your free pint. One of the bar's first clients was one William Jefferson Clinton. You'll find the Guinness logo on everything from piggy banks to underpants in the Guinness Store on the ground floor.

■ TIP→ The "Connoisseur Experience" guided tour (3 hours, €95) takes travelers behind the scenes. ✉ *St. James' Gate, Dublin West* ☎ *01/408–4800* 🌐 *guinness-storehouse.com* 🎫 *From €26.*

Irish Museum of Modern Art

ART MUSEUM | **FAMILY** | Housed in the Royal Hospital Kilmainham, the Irish Museum of Modern Art concentrates on the work of contemporary Irish artists along with regular international exhibitions. Artists such as Richard Deacon, Richard Gorman, Dorothy Cross, Sean Scully, Matt Mullican, Louis le Brocquy, and James Coleman are included in the collection. The museum also displays works by some non-Irish 20th-century greats, including Picasso and Miró, plus recent hotshots like Damien Hirst, and regularly hosts touring shows from major European museums. The café serves light fare including soups and sandwiches, and has a cool kids' play area. It's a short ride by taxi or bus from the city center and there is a LUAS stop nearby. ✉ *Kilmainham La., Dublin West* ☎ *01/612–9900* 🌐 *imma.ie* 🎫 *Free* 🕓 *Closed Mon.*

★ Kilmainham Gaol

JAIL/PRISON | Leaders of many failed Irish rebellions spent their last days in this grim, forbidding structure, and it holds a special place in the myth and memory of the country. The 1916 commanders Pádraig Pearse and James Connolly were held here before being executed in the prison yard. Other famous inmates included the revolutionary Robert Emmet and Charles Stewart Parnell, a leading politician. You can visit the prison only as part of a very moving and exciting guided tour, which leaves every hour on the hour. The cells are a chilling sight, and the guided tour and a 30-minute audiovisual presentation relate a graphic account of Ireland's political history over the past 200 years—from an Irish Nationalist viewpoint. A newer exhibition explores the history of the prison and its restoration. A small tearoom is on the premises. ■ **TIP→ It is almost essential to book ahead for the guided tour, especially during high season. You really don't want to chance a three-hour wait.** ✉ *Inchicore Rd., Dublin West* ☎ *01/453–5984* 🌐 *kilmainhamgaolmuseum.ie* 🎟 *€8.*

Marsh's Library

LIBRARY | When Ireland's first public library was founded and endowed in 1701 by Narcissus Marsh, the archbishop of Dublin, it was made open to "All Graduates and Gentlemen." The two-story brick Georgian building has remained virtually the same since then. It houses a priceless collection of 250 manuscripts and 25,000 15th- to 18th-century books. Many of these rare volumes were locked inside cages, as were the readers who wished to peruse them. The cages were to discourage the often impecunious students, who may have been tempted to make the books their own. The library has been restored with great attention to its original architectural details, especially in the book stacks. It's a short walk west from St. Stephen's Green and is accessed through a charming little cottage garden. ✉ *St. Patrick's Close, off Patrick St., Dublin West* ☎ *01/454–3511* 🌐 *marshlibrary.ie* 🎟 *€5* ⏱ *Closed Sun. and Mon.*

The National College of Art & Design

COLLEGE | The delicate welding of glass and iron onto the redbrick Victorian facade of this onetime factory makes this school worth a visit. A walk around the cobblestone central courtyard often gives the added bonus of viewing students working away in glass, clay, metal, and stone. The glass-fronted gallery combines work by local, national, and international avant-garde artists. ✉ *100 Thomas St., Dublin West* ☎ *053/1636–4200* 🌐 *ncad.ie* 🎟 *Free* ⏱ *Closed weekends.*

Old Jameson Distillery

DISTILLERY | Founded in 1791, this distillery produced one of Ireland's most famous whiskeys for nearly 200 years, until 1966, when local distilleries merged to form Irish Distillers and moved to a purpose-built, ultramodern distillery in Middleton, County Cork. A major recent renovation has turned this original distillery into a state-of-the-art museum and whiskey experience to rival Guinness's storehouse. In fact, Jameson claims to be the most visited distillery in the world. Tours focus on either exploring the history of the old place, blending your own whiskey, or honing your whiskey-cocktail-making skills. Tours include a complimentary tasting; four attendees are invited to taste different brands of Irish whiskey and compare them against bourbon and Scotch. If you have a large group and everyone wants to do this, phone in advance to arrange it. You can even bottle your own whiskey, with a personalized label. ✉ *Bow St., Dublin West* ☎ *01/807–2348* 🌐 *jamesonwhiskey.com* 🎟 *From €25.*

★ **Roe & Co. Distillery**

DISTILLERY | Not content to have the busiest tourist attraction in the country with the Storehouse, Guinness (or rather, its parent company, mega-liquor brand Diageo) has launched a new whiskey distillery on the site of the former brewery powerhouse, across the street from the Guinness Open Gate Brewery taproom. It's named after a long-forgotten whiskey made on-site, but all that remains of that original distillery is the beautiful windmill tower and a single pear tree (both of which are nodded to in the design of the bottle). A passionate guide leads you on an excellent whiskey tour through this state-of-the-art facility. Explore the science of distillation and the guesswork of blending, and try your hand at tasting and cocktail-making workshops. Finish it all with a whiskey cocktail at the fun Power House Bar. ✉ *92 James St., Dublin West* ☎ *01/643–5999* 🌐 *roeandcowhiskey.com* 🎫 *€25.*

Royal Hospital Kilmainham

NOTABLE BUILDING | This replica of Les Invalides in Paris is regarded as the most important 17th-century building in Ireland. Commissioned as a hospice for disabled and veteran soldiers by James Butler—the Duke of Ormonde and viceroy to King Charles II—it was completed in 1684, making it the first building erected in Dublin's golden age. It survived into the 1920s as a hospital, but after the founding of the Irish Free State in 1922, the building fell into disrepair. The entire edifice has since been restored. The architectural highlight is the hospital's Baroque chapel, distinguished by its extraordinary plasterwork ceiling and fine wood carvings. The hospital also houses the Irish Museum of Modern Art. ✉ *Kilmainham La., Dublin West* ☎ *01/612–9900* 🌐 *rhk.ie.*

St. Michan's Church

CHURCH | However macabre, St. Michan's main claim to fame is down in the vaults, where the totally dry atmosphere has preserved several corpses in a remarkable state of mummification. They lie in open caskets. Most of the resident deceased are thought to have been Dublin tradespeople (one was, they say, a religious crusader). Except for its 120-foot-high bell tower, this Anglican church is architecturally undistinguished. The church was built in 1685 on the site of an 11th-century Danish church (Michan was a Danish saint). If preserved corpses are not enough of a draw, you can also find an 18th-century organ, which Handel supposedly played for the first performance of *Messiah.* Don't forget to check out the Stool of Repentance—the only one still in existence in the city. Parishioners judged to be "open and notoriously naughty livers" used it to do public penance. ✉ *Lower Church St., Dublin West* ☎ *01/872–4154* 🌐 *visitdublin.com* 🎫 *Crypts €6.*

★ St. Patrick's Cathedral

CHURCH | The largest cathedral in Dublin and also the national cathedral of the Church of Ireland, St. Patrick's was built in honor of Ireland's patron saint, who—according to legend—baptized many converts at a well on this site in the 5th century. The original building, dedicated in 1192 and early English Gothic in style, was an unsuccessful attempt to assert supremacy over the capital's other Protestant cathedral, Christ Church Cathedral. At 305 feet, this is the longest church in the country, a fact Oliver Cromwell's troops found useful, as they made the church's nave into their stable in the 17th century.

■ TIP→ While in the shadow of St. Patrick's Cathedral, head from Patrick Close to Patrick Street; look down the street toward the Liffey for a fine view of Christ Church.

Make sure you see the gloriously heraldic Choir of St. Patrick's, hung with colorful medieval banners, and find the tomb of Jonathan Swift, most famous of St. Patrick's many illustrious deans and immortal author of *Gulliver's Travels,* who held office from 1713 to 1745. Swift's tomb is in the south aisle, not far from that of his beloved "Stella," Mrs. Esther Johnson. Swift's epitaph is inscribed over the robing-room door. W.B. Yeats—who translated it thus: "Swift has sailed into his rest; Savage indignation there cannot lacerate his breast"—declared it the greatest epitaph of all time. Other memorials include the 17th-century Boyle Monument, with its numerous painted figures of family members, and the monument to Turlough O'Carolan, the last of the Irish bards and one of the country's finest harp players. *Living Stones* is the cathedral's permanent exhibition celebrating St. Patrick's place in the life of the city. If you're a music lover, you're in for a treat; matins (9:40 am) and evensong (5:45 pm) are still sung on many days. ✉ *Patrick St., Dublin West* ☎ *01/453–9472* 🌐 *stpatrickscathedral.ie* 🎟 *€9.*

Smithfield

MARKET | Bordered on the east by Church Street, on the west by Blackhall Place, to the north by King Street, and to the south by the Liffey, Smithfield is Dublin's old market area where flowers, fruit, vegetables, and even horses have been sold for generations. Chosen as a flagship for north inner-city renovation during the boom, the area saw a major face-lift—with mixed reactions from the locals. Some of the beautiful cobblestones of its streets have been taken up, refinished, and replaced, and giant masts topped with gaslights used to send 6-foot-high flames over Smithfield Square. Unfortunately, they don't light the gas anymore, and there's the air of a white elephant about the whole thing. But the area is still worth a visit, especially in the early morning, as the wholesale fruit and vegetable sellers still ply their trade in the wonderful 19th-century covered market. It's also home to the Lighthouse cinema and a twice-yearly horse-trading market. ✉ *Smithfield, Dublin West.*

Teeling Whiskey Distillery

DISTILLERY | While this state-of-the-art whiskey distillery in Dublin's historic Liberties neighborhood is relatively new, it's only a stone's throw from the 1782 site of the original Teelings. Part of the modern Irish renaissance in whiskey making, this pot-still operation offers one of the best and most inclusive whiskey tours in the country. You get to see the nuts and bolts of how the *uisce beatha* or "water of life" is made, and there's a delicious tasting waiting for you at the end. The little café out front is usually lively.

■ TIP→ **Prices of tours vary greatly depending on the quality of the whiskey you will be tasting at the end.** ✉ *13–17 Newmarket Sq., The Liberties* ☎ *01/531–0329* 🌐 *teelingwhiskey.com* 🎟 *From €17.*

Restaurants

★ Bastible

$$$$ | BISTRO | Even with its location in a relatively unfashionable corner of the city, this high-end bistro has the natives traveling miles to get a treasured table. The five-course set menu manages to be daring and traditional at the same time, with game and fish transformed in particularly ingenious ways. **Known for:** trendy crowd; booking up; ample wines by the glass, pairings offered. Ⓢ *Average main: €85* ✉ *111 S. Circular Rd., Dublin West* ☎ *01/473–7409* 🌐 *bastible.com* ⊙ *Closed Sun.–Tues. No lunch.*

★ Fish Shop

$$ | SEAFOOD | Irish seafood is finally getting the royal treatment it deserves at this simple but brilliant new eatery in the old market, Smithfield district. The award-winning kitchen serves inventive treasures like whipped hake and dillisk (native seaweed) on sourdough, but don't expect a choice in seafood: you're served a three-course menu focused on what was caught that morning. **Known for:** elevated fish-and-chips; fun, casual atmosphere; local oysters. Ⓢ *Average main: €22* ✉ *6 Queen St., Dublin North* ☎ *01/430–8594* 🌐 *fish-shop.ie* ⊙ *Closed Tues.*

★ The Fumbally

$ | MODERN IRISH | FAMILY | Opened by a group of friends, the Fumbally started out with a market stall but quickly became the vanguard of true slow food in Dublin, finding its roots in a spacious, light-filled space smack in the middle of the Liberties area, the heart of the old city. Menus are simple but clever, with the Fumbally eggs, lightly scrambled with Gubeen cheese and sautéed kale, a classic. **Known for:** fun lunch specials; pleasant, friendly staff; can get busy. Ⓢ *Average main: €14* ✉ *Fumbally La.,*

Dublin West ☎ *01/592–8732* 🌐 *thefumbally.ie* ⏲ *Closed Mon. No dinner.*

★ Hen's Teeth

$$ | **TAPAS** | This effortlessly cool, award-winning eatery slots neatly into the gallery/shop that makes up the rest of the Hen's Teeth empire. Located in the working-class Blackpitts area of the Liberties, the atmosphere is diner casual, while the food is a tapas-inspired trip into small-plate adventure. **Known for:** Sunday roast dinners; DJs on weekends; fun cocktails. [$] *Average main: €21* ✉ *Blackpits, Merchant Quay, The Liberties* ☎ *01/561–3036* 🌐 *hensteethstore.com* ⏲ *Closed Mon. and Tues.*

Leo Burdock

$ | **IRISH** | Old man Burdock has moved on and the place hasn't been the same since, but the hordes still join the inevitable queue at Dublin's famous 100-year-old takeout fish-and-chips shop. You can't eat here, but why would you anyway, when you can sit in the gardens of St. Patrick's Cathedral a few minutes away. **Known for:** fresh cod and chips; battered sausage; a line outside. [$] *Average main: €14* ✉ *2 Werburgh St., Christchurch, Dublin West* ☎ *01/454–0306* 🌐 *leoburdock.com.*

★ Variety Jones

$$$$ | **FRENCH FUSION** | Unassuming Thomas Street is the last place you'd expect to find a Michelin-starred restaurant, but that's exactly where celebrated chef Keelann Higgs set up shop. Inside, you're greeted by the smell of wood smoke, and the narrow dining room is dominated by an open kitchen where cooking is done over a blazing fire. **Known for:** open-fire cooking; great wine list; creative takes on classic dishes. [$] *Average main: €36* ✉ *78 Thomas St., Dublin West* ☎ *01/516–2470* 🌐 *varietyjones.ie* ⏲ *Closed Sun.–Tues. No lunch.*

Coffee and Quick Bites

Bibi's

$ | **CAFÉ** | The small menu at this tiny café in the middle of a quiet, off-the-beaten-track residential street emphasizes creative breakfasts and lunch (and brunch on the weekend) with a local twist. It's a good spot to sit and watch locals go about their everyday lives as you eat black rice quinoa porridge with coconut milk, miso, and banana or their wonderful spicy cannellini beans with chorizo, crème fraîche, and thyme. **Known for:** true neighborhood feel; healthy breakfasts; popular, so can be hard to get a table. [$] *Average main: €11* ✉ *14b Emorville Ave., Dublin West* ☎ *01/454–7421* 🌐 *bibis.ie* ⏲ *Closed Mon. and Tues. No dinner.*

Lovin Catering

$ | **CAFÉ** | This unassuming little shop on Francis Street conjures up some of the best pastries in town. There's no seating in this powerhouse patisserie, but long counters allow space for perching your coffee and tucking into the finest sweet and savory treats. **Known for:** great quiches and pastries; quality coffee; fast service. [$] *Average main: €12* ✉ *49 Francis St., Dublin West* ☎ *01/454–4912* 🌐 *lovincatering.com* ⏲ *Closed Sun. No dinner.*

The Silk Road Café

$ | **MIDDLE EASTERN** | A great-value, Middle Eastern delight hidden away in the Chester Beatty Library, the Silk Road Café has a buffet-style menu always full of exotic surprises. The light-filled atrium (Tuesday–Friday 10 am–4:45 pm, Saturday 11 am–4:45 pm, and Sunday 1–4:45 pm) and serene atmosphere make you want to linger longer than you should. **Known for:** outdoor seating overlooking Dublin Castle garden; decadent cakes; halal and kosher. [$] *Average main: €16* ✉ *Chester Beatty Library, Castle St., Dublin West* ☎ *01/407–0770* 🌐 *silkroadcafe.ie* ⏲ *Closed Mon. No dinner.*

Hotels

The Hendrick

$$ | **HOTEL** | Smithfield's newest hotel might look a little mundane with its red-brick, officelike exterior, but inside it's a lot more fun. **Pros:** original art throughout; clever room design; warm and friendly staff. **Cons:** no closet, just a few hangers on the wall; lack of amenities; not cheap for size. *Rooms from: €205* *6–11 Hendrick St., Dublin West* *01/482–6500* *hendrickdublin.ie* *146 rooms* *Free Breakfast.*

Hilton Dublin Kilmainham

$$ | **HOTEL** | While the exterior of this no-nonsense chain hotel in the historic Kilmainham district is distinctly functional, the higher-floor rooms have some of the most stunning panoramas in the whole city. **Pros:** some rooms have balconies; close to Heuston train station; rooms large by Dublin standards. **Cons:** uninspiring exterior; outside city center; attracts a business crowd. *Rooms from: €220* *Kilmainham, Dublin West* *01/420–1800* *hilton.com* *120 rooms* *No Meals.*

Hyatt Centric the Liberties Dublin

$$ | **HOTEL** | While the exterior of redbrick and office-block glass might be a tad mundane, Dublin's first Hyatt delivers a boutique-quality hotel that won't break the bank. **Pros:** secure underground parking; 24-hour fitness center; friendly, knowledgeable staff. **Cons:** some rooms look out over a parking lot; a fairly long walk to city center; limited amenities and services. *Rooms from: €230* *Dean St., The Liberties* *01/708–1999* *hyatt.com* *234 rooms* *No Meals.*

Jurys Inn Christchurch

$$$ | **HOTEL** | **FAMILY** | Expect few frills at this functional budget (at least, budget by city-center standards) hotel, on a hill facing Christ Church Cathedral and within walking distance of most city-center attractions. **Pros:** restaurant offers excellent buffet breakfast; warm and friendly staff; near Temple Bar. **Cons:** ugly building; basic, functional room design; tends to be popular with bachelor(ette) parties. *Rooms from: €229* *Christ Church Pl., Dublin West* *01/454–0000* *leonardo-hotels.co.uk/hotels/dublin/christchurch* *182 rooms* *No Meals.*

Maldron Hotel Newlands Cross

$$ | **HOTEL** | This four-story franchise hotel on the southwest outskirts of the city is cheap, cheerful, and especially ideal if you're planning to travel to the west or southwest of Ireland and you don't want to deal with Dublin's crazy morning traffic. **Pros:** great for families; excellent breakfasts at the hotel restaurant; delicious Bewley's coffee in the morning. **Cons:** mainly business clientele; not convenient to the city center; overlooks the expressway. *Rooms from: €180* *Newlands Cross at Naas Rd., Dublin West* *01/464–0140* *maldronhotel-newlandscross.com* *299 rooms* *No Meals.*

Radisson Blu Royal Hotel, Dublin

$$$ | **HOTEL** | The sleek glass-and-concrete Radisson, just off South Great George's Street, offers to-the-point business accommodations with a dash of cool contemporary style, proof positive that it is possible to be elegant and functional at the same time. **Pros:** right in the heart of "real Dublin"; stylish, understated decor; landscaped rooftop terrace. **Cons:** looks out over a block of flats; restaurant is hit or miss; mostly business clientele. *Rooms from: €299* *Golden La., Dublin West* *01/898–2900* *radissonhotels.com/en-us/hotels/radisson-blu-dublin* *150 rooms* *No Meals.*

Nightlife

PUBS

Anti Social

BARS | A clever and cool addition to the Dublin nightlife scene, an evening at Anti Social can mean some serious dancing to live DJs, or a laid-back gaming session on the old-school arcade machines. ✉ *101 Francis St., The Liberties* ☏ *01/498–8855* 🌐 *antisocial.ie.*

Brazen Head

PUBS | Reputedly Dublin's oldest pub (the site has been licensed since 1198), the Brazen Head doesn't have much of a time-burnished decor, with one big exception: an enchanting stone courtyard that is intimate, charming, and delightful. The front is a faux one-story castle, complete with flambeaux, while the interior looks modern-day (except for the very low ceilings). People love to jam the place not for its history but for its traditional-music performances and lively sing-along sessions on Sunday evening. On the south side of the Liffey quays, it's a little difficult to find—turn down Lower Bridge Street and make a right onto the old lane. ✉ *20 Lower Bridge St., Dublin West* ☏ *01/677–9549* 🌐 *brazenhead.com.*

★ Cobblestone

LIVE MUSIC | A glorious house of ale in the best Dublin tradition, the Cobblestone is popular with Smithfield Market workers. Its chatty imbibers and high-quality, nightly, live traditional music are attracting a more varied, younger crowd from all over town. ✉ *N. King St., Dublin West* ☏ *01/872–1799* 🌐 *cobblestonepub.ie.*

★ Fallons

PUBS | Somehow you always get a seat in this tiny sliver of a pub—a warm, old-school boozer at its best—tucked away on a corner near St. Patrick's Cathedral. Pure Dublin class. ✉ *129 The Coombe, Dublin West* ☏ *01/454–2801.*

Performing Arts

St. Patrick's Cathedral

CONCERTS | Along with some regular concert performances, you can catch some beautiful church singing at evensong at St. Pat's most weekdays around half past 5 pm. ✉ *St. Patrick's Close, Dublin West* ☏ *01/453–9472* 🌐 *stpatrickscathedral.ie* 🎟 *€6.*

LIVE MUSIC

Vicar Street

MUSIC | Across from Christ Church Cathedral, Vicar Street is a venue for intimate concerts. It often plays host to folk music, jazz, and comedy, as well as rock performances. ✉ *58–59 Thomas St., Dublin West* ☏ *01/775–5800* 🌐 *vicar-street.com.*

Shopping

ANTIQUES

Christy Bird

ANTIQUES & COLLECTIBLES | Dublin's oldest furniture shop, Christy Bird was recycling household items before anyone else dreamed of it. You have to hunt for anything that is true quality and most of the goods here are now repro and mass-market. ✉ *32 S. Richmond St., Dublin West* ☏ *01/475–4049* 🌐 *christybird.com.*

Martin Fennelly Antiques

ANTIQUES & COLLECTIBLES | A stalwart of Dublin's traditional antiques quarter around Francis Street, Fennelly's specializes in early furniture and decorative items like candlesticks, tea caddies, and fitted jewelry caskets. ✉ *60 Francis St., Dublin West* ☏ *01/473–1126* 🌐 *fennelly.net.*

★ O'Sullivan Antiques

ANTIQUES & COLLECTIBLES | Specializing in 18th- and 19th-century furniture, with a high-profile clientele (including Mia Farrow and Liam Neeson), the O'Sullivan "look" has been so successful that it now runs a full-time sister shop in New York. ✉ *43–44 Francis St., Dublin West* ☏ *01/454–1143* 🌐 *osullivanantiques.com.*

OUTDOOR MARKETS

Liberty Market

MARKET | Just minutes from Christ Church Cathedral, this working-class favorite is a great place to get a feel for Dubliners at play. The stalls vary from knickknacks to children's clothing and candy. Open Thursday to Saturday.

✉ *Meath St., Dublin West* 🌐 *libertymarket.ie.*

GOLF

Hermitage Golf Club

GOLF | Set in a part of the Liffey Valley idyllically titled the Strawberry Beds, this rolling parkland course has been a feature of West Dublin golf since 1905. The gentle terrain of the front nine stands in stark contrast to the stern, water-featured test that awaits you on the way home. The signature hole is the picturesque 10th, which looks down on the river as it winds through a spectacular treescape. The course has seen some big personalities walk its fairways over the years, including Bing Crosby, Seve Ballesteros, and Colin Montgomerie. A sense of history pervades the place. ✉ *Ballydowd, Lucan* ☎ *01/626–8491* 🌐 *hermitagegolf.ie* *Weekdays €80, weekends €100* *18 holes, 6596 yards, par 71.*

Phoenix Park and Around

Far and away Dublin's largest park, Phoenix Park (the name is an anglicization of the Irish *Fionn Uisce,* meaning "clear water") is a vast, green, arrowhead-shape oasis north of the Liffey, about a 20-minute walk from the city center. It's the city's main escape valve and sports center (cricket, soccer, Gaelic games, and polo), and the home of the noble creatures of the Dublin Zoo. A handful of other cultural sights near the park also merit a visit.

Arbour Hill Cemetery

CEMETERY | All 14 Irishmen executed by the British following the 1916 Easter Rising are buried here, including Pádraig Pearse, who led the rebellion; his younger brother Willie, who played a minor role in the uprising; and James Connolly, a socialist and labor leader wounded in the battle. Too weak from his wounds to stand, Connolly was tied to a chair and then shot. The burial ground is a simple but formal area, with the names of the dead leaders carved in stone beside an inscription of the proclamation they issued during the uprising. ✉ *Arbour Hill, Dublin West* ☎ *01/821–3021* 🌐 *heritageireland.ie/places-to-visit/arbour-hill-cemetery/* *Free.*

Dublin Zoo

ZOO | **FAMILY** | Founded in 1830, Dublin Zoo may be the third-oldest public zoo in the world but the modern incarnation is an exciting, humane, and well-thought-out wildlife adventure. Animals from tropical climes are kept in unbarred enclosures, and Arctic species swim in the lakes close to the reptile house. Some 700 lions have been bred here since the 1850s, one of whom became familiar to movie fans the world over when MGM used him for its trademark. (As they will tell you at the zoo, he is in fact yawning in that familiar shot: an American lion had to be hired to roar and the "voice" was dubbed.) The African Plains section houses the zoo's larger species; the Nakuru Safari is a 25-minute tour of this area. Sea Lion Cove is one of the most popular destinations, especially at feeding time. In summer the Lakeside Café serves ice cream and drinks. ✉ *Phoenix Park, Dublin West* ☎ *01/474–8900* 🌐 *dublinzoo.ie* *€19.*

Farmleigh

FARM/RANCH | This 78-acre Edwardian estate, situated northwest of Phoenix Park and accessed via the main park road, includes Farmleigh House (which is full of antique furnishings and historic art, now used to accommodate visiting dignitaries), a working farm, walled and sunken gardens, wonderful picnic-friendly grounds, a regular organic food market, and a restaurant in the boathouse. Guided tours of the house last 45 minutes

Sports Mad

The Five Sports Dubliners Love

If the Irish love their sporting pastimes, the Dubs are literally mad for them.

GAA. While the majestic, stick-and-ball game of hurling is popular at a club level (check out the successful Cula club in southside Dalkey), there is a deep love affair between Dublin and Gaelic football. Devised during the 19th-century Celtic Revival as an Irish pastime for Irish people, the kicking and catching game took off like wildfire in the capital. "The Dubs," as the still-amateur county team is affectionately known, regularly packed the 80,000-seat Croke Park stadium on the way to a record-breaking six All Ireland titles in a row in 2020. To really experience the community spirit, check out a club match at St. Vincent's in Marino.

Soccer. The most-played sport in the capital, but very much the poor sister to the GAA when it comes to funding and attendance. The men's and women's national teams have had some noted victories, but the semiprofessional League of Ireland struggles for cash and fans. But a short LUAS trip to Phibsborough's Dalymount Park to see Bohemians FC will illustrate that there's plenty of passion in the stands. It's at a younger level that the sport thrives, and a weekend visit to the Fifteen Acres section of the Phoenix Park will reveal hundreds of kids living out their goal-scoring dreams.

Rugby. The success of the men's and women's national teams (who play at Dublin's Aviva stadium) has widened rugby's appeal, but in Dublin, the sport still revolves around a few posh, fee-paying schools in the Southside suburbs. The majority of the professional players who line out for the hugely successful Leinster team (at their RDS stadium in Donnybrook) graduated from these same schools. In early spring these school teams face off for the Senior Cup, and hordes of chanting teens show up to cheer on their schoolmates.

Horse Racing. The Irish love horses a great deal; and betting on them even more. It's hard to stroll through Dublin without passing a pub, but the same might be true for a bookmaker. These "betting shops" heave with great characters and tall tales. But it's at the green and elegant racecourses that surround the capital that the sport truly comes into its own. Leopardstown, in the Southside suburbs, is the home to some of the best racing year-round, with the Christmas national hunt (the horses jump fences) meeting a wonderful day out.

Cricket. Before soccer, rugby, and the GAA, cricket was the big thing in Ireland, with nearly every parish having a team. That was a long time ago, and the slow, gentle game is definitely a minority sport in Dublin now. But it does have the advantage of being played at some of the most picturesque old grounds and scenic locations around the city. Head to Phoenix Park on a weekend where the oldest continuous cricket club in the world (called Phoenix, of course) still plays. Grab a beer in the tiny Victorian clubhouse, take a seat on the grass, and watch the men and women in their crisp whites bat and bowl with passion and a deep sense of fair play.

and are offered hourly on a first-come, first-served basis but are limited in size; moreover, the house may be closed on short notice if it is in use by the government. ✉ *Castleknock, Dublin West* ☎ *01/815–5900 for hrs, 01/815–7255* 🌐 *farmleigh.ie* 🎫 *Free, €8 guided tour* ⏲ *Closed Jan. and Feb.*

★ National Museum of Decorative Arts and History

HISTORY MUSEUM | Here, in one gigantic treasure chest, is the full panoply of the National Museum's collection of glass, silver, furniture, and other decorative arts, along with some items from the country's military history. The setting is spectacular: the huge Collins Barracks, named for the assassinated Irish Republican leader Michael Collins (1890–1922). Built in the early 18th century, and designed by Captain Thomas Burgh, these erstwhile "Royal Barracks" were stylishly renovated to become a showcase for the museum, which opened in 1997. The displays are far-ranging, covering everything from one of the greatest collections of Irish silver in the world to Irish period furniture—you'll see that the country's take on Chippendale was far earthier than the English mode. *Soldiers and Chiefs: The Irish at War* and a thousand years of Irish coins are other highlights. Headlining the collections are some extraordinary objects, including the Fonthill Vase, the William Smith O'Brien Gold Cup, and the Lord Chancellor's Mace. There is also a small military museum. ✉ *Benburb St., Phoenix Park and Environs* ☎ *01/677–7444* 🌐 *museum.ie* 🎫 *Free* ⏲ *Closed Mon.*

★ Phoenix Park

CITY PARK | FAMILY | Europe's largest enclosed public park, which extends about 5 km (3 miles) along the Liffey's north bank, encompasses 1,752 acres and holds a lot of verdant green lawns, woods, lakes, and playing fields. Sunday is the best time to visit: games of cricket, football (soccer), polo, baseball, hurling (a traditional Irish sport that resembles a combination of lacrosse, baseball, and field hockey), and Irish football are likely to be in progress. Old-fashioned gas lamps line both sides of Chesterfield Avenue, the main road that bisects the park for 4 km (2½ miles), which was named for Lord Chesterfield, a lord lieutenant of Ireland who laid out the road in the 1740s. The beautiful, pristine 1896 Victorian Tea Rooms near the Avenue still serve dainty dishes for park visitors. To the right as you enter the park is the People's Garden, a colorful flower garden designed in 1864. Rent bikes (including tandems) at the main gate to get the most from the park's hidden corners. Within Phoenix Park is a visitor center, in the 17th-century fortified Ashtown Castle; it has information about the park's history, flora, and fauna. Admission to the center is free, and it runs guided tours of the park throughout the year. There is also the wonderful Phoenix Cafe beside the old walled garden. ☎ *01/677–0095 visitor center* 🌐 *phoenixpark.ie* ⏲ *Visitor center closed Mon. and Tues. in Jan. and Feb.*

Need A Break?

Ryan's Pub. One of Dublin's last remaining genuine late-Victorian era pubs, Ryan's has changed little since its last remodeling—in 1896. It's right near the entrance to Phoenix Park. ✉ *28 Parkgate St., Phoenix Park and Environs* ☎ *01/677–6097* 🌐 *thebuckleycollection.ie/ryan-s-victorian-pub.*

Restaurants

Nancy Hands Bar & Restaurant

$$ | ECLECTIC | There's a fine line between re-creating tradition and looking like a theme bar, but Nancy Hands just about pulls it off. A galleylike room juxtaposes old wood, raw brick, and antiques with contemporary art to create a convivial, cozy dining area. **Known for:** great-value food and cheap pints of Guinness; hearty Irish dishes; warm and friendly staff. *Average main: €23 30–32 Parkgate St., Phoenix Park and Environs 01/677–0149 nancyhands.ie.*

Phoenix Cafe

$ | CAFÉ | FAMILY | A pastry-laden café in the middle of a huge park and next door to a playground—it's no wonder kids love the Phoenix Cafe. This gem is overlooked by a lot of locals, but when the sun is shining and you can sit outdoors there are few more tranquil and idyllic spots in the capital. **Known for:** house-made jams; offers yoga classes in the park; famous gluten-free brownies. *Average main: €14 Ashtown Castle, Phoenix Park Visitors Centre, Phoenix Park and Environs 01/677–0090 phoenixcafe.ie No dinner.*

Side Trips: North County Dublin

Dublin's northern suburbs remain largely residential, but there are a few places worth the trip, such as the historic Glasnevin Cemetery. As with most suburban areas, walking may not be the best way to get around. It's good, but not essential, to have a car. Buses and trains serve most of these areas.

Glasnevin

Drive from north city center by Lower Dorset St., as far as bridge over Royal Canal. Turn left; go up Whitworth Rd., by side of canal, for 1 km (½ mile); at its end, turn right onto Prospect Rd. and then left onto Finglas Rd. (N2). You can also take Bus 40 or Bus 40A from Parnell St., next to Parnell Sq., in northern city center.

Sights

Glasnevin Cemetery and Museum

CEMETERY | Glasnevin Cemetery, on the right-hand side of Finglas Road, is the best-known burial ground in Dublin. It's the site of the graves of many distinguished Irish leaders, including Eamon de Valera, a founding father of modern Ireland and a former Irish *taoiseach* (prime minister) and president, and Michael Collins, the celebrated hero of the Irish War of Independence. Other notables interred here include the late-19th-century poet Gerard Manley Hopkins and Sir Roger Casement, a former British consul turned Irish nationalist, hanged for treason by the British in 1916. The large column to the right of the main entrance is the tomb of "The Liberator" Daniel O'Connell, perhaps Ireland's greatest historical figure, renowned for his nonviolent struggle for Catholic Emancipation, achieved in 1829. The cemetery is freely accessible 24 hours a day. An impressive museum has a *City of the Dead* permanent exhibition that covers the burial practices and religious beliefs of the 1.5 million people buried in Glasnevin. The Milestone Gallery has exhibits on key historical figures buried here. They also run great tours of the cemetery itself. You can also climb the refurbished Round Tower, Ireland's tallest, with views of the whole city. *Glasnevin 01/882–6550 dctrust.ie/location/glasnevin.html Museum €9, tour €13.*

National Botanic Gardens

GARDEN | The National Botanic Gardens, on the northeastern flank of Glasnevin Cemetery and the south bank of the Tolka River, date from 1795 and have more than 20,000 varieties of plants, a rose garden, and a vegetable garden. The main attraction is the beautifully restored Curvilinear Range—400-foot-long greenhouses designed and built by a Dublin ironmaster, Richard Turner, between 1843 and 1869. The Great Palm House, with its striking double dome, was built in 1884 and houses orchids, palms, and tropical ferns. Inspiring free guided tours are offered Sunday at noon and 2:30. ✉ *Glasnevin Rd., Glasnevin* ☎ *01/804–0300* 🌐 *botanicgardens.ie* 🎫 *Free.*

Activities

GOLF

Island Golf Club

GOLF COURSE | Talk about exclusive—until 1960, the only way to reach this club was by boat. It was about as remote as you could get and still be only 24 km (15 miles) from Dublin. But things have changed. The Island has opened its doors to reveal a fine links course with holes that force you to navigate between spectacular sand dunes toward small, challenging greens. ✉ *Corballis, Donabate* ☎ *01/843–6205* 🌐 *theislandgolfclub.com* 🎫 *Nov.–Mar. daily €90; Apr.–Oct. from €200.*

Portmarnock Golf Club

GOLF | Portmarnock is arguably the most famous of Ireland's "Big Four" (Ballybunion, Royal County Down, and Royal Portrush are the others). This links course, on a sandy peninsula north of Dublin, has hosted numerous major championships and Tom Watson often used it as a preparation for the Open. Known for its flat fairways and greens and its 100-plus bunkers, it provides a fair test for any golfer who can keep it out of the heavy rough. Greens fees include lunch. ✉ *Portmarnock* ☎ *01/846–2968* 🌐 *portmarnockgolfclub.ie* 🎫 *Nov.–Mar. daily €165; Apr.–Oct. from €275* ⛳ *Championship Course: 18 holes, 7382 yards, par 72; Yellow Course: 9 holes, 3449 yards, par 37.*

North Bull Island

From Dublin's north city center, take Clontarf Rd. for 4 km (2½ miles) to causeway.

A 5-km-long (3-mile-long) island created in the 19th century by the action of the tides, North Bull Island is one of Dublin's wilder places—it's a nature conservancy with a vast beach and dunes that attract thousands of varied seabirds year-round. The island is linked to the mainland via a wooden causeway that leads to Bull Wall, a 1½-km (1-mile) walkway that stretches as far as the North Bull Lighthouse. The island is also accessible via a second, northerly causeway, which takes you to Dollymount Strand. (The two routes of entry don't meet at any point on the island.) You can reach this causeway from the mainland via James Larkin Road.

Sights

St. Anne's Park

CITY PARK | On the mainland directly across from North Bull Island is St. Anne's Park, a public green with extensive rose gardens (including many prize hybrids), woodland walks, a farmers' market, and a scrumptious café. ✉ *James Larkin Rd. and Mt. Prospect Ave., Dublin North.*

Activities

GOLF

★ **The Royal Dublin Golf Club**

GOLF | Links courses are usually in remote, even desolate areas, but this captivating example is only 6 km (4 miles) from the center of Dublin—on Bull Island, a bird sanctuary. Ireland's third-oldest club has always been challenging, but Martin Hawtree's ongoing redesign is making things even trickier. Watch out for the 5th, the 13th, and the infamous 18th—a par-4 dogleg with plenty of opportunities to shoot out-of-bounds. ✉ *Dollymount* ☎ *01/833–6346* 🌐 *theroyaldublingolfclub.com* 🎫 *Nov.–mid-Mar., from €110; mid-Mar.–Oct., from €160* ⛳ *18 holes, 7296 yards, par 72.*

Howth

From Dublin, take DART train, or Bus 31B from Lower Abbey St. in city center. Or, by car, take Howth Rd. from north city center for 16 km (10 miles).

A quick DART ride from the city takes you to the vibrant, upmarket coastal town of Howth. A fishing village at the foot of a long peninsula, Howth (rhymes with "both," and derived from *hoved,* Norse for "head") was an island inhabited as long ago as 3250 BC. Between 1813 and 1833, Howth was the Irish terminus for the sea crossing to Holyhead in north Wales, but it was then superseded by the newly built harbor at Kingstown (now Dun Laoghaire). Today, its harbor, which supports a large fishing and sailing fleet, includes a marina. Both arms of the harbor pier form extensive walks with lots of great seafood options along the way.

Sights

Baily Lighthouse

LIGHTHOUSE | At the King Sitric restaurant on the East Pier, a 2½-km (1½-mile) cliff walk begins, leading to the white Baily Lighthouse, built in 1814. In some places, the cliff path narrows and drops close to the water, but the views out over the Irish Sea are terrific. Some of the best views in the whole Dublin area await from the parking lot above the lighthouse, looking out over the entire bay as far south as Dun Laoghaire, Bray, and the north Wicklow coast. You can also see quite a bit of the city. ✉ *Howth Summit, Howth* 🌐 *www.irishlights.ie.*

Howth Castle Gardens

GARDEN | The Howth Castle Gardens, next door to the Transport Museum and accessible from the Deer Park Hotel, were laid out in the early 18th century. The many rare varieties in the fine rhododendron garden are in full flower April through June; there are also high beech hedges. The rambling castle, built in 1654 and considerably altered in the following centuries, is not open to the public, but you can access the ruins of a tall, square, 16th-century castle and a Neolithic dolmen. ✉ *Deer Park Hotel, Howth* ☎ *01/832–2624* 🌐 *howthcastle.ie* 🎫 *Free.*

Ireland's Eye

ISLAND | Separated from Howth Harbour by a channel nearly 1½ km (1 mile) wide is the little island of Ireland's Eye, with an old stone church on the site of a 6th-century monastery, and an early-19th-century Martello tower. In calm summer weather, local boatmen make the crossing to the island from the East pier in Howth Harbour. Check the notice board in the harbor for the number of a boat owner willing to do the trip. ✉ *Howth, Howth.*

National Transport Museum Of Ireland

OTHER MUSEUM | **FAMILY** | Until 1959, a tram service ran from the railway station in Howth, over Howth Summit, and back down to the station. One of the open-top Hill of Howth trams that plied this route is now the star at the National Transport Museum, a short 800-yard walk from Howth's DART station. Volunteers spent several years restoring the tram, which stands alongside other unusual vehicles, including horse-drawn bakery vans. ✉ *Heritage Depot, Howth Demense, Howth* ☎ *01/832–0427* 🌐 *nationaltransportmuseum.org* 🎫 *€3* 🕐 *Closed weekdays.*

Restaurants

Aqua

$$$ | **SEAFOOD** | Stunning views over Howth Harbor are your first reward for choosing this impressive seafood restaurant located in the old yacht club building only a few yards from where local fishermen still land their catch. The open, modern interior is awash with light that pours in the huge windows—definitely get a seat beside one of these. **Known for:** perfect rib eye; decadent desserts;

friendly and attentive staff. *Average main: €27* *1 West Pier, Howth* *01/832–0690* *www.aqua.ie* *Closed Mon. No lunch Tues.*

King Sitric

$$ | SEAFOOD | Joan and Aidan MacManus's well-known seafood bar down by the harbor attracts many contemporary visitors to the old town. It's in a Georgian house, with the yacht marina and port on one side and sea views from which you can watch the boats land the very fish that might be tomorrow's special. **Known for:** warm, friendly atmosphere; fillet of turbot with crab mash and caviar cream sauce; tempura prawns. *Average main: €21* *East Pier, Howth* *01/832–5235* *kingsitric.ie.*

Malahide

By car, drive from north city center on R107 for 14½ km (9 miles). Or catch hourly train from Connolly Station. Or board Bus 42 to Malahide, which leaves every 15 minutes from Beresford Place behind Custom House.

Sights

Malahide Castle

CASTLE/PALACE | FAMILY | This township is chiefly known for its glorious Malahide Castle, a picture-book castle occupied by the Talbot family from 1185 until 1976, when it was sold to the local County Council. The great expanse of parkland around the castle has more than 5,000 different species of trees and shrubs, all clearly labeled. The castle itself combines styles and crosses centuries; the earliest section, the three-story tower house, dates from the 12th century. The stunning walled gardens are now open to the public, with a fairy trail for kids and a butterfly house. Hung with many family portraits, the medieval great hall is the only one in Ireland that is preserved in its original form. Authentic 18th-century pieces furnish the other rooms. An impressive new addition includes a visitor center, the Avoca restaurant, and a shop. *10 km (6 miles) north of Howth on Coast Rd., Malahide* *01/846–2184* *malahidecastleandgardens.ie* *€15.*

★ Newbridge House and Farm

HISTORIC HOME | FAMILY | One of the greatest stately homes of Ireland, Newbridge House, in Donabate, was built between 1740 and 1760 for Charles Cobbe, archbishop of Dublin. A showpiece in the Georgian and Regency styles, the house is less a museum than a home because the Cobbe family still resides here, part of a novel scheme the municipal government allowed when they took over the house in 1985. The sober exterior and even more sober entrance hall—all Portland stone and Welsh slate—don't prepare you for the splendor of Newbridge's Red Drawing Room, perhaps Ireland's most sumptuous 18th-century salon. Cobbe's son, Thomas, and his wife, Lady Betty Beresford, sister of the marquess of Waterford, had amassed a great collection of paintings and needed a hall in which to show them off, so they built a back wing on the house to incorporate an enormous room built for entertaining and impressing others. That it does, thanks to its crimson walls, fluted Corinthian columns, dozens of old masters, and glamorous rococo-style plaster ceiling designed by the Dublin stuccadore Richard Williams. Beyond the house's walled garden are 366 acres of parkland and a restored 18th-century animal farm. The coffee shop is renowned for the quality and selection of its homemade goods. You can travel from Malahide to Donabate by train, which takes about 10 minutes. From the Donabate train station, it's a 15-minute walk to the Newbridge House grounds. *Donabate, 8 km (5 miles) north of Malahide, signposted from N1, Malahide* *01/843–6534* *newbridgehouseandfarm.com* *From €9* *Closed Mon. Oct.–Mar.*

Chapter 4

DUBLIN ENVIRONS

Updated by
Anto Howard

Sights	Restaurants	Hotels	Shopping	Nightlife
★★★★★	★★★★☆	★★★★☆	★★★☆☆	★★★☆☆

WELCOME TO DUBLIN ENVIRONS

TOP REASONS TO GO

★ **Newgrange:** Just standing amid these 5,000-year-old tombs (which predate the pyramids), you'll wonder: how did they build them?

★ **A Day at the Races:** The Irish may be known to enjoy a sociable drink, but they really love to gamble, as you'll discover in Kildare, center of the Irish bloodstock world. Punchestown in spring and the Curragh in summer are both unique, passionate racecourse experiences.

★ **Spectacular Georgian Country Houses:** Modesty was not a feature of the Anglo-Irish class, whose propensity to flaunt their riches led to such over-the-top stately homes as Castletown, Russborough, and Powerscourt.

★ **Wicklow Is for Walkers:** There's no better way to meet the locals and see the land than trekking out on the 137-km-long (85-mile-long) Wicklow Way, Ireland's most popular trail.

★ **Early Morning at Glendalough:** Channel the spirit of the 6th-century, isolation-seeking St. Kevin.

1 **Hill of Tara.** This hill and its ancient monuments were the seat of power for ancient High Kings.

2 **Kells.** While the *Book of Kells* is no longer here, this town has High Crosses, a Round Tower, and immense history.

3 **Newgrange.** A Neolithic burial ground and solar observatory that's still evocative of the mysteries of pre-Celtic civilization.

4 **Slane.** Slane Castle is the main draw in this small Georgian village.

5 **Drogheda.** Georgian architecture, a medieval town gate, and lots of churches are the draw to this riverside town.

6 **Mellifont Abbey.** The first Cistercian monastery in Ireland.

7 **Dundalk.** The main town of Ireland's smallest county is a perfect base for exploring both north and south of the border.

8 **Blessington.** A charming Georgian village near the impressive Poulaphouca reservoir.

9 **Bray.** One of Ireland's oldest seaside resorts, this trim little town has a 2-km (1-mile) sand-and-shingle beach.

10 **Powerscourt House, Gardens, and Waterfall.** Sitting in more than 14,000 acres, this remains one of the great Georgian houses of Ireland and Britain.

11 **Glendalough.** This 6th-century monastic site is so serene you may be tempted to renounce the profane world.

12 **Mount Usher Gardens.** This Victorian walled garden has a great café and craft shops.

13 **Wicklow Town.** A historic town and gateway to the wild Wicklow Mountains.

14 **Maynooth.** The serene university town is near the Georgian splendor of Castletown House.

15 **Straffan.** This small town boasts a butterfly farm and the luxury K Club resort.

16 **Naas.** The market town is at the heart of Irish Thoroughbred country.

17 **The Curragh.** Broad and wild, these plains are home to hundreds of galloping racehorses.

18 **Kildare Town.** The Irish National Stud and Japanese Gardens are big draws in this midsize town.

NORTHERN IRELAND
Annayalla
Castleblayney
MONAGHAN
Omeath
Carlingford Lough
N53
Dundalk
7
Inniskeen
N2
Cavan
CAVAN
Dundalk Bay
New Inn
M1
Ardee
LOUTH
Irish Sea
N3
N52
N2
BOYNE VALLEY
Mellifont Abbey
5
6
Kells
Drogheda
Slane
2
N3
4
Newgrange
3
M1
N52
Navan
N51
1
Hill of Tara
N2
WESTMEATH
Cloghan
DUBLIN
Lambay Island
MEATH
M3
Swords
Kinnegad
N4
M1
14
Drumleck Point
Tyrrellspass
Maynooth
DUBLIN
Dublin Bay
Straffan
Castletown House
15
OFFALY
KILDARE
M11
16
M7
Russborough House
9
Bray
Naas
Punchestown Racecourse
Powerscourt House
18
17
10
Cherryville
The Curragh
Blessington
Kilmacanogue
Kildare Town
Kilcullen
8
WICKLOW
N11
N7
Wicklow Way
WICKLOW MOUNTAINS
Roundwood
Portlaoise
N78
12
Mount Usher Gardens
Glendalough
11
Athy
LAOIS
M9
Wicklow Town
Wicklow Head
13
Abbeyleix
N11
Durrow
CARLOW
Arklow
0
10 mi
0
10 km
WEXFORD

THE RIVER BOYNE VALLEY: IRELAND'S HISTORIC HEART

Newgrange is a spectacular passage tomb.

Stone Age, Celtic, early Christian, and Norman: the country is scattered with sites that act as signposts in the long and twisting story called "Ireland." But by circumstance of geography and mystical significance many of the great stone ghosts of ancient Ireland are concentrated in the counties immediately surrounding Dublin.

Here, often so closely thrown together as to make a mockery of the vastness of time and history, stand the man-made wonders that are impressive but slightly melancholic reminders of more heroic and more savage ages. In fact, a tour down the valley of the River Boyne is a trip into the past, back beyond history, to the Neolithic tombs of Newgrange, the Druidic holy place of the Hill of Tara, the monasteries of early Christianity, and the Norman castles of the chain-mailed invaders who brought a bloody end to so much of Celtic Ireland. Not far from Dublin, chart the rise and fall of Irish culture at their glorious monuments.

THE HIGH CROSS

The Celtic High Cross is an endearing symbol of Ireland, and Monasterboice has more of them than anywhere in Ireland. Dating to AD 923, the 20-foot-high Muireadach Cross is the best preserved, as its panels depicting the slaying of Abel, David and Goliath, and the Last Judgment prove. The nearby 110-foot Round Tower gives you a view of the once-glorious monastic site.

NEWGRANGE

Built in the 4th millennium BC, a thousand years before Stonehenge, Newgrange is not only one of the world's pristine surviving passage tombs but also a great granite reminder of the ingenuity, spirituality, and perseverance of modern Ireland's Neolithic ancestors. How did they move 250,000 tons of stone? How did they align it to perfectly capture the first rays of the dawn sun on the winter solstice? The thrill of visiting and entering the somber tomb at Newgrange lies not only in what you discover but in the awesome mysteries that can only be answered by the imagination.

GLENDALOUGH

A single early-morning hour spent in the isolated and serene Glendalough Valley—a green jewel in the Wicklow Mountains—should be enough to convince you that St. Kevin made the perfect choice when he was searching for 6th-century solitude and peace. The simplicity, separation, and sparseness that were at the heart of early Christianity in Ireland are sublimely apparent in the hermit's cave called St. Kevin's Bed and the ruins of the tiny Church of the Oratory.

The Stone of Destiny rests on the Hill of Tara.

Graves and High Crosses hallow the grounds of Glendalough.

HILL OF TARA

First-timers are sometimes disappointed when they finally see the mythical Hill of Tara, spiritual and regal heart of Celtic and Druidic Ireland. It is now just a hill: 300 feet high, with awesome views out over the flat central plains of Ireland and all the way to Galway in the west. But with a little reading at the interpretive center and a lot of imagination, you can picture the Iron Age fort that once stood here and the huge *feis,* or national assembly, where Celtic Ireland passed its laws and settled its tribal disputes. It is a place that is both beyond history and made of it.

MELLIFONT ABBEY

As well as war, the Normans brought great stone-church building to Ireland; one of their greatest religious monuments is Mellifont Abbey. Founded in 1142 by St. Malachy, the main parts of the abbey were built a little later in the Norman style, including the two-story chapter house and the octagonal lavabo, where the monks used to wash. Although much of the abbey is in ruins, it still manages to illustrate the medieval church's rise to wealth and power in Ireland. Incidentally, the term "Celtic" is derived from the tribes that arrived on Irish shores around 700 BC, first called Galli by the Romans and then named Gaels in Ireland.

Walt Disney himself couldn't have planned it better. The small counties immediately north, south, and west of Dublin—historically known as the Pale—seem expressly designed to entertain and enchant sightseers. The entire region is rich with legendary Celtic sites, gorgeous gardens, and the most elegant Palladian country estates in Ireland.

Due to its location on the Irish Sea, facing Europe, the region was the first to attract the earliest "tourists"—conquerors and rulers—and the first over which they exercised the greatest influence. Traces of each new wave remain: the Celts chose Tara as the center of their kingdom; the Danes sailed the Rivers Boyne and Liffey to establish many of today's towns; and the region's great Protestant-built houses of the 18th century remind us that the Pale (originally the area of eastern Ireland ruled directly by the Normans) was the starting point and administrative center for the long, violent English colonization of the whole island.

The Dublin environs include three basic geographical regions. North of Dublin lies the Boyne Valley, with its abundant ruins of Celtic Ireland extending from counties Meath to Louth. In pagan times this area was the home of Ireland's High Kings and the center of religious life. All roads led to Tara, the fabled Hill of Kings, the royal seat, and the place where the national assembly was held. Today, time seems to stand still—and you should, too, for it's almost sacrilegious to introduce a note of urgency here.

South of the capital is the mountainous county of Wicklow, where the gently rounded Wicklow Mountains contain the evocative monastic settlement at Glendalough, many later abbeys and churches, and the great 18th-century estates of the Anglo-Irish aristocracy, such as Castletown, Powerscourt, and Russborough.

Southwest of Dublin are the pastoral plains of County Kildare, which stretch between the western Midlands and the foothills of the Dublin and Wicklow mountains—both names refer to the same mountain range, but each marks its county's claim to the land. Kildare is the flattest part of Ireland, a natural playing field for breeding, training, and racing some of the world's premier Thoroughbreds.

Rapid, omnivorous expansion of the capital city in the last 30 years has seen its suburban limits spread deep into the once-bucolic areas of Meath and Kildare, so don't be surprised to hear Dublin accents starting to dominate in towns like Navan and Naas. The booming economy and the parallel hike in house prices have been strongly felt in these satellite towns so dependent on the economy of Dublin.

MAJOR REGIONS

Set 48 km (30 miles) north of Dublin, this entire area is packed with prehistoric and pagan sites. You don't have to be an Indiana Jones to be awed by the Hill of Tara or Newgrange, a Neolithic burial ground and solar observatory still evocative of the mysteries of pre-Celtic civilization.

The Boyne Valley. For every wistful schoolchild in Ireland, the River Boyne is a name that resonates with history and adventure. It was on the banks of that river in 1014 that the Celtic chieftain Brian Boru defeated the Danish in a decisive battle that returned the east of Ireland to native rule. It was also by this river that Protestant William of Orange defeated the Catholic armies of exiled James II of England in 1690. In fact, this whole area, only 48 km (30 miles) north of cosmopolitan Dublin, is soaked in stories and legends that predate the pyramids. You can't throw a stick anywhere in the valley without hitting some trace of Irish history. The great prehistoric, pagan, and Celtic monuments of the wide arc known as the Boyne Valley invariably evoke a sense of wonder. You don't have to be an archaeologist to be awed by Newgrange and Knowth—set beside the River Boyne—or the Hill of Tara, Mellifont Abbey, or the High Cross of Monasterboice. One way to explore this area is to start at Trim, the town closest to Dublin, and work your way north. Keep in mind that Omeath and the scenic Cooley Peninsula are on the border of Northern Ireland.

County Kildare. Horse racing is a passion in Ireland—just about every little town has at least one betting shop—and County Kildare is the country's horse capital. Nestled between the basins of the River Liffey to the north and the River Barrow to the east, its gently sloping hills and grass-filled plains are perfect for breeding and racing Thoroughbreds. For some visitors, the fabled National Stud Farm just outside Kildare Town provides a fascinating glimpse into the world of horse breeding. And don't forget the Japanese Gardens, adjacent to the National Stud, which are among Europe's finest. You may want to head to this area from Glendalough—the spectacular drive across the Wicklow Gap, from Glendalough to Hollywood, makes for a glorious entrance into Kildare.

County Wicklow. Make your way to the fourth or fifth story of almost any building in Dublin that faces south, and you can see off in the distance—amazingly, not *that* far off in the distance—the green, smooth hills of the Dublin and Wicklow mountains. On a clear day, the mountains are even visible from some streets in and around the city center. If your idea of solace is green hills, and your visit to Ireland is otherwise limited to Dublin, County Wicklow—or Cill Mhantáin (pronounced "kill *wan*-tan"), as it's known in Irish—should be on your itinerary.

Not that the secret isn't out; rugged and mountainous with dark, wooded forests, central Wicklow, known as the "garden of Ireland," is a popular picnic spot among Dubliners. It has some of Ireland's grandest 18th-century mansions, including Russborough and Powerscourt, and cradles one of the country's earliest Christian retreats: Glendalough. Nestled in a valley of dense woods and placid lakes, Glendalough and environs can seem (at least during the off-season) practically untouched since their heyday 1,000 years ago. The granite mountains that have protected Glendalough all these years run into the sea along the east coast, which has several popular sandy beaches.

Planning

When to Go

While certainly not the wettest part of Ireland (the West gets that dubious distinction), the counties around Dublin do get their fair share of rain. June, July, August, and September tend to be the driest months, and the good news is that the summer showers are usually light and short-lived. Wicklow, with all its hills and valleys, seems to have an obscure microclimate of its own, so don't rely too much on the weather forecast to get it right.

Planning Your Time

Most people who explore Dublin Environs base themselves in the capital and sample the very different landscapes on day trips. Driving distances from downtown are less than two hours (in decent traffic). Just don't plan on visiting both the north and south of Dublin in the same day—each region is worth its own day or half-day trip.

Visits to Newgrange and Glendalough are musts, and the latter could be combined with a country house visit to Powerscourt. For more active visitors, a one-day walk along the Wicklow Way might pair best with an overnight stay in the cozy Hunter's Hotel.

Getting Here and Around

BUS

Bus Éireann links Dublin with towns in the area. Dublin Bus serves some towns and estates in the region as well. All buses for the region depart from Dublin's Busáras, the central bus station, at Store Street. St. Kevin's Bus Services offers regular trips from Dublin to numerous towns and sights in Wicklow, including Glendalough, Roundwood, Laragh, and Bray.

CONTACTS Bus Éireann. ☎ *01/836–6111* 🌐 *buseireann.ie.* **Dublin Bus.** ☎ *01/873–4222* 🌐 *dublinbus.ie.* **St. Kevin's Bus.** ☎ *01/281–8119* 🌐 *www.glendaloughbus.com.*

CAR

The easiest and best way to tour Dublin's environs is by car, because many sights are not served by public transportation. What service there is, especially to outlying areas, is infrequent. To visit destinations in the Boyne Valley, follow N3, along the east side of Phoenix Park, out of the city and make Trim and Tara your first stops. Alternatively, leave Dublin via N1/M1 toward Belfast. To reach destinations in County Kildare, follow the quays along the south side of the River Liffey (they are one-way westbound) to St. John's Road West (N7/M7); in a matter of minutes you're heading for open countryside. Avoid traveling this route during the evening rush hour, especially on Friday, when Dubliners are making their weekend getaways. To reach destinations in County Wicklow, N11/M11 is the fastest and most clearly marked route. The two more scenic routes to Glendalough are R115 to R759 to R755, or R177 to R755. All major roads can be congested during rush hours, and like most major cities, Friday afternoon is a busy time to leave the city.

TRAIN

Irish Rail (Iarnród Éireann) trains run the length of the east coast, stopping at towns between Dundalk to the north in County Louth to Arklow along the coast in County Wicklow. From Heuston Station, the Arrow, a commuter train service, runs westward to Celbridge, Naas, Newbridge, Athy, and Kildare Town.

CONTACTS Irish Rail–Iarnód Éireann. ☎ *01/836–6222 in Dublin, 041/983–8749 in Drogheda* 🌐 *irishrail.ie.*

Hotels

When exploring the region around Dublin, many people opt to stay in the capital and take day trips. The city center is obviously a favorite option but does leave you subject to some heavy rush-hour traffic; in general, you can still get in and out of Dublin quite quickly. A hotel on the Southside of the city or in South County Dublin might be a good idea if you're planning to spend time in Wicklow or East Kildare. For Meath and Louth, a hotel on the Northside or to the west of the city might work better.

If you don't want to "commute" from the city, the noted country-house hotels around Kildare and Wicklow are great options. They are a surprisingly good value given their unique, luxurious atmospheres. Bed-and-breakfasts are another good option, and although those in this region tend to be a little more expensive than in other parts of Ireland, they also are more stylish. Like in Dublin, hotel prices have increased over the last few years.

Restaurants

Dining out in the area is usually a casual affair, but Dublin's top restaurateurs are influencing the cooking—and the prices—at the finer establishments outside the capital, culminating in Kildare's new dining sensation, Aimsir, winning two Michelin stars. But cheaper overheads also allow smaller, innovative, and, above all, good-value restaurants like Las Radas to spring up in unlikely places like Naas. Chefs hereabouts have a deep respect for fresh, locally grown and raised produce. You'll find everything from continental-style meals to hearty ploughman's lunches.

RESTAURANT AND HOTEL PRICES

⇨ *Restaurant prices are the average cost of a main course at dinner or, if dinner is not served, at lunch. Hotel prices are the lowest cost of a standard double room in high season. Restaurant and hotel reviews have been shortened. For full information, visit Fodors.com.*

What It Costs in Euros

	$	$$	$$$	$$$$
RESTAURANTS	under €19	€19–€24	€25–€32	over €32
HOTELS	under €150	€150–€200	€201–€270	over €270

Tours

Finn McCools Tours

GUIDED TOURS | Their one-day, guided tour takes in Glendalough and the Wicklow Mountains and even includes a demonstration of a sheepdog at work. They pick you up and drop you back from outside the Hugh Lane Gallery. ☎ *01/882–8344* 🌐 *finnmccoolstours.com* 🎫 *€80.*

Tourism Ireland

DRIVING TOURS | The website for Tourism Ireland has a Grand Tour section that outlines a number of cleverly themed driving tours in the area. ☎ *800/242–473* 🌐 *ireland.com.*

Wild Wicklow Tours

BUS TOURS | For smaller private groups of any size, family-run Wild Wicklow Tours takes you off the beaten track. Day trips to Glendalough also take in Avoca Handweavers and a Dublin coastal drive. ☎ *01/280–1899* 🌐 *wildwicklow.ie* 🎫 *Contact for rates for private group.*

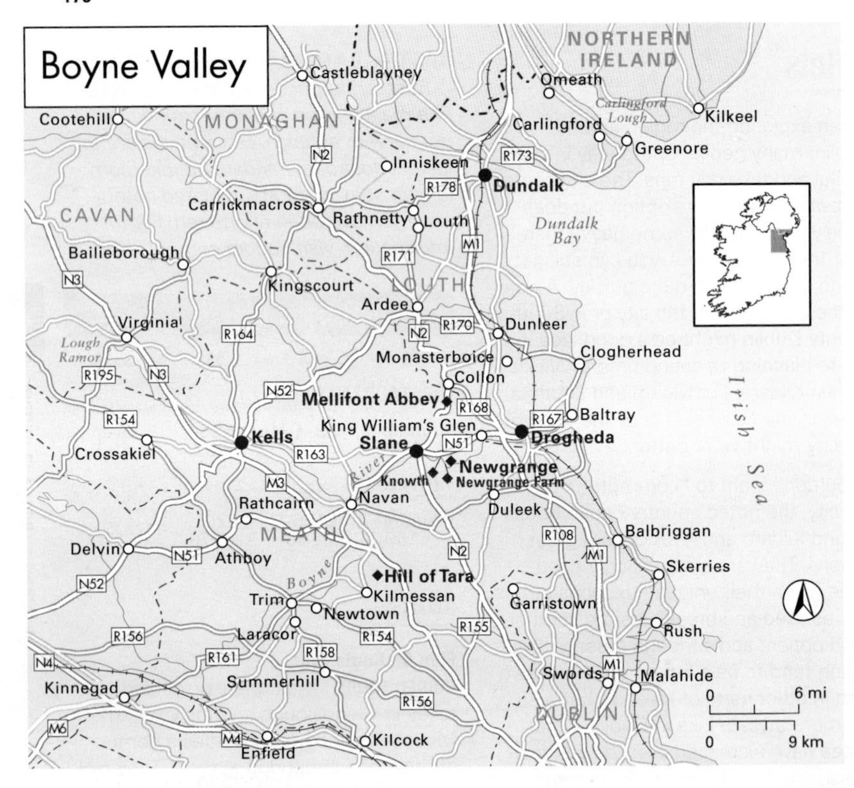

Visitor Information

You're likely to encounter signs and other promotional materials for the country's newest tourism initiative, "Ireland's Ancient East," which is designed to link many of the great sites in this half of the country. Like the hugely successful "Wild Atlantic Way" initiative before it, the resources developed to promote and support the campaign are a huge benefit to visitors. Be sure to check the Ireland's Ancient East website as it is a great source for current events and suggested stops. County Kildare, County Louth, and County Meath all have offices that offer year-round tourism advice. Some are run by Tourism Ireland while others are locally operated. In summer, temporary offices are open in such towns as Trim in County Meath, Drogheda and Dundalk in County Louth, and Kildare Town in County Kildare.

CONTACTS County Kildare Tourism. ☎ *045/898–888* 🌐 *intokildare.ie.* **County Louth Tourism.** ☎ *042/933–5457* 🌐 *visitlouth.ie.* **County Meath Tourism.** ☎ *046/909–7060* 🌐 *meath.ie/discover.* **Ireland's Ancient East.** ☎ *1850/230–330* 🌐 *www.irelandsancienteast.com.* **Wicklow Tourism.** ☎ *0404/69118* 🌐 *visitwicklow.ie.*

Hill of Tara

40 km (25 miles) northwest of Dublin.

In legends and in the popular imagination, the "seat of the High Kings of Ireland" has taken on mythic proportions. As with much of the Celtic past, it was the 19th-century revival led by W.B. Yeats and Lady Gregory that was responsible for the near-religious veneration of this site, set at the junction of the five ancient roads of Ireland. Today, its ancestral banqueting hall and great buildings (one was the former palace of the *Ard Rí*, or High King) have vanished except for a few columns. Still, the site is awe-inspiring.

GETTING HERE AND AROUND

An hour's drive from Dublin, the Hill of Tara is just off the N3/M3 motorway. From Belfast it's a 1½-hour drive; take the M1 and connect with the N51 at Drogheda. There's ample parking near the site. You can also take a Navan-bound Bus Éireann, which passes within 2 km (1 mile) of the site and walk; ask the driver to drop you at the Tara Cross and follow the signs. A taxi from Navan to Tara costs about €18.

TOURS

Newgrange Tours

BUS TOURS | Bus tours run from Dublin Monday through Saturday. The company charges €40, which includes admission to the Hill of Tara and Newgrange. Tours depart from outside the Visit Dublin Centre on Suffolk Street, as well as from some major hotels. *086/335–1355* *newgrangetours.com* *Tours €75.*

Sights

★ Hill of Tara

HISTORIC SIGHT | One of the most sacred places in pre-Christian Ireland, and the seat of power for ancient High Kings, the Hill of Tara is at the nexus of Celtic myth and history. You are free to roam across the site, but it might require a little research and imagination to bring it all to life. From the top of the Hill—it rises more than 300 feet above sea level—you can see across the flat central plain of Ireland, with the mountains of East Galway visible from a distance of nearly 160 km (100 miles). At the summit you will also find an oval Iron Age hilltop enclosure, a massive "hill fort," which became known as the Fort of the Kings (Ráith na Ríogh). Within the fort are further earthworks, a ring fort and a ring barrow—Cormac's House (Teach Chormaic) and the Royal Seat (Forradh). In the middle of the Forradh you'll notice a solitary standing stone. This is believed to be the Stone of Destiny (Lia Fáil), the ancient crowning place of the High Kings. Wander farther to find other earthworks, a massive ring fort known as Rath Maeve, and a Holy Well. The legend of St. Patrick claims he came to the Hill of Tara to confront the ancient pagan religion at its most important site. In the mid-19th century, the nationalist leader Daniel O'Connell staged a mass rally here that supposedly drew more than a million people.

TIP→ Before you wander, stop at the Interpretative Center, housed in an old church on the hillside, where you can learn the story of Tara and its legends and watch a short movie showing stunning aerial views. Without this background it will be difficult to get your bearings or to identify many of the earthworks outside.

After systematic excavations in the 20th century, archaeologists have concluded that the Iron Age fort was ruined in the 19th century by religious zealots searching for the Ark of the Covenant. The Mound of the Hostages, a Neolithic passage grave, most likely gave the place its sacred air. *Navan* *12 km (7 miles) south of Navan off N3* *046/902–5903* *heritageireland.ie/visit/places-to-visit/hill-of-tara* *Free* *Visitor center closes early Sept.–late May.*

Hotels

Bellinter House

$$$ | **HOUSE** | Surrounded by 12 acres on the banks of the Boyne, this splendid 1750 country house retains the glories of the original architecture while adding a few modern twists. **Pros:** stunningly authentic original rooms; impressive spa; relaxing atmosphere. **Cons:** newer rooms not as grand; dining room decor is a bit stuffy; can book up in summer. $ *Rooms from: €220* ✉ *Navan* ⊕ *4 km (2½ miles) northwest of Hill of Tara* ☎ *046/903–0900* 🌐 *bellinterhouse.com* *42 rooms* *Free Breakfast.*

Activities

GOLF

Killeen Castle Golf Club

GOLF | The great Jack Nicklaus had a hand in the design and construction of this championship-level course and golf school set in the serene woodlands of Norman Killeen Castle in Meath. Covering twice the acreage of an average championship course—you might need a buggy to get around—Nicklaus really had room to let his imagination run free, and the natural water features and stonework are a special treat.

■ TIP→ Check out the wonderful Paul Ferriter sculpture of the great man himself near the first tee box. ✉ *1 Loughmore Ave., Dunsany* ☎ *01/689–3000* 🌐 *killeencastle.com* *May–Sept. from €70; Apr. and Oct. from €60; Nov.–Mar. from €50* *18 holes, 7700 yards, par 72.*

Kells

67 km (41 miles) northwest of Dublin.

In the 9th century, a group of monks from Scotland took refuge at Kells (Ceanannus Mór), where St. Columba had founded a monastery 300 years earlier. Although some historians think it was indigenous monks who wrote and illustrated the *Book of Kells*—the Latin version of the four Gospels, and one of Ireland's greatest medieval treasures—most now believe that the Scottish monks brought it with them. Reputed to have been fished out of a watery bog at Kells, the legendary manuscript was removed for safekeeping during the Cromwellian wars to Trinity College, Dublin, where it remains.

Fires of Faith

The Hill of Tara's decline was predicted one Easter Eve in the 5th century when, in accordance with the Druid religion, the lighting of fires was forbidden. Suddenly, on a hillside some miles away, flames were spotted. "If that fire is not quenched now," said a Druid leader, "it will burn forever and will consume Tara." The fire had been lighted by St. Patrick at Slane to celebrate the Christian Paschal rites.

GETTING HERE AND AROUND

Kells is a 50-minute drive northwest of Dublin on the M3 motorway. There is ample parking in and around the town. Bus Éireann has regular service from Dublin; the trip takes 1 hour and 25 minutes.

Sights

Kells Courthouse Tourism and Cultural Hub

VISITOR CENTER | Located in Kells Town Hall, the office is also home to a brilliant copy of the *Book of Kells*—it's a more pleasant, less rushed, and less expensive way to see this medieval masterpiece compared with the madness of Trinity College in high season. They also have a diorama of Kells Town around AD 815. ✉ *Headfort Pl., Kells* ☎ *046/924–8856* 🌐 *discoverboynevalley.ie* *Free* *Closed Sun.*

Round Tower

HISTORIC SIGHT | The nearly 100-foot-high Round Tower, adjacent to St. Colmcille's House, dates back to 1076 and is in almost perfect condition. The tower was likely used as a defensive hideout by local monks during an invasion; they would climb up the rope ladder with their valuables and pull it up after them. Its top story has five windows, not the usual four, each facing an ancient entrance into the medieval town. You can't go inside, but just standing beside it gives a real sense of the inventiveness and desperation of the Viking-fearing monks. ✉ *R163, west of intersection of N3 and N52, Kells.*

St. Colmcille's House

CHURCH | Similar in appearance to St. Kevin's Church at Glendalough and Cormac's Chapel at Cashel, St. Colmcille's House is an 11th-century church on a much older site. It measures about 24 feet square and nearly 40 feet high, with a steeply pitched stone roof. The nearby tourist office can help you get inside and it's well worth it to feel what the ancient monastic life was like. ✉ *R163, west of intersection of N3 and N52, Kells.*

St. Columba's

RELIGIOUS BUILDING | Four elaborately carved High Crosses stand in the church graveyard; you'll find the stump of a fifth in the marketplace—it was used as a gallows during the 1798 uprising against British rule. ✉ *Off Cannon St. and Church St., Kells.*

Newgrange

21 km (13 miles) east of Kells, 28 km (17 miles) northwest of Dublin.

Expect to see no less than one of the most spectacular prehistoric tombs in Europe when you come to Newgrange. Built in the 4th millennium BC—which makes it roughly 1,000 years older than Stonehenge—Newgrange was constructed with some 250,000 tons of stone, much of which came from the Wicklow Mountains, 80 km (50 miles) to the south. The Brú na Bóinne (loosely translated as "Palace of the Boyne") Visitor Centre, near the village of Donore, is the starting point for all visits to Newgrange and Knowth. Newgrange often sells out in high season.

Winter Solstice at Newgrange

A visit to Newgrange's passage grave during the winter solstice is a memorable experience. You'll have to get on the nine-year waiting list to reserve one of the 24 places available on each of the five mornings (December 19–23). And then pray that no clouds obscure the sun and ruin the light show the Bronze Age builders intended.

GETTING HERE AND AROUND

From Dublin it's about a 50-minute drive to Newgrange: take the M1 motorway north to the Donore exit before Drogheda; Brú na Bóinne is clearly signposted before the exit. Drive about 6 km (4 miles) to the village of Donore, turn right and travel about half a mile to the visitor center. There is ample parking at the center. The Bus Éireann route from Dublin to Drogheda stops at Newgrange, and Newgrange Tours combines a visit to this site with the Hill of Tara on its bus tour.

VISITOR INFORMATION

CONTACTS Brú na Bóinne Visitor Centre. ✉ *Off Staleen Rd., near Donore Village, Slane* ☎ *041/988–0300* 🌐 *heritageireland.ie/visit/places-to-visit/bru-na-boinne-visitor-centre-newgrange-and-knowth.*

Sights

★ **Newgrange**

HISTORIC SIGHT | One of the most spectacular prehistoric sites in the world, Newgrange's Neolithic tomb inexplicably remains something of a hidden gem when compared with less-ancient Stonehenge. The wondrous site is shrouded in myth and mystery, including how the

Built between 3100 and 2900 BC, Newgrange is strikingly adorned with boulders carved with Neolithic triple spirals and diamonds.

people who built Newgrange transported the huge stones to the spot. The mound above the tomb measures more than 330 feet across and reaches a height of 36 feet. White quartz was used for the retaining wall, and egg-shape gray stones were studded at intervals. The passage grave may have been the world's earliest solar observatory. It was so carefully constructed that, for five days on and around the winter solstice, the rays of the rising sun still hit a roof box above the lintel at the entrance to the grave. The rays then shine for about 20 minutes down the main interior passageway to illuminate the burial chamber. The geometric designs on some stones at the center of the burial chamber continue to baffle experts. Tours of the site depart from the Brú na Bóinne Visitor Centre.

■ TIP→ Reserving tickets in advance is a must. Walk-in tickets are rarely available. ✉ *Off N2, 2 km (1 mile) west of Donore Village, Slane* ☎ *041/988–0300 for Brú na Bóinne Visitor Centre* 🌐 *heritageireland.ie/visit/places-to-visit/bru-na-boinne-visitor-centre-newgrange-and-knowth* 🎫 *€10 tour and visitor center exhibit, €5 visitor center exhibit.*

Slane

2½ km (1½ miles) north of Newgrange, 46 km (29 miles) northwest of Dublin.

Slane Castle is the draw at this small Georgian village, built in the 18th century around a crossroads on the north side of the River Boyne.

GETTING HERE AND AROUND

Slane is 46 km (29 miles) northwest of Dublin on the N2 major road. There is plenty of parking around the town and at the castle. Bus Éireann runs a regular service from Dublin; it takes about an hour and 10 minutes.

Sights

Hermitage

RUINS | The 16th-century Hermitage was constructed on the site where St. Erc, a local man converted to Christianity by St. Patrick himself, led a hermit's existence. All that remains of his original monastery is the faint trace of the circular ditch, but the ruins of the later church include a nave and a chancel with a tower in between, and a stroll through them can evoke a little of the atmosphere of medieval Ireland. ✉ *Slane Castle Demesne, Slane.*

★ Knowth

RUINS | Under excavation since 1962, the prehistoric site of Knowth is comparable in size and shape to Newgrange, standing at 40 feet and having a diameter of approximately 214 feet. Some 150 giant stones, many of them beautifully decorated, surrounded the mound. More than 1,600 boulders, each weighing from one to several tons, were used in the construction. The earliest tombs and carved stones date from the Stone Age (3000 BC); and in the early Christian era (4th–8th centuries AD), it was the seat of the High Kings of Ireland. Much of the site is still under excavation, and you can often watch archaeologists at work. Tours of the site depart from the Brú na Bóinne Visitor Centre. ✉ *Off N2, near Donore Village, Slane* ☎ *041/988–0300 for Brú na Bóinne Visitor Centre* 🌐 *heritageireland.ie/visit/places-to-visit/bru-na-boinne-visitor-centre-newgrange-and-knowth* 🎫 *€10.*

Newgrange Farm

FARM/RANCH | **FAMILY** | A two-hour tour of farmer Willie Redhouse's fully functioning farm includes feeding the ducks, bottle-feeding the lambs, a visit to aviaries stocked with exotic birds, and a straw maze and go-karts for the kids. A blacksmith gives demonstrations of his ancient art, and there's a nice tractor ride around the farm. Every Sunday at 3 pm the Sheep Derby takes place, with teddy bears tied astride the animals in the place of jockeys. ✉ *N51, Slane* ✣ *3 km (2 miles) east of Slane* 🌐 *newgrangefarm.com* 🎫 *€10* 🕓 *Closed early Sept.–late Mar.*

★ Slane Castle

CASTLE/PALACE | The stately 18th-century Slane Castle overlooks a natural amphitheater, a bowl-shape hollow formed by surrounding hills. In 1981 the castle's owner, Anglo-Irish Lord Henry Mount Charles, staged the first of what have been some of Ireland's largest outdoor rock concerts; up to 100,000 fans have gathered to watch stars including U2, Bob Dylan, and the Rolling Stones. A tour of the Gothic-style castle includes the main hall, with its delicate plasterwork and beautiful stained glass, and the dazzling neo-Gothic ballroom completed in 1821 for the visit of King George IV. The stunning parklands were laid out by Capability Brown, a famous 18th-century landscape gardener. Slane Castle produces its own whiskey and has fun tasting tours, including a how-to-make-an-Irish-coffee tour. ✉ *Off N51, Slane* ☎ *041/988–4477* 🌐 *slanecastle.ie* 🎫 *Castle €14, Distillery Tour from €20* 🕓 *Castle: closed Sept. 2–Feb., and Fri. and Sat. Mar.–Aug.*

Slane Hill

VIEWPOINT | North of Slane is the 500-foot-high Slane Hill, where St. Patrick proclaimed the arrival of Christianity in 433 by lighting the Paschal fire. From the top you have sweeping views of the Boyne Valley. On a clear day, the panorama stretches from Trim to Drogheda, a vista extending 40 km (25 miles). ✉ *Off N2, Slane* ✣ *1½ km (1 mile) northeast of Slane Castle.*

Restaurants

Brabazon Restaurant

$$$$ | **BISTRO** | Located in the cozy ground floor of a long stone outbuilding at Georgian Tankardstown House, this bistro-style eatery mixes country comfort with a touch of class. The set menu includes dishes like panfried quail breast with baked salsify, quail egg, and garlic and parsley puree. **Known for:** tasting menu; impressive gin menu; views of extensive gardens. $ *Average main:*

€70 ✉ *Tankardstown House, Rathkenny, Slane* ☎ *041/982–4621* 🌐 *www.tankardstown.ie/brabazon-restaurant.html* ⊗ *Closed Mon. and Tues. No dinner Sun. No lunch Wed. and Thurs.*

Hotels

★ **Tankardstown House**

$$$$ | **B&B/INN** | A sumptuous Georgian-era manor house with a classic walled garden and 80 acres of breathtaking parkland, no expense was spared in the loving restoration of what is often lauded as Ireland's best private house hotel. **Pros:** authentic Georgian exterior and interiors; idyllic setting; great restaurant. **Cons:** can only book three months in advance; limited facilities; cottages lack style of house rooms. $ *Rooms from: €290* ✉ *Slane* ✥ *2½ km (1½ mile) from gates of Slane Castle* ☎ *041/982–4621* 🌐 *tankardstown.ie* *7 rooms, 7 cottages* *Free Breakfast.*

Drogheda

15½ km (9 miles) east of Slane, 45 km (28 miles) north of Dublin.

Drogheda (pronounced "*dra*-he-da") is one of the most enjoyable and historic towns on the east coast of Ireland—and a setting for one of the most tragic events in Irish history, the siege and massacre wrought by Oliver Cromwell's English army. The town was colonized in 911 by the Danish Vikings; two centuries later, it was taken over by Hugh de Lacy, the Anglo-Norman Lord of Meath, who was responsible for fortifying the towns along the River Boyne. At first, two separate towns existed, one on the north bank, the other on the south. In 1412, already heavily walled and fortified, Drogheda was unified, making it the largest English town in Ireland. Today, 18th-century warehouses line the northern bank of the Boyne. The center of town, around West Street, is the historic heart of Drogheda.

GETTING HERE AND AROUND

Thanks to the M1 motorway, Drogheda is a 45-minute trip north of Dublin. Paid parking is available throughout the town. Bus Éireann operates express and regular service connecting Drogheda to Dundalk (30 minutes), Dublin (40 minutes), Navan (40 minutes), and Belfast (1 hour, 30 minutes), while Irish Rail connects the town to Hueston Station in Dublin (51 minutes), Belfast (1 hour, 40 minutes), and Dundalk (20 minutes) on the same line. The bus station is south of the river on the corner of John Street and Donore Road, and the train station is south of the river and east of the town center on the Dublin Road.

VISITOR INFORMATION

CONTACTS Drogheda Tourist Office. ✉ *The Tholsel, West St., Drogheda* ☎ *041/987–2843* 🌐 *drogheda.ie.*

Sights

Butler's Gate

HISTORIC SIGHT | One of the city's original 11 entrances, Butler's Gate predates St. Laurence's Gate by 50 years or more, making it one of the country's oldest surviving Norman urban structures. It's near the Drogheda Museum Millmount. ✉ *Off Mt. Saint Oliver, Millmount.*

★ **Drogheda Museum Millmount**

HISTORY MUSEUM | It was in Millmount that the townsfolk made their last stand against the bloodthirsty Roundheads of Cromwell. Perhaps in defiance of Cromwell's attempt to obliterate the town from the map, the museum contains relics of eight centuries of Drogheda's commercial and industrial past, including painted banners of the old trade guilds and a circular willow-and-leather coracle (the traditional fishing boat on the River Boyne). Most moving are the mementos of the infamous 1649 massacre of 3,000 people by Cromwell. The exhibit inside the Martello Tower, adjacent to the museum on the site of the old fort, focuses on the town's military history. The museum shares space in a renovated British Army barracks with several crafts workshops and other exhibitions including a re-created folk kitchen and a geological collection. ✉ *Off Mt. Saint Oliver, Millmount* ✣ *Off N1, south of Drogheda* ☎ *041/983–3097* 🌐 *droghedamuseum.ie* 🎫 *€6.*

St. Laurence's Gate

NOTABLE BUILDING | There were once 11 passages through the city walls, but the 13th-century St. Laurence's Gate is one of the last that remains. With two four-story drum towers, it's one of the most perfect examples in Ireland of a medieval town gate. ✉ *St. Laurence St., Drogheda.*

St. Peter's

CHURCH | A severe church within an enclosed courtyard, the 18th-century Anglican St. Peter's is rarely open except for Sunday services. It's worth a peek for its setting and for the fine views of the town from the churchyard. ✉ *Peter St. off Fair St., Drogheda* 🌐 *drogheda.armagh.anglican.org.*

St. Peter's Church

CHURCH | The Gothic Revival Roman Catholic St. Peter's Church houses the preserved head of St. Oliver Plunkett. Primate of all Ireland, he was martyred in 1681 at Tyburn in London; his head was pulled from the execution flames. ✉ *West St., Drogheda* 🌐 *saintpeters-drogheda.ie.*

Tholsel

BANK | This bank building has an 18th-century square granite edifice with a cupola. It now contains the tourist office. ✉ *West St. and Shop St., Drogheda.*

Victorian Railway Viaduct

BRIDGE | Among the town's landmarks is its long railway viaduct, which towers over the river. Built around 1850 as part of the railway line from Dublin to Belfast, it's still in use and is a splendid example of Victorian engineering. Its height above the River Boyne makes the viaduct Drogheda's most prominent landmark. ✉ *Drogheda* ✣ *Crosses Marsh Rd. on south side of river, and N. Strand on north side of river.*

Hotels

Boyne Valley Hotel and Country Club

$ | **B&B/INN** | Once owned by a Drogheda brewing family, this 19th-century mansion has been restored in period fashion with Neoclassical pillars, intricate plasterwork, and crystal chandeliers. **Pros:** great facilities; lovely grounds; renowned breakfast. **Cons:** newer building a touch functional; can attract a business crowd; some rooms can be noisy. 💲 *Rooms from: €128* ✉ *Dublin Rd., Drogheda* ☎ *041/983–7737* 🌐 *boyne-valley-hotel.ie* 🛏 *71 rooms* 🍽 *Free Breakfast.*

The D Hotel

$ | **HOTEL** | A dramatic location on the south bank of the Boyne easily makes up for the slightly functional exterior of this trendy hotel in the center of medieval Drogheda. **Pros:** dramatic riverside location; great value year-round; great terrace for people-watching. **Cons:** only some rooms have great views; restaurant is nothing special; attracts a business crowd. 💲 *Rooms from: €129* ✉ *Marsh Rd., Drogheda* ☎ *041/987–7700* 🌐 *thedhotel.com* 🛏 *111 rooms* 🍽 *Free Breakfast.*

Activities

GOLF

County Louth Golf Club

GOLF | How do they keep this links treasure such a secret? Covering 190 acres by the Irish Sea at the mouth of the River Boyne, this wonderful links course really has flown under the radar of the golfing world, which means smaller crowds in summer. Long hitters will love the atypical layout, a par-72 that features five par-5s, but beware the well-protected, undulating greens. ✉ *Off R167, Baltray* ✣ *8 km (5 miles) east of Drogheda* ☎ *041/988–1530* 🌐 *countylouthgolfclub.com* 🎟 *Nov.–Mar. Mon.–Fri. €100; Apr.–Oct. Mon.–Thurs. €220, Fri.–Sun. €240* ⛳ *18 holes, 6936 yards, par 72.*

Mellifont Abbey

10 km (8 miles) northwest of Drogheda.

On the eastern banks of the River Mattock, which creates a natural border between Counties Meath and Louth, lie the remains of Mellifont Abbey, the first Cistercian monastery in Ireland.

GETTING HERE AND AROUND

The abbey is a 13-km (8-mile) drive northwest of Drogheda off the R168. There is ample parking at the site. There is no public transport to the abbey, but you can get a taxi from Drogheda.

Sights

★ Mellifont Abbey

RUINS | Founded in 1142 by St. Malachy, Mellifont Abbey was inspired by the formal structure surrounding a courtyard of St. Bernard of Clairvaux's monastery, which St. Malachy had visited. Among the substantial ruins are the two-story chapter house, built in 12th-century English–Norman style and once a daily meeting place for the monks; it now houses a collection of medieval glazed tiles. Four walls of the 13th-century octagonal lavabo, or washing room, still stand, as do some arches from the Romanesque cloister. At its peak, Mellifont presided over almost 40 other Cistercian monasteries throughout Ireland, but all were suppressed by Henry VIII in 1539 after his break with the Catholic Church. Adjacent to the parking lot is a visitor center with a museum depicting the history of the abbey and the craftsmanship that went into its construction. ✉ *Off Old Mellifont Rd., off N2, Collon* 🌐 *heritageireland.ie/visit/places-to-visit/old-mellifont-abbey* 🎟 *€5* 🕒 *Visitor center closed late Aug.–late June.*

Dundalk

80 km (53 miles) north of Dublin.

Perfectly positioned as a hub to explore the region north and south of the border, Dundalk—only 9½ km (6 miles) from Northern Ireland—is the main town of County Louth, Ireland's smallest county. Its earliest settlement dates from the early Christian period, around the 7th century. In May the town hosts an avant-garde "fringe" drama and visual arts festival that includes a nice schedule of children's events.

GETTING HERE AND AROUND

From Dublin, take the M1 north and exit at junction 16 onto the roundabout. Take the first exit onto the N52 to Dundalk. Bus Éireann runs regular buses from Dublin to the town's bus station on Long Walk; the trip takes one hour and 30 minutes. Routes from Belfast and Drogheda also connect to Dundalk. Serviced by Irish Rail, Clarke Train Station is on Carrickmacross Road. There are daily trains from Dublin (1 hour, 20 minutes); Belfast (1 hour, 20 minutes); and Drogheda (20 minutes).

VISITOR INFORMATION

CONTACTS Dundalk Tourist Office. ✉ *Market Sq., Dundalk* ☎ *042/935–2111* 🌐 *dundalktown.ie.*

Sights

Bell Tower

NOTABLE BUILDING | This bell tower of a Franciscan monastery dates back to the 13th century. Keep an eye out for the lovely Gothic windows. ✉ *Mill St., Dundalk.*

Did You Know?

Ireland has more medieval, carved-stone High Crosses than any other European country, and an outstanding collection—lorded over by the 110-foot-high Round Tower and crowned by the 20-foot-high Muireadach Cross—is in the small, secluded village of Monasterboice, a former monastic settlement found on the road to Ardee.

County Museum Dundalk

HISTORY MUSEUM | Set in a beautifully restored 18th-century warehouse, this museum is dedicated to preserving the history of the dying local industries, such as beer brewing, cigarette manufacturing, shoe and boot making, and railway engineering. Other exhibits deal with the Irish in World War I, and the history of Louth from 7500 BC to the present, including Oliver Cromwell's shaving mirror. ✉ *Carroll Centre, Joycelyn St., Dundalk* ☎ *042/932–7056* 🌐 *louthcoco.ie/en/services/county-museum* 🎫 *€2* 🕑 *Closed Sun. and Mon.*

St. Patrick's Cathedral

CHURCH | Built between 1835 and 1847, this grand cathedral was designed when the Gothic Revival was at its height. With its buttresses and mosaics lining the chancel and the side chapels, it was modeled on the 15th-century King's College Chapel at Cambridge, England. The fine exterior was built in Newry granite, and the high altar and pulpit are of carved Caen stone. ✉ *Roden Pl., Dundalk* ☎ *042/933–4648* 🌐 *stpatricksdundalk.com.*

Restaurants

★ **Square Restaurant**

$$$ | **MODERN IRISH** | Award-winning young chef Conor Halpenny returned to his hometown to open this impressive little eatery right on the Market Square. The setting is simple and cozy, with a small room dominated by the big window looking out onto the bustling square. **Known for:** exceptional service; best food for miles around; great vegetarian options. 💲 *Average main: €27* ✉ *6 Market Sq., Dundalk* ☎ *042/933–7969* 🌐 *squarerestaurant.ie* 🕑 *Closed Mon.–Wed. No lunch.*

The Legendary Cuchulainn

The area around Dundalk is closely connected with Cuchulainn (pronounced "*coo*-chu-lain")—"a greater hero than Hercules or Achilles," as Frank McCourt, in *Angela's Ashes*, quotes his father. Cuchulainn, the warrior of the Irish epic *Táin Bó Cuailnge* (Cattle Raid of Cooley), heroically defended this area of ancient Ulster against invaders.

Hotels

Ballymascanlon House Hotel

$$$ | **HOTEL** | Just north of Dundalk, this Victorian mansion with a slightly severe but elegant modern addition sits on 130 acres on the scenic Cooley Peninsula. **Pros:** large guest rooms; discount golf for guests; good weekend deals. **Cons:** outside of town; in-room facilities sparse; sometimes crowded with wedding parties. 💲 *Rooms from: €225* ✉ *Off R173, 3 km (2 miles) north of Dundalk, Dundalk* ☎ *042/935–8200* 🌐 *ballymascanlon.com* *97 rooms* 🍽 *Free Breakfast.*

Innisfree House

$ | **B&B/INN** | An early-20th-century red-brick gem in the heart of Dundalk, Innisfree House is a shockingly good value considering the genteel, stylish atmosphere created by the beautiful Edwardian furniture and antiques throughout. **Pros:** afternoon tea in the cute tearoom; hearty breakfasts; warm and attentive staff. **Cons:** not in the most picturesque area; maybe a little overdecorated; short on facilities. 💲 *Rooms from: €125* ✉ *Carrickmacross Rd., Dundalk* ☎ *042/933–4912* 🌐 *innisfreehouse.ie* *9 rooms* 🍽 *Free Breakfast.*

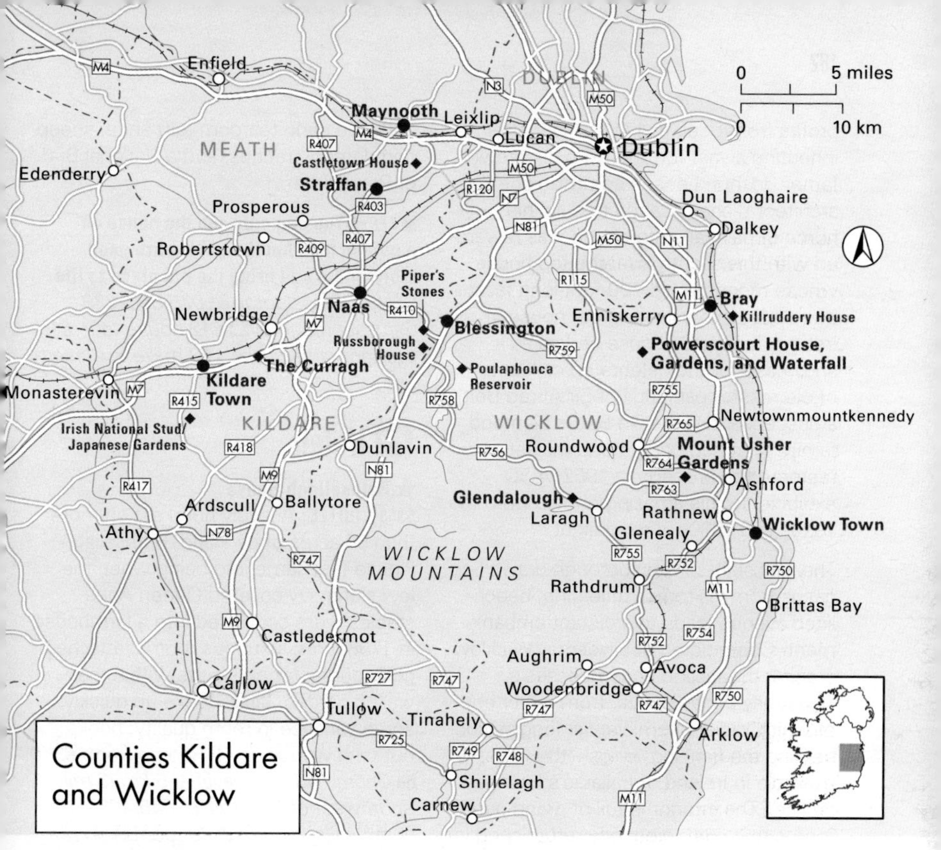

Blessington

23 km (14 miles) southwest of Dublin.

With its wide main street lined on both sides by tall trees and Georgian buildings, Blessington is one of the most charming villages in the area. It was founded in the late 17th century, and was a stop on the Dublin–Waterford mail coach service in the mid–19th century. Until 1932, a steam train ran from here to Dublin. Just outside the village are two of the marvels of Ireland: the 18th-century Russborough House and the adjacent Poulaphouca Reservoir.

GETTING HERE AND AROUND

You can reach Blessington by car from Dublin via the N81; the drive takes half an hour. Dublin Bus runs a daily service to Blessington.

 Sights

Poulaphouca Reservoir

BODY OF WATER | Known locally as the Blessington Lakes, Poulaphouca (pronounced "pool-a- *fook*-a") is a large, meandering reservoir that provides Dublin's water supply. You can drive around the entire perimeter of the artificial lake on minor roads; on its southern end lies Hollywood Glen, a particularly beautiful natural spot. The whole area is great for a walk or a picnic. ✉ *R758, Blessington* ✣ *6½ km (4 miles) southwest of Blessington* 🌐 *visitwicklow.ie.*

★ **Russborough House**

HISTORIC HOME | **FAMILY** | A conspicuously grand house rising seemingly in the middle of nowhere—actually the western part of County Wicklow—Russborough was an extravagance paid for by the profits from beer. In 1741, a year after inheriting a vast fortune from his brewer father, Joseph Leeson commissioned architect Richard Castle to build him a home of palatial stature, and was rewarded with this slightly over-the-top house, whose monumental 700-foot-long facade one-upped every other great house in Ireland. Today, the house serves as a showcase for the celebrated collection of old master paintings of Sir Alfred Beit, a descendant of the De Beers diamond family, who had bought and majestically restored the property in 1952. A 3D exhibition of his amazing photos from the 1920s and 1930s is a highlight.

The first sight of Russborough draws gasps from visitors: a mile-long, beech-lined avenue leads to a distant embankment. Constructed of silver-gray Wicklow granite, the facade encompasses a seven-bay central block, from either end of which radiate semicircular loggias connecting the flanking wings—the finest example in Ireland of Palladio's "winged device." The interior is full of grand period rooms that were elegantly refurbished in the 1950s under the eye of the legendary 20th-century decorator, Lady Colefax. The Hall is centered on a massive black Kilkenny marble chimneypiece and has a ceiling modeled after one in the Irish Parliament. Four 18th-century Joseph Vernet marine landscapes grace the glorious stucco moldings created to frame them in the Drawing Room. The grandest room, the Saloon, is famed for its 18th-century stucco ceiling by the Lafranchini brothers; fine old masters hang on walls covered in 19th-century Genoese velvet. The views out the windows take in the foothills of the Wicklow Mountains and the famous Poulaphouca Reservoir in front of the house. Kids will love getting lost in the huge hedge maze on the grounds and wandering the fairy trail. Additional attractions include a 200-acre park, tearoom, gift shop, sheepdog demonstrations, and a National Bird of Prey center.

TIP→ You can only see the house on a guided tour, but the guides are good storytellers and bring the old place to life. ✉ *N81, Blessington* ☎ *045/865–239* 🌐 *russborough.ie* *€12 house tour, €15 outdoor family ticket, €3 maze* ⏲ *Closed Jan.*

Hotels

★ Rathsallagh House

$$$$ | **HOTEL** | A lovely hotel set on more than 50 acres of parkland, Rathsallagh House first came into being when the low-slung, ivy-covered Queen Anne stables were converted into a farmhouse in 1798. **Pros:** luxurious rooms; attached golf course; tennis courts within the walled garden. **Cons:** books up quickly; some variance in room quality; books out with weddings. $ *Rooms from: €350* ✉ *Church Rd., Dunlavin* ✣ *5 km (3 miles) southwest of Dunlavin* ☎ *045/403–112* 🌐 *rathsallagh.com* *39 rooms* *Free Breakfast.*

Activities

HIKING

Church Mountain

HIKING & WALKING | You can take in splendid views of the Blessington Lakes from the top of Church Mountain, which you reach via a vigorous walk through Woodenboley Wood, at the southern tip of Hollywood Glen. Follow the main forest track for about 20 minutes, and then take the narrow path that heads up the side of the forest to the mountaintop for about another half hour. ✉ *R756, Blessington* ✣ *19 km (12 miles) southwest of Poulaphouca Reservoir.*

Bray

22 km (14 miles) south of Dublin on N11, 8 km (5 miles) east of Enniskerry on R755.

One of Ireland's oldest seaside resorts, Bray is known for its summer cottages and sand-and-shingle beach, which stretches for 2 km (1 mile). When the trains first arrived from Dublin in 1854, Bray became the number one spot for urban vacationers and subsequently took on the appearance of an English ocean-front town. Some Dubliners still flock to the faded glory of Bray's boardwalk to push baby carriages and soak up the sun. Uncrowded trails for hiking and mountain biking crisscross the mountains bordering Bray to the south.

GETTING HERE AND AROUND

From Dublin, take the N81 south to the M50 southbound. Exit onto the M11, and at junction 5 take the second exit at the roundabout to the R761 (signposted "Bray"). The drive takes about half an hour. The DART train runs regularly from Dublin to Bray, as do a number of city buses. There is plenty of parking around the town. St. Kevin's Bus from Dublin also stops in Bray.

Sights

★ Killruddery House

HISTORIC HOME | FAMILY | The 17th-century formal gardens at Killruddery House are precisely arranged, with fine beech hedges, Victorian statuary, and a parterre of lavender and roses. The Brabazon family, the earls of Meath, have lived here since 1618. In 1820 they hired William Morris to remodel the house as a revival Elizabethan mansion. The estate also has a Crystal Palace conservatory modeled on those at the botanic gardens in Dublin. Killruddery Arts organizes year-round events including an old-fashioned Easter egg hunt. You have to take one of the twice-daily tours to see the house itself, but the real draw is the gardens, which you are free to roam at your leisure. The teahouse in the old dairy is a perfect spot for a light snack and kids will love watching the sheep shearing and the chickens being fed on the adjoining farm. There's a wonderful farmers' market every Saturday. ✉ *Bray–Greystones Rd., Bray* ⊕ *3 km (2 miles) south of Bray, off R768* ☎ *01/286–3405* 🌐 *killruddery.com* 🎫 *Gardens €9, house and gardens €16* 🕑 *Closed Nov.–Mar. Closed Mon.*

National SEA LIFE

AQUARIUM | FAMILY | Dedicated to the creatures of the sea, National SEA LIFE emphasizes those that occupy the waters around Ireland. Besides massive tanks that contain all manner of swimming things, there are major conservation projects focusing on breeding seahorses and stingrays. The Tropical Shark Lagoon is always a thrill for kids. Touch-screen computers and video games give the place a high-tech feel. There are also regular feeding demonstrations during the day. In winter, call ahead to confirm opening times. ✉ *Strand Rd., Bray* ☎ *01/286–6939* 🌐 *visitsealife.com/bray* 🎫 *€15.*

Restaurants

★ The Hungry Monk

$$ | SEAFOOD | The cloisters-and-refectory-style decor is definitely tongue-in-cheek at this upbeat, fun restaurant in sleepy Greystones, an old-fashioned seaside resort a couple of miles south of Bray. Dinner is served by candlelight and the menu specializes in uncluttered seafood dishes in summer and wild game on cold winter nights. **Known for:** delicious seafood symphony; Wicklow game pie with champ potato; fun and friendly atmosphere. 💲 *Average main: €24* ✉ *1 Church Rd., Greystones* ☎ *01/287–5759* 🌐 *thehungrymonk.ie* 🕑 *Closed Mon. and Tues. No lunch Wed.–Sat.*

HIKING

Bray Head

HIKING & WALKING | A well-marked path leads from the beach to the 10-foot-tall cross that crowns the spiny peak of Bray Head, a rocky outcrop that rises 791 feet from the sea. The fairly difficult one-hour climb affords stunning views of Wicklow Town and Dublin Bay. ✉ *Bray* ✣ *South end of Bray, off Raheen Park.*

★ **Wicklow Way**

HIKING & WALKING | Devoted hikers come from all over the world to traverse the 137-km (85-mile) Wicklow Way, the first long-distance trail to open in Ireland, and still one of the best. Much of the route lies above 1,600 feet and follows rough sheep tracks, forest firebreaks, and old bog roads, so rain gear, windproof clothing, and sturdy footwear are essential. The trail starts in Marlay Park, just south of central Dublin, then ascends into the Wicklow mountain foothills, before passing glens, farms, and historic sights like Rathgall, home to the Kings of Leinster, and the Mill of Purgatory—a venerated "wardrobe" in Aghowle Church—before finishing up in Clonegal. If your feet are less than bionic, you can opt for any number of the short walks, or hop on a bike. ☎ *0404/45152* 🌐 *wicklowway.com.*

Powerscourt House, Gardens, and Waterfall

25 km (16 miles) south of Dublin on R117, 22 km (14 miles) north of Glendalough on R755.

One of the grandest estates and gardens in Ireland, Powerscourt is one of the main reasons that people head to Enniskerry. Within the shadow of the Great Sugar Loaf Mountain, Enniskerry remains one of the prettiest villages in Ireland. It's built around a sloping central triangular square with a backdrop of the wooded Wicklow Mountains. But the real draw is the majesty of Powerscourt.

GETTING HERE AND AROUND

Powerscourt is about a half-hour drive from Dublin. Head south from Dublin on the N81 to the M50 southbound. Take the exit for the M11, which becomes the N11; then take the R117 for Enniskerry and continue on to Powerscourt House and Gardens. You can also take the bus from Dublin to Enniskerry and walk the mile to Powerscourt. Alternatively, you can take the Irish Rail's DART train line from Dublin to Bray and then take Dublin Bus 185c (€1.80) to Powerscourt. Not all No. 185 buses go to Powerscourt, only the 185c buses; ask the driver whether you have the right bus.

Sights

★ **Powerscourt House & Gardens**

GARDEN | **FAMILY** | At more than 14,000 acres, including stunning formal gardens and a 400-foot waterfall, Powerscourt was truly one of the great houses of Ireland and Britain in its day. Unfortunately, you won't be able to see much of it. A terrible fire almost completely destroyed the house in 1974, cruelly on the eve of a huge party to celebrate the completion of a lengthy restoration. The original ballroom on the first floor—based on Palladio's version of the "Egyptian Hall" designed by Vitruvius, architect to Augustus, emperor of Rome—is the only room that still gives a sense of the place's former glory.

The real draw here is not the house but Powerscourt Gardens, considered among the finest in Europe. They were laid out from 1745 to 1767, following the completion of the house, and radically redesigned in the Victorian style from 1843 to 1875 by Daniel Robertson. The Villa Butera in Sicily inspired him to set these gardens with sweeping terraces, antique sculptures, and a circular pond and fountain flanked by winged horses. The grounds include many specimen trees (plants grown for exhibition), an avenue of monkey puzzle trees, a parterre of brightly colored summer flowers, and a Japanese garden. The kitchen gardens, with their modest rows of flowers, are a striking antidote to the classical formality of the main sections. A cute café, crafts and interior design shops, a garden center, and a children's play area are also in the house and on the grounds. Kids love Tara's Palace, a 22-room Georgian-style dollhouse. ✉ *Enniskerry* ✢ *Off R760* ☎ *01/204–6000* 🌐 *powerscourt.com* 🎫 *Gardens €13, waterfall €7, cool planet €11.*

Powerscourt Waterfall

WATERFALL | One of the most inspiring sights to the writers and artists of the Romantic generation, the 400-foot Powerscourt Waterfall is the highest in Ireland or Britain. ✉ *Enniskerry* ✢ *5 km (3 miles) south of Powerscourt Gardens* ☎ *01/204–6000* 🌐 *powerscourt.com* 🎫 *€7* ⏲ *Closed Dec. 11–25.*

Restaurants

Poppies Country Cooking

$ | **IRISH** | This cozy café—with a pine-panel ceiling, farmhouse furniture, and paintings of poppies on the walls—is a great place for breakfast, lunch, or late-afternoon tea. Expect potato cakes, shepherd's pie, lasagna, vegetarian quiche, house salads, and soups. **Known for:** farm-fresh produce; irresistible desserts; healthy choices. $ *Average main: €13* ✉ *The Square, Enniskerry* ☎ *01/282–8869* 🌐 *poppies.ie* ⏲ *No dinner.*

Sika

$$$$ | **FRENCH** | Local produce and stunning views are the stars of this hotel restaurant, with the Wicklow lamb a thrilling house specialty in season. Low ceilings give the very formal dining room a slightly overbearing feel, but floor-to-ceiling windows look out onto the serene Sugar Loaf mountain. **Known for:** wild game on menu; excellent service; great wine list. $ *Average main: €33* ✉ *Powerscourt Hotel, Powerscourt Estate, Enniskerry* ☎ *01/274–9377* 🌐 *powerscourthotel.com/dining/sika-restaurant-wicklow.*

Hotels

★ Powerscourt Hotel

$$$$ | **RESORT** | The gargantuan Palladian-style exterior of this Xanadu may seem out of place in the bucolic surroundings, but luxury always makes itself at home, and the views of the fabled Sugar Loaf peak outside the soaring windows are breathtaking. **Pros:** sumptuous pool and spa; excellent dining options; beautiful setting in Powerscourt grounds. **Cons:** over-the-top exterior is not for everyone; garden rooms don't have a great view; pricey even for the region. $ *Rooms from: €400* ✉ *Powerscourt Estate, Enniskerry* ☎ *01/274–8888* 🌐 *powerscourthotel.com* *194 rooms* *Free Breakfast.*

Activities

GOLF

★ Druids Glen Resort

GOLF | Known in golfing circles as the "Augusta of Europe," the beautiful Druids Glen Golf Course has hosted the Irish Open on four occasions since it opened in 1995. The wonderful landscaping and the extensive use of water in the layout explain the comparisons to the home of the Masters. It's essentially an American-style target course incorporating some delightful changes in elevation, and its forbidding, par-3 17th has an island green, like the corresponding hole at the Tournament Players Club at Sawgrass. A second course, Druids Heath, is a marvelous attempt to combine the best of links, heathland, and parkland golf. ✉ *Newtownmountkennedy* ☎ *01/287–3600* 🌐 *druidsglenresort.com* 🎫 *From €70* *Glen Course: 18 holes, 7046*

Did You Know?

While the palatial house of Powerscourt was devastated by fire after a 1974 renovation, its gardens remain as one of the finest examples of the Victorian style. Designed by the often-drunk Daniel Robertson, his creation remains a marvel of order cut from chaos. Nature, as if in approval, supplies the stunning backdrop of the famed Sugar Loaf Mountain.

yards, par 71; Heath Course: 18 holes, 7434 yards, par 71.

Powerscourt Golf Club
GOLF | This pair of courses is nestled in the foothills of the Wicklow Mountains on the grounds of the legendary 18th-century stately home and garden. Panoramic views to the sea and Sugar Loaf Mountain—and all those 200-year-old trees—give the impression that the course has been here for years. The older East Course is a parkland course, but some holes have certain links characteristics. The course's tiered greens test even the best golfers. The newer West Course is even more challenging and is designed with top-class tournament play in mind. ✉ *Enniskerry* ☎ *01/204–6033* 🌐 *powerscourtgolfclub.com* 🎫 *From €55* 🏌 *East Course: 18 holes, 7022 yards, par 72; West Course: 18 holes, 6938 yards, par 72.*

Glendalough

9 km (6 miles) southwest of Roundwood via R755 and R756.

One of Ireland's best monastic sites, Glendalough also has a stunningly photogenic lakeside setting. It's a popular destination for day trips.

GETTING HERE AND AROUND

If you're driving, consider taking the scenic route along the R115, but be prepared for awesome, austere mountain passes. Don't take this route if you're in a hurry—it takes about an hour and 45 minutes, compared to an hour on the N11—and don't expect a lot of signposting. Just concentrate on the nifty views.

St. Kevin's Bus has daily service between Dublin and Glendalough, with a stop in Bray. The trip takes 1½ hours. There is no direct train to Glendalough, but you can take the Irish Rail train from Dublin as far as Rathdrum (1 hour, 20 minutes) and then take a taxi (approximately €13) the 11 km (7 miles) from there to Glendalough.

Genius in a Bottle

Powerscourt's grand Victorian gardens were designed by an eccentric boozer, Daniel Robertson, who liked to be tooled around the gardens-in-progress in a wheelbarrow while taking nips from a bottle of sherry.

Sights

★ **Glendalough**
RUINS | Nestled in a lush, quiet valley deep in the rugged Wicklow Mountains, among two lakes and acres of windswept heather, Gleann dá Loch ("glen of two lakes") is one of Ireland's premier monastic sites. The hermit monks of early Christian Ireland were drawn to the Edenic quality of some of the valleys in this area, and this evocative settlement remains to this day a sight to calm a troubled soul. Stand here in the early morning (before the crowds and the hordes of students arrive), and you can appreciate what drew the solitude-seeking St. Kevin to this spot.

Probably the oldest building on the site, presumed to date from St. Kevin's time, is the Teampaill na Skellig (Church of the Oratory), on the south shore of the Upper Lake. A little to the east is St. Kevin's Bed, a tiny cave in the rock face, about 30 feet above the level of the lake, where St. Kevin lived his hermit's existence. It's not easily accessible; you approach the cave by boat, but climbing the cliff to the cave can be dangerous. At the southeast corner of the Upper Lake is the 11th-century Reefert Church, with the ruins of a nave and a chancel.

Even though it was destroyed by Viking raids and then disbanded as a monastery by the Reformation, medieval Glendalough remains magical and magnificent.

The ruins by the edge of the Lower Lake are the most important of those at Glendalough. The gateway, beside the Glendalough Hotel, is the only surviving entrance to an ancient monastic site anywhere in Ireland. An extensive graveyard lies within, with hundreds of elaborately decorated crosses, as well as a perfectly preserved six-story Round Tower. Built in the 11th or 12th century, it stands 100 feet high, with an entrance 25 feet above ground level. ✉ *Glendalough* ✣ *Visitor center car park off R757* ☎ *040/445–325* 🌐 *heritageireland.ie/visit/places-to-visit/glendalough-visitor-centre* 🎫 *Ruins free, visitor center €5.*

Hotels

Tudor Lodge

$ | **B&B/INN** | This 1990s lodge may not be genuine Tudor, but it's a wonderfully cozy and serene B&B only half a mile from the entrance to Glendalough. **Pros:** delicious breakfasts; has several self-catering log cabins; great hosts. **Cons:** not cheap for a B&B; limited facilities; books up quickly. $ *Rooms from: €116* ✉ *Tudor Lodge, R755, Glendalough* ✣ *3 km (2 miles) west of Glendalough visitor center* ☎ *040/445–554* 🌐 *tudorlodgeireland.com* ⏲ *Closed Jan.* 🛏 *8 rooms* 🍽 *Free Breakfast.*

Nightlife

Wicklow Brewery

BREWPUBS | Located a few miles southeast of Glendalough in Redcross, this little brewery and beer hall is the home of St. Kevin's Red Ale and a great place to hear traditional and folk music on the weekend. They also have regular tastings and you can call in advance to book a brewery tour. ✉ *Mick Finn's Pub, Redcross, Glendalough* ☎ *040/441–661* 🌐 *wicklowbrewery.ie.*

Roundwood

At 800 feet above sea level, Roundwood is the highest village in Ireland. It's also surrounded by spectacular mountain scenery. The Sunday afternoon market in the village hall, where cakes, jams, and other homemade goods are sold, livens up what is otherwise a sleepy place. From the broad main street, a minor road leads west for 8 km (5 miles) to two lakes, Lough Dan and Lough Tay, lying deep between forested mountains like Norwegian fjords.

Drive south from Dublin on the N81 to the M50 southbound, then take the exit for the M11, which becomes the N11. At junction 12, exit onto the R772 into Newtownmountkennedy. Turn right onto the R765 for Roundwood.

Mount Usher Gardens

18 km (11 miles) east of Glendalough via R755 and R763.

Close to both Ashford and Rathnew villages, these extensive gardens are a popular day trip from Dublin. The excellent café is run by Avoca, and shouldn't be missed on a visit here.

GETTING HERE AND AROUND

From Dublin, Mount Usher Gardens is less than an hour's drive. Take the N81 to the M50 southbound and exit onto the M11. At junction 15, exit onto the R772 to Ashford and turn left to the signposted Mount Usher Gardens. Bus Éireann runs regular service to Ashford from Dublin.

Sights

Mount Usher Gardens

GARDEN | Covering more than 20 acres on the banks of the River Vartry, the gardens were first laid out in 1868 by textile magnate Edward Walpole. Succeeding generations further planted and maintained the grounds, which today include more than 5,000 types of native and nonnative plants. The gardener has made the most of the riverside locale by planting eucalyptus, azaleas, camellias, and rhododendrons. The river is visible from nearly everywhere in the gardens; miniature suspension bridges bounce and sway underfoot as you cross the river. Near the entrance, you'll find a cluster of crafts shops (including a pottery workshop) as well as a country clothing shop and café. The twin villages of Ashford and Rathnew are to the south and east, and Newtownmountkennedy is to the north. ✉ *Ashford* ✣ *Off R772* ☎ *404/40205* 🌐 *mountushergardens.ie* 🎫 *€10.*

Hotels

★ Hunter's Hotel

$$ | **HOTEL** | On 2 acres of flower gardens (the Knot Garden is an award winner) beside the Vartry River, the beautiful Hunter's Hotel is the oldest coaching inn in Ireland. **Pros:** pleasing period atmosphere; enchanting gardens; fine restaurant. **Cons:** books up easily; limited amenities; bedrooms aren't huge. [$] *Rooms from: €190* ✉ *Newrath Bridge, Rathnew* ☎ *404/40106* 🌐 *hunters.ie* ⏲ *Closed Jan. and Feb.* 🛏 *16 rooms* 🍽 *Free Breakfast.*

Wicklow Town

26 km (16 miles) east of Glendalough, 51 km (32 miles) south of Dublin.

At the entrance to the attractive, tree-lined Main Street of Wicklow Town sprawl the extensive ruins of a 13th-century

Franciscan friary. Wicklow, from the Danish *wyking alo,* means "Viking meadow," testifying to the region's very ancient roots.

The streets of Wicklow ran with blood during the 1798 rebellion when Billy Byrne, member of a wealthy local Catholic family, led rebels from south and central Wicklow against the forces of the Crown. Byrne was eventually captured and executed at Gallow's Hill just outside town. There is a memorial to him in the middle of Market Square.

GETTING HERE AND AROUND

A 50-minute drive south on the N81 and then the N11/M11 takes you from Dublin straight into Wicklow Town. Parking is available throughout the town. There are also daily trains and buses from Dublin.

VISITOR INFORMATION

CONTACTS Wicklow Tourist Office. ✉ *Railto House, Fitzwilliam Sq., Wicklow* ☎ *040/469–117* 🌐 *visitwicklow.ie.*

Sights

Black Castle

RUINS | Immediately south of the harbor, perched on a promontory that has good views of the coastline, are the ruins of the Black Castle. This structure was built in 1169 by Maurice Fitzgerald, an Anglo-Norman lord who arrived with the English invasion of Ireland. The freely accessible ruins extend over a large area; with some difficulty, you can climb down to the water's edge. ✉ *Off South Quay, Wicklow Head.*

Friary

RUINS | Closed down during the 16th-century dissolution of the monasteries, the Friary is a reminder of Wicklow's stormy past, which began with the unwelcome reception given to St. Patrick on his arrival in AD 432. Inquire at the nearby priest's house to see the ruins. ✉ *Abbey St., N.W. corner of Wicklow Town, across road from Old Forge Pub, Wicklow* ☎ *040/467–196 for priest's house.*

St. Thomas Church

CHURCH | Between the River Vartry and the road to Dublin stands the Protestant church, which incorporates various unusual details: a Romanesque door, 12th-century stonework, fine pews, and an atmospheric graveyard. The church is topped by a copper, onion-shape cupola, added as an afterthought in 1771. ✉ *Church Hill, off Dublin Rd., Wicklow* 🌐 *wicklowchurchofireland.com* 🎫 *Free.*

Wicklow Harbour

BEACH | The town's most appealing area is Wicklow Harbour. Take South Quay down to the pier; Bridge Street leads you to a bridge across the River Vartry leading to a second, smaller pier at the northern end of the harbor. From this end, follow the shingle beach, which stretches for 5 km (3 miles); behind the beach is the Broad Lough, a lagoon noted for its wildfowl. ✉ *South Quay, Wicklow.*

Wicklow's Historic Gaol

JAIL/PRISON | **FAMILY** | Just above Market Square, the town's old jail has been converted into a museum and heritage center where it's possible to trace your genealogical roots. The "gruff gaoler" escorts you to your prison cell before computer displays, actors, and life-size models tell the gruesome history of the prison, from the 1798 rebellion to the late 19th century. The new "Gates of Hell" virtual reality experience adds an extra thrill. ✉ *Market Sq., Wicklow* ☎ *404/61599* 🌐 *wicklowshistoricgaol.com* 🎫 *Tour €12; Gates of Hell €17.*

Restaurants

★ The Strawberry Tree

$$$$ | **FRENCH** | Claiming to be Ireland's first "certified organic restaurant," this idyllic spot is tucked away in a rural valley as part of the BrookLodge Hotel. Dunmore East cod with dillisk and wild woodruff, and wood pigeon with crispy coppa and white tomato foam are part of the feast. **Known for:** offers a spectacular nine-course tasting menu; fantastic vegetarian options; great wine list. *$ Average main: €50 ✉ BrookLodge Hotel, Macreddin Rd., Macreddin ☎ 040/236–444 🌐 brooklodge.com ⏲ Closed Mon. and Tues. No lunch.*

Hotels

BrookLodge

$$$ | HOTEL | Located in a spectacular valley, 30 km (18 miles) from Wicklow Town, this serene country house has a get-away-from-it-all feel, but that doesn't mean it skimps on the luxury. **Pros:** great amenities; outstanding levels of service; excellent dining options. **Cons:** a little out of the way; can get very busy; popular with weddings. *$ Rooms from: €265 ✉ Off Aughrim Oaks Rd., Macreddin ☎ 040/236–444 🌐 brooklodge.com 86 rooms Free Breakfast.*

★ **Wicklow Head Lighthouse**

$$$$ | HOUSE | This 95-foot-high stone tower—first built in 1781—once supported an eight-sided lantern, and has been renovated by the Irish Landmark Trust as a delightfully quirky lodging. **Pros:** a photographer's dream location; pet-friendly; great for groups. **Cons:** a lot of stairs; books up quickly; minimum stay is two nights. *$ Rooms from: €370 ✉ Dunbar Head, Wicklow Head ☎ 01/670–4733 🌐 irishlandmark.com/property/wicklow-head-lighthouse 2 rooms No Meals.*

Maynooth

21 km (13 miles) west of Dublin.

Maynooth itself is a serene university town named for a pre-Christian king of Ireland. The mighty Fitzgerald family inherited the local manor in the 12th century and founded the original Catholic college. A few minutes south of the tiny Georgian town is the hamlet of Celbridge, official address to Ireland's largest country house, Castletown.

GETTING HERE AND AROUND

From Dublin take the N4/M4 in the direction of Galway/Sligo, then exit at junction 7 and take the R406 to Maynooth. The drive takes around half an hour. Dublin Bus serves Maynooth from Merrion Square in the city center, and there is a regular train service from Connolly Station in Dublin.

Sights

★ **Castletown House**

HISTORIC HOME | In 1722, William Conolly (1662–1729) decided to build himself a house befitting his new status as the speaker of the Irish House of Commons and Ireland's wealthiest man. On an estate 20 km (12 miles) southwest of Dublin, he began work on Castletown, designed in the latest Neoclassical fashion by the Florentine architect Alessandro Galilei. As it turns out, a young Irish designer and Palladian-style aficionado by the name of Sir Edward Lovett Pearce (1699–1733) was traveling in Italy, met Galilei, and soon signed on to oversee the completion of the house. Inspired by the use of outlying wings to frame a main building—the "winged device" used in Palladio's Venetian villas—Lovett Pearce added Castletown's striking colonnades and side pavilions in 1724. It is said that between them a staggering total of 365 windows were built into the overall design of the house. Conolly died before the interior of the house was completed, and work resumed in 1758 when his great-nephew Thomas and his 15-year-old wife, Lady Louisa Lennox, took up residence there. Little of the original furnishings remain today, but there is plenty of evidence of the ingenuity of Louisa and her artisans, chief among whom were the Lafranchini

Continued on page 198

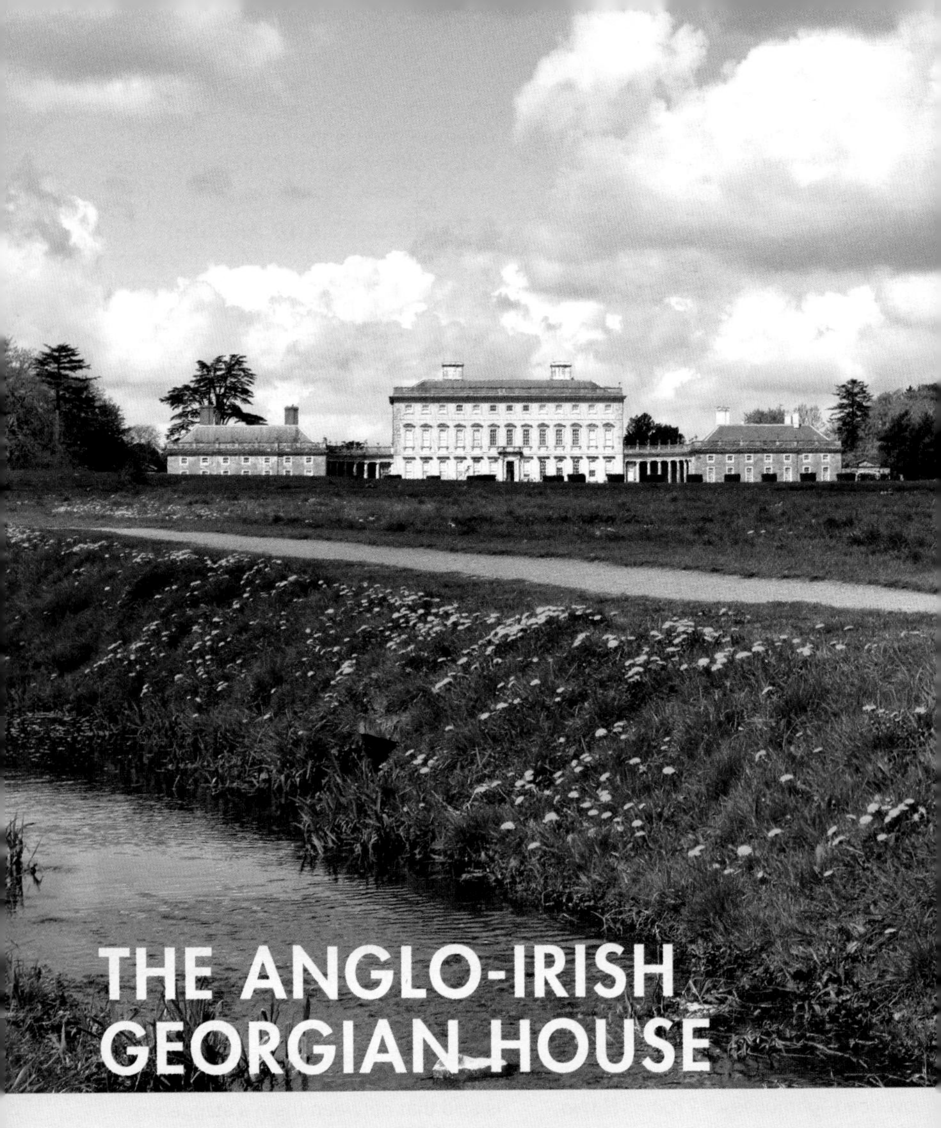

THE ANGLO-IRISH GEORGIAN HOUSE

For an up-close look at the lifestyles of the rich and famous, 18th-century style, nothing beats a visit to the great treasure houses of Castletown and Russborough. Set just a half-hour south of Dublin and located only 20 miles apart, they offer a unique peek through the keyhole into the extravagant world of Ireland's "Princes of Elegance and Prodigality."

Castletown House and its impressive grounds.

When the Palladian architectural craze swept across England, the Anglo-Irish—determined not to be outdone—set about building palaces in their own domain that would be the equal of anything in the mother country. Both Castletown House and Russborough House set new benchmarks in symmetry, elegance, and harmony for the Georgian style, which reigned supreme from 1714 to 1830 and was named after the four Georges who successively sat on the English throne. This style was greatly influenced by the villa designs of the 16th-century Italian architect Andrea Palladio.

Although Castletown remains the largest private house in Ireland, and Russborough has the longest façade of any domicile in the country, Georgian groupies know that the real treasures lie inside: ceilings lavishly worked in Italianate stuccowork, priceless Old Master paintings, and an intimate look at the glory and grandeur of the Anglo-Irish lords.

CASTLETOWN: A GEORGIAN VERSAILLES

Reputedly the inspiration for a certain building at 1600 Pennsylvania Avenue, Castletown remains the finest example of an Irish Palladian–style house.

In 1722, William Conolly (1662–1729) decided to build himself a house befitting his new status as the speaker of the Irish House of Commons and Ireland's wealthiest man. On an estate 20 km (12 miles) southwest of Dublin, he began work on Castletown, designed in the latest Neoclassical fashion by the Florentine architect Alessandro Galilei. As it turns out, a young Irish designer and Palladian aficionado by the name of Sir Edward Lovett Pearce (1699–1733) was traveling in Italy, met Galilei, and soon signed on to oversee the completion of the house. Inspired by the use of outlying wings to frame a main building—the "winged device" used in Palladio's Venetian villas—Lovett Pearce added Castletown's striking colonnades and side pavillons in 1724. It is said that between them a staggering total of 365 windows were built into the overall design of the house—legend has it that a team of four servants were kept busy year-round keeping them all clean.

Conolly died before the interior of the house was completed, and work resumed in 1758 when his great nephew Thomas, and more importantly, his 15-year-old wife, Lady Louisa Lennox, took up residence there. Luckily, Louisa's passion for interior decoration led to the creation of some of Ireland's most stunning salons, including the Print Room and the Long Gallery. Little of the original furnishings remain today, but there is plenty of evidence of the ingenuity of Louisa and her artisans, chief among whom were the Lafranchini brothers, master craftsmen who created the famous wall plasterwork, considered masterpieces of their kind. Rescued in 1967 by Desmond Guinness of the brewing family, Castletown was deeded to the Irish state and remains the headquarters for the Irish Georgian Society.

Above left: Castletown House facade
Above right: The family crest of William Conolly.

THE ENTRANCE HALL

Studded with 17th-century hunting scenes painted by Paul de Vos, this soaring white-on-white entryway showcases one of Ireland's greatest staircases. Also extraordinary are the walls festooned with plasterwork sculpted by the Brothers Lafranchini, famous for their stuccoed swags, flora, and portraits.

THE LONG GALLERY

Upstairs at the rear of the house, this massive room—almost 80 feet by 23 feet—is the most notable of the public rooms. Hued in a vibrant cobalt blue and topped by a coved ceiling covered with Italianate stuccowork and graced by three Venetian Murano glass chandeliers, it is a striking exercise in the antique Pompeian style.

THE PRINT ROOM

Smaller but even more memorable is the Print Room, the only example in Ireland of this elegant fad. Fashionable young women loved to glue black-and-white prints—here, looking like oversize postage stamps in a giant album—onto salon walls. This was the 18th-century forerunner of today's teens covering their walls with posters of rock-star icons.

Above left: The Grand Staircase. Upper right: 18th–century Italian engravings decorate the Print Room. Bottom right: A marble statue within the Long Gallery. Far right: Mahogony bureau made for Lady Louisa, circa 1760.

WHAT A WAY TO GO

"I do not get any idea of the beauty of my house if I live in it . . . only if I can gaze upon the house from far off," proclaimed Lady Louisa in 1821 of her beloved Castletown. In her late seventies, she had a tent built on the front lawn so she could study the house at her leisure. After one evening on the lawn she caught a chill and promptly died.

5 OTHER GREAT GEORGIAN HOUSES

Newbridge, County Dublin

Emo Court, County Laois

Westport House, County Mayo

Florence Court, County Fermanagh

Castle Coole, County Fermanagh

RUSSBOROUGH: A TEMPLE TO ART

An Irish Xanadu, Russborough House pulls out all the stops to achieve Palladian perfection.

Another conspicuously grand house rising seemingly in the middle of nowhere—actually the western part of County Wicklow—Russborough was an extravagance paid for by the wages of beer. In 1741, a year after inheriting a vast fortune from his brewer father, Joseph Leeson commissioned architect Richard Castle to build him a home of palatial stature, and was rewarded with this slightly over-the-top house, whose monumental 700-foot-long façade one-upped every other great house in Ireland. Following Castle's death, the project was taken over and completed by his associate, Francis Bindon. Today, the house serves as a showcase for the celebrated collection of Old Master paintings of Sir Alfred Beit, a descendant of the De Beers diamond family, who had bought and majestically restored the property in 1952.

PRINCELY MAGNIFICENCE

The first sight of Russborough draws gasps from visitors: a mile-long, beech-lined avenue leads to a distant embankment on which sits the longest house frontage in Ireland. Constructed of silver-gray Wicklow granite, the façade encompasses a seven-bay central block, from either end of which radiate semicircular loggias connecting the flanking wings—the finest example in Ireland of Palladio's "winged device."

The interiors are full of grand period rooms that were elegantly refurbished in the 1950s by their new, moneyed owner under the eye of the legendary 20th-century decorator, Lady Colefax. The Hall is centered around a massive black Kilkenny marble chimneypiece and has a ceiling modeled after one in the Irish Parliament. Four 18th-century Joseph Vernet marine landscapes—once missing but found by Sir Alfred—once again grace

Top left: A look at the 700–foot façade of Russborough House. Bottom left: The grand Saloon. Above right: The Hall. Opposite, top: Drawing Room. Opposite: Vermeer's *Lady Writing a Letter.*

the glorious stucco moldings created to frame them in the Drawing Room. The grandest room, the Saloon, is famed for its 18th-century stucco ceiling by the Lafranchini brothers; fine Old Masters hang on walls covered in 19th-century Genoese velvet. The views out the windows take in the foothills of the Wicklow Mountains and the famous Poulaphouca reservoir in front of the house.

VERMEER, DIAMONDS, AND GANGSTERS

If it can be said that beer paid for the house, then diamonds paid for the paintings. Russborough House is today as famed for its art collection—and the numerous attempts, some successful, to steal it—as for its architecture. Credit for this must go to Sir Alfred Beit (1903—1994), nephew of the cofounder of De Beers Diamonds. One evening in 1974 while Alfred was enjoying a quiet dinner with his wife, the door burst open and in marched Rose Dugdale, an English millionaire's daughter turned IRA stalwart. Her gang "liberated" 19 of the Beit masterpieces, including Vermeer's fabled *Lady Writing a Letter*, hopefully to bargain for the release of two IRA members jailed in London. Once the paintings were recovered a week later, Sir Alfred decided to donate 17 works to the National Gallery of Ireland. Alas, a week before the handing-over ceremony in 1986, Sir Alfred and his wife were again settling down to dine when in marched Martin Cahill, a.k.a. "The General," Dublin's most notorious underworld boss (and subject of three major movies). He made off with the Vermeer and 16 other paintings. They were returned and now sit safely (we hope) in the National Gallery.

STUCCADORES

Sounds better than plaster-workers, no? Baroque exuberance reigns in the house's lavishly ornamented plasterwork ceilings executed by celebrated stuccadores the Brothers Lafranchini, who originally hailed from Switzerland and worked in other great houses in Ireland, including Castletown. Their decorative flair adorns the Music Room and Library, but even these pale compared to the plasterwork done by an unknown artisan in the Staircase Hall—an extravaganza of whipped-cream moldings, cornucopias, and Rococo scrolls: "the ravings of a maniac," according to one 19th-century critic, who guessed that only an Irishman would have had the blarney to pull it off.

Reputedly the inspiration for a certain building at 1600 Pennsylvania Avenue, Castletown remains the finest example of the Irish Palladian-style house.

brothers, master craftsmen who created the famous wall plasterwork, considered masterpieces of their kind. ✉ *Celbridge* ✣ *Exit 6 off M4* ☎ *01/628–8252* 🌐 *castletown.ie* 🎫 *€10* 🕒 *Closed mid-Dec.–Feb.; Nov.–mid-Dec. closed Mon. and Tues.*

Restaurants

★ Aimsir

$$$$ | **IRISH** | This new sensation of Irish cuisine was awarded not one but two Michelin stars only months after it opened. It didn't come as a surprise to those in the know, with the husband-and-wife team of Jordan and Majken Bech Bailey both having worked in some of Europe's most feted eateries. **Known for:** unique nonalcoholic pairing menu (as well as wine, beer, and cider pairings); impeccable service; bucket-list dining experience with 18 small courses. 💲 *Average main: €220* ✉ *Cliff at Lyons, Lyons Rd., Celbridge* ☎ *01/630–3500* 🌐 *aimsir.ie* 🕒 *Closed Sun.–Tues. No lunch.*

Bistro 53

$ | **ITALIAN** | **FAMILY** | This cozy, affordable eatery right on main street has quickly established itself as a favorite with the locals. Exposed beams and leather banquettes create the bistro setting, but the menu is more Italian inspired than French. **Known for:** generous portion sizes; great selection of vegetarian menu items; warm, friendly atmosphere. 💲 *Average main: €18* ✉ *53 Main St., Maynooth* ☎ *01/628–9001* 🌐 *bistro53.ie.*

Hotels

★ Cliff at Lyons

$$$$ | **HOTEL** | The team from the celebrated Cliff House in Ardmore have brought their modern Irish style to bear at this carefully restored tiny village of 18th-century buildings in the rolling Kildare countryside, a half hour from Dublin. **Pros:** Michelin-starred Aimsir restaurant on-site; excellent room amenities; historic and serene setting. **Cons:** rooms vary; restaurant is very popular and books up quickly; popular wedding venue.

Rooms from: €380 Cliff at Lyons, Lyons Rd., Celbridge 01/630–3500 cliffatlyons.ie 38 rooms No Meals.

Activities

GOLF

Carton House Golf Club

GOLF | This just-outside-of-Dublin estate has quickly become one of the brightest stars in the Irish golfing universe. The parkland Mark O'Meara course makes use of the estate's rolling hills, specimen trees, and the River Rye. The stretch of the 14th, 15th, and 16th holes is a highlight: a pair of classy par-3s wrapped around a heroic par-5. The second 18 holes, created by Colin Montgomerie, are an inland links–style course that is flatter and virtually treeless. There's a good mix of long par-4s backed up with tricky short ones. Recessed pot bunkers lie in wait to pick up off-line shots. *Off R148, Maynooth 01/651–7720 cartonhouse.com/golf May–Sept., from €120; Oct.–Apr., from €60 O'Meara Course: 18 holes, 7006 yards, par 72; Montgomerie Course: 18 holes, 7301 yards, par 72.*

Straffan

5 km (3 miles) southwest of Castletown House, 25½ km (16 miles) southwest of Dublin.

Its attractive location on the banks of the River Liffey and the Kildare Hotel and Country Club—where Arnold Palmer designed the K Club, one of Ireland's most renowned 18-hole golf courses—are what make Straffan so appealing.

GETTING HERE AND AROUND

To get here by car from Dublin, take the N4/M4 toward Galway and exit at junction 7 to the R406 (toward Naas). At the roundabout take the second exit onto Barberstown Road (signposted "Straffan"). Bus Éireann runs a regular service here from Dublin.

Sights

The Steam Museum

OTHER MUSEUM | This museum covers the history of Irish steam engines, handsome machines used both in industry and agriculture—for churning butter or threshing corn, for example. There's also a fun collection of model locomotives. Engineers are present on "live steam days" every Sunday and on bank holidays. The adjoining Lodge Park Walled Garden is included in the price and is open year-round for a leisurely summer stroll. *Lodge Park, off Baberstown Rd., Straffan 01/627–3155 steam-museum.com €8 Closed Oct.–Apr.; June–Aug., closed Mon.–Thurs.; May and Sept., closed weekdays.*

Hotels

Barberstown Castle

$$$ | HOTEL | With a 13th-century castle keep at one end, an Elizabethan section in the middle, a large Georgian country house at the other end, and a modern wing, Barberstown Castle represents 750 years of Irish history. **Pros:** welcoming and attentive staff; 20 acres of serene gardens; real fires in public spaces. **Cons:** prices a little inflated; popular wedding venue; newer wings have less charm. *Rooms from: €240 Baberstown Rd., Straffan 01/628–8157 barberstowncastle.ie 55 rooms Free Breakfast.*

★ **The K Club**

$$$$ | RESORT | Manicured gardens and the renowned Arnold Palmer–designed K Club golf course surround this mansard-roof country mansion. **Pros:** restaurant has one of Ireland's finest wine cellars; luxurious spa; championship golf course. **Cons:** attracts golf crowd; rooms vary in quality; can get very busy in summer. *Rooms from: €450 Off Baberstown Rd., Straffan 01/601–7200* *kclub.ie 69 rooms, 23 apartments Free Breakfast.*

GOLF

★ The K Club

GOLF | "Home to the 2006 Ryder Cup" says all a golfer needs to know about the pedigree of the K Club. The Ryder Cup Course (formerly the Palmer Course) was designed by the legendary Arnold Palmer, and offers a round of golf in lush, wooded surroundings bordered by the River Liffey. The generous fairways and immaculate greens are offset by formidable length, which makes it one of the most demanding courses in the Dublin vicinity. The Smurfit Course is essentially an inland links course. The signature 7th hole wows visitors with its water cascades and rock-quarry feature. *Kildare Country Club, off Baberstown Rd., Straffan 01/601–7321 kclub.ie May–Sept. €250; Nov.–Mar. €120; Apr. and Oct. €180 Ryder Cup Course: 18 holes, 7350 yards, par 72; Smurfit Course: 18 holes, 7277 yards, par 72.*

Naas

13 km (8 miles) south of Straffan, 30 km (19 miles) southwest of Dublin.

The seat of County Kildare and a thriving market town in the heartland of Irish Thoroughbred country, Naas (pronounced "nace") is full of pubs with high stools where short men (apprentice jockeys) discuss the merits of their various stables.

GETTING HERE AND AROUND

To get here from Dublin, take the N81 to the N7 toward Limerick. Exit at junction 9 to the R445 (signposted Naas). The drive takes about 35 minutes. Bus Éireann runs a regular service from Dublin. Parking is available throughout the town.

Restaurants

Las Radas

$$ | **WINE BAR** | Experienced foodies Jules and Joanne Bradbury have taken a creative approach to tapas adding local flavor to their Moorish-inspired, brightly decorated bar and restaurant. Tapas choices include wonderful sweet potatoes with truffle mayo and cheese, and roasted red peppers stuffed with salmon and crab. **Known for:** excellent separate vegan and vegetarian menu; lively atmosphere; decadent desserts. *Average main: €24 New Row, Naas 045/879–978 lasradas.ie Closed Mon. and Tues. No lunch.*

HORSE RACING

Punchestown Racecourse

HORSE RACING | A wonderful setting amid rolling plains distinguishes the Punchestown Racecourse, with the Wicklow Mountains providing a spectacular backdrop. Horse races are held regularly, but the most popular event is the Punchestown National Hunt Festival in April, a real pilgrimage for fans of steeplechase racing. *R411, Naas 3 km (2 miles) south of Naas 045/897–704 punchestown.com.*

The Curragh

8 km (5 miles) southwest of Naas, 25½ km (16 miles) west of Poulaphouca Reservoir.

The broad plain of the Curragh, bisected by the main N7 road, is the biggest area of common land in Ireland, encompassing about 31 square km (12 square miles) and devoted mainly to grazing.

Restaurants

Dubh Cafe
$$ | **MODERN IRISH** | This little foodie gem at the center of Newbridge takes casual lunch to a whole new level. Try the outrageously good kimchi fried chicken sandwich with phat boy mayo, coriander, carrot, pickled red onion, and baby gem lettuce all on toasted Irish batch bread. **Known for:** hearty breakfast baps; warm and friendly atmosphere; delicious pastries and excellent coffee. *Average main: €23* *10 Georges St., Newbridge* *085/766–7911* *wearedubh.ie* *Closed Mon and Tues. No dinner Sun.*

Activities

HORSE RACING

★ Curragh Racecourse
HORSE RACING | A day out at the Curragh, especially on Derby day, is an Irish summer ritual. The area is Ireland's major racing center, and the Curragh Racecourse is its main showplace. It's a flat racing mecca for enthusiasts from all over the world, and the Irish Derby and other international horse races are run here. *N7, Naas* *045/441–205* *curragh.ie* *€20.*

Kildare Town

5 km (3 miles) west of the Curragh, 51 km (32 miles) southwest of Dublin.

Horse breeding is the cornerstone of County Kildare's thriving economy, and Kildare Town is the place to come if you're crazy about horses. But, in addition to all things equine, Kildare boasts other stellar attractions, including the famous Japanese Gardens.

GETTING HERE AND AROUND

Kildare Town is about 45 minutes from Dublin; take the N81 south to the N7/M7, exit at junction 13, and take the third exit at the roundabout to the R415 (signposted "Kildare"). Parking is available throughout the town. Kildare Town is a major junction stop for Irish Rail, which has trains to Dublin (45 minutes), Cork (2 hours, 25 minutes), Limerick (1 hour, 45 minutes), and Galway (2 hours).

VISITOR INFORMATION

CONTACTS Kildare Tourist Office. *Heritage Centre, Market Sq., Kildare* *045/521–240* *intokildare.ie.*

Sights

Irish National Stud
FARM/RANCH | If you're a horse aficionado, or even just curious, check out this stud farm, a main center of Ireland's racing industry. The Stud was founded in 1900 by brewing heir Colonel William Hall-Walker. It's here that breeding stallions are groomed, exercised, tested, and bred. Spring and early summer, when mares have foals, are the best times to visit. The **National Stud Horse Museum,** also on the grounds, recounts the history of horses in Ireland. Its most outstanding exhibit is the skeleton of Arkle, the mighty Irish racehorse that won major victories in Ireland and England during the late 1960s. The museum also contains medieval evidence of horses, such as bones from 13th-century Dublin, some early examples of equestrian equipment, and "Living Legends" or recently retired equine stars of the racing game. *Tulley Rd., Kildare* *1½ km (1 mile) south of Kildare Town* *045/521–617* *irishnationalstud.ie* *€17, includes Japanese Gardens* *Closed Jan.–mid-Feb.*

Japanese Gardens
GARDEN | Adjacent to the Irish National Stud, the Japanese Gardens were created between 1906 and 1910 by the horse breeder's founder, Colonel Hall-Walker, and laid out by a Japanese gardener, Tassa Eida, and his son Minoru. Although quite small and cramped, the gardens are recognized as among the finest Asian gardens in the world, although they're

more of an East–West hybrid than authentically Japanese. The Scots pines, for instance, are an appropriate stand-in for traditional Japanese pines, which signify long life and happiness. The gardens symbolically chart the human progression from birth to death, although the focus is on the male journey. ✉ *Tully Rd., Kildare* ✣ *About 2½ km (1½ miles) south of Kildare Town* ☎ *045/521–617* 🌐 *irishnationalstud.ie* 🎫 *€17, includes Irish National Stud* ⏲ *Closed Jan.–mid-Feb.*

Round Tower

MILITARY SIGHT | The 108-foot-high Round Tower, dating from the 12th century, is the second-highest in Ireland (the highest is in Kilmacduagh in County Galway). Extraordinary views across much of the Midlands await if you're energetic enough to climb to the top. ✉ *St. Brigid's Cathedral, off Market Sq.* ☎ *045/521–229* 🎫 *€6* ⏲ *Closed Oct.–Apr.*

St. Brigid's Cathedral

CHURCH | The Church of Ireland St. Brigid's Cathedral is where the eponymous saint founded a religious settlement in the 5th century. The present cathedral, with its stocky tower, is a restored 13th-century structure. It was partially rebuilt around 1686, but restoration work wasn't completed for another 200 years. The stained-glass west window of the cathedral depicts three of Ireland's greatest saints: Brigid, Patrick, and Columba. ✉ *Off Market Sq., Kildare* 🌐 *kildare.ie* 🎫 *€2* ⏲ *Closed Oct.–Apr.*

Restaurants

★ The Green Barn

$$$ | **MODERN IRISH** | **FAMILY** | Look out the floor-to-ceiling windows and see the veggies that you're about to eat growing in front of you at this family-run, organic restaurant in a revamped barn on the rolling grounds of gorgeous Burtown House. Seasonal and homegrown are the buzzwords on the small, ever-changing menu, where Irish beef ribs with sautéed Savoy cabbage and herb mash is melt-in-the-mouth perfect. **Known for:** stunning setting; family-friendly junior menu; heated outdoor dining. 💲 *Average main: €27* ✉ *Burtown House, Kildare* ☎ *059/862–3865* 🌐 *burtownhouse.ie* ⏲ *Closed Mon. and Tues., and Jan. No dinner Wed.–Thurs. and Sun.*

Hotels

Keadeen Hotel

$$ | **HOTEL** | **FAMILY** | The luxurious spa and health center are the big attractions at this family-owned hotel on 10 acres of flower-filled gardens. **Pros:** very family-friendly; gorgeous Atrium cocktail lounge; welcoming and attentive staff. **Cons:** uninspired architecture; crowded with weddings; can feel very busy at times. 💲 *Rooms from: €190* ✉ *Off Ballymany, Newbridge* ☎ *045/431–666* 🌐 *keadeenhotel.ie* 🛏 *71 rooms* 🍽 *Free Breakfast.*

Chapter 5

THE MIDLANDS

Updated by
Alexandra Pereira

Sights	Restaurants	Hotels	Shopping	Nightlife
★★★★★	★★★★☆	★★★☆☆	★★☆☆☆	★★☆☆☆

WELCOME TO THE MIDLANDS

TOP REASONS TO GO

★ **Clonmacnoise:** Atmospheric and still seemingly spirit-warmed, this great early Christian monastery survived Viking, Norman, and English invaders over the centuries.

★ **Stately Houses:** While known for its rich farmlands, the Midlands is also home to stately homes and gardens, including fairy-tale Tullynally Castle, Charleville Castle, and Birr Castle.

★ **Hiking the Riverside and Slieve Bloom Mountains:** Dip in and out of Blue Trails along the Shannon River or the 32-km (20-mile) Slieve Bloom Trail, ideal hiking country for those with a yen to rise above their surroundings.

★ **Athlone:** The restored 13th-century castle along with the quirky shops and Europe's oldest pub are worth taking time to visit, as is the Luan Gallery.

★ **Cruise the River Shannon:** The longest river in both Ireland and Britain is a veritable playground for cruisers meandering through locks and quays from County Cavan to the Atlantic Ocean.

Perfect for the relaxed visitor who values the subtle over the spectacular, the flat, fertile plain at the center of Ireland is teeming with underrated historic towns, abbey ruins, and grand houses.

1 Abbeyleix. An elegant tree-lined town with original shop facades and Georgian stone homes.

2 Portlaoise. The busy county town of Laois boasts historic architecture and stands at a crossroads linking major cities.

3 Portarlington. A delightful riverside town set amid rich agricultural hinterland.

4 Tullamore. A vibrant place and county seat of Offaly noted for its whiskey.

5 Kilbeggan. A small town founded on a 6th-century monastery and the home of another major whiskey distiller.

6 Mullingar. One of the biggest towns in Westmeath, pleasantly situated on the Grand Canal.

7 Castlepollard. A village laid out around a triangular green and renowned for its colorful shop fronts.

8 Fore. Lying in a valley between two hills, the village is a bona fide example of an early Christian settlement.

9 Longford Town. A market town known for its literary associations and its historic cathedral restored after being destroyed by fire.

10 Anthony Trollope Trail. A trail with 27 locations celebrating the English author who introduced pillar boxes to Ireland.

11 Athlone. A thriving town on the River Shannon, its imposing castle is a major attraction.

12 Clonmacnoise. One of Ireland's most important ecclesiastical sites set in an atmospheric landscape.

13 Boyle. A small, hilly town at the base of Curlew Mountains near Lough Key.

14 Banagher. A small crossroads town on the river with a lively marina.

15 Birr. An outstanding heritage town dating from the 6th century where exquisite Georgian buildings are the main feature.

16 Roscrea. The past is all around you in this Tipperary town of ancient castles, towers, and churches.

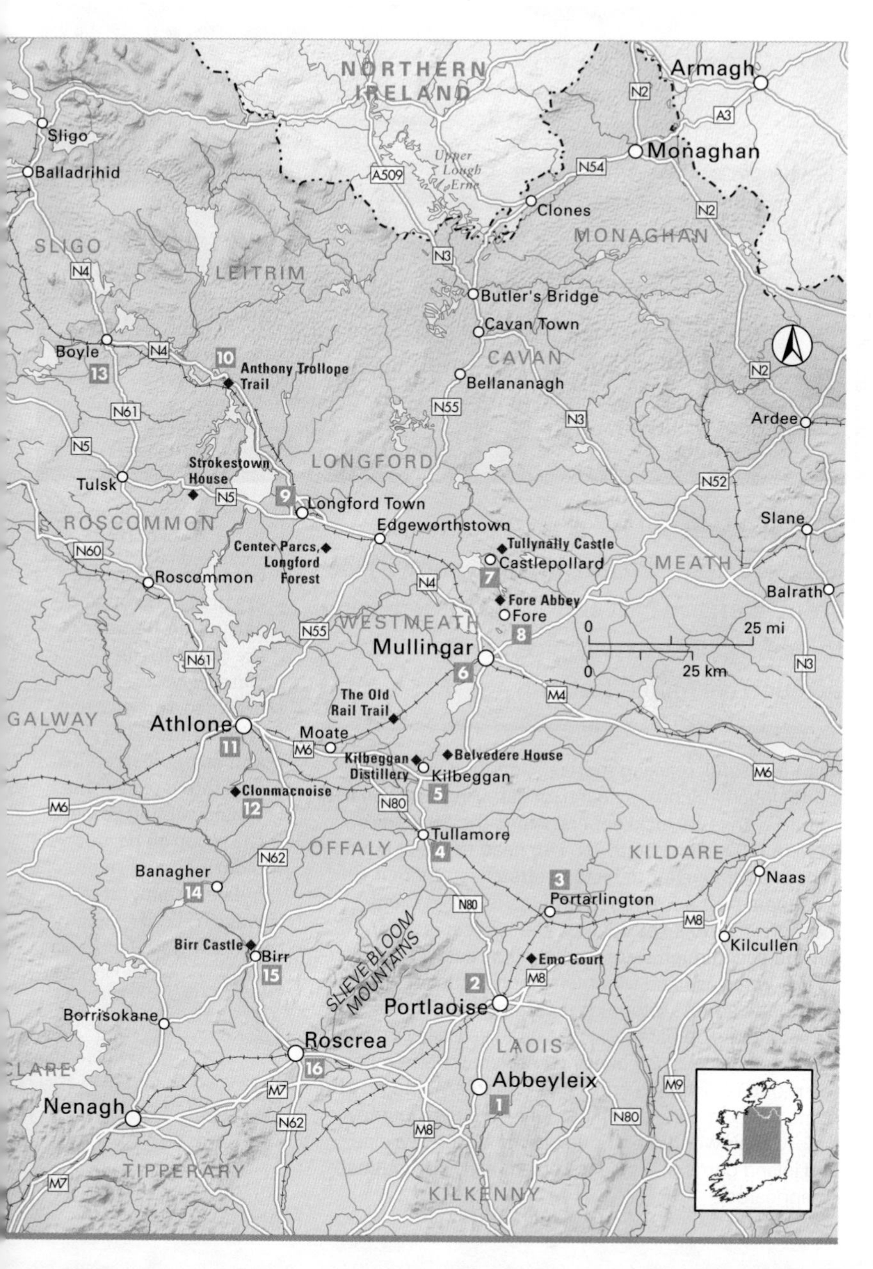
NORTHERN IRELAND
Armagh
Sligo
Balladrihid
Monaghan
Upper Lough Erne
A509
N54
N2
A3
Clones
MONAGHAN
SLIGO
LEITRIM
N4
N3
Butler's Bridge
Cavan Town
CAVAN
Boyle
13
10
Anthony Trollope Trail
Bellananagh
N55
N61
N5
Ardee
Strokestown House
LONGFORD
Tulsk
9
Longford Town
N52
ROSCOMMON
Edgeworthstown
Slane
N60
Center Parcs, Longford Forest
Tullynally Castle
Castlepollard
7
MEATH
Roscommon
Balrath
Fore Abbey
Fore
8
WESTMEATH
0
25 mi
25 km
Mullingar
6
The Old Rail Trail
M4
GALWAY
Athlone
11
Moate
M6
Kilbeggan Distillery
Belvedere House
Kilbeggan
5
Clonmacnoise
12
N80
Tullamore
4
OFFALY
KILDARE
N62
Banagher
14
3
Portarlington
Naas
M8
Kilcullen
Birr Castle
Birr
15
SLIEVE BLOOM MOUNTAINS
Emo Court
2
Portlaoise
Borrisokane
Roscrea
LAOIS
16
CLARE
Abbeyleix
1
M9
M7
Nenagh
TIPPERARY
KILKENNY

CRUISING ON THE SHANNON

A great vacation along the Shannon River

Whether you opt for a one-hour or one-week journey, cruising privately or with a group along the River Shannon is a never-to-be-forgotten experience, giving a new perspective on old Ireland.

Picture blissful, relaxing mornings on the river, mooring for lunch at a quayside inn, or sampling traditional culture with jovial lockkeepers. Along the Shannon's 334-km (207-mile) length you can head to major boating hubs like Athlone, or to historic stretches where it meanders past ancient settlements (such as Clonmacnoise), or to lakes aplenty. The biggest is Ireland's "inland sea," Lough Derg, bordered by easygoing villages like Terryglass and Mountshannon that offer appealingly quiet streets, stone-built cottage restaurants, and rustic harborside bars with picnic tables (many with evening music or Irish dancing sessions). Remember, the motto of Shannon cruising is "There's no hurry": the boats travel at only 11 kph (7 mph), so a river journey is a slow affair with time to drink in the history, wildlife, and inland gems of an older Ireland many thought had disappeared.

WHEN TO GO

Good times to cruise are in May through early June. Rentals are cheaper, the waterways are less crowded, the weather is generally favorable, and daylight stretches well into late evening. Whenever you go, get the scoop on permits, moorings, and river bylaws from Waterways Ireland (🌐 *www.waterwaysireland.org*).

A WONDERFUL DAY ON THE WATER

On the map, the scale of the Shannon may look daunting, but that's one reason many people opt for an idyllic daylong exploration. If you only have time for a short guided journey, then one of the best is upriver from Athlone to Lough Ree on a three-hour trip on board the signature *Viking* boat (€15–€20). Or opt to go downriver to magnificent Clonmacnoise. You can also board pleasure cruisers at Killaloe and Dromineer. If you're feeling romantic, try an evening cruise with the Moon River company, which operates a 100-seater from Carrick-on-Shannon.

Killaloe River Cruises ✉ *The Quay, Lakeside Dr., Killaloe* ☎ *086/814–0559* 🌐 *www.killaloerivercruises.com* 🎟 *€15.*

Moon River ✉ *Marina, Carrick-on-Shannon waterfront* ☎ *071/962–1777* 🌐 *www.moonriver.ie.*

Silver Line Cruisers ✉ *The Marina, Banagher* ☎ *057/915–1112* 🌐 *www.silverlinecruisers.com.*

Viking Ship Cruises ✉ *The Quay at Athlone Castle, Athlone* ☎ *086/262–1136* 🌐 *www.vikingtoursireland.ie* 🎟 *€25.*

Many travelers opt to boat 'n' bike downriver to the boating hub of Athlone.

Ireland's "inland sea," Lough Derg

GOING WITH THE SHANNON FLOW

As the Shannon has its own slow pace, why not consider your own boat hire? The beauty of a personal cruise is that you can concoct your own itinerary, moving at your own speed and stopping off where the notion takes you.

There are four main boating towns for hiring cruisers: Carrick-on-Shannon, Portumna, Banagher, and Williamstown. From luxury cabin cruisers to barges or smaller boats, a glittering array of vessels is available for rent. Prices range from €700 for a two- to four-berth cruiser for one week in the quieter off-season, and from €1,650 in the summer. With most companies, you can also rent for three-night/four-day short breaks. In addition to guided tours, Silver Line Cruisers offers boat rentals.

Carrick Craft ✉ *The Marina, Carrick-on-Shannon* ☎ *071/962–0236* 🌐 *www.carrickcraft.com.*

Emerald Star ✉ *Portumna* ☎ *071/962–3711* 🌐 *www.emeraldstar.ie.*

Silver Line Cruisers ✉ *The Marina, Banagher* ☎ *057/915–1112* 🌐 *www.silverlinecruisers.com.*

For a slice of authentic Ireland, this region is worth a detour from the busy motorway that links Dublin to the West of Ireland. Visitors can sample hearty, artisanal produce and rural peace in spa hotels or farmhouses, experience festivals, walk or cycle through lush countryside, and follow well-developed tourist trails—all in an area where life moves at a different pace.

The region's artery, the Shannon, is the longest river in both Britain and Ireland and from it flows a series of delightful lakes where cruisers idle along at their own pace. Along its bank a new network of waymarked trails—the Blueways—offers visitors an opportunity to explore the region's lesser-seen landscape on foot, bike, horse, or canoe.

On firm land, the flat plains of the center of Ireland are made up of elegant places rich in delights that attract the culturally curious. Art galleries and heritage museums cluster around the town centers of Birr, Athlone, Portlaoise, Tullamore, and Cavan. You won't find many international coffee chains or behemoth brands, but you will discover age-old industries such as lace making, crystal making, and whiskey making. Slow down and appreciate the gentle pace of time-burnished G&G (Grocery & Guinness) pubs, old-school barbers, or hardware and drapery stores complete with high shelves, long counters, and garrulous owners. With blink-and-you'll-miss-them one-tractor villages, half the fun is in driving down a back road and stumbling on a teddy-bear shop or craft workers sculpting wood. Spend enough time in the region and you might even get to recognize the difference between a Cavan twang and a Tipperary brogue.

The big set pieces are here, too. Among them are Clonmacnoise, Ireland's most important monastic ruins; the gorgeous gardens of Birr Castle, now open to the public for tours for the first time in its history; and some of Ireland's finest Anglo-Irish houses, including Strokestown Park House and Emo Court. As for scenic pleasures, this region has its fair share of Ireland's 800 bodies of water, and much of the landscape is blanket bog. The River Shannon, one of the longest rivers in Europe and the longest in Britain or Ireland, bisects the Midlands from north to south, piercing a series of loughs (lakes): Lough Allen, Lough Ree, and Lough Derg. The Royal Canal and the Grand Canal cross the Midlands from east to west, ending in the Shannon north and south of Lough Ree. The Midlands comprises nine counties: Tipperary, Laois (pronounced "leash"), Offaly,

Westmeath, Longford, Roscommon, Leitrim, Cavan, and Monaghan.

Tourism authorities have hatched a plot to entice more visitors to the Midlands with the launch by Fáilte Ireland of a new €2 million program called Ireland's Hidden Heartlands. The campaign drove mindful travelers to explore the region's natural delights through what marketing gurus describe as "the power of quiet," "slow tourism," and "great escapes."

MAJOR REGIONS

The Eastern Midlands. Just an hour from Dublin, this region is essentially rich farmland but is studded with even richer sights: grand homes such as Emo Court, Belvedere House, and Tullynally Castle; once-upon-a-time villages such as Abbeyleix; and the historic treats of Fore Abbey and Kilbeggan Distillery. Leaving the ancient kingdom of Leinster, you come to two counties of Ulster: Cavan and Monaghan. Beyond Cavan Town you enter the heart of the Northern Lakelands, dotted with hundreds of beautiful lakes.

The Western Midlands. One of the corners of "hidden Ireland," this region is unblighted by crowds—although if the tourist board has its way, this may soon change. This section of the Midlands covers the area's western fringe, making its way from the heart of the region, the town of Longford, and skirting the hilly landscape of County Leitrim, dappled with lakes and beloved by anglers for its fish-filled waters. Moving south through Roscommon, western Offaly, and the northern part of Tipperary, the scenery is generally low on spectacle but high on unspoiled, lush, and undulating countryside. The towns are small and undistinguished, except Birr and Strokestown, both designed to complement the "big houses" that share their names. The historic highlight of this region is the ancient site of Clonmacnoise, an important monastery of early Christian Ireland, while Birr Castle, now opened to the public for the first time in 400 years, is an essential part of any visitor's itinerary.

Planning

Getting Here and Around

AIR

Dublin Airport is the principal international airport that serves the Midlands; car-rental facilities are available here.

BIKE

One of the best ways to immerse yourself in the Midlands is to meander through the region on a bike. Although the area may not offer the spectacular scenery of the more hilly coastal regions, its level, Netherlands-like terrain means a less strenuous ride. New cycling blueways and greenways capitalize on this, as does the recent opening of the Old Rail Trail as a major cycle route leading from Athlone to Mullingar.

The twisting roads are generally in good (well, good enough) condition. There are picnic spots galore in the many state-owned forests just off the main roads. The more rural regions of Laois allow you to spend days exploring beautiful glens, waterfalls, nature trails, and wooded regions around the Slieve Bloom Mountains. Avoid the motorways that bisect the region—after all, this is an area that deserves thorough and leisurely exploration. Contact regional and township tourist offices for all the details.

BUS

With a much more extensive network than trains, buses are a better bet for exploring much of the Midlands. Most small towns and villages are serviced by at least one bus per day, while trains are generally limited to towns on main lines linking cities. Bus Éireann runs express buses from Dublin to many Midlands towns, and regular-speed buses connect

Walk the Slieve Bloom Mountains

Crystal clear freshwater streams, gushing waterfalls, lush forests, and no fewer than 27 glens are all part of the Slieve Bloom Mountains experience. The mountains stretch across the southern end of Offaly and are shared with neighboring County Laois. At one time, the summit—Arderin—was considered to be the highest point in Ireland. Whether you come for serious hiking, a gentle stroll, or just to drink in the spectacular views, you won't be disappointed. Looped walks, some led by guides, range from 4 km (2.5 miles) to 15 km (9 miles). Popular trailheads start from the villages of Kinnitty, Cadamstown, and Clonaslee, or you can make your base in the beautiful heritage town of Birr. Information and guided walking leaflets are available from tourist info offices in Birr, Portlaoise, and Tullamore.

others. The train stations for Athlone and Longford also act as their bus depots.

CAR

The roads of the Midlands offer an easier intro to Irish driving than the hairpin bends of West Cork and Connemara. Because the area has a decent network of main arteries and off-the-beaten-track byroads, a car may be your best option for covering the widest itinerary.

Don't be surprised to round a bend only to confront a herd of sheep idly grazing with little hurry about them—do what the locals do, slow to a stop and wait for an opening in the woolly mass to occur. The same goes for cows. Refrain from honking your horn on these occasions—it will only confirm your status as an impatient tourist, and, besides, the cows won't take a bit of notice.

TRAIN

All trains are run by Irish Rail. The main Midlands towns, such as Athone, have train connections that lie on cross-country routes linking the cities, either east–west or north–south. Intercity trains make only a few stops at smaller towns, while slower trains stop at small towns and some villages. You can connect from one Midlands town to another by train, but check in advance on the regularity of services. There are no exclusively local train services—they all continue on to larger cities.

CONTACTS Athlone Railway Station. ✉ *Southern Station Rd., Athlone* ☎ *090/647–3300* 🌐 *www.irishrail.ie/en-ie.*

Hotels

As commercial progress has blossomed in the Midlands, so, too, have the options in hotels, country houses, and cottage rentals. There is an acute lack of hotel accommodation in the smaller Shannon-side towns, but on the plus side, the Irish bed-and-breakfast offers great value in the Midlands—farmhouses and homes geared to paying guests provide direct contact with local families and the lore of their area. Good beds, decent heating, en suite bathrooms, and the legendary Irish breakfast are the norm.

■ TIP→ **While most properties have Internet access, Wi-Fi is not a given at B&Bs in the Midlands.**

From June to early September, tourism gets into serious stride, bolstered by the many Irish families using their holiday homes and getaway cottages in the region. Finding accommodations is never a major problem—except for those weekends when a town is holding an annual music festival.

Restaurants

The Midlands town of Birr is known as the "belly button of Ireland" because of its central location, not because this region is regarded as one of the cuisine centers of Ireland. No matter that Ireland's oft-dubbed best restaurant and cookery school—Neven Maguire's MacNean's near Cavan town (⇨ *see Chapter 12 for more*)—is in the Midlands, nor the fact that the region is also home to Wineport Lodge, Ireland's first "wine hotel," you'll find that many are simple eateries, ranging in price from inexpensive to moderate, but in recent times Athlone has become especially noted for its high-end restaurants.

Nevertheless, there are those restaurants that will entice you right in off the street, especially those offering beef—Mullingar, in the center of the Midlands, is the beef capital of Ireland—and fish specialties, as the many lakes and rivers of the region provide an abundance of fresh salmon and trout (in fact, since no place is more than an hour and a half from the sea, expect to find lots of fresh ocean fish).

RESTAURANT AND HOTEL PRICES

⇨ *Restaurant prices are the average cost of a main course at dinner or, if dinner is not served, at lunch. Hotel prices are the lowest cost of a standard double room in high season. Restaurant and hotel reviews have been shortened. For full information, visit Fodors.com.*

What It Costs in Euros

	$	$$	$$$	$$$$
RESTAURANTS				
	under €19	€19–€24	€25–€32	over €32
HOTELS				
	under €120	€120–€170	€171–€210	over €210

Planning Your Time

The Midlands is a slice of old Ireland. Spend a few days traveling around the unspoiled countryside with its traditional hay meadows and you'll be Instagramming ancient humped bridges, handsome square tower-houses, and curious-looking castles.

IF YOU HAVE THREE DAYS

If you come from the Greater Dublin area (the Midlands is easily accessible from the city in just over an hour) or surrounding counties such as Wicklow and Kildare, then a grand kickoff to a tour is at Kelbeggan Distillery to discover the art of whiskey production in an 18th-century premises, with its old waterwheel and giant copper pot stills.

From there, head west to Athlone on the River Shannon, the unofficial capital of the Midlands region—and an excellent base to explore the area's main attractions. Walk around Athlone's quirky Left Bank, which is full of crafts and antiques shops as well as secondhand bookshops, restaurants, and cafés. Wind off the night in Sean's Bar—the oldest public premises in Ireland.

Day 2, Athlone Castle calls. Spend an hour or two touring the exhibits in the wonderfully restored fortress—part of which dates back to the 13th century—before visiting the nearby Luan Gallery. Then make time for a two-hour cruise along the Shannon to get a different perspective on the Midlands.

Day 3, drive to Birr for a morning's exploration of its Georgian architecture and a wander around the castle grounds. The formal gardens contain the tallest box hedges in the world; in spring you will see a dazzling display of flowering magnolias, cherries, crab apples, and naturalized narcissi. Guided tours of the Gothic Revival castle, opened to the public in 2013 for the first time in its 400-year history, take place in the summer, pulling back a curtain into a previously unseen world. A half-hour drive takes you to Clonmacnoise, Ireland's most important monastic settlement, where it's worthwhile to join a guided tour that will give you a sense of the place and its past in less than an hour.

John McGahern

Until his death in 2006, the Midlands was the home of one of Ireland's leading writers, John McGahern; at the end of July, the John McGahern International Seminar and Summer School—a series of lectures, workshops, and tours—is held in Carrick-on-Shannon in his honor.

Festivals and Events

JULY

Percy French Summer School

MUSIC FESTIVALS | During the first week of July, one of Ireland's best-loved songwriters, Percy French, is celebrated in Roscommon town and at Castlecoote House with a summer school, complete with concerts and lectures. ✉ *Castlecoote House, Castlecoote, Elphin* ☎ *090/666–3794* 🌐 *www.percyfrench.ie.*

AUGUST

★ **Tullamore Show**

FESTIVALS | **FAMILY** | Ireland's biggest agricultural gathering (and one of its longest established) attracts 60,000 annually in the second week of August, when the largest assembly of cattle anywhere in the country compete in 1,000 classes for 42 national titles. ✉ *Butterfield Estate, Birr Rd., near Blueball, Tullamore* ✣ *Free shuttle buses to venue run from Tullamore train station every hr from 9 am* ☎ *057/935–2141* 🌐 *www.tullamoreshow.com.*

SEPTEMBER

Electric Picnic

ARTS FESTIVALS | In the first weekend of September the historic grounds of Stradbally Hall come alive with a music and arts festival at one of Ireland's biggest outdoor gigs. Running since 2004, the festival attracts big-name performers and up to 50,000 picnickers who come not only for the music but also comedy, theater, and food. Book tickets early if you wish to attend. ✉ *Stradbally Hall, Stradbally* ☎ *01/497–0313* 🌐 *www.electricpicnic.ie.*

Visitor Information

The TIO in Athlone in the grounds of the castle is open from April–October.

⇨ *Find tourist office contact info listed under the main town sections throughout this chapter.*

Abbeyleix

99 km (61 miles) southwest of Dublin.

Abbeyleix has retained its Georgian feel, and its wide high street is lined with trees and well-appointed stone-cut buildings and original shop fronts in the traditionally ornate Irish style. The town was built in the 18th century, on the orders of the Viscount de Vesci, to house servants and tradesmen working on his nearby estate. Many town houses and vernacular buildings date from the 1850s, but more recent buildings, including the Market House, erected in 1906, and the Hibernian Bank, from 1900, contribute greatly to the town's refined character.

GETTING HERE AND AROUND

Drivers between Cork and Dublin can now bypass Abbeyleix via the N8, which has partially alleviated the town's traffic problems. However, on busy summer holiday weekends, congestion still occurs, so add a little extra time in case of delays. Allow 75 minutes driving time to Dublin or 90 minutes to Dublin Airport. The nearest large town is Portlaoise, a 10-minute drive, while Kilkenny is 30 minutes south on the N77. Free on-street car parking and several car parks are available in town. Daily buses connect Abbeyleix to Dublin or Cork; the former is just less than two hours away, the latter a 2¾-hour trip.

Sights

Heritage House

HISTORIC HOME | Remodeled interpretation, time lines, and new infographics were added during 2020 at the Heritage House, also known as the former North Boys School. The displays feature a variety of aspects of Laois life as well as the history of Abbeyleix and the de Vescis, an Anglo-Norman family who, in 1699, came to live at an estate nearby. They were instrumental in building and developing the new town of Abbeyleix in 1770. The school was originally constructed for the education of Catholics (at the other end of the town you'll find the South School, built for Protestants). Hour-long guided walking tours of the town are held in the summer while another tour links the center with new boardwalks at Abbeyleix Bog on the southern outskirts of the town that encompasses a 500-acre area of diverse habitats. Both tours costs €7, which includes admission to the house. Check the website for details of tour dates and times. ✉ *Main St., Abbeyleix* ☎ *057/873–1653* 🌐 *www.abbeyleixheritage.com* 🎫 *From €5* 🕐 *Closed Sun. in Mar.–Oct.; closed Sun. and Mon. in Nov.–Feb.*

Heywood Gardens

GARDEN | The Lutyenses' house, once in the pretty Georgian village of Ballinakill, burned down in 1950 due to an electrical fault, but the gardens, with landscaping most likely attributable to the famed Gertrude Jekyll, are still worth a detour. Guided one-hour tours by prior booking (Monday–Thursday) are available through this gardener's paradise, where a formal lawn flanked by traditional herbaceous borders leads to a sunken Italian garden. Highlights include a rose called Natalie Naples and Johnston's Blue geraniums. ✉ *About 5 km (3 miles) south of Abbeyleix* ☎ *057/873–3563* 🌐 *www.heritageireland.ie* 🎫 *Free.*

Morrissey's Pub

RESTAURANT | Don't miss Morrissey's. A working public house since 1775, this is one of Ireland's best-loved drinking emporiums and has a dark, wood-panel interior furnished with antique bar fittings. Customers can warm themselves by an ancient potbelly stove. Until 2005, this establishment still functioned as a shop, and while it retains its stocks of groceries, they are no longer for sale. An evocative time capsule, it serves as a reminder of times when you could purchase a pound of butter, the newspaper, and cattle feed while enjoying the obligatory pint of Guinness. They serve sandwiches in the afternoon, which you can enjoy alfresco at picnic tables at the front of the bar, and pizzas are available into the late evening. ✉ *10 Main St., Abbeyleix* ☎ *057/873–1281.*

Portlaoise

14 km (9 miles) north of Abbeyleix.

Portlaoise's name is derived from the Irish for "Fort of Laois" and refers to the town's strife-filled history. It's a large

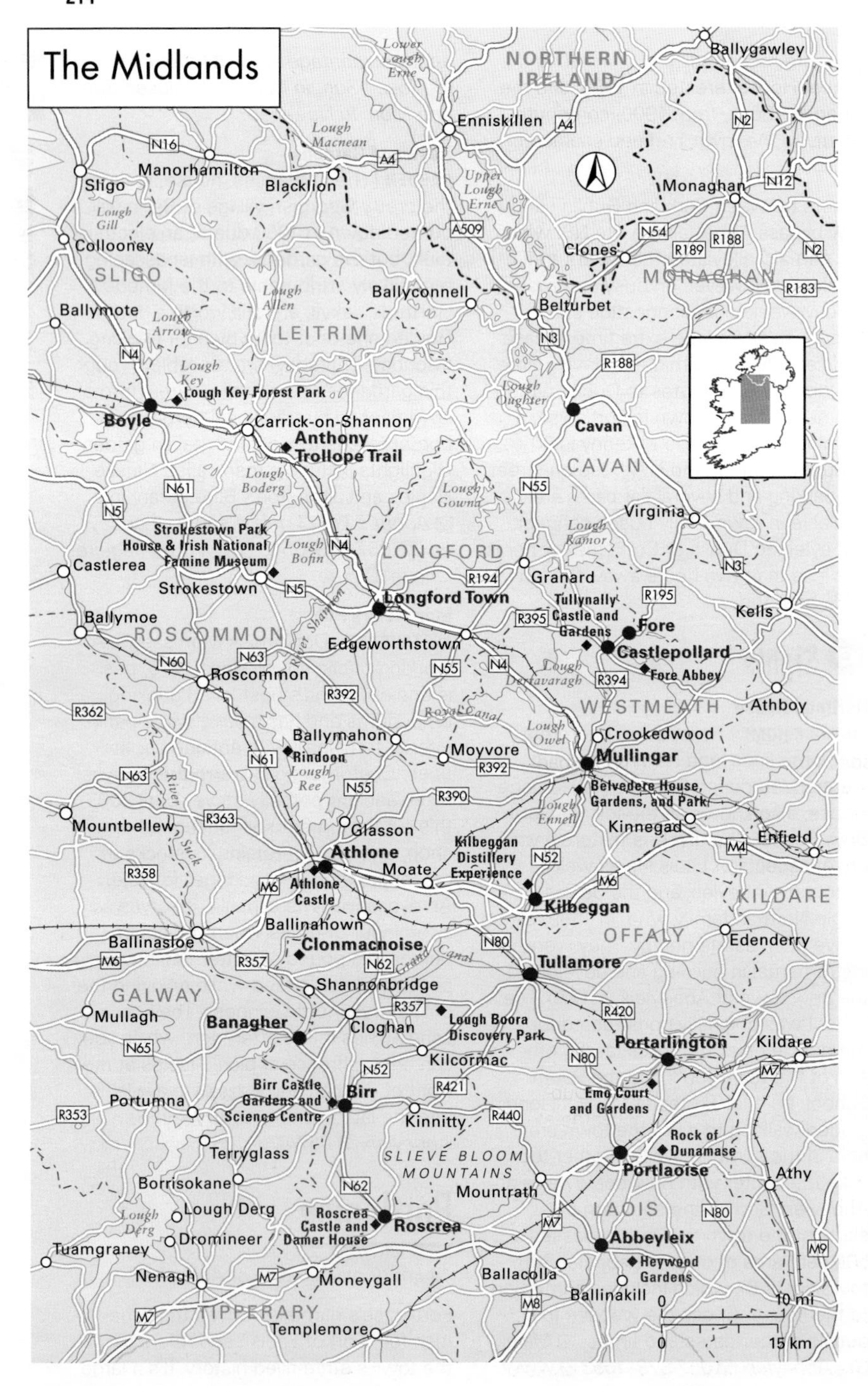
The Midlands
NORTHERN IRELAND
Lower Lough Erne
Enniskillen
Ballygawley
Lough Macnean
Manorhamilton
Sligo
Blacklion
Upper Lough Erne
Monaghan
Lough Gill
Collooney
Clones
SLIGO
MONAGHAN
Lough Allen
Ballyconnell
Belturbet
Ballymote
Lough Arrow
LEITRIM
Lough Key
Lough Key Forest Park
Lough Oughter
Boyle
Carrick-on-Shannon
Cavan
Anthony Trollope Trail
Lough Boderg
CAVAN
Lough Gowna
Virginia
Strokestown Park House & Irish National Famine Museum
Lough Bofin
LONGFORD
Lough Ramor
Castlerea
Strokestown
Granard
Longford Town
Tullynally Castle and Gardens
Fore
Kells
Ballymoe
ROSCOMMON
River Shannon
Edgeworthstown
Castlepollard
Fore Abbey
Roscommon
Lough Derravaragh
WESTMEATH
Athboy
Royal Canal
Ballymahon
Lough Owel
Crookedwood
Rindoon
Moyvore
Mullingar
Lough Ree
Belvedere House, Gardens, and Park
River Suck
Lough Ennell
Kinnegad
Mountbellew
Glasson
Enfield
Kilbeggan Distillery Experience
Athlone
Moate
Athlone Castle
Kilbeggan
KILDARE
Ballinahown
OFFALY
Edenderry
Ballinasloe
Clonmacnoise
Grand Canal
Tullamore
GALWAY
Shannonbridge
Mullagh
Lough Boora Discovery Park
Banagher
Cloghan
Portarlington
Kildare
Kilcormac
Birr Castle Gardens and Science Centre
Birr
Emo Court and Gardens
Portumna
Kinnitty
Rock of Dunamase
Terryglass
SLIEVE BLOOM MOUNTAINS
Portlaoise
Borrisokane
Mountrath
Athy
Lough Derg
Roscrea Castle and Damer House
Roscrea
LAOIS
Dromineer
Abbeyleix
Tuamgraney
Heywood Gardens
Nenagh
Moneygall
Ballacolla
Ballinakill
TIPPERARY
Templemore
0
10 mi
0
15 km

town with an industrial feel—sprawling in all directions from the town center with warehouses and retail outlets. At best, its architecture can be described as eclectic—it feels as if bits of other towns were picked up and dropped randomly onto the site. It was once best known for having Ireland's highest-security prison, which housed the IRA's most notorious members during the 1970s and '80s and still looms over the town. Its saving grace is its main street, which is now largely given over to pedestrians, and so pubs and restaurants are flourishing. The thriving Dunamaise Arts Centre, where the Portlaoise tourist office resides, adds an extra dash of culture. In 2020, the town embarked on a large biodiversity project which saw 5,000 trees planted along with shrubs and pollinator-friendly flower beds on roadside verges and hedgerows with the aim of making Portlaoise "A Town in a Garden."

GETTING HERE AND AROUND

Portlaoise is an hour by train, bus, or car from Dublin. Kilkenny is 45 minutes south on the N8 and then N77. Roads from Portlaoise also lead south and west to Cork, Galway, and Limerick. There is no free parking anywhere in town; paid parking is available on James Fintan Lalor Avenue, next to County Hall, and at shopping centers.

Portlaoise has several daily Irish Rail trains to the capital and is on the main line linking it with Cork, Limerick, and Tralee. The small station is five minutes from the town center. Bus routes leading to Ireland's three main cities—Dublin, Cork, and Limerick—converge at Portlaoise. In addition to Bus Éireann, an independent operator named J. J. Kavanagh & Sons serves the town, and Dublin Coach offers a route to Dublin Airport.

CONTACTS Dublin Coach. ✉ *James Fintan Lalor Ave., Portlaoise* ✣ *Pickup/drop-off at bus shelter* ☎ *01/465–9972* 🌐 *www.dublincoach.ie.* **J.J. Kavanagh.** ✉ *James Fintan Lalor Ave., Portlaoise* ✣ *Buses stop and pick up at bus shelter* ☎ *056/883–1106* 🌐 *www.jjkavanagh.ie.*

TOURS

Experiencing Laois

GUIDED TOURS | Discover and explore more of County Laois in these two-hour tours led by Trudy Earls. They can be tailored to suit your interests, whether it's history, heritage, culture, or family ancestry. The most popular tour is on Sunday at 2 pm. Ask at the tourist office in the Dunamaise Arts Centre in Portlaoise for more details. ✉ *Dunamaise Arts Centre, Church St., Portlaoise* ☎ *087/792–3367* 🌐 *www.experiencinglaois.com* 🎫 *€5.*

VISITOR INFORMATION

CONTACTS Portlaoise Tourist Office. ✉ *Dunamaise Arts Centre, Church St., Portlaoise* ☎ *057/862–1178* 🌐 *www.laoistourism.ie.*

Sights

Laois Garden Trail

GARDEN | Connecting 10 of the county's celebrated formal gardens and expertly maintained privately owned ones, this driving route promotes the area's horticultural heritage. There's no trailhead for the tour so start the trail wherever you wish and spend as long as you'd like in each garden. Stops include the state-run gardens at Emo Court and Heywood House, as well as Gash Gardens in Castletown, which offers a delightful river walk along the banks of the Nore; the demesne gardens of Castle Durrow, with its glorious scented roses; and the organically managed potager-style kitchen garden of Dunmore Country School, just outside Durrow. For those interested and with time to spare, the Dunmore School also holds one-day gardening courses. There is a charge for only one garden, at Ballintubbert (around €10); admission to the others is free.

■ TIP→ Maps of the trail are available in Portlaoise Tourist Office based in the Dunamaise Arts Centre in Church Street.

✉ *Church St., Portlaoise* 🌐 *www.laois-tourism.ie.*

Laois Heritage Trail

SCENIC DRIVE | Stop by the Portlaoise Tourist Office in the Dunamaise Arts Centre to pick up a map of the Laois Heritage Trail, a signposted, daylong drive on quiet back roads that takes in 13 heritage sites, ranging from Abbeyleix to Emo Court. The circular trail starts in Borris-in-Ossory on the N7.

■ TIP→ Some sites along the trail charge an admission fee. ✉ *Portlaoise Tourist Office, Dunamaise Arts Centre, Church St., Portlaoise* 🌐 *www.laoistourism.ie.*

Rock of Dunamase

RUINS | A dramatic 150-foot-high limestone outcrop, the famous Rock of Dunamase dominates the landscape east of Portlaoise. For this reason, it was used as a military stronghold. As far back as AD 140, its occupants kept watch against marauders, and it was fought over in turn by the Vikings, Normans, Irish, and English. Today it's crowned by the ruins of a 12th-century castle, once home to Diarmuid MacMurrough, king of Leinster, who precipitated the Norman invasion when he invited the famed and feared Norman leader Strongbow to Ireland to marry his daughter. Some of the castle's thick walls still stand after it was largely destroyed during the Cromwellian invasion in 1650.

■ TIP→ Take the short walk to its summit to enjoy the view of the Slieve Bloom Mountains to the north and the Wicklow Mountains to the south. ✉ *N80 (Stradbally Rd.), Portlaoise* ✣ *5 km (3 miles) east of Portlaoise.*

Restaurants

Kelly's Steakhouse

$$$ | **STEAKHOUSE** | Just across the road from the Midlands Park Hotel, Kelly's Steakhouse expertly prepares cuts of Irish beef in all shapes and sizes, from a 20-ounce porterhouse T-bone to a more modest 10-ounce rib eye. The chef knows a thing or two about gradations, but if you want to try your own hand, the steak house offers the unique chance to cook the meat yourself over a volcanic black rock hot stone. **Known for:** prime cuts of Irish meat; cooking your own steak over a black rock hot stone; Ma Kelly's cheesecake. ⑤ *Average main: €27* ✉ *Jessop St., Portlaoise* ✣ *Opposite Midlands Park Hotel* ☎ *057/867–8588* 🌐 *www.midlandsparkhotel.com/kellys-steakhouse* ⊙ *Closed Mon. No lunch.*

Hotels

The Heritage Killenard

$$$$ | **RESORT** | This modern hotel looks out over the parkland setting of an 18-hole golf course and across to the distant Slieve Bloom Mountains. **Pros:** dazzling freshness to public areas; 5-km (3-mile) walking trail with exercise stations; haven of peace and calm. **Cons:** in summer the grass cutters start early; isolated from any nearby towns; five-minute walk to the spa. ⑤ *Rooms from: €249* ✉ *Killenard* ✣ *5 km (3 miles) south of Portarlington* ☎ *057/864–5500* 🌐 *www.theheritage.com* ⇨ *98 rooms* 🍽 *Free Breakfast.*

Ivyleigh House

$$ | **B&B/INN** | "The best of everything" is the maxim of affable owners Dinah and Jerry Campion and that is certainly evident the minute you step inside this elegant Georgian town house next to the Portlaoise train station—open fires, antiques, and sumptuously cozy sofas await you in the beige-on-brown, wood-accented sitting room. **Pros:** lavish breakfasts; rococo feel; convenient location for town. **Cons:** no baths, power shower only; pricey for this area; few extra frills. ⑤ *Rooms from: €125* ✉ *Intersection of Bank Pl. and Church St., Portlaoise* ☎ *057/862–2081* 🌐 *www.ivyleigh.com* ⇨ *6 rooms* 🍽 *Free Breakfast.*

Nightlife

Ramsbottoms Bar

BARS | For a glimpse of old Ireland, call into Ramsbottoms in Lower Main Street where a log fire burns brightly beside comfy settees. It started out in the 1870s selling animal feed and importing the finest teas, wines, and brandies, but this former grocery-cum-bar now sells only alcohol, although reminders of its past are all around. The original bacon-slicing machine from the grocery shop is on display; walls are adorned with sepia-tinted photographs, whiskey and cigarette signs, and record sleeves featuring John McCormack and Bing Crosby, and banknotes from around the world are pinned to the bar. For €2, you can select your own five tunes from the jukebox, sit back, and enjoy a flawless pint. ✉ *101 Lower Main St., Portlaoise* ☎ *057/866–1298.*

Performing Arts

Dunamaise Arts Centre

ARTS CENTERS | This lively arts center has a 240-seat theater, an art gallery, and a friendly coffeehouse (closed Sunday). You may catch a professional production on tour or a local amateur show; anything from a meditation workshop to a panto to an arthouse movie marathon. The exhibition space displays the work of contemporary Irish artists. It's built into the back of the 18th-century stone courthouse on Church Street in a space that used to be the town jail. There's a small café. ✉ *Church St., Portlaoise* ☎ *057/866–3355* 🌐 *www.dunamaise.ie.*

Activities

GOLF

The Heath Golf Club

GOLF | From early spring, the dazzling blaze of yellow furze—also known as gorse—decorates the open heathland at this 18-hole course. The area has a colorful history, too, as the popular Irish politician Daniel O'Connell held meetings here in the mid-1830s. They've been playing golf on the Heath since the 1890s and the club dates from 1930. The course, open to the public, incorporates three natural lakes and is referred to as an "inland links." Good-value deals for visitors include special rates combining golf with a meal; or you can settle for a drink in the friendly "19 Hole" bar. ✉ *The Great Heath of Maryborough* ✣ *5 km (3 miles) northeast of Portlaoise on main Dublin Rd.* ☎ *057/864–6533* 🌐 *www.theheathgc.ie* 🎫 *Feb.–July, Oct., and Nov., from €15; Aug., Sept., Dec., and Jan., from €17* ⛳ *18 holes, 6120 yards, par 72.*

The Heritage Golf Resort

GOLF | Millions of dollars were spent on developing this 18-hole championship course—and it shows. A challenge for the pros, but somehow forgiving to the amateur at the same time, Heritage has second-to-none facilities including a 38,000-square-foot clubhouse. A life-size bronze of Seve Ballesteros (by the renowned sports sculptor Paul Ferriter) greets you at the entrance to the course he designed here, which is noted for its mix of challenging doglegs and water traps (including five on-course lakes). Add four demanding par-5s to the mix and the result is a truly world-class parkland course. It's known for its 96 beautifully arranged bunkers set amongst 7,000 trees—during 2019 several bunkers were reshaped on the 14th. The development of luxury on-site accommodations has also increased the club's attractiveness to the visiting golfer. ✉ *Killenard* ✣ *5 km (3 miles) south of Portarlington* ☎ *57/864–2321* 🌐 *www.heritageresort.ie* 🎫 *Apr.–Oct., from €45; Nov.–Mar., from €39* ⛳ *18 holes, 7319 yards, par 72.*

Portarlington

13 km (8 miles) northeast of Portlaoise.

Built on the River Barrow in the late 17th century, Portarlington was originally an English settlement. Later, a displaced Huguenot colony secured lands in payment for loyalty to the Williamite forces, so French surnames are still common in the area. It has a plain and wholesome town center with decent examples of Georgian architecture scattered throughout.

GETTING HERE AND AROUND

On the road between Mullingar and Portlaoise, Portarlington is a small crossroads town relatively free of traffic—it's well clear of the N7, so it misses out on the motorway trade. Tullamore is a 30-minute drive away, Portlaoise is 20 minutes, and Dublin is a 45-minute drive. There are several free parking lots in town. The Dublin–Cork train stops at Portarlington and there are regular Bus Éireann connections to the bigger towns, and Dublin.

Coolbanagher Church

RELIGIOUS BUILDING | Coolbanagher Church, the familiar name for the exquisite Church of St. John the Evangelist, was, like Emo Court and Gardens, designed by James Gandon. It means "hill of the pointed nooks." On view inside are Gandon's original 1795 plans and an elaborately sculpted 15th-century font from an earlier church that stood nearby. Adjacent to the church is Gandon's mausoleum for Lord Portarlington, his patron at Emo.

The church is open only by advance telephone arrangement. The 1960s, '70s, and '80s saw extensive renovations take place, with parishioners themselves working on infrastructure, such as slating and window work, while staining and elaborate painting was carried out by professionals. ✉ *Portarlington* ✣ *8½ km (5 miles) south of Portarlington on R419* ☎ *057/862–4143* 🌐 *www.mountmellick-groupofparishes.ie* 🎫 *Free.*

Emo Court and Gardens

HISTORIC HOME | History, architecture, and nature merge in a happy commingling at Emo Court, a quintessential landmark of Irish Palladian elegance and a fine large-scale country house. The house is currently closed to the public—expected to reopen in 2023—although the extensive grounds may still be visited free of charge. Built in the late 18th century and designed by architect James Gandon—it's thought to be his only domestic work matching the grand scale of his Dublin civic buildings such as the Custom House and the Four Courts.

The ground-floor rooms have been beautifully restored and decorated and are prime examples of life on a grand scale. Among the highlights are the entrance hall, with trompe-l'oeil paintings in the apses on each side, and the library, which has a carved Italian-marble mantel. Emo's 55 acres of grounds include a 20-acre lake, lawns planted with yew trees, a small garden (the Clocker) with Japanese maples, and a larger one (the Grapery) with rare trees and shrubs. ✉ *Emo* ✣ *7 km (4½ miles) south of Portarlington* ☎ *057/862–6573* 🌐 *www.heritageireland.ie* 🎫 *Gardens free, house €8* 🕙 *House closed Oct.–Mar.*

★ **Roundwood House**

$$$ | **B&B/INN** | There's a dreamy beauty to this chateaulike mansion set on the slopes of the Slieve Bloom Mountains—as you arrive, a dark, tree-lined avenue suddenly opens up to reveal a dramatically gorgeous Palladian villa, while some ducks, hens, and a Labrador called Rococo often form the welcoming party. **Pros:** characterful house filled with history; mature woodland is ideal for

In the spring, the gardens at Emo Court rival the splendor of its Neoclassical-style salons.

walks; elegant and airy rooms in the main house. **Cons:** remote; no TVs; so many books, so little time. $ *Rooms from: €190* ✉ *Mountrath* ✣ *5 km (3 miles) from Mountrath on scenic road to Kinnitty* ☎ *057/873–2120* 🌐 *www.roundwood-house.com* ⇆ *10 rooms, 2 self-catering cottages* 🍽 *Free Breakfast* ☞ *4-course dinner €60.*

Tullamore

27 km (17 miles) northwest of Portarlington.

The county seat of Offaly, Tullamore is a bustling market town that thrived during Ireland's economic boom that lasted from the mid-1990s until 2008; like many parts of Ireland it has suffered in the downturn, but with the arrival of the third decade of the 21st century it has experienced an upturn in its fortunes with several excellent hotels, the Bridge Shopping Centre, and an enhanced town square housing a newly opened tourism office. The county council has created a marketing slogan, branding Offaly "Ireland's Hidden Gem," and while it is hardly the most charismatic phrase, it points to a more coherent identity and renewed collective effort to improve the public realm and promote tourism in both the town and county. Tullamore's historical success was based on its location on the Grand Canal, one of Ireland's most important trading links during the 18th and 19th centuries. Many of the town's most notable older buildings—erected in the 50-year period 1785–1835—have been preserved, and a leisurely stroll along the streets is a rewarding experience where you can follow signposted trails beside the cana.

GETTING HERE AND AROUND

A medium-size Midlands town, Tullamore is a transportation hub. Six roads converge here, meaning that market days at the end of the week are especially busy and free street parking is first-come, first-served. Dublin is just over an hour's drive, while the neighboring towns of

Athlone, Mullingar, and Portlaoise are approximately 30 minutes away. Travelers are reasonably well served by Bus Éireann; routes connect to Dublin (two hours east) as well as towns north, south, and west of Tullamore. By train, Tullamore is 70 minutes from Dublin, 90 minutes from Galway, and two hours from Sligo. Train and bus services coalesce at Cormac Street in town.

TOURS

Offaly Enchanting Tours

GUIDED TOURS | "Five castles in one day" is the sales tag utilized by Offaly Enchanting Tours, which operates fascinating guided history, culture, and heritage trips to some of the county's premier sites. Incorporating battlement towers and castellated mansions, as well as inspirational monastic and archaeological places of interest, the one-day package tour leaves from the car park of the Tullamore Court Hotel at 9:30 am and returns around 6 pm. The price of €95 covers transfers to and from sites, tea/coffee, and scones at one castle, all admission fees, and guided tour with a dash of fun thrown in for good measure. Reservations are essential as places are limited. ✉ *Tour meets at rear parking lot of Tullamore Court Hotel, O'Moore St., Tullamore* ☎ *085/283–1591* 🌐 *www.offalyenchantingtours.com* 🎫 *€95.*

VISITOR INFORMATION

Offaly History Centre

VISITOR INFORMATION | Based in a former wine warehouse, this combination of bookshop—with several thousand new and secondhand books on Offaly—and an adjoining library and archive is the local history center and a fascinating resource for the culturally curious and anyone remotely interested in their Irish past. The shop promotes the rich heritage and diverse culture of the county, as well as stocking an extensive selection of books for sale on the Midlands and Ireland in general. Look out for *Tullamore: A Portrait*, by Michael Byrne with exquisite watercolor sketches of historic buildings by Fergal MacCabe. Staff will also help with queries on family ancestry. It is well worth 30 minutes of your time. ✉ *Bury Quay, Banagher* ✣ *200 meters from Tullamore Whiskey Distillery* ☎ *057/932–1421* 🌐 *www.offalyhistory.com.*

Offaly Tourism Office

VISITOR INFORMATION | Set on the main square, this tourism office is a veritable treasure trove of hard-copy information consisting of town maps, accommodations, attractions, outdoor pursuits, shopping and dining guides, and details on Offaly's hidden gems. For the tech savvy, this is complimented with an app courtesy of Tullamore town, a historical narrated walking tour that can be downloaded for free. The knowledgeable staff will help with any queries relating to Tullamore, surrounding towns in the county, and the wider Irish Midlands. ✉ *O'Connor Sq., Tullamore* ☎ *057/935–7295* 🌐 *www.visitoffaly.ie.*

Sights

Charleville Castle

CASTLE/PALACE | One relic of Tullamore's prefamine era is found on the southwestern edge of town, where you'll find a storybook neo-Gothic 19th-century castle. Its flag tower and turrets rise above its domain of 30 acres of woodland walks and gardens. The Georgian–Gothic Revival house was built as a symbol of English oppression over French and Irish (the French revolutionary forces had become a little too cozy with the Irish locals). In fact, the floor plan is even modeled on the Union Jack. Commissioned by Baron Tullamore and dating from 1812, the castle is a rural example of the work of architect Francis Johnston, who was responsible for many of Dublin's stately Georgian buildings. The interiors are somewhat the worse for wear and parts of the castle, such as the stairwell restoration project (also known as Harriet's Staircase), are works in progress, but the

William Morris–designed dining room ceiling has its original stenciled wallpaper with gold leaf. And the building still holds wide appeal: paranormal groups hold investigations in it, filmmakers are attracted to it (castle scenes were used in 2019 for the Netflix comedy *The Knight Before Christmas* and for the biographical romantic drama *Becoming Jane* about the life of Jane Austen), and tourists love to hear the stories of previous owners and its secret passage.

⚠ **To reach the castle by car it is a 2-km (1-mile) drive on a rough narrow lane off the main road, so be aware of ramps and potholes along part of it. Look out also for the King Oak in the grounds—estimated to be between 400 and 800 years old—which stands just inside the main entrance.** ✉ *Tullamore* ✣ *1½ km (1 mile) outside Tullamore on N52 to Birr* ☎ *057/932-3040* 🌐 *www.charlevillecastle.ie* 🎫 *Tour from €20.*

Clara Bog Visitor Centre

VISITOR CENTER | FAMILY | As one of the best remaining examples of an intact raised bog in western Europe, Clara Bog is home to protected wildlife species, including the rare dark tussock moth, the keeled skimmer, and a powder-blue dragonfly as well as two rare midges and a click beetle. Unique bog plants, such as sphagnum mosses and the pink rosemary (Offaly's county flower), can be seen. A five-minute walk from Clara railway station, Clara Bog is a wet environment (deep pools and quaking surfaces), so dress appropriately and stay on the boardwalk. While its long-running visitor center is currently closed, the 1 km looped boardwalk on Clara Bog Nature Reserve is accessible at all times. ✉ *Clara, Ballycumber Rd., Tullamore* ✣ *2 km (1 mile) southeast of Clara town* ☎ *57/936-8878* 🌐 *www.npws.ie* ⏲ *Closed Nov.–Apr.; May–Sept., closed weekends.*

★ **Lough Boora Discovery Park**

CITY PARK | FAMILY | This open expanse of once commercial, now exhausted, bog has been restored for a variety of leisure activities, from hiking and cycling to coarse angling and bird-watching (more than 150 species make their home here). When it was first established as a sanctuary in 2001, there were just 11 breeding pairs of gray partridge in the parkland—now there are several hundred of these ground-nesting birds, the last remaining population of them in Ireland. You're unlikely to see them, however, as they spend only one minute of each day in the air. Best of all, Lough Boora is home to one of Ireland's most unique sculpture parks. Along the Sculpture Walk, where golden plovers, lapwings, and starlings may accompany you, 24 large-scale sculptures made from local materials (including glacial stone, water, and willow) have been created by artists influenced by the legacy of the bogs. The result is some of the most creative environmental outdoor artwork anywhere in Ireland. To cite one example, the installation artist Mike Bulfin has turned a rusty old bog train into a cartoonish curve whose image will remain imprinted in your mind long after your visit to this magical place. The most recent sculpture, the *Gathering of Stones,* features a different type of stone from each of the four provinces in Ireland, creating a ring fort and circular wall. It reflects the Irish diaspora through "emigrant stones" laid out in a cruciform shape embracing people from all corners of the world. An organic café serves snacks from 10 am to 6 pm. An off-road bike trail runs for 22 km (13 miles). You can choose from five different looped color-coded walks, while guided walking tours run April–September.

■ **TIP→ Bring your binoculars: bird blinds are located throughout the park to provide the opportunities to spy on birds such as golden plover and lapwing.** ✉ *Boora, 3 km (2 miles) north of Kilcormac, Tullamore* ✣ *Turn off R537; Lough Boora is in* *townland of Leabeg ☏ 57/934–0010 🌐 www.loughboora.com 🎫 Free; bike rental €5 per hr, parking €4 full day.*

★ Tullamore Dew Visitor Centre
DISTILLERY | Recently moved from its town center location in a bonded warehouse, the visitor center is now located at its modern plant at Clonminch outside Tullamore. Highlights include whiskey tours, tasting sessions, and a whiskey master class. In 2014, a €35 million distillery opened at Clonminch on the outskirts of town, bringing whiskey production back to the area after a gap of 60 years. The company embarked on a €10 million global marketing campaign, and today it's the world's second-largest and fastest-growing Irish whiskey brand—just behind Jameson. It's all a far cry from humble beginnings in 1829 when Tullamore Distillery was founded. It was greatly expanded under the aegis of Daniel E. Williams, whose family became joint shareholders, and his own initials (D. E. W.) were added to the whiskey's name, inspiring the slogan "Give every man his Dew" (which appeared on the bottles for many years). Triple distilled, and made from a unique blend of single malt, pot still, and grain whiskey, it is regarded by connoisseurs as exceptionally smooth. The visitor center shows several short videos on the history of the company and guided tours reflect the aroma aspects of the whiskey alongside infographics panels. The tour includes a 105-minute "behind-the-scenes" visit of the working distillery, an Irish coffee, still house visit, and experiment in the blending lab—where you can "dip the dog" and taste whiskey straight from the cask in the so-called secret warehouse snug. *✉ Clonminch, Tullamore ✥ 3 km (2 miles) south of Tullamore ☏ 057/932–5015 🌐 www.tullamoredew.com 🎫 From €17.*

Hotels

Annaharvey Farm
$ | **B&B/INN** | Dedicated to all things equestrian, this family farmhouse, now in the fifth generation of the same family, was once an old-world grain barn but has been converted into elegant accommodations, with pitch-pine floors, massive roof beams, and open fireplaces. **Pros:** secluded location; horse-riding packages; convenient to Clonmacnoise and Birr Castle. **Cons:** bathrooms are small; not one for those with animal allergies; meals must be booked in advance. *$ Rooms from: €90 ✉ Tullamore ✥ 6 km (4 miles) outside of Tullamore town on the Portarlington road ☏ 057/934–3544 🌐 www.annaharveyfarm.ie ⏲ Closed Nov.–mid-Mar. 7 rooms 🍴 Free Breakfast.*

Tullamore Court Hotel
$$ | **B&B/INN** | Situated on the edge of town, its 103 guest rooms are attractively presented in cream with wood fittings, while the executive rooms are decorated in pleasing dark red furnishings. **Pros:** excellent location; friendly and efficient staff; free parking. **Cons:** heavy breakfast traffic from 9:30 am; gets busy with conferences and weddings; can be noisy with large events. *$ Rooms from: €139 ✉ O'Moore St., Tullamore ✥ About 800 feet from main street ☏ 057/934–6666 🌐 www.tullamorecourthotel.ie 103 rooms 🍴 Free Breakfast.*

Activities

GOLF

Esker Hills Golf Club
GOLF | This small Midlands golf club, near the village of Clara, was thrust into the international media spotlight in 2019 when one of its members, 32-year-old Shane Lowry, triumphed at the British Open at Royal Portrush on the north coast of Ireland. The 18-hole championship course where Lowry learned those vital early skills as a child—excelling at pitch and putt—is studded with natural

lakes and woodlands, as well as superb sand-based greens. Masterfully designed by Christy O'Connor Jr., it is regarded as one of Ireland's leading inland links–type courses. The full greens are playable all year round and welcomes visitors. The club takes its name from eskers, or mounds of sand or gravel left by streams of melted ice, which provide the dramatic undulations of the course. ✉ *N52, Esker Hills* ✣ *5 km (3 miles) north of Tullamore* ☎ *057/935–5999* 🌐 *www.eskerhillsgolf.com* 🎟 *From €35* 🏌 *18 holes, 6626 yards, par 71.*

Kilbeggan

11 km (7 miles) north of Tullamore.

GETTING HERE AND AROUND

The small town of Kilbeggan is on the main M6 Dublin–Athlone route; the nearest large town is Tullamore, 15 minutes south on the N52. There is free parking in town. Regular buses serving the busy Dublin–Galway route stop at Kilbeggan. Athlone is a 15-minute journey by bus, and Dublin is an 80-minute ride.

Sights

★ Kilbeggan Distillery Experience

DISTILLERY | It's the whiskey (the Irish spell their traditional tipple with an "e") that brings most people to the unassuming little town of Kilbeggan, home of the Kilbeggan Distillery Experience, the oldest pot-still distillery in the world and the last of its type in Ireland. Established in 1757, it closed as a functioning distillery in 1954, but has since found new life as a museum of industrial archaeology, illustrating the process of Irish pot-whiskey distillation and the social history of the workers. The distillery's original old stone and whitewashed buildings have been carefully tended, and the glorious timber waterwheel has been restored and repainted and is now creaking again. Multiple different types of tours are available. The one-hour Apprentice tour (€15) includes tasting three whiskeys; on the 90-minute Distillers tour (€30), you get to taste all four Kilbeggan core brands: Kilbeggan single grain, Kilbeggan Irish whiskey, Tyrconnell single malt, and Connemara peated single malt.

■ TIP→ If you're looking for a present, the new Kilbeggan single pot-still whiskey—launched in 2019 at €60—is soft and mellow with citrusy summer fruits, or you could opt for handmade dark chocolate whiskey truffles or fudge in the shop. ✉ *Lower Main St., Kilbeggan* ☎ *057/933–2134* 🌐 *www.kilbegganwhiskey.com* 🎟 *Shop and bar free; tours from €15.*

Mullingar

24 km (15 miles) northeast of Kilbeggan.

Probably most famous internationally as the hometown of Niall Horan of pop band One Direction fame, Mullingar's title as Ireland's beef capital is what, historically, has put it on the map in Ireland. It's largely attributed to the surrounding rich countryside where cattle trading has historically been one of the townsfolk's chief occupations. It's also County Westmeath's major town—a busy commercial and cattle-trading center on the Royal Canal, midway between two attractive lakes, Lough Owel and Lough Ennel.

GETTING HERE AND AROUND

Mullingar is a busy town on the N4 Longford–Dublin route. Although it is bypassed by the highway, traffic in town can still come to a standstill at certain times of the day. The Dublin–Sligo train stops at Mullingar, and buses run to Athlone (one hour) and Dublin (90 minutes).

Sights

★ Belvedere House, Gardens, and Park

CITY PARK | **FAMILY** | A stately mid-18th-century hunting lodge with extensive gardens, Belvedere House occupies a beautiful spot on the northeast shore of Lough Ennell. Access to the mansion is through the servants' entrance—so you can see what life behind the scenes was like back then. The interiors are a quirky mix of Georgian stateliness and Victorian charm. The noted bow and Palladian windows have great parkland views sloping down to the lake and its islands.

It was built in 1740 by architect Richard Cassels for Robert Rochfort, first earl of Belvedere, and his wife, Mary. She was accused of having an affair with Robert's brother Arthur, which was denied, but she was locked away in the Rochfort's ancestral home at Gaulstown House for 31 years on a charge of adultery. During this time, Robert had considerable work carried out on Belvedere House to make it more homey; one of the most impressive features he commissioned was the rococo plasterwork ceiling by the renowned stucco artist Bartholomew Cramillion. He spent much of his family fortune dotting the gardens of the estate with "follies," including the Jealous Wall, a gigantic mock-castle ruin that served to cover up a view of the adjoining estate, owned by another brother, also hated. It now stands as Ireland's largest folly and is loved by Instagrammers.

You can walk around the 160 acres of the estate and 10 km (6 miles) of woodland trails; some walks take you past the Gothic arch folly. Belvedere rebranded its historical interpretation in 2019 to add interactive panels, audio guides covering both the house and grounds bringing history to life in a new way through illustrated characters, and even talking portraits. In the dining room, for example, you can listen to the commentary of the Wicked Earl, known for his extreme jealousy, hosting a lavish dinner party for his friends. Also on the grounds are a café and four children's play areas, which include a zipline and a fairy garden. At the back of the house, look out for the sculpture of King Malachy, the last High King of Ireland, made from the stump of an old oak tree whose story is recounted in the audio tour. ✉ *N52, Mullingar* ✣ *5 km (2½ miles) south of Mullingar* ☎ *044/933–8960* 🌐 *www.belvedere-house.ie* 🎫 *House and parkland €8 standard.*

Cathedral of Christ the King

CHURCH | The town's largest structure is the Renaissance-style Catholic Cathedral of Christ the King, completed in 1939. Note the facade's finely carved stonework, and the mosaics of St. Patrick and St. Anne by the Russian artist Boris Anrep in the spacious interior. There's a museum in the cathedral, and you can wander through the building anytime the doors are open, knowing you will be restricted when mass is in session. ✉ *Mary St., Mullingar* ☎ *044/934–8338* 🌐 *www.mullingarparish.ie.*

Hotels

Mullingar Park Hotel

$$ | **HOTEL** | On the outskirts of Mullingar, this stylish hotel has built up a solid reputation, both for its inviting accommodations and the high quality of its cuisine. **Pros:** amenities including gym, pool, and sauna; free parking; conveniently situated. **Cons:** business conferences can take over; popular with weddings; twin rooms are small. 💲 *Rooms from: €155* ✉ *Dublin Rd., Mullingar* ☎ *044/933–7500* 🌐 *www.mullingarparkhotel.com* 🛏 *95 rooms* 🍽 *Free Breakfast.*

Activities

GOLF

Mullingar Golf Club

GOLF | Mullingar Golf Club is a demanding—some say roller-coaster—18-hole course designed by James Braid. Mature oak, beech, and ash trees surround the idyllic course in undulating parkland, making precision a priority with every shot. Many holes have special features but the trees are common to all of them, presenting an old-style arboreal challenge, which visiting golfers enjoy. You can book your tee time online. The club is open to visitors from Monday to Saturday and is noted for the warmth of its welcome. ✉ *Belvedere, Mullingar* ✣ *Take Exit 15 off M4 and follow signs for Belvedere House along R400; club is 7 km (4 miles) along this road on right* ☎ *044/934–8366* 🌐 *www.mullingargolfclub.ie* 🎫 *From €20* *18 holes, 6685 yards, par 72.*

Castlepollard

21 km (13 miles) north of Mullingar.

A pretty village of multihued 18th- and 19th-century houses laid out around a large, triangular green with a church spire, Castlepollard is also home to the memorable Tullynally Castle and Gardens, the largest castle in Ireland that still functions as a family home.

GETTING HERE AND AROUND

The small rural town of Castlepollard sits at a crossroads between Cavan and Mullingar, which is the nearest large town, 20 minutes south on the narrow R394. Free parking is available in the square or on side streets. There is a daily bus service to Dublin (the trip takes two hours) and a route once a week to Mullingar.

Sights

Tullynally Castle and Gardens

CASTLE/PALACE | It's hard to figure out which is more famous: Tullynally's storybook castle or the magical parklands that surround it. Tullynally—the name, literally translated, means "Hill of the Swans"—has been the home of 10 generations of the Pakenham family which has produced Elizabeth Longford (the well-known biographer of England's Queen Victoria) and Antonia Fraser—the best-selling biographer of Mary, Queen of Scots. Her brother Thomas, a historian, is the current earl but does not use the title. He inherited Tullynally from his uncle and has planted 90,000 trees.

As a result of an 18th-century "Gothicization," the former Georgian house was transformed into a faux castle by architect Francis Johnston. The resulting 600 feet of battlements were not just for show, as the earls vehemently opposed civil rights and the freedom for Catholics to vote and hold land in Ireland. The total circumference of the building's masonry adds up to nearly ½ km (¼ mile) and includes a motley agglomeration of towers, turrets, and crenellations that date from the first early fortified building (circa 1655) up through the mid-19th century, when additions in the Gothic Revival style went up one after another.

Today, more attention is given to the beautiful parkland, in part due to the passion of Thomas Pakenham, a tree-hugger extraordinaire who founded the Irish Tree Society in 1992 and authored several books. The estate's rolling parkland was laid out in 1760, much along the lines you see today, with fine rhododendrons, numerous trees (oak, ash, sycamore, Scots pine, beech, silver fir, larch, and spruce, among others), and two ornamental lakes. A walk through the grounds in front of the castle leads to a spacious flower garden, a pond, a grotto, and walled gardens. You'll also find a Tibetan garden, a Chinese garden, and a kitchen garden, one of the largest in Ireland, with a row of old Irish yew trees.

TIP→ Don't miss the forest path, which takes you around the perimeter of the parkland and affords excellent views of the romantic castle. After your walk, enjoy a visit to the Tullynally Tea Rooms in a renovated Georgian stable block, which serves lunches such as lasagna, quiche, and preconcert supper roasts. ✉ *Castlepollard* ✣ *1½ km (1 mile) west of Castlepollard on R395 road to Granard* ☎ *044/966–1856* 🌐 *www.tullynallycastle.com*

Tullynally Castle, the largest in Ireland—just a small portion is shown here—is surrounded by spectacular parkland, forest paths, and kitchen gardens.

Garden only €8. House tour €16 with limited access, includes entry to garden. Prebooking advisable Closed Oct.–Mar. and Mon.–Wed. Not wheelchair-friendly or suitable for kids under 10.

Fore

5 km (3 miles) east of Castlepollard.

You've heard of the seven wonders of the ancient world, but here in the heart of the Irish Midlands is a tiny but bold village with seven wonders all to itself. According to an Irish myth, this is the place where water runs uphill, where there's a tree that will not burn and water that will not boil, among other fantastical occurrences. The village is known not only for its legend but also for its medieval church and the remains (supposedly the largest in Ireland) of a Benedictine abbey.

GETTING HERE AND AROUND

Fore is on a quiet country road between Castlepollard and Oldcastle on the R195. The nearest main town is Mullingar, a 30-minute drive. There's free parking in the village. Fore cannot be reached by train or bus.

Sights

★ Fore Abbey

RUINS | Close to the shores of Lough Lene is the spectacular remains of Fore Abbey—its structure is massive, and its imposing square towers and loophole windows make it resemble a castle rather than an abbey. Cast an eye over Greek masonry at the entrance to discover a 3-ton limestone lintel carved with cross—believed to have floated into place by the power of prayer. There are Seven Wonders of Fore, which include water flowing uphill, a tree that will not burn, and a mill without a millrace. Number six is an "anchorite in a stone"—a tiny hermitage connected to the abbey by a pathway. It is worth taking time to explore the 3-km (2-mile) looped walk, St. Feichin's Way—which includes his namesake's well. The views across the valley are sublime and magical. ✉ *Fore* ✣ *From Castlepollard take R195 eastbound and 4 km (2½ miles) along this road take minor road signposted to Fore and follow it for 3 km (2 miles)* 🌐 *www.voicesfromthedawn.com.*

Longford Town

37 km (23 miles) southwest of Cavan, 124 km (77 miles) northwest of Dublin.

Longford, the seat of County Longford and a typical, small, market-town community, is rich in literary associations, though after Oliver Goldsmith, the names in the county's pantheon of writers may draw a blank from all but the most dedicated Irish literature enthusiasts. Longford town provides a good base for exploring the countryside surrounding it. A day trip to the pretty heritage village of Ardagh (10 km [7 miles] southeast of Longford town), with its quaint houses and village green, is a popular option. Tours of the village may be booked through Ardagh Heritage Centre (☎ *086/302–7602*). The talk of the county, however, has been the opening of the glitzy new Center Parcs near Ballymahon, which has turned a forest into a playground and has been a game changer for family tourism in this quiet backwater.

GETTING HERE AND AROUND

Longford is on the N4 linking Mullingar and Carrick-on-Shannon. It's easily accessible by car, and town parking is generally not a problem. Shop around, as some parking is free, while other streets are metered. Unlike many Midlands towns, Longford is doubly blessed with both train and bus links. Convenient for making connections, buses stop outside Longford train station. Bus Éireann routes fan out in all directions. Dublin Airport and the city are 2¼–2½ hours away, and Belfast is a four-hour ride. There's also a cross-border bus from Longford to Derry operated in conjunction with Ulsterbus; journey time is four hours. The town is on the main Irish Rail Dublin–Sligo railway line: Dublin is 1¾ hours away and Sligo is 1¼ hours.

CONTACTS Longford Railway Station. ✉ *Convent Rd., Longford* ☎ *043/334–5208.*

VISITOR INFORMATION

CONTACTS Longford Tourism Office. ✉ *Market Sq., Longford* ☎ *043/334–3509* 🌐 *www.longford.ie/en.*

Strokestown Park House & Irish National Famine Museum

HISTORY MUSEUM | The highlight of a trip to Strokestown in County Roscommon is the Irish National Famine Museum in the stable yard of Strokestown Park House. The museum tells the story of the devastating Irish potato blight in the 1840s, which is now regarded as one of the greatest social disasters in 19th-century Europe. Two million people—about a quarter of the population of Ireland—either died or emigrated and their harrowing story is well worth exploring. Museum exhibits include original famine documents found during the restoration of the house; it's a remarkable contrast to the opulent surroundings of the Georgian Palladian mansion and its 6 acres of restored garden, which includes a fernery, rose garden, and lily pond representative of horticultural practices and garden architecture from the 1740s. The Strokestown Park House landlord, Major Denis Mahon, was assassinated in November 1847 at the height of the famine. A poignant glass memorial wall bears the names of 1,492 tenants from the estate who boarded famine ships to Quebec. Almost half died on their way to Canada. Guided tours of the house are held three times daily (at noon, 2:30, and 4 pm) in the main tourist season, and once in winter at 2 pm. In 2021, an investment of more than €5 million transformed the famine museum using cutting-edge technology along with new projects and soundscapes. The money, provided by Fáilte Ireland, the Irish Heritage Trust, and the owners of Strokestown Park House, is part of the Hidden Heartlands scheme to attract more visitors to the Midlands. While the work is in progress, the museum and house will remain open as normal.

■ **TIP→ It is not possible to tour the house on your own—all visitors must join a guided tour.** ⊠ *Strokestown* ✣ *30-min drive west of Longford Town on N5* ☏ *071/963–3013* 🌐 *www.strokestownpark.ie* *House, museum, and gardens €13.*

Restaurants

★ The Purple Onion

$$$ | **IRISH** | Originally a standard public house with low ceilings, this Shannon-side resting place on the main street of a tiny village to the west of Longford Town has been transformed into a gourmet's delight—a special gastropub, bustling with locals and tourists alike. Specialties include Thornhill duck, renowned local steaks from a butcher specializing in Irish grass-fed beef, and a famous Bakewell tart. **Known for:** duck and artisanal-butcher steaks; delicious Toblerone cheesecake; good-value early-bird menu. $ *Average main: €25* ⊠ *Main St., Tarmonbarry* ✣ *From Longford Town drive 10 km (6 miles) west on N5* ☏ *043/335–9919* 🌐 *www.purpleonion.ie* ☞ *Great value Irish fare served until 9:15 pm Wed.–Sat., until 7:15 Sun.*

Hotels

Center Parcs Longford Forest

$$$$ | **RESORT** | **FAMILY** | Rising out of the flat bogland and forest, Center Parcs is a huge new family-friendly resort that may have been developed for the Irish family travel market, but its wide variety of accommodations, amenities, and more than 100 activities make it a great option for visiting families with children who might want a break from the typical castles-and-cliffs Irish vacation. **Pros:** luxury accommodation; biggest water park in Ireland; wide range of activities. **Cons:** minimum three-night stay; restaurant reservations essential; many activities cost extra. $ *Rooms from: €339* ⊠ *Center Parcs, Newcastle Rd., Ballymahon, Longford* ✣ *3 km (2 miles) east of Ballymahon on Newcastle Rd.* ☏ *1890/995–588* 🌐 *www.centerparcs.ie* *466 cottages, 30 apartments* *No Meals.*

★ Keenan's Boutique Hotel

$$ | **HOTEL** | Barry Keenan is the fifth generation of his family since 1838 to run this first-rate hotel overlooking the Shannon, with a quality restaurant perfectly capable of challenging the Purple Onion next door for culinary polish and panache. **Pros:** hospitable family-run operation; great tree-lined walks along the riverbank; good bar and restaurant. **Cons:** Tarmonbarry is best for just one night on your way east or west; a long way from the bright lights; rooms are on the small side. $ *Rooms from: €120* ⊠ *On main N5* ✣ *8 km (5 miles) west of Longford Town* ☏ *043/332–6052* 🌐 *www.keenanshotel.ie* *12 rooms* *Free Breakfast.*

Performing Arts

Backstage Theatre

THEATER | This theater, the center of a thriving local arts scene, is on the grounds of the local Gaelic Athletic Association club. Catch a local match before heading into the theater for a dose of drama, dance, classical music, or opera. The theater and club are located a mile outside Longford on the road to Athlone. ⊠ *Farneyhoogan, Longford* ☏ *043/334–7888* 🌐 *www.backstage.ie.*

Shopping

Casey's Bogwood Sculptures

CRAFTS | A lovely spot near Longford Town is Newtowncashel, on the banks of Lough Ree, where you can visit Casey's Bogwood Sculptures, a fascinating workshop and showroom run by sculptors Michael and Kevin Casey. The center displays sculptures and keepsakes made from bog oak and bog yew, which is hewn from the 5,000-year-old trees submerged and ultimately preserved by the area's ancient peatlands. Their handiwork includes birds and fish, while other pieces furnish churches and sanctuaries. The owners will tell you the story of how they re-created froglike creatures called the *lucht na fathi* (the swamp people), inspired by a mix of local tales and Celtic mysticism. ✉ *Barley Harbour, Newtowncashel* ✣ *From Longford, drive 14 km (9 miles) on N63 to Lanesborough, then take R392 for 2 km (1 mile) and follow signs for Turreen–Newtowncashel* ☎ *043/332–5297* 🌐 *www.bogwood.net* ⏱ *Closed Sun.*

Anthony Trollope Trail

Trail starts in the village of Drumsna, 16 km (10 miles) north of Longford Town.

GETTING HERE AND AROUND

The Trollope Trail is centered on Drumsna, a village 10 minutes from Carrick-on-Shannon and 30 minutes from Longford Town. Dublin is a two-hour drive along the N4. Sligo lies 30 minutes north on the N4. Head west across the Plains of Mayo and two hours' driving will take you to breathtaking Galway.

Sights

Anthony Trollope Trail

TRAIL | This trail, created to honor the celebrated English Victorian novelist Anthony Trollope (1815–82), takes in 27 locations throughout Leitrim and incorporates many fascinating topographical spots, including an area along the River Shannon known as Flaggy Bottoms. Trollope, a senior civil servant, was sent to Drumsna in 1843 to investigate the financial affairs of the postmaster. While living there he wrote his first novel, *The Macdermots of Ballycloran,* drawing inspiration from the nearby ruin of Headford House. A leaflet and information on the trail is available from the tourist office in Carrick-on-Shannon (☎ *071/962–0170*). A series of events was held in 2015 to mark his bicentenary and helped rekindle interest in the man who introduced pillar boxes to both Ireland and Britain. 🌐 *leitrimtourism.com/walks-and-trails/town-village-walks/anthony-trollope-trail.*

Athlone

34 km (21 miles) southwest of Longford Town, 127 km (79 miles) west of Dublin, 121 km (75 miles) east of Limerick.

The mighty Shannon—the longest river in both Britain and Ireland—flows majestically through the heart of Athlone, yet for years it seemed as if the town was happy to turn its back on one of Europe's great waterways. That trend has been well and truly reversed, and there is a real buzz of regeneration. The area around Athlone Castle has been transformed into a veritable "Left Bank," with the Luan Gallery attracting culture vultures from all over Ireland. On both sides of the Shannon, new restaurants and stylishly modern architecture have sprung up on streets lined with 200-year-old buildings that have been given some imaginative repurposing alongside one of Ireland's most architecturally dazzling churches. Look out, too, for the stunning sculpture of the singer John Count McCormack, a famous Athlonian. Once upon a time, tourists were few and far between in what was cuttingly termed the "dead center" of Ireland, but the renaissance has made Athlone an increasingly attractive destination.

GETTING HERE AND AROUND

Athlone is one of the Midlands' largest towns and on busy days its long main street can take 30 minutes to drive end to end. Although the main Dublin N6 motorway has considerably eased congestion, this is still a place where delays are inevitable. Parking is available on the street, in paid lots, and at shopping centers. The drive to Dublin takes two hours, while Galway is 90 minutes west.

With its central location, Athlone is an important Bus Éireann hub with connecting expressway services to more than 20 principal towns and cities as well as dozens of smaller destinations across Ireland. Some routes are operated in conjunction with Ulsterbus. As a major rail connector, trains branch out in three main directions from Athlone: southwest to Galway, west to Westport, and east to Dublin. The east–west intercity Irish Rail Galway–Dublin service takes 1¾ hours to reach Dublin.

CONTACTS Athlone Railway Station. ✉ *Southern Station Rd., Athlone* ☎ *090/647–3300* 🌐 *www.irishrail.ie/en-ie.*

VISITOR INFORMATION

CONTACTS Athlone Tourist Office. ✉ *Athlone Castle, Castle St., Athlone* ☎ *090/649–4630* 🌐 *www.athlone.ie.*

★ Athlone Castle

CASTLE/PALACE | FAMILY | Bold and imposing, Athlone Castle stands beside the River Shannon. A raft of dazzling exhibitions are housed inside this 13th-century Norman stronghold. After their defeat at the Battle of the Boyne in 1691, the Irish retreated to Athlone and made the river their first line of defense. The castle, which is now more than 800 years old, has played a strategic role in Irish history. Eight exhibition spaces—in the main building as well as the keep and the armory—detail this enthralling chronological story and that of the town from the earliest settlement up to modern trading times. Sculptural forms convey human figures that bring the characters of Athlone to life in an engaging way. They sit cheek by jowl with 3D maps, audiovisuals, and weapons, like a bow and arrow, that allow hands-on experiences for both children and adults.

You will feel right at the center of things with the 360-degree view of events of the Siege of Athlone in 1690. It's not your typical Irish fairy-tale castle, but it is fun, and kids especially love the interactive game "How to Capture a Castle." It's hard to beat on a wet day in the Midlands. A fascinating permanent exhibition focuses on the life of the singer John Count McCormack, who was born in Athlone in 1884. Programs from the Dublin Amateur Operatic Society, his papal chain presented to him in 1928, a montage of photographs, and HMV records with his signature song, "I Hear You Calling Me," are on show. Cabinets contain a silver cup from his admirers in Philadelphia and a cup presented by the Friendly Sons of St. Patrick, New York.

McCormack sang in the Metropolitan Opera House in New York opposite Dame Nellie Melba in 1910 and continued to sing at the Met until 1918. During 2019, the first phase of a major €500,000 project to restore the castle walls took place and continuing maintenance work is needed, but this will not affect the opening of the attraction. The castle gatehouse serves as the town's tourist office.

■ TIP→ If you are here in summer the castle hosts a two-day medieval fair in the courtyard and upper battlements held in conjunction with the Athlone River Festival. Dates vary (it has been held in June and in August) so it is best to check the website for exact details. ✉ *St. Peter's Sq., Athlone* ☎ *090/644–2130* 🌐 *www.athlone-castle.ie* 🎫 *€10* 🕓 *Closed Mon. and Tues.*

A Great Irish Tenor

John Count McCormack (1884–1945) was perhaps the finest lyric tenor Ireland has produced. Born in Athlone, he recorded 600 records and made the Hollywood film *Song of My Heart*. A magnificent bronze sculpture of McCormack stands as the centerpiece of a civic park dedicated as a permanent memorial to him in 2014 beside Athlone Civic Centre. Created by the Irish artist Rory Breslin and depicting McCormack in a relaxed pose, the sculpture stands atop a 4-ton plinth. It marks the starting point of a self-guided walking trail covering 12 stops including the house in which he was born and his old school. It also takes in a memorial bust on Grace Road by the Shannon unveiled in 1970.

Nov.–Feb.; closed Mon. Mar.–May, Sept., and Oct.

Luan Gallery

ART GALLERY | The Luan Gallery has created a much-needed municipal space to showcase the work of local artists from throughout the Midlands. Since its opening in 2012, Athlone's cultural status has risen a few notches, and this contemporary visual-arts gallery, idyllically sited on the River Shannon, has been well supported by both townspeople and tourists. While it organizes exhibitions and guided tours featuring both emerging and established local artists, the Luan also draws on the national and international permanent collection of the Irish Museum of Modern Art in Dublin. ✉ *Grace Rd., Athlone* ☎ *090/644–2154* 🌐 *www.athloneartsandtourism.ie* ⏲ *Closed Mon.*

Rindoon

RUINS | Coined the "Camelot on the Shannon" by romantic souls, Rindoon was built in 1227 and the population at its height was 1,000 people—a significant town in its day. By the late 13th and early 14th centuries the town was destroyed—and forgotten as the centuries passed. Today, its town wall, castle, bee bole, medieval hospital, windmill, gatehouse, church, and mill are quite remarkably preserved. ✉ *Lisnageeragh* ✥ *18 km (11 miles) north of Athlone on N61.*

St. Peter and St. Paul Catholic Church

RELIGIOUS BUILDING | Sparkling with its restored granite walls, St. Peter and St. Paul Catholic Church is a striking Baroque ecclesiastical landmark that many come to see. Built in a completely different style from that generally adopted in Ireland, the church opened on June 29, 1937 (the feast day of the patron saints of St. Peter and St. Paul). Repair work on the impressive interior included redecoration of the vaulted ceiling, walls, floors, and pews. Dominating the skyline for many miles around, the twin campaniles symbolize the saints, while the squat copper dome adds to the overall grace of this much-loved building. Look out for the six fine stained-glass windows from the famed Harry Clarke Studios in Dublin. The tribute window to St. Patrick is a riot of glorious color. ✉ *Market Sq., Athlone* ☎ *090/649–2171* 🌐 *www.sspeterandpaulsparishathlone.com.*

Restaurants

The Fatted Calf

$$$ | **IRISH** | One of the Midlands food heroes, chef-owner Feargal O'Donnell uses fresh, locally sourced ingredients and gives them an global spin at his popular Irish restaurant in the town center, where you can sink into comfortable orange chairs made of cowhide leather for signature dry-aged steak. Starter nibbles to excite the taste buds might be crispy Garryhinch garlic oyster mushroom or silver darlings (herring), while starters may include Burren Smokehouse mackerel, lemon horseradish, toasted onion paratha, dill pickle beetroot, or crispy beef with pineapple. **Known for:** John Stone dry-aged Irish steaks; Young Buck blue cheese; calm, contemporary atmosphere. *Average main: €26 ✉ Church St., Athlone ☎ 090/643–3371 🌐 www.thefattedcalf.ie ⏲ Closed Sun. and Mon.*

Kin Khao Thai Restaurant

$$ | **THAI** | Many regard this as the leading Thai restaurant in the Midlands, if not all of Ireland. Adam Lyons runs a slick first-floor operation in a 650-year-old building on the west bank where the extensive menu features dishes from the Isaan region of northeast Thailand, including the Crying Tiger (grilled fillet of beef on a sizzling hot platter with a hot chili sauce). **Known for:** flaming curries; extensive menu of authentic dishes; best Thai food in the Midlands. *Average main: €20 ✉ 1 Abbey La., Athlone ☎ 090/649–8805 🌐 www.kinkhaothai.ie ⏲ Closed Mon. and Tues.*

★ The Left Bank Bistro

$$$ | **ASIAN** | One of Athlone's culinary highlights, this bistro is noted for its pretheater menu, which runs through the evening (except Saturday, when it ends at 6 pm), filled with such delights as bacon and colcannon mash with cider sauce, or chargrilled pork fillet. Later on, the beige-on-brown dining room fills up for the main dinner menu, which favors steaks, monkfish, duck, and rack of lamb. **Known for:** value prix fixe menu; innovative food; minimalist style. *Average main: €26 ✉ Fry Pl., Athlone ☎ 090/649–4446 🌐 www.leftbankbistro.com ⏲ Closed Sun. and Mon.*

Thyme

$$ | **IRISH** | Clusters of smoked glass pendant lights, aromatic candlelit tables, green banquette furnishings, and smooth music add luster to this always-busy riverside restaurant hidden down a side street beside the bridge. Tuck into some truly creative Athlonian food which might include glazed ham hock, goat or venison loin, or featherblade of beef (sourced from the shoulder blade of the cow). **Known for:** Wagyu beef; sticky toffee pudding; craft beers. *Average main: €23 ✉ Custume Pl., Athlone ✣ Just off main street, close to bridge on western side of town ☎ 090/647–8850 🌐 www.thymerestaurant.ie.*

Hotels

The Bastion

$ | **B&B/INN** | An inviting glow hits you as you step into the long, narrow corridor of this unconventional B&B, all nooks and little staircases, an easygoing place to chill for a few days. **Pros:** minimalist chic and no clutter; excellent value; great pubs and restaurants nearby. **Cons:** modest bathrooms; no phones, TVs; no elevator. *Rooms from: €65 ✉ 2 Bastion St., Athlone ☎ 090/649–4954 🌐 www.thebastion.net 7 rooms, 1 self-catering cottage 🍽 No Meals.*

Glasson Lakehouse

$$$ | **HOTEL** | The sumptious rooms and suites have a soothing palette of autumnal greens, reds and beiges that make leaving them difficult. **Pros:** outstanding views from spacious guest rooms; complimentary bike hire; top-class golf facilities and spa. **Cons:** strong winds whip in off the lake; Netflix TVs make it hard to leave bed; sometimes crowded with meetings and parties. *Rooms from: €188 ✉ Glasson ✣ 7 km (4 miles) north of Athlone on N55 Cavan–Longford road ☎ 090/648–5120 🌐 www.glassonlakehouse.ie 75 rooms 🍽 Free Breakfast.*

Radisson Blu Hotel, Athlone

$$$ | **HOTEL** | In a prime location on the banks of the Shannon, this property has a distinctive water theme; not surprising, as more than half the bedrooms have superb views of the meandering river

with a lovely look at Sts. Peter and Paul across the way. **Pros:** stunning views; great location for exploring the town, castle, and Left Bank; rooms are clean and modern. **Cons:** precooked breakfasts are mediocre; good pool but no spa; can be noisy during family communion and confirmation lunches. *Rooms from: €190 Northgate St., Athlone 090/644–2600 www.radissonblu.ie/hotel-athlone 128 rooms Free Breakfast.*

Sheraton Athlone Hotel
$$$ | HOTEL | Right in the heart of town, this distinctive 12-story tower hotel comes not only with outstanding comfort but also top-class views of the Midlands, making it one of the highest points in Westmeath—a county not noted for many mountains. **Pros:** central location with parking; rooms with inspiring views; luxurious spa and swimming pool. **Cons:** stairwell carpet showing some wear; easy to lose yourself in complex of corridors; less intimate than some Midland boutique hotels. *Rooms from: €200 Gleeson St., beside Athlone Shopping Center, Athlone 090/645–1000 www.sheratonathlonehotel.com 167 rooms Free Breakfast.*

★ **Wineport Lodge**
$$$ | HOTEL | Ireland's first "wine hotel" began life as a humble boathouse, but today it is one of the country's most enchanting hideaways—stylishly modern and light-filled, with log fires and billowy sofas, and rooms opening out onto the placid waters of Killinure Lough. **Pros:** magical lake and forest setting; underfloor bathroom heating; water views. **Cons:** serenity is occasionally broken by Jet Skis on the lake; meat-heavy menu may be overwhelming for plant-based diets; only some rooms have balconies. *Rooms from: €210 Glasson, Athlone 5 km (3 miles) north of Athlone 090/643–9010 www.wineport.ie 29 rooms Free Breakfast.*

Nightlife

★ **Sean's Bar**
PUBS | In Athlone's buzzing Left Bank sector, Sean's Bar styles itself as Ireland's oldest pub (a claim some cynics dispute, although a framed certificate from *Guinness World Records* says otherwise), dating to AD 900. This date has inspired the house beer, AD 900, a pale lager brewed in County Carlow. In 2018, Sean's produced two new whiskeys specially blended for the bar: one is dedicated to Luain, the first innkeeper, and is a blend of grain and malt, while the other is a malt whiskey called Clonmacnoise, a tribute to the monks who perfected the art of distillation, and with which you can wash down a complimentary dark chocolate whiskey-infused truffle. Sawdust on the floor of this dimly lighted, low-ceiling, long, narrow bar helps give it a rustic look and soaks up spills. Framed pictures and prints line the walls alongside maps of the Shannon navigation system, and the beer garden stretches almost down to the water. There's traditional music—or on Wednesday, jazz and folk—most nights of the year. **TIP→ Note the slight tilting of the floor; this was an early medieval feat of engineering—when the Shannon River's water rose and spilled into town, it would flow in one door and out the other.** *13 Main St., Athlone 090/649–2358 www.seansbar.ie.*

Shopping

★ **Bastion Gallery**
SOUVENIRS | Michael Jackson once had a shopping spree here. An Aladdin's cave of a place in which to browse, the funky Bastion Gallery sells quirky gifts, books, and toys. The owner, Katie McCay, designs and handcrafts jewelry designed with ogham, the first written form of Gaelic, sculpting words onto chains, pendants, and earrings. The shop opens in the afternoons from 12:30 to 6. *6 Bastion St., Athlone Around corner and*

Goldsmith Country

All that glitters may not be Goldsmith, but that hasn't prevented the Irish tourist board from promoting the Northern Lakelands to the burgeoning literary tourism market as "Goldsmith Country."

Yes, this is the region that gave birth to the writer Oliver Goldsmith (1728–74), celebrated for his farcical drama *She Stoops to Conquer* and his classic novel *The Vicar of Wakefield.* Goldsmith left his homeland as a teenager and returned rarely. However, he is thought to have drawn on memories of his native Longford for his most renowned poem, "The Deserted Village." At Goldsmith's childhood home in Lissoy in County Longford, only the bare walls of the family house remain standing. At Pallas, near Ballymahon in County Longford, his birthplace, there's a statue in his memory but little else. The plot of *She Stoops to Conquer* involves a misunderstanding in which a traveler mistakes a private house for an inn. This actually happened to Goldsmith at Ardagh House, now a college, in the center of the village of Ardagh (just off the N55) in County Longford. In the same play the character Tony Lumpkin sings a song about a pub called the Three Jolly Pigeons; today the pub of the same name, on the Ballymahon road (N55) north of Athlone, is the headquarters of the Oliver Goldsmith International Literary Festival.

Every year on the first weekend in June, leading academics from around the world speak on Goldsmith at this pub and other venues, and there are readings by Ireland's contemporary poets and evening traditional-music sessions in the tiny, atmospheric, country pub. Call the Athlone Tourist Office (☎ *090/649–4630*) for more information, or visit the website.

up hill from Sean's Bar ☎ *086/843–7802* 🌐 *www.thebastiongallery.com* ☞ *Opening times change from season to season; check website.*

Celtic Roots Studio

CRAFTS | *Looking for lost pieces of yourself?* reads the ethereal text on the website. But come find it for yourself. Combining a workshop and gallery, the Celtic Roots Studio in Ballinahown specializes in hand-carved sculptures and personalized jewelry from 5,000-year-old bogwood in the nearby Lough Boora bog, where the wood was preserved in the peat. The owner engraves her work, creating wish stones and all manner of carvings evocative of the natural world and Irish mythology, which make special keepsakes. Ballinahown is the last village in Westmeath as you travel to Clonmacnoise. ✉ *N62, south from Athlone to Limerick, Athlone* ✥ *Ballinahown is 12 km (7½ miles) south of Athlone* ☎ *090/643–0404* 🌐 *www.celticroots.ie.*

John's Bookshop

BOOKS | Owned and run since 1997 by the affable John Donohoe, this bookshop is exactly the way a secondhand bookstore should be: cluttered, disorganized, and heaving with rare and signed Irish-related and general books (up to 10,000 titles at any one time). Also rare movie posters and signed author portraits. ✉ *9 Main St., Athlone* ☎ *090/649–4151* 🌐 *www.johnsbookshop.com.*

Activities

BICYCLING

Buckleys Cycles

BIKING | A combination of unfrequented back roads, lakeside scenery, and flatlands makes this attractive biking country, so head to this place to rent a bike. ✉ *Kenna Centre, Dublin Rd., Athlone* ☎ *090/647–8989* 🌐 *www.buckleycycles.ie* ⏲ *Closed Sun.*

BOATING

Viking Tours

BOATING | For a unique way to cruise the Shannon, take a ride on the *Viking*. A replica of a Viking longboat, it travels upriver to nearby Lough Ree. Originally built in 1923, it's the longest-serving timber passenger boat in Ireland or the United Kingdom. The cost is €20 for a 75-minute round-trip sailing; they take place March through October. You can also sail southbound from Athlone to the ecclesiastical site of Clonmacnoise for €25; it takes 90 minutes one-way, with return by bus. Check the website for schedules. ✉ *The Quay at Athlone Castle, Athlone* ☎ *086/262–1136* 🌐 *www.vikingtoursireland.ie.*

GOLF

Athlone Golf Club

GOLF | An 18-hole parkland course, founded in 1892, Athlone is one of Ireland's oldest clubs. The course stretches along the shores of Lough Ree at Hodson Bay with stunning views of the Shannon. Tree-lined fairways, sandy greens, and undulating terrain make for an idyllic location that visitors hold in high regard. A fertilizer program has improved the quality of the fairway and rough by producing a thicker sward—resulting in a much more playable course. The club hosts national and provincial competitions, and the resident head pro, Irish golfer Kevin Grealy, offers lessons to players of all abilities and specializes in tuition on the short game.

■ TIP→ Every Wednesday, throughout the year, the club holds popular "Open Wednesday" competitions, as well as open competitions on bank holiday weekends. ✉ *Hodson Bay, Athlone* ☎ *090/649–2073* 🌐 *www.athlonegolfclub.ie* 🎫 *From €35* ⛳ *18 holes, 6001 yards, par 72.*

HIKING AND WALKING

The Old Rail Trail

BIKING | FAMILY | Westmeath's Old Rail Trail is a newly established off-road route through the heart of the Midlands, ideal for cyclists and walkers. In the days of the Midland Great Western Railway, the line linked Dublin to both Galway and Sligo. Now the 40-km (25-mile) journey running between Athlone and Mullingar has been converted into a popular flat rural trail—with just a few gentle slopes—forming part of a proposed Galway-to-Dublin cycleway. Starting at Garrycastle on the eastern edge of Athlone, the trail leads through Moate and Castletown Station, as well as arched bridges, a tunnel, and farmland to Mullingar, where you can continue your journey by joining the Royal Canal. ✉ *Starting point: Garrycastle, Athlone, Athlone* ☎ *044/932–2000* 🌐 *www.greenway.westmeathcoco.ie.*

Shannon Banks Nature Trail

HIKING & WALKING | Along the newly established Shannon Banks color-coded nature trail, wildflowers such as herb Robert, stitchwort, speedwell, and silverweed are all prominent. The looped, bidirectional trail starts at the main bridge of the Shannon at the back of Athlone castle. To the west, follow the promenade that runs parallel with Grace Road and you will come across a park filled with multilimbed trees such as silver birch, horse chestnut, red oak, common limes, and Norway maple, all of which attract rich birdlife. The other direction leads along the quay to Athlone docks. Along the way, signposts detail flora, fauna, wildlife, and fish to look for. The route takes about 45 minutes in either direction. ✉ *Athlone* 🌐 *www.*

One of Ireland's greatest monastic settlements, Clonmacnoise was nearly leveled in places—including the Norman Castle seen above—but has other ruins that still inspire awe.

athlone.ie/visit/shannon-banks-nature-trail; www.visitwestmeath.ie/westmeath-things-to-do/irelands-hidden-heartland/outdoor-adventure/shannon-banks-walk-nature-trail.

Clonmacnoise

20 km (12 miles) south of Athlone, 93 km (58 miles) east of Galway.

Many ancient sites dot the River Shannon, but Clonmacnoise is early Christian Ireland's foremost monastic settlement and, like Chartres, a royal site—a burial location for many great Gaelic kings and chieftains. The monastery was founded by St. Ciarán between AD 543 and 549 at a location that was not as remote as it now appears to be, near the intersection of what were then two of Ireland's most vital routes: the Shannon River, running north–south, and the Eiscir Riada, running east–west. Like Glendalough, Celtic Ireland's other great monastic site, Clonmacnoise benefited from its isolation; surrounded by bog, it's accessible only via one road or via the Shannon or from the river on a small lock.

GETTING HERE AND AROUND

It takes dedication to get here. As the easiest way to Clonmacnoise is by car, it can be crowded in high season, although many visitors also arrive on tour buses with the same gusto as for Mayan ruins. Get here early—the main parking lot fills up quickly. The site is 20 minutes south of Athlone; take the N62 then turn off onto the narrow R444 in the direction of Shannonbridge. Birr is 35 minutes by car south along the R357 and then the N52. Parking here is free.

Clonmacnoise is well-nigh impossible to reach by public transport. If you don't have a car, it's best to book a trip with companies such as CIE Tours, Paddywagon, Shamrocker, or Midlands Tours. Or opt to board a boat in Athlone for a 90-minute journey to the jetty beside Clonmacnoise visitor center. Trips are run on the *Viking*, and advance booking is necessary. The round-trip is €17.

Sights

★ Clonmacnoise

RUINS | Thanks to its location, this legendary monastery survived almost everything thrown at it, including raids by feuding Irish tribes, Vikings, and Normans. But when a savage English garrison arrived from Athlone in 1552, they ruthlessly ransacked and reduced the site to ruin—one account that "not a bell, large or small, an image or an altar, a book or a gem, or even a glass in a window, was left which was not carried away." A hundred years later more English tribes arrived under Cromwell to cannon-ball the infrastructure. Still, with a little imagination, you can picture life here in medieval times, when the nobles of Europe sent their sons to be educated by the local monks. The monastery was founded on an esker (natural gravel ridge) overlooking the Shannon and a marshy area known as the Callows, a distinctive landscape of shallow waters and grassy meadow land on the river's floodplains, which overflows heavily during wet winters. It was, geographically, the crossroads of Ireland in the very center of the country and The Shannon River—so logistically and strategically, very important.

Numerous buildings and ruins remain. The small cathedral dates as far back as the 10th century but has additions from the 15th century. It was the burial place of kings of Connaught and of Tara, and of Rory O'Conor, the last High King of Ireland, who was buried here in 1198. The two Round Towers include O'Rourke's Tower, which was struck by lightning and subsequently rebuilt in the 12th century. There are eight smaller churches, the littlest of which is thought to be the burial place of St. Ciaran.

Set in a field on its own, a 10-minute walk from the main site, this serene church is the quietest place to experience some peace. The High Crosses have been moved into the visitor center to protect them from the elements (copies stand in their original places); the best preserved of these is the Cross of the Scriptures, also known as Flann's Cross. Some of the treasures and manuscripts originating from Clonmacnoise are now housed in Dublin, most at the National Museum. A 20-minute audiovisual presentation tells the history of the settlement in English, German, Italian, and French. ✉ *5 km (3 miles) north of Shannonbridge, 21 km (13 miles) south of Athlone, Clonmacnoise* ✣ *Take N62 from Athlone and turn off at Doon Cross Roads on to R444 following signposts* ☎ *090/967–4195, 090/967–4134 for Shop at Clonmacnoise* 🌐 *www.heritageireland.ie* 🎫 *From €8* ⏲ *Closed Dec. 23–29.*

Boyle

72 km (45 miles) northwest of Athlone.

Hollywood legend Maureen O'Sullivan, mother of actress Mia Farrow and grandmother of journalist Ronan Farrow—along with other notables such as actor Chris O'Dowd—hail from this small town that architecturally punches far above its weight. Its centerpiece is a handsome, balustraded bridge that links the town center over the Boyle River—but the most impressive feature is the ruin of Boyle Abbey that lies on the east side of town. The town also played a starring role in one of Ireland's few triumphs against conquering forces in 1599.

Despite all this, and the village's undeniable pastoral charm, sleepy Boyle is still one step behind modern-day Ireland. Tractors putter through town and there's a noticeable absence of coffeehouses, gift shops, and franchise outlets. It seems that, unlike its famous townsfolk and their families, Boyle is still waiting to be discovered.

GETTING HERE AND AROUND

Boyle is remote and loosely connected by the N4 and N61 to the rest of the county—Dublin is 169 km (105 miles) southeast and Limerick City lies 188 km (117 miles) due south. Rail is a surprisingly easy way to discover Boyle on the Dublin to Sligo intercity route. Bus Éireann Route 23 passes through Boyle from Dublin to Sligo.

VISITOR INFORMATION

CONTACT Úna Bhán Tourism. ✉ *Main St., Boyle, Roscommon* ☎ *071/966–3033* 🌐 *www.unabhan.ie.*

Sights

King House

HISTORIC HOME | FAMILY | The mannequins that recite the backstory of the King clan haven't a cheerful disposition, but then again, neither did the family they depict, and many of them have a grim tale to tell in this large, white-painted Georgian mansion. The often brutal, sometimes glorious stories of Connaught chieftains, sibling squabbles, and the tragedy and evictions during the famine are just some of the topics recounted. Many of the props are interactive and child-friendly—and *Tarzan The Ape Man* (1934) and *Hannah and Her Sisters* (1986) star Maureen O'Sullivan, who was born in Boyle, has a room devoted to her story. The King family moved to Lough Key until it burned down in 1957, while King House fell into disuse after it had a stint as an army barracks. The courtyard has a crafts shop, café, and weekly farmers' market. ✉ *King's House, Boyle* ☎ *087/144–4739* 🌐 *www.visitkinghouse.ie* *€7* *Closed Oct.–mid-Apr.*

★ Lough Key Forest Park

FOREST | FAMILY | A shuttle bus operates from King House in Boyle for the 4-km (2-mile) trip to 350-hectare Lough Key Estate where you can camp, caravan or moor. It's a natural, nautical wonderland with a scattering of small islands, some with fabulously picturesque ruins, like Castle Island with its 19th-century McDermott's Castle. It's especially popular with families due to its fairy bridge, ziplines, boat trips, orienteering, a wishing chair, bog gardens, and a panoramic, 300-meter-long treetop canopy walk. Marked walking and electric-bike trails cut through the park, which was once part of the King family's estate from the 17th century until 1957, when their Rockingham House was destroyed by a fire. There still remains the shell of stables, and sinister, dark tunnels that lead to Key Lake—designed to obscure the servants from their affluent, fainthearted guests. ✉ *Lough Key* ☎ *71/967–3122* 🌐 *www.loughkey.ie* *From €10.*

Restaurants

Gate Lodge

$ | CONTEMPORARY | "Lovage at the Gate Lodge," as it's known locally, overlooks the river and serves the best coffee in town. Pastries, wraps, baps, and burgers are common on the menu, but make sure to check the blackboard for daily specials. **Known for:** generous portion sizes; beautiful riverside location; wide variety of coffees. *Average main: €12* ✉ *Knocknashee, Bridge St., Boyle* ☎ *087/161–7564* *lovagecompany@gmail.com.*

Hotels

Kilronan Castle Estate

$ | HOTEL | Overlooking Lough Meelagh deep in a 40-acre estate, this restored 18th-century castle offers keenly priced luxury in a romantic setting. **Pros:** beautiful grounds; good leisure facilities; four-poster beds and antique-style furnishings. **Cons:** limited dining; attracts a wedding trade; remote—car an advantage. *Rooms from: €110* ✉ *Kilronan Castle, Ballyfarnon* *19 km (11 miles) northeast via R285* ☎ *71/961–8000* 🌐 *www.kilronancastle.ie* *85 rooms* *Free Breakfast.*

Banagher

31 km (19 miles) south of Clonmacnoise.

"Well, that beats Banagher!" This small Shannon-side town is best known in Ireland because of this common phrase, which dates from the 19th century when the town was the very worst example of a pocket or "rotten borough"—a corrupt electoral area controlled by the local landed gentry who blackmailed tenants into voting for them during parliamentary elections. In short, if something "beats Banagher and Banagher beat the band," it's either pretty bad or rather extraordinary. Nowadays, Banagher is a lively marina town that is a popular base for water-sports enthusiasts. Charlotte Brontë (1816–55) famously spent her honeymoon here. On the second Sunday in September each year one of Ireland's oldest horse fairs takes over the town. Buyers and sellers come from all over the country to take part in the horse trading that gives the town a raffish air thick with the fragrance of horse odor and horse leather.

TIP→ Pick up a copy of the Banagher Heritage Trail, available in shops, pubs, and B&Bs. It will guide you around 17 buildings, sculptures, and sites of interest in the town and along the riverside, including places with a Brontë connection.

GETTING HERE AND AROUND

Midway between Athlone and Roscrea, Banagher is a small crossroads town. Athlone and Birr are both a 40-minute drive, and although the town is busy in summer, parking is generally not a problem. Kearns Transport operates daily services with links from Banagher to Birr (15 minutes), Tullamore (35 minutes), and Dublin (three hours).

CONTACTS Banagher Tourist Information. *Crank House, Main St., Banagher* *057/915–2155.* **Kearns Transport.** *Harper Rd., Banagher* *Pickup and drop-off is at square in Banagher* *057/912–0124* *www.kearnstransport.com.*

Restaurants

Flynn's Bar & Lounge

$ | **MODERN IRISH** | **FAMILY** | In the center of town, Flynn's is worth visiting to appreciate its light and spacious Victorian-style design. The lunch menu includes sandwiches, salad platters, and dishes such as red Thai curry, chicken Milanese, or Irish lamb stew. **Known for:** quality roast beef; scrumptious apple pie; Irish coffees. *Average main: €13* *Commercial House, Main St., Banagher* *057/915–1312* *www.flynnsbar.ie.*

Hotels

Charlotte's Way

$ | **B&B/INN** | The sweet aroma of turf smoke percolates in the living room of this historic B&B, where the delightful Nicola Daly welcomes guests to her "home from home," an 18th-century house that has a connection to Charlotte Brontë, whose husband lived here after her death. **Pros:** Victorian history seeps from its pores; homemade jams from the property; countryside views. **Cons:** quiet; short walk into town; no credit cards. *Rooms from: €80* *Birr Rd., Kylebeg* *057/915–3864* *www.charlottesway.com* *No credit cards* *Closed Nov.–mid-Mar.* *6 rooms* *Free Breakfast.*

Nightlife

J. J. Hough's

PUBS | Travelers love Hough's, which calls itself "a singing pub" and where on many an eve there's usually an almighty sing-along around the German piano. Try the cocktails or the house special, Shakalaka Boom, a mix of Irish whiskey and Bailey's cream liqueur. Note the walls decorated with business cards, testifying to the pub's popularity the world over. Side rooms lead to a beer garden with wooden chairs and tables. You can also join in card games with the locals, and there's generally traditional music on Saturday night and most nights between April and October. The owner, Mick Hough, has been known to launch into song himself on occasion. If you're feeling peckish, 10 different styles of pizza are served from lunchtime to closing time. ✉ *Main St., Banagher* ☎ *087/935–7312* *geraldhough@yahoo.com.*

Birr

12 km (7 miles) southeast of Banagher, 130 km (81 miles) west of Dublin.

Beautifully reminiscent of an English country town with its tree-lined malls and well-preserved houses, the heritage town of Birr has roots that date to the 6th century. Still, the mid-18th-century Georgian buildings set the tone. Birr Castle is the pièce de résistance and an ideal place to while away a morning on a guided tour or spend the afternoon in an idyllic setting. For those who enjoy a riparian ramble, head to the Camcor River Walk. Birr is also noted for its variety of festivals throughout the year, including the longest-running hot-air-balloon championships in the world, held at the end of September.

GETTING HERE AND AROUND

Six main roads meet at Birr. Limerick is 90 minutes south on the N52 and then the N7, while Athlone is 30 minutes north on the N52. There may be traffic delays along the town's narrow central streets. Several paid lots and on-street metered spaces provide parking. Buses leave from Emmet Square for Dublin (3½ hours away) and west for Limerick (75 minutes).

Sights

★ Birr Castle Gardens and Science Centre
CASTLE/PALACE | FAMILY | Summer visitors can join a guided tour of one of Ireland's most elegant stately homes and peer behind the scenes of a previously closed-off world. Although relatively recently constructed, during the great famine in the mid-19th century, this Gothic Revival castle (built around a series of castles since the 12th century—including one that was damaged by fire in 1823) has been the home of the earls of Rosse or Parson family since the turbulent 17th century. Castle tours, usually given by family members, bring you through the spectacular Gothic music saloon, the library, the yellow drawing room, and reception rooms. Held from May to August, Monday–Saturday, the tours run at 10, 11:30, and 1, and last around 60 minutes. Note that the castle has more than 100 rooms and the tour takes in just a small number of them.

The Parson family continue the tradition of making botanical expeditions for specimens of rare trees, plants, and shrubs to fill the demesne's 150 acres. The formal gardens contain the tallest box hedges in the world (at 32 feet) and vine-sheltered hornbeam allées. In spring, check out the wonderful display of flowering magnolias, cherries, crab apples, and naturalized narcissi; in autumn, the maples, chestnuts, and weeping beeches blaze red and gold.

TIP→ If you are joining a house tour, book in advance; allow at least three hours to see everything in the demesne—there are 3,400 plants and 3,860 varieties of trees from 40 countries. ✉ *Rosse Row, Birr* ☎ *057/912–0336* 🌐 *www.birrcastle.com* *€10* ⏲ *Castle closed Sept.–May and Sun.*

Birr Library
NOTABLE BUILDING | In keeping with the historic townscape character, it's worth calling in here to see what ranks as one of Ireland's most spectacular locations for a library. Based in the ground floor of

the Birr municipal offices (and a former convent), the building was designed by A. W. N. Pugin and completed by his son Edward in the mid–19th century. The former chapel—which is now the library—has retained the exquisite Gothic-style stone and mullioned, stained-glass windows. Upstairs you will find a facsimile of an early Christian illuminated manuscript, the *Gospel Book of MacRegol,* also known as the *Book of Birr* and the *Rushworth Gospels,* on permanent display. MacRegol was a scribe, bishop, and abbot in Birr. The original manuscript, which is now in Oxford's Bodleian Library, was produced around AD 800 and consists of 169 vellum folios or leaves. The library also offers Internet service and you can pick up some local tourist information leaflets and brochures here, too. ✉ *Wilmer Rd., Birr* ☎ *057/912–4950* 🌐 *www.offaly.ie* ⏲ *Closed Sun. and Mon.*

Restaurants

Emma's Café and Deli

$ | **IRISH** | A tempting array of both savory and sweet delights are on display at this central daytime café and deli counter. Nourishing soups at lunchtime, such as colcannon (cabbage and potato) or mushroom come with freshly baked brown bread. **Known for:** colcannon soup; meat-filled sandwiches; superfresh scones. $ *Average main: €11* ✉ *31 Main St., Birr* ☎ *057/912–5678.*

The Thatch Bar

$$ | **IRISH** | Imaginative food and a warm welcome await at this 300-year-old bar and restaurant, its thatched roof (completely redone in 2017), exposed wooden beams, and brick walls adding to the intimate country atmosphere. Main courses may include half honey roast duck, braised lamb shank, grilled aubergine with goat cheese, or chicken with black pudding. **Known for:** steaks; huge portions; flawless service. $ *Average main: €19* ✉ *Military Rd., Crinkill* ✣ *2 km (1 mile) south of Birr, just off N62 Roscrea road* ☎ *057/912–0682* 🌐 *www.thethatchcrinkill.com* ⏲ *Closed Mon. and Tues. No lunch Wed.–Fri.*

Hotels

Dooly's Hotel

$ | **HOTEL** | Originally a coach house, this unpretentious country hotel in Birr's central square, just a five-minute walk to Birr Castle, began life in 1747 and has retained its old-style homeyness with well-appointed rooms decorated with neutral furnishings. **Pros:** huge rooms; a handy Midlands stopover, if you're on your way to the west coast; short walk to Birr Castle. **Cons:** attached nightclub can be noisy; stairs can be difficult for the disabled or elderly; no pool. $ *Rooms from: €80* ✉ *Emmet Sq., O'Connell St., Birr* ☎ *057/912–0032* 🌐 *www.doolyshotel.com* *17 rooms* *Free Breakfast.*

Roscrea

19 km (12 miles) south of Birr.

Every corner you turn in this charming town will offer reminders of its rich and sometimes turbulent past. Ancient castles, towers, and churches dot the skyline, proof of a rich heritage that dates to the 7th century. The road through town cuts right through the remains of a monastery founded by St. Cronan. It also passes the west facade of a 12th-century Romanesque church that now forms an entrance gate to a modern Catholic church. Above the structure's rounded doorway is a hood mold enclosing the figure of a bishop, probably St. Cronan.

GETTING HERE AND AROUND

Roscrea is on the main N7 road between Dublin and Cork, making it ideal as a stopover en route to the south. Limerick is one hour south on this route, and roads from the town lead to all points of the Midlands compass. There is ample parking on side streets and in designated areas.

Presidential Roots

The village of Moneygall (population 320) is an unassuming place on the main N7 Dublin–Limerick road, but it was thrust into the spotlight in 2011 when President Barack Obama paid a visit to check on his ancestors and since then, Moneygall has forced itself onto the map as the ancestral homeland of the 1/32nd-Irish former president. His great-great-great grandfather came from the village and his maternal ancestors lived and worked in the Moneygall area more than 160 years ago. Ollie Hayes' Bar on the main street has an "Obama Corner," and on a Thursday evening you may see the Obama Set Dancers strutting their Cashel and Ballycommon sets and practicing a mix of jigs, reels, polkas, and hornpipes. In 2014, the President Barack Obama Visitor Centre was opened, which explores the links between the village and the president. It's based in Barack Obama Plaza, a service station at junction 23 of the M7. Tour companies passing through from Dublin stop here regularly to offer an opportunity to drink at the pub where the former president took a healthy swig of Guinness, and, of course, shop the presidential plaza for Obama swag. Kitsch-factor alone makes this a worthy stop if you happen to be driving through.

The Bus Éireann Expressway from Dublin to Limerick stops in Roscrea, a 2½-hour journey. The Roscrea–Limerick leg of the route is 70 minutes. From Roscrea, you can also catch a bus south to Cashel (2¼ hours) and Cork (three hours), as well as north to Athlone (70 minutes) or as far northwest as Sligo, a journey of nearly five hours. The Irish Rail Dublin–Limerick train stops in Roscrea as well; the town is 90 minutes from each city.

Sights

Roscrea Castle and Damer House

CASTLE/PALACE | In the very center of town is Roscrea Castle, a Norman fortress dating from 1314, given by King Richard II to the Duke of Ormonde. Inside are vaulted rooms graced with tapestries and 16th-century furniture. A ticket to the castle gains entry to the adjacent Damer House, a superb example of an early-18th-century town house on the grand scale. The house has a plain, symmetrical facade and a magnificent carved-pine staircase inside; on display are exhibits about local history. The Damer Art Gallery is on the second floor, while on the third the Kelly Exhibition showcases furniture and farm implements donated from a local farmhouse. Guided 45-minute tours are held in spring and summer. Your ticket also includes entry to the restored Black Mills in Church Street, a small museum with local artifacts, of which the star attraction is St. Cronan's High Cross. ✉ *Castle St., Roscrea* ✣ *To get here, start with your back to St. Cronan's Monastery, turn left, and then turn right onto Castle St.* ☎ *050/521850* 🌐 *www.heritageireland.ie* 🎫 *€5* ⏲ *Closed Oct.–Easter.*

Shopping

Roscrea Country Market

MARKET | For a real taste of some honest-to-goodness Tipperary home baking, try to catch the Roscrea Country Market, held every Friday 10–1 at the Abbey Hall, for whole-grain scones and breads, apple and rhubarb tarts, fruit and sponge cakes, and homemade jams. Potatoes, vegetables, eggs from free-range chickens, and flowers are also on offer. The market has been running since 1962. ✉ *Abbey Hall, Roscrea.*

Chapter 6

THE SOUTHEAST

Updated by
Anto Howard

Sights	Restaurants	Hotels	Shopping	Nightlife
★★★★★	★★★★★	★★★★★	★★★★★	★★★★★

WELCOME TO THE SOUTHEAST

TOP REASONS TO GO

★ **Sacred Ardmore:** St. Declan founded Ireland's first Christian settlement near this beautifully situated fishing village on the Waterford coast.

★ **Kilkenny, Ireland's Medieval Capital:** With its famous 14th-century "witch," Petronilla, Camelot-worthy Black Abbey, and fairy-tale Kilkenny Castle, the city still conjures up the days of knights and damsels.

★ **Pretty-as-a-Postcard Lismore:** Presided over by the neo-baronial castle of the dukes of Devonshire, this storybook village has attracted visitors ranging from Sir Walter Raleigh to Fred Astaire.

★ **Cashel of the Kings:** Ireland's "Rock of Ages," this spectacular 200-foot-tall rock bluff was the ancient seat of the kings of Munster.

★ **Wexford and Waterford:** Big-city lights shine brightest here, thanks to such attractions as the famed Wexford Opera Festival and the reborn House of Waterford Crystal factory and visitor center.

Set around Tipperary—Ireland's largest inland county—the Southeast is a vast region that stretches from the town of Carlow near the border of County Wicklow in the north to Ardmore near the border of County Cork in the south. Although main towns can be packed with camera-wielding tourists, you can easily escape the tour buses thanks to endless expanses of tranquil countryside.

1 Kilkenny City. A picturesque city with a medieval castle, a lively pub scene, and quality Irish crafts.

2 Thomastown. This pretty riverside village is known for Jerpoint Abbey and Mount Juliet Golf Course.

3 Enniscorthy. On the road between Dublin and Wexford with an imposing Norman castle worth visiting.

4 Wexford Town. A compact coastal town famous for its opera festival and beautiful Johnstown Castle Gardens.

5 Rosslare. A seaside town and port for the ferry to Wales and France.

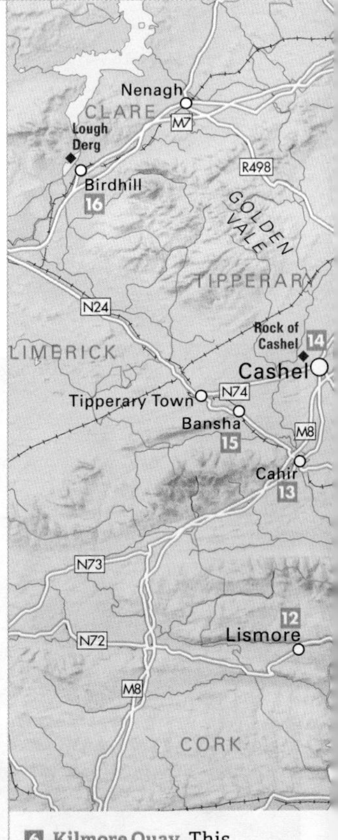

6 Kilmore Quay. This quiet and pretty fishing village has thatched cottages and the Saltee Islands.

7 Ballyhack. A picturesque village with a square castle keep, thatched cottages, and one of Ireland's finest country houses.

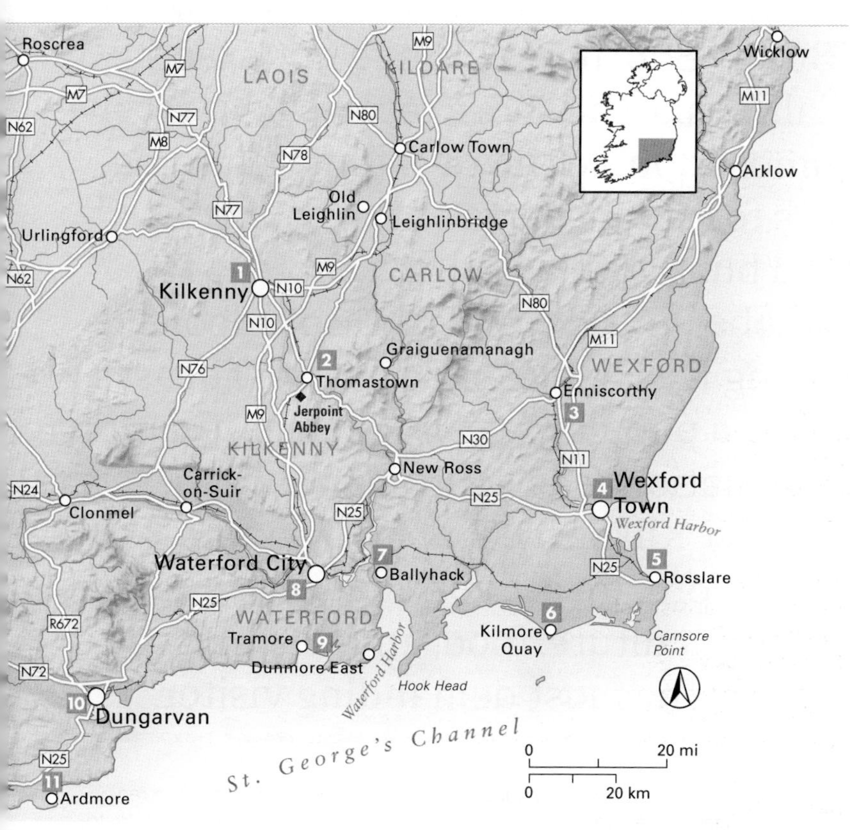

8 Waterford City. Ireland's oldest city offers preserved city walls, the Waterford Crystal factory, and a fairy-tale castle.

9 Tramore. The most popular beach in the "sunny Southeast."

10 Dungarvan. A great base for climbers and hikers and a must-visit for the new Waterford Greenway and one of Ireland's top restaurants.

11 Ardmore. A picture-postcard little town with an award-winning restaurant and a famous Irish pottery studio and shop.

12 Lismore. Highlights here include the Knockmealdown Mountains and Lismore Castle and Gardens.

13 Cahir. A compact and attractive town with a beautiful castle.

14 Cashel. Home to one of Ireland's top attractions, the Rock of Cashel.

15 Bansha. Great for mountain walking, fishing, horseback riding, and generally soaking in the Glen of Aherlow.

16 Birdhill. A charming little town on the shores of Lough Derg.

Going to Ireland for the sunshine might sound like a joke, but not if you head to the golden beaches and blue surf of the "Sunny Southeast." While not exactly California, the shore resorts here receive almost double the rays found in some less fortunate parts of the country, and buzz with activity from May to October. Little wonder the outdoors-loving Irish have made the Southeast's coast a popular warm-weather vacation destination. The counties Wexford, Carlow, Kilkenny, Tipperary, and Waterford are also packed with enough history, culture, food, and festivals to satisfy the most demanding visitor.

Thousands of families take their annual summer holidays here, where picnics and barbecues—often a rain-washed fantasy elsewhere in Ireland—are a golden reality.

The entire Southeast is rich with natural beauty—not the rugged and wild wonders found to the north and west, but a coast that alternates between long sandy beaches and rocky bays backed by low cliffs, and an inland landscape of fertile river valleys and lush undulating pastureland. The landscape of the region is diverse, the appeal universal: you'll find seaside fishing villages with thatched cottages and Tipperary's verdant, picturesque Golden Vale. The region doesn't lack for culture, either. History-rich Ardmore, Carlow Town, the cities of Kilkenny and Waterford, and Wexford Town have retained traces of their successive waves of invaders—Celt, Viking, and Norman.

The most important of these destinations is Kilkenny City, a major ecclesiastic and political center until the 17th century and now a lively market town. Its streets still hold remnants from medieval times—most notably St. Canice's Cathedral—and a magnificent 12th-century castle that received a sumptuous Victorian makeover. Wexford's narrow streets are built on one side of a wide estuary, giving it a delightful maritime air. Waterford, although less immediately attractive than Wexford, is also built at the confluence of two of the region's rivers, the Suir and the Barrow. It offers a rich selection of Viking and Norman remains, some attractive Georgian buildings, and the visitor center and shop at the famed House of Waterford Glass Factory.

Deeper into the countryside, rustic charms beckon. The road between Rosslare and Ballyhack passes through quiet, atypical, flat countryside dotted with thatched cottages. In the far southwest of County Waterford, near the Cork border, Ardmore presents early Christian ruins on an exposed headland, while, in the wooded splendor of the Blackwater Valley, the tiny cathedral town of Lismore has a hauntingly beautiful fairy-tale castle.

MAJOR REGIONS

Kilkenny City. Creativity is evident in every aspect of this town, from its medieval stonework to its array of modern and traditional craft and design found in galleries and studios. Many festivals and events are held here year-round.

Southeast Inlands. North of Kilkenny City is a region notably rich in historical sights. Travel through the farmlands of the Barrow Valley to the small county seat of Carlow Town, with scenic detours to Thomastown and the historic Jerpoint Abbey.

The Southeast Coast. This journey takes you along mainly minor roads through the prettiest parts of the coast in counties Wexford and Waterford, pausing midway to explore Waterford City—home of the dazzling cut glass—on foot. Along the way expect to see long golden beaches, quaint fishing villages like Kilmore Quay and Ballyhack, some of the country's best nature reserves, and the family seaside resort of Tramore. If you're coming from the Continent or England, chances are you'll end up on a ferry bound for Rosslare Harbor, one of Ireland's busiest ferry ports.

County Tipperary and Around. "It's a long way to Tipperary ..." So run the words of that famed song sung all over the world since World War I. Actually, Tipperary is *not* so far to go, considering that, as Ireland's biggest inland county, it's within easy striking distance of Waterford and Cork. Moving in from the coastline, you can travel through some of Ireland's lushest pasturelands and to some of its most romantic sights, such as Lismore Castle in the enchanting town of Lismore. The Blackwater Valley is renowned for its peaceful beauty and excellent fishing. Some of the finest racehorses in the world are raised in the fields of Tipperary, which is also where you can find the Rock of Cashel—the greatest group of monastic ruins in all Ireland.

Planning

Getting Here and Around

BOAT AND FERRY

If you are coming into Ireland from England, chances are you'll leave from Wales on a ferry bound for Rosslare Harbour, 19 km (12 miles) south of Wexford, one of Ireland's busiest ferry ports. There are two main companies that service Rosslare. Irish Ferries connects Rosslare to Pembroke, Wales (four hours). Stena Line sails directly between Rosslare Ferryport and Fishguard, Wales (three hours), and to Cherbourg in France (19½ hours). Brittany Ferries, a smaller company, also sails to Cherbourg and twice a week to Bilbao in Spain (28 hours). They all have small information kiosks in the ultramodern terminal, which also has lockers and a sprawling waiting room. Passage East Car Ferry is a short-cut across the Suir Estuary, connecting Ballyhack in Wexford with Passage East in Waterford.

The bypass and bridge around New Ross mean drive times to the rest of the Southeast have been cut by half an hour or more.

You can purchase ferry tickets at the terminal, but try to reserve a space in advance online to avoid the frequent sell-outs, particularly in summer and anytime the Irish soccer team is playing in a major tournament abroad.

Reservations are a must if you're traveling by car or motorcycle because onboard parking space is at a premium. Eurail Pass holders get a discount on ferries from France. Departure times vary from season to season, so call ahead.

CONTACTS Brittany Ferries. ✉ *Cork City* ☎ *021/427–7801 in Ireland* 🌐 *brittany-ferries.ie.* **Irish Ferries.** ☎ *0818/300–400* 🌐 *irishferries.com.* **Passage East Ferry Company.** ☎ *051/382–480* 🌐 *passageferry.ie.* **Stena Line.** ☎ *01/907–5555* 🌐 *stenaline.ie.*

BUS

Bus Éireann runs frequent buses between Waterford and Dublin, Limerick, Cork, and Rosslare. J.J. Kavanagh & Sons runs daily buses from Dublin to Carlow, Waterford, and Kilkenny.

CONTACTS Bus Éireann. ☎ *01/836–6111* 🌐 *buseireann.ie.* **J.J. Kavanagh & Sons.** 🌐 *jjkavanagh.ie.*

CAR

With quality highways to Waterford and Kilkenny, a car is the best option for covering ground quickly and easily. Waterford City, the regional capital, is easily accessible from all parts of Ireland.

From Dublin, take the M7 southwest, change to the M9, and continue along as it bypasses Carlow Town and Thomastown until it ends in Waterford. N25 travels east–west through Waterford City, connecting it with Cork in the west and Wexford Town in the east. From Limerick and Tipperary Town, N24 stretches southeast until it, too, ends in Waterford City.

For the most part, the main roads in the Southeast are of good quality and are free of congestion. Side roads are generally narrow and twisting, and you should keep an eye out for farm machinery and animals on country roads.

TAXI

It costs €3.80 to hire a taxi on the street (€4.20 by night) in the larger towns: add €2 to book by phone, and €1.14 per kilometer or part of a kilometer for the first 15 km (9 miles). Reputable companies include Wexford Cabs in Wexford, Rapidcabs in Waterford, and Kilkenny Taxi.

CONTACTS Kilkenny Taxi. ☎ *087/225–5333* 🌐 *kilkennytaxi.com.* **Rapidcabs.** ☎ *051/858–585* 🌐 *rapidcabs.com.* **Wexford Cabs.** ☎ *053/912–3123* 🌐 *wexfordcabs.ie.*

TRAIN

Waterford City is linked by daily Irish Rail service to Dublin, with trains making stops at Thomastown, Kilkenny, Bagenalstown, and Carlow Town. The daily train between Waterford City and Limerick makes stops at Carrick-on-Suir, Clonmel, Cahir, and Tipperary Town. The daily trail from Dublin to Rosslare port travels through Wexford.

CONTACTS Irish Rail. ☎ *01/836–6222* 🌐 *irishrail.ie.* **MacDonagh Station.** ✉ *St. John's St., Kilkenny.* **O'Hanrahan Station.** ✉ *Redmond Pl., Wexford.* **Plunkett Station.** ✉ *Dock Rd., Waterford.*

Hotels

Festivals, the good weather, and commerce make the Southeast popular, so plan way ahead for a stay in any of the main towns (or in many country manors, which usually have fewer than six bedrooms and fill up fast). As always, the local tourist offices can offer assistance if you arrive without reservations.

Restaurants

Food is usually prepared in a simple, country-house style, though pleasant surprises abound. A number of ambitious Irish chefs are at work in the Southeast's restaurants and hotels, and at newer joints with inventive offerings that offer a great value. The best of the region's cuisine rests on modern, international interpretations of classic Irish dishes. Leading lights in the area include chef Kevin Dundon at Dunbrody Country House, Paul Flynn of the Tannery, and Gareth Byrne at the Michelin-starred Campagne in Kilkenny.

Other than its fabled strawberries, the Southeast is probably best known for its rich seafood, especially Wexford mussels, crabs, and locally caught salmon. Kilmore Quay, noted for lobster and deep-sea fishing, hosts an annual Seafood Festival the second week of July. Many restaurants serve local lamb, beef, and game in season.

RESTAURANT AND HOTEL PRICES

⇨ *Restaurant prices are the average cost of a main course at dinner or, if dinner is not served, at lunch. Hotel prices are the lowest cost of a standard double room in high season. Restaurant and hotel reviews have been shortened. For full information, visit Fodors.com.*

What It Costs In Euros

	$	$$	$$$	$$$$
RESTAURANTS				
	under €19	€19–€24	€25–€32	over €32
HOTELS				
	under €150	€150–€200	€201–€270	over €270

Tune In to the Southeast

If you want to feel the true pulse of the nation, check out any of RTÉ Radio 1's morning and afternoon shows. With a falloff in religious attendance and a new liberal social outlook, the radio has become Ireland's modern confessional and a serious insight into what makes the Irish tick. Waterford Local Radio (95.1/97.5 FM) and South East Radio (95.6/96.4 FM) are the popular options around Waterford and Wexford, respectively.

Tours

Burtchaell Tours of Waterford City

WALKING TOURS | The knowledgeable and delightful Jack Burtchaell and his associates lead a Waterford City walk daily at noon and 2 pm (departing from Granville Hotel) and 11:45 am and 1:45 pm (departing from the tourist office). They run from mid-March through mid-October. ☎ *051/873–711* 🌐 *jackswalkingtours.com* 🎫 *From €7.*

A Rural Experience

GUIDED TOURS | This outfit runs day excursions and extended private chauffeur tours all over the Southeast, and the County Kilkenny tour is especially popular. ☎ *056/772–7590* 🌐 *aruralexperience.com* 🎫 *From €220.*

Tynan Tours of Kilkenny City

WALKING TOURS | These walking tours of Kilkenny take place Monday to Saturday, April through October, and by appointment November to March. ☎ *087/265–1745* 🌐 *kilkennywalkingtours.ie* 🎫 *From €20.*

When to Go

As well as having some of the richest land in the country, the Southeast is the envy of all Ireland for that most elusive element—sunshine. The region is also one of the driest in Ireland, which is saying something in a country where seldom do more than three days pass without some rain. Compared with an average of 80 inches on parts of the west coast, the Southeast gets as little as 40 inches of rainfall per year, varying from the finest light drizzle (a soft day, thank goodness!) to full-blown downpours.

Festivals and Events

With practically every hamlet and village across the country glorying in its own festival (an excuse for keeping pubs open later), the Southeast delivers some of Ireland's most popular gatherings. Check with the tourist boards for listings and dates of all events, big and small.

APRIL

West Waterford Festival of Food

FESTIVALS | With the Southeast gaining a reputation as a hotbed of inventive Irish cuisine, this foodie's festival has rapidly grown into one of the best in the country. Local and international chefs, bakers, picklers, brewers, and a host of other food artists take over the bustling seaside town of Dungarvan for four days in April. ✉ *Dungarvan* ☎ *058/21433* 🌐 *westwaterfordfestivaloffood.com.*

JUNE

Carlow Arts Festival

ARTS FESTIVALS | The Carlow Arts Festival is a five-day celebration of visual arts held every June. ☎ *059/917–2400* 🌐 *carlowartsfestival.com.*

AUGUST

Kilkenny Arts Festival

ARTS FESTIVALS | Every August, Kilkenny becomes the focus for Ireland's culture vultures when the Kilkenny Arts Festival takes over the city for about two weeks. Street theater, elaborate parades, and even a rock concert set the mood. ✉ *Kilkenny* ☎ *056/775–1704* 🌐 *kilkennyarts.ie.*

Spraoi

ARTS FESTIVALS | Every August, the Spraoi street arts festival presents an exuberant display of music, theater, and other entertainment in Waterford City. You'll find it around the city's extensive pedestrian areas. ✉ *Waterford* 🌐 *spraoi.com.*

OCTOBER

Wexford Fringe Festival

ARTS FESTIVALS | Running alongside the opera festival from late October to early November, the chaotic and theatrical Wexford Fringe Festival is an eclectic mix of theater, literature, music, dance, and street events. ✉ *Wexford* 🌐 *wexfordfringe.ie.*

Wexford Opera Festival

FESTIVALS | From late October to early November, the two-week-long Wexford Opera Festival is the biggest social and artistic event in the entire Southeast. From mid-September until the final curtain comes down, Wexford becomes home to a colorful cast of international singers, designers, and musicians as they prepare for the annual staging of three grand operas at the Wexford Opera House. Along with an ever-expanding offering of more populist fare performed in small venues and pubs, the festival supplies a feast of concerts and recitals that start at 11 am and continue until midnight. The bad news: nearly every single bed within miles is booked during the festival, and usually months ahead of time. ✉ *Wexford* 🌐 *wexfordopera.com.*

Planning Your Time

IF YOU HAVE THREE DAYS

Distances are not great, but if you are here for a short stay—three days or fewer—you might want to base yourself in one of the region's cities or larger towns: Waterford, Kilkenny, or Wexford. All three are historic locations with plenty of places of cultural and historical interest accessible on foot. They are also growing shopping destinations. Day trips from Waterford and Wexford could include idyllic coastal villages like Ardmore, Dunmore East, and Kilmore Quay. From Kilkenny and Waterford the mountains, glens, and lakes of Tipperary are only a short drive away. Spend a night at a coastal hotel like the Cliff House in Ardmore or the country manor of Ballyduff House in Thomastown.

IF YOU HAVE FIVE DAYS

If you have more time in the region, you might want to drive the whole of the scenic coast from Wexford down around spectacular Hook Head to Waterford and on to the winding road to Ardmore and Dungarvan. Take your time, avoid the motorway, and stop off at any village or watering hole that takes your fancy. You'll still have plenty of time for a detour north into Tipperary along some beautiful mountain back roads and on to the historic town of Cashel to see the legendary Rock. From there, head northwest for a touch of water sports on Lough Derg or take the short, scenic hop back to medieval Kilkenny City.

Visitor Information

Eight tourist information offices of varying quality in the Southeast are open all year. They are in Carlow Town, Dungarvan, Gorey, Kilkenny, Lismore, Waterford City, Tramore, and Wexford Town. Another four TIOs are open seasonally: Cahir (April–October); Cashel (April–September); Rosslare (April–September); and Tipperary Town (May–October). If traveling extensively by public transportation, be sure to load up on information (schedules, the best taxi companies, etc.) upon arriving at the train and bus stations in Kilkenny City, Wexford Town, and Waterford City.

Kilkenny City

101 km (63 miles) southwest of Dublin.

Dubbed "Ireland's Medieval Capital" by its tourist board, and also called "the Oasis of Ireland" for its many pubs and watering holes, Kilkenny is one of the country's most alluring destinations. It demands to be explored by foot or bicycle, thanks to its easily circumnavigated town center, a 900-year-old Norman citadel that is now a lovely place of Georgian streets and Tudor stone houses. The city (population 24,500) is impressively preserved and attractively situated on the River Nore, which forms the moat of the magnificently restored Kilkenny Castle. In the 6th century, St. Canice (known as "the builder of churches") established a large monastic school here. The town's name reflects Canice's central role: Kil Cainneach means "Church of Canice." Kilkenny did not take on its medieval look for another 400 years, when the Anglo-Normans fortified the city with a castle, gates, and a brawny wall. Kilkenny City's central location means that it's not too far from anywhere else in Ireland.

GETTING HERE AND AROUND

From Dublin, take the N7/M7 to the M9 and exit at junction 8 for the N10 to Kilkenny. These are major motorways, so the 101-km (62-mile) trip takes only an hour and a half. Cork is a two-hour drive, while Waterford City is only a 40-minute hop. There is plenty of paid parking around the town.

The bus stop is a bit down from the train station on St. John's Street, and Bus Éireann runs eight buses a day from Dublin, but you have to change at Carlow. Prices vary but the three-hour, 10-minute trip generally costs around €17 one-way, €23 round-trip. J.J. Kavanagh & Sons runs five direct buses a day from Dublin city center and airport. The two-hour journey costs from €15 one-way, €21 round-trip.

MacDonagh Station, the city train station, is a short walk from the city center at the top of St. John's Street. The station is on the Dublin–Waterford City line, which also serves Athy, Carlow, Bagenalstown, and Thomastown. Irish Rail runs six trains a day from Dublin, and the trip takes about one hour, 45 minutes and costs approximately €21 one-way and €29 round-trip. You can save money if you book online.

VISITOR INFORMATION

CONTACTS Kilkenny Tourist Office. ✉ *79A High St. Gardens, Kilkenny* ☎ *1850/230–330* 🌐 *visitkilkenny.ie.*

Sights

Kilkenny's city center is small, and despite the large number of historic sights and picturesque streets—in particular, Butter Slip and High Street—you can easily cover it in less than three hours. The "Medieval Mile" runs from the iconic castle to St. Canice's Cathedral and contains many of the oldest buildings. One of the most pleasant cities south of Dublin (and one of its most sports-minded—from July to September practically the only topic of conversation is the fate of the city's team at the All-Ireland Hurling Championship), Kilkenny City has become in recent years something of a haven for artists and craft workers seeking an escape from Dublin. At such venues as the Kilkenny Design Centre you can find an array of quality Irish crafts.

The city has more than 60 pubs, many of them on Parliament and High Streets, which also support a lively music scene. Many of the town's pubs and shops have old-fashioned, highly individualized, brightly painted facades, created as part of the town's 1980s revival of this Victorian tradition. So, after taking in Kilkenny Castle and the Riverfront Canal Walk—an overgrown pathway that meanders along the castle grounds—mosey down High and Kieran Streets. These parallel avenues, considered the historic center of Kilkenny, are connected by a series of horse cart–wide lanes and are fronted with some of the city's best-preserved pubs and Victorian flats. Be sure to look up over the existing modern storefronts to catch a glimpse of how the city looked in years past, as many of the buildings still have second-floor facades reflecting historic decorative styles.

Black Abbey

CHURCH | With a stained-glass, carved-stone interior that seems right out of the musical *Camelot,* the 13th-century Black Abbey is one of the most evocative and beautiful Irish medieval structures. Note the famous 1340 five-gabled Rosary Window, an entire wall agleam with ruby and sapphire glass, depicting the life of Christ. Home to a Dominican order of monks since 1225, the abbey was restored as a church by the order, whose black capes gave the abbey its name. Interestingly, it's also one of the few medieval churches still owned by the Roman Catholic Church, as most of the oldest churches in Ireland were built by the Normans and reverted to the Church of Ireland (Anglican) when the English turned to Protestantism. Nearby is the Black Freren Gate (14th century), the last remaining gateway to the medieval city. ✉ *South of St. Canice's Cathedral, Kilkenny* ☎ *056/772–1279* 🎫 *Free.*

★ Kilkenny Castle

CASTLE/PALACE | Built in 1172 and set amid 50 acres of rolling lawns beside the River Nore, Ireland's most recognizable castle is a bewitching marriage of Gothic and Victorian styles. It conjures images of knights and damsels, dukes and duchesses. For more than 500 years, beginning in 1391, Kilkenny Castle served as the seat of one of the more powerful clans in Irish history, the Butler family, members of which were later designated earls and dukes of Ormonde. Around 1820, William Robert, son of the first

While studded with plenty of historic sights, Kilkenny also welcomes the traveler with traditional and "characterful" pubs.

marquess of Ormonde, overhauled the castle to make it a wonderland in the Victorian Feudal Revival style. In 1859, John Pollen was called in to redo the aptly named Long Gallery—a refined, airy hall with dazzling green walls hung with a vast collection of family portraits and frayed tapestries, and a marvelously decorated ceiling, replete with oak beams carved with Celtic lacework and brilliantly painted animal heads. The main staircase was also redone in the mid-1800s to become a showpiece of Ruskinian Gothic.

The castle's Butler Gallery, formerly the servants' quarters, houses a superb collection of Irish modern art, including examples by Nathaniel Hone, Jack B. Yeats, Sir John Lavery, Louis Le Brocquy, and James Turrell. Be sure to stroll the grounds, and the Celtic cross–shape rose garden, after a spot of tea in the old Victorian kitchen. ✉ *The Parade, Kilkenny* ☎ *056/770–4100* 🌐 *kilkennycastle.ie* 🎫 *From €8.*

Kyteler's Inn

RESTAURANT | The oldest inn in town, Kyteler's is notorious as the place where Dame Alice Le Kyteler, a member of a wealthy banking family and an alleged witch and "brothel keeper," was accused in 1324 of poisoning her four husbands. So, at least, said the enemies of this apparently very merry widow. The restaurant retains its medieval aura, thanks to its 14th-century stonework and exposed beams down in the cellar, built up around Kieran's Well, which predates the house itself. Food and drink in this popular pub are as simple and plentiful as they would have been in Dame Alice's day—minus her extra ingredients. ✉ *Kieran St., Kilkenny* ☎ *056/772–1064* 🌐 *kytelersinn.com.*

Rothe House

HISTORIC HOME | There's a feeling of time travel as you step off the busy main street and into one of Ireland's finest examples of a Tudor-era merchant's house. Built by John Rothe between 1594 and 1610, this medieval complex with stone-wall courtyards (one of which

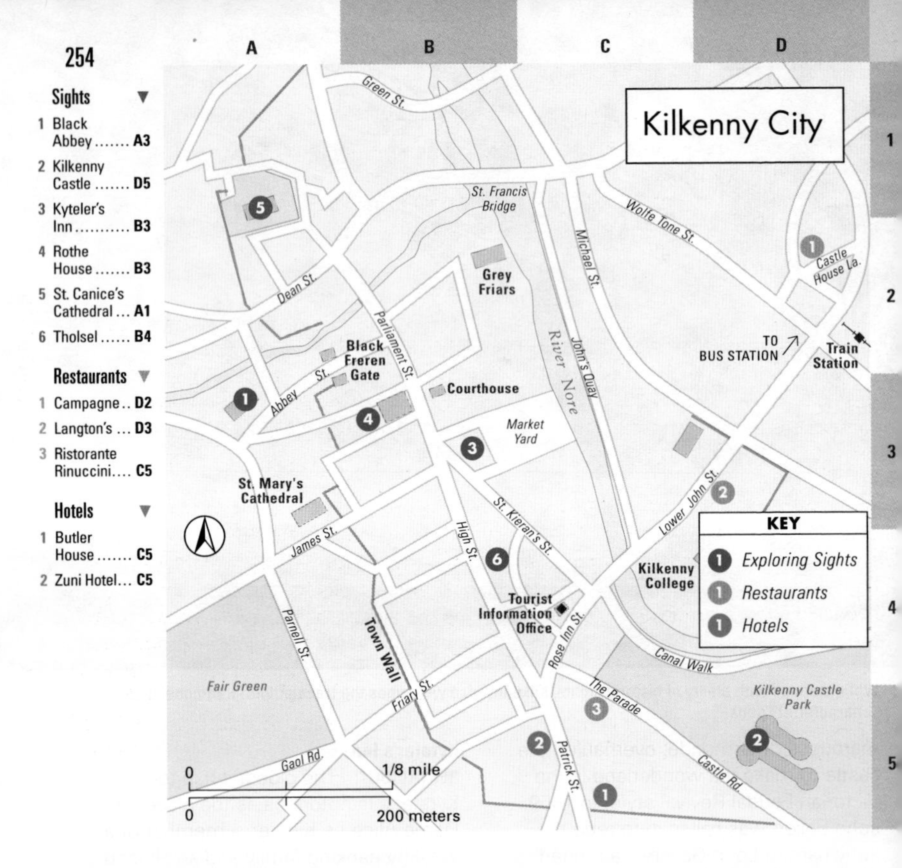

houses a medieval well) is owned by the Kilkenny Archaeological Society and houses a collection of Bronze Age artifacts, ogham stones (carved with an early Celtic alphabet), and period costumes. The Burgage Garden re-creates, down to the plant types themselves, a typical 17th-century Irish merchant's garden. There's also a genealogical research facility to help you trace your ancestry. ✉ *Parliament St., Kilkenny* ☎ *056/772–2893* 🌐 *rothehouse.com* 🎫 *€8.*

★ St. Canice's Cathedral

CHURCH | In spite of Cromwell's defacements, this is still one of the finest cathedrals in Ireland and the country's second-largest medieval church, after St. Patrick's Cathedral in Dublin. Behind the massive walls of this 13th-century structure (restored in 1866) is an exuberant Gothic interior, given a somber grandeur by the extensive use of a locally quarried black marble. Many of the memorials and tombstone effigies represent distinguished descendants of the Normans, some depicted in full suits of armor. Look for a female effigy in the south aisle wearing the old Irish, or Kinsale, cloak; a 12th-century black-marble font at the southwest end of the nave; and St. Ciaran's Chair in the north transept, also made of black marble, with 13th-century sculptures on the arms.

In recent years, St. Canice's has achieved notoriety as the resting place of President Obama's great-great-great uncle, the Bishop of Ossory. The biggest attraction on the grounds is the 102-foot-high Round Tower, which was built in 847 by King O'Carroll of Ossory; if you have the energy, climb the tower's 167 steps for the tremendous 360-degree view from the top, as well as for the thrill of mounting 102 steps on makeshift wooden stairs. Next door is St. Canice's Library, containing some 3,000 16th- and 17th-century volumes. ✉ *Dean St., Kilkenny* ☎ *056/776–4971* 🌐 *stcanicescathedral.ie* 🎫 *From €6.*

Tholsel

GOVERNMENT BUILDING | With its distinctive clock tower and grand entrance portico, this limestone-marble building on Parliament Street stands on the site of the execution of poor Petronilla, the "witch" burned at the stake in the 14th century in lieu of her mistress, Dame Alice Le Kyteler. Built in 1761, burned down in 1985, and then completely rebuilt, Tholsel now houses the city's municipal archives and council offices. Musicians often busk in the portico, and city walking tours are sometimes allowed inside to explore. Adjacent to the Tholsel is Alice's Castle, a town jail rather grandly fitted out in 18th-century architectural ornamentation. ✉ *Parliament St., Kilkenny.*

Restaurants

★ Campagne

$$$$ | **FRENCH** | When Garrett Byrne, the former head chef of Dublin's celebrated Chapter One, returns home and opens a restaurant, people take notice, and the awards (including a Michelin star)—and diners from all of Ireland—start flooding in. The menu is a work of art, with common French themes toyed with and expanded. **Known for:** modern French cuisine; destination dining; relaxed contemporary setting. $ *Average main: €38* ✉ *5 The Arches, Gashouse La., Kilkenny* ☎ *056/777–2858* 🌐 *campagne.ie* ⏲ *Closed Mon. and Tues. No dinner Sun. No lunch Wed.–Sat.*

★ Langton's

$$ | **IRISH** | A landmark since the 1940s, Langton's is a labyrinth of interconnected bars and eateries. Up front is one of Ireland's most famous "eating pubs," often crammed to the rafters of its low ceiling with a lively crowd. **Known for:** variety of seating options; great location; lively scene. $ *Average main: €21* ✉ *69 John St., Kilkenny* ☎ *056/776–5133* 🌐 *langtons.ie.*

Ristorante Rinuccini

$$$ | **ITALIAN** | A warm glow emanates from this Georgian town-house restaurant, where owner-chef Antonio Cavaliere is intensely involved in preparing such luscious Italian dishes as rigatoni *all' arrabbiata* (tubes of homemade egg pasta in a fresh tomato sauce with chili and garlic). Other specialties, such as medallions of fresh Kilmore Quay monkfish with roasted cherry tomatoes, garlic, white wine, and a touch of fresh chili, go particularly well with Antonio's garlic roasted potatoes—highly recommended as a side dish. **Known for:** best Italian in town; excellent Italian wine list; Kilmore Quay monkfish. $ *Average main: €29* ✉ *1 The Parade, across from Kilkenny Castle, Kilkenny* ☎ *056/776–1575* 🌐 *rinuccini.com.*

Hotels

Butler House

$$ | **HOTEL** | Who needs Kilkenny Castle when you can stay at the Dowager Duchess of Ormonde's 18th-century town house, a charming piece of Georgian grandeur with an ivy-covered three-bay facade and an elegant walled garden? (There's even a private entrance to Kilkenny Castle.) Inside, the reception salon has a magnificent plaster ceiling and marble fireplaces. **Pros:** classic castle feel; serene walled garden; breakfast in the old stables of Kilkenny Castle. **Cons:** books up quickly; no restaurant or bar; some rooms a lot smaller than others. $ *Rooms from: €195* ✉ *16 Patrick St., Kilkenny* ☎ *056/776–5707* 🌐 *butler.ie* *17 rooms* 🍽 *Free Breakfast.*

Extending 150 feet, Kilkenny Castle's Long Gallery is lined with family portraits and has a hammer-beam ceiling supported on carved stone corbels with gilded animal and bird heads on the crossbeams.

Zuni Hotel

$$ | **HOTEL** | This popular family-owned hotel in the center of Kilkenny boasts the gloss of a big-city boutique lodging but not the icy-cool reception you get in some fashionable joints. **Pros:** in the heart of the city; family owned and run; tasty eatery. **Cons:** books up quickly; limited one-night stays in summer; can get noisy outside on weekends. *Rooms from: €180* *26 Patrick St., Kilkenny* *056/772–3999* *zuni.ie* *13 rooms* *Free Breakfast.*

 Nightlife

John Cleere's

PUBS | If you're craving a pint, you have a choice of pubs along Parliament and High Streets. John Cleere's is the best in town for a mix of live traditional music, poetry readings, and theatrical plays. *22 Parliament St., Kilkenny* *056/776–2573* *cleeres.com.*

Lenehan's

PUBS | A pristine, classic Irish pub that dates back to the 18th century, Lenehan's has been at the heart of Kilkenny social life for generations. Settle into the private snug in the front bar section and enjoy the view. *10 Castlecomer Rd., Kilkenny* *056/772–1621.*

★ **Tynan's Bridge House**

PUBS | Set on one of Kilkenny's famous "slips," Tynan's Bridge House was first used as an exercise run for dray horses. Inside, you can guess that the pub is more than 200 years old from all the gas lamps, silver tankards, and historic teapots on display. Behind the horseshoe-shape bar, you'll find antiquities from its time as a grocery and pharmacy, but it's best known these days for its Guinness and good conversation. *2 Horseleap Slip, Kilkenny* *056/772–1291* *facebook.com/TynansBarKilkenny.*

Performing Arts

Watergate Theatre

THEATER | With a roster of operas, plays, concerts, and comedy shows, the Watergate hosts affordable local, national, and international productions. ✉ *Parliament St., Kilkenny* ☎ *056/776–1674* 🌐 *watergatetheatre.com.*

Shopping

CLOTHING

Sweater Shop

MIXED CLOTHING | You'll find a great selection of Irish knitwear and accessories for men, women, and children at this popular shop. ✉ *81 High St., Kilkenny* ☎ *056/776–3405* 🌐 *sweatershop.ie.*

CRAFTS

Jerpoint Glass Studio

CRAFTS | You can see glass being blown at this noted family-run studio, where the glass is heavy, modern, uncut, and hand-finished using traditional tools and methods. The studio's factory shop, 16 km (10 miles) south of Kilkenny, is a good place to pick up a bargain. ✉ *Main St., Stoneyford* ☎ *056/772–4350* 🌐 *jerpointglass.com.*

★ **Kilkenny Design Centre**

CRAFTS | One of Ireland's favorite sources for Irish handicrafts, the Kilkenny Design Centre sells ceramics, jewelry, sweaters, and handwoven textiles. This spot in the old stable yard opposite the castle also has a restaurant specializing in hearty Irish fare. ✉ *Opposite Kilkenny Castle, Kilkenny* ☎ *056/772–2118* 🌐 *kilkennydesign.com.*

★ **Nicholas Mosse Pottery**

CERAMICS | One of the best-known names in Irish ceramics, Mosse first set up his potter's wheel in an old flour mill in 1975. Since then, the shop's rustic floral-pattern pottery has become instantly recognizable for its "spongeware" designs. A visit to the shop, in a quiet village 16 km (10 miles) south of Kilkenny, allows you to see the pottery being made, and the adjoining factory shop often has good bargains. ✉ *Off Annamult Rd., Bennettsbridge* ☎ *056/772–7505* 🌐 *nicholasmosse.com.*

JEWELRY

Murphy Jewellers

JEWELRY & WATCHES | This county favorite specializes in silver and diamond jewelry. ✉ *85 High St., Kilkenny* ☎ *056/772–1127* 🌐 *murphyjewellers.ie.*

Rudolf Heltzel

JEWELRY & WATCHES | German-born but living in Kilkenny since the 1960s, Rudolf Heltzel is known for striking, modern designs and mostly showcases gold and silver jewelry. ✉ *10 Patrick St., Kilkenny* ☎ *056/772–1497* 🌐 *rudolfheltzel.com.*

Activities

HURLING

★ **Kilkenny GAA Grounds**

LOCAL SPORTS | The 1366 Statutes of Kilkenny expressly forbade the ancient Irish game of hurling. No matter: today, Kilkenny is considered one of the great hurling counties. Like its neighbor and archenemy, Wexford, Kilkenny has a long history of success in hurling, and as the annual All-Ireland Hurling Championships draws to its final stages during July and August, interest in the county's team runs to fever pitch. Catch the home team at matches held at Kilkenny GAA Grounds. ✉ *Nowlan Park, Kilkenny* ☎ *056/776–5122* 🌐 *kilkennygaa.ie.*

Thomastown

14½ km (9 miles) south of Kilkenny.

Originally the seat of the kings of Ossory (an ancient Irish kingdom), Thomastown is a pretty, stone-built village on the River Nore. It takes its name from Thomas FitzAnthony of Leinster, who encircled the town with a wall in the 13th century. Fragments of this medieval wall remain,

Hurling: A Fast and Furious Sport

Get chatting with the locals in almost any pub across the Southeast, mention the sport of hurling, and an enthusiastic and often passionate conversation is bound to ensue. The region is the heartland of this ancient sport, whose followers have an almost religious obsession with the game.

Hurling is a kind of aerial field hockey with players wielding curved sticks. Its history comes from Ireland's Celtic ancestors, but it bears about the same relation to field hockey as ice hockey does to roller-skating. It's no accident that prowess on the hurling field is regarded as a supreme qualification for election to public office. A man who succeeds at hurling is eminently capable of dealing with anything that fate and the spite of other politicians can throw at him. Hurling is also an extremely skillful sport. A player must have excellent hand-eye coordination combined with an ability to run at high speeds while balancing a small golf-ball-size ball on his *camán* (hurling stick). Fans will proudly tell you it's also the world's fastest team sport.

Ireland's other chief sporting pastimes, including soccer and hurling's cousin, Gaelic football, take a back seat in this part of the country. Stars like Kilkenny's TJ Reid, rather than professional soccer players, are sporting icons for local kids. Counties Tipperary, Wexford, and Waterford are among the top teams in the region, but Kilkenny (nicknamed "The Cats") dominated the national scene over the last two decades before a dip in form in recent years. That team won 11 of 20 All-Ireland Hurling Championships and was considered by many the greatest of all time.

There's an intense rivalry between the counties, especially between old foes Tipperary and Kilkenny. When it gets down to club level, passions run even higher. Almost every parish in the region has a hurling club, and a quick inquiry with locals will usually be enough to find out when the next game is on. Even for the uninitiated, hurling is a great spectator sport. Sporty types wishing to give it a go, be warned; it's fast, furious, and entails more than a hint of danger, as players flail the air to capture the bullet-fast *sliotar* (hurling ball).

as do the partly ruined 13th-century church of St. Mary. Mullins Castle sits adjacent to the town bridge.

GETTING HERE AND AROUND

From Kilkenny, take the N77 to the Thomastown exit. The 14½-km (9-mile) trip should take 20 minutes. Bus Éireann runs regular services from Dublin and Kilkenny. There is also regular train service from Dublin, Kilkenny, and Waterford.

Sights

★ **Jerpoint Abbey**

RUINS | Known for its rearing and massive 15th-century tower, Jerpoint Abbey is one of the most notable Cistercian ruins in Ireland, dating from about 1160. The church, tombs, and the restored cloister are must-sees for lovers of the Irish Romanesque. The vast cloister is decorated with affecting carvings of human figures and fantastical mythical creatures, including knights and knaves (one with a stomachache) and the assorted dragon or two. Dissolved in 1540, Jerpoint was taken over, as was so much around these parts, by the earls of Ormonde. The one part of the abbey that remains alive, so to speak, is its hallowed cemetery—the natives are still buried here. Guided tours are available or you can just wander at your leisure. ✉ *N9, 2 km (1 mile) south of Thomastown, Thomastown* ☎ *056/772–4623* 🌐 *heritageireland.ie/visit/places-to-visit/jerpoint-abbey* 🎫 *€5* ⏲ *Closed Dec.–Feb.*

Hotels

Ballyduff House

$ | **B&B/INN** | As the clematis-clad mansion comes into view at the top of a gently curving driveway you can understand why this wonderfully picturesque house was used as a location in the 1995 movie adaptation of Maeve Binchy's *Circle of Friends*. **Pros:** great river views from some rooms; stunningly authentic mansion; guests can use kitchen to prepare a picnic. **Cons:** fills up fast; few modern facilities; can attract a mostly golf crowd. $ *Rooms from: €130* ✉ *Off R700, Thomastown* ☎ *056/775–8488* 🌐 *ballyduffhouse.ie* *5 rooms* *Free Breakfast.*

★ **Mount Juliet**

$$$$ | **HOTEL** | For many, the Jack Nicklaus–designed golf course—which has hosted the Irish Open on three occasions—is the main draw, but this lush 1,500-acre estate beside the beautiful River Nore offers so much more. **Pros:** great golf on your doorstep; period elegance with modern amenities; Michelin-starred restaurant. **Cons:** rooms outside main house a little inferior; some charm sacrificed for modern comfort; restaurant books up quickly. $ *Rooms from: €275* ✉ *Off L4206, Thomastown* ☎ *056/777–3000* 🌐 *mountjuliet.ie* *125 rooms* *Free Breakfast.*

Activities

GOLF

★ **Mount Juliet Golf Course**

GOLF | Attached to a magisterial country-house hotel, this Jack Nicklaus–designed championship parkland course, 19 km (11 miles) from Kilkenny Town, includes practice greens, a driving range, and, for those who feel a little rusty, a David Leadbetter golf academy. The heavily forested course has eight holes that play over water, including the wonderful 3rd hole—a par-3 over a stream from an elevated tee. The back nine present a series of difficult bunker shots. Greens fees are above average, and although visitors are always welcome, a weekday round is best, since it's often crowded with members on weekends. ✉ *Mount Juliet Estate, off L4206, Thomastown* ☎ *056/777–3010* 🌐 *mountjuliet.ie* 🎫 *May–Sept., daily from €130; Nov.–Mar., daily from €62; Apr. and Oct., daily from €85* *18 holes, 7264 yards, par 72.*

Enniscorthy

32 km (20 miles) east of Graiguenamanagh.

On the sloping banks of the River Slaney and on the main road between Dublin and Wexford to the south of the popular resort of Gorey, Enniscorthy is a thriving market town that is rich in history.

GETTING HERE AND AROUND

From Wexford, take the N1 to the N30; the 32-km (20-mile) trip takes about half an hour. From Dublin, take the N11/M11 all the way to Enniscorthy; the trip takes about 90 minutes. There is regular bus and train service from Wexford and Dublin.

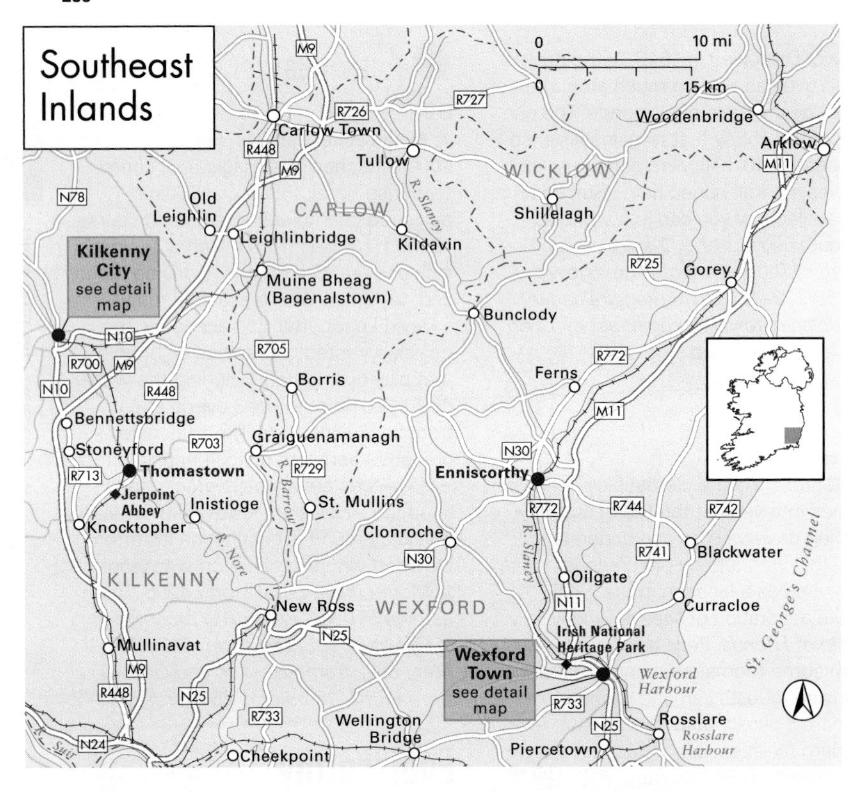

Sights

★ Enniscorthy Castle

CASTLE/PALACE | The town is dominated by Enniscorthy Castle, built in the first quarter of the 13th century by the Prendergast family. The imposing Norman castle was the site of fierce battles against Oliver Cromwell in the 17th century and during the Rebellion of 1798. There are exhibitions exploring the 1916 Rising in Enniscorthy and the work of furniture designer and architect Eileen Gray, who was born in 1878 just outside town. Gray went on to become one of the founding designers of the Modernist movement in the 1920s and now enjoys worldwide fame at staggering prices (one chair she designed brought $22 million at auction). The guided tour is a real treat, with a trip to the dungeon followed by a walk on the roof with impressive views out over the town and beyond and the bloody 1798 battlefield Vinegar Hill. ✉ *Castle Hill, Enniscorthy* ☎ *053/923–4699* 🌐 *enniscorthycastle.ie* 🎫 *€6.*

National 1798 Centre

HISTORY MUSEUM | This small museum tells the tale of the United Irishmen and the ill-fated 1798 rebellion. ✉ *Arnold's Cross, Enniscorthy* ☎ *053/923–7596* 🌐 *1798centre.ie* 🎫 *€6* ⏲ *Closed Nov.–Jan.*

St. Aidan's Cathedral

CHURCH | Standing on a commanding site overlooking the Slaney, the Gothic Revival structure of St. Aidan's was built in the mid-19th century under the direction of Augustus Welby Pugin, famed architect of the Houses of Parliament in London. ✉ *Cathedral St., Enniscorthy* ☎ *053/923–5777* 🌐 *staidanscathedral.ie* 🎫 *Free.*

Hotels

★ Monart

$$$$ | HOTEL | The Monart declares itself a "destination spa," and you can see why with an outdoor Finnish sauna and salt grotto, an award-winning thermal spa, a daring fine-dining restaurant, and luxe rooms to add to the pampering. **Pros:** luxurious wellness amenities; scenic setting and views; serene and peaceful. **Cons:** weekends book up quickly; can be pricey; no kids allowed. *Rooms from: €350* *Monart Destination Spa, The Still, Enniscorthy* *053/923–8999* *monart.ie* *68 rooms* *Free Breakfast.*

Wexford Town

19 km (12 miles) south of Enniscorthy, 62 km (39 miles) northeast of Waterford City, 115 km (72 miles) southwest of Dublin.

This coastal town is most famed for the Wexford Opera Festival, usually held in October, which has been seducing the world with wonderful productions of rare opera for more than 50 years. The warm and vivacious welcome, the narrow streets, and the atmospheric Theatre Royal add to the pleasure of this event and to any visit to Wexford Town.

From its appearance today, you would barely realize that Wexford is an ancient place, but in fact the Greek cartographer Ptolemy mapped it as long ago as the 2nd century AD. Its Irish name is Loch Garman, but the Vikings called it Waesfjord (the harbor of the mudflats), which became Wexford in English. Wexford developed into an English garrison town after it was captured by Oliver Cromwell in 1649.

Rising above the town's rooftops are the graceful spires of two elegant examples of 19th-century Gothic architecture. These twin churches have identical exteriors, their foundation stones were laid on the same day, and their spires each reach a height of 230 feet. The Church of the Assumption is on Bride Street. The Church of the Immaculate Conception is on Rowe Street.

GETTING HERE AND AROUND

From Dublin take the N11/M11 all the way to Wexford Town; the trip takes about two hours and 10 minutes.

Intercity buses arrive at O'Hanrahan Train Station on Redmond Place. Fares are approximate as prices vary depending on season and day of week. Bus Éireann has nine buses a day from Dublin (three hours; around €19 one-way, €27 round-trip), nine from Rosslare (30 minutes; around €8 one-way, €10 round-trip), and six (three on Sunday) from Waterford City (three hours; around €12.60 one-way, €17 round-trip).

Irish Rail trains arrive at O'Hanrahan Train Station, at the northern end of town on Redmond Place. Wexford is on the Dublin–Roslare line and three trains a day arrive from Dublin; the 2½-hour trip costs approximately €18 one-way, €30 round-trip. The short hop to Rosslare costs about €8 one-way, €10 round-trip, and takes 25 minutes. There are no direct trains to Cork or Waterford.

VISITOR INFORMATION

CONTACTS Wexford Tourist Office. *Crescent Quay, Wexford* *053/912–3111* *visitwexford.ie.*

Sights

The River Slaney empties into the sea at Wexford Town. The harbor has silted up since the days when Viking longboats docked here; nowadays only a few small trawlers fish from here. Wexford Town's compact center is on the south bank of the Slaney. Running parallel to the quays on the riverfront is the main street (the name changes several times) and its pleasant mix of old-fashioned bakeries, butcher shops, stylish boutiques, and a share of Wexford's many pubs. It can be explored on foot in an hour or two. Allow at least half a day in the area if you also intend to visit Irish National Heritage Park at nearby Ferrycarrig, and a full day if you want to take in Johnstown Castle Gardens or walk in the nature reserve at nearby Curracloe Beach.

★ Irish National Heritage Park

HISTORIC SIGHT | FAMILY | A 35-acre, open-air, living-history museum beside the River Slaney, this is one of Ireland's most successful and enjoyable family attractions. In about 90 minutes, a guide takes you through 9,000 years of Irish history—from the first evidence of humans on this island, at around 7000 BC, to the Norman settlements of the mid-12th century. Full-scale replicas of typical dwellings illustrate the changes in beliefs and lifestyles. Highlights include a prehistoric homestead, a *crannóg* (lake dwelling), an early Christian *rath* (fortified farmstead), a horizontal water mill, a Viking longhouse, and a Norman castle. There are also examples of pre-Christian burial sites and a stone circle. Most of the exhibits are "inhabited" by students in appropriate historic dress who will answer questions. The riverside site includes several nature trails and a falconry center. There's a family restaurant and you can even stay a night in a medieval ring fort. ✉ *N11, 5 km (3 miles) north of Wexford Town, Ferrycarrig* ☎ *053/912–0733* 🌐 *irishheritage.ie* 🎫 *€13.*

★ Johnstown Castle Gardens

GARDEN | Set in a beautiful garden estate, this Victorian Gothic castle looks like it was designed for a Disney movie but it was in fact built for the Grogan-Morgan family between 1810 and 1855. The magnificent parklands—with towering trees and ornamental gardens—offer a grand frame to the castle. Unfortunately, you can't tour the building (it houses an agricultural college) other than its entrance hall, but the well-maintained grounds are open to the public. The centerpiece is the 5-acre lake, one side of which has a statue-lined terrace where you can take in the panorama of the mirrored castle. Because there's such a variety of trees—Japanese cedars, Atlantic blue cedars, golden Lawson cypresses—there's color through much of the year. Nearby are the Devil's Gate walled garden—a woodland garden set around the ruins of the medieval castle of Rathlannon—and the Irish Agricultural Museum. The latter, housed in the quadrangular stable yards, shows what life was once like in rural Ireland. It also contains a 5,000-square-foot exhibition on the potato and the Great Famine (1845–49). ✉ *Off N25, 6 km (4 miles) southwest of Wexford Town, Wexford* ☎ *053/914–2888* 🌐 *johnstowncastle.ie* 🎫 *Gardens and museum €9, castle tour €4.*

Westgate Tower

MILITARY SIGHT | Of the five fortified gateways through the Norman and Viking town walls, Westgate is the only one remaining. The early-13th-century tower has been sensitively restored. Keep an eye out as you wander this part of town for other preserved segments of the old town walls. ✉ *Westgate, Wexford.*

Wexford Bull Ring

HISTORIC SIGHT | Once the scene of bull baiting, a cruel medieval sport that was popular among the Norman nobility, this arena was sad witness to other bloody crimes. In 1649, Cromwell's soldiers massacred 300 panic-stricken townspeople who had gathered here to pray as the army stormed their town. The memory of this heartless leader has remained a dark folk legacy for centuries and is only now beginning to fade. ✉ *Quay St., Wexford.*

Wexford Opera House

ARTS CENTER | Wexford's grand and hoary landmark, the Theatre Royal, has been entirely rebuilt to serve as the Wexford Opera Theatre for the world-famous Wexford Opera Festival, held here during the last two weeks of October and the beginning of November. The strikingly

Wexford Town's waterfront varies across the small city, from ports in the harbor to serene beaches along the quay, such as Curracloe Beach.

modern, Keith Williams–designed building is custom-built for opera and offers fabulous views out over Mt. Lenister to the northwest and Tuskar Rock lighthouse to the southeast. The surprisingly large main auditorium seats 749 with a smaller second space for 172. Year-round, touring companies and local productions are also seen at these venues. ⊠ *27 High St., Wexford* ☎ *053/912–2144* 🌐 *wexfordopera.com.*

Wexford Wildfowl Reserve

WILDLIFE REFUGE | A nature lover's paradise, Wexford Wildlife Reserve is just a short walk across the bridge from the main part of town. It shelters a third of the world's Greenland white-fronted geese. As many as 10,000 of them spend their winters on the mudflats (known locally as "slobs"), which also draw ducks, swans, and other waterfowl. Observation hides are provided for bird-watchers, and an audiovisual show and exhibitions are available at the visitor center. ⊠ *Wexford Harbour, Wexford* ☎ *053/912–3406* 🌐 *wexfordwildfowlreserve.ie* 🎫 *Free.*

Restaurants

D'Lush Cafe

$ | **CAFÉ** | Locals swear this cute little joint at the back of the Arts Centre is the home of Wexford's best coffee. The interior is simple but cozy with creative touches like local artwork visible throughout. **Known for:** quality snacks; delicious desserts; arty crowd. $ *Average main: €15* ⊠ *Wexford Arts Centre, Cornmarket, Wexford* ☎ *053/912–3795* 🌐 *facebook.com/dlushcafewexford* ⏲ *Closed Sun. and Mon. No dinner.*

La Côte

$$$ | **SEAFOOD** | Located on historic Custom Quay overlooking the Irish Sea, this buzzy little eatery is known for beautifully cooked seafood with a bit of flare. The menu adapts to the seasonal catch, working with local fishermen and farmers. **Known for:** friendly atmosphere; affordable fine dining; seasonal seafood.

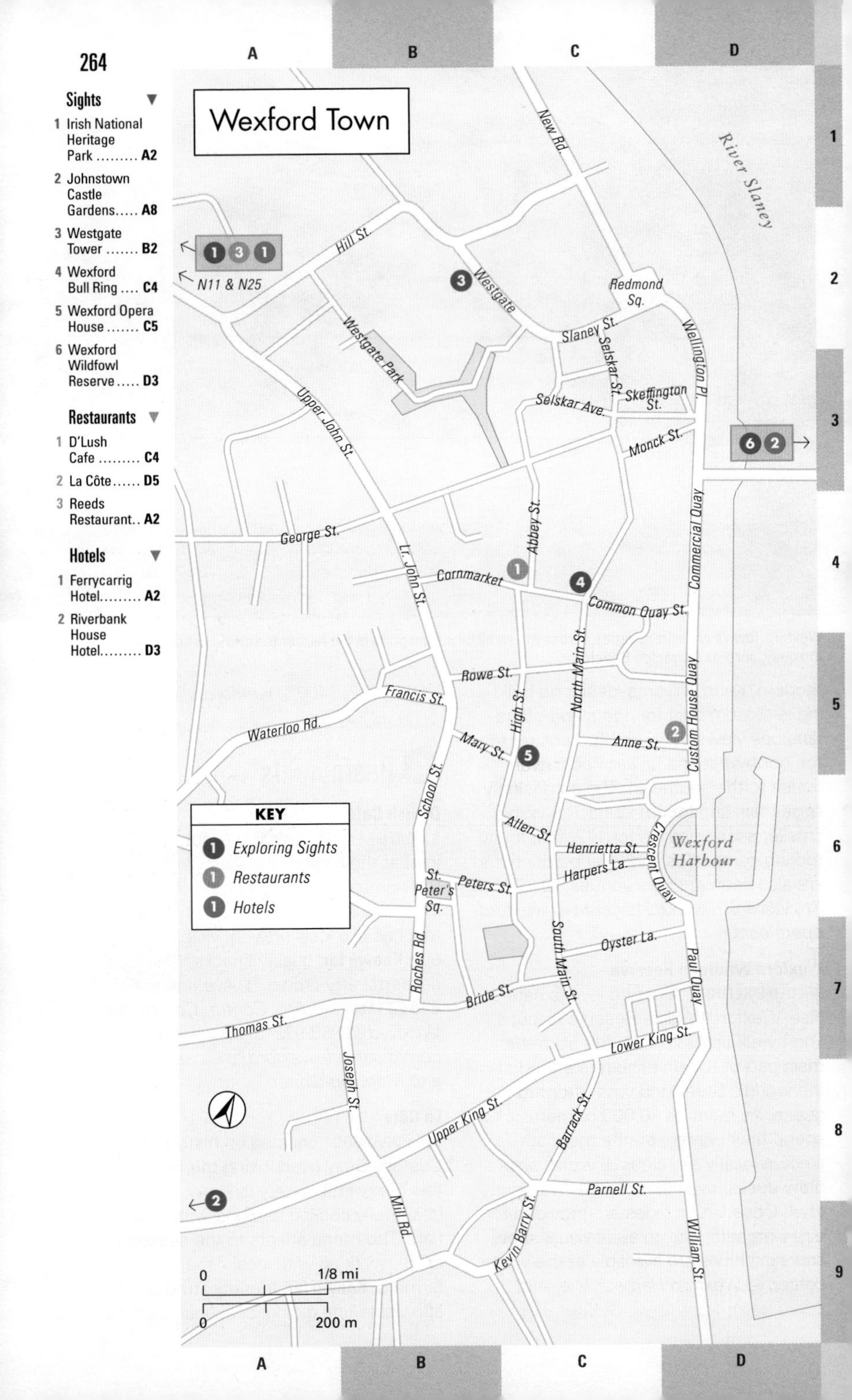
Sights
1 Irish National Heritage Park A2
2 Johnstown Castle Gardens..... A8
3 Westgate Tower B2
4 Wexford Bull Ring C4
5 Wexford Opera House C5
6 Wexford Wildfowl Reserve..... D3
Restaurants
1 D'Lush Cafe C4
2 La Côte...... D5
3 Reeds Restaurant.. A2
Hotels
1 Ferrycarrig Hotel......... A2
2 Riverbank House Hotel......... D3
Wexford Town
A
B
C
D
1
2
3
4
5
6
7
8
9
N11 & N25
New Rd.
River Slaney
Hill St.
Westgate
Redmond Sq.
Westgate Park
Slaney St.
Selskar St.
Wellington Pl.
Skeffington St.
Selskar Ave.
Upper John St.
Monck St.
Abbey St.
Commercial Quay
George St.
Lr. John St.
Cornmarket
Common Quay St.
North Main St.
Rowe St.
Francis St.
High St.
Custom House Quay
Waterloo Rd.
Mary St.
Anne St.
School St.
Allen St.
Crescent Quay
Wexford Harbour
Henrietta St.
Harpers La.
St. Peter's Sq.
Peters St.
KEY
Exploring Sights
Restaurants
Hotels
South Main St.
Oyster La.
Paul Quay
Roches Rd.
Bride St.
Thomas St.
Lower King St.
Joseph St.
Upper King St.
Barrack St.
Parnell St.
Mill Rd.
Kevin Barry St.
William St.
0
1/8 mi
0
200 m

Ⓢ *Average main: €25* ✉ *Custom House Quay, Wexford* ☎ *053/912–2122* 🌐 *lacote.ie* ⏲ *Closed Mon. and Tues. No lunch Wed.–Sat.*

Reeds Restaurant

$$$ | **IRISH** | Fresh-off-the-boat fish is the big draw at this restaurant at the family-friendly Ferrycarrig Hotel. Seafood from Kilmore Quay is a favorite, but the Killurin lamb is just as local and tasty, as is the wild Wicklow venison loin with red cabbage tatin, parsnip puree, red wine jus, and game chips (potatoes, flour-dusted then thinly sliced and fried). **Known for:** great selection of vegetarian and vegan options; romantic riverfront views; extensive wine list. Ⓢ *Average main: €27* ✉ *Ferrycarrig Hotel, off N11, 4 km (2½ miles) outside Wexford Town, Wexford* ☎ *053/912–0999* 🌐 *ferrycarrighotel.ie.*

Hotels

Ferrycarrig Hotel

$$ | **HOTEL** | **FAMILY** | A favorite with families, this spot offers a swimming pool for kids, a peaceful and tranquil riverside location for parents, and a well-equipped health center for both. **Pros:** warm and friendly atmosphere; superb buffet breakfast at the restaurant; large, well-appointed rooms. **Cons:** can get a bit hectic in summer; weekends more expensive; some rooms better than others. Ⓢ *Rooms from: €180* ✉ *Off N11, 4 km (2½ miles) outside Wexford Town, Wexford* ☎ *053/912–0999* 🌐 *ferrycarrighotel.ie* *102 rooms* *Free Breakfast.*

Riverbank House Hotel

$ | **HOTEL** | Located across a bridge from the center of town, with stunning views of the River Slaney, the Riverbank's perfectly manicured gardens and original Victorian furnishings add to the romantic vibe of this boutique hotel. **Pros:** friendly, attentive staff; comfortable public areas; minutes from town center. **Cons:** popular with weddings; prosaic room design; some noise from town. Ⓢ *Rooms from: €140* ✉ *The Bridge, Wexford* ☎ *053/912–3611* 🌐 *riverbankhousehotel.com* *23 rooms* *Free Breakfast.*

Nightlife

Centenary Stores

PUBS | As the saying goes, if you can find a street without at least one bar on it, you've left Wexford. Centenary Stores is a Victorian-style pub with an adjoining nightclub that makes it popular with the young crowd. Lunch is served daily, and there's traditional music every Sunday morning. ✉ *Charlotte St., Wexford* ☎ *053/912–4424* 🌐 *thestores.ie.*

The Sky & the Ground

PUBS | One of the best pubs in town, the Sky & the Ground is a hub for Irish music sessions, which pack in the crowds from Monday through Thursday. ✉ *112 S. Main St., Wexford* ☎ *053/912–1273* 🌐 *facebook.com/TheSkyAndTheGround.*

★ **Thomas Moore Tavern**

PUBS | Dating to the 13th century, the Thomas Moore Tavern is Wexford's oldest pub, named after the renowned Irish poet whose parents lived here. The pub has its original medieval walls and fine old beams along the ceiling, and a spot by the roaring fire is the perfect place for a quiet drink. There's a restaurant attached, and pub-grub dinners are served in the bar. ✉ *Cornmarket, Wexford* ☎ *053/917–4688* 🌐 *thomasmooretavern.com.*

Shopping

Barkers

HOUSEWARES | Established in 1848, Waterford crystal, Belleek china, local pottery, linens, and crafts are found here in tempting array. ✉ *36 S. Main St., Wexford* ☎ *053/912–3159* 🌐 *barkers.ie.*

Martin's Jewellers

JEWELRY & WATCHES | This popular shop specializes in bespoke Celtic jewelry. Have it made before your eyes in the attached workshop. ✉ *2 Lower Rowe St., Wexford* ☎ *053/912–2635* 🌐 *martinsjewellers.ie.*

Westgate Design

CRAFTS | A good selection of quality Irish crafts, clothing, pottery, candles, and jewelry is found at Westgate Design. There's also a restaurant and deli. ✉ *22A N. Main St., Wexford* ☎ *053/912–3787* 🌐 *westgatedesign.ie.*

Activities

GAELIC FOOTBALL

Wexford Park GAA

LOCAL SPORTS | Wexford is mostly a hurling county, but you can watch both Gaelic football and hurling at the Wexford Park GAA. ✉ *Clonard Rd., Wexford* ☎ *053/914–4808* 🌐 *wexfordgaa.ie.*

Rosslare

16 km (10 miles) southeast of Wexford Town.

Sometimes called Ireland's sunniest spot, the village of Rosslare is a seaside getaway with an attractive beach. Many vacationers head here to hike, golf, sun, and swim. But the truth is that most visitors are only here to take the ferry from the Rosslare Europort terminal, the only reason (some point out) you should find yourself in this otherwise unexciting little town.

GETTING HERE AND AROUND

As Rosslare is so well connected to the ferry port, the roads to major cities to and from here are very good: N81, N11, and N25. Rosslare is 16 km (10 miles) southeast of Wexford Town on the R470. The trip from Dublin takes around two hours, 12 minutes. A new bypass around New Ross means drive times from the rest of the Southeast have been cut by half an hour at least.

Bus Éireann has service from many cities and towns in Ireland, including Waterford City (around €19 one-way, €32 round-trip; 1½ hours) and Dublin (around €20 one-way, €28 round-trip; three hours). Irish Rail runs three trains daily on the Dublin–Rosslare Europort line via Wexford Town. The trip to Dublin takes three hours (around €24 one-way, €28 round-trip) and to Wexford Town only 25 minutes (around €8 one-way, €10 round-trip).

Stena Line Express sails from May to September between Rosslare Harbour and Fishguard in Wales (3½ hours; two sailings per day) year-round. The fare in summer starts from €42, or €180 for a car and driver. Irish Ferries sails to Pembroke in Wales (3¾ hours, twice daily). Single summer fares start at €42 for a foot passenger, €190 for a car and driver. There are also ferries to Cherbourg, France (19½ hours, up to three a week). Brittany Ferries sails twice a week to Bilbao, Spain (28 hours).

TIP→ Ferries to and from Rosslare sometimes sell out, so reserve your space in advance.

Sights

Rosslare Harbour

MARINA/PIER | The end of the line for car ferries to and from Fishguard (3½ hours) and Pembroke (3¾ hours) in Wales, Cherbourg (19½ hours) in France, and Bilbao in Spain (28 hours) is Rosslare Harbour, 8 km (5 miles) south of the village. Irish Ferries and Stena Sealink have small kiosks in the ultramodern terminal, which also has lockers, a café, and a sprawling waiting room. You can purchase ferry tickets at the terminal, but reservations are also a must if you're traveling by car, because space is at a premium. Connecting bus and rail stations are also here. ✉ *Rosslare* 🌐 *rosslareeuroport.ie.*

Hotels

Kelly's Resort Hotel & Spa
$$$$ | **HOTEL** | **FAMILY** | A local institution, Kelly's has been consistently entertaining families since 1895 with its winning formula of a stunning beachfront location, excellent entertainment and leisure facilities, a child-friendly approach, and a reputation for good food. **Pros:** great Irish art collection; ample on-site family activities; relaxing spa. **Cons:** lots of kids make it hectic; fairly basic amenities in rooms; summer weekends book up quickly. *Rooms from: €320* ✉ *Strand Rd., Rosslare* ☎ *053/913–2114* 🌐 *kellys.ie* *Closed Dec.–mid-Feb.* *118 rooms* *Free Breakfast.*

Nightlife

Portholes Bar
BARS | A trendy spot with designer decor, the Portholes Bar is the main hangout at the Hotel Rosslare. It's particularly popular for live music on weekends. ✉ *Hotel Rosslare, Rosslare Harbour* ☎ *053/913–3110* 🌐 *hotelrosslare.ie.*

Activities

GOLF

Rosslare Golf Club
GOLF | Opened in 1905, this 30-hole championship links sits on a narrow peninsula with the harbor on one side and the Irish Sea on the other. On the 18-hole Old Course, the "Barber's Pole" is the devilishly tricky par-4 11th hole. The 12-hole Burrow Course was designed by Irish legend Christy O'Connor Junior. The course is famous for its stunning flora and birdlife. ✉ *Rosslare Strand, Rosslare* ☎ *053/913–2203* 🌐 *rosslaregolf.com* *Apr.–Oct., from €55; Nov.–Mar., from €35* *Old Course: 18 holes, 6786 yards, par 72; Burrow Course: 12 holes, 3956 yards, par 48.*

Off The Beaten Path

Curracloe Beach. Steven Spielberg filmed the D-Day landing scenes from *Saving Private Ryan* along this strand. In real life it's a popular swimming place in summer and a quiet home to migratory birds in winter. It's 9 km (5½ miles) long, with a 1-km (½-mile) nature trail in the seashore sand dunes. Lifeguards are on duty only in summer on one stretch of the beach. **Amenities:** lifeguards; parking; showers. **Best for:** solitude in winter; swimming; walking; windsurfing. ✉ *R742, 11 km (7 miles) northeast of Wexford Town, Wexford* 🌐 *wexford.ie.*

St. Helens Bay Golf Resort
GOLF | With panoramic views of the south Wexford coastline and Tuskar Rock, 18-hole St. Helens Bay, a relatively new course, is a classic Irish golf experience. Designed by Irish Ryder Cup hero Philip Walton, it's famous for its challenging but stunning final two holes. There's a fun 9-hole golf course right next door if you feel like extending your day. ✉ *Off St. Helen's Dr., Kilrane* ☎ *053/913–3234* 🌐 *sthelensbay.ie* *Apr.–Oct., from €40; Nov.–Mar., from €30* *18 holes, 6715 yards, par 72.*

Kilmore Quay

22 km (14 miles) south of Rosslare.

Noted for its fishing industry, this quiet, old-fashioned seaside village of thatched and whitewashed cottages is also popular with recreational anglers and bird-watchers. From the harbor there's a pleasant view to the east over flat coast that stretches for miles. Recent

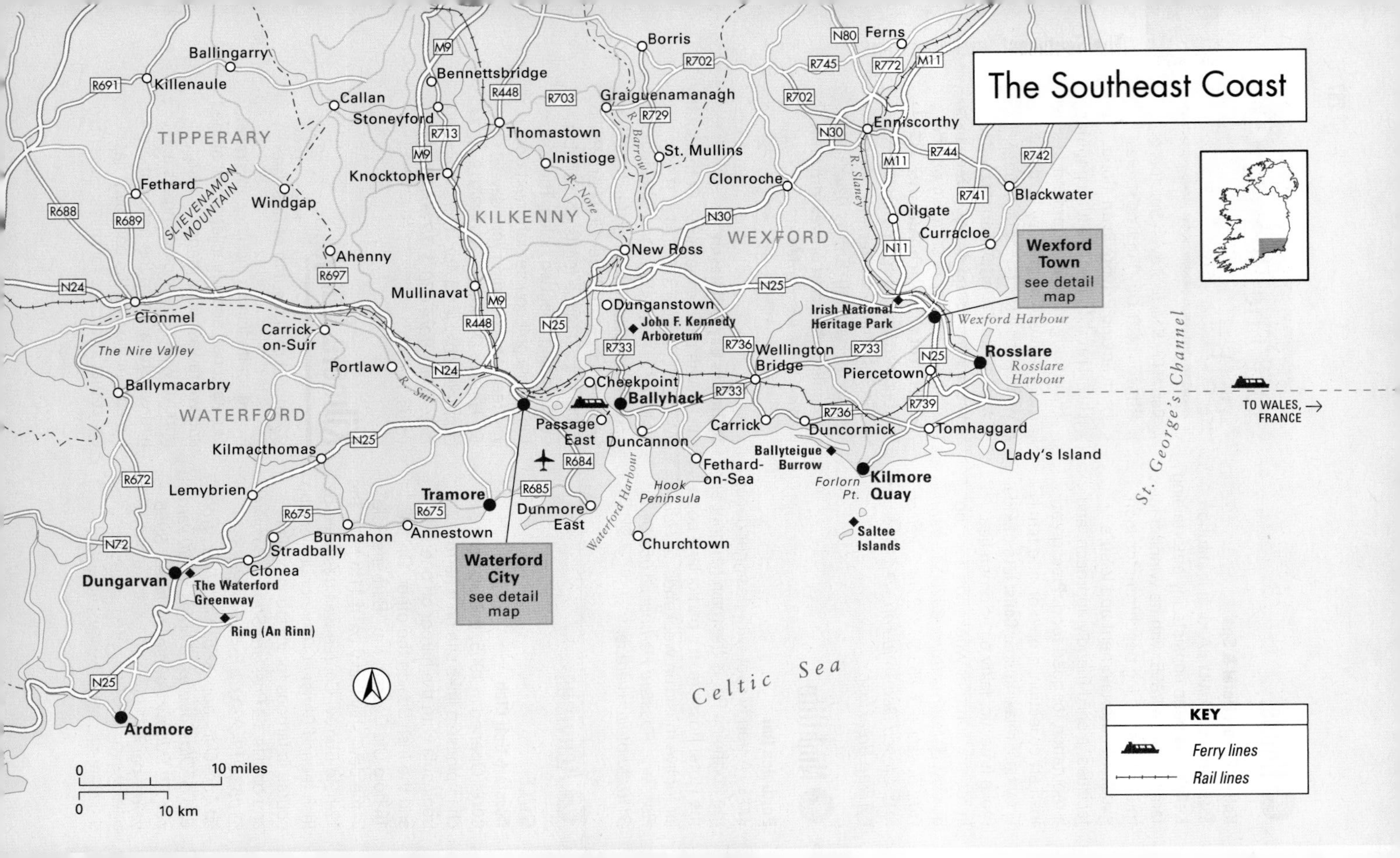

The Southeast Coast
KEY
Ferry lines
Rail lines
TO WALES, FRANCE
St. George's Channel
Celtic Sea
Wexford Town
see detail map
Waterford City
see detail map
TIPPERARY
KILKENNY
WEXFORD
WATERFORD
SLIEVENAMON MOUNTAIN
The Nire Valley
Ballingarry
Killenaule
Callan
Stoneyford
Bennettsbridge
Thomastown
Inistioge
Graiguenamanagh
Borris
St. Mullins
Ferns
Enniscorthy
Clonroche
Oilgate
Curracloe
Blackwater
Fethard
Windgap
Knocktopher
Ahenny
Mullinavat
New Ross
Dunganstown
John F. Kennedy Arboretum
Irish National Heritage Park
Wexford Harbour
Rosslare
Rosslare Harbour
Clonmel
Carrick-on-Suir
Portlaw
Ballymacarbry
Cheekpoint
Ballyhack
Wellington Bridge
Piercetown
Passage East
Duncannon
Carrick
Duncormick
Tomhaggard
Lady's Island
Kilmacthomas
Fethard-on-Sea
Ballyteigue Burrow
Kilmore Quay
Forlorn Pt.
Hook Peninsula
Waterford Harbour
Saltee Islands
Churchtown
Lemybrien
Tramore
Dunmore East
Bunmahon
Annestown
Stradbally
Clonea
Dungarvan
The Waterford Greenway
Ring (An Rinn)
Ardmore
R. Barrow
R. Nore
R. Slaney
R. Suir
R691
R688
R689
R697
M9
R448
R713
R703
R729
R702
R745
R772
M11
N80
N30
R744
R742
R741
N11
N24
N25
R733
R736
R739
R684
R685
R675
R672
N72
0
10 miles
0
10 km

development has turned the harbor into a popular leisure marina.

Sights

★ **Ballyteigue Burrow**

NATURE PRESERVE | Nature lovers and walkers flock to the 8-km-long (5-mile-long) Ballyteigue Burrow, one of the finest sand-dune systems in Europe. It runs all the way from Kilmore Quay to Cullenstown, and is perfect for a long summer stroll and a picnic, with trails through the rolling dunes or along the beautiful beach. The western end is an important nature reserve rich in butterflies, flowers, and wading birds. ✉ *Ballyteigue Burrow, Kilmore Quay.*

Kilmore Quay Seafood Festival

OTHER ATTRACTION | For three days in early July, Kilmore Quay hosts a lively Seafood Festival with a parade, live music, seafood barbecues, guided walks, and other events. ✉ *Kilmore Quay* 🌐 *kilmorequayseafoodfestival.com.*

Saltee Islands

NATURE PRESERVE | Ireland's largest bird sanctuary, the Saltee Islands make a fine day trip from Kilmore Quay. You can see kittiwakes, puffins, guillemots, cormorants, gulls, and petrels, especially in late spring and early summer when several million seabirds nest among the dunes and rocky scarp on the southernmost of the two islands. From mid-May to mid-September, look for boats at the village waterfront or on the marina to take you to the islands, weather permitting. ✉ *Saltee Islands, Kilmore Quay* 🌐 *saltee-islands.info.*

Restaurants

Marry Barry's

$$ | **SEAFOOD** | **FAMILY** | Kilmore Quay is an active fishing harbor, so it's no surprise this old-school pub does a sideline in quality seafood. The menu changes with the daily haul, but regulars include the fresh cold seafood platter with crab, smoked salmon, prawns, barbeque salmon, rollmop herring, and more. **Known for:** buzzing atmosphere; the freshest of seafood; live music. 💲 *Average main: €24* ✉ *Kilmore Village, Kilmore Quay* ☎ *053/913–5982* 🌐 *marybarrys.ie.*

Hotels

Quay House

$ | **B&B/INN** | A perfect base for those interested in boating or fishing, this family-run guesthouse is a three-minute walk from the pier. **Pros:** great angling and diving spot; year-round value; friendly host. **Cons:** rooms are not huge; few facilities; no breakfast served. 💲 *Rooms from: €120* ✉ *Quay House, Kilmore Quay* ☎ *053/912–9988* 🌐 *quayhouse.net* *10 rooms* *No Meals.*

Nightlife

PUBS

Kehoe's Pub and Parlour

PUBS | The hub of village activity, Kehoe's Pub has a collection of maritime artifacts as interesting as that of many museums. ✉ *Kehoe's Pub, Kilmore Quay* ☎ *053/671–0338.*

Ballyhack

39 km (24 miles) west of Kilmore Quay, 54 km (33 miles) west of Rosslare.

On the upper reaches of Waterford Harbour, this pretty village with a square castle keep, thatched cottages, and a green, hilly background is admired by painters and photographers.

GETTING HERE AND AROUND

A small car ferry makes the five-minute crossing from Passage East in County Waterford. Driving from Wexford, take the N25 west to the R373. The 48-km (30-mile) trip takes about an hour on these relatively narrow roads. There is regular bus service from Wexford Town.

Sights

Ballyhack Castle

CASTLE/PALACE | The gray stone keep of Ballyhack Castle dates from the 16th century. It was once owned by the Knights Templar of St. John of Jerusalem, who held the ferry rights by royal charter. The first two floors now house local-history exhibits. Guided tours are available by appointment. ✉ *Ballyhack Castle, Ballyhack* ☎ *051/389–468* 🌐 *heritageireland.ie/visit/places-to-visit/ballyhack-castle* 🎫 *Free* ⏲ *Closed Sept.–early May.*

John F. Kennedy Arboretum

GARDEN | About 12 km (8 miles) to the north of Ballyhack lies the John F. Kennedy Arboretum, with more than 600 acres of forest, nature trails, and gardens, plus an ornamental lake. The grounds contain some 4,500 species of trees and shrubs and serve as a resource center for botanists and foresters. The top of the park offers fine panoramic views. The arboretum is clearly signposted from New Ross on R733, which follows the banks of the Barrow southward for about 5 km (3 miles). The cottage where the president's great-grandfather was born is in Dunganstown; Kennedy relatives still live in the house. About 2 km (1 mile) down the road at Slieve Coillte you can see the entrance to the arboretum. ✉ *John F. Kennedy Arboretum, off R733, Dunganstown* ☎ *051/388–171* 🌐 *heritageireland.ie/visit/places-to-visit/the-john-f-kennedy-arboretum* 🎫 *€5.*

Restaurants

★ Harvest Room

$$$$ | **CONTEMPORARY** | Gourmands come in droves to the ruby-red dining room at Dunbrody House, where celebrity-chef Kevin Dundon serves up foie gras with toasted brioche and balsamic-marinated strawberries, pan-seared Hook Head monkfish with garden courgettes and lemon butter sauce, and a chocolate "selection of indulgences." The weekend eight-course tasting menu is a parade of culinary delights. If you're a hands-on type, you can learn how to cook the Harvest Room's delights yourself; Dundon runs a cooking school on weekends. **Known for:** culinary reputation; legendary Sunday lunch; cooking school. 💲 *Average main: €37* ✉ *Dunbrody House, off L4052, Arthurstown* ☎ *051/389–600* 🌐 *www.dunbrodyhouse.com* ⏲ *Closed Mon. and Tues. No lunch Wed.–Sat.*

Hotels

★ Dunbrody Country House

$$$$ | **HOTEL** | One of Ireland's finest country houses, Dunbrody is a sprawling, two-story 1830s Georgian manor house with beautiful gardens, cooking classes with an Irish celeb chef, guest rooms that charm with a judiciously luxe combination of period antiques and fine reproductions, and restful views over the Barrow Estuary. **Pros:** authentic Georgian feel; ideally positioned for exploring Wexford and the Hook Peninsula; great restaurant and lively bar. **Cons:** expensive for this region; spa is small; quality of rooms can vary. 💲 *Rooms from: €310* ✉ *Off L4052, Arthurstown* ☎ *051/389–600* 🌐 *dunbrodyhouse.com* 🛏 *22 rooms* 🍴 *Free Breakfast.*

★ Kilmokea Country Manor & Gardens

$$ | **B&B/INN** | Originally an 18th-century stone rectory, the authentic Georgian-country-house experience is promised and more than delivered at luxurious Kilmokea, known for its award-winning gardens. **Pros:** great for families; wonderful hosts; rooms boast gorgeous garden views. **Cons:** a little out of the way; occasionally booked up for private parties; two-night minimum in high season. 💲 *Rooms from: €180* ✉ *Great Island, Campile, Wexford* ☎ *051/388–109* 🌐 *kilmokea.com* 🛏 *7 rooms, 1 cottage* 🍴 *Free Breakfast.*

Waterford City

10 km (6 miles) west of Ballyhack by ferry and road, 62 km (39 miles) southwest of Wexford Town, 158 km (98 miles) southwest of Dublin.

The largest town in the Southeast and Ireland's oldest city, Waterford was founded by the Vikings in the 9th century and was taken over by Strongbow, the Norman invader, with much bloodshed in 1170. The city resisted Cromwell's 1649 attacks but fell the following year. It did not prosper again until 1783, when George and William Penrose set out to create "plain and cut flint glass, useful and ornamental," and thereby set in motion a glass-manufacturing industry long without equal. The famed glassworks closed some time back, but Waterford Crystal has triumphantly risen from the ashes in a smaller, leaner version.

GETTING HERE AND AROUND

From Dublin, take the N7/M7 to the N9/M9 and all the way to Waterford City. This motorway is often quiet, and the trip takes only two hours. The city is only 45 minutes from Kilkenny via the N9 and N10.

It can be a long drive around the coast from Wexford to Waterford and the Passage East Car Ferry Company operates year-round from Passage East in Wexford to Ballyhack, near Waterford City. The five-minute crossings are continuous from 7 am until 10 pm, April through September, and until 8 pm the rest of the year (with first sailing on Sunday at 9:30 am). The cost is €9 one-way and €13 round-trip for a car and passengers and €1.50 one-way, €2 round-trip for a foot passenger.

Bus Éireann has a station on the waterfront at Merchant's Quay and runs regular buses to cities and towns all over the country, including Tramore (around €4 one-way, €7 round-trip; 30 minutes); Dungarvan (around €4.80 one-way, €10 round-trip; 50 minutes); Wexford (around €12.60 one-way, €17 round-trip; 1½ hours); Cork (around €14.30 one-way, €21 round-trip; 2¼ hours); and Dublin (around €16 one-way, €23 round-trip; three hours). Bus Éireann also runs a local city bus service in Waterford City, with five routes that cover the city center.

On the north side of the river, Plunkett Station receives Irish Rail trains from Kilkenny (€11 one-way, €12 round-trip; 45 minutes); Dublin (€26 one-way, €29 round-trip; 2¾ hours); and Limerick (€19 one-way, €30 round-trip; 2¾ hours). Note: bus and rail fares fluctuate depending on when you travel.

VISITOR INFORMATION

CONTACTS Waterford City Tourist Office. ✉ *120 Parade Quay, Waterford* ☎ *051/875–823* 🌐 *visitwaterford.com.*

Sights

Waterford has better-preserved city walls than anywhere else in Ireland besides Derry.

■ TIP→ You can spot one of the remaining portions of the city walls along Spring Garden Alley, off Colbeck Street.

Initially, the slightly run-down commercial center doesn't look promising. You need to park your car and proceed on foot to discover the city's proudly preserved heritage, in particular the grand 18th-century Georgian buildings that Waterford architect John Roberts (1714–96) built, including the town's Protestant and Catholic cathedrals.

Waterford's compact town center can be visited in a couple of hours. Most visitors consider the Waterford Glass Visitor Centre and the impressive pair of history museums as must-sees in any city tour. The "Freedom of Waterford Pass" (€15) allows you access to most sites and will save you a lot of money. It's available from 🌐 *www.waterfordtreasures.com* or at any of the sites.

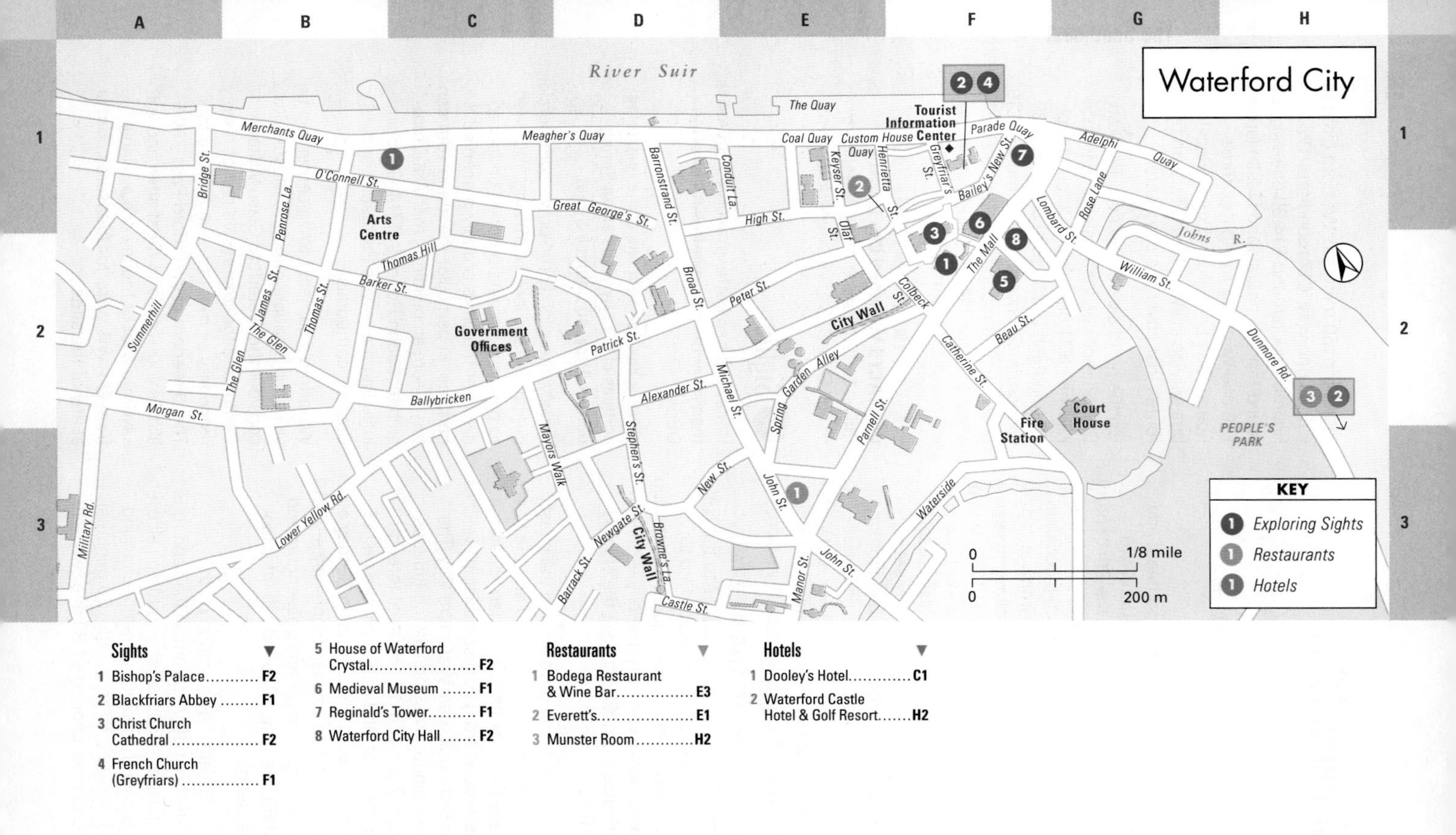

Sights

1 Bishop's Palace........... **F2**

2 Blackfriars Abbey **F1**

3 Christ Church Cathedral **F2**

4 French Church (Greyfriars) **F1**

5 House of Waterford Crystal...................... **F2**

6 Medieval Museum **F1**

7 Reginald's Tower.......... **F1**

8 Waterford City Hall **F2**

Restaurants

1 Bodega Restaurant & Wine Bar................ **E3**

2 Everett's.................... **E1**

3 Munster Room............**H2**

Hotels

1 Dooley's Hotel.............**C1**

2 Waterford Castle Hotel & Golf Resort.......**H2**

Bishop's Palace

HISTORIC HOME | Among the most imposing of the city's remaining Georgian town houses, the Bishop's Palace is the home to the Georgian part of the Waterford Treasures exhibition, mapping the history of what was Ireland's second city from 1700 to 1790. The most impressive part of the collection is the elegant silverware and, of course, fine glassmaking, including the oldest piece of Waterford crystal on the planet—a decanter from the 1780s. Try to catch one of the regular tours, where local actors play some well-known scenes from Waterford history. ✉ *The Mall, alongside Waterford City Hall, Waterford* ☎ *051/304–500* 🌐 *waterfordtreasures.com/bishops-palace* 🎫 *From €10.*

Blackfriars Abbey

HISTORIC SIGHT | While you can't go inside, you can get close to the remains of this genuinely medieval abbey and get a sense of how impressive it once was. This ruined tower belonged to a Dominican abbey that was founded in 1226 and returned to the Crown in 1541 after the dissolution of the monasteries. It was used as a courthouse until Cromwellian forces destroyed most of it in the 17th century. ✉ *High St., Waterford.*

Christ Church Cathedral

CHURCH | Lovers of Georgian decorative arts will want to visit this late-18th-century Church of Ireland cathedral, the only Neoclassical Georgian cathedral in Ireland, designed by local architect John Roberts. Inside, all is elegance—yellow walls, white-stucco florets and laurels, grand Corinthian columns—and you can see why architectural historian Mark Girouard called this "the finest 18th-century ecclesiastical building in Ireland." It stands on the site of a great Norman Gothic cathedral, which a bishop authorized knocking down after rubble fell in his path a few times (with a little help from potential builders). Medievalists will be sad, but those who prize Age of Enlightenment high style will rejoice. Try to catch one of the regular choral concerts to get the full atmospheric reward. ✉ *Henrietta St., Waterford* ☎ *051/858–958* 🌐 *christchurchwaterford.com* 🎫 *€3* 🕒 *Closed Sun. (except for normal services).*

French Church (Greyfriars)

RUINS | Roofless ruins are all that remain of French Church, a 13th-century Franciscan abbey. The church, also known as Greyfriars, was given to a group of Huguenot refugees (hence the "French") in 1695. A splendid east window remains amid the ruins. The key is available at Reginald's Tower. ✉ *Greyfriars St., Waterford.*

★ **House of Waterford Crystal**

FACTORY | Iconic Waterford crystal is once again being produced in the city, albeit on a much smaller scale than before. The factory tour, which includes the blowing, sculpting, and cutting departments, is a must for anyone who appreciates timeless craftsmanship and unique design. After watching a team of glassworkers create a twinkling masterpiece from a molten blob, you may have trouble resisting the retail store, where you can select from the world's largest collection of Waterford crystal. You can have your purchase engraved on the spot. They also offer a sumptuous afternoon tea served on fine bone china. ✉ *The Mall, Waterford* ☎ *051/317–000* 🌐 *waterfordvisitorcentre.com* 🎫 *Tour €17* 🕒 *Closed weekends in Nov.–Feb.*

Medieval Museum

HISTORY MUSEUM | Waterford's newest museum cleverly incorporates two medieval-era structures within its walls. Inside, the focus is on Waterford's rich Norman history. A collection of rare and beautiful artifacts includes the Charter Roll of 1372, a list of all charters granted to Waterford up to that time, written in Latin. Also here you'll find the sword of King Edward IV and 15th-century "Cloth of Gold" religious vestments—a true

The circular Reginald's Tower, originally built by the Vikings, is one of the eye-catching sights along Waterford's Merchant's Quay, long the center of the city's social and economic scene.

work of art. There's a detailed audiovisual display to add to the experience. ✉ *The Mall, Waterford* ☎ *051/304–500* 🌐 *waterfordtreasures.com/medieval-museum* 🎫 *From €10.*

★ Reginald's Tower

NOTABLE BUILDING | Restored to its original medieval appearance, Reginald's Tower—a circular structure on the east end of Waterford's quays—is a striking setting for a museum on Waterford's Viking history. Built by the Vikings for the city's defense in 1003, it has 80-foot-high, 10-foot-thick walls; an interior stairway leads to the top. The tower served in turn as the residence for a succession of Anglo-Norman kings (including Henry II, John, and Richard II), a mint for silver coins, a prison, and an arsenal. It's said that Strongbow's marriage to Eva, the daughter of Dermot MacMurrough, took place here in the late 12th century, thus uniting the Norman invaders with the native Irish. The impressive exhibits include the full weapon kit of a local Viking leader. On the top floor, there's an audiovisual display and objects to represent every century since the tower was built. ✉ *The Quay, Waterford* ☎ *051/304–500* 🌐 *waterfordtreasures.com/reginalds-tower* 🎫 *€5* ⏲ *Closed mid-Dec.–Jan 6., and Mon. and Tues. Jan. 7–mid-Mar.*

Waterford City Hall

GOVERNMENT BUILDING | One of Waterford's finest Georgian buildings, Waterford City Hall dates from 1783 and was designed by native son John Roberts. The arms of Waterford hang over the entrance, which leads into a spacious foyer that originally served as a town meeting place and merchants' exchange. The building contains an enormous 1802 Waterford glass chandelier, which hangs in the Council Chamber (a copy hangs in Independence Hall in Philadelphia). The Victorian horseshoe-shape Theatre Royal is the venue for the annual Festival of Light Opera in September. ✉ *The Mall, Waterford* ☎ *051/309–900* 🎫 *Free* ⏲ *Closed weekends.*

Waterford Crystal

Silica sand + potash + litharge = Waterford crystal. It reads like cold science, but something magical happens when the craftsmen of Waterford produce arguably the top crystal in the world (although France's Baccarat might have something to say about that).

When the Waterford Glass Factory opened in 1783, it provided English royalty and nobility with a regular supply of ornate handcrafted stemware, chandeliers, and decorative knickknacks. Since then, Waterford crystal has graced the tables of heads of state the world over, and Waterford's earlier pieces have become priceless heirlooms.

The best Waterford glass was produced from the late 18th century to the early 19th century. This early work, examples of which can be found in museums and public buildings all over the country, is characterized by a unique, slightly opaque cast that is absent from the modern product.

Crystal glass is not cheap: each piece is individually fashioned by almost two dozen pairs of hands before it passes final inspection and receives the discreet Waterford trademark.

The first thing on the itinerary of any visitor to Waterford was for many years a tour of the glass factory, a buzzing hive of master craftspeople. But the global downturn saw the landmark factory close. Happily, Waterford Crystal arose from the ashes in 2010 and now offers a smaller specialist facility at the Mall. The adjoining visitor center is already a must-see.

Restaurants

Bodega Restaurant & Wine Bar

$$ | **MODERN IRISH** | A casual, modern Irish eatery, Bodega Restaurant is known as the fun place to eat in town. Everything is prepared with locally sourced ingredients, with the Kilmore Quay haddock bake a hearty favorite, along with celeriac and baby carrot risotto with sherry vinegar caramel, crispy potato rosti, mascarpone, and Parmesan. **Known for:** superfresh fish; good wine menu; great live music. *Average main: €24 54 John's St., Waterford 051/844–177 bodegawaterford.com Closed Mon. and Tues. No lunch Wed.–Sat.*

★ Everett's

$$$ | **MODERN IRISH** | Located in an atmospheric, vaulted 15th-century house at the heart of the city, this new, award-winning bistro has a young local chef who trained with some of the best in Ireland. Start with seared Wexford scallops with broccoli, smoked bacon, and hazelnut. **Known for:** fantastic vegetarian options; wild meats; award winner. *Average main: €27 22 High St., Waterford 051/325–174 everetts.ie No lunch Sun.–Thurs.*

★ Munster Room

$$$$ | **FRENCH** | Inside the Waterford Castle Hotel, the Munster Room's luxe decor—with oak paneling darkened with age and ancestral portraits in gilt frames—hints at one of the most sophisticated menus around. Options include a fixed-price, three-course menu featuring adventurous starters such as ballotine of quail with celeriac foam, winter slaw, and cinnamon and apple jelly. **Known for:** quality service; killer dessert menu; smart dress code. *Average main: €40 Waterford Castle Hotel, The Island, 2 km (1 mile) south of Waterford, Ballinakill 051/878–203*

🌐 *waterfordcastleresort.com/munster-room-restaurant.html* ⏲ *No lunch.*

Hotels

Dooley's Hotel

$$ | **HOTEL** | **FAMILY** | A short stroll from all the main attractions, this unpretentious hotel on the banks of the River Suir is popular both with families and business travelers, while the traditional bar is packed with locals. **Pros:** downtown location; large guest rooms; excellent service. **Cons:** attracts a business clientele; you can get more for same price elsewhere; can be a little noisy. Ⓢ *Rooms from: €169* ✉ *30 The Quay, Waterford* ☎ *051/873–531* 🌐 *dooleys-hotel.ie* *112 rooms* *Free Breakfast.*

★ **Waterford Castle Hotel & Golf Resort**

$$$$ | **HOTEL** | **FAMILY** | Not only does this fairy-tale castle come with an 800-year history, its own 310-acre island, a private ferry, and a highly rated 18-hole golf course, it also caters to lucky guests with the best of Irish service and the grandest of Irish style. **Pros:** tennis and basketball courts; great golf course and driving range; traditional afternoon tea. **Cons:** expensive for this region; books up quickly in summer; popular with weddings. Ⓢ *Rooms from: €330* ✉ *The Island, 2 km (1 mile) south of Waterford, Ballinakill* ☎ *051/878–203* 🌐 *waterfordcastleresort.com* *19 rooms* *No Meals.*

Nightlife

The Gingerman

PUBS | Glass, brass, and dark wood identify this city-center hostelry as a genuine old-school classic. It's a great place to meet locals at rest, and the pub-grub menu offers excellent value. ✉ *6 Arundel La., Waterford* ☎ *051/879–522.*

Jack Meades

PUBS | Known to locals as "Meades under the Bridge," this place is indeed set beneath a time-stained stone bridge. In centuries past it was a stop on the coach road from Waterford to Passage East. There's a solid pub menu, and singalong sessions on Saturday. In winter the fireplaces roar, illuminating the wood beams and displayed bric-a-brac. ✉ *Halfway House, Cheekpoint Rd., Dunmore East* ☎ *051/873–187* 🌐 *jackmeades.com.*

Old Ground

PUBS | Housed in an 800-year-old building, this pub is highly popular with locals. Lunch is served daily, and it's a cozy spot on a rainy day. ✉ *10 The Glen, Waterford* ☎ *051/852–283.*

Performing Arts

Garter Lane Arts Centre

ARTS CENTERS | Culture buffs shouldn't miss the Garter Lane Arts Centre, which has a schedule filled with concerts, exhibits, and theater productions. ✉ *22A O'Connell St., Waterford* ☎ *051/855–038* 🌐 *garterlane.ie.*

Theatre Royal Waterford

THEATER | One of the oldest theaters in Ireland, the elegant Theatre Royal is devoted to large-scale productions and musicals, as well as live music. ✉ *Waterford City Hall, The Mall, Waterford* ☎ *051/874–402* 🌐 *theatreroyal.ie.*

Shopping

Penrose Crystal

CRAFTS | Check out the quality goods at the town's handmade-crystal factory. With a little notice, Penrose can have a personally engraved piece waiting for you when you arrive. ✉ *32 John St., Waterford* ☎ *051/876–537* 🌐 *penrosecrystal.com.*

Tower Gift Shop

SOUVENIRS | You'll find a mix of local arts and crafts and kitschy souvenirs, along with insights into what's going on around the city, in this fun little gift shop. ✉ *128 Parade Quay, Waterford* ☎ *086/407–3191.*

Activities

GAELIC FOOTBALL

Waterford GAA Grounds

LOCAL SPORTS | Watch exciting and spectacular Gaelic football and hurling at the Waterford GAA Grounds. ✉ *Walsh Park, Waterford* ☎ *051/591–5544* 🌐 *waterford-gaa.ie.*

GOLF

Waterford Castle Hotel & Golf Club

GOLF | Claiming to be Ireland's only true island course, Waterford Castle is completely detached from the mainland on a privately owned 310-acre island. Designed by Irish golfing great Des Smyth, the tricky but playable 18-hole course winds through mature woodland and features four internal water features in addition to the encroaching sea. There are plenty of opportunities to hit one into the drink. ✉ *The Island, 2 km (1 mile) south of Waterford, Ballinakill* ☎ *051/871–633* 🌐 *waterfordcastleresort.com* *Nov.–Mar., from €25; Apr.–Oct., from €50* *18 holes, 6372 yards, par 72.*

Tramore

11 km (7 miles) south of Waterford City on R675, 4 km (2½ miles) west of Dunmore East.

Tramore's 5-km-long (3-mile-long) beach is a popular escape for families from Waterford and other parts of the Southeast, as the many vacation homes indicate. The beach is adjacent to the "merries," aka Tramore Amusement Park, which features all the usual rides, including a Ferris wheel, roller coaster, and old-fashioned bumper cars. Kiddie heaven, in other words.

GETTING HERE AND AROUND

From Waterford City, take the R675 south to Tramore. The trip takes about 15 minutes. Bus Éireann runs frequent service from Waterford City (around €4 one-way, €7 round-trip; 30 minutes). The Bus Éireann bus stop is outside the tourist office near Splashworld.

Restaurants

The Beach House

$$$ | **SEAFOOD** | Situated on the ground floor of a Victorian house with a wonderful vegetable garden out back, the Beach House has rapidly become one of the hottest seafood restaurants in the country. Their shellfish bisque is a gorgeous starter, and while mains change with the daily catch, the brill with mussels and Muscadet and the black sole are two of the more popular. **Known for:** ever-changing menu; family-owned; award-winning chef. *Average main: €26* ✉ *Turkey Rd., Tramore* 🌐 *beachhousetramore.ie* *Closed Jan.–Mar.*

Dungarvan

42 km (26 miles) southwest of Tramore, 44 km (27 miles) southwest of Waterford.

With their covering of soft grasses, the lowlands of Wexford and eastern Waterford gradually give way to heath and moorland. The mountains responsible for the wetter climate rise up behind Dungarvan, the largest coastal town in County Waterford. This bustling fishing and resort spot sits at the mouth of the River Colligan where it empties into Dungarvan Bay. It's a popular base for climbers and hikers.

GETTING HERE AND AROUND

From Waterford, take the N25 west to Dungarvan. The trip takes 45 minutes. Bus Éireann drops off passengers on Davitt's Quay. It has regular daily services from Waterford (around €4.80 one-way, €10 round-trip; 55 minutes); Cork (around €8 one-way, €11 round-trip; 1½ hours; 13 daily); and Dublin (around €14 one-way, €27 round-trip; 1 hour 10 minutes).

VISITOR INFORMATION

CONTACTS Dungarvan and West Waterford Tourism. ✉ *Main St., Dungarvan* ☎ *058/41741* 🌐 *dungarvantourism.com.*

Sights

★ Ring (An Rinn)

TRAIL | FAMILY | Unusual in the south and east of the country, Ring (An Rinn) is an unspoiled Gaeltacht area on Dungarvan Bay where you will find the Irish language still in daily use. Courses in Irish have been taught at Coláiste na Rinne, a language college, since 1909. It's a lovely spot for bikers, walkers, and bird-watchers—the area includes An Cuinigear, a long, thin peninsula that thousands of seabirds call home. Helvic, a tiny fishing village, commands great views over the Waterford coastline, with the Comeragh Mountains as a backdrop. ✉ *Off N674F, 7 km (4½ miles) southeast of Dungarvan, Dungarvan.*

★ The Waterford Greenway

TRAIL | FAMILY | Running along a converted railway track between Dungarvan and Waterford City, the 46 km (29 miles) of the Waterford Greenway has quickly become a must-do destination for walkers and off-road cyclists. Passing through some of the region's most spectacular countryside, and crossing no fewer than three tall viaducts, you'll lose yourself in the natural surroundings. The flat, paved path is perfect for families, and you can take on the whole route or just do one of the many small sections. Bikes can be rented all along the way, and new, funky eateries are opening all the time. ✉ *Waterford Greenway, Dungarvan* ☎ *053/584–1741* 🌐 *greenwaysireland.org/waterford-greenway.*

Restaurants

The Old Bank

$$$ | ITALIAN | FAMILY | Set in a magnificent and grand Palladian-style bank in the center of Dungarvan, the Old Bank restaurant is *the* place to withdraw some delicious food and cocktails. The ground-floor Italian bistro menu has plenty of local twists, while the first-floor restaurant is more fine dining. **Known for:** local seafood; creative cocktails; historic building. $ *Average main: €30* ✉ *Davitts Quay, Dungarvan* ☎ *058/48189* 🌐 *theoldbankdungarvan.ie* ⏲ *Closed Mon. and Tues.*

★ The Tannery

$$$$ | ECLECTIC | Local culinary wizard Paul Flynn whets quite an appetite in the flocks of Dubliners who besiege every weekend what is commonly regarded as one of Ireland's leading restaurants. The menu is rustic but whimsical and always seasonal. **Known for:** celebrity chef; award-winning cuisine; culinary school attached. $ *Average main: €35* ✉ *10 Quay St., Dungarvan* ☎ *058/45420* 🌐 *tannery.ie* ⏲ *Closed Mon. and Tues. No dinner Sun. Sept.–May. No lunch Wed.–Sat.*

Hotels

Gold Coast Golf Hotel

$$ | HOTEL | FAMILY | Overlooking Dungarvan Bay, this hotel is part of a family-run and family-friendly property that includes self-catering holiday cottages and golf villas on the edge of a woodland course on a links setting. **Pros:** great location; owners love kids; great value even in high season. **Cons:** can be hectic and noisy; guest rooms are a little mundane; limited facilities. $ *Rooms from: €175* ✉ *Off Clonea Rd., Dungarvan* ☎ *058/42249, 058/42416* 🌐 *goldcoastgolfresort.com* *37 rooms, 16 cottages, 12 villas, 27 lodges* 🍴 *Free Breakfast.*

Performing Arts

Coláiste na Rinne

FOLK/TRADITIONAL DANCE | A few miles outside Dungarvan, you can sit/join in on a *ceilí* (traditional Irish dance), held most nights in summer at Coláiste na Rinne, the school in this Irish-speaking community known for its strong tradition in Irish language, heritage, and culture. ✉ *Ring* ☎ *058/46104* 🌐 *anrinn.com.*

Ardmore

29 km (18 miles) southwest of Dungarvan.

Historic spiritual sites, white beaches, dramatic cliff walks, local fishermen—little Ardmore is a picture-postcard Irish town that packs a whole lot of wonder into a small peninsula at the base of a tall cliff. With a few notable exceptions—including John F. Kennedy and Gregory Peck—the cute but very real village, with a highly lauded restaurant, is often overlooked by most overseas tourists.

GETTING HERE AND AROUND

From Waterford, take the N25 west and exit left onto the R673. The trip takes about an hour, with the last part traveled on a small country road. There are a few buses a day from Dungarvan and Youghal. Parking can be a problem in the high season.

Sights

Cathedral of St. Declan and Round Tower

RUINS | There's a story behind every ruin you pass in Ireland; behind many, there's a truly ancient story. Inside the ruined 12th-century Cathedral of St. Declan are some pillar stones decorated with ogham script (an ancient Irish alphabet) as well as weathered but stunningly abstract biblical scenes carved on its west gable. St. Declan is reputed to have disembarked here in the 5th century—30 years before St. Patrick arrived in Ireland—and founded a monastery. The saint is said to be buried in St. Declan's Oratory, a small early Christian church that has been partially reconstructed.

On the grounds of the ruined cathedral is the 97-foot-high Round Tower, which is in exceptionally good condition. Round Towers were built by the early Christian monks as watchtowers and belfries, but came to be used as places of refuge for the monks and their valuables during Viking raids. This is the reason the doorway is 15 feet above ground level—once inside, the monks could pull the ladder into the tower with them. ✉ *Tower Hill, Ardmore.*

Restaurants

★ **The House Restaurant**

$$$$ | **ECLECTIC** | The compact, award-winning dining room of the Cliff House looks out over the crashing sea, and the dramatic location clearly inspires the menu. The food is locally sourced—including foraging raids on nearby woods and beaches—but prepared with dashes of modern and experimental cuisine. **Known for:** dramatic setting; award-winning; creative menu. 💲 *Average main: €42* ✉ *Cliff House, Cliff Rd., Ardmore* ☎ *024/87800* 🌐 *thecliffhousehotel.com* ⏲ *No lunch weekdays.*

Hotels

★ **Cliff House**

$$$$ | **HOTEL** | Tucked into the cliffs overlooking the fishing village of Ardmore, ageless nature confronts modernist design at Cliff House—and this luxury hotel and spa remains one of the most innovative additions to Irish accommodations in the last few decades. **Pros:** the sea is everywhere; great spa and pool; up the road from the wonderful Ardmore Pottery shop. **Cons:** pricey for the region; sometimes has two-day minimum in summer; younger staff still learning the trade. 💲 *Rooms from: €450* ✉ *Cliff Rd., Ardmore* 🌐 *thecliffhousehotel.com* *39 rooms* *No Meals.*

Did You Know?

One of the earliest landmarks of Christianity in Ireland, St. Declan's Cathedral stands on a cliff top settled by the saint between 350 and 420—decades before St. Patrick arrived. On St. Declan's Day, July 24, pilgrims walk along the 80-km (50-mile) St. Declan's Way to the Rock of Cashel.

Shopping

★ **Ardmore Pottery & Craft Shop**
CRAFTS | Home to potter Mary Lincoln, a poll of *Irish Times* readers a few years back agreed this is one of the most beloved, creative, and cleverly stocked craft shops in the country, with everything from Lynsey de Burca's silver jewelry to McNutt's fine tweeds and linens. You can even watch Mary work at the wheel and purchase some of her own beautiful, delicate designs. ✉ *Ardmore Pottery and Gallery, Cliff Rd., Ardmore* ☎ *024/94152* 🌐 *ardmorepottery.com.*

Activities

Ardmore Adventures
WATER SPORTS | **FAMILY** | Ardmore and other nearby beaches have become meccas for water-sports lovers, and this shop organizes surfing, snorkeling, kayaking, paddleboarding, and anything else that involves fun and the sea. They run a great camp for kids in summer. ✉ *Ardmore* ☎ *083/374–3889* 🌐 *ardmoreadventures.ie.*

Lismore

20 km (13 miles) northwest of Dungarvan.

Lismore is one of Ireland's grandest places to get lost in. Popular with both anglers and romantics, the enchanting little town is built on the banks of the Blackwater, a river famous for its trout and salmon. From the 7th to the 12th century it was an important monastic center, founded by St. Carthac (or Carthage), and it had one of the most renowned universities of its time. The village has two cathedrals: a soaring Roman Catholic one from the late 19th century, and the Church of Ireland's St. Carthage's, which dates from 1633 and incorporates fragments of an earlier church.

Glamour arrived in the form of the dukes of Devonshire, who built their Irish seat here, Lismore Castle (their main house is Chatsworth in England); in the 1940s, Fred Astaire, whose sister, Adele, had married Lord Charles Cavendish, younger son of the ninth duke, would bend the elbow at the town's Madden's Pub. Other architectural jewels include a quaint library funded by Andrew Carnegie and the Ballysaggartmore "folly," a Gothic-style gateway to a 19th-century house that was so costly the house itself was never erected.

GETTING HERE AND AROUND

From Waterford take the N25 west to the N72. The trip takes about 55 minutes. There are regular buses from Dungarvan. In summer, parking spots are at a premium around the small town.

VISITOR INFORMATION

CONTACTS Lismore Tourist Office. ✉ *Lismore Heritage Centre, West St. and Chapel St., Lismore* ☎ *058/54975* 🌐 *discoverlismore.com.*

Sights

Knockmealdown Mountains
MOUNTAIN | Leaving Lismore, head east on N72 for 6½ km (4 miles), then north on R669 into the Knockmealdown Mountains. From the summit, called Vee Gap, you'll have superb views of the Galtee Mountains in the northwest and a peak called Slievenamon in the northeast. If the day is clear, you should be able to see the Rock of Cashel, ancient seat of the kings of Munster, some 32 km (20 miles) away. Just before you enter the Vee Gap, look for a 6-foot-high mound of stones beside the road. It marks the grave of Colonel Grubb, a local landowner who liked the view so much that he arranged to be buried here standing up so that he could look out over the scene for all eternity. ✉ *Vee Gap Rd., Lismore.*

The duke of Devonshire's Lismore Castle once sheltered Edmund Spenser when he was writing *The Faerie Queene;* today, his parklands are home to avant-garde artworks.

★ Lismore Castle and Gardens

CASTLE/PALACE | As you cross the bridge entering Lismore, you spot the magnificent Lismore Castle, a vast, turreted building atop a rock overhanging the River Blackwater. There has been a castle here since the 12th century, but the present structure, built by the sixth duke of Devonshire, dates from the mid–19th century. The house remains the estate of the Cavendish family, and most of it is not open to the public. You can see the contemporary-art gallery, designed by Cork architect Gareth O'Callaghan, in the west wing, as well as the upper and lower gardens, which consist of woodland walks, including an unusual yew walk said to be more than 800 years old (Edmund Spenser is said to have written parts of *The Faerie Queene* here), certain months of the year. The gardens have an impressive display of magnolias, camellias, and shrubs, and are adorned with examples of contemporary sculpture. ✉ *Off N72, Lismore* ☎ *058/54424* 🌐 *lismorecastlegardens.com* 🎟 *€9* 🕑 *Closed Nov.–mid-Mar.*

Lismore Heritage Center

VISITOR CENTER | **FAMILY** | In the former town courthouse, Lismore Heritage Center and its exhibits focus on the town's Celtic origins and its links to famous people from Sir Walter Raleigh to Prince Charles to Fred Astaire. Lismore Experience, an impressive video presentation, charts the history of the town from its monastic 7th-century origins up to the present day, with a virtual reality tour of the castle an additional option. The center also has a large crafts shop, and the Robert Boyle Escape Room is a fun way to uncover the great discoveries of the noted local 17th-century scientist. ✉ *West St. and Chapel St., Lismore* ☎ *058/54975* 🌐 *discoverlismore.com* 🎟 *From €3* 🕑 *Closed weekends in Nov.–Mar.*

Mount Melleray Abbey

CHURCH | The first post-Reformation monastery, Mount Melleray Abbey was founded in 1832 by the Cistercian Order in what was then a barren mountainside wilderness. Over the years the order has transformed the site into more than 600 acres of fertile farmland. The monks maintain strict vows of silence, but you're welcome to join in services throughout the day and are permitted into most areas of the abbey. It's also possible to stay in the guest lodge. There's a small heritage center about the history of Irish monasticism with a few ogham stones and a short film. ✉ *Off R669, 13 km (8 miles) from Lismore, Cappoquin* ☎ *058/54404* 🌐 *mountmellerayabbey.org* 🎫 *Free.*

Richmond House

$$ | **B&B/INN** | It's been 300 years since the earl of Cork and Burlington built this handsome country house, and it still retains its imposing aura of courtly elegance, thanks to owners Claire and Paul Deevy. **Pros:** great views; locally sourced restaurant; enchanting gardens. **Cons:** limited facilities; books up quickly; place is a little tattered around the edges. $ *Rooms from: €190* ✉ *Richmond House, off N72, Cappoquin* ☎ *058/54278* 🌐 *richmondhouse.net* ⏲ *Closed late Dec.–mid-Jan.* *10 rooms* *Free Breakfast.*

Cahir

37 km (23 miles) north of Lismore.

Cahir (pronounced "care") is a busy but easygoing market town with a pleasant Georgian square at its heart. It is built on the River Suir at the eastern end of the Galtee mountain range. The Suir is known for its good salmon and trout fishing, as is the Aherlow River, which joins it above town.

GETTING HERE AND AROUND

From Dublin, take the N7/M7 south to junction 19 and the N24. At junction 10, take the R670 to Cahir. The trip takes just over two hours. There is regular bus service from Kilkenny and Waterford, as well as train service from Dublin and Kilkenny.

VISITOR INFORMATION

CONTACTS Cahir Tourist Office. ✉ *Castle Car Park, Cahir* ☎ *052/744–1453* 🌐 *tipperary.com/listings/cahir-tourist-office.*

Cahir Castle

CASTLE/PALACE | The unavoidable focal point of the town, Cahir Castle is dramatically perched on a rocky island on the River Suir. Once the stronghold of the mighty Butler family and one of Ireland's largest and best-preserved castles, it retains its dramatic keep, tower, and much of its original defensive structure. An audiovisual show and guided tour are available upon request. ✉ *Castle St., Cahir* 🌐 *heritageireland.ie/visit/places-to-visit/cahir-castle* 🎫 *€5.*

★ Swiss Cottage

HISTORIC HOME | If there's little storybook allure to the brute mass of Cahir Castle, fairy-tale looks grace the first earl of Glengall's 1812 Swiss Cottage, a dreamy relic from the days when Romanticism conquered 19th-century Ireland. A mile south of town on a particularly picturesque stretch of the River Suir, this "cottage *orné*" was probably designed by John Nash, one of the Regency period's most fashionable architects. Half thatch-roof cottage, half mansion, it was a veritable theater set that allowed the lordly couple to fantasize about being "simple folk" (secret doorways allowed servants to bring food without being noticed). Inside, some of the earliest Dufour wallpapers printed in Paris charm the eye. A pleasant way to get here is to hike from Cahir Castle on a footpath along the river. In peak season, crowds can be fierce. ✉ *Off R670, Cahir* 🌐 *heritageireland.ie/visit/places-to-visit/swiss-cottage* 🎫 *Free* ⏲ *Closed Nov.–early Mar.*

Hotels

★ Aherlow House Hotel & Lodges
$ | HOTEL | Built in 1928 to replace a house destroyed in Ireland's Civil War, Aherlow is set on the slopes of Sliabh na Muc (Mountain of the Pigs) and comes with its own private forest and incredible views of the magnificent Galtee Mountains and the ancient Glen of Aherlow. **Pros:** rooms are big; families will love the lodges; stunning natural surroundings. **Cons:** popular with local weddings and parties; gets booked up summer weekends; weekend rates higher. *Rooms from: €120 Off R663, Aherlow 062/56153 aherlowhouse.ie 29 rooms, 15 lodges No Meals.*

Cashel

17 km (11 miles) north of Cahir.

Cashel is a market town on the busy Cork–Dublin road, with a lengthy history as a center of royal and religious power. From roughly AD 370 until AD 1101, it was the seat of the Kings of Munster, and it was probably at one time a center of Druidic worship. Here, according to legend, St. Patrick arrived in about AD 432 and baptized King Aengus, who became Ireland's first Christian ruler. One of the many legends associated with this event is that St. Patrick plucked a shamrock to explain the mystery of the Trinity, thus giving a new emblem to Christian Ireland.

GETTING HERE AND AROUND

Cashel is on the busy N8/M8 motorway between Dublin and Cork. Dublin is 162 km (100 miles) northeast of Cashel on the N8/M8 and N7/M7. Cork City is 97 km (60 miles) or one hour and 10 minutes south of Cashel on the N8/M8 and the N74. Bus Éireann runs buses from Dublin (around €14 one-way, €24 round-trip; three hours; six daily), Cork (around €14 one-way, €23.50 round-trip; 1½ hours) via Cahir (around €5 one-way, €9 round-trip; 15 minutes), and Fermoy (around €12 one-way, €25 round-trip; one hour, 20 minutes). The bus stop for Cork is outside the Bake House on Main Street. The Dublin stop is directly opposite.

To head to the Rock of Cashel directly from Dublin, many travelers use the Irish Rail route that heads to the small town of Thurles, then take a 20-minute bus or taxi ride to Cashel.

VISITOR INFORMATION

CONTACTS Cashel Tourist Office. *Cashel Heritage Centre, Main St., Cashel 062/62511 cashel.ie.*

Sights

Cashel Heritage Centre
VISITOR CENTER | In the same building as the tourism office, the Cashel Heritage Centre explains the historic relationship between the town and the Rock and includes a scale model of Cashel as it looked during the 1600s. *City Hall, Main St., Cashel 062/62511 cashel.ie Free Closed weekends Nov.–Feb.*

★ The Rock of Cashel
HISTORIC SIGHT | Seat of the kings of Munster and the hallowed spot where St. Patrick first plucked a shamrock to explain the mystery of the Trinity, the Rock of Cashel is Ireland's greatest group of ecclesiastical ruins. Standing in the middle of a sloped, treeless valley, the Rock's titanic grandeur and majesty creates what one ancient scribe called "a fingerpost to Heaven." Today, the great limestone mass still rises 300 feet to command a panorama over all it surveys—fittingly, the name derives from the Irish *caiseal,* meaning "stone fort," and this gives a good idea of its strategic importance.

Continued on page 291

THE ROCK OF CASHEL

Haunt of St. Patrick, Ireland's "rock of ages" is a place where history, culture, and legend collide.

Seat of the Kings of Munster and the hallowed spot where St. Patrick first plucked a shamrock to explain the mystery of the Trinity, the Rock of Cashel is Ireland's greatest group of ecclesiastical ruins. Standing like an ominous beacon in the middle of a sloped, treeless valley, the Rock has a titanic grandeur and majesty that create what one ancient scribe called "a fingerpost to Heaven."

Historians theorize the stupendous mass was born during the Ice Age. This being Ireland, however, fulsome myths abound: There are those who believe it was created when the Devil himself took a huge bite of the Slieve Bloom Mountains only to spit it out right in the middle of the Golden Vale. Today, the great limestone mass still rises 300 feet to command a panorama over all it surveys—fittingly, the name derives from the Irish *caiseal*, meaning stone fort, and this gives a good idea of the strategic importance of Cashel in days of yore.

For centuries, Cashel was known as the "city of the kings"—from the 5th century, the lords of Munster ruled over much of southern Ireland from here. In 1101, however, they handed Cashel over to the Christian fathers, and the rock soon became the center of the reform movement that reshaped the Irish Church. Along the way, the church fathers embarked on a centuries-long building campaign that resulted in the magnificent group of chapels, round towers, and walls you see at Cashel today. View them from afar on the N8 highway and the complex looks so complete you're surprised upon arriving to discover guides in modern dress and not knights in medieval uniform.

TIP→ You have to stay at the Cashel Palace Hotel on Main St. to enjoy the best approach to the rock; along the Bishop's Walk, a 10-minute hike that begins outside the drawing room.

SOUTHEASTERN VIEW OF THE ROCK

❶ HALL OF THE VICAR'S CHORAL

Built in the 15th century—though topped with a modern reconstruction of a beautifully corbeled medieval ceiling—this was once the domain of the cathedral choristers.

The Museum Located in the hall's undercroft, this collection includes the original St. Patrick's Cross and fast-forwards you to the present thanks to a striking audiovisual display on the Rock entitled the "Stronghold of the Faith."

❷ CORMAC'S CHAPEL

The real showpiece of Cashel is this chapel, built in 1127 by Cormac McCarthy, King of Desmond and Bishop of Cashel. A rare jewel in gleaming red sandstone, it is the finest example of Hiberno-Romanesque architecture. The entry archway carries a tympanum featuring a centaur in a helmet with a bow and arrow aimed at a lion, perhaps a symbol of good over evil. Such work was rare in Irish architecture and points to possible European influence. Preserved within the chapel is a splendid but broken sarcophagus, once believed to be Cormac's final resting place. At the opposite end of the chapel is the nave, where you can look for wonderful medieval paintings now showing through old plasterwork.

North Transept

ST. PATRICK'S CATHEDRAL

With thick walls that attest to its origin as a fortress, this now-roofless cathedral is the largest building on the site. Built in 1169, it was dedicated on March 17th—St. Patrick's Day. On the theory that ancient churches were oriented to the sunrise on the feast day of their dedicated saint, the cathedral points east, a direction agreeing closely with March 17th. The original cathedral, constructed in a flamboyant variation on Irish Romanesque style, was destroyed by fire in 1495. In ❸ **The Choir,** look for the noted Tomb of Myler McGrath. Note the tombs in the ❹ **North Transept** whose carvings—of the apostles, other saints, and the Beasts of the Apocalypse—are remarkably detailed. The octagonal staircase turret that ascends the cathedral's central tower leads to a series of defensive passages built into the thick walls—from the top of the tower, you'll have wonderful views. At the center of the cathedral is the area known as ❺ **The Crossing,** a magnificently detailed arch where the four sections of the building come together.

COMING OF AGE

AD 450—St. Patrick comes to Cashel, bringing the advent of Christianity when King Aengus accepts baptism from Ireland's patron saint.

990—Cashel is fortified by King Brian Boru, the legendary figure who broke the stranglehold of the Danes at the Battle of Clontarf in 1014.

1101—King Murtagh O'Brien, grandson of Brian Boru, proclaims the royal fortress "for God, St. Patrick, and St. Ailbe," making Cashel center of the Irish Church.

1317—The arrival of the Scots: Edward Bruce, brother of Robert I, is inaugurated king of Ireland, and attends Mass on the Rock where he later holds a parliament.

1749—Protestant archbishop Price earns undying infamy by pulling down the roof of the cathedral to rebuild his own church.

Detail of wooden ceiling in the Vicar's Choral, Rock of Cashel

NORTHERN VIEW OF THE ROCK

6 THE ROUND TOWER

As the oldest building on the Rock, the Round Tower rises 92 feet to command a panoramic view of the entire Vale of Tipperary. Dating back to 1101, its construction followed the grim reality of the Viking invasions. A constant lookout was posted here to warn of any advancing armies, and food was always provisioned in the tower so as to outlast any prolonged siege. Note the door 10 feet from the ground, allowing ladders to be pulled up to thwart attackers, some of whom attempted to chip the rock at the base, to little effect.

7 ST. PATRICK'S CROSS

Directly beyond the Rock's main entrance is this 7-foot-tall High Cross carved from one large block and resting upon what is said to have been the original coronation stone of the Munster kings. The cross was erected in the saint's honor to commemorate his famous visit to Cashel in 450. Upon both sides carved in high relief are two figures—the face of Christ crucified and a robed St. Patrick with his feet resting upon an ox head. Unique among High Crosses, this one has vertical supports on either side, perhaps allusions to the crosses of the good and bad thieves. A sort of early Irish bible class, these large stone crosses (which were sculpted from the 9th to the 12th centuries) were perfect teaching tools for a population that was largely illiterate. This cross is a faithfully rendered replica—the original now rests in the site museum.

THE ST. PATRICK CONNECTION

While many legends surround Saint Patrick, he was an actual historical figure—his writings, a Latin text dating from the 5th century AD, yield the few undisputed facts about him. Born into a wealthy family in Roman-occupied Britain, he was kidnapped as a young man by Irish marauders and enslaved for six years as a sheepherder on the slopes of Slemish in County Antrim. He escaped, and returned to Britain, but a vision called him back to Ireland to convert the people to Christianity. Arriving in 433, he defied the pagan priests of Tara by kindling the Easter fire on Slane but went on in a peaceful conversion of Ireland to Christianity—not a drop of blood was shed—until his death in AD 460.

St. Patrick's conversion of Ireland was characterized by clever diplomacy: his missionaries were careful to combine elements of then-current druidic ritual with new Christian practice. For example, the Irish Christian church popularized the Feast of all Saints, and arranged for it to be celebrated on November 1, the same day as the great Celtic harvest festival, Samhain. Today's Halloween evolved from this linking of Celtic and Christian holidays.

Clearly a skilled negotiator as well as missionary, St. Patrick wisely preserved the social structure of Ireland, converting the people tribe by tribe. He first attempted to establish the Roman system of dioceses and bishops, but—since Ireland had never been conquered by the Romans—this arrangement did not suit a society without large cities. Instead, the Celts preferred a religious institution introduced by the desert fathers: the monastery, an idea of a "family" of monks being easy to grasp in a tribal society. Over 70 monasteries were founded in the 5th and 6th centuries, and by AD 700 abbots had replaced bishops as the leaders of the Catholic church.

In 457 St. Patrick retired to Saul, where he died. The only relic that can be tied to him is the famous 5th-century iron bell in Dublin's National Museum. Even if it was not, as is traditionally believed, used by the saint, he carried one very like it, and used it to announce his approach.

Above: Dublin, St. Patrick's Day parade

Dating to 1101, the Round Tower is the oldest building on the Rock, rising to 92 feet and providing a panoramic view of the entire Vale of Tipperary.

For centuries, Cashel was known as the "city of the kings"—from the 5th century, the lords of Munster ruled over much of southern Ireland from here. In 1101, however, they handed Cashel over to the Christian fathers, and the rock soon became the center of the reform movement that reshaped the Irish Church. Along the way, the church fathers embarked on a centuries-long building campaign that resulted in the magnificent group of chapels, Round Towers, and walls you see at Cashel today.

Built in the 15th century—though topped with a modern reconstruction of a beautifully corbelled medieval ceiling—the Hall of the Vicar's Choral was once the domain of the cathedral choristers. Located in the hall's undercroft, the museum includes the original St. Patrick's Cross.

The real showpiece of Cashel is Cormac's Chapel, completed in 1134 by Cormac McCarthy, King of Desmond and Bishop of Cashel. It is the finest example of Hiberno-Romanesque architecture. Preserved within the chapel is a splendid but broken sarcophagus, once believed to be Cormac's final resting place. At the opposite end of the chapel is the nave, where you can look for wonderful medieval paintings now showing through old plasterwork.

With thick walls that attest to its origin as a fortress, the now roofless St. Patrick's Cathedral is the largest building on the site. In the choir, look for the noted tomb of Myler McGrath. Note the tombs in the north transept, whose carvings—of the apostles, other saints, and the beasts of the Apocalypse—are remarkably detailed. The octagonal staircase turret that ascends the cathedral's central tower leads to a series of defensive passages built into the thick walls—from the top of the tower, you'll have wonderful views. At the center of the cathedral is the area known as The Crossing, a magnificently detailed arch where the four sections of the building come together.

Directly beyond the Rock's main entrance is the 7-foot-tall High Cross, carved from one large block and resting upon what is

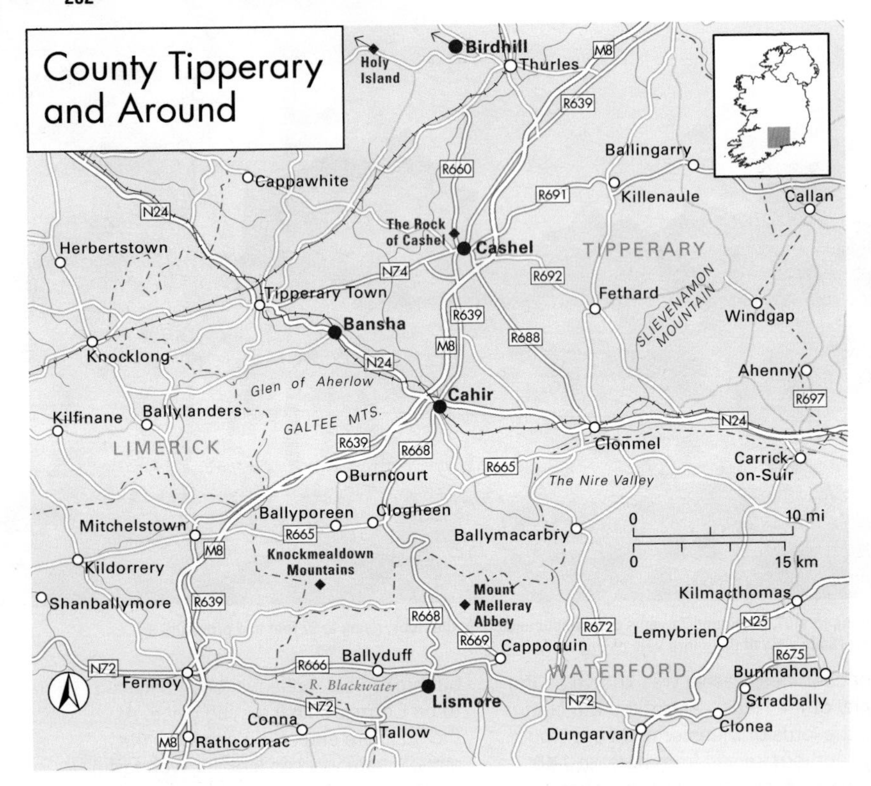

said to have been the original coronation stone of the Munster kings. The cross was erected in St. Patrick's honor to commemorate his famous visit to Cashel in AD 450. This cross is a faithfully rendered replica—the original now rests in the Rock's museum. As the oldest building on the Rock, the Round Tower rises 92 feet to command a panoramic view of the entire Vale of Tipperary. A constant lookout was posted here to warn of any advancing armies. ✉ *Rock of Cashel, Cashel* ☎ *062/61437* 🌐 *heritageireland.ie/places-to-visit/rock-of-cashel* 🎫 *€8.*

Restaurants

★ Chez Hans

$$$ | **FRENCH** | It's rather fitting that this restaurant is in a converted church, as it's become something of a shrine for foodies. Jason Matthia's cuisine is classic French with contemporary Irish twists. The seafood cassoulet—half a dozen varieties of fish and shellfish with a delicate chive velouté—is legendary. **Known for:** warm welcome; hearty menu; stunning dining room. $ *Average main: €31* ✉ *Moore La., Cashel* ☎ *062/61177* 🌐 *www.chezhans.net* 🕒 *Closed Mon.–Thurs. No lunch Fri. and Sat.*

Performing Arts

Brú Ború Cultural Centre

ARTS CENTERS | Enjoy folk singing, storytelling, trad music, and dancing at the Brú Ború Centre at the foot of the Rock of Cashel. The center also has the Sounds of History audiovisual exhibition open all day and regular arts and music events throughout the year. ✉ *Rocklane, Cashel* 🌐 *bruboru.ie.*

Bansha

16 km (10 miles) southwest of Cashel.

This prosperous little farming town at the foot of the Galtee Mountains is really of interest as a base for the beautiful Glen of Aherlow. The glen itself is a lush valley formed where the River Aherlow runs between the Galtees and the tree-covered ridge of Slievenamuck. Historically, it was a key passageway for the native Irish between Tipperary and Limerick.

GETTING HERE AND AROUND

From Dublin take the N7/M7 toward Cork. Exit onto the M8 and get off on the N24 to Bansha. From Cashel take the N74 west, then the N24 to Bansha. There are regular bus services from Dublin, Limerick, and Waterford.

Sights

The Glen of Aherlow is a hiking and horse-riding paradise, with a feast of national trails ranging from gentle loops to some serious climbs. The rewards for mountain walking are great, with Lough Curra and Lake Muskry, two stunning corrie lakes with views overlooking the whole of central and southern Ireland. The Glen hosts two walking festivals on the last weekend in January and the first weekend in June. For history buffs, the Tipperary Heritage Way (based on ancient pilgrim walks) from Cashel to Ardmore also passes through here. The walks will take you past a number of ancient sites, from St. Pecaun's Holy Well at the eastern end of the Glen to the fascinating and overlooked Darby's Bed passage tomb on the west side of Slievenamuck hill near the village of Galbally. This is also prime horse country, and the same trails can often be taken on a locally hired mount with an experienced guide to help along the way. For details of walks, activities, and events in the Glen, check *aherlow.com*.

Restaurants

★ Dooks Fine Foods

$ | **SANDWICHES** | Located about 20 minutes from Bansha in the unassuming market town of Fethard, this new deli restaurant has caused a stir with food lovers all over Ireland. Chef Richard Gleeson trained at Ballymaloe and with the revered Ottolenghi in London, and brings his precision and training to play at this bright and warm spot, with polished concrete floors, an open kitchen, and wood tables and chairs. **Known for:** quality affordable eats; rustic warmth and atmosphere; takeaway treats. *Average main: €14* *Kerry St., Fethard, Bansha* *dooksfinefoods.ie* *Closed Sun. and Mon. No dinner.*

Hotels

Foxford Farmhouse B&B

$ | **B&B/INN** | **FAMILY** | Honora and Philip Russel clearly love having visitors to their modern, simple house—a classic Irish B&B—on their family farm at the entrance to the hiker's paradise that is the Glen of Aherlow. **Pros:** family-run; great value; perfect hiking base. **Cons:** only three rooms; remote location; limited amenities. *Rooms from: €100* *Foxford, Bansha* *062/54552* *foxfordfarmhouse.net* *3 rooms* *Free Breakfast.*

Birdhill

62 km (38 miles) north of Bansha, 24 km (15 miles) northeast of Limerick City.

It's no coincidence that this picturesque little village in undiscovered north Tipperary always does well in the national "Tidy Towns" competition, a village beauty contest that the Irish take very seriously. But the real charm of this cute hamlet is its proximity to the majestic Lough Derg with the mysterious Holy Island at its center.

GETTING HERE AND AROUND

From Bansha take the N24 north to the R455. From Dublin take the N7/M7 south and exit at junction 21 to the R445.

VISITOR INFORMATION

CONTACTS Tipperary Tourist Information. ✉ *Cashel* ☎ *0818/065–000* 🌐 *tipperary.com.*

Sights

Lough Derg is the third-largest lake in Ireland and actually borders three counties: Clare, Tipperary, and Galway. The lake area near Birdhill is some of its least explored territory. It's a haven for anglers and water-sports enthusiasts, including windsurfers, sailors, and relaxed cruisers. The Lough Derg Drive is another undiscovered treasure of the area. It meanders around the lake, through gorgeous little villages in all three counties. You can pull over at numerous lookout points to appreciate the unique setting of the monastic settlement at the center of the lake. The Lough Derg section has a list of the best providers for waterskiing, wakeboarding, sailing, and other activities. The Watermark Ski Club (based in Terryglass) is one of the best places on the lake to get started and meet fellow water-sports enthusiasts.

Holy Island

HISTORIC SIGHT | The 6th-century monastic settlement of Holy Island (*Inis Cealtra* in Irish) sits in the middle of Lough Derg, slightly closer to the western shore. Around the year AD 520, St. Columba, seeking the type of solitude only an island can offer, founded his small monastery here. It was later expanded into a serious seat of Christian learning. The Vikings arrived in 836 and killed many of the monks before making off with most of their treasures, but the monastery survived in different forms until the Reformation. The ruins on the island include a Round Tower, St. Caimin's Romanesque church, and the Saints' Graveyard, which includes 11th-century grave markers in Irish, and one headstone for Cosrach, "the miserable one," who died in 898. Access to the island is via boats that leave from Mountshannon, on the western side of the lake. ✉ *Holy Island, Lough Derg.*

Hotels

Coolbawn Quay

$$$ | HOTEL | The main appeal of this collection of cottages built in the style of a 19th-century Irish village is the magical setting between Lough Derg and the surrounding rolling hills and forests. **Pros:** incredible natural setting; great choice of accommodation types; high-quality spa. **Cons:** can book up on weekends; remote location; popular with weddings. $ *Rooms from: €220* ✉ *Coolbawn Quay, Coolbawn, Lough Derg* ☎ *067/28158* 🌐 *coolbawnquay.com* *17 cottages* *Free Breakfast.*

Activities

BOATING

Killaloe River Cruises

BOATING | A cute, 12-seater passenger boat takes you on a serene, one-hour cruise of Lough Derg and into the River Shannon. It's a great chance to take in the unique wildlife and natural beauty of the region. Boats leave from the lakeshore at Killaloe, on the Clare bank of the lake. ✉ *Lakeside Dr., Killaloe* ☎ *086/814–0559* 🌐 *killaloerivercruises.com* *From €16.*

Chapter 7

COUNTY CORK

Updated by
Alexandra Pereira

WELCOME TO COUNTY CORK

TOP REASONS TO GO

★ **Cork City:** Ireland's second city is confident, cool, uncompromisingly Irish, and a must-go. At the edge of its hilly perimeter is Blarney Castle where visitors line up to kiss the Blarney Stone.

★ **Gougane Barra:** Tiny St. Finbarr's Church is perched on the edge of a promontory, so it almost appears to float over its reflection in the placid waters of the lake below.

★ **County Cork's Food Scene:** With Ireland's best pastures, heaving trawlers with fresh catch, happening craft beer scene, and creative chefs, Cork is enticing visitors to its busy eateries.

★ **The Launch Pad of the Wild Atlantic Way:** County Cork's shoreline is stuffed with secret coves and ridiculously pretty villages, along with the world's second-largest natural harbor at Cobh.

★ **The Beara Peninsula:** Rugged coastline, ancient stone circles, rich history, timeless pubs, and the home of Ireland's only over-water cable car make this one of Ireland's most rewarding destinations.

1 Cork City. Cork City is Ireland's second-largest city and, despite being significantly less populated than the capital, the city's frequent festivals and vibrant social scene bring an unquenchable energy throughout its grand Georgian parades and narrow medieval lanes at any time of year. The collection of pubs, restaurants, museums, and galleries reflect Cork's cultural revival, while Blarney Castle and its famous kissing stone on the northern rim of the city draw the crowds.

2 Cobh. This wide expanse of sea is bordered by the botanical gardens and parkland of Fota Island and the historic transatlantic port of Cobh where the RMS *Titanic* made its final, tragic departure.

3 Midleton. A lively market town dominated by its distillery.

4 Ballycotton. A gentle coastal haven with a fascinating maritime history and easy access to East Cork's best beaches and innumerable attractions.

5 Shanagarry. A small village famous for Ballmaloe Cookery School and Shanagarry Potters.

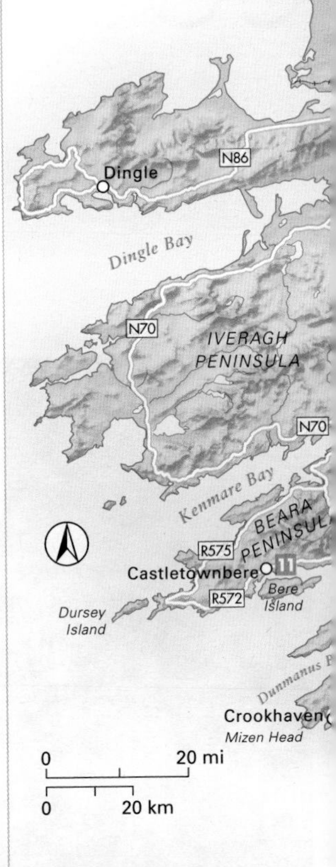

6 Kinsale. This historic small town on a picturesque harbor has a reputation for fine dining and attracts visitors year-round.

7 Clonakility and Nearby. Hometown of statesman Michael Collins and the gateway to West Cork, this picture-book-pretty market town has

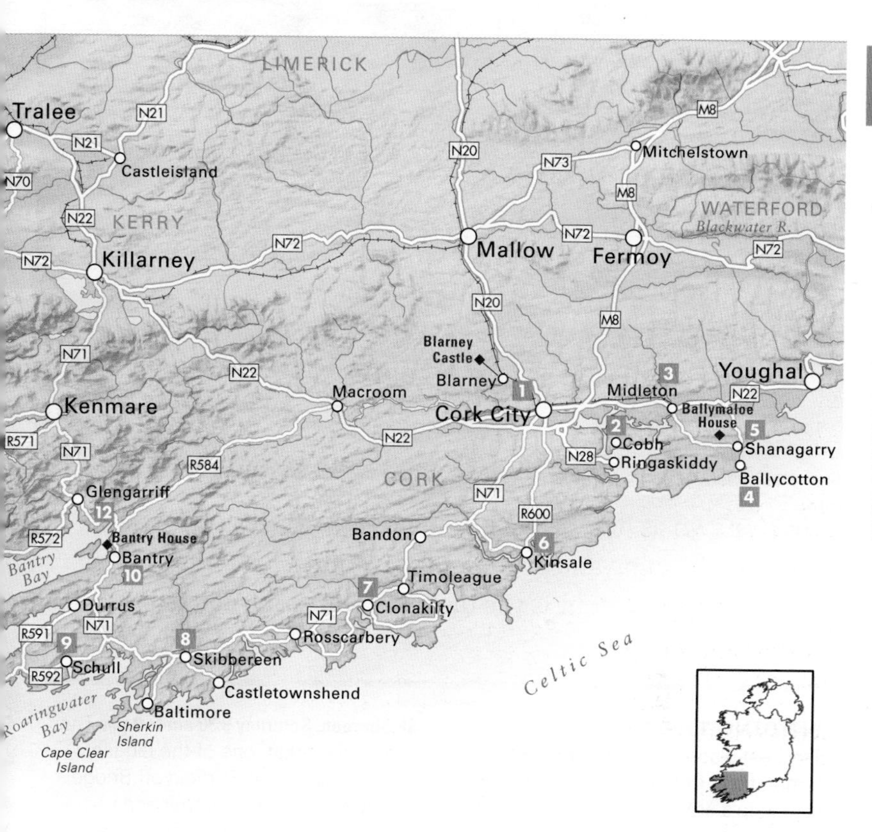

charming hand-painted shop fronts and a growing reputation for crafts and artisanal food.

8 Skibbereen. A practical hub for West Cork's scenic coast, Skib's Saturday market is a must in summer, while its Heritage Centre will put Ireland's Great Famine of the mid-19th century in perspective.

9 Schull. This small fishing village gives the essence of West Cork flavor, with the stunning Mizen Head Peninsula as a playground.

10 Bantry. This pretty market town that lies in the shadows of the Caha Mountains at the head of Bantry Bay is close to the hauntingly beautiful Gougane Barra.

11 Castletownbere. Home of famous McCarthy's Bar and an ideal place to explore the delights of the stunning Beara Peninsula.

12 Glengarriff. A small village with an island-studded harbor, its subtropical climate and sheltered location give rise to lush vegetation.

CORK'S FOOD MARKETS

Long known as "the belly of Ireland," West Cork is celebrated for its rich fishing and even richer farming. Like a world-class picnic, this cook's tour is the tastiest recipe for a day trip through the region.

FINDING THE FEAST

The best places to track down top temptations from Cork's gastronomic cornucopia are the area's food markets, often set in small villages and averaging only about a dozen stalls, and held one morning a week. Low overhead means bargains for the buyers, who enjoy an amazing array of artisanal foodstuffs. And the markets' festive atmosphere is complemented by the camaraderie of the stall holders—this is often their main contact with the buying public.

MARKETS

Bantry, Main Square, Friday 9:30 am to 1 pm. This traditional street market has a strong presence of growers of organic plants and vegetables.

Skibbereen, Saturday 9:30 am to 2 pm. The Saturday market, one of the biggest around, takes over Fairfield off Bridge Street, offering organic fruit and vegetables, excellent coffee, cut flowers, and crafts. It's also a great place to people-watch.

Kinsale, Market Square, Wednesday 9:30 am to 2:30 pm. Snack on a Breton crepe while stocking up on chutneys, smoked salmon, farmhouse cheeses, fresh fish, and organic fruit and vegetables at this cute piazza market.

Midleton, Saturday 9 am to 1 pm. One of the liveliest farmers' markets, it's held in a small parking lot, with buskers creating a festive vibe.

Schull, Sunday 10 am to 2 pm, Easter to December. At its best in summer and at Christmas, this foodie's market showcases superb products from local bakers, fish smokers, and cheese makers, and Gubbeen smoked pork products.

Cork City, The English Market, Monday to Saturday 8 am to 6 pm. Today this famous city-center covered market is a thriving hub of artisanal bakers, butchers, fishmongers, and greengrocers selling organic fruit and vegetables, top-quality meat and fresh fish, imported coffees and teas, locally made charcuterie, farmhouse cheeses—and even a champagne from the local wine merchant, Bubble Brothers.

OTHER FOODIE FAVES

The Irish deli is unlike any other, perhaps because there is no indigenous tradition of specialty-food shops, so those that do exist tend to be one-off expressions of their owners' personalities.

In Clonakilty head for **The Lettercollum Kitchen Project.** Both talented chefs and dedicated vegetable gardeners, Con McLaughlin and Karen Austin are masters of the vegetarian and ethnic repertory (and also offer cooking classes). Their bakery sells specialty breads, cooks' ingredients, sandwiches, and savory tarts.

Mannings' Emporium, with its open-air display of vegetables and outdoor picnic tables, looks as if it belongs on a Southern Italian roadside, rather than at Ballylickey, on the road between Bantry and Glengarriff. Val Manning has long championed West Cork's artisanal food producers, home bakers, and confectioners, and what was once a corner store selling milk and bread is now a renowned gastronomic outpost. Try the house-made charcuterie or cheese platters to get acquainted with local fare, including pungent Mileens, Ardsallagh goat's cheese, Knockalara sheep's milk cheese, and two local hard cheeses, Gabriel and Desmond.

SUPERMARKETS

In West Cork, local supermarkets make a point of supporting small, local food producers, and local people enjoy the chance to support their friends and neighbors by buying their produce. **Scally's** of Clonakilty and **Field's** of Skibbereen, both trading under the **SuperValu** logo, are prime examples of this trend.

With its deep-rooted history, more than a thousand kilometers of pristine coastline dotted with pretty harbor villages, and a gently lilting up-and-down accent that flows like the green hills that tumble to the ocean, the county of Cork and its abundance of character—and characters—is the essence of what makes Ireland special. Known locally as The People's Republic of Cork, Ireland's largest county is also home to the country's second-biggest city, and while you'll find huge festivals, a vibrant culinary scene, and big, breathtaking scenery, it feels small and friendly. The city is pleasantly compact and walkable, while the outlying towns are tiny and within easy reach along narrow, winding roads.

But as you look over the fuchsia-laden hedges that ring thriving dairy farms or stop at a wayside restaurant to sample locally sourced beef, it's difficult to imagine that a century and a half ago this area was decimated by famine. Thousands perished in fields and workhouses, and thousands more took "coffin ships" from Cobh in Cork Harbour to the New World. The region was battered again during both the War for Independence and the civil war that were fought with intensity in and around "Rebel Cork" between 1919 and 1921. Most Cork families have relatives who left for the USA on an emigrant liner back in the 1950s and '60s, and memories of the civil war years are kept alive, fueled by memorial events.

Cork City's locals will immediately charm you, as will the festive air that prevails in its streets, where many visitors assume that some kind of festival is going on, even on those rare occasions when it is not.

MAJOR REGIONS

The major metropolis of the South, **Cork City and its Environs** makes a great base from which to explore the whole southern region. Though it's Ireland's second-largest city, it runs a distant second, with a population of and a compact, walkable center. In the last decade, with high prices and overcrowding in Dublin, Cork became the new hot spot for short city breaks. Groups of Europeans frequently pop over for a weekend of partying, as the city is a spirited place with a formidable pub culture, a lively traditional-music scene, a respected and progressive university, attractive art galleries, and offbeat cafés. With the 2019 extension of the city boundary, Blarney Castle and Gardens now falls within the city's perimeter and makes for a rewarding afternoon excursion from midtown.

East Cork. The county's eastern portions—Cobh, Midleton, and Shanagarry—are less frequented by visitors to Cork but are worth exploring. Products of the rich farming land east of Cork City used to include whiskey: see how it was made at the Jameson Experience in Midleton, just a short drive from Ballymaloe House, pioneer of the New Irish cuisine. The long, flat, sandy beaches here—a summertime favorite with Irish holidaymakers—are great for windswept walks year-round.

West Cork. With a vast coast that harbors quiet villages and secret coves, this is arguably the prettiest corner of Ireland and the place where many Dubliners seek refuge from the capital. Start in the historic old port of Kinsale and navigate the West Cork shoreline with place-names that roll off the tongue, like Roscarbery or Clonakilty, while following the jagged contours of the county's three sister peninsulas that jut out into the ocean, where every twist in the road reveals something more spectacular than the last view. Bantry Bay, further to the west, is an oasis of subtropical growth due to its large natural harbor, and the place where 14,000 members of the French military attempted to land to help the Irish in their quest for freedom back in 1796, during the Napoleonic Wars. From whale-watching to fine dining, Cork's coast is brimful of delights, but dare to head inland to the quiet lanes that weave through the lush, hilly terrain where you might catch a leisurely game of bowls on the roadside, or Béal na mBláth, the place where Irish revolutionary and politician Michael Collins met his fate during an ambush on a summer's day in 1922. Gougane Barra, a lakeside monastic sanctuary in the heart of West Cork, is the place to recharge your soul in quiet wooded solitude, with little but the sound of lapping water and the whispers of ancient spirits to keep you company.

Planning

Getting Here and Around

AIR

Cork Airport, 5 km (3 miles) south of Cork City on the Kinsale road, has direct flights daily to London (Heathrow, Gatwick, and Stansted), Manchester, East Midlands, Paris, and Malaga, and direct flights to many other European cities. There are transatlantic flights once a week from Providence/Boston–T.F. Green. Shannon Airport, 124 km (76 miles) north of Cork City, is the point of arrival for a limited amount of seasonal transatlantic flights, including direct flights from Philadelphia, Toronto (summer only), and New York City (from both JFK and Newark), while Dublin Airport, which is 264 km (165 miles) northeast of Cork on a motorway, has frequent daily services from many North American hubs.

AIRPORTS Cork Airport. ☎ *021/431–3131* 🌐 *www.corkairport.com.* **Dublin Airport.** ✉ *Dublin* ☎ *1/814–1111* 🌐 *www.dublinairport.com.* **Shannon Airport.** ☎ *061/712–000* 🌐 *www.shannonairport.ie.*

AIRPORT TRANSFERS

Bus Éireann has a bus link between Cork Airport and the Cork Parnell Place Bus Station about every 30 minutes, and a route between the airport and Kinsale roughly every hour. Tickets for both destinations can be bought on the bus.

SHUTTLES Bus Éireann. ☎ *021/836–6111* 🌐 *www.buseireann.ie.*

BUS

Bus Éireann and Aircoach operate express buses from Dublin, Dublin Airport, Galway, Shannon Airport, Limerick, Tralee, and Killarney to Cork City. Most operators offer Wi-Fi and toilet facilities. From Shannon Airport, it takes two hours and 30 minutes, while from Dublin it is three hours and 15 minutes. GoBus offers a nonstop service from Dublin Airport. Citylink buses serve many Irish cities, including Cork City; book online for the best prices. Local buses tend to stop running in the early evening, which rules out many day trips—unless you want to spend most of the day on the bus. As a general rule, the smaller and more remote the town, the less frequent its bus service. Consult with hotel concierges, tourist board staffers, or the bus lines' websites for schedules.

CONTACTS Aircoach. ☎ *01/844–7118* 🌐 *www.aircoach.ie.* **Bus Éireann.** ☎ *01/836–6111 in Dublin, 021/450–8188 in Cork* 🌐 *www.buseireann.ie.* **Citylink.** ☎ *091/564–164* 🌐 *www.citylink.ie.* **Cork Bus Station Parnell Place.** ✉ *Parnell Pl. and Merchant's Quay, City Center South* ☎ *021/450–8188.* **GoBus.** ✉ *Forster Ct., Unit 8, Galway City* ☎ *091/564–600* 🌐 *www.gobus.ie.*

CAR

Scenery is the main attraction in County Cork, and unless you're a biker or hiker, the best option to explore the region's peninsulas, gorgeous towns, and major attractions is to rent a car, although regional buses do run on main roads. Once behind the wheel, plan to adopt the local pace: slow. Covering about 100 km (60 miles) a day is ideal, with many stops along the way. Speed is dictated to some degree by the roads—most are small, with one lane in each direction and plenty of bends and hills.

The main driving route from Dublin is the M7 motorway, connecting with the M8 in Portlaoise to continue 257 km (160 miles) on to Cork City. The journey from Dublin to Cork takes less than three hours. Except for Cork City, where you're best off using a garage, parking is relatively easy to figure out throughout County Cork.

ROAD CONDITIONS

County Cork has good, wide main roads (National Primary Routes) and better-than-average local roads (National Secondary Routes), both known as "N" routes. Regional ("R") routes can be narrow. They're also used by hikers and cyclists from Easter to October, as well as local traffic, which can include school buses and huge trucks serving the local agricultural co-ops. The speed limit on these regional routes is 80 kph (50 mph), but use your common sense and adjust your speed accordingly. If traffic builds up behind you, it is customary to signal to the left, and slow down (or pull off the road if there is space) to let the locals whizz past.

CONTACTS Europcar. ✉ *Cork Airport, Kinsale Rd., Arrivals Hall, Cork City* ☎ *21/240–0100* 🌐 *europcar.ie.* **GoCar.** ☎ *1/844–1969* 🌐 *welcome.gocar.ie.*

Car rental in County Cork, as all over Ireland, can get pricey depending on what vehicle you go for and for how long. Do you want a nippy little Ford, a prestige Volvo, or a minivan to haul your dear brood around, sheltered from those Irish winds and rains? The bright and clear website makes booking simple, and totally free of sneaky add-ons at the end of your booking when making payment.

Europcar seem to offer the best rates and deals for a shorter or longer break in Ireland, with airports generally being the best place to pick up your ride. Ease of collection of a huge array of vehicle options is made all the more smoother with Europcar usually having their offices and parking lots closest to the terminal, and the additional new service of "direct to car," where you can cut out the middle man and any pesky queues by unlocking your car directly and setting off on your journey.

They also operate an increasingly popular car sharing service in Ireland called GoCar that resembles other services worldwide: convenient and affordable rentals by the hour. Be sure to register and have your license validated in advance, as well as checking your insurance premiums and carrying both parts of your license as you would in the rest of Europe. You can swiftly book and access vehicles from simple economy hatchbacks to larger, more comfortable family cars and people carriers, all using a smartphone app.

You can get something like a Polo, Aygo, or Fiesta for as little as €30 a day, with a more luxe car like a BMW 3 Series for €77. Take care to book well ahead of time, especially in high season when everyone is driving from town to town taking in Cork's splendor.

TAXI

Taxis at Cork, Dublin, and Shannon airports are listed on the relevant sites, but expect to pay €17 from Cork Airport (ORK), €200 from Shannon Airport (SNN), and a whopping €350 from Dublin Airport (DUB). The National Transport Authority website has a fare estimator tool.

CONTACTS Cork Taxi Co-op. ☎ *021/427–2222* 🌐 *www.corktaxi.ie.*

TRAIN

Irish Rail–Iarnród Éireann runs direct hourly trains from Dublin Heuston Station to Cork's Kent Station; the trip takes just under three hours. Galway and Limerick City (a short bus ride to Shannon Airport) are connected to Cork via Limerick Junction. Suburban trains serve Fota Island, Midleton, and Cobh. The journey time to Midleton or Cobh is about 25 minutes.

CONTACTS Irish Rail–Iarnód Éireann. ☎ *01/836–6222 for inquiries and booking, 01/836–6222 in Ireland, 021/450–4777 in Cork* 🌐 *www.irishrail.ie.*

Hotels

County Cork's great country-house accommodations include Ballymaloe House in East Cork, along with the guest wing at magnificent Bantry House. There are many excellent family-owned and-run traditional hotels, such as the Blarney Castle Hotel on Blarney's village green and the Seaview in Ballylickey on Bantry Bay.

Restaurants

County Cork, home of the famous Slow Food Ireland movement, has become one of Ireland's top foodie destinations. Using the ample supply of national resources from sea and land, Cork's culinary landscape infuses those ingredients with traditional and happening techniques which is attracting an international fan base. Adventurous, well-traveled chefs throughout County Cork make the most of the first-rate local specialties: succulent beef and lamb, game in the winter, fresh seafood, and farmhouse cheeses. The best restaurants are not all in the larger towns: some of the county's best and most innovative restaurants and gastropubs are located in smaller villages along the coast.

RESTAURANT AND HOTEL PRICES

⇨ *Restaurant prices are the average cost of a main course at dinner or, if dinner is not served, at lunch. Hotel prices are the lowest cost of a standard double room in high season. Restaurant and hotel reviews have been shortened. For full information, visit Fodors.com.*

What It Costs in Euros

$	$$	$$$	$$$$
RESTAURANTS			
under €20	€20–€25	€26–€30	over €30
HOTELS			
under €120	€120–€170	€171–€200	over €200

Tours

With several good independent walking trails available to download, even a first-time visitor to the Rebel City will be able to get to grips with the city's layout and best walking or cycling routes without hiring a guide. Similarly, from the epic Wild Atlantic Way to the more manageable Sheep's Head Way, walkers, drivers, and hikers can follow signposted routes to embrace the incredible scenery this part of Ireland has on offer.

Cork City Tours

BUS TOURS | Cork City Tours is a convenient way to navigate the city, with a hop-on, hop-off service that stops at Cork City's major points of interest every 90 minutes from 9:30 am until 3:30 pm, with additional services on busy days. Stops include Cork City Goal and the English Market. The trailhead is at Grand Parade, but visitors can join the tour at any point. You can pay with cash on the bus, or with credit card in advance online. The same outfit offers tours of the Mizen Head Peninsula or an "Instagram Highlight" tour, which includes Gougane Barra, for €35. ✉ *Shannon Bldgs., Mallow Rd., Cork City* ✣ *Starts at Grand Parade* ☎ *21/430–9090* 🌐 *www.corkcitytours.com* 🎫 *€15* ☞ *Hop-on, hop-off tours operate Mar.–Nov. No service on some holidays.*

Cork City Walks

WALKING TOURS | Run by a troupe of mature Corkonians with years of experience in the field, these tour guides are as much storytellers as guides. The walking tour covers the city's key points of interest and how each one became a milestone in Cork's ancient history. Tours last two hours, and there are private tours available on request. ✉ *Tourist Information Centre, 125 St. Patricks St., Cork City* ☎ *877/223–9486* 🌐 *corkcitywalks.eu* 🎫 *€12.*

Ireland Walk Hike Bike

SPECIAL-INTEREST TOURS | Theme walks and bike routes take you along the coast of West Cork, around the Sheep's Head and Beara peninsulas in Bantry Bay. Self-guided hikes include accommodations, breakfasts, luggage-moving service, maps, tips, and other assistance. ✉ *Collis Sandes House, Tralee* ☎ *066/718–6181* 🌐 *www.irelandwalkhikebike.com* 🎫 *Self-guided hikes from €445.*

West Cork Walks

WALKING TOURS | West Cork Walks provide self-guided walking tours tailored to the individual hiker that take in a broad sweep of the stunning Beara Peninsula from the home base in the small, busy port of Castletownbere. The routes vary from 5 km (3 miles) to 25 km (15½ miles), and a shuttle is on hand to drop and collect guests at the trailhead and finishing point. ✉ *Beara Peninsula, Castletownbere* ☎ *27/70415* 🌐 *westcorkwalks.com.*

When to Go

The best times to visit County Cork are from mid-March to June and in September and October, when the Cork Jazz Festival is in full swing at the end of the month. July and August are the peak holiday periods. Roads are more crowded, prices are higher, and the best places are booked in advance. March can be chilly, with daily temperatures in the

40s and 50s. The average high in June is 65°F (18°C). May and June are the sunniest months, while May and September are the driest ones. From November to March, daylight hours are short, the weather is damp, and many places close.

Festivals and Events

Cork is known as Ireland's festival city, with a busy calendar of events, including a number of high-profile festivals. Elsewhere in the county there are annual festivals that are well worth planning your trip around, along with small community events that portray local heritage, local passions, and the character of the local people. These are just a selection.

JUNE AND JULY

Cork Harbour Festival

FESTIVALS | Celebrating Ireland's often turbulent maritime past in the world's second-largest natural harbor, this weeklong festival offers a range of activities that includes seaweed foraging and urban kayaking. It starts mid-May. ✉ *Cobh* ☎ *21/484–7673* 🌐 *corkharbourfestival.com.*

West Cork Chamber Music Festival

MUSIC FESTIVALS | Internationally renowned musicians perform in the library of Bantry House for nine days in late June–early July. ✉ *Bantry* ☎ *027/52788* 🌐 *www.westcorkmusic.ie.*

AUGUST

Masters of Tradition

MUSIC FESTIVALS | One very good reason to visit County Cork at any time is to hear authentic traditional music, but time your trip to coincide with this mid-August five-day festival in Bantry and you'll hear some of the finest. ✉ *Bantry* ☎ *027/52788* 🌐 *www.westcorkmusic.ie.*

OCTOBER

Cork International Short Story Festival

READINGS/LECTURES | Readings, author interviews, workshops, and award presentations are highlights of this four-day literary event in September. ✉ *Cork City* ☎ *021/431–2955* 🌐 *corkshortstory.net.*

A Taste of West Cork

FESTIVALS | **FAMILY** | A 10-day food festival in a region famed for its artisanal foods and top-class organic meat and seafood, it programs more than 230 events in 36 towns and on eight islands. These range from lectures and symposia by local foodies like Darina Allen of Ballymaloe, to cheese-making workshops, farm tours, and guest chefs cooking up a feast in local restaurants. ✉ *Skibbereen* ☎ *087/665–5567* 🌐 *www.atasteofwestcork.com.*

Guinness Cork Jazz Festival

MUSIC FESTIVALS | The highlight of Cork's festival calendar arrives in late October, which brings an international lineup of jazz and soul musicians to the city for four days of concerts in the big venues—Opera House, Everyman, Triskel Auditorium, and Triskel Christchurch. You can also hear music in pubs and hotels, on the street, and at various fringe events. ✉ *Cork City* 🌐 *www.guinnessjazzfestival.com.*

NOVEMBER

★ **Cork Film Festival**

FILM FESTIVALS | In the second week of November, this nine-day festival, established in 1956, puts on a lively program of world cinema at several city venues and includes feature films, documentaries, shorts, and other events. Expect some great characters, stories, and memories to unfold as filmmakers and cinephiles unite all over the city for the eclectic program and its after-parties. ✉ *Cork City* ☎ *021/427–1711* 🌐 *www.corkfilmfest.org.*

Planning Your Time

When you plan a trip to County Cork, you'll need to make a pick of the ports. The biggest one, Cobh, to the east of the Cork City, was the point of embarkation for most 19th-century Irish transatlantic passengers. Dominated by its tall-spired cathedral, the town, filled with 19th-century buildings, climbs vertiginously up- and downhill and faces southward out to sea. Ballycotton, farther to the east, is one of those soft, nostalgic towns set in the peaceful shoreline and still connected to its maritime past. Kinsale is more of a village than a town, built beside a hill at one end of an unspoiled fjord-like harbor. With its yacht marinas and tempting restaurants, Kinsale has a cosmopolitan air, but it also offers serious history at Charles Fort. Clonakilty, Schull, and Castletownbere are small and perfectly formed, while Bantry and Skibereen are larger market towns where the ghosts of the past still haunt the streetscape. Many visitors like to find a base in any of Cork's rugged three peninsulas, while others prefer the sheltered waters of subtropical Glengarriff.

IF YOU HAVE THREE DAYS

If you're here for a short stay—three days or fewer—you'd do well to base yourself in Cork City, which is easy to explore on foot. Allow a morning to take in the sights of the city center, including the Crawford Art Gallery and the indoor English Market. Take an afternoon amble from the city center to visit Blarney Castle and gardens, before settling into one of Cork's great pubs to sample the city's very own Murphy's Stout. In the morning head west to visit any of the county's stunning peninsulas, Mizen, Beara, or Sheep's Head, with their pretty villages, alluring coastlines, wide-open coves, and hidden pubs. On your last day, ramble close to home by visiting Cork's maritime past in both Kinsale and Cobh, where the *Titanic* and many emigrants caught the last glimpse of the magical Irish coastline. Return on your final night to Kinsale or Cork, both handy for the airport.

Visitor Information

Fáilte Ireland tourist information offices are open year-round in Bantry, Clonakilty, Cobh (Cork Harbour), Cork Airport (arrivals), Cork City, and Skibbereen. Those in Blarney, Glengarriff, Kinsale, and Midleton are open from mid-March to mid-September or the end of October. Fáilte Ireland's Discover Cork website page has details about locations and hours. Discovering Cork is another robust place to find help.

CONTACTS Cork Tourist Office. ✉ *125 Patrick St., City Center South* ☏ *021/425–5100* 🌐 *www.discoverireland.ie/places-to-go/cork*.

Cork City

253 km (157 miles) southwest of Dublin.

Cork's city center is in a valley that's spread over 13 islands where the River Lee splinters and meets again, while its suburbs are located in the surrounding hills like the seating of a giant amphitheater. With humble 6th-century origins as a monastic settlement, the major development occurred during the 17th and 18th centuries with the expansion of the butter trade, and many attractive Georgian-design buildings with wide bowfront windows were constructed during this time. As late as 1770, Cork's present-day main streets—Grand Parade, St. Patrick's Street, and the South Mall—were submerged under the Lee. Around 1800, when the Lee was partially dammed, the river divided into two streams that now flow through the city, leaving the main business and commercial center on an island, not unlike Paris's Île de la Cité. As a result, the city has a number of bridges and quays, which, although initially confusing, add greatly to the port's unique character.

Corkonians—as Cork City people are known—are famed for loyalty to their city, which has its own national newspaper, The *Irish Examiner;* its own stout, Murphy's; a lively artistic and literary community; and famous offspring, from the labor organizer Mother Jones (1837–1930) to rock guitarist Rory Gallagher (1948–95), actor Cillian Murphy, and soccer manager Roy Keane. But depending on what part of town you're in, Cork can also be distinctly itself—the sort of place where hipsters, accountants, and farmers drink at the same pub.

PLANNING YOUR TIME

You can tour the city's center in a morning or an afternoon, depending on how much you plan to shop along the way. To really see everything, however, allow a full day, with a break for lunch at the Farmgate Café in the English Market. Note that the English Market is closed on Sunday.

GETTING HERE AND AROUND

The drive from Dublin to Cork City on the M7/M8 motorway takes two and a half hours and about a 1½-hour drive from Killarney. The drive from Shannon Airport to Cork takes less than two hours, with motorway for some stretches. Use the tunnel (toll €2) to avoid traveling through the center of Limerick. Cork is well served by express buses. Irish Rail–Iarnród Éireann direct trains from Dublin Heuston Station to Cork's Kent Station run hourly. The trip takes just less than three hours.

If you're driving within Cork City, it's advisable to use a multistory parking garage, as on-street parking can be hard to find and the process of paying for it can be difficult to master. Cork's city center is compact and walkable, but if you want to bus the mile to the university campus, pick up a No. 8 on St. Patrick's Street. A great introductory tour is the hop-on, hop-off Cork City Tour, a double-decker bus that departs (March–October, €18) from the tourist information office on St. Patrick's Street between 9:30 am and 5 pm.

CONTACTS Cork Bus Station Parnell Place. ✉ *Parnell Pl. and Merchant's Quay, City Center South* ☎ *021/450–8188.* **Cork City Tour Bus.** ☎ *021/430–9090* 🌐 *www.corkcitytour.com.* **Kent Station.** ✉ *Lower Glanmire Rd., City Center North* ☎ *021/836–6222* 🌐 *www.irishrail.ie.*

Sights

Blackrock Castle and Observatory

CASTLE/PALACE | To the east of the city center, the past and present are fused together in this ornate riverfront castle that was constructed in 1829, when the original buildings were destroyed by a series of fires—the last happened when a boozy banquet hosted by the local council in 1827 got out of control. Today, the castle sits perched on a rock (hence its name), and visitors can explore its dungeons and murky past with smugglers and pirates—or take in one of the interplanetary shows hosted throughout the day. If all else fails, skip to the top of the tower and battlements for a rewarding view of the city. There is a café on-site. ✉ *Castle Rd., Blackrock, Cork City* ✣ *Catch the 202 bus from Parnell Pl.* ☎ *021/432–6120* 🌐 *bco.ie* 🎫 *Adults €7.*

★ Blarney Castle

CASTLE/PALACE | In the center of Blarney, the ruined central keep is all that's left of this mid-15th-century stronghold. The castle contains the famed Blarney Stone; kissing the stone, it's said, endows the kisser with the fabled "gift of the gab." It's 127 steep steps to the battlements. To kiss the stone, you must lie down on the battlements, hold on to a guardrail, and lean your head way back. It's good fun and not at all dangerous. Expect a line from mid-June to early September. You can take pleasant walks around the castle grounds. Rock Close contains oddly shaped limestone rocks landscaped in the 18th century and a grove of ancient

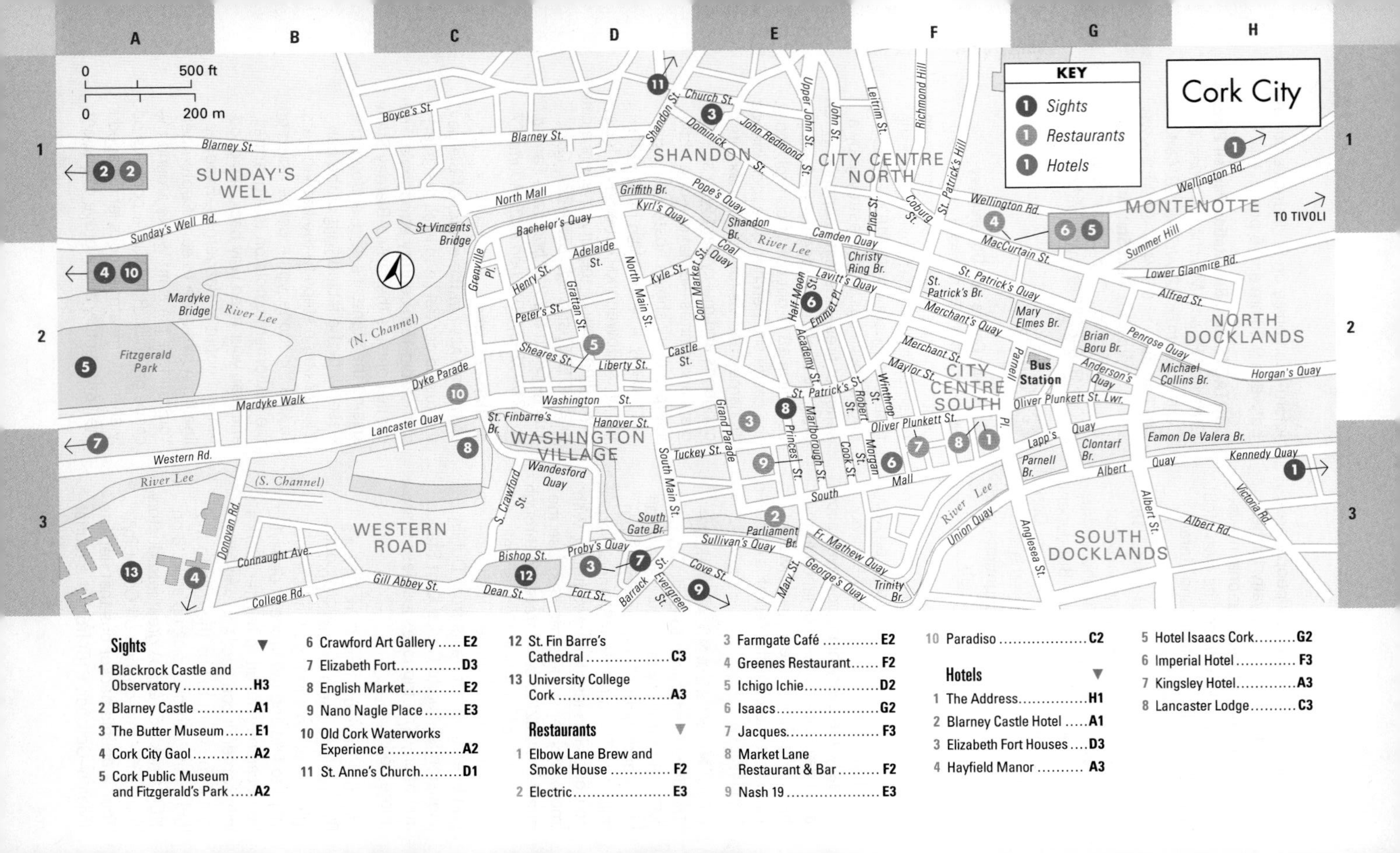

Sights

1 Blackrock Castle and Observatory H3
2 Blarney Castle A1
3 The Butter Museum E1
4 Cork City Gaol A2
5 Cork Public Museum and Fitzgerald's Park A2
6 Crawford Art Gallery E2
7 Elizabeth Fort D3
8 English Market E2
9 Nano Nagle Place E3
10 Old Cork Waterworks Experience A2
11 St. Anne's Church D1
12 St. Fin Barre's Cathedral C3
13 University College Cork A3

Restaurants

1 Elbow Lane Brew and Smoke House F2
2 Electric E3
3 Farmgate Café E2
4 Greenes Restaurant F2
5 Ichigo Ichie D2
6 Isaacs G2
7 Jacques F3
8 Market Lane Restaurant & Bar F2
9 Nash 19 .... E3
10 Paradiso C2

Hotels

1 The Address H1
2 Blarney Castle Hotel A1
3 Elizabeth Fort Houses D3
4 Hayfield Manor A3
5 Hotel Isaacs Cork G2
6 Imperial Hotel F3
7 Kingsley Hotel A3
8 Lancaster Lodge C3

yew trees that is said to have been a site of Druid worship. In early March, there's a wonderful display of daffodils. ✉ *Village Green, Blarney* ✥ *Blarney is about a 20-min drive west of Cork City Center, midway between the N22 Killarney road and the N20 to Limerick. Local buses that depart from Cork Bus Station Parnell Pl. drop you at the Blarney Green, adjacent to the castle and the crafts shops. There is a large parking lot (no fee). Taxis are available from Castle Cabs by phone reservation.* ☎ *021/438–5252* 🌐 *www.blarneycastle.ie* 🎟 *€18* ☞ *Discounted rates online.*

The Butter Museum

FACTORY | Once the bread and butter of Cork City's economy, the creamy product from the Rebel County's lush countryside and beyond—butter—dominated the world market with distribution in every corner of the former British Empire. Today, in a quirky Shandon neighborhood near St. Anne's Church on a square that once housed the Butter Market and follows the contours of the large circular Firkin Crane building (where casks were once weighed), visitors can trace that history and discover the merchant's artifacts and tools in this pint-sized museum. ✉ *O'Connell Sq., Shandon, City Center North* ☎ *021/430–0600* 🌐 *thebuttermuseum.com* 🎟 *€5* ⏲ *Closed Mon. and Tues.*

Cork City Gaol

JAIL/PRISON | **FAMILY** | The austere Georgian Gothic mansion in the center of the complex, with its castellated-style, three-story tower, was once the governor's residence. The two enormous gray wings that span symmetrically to the left and right detained prisoners for a century. Life-size wax figures occupy the cells, and they illustrate the wretched backstories of those incarcerated and those who held them captive, with suitably somber sound effects. Take note of the weighing chair near the governor's office—beneath its bright, timber surface lurks a dark secret—it was used to weigh prisoners before a suitable rope strength could be selected for their upcoming rendezvous with the gallows. Rebel leader Constance Markievicz and writer Frank O'Connor were former inmates. The Radio Museum Experience exhibits genuine artifacts from a 1923 radio station, 6CK, and tells the story of radio broadcasting in Cork. ✉ *Sunday's Well Rd., Sunday's Well* ☎ *021/430–5022* 🌐 *www.corkcitygaol.com* 🎟 *€10 (includes guidebook).*

Cork Public Museum and Fitzgerald's Park

CITY PARK | **FAMILY** | This picture-perfect riverside park a short walk west of the city center is accessed along the Mardyke, a tree-lined walkway overlooking a pitch where cricket is still played. Like the cricket pitch, the park is a remnant of Cork's Victorian past, and was the site of the 1902 Cork Exhibition. Its best-loved feature is the "Shakey Bridge," a famously unstable pedestrian suspension bridge linking the north and south banks of the Lee. The park is a popular venue for outdoor entertainment during the Midsummer Festival, and contains the **Cork Public Museum,** a Georgian mansion with displays of the city's history. ✉ *Western Rd., Western Road* ☎ *021/427–0679* 🌐 *www.corkcity.ie* 🎟 *Free* ⏲ *Museum closed Mon. and Sun. Oct.–Apr.*

★ **Crawford Art Gallery**

ART GALLERY | The large redbrick building was built in 1724 as the customs house and is now home to Ireland's leading provincial art gallery. An imaginative expansion has added gallery space for visiting exhibitions and adventurous shows of modern Irish artists. The permanent collection comprises more than 2,000 works and includes landscape paintings depicting Cork in the 18th and 19th centuries as well as contemporary video installations. Take special note of works by Irish painters William Leech (1881–1968), Daniel Maclise (1806–70), James Barry (1741–1806), and Nathaniel Grogan (1740–1807). The café is a good place for a light lunch or a house-made sweet. ✉ *Emmet Pl., City Center South* ☎ *021/480–5042* 🌐 *www.crawfordartgallery.ie* 🎫 *Free.*

★ Elizabeth Fort

MILITARY SIGHT | The tapestry of Cork's volatile past half millennium unfolds during a visit to this large star-shape fort, starting from the point when it was constructed as a stronghold after the Siege of Kinsale in 1601. It played a key role in history when it was fortified during Oliver Cromwell's invasion and later it was a prison depot for infamous Australia-bound convict ships. In the middle of the 19th century, it stored maize for the poor to buy and inflated prices before being shipped abroad as the great famine decimated the population. In the 20th century, it was occupied by British forces, and during World War II it was an air-raid shelter. It's worth a visit just to take in the commanding views over Cork City from its walls. ✉ *Elizabeth Fort, Barrack St., Cork City* ☎ *021/497–5947* 🌐 *www.elizabethfort.ie* 🎫 *Free; tour €3* ⏲ *Closed Oct.–Apr., Sun. morning* ☞ *Disability access is restricted.*

★ English Market

MARKET | Fetchingly housed in an elaborate, brick-and-cast-iron Victorian building with a decorative light-infused dome-shape ceiling, such is the fame of this foodie mecca that England's Queen Elizabeth II insisted on an impromptu walkabout here on her historic first visit to Ireland in 2011. Among the 140 stalls, keep an eye out for the Alternative Bread Company, which produces more than 40 varieties of handmade bread every day. Tom Durcan's Meats Limited sells vacuum-packed local specialties including spiced beef and dry-aged beef. The Olive Stall sells olive oil, olive-oil soap, and olives from Greece, Spain, France, and Italy. Kay O'Connell's Fish Stall, in the legendary fresh-fish alley, purveys local smoked salmon. O'Reilly's Tripe and Drisheen is the last existing retailer of tripe, a Cork specialty, and *drisheen* (blood sausage). Upstairs is the Farmgate, an excellent café. ✉ *Entrances on Grand Parade and Princes St., City Center South* ☎ *021/492–4182* 🌐 *corkcity.ie/en/english-market* ⏲ *Closed Sun.*

Nano Nagle Place

GARDEN | Nano Nagle (1718–84) founded the Presentation order of nuns, and was a pioneer in the education of the poor. The convent that was her Cork headquarters has been transformed into a delightful heritage center and provides a welcome oasis of calm in the city center. Visit her tomb, with its water fountain, graveyard, and garden before discovering the ornate Victorian Gothic Revival chapel ("The Goldie Chapel"), a popular new venue for readings and other events. The oldest buildings on-site, dating from the early 18th century, including Miss Nagle's parlor, can be visited only on guided tours, which depart daily at 11 am and 3 pm. ✉ *60–61 Douglas St., City Center South* ✥ *A short walk from Grand Parade or South Mall, across Nano Nagle Bridge and up Mary St.* ☎ *021/419–3580* 🌐 *www.nanonagleplace.ie* 🎫 *Garden and graveyard free, heritage center €8* ⏲ *Closed Mon.*

Old Cork Waterworks Experience

FACTORY | **FAMILY** | Set on the banks of the River Lee with a redbrick chimney that towers over the network of handsome sandstone Victorian buildings that house 100-year-old engine rooms, boilers, and steam centers, this fascinating experience takes you behind the mechanics that generated three centuries of local hydraulic innovation. With interactive exhibitions and informative tours, visitors explore Cork's industrial heritage and get some insight into the science behind water supply and the challenges facing the environment today. Tours are held every 30 minutes. ✉ *Lee Rd., Cork City* ☎ *021/494–1500* 🌐 *lifetimelab.ie* 🎫 *€5* ⏲ *Closed weekends Sept.–May.*

Great resources like the English Market have made Cork a foodie mecca. Her Majesty Queen Elizabeth II's walkabout here was a highlight of her first visit to Ireland in 2011.

St. Anne's Church

CHURCH | The church's pepper-pot steeple, which has a four-sided clock and is topped with a golden, salmon-shape weather vane, is visible from throughout the city and is the chief reason why St. Anne's is so frequently visited. The Bells of Shandon were immortalized in an atrocious, but popular, 19th-century ballad of that name. Your reward for climbing the 120-foot-tall tower is the chance to ring the bells out over Cork, with the assistance of sheet tune cards—and, of course, the magnificent views over the city. The famous clock tower with its red sandstone and white ashlar finish is a city landmark and supposedly the inspiration for the county's renowned red-and-white sports colors, while the clock's notoriously unreliable timekeeping gained it the nickname of the "Four Faced Liar." Beside the church, Firkin Crane, Cork's 18th-century butter market, houses two small performance spaces. ✉ *Church St., Shandon* ☎ *021/450–5906* 🌐 *www.shandonbells.ie* 🎫 *Church free, tower €5.*

St. Fin Barre's Cathedral

RELIGIOUS BUILDING | On the site that was the entrance to medieval Cork, this compact, three-spire Gothic cathedral, which was completed in 1879, belongs to the Church of Ireland and houses a 3,000-pipe organ. According to tradition, St. Fin Barre established a monastery on this site around AD 650 and is credited with being the founder of Cork. The cathedral was designed by William Burges, one of the greatest of the Victorian art–architects, and everything here, including the church fittings, furnishings, mosaics, ironwork, and stained glass, shows his distinctive "Burgesian Gothic" hand. ✉ *Bishop St., City Center South* ☎ *021/496–3387* 🌐 *corkcathedral.webs.com* 🎫 *€6.*

University College Cork

COLLEGE | The Doric-porticoed gates of UCC stand about 2 km (1 mile) from the city center. The college, which has a student body of roughly 10,000, is a constituent of the National University of Ireland. The main quadrangle is a fine example of 19th-century university architecture in the Tudor-Gothic style, reminiscent of many Oxford and Cambridge colleges. Several ancient ogham stones are on display in the North Quadrangle (near the visitor center), and the renovated Crawford Observatory's 1860 telescope can be visited. The Honan Collegiate Chapel, east of the quadrangle, was built in 1916 and modeled on the 12th-century Hiberno-Romanesque style, best exemplified by the remains of Cormac's Chapel at Cashel. The UCC chapel's stained-glass windows, as well as its collection of art and crafts, altar furnishings, and textiles in the Celtic Revival style, are noteworthy. ✉ *College Rd., Western Road* ☎ *021/490–1876* 🌐 *www.ucc.ie* *Free; guided tours €4* ⏲ *Visitor center closed Sun., and Dec. and Jan.*

Granddad of the Computer

George Boole (1815–64), a University College professor, is one of the heroes of the computer age. Despite growing up in poor circumstances, he developed into a mathematical genius, inventing Boolean algebra—the foundation upon which computer science was built. University College Cork raised his profile considerably during 2015, the bicentenary of his birth. See 🌐 *www.georgeboole.com*

Restaurants

Elbow Lane Brew and Smoke House

$$ | **IRISH** | The small, dark, L-shape room (hence the name) on the ground floor of a handsome town house is dominated by a blue-tiled chimney with a wood-smoke grill, whose aroma pervades the room. There's a masculine ambience here, as befits a brewery and smokehouse renowned for hearty portions of grilled food and triple-cooked chips. **Known for:** slow-smoked pork ribs, jerk quail, house brews; open 7 days a week; no reservations, creating a wait at peak times. *Average main: €20* ✉ *4 Oliver Plunkett St., City Center South* ☎ *021/439–0479* 🌐 *www.elbowlane.ie* ⏲ *No lunch.*

Electric

$ | **MODERN IRISH** | In front of a fast-flowing, urban stretch of the River Lee, the neon-clad exterior of a snazzy Art Deco building announces a casual city-center venue that combines a sense of dining as theater with a friendly staff that puts everyone at ease. The ground floor has a square bar with booths and dining niches around the perimeter, while upstairs is a more conventional dining room. **Known for:** hearty lunchtime stews: local, fresh, and made to order; Asian brunch weekends noon–3:30; river view with seats outside in summer. *Average main: €15* ✉ *41 South Mall, City Center South* ☎ *021/422–2990* 🌐 *www.electriccork.com* *No credit cards.*

Farmgate Café

$ | **IRISH** | One of the best—and busiest—informal lunch spots in town is on a terraced gallery above the fountain at the Princes Street entrance to the atmospheric English Market. All ingredients used at the café are purchased in the market below. **Known for:** delicious traditional Irish comfort food like corned beef and colcannon; separate weekend dinner menu; an artistic clientele including many poets. *Average main: €16* ✉ *English Market, Princes St., City Center South* ☎ *021/427–8134* 🌐 *www.farmgate.ie* ⏲ *Closed Sun.*

★ Greenes Restaurant

$$$ | **FUSION** | Tucked away on a cobbled patio, this surprising haven is part of a Victorian warehouse conversion that houses Hotel Isaacs. Stone and redbrick

As the River Lee flows through Cork's center, delightful bridges and quays add to the city's unique character.

walls are the backdrop to a minimalist modern interior, while out back a gigantic rock-wall waterfall makes a stunning backdrop to the dining area. **Known for:** creative cuisine using local produce; seven- and nine-course tasting menus; buzzy atmosphere. *Average main: €26 Hotel Isaacs, 48 MacCurtain St., City Center North 021/455–2279 www.greenesrestaurant.com No lunch Mon.–Wed.*

★ Ichigo Ichie

$$$$ | JAPANESE | "Ichigo Ichie" translates as "a once-in-a-lifetime encounter" and a special, once-in-a-lifetime dining experience is exactly what this dramatic, Michelin-starred kaiseki restaurant delivers. Japanese chef-owner Takashi Miyazaki brings the traditional Japanese multicourse tasting ritual to Cork in the *kappou* style (meaning the sushi and sashimi is prepared by the chef in front of the diner) and infuses the 12-course menu with Irish fish and produce. The Mushimono dish comprises a gorgeous egg dashi pot, Castletownbere Lagoustine, Gubbeen guanciale, and tomato foam. **Known for:** interesting and unique menu and experience; seasonal menu; very difficult to get a reservation. *Average main: €135 5 Fenns Quay, City Center South 021/427–9997 ichigoichie.ie Closed Mon.*

Isaacs

$$ | CONTEMPORARY | Cross Patrick's Bridge to the River Lee's north side and turn right to reach this large, atmospheric brasserie in a converted 18th-century warehouse—a true Cork institution. Modern art, muted jazz, high ceilings, and well-spaced tables with colored wooden tops create a relaxed setting. **Known for:** group gathering spot; East-meets-Mediterranean fusion menu; beef fillet, curries and confits. *Average main: €22 48 MacCurtain St., City Center North 021/450–3805 www.isaacsrestaurant.ie Closed Mon. No lunch Sun.*

Jacques

$$$ | EUROPEAN | Tucked away near the GPO is one of Cork's favorite restaurants. Enter through a softly lit, curved Art

Did You Know?

Whether or not you intend to kiss the Blarney Stone found atop Blarney Castle, the view from the 120-foot-tall square tower is most impressive. The Kissing Stone is scrubbed with disinfectant several times a day so this is a completely hygienic feat.

Deco–style bar that combines exposed brick walls with caramel-shaded leather banquettes to create a soothing respite from the city center. **Known for:** elegant, intimate dining; good value; tapas and side plates menu. *Average main: €26 23 Oliver Plunkett St., City Center South 021/427–7387 www.jacques-restaurant.ie Closed Sun.–Tues.*

Market Lane Restaurant & Bar

$ | **MODERN IRISH** | All that remains of this building's former identity as a pub is the long mahogany bar; today, it is a bustling bistro-style restaurant serving robust, freshly prepared food from an open kitchen. Art Deco touches and a predominantly black-and-white theme set a Parisian mood, and light floods in from two walls of large windows on summer evenings. **Known for:** Irish comfort food; homemade sausages with colcannon; variety of vegetarian options. *Average main: €18 5–6 Oliver Plunkett St., City Center South 021/427–4710 www.marketlane.ie.*

Nash 19

$ | **INTERNATIONAL** | Easily missed, tucked into a quiet lane close to the renowned English Market, Nash 19 is one of Cork's secret gems, popular with locals for its wholesome, unpretentious cooking using local, seasonal ingredients. Highlights include a decadent signature platter that features the best of Cork's artisanal produce. **Known for:** hearty soups; delicious breakfasts and scones; takeaway meals. *Average main: €15 19 Princes St., City Center North 21/427–0880 www.nash19.com Closed Sun. and Mon. No dinner.*

Paradiso

$$$$ | **VEGETARIAN** | Irish owner–chef Denis Cotter has won awards for his cookbooks, which have added greatly to the fame of this simple, café-style restaurant. The Mediterranean–Eastern fusion-style food is locally grown, and is known for its imaginative combinations, such as dandan tofu minco or pumpkin seed chocolate mole and squash. **Known for:** risottos of seasonal vegetables; attractively plated combinations; local cheeses and vegetables. *Average main: €40 16 Lancaster Quay, Western Road 021/427–7939 paradiso.restaurant Closed Sun. and Mon.*

Hotels

The Address

$$$$ | **HOTEL** | An imposing redbrick and cut-limestone Victorian-era nursing home is now a comfortable hotel with character and some of the best views in Cork, encompassing the city and surrounding hills. **Pros:** patronized by lively clientele; amazing views from its hilltop perch over the river and docks; generous-size bedrooms. **Cons:** steep hike up from city; in a residential area with few other pubs or cafés; decor fusty and unadventurous. *Rooms from: €210 Military Hill, St. Luke's, City Center North 021/453–9000 www.theaddresscork.com 70 rooms Free Breakfast.*

Blarney Castle Hotel

$$$ | **HOTEL** | Set on the village green only a minute's walk from the famed castle, this 1837 hotel occupies a traditional gabled building, with guest rooms on two stories above the bar and a quiet residents' lounge on the first floor. **Pros:** ideal touring base; good alternative to Cork City (8 km [5 miles]); restaurant on premises. **Cons:** bar can get busy on Sunday night; no elevator; some rooms overlook parking lot and yard. *Rooms from: €179 Blarney Village Green, Blarney 021/438–5116 www.blarneycastlehotel.com 13 rooms Free Breakfast.*

Elizabeth Fort Houses

$$$$ | **HOUSE** | Two early-17th-century houses within the walls of Elizabeth Fort, one of the oldest and most historic sites in Cork, have been sensitively restored by the Irish Landmark Trust to offer a

unique and historical Cork City experience. **Pros:** oozing historic charm; central location; city views. **Cons:** no parking; two-night minimum stay; located in a busy tourist attraction. *Rooms from: €207 Elizabeth Fort, City Center South 1/670–4733 www.irishlandmark.com 2 rooms in each house No Meals.*

Hayfield Manor
$$$$ | **HOTEL** | An elegant Georgian-style house, its red brick exterior brightened by white-sash windows hints at the comfort that lies within. **Pros:** modern country-house style; a good value for luxury accommodations; great dining options. **Cons:** 15-minute walk to city center; unremarkable location; nearby streets busy with students by day. *Rooms from: €435 Perrott Ave., Western Road 021/484–5900 www.hayfieldmanor.ie 88 rooms Free Breakfast.*

★ **Hotel Isaacs Cork**
$$ | **HOTEL** | A stylish renovation transformed an old city-center warehouse into a contemporary boutique hotel, which is accessed via a cobblestone arch and includes original features like exposed stone walls as well as a courtyard patio with a waterfall. **Pros:** convenient location; courtyard dining; historic hotel. **Cons:** heavy through-traffic outside; parking is not on-site; breakfast not included. *Rooms from: €139 48 MacCurtain St., City Center North 021/450–0011 www.hotelisaacscork.com 47 rooms, 11 apartments No Meals.*

Imperial Hotel
$$ | **HOTEL** | Though it cannot compete in size with the grande-dame hotels of bigger cities, the Imperial, which dates to 1813, plays the part with conviction, with its marble lobby, opulent finishes, and traditional concierge. **Pros:** central location; genuine Cork character; elegant dining options. **Cons:** some standard bedrooms are very small; quiet rooms have no view; popular venue for wedding receptions. *Rooms from: €160 South Mall, City Center South 021/427–4040 www.imperialhotelcork.com 126 rooms, 1 suite Free Breakfast.*

Kingsley Hotel
$$$ | **HOTEL** | A 15-minute walk (or short taxi ride) from the city center, the Kingsley has an idyllic riverside location, overlooking a rowing club on a pretty section of the River Lee and beside the Lee Fields, a big meadow with paths that are popular with joggers. **Pros:** highest standard of comfort; impeccable service; excellent leisure facilities. **Cons:** bland exterior; only half the rooms have river views—the rest overlook the car park; 15-minute walk from city center. *Rooms from: €179 Victoria Cross, Western Road 021/480–0500 www.thekingsley.ie 131 rooms Free Breakfast.*

Lancaster Lodge
$$ | **B&B/INN** | Free city-center parking, a great location midway between the shopping district and the university, and good value are the main reasons to stay at this modern, four-story inn. **Pros:** central location; free parking; good value. **Cons:** no bar or wine license; poor views; budget design. *Rooms from: €141 Lancaster Quay, Western Road 021/425–1125 www.lancasterlodge.com 48 rooms Free Breakfast.*

Nightlife

★ **Charlies Bar**
BARS | Opens 7 am for that early Guinness thirst. Raucous nightly music sessions are held here, with traditional Irish showcased on Sunday from 3 pm and nightly in between. Tuesday and Wednesday they shut down the bar for some deserved shut-eye. *2 Union Quay, South Docklands 021/431–8342 www.charliesbarcork.com Closed Tues. and Wed.*

Thanks to streets lined with cafés, pubs, and shops, a simple stroll around Cork can be a delightful way to while away the hours.

Corner House

BARS | This popular bar, Cork's best local in the opinion of many regulars, is open daily and hosts Cajun, folk, or Irish music from Thursday to Sunday. ✉ *7 Coburg St., City Center North* ☎ *021/450–0655* 🌐 *www.thecornerhouse.ie* ⏲ *Closed Tues.*

★ **Franciscan Well Brewery**

BREWPUBS | With giant multinational Molson Coors at the helm of this establishment, Franciscan Well's microbrewery status is debatable, but every effort has been made to retain the flavor of the beer. On the site of an ancient Franciscan monastery (in fact, the story goes that there are monks buried beneath the flooring), it has a heated beer garden and an atmospheric candlelit bar, open daily from 3 pm. Share a pizza fresh from the wood-burning oven. ✉ *North Mall, Shandon* ☎ *021/439–3434* 🌐 *www.franciscanwellbrewery.com.*

★ **Mutton Lane Inn**

PUBS | Down a narrow, mural-coated lane off the main drag near the English Market, this cavernous little candlelit pub is the perfect setting for a clandestine pirate meeting, and given its 1787 vintage—making it one of Cork City's oldest inns—that may well have been the case in the misty past. A roaring fire welcomes guests during the winter months, while Rising Brew craft beer quenches the thirst in summer. Get in early for seating; it really is that small. ✉ *Market La., Cork City* ✣ *Off Patrick's St.* ☎ *21/427–3471.*

The Oliver Plunkett

LIVE MUSIC | You can hear live music here nightly—trad, blues, rock, swing, and soul. ✉ *116 Oliver Plunkett St., City Center South* ☎ *021/422–2779* 🌐 *www.theoliverplunkett.com.*

Sin é

LIVE MUSIC | Pronounced "*shin*-ay" (Irish for "that's it"), this is the place for live Irish music—fiddles, flutes, banjos, and bodhráns. Sessions are Friday and Sunday at 6:30 pm and Tuesday at 9:30 pm. ✉ *8 Coburg St., City Center North* ☎ *021/450–2266* 🌐 *www.facebook.com/sinecork.*

 Performing Arts

Cork Opera House

MUSIC | The city's major hall for touring productions also presents dance, theater, panto, comedy, and music events. ✉ *Emmet Pl., City Center South* ☎ *021/427–0022* 🌐 *www.corkoperahouse.ie.*

Everyman Palace Theatre

THEATER | Modest-size theatrical productions are staged at this theater, which has an ornate Victorian interior. ✉ *15 MacCurtain St., City Center North* ☎ *021/450–1673* 🌐 *www.everymancork.com.*

Triskel Arts Centre

ARTS CENTERS | The popular venue presents live music, classic and contemporary films, and readings in the former Christchurch (dating from 1717), and hosts art exhibitions. ✉ *Tobin St., off S. Main St., Washington Village* ☎ *021/427–2022* 🌐 *www.triskelartscentre.ie.*

BOOKS AND VINYL

Records and Relics

ANTIQUES & COLLECTIBLES | Whether you're hunting for early '20s jazz, '80s punk, or vintage Irish records, you'll find something of interest in the stacks of formerly loved records in this place. Stocks include the paraphernalia to accompany the records, from checked flannel shirts to bowler hats. ✉ *14 Lancaster Quay, City Center North* ☎ *21/229–1594* ⏲ *Closed Sun.*

Vibes and Scribes Bookshop

BOOKS | Rare secondhand books, graphic novels, and a wide range of photography and art illustrations cram this popular shop on Lavitt's Quay. ✉ *21 Lavitt's Quay, City Center South* ☎ *21/427–9535.*

DEPARTMENT STORES

★ Blarney Woollen Mills

CRAFTS | With the largest stock and the highest turnover of Blarney's crafts shops, this noted emporium sells everything from Irish-made fashion for men and women to Aran hand-knitted items to leprechaun key rings. ✉ *The Square, Blarney* ☎ *021/451–6111* 🌐 *www.blarney.com.*

Brown Thomas

DEPARTMENT STORE | Ireland's best high-end department store carries items by Irish and international designers. The ground floor has an excellent cosmetics hall and a good selection of menswear and Irish crystal. Refuel at the coffee shop, which sells healthful open sandwiches and house-made soups. ✉ *18–21 St. Patrick's St., City Center South* ☎ *021/480–5555* 🌐 *www.brownthomas.com.*

GALLERIES

Lavit Gallery

ART GALLERIES | This ground-floor space exhibits works by members of the long-established Cork Arts Society and others. ✉ *Wandesford Quay, Clarkes Bridge, Washington Village* ☎ *021/427–7749* 🌐 *www.lavitgallery.com.*

JEWELRY

Designworks Studio

JEWELRY & WATCHES | A local favorite, this store is not only a showcase for imaginative, modern Irish jewelry but home to a thriving open-view workshop with three full-time goldsmiths. ✉ *Cornmarket St., City Center South* ☎ *021/427–9420* 🌐 *designworksstudio.ie* ⏲ *Closed Sun.*

Silverwood

JEWELRY & WATCHES | A large selection of Celtic-inspired silver jewelry is sold here, including traditional claddagh rings. ✉ *84a Oliver Plunkett St., City Center South* ☎ *021/427–8150* 🌐 *www.silverwoodjewellery.com.*

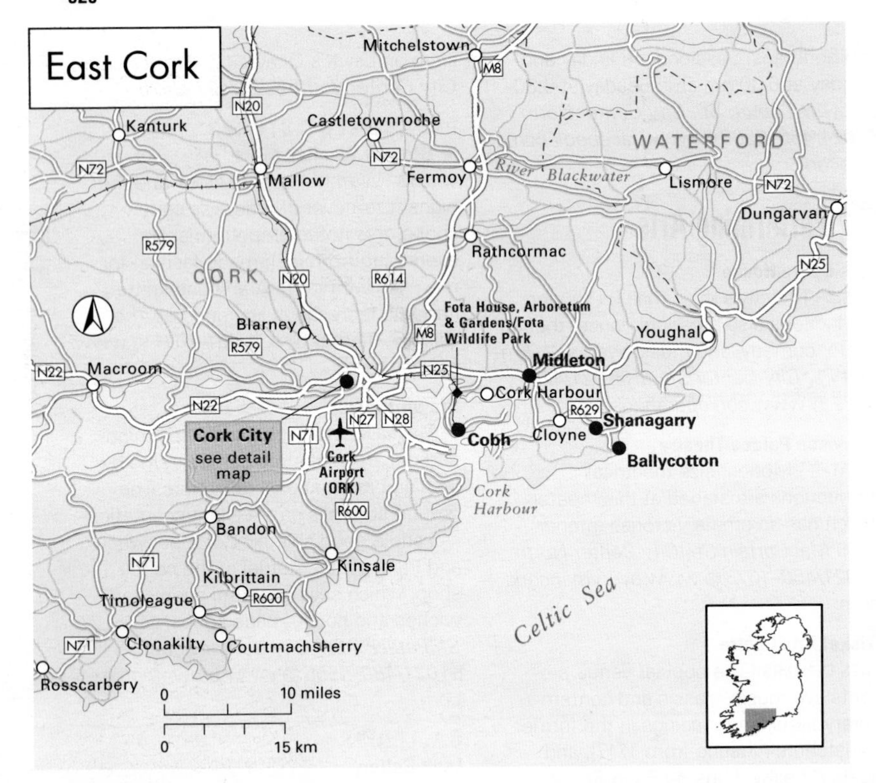

Cobh

16 km (10 miles) east of Cork City.

On a fine day, with visitors milling along Cobh's colorful harbor front at the foot of its hilly terrain, it's hard to imagine that millions of emigrants funneled through the ticket booths (most famously the RMS *Titanic*) to bid a final farewell to Ireland aboard ships destined for the USA. Pretty cafés and hanging baskets line the quayside in Cobh today—catch a southerly, unforgettable view of the town's brightly painted "Deck of Cards" houses lined up a steep street as far as St. Colman's Cathedral, which towers high over Cobh's hilly terrain.

GETTING HERE AND AROUND

Cobh lies 16 km (10 miles) east of Cork City, and is signposted from the N25 (follow signs for Waterford). A suburban train from Cork's Kent Station stops at Fota Island and Cobh, and offers better harbor views than the journey by road.

TOURS

★ Spike Island

WALKING TOURS | FAMILY | Call it Ireland's Alcatraz. A scenic 15-minute boat ride from Cobh, Spike Island was originally the site of a 6th-century monastery, then a British artillery fortification in the 18th century, and a holding for convicts awaiting deportation to Australia in the mid-19th century. Ten times the size of Alcatraz, it remained a prison until the late 20th century, and now contains interpretative displays and a café. The island itself has plenty to see, from the abundant wildlife to the museum building and much more. The island also offers great views of Cork Harbour, especially lovely when the weather cooperates. The regular tour takes 3½ hours including boat trips, but there are shorter "after dark" tours, fully guided, with no costumed actors or forced scares, just the grim reality of the island fortress prison to strike a chill in your soul. ✉ *Cobh* ✣ *Kennedy Pier is in center of Cobh's waterfront, below cathedral* ☎ *021/237–7355* 🌐 *www.spikeislandcork.ie* 🎫 *From €23.*

The *Titanic* Trail
WALKING TOURS | A 60-minute guided walking tour of Cobh by local historian and author, Dr. Michael Martin, covers *Titanic* sites and history. The tour departs daily at 11 am from the Commodore Hotel. No advance booking required. The *Titanic* crew also offer ghost tours of Cobh, a Titantic Excursion from Cork by train, and more. ✉ *Mellieha, Carrignafoy, Cobh* ☎ *087/276–7218* 🌐 *www.titanic.ie* 🎫 *From €16.*

VISITOR INFORMATION

CONTACTS Cobh Tourist Office. ✉ *Sirius Arts Centre, Lower Rd., Cobh* ☎ *021/481–3301* 🌐 *www.visitcobh.com.*

Sights

Fota House, Arboretum & Gardens
GARDEN | The name of the Smith-Barry ancestral estate is derived from the Irish *Fód te,* which means "warm soil," a tribute to the unique tidal estuary microclimate here and the reason why one of Ireland's most exotic botanical gardens was established here. The original lodge house was built in the mid-18th century for the family, which owned vast tracts of land in South Cork, including the whole of Fota Island. The next generation of the powerful family employed the renowned architects Richard and William Vitruvius Morrison to convert the structure into an impressive Regency-style house that has now been painstakingly restored. The symmetrical facade is relatively unadorned and stands in contrast to the resplendent Adamesque plasterwork of the formal reception rooms (somewhat denuded of furniture). The servants' quarters are almost as big as the house proper. Fota's glories continue in the gardens, which include an arboretum, a Victorian fernery, an Italian garden, an orangerie, and a special display of magnolias. You can also (for an extra charge) visit the Victorian working garden. There's a tearoom, and the house hosts a program of concerts and exhibitions. ✉ *Fota Island* ☎ *021/481–5543* 🌐 *www.fotahouse.com* 🎫 *House tour €10* 🕒 *House closed Oct.–mid-Feb.*

Fota Wildlife Park
WILDLIFE REFUGE | **FAMILY** | The 70-acre park is 12 km (7 miles) east of Cork via N25 and R624, the main Cobh road, and also accessible by rail from Cork's Kent Station. It's an important breeding center for cheetahs and wallabies, and also is home to monkeys, zebras, giraffes, ostriches, flamingos, emus, and kangaroos. ✉ *Fota Island* ☎ *021/481–2678* 🌐 *www.fotawildlife.ie* 🎫 *€18.*

The Queenstown Story at Cobh Heritage Centre
HISTORIC SIGHT | Many of the people who left Ireland on immigrant ships for the New World departed from Cobh, which was formerly known as Queenstown. The exhibit, in the old Cobh train station, re-creates the experience of the 2½ million emigrants who left from here between 1848 and 1960. It also tells the stories of great transatlantic liners, including the ill-fated *Titanic,* whose last port of call was Cobh, and the *Lusitania.* ✉ *Lower Rd., Cobh* ☎ *021/481–3591* 🌐 *www.cobhheritage.com* 🎫 *€13* 🕒 *Closed Dec. 23–27 and Dec. 31–mid-Jan.*

The Sinking of the *Lusitania*

On May 7 every year, an event is held on the quayside in Cobh at the *Lusitania* Peace Memorial to commemorate the 1,198 innocent civilians lost at sea on May 7, 1915. The Cunard liner *Lusitania* was torpedoed off the Old Head of Kinsale, 40 km (25 miles) west of Queenstown (as Cobh was then known). This attack on a nonmilitary target was a major factor in the decision by the United States to enter World War I in 1917.

The *Lusitania* was the pride of the Cunard fleet. It had set a record in 1907, crossing the Atlantic in four days, 19 hours, 52 minutes, and the transatlantic service continued, despite the outbreak of war in 1914. The vessel was on a voyage from New York to Liverpool when it was struck by a torpedo from the German submarine U20 shortly after 2 pm. It quickly listed to one side, making it difficult to launch the lifeboats, and 18 minutes later, the mighty liner had sunk, leaving hundreds struggling in the water. A flotilla of local boats, tenders, tugs, and fishing vessels rushed to the rescue, while those onshore worked tirelessly to cope with the sudden disaster. Of the 1,959 passengers and crew aboard, only 761 survived. Of the 289 bodies recovered, 169 are buried in Cobh, 45 of them unidentified.

St. Colman's Cathedral

RELIGIOUS BUILDING | The best view of Cobh, well worth the uphill stroll, is from St. Colman's Cathedral, an exuberant neo-Gothic granite church designed by the eminent British architect E.W. Pugin in 1869, and completed in 1919. Inside, granite niches portray scenes of the Roman Catholic Church's history in Ireland, beginning with the arrival of St. Patrick. The row of colorful "Deck of Cards" Houses that lead the way up the hill add a unique backdrop to the cathedral. ✉ *Cathedral Close, Cobh* ☎ *021/481–3222* 🌐 *www.cobhcathedralparish.ie.*

★ The *Titanic* Experience Cobh

MARINA/PIER | **FAMILY** | Cobh was the last port of call for the ocean liner *Titanic.* At 1:30 pm on April 11, 1912, tenders carried 123 passengers out to the ship from the offices of the White Star Line. These offices have now been converted into an interactive exhibition (cinema, holographs, touch-screen displays), allowing visitors to follow, literally, in the footsteps of the passengers as they embarked on the fateful voyage. Visitors assume the identity of one passenger and discover if that passenger survived at the end of the tour. ✉ *The Promenade, Cobh* ☎ *021/481–4412* 🌐 *www.titanicexperiencecobh.ie* 🎟 *€10.*

Midleton

12 km (8 miles) east of Cork City.

Midleton is famous for its school, Midleton College, founded in 1696, and its distillery, founded in 1825 and modernized in 1975, which manufactures spirits—including Irish whiskey—for distribution worldwide. A pleasant market town set at the head of the Owenacurra River estuary, near the northeast corner of Cork Harbour, Midleton has many gray-stone buildings dating mainly from the early 19th century.

GETTING HERE AND AROUND

Midleton is 12 km (8 miles) east of Cork City on the main N25. It also has regular bus and train connections with the city.

If you're going to visit the Jameson distillery, it runs a daily shuttle, April through October, from St. Patrick's Quay in Cork. In other months, Bus Éireann's daily service from Cork Bus Station Parnell Place is the best option because it stops right outside the distillery (€9.60 round-trip, 30 minutes). Many trains run from Cork's Kent Station every day (€6.50 round-trip); the Midleton train station is about 25 minutes' walk from the distillery.

CONTACTS Bus Éireann. ✉ *Parnell Pl., City Center South* ☎ *021/450–8188* 🌐 *www.buseireann.ie.* **Irish Rail.** ✉ *Kent Station, City Center North* ☎ *021/450–6766 for timetable* 🌐 *www.irishrail.ie.*

Sights

Jameson Experience
DISTILLERY | On a tour of the Old Midleton Distillery, you'll learn how this now-world-renowned whiskey (*uisce beatha*, or "the water of life") was made in the old days. The old stone buildings are excellent examples of 19th-century industrial architecture, the impressively large old waterwheel still operates, and the pot still—a copper dome that can hold 32,000 imperial gallons of whiskey—is the world's largest. Tours end with a complimentary glass of Jameson's Irish whiskey (or a soft drink). A gift shop and café are also on the premises. From April to October there is a daily shuttle bus service from St. Patrick's Quay Cork; inquire when booking. **TIP→ Early in the tour, requests are made for a volunteer "whiskey taster," so be alert if this option appeals.** ✉ *Old Midleton Distillery, Old Distillery Walk, Midleton* ✣ *18 km (10 miles) northwest of Ballycotton on R629, 20 km (12½ miles) northeast of Cobh on R624* ☎ *021/461–3594* 🌐 *www.jamesonwhiskey.com* 🎟 *From €23.*

Hotels

Castlemartyr Resort
$$$$ | **RESORT** | **FAMILY** | A gracious 18th-century manor house is the centerpiece of this resort overlooking ancient pastures grazed by Kerry Bog ponies, and adjacent to a 12th-century castle. **Pros:** luxurious period-style suites; excellent spa and golf course; 220-acre grounds include a lake and woodland paths. **Cons:** off the beaten track; popular as a wedding and conference venue; some of the new bedrooms are a bit far from main amenities. $ *Rooms from: €319* ✉ *Castlemartyr* ✣ *12 km (8 miles) north of Ballycotton by R629* ☎ *021/421–9000* 🌐 *www.castlemartyrresort.ie* *103 rooms, 45 lodges* *Free Breakfast.*

Ballycotton

36 km (20 miles) southwest of Cobh on the R624 and R629, 40 km (25) miles southwest of Cork City.

Perched on a rocky spur over the Atlantic, this pretty bay-front village with its famous lighthouse has a cliff-side track that connects it to a series of sandy beaches. Seafood is the local specialty, which is served fresh in restaurants and watering holes throughout its steep streetscape. Keep an eye out for the RNLB *Mary Stanford*, a lifeboat with an illustrious past that sits on a pedestal by the pier. Her crew saved 122 lives over her career, and her prominence in Ballycotton reflects the pride locals take in the town's maritime history. With oodles of Cork charm, as its name suggests, Ballycotton is a cozy base to discover the East Cork coastline and countryside.

GETTING HERE AND AROUND

Ballycotton harbor is a cul-de-sac, a coastal outpost that lures visitors who want to escape from the crowds during peak season at the end of Road R629.

It has a proud maritime past. Bus Éireann service 240 regularly connects Ballycotton to Cork City, Midleton, and Ballymaloe, with the last bus departing from Ballycotton at 4:50 pm.

Sights

Ballycotton Cliff Walk

BEACH | The trailhead of this invigorating walk is close to the pier in Ballycotton. Passing sandy beaches, a small stone bridge that crosses a stream, and wonderful animal and plant life, this trail also offers magnificent views across the bay, with rambling meadows and fragrant growth on land side. As the trails cut through a bird sanctuary visitors can linger on benches to enjoy the feathered company or just to breathe in those views. The trail ends at Ballyandreen Beach.

Ballycotton Lighthouse

LIGHTHOUSE | After *Sirius*, the first vessel to cross the Atlantic completely under steam, sank off Ballycotton Bay on a foggy night in the mid-19th century, the lighthouse was constructed in its wake. Tours starting at 10 am in season take in 360-degree panoramic views of the bay, as far as Kinsale Head. The 90-minute tour includes a visit to one of Ireland's rare black lighthouses and the recounting of legends that surround the local maritime community. ✉ *Ballycotton Pier, Ballycotton* ☎ *87/396–3998* 🌐 *ballycottonseaadventures.com* 🎫 *€25* 🕒 *Closed Nov.–Mar. Weather-dependent in season.*

Restaurants

Cush

$$ | **IRISH** | Expect fresh, in-season catch from the pier—hake; or shrimp, prawns, scallops, lobster, and crab—to feature on the menu. For meat lovers there's the likes of pheasant or short rib, and a three-course menu for just €40. **Known for:** contemporary and modern menu; stunning lighthouse views; comfortable B&B. 💲 *Average main: €20* ✉ *The Pier* ☎ *21/464–6768* 🌐 *www.cush.ie* 🕒 *Closed Mon. and Tues. No lunch Wed.*

Shanagarry

15 km (8 miles) southeast of Midleton, 17 km (11 miles) southeast of Cork Harbour.

Shanagarry (meaning Old Garden) was the childhood home of William Penn, founder of Pennsylvania. He discovered Quakerism here—and some of that old faith still lingers in this farming village.

GETTING HERE AND AROUND

Shanagarry, on a rural back road, is about an hour's drive from Cork City or Cork Harbour on the N25 to the R632; from Midleton, take the R629. Or take the Ballycotton bus (there are five runs daily) from Cork Bus Station Parnell Place. The trip takes an hour and a quarter. The last bus back to Cork leaves Shanagarry at 4:54 pm.

Sights

Ballymaloe Cookery School and Gardens

GARDEN | **FAMILY** | The extensive organic gardens here provide herbs and vegetables for the school and the restaurant, and visitors can ramble through wildflower meadows and admire herbaceous borders leading to an ornately crafted shell house, the potager vegetable garden, rustic tree house, and a Celtic maze. A farm walk visits cows in their clover field, rare-breed pigs, and some 400 hens. Conclude your visit in the Farm Shop, open the same hours as the garden. ✉ *Kinoith House, Shanagarry* ☎ *021/464–6785* 🌐 *www.ballymaloecookeryschool.ie/* 🎫 *Garden €9* 🕒 *Closed Sun.*

Shanagarry Design Centre

STORE/MALL | Run by the Kilkenny Shop, the spacious gallery and showroom (with scrumptious home baking in the café) is in the village center. On display are high-end Irish-made crafts including Newbridge silverware, Orla Kiely handbags, and potter Louis Mulcahy's huge bowls and lamps, as well as Irish-made clothing, woolen goods, Irish linen, and jewelry. Several artists and craft makers have studios in the basement, where their work is also for sale. ✉ *Next to Shanagarry Parish Church, Shanagarry* ☎ *021/464–5838* 🌐 *www.kilkennyshop.com/shanagarrydesigncentre* 🎫 *Free.*

★ **Shanagarry Potters**

STORE/MALL | Now returned to the village where he grew up, potter Stephen Pearce has reopened the traditional craft pottery that launched his career in the late 1960s. The showroom sells his distinctive, contemporary hand-thrown black-and-cream earthen tableware and the terra-cotta-and-white line, made from organic local clay and both beloved of collectors. The tearoom opens daily from May to September, weekends only in winter. Book a pottery tour in advance, and ask about workshops.

■ **TIP→ Pearce's simple, practical, but beautiful pottery makes for great, contemporary Irish gifts and souvenirs. U.S. shipping is available if you can't limit yourself to something packable!** ✉ *The Old Pottery, Shanagarry* ✥ *5 km (3 miles) on R629 from Ballycotton* ☎ *021/464–6807* 🌐 *www.shanagarrypotters.com.*

Hotels

★ **Ballymaloe House**

$$$$ | **B&B/INN** | This Georgian manor is a symphony of whites and beiges, its drawing room beckoning with fine modern Irish paintings—a lovely touch for what is basically a farmhouse family home, albeit a world-famous one: Ballymaloe is the fountainhead of New Irish cuisine. **Pros:** run by Ireland's famous foodie family; country-house charm; quiet rural location. **Cons:** advance booking essential; splurge in comparison to other B&Bs; rural location means you will need a car. 💲 *Rooms from: €320* ✉ *Off R629, Shanagarry* ✥ *6 km (4 miles) northwest of Ballycotton on R629* ☎ *021/465–2531* 🌐 *www.ballymaloe.ie* 🛏 *29 rooms* 🍽 *Free Breakfast.*

Kinsale

29 km (18 miles) southwest of Cork City.

Kinsale—with its narrow, winding cobbled streets, seaside setting, striking architecture, and old-world charm—ranks as one of the most beautiful villages in Ireland, but that's not its only appeal. Foodies flock to this picturesque port that pioneered the Irish small-town tradition of fine dining in unbelievably small restaurants. While the town has grown over the last few decades, its charm and quality of dining has remained constant. Year-round, head to Market Square (Wednesday 10 am–1 pm) to find Kinsale Market, a cute piazza market where you can snack on a Breton crepe while stocking up on chutneys, smoked salmon, farmhouse cheeses, fresh fish, and organic goodies.

In Kinsale's town center, at the tip of the wide, fjord-like harbor that opens out from the River Bandon, upscale shops and eateries with brightly painted facades line small streets. Kinsale has two yacht marinas, and skippers with deep-sea angling boats offer day charters. The Kinsale Yacht Club hosts racing and cruising events during the sailing season, which runs from March to October for hardy souls and from June to August for everyone else.

GETTING HERE AND AROUND

Kinsale is 29 km (18 miles) southwest of Cork City on the R600, a half-hour drive, and is only a 15-minute drive from Cork Airport. Ground-level parking is easily available. Buses from Cork City stop at the airport and run every hour. Kinsale's town center is compact, and there is no

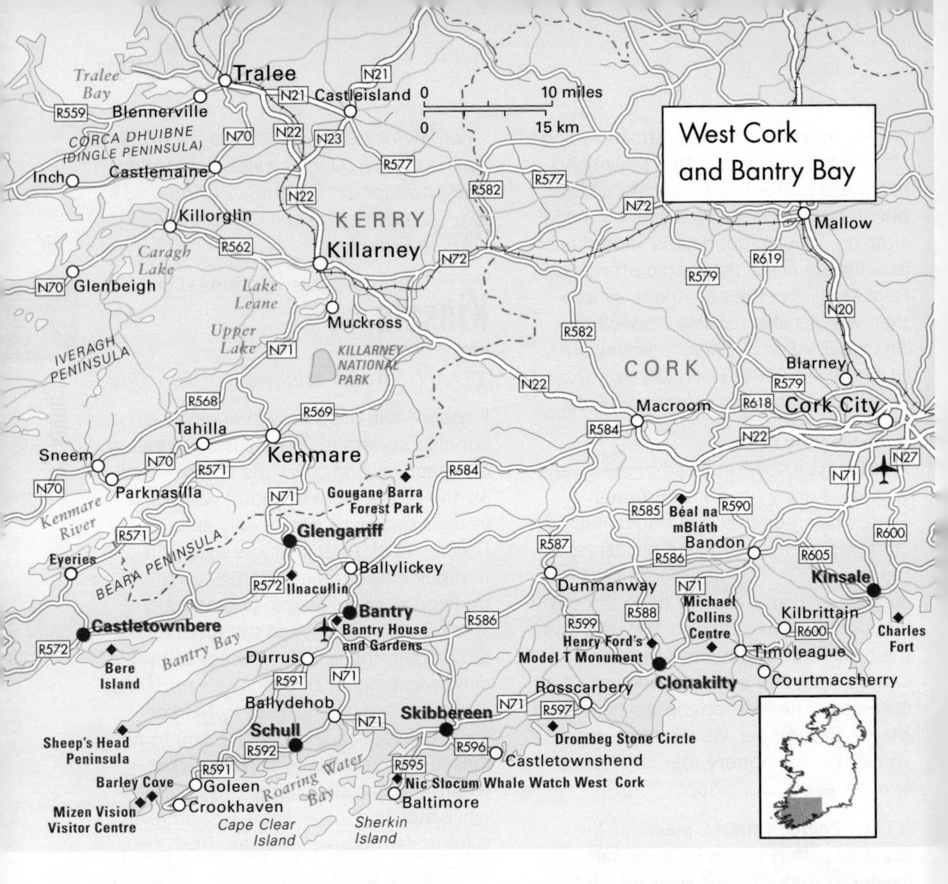

public transport, but taxis can be booked from Kinsale Cabs.

CONTACTS Kinsale Cabs. ✉ *Market Sq., Kinsale* ☎ *021/477–2642* 🌐 *www.kinsale-cabs.com.*

TOURS

Don & Barry's Kinsale Historic Stroll

GUIDED TOURS | On this tour of Old Kinsale you'll learn about the town's links to "Man Friday" and the truth about Kinsale Hookers pirates. It departs from the town's tourist office daily at 11:15 am; there's an additional tour at 9:15 am Monday to Saturday from May to September. ✉ *Kinsale* ☎ *021/477–2873* 🌐 *www.historicstrollkinsale.com* 🎫 *€8.*

Kinsale Harbour Cruises

BOAT TOURS | **FAMILY** | For an overview of Kinsale's great natural harbor, take an hour-long cruise on the *Spirit of Kinsale*, offered by Kinsale Harbour Cruises. You'll hear informative commentary and view wildlife, including herons, seals, and otters. ✉ *Pier Rd., Kinsale* ☎ *086/250–5456* 🌐 *www.kinsaleharbourcruises.com* 🎫 *€14* 🕒 *Closed Nov.–Apr.*

Kinsale Heritage Town Walks

GUIDED TOURS | Dermot Ryan, a native of Kinsale and a local-history enthusiast, leads guided town walks daily at 10:30 am. ✉ *Kinsale* ☎ *021/477–2729* 🌐 *www.kinsaleheritage.com* 🎫 *€5.*

VISITOR INFORMATION

CONTACTS Kinsale Tourist Office. ✉ *Pier Rd., Kinsale* ☎ *021/477–2234* 🌐 *www.kinsale.ie.*

Sights

★ Charles Fort

MILITARY SIGHT | FAMILY | Built—almost symbolically—on the site of the ruins of an earlier Irish castle, Charles Fort on the east side of the Bandon River estuary in the late 17th century was constructed by the British after they defeated the Spanish and Irish forces. One of Europe's best-preserved "star forts" encloses some 12 clifftop acres and is similar to Fort Ticonderoga in New York State. If the sun is shining, take the footpath from Kinsale signposted Scilly Walk; it winds along the harbor's edge under tall trees and then through the village of Summer Cove. ✉ *3 km (2 miles) east of town, Kinsale* ☎ *021/477–2263* 🌐 *www.heritageireland.ie* 🎫 *€5.*

Courthouse and Regional Museum

HISTORY MUSEUM | Memorabilia from the wreck of the *Lusitania* are among the artifacts in this museum, housed in a 17th-century, Dutch-style courthouse. The 1915 inquest into that ship's sinking took place in the wood-paneled courtroom. Downstairs is a fascinating collection of antique tradesman's tools. Because the staff consists of volunteers, it's best to call to confirm opening times. ✉ *Old Courthouse, Market Sq., Kinsale* ☎ *021/477–2234* 🌐 *kinsale.ie* ⏲ *Closed Nov.–Mar.*

Restaurants

★ Bastion

$$$$ | CONTEMPORARY | Prosecco on tap sets the tone for fun at this wine bar and restaurant in the heart of Kinsale. There's a bar in the funky front parlor along with some tables beside its street windows, supplemented by a more private back room. **Known for:** experimental small plates; more than 100 wines; range of prix-fixe and tasting menus. $ *Average main: €100* ✉ *5 Main St., Kinsale* ☎ *021/470–9696* 🌐 *www.bastionkinsale.com* ⏲ *Closed Mon. and Tues. Closed last wk of Nov. and all Feb.*

The Black Pig

$ | WINE BAR | A small 18th-century coach house on a backstreet was an unlikely candidate to become the hottest place in a town famed for sophisticated eateries, but that's what happened here, and the uncluttered, minimalist premises and cobbled courtyard are buzzing with life. Reserve and your name is chalked on the wall beside your table, but the tall squeaky bar stools are just as popular. **Known for:** up to 100 wines available by the glass; daily hot special; local coffee and chocolates. $ *Average main: €16* ✉ *66 Lower O'Connell St., Kinsale* ☎ *021/477–4101* 🌐 *www.theblackpigwinebar.com* 💳 *No credit cards* ⏲ *Closed Mon. and Tues., and mid-Jan.–Mar. No lunch.*

The Bulman Bar and Toddies

$ | CONTEMPORARY | Kinsale has other pub–restaurants, but none with such an idyllic waterside location. In summer, bar food is served on the big stone quay right beside the ocean. **Known for:** half-grilled lobster in summer months; slow-cooked pork ribs with house barbecue sauce; deep-fried calamari salad. $ *Average main: €16* ✉ *Summercove, Kinsale* ☎ *021/477–2131* 🌐 *www.thebulman.ie* ⏲ *No food Mon. and Tues. No dinner Sun.* ☞ *Lunch available in the bar Tues.–Sun.*

Finns' Farmcut

$$$$ | CONTEMPORARY | A must-stop for Kinsale's more carnivorous visitors, but while locally sourced meat (directly from the owner's farm) is center stage on the Finn family's menu, there's a good offering of fresh catch, and a vegan option "from the soil," too. Talented owner-chef John Finn runs the restaurant with his wife, Julie—but "Bertha" (an imported charcoal-burning oven) is second-in-command. **Known for:** roast rack of lamb; locally sourced meat; excellent wine list.

$ *Average main: €34* ✉ *6 Main St., Kinsale* ☎ *021/470–9636* 🌐 *www.finnsfarmcut.com* ⏲ *No dinner Sun. and Mon.*

★ Fishy Fishy Café
$$$$ | SEAFOOD | FAMILY | Originally a café in a fish shop, this place has moved up in the world, now located in a sumptuous two-story former art gallery in the town park. TV chef Martin Shanahan, who trained in San Francisco, brings California pizzazz to his dishes. **Known for:** surf 'n' turf of scallops and black pudding on parsnip puree; "fishy fish pie" served with mash au gratin in a hot cream sauce; spicy seafood chowder. $ *Average main: €45* ✉ *Crowley's Quay, Kinsale* ☎ *021/470–0415* 🌐 *www.fishyfishy.ie* ⏲ *No dinner Sun.–Wed. in Nov.–Feb.* ☞ *Nonfish options available on the menu.*

Jim Edwards
$$ | EUROPEAN | One of Ireland's original bar–restaurants, this is a Kinsale institution that serves local steak, lamb, duck, and fresh seafood. Choose from the inexpensive daily specials in the busy bar, or have a more leisurely meal among the mahogany tables, dark red decor, and oil lamps of the somewhat baronial restaurant. **Known for:** generous portions of fresh seafood; top-quality local steak; good-value set menu. $ *Average main: €22* ✉ *Market Quay, Kinsale* ☎ *021/477–2541* 🌐 *www.jimedwardskinsale.com* ⏲ *Closed Thurs.*

Max's
$$$ | FRENCH | Polished tables, a large stone chimney, and bay windows are the cornerstone of this contemporary space behind this double-fronted town house. At dinner, owner-chef Olivier Queva's classical French background is evident in his treatment of the daily catch directly from the pier, including fresh grilled lobster in the summer, and clever ways with unusual cuts of meat. **Known for:** good-value early-bird menu; excellent seafood; reservations required on summer weekends. $ *Average main: €28* ✉ *48 Main St., Kinsale* ☎ *021/477–2443* 🌐 *www.maxs.ie* ⏲ *Closed Dec.–Feb.*

Hotels

★ Actons
$$ | HOTEL | Opened by sisters Sidney and Sheila Acton in 1946, this was originally the home of the entrepreneurially renowned Acton family since the 1860s. **Pros:** interior design hits the tricky mark of quirky but elegant; Kinsale's only pool, plus spa and gym; top-notch location for dining out, bar crawls, and shopping. **Cons:** not the best staff service; feels like five-stars, some prices reflect that; garden feels cut off from the seaviews. $ *Rooms from: €165* ✉ *Pier Rd., Kinsale* ☎ *021/477–9900* 🌐 *www.actonshotelkinsale.com* *77 rooms* *Free Breakfast.*

Friar's Lodge
$$ | B&B/INN | A large Georgian town house has been tastefully converted into this cheerful guesthouse, with an array of amenities that would do a hotel proud. **Pros:** quiet location yet close to town; pleasant, spacious rooms; private parking. **Cons:** no restaurant or bar; some rooms are small; decor may feel dated. $ *Rooms from: €150* ✉ *Friar's St., Kinsale* ☎ *021/477–7384* 🌐 *www.friars-lodge.com* ⏲ *Closed Christmas wk* *18 rooms* *Free Breakfast.*

★ Giles Norman Gallery Townhouse
$$ | B&B/INN | The gallery sells striking black-and-white photos, so it's fitting that the rooms in this carefully restored Victorian house are decked out in black, white, and gray contemporary furnishings, with large photo murals on the walls. **Pros:** town-center location; comfortable, spacious rooms; sea views. **Cons:** no breakfast; up two or three flights of stairs and no elevator; no dedicated parking. $ *Rooms from: €160* ✉ *45 Main St., Kinsale* ☎ *021/477–4373* 🌐 *www.gilesnorman.com* ⏲ *Closed mid-Dec.–Feb.* *4 rooms* *No Meals.*

Thanks to locals painting their houses with bright colors, the historic seaside village of Kinsale has become one of Ireland's most picturesque photo ops.

Perryville House

$$$$ | B&B/INN | This strikingly handsome, early-19th-century pier-front property with its black, iron-laced facade looks like it belongs in a French colony; inside, the elegance continues with a quintessential Irish edge. **Pros:** breakfast featuring ingredients from Cork's food producers; stunning harbor views; comfortable beds. **Cons:** pricey; closed in the winter; not really child-friendly. *Rooms from: €300 Long Quay, Sleveen, Kinsale 21/477–2731 www.perryvillehouse.com Closed late Oct.–mid-Apr. 25 rooms No Meals.*

Trident Hotel

$$$ | HOTEL | The modern three-story building may lack old-world charm, but the waterfront location—built around three sides of a former dockyard on the edge of Kinsale's magnificent harbor—more than compensates. **Pros:** great sea views; working harbor setting; lively tavern. **Cons:** not the best on-site restaurant; bland interiors; pool and spa are at a sister hotel a five-minute walk away. *Rooms from: €200 Pier Rd., World's End, Kinsale 021/477–9300 www.tridenthotel.com 75 rooms Free Breakfast.*

Nightlife

The Folk House

PUBS | This friendly pub presents live music on weekends year-round, and also midweek from May through October. *Guardwell, Kinsale 021/477–2382 folkhousevenue.com.*

Spaniard Inn

LIVE MUSIC | Check out the Spaniard Inn for rock and folk groups. There's a traditional Irish session on Wednesday from 10 pm year-round. *Scilly, Kinsale 021/477–2436 www.thespaniard.ie.*

Shopping

ART

The Boathouse Gallery

ART GALLERIES | Many of the works by locally based contemporary artists sold here are small enough to carry home. ✉ *68 Main St., Kinsale* ☎ *021/470–9981* 🌐 *www.theboathousegallery.ie.*

Giles Norman Photography Gallery
ART GALLERIES | Black-and-white photographs of Irish scenes are featured at this local gallery. ✉ *44 Main St., Kinsale* ☎ *021/477–4373* 🌐 *www.gilesnorman.com* ⏲ *Closed Sun. and Mon.*

BOOKS

bookstór
BOOKS | This popular local hangout stocks new and vintage books, and a great selection of local interest reads. They've won awards for their children's section, and the staff has plenty of helpful tips. ✉ *1 Newman's Mall, Kinsale* ☎ *021/477–4966* ⏲ *Closed Sun.–Tues.*

FOOD

Koko Chocolates
CHOCOLATE | Just across the road from the tourist office, the aroma of hot chocolate will lead you to Kinsale's tempting little chocolate shop. Truffles are handmade on the premises, along with a range of novelty chocolates (including a chocolate iPhone) and hot drinks to go. ✉ *Pier Rd., Kinsale* ☎ *087/611–0209* 🌐 *kokokinsale.com.*

HOME

Granny's Bottom Drawer
MIXED CLOTHING | A selection of fine Irish linen and hand weaving, in classic and contemporary styles, is carried at this shop, together with Irish-made luxury knitwear in cashmere and silk. ✉ *53 Main St., Kinsale* ☎ *021/477–4839* 🌐 *www.grannysbottomdrawer.com.*

Hilary Hale
HOUSEWARES | Hilary Hale uses storm-felled, locally grown timber to make lamps, bowls, and platters. ✉ *Rincurran Hall, Summercove, Kinsale* ☎ *021/477–2010* 🌐 *www.hilaryhale.com.*

Kinsale Crystal
GLASSWARE | This family-run studio sells handblown, hand-cut Irish crystal. ✉ *Market St., Kinsale* ☎ *21/477–4493* 🌐 *www.kinsalecrystal.ie.*

JEWELRY

Kinsale Silver
JEWELRY & WATCHES | Dominic Dolan is the silversmith who crafts fine jewelry on the premises here. ✉ *Pearse St., Kinsale* ☎ *021/477–4020* 🌐 *www.kinsalesilver.ie.*

Activities

BICYCLING

Mylie Murphy's
BIKING | Rent a bike here to explore Kinsale's picturesque hinterland. If you prefer to lie back on a boat—they also sell fishing tackle. ✉ *Pearse St., Kinsale* ☎ *021/477–2703* ⏲ *Closed Sun.*

GOLF

★ **Old Head Golf Links**
GOLF | Golf doesn't get much more spectacular than this. On a celebrated 215-acre peninsula, which juts out into the wild Atlantic nearly 300 feet below, you can find an awe-inspiring spectacle that defies comparison. The only golfing stretches that could be likened to it are the 16th and 17th holes at Cypress Point and small Pacific sections of Pebble Beach, from the 7th to the 10th, and the long 18th. Even if your golf is moderate, expect your pulse to race at the stunning views and wildlife. They've added 15 suites and a spa, so you can now stay at the course for a few days. ✉ *Old Head, off R604, Kinsale* ☎ *021/477–8444* 🌐 *www.oldhead.com* *€375 May–mid-Oct.; €225 mid-Apr. and late Oct.* *18 holes, 7215 yards, par 72* ⏲ *Closed late Oct.–mid Apr.*

Clonakilty and Nearby

28 km (19 miles) west of Kinsale.

Clonakilty is a small market town and famous for being the hometown of statesman and revolutionary Michael

Collins. His significance still resonates throughout the town, with a bronze statue located in the square and two museums dedicated to his legacy. Clonakility black pudding and sausages are generally considered the best in Ireland. The town is west of Kinsale on a scenic, largely coastal road that passes through the village of Timoleague. Many of the storefronts in Clonakilty have charmingly traditional hand-painted signs and wooden facades. Clonakilty marks the western edge of the Seven Heads Peninsula, which stretches back eastward to Timoleague, whose ruined abbey dominates the view. Timoleague sits on the Argideen River estuary, renowned for its birdlife, especially great flocks of wintering migrants. From the abbey, you can see the road to Courtmacsherry across the water. The sandy beach of this postcard-pretty village attracts many vacationers.

GETTING HERE AND AROUND

Clonakilty is 28 km (19 miles) west of Kinsale on the R600, Timoleague 19 km (12 miles). Follow the signposts from Timoleague to reach Courtmacsherry. Parking is easy in all three towns. There is no public transit between Kinsale and Clonakilty, but you can take a bus (about an hour) from Cork City.

VISITOR INFORMATION

CONTACTS Clonakilty Tourist Information Office. ✉ *25 Ashe St., Clonakilty* ☎ *023/883–3226* 🌐 *www.clonakilty.ie.*

Sights

Béal na mBláth

HISTORIC SIGHT | The peaceful setting along this country road was shattered by the sound of gunfire on the 22nd of August, 1922. The ambush resulted in the death of one of Ireland's most famous statesmen—Michael Collins—and the assassination is still shrouded in uncertainty. A large limestone cross and other monuments mark the spot where this happened, which is frequently visited by a steady stream of people to this date. Expect to discover the unique game of road bowling—an Irish sport where competitors throw a metal ball along a predetermined course—along this stretch of country lanes. ✉ *Béal na mBlath, Clonakilty* ✣ *28 km (17 miles) north of Clonakility via R588.*

Drombeg Stone Circle

RUINS | On a windswept hill that tumbles down as far as the coast, this huddled gathering of megalithic standing stones has marked the changing seasons and braced the elements for thousands of years. Nearby, an ancient outdoor barbeque (*fulacht fia*) popular with Bronze Age alfresco diners has revealed its prehistoric culinary secrets to scientists—but modern-day travelers will find more convenient options available a few kilometers away, at the pretty, billowy, sailboat haven of Rosscarbery. ✉ *Drombeg, Clonakilty.*

Henry Ford's Model T Monument

HISTORIC SIGHT | Just 8 km (5 miles) north of Clonakilty, in the "blink and miss it" hamlet of Ballinascarty (it's really just a crossroads) an unsuspecting traveler might pause to inspect the stainless steel, fully-to-scale Model T that's perched on a limestone pedestal on the side of a road. Across the street, the Henry Ford Tavern is open for business—because this is the cradle of a modern-day basic—the car. Henry Ford's father, William, was born in this tiny townland, and fled to the safer shores of America during the Great Famine that decimated Ireland's population. In fact, both of Henry's parents were of County Cork stock, which is why the European Ford production line for Ford Cars was located in the Rebel City until its fortunes changed back in 1984. ✉ *Ballinascarty, Clonakilty* 🌐 *www.thehenryford.org/collections-and-research/digital-collections/artifact/366483.*

Michael Collins Centre

VISITOR CENTER | It was in the village of Woodfield, 9 km (6 miles) west of Timoleague, that Michael Collins (1890–1922) had his last drink before he was shot in an ambush. The enthusiastic guide at this cottage-museum, signposted off the R600 east of Clonakilty, offers a lively introduction to the controversial hero of Irish independence, using slides, large photos, and film clips. Outside is a reconstruction of the ambush site, complete with Collins's armored Rolls-Royce and a Crossley tender. Directions to other Collins sites in the area are available, as are guided tours (prebooking essential mid-September to mid-June). ✉ *7 Emmet Sq., Maulnaskehy, Clonakilty* ✣ *8 mins from Clonakility. Take R600 for about 2 km (1¼ miles) then take 2nd road to left (L8085-27)* ☎ *023/884–6107* 🌐 *www.michaelcollinscentre.com* 🎫 *€7* 🕒 *Closed Sun. Reservations only mid-Sept.–mid-June.*

Michael Collins House

HISTORIC HOME | **FAMILY** | Located in one of Ireland's few planned squares—an area where Collins lived as a boy—this museum maps the struggle for Irish independence from early days until 1922. History comes alive through interactive displays, audiovisuals, information boards, and artifacts. Although Collins, the famous statesman and politician, is the focus here, other periods—such as the rebellion of 1798—are also included. ✉ *7 Emmet Sq., Clonakilty* ☎ *23/885–8676* 🌐 *www.michaelcollinshouse.ie* 🎫 *€5* 🕒 *Closed Sun. and Mon. May–Sept. Also closed Wed. off-season.*

Timoleague Abbey

RELIGIOUS BUILDING | A mid-13th-century Franciscan abbey at the water's edge is Timoleague's most striking monument. The abbey was built before the estuary silted up, and its main business was the importing of wine from Spain. A tower and walls with Gothic-arch windows still stand, and you can trace the ground plan of the old friary—chapel, refectory, cloisters, and the extensive wine cellar. The English sacked the abbey in 1642, but like many other ruins of its kind it was used as a burial place until the late 20th century, hence the modern gravestones.

■ TIP→ Walk around the back to find the entrance gate. The view of the sea framed by the structure's ruined Gothic windows is a don't-miss photo op. ✉ *The Quay, Timoleague* 🎫 *Free.*

Beaches

Inchydoney Beach

BEACH | The beach is on an island connected to the mainland by causeways, and accessible by car. It consists of two flat, wide stretches of fine white sand divided by a rocky promontory. The east side is the most sheltered and has dunes that can be walked. The slope to the sea is so gentle that at low tide it's a long walk to find deep water. Busy in July and August, its vast expanses offer exhilarating walks the rest of the year. And then there's Inchydoney Island Lodge & Spa, for those that want to bask in the tranquility here a little while longer. **Amenities:** parking (no fee); toilets; water sports. **Best for:** surfing; swimming; walking. ✉ *Inchydoney Island, 3 km (2 miles) south of town, Clonakilty.*

Restaurants

The Pink Elephant

$ | **EUROPEAN** | **FAMILY** | The legendary Pink Elephant looks out to sea and across the bay to wooded slopes. Huge windows frame the stunning view, and in good weather there is seating outside. **Known for:** local meat, fresh fish, organic produce; traditional Sunday lunch; served in a room with a great view. [$] *Average main: €16* ✉ *R600 between Kinsale and Timoleague, Harbour View, Kilbrittain* ☎ *023/884–9608* 🌐 *www.pinkelephant.ie* ▬ *No credit cards* 🕒 *Closed most Jan. and Feb. for winter break; call ahead.*

Hotels

Dunmore House Hotel

$$$ | HOTEL | Just 8 km (5 miles) from Clonakility with a private beach and nine-hole golf course, this fourth generation family-operated property is an intimate place to wind down for a few days—without the busy vibe of a larger property. **Pros:** decor is thoughtful, accented with seascape and earthy tones; the ocean views are hard to match; small private beach for optimal fresh dips. **Cons:** no leisure facilities; out of town so a car is handy; can be weddings. *Rooms from: €189 Clonakilty 8 km (5 miles) south of Clonakility 23/883–3352 www.dunmorehousehotel.ie 30 rooms Free Breakfast.*

Inchydoney Island Lodge & Spa

$$$ | HOTEL | A palatial and breezy four-star hotel facing out onto the far west ocean. **Pros:** light and airy oceanfront suites; top-tier room service; romantic island getaway on the water. **Cons:** no kids club; need a car; quieter than the town/city stays. *Rooms from: €190 Inchydoney Island Lodge & Spa, Inchydoney Island, Clonakilty 23/883–3143 www.inchydoneyisland.com 67 rooms Free Breakfast.*

Shopping

Edward Twomey

FOOD | This butcher's shop is known the world over (at least with Irish expats) for its Clonakilty Black Pudding, a breakfast product that's prominently featured on the shop's T-shirts—the ultimate West Cork souvenir. *16 Pearse St., Clonakilty 023/883–3365 www.clonakiltyblackpudding.ie.*

Lettercollum Kitchen Project

FOOD | Owners Con McLaughlin and Karen Austin are masters of the vegetarian and ethnic repertory. Their bakery and deli sells specialty breads, cooks' ingredients, sandwiches, and savory herb tarts. You can assemble a superior picnic here. *Lettercollum Timoleague, Clonakilty 023/884–6251 www.lettercollum.ie.*

Spiller's Lane Gallery

JEWELRY & WATCHES | Set in a converted grain store at a pretty mews, this shop sells Irish-made jewelry, cutlery, pottery, and paintings. *Spiller's La., Bridge St., Clonakilty 023/883–4815 www.instagram.com/spillerslane.*

Urru

OTHER ACCESSORIES | After taking the Ballymaloe certificate cookery course, Ruth Healy left the corporate treadmill behind to open the ultimate cooks' shop, which aims to bring urban chic to rural Ireland. It's worth a stop en route if you're driving from Cork or Kinsale to Clonakilty. Sip a latte while browsing among locally made foodstuffs, including pâtés and patisserie, and a tempting range of cookbooks, cookware, and chocolates. *The Mill, MacSwiney Quay, Bandon 023/885–4731 www.urru.ie Closed Sun. and Mon.*

Skibbereen

33 km (20 miles) west of Clonakilty.

Skibbereen is the main market town in this neck of southwest Cork. The Saturday country market and the plethora of pubs, punctuated by bustling shops, supermarkets, and coffeehouses, keep the place jumping year-round. It's just 15 minutes or 12 km (8 miles) from the glorious seaside village of Baltimore, so visitors have a wonderful choice of scenic locations on their doorstep.

GETTING HERE AND AROUND

Skibbereen is 85 km (53 miles) southwest of Cork City, a drive of an hour and 20 minutes on the N71, the main Bantry road. The town lies 33 km (20 miles) west of Clonakilty, about a half-hour drive. There is free parking on the street and in several parking lots. Buses depart from Cork Bus Station Parnell Place, but there's no local public transportation. For local excursions, contact Long's Taxis. Skibbereen is a designated hub of the National Cycle Network, with three signposted routes of one-day and half-day trips. Book a bike in advance from Roycroft Cycles.

CONTACTS Skibbereen Cabs & Taxi Service. ✉ *55 Bridge St., Skibbereen* ☎ *028/21258.*

VISITOR INFORMATION

CONTACTS Skibbereen Tourist Office. ✉ *North St., Skibbereen* ☎ *028/21766* 🌐 *www.skibbereen.ie.*

Nic Slocum Whale Watch West Cork

NAUTICAL SIGHT | More than 24 species of whale and dolphin have been spotted off the coast of West Cork. Trips to see at least some of them last three to four hours, with commentary on other local bird and wildlife, and leave from the harbor at Baltimore, about 13 km (8 miles) southwest of Skibbereen. Reservations are recommended in peak season. ✉ *Baltimore* ☎ *086/120–0027* 🌐 *www.whalewatchwestcork.com* 🎫 *€55* 🕓 *Closed Sept.–Mar.*

Skibbereen Heritage Centre

HISTORY MUSEUM | A thoughtful renovation of a stone gasworks building has created an attractive, architecturally appropriate home for the Skibbereen Heritage Centre. An elaborate audiovisual exhibit on the Great Famine presents dramatized firsthand accounts of what it was like to live in this community when it was hit hard by hunger. Other attractions include displays on area marine life, walking tours, access to local census information, and a varying schedule of special programs. ✉ *Old Gasworks Bldg., Upper Bridge St., Skibbereen* ☎ *028/40900* 🌐 *www.skibbheritage.com* 🎫 *€6* 🕓 *Closed Nov.–mid-Mar.; mid-Mar.–Apr. and Oct., closed Sun. and Mon.; May–Sept. closed Sun.*

The Baltimore Room

$$ | IRISH | When it comes to an organically sourced menu, it's hard to match the offerings at the Casey family's wonderful oceanfront restaurant close to the tiny roadside hamlet of Baltimore. The mussels come from their farm at Roaring Bay, water from the property's spring well, and root vegetables travel a couple of feet from their garden to the kitchen, while the bread arrives warm to the table as it's freshly baked on-site. **Known for:** views of Ilen River Estuary; fresh seafood; craft beer. $ *Average main: €21* ✉ *Casey's of Baltimore, Baltimore* ✥ *13 km (7 miles) south of Skibereen on R595* ☎ *28/20197* 🌐 *www.caseysofbaltimore.com.*

★ **Dede at The Customs House**

$$$$ | CONTEMPORARY | Ahmet Dede, formerly of the exquisite Mews just down the street, bestows his culinary magic on his in-season tasting menu that can include Wagyu beef, black sole, red mulberry, and brown butter—or even brown butter ice cream for that matter. This chef is living proof that with talent, a restaurant does not need the pomp and trappings of fine dining to offer a feast of flavor—because he's wowing critics both nationally and globally with his local ingredients served with Turkish flair in his stripped-back, fine yet relaxed eatery in the delightful seaside village of Baltimore. **Known for:** reservations are essential; guided wine pairings; seasonal menu. $ *Average main: €130* ✉ *Customs House Baltimore, Baltimore* ☎ *28/48248* 🌐 *www.customshousebaltimore.com* 🕓 *No dinner Sun.–Wed. Closed Jan. and Feb.* ☞ *Phone ahead; owner Dede changes the schedule regularly.*

Hotels

★ Liss Ard Estate

$$$$ | HOTEL | A Victorian mansion set on a 163-acre estate—which includes a lake for canoe enthusiasts, running tracks, a waterfall, and the James Turrell Irish Sky Garden, an ancient stone fort that has become a magnificent crater garden with a delicate balance of light and space. **Pros:** rolling private estate and gardens; wellness rituals such as acupuncture, tea ceremony, and sound bath; entirely unique and exclusive concept in Cork. **Cons:** car advisable; gets pricer with add-ons; an abundance of options. *Rooms from: €225* ✉ *Skibbereen* ✢ *2½ km (1½ miles) south of Skibbereen* 🌐 *www.lissardestate.ie* *26 rooms* *No Meals.*

Performing Arts

Ulllinn West Cork Arts Center

ARTS CENTERS | This massive €3.4 million corten steel–clad building, dating from 2015, exhibits the works of local artists and distinguished visiting artists. ✉ *Skibbereen town center, Skibbereen* ☎ *028/22090* 🌐 *www.westcorkartscentre.com* *Closed Sun.*

Schull

105 km (66 miles) west of Cork.

Teeming with the brightly painted facades of craft and book stores, galleries, and pubs, this pretty village is alive with schooners in season and attracts an artsy crowd year-round from the capital and farther afield, which creates a uniquely West Cork boho vibe. It's also the main hub and gateway to the greater Mizen Head Peninsula and Ireland's most southerly point, with all its attractions. A sprinkling of small islands is the only thing that separates the harbor front from the expanse of ocean that gently laps against the small wharf.

GETTING HERE AND AROUND

Perched on the coast in the northern territory of the Mizen Head Peninsula, Schull is best accessed by car from Cork City via the N71 that skirts along the ribbon of West Cork seaside villages, like Clonakilty and Rosscarbery. There are three free car parking locations in the village, so it is better to avoid the busy streets. The 237 bus (Bus Éireann) provides a three-times-daily service between Cork and Schull.

TOURS

Cape Clear Ferry Tours

BOAT TOURS | A 25-minute crossing in comfort to one of Ireland's most southerly islands aboard the new fast service to Cape Clear gives visitors the opportunity to sample *Gaeltacht* (Irish-speaking) life in a rugged, off-radar setting. To get an overview of this 5-km-long (3-mile-long) by 1½-km-wide (1-mile-wide) oasis of solitude, take the Gleann Loop Trail and linger by the heather-scented cliff tops to breathe in the ocean views, or idle by the north harbor to pass time on the island's only sandy beach, where there is a small selection of hospitality and a castle ruin. For those who fall in love with the place, there are small guesthouses available. A year-round service operates from the mainland, a stone's throw away from Schull, at Baltimore Pier. ✉ *Schull Harbour, Schull* ☎ *28/39159* 🌐 *www.capeclearferries.com* *€40 return fast ferry, €18 regular ferry from Baltimore.*

VISITOR INFORMATION

Visitors move freely among locals, as can be witnessed by the diversity of far-reaching accents that rise and fall at the weekly craft and artisan market in the village square. A tourist office with typically free-spirited opening times is located on the Main Street, and when closed visit 🌐 *www.schull.ie* for more details.

CONTACTS Schull Tourist Office. ✉ *Schull* ☎ *28/28600* 🌐 *www.schull.ie.*

Sights

Barley Cove

BEACH | One of the most photographed beaches in Ireland, this expanse of soft flaxen-colored dunes that curls around the sapphire and turquoise shades of the Atlantic's water is a West Cork Instagrammable highlight. A river cuts through the sand and spills into the ocean, giving a fresh flow of cool water on either side of the green, tufty headlands. There are public facilities and car parking. A nearby inn opens seasonally, where visitors can stop by for a beachfront beverage. ✣ *24 km (15 miles) southwest on R592 and R591 from Schull.*

★ Mizen Vision Visitor Centre

VISITOR CENTER | Travel to this visitor center, set in a lighthouse at the tip of the Mizen Head (follow the R591 through Goleen to the end of the road), and you'll wind up reaching the Irish mainland's most southerly point. The lighthouse itself is on a rock at the tip of the headland; to reach it, you must cross a dramatic 99-step suspension footbridge—which has become a famous landmark over time. The lighthouse was completed in 1910; the Engine Room and Keepers' House have been restored by the local community. The exhilaration of massive Atlantic seas swirling 164 feet below the footbridge and the great coastal views and scenic drive here guarantee a memorable outing. ☒ *Harbour Rd., Goleen* ☎ *028/35115* ⊕ *www.mizenhead.ie* 🎫 *€8* ⊙ *Closed weekdays and Nov.–Feb.*

Schull Market

MARKET | From Easter to September, this foodie's Sunday market showcases superb products from local bakers, fish smokers, cheese makers, and Gubbeen smoked pork products, all sold by their makers. Hours 10–2. ☒ *Pier Rd., Schull* ⊙ *Closed Jan.–Easter, Oct., and Nov.; closed Mon.–Sat. Easter–Sept. and Dec.*

Restaurants

Heron's Cove

$$$$ | **SEAFOOD** | Although only minutes by foot from the main road and Goleen's village center, this harborside retreat is a peaceable kingdom—expect to see herons outside the window. "Fresh fish and wine on the harbor" is the motto here. The restaurant, in Sue Hill's modern house (she also offers B&B) is well run with great service. **Known for:** fresh, local seafood served by the waterside; lobster from the harbor; an interesting selection of wine, chosen from bottles on wall racks. $ *Average main: €33* ☒ *The Harbour, Goleen* ☎ *028/35225* ⊕ *www.heronscove.com* ⊙ *Closed Oct.–Apr.*

★ Restaurant Chestnut

$$$$ | **IRISH** | The last thing you would expect to find behind the typical, small pub facade located along a long street filled with a row of modest vernacular buildings is a heightened level of dining experience with a sophisticated, inventive menu. Schull man Rob Krawczyk runs the kitchen a few miles from his hometown in Ballydehob, and he's impressing professional food critics and novices alike with his inventive taster menus. **Known for:** tasting menu; locally sourced produce; creative and often experimental menu. $ *Average main: €140* ☒ *Staball Hill, Ballydehob, Schull* ✣ *8 km (5 miles) northeast of Schull* ☎ *28/25766* ⊕ *www.restaurantchestnutwestcork.ie* ⊙ *Closed Mon., Tues., and Jan.–mid-Mar.*

Hotels

★ Blairscove House

$$$ | **B&B/INN** | Set on the northwesterly side of Mizen Head, directly across from Schull, this elegant Georgian house offers a variety of self-catering options and sea views. **Pros:** stunning sea views; gourmet restaurant in barn; perfect nature-filled escape. **Cons:** remote, so a car is needed; rooms are not in the main house; no lunch on-site. *Rooms from: €190* ✉ *Durrus, Schull* ✣ *15 km (9 miles) northwest of Schull on R591* ☎ *27/61127* 🌐 *blairscove.ie* ⏲ *Closed Nov.–early Mar. No dinner Sun. and Mon.* *4 rooms* *Free Breakfast.*

Bantry

25 km (16 miles) northwest of Skibbereen.

The town of Bantry is at the head of Bantry Bay, between the Sheep's Head Peninsula to the southwest and the Beara Peninsula to the northwest. A somewhat unprepossessing town at first sight, Bantry is centered on a large square that attracts artisans, craftspeople, and musicians to its Friday-morning market in summer. If you approach Bantry heading west on the seaside road, before you reach town you'll spot the parking lot and visitor's entrance to the area's big attraction, Bantry House and Gardens.

GETTING HERE AND AROUND

Bantry is on the N71, midway between Skibbereen and Kenmare, a 1½-hour drive from Cork and an hour from Killarney. There is a large parking lot (free) in the main square. Buses from Cork Bus Station Parnell Place continue on to Glengarriff. There is no other local public transportation.

VISITOR INFORMATION

Ireland can be expensive, but in this part of the country many of the best things are free. Ask at tourist information offices about the many coves and small beaches or the looped walks along sections of the Sheep's Head Walking Route. Information on looped walks in Bantry Town can be found in local bars and hotels.

CONTACTS Bantry Tourist Office. ✉ *The Old Courthouse, Wolfe Tone Sq., Bantry* ☎ *027/50229* 🌐 *www.bantry.ie.*

Sights

Bantry House and Gardens

GARDEN | One of Ireland's most famed manors is noted for its picture-perfect perch on a hillock above the south shore of Bantry Bay. The fine Georgian mansion is surrounded by a series of stepped gardens and parterres that make up "the stairway to the sky." Spreading out below lies the bay and, in the far distance, the spectacular range of the Caha Mountains—one of the great vistas of Ireland. Built in the early 1700s and altered and expanded later that century, the manor became the ancestral seat of the White family from that period. The decor of the house was largely the vision of Richard White, second earl of Bantry, whose father—having hailed from farming stock—had secured extensive land as a thank-you for supporting England when Irish and French rebel forces failed in their bid for Ireland's freedom. Richard traveled extensively throughout Europe and brought a lot back to Ireland with him: fabulous Aubusson tapestries said to have been commissioned by Louis XV adorn the Rose Drawing Room, while state portraits of England's King George III and Queen Charlotte glitter in floridly, flamboyant rococo gilt frames in the Wedgwood blue–and-gold dining room. Never shy about capitalizing on the flow of history, he acquired an antique or two thought to have belonged to Marie Antoinette—sometime after her execution in 1793. Throughout the famine years in the mid-18th century the estate carried out extensive manual work. After Irish independence the house was used as a hospital during the Irish Civil War from 1922 and later the estate was occupied by the Irish Army.

Outside, the drama continues in the garden terraces, set with marble statues, framed by stone balustrades, and showcasing such delights as an embroidered parterre of dwarf box trees. The tearoom serves light lunches and features local

Divided by the Hundred Steps, the gardens of Bantry House are adorned with exotic plants due to the microclimate of its bay setting.

artisanal foods. In summer the house hosts concerts in the grand library, notably the West Cork Chamber Music Festival (held during the first week of July). The house also doubles as a B&B. ✉ *N71, Bantry* ☎ *027/50047* 🌐 *www.bantryhouse.com* 🎟 *€14 house and garden, €5 garden only* ⏲ *House closed Nov.–Mar.*

★ Gougane Barra Forest Park

FOREST | This secluded little spot conjures up all things mythical and magical you have been dreaming of in Ireland. The tiny oratory or chapel, accessed by a causeway, was the location of St. Finbarr's hermitage in the 6th century and it is one of the most sought-after places for wedding couples in Ireland, for good reason. The location is hard to match, lying beneath craggy mountains with an evergreen forest that cascades down to its location at the very edge of a still, crystal clear lake. The view is reflected upon the lake, doubling the impact and creating an otherworldly impression to the first-time visitor. St. Finbarr's oratory dates back to the 19th century and the ruins on the approach to the park are from 1700. ✉ *Garrynapeaka, Gougane Barra, Bantry* ✣ *25 km (16 miles) north of Bantry along R584* 🎟 *Free.*

Sheep's Head Peninsula

SCENIC DRIVE | Jutting into the ocean like a bony, accusatory finger, this 28-km-long (17-mile-long) peninsula is 4 km (2½ miles) at its widest and is the place to go way off-grid in West Cork because of its restricted access on two minor roads. With a network of 20 looped trails, the most famous being the 88-km (54½-mile) Sheep's Head Way, the ocean is never more than a short hike away. Views of the neighboring peninsulas of Mizen and Beara unfold further into Sheep's Head, along with hairpin bends, cliff-side walks, castles, deep valleys, blowholes, and wide-open bays. A small shrine dedicated to the 329 lost souls aboard an ill-fated Air India aircraft back in 1985 provides a somber respite along the way. At the southerly tip is Bernie's Cupán Tae, a stalwart of Irish hospitality for decades, offering freshly baked scones and sandwiches that taste all the better after a hike in the fresh sea air. ✉ *Seamount, Glenlough West.*

Hotels

The Maritime Hotel

$$ | **HOTEL** | **FAMILY** | A legacy of Ireland's boom years, this gleaming, modern, waterfront hotel recalls times when building budgets were lavish, and it's a stylish addition to the town, with state-of-the-art leisure facilities that make it a good all-weather touring base. **Pros:** great location; most rooms have stunning views; high comfort levels. **Cons:** long, dimly lit internal corridors; some rooms accessible only via two elevators with a longish walk in between; popular (and sometimes noisy) spot for events. *Rooms from: €145* ✉ *The Quay, Bantry* ☎ *027/54700* 🌐 *www.themaritime.ie* *110 rooms* *Free Breakfast.*

Seaview House Hotel

$$$ | **HOTEL** | Among private, wooded grounds overlooking Bantry Bay, this large, three-story, 19th-century country house is an oasis of calm, nestled in its own gardens well away from the main road. **Pros:** sea views; unostentatious comfort; good food. **Cons:** may feel eerily quiet at times; make your own entertainment; the "village" is more a suburb of Bantry, with only one pub. *Rooms from: €190* ✉ *N71, Ballylickey* ☎ *027/50073* 🌐 *www.seaviewhousehotel.com* ⏲ *Closed Nov.–mid-Mar.* *25 rooms* *Free Breakfast.*

Shopping

Dunbeacon Pottery

CERAMICS | Europe's most southwesterly pottery workshop can be found on the scenic Durrus–Mizen Head road just west of Bantry. Helen Ennis produces handmade ceramic tableware in a variety of glazes. ✉ *Durrus, R591, Bantry* ☎ *027/61036* 🌐 *www.dunbeaconpottery.com.*

Forest & Flock

ART GALLERIES | A group of local artists and craftspeople sell their wares at this large retail premises in the town center. Wood turning from storm-felled timber, knitwear, local ceramics, small artworks, candles, and jewelry are among the handcrafted items on offer. ✉ *New St., Bantry* ☎ *087/386–1799* 🌐 *www.forestandflock.ie* ⏲ *Closed Tues.*

Manning's Emporium

FOOD | On the road between Bantry and Glengarriff, this deli (and wine bar) is a showcase for locally made farmhouse cheeses, pâtés, and salamis, served on attractive sampling platters. It's also an excellent place to assemble a picnic or just to browse. ✉ *Ballylickey* ☎ *027/50456* 🌐 *www.manningsemporium.ie* ⏲ *Closed Mon.–Wed.*

Castletownbere

124 km (77 miles) southwest from Cork, 51 km (31 miles) south of Bantry on R572.

Castletownbere is one of Ireland's busiest whitefish ports and a good place to set down the anchor for touring the magnificent Beara Peninsula. The village is almost burrowed into the foothills of the Caha Mountains and has a market square with a traditional Irish town streetscape that's lined with low-lying architecture. It has a reasonable supply of grocery stores, restaurants, inns, and pubs. Look out for the famous McCarthy's Bar that's always freshly painted in the county colors of red and white. The Healy Pass, which cuts through the Caha Mountain Range, is one of the most scenic drives in Ireland.

GETTING HERE AND AROUND

Castletownbere is a 50-minute drive from Bantry along the R572, where hikers can outnumber cars in season. Bus 236 (Bus Éireann) connects the town to Cork City, Bantry, and Dunmanway. There's an adequate supply of parking spaces by the harbor, near the tourist office.

VISITOR INFORMATION Beara Tourist Office. ✉ *St. Peter's Church Castletownbere, Beara* ☎ *27/70054* 🌐 *bearatourism.com.*

TOURS

★ The Beara Way

SELF-GUIDED TOURS | With an expanse of more than 200 km (124 miles), this way-marked route takes in highs, like Healy Pass, a famine road that slits through the Caha Mountains with vertiginous views across the peninsula and bay islands, and lows where the landscape dips into the lush valleys that harbor pretty, brightly painted villages like Eyeries and Allihies. There's no set trailhead and it is still off-radar for the bulk of visitors to Cork shores, so many visitors get to enjoy the views in peace under the watchful gaze of the hulking and bare Hungry Hill, the nemesis of Daphne du Maurier's sweeping 1946 family saga, *Hungry Hill.* ✉ *Beara Peninsula* 🌐 *www.bearatourism.com.*

★ Dursey Island Cable Car

SPECIAL-INTEREST TOURS | Ireland's only cable car has more going for it than the usual nip across a city or up a mountain—this cable car crosses over the ferocious ocean waters over Dursey Sound, and is a rarity in Europe. Used to transport sheep, today it's available for visitors who want to ramble, unhurriedly, around Dursey island in the company of puffins, gannets, and razorbills, and, if you're lucky, catch a glimpse of a passing whale. The island has a forlorn beauty, with just a handful of residents and few facilities. ✣ *22 km (14 miles) south of Castletownbere* ☎ *27/73851* 🌐 *www.durseyisland.ie.*

Sights

★ Bere Island

ISLAND | Bere is one of Ireland's largest islands and took a decade to hand back to the republic after independence due to its strategic and imposing location on Bantry Bay—but it is still navigable within a day. Unlike other islands that have seen their population dwindle over the years, Bere has retained its residents who live alongside the island's distant past, and are reminded of it daily with the abundance of historical monuments etched into the hilly terrain: a round Martello tower, standing stones, and wedge tombs are local landmarks, with the mainland's Hungry Hill across the sea as a backdrop. A scattering of pubs and facilities in the village offers guests the option to recharge their batteries after a brisk hike or cycle (bike rental is available on the island) around the island. Ferries run every day, year-round, with trips almost every hour. ☎ *27/75009* 🌐 *www.bereislandferries.com.*

Dunboy Castle

CASTLE/PALACE | The Beara Peninsula was the cradle of the most powerful O'Sullivan clan, and the crumbling walls of Dunboy Castle that lie wasting away by the ocean shore just south of Castletownbere were once its stronghold. Of enormous historical significance, the castle was the last bastion of strength held by the O'Sullivan chieftain, Donal Cam O'Sullivan, until it was laid waste by Elizabethan forces shortly after the Battle of Kinsale in 1601. Almost the entire clan of mostly women and children perished in a massacre at a failed hideout on nearby Dursey Island in the aftermath, the rest along the 804-km (500-mile) infamous odyssey due north in a bid to safeguard the clan. This is now waymarked and coined the O'Sullivan Way or Beara-Breifne Way, and is Ireland's longest walking and cycling trail. It can start at either Dursey or Castletownbere. Keep an eye out for Dunboy's neighboring ruin, Puxley Manor, a Victorian Gothic manor that was subjected to a botched development project during Ireland's Celtic Tiger period—in 2022, it was decided that a multimillion-euro deal would transform Dunboy into a hotel, incorporating the already-84-bedroom original castle quarters. ✉ *Dunboy Castle, Castletownbere.*

Eyeries and Allihies

OTHER ATTRACTION | These two brightly painted villages on the southern tip of the Beara Peninsula are regularly featured on tourism posters for their perfect, vernacular streetscapes—and dramatic settings. Allihies has an interesting mining backstory and pretty beach.

★ McCarthy's Bar

BARS | Instantly recognizable by fans of writer Pete McCarthy as the bar in the cover photograph of his hilarious and best-selling travelogue, *McCarthy's Bar,* which bore the motto "never pass a bar with your name on it." It's an old-fashioned pub in the real sense, which means it doubles as a shop, so guests can buy a packet of cereal from behind the wood counter or order a pint of the black stuff (or do both). A Japanese katana sword hangs self-consciously on the wall, uncomfortable in its old Irish world setting, but it's a good talking point with the McCarthy family members from the snug at the other side of the counter. The late Dr. Aidan McCarthy, father of the current owners, was a survivor of Dunkirk, a World War II prisoner of war camp, and the bombing of Nagasaki. ✉ *The Square* ☎ *27/70014* 🌐 *www.maccarthysbar.com.*

Glengarriff

14 km (8 miles) northwest of Bantry.

One of the jewels of Bantry Bay is Glengarriff, the "rugged glen" much loved by the writers William Thackeray and Sir Walter Scott. The drive from Bantry along the cliff top, with views of the islands of the bay and its shelter belt of mountains, is one of the scenic highlights of West Cork. The descent into the sheltered, wooded village reveals yet another landscape: thanks to the Gulf Stream, it's mild enough down here for subtropical plants to thrive. Trails along the shore are flanked by rhododendrons and offer beautiful views of the nearby inlets, loughs, and lounging seals. You're very much on the beaten path, however, with crafts shops, tour buses, and boatmen soliciting your business by the roadside.

GETTING HERE AND AROUND

Glengarriff is a 10-minute drive, 14 km (8 miles) from Bantry on the N71. There is a large public parking lot at Quill's Woolen Mills; on-street parking is easily found, too. Buses from Cork City stop here, and some continue to the Beara Peninsula. There is no public transportation locally, but you can take a boat trip around the harbor, where huge seals bask in fine weather.

Blue Pool Ferry

BOAT TOURS | Buy a ticket at the kiosk beside the Quill's Woolen Mills car park, and follow the trail to an enchanting hidden harbor that's surrounded by rocks and overhanging trees. Boats leave from here for Garinish Island and Illnacullin Gardens, traveling via Seal Island. No need to land—you can take a round-trip tour and enjoy the wildlife of the bay, which includes a colony of comical basking seals. Cameras at the ready! First departure of the day is at 9:45 am. ✉ *N71, Glengarriff* ☎ *027/63333* 🌐 *bluepoolferry.ie* 🎫 *€13, €5 island access.*

Sights

★ Ilnacullin

GARDEN | Many visitors head to Glengarriff because of that Irish Eden, Ilnacullin. On Garnish Island, offshore from Glengarriff and beyond islets populated by comical-looking basking seals, you can find one of the country's horticultural wonders. In 1910, a Belfast businessman, John Annan Bryce, purchased this rocky isle, and, with the help of famed English architect Howard Peto and Scottish plantsman Murdo Mackenzie, transformed it into a botanical wonderland. The main showpiece is a wisteria-covered "Casita"—a roofed-over viewing point that overlooks a sunken Italian garden and pool. The modest Bryce family home is open to visitors, presented as it would have been in the early 20th century.

You get to Ilnacullin by taking a Blue Pool ferry (10 minutes), which departs for the island from Glengarriff. George Bernard Shaw found Ilnacullin peaceful enough to allow him to begin his *St. Joan* here; maybe you'll find Garnish inspiring, too.

TIP→ Credit cards are not accepted on the island. *Garnish Island* *027/63040* *www.garinishisland.com* *Gardens €5, ferry €10 round-trip* *Closed Nov.–Mar.*

Hotels

Glengarriff Eccles Hotel and Spa

$$ | **HOTEL** | This high-peaked Victorian landmark has peered out over the calm water of Glengarriff's harbor for more than 250 years, and in that time it has welcomed literary legends such as George Bernard Shaw, William Butler Yeats, and novelist William Thackeray. **Pros:** water's edge location; great sense of history; locals use the bar. **Cons:** five-minute walk from village; rooms can feel small; a bit eerie when not busy. *Rooms from: €160* *Harbour, Glengarriff* *027/63003* *www.eccleshotel.com* *Closed Nov.–mid-Mar.* *66 rooms* *Free Breakfast.*

Glengarriff Park Hotel

$$ | **HOTEL** | Smack-dab in the middle of the scenic and busy village of Glengarriff, this small, family-run hotel is an excellent base for touring, with some great scenic walks on the doorstep, and sits alongside its sister establishments MacCarthy's Bar and the Park Bistro. **Pros:** great value; knowledgeable local staff; handy one-stop shop for bed, food, and drink; popular destination for Irish people on short breaks. **Cons:** views from bedrooms are disappointing; in high season the village is busy with tourists and tour buses en route to Killarney and the Ring of Kerry. *Rooms from: €149* *Village Center, Glengarriff* *027/63000* *www.glengarriffpark.com* *No credit cards* *26 rooms* *Free Breakfast.*

Chapter 8

THE SOUTHWEST

Updated by
Vic O'Sullivan

Sights ★★★★★ | Restaurants ★★★★★ | Hotels ★★★★★ | Shopping ★★★★★ | Nightlife ★★★☆☆

WELCOME TO THE SOUTHWEST

TOP REASONS TO GO

★ **The Ring of Kerry:** The most brazenly scenic coastal drive in Ireland might have been designed with the visitor in mind—cameras and videos at the ready!

★ **Skellig Michael:** Kerry's end-of-world beauty on display at this UNESCO World Heritage site is captured in *Star Wars: The Force Awakens* and can be visited by boat from the mainland.

★ **The Dingle Peninsula:** This narrow strip of land with its miles of dramatic coastline and hair-raising views draws a steady stream of visitors throughout the year.

★ **Adare:** Discover one of Ireland's prettiest villages by walking past its thatched cottages to the banks of the River Maigue, where the remains of priories established by medieval monks still stand.

★ **Limerick City:** Limerick has become one of the finest urban locations in Europe, with excellent pubs, hotels, and restaurants nestled between world-class attractions, set with a Shannon River backdrop.

1 **Killarney and Nearby.** Nineteenth-century visitors found the views of Killarney every bit as romantic and uplifting as the mountains of Switzerland; the unique combination of glacial landscape and abundant subtropical vegetation, studded by the bright blue waters of the lakes, creates an unforgettable vista—and it smells good, too, with peat-fire smoke mingling with fresh mountain air.

2 **Kenmare.** A lively little town, its streets lined with restaurants and boutiques, Kenmare is a natural stopping place where the roads from Bantry and Killarney intersect.

3 **Sneem.** This small, lively village with brightly colored houses is a highlight of the lush, sheltered southern route of the Ring of Kerry.

4 **Waterville.** Popular with golfers and anglers, and boasting spectacular sea views on its eastern approach, this is a popular holiday spot for outdoors types.

5 **The Skelligs and Valentia.** Two of Ireland's most westerly points, sheltered Valentia Island contrasts with the wild offshore vista of the rocky, twin-peaked Skelligs of Star Wars fame.

6 **Cahirciveen.** Its main market town, Cahirciveen has the Ring's only sizeable supermarket and an interesting heritage center.

7 **Glenbeigh.** Blink and you miss the village, it's so tiny, but follow the signs for Rossbeigh on its outskirts for a walk on its superb, wild, sandy beach.

8 **Killorglin.** Famous for the annual Puck Fair in August, this little market town on the River Laune is especially lively in summer.

9 **Ring of Kerry.** A stunning 179-km (111-mile) circular route around Kerry's Iveragh Peninsula.

10 **Annascaul.** The wide road in this quiet little village is a relic of its importance as a cattle-trading center in the past century; most visitors today seek out the pub once owned by Polar explorer Tom Crean.

11 **An Daingean (Dingle Town).** Beware, this little Irish-speaking town on a sheltered harbor backed by mountains and abounding in friendly pubs and restaurants just might steal your heart away.

12 **Ceann Tra (Ventry).** More a village than a town, Ventry is chiefly known for its long, sandy beach.

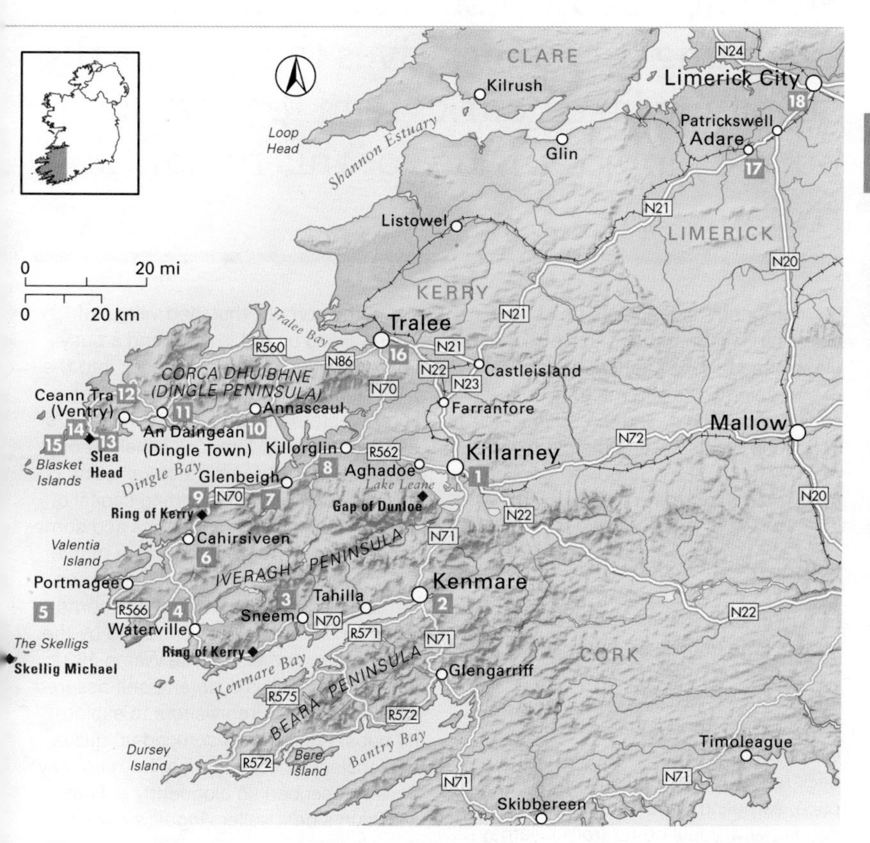

13 Ceann Sléibhe (Slea Head). The rocky southwest extremity of the peninsula boasts dramatic coastal scenery and deserted beaches.

14 Dún Chaoin (Dunquin). Once the mainland harbor for the Blasket islanders, Dún Chaoin now attracts many students of Irish language and folklore.

15 Great Blasket Island. The nimble-footed will enjoy an excursion to this rocky offshore island, which was inhabited by hardy souls until 1953.

16 Tralee. The largest town in County Kerry, Tralee is the county's main business and shopping destination, worth visiting chiefly for its folk theater and excellent museum.

17 Adare. The thatched cottages make this one of Ireland's prettiest villages, but don't miss the monastic remains and imposing manor house, now a luxury hotel.

18 Limerick City. Ireland's third-largest city, and the nearest to Shannon Airport, is located on the wide River Shannon, and has a riverside walk that visits most of its historic attractions.

Ever since Killarney was first "discovered" by William Thackeray and Sir Walter Scott, visitors have been searching for superlatives to describe the deep blue lakes, dark green forests, and purple mountainsides of this romantic region.

While modern-day tour-bus traffic and increased visitor numbers have slightly diminished the experience, the appeal of sweeping lakes and mountains, the ever-changing light, and the unusual flora and fauna persists—and the old tales resurrected by the tour guides continue to cast a mesmerizing spell.

The region stretches from the Ring of Kerry in the south, the Dingle Peninsula in the west, through Killarney and north to Adare, and Limerick City—and is replete with unpolluted beaches and rivers, easy access to golf, wild scenery, and, above all, places where locals still take time to stop and talk. So take your cue from them and venture onto the back roads. Meander along at your own pace, sampling wayside delights. Before you know it, you'll be far from Killarney town's crowds and in the middle of the region's tranquil and incredibly stunning landscapes.

If Mother Nature doesn't cooperate, there is always the bounty of historic and man-made attractions. Move northward towards south County Limerick's wild Ballyhoura country. It's the homeland of President John F. Kennedy's ancestors (Fitzgerald side)—a mountainous landscape with adrenaline-pumping bike trails, which plateau as the scenery becomes less dramatic but much cozier, like in the comely, thatched village of Adare. Head up to Limerick and a busy four-lane highway hurls you back into the 21st century. The metropolitan hub of southwestern Ireland (and the republic's third-largest city), Limerick is half Georgian, half medieval architecturally, and is quickly becoming the sporting capital of Ireland. It hosts city marathons and some of the greatest rugby and hurling matches in the country, having shed its down-at-the-heels backstory that it has borne since its city walls were besieged by the English during the Jacobite War in 1691. Today's Limerick is a vibrant, self-assured metropolis that lures visitors to explore its pubs, restaurants, spruced-up quays, and ancient lanes—a far cry from its gray days—described so eloquently in Frank McCourt's best seller *Angela's Ashes*.

MAJOR REGIONS

The Ring of Kerry. One of Europe's great scenic drives, a highlight of the Wild Atlantic Way, the route runs around the edge of this rocky peninsula, passing from the subtropical splendor of Sneem, on the sheltered Kenmare River, past Waterville and onward to Portmagee where ferries depart for UNESCO World Heritage site Skellig Michael. Travel to the north for the starker views of Dingle Bay, where stunning mountain and coastal views are around almost every turn. The only drawback: on a sunny day, it seems like half the nation's visitors are traveling along this two-lane road, packed into buses, riding bikes, or backpacking. The route is narrow and curvy, and the local sheep think nothing of using it for a nap: take it slowly.

The gorgeously scenic **Dingle Peninsula** stretches for some 48 km (30 miles) between Tralee (pronounced "tra- *lee*") in the east and Ceann Sléibhe (Slea Head) in the west. Often referred to by its Irish name, Corca Dhuibhne (pronounced "cor-kah-guy-nay"), the peninsula is made up of rugged mountains, seaside cliffs, and softly molded glacial valleys and lakes. Long, sandy beaches and Atlantic-pounded cliffs unravel along the coast. Drystone walls enclose small, irregular fields, and exceptional prehistoric and early Christian remains dot the countryside. As you drive over its mountain passes, looking out past prehistoric remains to the wild Atlantic sea, the raw scenery casts a peaceful lost-in-time spell. Unfortunately, the peninsula is notorious for its heavy rainfall and impenetrable sea mists, which can strike at any time of year. If they do, sit them out in An Daingean (Dingle Town) and enjoy the friendly bars, cafés, and crafts shops.

■ TIP→ **West of Annascaul, the peninsula is Irish-speaking: English is considered a second language. A good Irish–English map can prove handy.**

North Kerry and County Limerick have rich green pastures, known as the Golden Vale, with rolling hills and crystal clear streams that flow through its valleys. Quaint villages often appear unexpectedly around the bend of a country lane—like Adare, coined "Ireland's Prettiest Village," with its charming thatched cottages (and Adare Manor, one of Ireland's most grand and ostentatious hotels). Confident and alluring, Limerick City is the area's capital that straddles the Shannon, the longest river in both Ireland and Britain. It's a tale of two cities—a medieval network of narrow lanes that gushes into a broad, wide-open Georgian grid with redbrick town houses and broad avenues. It was once the sad backdrop to Frank McCourt's international best seller, *Angela's Ashes*; but after a billion-euro makeover, it's basking in the glow of a metropolitan renaissance.

Planning

Getting Here and Around

AIR

The Southwest can be accessed most conveniently from two international airports: Cork (ORK) on the southwest coast, and Shannon (SNN) in the west (26 km [16 miles] west of Limerick City). Cork Airport is about 80 minutes drive from both Killarney and Kenmare. Shannon Airport is 135 km (84 miles) from Killarney via Limerick, a journey that takes about two hours. Dublin Airport is 312 km (195 miles) from Killarney and 208 km (130 miles) from Limerick City. Kerry County Airport (KIR) at Farranfore, 16 km (10 miles) from Killarney, has daily flights from Dublin and London (Stansted and Luton), with twice-weekly flights from Frankfurt (Hahn), Berlin Schönefeld, and Manchester.

AIRPORT INFORMATION Kerry County Airport. ✉ *N23, Farranfore, Killarney* ☎ *066/976–4644* 🌐 *kerryairport.ie.*

AIRPORT TRANSFERS

You'll find taxis directly outside the terminal building. Bus Éireann runs direct bus services to Killarney, Tralee, and Limerick, connecting to a nationwide bus and rail network. Tickets may be bought on board.

CONTACTS Bus Éireann. ☎ *01/836–6111* 🌐 *buseireann.ie.*

BUS

Bus Éireann operates express services from Dublin and Cork to Limerick City and Tralee. Buseireann's Expressway Service links Limerick, Tralee, and Killarney and bus stations are located outside the railway stations in all towns. Dublin Coach–M7 Express 300 links Dublin, Limerick, Killarney, and Tralee with a regular daily service from 6 am until late. Bus Éireann runs a regular local bus service from Tralee to Dingle and around the Ring of Kerry between mid-June and mid-September with a scaled-back service in winter. Check ahead as these frequently change. A Leap Card (🌐 *leapcard.ie*) bought online saves money on fares.

CONTACTS Bus Éireann. ☎ *01/836–6111 in Dublin, 061/313–333 in Limerick, 066/716–4700 in Tralee* 🌐 *buseireann.ie.*

CAR

Despite high costs of rental and fuel, a car is still a popular way to explore this region, packed as it is with scenic routes, attractive but remote towns, and a host of out-of-the-way restaurants and hotels that deserve a detour.

The main driving route from Dublin is the N7 Motorway, which goes 192 km (120 miles) directly to Limerick City. If you land at Shannon Airport, access to the Southwest is also via Limerick City; from there, pick up the N21 to Killarney. From Limerick it is about two hours to Killarney (111 km [69 miles]), and another half hour to Kenmare. Many people prefer to fly from Dublin to Kerry Airport (40 minutes) and pick up a rental car there.

TAXI

A taxi from Shannon Airport to Limerick City costs between €40 and €55. It costs €4.10 to hire a taxi on the street (€4.45 at night); add €2 to book one by phone and €1.14 per kilometer. Full details of fares and conditions are on the National Transport Authority's website.

Taxis are also found in town centers and at train stations in Tralee, Killarney, and Limerick, and at Shannon and Kerry airports. Otherwise, they must be prebooked by phone: ask for the number of the local company at your hotel or bed-and-breakfast.

CONTACTS Killarney Cabs. ✉ *Killarney* ☎ *087/228–8822* 🌐 *killarneycabs.com.* **Tralee Radio Taxis.** ✉ *Tralee* ☎ *066/712–5451* 🌐 *traleeradiotaxis.com.*

TRAIN

The region is accessible by train from Dublin Heuston Station and from Cork's Kent Station. From Dublin the region is served by two direct rail links, to Limerick Junction (where you change trains for Limerick City), and on to Tralee (via Mallow). The rail network is useful for moving from one touring base to another. Buy a Leap Card online for steeply discounted fares.

⇨ *For more information on getting here and around, see "Travel Smart Ireland."*

Hotels

For accommodations, the Southwest has some of the great country houses, including Adare Manor in County Limerick; Kenmare's unique duo of the magnificent Sheen Falls Lodge and the stately Park Hotel and finally the rambling landmark resort, the Parknasilla Resort in Sneem, a great place for a family break. At the other end of the spectrum is the uniquely Irish experience of a farmhouse B&B, such as Lakelands Farm Guesthouse in Waterville, with rowboats bobbing on Lough Currane at the bottom of the garden. In between is a range of excellent family-owned and-run traditional hotels, such as the Brook Lane Hotel in Kenmare, the Butler Arms in Waterville, and the secluded Carrig Country House at Glenbeigh near Killorglin. Limerick City has top-of-the-range modern hotels like The Strand, which overlooks the River Shannon, or The Savoy in the city center.

Restaurants

Kenmare, Dingle, and Killarney all have a high density of restaurants serving locally raised meat, artisanal cheeses, and local seafood. Kerry mountain lamb has a unique flavor imparted by the wild herbs and grasses that those sheep you see on every hillside are busy munching. Adare also has an array of tempting restaurants; the elegant comfort food of Restaurant 1826 or the sophisticated offerings in a clubby backdrop at The Carriage House in Adare Manor's rambling estate. Limerick City has a pedigree of fine Italian dining stretching back to World War II and top-notch cooking in arguably the finest selection of gastropubs in Ireland.

RESTAURANT AND HOTEL PRICES

⇨ *Restaurant prices are the average cost of a main course at dinner or, if dinner is not served, at lunch. Hotel prices are the lowest cost of a standard double room in high season. Restaurant and hotel reviews have been shortened. For full information, visit Fodors.com.*

What It Costs in Euros

$	$$	$$$	$$$$
RESTAURANTS			
under €19	€19–€24	€25–€32	over €32
HOTELS			
under €120	€120–€170	€171–€210	over €210

Tours

BUS TOURS

Many of the tours listed here can be booked through the Killarney Tourist Office.

Bus Éireann

BUS TOURS | A range of daylong and half-day guided tours are offered from June to September. You can book them at the bus station in Killarney, or at any tourist office. The memorable Gap of Dunloe Tour includes a coach; you can add on a private horse-drawn jaunting-car ride through the Gap. More conventional day trips can also be made to the Ring of Kerry, An Daingean (Dingle), and Ceann Sléibhe (Slea Head), and to Caragh Lake and Rossbeigh. Full-day tours depart at 10:30 am and return at 5 pm, and the price does not include lunch and refreshments. ☎ *061/313–333 in Limerick, 066/716–4700 in Tralee, 064/663–0011 in Killarney* 🌐 *buseireann.ie* 🎫 *From €25.*

SPECIAL-INTEREST TOURS

Hidden Ireland Tours

SPECIAL-INTEREST TOURS | Cultural hiking trips by knowledgeable guides Con Moriarty and Ann Curran are some of the highlights on offer from long-running Hidden Ireland Tours. Providing personalized journeys to couples, families, and small groups, each trip is customized with hidden, local gems at its heart. Independent travelers wishing to hike or explore with a Hidden Ireland Tours guide for a day can also be accommodated. ☎ *087/221–4002* 🌐 *www.hiddenirelandtours.com.*

When to Go

The best times to visit the Ring of Kerry, Killarney, and Dingle are mid-March to June, and September and October. In July and August it's the peak holiday period, meaning roads are more crowded, prices are higher, and the best places are booked in advance. March can be chilly, with daily temperatures in the 40s and 50s. The average high in June is 65°F (18°C), and the temperature varies little from that. May and June are the sunniest months, while May and September are the driest months. The farther west you go, the more likely you'll get rain. The weather is not such a crucial factor in Adare and the Limerick area, but from November to mid-March daylight hours are short, the weather is damp, and

Walking Tours

Gap of Dunloe. A full-day bus, bike, and jaunting-car tour allows you to experience the best of Killarney, including a beautiful boat trip across the three Lakes of Killarney, followed by a 90-minute journey off-road through the Gap of Dunloe in a trap—a horse-drawn carriage. A shorter bus and boat option allows you to go at your own pace and enjoy the 2½- to 3-hour walk through the Gap. ✉ *O'Connor's Pub, 7 High St., Killarney* ☎ *064/663–0200* 🌐 *gapofdunloetours.com* 🎫 *From €25.*

Ireland Walk Hike Bike. A Kerry-based active holiday provider specializing in guided and self-guided hiking and cycling tours of the county and country. Self-drive holidays with or without a specific focus on activity can also be arranged. ✉ *Box 372, Tralee* ☎ *066/718–6181, 087/250–2434* 🌐 *irelandwalkhikebike.com.*

Killarney Guided Walks. Run by Richard Clancy, a noted historian, these tours feature a two-hour walk in Killarney National Park daily at 11 am; departures are from outside O'Shea's Funeral Home, opposite the cathedral in Killarney. No booking is required except November through April when you should phone ahead of time. ✉ *New St., Killarney* ☎ *087/639–4362* 🌐 *killarneyguidedwalks.com* 🎫 *€12.*

many smaller places on the Kerry coast and in Killarney are closed.

Festivals and Events

In common with many areas of Ireland, there's plenty going on in the Southwest, with a number of high-profile festivals that are well worth taking into account when deciding when to visit. These are just a few of the highlights; tourist offices will have details of others.

Listowel Writers' Week

FESTIVALS | Big names and beginners rub shoulders at this major event on the Irish literary calendar, which takes over the small North Kerry town for five days in late May and early June. Workshops for all levels combine with readings and panel discussions with national and international writers, cultural tours, and prize-giving events, including the National Poetry Award. ✉ *Listowel* ☎ *068/21074* 🌐 *writersweek.ie.*

Puck Fair

FESTIVALS | Expect big crowds at one of Ireland's oldest fairs—it celebrated its 405th year in 2018. It's held over three days starting August 10 in the streets of Killorglin. On day one, a goat is crowned King Puck, and horses are traded in the traditional manner. All three days feature street stalls, a fun fair (midway), and free entertainment, including traditional music and dancing. ✉ *Killorglin* ☎ *066/976–2366* 🌐 *puckfair.ie.*

Rose of Tralee International Festival

FESTIVALS | The town of Tralee is en fête for five days in mid-August with street theater, parades, fireworks, and big-name concerts. The highlight is a televised two-evening show in which young women from the Irish diaspora compete for the title of Rose, as they have done since 1959, with very few concessions to changing times. ✉ *Tralee* ☎ *066/712–1322* 🌐 *roseoftralee.ie.*

Planning Your Time

If you're here for a short stay—three or fewer days—you'd do well to base yourself in Killarney and devote your time to exploring the surrounding area, then heading out to the Ring of Kerry or the Dingle Peninsula. With more time at your disposal, consider a half-day trip to Skellig Michael, an unforgettable remote, rock-hewn monastery, or Adare, one of Ireland's prettiest villages.

You will also want to pick your peninsula, for two of Ireland's most scenic destinations sit side by side on the map: the Iveragh Peninsula (also known as the Ring of Kerry) and Dingle. If you like wild landscapes, white sandy beaches, archaeological remains, and dramatic ocean views, them Dingle is for you. In contrast, the Ring of Kerry is a longer drive with more varied scenery punctuated by a series of small villages, with views that range from lush subtropical vegetation to rocky coves and long sandy beaches near Glenbeigh.

IF YOU HAVE THREE DAYS

Spend the first day driving the Ring of Kerry, pausing often to take in the varied coastal scenery. Spend the night in Kenmare or Killarney, then head out the next morning to explore Killarney National Park either on a boat trip or in a horse-drawn jaunting car. Next head for Dingle and drive the Slea Head loop, before enjoying fresh seafood and live traditional music in Dingle Town, a good overnight stop. On your third morning, drive the Conor Pass to Tralee, heading away from the rugged coast to rich farmlands and toward the pretty village of historic Adare. Finish the day with a riverside walk before winding down the night in the shadow of St. Mary's Cathedral at George's Quay in Limerick City.

Visitor Information

Fáilte Ireland (🌐 *failteireland.ie*) provides a free information service in its tourist information offices (TIOs) which also sell a selection of tourist literature. Fáilte Ireland's TIOs will book accommodations for you anywhere in Ireland. Seasonal TIOs in Waterville, Cahirciveen, and Valentia are open from June to September; the TIO in Kenmare is open from Easter to October. Opening times vary, but many are generally open Monday to Saturday 9–6; in July and August they are also open Sunday 9–6. Year-round TIOs can be found in Adare, An Daingean/Dingle, Killarney, Limerick, Shannon Airport, and Tralee. These offices are usually open Monday to Saturday 9–6 and also Sunday 9–6 in July and August.

Killarney and Nearby

87 km (54 miles) west of Cork City, 19 km (12 miles) southeast of Killorglin, 24 km (15 miles) north of Glengarriff.

One of Southwest Ireland's landmark locales, Killarney is also the most heavily visited town in the region (its proximity to the Ring of Kerry and the Dingle Peninsula helps to ensure this).

Killarney is famous for its setting, not for the town, a point to bear in mind in order to avoid disappointment. Killarney town was one of the first places in Europe to owe its existence almost entirely to the tourism industry. Victorian visitors came for the region's dramatic lake scenery and the arrival of the railroad ensured its growing popularity. Today Killarney is a small, low-key town lined with shops and eateries firmly targeted at the numerous visitors; it's also a popular holiday destination for Irish visitors, yet it retains the traditional friendliness of less-famous towns. There's a lively restaurant scene, and a range of crafts and clothing shops, but you may want to limit time spent there if jaded nightclubs, Irish cabarets, amateur drama and singing pubs—a local specialty—aren't your thing.

The nightlife is at its liveliest from May to September. At other times, particularly from November to mid-March, when many of the hotels are closed, the town is quiet to the point of being eerie. Given the choice, go to Killarney in April, May, or early October.

Light rain is typical of the area, but because of the topography, it seldom lasts long. And the clouds' approach over the lakes and the subsequent showers can actually add to the scenery. The rain is often followed within minutes by brilliant sunshine and, yes, sometimes even a rainbow.

GETTING HERE AND AROUND

Killarney is about 1½ hours from Cork on the N22, about two hours from Shannon Airport via Limerick on the N21/23/22. From Shannon Airport be sure to take the tunnel (toll €2) route when approaching Limerick, rather than driving through the center of the city. The main car park in Killarney is near the tourist information office in the town center, and there are others around the town, all operated on a "pay-and-display" basis during business hours. The town is well served by Expressway buses and has a rail link to Dublin (three hours, 20 minutes) and Cork (two hours, 30 minutes). The bus and train stations are adjacent to each other, in the center of town, with taxi ranks. Most B&Bs and hotels offer a pickup service. Elsewhere, taxis should be prebooked by phone.

There is no local bus service in Killarney town; the traditional way to get around, especially if you plan to visit the car-free Muckross Park, is to hire one of the famous ponies and traps, known as "jaunting cars." The leading jaunting, bus, and boat tour operator is Killarney Jaunting Cars. An hour's "jaunt" for four people costs about €80. Jaunting cars can be prebooked and will collect you at your hotel (see below for booking information) or hired at the junction of Main Street and East Avenue. From April to October a shuttle bus service operates from the Killarney Tourist Office and is a good way to see out-of-town sights including Muckross House and Farms, the Gap of Dunloe, and Ladies' View.

TIP→ From mid-March to September you can view the national park by taking a water-coach cruise on the Lily of Killarney boat from Ross Castle (one hour, €12); book at the Killarney Tourist Office.

CONTACTS Killarney Bus and Train Station. ✉ *East Ave., Killarney* ☎ *064/663–0011 bus station, 064/663–1067 train station.* **Killarney Jaunting Cars Ltd/Tangney Tours.** ✉ *Gilhuys, 10B Muckross Close, Killarney* ☎ *064/663–3358* 🌐 *killarneyjauntingcars.ie.*

VISITOR INFORMATION

CONTACTS Discover Ireland Centre. ✉ *Aras Fáilte, Beech Rd., Killarney* ☎ *064/663–1633* 🌐 *killarney.ie.*

Sights

Yes, the Lakes of Killarney really are sapphire blue (at least when the sun is out), and, seen from a distance, the MacGillicuddy's Reeks really are purple. Add a glacial landscape with a glorious waterfall, and acres of subtropical flora and trees, and you're starting to get the picture.

Aghadoe

RUINS | This is an outstanding place to get a feel for what Killarney is all about: lake and mountain scenery. Stand beside Aghadoe's 12th-century ruined church and Round Tower, and watch the shadows creep gloriously across Lower Lake, with Innisfallen Island in the distance and the Gap of Dunloe to the west. ✉ *Killarney* ✣ *5 km (3 miles) west of Killarney on Beaufort–Killorglin road.*

★ Gap of Dunloe

NATURE SIGHT | Massive, glacial rocks form the sides of this narrow mountain pass that stretches for 6½ km (4 miles) between MacGillicuddy's Reeks and the Purple Mountains. The Gap is a natural auditorium where sound waves can bounce from stone to return—creating almost an echo chamber, which can be fun to test out with a short sharp shout. Five small lakes lie along the route. Cars are banned from the Gap, but in summer the first 3 km stretch (2 miles) is busy with horse and foot traffic, much of which turns back at the halfway point. The entrance to the Gap is 10 km (7 miles) west of Killarney at Beaufort on the N72 Killorglin Road. If you drive or are on a tour bus, stop here and either hire a pony and trap or opt to walk. One advantage to an organized tour—and a popular option—is that, without the need to get back to your car, you can amble through the parkland as far as Lord Brandon's Cottage, then get a prebooked boat back to Killarney town. ✉ *N72 (Killorglin Rd.), Beaufort.*

Innisfallen Island

ISLAND | The monastic ruins on Innisfallen Island include a Celtic cross and date from the 6th or 7th century. Between AD 950 and 1350 the *Annals of Innisfallen* were compiled here by monks. (The book survives in the Bodleian Library in Oxford.) There is a rough walking trail around the island, a wishing stone, and wild deer, but don't expect any facilities. On a sunny day, this is a charming place to take a picnic. From Ross Castle, row yourself over or let a boatman-guide take you out to the island (both options €12), or you can join a cruise (€12) from the castle, in a covered, heated launch. ✉ *Killarney.*

Kate Kearney's Cottage

RESTAURANT | At the entrance to the Gap of Dunloe, Kate Kearney's Cottage is a good place to rent a jaunting car or pony. Kate was a famous beauty who sold illegal *poitín* (moonshine) from her home, contributing greatly, one suspects, to travelers' enthusiasm for the scenery. Appropriately enough, Kearney's is now a pub and restaurant, and a good place to pause for an Irish coffee. ✉ *Gap of Dunloe, Beaufort* ☎ *064/664–4146* 🌐 *katekearneyscottage.com* ⏲ *Closed 2 wks from Jan. 6.*

Killarney House and Gardens

GARDEN | FAMILY | Once hidden away for many years behind tall walls in the center of town, Killarney House is now the official visitor center to Killarney National Park. Dating from the early 1700s, the house was originally the stable block of a more imposing manor that burned down in 1913. Today it contains a museum with information about Killarney Town and an interactive exhibition about the flora and fauna of Killarney National Park, as well as changing art exhibits relating to the area. The long-established formal gardens, spread over 30 acres, have been restored to their original 1720s French layout, and are enhanced by the natural backdrop of Killarney's wild mountains under a huge, ever-changing sky. There are easily accessible walks laid out in the grounds, and free guided tours every half hour. ✉ *Killarney House, Dromhale, Killarney National Park, Killarney* ✣ *Enter by Countess Gates beside Kenmare Pl. (where pony and traps wait), or 2 smaller gates on Mission Rd. (R877)* ☎ *01/539–3620, 076/100–2620* 🌐 *killarneynationalpark.ie.*

Killarney National Park

NATIONAL PARK | The three Lakes of Killarney and the mountains and woods that surround them make up this beautiful national park. It extends to nearly 25,000 acres, which includes oak, holly, and yew woodlands, and is populated by red deer. The National Park Visitor Centre in town offers an audiovisual presentation that is a good introduction to what you can explore on the signposted self-guiding trails that thread the park.

The heart of the park is Muckross House & Gardens, which is 6 km (4 miles) from

Killarney on N71. You can drive, walk, rent a bicycle, or take a traditional jaunting car (pony and a cart) to the house and from there explore this amazing landscape by foot or bicycle.

The air here smells of damp woods and heather moors. The red fruits of the Mediterranean strawberry tree (*Arbutus unedo*) are at their peak in October and November, which is also about the time when the bracken turns rust color, contrasting with the evergreens. In late April and early May, the purple flowers of the rhododendron *ponticum* put on a spectacular display. ✉ *Muckross Rd., Killarney* 🌐 *killarneynationalpark.ie* 🎫 *Free* 🕒 *Hrs vary seasonally.*

★ Ladies' View

VIEWPOINT | This famed viewpoint, with a stunning panorama of the three lakes and the surrounding mountains, is especially glorious on a sunny day, but worth a visit in any weather. The name goes back to 1861, when Queen Victoria was a guest at Muckross House. Upon seeing the view, her ladies-in-waiting were said to have been dumbfounded by its beauty. You may find yourself speechless, too, so be sure to bring your camera. ✣ *19 km (12 miles) southwest of Killarney on N71 in Kenmare direction.*

Lord Brandon's Cottage

RESTAURANT | The Gap of Dunloe's southern end, 7 km (4½ miles) west of Killarney, is marked by Lord Brandon's Cottage, a 19th-century hunting lodge that is now a basic tea shop serving soup and sandwiches. From here, a path leads to the edge of Upper Lake, where you can journey onward by rowboat (a traditional wooden boat with a motor)—but only if you have booked it in advance. It's an old tradition for the boatman to carry a bugle and illustrate the echoes. The boat passes under Brickeen Bridge and into Middle Lake, where 30 islands are steeped in legends, many of which your boatman is likely to recount. Look out for caves on the left-hand side on this narrow stretch of water. ✉ *Gap of Dunloe, Beaufort* 🕒 *Closed Oct.–Apr.*

Muckross Friary

RUINS | The monks were driven out of this 15th-century Franciscan friary by Oliver Cromwell's army in 1652, but it's amazingly complete (rare among Irish ruins), although roofless. An ancient yew tree rises above the cloisters and breaks out over the abbey walls. Three flights of stone steps allow access to the upper floors and living quarters, where you can visit the cloisters and what was once the dormitory, kitchen, and refectory. ✉ *Muckross Rd. (N71), Killarney* ✣ *4 km (2½ miles) south of Killarney—a short walk from car park on N71* ☎ *076/100–2620* 🌐 *killarneynationalpark.ie* 🎫 *Free.*

★ Muckross House

FARM/RANCH | FAMILY | This ivy-clad Victorian manor is located next door to Killarney National Park Visitor Center. Upstairs, elegantly furnished rooms are stuffed with, in typical Victorian fashion, rugs, animal wall mounts, and idiosyncratic decorative furnishing and, of course—china—which was commissioned for England's Queen Victoria's visit back in 1861. Paintings are original—and include the works of John Butler Yeats (father of artist Jack and poet William) and John Singer Sargent. The upstairs lifestyle of the landed gentry in the 1800s contrasts with the conditions of servants employed in the basement of Muckross House.

The magnificent informal grounds are noted for their rhododendrons and azaleas, the water garden, and the outstanding limestone rock garden. In the park beside the house, the Muckross Traditional Farms include reconstructed farm buildings and outbuildings, a blacksmith's forge, a carpenter's workshop, and a selection of farm animals. It's a reminder of the way things were done on the farm before electricity and the mechanization of farming. Meet and chat with the farmers and their wives as they go about their work. You'll also find folk displays where potters, bookbinders, and weavers demonstrate their crafts. The visitor center has a shop and a restaurant. ✉ *Muckross Rd. (N71), Killarney ✣ 5 km (3 miles) south of Killarney, signposted from N71 ☎ 064/667–0144 🌐 muckross-house.ie 🎫 From €7; visitor center free ⏲ Farms closed Nov. 21–Mar.; Apr. and Oct., closed weekdays.*

Ross Castle

CASTLE/PALACE | A fully restored 15th-century stronghold of the O'Donoghue Ross clan, sited on the lower lake 2 km (1 mile) south of town, this castle was the last place in the province of Munster to fall to Oliver Cromwell's forces in 1652. You can see its curtain walls, towers, and display of 16th- and 17th-century furniture on a 40-minute guided tour. ✉ *Knockreer Estate, Muckross Rd. (N71), Killarney ☎ 064/663–5851 🌐 heritageireland.ie/places-to-visit/ross-castle 🎫 €5 ⏲ Closed Nov.–Feb.*

Torc Waterfall

WATERFALL | FAMILY | You reach this roaring, 65-foot-high cascade by a footpath that begins in the parking lot outside the gates of the Muckross Park, 8 km (5 miles) south of Killarney. After your first view of the Torc, which will appear after about a 10-minute walk, it's worth the climb up a long flight of stone steps to the second, less-frequented clearing. ✉ *Muckross Rd. (N71), Killarney ✣ 300-meter walk from car park on N71.*

 Restaurants

Bricín

$$ | IRISH | Candles and an open fire cast a warm light on Persian-style rugs and dark red walls hung with antique engravings of Killarney at this cozy little eatery set above a ground-floor craft emporium on the main street, while simple country-style wooden tables and stick-back chairs are set within "snug" areas created by stained-glass panels. The good-value menu features boxty (Irish potato pancake) with a choice of fillings, including vegetarian. **Known for:** warm and friendly staff; offers a great €40 set menu; amazing dessert selection. Ⓢ *Average main: €20 ✉ 26 High St., Killarney ☎ 064/663–4902 🌐 bricin.ie ⏲ Closed Jan. 7–early Mar.; closed Sun. and Mon. Mar.–Nov., and Sun.–Wed. Nov.–Jan.*

Treyvaud's

$$$ | EUROPEAN | FAMILY | Step behind the Victorian arched facade here and you'll discover a buzzing contemporary restaurant, masterminded by the two Treyvaud brothers (one a popular TV chef), that features classic Irish dishes (e.g., fish cakes, sausages, or bacon and cabbage) with a continental twist. The interior is simple—pine floorboards, wood-beam ceiling, lines of red-back chairs—so the food takes center stage. **Known for:** wide selection of game, including rabbit, wild boar, pheasant, and quail; fantastic levels of service; melt-in-your-mouth duck confit. Ⓢ *Average main: €25 ✉ 62 High St., Killarney ☎ 064/663–3062 🌐 treyvaudsrestaurant.com.*

Killarney has a vast array of accommodations, from five-star, fully serviced properties to basic quarters located in the town and park.

★ Cahernane House Hotel

$$$$ | HOTEL | Dating from 1877, this imposing gray-stone house, once the residence of the earls of Pembroke, sits at the end of a long private avenue through a tunnel of trees—a refuge from the touristy buzz of Killarney town. **Pros:** great old-world atmosphere; very luxe; fantastic views. **Cons:** standard rooms are disappointingly plain; lots of weddings; rooms in new wing lack character of those in main house. Ⓢ *Rooms from: €309 ✉ Muckross Rd., Killarney ☎ 064/663–1895 🌐 cahernane.com ⏲ Closed Jan. and Feb. 🛏 48 rooms 🍽 Free Breakfast.*

The beauty gauge buries the needle at the Gap of Dunloe, considered by many to be the scenic star of the Lakes of Killarney region.

Hotel Europe

$$$$ | **HOTEL** | **FAMILY** | The rooms at the Europe are chic and most have private balconies with commanding views over gardens, mountains and Killarney's largest lake. **Pros:** solid on-site dining options (with plenty of kids' options); warm, attentive staff; spacious rooms. **Cons:** outside Killarney; architecturally of its time (1965); can be expensive for the area. *Rooms from: €320 ✉ Ring of Kerry, Killarney ✣ 6½ km (4 miles) west of Killarney Town on N72 (Ring of Kerry) ☎ 064/667–1300 🌐 theeurope.com ⊙ Closed Christmas and Easter 187 rooms 🍴 Free Breakfast.*

★ **Killarney Park Hotel**

$$$$ | **HOTEL** | This luxurious hotel, a distinctive yellow-painted building in landscaped grounds, is a few minutes' walk from the train station, shops, and restaurants, making it an excellent base for visitors without a car. **Pros:** spa with 20-meter pool and outdoor hot tub; drawing room and library host full afternoon teas in front of an open fire; warm and welcoming staff. **Cons:** no lake or mountain views; popular wedding venue; sells out well in advance July and August. *Rooms from: €365 ✉ East Ave. (N71), Killarney ☎ 064/663–5555 🌐 killarneyparkhotel.ie 68 rooms 🍴 Free Breakfast.*

Killarney Plaza Hotel

$$$$ | **HOTEL** | **FAMILY** | Pushing hard against the standard magnolia and MDF craze that has gripped many of Ireland's midrange properties over the last decade—the Killarney Plaza Hotel is all about glamour and high-quality finish. **Pros:** leisure center with gym, hot tub, and swimming pool; beautiful full-service spa; excellent location. **Cons:** area can be gridlocked with visitors in season; classic interiors give little indication of location; limited underground parking spots. *Rooms from: €348 ✉ Killarney ☎ 064/662–1111 🌐 killarneyplaza.com 198 rooms 🍴 Free Breakfast.*

Nightlife

BARS AND PUBS

★ Courtney's Bar

PUBS | With its selection of more than 60 Irish and 30 Scottish whiskeys and a vast range of Irish craft beers, this family-run traditional bar in the town center is an excellent spot for discovering Ireland's distilling and brewing traditions. A favorite of local and visiting musicians, it hosts live traditional sessions Monday to Thursday in season, with live contemporary music every Friday night. ✉ *24 Plunkett St., Killarney* ☎ *064/663–2689* 🌐 *courtneysbar.com.*

★ JM Reidy's

PUBS | Informally known as "the Sweetshop Pub" this much-loved Killarney landmark, bang in the center of town, dates from 1870 and was recently given a sensitive makeover. The sweets are still there in jars, but one side of the pub now serves coffee, cakes, and light snacks, while the other is a regular pub. Both sides of the establishment are decorated with a fascinating collection of memorabilia. It's a great place to meet the locals. ✉ *4–5 Main St., Killarney* ☎ *066/663–2546* 🌐 *reidyskillarney.com.*

Performing Arts

LIVE MUSIC

Gleneagles

LIVE MUSIC | This is the place for big-name Irish acts to local amateur drama productions—comedian Dara O'Briain, singer Hozier and dance trope Riverdance appear regularly—at the Irish National Events Centre (INEC) within the hotel. Gleneagles also has a bar with nightly live music. ✉ *Muckross Rd., Killarney* ☎ *064/667–1555* 🌐 *inec.ie.*

Shopping

CLOTHING

Aran Sweater Market

KNITTING | Traditional fisherman's knitwear, designed and knitted in the Aran Islands, can be purchased here. You can acquire an heirloom-quality piece or buy knitting wool and patterns and make your own. ✉ *College Sq., Killarney* ☎ *064/662–3102* 🌐 *aransweatermarket.com.*

Kerry Woollen Mills

MIXED CLOTHING | This mill was established here in the 17th century and still uses the original buildings. Its traditional woolen products, from knitting yarns to hats and capes, make great gifts. The property is signposted off the main road between Killarney and Killorglin. ✉ *Off N72, Beaufort* ☎ *064/664–4122* 🌐 *kerrywoollenmills.ie.*

MacBee's

WOMEN'S CLOTHING | This contemporary boutique stocks the best of high-end Irish and international fashion. ✉ *26 New St., Killarney* ☎ *064/663–3622* 🌐 *macbees.ie.*

Quills Woollen Market

MEN'S CLOTHING | Stop here for the town's largest selection of Irish woolen goods. Quills carries Aran knitwear, tweeds, linens, Celtic jewelry, and Irish gifts. ✉ *1 High St., Killarney* ☎ *064/663–2277* 🌐 *irishgiftsandsweaters.com.*

CRAFTS

The Kilkenny Shop

CRAFTS | Stocking a best-in-class offering of contemporary Irish craft that includes pottery, ironwork, woodwork, art, cut glass, and jewelry. ✉ *3 New St., Killarney* ☎ *064/662–3309* 🌐 *kilkennyshop.com.*

Muckross Craft Center

CRAFTS | Adjacent to Muckross House, the craft center has a wide range of gifts and clothing, as well as a resident weaver, a bookbindery, and Muckross Pottery where Margaret Phelan works on-site producing tableware in attractive glazes including her signature honey and blue collection. ✉ *Muckross House, N71, Killarney* ☎ *064/667–0147* 🌐 *muckross-house.ie.*

MUSIC

Variety Sounds

MUSIC | Visit this specialist music shop for Irish music and songbooks and a collection of Irish musical instruments including tin whistles and bodhrans. ✉ *7 College St., Killarney* ☎ *064/663–5755* 🌐 *facebook.com/VarietySoundsKillarney.*

Activities

BICYCLING

O'Sullivan's Cycles

BIKING | A bicycle is the perfect way to enjoy Killarney's mild air, whether within the confines of the national park or farther afield in the Kerry Highlands, and O'Sullivan's (opposite the tourist office) is a top place to rent bicycles—classic, hybrid, or e-bikes—for either the day or the week. ✉ *Lower New St., Killarney* ☎ *064/663–1282* 🌐 *killarneyrentabike.com* *€20 a day.*

FISHING

Salmon and brown trout populate Killarney's lakes and rivers.

O'Neill's

FISHING | To bag your own salmon or brown trout in Killarney's wondrous lakes and rivers, check out this longtime outfitter of fishing tackle, bait, and licenses. ✉ *6 Plunkett St., Killarney* ☎ *064/663–1970* 🌐 *facebook.com/oneillsofkillarney.*

GOLF

★ Killarney Golf and Fishing Club

GOLF | Located in Killarney's national park, this club is set amid a stunning mixture of mountains, lakes, and forests. There are two 18-hole courses: Mahony's Point, along the shores of Lough Leane, and—the jewel in the crown—water-feature-packed Killeen, four-time host of the Irish Open. Despite the abundance of seaside links, many well-traveled golfers name Killarney their favorite place to play in Ireland. Freshwater fishing is also available here. ✉ *Mahony's Point, N72, Killarney* ✣ *3 km (2 miles) west of Killarney on Kilorglin road* ☎ *064/663–1034* 🌐 *killarneygolfclub.ie* *Killeen from €65 mid-Apr.–mid-Oct.; from €50 mid-Oct.–mid-Apr.; Mahony's Point from €50 mid-Apr.–mid-Oct.; from €40 mid-Oct.–mid-Apr.* *Killeen: 18 holes, 7252 yards, par 72; Mahony's Point: 18 holes, 6780 yards, par 72.*

Ring of Kerry Golf Club

GOLF | Set in 150 acres of rolling South Kerry countryside with magnificent views of the ocean over Kenmare Bay, this mature golf course is fresh from a multimillion-euro makeover under new stewardship. A new clubhouse offers top-notch food. A mix of subtropical characteristics along the parkland, generous sandy fairways and heathland terrain offer a good and challenging game. Guests of The Sheen Falls Hotel have discounted green fees and transport. ✉ *Blackwater, Killarney* ☎ *064/664–2000* 🌐 *www.ringofkerrygolf.com* *Green fees €110.*

HIKING

★ Cronin's Yard

HIKING & WALKING | This is the gateway to the MacGillicuddy's Reeks and traditional starting point for the ascent of Ireland's highest mountain, Carrauntoohil (3,406 feet). Outdoors types will definitely fall in love with Killarney here. Parking at the yard is €2 for the whole day. You can prebook a guide for the ascent, which is about six hours round-trip. For a less strenuous outing, there is a self-guided, signposted 8-km (5-mile) loop of sandy paths and mountain tracks. Lough Cummeenoughter is halfway to the way to the top (or bottom)—at 2,319 feet, it's Ireland's highest lake and a dramatic setting for a swim beneath enormous twin peaks. On your return, enjoy a hot bowl of soup in the tearoom and, especially if the Irish weather has not been kind, luxuriate in a hot shower (small fee). Sleeping bags are available for those who wish to stay in one of the wooden "sleeping pods," and wake up to a stunning view. ✉ *Mealis, Beaufort* ✣ *Drive 10 km (7 miles) west of Killarney to Beaufort on N72 and follow signs to Cronin's Yard* ☎ *064/662–4044* 🌐 *croninsyard.com.*

Kerry Way

HIKING & WALKING | This long-distance walking route—it takes about eight days, start to finish—passes through the Killarney National Park on its way to Glenbeigh. You can get a detailed leaflet about the beautiful but challenging route from the Kerry tourist information office. 🌐 *kerryway.com.*

Mangerton Walking Trail

HIKING & WALKING | You can reach the small tarred road leading to this scenic trail that circles Mangerton Lake (aka Devil's Punch Bowl) by turning left off N71 midway between Muckross Friary and Muckross House (follow the signs).

Muckross Park

HIKING & WALKING | A car-free zone frequented by pony and traps, this park within the Killarney National Park has five signposted nature trails for walkers. Try the 5½-km (3½-mile) Arthur Young's Walk, which passes through old yew and oak woods frequented by sika deer. For a longer hike, take an open boat from Ross Castle to the head of the Upper Lake, then walk back along the lakeside to Muckross House, about 10 km (6 miles). ✉ *Killarney* 🌐 *killarneynationalpark.ie.*

HORSEBACK RIDING

Killarney Riding Stables

HORSEBACK RIDING | **FAMILY** | Trails from one- to three hours into Killarney National Park. Alternatively, book a day or half day of horseback riding on a quiet cob in Killarney National Park, or embark on a three- or six-day Reeks Trail ride through the mountains and woodlands of MacGillicuddy's Reeks. ✉ *N72, Ballydowney* ☎ *064/663–1686* 🌐 *killarneyridingstables.com* 💳 *From €50.*

Kenmare

34 km (21 miles) south of Killarney, 336 km (209 miles) southwest of Dublin.

Located slightly inland without a clear view of Kenmare Bay, Kenmare is a natural stopover for both the Ring of Beara and The Ring of Kerry. Set at the head of the sheltered Kenmare River estuary, this small but bustling market town makes a lively touring base for those who wish to skip its hectic coach-bus-choked neighbor, Killarney, altogether. Galleries, quality restaurants, and gastropubs line the streets while Holy Cross Church Spire is visible from every corner. The town was founded in 1670 by William Petty (Oliver Cromwell's surveyor general, a multitasking entrepreneur), and most of its buildings date from the 18th century, making it one of Ireland's first planned towns.

Kenmare also boasts the top-rated Kenmare Market, with purveyors of organic goods and foodstuffs (March to December, Wednesday 10–5). The shopping is pretty good, too, with Irish high fashion, crafts, and original art vying for your attention.

GETTING HERE AND AROUND

Kenmare is at the intersection of the N71 road that links Bantry and Glengarriff with Killarney, and the N70, which continues around the perimeter road known as the Ring of Kerry. Killarney and Glengarriff are both about 40 to 45 minutes away on scenic mountain roads. Kenmare is a natural stopover between Glengarriff (21 km [13 miles] south) and Killarney (34 km [21 miles] to the north). The mountain pass (N71) from Kenmare to Killarney via Ladies' View is a scenic highlight, offering a stunning first view of the lakes. There is ample parking in Kenmare town center.

A bus route, operated by Bus Éireann, connects Killarney to Kenmare; in summer it continues on around the Ring of Kerry, stopping in all the villages between Kenmare and Killorglin before returning

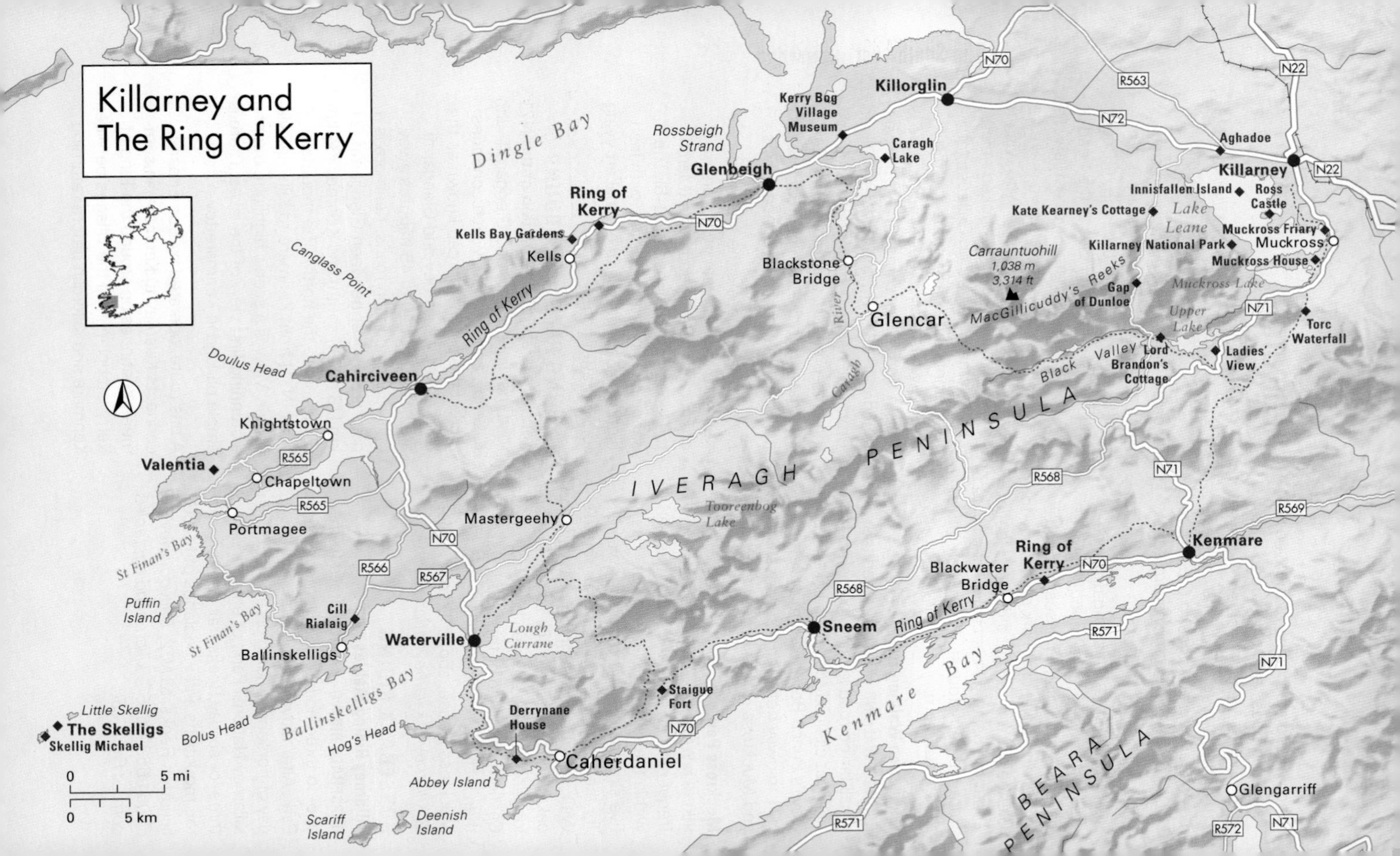
Killarney and
The Ring of Kerry
Dingle Bay
Rossbeigh Strand
Kerry Bog Village Museum
Killorglin
N70
R563
N72
N22
Aghadoe
Killarney
Caragh Lake
Glenbeigh
Ring of Kerry
Kells Bay Gardens
Kells
Canglass Point
Ring of Kerry
Doulus Head
Cahirciveen
Knightstown
Valentia
R565
Chapeltown
Portmagee
St Finan's Bay
Puffin Island
Cill Rialaig
Ballinskelligs
Waterville
Little Skellig
The Skelligs
Skellig Michael
Bolus Head
Ballinskelligs Bay
Hog's Head
Abbey Island
Scariff Island
Deenish Island
0
5 mi
5 km
R566
R567
Mastergeehy
Lough Currane
Derrynane House
Caherdaniel
Staigue Fort
Blackstone Bridge
River
Caragh
Glencar
IVERAGH PENINSULA
Tooreenbog Lake
Carrauntuohill
1,038 m
3,314 ft
MacGillicuddy's Reeks
Gap of Dunloe
Kate Kearney's Cottage
Innisfallen Island
Ross Castle
Lake Leane
Muckross Friary
Muckross
Killarney National Park
Muckross House
Muckross Lake
Upper Lake
N71
Torc Waterfall
Lord Brandon's Cottage
Black Valley
Ladies' View
R568
Kenmare
R569
Ring of Kerry
Blackwater Bridge
Sneem
R571
Kenmare Bay
BEARA PENINSULA
Glengarriff
R572

Bright Waters and Dark Skies

When planning a day out on the water, bear in mind the long days of the Irish summer. In mid-May, the sun rises at 5:40 am and doesn't set until 9:29 pm, while by July the sun is rising at 5:24 am and setting at 9:59 pm. The light will linger for another hour or so on clear evenings.

Once the sun has set, you will be beneath some of the clearest night skies in Europe—providing the mist holds off. Southwest Kerry is recognized as the Kerry International Dark Sky Reserve due to the lack of light pollution in the area—and is one of only two of its kind in Ireland—the other being Ballycroy National Park in County Mayo. Over the Ring of Kerry an unusual array of phenomena are visible, including a great view of the Milky Way. Anyone with even a slight knowledge of astronomy will be thrilled at the array of stars.

to Killarney. A summer service also connects the Ring of Beara and Cork City and Airport.

TOURS

Kenmare Coach and Cab

BUS TOURS | You can opt to base yourself in Kenmare and take a guided tour of the Ring by minibus (June to August) with this local taxi company. Its minibuses depart from the square for the Ring on Monday, Wednesday, and Friday at 10 am. Other destinations include the Ring of Beara and Glengarriff (Tuesday and Thursday). It is best to reserve by 10 pm the night before and trips are subject to minimum numbers. ✉ *Longfin House, Kenmare* ☎ *064/664–1491* 🌐 *kenmarecoachandcab.com.*

Kenmare Foodie Tours

SPECIAL-INTEREST TOURS | Join local TV cook and blogger Karen Coakley on a fun and interactive guided walking tour of Kenmare's thriving food scene. Meet chefs, producers, and traders and enjoy many samples and local treats along this delicious half-day tour. ✉ *Maison Gourmet, 24 Henry St., Kenmare* ✣ *Meet in back garden* ☎ *087/640–1531* 🌐 *kenmarefoodies.com* 🎫 *€69.*

VISITOR INFORMATION

CONTACTS Kenmare Tourist Office. ✉ *The Square, Kenmare* ☎ *064/664–1233* 🌐 *kenmare.ie.*

Sights

Kenmare Heritage Centre

VISITOR CENTER | Come to this center in the tourist office to learn about the town's history. They can outline a walking route to Kenmare's places of interest. ✉ *The Square, Kenmare* ☎ *064/664–1233* 🌐 *discoverireland.ie/kerry/kenmare-heritage-centre* 🎫 *Free* 🕒 *Closed Nov.–Easter; Easter–Oct., closed Sun.*

Kenmare Market

MARKET | Each Wednesday a small group of outdoor vendors offer local organic produce and a few exotic imports to an appreciative local clientele. Look out for Olivier's On the Wild Side's handmade charcuterie and smoked trout from Killorglin, local organic veggies, homemade pâtés, preserves from Caherdaniel, and wonderful duck and quail eggs. ✉ *The Square, Kenmare* 🌐 *facebook.com/kenmaremarket18* 🕒 *Closed Jan. and Feb.; Mar.–Dec., closed Thurs.–Tues.*

Stone Circle

RUINS | Perhaps the town's most notable historic sight is this 3,000-year-old monument that dates from the early Bronze Age. Sometimes called the Druid Circle, it is within five minutes' walk of the village square (head down Market Street in front of the tourist office). It consists of 15 large stones arranged in a circle around a huge central boulder, which marks a rare Bronze Age burial site. ✉ *Market St., Kenmare.*

Ring Strategy

Tour buses tend to start in Killarney between 9 am and 10 am and head for Killorglin to ply the Ring counterclockwise, so consider jumping ahead and starting in Killorglin ahead of the Killarney buses, or following the route clockwise, starting in Kenmare (although this means you risk meeting tour buses head-on on narrow roads).

Restaurants

★ The Falls Restaurant

$$$$ | **MODERN IRISH** | The setting of this restaurant overlooking cascades and a twin arched bridge is almost enough to draw pundits to Kenmare's premier dining venue, but even that vista is eclipsed by the offerings on the menu. The three-course meal comes with a hefty price tag of €85, but even at that price it offers value. **Known for:** excellent service; views; fresh, locally sourced produce from the land and sea. *Average main: €85* ✉ *Kenmare* ☎ *064/664–1600* 🌐 *sheenfallslodge.ie/dine/the-falls-restaurant.*

Lime Tree

$$$ | **EUROPEAN** | An open fire, stone walls, and a minstrel's gallery above the main room lend considerable character to this restaurant, while the chef-owner's imaginative ways with local produce result in memorable fare. Built in 1823 as a schoolhouse, it is located in its own leafy gardens near the Park Hotel (where many of its staff trained). **Known for:** delicious seafood chowder; healthy options on the children's menu; inventive desserts such as upside-down lemon-and-lime cheesecake. *Average main: €28* ✉ *Shelburne St., Kenmare* ☎ *064/664–1225* 🌐 *limetreerestaurant.com* ⏲ *Closed Mon.–Thurs., closed winter–early Mar. No lunch.*

Mulcahy's

$$ | **ECLECTIC** | Previously a pub, the wood-clad restaurant is intimate and contemporary chic with brown leather seats at small wooden tables, and a menu starring fresh Irish produce and Asian influence. Start with sushi and sashimi, or wild-mushroom pearl-barley risotto with aged Parmesan, and follow with roast halibut with mussel, bacon, and clam cream or veal cheek ravioli. **Known for:** delicious homemade Guinness bread; warm, welcoming staff; friendly, widely traveled owner-chef. *Average main: €24* ✉ *Main St., Kenmare* ☎ *064/664–2383* 🌐 *mulcahyskenmare.ie* ⏲ *Closed Tues. and Wed. in Oct.–May, and last 2 wks in Jan. No lunch.*

O Donnabhain`s Townhouse and Gastro Bar

$ | **MODERN IRISH** | **FAMILY** | One of the cornerstones of the village since it first appeared in 1774, this building has welcomed a local clientele since it opened its doors for local trade. The current owners have developed a busy bar over 30 years and in that time have kept in line with the fine dining that hails from first-class pubs throughout the country. **Known for:** crab claws and Guinness; famous facade is used in marketing campaigns. *Average main: €15* ✉ *10 Henry St., Kenmare, Kenmare* ☎ *64/664–2106* 🌐 *odonnabhain-kenmare.com* ⏲ *Closed Nov.–Feb.*

Hotels

Park Hotel Kenmare
$$$$ | HOTEL | One of Ireland's premier country-house hotels, this 1897 stone château has spectacular views of the Caha Mountains and its 11-acre parkland, where every tree seems manicured. **Pros:** 25-meter lap pool; immaculate decor; one of Kenmare's best restaurants. **Cons:** a bit like living in a museum; basic room rates are quite steep; extra charge for Jacuzzi and thermal suite. *Rooms from: €555* *Shelburne Rd., Kenmare* *064/664–1200* *parkkenmare.com* *Closed mid-Dec.–Dec 23 and Jan. 2–early Feb.* *43 rooms* *Free Breakfast.*

★ **Sheen Falls Lodge Kerry Hotel**
$$$$ | HOTEL | The magnificence of this bright-yellow, slate-roofed former hunting lodge is matched only by its setting on 300 secluded acres of lawns, gardens, and forest between Kenmare Bay and the falls of the River Sheen. **Pros:** impeccable service from attentive staff; gourmet picnics available from the lodge; Skellig Island trips (boat or helicopter) by arrangement. **Cons:** Less than 2 km (1 mile) from the village; small swimming pool; spa gets busy, book in advance. *Rooms from: €615* *Off N71, Kenmare* *064/664–1600* *sheenfallslodge.ie* *Closed Jan. 3–Feb. 4* *66 rooms* *Free Breakfast.*

Shopping

Avoca Handweavers
DEPARTMENT STORE | At this scenic spot, midway between Kenmare and Killarney, you'll find stylish wool clothing, mohair throws, and rugs in remarkable palettes and a variety of weaves, alongside a café with superb views, serving Avoca's famous baked goods and salads. There's a new food market on the ground floor. *Moll's Gap (N71), Kenmare* *064/663–4720* *avoca.ie.*

The Cashmere Shop
MIXED CLOTHING | Here you'll find Irish-made knitwear in lambswool and cashmere in this town center shop. *20 Henry St., Kenmare* *064/664–8986* *thecashmereshop.ie.*

Kenmare Bookshop
BOOKS | A good selection of books of local interest and all the best sellers can be found here. *Shelburne St., Kenmare* *064/664–1578* *facebook.com/kenmarebookshop.*

Norman McCloskey Photography
ART GALLERIES | Norman has been photographing this area since 1992. He has created some breathtakingly beautiful images, many of them large-scale landscapes that can be seen and purchased here. *4 Main St., Kenmare* *087/274–4879* *normanmccloskey.com.*

Paul Kelly Jewellers
JEWELRY & WATCHES | Local master goldsmith, Paul F. Kelly, makes and sells his striking, modern jewelry in gold and silver here. *33 Henry St., Kenmare* *064/664–2590* *pfk.ie.*

The White Room
HOUSEWARES | Candles, fragrances, Irish lace, bed linen, and throws both new and antique are the specialty here. *21 Henry St., Kenmare* *064/664–0600* *thewhiteroomkenmare.com.*

Activities

BICYCLING

Finnegan's Cycles
BIKING | Pick up a free copy of the Ring of Kerry Cycle Route brochure from the tourist information office on the Square, and then explore the Ring using quiet country roads. The full trip is a blister-inducing 213 km (133 miles). Bikes, including hybrids and electric bikes, are available for rent at this shop in town. *37 Henry St., Kenmare* *064/664–1083* *finneganscycles.com* *€35 a day.*

Gifts From Kerry

You will soon notice that parts of County Kerry have more sheep than people. Sheep mean wool, and in this part of Ireland wool means suits, sweaters, scarves, socks, and woolen hats. All four will come in very useful during your stay, and make great gifts, too.

Louis Mulcahy Pottery. Ceramics are a strong point, too, with the Louis Mulcahy Pottery ceramics workshop and showrooms on Slea Head being the most western pottery in Europe. ✉ *Clogher, Ballyferriter, Dingle, Co. Kerry 066/915–6229.*

Quills Woollen Market. This top gifts-and-souvenirs resource has outlets in Killarney, Kenmare, Sneem, and Dingle. Look out for "blackthorns": a traditional, craggy walking stick made from branches of the blackthorn tree, a handy accessory to have while you're here, and a cool souvenir to take home. ✉ *Market Cross, Killarney, Co. Kerry 064/663–2277.*

WILDLIFE-WATCHING

Seafari Seal and Eagle Watching Cruises
WILDLIFE-WATCHING | FAMILY | With complimentary tea and coffee for adults, plus lollipops (suckers) for the kids, Seafari's popular nature cruises feature fun two- to three-hour ecotours with regular sightings of seals and white-tailed sea eagles. Reservations are essential, and there are special family rates ✉ *Kenmare Pier, 3 Pier Rd., Kenmare* ☎ *064/664–2059* 🌐 *seafariireland.com* *From €20.*

Sneem

27 km (17 miles) southwest of Kenmare.

The pretty little village of Sneem (from the Irish for "knot") is settled around a green on the Ardsheelaun River estuary, and its streets are crammed with vibrantly painted houses. The effect has been somewhat diminished by a cluster of new holiday home developments.

GETTING HERE AND AROUND

It takes about 15 minutes to reach Sneem from Kenmare on the N70. There's plenty of free street parking in the town's main square.

TIP→ To see the best of Sneem, park near the Blue Bull pub, and walk down the narrow road beside it, signposted "Pier." This quiet byway leads past a carefully tended community garden, terminating about 300 yards farther on at the village pier. Take a seat and look back toward the village to appreciate Sneem's unique location, nestled amid lush subtropical growth between the sea and the hills.

★ Derrynane House
HISTORIC HOME | The Ring of Kerry has very few historic country houses, so many visitors here enjoy making a special excursion to Derrynane House. Famed as the home of Daniel O'Connell ("The Liberator," 1775–1847), the man who fought for liberal reform and easing of the often cruel penal laws imposed by England and those involved in the slave "industry" on Roman Catholics. His surname appears on major street names in most of Ireland's cities as recognition of his work. He campaigned for Catholic Emancipation (the granting of full rights of citizenship to Catholics), which became a reality in 1829. The house's south and

The Ring of Kerry—one of Ireland's most popular scenic routes—is also one of Europe's great drives.

east wings—which O'Connell himself remodeled—are decorated with original furniture and fittings. Take a self-guided tour: every piece has a genuine connection to O'Connell. The 300-acre estate of Derrynane House is freely accessible and has trails (including a woodland fairy trail) running through mature woodland, bordering on rocky outcrops that lead to wide sandy beaches and dunes. At low tide, you can walk to Abbey Island offshore. Look out for the chariot built by his supporters to draw him through Dublin streets upon his release from jail in 1844 for his efforts to repeal the union with England.

⚠ **Signposting is poor.** ✉ *Off N70, Sneem* ✣ *30 km (18 miles) west of Sneem, near Caherdaniel* ☎ *066/947–5113* 🌐 *derrynanehouse.ie* 🎫 *From €5* 🕒 *Closed mid-Dec.–mid-Mar.; closed weekdays Nov.–mid-Dec.*

Staigue Fort

RUINS | Take a 4-km (2½-mile) detour off the N70 Ring of Kerry road to visit Staigue Fort. Approximately 2,500 years old, the mortar-free stone fort is almost circular and about 75 feet in diameter, with a single south-side entrance. From the Iron Age (from 500 BC to the 5th century AD) and early Christian times (6th century AD), such "forts" were, in fact, fortified homesteads for several families of one clan and their cattle. The walls at Staigue Fort are almost 13 feet thick at the base and 7 feet thick at the top; they still stand 18 feet high on the north and west sides. Within them, stairs lead to narrow platforms on which the lookouts stood.

TIP→ Private land must be crossed to reach the fort, and a "compensation for trespass" of €1 is often requested by the landowner.

The site has free parking and is freely accessible, but it has no facilities. ✉ *Sneem* ✣ *12 km (7½ miles) northeast of Derrynane on N70.*

Hotels

Parknasilla Resort

$$$$ | **RESORT** | **FAMILY** | This limestone custom-built hotel was constructed in the mid-19th century to facilitate the growth in local tourism at that time. **Pros:** excellent sports amenities and spa; sheltered coastal location; great family destination. **Cons:** grounds and hotel big enough to get lost in; busy in July and August; some rooms could do with an update. *Rooms from: €289 ✉ N70, Sneem ☎ 064/667–5600 🌐 parknasillaresort.com ⏲ Closed Nov.–early Mar. 83 rooms Free Breakfast.*

Sneem Hotel

$$ | **HOTEL** | **FAMILY** | Meet the locals and enjoy spacious accommodations at this waterfront hotel and apartment complex on Goldens Cove, a rocky, sheltered spot with views of distant mountains. **Pros:** offers spacious family rooms; sauna, hot tub, and gym; good value for the Ring of Kerry. **Cons:** some new development detracts from the views; 10-minute walk from the village; no pool. *Rooms from: €160 ✉ Goldens Cove, Sneem ☎ 064/667–5100 🌐 sneemhotel.com 69 rooms, 28 apartments Free Breakfast.*

Waterville

35 km (22 miles) west of Sneem.

Waterville, a seaside village facing Ballinskelligs Bay, is famous for its sportfishing, its 18-hole championship golf course (adopted as a warm-up spot for the British Open by Tiger Woods), and for the fact that Charlie Chaplin and Charles de Gaulle spent summers here. The village, like many others on the Ring of Kerry, has a few restaurants and pubs, but little else. There's excellent salmon and trout fishing at nearby Lough Currane, and the area offers challenging hikes with stunning vistas.

GETTING HERE AND AROUND

Waterville, part of the Ring of Kerry driving loop, is a short half-hour drive from Sneem on the N70. You approach the town driving through the dramatically rocky Coomakesta Pass and Hog's Head. Stop at one of the viewing areas to take in the panoramic sea views, which look out at the distinctive Skellig Rocks. There is plenty of free parking in the village.

VISITOR INFORMATION

CONTACTS Waterville Tourist Information Point. *✉ Town Center, Waterville ☎ 066/947–8818 🌐 visitwaterville.ie.*

Sights

Cill Rialaig

STORE/MALL | West of Waterville and 1 km (½ mile) before the Irish-speaking village of Ballinskelligs is the Cill Rialaig Arts Centre. This is the best place in Kerry to see Irish and international art, along with fine crafts and gifts. Its attractive, thatched, beehive-shape roof is hard to miss. There's also a café with wholesome homemade food and a wood-burning pizza oven. *✉ R566, Waterville ↔ 14 km (9 miles) east of Portmagee on R565 ☎ 066/947–9277 🌐 cillrialaigartscentre.com Free ⏲ Call in advance Oct.–May. Café closed Mon. and Tues.*

Shopping

Skelligs Chocolate

CHOCOLATE | The wild coastal road between Ballinskelligs and Portmagee is an unusual location for a chocolate factory, café, and shop, but then this is unusual chocolate, handmade in small batches and acclaimed by connoisseurs for its excellence. A visit to the chocolate factory is also the perfect rainy-day treat: taste the freshly made samples, buy some to take home, then sip a hot chocolate in the café while enjoying the stormy sea view of the Wild Atlantic Way. *✉ The Glen, The Glen Skelligs Ring (R566), Portmagee ↔ 8 km (5 miles)*

Did You Know?

Due to choppy seas at the best of times, June, July, and early August are the best months to take the boat tour to the Little Skellig and Great Skellig isles. Access is limited—and has not been increased following the Skelligs' appearance in recent Star Wars movies—so be sure to book ahead. But even if you need a lot of Dramamine, don't miss the rocky pinnacles of this ancient Christian community—the Skelligs will haunt you for days.

south of Portmagee on Skellig's Ring Rd. ☎ *066/947–9119* 🌐 *skelligschocolate.com.*

Activities

GOLF

★ Waterville Golf Links

GOLF | Famously adopted by Tiger Woods and Mark O'Meara to practice their swings, this 18-hole championship links course remains one of the toughest and most scenic in Ireland or Britain, and as one of Ireland's top five courses, it is considered to be among the best in the world. Consisting of sand dunes, gorse, native grass, and sod-faced bunkers linked by firm fairways and carefully tended greens, Waterville is bordered by the wild Atlantic on two of its three sides. Gary Player described the 11th hole, which runs for 500 yards through majestic dunes, as "the most beautiful and satisfying par-5 of them all." Caddies must be booked in advance. ✉ *N70, on Cahirciveen side of village, Portmagee* ✣ *20 (12 miles) km east of Portmagee on R485/N70* ☎ *066/947–4102* 🌐 *watervillegolflinks.ie* 💳 *Apr.–Oct., €300; Nov.–Mar., contact for availability and rates* 🏌 *18 holes, 7378 yards, par 72.*

The Skelligs and Valentia

Islands off the coastal town of Portmagee, 21 km (13 miles) northwest of Waterville; Valentia Island is across a road bridge from Portmagee.

Visible from Valentia, and on a clear day from Waterville and other points along the coast, are the Skelligs, one of the most spectacular sights in Ireland. Sculpted as if by the hand of God, the islands of Little Skellig, Skellig Michael (or the Great Skellig), and the Washerwoman's Rock are distinctively cone-shape, surrounded by blue swirling seas. The largest island, Skellig Michael, distinguished by its twin peaks and ancient monastic site, rises 700 feet from the Atlantic. During the journey to these islands you'll pass Little Skellig, the breeding ground of more than 22,000 pairs of gannets. Puffin Island, to the north, has a large population of shearwaters and storm petrel. Puffins nest in sand burrows on the Skellig Michael in the month of May. Skellig Michael can be visited by boat, but it is an arduous journey that should be booked in advance and attempted in good weather.

■ TIP→ In spite of the Skelligs' increased fame following the last two Star Wars movies, visitor access is limited by law: consider a cruise around the islands, without landing, which provides some great photo ops, or if weather prohibits, opt for a visit to the Skellig Experience Visitor Centre instead.

VISITOR INFORMATION

CONTACTS The Skelligs Experience. ✉ *Skellig Experience, Valentia Island* ☎ *066/947–6306* 🌐 *www.skelligexperience.com.*

Sights

★ Skellig Michael

ISLAND | The masterpiece of the Skellig Islands is the phenomenal UNESCO World Heritage site of Skellig Michael, with its amazing remains of a 7th- to 12th-century village of monastic beehive dwellings that were home to early Christian monks. In spite of a thousand years of battering by Atlantic storms, the church, oratory, and living cells are surprisingly well preserved. The site is reached by climbing more than 600 increasingly precipitous steps, offering vertigo-inducing views. The Skelligs boat trip includes 1½ hours on Skellig Michael. Despite the publicity following the island's pivotal appearance in two Star Wars movies, *The Force Awakens* and *The Last Jedi,* access to this fragile site is still limited to 180 visitors a day, so book in advance (booking opens in early spring) and hope for good weather. Because of the choppy seas, stiff climb, and lack of facilities, the trip is not recommended for small children or those with mobility issues. ✉ *Skellig Islands* 🌐 *heritageireland.ie/places-to-visit/skellig-michael* 🎟 *Free (charge for boat trip)* ⏲ *Closed Oct.–mid-May.*

Restaurants

★ The Moorings-Bridge Bar

$ | **IRISH** | The dramatic location of this simple bar on the windswept waterfront of the tiny fishing village of Portmagee draws year-round visitors to this corner of the Iveragh Peninsula. A simple menu with the emphasis on local seafood, fish-and-chips, and lamb is served in the low-beamed bar's rustic pine interior. **Known for:** local seafood chowder; unpretentious hospitality; popularity with locals. $ *Average main: €15* ✉ *Main St., Portmagee* ☎ *066/947–7108* 🌐 *moorings.ie.*

Hotels

Royal Valentia Hotel

$$ | **HOTEL** | A grand dame of sorts, this Victorian era hotel occupies a commanding site overlooking the island's quay and it's a cornerstone of Knightstown's village streetscape. **Pros:** good touring base; historical building; friendly-family service. **Cons:** no frills; weddings occasionally; no gym. $ *Rooms from: €130* ✉ *Knightstown, Valentia Island, Valentia Island* ☎ *66/947–6144* 🌐 *royalvalentia.ie* 🛏 *29 rooms* 🍽 *Free Breakfast.*

Cahirciveen

18 km (11 miles) north of Waterville.

Cahirciveen (pronounced "cah-her-si-*veen*"), at the foot of Bentee Mountain, is the gateway to the western side of the Ring of Kerry and the main market town for southern Kerry. Following the tradition in this part of the world, the modest, terraced houses are each painted in varying vibrant colors (sometimes two or three per unit)—the brighter the better.

GETTING HERE AND AROUND

Cahirciveen is about a 15-minute drive from Waterville on the N70, double that if you choose to detour to Portmagee for a visit to the Skellig Rock and Valentia Island. In summer you can return from Knightstown on Valentia Island to Cahirciveen by ferry. There is free parking on the side streets off the main road and outside the local tourist office.

TIP→ If the tourist office is closed, contact the Old Barracks Heritage Centre with any questions as it's run by helpful local people who know everything that's going on in and around Cahirciveen.

Sights

Caherciveen Parish Daniel O'Connell Memorial Church

CHURCH | This large, elaborate, neo-Gothic structure dominates the main street. It was built in 1888 of Newry granite and black limestone to honor local hero Daniel O'Connell—the only church in Ireland named after a layman. ✉ *Church St., Cahirciveen* ☎ *066/947–2210* 🌐 *facebook.com/oconnellmemorialchurch.*

Kells Bay Gardens

GARDEN | **FAMILY** | The subtropical gardens teeming with ferns and exotic plants date from 1838 and have been fully restored and greatly improved by the present owners, Billy and Penn Alexander. The Skywalk rope bridge is the longest in Ireland and takes half an hour to navigate. The front-gate waterfall and the giant Chilean wine palm compete for your attention with carved wooden dinosaurs and giant Dicksonia Antarctica (Tasmanian fern trees) dating from the 1890s, so allow at least an hour for the rest of the garden. Penn, a former chef, has opened a Thai restaurant that is very popular locally and opens for lunch, dinner, and takeaway. Do not let the rain put you off visiting: Kells receives more than 60 inches of rain annually, and it actually enhances the plants and the waterfall. But do wear sensible shoes as it is usually damp underfoot. ✉ *Kells Bay Gardens, Cahirciveen* ✣ *Signposted off N70 13 km (8 miles) north of Cahirciveen* ☎ *066/947–7975* 🌐 *kellsbay.ie* 🎫 *€9* ☞ *Call ahead in Jan. when gardens may be subject to closures.*

Glenbeigh

27 km (17 miles) northeast of Cahirciveen.

The road from Cahirciveen to Glenbeigh is one of the Ring's highlights. To the north is Dingle Bay and the jagged peaks of the Dingle Peninsula, which will, in all probability, be shrouded in mist. If they aren't, the gods have indeed blessed your journey. The road runs close to the water here, and beyond the small village of Kells it climbs high above the bay, hugging the steep side of Drung Hill before descending to Glenbeigh. Note how different the stark character of this westerly stretch of the Ring is from the gentle, woody Kenmare Bay side.

On a boggy plateau by the sea, the block-long village of Glenbeigh is a popular holiday base—the hiking is excellent in the Glenbeigh Horseshoe, as the surrounding mountains are known, and the trout fishing exceptionally good in Lough Coomasaharn. The area south of Glenbeigh and west of Carrantouhill Mountain, around the shores of the Caragh River and the village of Glencar, is known as the Kerry Highlands. The scenery is wild and rough but strangely appealing. A series of signposted loop walks and parts of the Kerry Way pass through here. The area attracts serious climbers who intend to scale Carrantouhill, Ireland's highest peak (3,408 feet).

GETTING HERE AND AROUND

The tiny roadside village of Glenbeigh is about 40 minutes from Cahirciveen on the N70. There's free parking on the streets.

Caragh Lake

BODY OF WATER | A signpost to the right outside Glenbeigh points to Caragh Lake, a tempting excursion south to a beautiful expanse of water set among gorse- and heather-covered hills and majestic mountains. The road hugs the shoreline much of the way. ✉ *Glenbeigh.*

Kerry Bog Village Museum

MUSEUM VILLAGE | FAMILY | Worth a quick look, this museum, between Glenbeigh and Killorglin on the Ring of Kerry, is a cluster of reconstructed, fully furnished cottages that vividly portray the daily life of the region's agricultural laborers in the early 1800s. The adjacent Red Fox Bar is famous for its Irish coffee. ✉ *Ballincleave, N70, Shronowen Bog* ☎ *066/976–9184* 🌐 *kerrybogvillage.ie* 🎫 *€8.*

Rossbeigh

BEACH | FAMILY | On the coast, Rossbeigh consists of a tombolo (sand spit) of about 3 km (2 miles) backed by high dunes. It faces Inch Strand, a similar formation across the water on the Dingle Peninsula. Popular with families for its safe swimming, it also attracts walkers. **Amenities:** food and drink; parking (no fee). **Best for:** swimming; walking. ✉ *Rossbeigh Rd.* ✣ *2 km (1 mile) west of Glenbeigh.*

Carrig Country House

$$$$ | HOTEL | A rambling two-story Victorian house covered in flowering creepers and set on 4 acres of lush gardens along the secluded shore of Caragh Lake on Kerry's Wild Atlantic Way, this comes pretty close to most people's dream rural retreat. **Pros:** lovely secluded location; real country-house atmosphere; excellent restaurant. **Cons:** closed off for two-night stays for many periods; only croquet and fishing on-site; no air-conditioning. *Rooms from: €270* ✉ *Caragh Lake, off Ring of Kerry, Killorglin* ✣ *From Killorglin, take Ring of Kerry toward Glenbeigh. After 4 km (2½ miles) turn left, signposted "Caragh Lake"; at Caragh Lake School and Shop, turn sharp right and continue to hotel. From Glenbeigh, turn right before Red Fox Inn onto Caragh Lake road (signposted)* ☎ *066/976–9100* 🌐 *carrighouse.com* *Closed Nov.–Mar. Restaurant closed Sun.–Tues. Oct.–Apr.* *17 rooms* *Free Breakfast.*

Activities

BICYCLING

Caragh Lake Cycling Route

BIKING | Cyclists love this circuit, which is about a 35-km (22-mile) round-trip from Glenbeigh. It is relatively traffic-free compared to the Ring of Kerry, and runs through truly remote bog and mountain landscape that's rich in wildlife. You might spot a herd of long-bearded wild goats, or a peregrine falcon soaring above. But bring your own drinks and snacks: retail outlets are scarce in these parts. ✉ *Blackstones Bridge, Glenbeigh.*

HIKING

Blackstones Bridge

HIKING & WALKING | **FAMILY** | In this partially wooded area near Glencar, in the shadow of Carrauntuohill, Ireland's highest mountain, and the MacGillicuddy Reeks, a series of looped walks from 2 km (1.2 miles) upward, are mapped out on picture boards in the parking areas. ✉ *Off N70, Glenbeigh* ✣ *About 12 km (7 miles) southeast of Glenbeigh.*

HORSEBACK RIDING

Rossbeigh Beach Riding Center

HORSEBACK RIDING | **FAMILY** | Gallop a 5-km (3-mile) stretch of Rossbeigh Strand, or take a trek around quiet country roads on a horse from this long-established family business. They use mainly quiet colored cobs (black-and-white long-haired all-rounders). Hats and boots are included in the price. Book 24 hours in advance to avoid disappointment. ✉ *R564, Glenbeigh* ☎ *087/237–9110* 🌐 *beachtrek.ie* *From €50.*

Killorglin

14 km (9 miles) east of Glenbeigh, 22 km (14 miles) west of Killarney.

Killorglin is on top of a hill beside the River Laune. At the "top of the town" is a continental-style piazza, with outdoor tables in good weather and free entertainment in summer. (This is also the location of the tourist information office.) Venture down the hill to find old-style traditional pubs where you can savor a pint.

Killorglin is famed as the scene of the Puck Fair (🌐 *puckfair.ie*), three days of merrymaking during the second weekend in August and the oldest gathering festival in Ireland. A large billy goat with beribboned horns, installed on a high pedestal, presides over the fair. The origins of the tradition of King Puck are lost in time. Horse dealing takes place in an open field on the first morning of the fair. In the village, the main attractions are funfair rides, street traders, street performers, free outdoor concerts, and extended drinking hours. The crowds can be huge, so avoid Killorglin at fair time if you've come for peace and quiet. On the other hand, if you intend to join in the festivities, be sure to book accommodations well in advance.

GETTING HERE AND AROUND

The town is a 15-minute drive on the R70 from Glenbeigh. Street parking is available and there is a free parking lot near the tourist information office.

VISITOR INFORMATION

CONTACTS Reeks District Visitor Centre. ✉ *Library Pl., Iveragh Rd., Killorglin* ☎ *066/976–1451* 🌐 *reeksdistrict.com.*

Restaurants

The Bianconi

$$ | **IRISH** | This busy Victorian-style pub (with guest rooms) was once the coaching inn for the national network of horse-drawn coaches known as Bianconis; today, it serves local seafood and traditional Irish food. Its dark-wood interior has a rambling barroom with a tile floor, leatherette banquettes, and ancient stuffed animals above the booths. **Known for:** hearty portions of bistro-style food; warm, friendly atmosphere; divine desserts. *Average main: €21* ✉ *Lower Bridge St., Killorglin* ☎ *066/976–1146* 🌐 *bianconi.ie* *No lunch Sun.*

Kingdom 1795

$$$$ | **MODERN IRISH** | A paired-back, well-thought-out menu works in harmony with the simple whitewashed facade of this vernacular building in the center of the village. A former pub now houses a chic brasserie with an uncluttered cooking that includes scallops, cod, beef, and duck along with a vegan choice. **Known for:** local produce; friendly service. *Average main: €47* ✉ *Main St., Killorglin* ☎ *66/979–6527* 🌐 *kingdom1795.com* *Closed Mon. and Tues.*

10 Bridge Street

$ | **SPANISH** | Located in a former church, 10 Bridge Street is a spacious and atmospheric restaurant and wine bar with beautiful stained-glass windows illuminating the room. The menu is split into nibbles, small plates, and larger portion sizes and features quality Irish produce like hake, braised beef, and Glenbeigh mussels—and mixes contemporary regulars such as skewers with old Irish favorites like colcannon or Guinness bread. **Known for:** atmospheric setting; exciting wine list; flavorsome traditional cooking. *Average main: €13* ✉ *Lower Bridge St., Killorglin* ☎ *066/976–2347* 🌐 *10bridgestreet.ie* *Closed Jan., Feb., Sat., and bank holidays Mar. 17–May, and Sun.–Wed.*

The Ring of Kerry

The Ring of Kerry is a 179-km (111-mile) circular route around Kerry's Iveragh Peninsula. It takes in the towns of Killarney, Beaufort, Killorglin, Glenbeigh, Caherciveen, Waterville, Caherdaniel, Sneem, and Kenmare.

Sights

★ The Ring of Kerry

SCENIC DRIVE | Along the perimeter of the Iveragh Peninsula, the dramatic coastal road from Kenmare to Killorglin known as the Ring of Kerry is probably Ireland's single most popular tourist route. Stunning mountain and coastal views are around almost every turn. The only drawback: on a sunny day, it seems like half the nation's visitors are traveling along this two-lane road, driving, packed into buses, riding bikes, or hiking. The route is narrow and curvy, and the local sheep think nothing of using it for a nap; take it slowly. Tour buses tend to start in Killarney and ply the Ring counterclockwise, so consider jumping ahead and starting in Killorglin or following the route clockwise, starting in Kenmare (although this means you risk meeting tour buses head-on on narrow roads). Either way, bear in mind that most of the buses leave Killarney between 9 and 10 am. The trip covers 179 km (111 miles) on N70 (and briefly R562 and N71) if you start and finish in Killarney. The journey will be 40 km (25 miles) shorter if you only venture between Kenmare and Killorglin. Because rain blocks views across the water to the Beara Peninsula in the east and the Dingle Peninsula in the west, hope for sunshine. It makes all the difference.

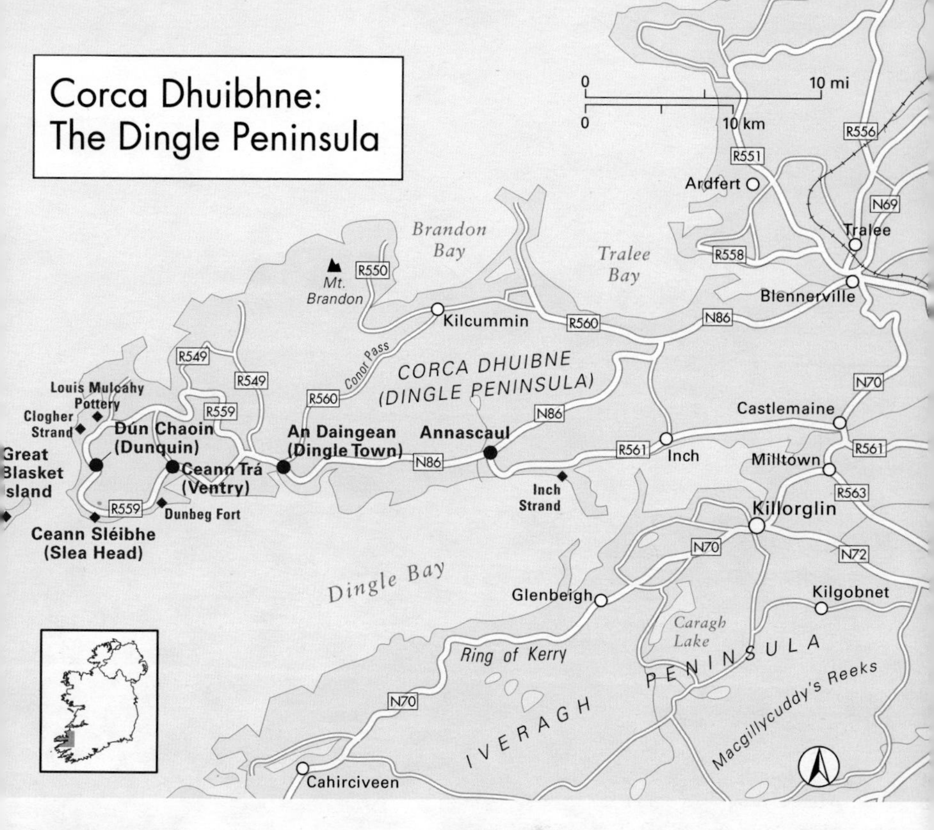

Annascaul

47 km (30 miles) northwest of Killarney.

An important livestock center until the 1930s, this village near the junction of the Castlemaine and Tralee roads has a broad road, as cattle trading was once carried out in the streets. The town also has many pubs. It is a popular base for walkers tackling the Dingle Way (179 km [111 miles]) or the shorter (57-km [35-mile]), three-day guided Kerry Camino (🌐 *kerrycamino.com*).

GETTING HERE AND AROUND

Annascaul is about 45 minutes from Tralee on the N86, about an hour from Killarney (take N70 then R561), and less than 20 minutes' drive from Dingle Town continuing on the main N86. There is abundant free parking in town.

Sights

Inch Strand

BEACH | Despite its diminutive name, Inch is a 5-km (3-mile) stretch of sand and sea that extends as far as Dingle Bay. Its vast and glorious setting created pivotal backdrops for movies like *Ryan's Daughter* (1970), *Excalibur* (1981), and *Far And Away* (1992)—but in Ireland it's famous for its summer surf schools and the 3-meter-high waves that can approach its westerly coastline. ✉ *Anascaul* ✣ *6 km (3 miles) east from Annascaul on the R561.*

★ The South Pole Inn

PUBS | This fascinating landmark pub was built by local hero Tom Crean (1877–1938). Crean enlisted in the English navy at the age of 15, and served on three

Continued on page 381

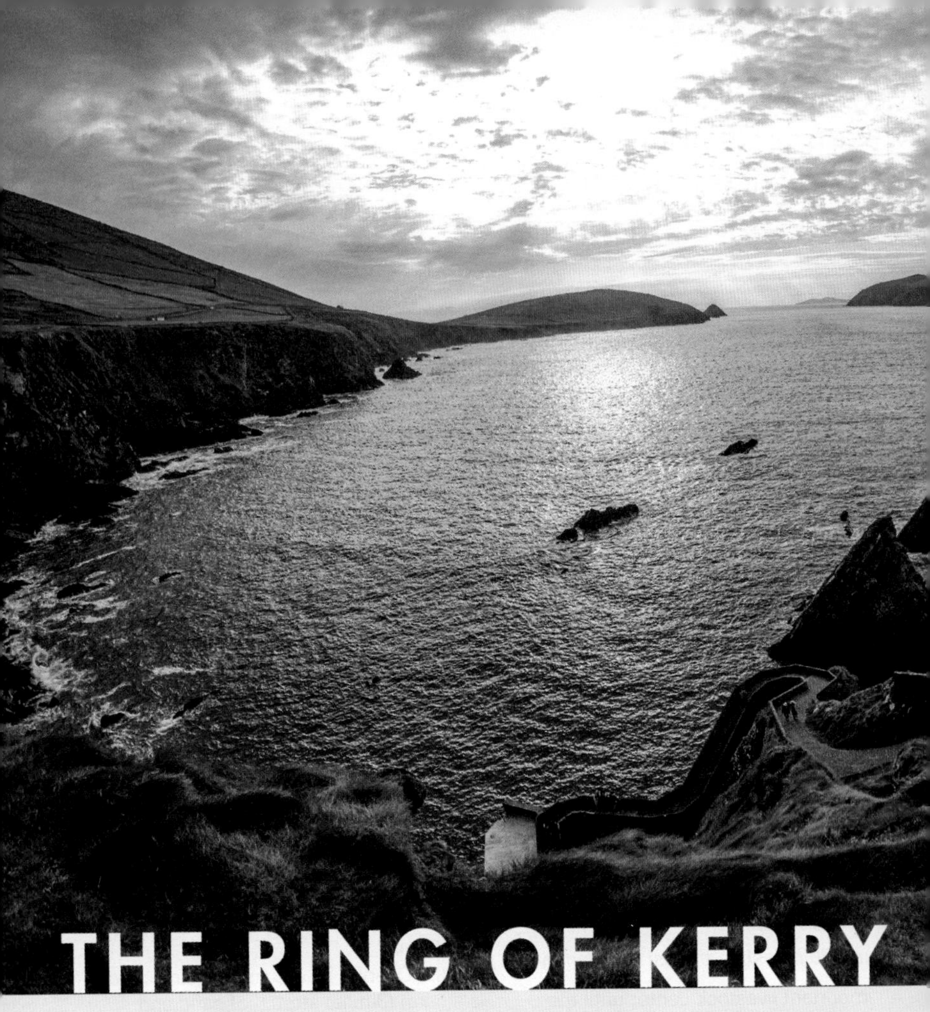

THE RING OF KERRY

When you travel Ireland's most popular scenic route, leaving your car behind makes all the difference. Here's how to get far from the madding crowd.

The Ring of Kerry is one of Europe's great drives. The common wisdom, though, is that it suffers from its own popularity: tour buses dominate the road from sunup to sundown. There's more than a grain of truth to this reputation, but that doesn't mean you should scratch the Ring from your itinerary. While most savvy drivers travel in May or September or rise early and navigate the full loop clockwise, in the opposite direction of tour buses, there are other options." before itinerary. Plan to turn off the main road and get out of your car. You'll make a blissful discovery: the Iveragh Peninsula—one of the most beautiful locations in all of Ireland—remains largely unspoiled. It's full of fabulous places to hike, bike, and boat—and best of all, there are views the tour bus passengers can only dream of.

Top, Elevated coastal view from the Ring of Kerry; Below left, on horseback in Rossbeigh Strand, Kerry; Below right, cycling around the Ring

AROUND THE RING BY FOOT AND BY BIKE

HIKING THE RING

Option number one for getting outdoors around the Ring of Kerry is to go by foot. As the peninsula's Greenway, an off-road trek that follows an old railway line, expands year on year, it's a good time to dust off the hiking boots and plan ahead. There are staggeringly beautiful walking options for every degree of fitness and experience, from gentle, paved paths to an ascent up Ireland's tallest mountain.

THE KERRY WAY

The main hiking route across the peninsula is the Kerry Way, a spectacular 133-mile footpath that's easily broken down into day-trip-size segments. The path winds from Killarney through the foothills of the MacGillicuddy's Reeks and the Black Valley to Glencar and Glenbeigh, from where it parallels the Ring through Cahirciveen, Waterville, Caherdaniel, and Sneem, before ending in Kenmare. The route, indicated by way markers, follows grassy old paths situated at higher elevations than the Ring—meaning better, and more tranquil, views. Hiking the entire Kerry Way can take from 10 to 12 days. Numerous outfitters organize both guided and unguided tours. For a great day trip, hike the 10 km (6 miles) section from Waterville to Caherdaniel, which has great views of small islands and rocky coves. In the Glencar area near Blackstones Bridge, a series of shorter signposted walks, from 3 km (2 miles) upward, put you in the shadow of Carrauntuohill, Ireland's highest mountain.

TAKING IT EASY: THREE GENTLE STROLLS

Muckross Park in Killarney is a car-free zone with four signposted nature trails. Try the 4 km (2½ miles) Arthur Young's Walk through old yew and oak woods frequented by sika deer. You can also take an open boat from Ross Castle to the head of the Upper Lake, then walk back along the lakeside to Muckross House—about 10 km (6 miles).

The trails in **Derrynane National Park**, a 320-acre estate, run through mature woodland, bordering on rocky outcrops that lead to wide sandy beaches and dunes. At low tide, you can walk to Abbey Island offshore.

Even in high summer, **Valentia Island** is a peaceful spot for walking, with little traffic. Walk the road from Knightstown through the sub-tropical vegetation of the Knight of Kerry's estate, to the historic **Slate Quarry** (3 km/2 miles), 900 ft above the sea, with views of the Skelligs offshore.

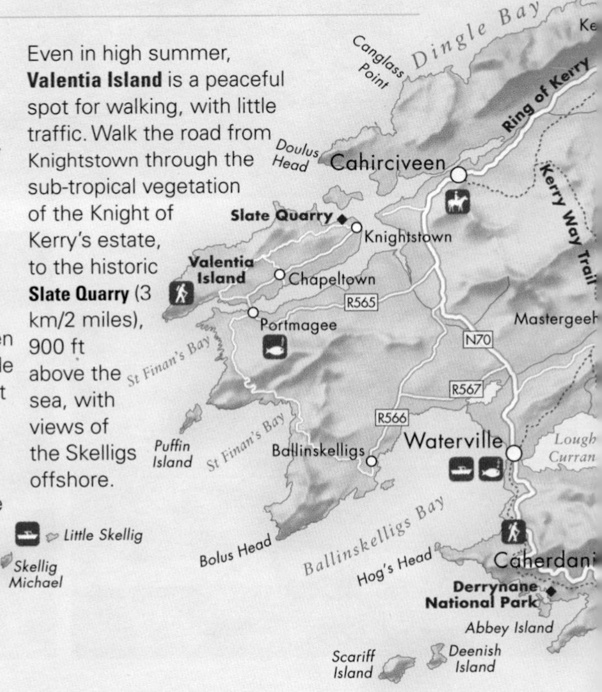

CYCLING THE RING

The Ring of Kerry Cycle Route follows the main road for about a third of its 134 miles, but the rest is on deserted roads, including a long, scenic loop through Ballinskelligs, Portmagee, and Valentia Island. There are significant climbs and strong winds along the way, so good fitness is a prerequisite.

EASY RIDES

From Killarney, the N71 road past **Muckross Park** and the **Upper Lake** takes you through ancient woodlands to Ladies' View (about 12 km/7.5 miles). From here you have one of the area's best panoramas, with the sparkling blue lakes backed by purple mountains. The scene will be in front of you as you make the ride back.

From **Glenbeigh,** escape the traffic by riding inland to peaceful Caragh Lake through a bog and mountain landscape that's rich in wildlife. You might spot a herd of long-bearded wild goats, or a peregrine falcon hovering above its prey. The full circuit of the lake, returning to Glenbeigh, is about 35 km (22 miles).

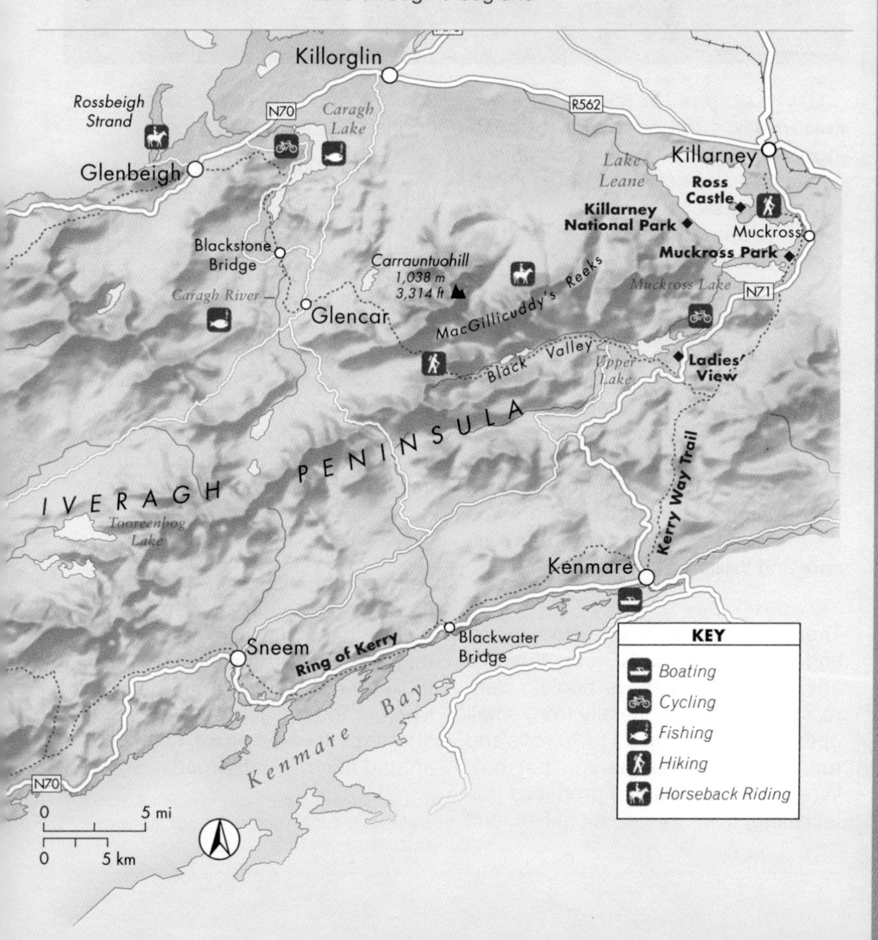

RING ACTIVITIES

BOATING AROUND THE RING ...

Kenmare Bay is the best spot for boating expeditions, on which you can see castles, seals, dolphins, and salmon farms. Boats can take up to 10 people. For something gentle head to Lough Leane near Killarney.

... AND SWIMMING

Swimming off the beaches around the coast is at its best in July and August, when the water temperatures reach 55 to 60 degrees. Rossbeigh, Derrynane and Valentia Island Pool are the best coastal swimming spots while Cummeenoughter Lake is the highest lake in Ireland for a swim. There are dive centers at **Kenmare** and **Valentia Island.**

... AND FISHING

There's good fishing here, both inland and at sea. **Portmagee** and **Waterville** are the main deepsea angling centers; outings are generally from small open boats carrying up to 10 rods and run about €30 per person per day. Wreck and reef fishing promises pollock, ling, cod, conger, monkfish, and shark. Inshore there are bass, turbot, dogfish, flounder, and tope.

The **Caragh Lake** and the rivers **Laune**, **Inny**, **Roughty**, and **Caragh** are all excellent for wild salmon—and all are beautiful wilderness locations. **Lough Currane** near Waterville is one of the great sea trout fisheries. The season runs from March to September, and fishing permits are available locally from hotels. You'll find tackle shops in Killarney and Waterville. For detailed information before you go, check out the website of the Inland Fisheries Ireland (🌐 www.fishinginireland.info).

... AND EQUITREKKING

Horses hold a special place in the hearts of the Irish. Horsemanship and breeding are sources of national pride. If you share the Irish passion for all things equine, there's no better way to see the Ring than from the back of a horse. You can gallop along the 3mile stretch of **Rossbeigh Strand**, or take a trek around quiet country roads.

Top left, horses at the Lakes of Killarney; Right, trout fishing; Bottom left, fishing boats in the Dingle harbor

WEATHER, FLORA, AND TOURING TIPS

Swimming at the Ring

THANKS TO THE GULF STREAM . . .

The warm waters flowing from the Gulf of Mexico across the Atlantic, known as the Gulf Stream, give Ireland a mild climate, and the effects are particularly felt along the Ring of Kerry. The area is frost-free year round, with temperatures averaging 45 degrees Fahrenheit in winter and 60 in summer. But rain is a constant threat, brought in from the Atlantic by the prevailing southwesterly winds. Console yourself with this though: it may be wet, but it is never freezing.

Don't bother touring the Ring in heavy sea mist: you won't see a thing. But don't let other forms of rain deter you. Part of the attraction of the Ring is the interplay of light with sea, mountain, and distant horizons. Rain often enhances the view, and can give delightful effects. The sun is often shining before the rain has finished, so rainbows abound. Any weather, good or bad, seldom lasts more than half a day: if it's wet in the morning, it will probably be sunny in the afternoon, and vice versa.

SOCK IT TO ME

Bring a rain jacket and a warm fleece or sweater: sea winds can be chilly. Above all, wear sensible footwear. If you're venturing off-road, even in summer, you will be glad of strong, waterproof shoes. And bring plenty of socks. There's nothing more miserable than wet feet!

LAND OF EXOTIC PALMS

With no frost, Killarney and the Iveragh Peninsula are havens for subtropical vegetation. The New Zealand fern tree and the banana tree thrive. The "palm trees" you see here are usually yuccas that have been allowed to grow tall. Flax also grows to enormous size, and is often used as a shelter belt. The leaves of the gunnera can grow to the size of a compact car—look for them in Muckross Park. The lakes of Killarney are surrounded by luxuriant woods of oak, arbutus, birch, holly, and mountain ash, with undergrowth of ferns, saxifrages, and mosses. Rhododendron and azaleas thrive on pockets of acid soil, and are at their best from mid-April to May.

THE ICE AGE COMETH, AND GOETH

Some 60 million years ago, the great rias, or drowned rivers, that became the bays of Bantry, Kenmare, and Dingle were formed. The sea penetrated far inland, forming the peninsulas of Beara, Iveragh, and Dingle. A million years ago, these lands were gripped by the Ice Age. When the ice receded, some 10,000 years ago, it left corries (or glacial hollows) gouged out of the mountains, great rocks scattered on the landscape (giving rise to legends of giants throwing stones), and outcrops of ice-smoothed sandstone.

Valentia Island

THE TWIN PEAKS OF YOUR TRIP

Above and below left, ancient monastic site on Skellig Michael with Little Skellig in the background.

The distinctive conical **Skellig Rocks** hover offshore at the western end of the Iveragh Peninsula, surrounded by swirling blue sea. They're a haunting presence that seems to follow along as you travel the mainland from Valentia to Waterville and Caherdaniel.

A venture out to the twin peaks of **Skellig Michael** (shown above, also known as Great Skellig) is a truly awesome experience. Boats leave from Waterville, Ballinskelligs, and Portmagee for a white-knuckle ride lasting about 45 minutes. Along the way you pass Michael's companion, **Little Skellig,** where people aren't allowed but gannets flourish.

Skellig Michael rises steeply for 700 feet; you reach the summit by climbing 600 steps cut into the rockface. Once there, you find, amazingly, the remains of a monastery, occupied by hermit monks from the 7th to 12th century. Looking back to the mainland and out at the wild expanse of open sea, you get an inkling of the monks' isolation from all things worldly. A visit to Skellig Michael may not be the most comfortable outing of you trip, but it will probably be the most memorable.

BIRDS OF THE SKELLIGS

The Ring of Kerry is one of the best places in Europe for observing seabirds, and the Skelligs are a particular treasure for birders. The gannet, with a wing span of 2 yards, is Ireland's largest seabird and up to 22,000 nesting pairs reside on Little Skellig, where they dive for food from heights of up to 120 feet.

If you are lucky enough to get out to Skellig Michael in May, you'll be warned to watch out for comical-looking **puffins** (*below*) nesting in burrows underfoot.

Below, two puffins standing on Skellig rocks

expeditions to Antarctica—the *Discovery* (1901–04) and the *Terra Nova* (1910–13), both under the command of Captain Robert Falcon Scott, and the *Endurance* (1914–16), where he was second officer to Ernest Shackleton. Crean himself failed to reach the South Pole on any of these expeditions and named his pub so that in his retirement he could go to work at the South Pole every day.

Memorabilia at the pub fill in the details of Crean's Antarctic adventures. Famed for his amazing strength and resilience, he walked 56 km (35 miles) through an Antarctic blizzard to bring help to his colleagues, with only two bars of chocolate and three cookies for sustenance. For this he received the Albert Medal for Bravery. On another occasion he survived a 15-day journey across 1,280 km (800 miles) of ocean in an open boat.

Today the South Pole Inn offers heart-warming fare and a selection of local craft beer along with the usual brands. ✉ *Off N86, Anascaul* ☎ *066/915–7388* 🌐 *southpoleinn.com* ☞ *No reservations.*

An Daingean (Dingle Town)

18 km (11 miles) west of Annascaul, 67 km (42 miles) west of Killarney, 45 km (28 miles) west of Killorglin.

Backed by mountains and facing a sheltered harbor, An Daingean, the chief town of its eponymous peninsula, has a year-round population of 1,400 that more than doubles in summer. Although many expect Dingle (to use its English name) to be a quaint and undeveloped Gaeltacht village, it has many crafts shops, seafood restaurants, and pubs.

Still, you can explore its main thoroughfares—the Mall, Main and Strand streets, and the Wood—in less than an hour. Celebrity hawks, take note: off-season Dingle is favored as a hideaway by the likes of Julia Roberts, Paul Simon, Tom Cruise, and Dolly Parton. These and others have their visits commemorated on Green Street's "path of stars."

The latest addition to the annual calendar is the Dingle Food Festival.

■ TIP→ In peak season avoid the frustration of trying to park in town; instead find your way to the peripheral parking lot 200 yards from the town center.

GETTING HERE AND AROUND

Dingle Town is about an hour's drive from Tralee on the N86, and about 1½ hours west of Killarney via Killorglin and Castlemaine. There are daily buses from Tralee, which also has the nearest train station.

There is no public transportation west of Dingle Town, around Slea Head, where some of the best scenery is found. If you don't have a car, the 30-km (18-mile) circuit can be toured by minibus. If you are driving, bear in mind that there are no gas stations and no ATMs west of Dingle Town, so load up on supplies before you leave.

Most boats to the Blasket Islands leave from Dunquin, 21 km (13 miles) west of town, but Dingle Boat Tours leaves from the Dingle Town marina.

TOURS

Coastline Tours

BUS TOURS | If you don't have a car, this company offers minibus tours of the 30-km (18-mile) route around Slea Head. ☎ *087/998–2230* 🌐 *coastline-tours.com* 🎫 *€30 per person for 3-hr tour.*

Dingle Bay Charters

BOAT TOURS | Dingle Boat Tours operates a 45-minute ferry ride from the marina in Dingle Town to the Great Blasket island (€60) as well as a 4½-hour guided ecotour around the Blasket Islands daily between March and October, weather permitting (€60). They also run a harbor cruise (€10 for one hour) several times daily, and a 2½-hour Blasket Island

The coastal tip of the Dingle Peninsula provides a dramatic seascape whatever the weather.

RIB sea safari (from €46 per person). ✉ *Dingle Marina, Dingle* ☎ *087/672–6100* 🌐 *dingleboattours.com* 🎟 *€10 for Dingle Bay.*

VISITOR INFORMATION

CONTACTS An Daingean (Dingle Town) Tourist Office. ✉ *Strand St., Dingle* ☎ *066/915–2448* 🌐 *dingle-peninsula.ie.*

Restaurants

Ashe's

$$$ | **SEAFOOD** | This pub has been sitting here since it opened in 1849 as a drapery with a liquor license, and its history over the years has included its location as the unofficial base for the cast of *Ryan's Daughter,* which filmed in the town in 1968. In fact, it was for this crew that Ashe's first started serving food, and while the bar has expanded to accommodate more visitors with two additional cozy, no-frills rooms, the fare served on the plain wooden tables remains the freshest seafood, cooked to order, and a small selection of meat and vegetarian dishes—all hearty and good. **Known for:** good-value early menu 5:30–6:30 (booking advised); Blasket Island lobster, steamed with lemon or garlic butter; Glenbeigh mussels in Thai-style broth. 💲 *Average main: €27* ✉ *6 Main St., Dingle* ☎ *066/915–0989* 🌐 *facebook.com/Ashesbardingle* ⏲ *Closed Dec. 1–14 and Jan.–mid-Mar.*

★ Chart House

$$$ | **IRISH** | Host Jim McCarthy is often found in the early evening leaning over the red half door of this low, cabinlike stone building. The atmosphere is pleasantly informal (nautical artifacts complement the rusty-red walls and matching tablecloths), but both food and service are polished and professional. **Known for:** warm, attentive staff and atmosphere; Annascaul black pudding; perfect spot for a romantic dinner. 💲 *Average main: €28* ✉ *The Mall, Dingle* ☎ *066/915–2255* 🌐 *thecharthousedingle.com* ⏲ *Closed Jan. 2–mid-Mar. and Mon.–Wed. Dec.–Apr. (call to confirm). No lunch.*

★ Out of the Blue

$$$ | **SEAFOOD** | Every fishing port should have a simple waterfront bistro like this one, serving the best seafood (the owner won't open up if there's no fresh-caught seafood available—which is almost never). Lobster, scallops, and crayfish are specialties, but also expect turbot, black sole, plaice, brill, monkfish, and even the humble pollack on the daily blackboard menu of this unpretentious shack. **Known for:** no chips or deep-fried seafood; tasty chowder; the bargain "Fish Deal" set menu. *Average main: €27 The Pier, Dingle 066/915–0811 outoftheblue.ie Closed mid-Nov.–mid-Mar. No lunch Mon.–Sat.*

Coffee and Quick Bites

Murphy's Ice Cream

$ | **ICE CREAM** | **FAMILY** | One of Ireland's more unusual culinary success stories, Murphy's has won international awards for its delightfully creamy ice cream, including flavors like Dingle sea salt and Irish brown bread. Grab a scoop or two at this flagship parlor. **Known for:** tasty Aztec hot chocolate; you can sample flavors before you buy; unexpected flavors such as Irish gin, or fennel. *Average main: €4 Strand St., Dingle 066/915–2644 murphysicecream.ie.*

Hotels

Dingle Skellig Hotel and Peninsula Spa

$$$ | **HOTEL** | **FAMILY** | This rambling modern hotel's setting on Dingle Bay enjoyed extensive refurbishment in 2019 and offers panoramic views of the bay, most notably from the restaurant. **Pros:** waterfront location; outdoor hot tub with sea view; separate floors for child-free guests. **Cons:** mostly undistinguished architecture; on the edge of town; bar very busy on weekends. *Rooms from: €180 Dingle Harbor, Dingle 066/915–0200 dingleskellig.com Closed Jan., and Mon.–Thurs. in Nov. and Dec. 152 rooms Free Breakfast.*

Greenmount House

$$ | **B&B/INN** | More like a modern boutique hotel than a B&B, the combination of comfort and elegance in the lobby sets the tone, as do the wonderful views of the town and harbor. **Pros:** rooms both stylish and comfortable; wine license; wonderful breakfasts. **Cons:** new developments mar an otherwise great view; short walk uphill from town center; can fill up quickly: book well ahead. *Rooms from: €130 Upper John St., Dingle 066/915–1414 greenmounthouse.ie Closed Christmas Day–New Year and mid-Jan.–early-Feb. 14 rooms Free Breakfast.*

Heaton's Guesthouse

$$ | **B&B/INN** | On the Slea Head edge of Dingle Town, but just a short walk to the center, this traditional-style yellow house is right on the water's edge. **Pros:** voted one of the best places to stay in Ireland; outstanding breakfast; only a short walk from town. **Cons:** if it rains you'll be driving, not walking, to nearest bars and restaurants; no leisure facilities; limited menu selection. *Rooms from: €170 The Wood, Dingle 066/915–2288 heatonsdingle.com Closed Dec. 1–27 and Jan. 7–31 16 rooms Free Breakfast.*

Nightlife

Nearly every bar on the Corca Dhuibhne (Dingle Peninsula), particularly in the town of An Daingean, offers live music nightly in July and August.

An Droichead Beag (The Small Bridge)

LIVE MUSIC | For a lively nighttime spot, try this large, busy pub in the town center, known for live Irish music and late hours. *Main St., Dingle 066/915–1723 androicheadbeag.com.*

★ **Dick Mack's**

LIVE MUSIC | Part cobbler's shop, part bar, this tiny pub has been quenching thirsts since 1899. Offering a quintessential Dingle experience, with music nightly and a big selection of whiskeys. It has its own food truck and microbrewery by the beer garden, where tours and tastings take place daily in the taproom. ✉ *Green St., Dingle* ☎ *066/915–1787* 🌐 *dickmackspub.com.*

O'Flahertys

PUBS | An Daingean's pubs are well-known for their music, but among them O'Flaherty's, a simple, stone-floor bar at the entrance to town, is something special and a hot spot for traditional musicians. Spontaneous sessions occur most nights in July and August, less frequently at other times. Even without music, this pub is a good place to compare notes with fellow travelers. ✉ *Bridge St., Dingle* ☎ *066/915–1983* 🌐 *oflahertysdingle.com.*

Shopping

★ **Original Kerry Gift Shop and Craft Center**

CRAFTS | This is a cooperative venture that provides a retail outlet for 32 Kerry-based craft workers. From jewelry to soap, wood turning to rain hats, glass to knitwear, and textile art to ceramics, you will find all things handmade here. ✉ *Goat St., Dingle* ☎ *083/852–0705* 🌐 *originalkerry.shop.*

Weaver's Shop

CRAFTS | Weaver and tapestry artist Lisbeth Mulcahy's combined studio and shop sells her outstanding scarves, stoles, throws, and wall hangings in unique color combinations alongside her one-off tapestries. The shop also stocks work from other Irish creatives. ✉ *Green St., Dingle* ☎ *066/915–1688* 🌐 *lisbethmulcahy.com.*

Activities

BICYCLING

Dingle Electric Bike Experience

BIKING | You'll remember your bike ride around Slea Head for a long time, but given gradients and headwinds in this area, you might be inclined to remember it more favorably with the benefit of an electric bike. Dingle Electric Bike Experience will deliver to your lodgings, provide luggage transfers on request, self-guiding maps, free helmets, locks, and high-visibility gear, plus a choice of electric or conventional bike to suit your needs. ✉ *Curran's Pub, Main St., Dingle* ☎ *086/084–8378* 🌐 *dinglebikes.com* 🎟 *Electric bike rentals from €45, regular bikes from €20.*

HORSEBACK RIDING

Dingle Horse Riding

HORSEBACK RIDING | Up in the hills behind Dingle Town, this stable offers some unforgettable treks, suited to many different abilities. Riders might choose the 2½-hour Shamrock Trail (€125) following mountain tracks close to the coastline. Full-day trail options (from €280) are suited to intermediate and advanced riders, exploring the wider terrain of the Dingle Peninsula. Three-day to full-week trail rides with accommodations are also available. ✉ *Baile na Buaile, Dingle* ☎ *086/821–1225* 🌐 *dinglehorseriding.com* 🎟 *From €150 for a 2½-hr trek.*

Ceann Trá (Ventry)

8 km (5 miles) west of An Daingean (Dingle Town) on the R561.

The next town after An Daingean along the coast, Ceann Trá has a small outcrop of pubs and small grocery stores (useful, since west of Dingle Town you'll find few shops of any kind), and a long, sandy beach. Between Ventry and Dún Chaoin (Dunquin) are several interesting archaeological sites on the spectacular cliff-top road that coasts along Ceann Sléibhe (Slea Head).

GETTING HERE AND AROUND

It takes about 10 minutes to reach Ventry by car on the R561 from Dingle Town. Take extra care when driving these narrow scenic roads, which can be busy with cyclists, walkers, and sometimes even sheep, as well as many other drivers unfamiliar with the locality.

Sights

Dunbeg Fort

RUINS | Perched on the very edge of a Dingle Bay cliff, and set in the small district of Fahan (which is part of the larger township of Ventry), this small, well-weathered fort was an important Iron Age defensive promontory site, inhabited from about AD 800 until around 1200. It was badly damaged by storms in the winter of 2017–18, and it is unlikely full access will be restored, but you can still view it from above. Its drystone mound was defended against cattle raiders by four earthen rings—note the *souterraine* (underground) escape route, by the entrance. In addition, there are a number of archaeological artifacts here to interest the time traveler.

There is a 10-minute audiovisual show in the adjacent visitor center, but just as fascinating is the building itself, a modern replica of the drystone construction of the clochán s (pronounced "cluk- *awns*"), the famous prehistoric "beehive" cells first used by hermit monks in the early Christian period. Beside it is a typical *naomhóg* (pronounced "na- *vogue*"), a tarred canvas canoe, resting upside down.

About 1 km (½ mile) farther on is another parking lot, and an interesting group of clocháns can be visited (€3 fee to resident farmer), built of drystone and set on the southern slopes of Mt. Eagle looking out directly across the sea to Skellig Michael. Far from being only prehistoric relics, as the signposts claim, clocháns were being built until a century ago; wood was scarce and stone abounded, so you'll find more than 400 of them between Ceann Sléibhe and Dún Chaoin. ✉ *Fahan, Ventry* ✣ *8 km (5 miles) west of Ventry* ☎ *066/915–9070* 🌐 *dunbeagfort.com* 🎫 *€4.*

Beaches

Ventry Beach

BEACH | Ventry Beach (or Ventry Strand) is just southwest of the village of Ceann Trá (Ventry). This lovely stretch of golden sand, said by many to be one of Ireland's most beautiful beaches, runs for 8 km (5 miles) and is part of the Dingle Way walking route. There is a dune system with a small lake, wetlands, and a reed swamp, and abundant wildlife. In July and August it attracts families and swimmers. **Amenities:** food and drink; parking (no fee); toilets; water sports. **Best for:** surfing; swimming; walking; windsurfing. ✉ *Ventry.*

Ceann Sléibhe (Slea Head)

16 km (10 miles) west of An Daingean (Dingle Town), 8 km (5 miles) west of Ceann Trá.

From the top of the towering cliffs of Ceann Sléibhe (pronounced "kyeown *shla*-va") at the southwest extremity of the Dingle Peninsula, the view of the Blasket Islands and the Atlantic Ocean is guaranteed to stop you in your tracks. Alas, Slea Head—to use its English name—has become so popular that tour buses, barely able to negotiate the narrow road, are causing traffic jams, particularly in July and August. Coumeenoole, the long, sandy strand below, looks beautiful and sheltered as it did in the movie *Ryan's Daughter*, but swimming here is extremely dangerous. This treacherous stretch of coast has claimed many lives in shipwrecks—most recently in 1982, when a large cargo boat, the *Ranga,* foundered on the rocks and sank. In 1588 four ships of the Spanish Armada were driven off course through the Blasket Sound; two made it to shelter, and two sank here.

GETTING HERE AND AROUND

Slea Head is a 10-minute drive from Ventry on R559.

Clogher Strand

BEACH | This dramatic, windswept stretch of rocks and sand visible below the coast road to the north of Slea Head is not a safe spot to swim, but it's a good place to watch the ocean dramatically pound the rocks when a storm is approaching or a gale is blowing. It may also be familiar from David Lean's 1970 film *Ryan's Daughter.* **Amenities:** none. **Best for:** walking. ✉ *Dunquin* ✣ *On left as you travel from Dunquin to Ballyferriter on R559, across from Louis Mulcahy Pottery.*

Dún Chaoin (Dunquin)

13 km (8 miles) west of Ceann Trá, 5 km (3 miles) north of Ceann Sléibhe (Slea Head).

Once the mainland harbor for the Blasket islanders (when there *were* islanders, as the Blaskets are deserted now), Dún Chaoin is at the center of the Corca Dhuibhne Gaeltacht, and it attracts many students of Irish language and folklore.

GETTING HERE AND AROUND

Dunquin is on R559 at the western end of the Dingle Peninsula. Bus Éireann's Dingle–Ballyferriter service (Monday and Thursday only) calls at Dunquin.

★ Blasket Centre

VISITOR CENTER | **FAMILY** | Fully refurbished and extended with high-spec interactive gadgetry and new displays and a first-rate café, this museum is a worthy stop to discover life on the Blasket Islands (An Bhlascaoid Mhóir), which are among Ireland's most extraordinary islands. The largest visible from Ceann Sléibhe is the Great Blasket, inhabited until 1953. The Blasket islanders were great storytellers and were encouraged by Irish scholars to write their memoirs. The Blasket Centre explains the heritage of these islanders and celebrates their use of the Irish language with videos and exhibitions. The new viewing platform (free) alone makes this center an essential part of the Dingle itinerary. ✉ *Dunquin* ☎ *066/915–6444* 🌐 *www.heritageireland.ie* 🎫 *€5* ⏲ *Closed Nov.–early Mar.*

★ Dún Chaoin Pier

MARINA/PIER | Signposted from the main road, and accessed via a dramatic corkscrew walkway, Dún Chaoin pier is surrounded by cliffs of colored Silurian rock, more than 400 million years old and rich in fossils. Down at the pier you can see *naomhóga* (open fishing boats traditionally made of animal hide stretched over wooden lathes and tarred) stored upside down. Traditionally, three or four men walk these currachs out to the sea, holding them over their heads. Similar boats are used in the Aran Islands, and when properly handled they're extraordinarily seaworthy. Five minutes south on the R559 don't miss an opportunity to visit staggeringly beautiful (but lethal for swimming) Coumeenoole Beach at the foot of a curving stepway. Like many landmarks on the Dingle Peninsula, it featured in *Ryan's Daughter* in 1970. ✉ *R559, Dunquin.*

★ Louis Mulcahy Pottery

STORE/MALL | Overlooking the beach is the pottery studio of one of Ireland's leading ceramic artists. Louis Mulcahy produces large pots and urns that are both decorative and functional. You can watch the work in progress and buy items at workshop prices. There's also a coffee shop. ✉ *Clogher Strand, Ballyferriter* ☎ *066/915–6229* 🌐 *www.louismulcahy.com.*

Great Blasket Island

The Great Blasket, which measures roughly 3 km by 1 km (2 miles by ½ mile), has no traffic, no pub, no hotel, and no electricity. Yet this island—centerpiece of the An Bhlascaoid Mhóir (Blasket Islands)—is one of the most memorable places in Ireland to visit.

Visitors are usually attracted by the literary heritage of the island—the Irish-language writings of Tomás Ó Criomhthain, Muiris Ó Suilleabhain (also known in English as Tomás O'Crohán and Maurice O'Sullivan), and Peig Sayers—but what makes people return is something else: a rare quality of light and an intense peace and quiet in beautiful, hauntingly unspoiled surroundings.

The inadequacy of the existing piers limits visitors to the island to a maximum of about 400 per day, a figure that is reached only rarely, with the average less than 200. Most visitors stay for three or four hours, walking, sketching, or taking photographs. Five simple self-catering cottages are available to rent and a small coffee shop serves refreshments during the season.

The silence strikes you at once. The seabirds, stonechats, and swallows sound louder than on the mainland; sheep graze silently on the steep hillside. The simple domestic ruins are very touching; you do not need to know the history to work out what happened to their owners (most departed for other places, with many settling in Springfield, Massachusetts).

■ TIP→ Before you go, read Maurice O'Sullivan's *Twenty Years a-Growing*, a fascinating account of a simple way of life that has only recently disappeared on the Blaskets. For an overview of the island's more recent history, read *Hungry for Home: Leaving the Blaskets—A Journey from the Edge of Ireland* by Cole Moreton.

GETTING HERE AND AROUND

These days it takes just 15 minutes from Dún Chaoin (Dunquin) Pier to make the 3-km (2-mile) crossing of the Blasket Sound, but even on a calm day the swell can be considerable. In summer, the island is usually accessible most days; in winter the island can be cut off for weeks.

CONTACTS Dingle Boat Tours. ✉ *Dingle* ☎ *066/915–1344* 🌐 *www.dingleboattours.com.*

Great Blasket Island Accommodation

$$ | **HOUSE** | Three restored self-catering cottages offer the magical opportunity to overnight on this wild and remote island. **Pros:** a wild escape from the modern world; experience the silence after the day-trippers leave; unique, bragging-rights-type stay. **Cons:** no electricity; sailings are weather-dependent; must bring own food supplies. $ *Rooms from: €130* ✉ *Great Blasket Island, Dunquin* ☎ *086/313–5098* 🌐 *www.greatblasketisland.net* ⏲ *Closed Oct.–Apr.* *3 cottages (each cottage sleeps up to 7)* *No Meals* ☞ *Price is for 1 person, each extra person pays €50.*

Tralee

50 km (31 miles) northeast of An Daingean (Dingle Town) on R559.

County Kerry's capital and its largest town, Tralee (population 24,000) is the main shopping and business destination for North and West Kerry. It's a transport

Almost as memorable as the boat ride to the Skellig isles is the excursion out to the unspoiled Blasket Islands, a favorite escape for poets and writers.

hub for the region and has a large student population. More of a commercial draw than tourism hot spot, it nevertheless offers a few quality attractions, including the town museum, wetlands center, and the Siamsa Tíre—the National Folk Theatre of Ireland—which stages impressive dances and plays based on Irish folklore.

The town has long been associated with the popular Irish song "The Rose of Tralee," the inspiration for the annual Rose of Tralee International Festival. The second week of August, Irish communities worldwide send young women to join native Irish competitors; one of them is chosen as the Rose of Tralee. Visitors, musicians, and entertainers pack the town then. A two-day horse-racing meet—with seven races a day—runs at the same time, which contributes to the crowds.

GETTING HERE AND AROUND

Tralee is at the junction of the N21 from Limerick (about 1½ hours away), the N21 and N22 from Killarney (about a half hour away), and the N86 from Dingle (an hour away). Cork is 116 km (72 miles) away. It's also the terminus for the train from Dublin (the trip takes just under four hours) and is well served by buses from Shannon Airport, Limerick, Galway, Killarney, and Dingle. There's a bus service that circles the town every hour, mainly to facilitate students; visit the tourist information office for details.

CONTACTS Tralee Bus Station. ✉ *John Joe Sheehy Rd., Tralee* ☎ *066/716–4700.* **Tralee Rail Station.** ✉ *Casement Station, John Joe Sheehy Rd., Tralee* ☎ *066/712–3522* 🌐 *www.irishrail.ie.*

VISITOR INFORMATION

CONTACTS Tralee Tourist Office. ✉ *Ashe Memorial Hall, Denny St., Tralee* ☎ *066/712–1288* 🌐 *www.discoverireland.ie.*

Sights

Kerry County Museum

HISTORY MUSEUM | FAMILY | Tralee's major cultural attraction traces the history of Kerry's people since 5000 BC, using dioramas and an entertaining audiovisual show. There is an excellent display on Tom Crean and Roger Casement, the celebrated humanitarian activist whose brief sojourn in Kerry during Ireland's Easter Rising had a huge impact locally and internationally. You can also walk through a life-size reconstruction of a Tralee street of the Middle Ages. ✉ *Ashe Memorial Hall, Denny St., Tralee* ☎ *066/712–7777* 🌐 *www.kerrymuseum.ie* 🎟 *€5* ⏲ *Closed Sun., Mon., and Sept.–May.*

Tralee Bay Wetlands Center

VISITOR CENTER | FAMILY | Get to know the birdlife of the area before venturing on to Kerry's many beaches by visiting this small but effective center, just a short drive from town. The trail offers bird blinds, and the nature zone will help you identify the many wading birds of the area, while the viewing tower reveals the vast expanse of Tralee Bay and the Slieve Mish mountains. The activity zone and lake offer boating (from €10) and an outdoor climbing wall (€15). The center is also a good spot for lunch. ✉ *Ballyard Rd, Tralee* ✣ *Off main N86 Dingle road on Wild Atlantic Way* ☎ *066/712–6700* 🌐 *www.traleebaywetlands.org* 🎟 *€3, café free* ☞ *Last admission 3:30 pm Sept.–Mar; 4:30 pm Apr.–Aug. Car park closes 5 pm.*

Restaurants

Quinlans' Seafood Bar

$ | FAST FOOD | Cutting the supply chain to the minimum, Quinlan's fleet of vessels transport its catch from ocean to plate on the same day. The cod, squid, and scampi are fresh and cooked to order with light panfry options. $ *Average main: €9* ✉ *1 The Mall, Tralee* ☎ *066/712–3998* 🌐 *kerryfish.com/seafood-bars.*

Hotels

Ballygarry House Hotel

$$$ | HOTEL | A mile and a half outside town, this family-run hotel with 10 acres of gardens and supremely stylish guest rooms is an excellent choice if you're touring by car. **Pros:** next to a woodland amenity area for runners; free access to spa, gym, and outdoor hot tub; Restaurant 58 is highly reputed. **Cons:** no shops or cafés within walking distance; uninspiring exterior and older "classic" rooms a bit plain, so it's worth upgrading to "superior"; often hosts large weddings. $ *Rooms from: €185* ✉ *Leebrook, Tralee* ☎ *066/712–3322* 🌐 *www.ballygarryhouse.com* *64 rooms* 🍽 *Free Breakfast.*

★ Ballyseede Castle

$$$$ | HOTEL | Originally dating back to the 15th century, Ballyseede Castle is just a side step away from modern times, operating in its own gorgeous, eccentric zone where you might chance upon a Shakespearean production taking place on the property in summer, or a docile Irish wolfhound might appear from around the corner. **Pros:** peaceful location on own gounds; excellent restaurants; charming bedroom furnishings. **Cons:** 10-minute drive from center of Tralee; popular with weddings; no leisure facilities. $ *Rooms from: €290* ✉ *Tralee* ✣ *5 km (3 miles) from Tralee center via N21 and R875* ☎ *066/712–5799* 🌐 *www.ballyseedecastle.com* ⏲ *Closed Jan. and Feb.* *45 rooms* 🍽 *Free Breakfast.*

Performing Arts

★ National Folk Theater of Ireland (Siamsa Tíre)

THEATER | Language is no barrier to the supremely colorful entertainment offered by this theater, which re-creates traditional rural life through music, folk theater, and dance. There are nightly shows May to September, with year-round visual arts exhibitions and less frequent evening

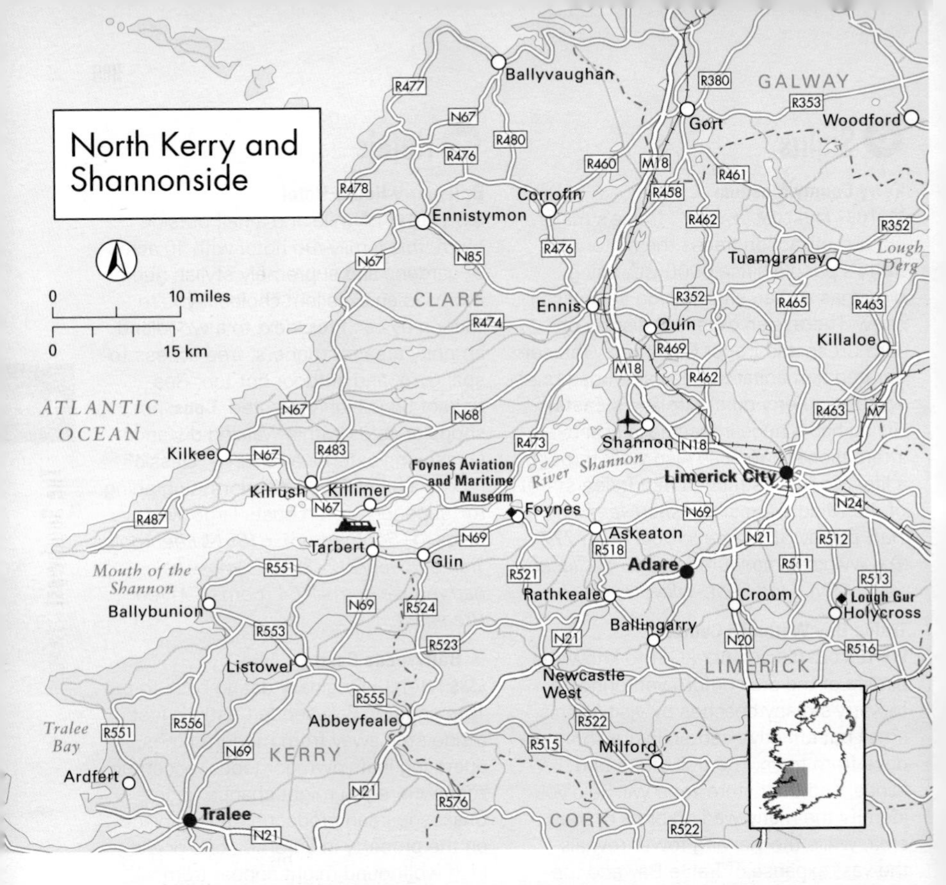

shows. ✉ *Town Park, Tralee* ☎ *066/712–3055* 🌐 *www.siamsatire.com.*

Activities

GOLF

★ Ballybunion Golf Club

GOLF | President Bill Clinton will be eternally associated in Irish golfers' minds with this revered course. In fact, there's even a brass statue of him teeing off in the nearby village, to commemorate his visit here in 1999. On the shore of the Atlantic where the Shannon Estuary meets the open sea, Ballybunion has the huge dunes of County Clare's Lahinch courses without the blind shots. It's no pushover, but every hole is pleasurable. Watch out for "Mrs. Simpson," a double fairway bunker on the 1st hole, named after the wife of Tom Simpson, the architect who remodeled the course in 1937. (Tom Watson did the same in 1995.) The Cashen Course, which opened in 1985, was designed by Robert Trent Jones Sr. and currently is available at a bargain rate if you've paid for a round on the Old Course. ✉ *Sandhill Rd., Ballybunion* ✣ *32 km (20 miles) north of Tralee on R556* ☎ *068/27146* 🌐 *www.ballybuniongolf-club.ie* 🎫 *Old Course: mid-Apr.–early Oct. €300; Cashen Course: Apr. 6–Oct. 9 from €125* ⛳ *Old Course: 18 holes, 6568 yards, par 72; Cashen Course: 18 holes, 6306 yards, par 70* ⏲ *Members-only weekends.*

Adare

19 km (12 miles) southwest of Limerick City, 82 km (51 miles) northeast of Tralee.

On the banks of the River Maigue, this once-upon-a-time-ified village dotted with thatched cottages is famed as one of Ireland's prettiest spots. It was given a beauty makeover by a wealthy local landowner, the 3rd Earl of Dunraven, in the 1820s and 1830s, in an effort to create the "perfect rustic village." To an extent, Adare is a victim of its own success, with its constant bottleneck of traffic along the village's main artery from both ends due to day visitors and the stream of commuters that pass through from the south to nearby Limerick City.

The town's historic sights include the remains of two 13th-century abbeys, a 15th-century friary, and the keep of the 13th-century Desmond Castle (now the centerpiece of a private golf course). Adjacent to the Adare Heritage Centre you'll find the Trinitarian Priory, founded in 1230 and now a convent. From the main bridge (where you can best view the castle), head to the Augustinian Priory and its gracious cloister. The most fetching time-burnished allure is provided by Adare's stone-built, thatched-roof cottages, often adorned with colorful, flower-filled window boxes and built for the earl's estate tenants. Some now house boutiques selling Irish crafts and antiques, along with several fine restaurants. Adare Manor, an imposing Tudor–Gothic Revival mansion, which was once the grand house of the Dunraven peerage, is now a celebrated hotel; on its grounds you can view two 12th-century ruins, the St. Nicholas Chapel and the Chantry Chapel.

The Listowel Ferry

Shannon Ferry Group. The Listowel Ferry offers a convenient and scenic 20-minute shortcut if you're heading for the West of Ireland. From Listowel, head north on N69 18 km (11 miles) to Tarbert, the terminus for the Shannon Ferries crossing to Killimer in West Clare. Reduced service on Sunday. ✉ *Tarbert* ☎ *065/905–3124* 🌐 *shannonferries.com* 🎫 *€23* ☞ *Discounted rates online.*

Sights

Adare Heritage Centre

VISITOR CENTER | This center is home to an array of helpful facilities, including a restaurant and three retail outlets (one sells sweaters, another crafts, and the third heraldry items). There is also an exhibition on Adare's history since 1223, complete with a 15-minute audiovisual display, but some may feel it is not worth the extra fee. Guided tours of Desmond Castle (June–September; €6) can be booked in advance online, and leave the center by bus. ✉ *Main St., Adare* ☎ *061/396–666* 🌐 *www.adareheritagecentre.ie* 🎫 *Heritage center free, exhibition €5.*

Restaurants

★ 1826 Adare

$$$ | **MODERN IRISH** | Bringing his classical training to County Limerick, critically acclaimed chef Wade Murphy opened 1826 Adare with his wife, Elaine, in 2013. Since then, his elegant comfort food has been in high demand, served in a pretty thatched cottage with whitewashed walls and cozy decor. **Known for:** clever,

As cute as a storybook village, Adare is a thatched-roof jewel laid out with characteristics that conjure up the English rather than the Irish countryside.

accomplished Irish cooking; legendary late Sunday lunches; excellent service. *Average main: €26 Main St., Adare 061/396–004 www.1826adare.ie Closed Mon.–Wed. No lunch Mon.–Sat.*

The Maigue Restaurant

$$$ | **IRISH** | If you like good, old-fashioned country service from a bygone era, with a tried and tested traditional menu that pleases guests across the generational divide, the Maigue Restaurant fits the bill. It offers some of the finest local ingredients in a short but crowd-pleasing menu. *Average main: €30 Main St., Adare 61/605–900 www.dunravenhotel.com/dining/the-maigue-restaurant/57-1.*

 Hotels

★ **Adare Manor Hotel**

$$$$ | **HOTEL** | This spectacular, recently overhauled, Victorian mansion, once the abode of the Quin family (earls of Dunraven) is an ostentatious Gothic wonderland, thanks to 840 well-manicured acres outside and the 26-foot-high, 100-foot-long Minstrels' Gallery with its decorated ceiling and stained-glass windows inside. **Pros:** fully updated Gothic mansion; one of Ireland's best golf courses; excellent amenities including a cinema, spa, and pool. **Cons:** off the beaten track as a touring base; fitness facilities and pool are modest in size; expensive. *Rooms from: €850 Limerick Rd., Adare 061/396–566 www.adaremanor.ie 108 rooms Free Breakfast.*

★ **Mustard Seed at Echo Lodge**

$$ | **B&B/INN** | This is the small country hotel of your dreams: a Victorian yellow-stucco jewel set atop a small hill overlooking Ballingarry, a village that time forgot, deep in rural Ireland, yet only 13 km (8 miles) southwest of Adare. **Pros:** stylish flair; extremely comfortable; acclaimed restaurant also open to nonresidents. **Cons:** in the middle of nowhere; rooster crows at dawn.

Rooms from: €140 ✉ Village Center, Ballingarry ☎ 069/68508 🌐 www.mustardseed.ie ⏲ Closed last 2 wks in Jan. 16 rooms 🍴 *Free Breakfast.*

Shopping

Draiocht Art Gallery

ART GALLERIES | *Draiocht* means "magic" in Irish, and this gallery is described by its owner as "a magical store of crafts and gifts." Many of the crafts and ceramics are Irish-made, and the colorful paintings in its large gallery come from all over Ireland. ✉ *Station Rd., Blackabbey, across side road from Heritage Centre, Adare* ☎ *061/395–539* 🌐 *www.draiochtadare.ie.*

Lucy Erridge

JEWELRY & WATCHES | Designer Irish knitwear, crafts, and original artwork are all for sale in this thatched-cottage boutique. ✉ *Main St., Adare* ☎ *061/396–898* 🌐 *www.lucyerridge.com.*

Activities

Limerick Greenway

HIKING & WALKING | **FAMILY** | The old, disused Limerick-to-Tralee railway line is now a pedestrian and cycleway stretching 40 km (25 miles) through some of the richest pastures in Ireland. The Greenway starts in Rathkeale and links the pretty county of Newcastle West to Abbeyfeale on a route that passes through meadows, woods, restored Victorian stations, a viaduct, and a 115-meter-long tunnel. Each town has a selection of cafés, castles, bars, and inns—and finishes at the County Kerry border. Cycle hire available. ✉ *Adare* ✣ *The Greenway starts in Rathkeale, which is 12 km (7 miles) south west of Adare on N21.*

Limerick City

19 km (12 miles) northeast of Adare, 26 km (15 miles) east of Shannon Airport, 198 km (123 miles) southwest of Dublin.

Limerick City is, historically, an island settlement accessible by a series of bridges that cross a wide bend of the Shannon River shortly before it flows into the Atlantic Ocean. It's the republic's third-largest city (population 94,000) and, after years in the doldrums, it has emerged over the last couple of decades to become one of the most dynamic cities in Ireland. High employment rates, the rejuvenated city center, state-of-the-art universities, low crime rate and success in the performing arts and sport—particularly rugby and hurling—have brought a renewed confidence that blows through its narrow lanes and broad avenues. Its recent designation as a gateway city to the Wild Atlantic Way driving route by the national tourism board is yet another bow to its resurgence.

TOURS

Limerick City Walking Tours

WALKING TOURS | City walks are scheduled from 10 am with an extra 2 pm slot in summer and can be booked online or at the tourist office, near the departure point. Choose between Georgian Limerick, including sites associated with Frank McCourt's *Angela's Ashes,* and medieval Limerick. At other times of the year small groups can book in advance. ✉ *Limerick City Tourist Office, Arthur's Quay, Limerick City* ☎ *61/484–911 Noel Curtin (mid-Oct.–Apr.)* 🌐 *limerickcitywalkingtours.com.*

★ **Limerick Civic Trust Walking Tours**

WALKING TOURS | To appreciate Limerick's long and eventful history, take a guided walking tour of medieval Limerick's English Town, People's Park, or the Masonic Lodge with Limerick Civic Trust. Advance

Looming over Adare's Desmond Castle is the regal Adare Manor Hotel, once home to the town's lord of the manor, the earl of Dunraven.

booking is required. ✉ *Church St., Limerick City* ☎ *061/313–399* 🌐 *www.limerickcivictrust.ie* 🎫 *€10.*

VISITOR INFORMATION

CONTACTS Limerick City Tourist Office. ✉ *20 O'Connell St., Limerick City* ☎ *061/317–522* 🌐 *www.failteireland.ie.*

Sights

There has been a large-scale investment in Limerick's city center in recent years, and it is finally starting to pay off. An attractive riverside walk now leads visitors past the city's three bridges that span the Shannon River, passing through the medieval center, which is situated, as in Paris, on a small island surrounded by rushing water. Bars and restaurants have started to colonize the quiet riverside quays across from the Hunt Museum, while the Georgian Quarter has a focal point in the People's Park, an elegant 19th-century city oasis which is ablaze in colorful bloom at any time of year. Large-scale pedestrianization has funneled traffic away from the main streets leaving fresh space for alfresco dining and a slower pace of life.

The good-nature sporting passion of Limerick's rugby and hurling supporters is legendary, and if you are in town on a match day it will never be forgotten. At any time of year, Limerick's reputation for friendliness is a genuine phenomenon: total strangers will engage you in conversation on the street—relax and enjoy!

Foynes Aviation and Maritime Museum

OTHER MUSEUM | FAMILY | Foynes was the crossroads between American and European skies in the early, glamorous days of flying. In fact, it was on this very site that an innovative chef called Joe Sheridan created the Irish coffee on a chilly night in 1943 to warm the bones of shivering passengers. The airport would soon move across the river to become Shannon Airport, but in that brief period in the middle of the 20th century, this little village welcomed dignitaries like Eleanor Roosevelt, John F. Kennedy, King George of Greece, novelist Ernest

Hemingway, and from the golden age of Hollywood, Douglas Fairbanks, Bob Hope, actress Gracie Fields, Bill Rogers, Edward G. Robinson, and Humphrey Bogart. The museum has the only B314 flying boat replica in the world, and it also explores the area's maritime history. There is a café on-site along with an Irish coffee lounge. ✉ *Aras Ide, Main St.* ✣ *36 km (20 miles) west of Limerick City on N69* ☎ *69/65416* 🌐 *www.flyingboatmuseum.com* 🎫 *€12* ⏲ *Closed Nov.–Mar.*

Hunt Museum

OTHER MUSEUM | Designed by architect Davis Ducart—the man who modeled the city's entire Georgian grid—this handsome limestone building was once the Old Custom House. Located on the banks of the Shannon in the city center, the Hunt Museum has the finest collection of Celtic and medieval treasures outside the National Museum in Dublin. Ancient Irish metalwork, European objets d'art, and a selection of 20th-century European and Irish paintings—including works by Jack B. Yeats—are on view. The museum has regular high-profile exhibitions. Free tours are offered and a café overlooks the river. ✉ *The Custom House, Rutland St., Limerick City* ☎ *061/312–833* 🌐 *www.huntmuseum.com* 🎫 *From €8 online (free Sun.)* ⏲ *Closed Mon.*

International Rugby Experience

VISITOR CENTER | **FAMILY** | If someone in your family has ambitions to play sports professionally, this interactive museum will test your budding athlete's aspiration with an immersive, linear voyage through the steps in that journey. Focused on rugby (it is Limerick, after all), the museum charts the journey from the grass roots of the game through training and team participation, and culminates in the greatest rugby moments on the global stage. The building has commanding views of the city, a café, and retail—and is bang in the heart of the city. ✉ *40 O'Connell St., Limerick City* 🌐 *www.internationalrugbyexperience.com.*

★ **King John's Castle**

CASTLE/PALACE | **FAMILY** | First built by the Normans in the early 1200s, King John's Castle still bears traces on its north side of a 1691 bombardment. If you climb the drum towers (the oldest section), you'll have a spectacular view of the city and the Shannon. Inside, an audiovisual show illustrates the history of Limerick and Ireland; an archaeology center has three excavated, pre-Norman houses to explore; and interactive exhibitions include scale models of Limerick from its founding in AD 922. ✉ *King's Island, Limerick City* ☎ *061/711–222* 🌐 *www.kingjohnscastle.com* 🎫 *€13.*

★ **Lough Gur**

HISTORIC SIGHT | The visitor center is a thatched replica of a Neolithic hut and it has excellent prehistoric exhibits and a small museum that displays Neolithic pieces and replicas of Bronze Age finds in the Lough Gur area (originals are displayed in Dublin's National Museum). The center gives context to the fascinating historical merit of the ancient settlements in the surrounding area. Of most significance is Grange, a magnificent 4,000-year-old circular enclosure made up of 113 upright stones. It's the largest prehistoric circle of its kind in Ireland and worth the detour from Limerick City. It's a 3-km (2-mile) walk from the heritage center with free roadside parking and access to the site. ✉ *Lough Gur, Limerick* ✣ *20 km (12 miles) south of Limerick City on R512* ☎ *061/385–186* 🌐 *www.loughgur.com* 🎫 *€5* ⏲ *Closes at 4 pm Oct.–Feb.*

★ **The Milk Market**

MARKET | One of Ireland's oldest and biggest—and arguably best—markets, with a fine collection of artisanal food producers, many direct from the rich pastures in County Limerick's Golden Vale. Cheese, breads, pastries, and meat stalls mix with with fresh fruit and vegetable traders along with sushi and garnish producers. They all sell their wares beneath a sturdy, all-weather canvas roof with a café upstairs in a mezzanine. Boho vintage clothing retailers and restaurants operate around the perimeter. The market takes place over the weekend, although Saturday morning is the time to see local citizens arrive in droves. For a sweet break, head around the corner to Cruise's Street for a selection of bakeries selling fresh cream cakes, pies, and coffee. ✉ *Market House, Mungret St., Limerick City* ☎ *061/214–782* 🌐 *www.milkmarketlimerick.ie.*

★ St. Mary's Cathedral

CHURCH | St. Mary's Cathedral is the city's oldest building in daily use. It was founded in 1168 on the site of an elaborate palace, some of which can still be seen today, such as the intricately carved Romanesque-style door that was once the entrance to original building. Inside, the black-oak carved misericords in the choir stalls are unique to Ireland and are from this period, while the altar in the Lady' Chapel is 13 feet long, and it is the cathedral's original pre-Reformation (from when the church was a Catholic place of worship) masterpiece. Oliver Cromwell's troops had unceremoniously dumped it, but it resurfaced in the 1960s in remarkably good shape. Donal Mór O'Brien, the last king of Munster and the man who constructed the cathedral, is believed to be buried in St. Mary's; a stunning carved sculpture of O'Brien prince stands on the grounds.

Other notable features include cannonballs that have remained since the siege of Limerick by the Williamites in 1691, exquisite stained glass windows, and a leper's squint—a slot where the sick could hear mass and receive communion from the streets outside. The bells of the cathedral's bells have cast a spellbinding melody across the city for decades. Bear in mind this is a fully functioning church with daily Church of Ireland services throughout the week. ✉ *Bridge St., Limerick City* ☎ *061/310–293* 🌐 *www.stmaryscathedral.ie* 🎫 *€5.*

Thomond Park

SPORTS VENUE | FAMILY | Thomond Park is a giant edifice to the city's passion for sport. It dominates the skyline with giant proportions that rise over its low valley backdrop. With a capacity of 26,000 people it attracts all the big rugby matches and high-profile performers like Pink, Ed Sheeran, Elton John, Bob Dylan, and Bruce Springsteen. Guests can take a tour to the innards of the stadium—the home of Munster Rugby—to discover significant milestones and the places normally only seen by players, officials, and artists. ✉ *Thomond Park, Cratloe Rd., Limerick City* ☎ *061/421–109* 🌐 *www.thomondpark.ie.*

Treaty City Brewery

BREWERY | Learn about the local brewing history from the 1700s and flavor process from master brewers in the heart of Limerick's medieval quarter. Treaty distributes Harris Pale Ale (named after Hollywood actor and local man Richard Harris), Thomond Red Ale, and Shannon River IPA to all the major pubs in Limerick City. ✉ *24 and 25 Nicholas St., Limerick City* ☎ *061/546–549* 🌐 *www.treatycitybrewery.ie.*

The Treaty Stone

MONUMENT | If you want to understand Irish history in one small nugget—or rather, a giant limestone block overlooking the Shannon River and King John's Castle—then cross over to the Treaty Stone, close to the Curragower Restaurant. Limerick's nickname (the Treaty City) is derived from this monument, set upon a hefty, stepped plinth, the site where the Williamite-Jacobite War ended in 1691 after the last stand by supporters of King James at the end of the Siege of Limerick. The Jacobites signed an agreement on the Treaty Stone that the Catholic Irish would be treated in a fair and dignified manner by the Williamites after their departure to mainland Europe. It was not honored and the country descended into unrest, a land free of civil rights, when those who remained in Ireland were held to the mercy of the conquerors. It didn't end well. ✉ *The Treaty Stone, Clancy Strand, Limerick City.*

University of Limerick
COLLEGE CAMPUS | **FAMILY** | Linked to the city by a river walk, the University of Limerick (UL) is a metropolis of redbrick buildings and wide-open spaces. It's the home of Ireland's first and only Olympic-sized swimming pool outside of the capital and the largest indoor sports complex, and, in keeping with its home base, it's the only university in the country to get five stars for its impressive sports facilities. The university's on-campus concert hall has attracted a wide range of performers from Johnny Cash to Van Morrison over the years. Its Living Bridge—a curving white feat of engineering—is the longest pedestrian bridge in Ireland, and it connects County Limerick to County Clare. Art lovers will appreciate the phenomenal collection of work in the Visual Art Collection in Plassey House. There are a number of quality restaurants on-site. ✉ *University of Limerick, Limerick City* ☎ *061/202–700* 🌐 *www.ul.ie.*

Restaurants

Bobby Byrnes
$ | **IRISH** | Operated by the same family for decades, this is the pub for a good old-fashioned Sunday roast with good portion sizes and all week breakfasts. Expect a typical pub menu cooked with flair, which includes burgers, steak, fish-and-chips with surprisingly good vegan options. **Known for:** Sunday roasts. [$] *Average main: €10* ✉ *1–3 O'Connell Ave., Limerick City* ☎ *61/316–949* 🌐 *bobbybyrnes.ie.*

The Buttery
$ | **CAFÉ** | This eatery is very popular, with a predominantly local clientele, so book ahead or arrive early before the queues. Sensible pricing, fresh organic food, and a social buzz come with good service and a quick turnover of guests. **Known for:** all-day weekend brunch; full Irish breakfast; fresh juices. [$] *Average main: €10* ✉ *10 Bedford Row, Limerick City* ☎ *061/597–668* 🌐 *www.thebuttery.ie.*

Canteen
$ | **CONTEMPORARY** | Paul William's smart, low-key restaurant in a pretty part of Georgian Limerick is all about good food, sustainability, and coffee. Flahavan's porridge with organic yogurt and fruit, organic eggs, and locally sourced onion sausage and bagels feature in the breakfast menu, while wraps, salads, freshly made soups, and vegetarian dishes are some of the other options available. **Known for:** Gobi vegetable curry lunchbox; local ingredients; refreshing change from fried foods. [$] *Average main: €10* ✉ *26 Catherine St., Limerick* ☎ *085/215–3212* 🌐 *www.wearecanteen.com.*

★ **The Curragower Bar and Restaurant**
$ | **IRISH** | It's not just the food that's made this restaurant the most popular in town: guests also like to drink in the views of King John's Castle (particularly when lit up in the evening) from under the heated terrace over sea bass served with crab beignets, salsa verde, and baby potatoes. Scampi comes with big planks of chips and lemon sole arrives in a bed of leek and onion. **Known for:** vegetarian options; excellent views; good selection of beers on draft. [$] *Average main: €15* ✉ *Clancy Strand, Limerick City* ☎ *087/701–4723* 🌐 *www.curragower.com.*

★ **The East Room**
$$$$ | **IRISH** | Chef Derek Fitzpatrick creates a refined and concise menu from local ingredients that have been foraged, or grown by local artisanal suppliers or on the restaurant's rooftop garden. There's a choice between an evening tasting menu (sensibly priced at €60 given the options) with six courses that could include

scallops, beef, or fresh catch. **Known for:** views of the waters of the Shannon River; à la carte menu options as well; elegant ambience. *$ Average main: €60 ✉ Plassey House, University of Limerick, Limerick City ☎ 061/202–186 🌐 www.eastroom.ie ⏲ Closed Mon. and Tues. No dinner Sun.*

Hotels

The Bedford Townhouse

$ | **B&B/INN** | This thin sliver of Bedford Row is in a quiet area in Limerick, while being in the very heart of the city. **Pros:** quiet retreat; small gym and café on-site; city center location. **Cons:** colors are quite dark; no car park; max two rooms per reservation. *$ Rooms from: €110 ✉ Bedford Row, V94 NNPO, Limerick City ☎ 061/204–400 🌐 www.thebedford.ie ⏲ Closed Christmas ⇨ 12 rooms 🍽 No Meals.*

Glenstal Abbey Guesthouse

$$ | **B&B/INN** | Glenstal Abbey has lured guests from presidents of countries to movie stars in search of a spiritual reboot—or just undiluted peace—for decades. **Pros:** free car parking; peaceful and secure location; beautiful setting. **Cons:** remote location for exploring; long hilly avenue to exit of grounds; a working monastery, education center, and farm. *$ Rooms from: €120 ✉ Murroe, County Limerick, Limerick ✥ 16 km (10 miles) east of Limerick City via R506 (watch for signposting) ☎ 61/621–005 🌐 glenstal.com/abbey/stay ⇨ 12 rooms 🍽 Free Breakfast.*

Glin Castle

$$$$ | **HOUSE** | **FAMILY** | With 800 years of ancestry in Glin, owner Catherine Fitzgerald and husband, actor Dominic West, have created a unique space at the point where the longest river in Ireland and Britain, the Shannon, meets the Atlantic Ocean. **Pros:** excellent touring base for the Wild Atlantic Way; peace and solitude with a walled garden; authentic castle backdrop. **Cons:** expensive; can only hire the castle in its entirety; need a car. *$ Rooms from: €5000 ✉ Glin Castle ✥ 48 km (30 miles) west of Limerick City on N69 ☎ 087/329–4575 🌐 www.glin-castle.com ⇨ 15 rooms 🍽 No Meals.*

No. 1 Pery Square

$$ | **HOTEL** | One of Limerick's finest Georgian houses—a tall redbrick structure with classical cut-stone portico, overlooking leafy People's Park—has been converted into a sumptuous boutique hotel with a reputation for attentive service. **Pros:** genuinely stylish; private parking; excellent service. **Cons:** you need to book well in advance; no air-conditioning. *$ Rooms from: €140 ✉ 1 Pery Sq., Limerick City ☎ 061/402–402 🌐 www.oneperysquare.com ⇨ 20 rooms 🍽 Free Breakfast.*

The Savoy Hotel

$$ | **HOTEL** | This gleaming black and glass building is a central as it gets in Limerick City—right across from a bus hub on busy Henry Street, close to pubs, restaurants, and clubs. **Pros:** city center across from bus hub; state-of-the-art room facilities; good dining facilities. **Cons:** no parking immediately on-site; no gym; gives little local flavor to architecture or furnishings. *$ Rooms from: €165 ✉ Henry St., Limerick City ☎ 61/448–700 🌐 www.thesavoycollection.com/the-savoy ⇨ 110 rooms 🍽 No Meals.*

The Strand

$$ | **HOTEL** | **FAMILY** | The Strand, a seven-story cube of glass, has become a city landmark since its construction during the Celtic Tiger economic boom. **Pros:** leisure facilities; on-site parking; views. **Cons:** guests must cross adjoining bridge to reach the city; decor lacks imagination or local flair; popular for weddings, rugby games, and local events. *$ Rooms from: €130 ✉ Ennis Rd., V94 03F2, Limerick City ☎ 061/421–800 🌐 www.strandhotellimerick.ie ⇨ 204 rooms 🍽 No Meals.*

Nightlife

Dolan's Pub

LIVE MUSIC | A lively waterfront spot, Dolan's has traditional Irish music every night, and dancing classes from September to May. Dolan's Warehouse, under the same management and in the same location, is a live-music venue with top national and international acts. Kasbah—one of Dolan's venues—has regular mixed straight and LBGTQ+ nights. ✉ *3–4 Dock Rd., Limerick City* ☎ *061/314–483* 🌐 *www.dolans.ie.*

JJ Bowles Pub

PUBS | Supposedly the oldest inn in town—it has served ale to locals from its low-ceiling quarters in a narrow slip lane by the west end of Thomond Bridge since 1794 (the building dates back over a hundred years earlier). JJ Bowles offers wonderful views from its riverside beer garden. It has a good reputation for the quality of its Guinness, making it a good stop on a chilly day if you can find a seat by the warm glow from its fireplace. And, being midway between the city center and Thomond Park Stadium, expect lively crowds during rugby season. ✉ *8 Thomondgate, Limerick City* ☎ *061/454–261* 🌐 *www.jjbowlespub.com.*

The Lime Tree and Belltable Theatre

CAFÉS | **FAMILY** | The Belltable Theater, a former Georgian town house, was remodeled with an Arts and Crafts facade in the early 19th century when it became a pioneering cinema. It has a gorgeous tapestry of wrought iron, stained glass, and limestone materials that stand apart from its neat redbrick neighbors on O'Connell Avenue. Just one block north of the oval-shaped Crescent with its large statue of the liberator, Daniel O'Connell, this building has entertained Limerick's citizens with plays and movies for more than a century. Intimate, with just 200 seats, it hosts many touring productions of stand-up comics, art-house movies, or the works of Irish playwrights like John B. Keane. It has a small café.

For larger productions, head 2 km (1 mile) south to the recently constructed, ubermodern Lime Tree Theatre on the grounds of the city's Mary Immaculate College. ✉ *Limerick* ☎ *061/953–400* 🌐 *www.limetreetheatre.ie.*

The Locke Bar

LIVE MUSIC | Set on the riverside, this is one of Limerick's oldest bars, dating from 1724, and has live music every night. It's also a great place for outdoor drinking in summer or a simple bar food meal. ✉ *3 George's Quay, Limerick City* ☎ *061/413–733* 🌐 *www.lockebar.com.*

Nancy Blake's Pub

PUBS | There's traditional fireside music at this busy pub year-round on Monday, Tuesday, and Wednesday in the front bar starting at 9 pm. ✉ *19 Denmark St., Limerick City* ☎ *061/416–443.*

Tom Collin's Bar

BARS | Tom Collin's Bar has managed to retain all of its authentic Victorian charm, which you'll see from its bright red-and-white timber facade or its arched doorway with tiny lion medallions and white metal fanlight. It paves the way for the old shopfront character inside, where it's as though a clock stopped ticking sometime in the distant past on the wall behind the ruby shades and mahogany finish of the bar counter. Service is second to none and the Guinness is legendary in this quiet premises, just a stone's throw from busy O'Connell Street. ✉ *34 Cecil St., Limerick City* ☎ *061/415–749.*

W.J. South's Pub

PUBS | An old-fashioned pub, this one is typical of the age of Frank McCourt's *Angela's Ashes*. There's no music, but you'll find big-game rugby matches playing live on TV. Drop by for hearty bar food and a drink while the local side, Munster, is playing. ✉ *4 Quinlan St., Limerick City* ☎ *061/318–850.*

Shopping

Brown Thomas Department Store

DEPARTMENT STORE | One of the largest department stores in Ireland has offered the best of local and international brands since 1874. Brown Thomas spans almost a full block of Limerick City's O'Connell Street. Upstairs gift and home wear ranges from quirky to brands like Waterford Crystal. Brown's Restaurant is a popular brunch, lunch, or coffee-and-scone stop. ✉ *O'Connell St., Limerick City* ☎ *061/417–222* 🌐 *www.brownthomas.com.*

Carraig Donn

WOMEN'S CLOTHING | Carraig Donn stocks a fashionable twist in Irish design with a variety of brands using fine-quality material. Women's clothing, gifts, candles, throws, and jewelry are the mainstay of this store. ✉ *O'Connell Mall, Limerick City* ☎ *061/418–011* 🌐 *www.carraigdonn.com.*

Crescent Shopping Centre

MALL | The largest and oldest shopping mall outside of Dublin and its environs is within close walking distance of the city center, and it draws the crowds seven days a week. Cafés, a cinema, boutiques, and gift stores make for a good rainy-day excursion—particularly with free, easy parking. ✉ *Dooradoyle Rd.* ☎ *061/228–560* 🌐 *www.crescentshoppingcentre.ie.*

Irish Handcrafts

CRAFTS | Beautifully crafted woolen clothing for men, women, and children—from Aran sweaters, throws, caps, and scarves to Donegal tweed—are all in full supply in the cramped, well-stocked store on Patrick Street. Owned and operated by the same family for decades, expect the service to be personable and insightful; be sure to ask about the intricate backstory of each pattern. ✉ *26 Patrick St., Limerick City* ☎ *061/415–504* 🌐 *www.irishhandcraft.com.*

Chapter 9

COUNTY CLARE, GALWAY CITY, AND THE ARAN ISLANDS

Updated by
Vic O'Sullivan

Sights ★★★★★ | Restaurants ★★★★★ | Hotels ★★★★☆ | Shopping ★★★★☆ | Nightlife ★★★★★

WELCOME TO COUNTY CLARE, GALWAY CITY, AND THE ARAN ISLANDS

TOP REASONS TO GO

★ **Burren and Cliffs of Moher UNESCO Global GeoPark:** This is one of Earth's most evocative landscapes with its endless miles of limestone slabs etched with ancient monuments and rare fauna as far at the Atlantic Ocean.

★ **Galway City:** With its top-notch restaurants and bars, vibrant arts scene, free-spirit boho vibe, and magnificent medieval center, Galway is arguably the most tourist-friendly city in Ireland.

★ **Dun Aengus, Aran Islands:** Dun Aengus Fort on Inis Mór, the largest of the Aran Islands, stands 100 meters high and barrier-free above the Atlantic Ocean.

★ **East County Clare:** The lush landscape is dotted. Lough Derg, Ireland's prettiest lake, defines the county's easterly contour.

★ **Loop Head Peninsula:** At the southerly tip of County Clare's 75-mile slice of the Wild Atlantic Way is a cliff-edge driving route filled with dramatic seascapes, blow holes, quirky pubs, and a lighthouse.

Without ever passing beyond the perimeter of this region, visitors get to sample the best of Ireland's attributes like a well-thought-out tasting menu. The west coast of County Clare and the Aran Islands offer cinematic seascapes, music, age-old Irish traditions, and, of course, the giant Cliffs of Moher and mysterious rocky Burren Park. The rural villages, country castles, lakes, and pastures of Clare match every preconception of Ireland's varied green landscape while Galway City is easily the liveliest city in Ireland after Dublin.

1 **Bunratty Village.** A tiny medieval village with the original Durty Nelly's Pub nestled by historic Bunratty Castle.

2 **Quin.** A rural village home to a worth-visiting abbey, fort, early-Celt dwellings, and a stunning castle-hotel.

3 **Ennis.** The lively county town with good pubs and live music.

4 **Killaloe.** A good base to explore the Lower River Shannon by boat.

5 **Kilkee.** A quiet seaside town with a crescent-shape beach and the stunning Loop Head Peninsula.

6 **Lahinch.** A popular seaside town for surfers and walkers and a good base to explore area attractions.

7 **The Cliffs of Moher.** One of Ireland's top attractions.

8 **Doolin.** A tiny fishing village known for its live music and pubs and a launchpad to the Aran Islands.

9 **The Burren.** A dramatic landscape home to forts, megalithic tombs, and rare flora and fauna.

10 **Ballyvaughan.** A pretty village on the water and good base for exploring the Burren.

11 **Kinvara.** Set on a pretty harbor and known for its good pubs, festivals, and oysters.

12 **Coole Park.** A nature reserve and popular haunt for W.B. Yeats fans.

13 **Galway City.** Ireland's liveliest city, named European Capital of Culture 2020.

14 **The Aran Islands.** A short ferry ride from Galway or Doolin, these rocky isles are home to prehistoric sites and beautiful scenery.

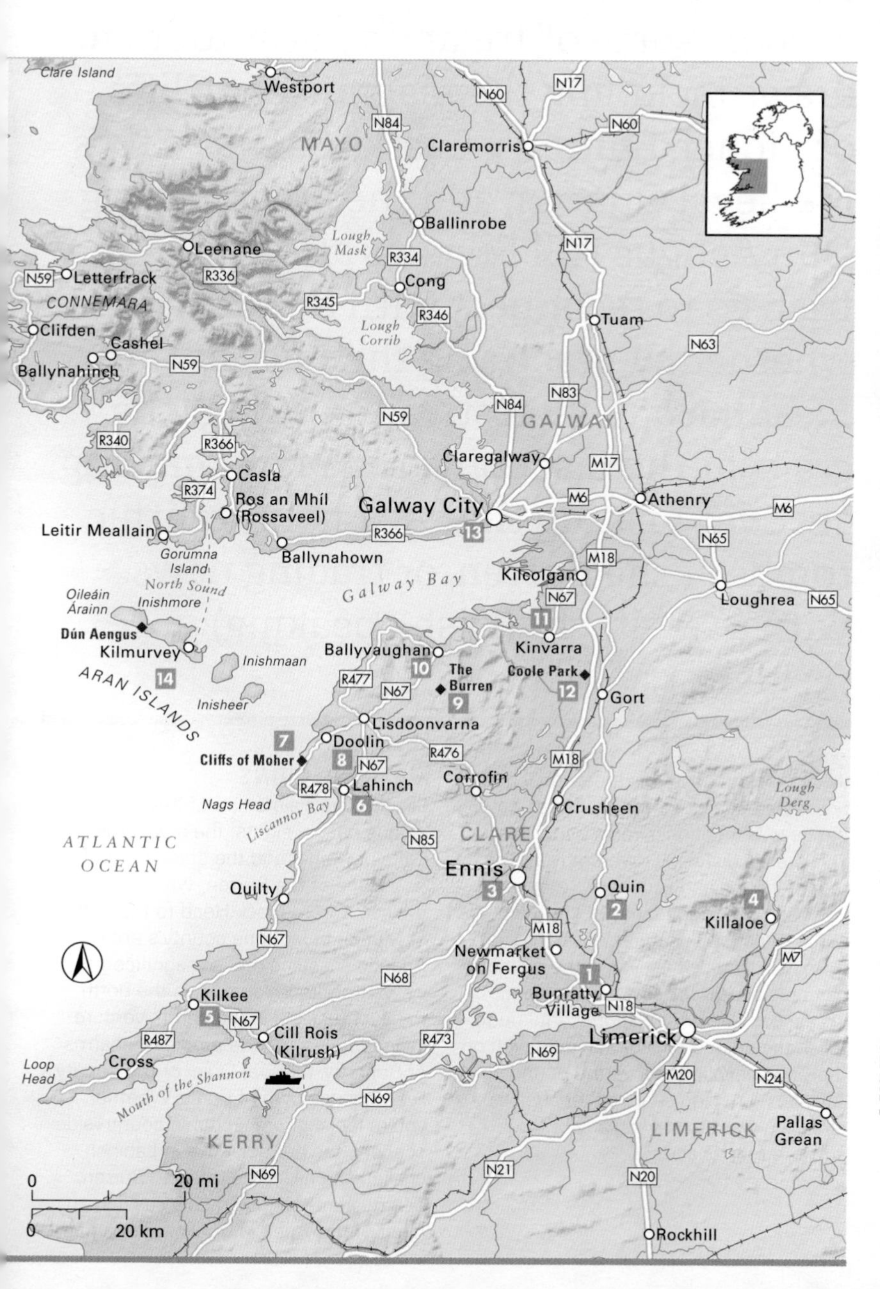
Clare Island
Westport
MAYO
Claremorris
Ballinrobe
Lough Mask
Leenane
Letterfrack
CONNEMARA
Cong
Clifden
Cashel
Ballynahinch
Lough Corrib
Tuam
GALWAY
Claregalway
Casla
Ros an Mhíl (Rossaveel)
Galway City
Athenry
Leitir Meallain
Ballynahown
Gorumna Island
North Sound
Galway Bay
Kilcolgan
Loughrea
Oileáin Árainn
Inishmore
Dún Aengus
Kilmurvey
ARAN ISLANDS
Inishmaan
Inisheer
Ballyvaughan
The Burren
Kinvarra
Coole Park
Gort
Lisdoonvarna
Doolin
Cliffs of Moher
Lahinch
Corrofin
Crusheen
Nags Head
Liscannor Bay
Lough Derg
ATLANTIC OCEAN
CLARE
Ennis
Quilty
Quin
Killaloe
Newmarket on Fergus
Bunratty Village
Kilkee
Cill Rois (Kilrush)
Limerick
Loop Head
Cross
Mouth of the Shannon
Pallas Grean
LIMERICK
KERRY
Rockhill
N17
N60
N84
R334
R336
N59
R345
R346
N63
N83
R340
R366
M17
R374
M6
N65
M18
N67
R477
R476
R478
N85
M7
N68
N18
R487
R473
N69
M20
N24
N21
N20
1
2
3
4
5
6
7
8
9
10
11
12
13
14
0
20 mi
20 km

The sweet spot midway along Ireland's 1,500-mile Wild Atlantic Way, this area harbors some of Ireland's finest tourism draws including the magnificent Cliffs of Moher, Bunratty Castle, Galway City's Medieval Quarter, and the breathtaking Dun Aengus Hill Fort. It's also where the Irish go to reconnect with their heritage, whether by practicing their jigs at the Fleadh Nua folk festival, enjoying "the craic" at the Lisdoonvarna Matchmaking Festival, visiting the ancient megalithic tombs of the Burren, or trading news with a Gaeltacht (Irish-speaking) resident.

Wherever you go in this area, you'll not only see, but more important *hear,* how the best of traditional Ireland survives. This area is distinctly different from the rest of Ireland and is bent on retaining its unspoiled, rugged way of life. With much of nature's magnificence on display from its Atlantic coastline to the rolling pastures on its lake lands to the east, it's easy to see why. Visitors continue to relish the unique thrill of standing high on the Cliffs of Moher above the pounding Atlantic, watching seabirds reel below, or sailing west to stay on any of three sublime Aran Islands.

MAJOR REGIONS

County Clare claims two of Ireland's unique natural sights: the awesome Cliffs of Moher and the stark, mournful landscape of the Burren, which hugs the coast from Black Head to the Cliffs of Moher. In fact, the county's entire Atlantic coastline offers magnificent views from Ballyvaughan in the north to beyond Kilkee in the south. Venture inland to discover the medieval charms of Bunratty, Killaloe, Quin, or the county's lively capital town of Ennis. Whether you're looking for inimitable countryside scenery, the perfect wave in Lahinch, challenging hiking trails in the Burren, or a guaranteed Irish music session any night of the week in Doolin, you can find it in Clare. Just beyond the county border in South Galway is the heartland of the Irish literary revival which took place in Kinvara, with its famous medieval tower house and Coole Park.

Galway City. Just an hour's drive north from Ennis in County Clare, historic Galway is one of Ireland's prettiest cities and definitely one of its liveliest. The short drive to Clare and surrounding Galway attractions like Connemara makes Galway City an ideal base for exploring the West of Ireland.

The Aran Islands. An hour or less from the mainland via ferry are the ageless Aran Islands. Once famed for their isolation, they are now attracting some 60,000-plus curious visitors every summer, but even so, they retain a distinctive identity, with traditional communities where Irish is still the daily language. Swap the car for a bike to discover the drystone walls and ocean views from the deserted lanes of these three islands, Inis Mor (Inishmore), Inis Meain (Inishmaan), and Inis Oirr (Inisheer).

Planning

Getting Here and Around

AIR

Shannon Airport, 93 km (55 miles) south of Galway in County Clare is the most accessible point of entry for international travelers to this region. Flying time from Dublin is about 30 minutes. Connemara Airport at Inverin is the base for Aer Arann, which services all three Aran Islands. It's 27 km (16 miles) west of Galway on the R336. Ask about transport to the airport when buying your ticket: there is usually a courtesy bus from the center of Galway City.

Dublin Airport offers a wider range of international routes and is 216 km (134 miles) east of Galway by motorway.

AIRLINE CONTACTS Aer Arann Islands. ☎ *091/593–034* 🌐 *aerarannislands.ie.*

AIRPORTS Aerfort Chonamara/Connemara Airport. ✉ *Caislean Inveran Inverin, Co. Galway* ✣ *30 km (19 miles) due west on R336* ☎ *091/593–034* 🌐 *aerarannislands.ie.* **Shannon Airport.** ✣ *235 km (149 miles) west of Dublin Airport on M7* ☎ *061/712–000* 🌐 *shannonairport.ie.*

AIRPORT TRANSFERS

With all the major car rental companies in its concourse and frequent bus transport on-site, Shannon Airport is well connected to Galway, Limerick, and Ennis by road. The drive to Galway is just one hour on the M18. The airport is 25 km (16 miles) south of Ennis, 24 km (15 miles) west of Limerick City, 84 km (52 miles) south of Galway, and 64 km (40 miles) southeast of Doolin, the seasonal port for the Aran Islands.

BOAT AND FERRY

FROM KERRY TO CLARE

The Tarbert–Killimer Ferry leaves every hour on the half hour and takes 20 minutes to cross the Shannon Estuary from North County Kerry to West County Clare. Alternatively, the Shannon tunnel, which bypasses Limerick City, is a quicker route to north Clare from Dingle and Killarney. The ferry runs every day of the year except Christmas and costs €23 one-way, €36 round-trip (discounted online). Cyclists, pedestrians, and motorcyclists pay €6 one-way. (Ferries return from Killimer every hour on the hour with a reduced service on Sunday and off-season.)

SHANNON FERRY GROUP Shannon Ferry Group. ✉ *Tarbert* ☎ *065/905–3124* 🌐 *shannonferries.com.*

TO THE ARAN ISLANDS

The spell of the famed Oileáin Árainn (Aran Islands) is such that many travelers can't resist their siren call and make for the first ferry leaving from Doolin, which offers rates from €25 one-way. There are two ferry operators on the pier. The addition of new boats to both services cuts the transfer time from Doolin to the smallest island in half, to 20 minutes.

Departures from Doolin to Inis Oirr are at 10, 11 (am), and 1, 4, and 5:30 pm. The last ferry back to Doolin leaves at 4:45 pm. In Doolin, you can book your trip in advance online or just walk down to the pier and book a seat. Sailing season is generally March to early November.

A seasonal service direct from Galway City Docks departs for Inis Mor at 9:30 am and returns at 5:30 pm the same day via The Cliffs of Moher (€49). One way Inis Mor is €30.

Day trips from Galway City to Rossaveal for a more regular service to the islands leave the city at 9:30 am or noon and return by 6:30 pm. Various licensed, escorted tours are available at Galway Tourist Information Office in Forster Place.

The standard ferry deal in Galway City costs €30 round-trip and €9 for bus transfer to the ferry port at Ros an Mhíl (Rossaveal). Look out for money-saving offers that may include bed-and-breakfast accommodations, free transfers to Ros an Mhíl or Connemara Airport (both 40 minutes away), bicycle rental on the islands, or a ferry-out, flight-back plan. There are three different ferry operators, and tickets are not transferable, so check the return sailing times of your operator when you get on board. If you opt for the five-minute flight, for safety reasons, you (yes, you—not your bags) will be weighed at check-in, and allocated an appropriate seat. There are similar combo tickets available from Doolin, with options that include a cruise of nearby Cliffs of Moher, interisland transfers, and overnight stays.

CONTACTS Aran Island Ferries. ✉ *37–39 Forster St., Galway, Center* ☎ *091/568–903* 🌐 *aranislandferries.com.* **Doolin Ferry Co.** ✉ *No. 1 Doolin Pier, Doolin* ☎ *065/707–5555, 087/958–1465* 🌐 *doolinferry.com.* **Doolin2Aran Ferries.** ✉ *Doolin Pier, Doolin* ☎ *065/707–5949, 087/245–3239* 🌐 *doolin2aranferries.com.*

BUS

Shannon Airport, Ennis, and Galway City have excellent connections to and from other regions in Ireland. Bus Éireann has the greatest network of bus routes in Ireland. Its Expressway 51 service connects Cork to Galway via Limerick City, Shannon Airport, and Ennis.

Bus Éireann's regional services can take you from Ennis and Galway to smaller towns and villages throughout the district. Regional service 343 connects Shannon Airport to Limerick and Ennis. For those heading to the coast, regional service 350 connects Ennis and Galway via Lahinch, Doolin, the Cliffs of Moher, and Kinvara.

Dublin Coach's 300 M7 Express brings passengers to Bunratty and Ennis from Dublin and Kerry. City Link connects Galway to Dublin, Cork, and Limerick and Dublin Airport via Red Cow Inn in Dublin. For best value and flexibility on state-funded transport like Bus Éireann, purchase a Leap Card at 🌐 *www.leapcard.ie.*

BUS CONTACTS Bus Éireann. ☎ *01/836–6111 in Dublin* 🌐 *buseireann.ie.* **Citylink.** ☎ *091/564–164* 🌐 *citylink.ie.* **Dublin Coach.** ☎ *01/465–9972* 🌐 *dublincoach.ie.* **GoBus.ie.** ✉ *Gobus Unit 8, Forster Ct., Center* ☎ *091/564–600* 🌐 *gobus.ie.*

BUS STATIONS Ennis Bus Station. ✉ *Station Rd., Ennis* ☎ *065/684–0444* 🌐 *buseireann.ie.* **Galway Bus Station.** ✉ *Station Rd., Galway City* ☎ *091/562–000.*

CAR

A car is the best mode of transport to navigate all that this region has to offer. Irish airports (Shannon, Dublin, Cork, and Belfast) have an ample supply of car rentals available.

There are three main access points to this area by car from anywhere in Ireland. The M6 (expressway) connects the region to the north and east, including Dublin. The N18 (highway) filters in traffic through County Clare from the south in a tunnel beneath the River Shannon (bypassing Limerick City) and onward to Galway. For those following the Wild Atlantic Way driving route, Shannon Ferries offers an hourly ferry service from Tarbert in County Kerry to Killimer, near the Loop Head peninsula in County Clare. A series of coastal roads lead to the N67 and onward to Galway City.

■ TIP→ Time permitting, pull off the M18 at the N85 exit and meander through the Burren. The M18 also has direct access to Bunratty Castle via junction 6.

ROAD CONDITIONS

The West has good, wide main roads (National Primary Routes) and better-than-average local roads (National Secondary Routes), both known as "N" routes. Since 2017 the M18 has connected the M6 to Galway City, bypassing all towns in between. If you follow the Wild Atlantic Way touring trail on the smaller Regional (R) routes, particularly in West Clare, you may encounter some challenging roads. Narrow and twisty, they are also used by hikers and cyclists from April to October, as well as local traffic (which can take the form of huge trucks serving the local agricultural co-ops, school buses, and tractors). The speed limit on these Regional routes is 80 kph (50 mph), even for trucks and buses, so use your common sense and adjust your speed accordingly.

■ TIP→ If traffic builds up behind you, it is customary to signal to the left and slow down or pull over to let the locals fly by. Your kind gesture will usually be acknowledged with a flash of lights, nod, or a wave.

TAXI

Taxis operate on the meter for journeys of up to 30 km (22 miles). For longer journeys, agree on the fare in advance. A Shannon Airport to Galway City journey will cost you about €150.

CONTACTS AAA Taxis. ✉ *Ennis* ☎ *065/689–2999* 🌐 *aaataxisennis.ie.* **Big O Taxis.** ✉ *17 Eyre Sq., Center* ☎ *091/585–858* 🌐 *bigotaxis.com.* **Burren Taxis.** ✉ *Fergus Row, Ennis* ☎ *065/682–3456.* **Galway Taxis.** ✉ *57 Dominick St. Lower, Galway City* ☎ *091/561–111* 🌐 *galwaytaxis.ie.*

TRAIN

The region's main rail stations are in Galway City and Ennis. Trains for Galway and Ennis leave from Dublin's Heuston Station (on different lines). Fares vary depending on time and season; tickets are generally cheaper if purchased online. For the best value and flexibility buy a Leap Card at 🌐 *www.leapcard.ie.*

Trains run to Galway via Athlone, taking about 2½ hours. The cost of an adult one-way ticket from Dublin to Galway is €29 (adult same-day return is €32 from the booking office or ticket vending machine (TVM). There are very steep discounts by buying online and even better value by using a Leap Card. There is no direct train to Ennis from Dublin. The trip requires transfers at Limerick Junction and Limerick and (including transfers) can take more than 4½ hours.

The Limerick-to-Galway train stops at Sixmilebridge and Ennis in County Clare and Gort, Ardrahan, Craughwell, Athenry, and Oranmore in County Galway before arriving at its destination. Limerick Station connects the region to the south, while Galway connects to Dublin.

■ TIP→ Check out the deeply discounted online fares on Irish Rail's website, which also allows for a free seat reservation. Online tickets go on sale 60 days before the date of travel.

CONTACTS Ennis Station. ✉ *Quin Rd., Ennis* ☎ *065/684–0444* 🌐 *irishrail.ie.* **Galway Station–Ceannt Railway Station.** ✉ *Eyre Sq., Center* ☎ *091/537–582* 🌐 *irishrail.ie.* **Irish Rail–Iarnod Éireann.** ✉ *Iarnród Éireann HQ, Connolly Station, Amien St., Dublin 1* ☎ *01/836–6222* 🌐 *irishrail.ie.*

Hotels

Since the arrival of Airbnb, a host of quirky properties from medieval tower houses to thatched coastal cottages are now available to rent in this region. Still, some of Ireland's finest country-house and castle hotels are in this area and worth a stay. Indoor pools and tennis courts are the exception rather than the rule outside of Galway City, where business is largely seasonal and the emphasis is on outdoor pursuits. Guest-house properties are in abundance on the Aran Islands and in rural areas, while the region also has its fair share of luxurious retreats. Festivals and events can have an impact on occupancy and rates. Booking ahead for popular locations like Doolin or Galway in July and August is always a good idea.

■ TIP→ Many properties use a popular tourist destination as their address, but these are often miles away from the main drag, on pathless roads. Every building in Ireland has an Eircode (🌐 *www.eircode.ie*), which you should ask for to get an exact location before booking.

Restaurants

Although some restaurants in remote areas close off-season, the larger towns and main tourism centers offer year-round service. Galway City has one of Ireland's finest dining scenes, which is gaining recognition nationally and around the globe. There are culinary landmarks in the region, including the award-winning Wild Honey Inn in Lisdoonvarna, County Clare, where the artisanal fare is simple but sublime. At the other extreme are more dazzling experiences, like Bunratty Castle's medieval banquet or the superb formal restaurant at Dromoland Castle. For impromptu dining, wander the towns of Ennis or Galway and you will easily find satisfying and hearty pub fare to restore you.

RESTAURANT AND HOTEL PRICES

⇨ *Restaurant prices are the average cost of a main course at dinner or, if dinner is not served, at lunch. Hotel prices are the lowest cost of a standard double room in high season. Restaurant and hotel reviews have been shortened. For full information, visit Fodors.com.*

What It Costs in Euros

$	$$	$$$	$$$$
RESTAURANTS			
under €19	€19–€30	€30–€45	over €45
HOTELS			
under €120	€120–€170	€171–€210	over €210

Tours

Heart of Burren Walks

WALKING TOURS | Heart of Burren Walks has a 2½-hour guided walk with author Tony Kirby in June, July, and August. The trail starts at U.C.G. Research Station, Crughwill (Eircode V95CY89), Carran at 10 am Tuesday to Thursday and at 2 pm on Friday. Highlights include the region's rare global landform (limestone pavement), the renowned Burren wildflower mix, and several archaeological monuments. ☎ *087/292–5487* 🌐 *heartofburrenwalks.com* 🎫 *From €35* ⊙ *Closed Sept.–May* ☞ *Contact for private tours.*

Lally Tours

BUS TOURS | A vintage double-decker bus departs every 45 minutes from Eyre Square in June, July, and August (every 90 minutes in spring and fall). Lally offers hourly tours of Galway City from 10:30 am until 3:30 pm from mid-March to October (€15). It also offers daily tours to the Cliffs of Moher and the Burren, returning to Galway around 4:30 pm (€45). ✉ *Eyre Sq., Galway City* ☎ *091/562–905* 🌐 *lallytours.com* 🎫 *From €15.*

When to Go

Like everywhere in Ireland, the weather in this region is unpredictable but rarely extreme. A downpour can last a week in July, while October can offer crisp blue skies ideal for trekking the Burren. Rainproof gear, layers of clothing, and hiking boots are the key to enjoying the great outdoors. From November to February the days are short, road conditions unreliable in remote areas, and many of the attractions, hotels, restaurants, and ferry services are scaled back or closed—yet there is good value and service is very personable. During these months, unless you're looking for an off-grid experience, stay in the larger areas like Galway or Ennis. July and August are peak travel times, justifiably so, and with 17 hours of daylight and an abundance of festivals, the opportunities to explore and experience Ireland are endless. If you don't want to contend with crowds and high hotel rates, like during Galway Race week at the beginning of August when demand outstrips supply for hotel rooms, then try the shoulder seasons from March to June or September and October instead. Mid-spring and early summer are when the Burren is in full bloom and service in the region is unhurried. Most attractions open for St. Patrick's Day, when days begin to stretch. In September and October the pace slows, and landscapes are ablaze with color.

■ TIP→ To catch a flavor of local community and team sport passion, catch one of the planet's fastest field games—a hurling match—during your stay. Check schedules at www.gaa.ie.

Festivals and Events

For visitors and locals alike, festivals provide both free entertainment and a chance to meet people from all backgrounds who share a common interest.

MAY

Fleadh na gCuach

MUSIC FESTIVALS | During the first weekend in May, the scenic harbor village of Kinvara hosts the hugely popular three-day traditional music festival, Fleadh na gCuach (the Cuckoo Fleadh), attracting musicians from far and wide. ✉ *Main St., Galway City* 🌐 *galwaytourism.ie/event/fleadh-na-gcuach-festival.*

★ Fleadh Nua

FESTIVALS | Ennis comes alive with the beat of the bodhrán for eight days at the end of May in one of Ireland's greatest traditional music festivals. It offers workshops, concerts, trad sessions, parades, and street performances, as well as the opportunity to mix with locals.

■ TIP→ Book ahead to avoid staying in the periphery.

✉ *Fleadh Nua Office, The Market, Ennis* ☎ *065/682–4276* 🌐 *fleadhnua.com.*

JULY

Galway Arts Festival

ARTS FESTIVALS | Held for two weeks in mid- to late July, the Galway Arts Festival hosts an international array of the best of contemporary theater, film, rock, jazz, traditional music, poetry readings, comedy acts, and visual arts exhibitions. ☎ *091/509–700* 🌐 *giaf.ie.*

The Galway Races

FESTIVALS | Known as the place where shady deals took place between politicians and developers during the boom times, the Galway Races is a high-profile event that brings the city to a standstill and brings out all of Ireland's aspiring socialites, horse-racing enthusiasts, and ostentatious hats. Room rates skyrocket around this festival, so plan accordingly. ✉ *Galway City* 🌐 *galwayraces.com.*

The Willie Clancy Summer School

MUSIC FESTIVALS | **FAMILY** | The sleepy town of Miltown Malbay has woken up every July since 1973 to the sound of harps, tin whistles, and uilleann pipes.

The weeklong Willie Clancy Summer School, named after the legendary piper, is the largest of its kind in Ireland, with 135 daily workshops and a full program of recitals, concerts, and dances open to the public. ☎ *065/708–5107* 🌐 *scoilsamhraidhwillieclancy.com.*

AUGUST

Cruinniú na mBád Festival

FESTIVALS | Kinvara's Cruinniú na mBád, meaning "the gathering of the boats," in late August commemorates a time when the Galway hookers—red-sailed, black-hulled timber boats—hauled turf to trade in Galway. It's a great opportunity to see restored craft in all their glory and remember a time gone by. ✉ *Kinvara* 🌐 *facebook.com/KinvaraCruinniu.*

SEPTEMBER

Galway International Oyster and Seafood Festival

FESTIVALS | Ireland's significance as the cradle of fresh oysters might have gone under the radar if it weren't for this late-September festival, culminating in a masquerade ball with flowing Guinness and champagne. ✉ *Center* ☎ *091/394–637* 🌐 *galwayoysterfestival.com.*

Lisdoonvarna Matchmaking Festival

FESTIVALS | Held in September in the spa town of Lisdoonvarna in the Burren, Europe's largest matchmaking fest is a monthlong festival of music, dancing, craic, and—if you're lucky—love. Its LGBTQ+ cousin, The Outing, takes place in south County Clare in February. ✉ *Lisdoonvarna* 🌐 *matchmakerireland.com.*

OCTOBER

★ **Galway Aboo Halloween Festival**

FESTIVALS | Galway's Latin Quarter hosts Ireland's biggest Halloween event on the last weekend of October. The highlight is the Sunday parade performed by the theatrical troupe Macnas, who add vibrant color in the early-evening darkness. ✉ *Center* 🌐 *macnas.com.*

Planning Your Time

There's much to see between Clare and Galway, so prioritizing your time means prioritizing your interests: if you want quintessential Irish castles, scenery, music, and history, spend all three days in County Clare, allowing yourself time to stop and explore everything from Bunratty to the Burren and Craggaunowen to the Cliffs, as well as a night on the Aran Islands from Doolin. If you want a little city buzz with your scenery, save the third day for vibrant Galway City—rich in history and alive with artistic activity and festivals—and plan to spend the night so that you can sample the lively pub and music scenes.

IF YOU HAVE THREE DAYS

With three days in this region, start with the Cliffs of Moher, the region's most breathtaking attraction, best enjoyed early in the day. Allow the rest of the day for exploring the Burren Park. Your first stop should be the pretty village of Kilfenora where you will find an unrivaled collection of High Crosses and the Burren Center Museum, the place for an overview of the park's evolution. Then head north along Corkscrew Hill, a road that's etched into a mountainside with panoramic views of the Burren's karst landscape. From here drive the short distance to Ailwee Cave and the Burren's famous landmark, the Poulnabrone Dolmen—an ancient portal tomb. Settle down for the night at O'Loclainn's Bari n Ballyvaughan, one of Ireland's most famous whiskey bars.

On Day 2, take the coastal route south with the Burren's rocky contours to the left and the blue ocean to the right, and pause by the roadside as the Cliffs of Moher come into view. Move onto Doolin Pier to catch the first ferry to the Aran Islands, which departs at 10 am. The boats sail to all three islands, but for a day trip, Inis Oírr is the closest, which gives you the most island time to seek out its hidden beaches and meandering pathways that carve through the neat stone-walled fields. Upgrade your ferry ticket to stay on board to cruise the Cliffs of Moher from the ocean, where you can fully appreciate their vast scale. Spend the evening in Doolin, where there's a guaranteed opportunity for a lively traditional music session in any of the pubs.

On Day 3, head to Galway City. It's Ireland's most charming city, with a bohemian attitude, fine dining, and an invigorating pub scene. Stay anywhere between the Quays and Eyre Square and explore the city's medieval quarter on foot before selecting one of its fine restaurants to round off the evening.

Visitor Information

Fáilte Ireland provides free information service, tourist literature, and accommodation booking service at its TIOs (tourist information offices). The following offices are open all year, generally weekdays 9 am–6 pm (daily during the high season): Aran Islands (Inis Mór), Ennis, and Galway City. Other TIOs that operate seasonally, generally weekdays 9 am–6 pm and Saturday 9 am–1 pm, include: Cliffs of Moher (April–October; a concession within the main visitor center, which opens year-round) and Salthill (May–September).

Information on Kinvara, Galway City, County Clare and the Aran Islands can be found at Discover Ireland (🌐 *discoverireland.ie*).

CONTACTS Ennis Tourist Information Office. ✉ *Arthur's Row, Ennis* ☎ *065/682–8366* 🌐 *discoverireland.ie/ennis.* **Galway City Discover Ireland Centre.** ✉ *Galway City Museum, Spanish Parade, Spanish Arch* ☎ *1800/230–330* 🌐 *discoverireland.ie/places-to-go/galway.*

Bunratty Village

18 km (10 miles) west of Limerick City on the N18 road to Galway City and Shannon Airport.

Bunratty was a thriving village until its population was decimated by the great famine in the middle of the 19th century. A hundred years later, Bunratty returned to prosperity with the development of nearby Shannon Airport, and that's when Bunratty Castle became one of Ireland's first major tourist attractions. The Celtic Tiger economy brought back the population with the construction of high-end housing and hospitality properties, but its medieval castle still takes center stage. The village has become the entertainment hub for the wider area, with a good mix of restaurants and pubs. The original Durty Nelly's Pub close to Bunratty Castle attracts older characters and tourists, while locals head down to JP Clarke's Pub on the weekends. An alfresco dining hub outside the Woollen Mills attracts visitors all week.

GETTING HERE AND AROUND

Bunratty is about 15 minutes from Limerick's center on the N18 Galway road. Bus Éireann Bus 343 connects Bunratty to Shannon Airport, Ennis, and Limerick City. Dublin Coach offers an M7 Express service that links Bunratty directly to Dublin, Limerick, and Killarney.

Sights

★ **Bunratty Castle and Folk Park**

CASTLE/PALACE | FAMILY | After a number of tit-for-tat burning of castles by the Normans and local chieftains on or nearby the current castle, the McNamara clan built the existing 15th-century Bunratty Castle. It was once the stronghold of the O'Brien family who became the earls of Thomond before they left Ireland in the 17th century for a change of identity and cozier lifestyle in England, but the castle is the park's highlight. It's now fully restored to its former glory, including everything from its carefully chosen period furniture to its "murder holes" that allowed defenders to pour boiling oil on attackers below. The views across the Shannon River from over the battlements are spectacular. Bunratty Folk Park has a carefully planned reconstruction of a typical 19th-century village, which comes complete with school, retail, haberdashery, and, of course, a fully stocked Mac's Pub. Other highlights scattered about the park include the Shannon Farmhouse, the park's first exhibit, which was transported stone by stone from a site earmarked for Shannon Airport's main runway, and the 1898 Hazelbrook House, which was the home of Ireland's most famous ice-cream producers. Pa's Pet Farm and the Fairy Trail keep younger visitors intrigued. The castle runs epic annual events at Halloween and Christmastime. A café and high-end gift store at the entrance to the park has good-quality lunch bites.

TIP→ Visit Bunratty Castle first as it is the earliest attraction to close (at 4 pm, to facilitate the evening banquets). ✉ *Bunratty* ☎ *061/711–222* 🌐 *bunrattycastle.ie* 🎫 *From €10.*

Restaurants

JP Clarke's Country Pub

$$ | **CONTEMPORARY** | **FAMILY** | A well-known gastropub, JP Clarke's has an airy, mountain-lodge-style interior with a brightly painted, vernacular exterior. On a sunny day, diners eat in the front garden space or can request seating under a glass roof. **Known for:** lunchtime and evening meals; country setting close to Bunratty Castle; nightly specials. $ *Average main: €20* ✉ *Old Bunratty Rd., Bunratty* ☎ *061/363–363* 🌐 *jpclarkes.ie.*

Noel's at the Manor

$$ | **MODERN IRISH** | This fine little eatery packs a punch in the local dining scene, harvesting the best of local produce from the sea and land. It's managed by the Wallace family in a modern, stone-and-plaster inn on the western perimeter of the village, but the style and presentation of the food comes with five-star finesse. **Known for:** delicious seafood chowder; great selection of vegan and vegetarian options; warm, relaxed atmosphere. $ *Average main: €25* ✉ *Bunratty Village, Bunratty* ☎ *61/707–984* 🌐 *bunrattymanor.ie/dining* ⏲ *Closed Sun. and Mon.*

Coffee and Quick Bites

Jilly and Joe's

$ | **MODERN IRISH** | Located in a courtyard outside of Bunratty Mills and spread out over a number of food trucks and kiosks, Jilly and Joe's was created to satisfy the demand for alfresco dining and has since become a local staple in the dining scene. Outside, guests huddle close to flames heaters on a chilly day—beneath an awning or canopy—and order pizza, sandwiches, daily specials, or a burger. **Known for:** carvery restaurant upstairs; excellent coffee spot; fun for families. $ *Average main: €9* ✉ *Blarney Woollen Mills, Bunratty* 🌐 *jillyandjoes.com.*

Hotels

Bunratty Castle Hotel

$ | **HOTEL** | **FAMILY** | This 144-room quality property is one of the few full-facilities hotels in the region, with a gym, spa, and the same in-room facilities you would expect from a quality-brand hotel. **Pros:** excellent buffet breakfast; small pool and gym; on-site parking. **Cons:** can be busy with weddings and tours; generic design; some rooms overlook a local graveyard. $ *Rooms from: €119* ✉ *Bunratty West, Bunratty* ☎ *061/478–700* 🌐 *bunrattycastlehotel.com* *144 rooms* 🍽 *Free Breakfast.*

Carrygerry Country House

$$ | **B&B/INN** | Modest and gabled, this 1793 country house is 12 km (7 miles) from Bunratty Village and despite being

its proximity it is an 8-km (5-mile) drive from Shannon Airport and is also a world apart, with views across the plains where horses calmly graze, as they have done for centuries, to the distant Shannon Estuary. **Pros:** real Irish character; abundant wildlife, birdsong, peace and quiet; excellent restaurant. **Cons:** tricky to find; no other facilities in the immediate area; bar menu only some nights. $ *Rooms from: €140* ✉ *Carrygerry, Shannon, Newmarket on Fergus* ☎ *061/360–500* 🌐 *carrygerryhouse.com* ⏲ *Call to confirm dinner Sun.–Tues. (bar menu only when quiet)* 🛏 *11 rooms* 🍽 *Free Breakfast.*

Nightlife

Durty Nelly's Pub
PUBS | Brimming with character, the low ceilings and stone flooring of this popular haunt next to Bunratty Castle draw back to earlier centuries. The pub was formerly known as "the Pike" (short for "turnpike") due to its role as the tollgate for the arched stone bridge that connects it to the other side of the Ratty River. Clients clamor for service at the small bar, where bar food and heartier restaurant-style portions are available. Recent additions include a large canopied dining area on the local bridge.

TIP→ Durty Nelly's is bang in the middle of the well-beaten tourist trail, so expect as many visitors as locals. ✉ *Bunratty Village, Bunratty* ☎ *061/364–861* 🌐 *www.durtynellys.ie.*

Performing Arts

Bunratty Castle Medieval Banquets
THEATER | Filled with music and storytelling, Bunratty Castle's medieval banquets have been entertaining guests since 1963. Guests are heralded over a drawbridge by a kilt-wearing bagpiper before being ushered by courtiers and ladies-in-waiting to a banquet featuring spare ribs and mead, a locally produced honey wine. The meal pauses for a melody, tale of woe, or the strumming of a harp. The congregation sits on benches while two unsuspecting guests are crowned Earl and Lady Thomond and allotted the responsibility of tossing someone into the great hall's dungeon. Banquets are held subject to demand at 5:30 and 8:45 nightly. ✉ *Bunratty Castle and Folk Park, Low Road, Bunratty Village, Bunratty* ✣ *Car park is on access road between castle and Durty Nelly's Pub* ☎ *061/711–222* 🌐 *bunrattycastle.ie/medieval-banquet* 🎫 *From €63.*

Shopping

Blarney Woolen Mills
SOUVENIRS | Tweeds, caps, rainproof gear, and a large selection of gifts, Irish clothing and souvenirs make this a good one-stop shop to buy gear without the garish hues in other tourist-centric stores. Next door (or by upstairs annex) Meadow's and Byrne offers tasteful home furnishings and appliances. A daytime restaurant upstairs offers sandwiches and reasonably priced mains. ✉ *Bunratty Village, Bunratty* ☎ *061/364–321* 🌐 *blarney.com.*

Bunratty Mead and Liqueur Company
WINE/SPIRITS | Just a five-minute walk past the entrance to Bunratty Castle and Folk Park on the Low Road is this unexpected find, which sells unique Irish alcoholic beverages such as mead (a fermented honey drink that was the beverage of choice at the castle banquets) and *poitín* (or potcheen). The latter is a potent liquor that was legalized in 2008 in a somewhat diluted form; however, its original ingredients of potatoes (of course), molasses, and beets remain. ✉ *Low Rd., Bunratty E, Bunratty* ✣ *1 km (½ mile) past Bunratty heading north on Low Rd.* ☎ *061/362–222* 🌐 *bunrattymead.net.*

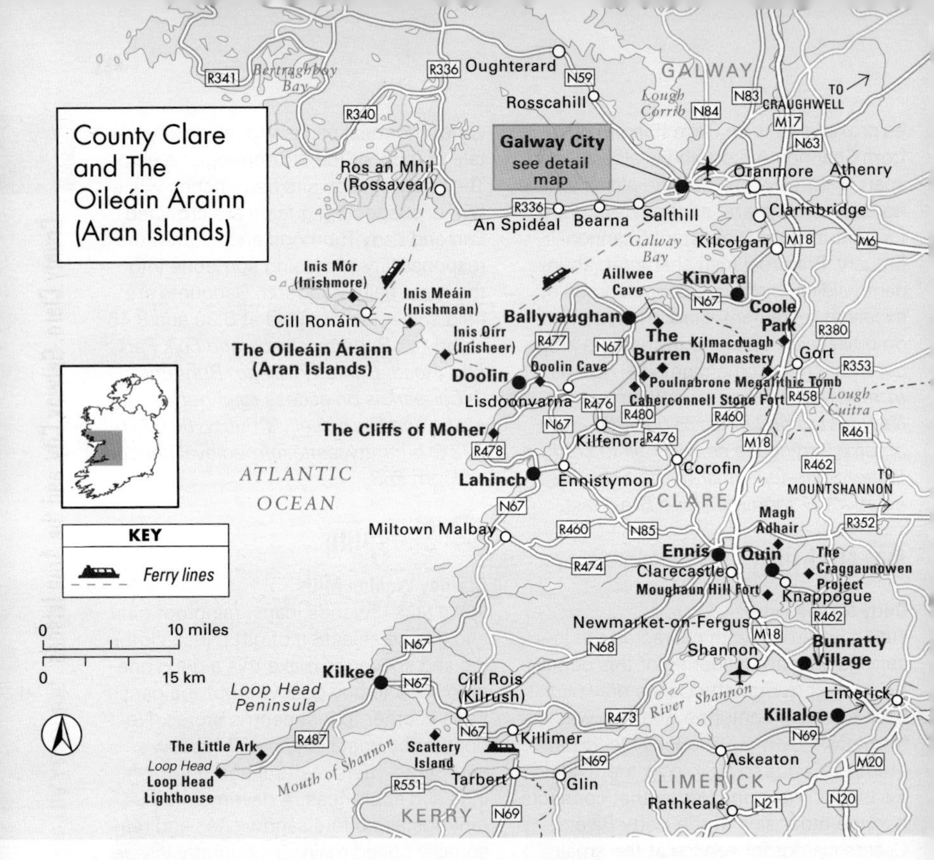

 Activities

12 O'Clock Hills

HIKING & WALKING | FAMILY | Locals could tell the time from the position of shadows cast along the valleys, fields, and brooks that lie on the circumference of these hills. While the highest is just 309 meters (1,013 feet)—the views from the apex are stunning, offering a panorama that includes the Burren National Park to the west, the River Shannon Estuary to the south, and Limerick City to the east. Within the folds of the hills is a sweeping view of Cullane Lake and a network of three looped trails (5 km [3 miles], 8 km [5 miles], and 13 km [8 miles]) that weave through famine roads, ancient bridges, and restored cottages. ✉ *Belvoir, Sixmilebridge, Bunratty* ✣ *13 km (8 miles) north of Bunratty on R471* 🌐 *12oclockhills.com.* 12 O'Clock Hills

Quin

21 km (13 miles) north of Bunratty.

Quin Village has retained the essence of old Ireland despite being only a 20-minute drive from Shannon Airport and less than 6½ km (4 miles) from iconic Dromoland Castle. "Blow-ins" have infiltrated village life with the development of smaller units in the village center and sprawling family homes on the periphery, but little else has changed in Quin over the last century. Dominated by its 14th-century Franciscan abbey and church ruins, its line of vernacular low-rise buildings is broken only by a narrow bridge over the Rine River. A plaque pays tribute to the village's only celebrity, Paddy Hannan. He was credited with Australia's Kalgoorlie gold rush and the subsequent prosperity of the area, where he lends his name to a main street. The village has a collection of pubs and supermarkets and is devoid of a public bus service, compounding its off-radar charm.

Sights

The Craggaunowen Project

CASTLE/PALACE | FAMILY | It's a strange experience to walk across the little wooden bridge above reeds rippling in the lake into Ireland's Celtic past as an aircraft passes overhead on its way into Shannon Airport—1,500 years of history compressed into an instant. But if you love all things Celtic, you'll have to visit the Craggaunowen Project. The romantic centerpiece is Craggaunowen Castle, a 16th-century tower house restored with furnishings from the period. It was a retreat for "Honest" Tom Steele, a local squire who famously canvassed Pope Pius VII to change his religion before he had a change of heart and became a key figure in Catholic Emancipation. Look for Steele's initials carved into a stone quoin outside the castle. Huddling beneath its battlements are two replicas of Bronze Age dwellings. On an island in the lake, reached by a narrow footbridge, is a clay-and-wattle *crannóg,* a fortified lake dwelling; it resembles what might have been built in the 6th or 7th century, when Celtic influence still predominated in Ireland. The reconstruction of a small ring fort shows how an ordinary soldier would have lived in the 5th or 6th century, at the time Christianity was being established here. Characters from the past explain their Iron Age (500 BC–AD 450) lifestyle, show you around their small holding stocked with animals, and demonstrate crafts skills from bygone ages. Be sure to check out the Brendan boat, a hide vessel used by explorer Tim Severn to test, and prove, the legend that Irish St. Brendan discovered America in a curragh boat almost a millennium before Christopher Columbus.

TIP→ The park is hilly in parts, particularly near the wild boar compound. Bring comfortable walking shoes. ✉ *Craggaunowen, Kilmurry* ☎ *061/711–222* 🌐 *craggaunowen.ie* 🎫 *From €10* ⏲ *Closed Sept.–Mar.*

Magh Adhair

HISTORIC SIGHT | Wander off the beaten path to discover the inauguration site of Ireland's greatest king, Brian Boru. Weaving through narrow country lanes from Quin Village, Magh Adhair appears to the left in the shape of a large grass-coated mound of earth, just past a small stone bridge that crosses Hell River. The mound is in fact a natural amphitheater where a lone voice could cut through large crowds during important regional ceremonies. It's one of the most sacred druid sites in Munster and believed to be the final resting place of Adhar, whose brother, Aengus, built Dun Aengus—a giant hill fort overlooking the ocean in the Aran Islands. Watch out for the *bullaun* (basin) stone altar, which looks like a giant's molar with a smooth, bowl-shape top. The druids believed that this altar captured hallowed water that protected their chieftains during and after life.

TIP→ Park the car before reaching the site as the road is very narrow. ✥ *About 6 mins northwest on R469 from Quin village* 🎫 *Free.*

Moghaun Hill Fort

RUINS | This prehistoric hill fort, once populated with the most powerful chieftains in the region, is the largest of its kind in Ireland. It commands a sweeping view of the Shannon, Ireland's longest river, which made it a strategic outlook for enemies navigating the main transport artery into the region. Today, a series of sturdy concentric walls set into a deep hilly thicket that hugs the northern territory of Dromoland Estate are what remain of this former dynasty's stronghold, constructed around 1000 BC. Information markers guide visitors past significant landmarks over the 27 acres, and a stone tower at the summit of the hill offers a rewarding view over the countryside. While much of the experience here is in your imagination (as in, imagining what would have once taken place on this very ground), the site makes for a truly beautiful and serene woodland walk, and it is particularly attractive in early autumn when the oak, horse chestnut, and beech trees turn every shade of crimson and amber.

■ TIP→ Turn to the left on leaving Mooghaun, and heading toward Quin, cast an eye over a humped-back bridge. It was the site of Europe's greatest gold find, many pieces of which are on display in Dublin and at the British Museum in London. The hoard belonged to the ancient residents of Mooghaun. ✉ *Mooghaun Hill Fort* ✣ *6 km (4 miles) south of Quin* 🎫 *Free.*

★ Quin Abbey

RELIGIOUS BUILDING | Set in a meadow by a crystal clear river in the heart of the village and beside the ruin of St. Mary's Church, Quin Abbey is one of Ireland's finest ancient monasteries. Legend has it that a McNamara chieftain built the abbey in 1402. The story goes that it was a gift offered to God for saving his son, who had survived a tumble into the icy river nearby and had resurfaced at the site of construction. The choice of location was most likely due to the giant, sturdy retaining walls and turrets of an old Norman castle that had remained intact, forming a practical foundation for the abbey. The bumpy terrain in the surrounding fields gives an insight to the old castle's scale. Despite Quin Abbey's desecration and damage during the turbulent 17th century, its bell tower, cloisters, and lady's chapel are well maintained. Take time to inspect the south-facing wall of the church: the shape of a crucifix will appear, etched onto the charred masonry after a Cromwellian visit. The founder of the monastery is interred here, while his descendant, "Fireball" McNamara, is buried around the corner in the lady's chapel. Other notable eternal guests of the abbey include the Dunboyne family from nearby Knappogue Castle, and the Blood Family, relatives of the great Crown Jewels thief, Thomas Blood. ✉ *Quin Abbey* 🌐 *clare.ie/do/quin-abbey* 🎫 *Free* 🕒 *Closed Nov.–Mar., but grounds open all yr.*

Hotels

The Abbey Tavern

$ | **B&B/INN** | The five basic rooms with all-modern facilities have the edge on other properties because of their location and view directly onto Quin Abbey. **Pros:** best food and drink option in town; traditional architecture; friendly, warm staff. **Cons:** basic rooms; have to use street parking; can be loud. [$] *Rooms from: €90* ✉ *Quin Rd., Ennis* ☎ *065/682–5525* 🌐 *abbeytavernquin.com* *5 rooms* *Free Breakfast.*

★ Dromoland Castle Hotel

$$$$ | **HOTEL** | **FAMILY** | With structures that date back to the 11th and 16th centuries, and now one of Ireland's grandest hotels, Dromoland Castle's picture-perfect setting and lavish finishes offer a classic fairy-tale feel but with modern comforts. **Pros:** old-fashioned luxury with modern amenities; high standard of service; beautiful grounds. **Cons:** in part, the grounds double as a golf course; some Queen Anne–section bedrooms have small windows facing a courtyard; lake-view rooms are in high demand and difficult to reserve. [$] *Rooms from: €535* ✉ *15 km (9 miles) southeast of Ennis via M18, Newmarket on Fergus* ☎ *061/368–144* 🌐 *dromoland.ie* *98 rooms* *Free Breakfast.*

Activities

★ Dromoland Golf Course

GOLF | Dromoland Golf Club is set in a 450-acre estate of rich woodland and rolling open pasture on the grounds of the famed Dromoland Castle hotel. The parkland course has a natural lake that leaves little room for error on a number of holes. Beginners, take note: a state-of-the-art golf academy can help you to improve your swing. ✉ *Newmarket on Fergus* ☎ *061/368–444* 🌐 *dromoland.ie/golf* 🎟 *Apr.–Oct. €150, Nov.–Mar. from €70* ⛳ *18 holes, 6824 yards, par 72.*

Mid Clare Way

HIKING & WALKING | Known as Slí na Méaracán in Irish (translated as the Foxglove Way), The Mid Clare Way is a 150-km (93-mile) looped walking route around the core of County Clare that is suited for visitors who want to take the path less traveled through Clare's lush valleys, lakes, and medieval estates. There are several trailheads along this moderate-to-easy marked route, but start at Dromoland near Newmarket on Fergus and follow through to Quin through the the streams and woodlands of Moohjaun, rising along the slopes of Slieve Aughty before descending into Dromore Woods near Ennis. The trail offers spectacular views of The Burren and Mullaghmore. ✉ *Quin* 🌐 *clarewalks.ie/home/the-mid-clare-way.*

Ennis

26 km (16 miles) north of Shannon Airport on M18.

Clare's main town, Ennis, has a medieval layout that follows the River Fergus with a network of narrow lanes and a one-way road system. Offload the car at the first opportunity and explore on foot. The vibrantly painted facades of its shop fronts are welcoming, even on the dullest day. That welcome is echoed later in the evening with a guaranteed trad-music session in one of the town's pubs in its myriad of narrow streets. A sculpture trail adds a novel way to navigate the streets and alleys, with anything from braying cattle in the marketplace to giant outstretched hands outside Ennis Cathedral to guide the way. The Fleadh Nua—a musical festival—at the end of May, brings the crowds.

GETTING HERE AND AROUND

Ennis is best served by Exit 12 from the M18 Limerick–Galway motorway. Dublin Coach M7 Express connects Dublin to Ennis. Bus Éireann connects Ennis to Cork, Limerick, Shannon Airport, and Galway. From Ennis the 350 Bus Éireann service stops at the Cliffs of Moher Visitor Center (50 minutes); Lahinch, Doolin, Lisdoonvarna, and Kinvarra on its way to Galway City. Ennis Railway Station can be accessed from Limerick City and Galway on the Irish Rail commuter route linking Limerick and Galway; the trip to Limerick takes 40 minutes, and Galway is one hour, 20 minutes.

VISITOR INFORMATION

CONTACTS Ennis Tourist Office. ✉ *Arthur's Row, Town Center, Ennis* ✥ *On narrow lane off O'Connell St.* ☎ *065/682–8366* 🌐 *discoverireland.ie/ennis.*

Restaurants

Eva's Cafe

$ | **CAFÉ** | For soup lovers, this modest, brightly painted café on a square in the heart of Ennis will hit all the right notes. With daily changing specials and a range of paninis and sandwiches, it's the perfect pit stop for a quality snack or budget lunch. **Known for:** daily soup specials; full Irish breakfast; French onion soup. 💲 *Average main: €9* ✉ *10 Merchants Sq., Ennis* ☎ *065/682–3901* 🌐 *facebook.com/EvasCafeEnnis* 🕒 *Closed Sun. No dinner.*

★ **The Town Hall Bistro**

$ | **IRISH** | Slate flooring, rich timber fixtures, a large bay window, and whitewashed walls hark back to an earlier time of midmorning scones and cakes or afternoon tea—both of which are available at this gorgeous former town hall, a local landmark right on the southern corner of O'Connell Street. Lunch and evening meals are special, too, making use of the rich County Clare produce like artisanal cheese or sea catch. **Known for:** great desserts; child-friendly atmosphere; delicious lamb shank. $ *Average main: €18* ✉ *The Old Ground Hotel, Station Rd., Clonroad Beg, Ennis* ☎ *065/682–8127* 🌐 *oldgroundhotelennis.com/town-hall-bistro.*

Hotels

Hotel Woodstock

$$ | **HOTEL** | This low-rise property packs a lot of personality inside of its modest exterior. **Pros:** on-site golf club with preferential play rates for residents; good leisure facilities; free parking. **Cons:** no public transport to the hotel; it's 4 km [2½ miles] away from Ennis town center through a residential road; contemporary exterior design lacks imagination. $ *Rooms from: €129* ✉ *Shanaway Rd., Ennis* ☎ *65/689–9800* 🌐 *hotelwoodstock.ie* *67 bedrooms* *No Meals.*

Old Ground Hotel

$$ | **HOTEL** | Understated modern bedrooms and a cornerstone location on O'Connell Street, right in the town center, is the key to the enduring success of this 18th-century ivy-clad landmark hotel. **Pros:** friendly and attentive staff; Nespresso machines in rooms; offers great breakfasts. **Cons:** some rooms could do with updating; finding parking can be a challenge; no leisure facilities. $ *Rooms from: €145* ✉ *O'Connell St., Ennis* ☎ *065/682–8127* 🌐 *oldgroundhotelennis.com* *83 rooms* *Free Breakfast.*

Nightlife

Ennis is one of the West's traditional-music hot spots. You're likely to hear sessions at many pubs, but keep in mind that sessions don't necessarily take place in the same pub every night and that the scene is constantly changing.

Brogans Bar and Restaurant

LIVE MUSIC | Enter through a side alley door to this large landmark pub that has served and entertained locals for decades, right in the town center. Musicians appear to crawl out of the handsome woodwork nightly and perform impromptu to an appreciative audience. Bar food is available. ✉ *24 O'Connell St., Ennis* ☎ *065/684–4365* 🌐 *brogansbarennis.com.*

Knappogue Castle Medieval Banquet

THEMED ENTERTAINMENT | Knappogue Castle's banquet is a feast of quaint pageantry with an inoffensive menu that still has a broad appeal. However, the setting on hilly pastures in a medieval limestone tower house in County Clare is sublime. Entertainers strum harps and sing old favorite Irish melodies and generally earn the €63 price tag for a night of poetry, sentimentality, and innocent fun. There's an elegant walled garden by the west side of the building and the castle is available to rent on Airbnb. ✉ *Knappogue Castle, Quin Rd., Knopoge, Ennis* 🌐 *knappoguecastle.ie/medieval-banquet* *Closed Sept.–Mar.*

Knox's Pub & Storehouse Restaurant

LIVE MUSIC | This Victorian-style bar, close to Ennis Friary, with a traditional plate-glass shop front with brick, timber, and bric-a-brac finishes, claims the title of the town's oldest pub. It serves bar food in its Storehouse Restaurant until 9 pm and offers live traditional music regularly from 9:30 pm. ✉ *18 Abbey St., Ennis* ☎ *065/682–2871* 🌐 *knoxs.ie.*

★ Nora Culligans Whiskey Bar

BARS | Behind the subtle, light-yellow timber-front entrance, this whiskey and tequila bar is a long warren of Victorian-bar idiosyncrasies, with lofty ceilings, barrel tables, and two-story-high whiskey cabinets that manifest like the love child of an old west saloon and a traditional Irish pub. The evening entertainment reflects the same hybrid, with jazz, blues, acoustic sessions, and the occasional bit of reggae offered back-to-back with

Where to Hear Traditional Irish Music

If you're interested in "trad" music, the beat of a *bodhrán* or the tap of a shoe will likely lead you to Galway and County Clare's great folk *fleadhs* (festivals) and pub *seisiúns* (sessions).

East Clare

East Clare takes its rich legacy of trad music seriously from Ennis to Killaloe, with some of the most powerful performances held in small rural villages. In Feakle check out **Peppers** (🌐 *peppersoffeakle.com*) or **Short's Bar**, which holds the title of the longest unbroken Thursday musical performance in Ireland: they haven't missed a beat in more than 45 years. **The Feakle Festival** (🌐 *feaklefestival.ie*) has five unbroken days of trad music on the Wednesday following the first weekend in August.

Ennis

During the last week in May, the pleasant country town of Ennis hosts the **Fleadh Nua** (🌐 *fleadhnua.com*), a massive eight-day-long celebration of dancing and song, with concerts, workshops, and competitions. Many of the events are open-air and free, and there is a great festive buzz. Ennis is home to a growing cadre of musicians: the Custys, Siobhán and Tommy Peoples, flute player Kevin Crawford, and accordion whiz kid Murty Ryan. Check out **Knox's Pub** (✉ *Abbey St.* ☎ *065/682–9264*) and **Cruise's Bar** (✉ *Abbey St.* ☎ *065/684–1800*) for lively evening sessions.

Doolin

The seaside village of Doolin hosts regular sessions in the pubs along the length of its short, ribbon layout. The best chance to catch a quality performance is at the **Russell Festival Weekend** (🌐 *michorussellweekend.ie*) at the end of February.

Miltown Malbay

Held during the first week in July, the **Willie Clancy Summer School** (🌐 *scoilsamhraidhwillieclancy.com*) is Ireland's biggest traditional music summer school. Classes, lectures, and recitals attract around 1,500 students from all over the world to this tiny village on the west coast of Clare near Spanish Point. Set dancing is a big draw here, and a surefire way to make friends.

trad-music sessions. It's the best place in town for a refreshing cocktail, and the antidote to an overindulgence in ballads and fiddles. ✉ *26 Abbey St., Ennis* ☎ *065/682–4954* 🌐 *facebook.com/noraculligans.*

The Poet's Corner

PUBS | The O'Connell Street door to the Old Ground Hotel leads directly to the Poet's Corner, a spacious, popular bar with pub grub in the day, and regular traditional music sessions on weekends from 9:30. ✉ *Old Ground Hotel, Main St., 58–60 O'Connell St., Ennis* ☎ *065/682–8127* 🌐 *oldgroundhotelennis.com/poets-corner-bar.*

Performing Arts

Glór—Irish Music Centre

CONCERTS | Ennis's venue for large concerts, Glór hosts popular touring acts, art-house cinema, stand-up comedy, and competitions of Irish music, song, and dance—including May's hectic Fleadh Nua. There's also an art gallery, a café, and free parking. ✉ *Causeway Link, Ennis* ☎ *065/684–3103* 🌐 *glor.ie.*

Shopping

Carraig Donn

WOMEN'S CLOTHING | A popular spot with locals for its own line of knitwear as well as its mix of Irish and international brands, Carraig Donn is also a sure thing for visitors looking for some contemporary Irish fashion, jewelry, crystal, and pottery. ✉ *Bank Pl., Ennis* ☎ *065/689–3433* 🌐 *carraigdonn.com.*

Custy's Traditional Music Shop

MUSIC | This is where Ennis's traditional musicians stock up on sheet music, specialist books, and musical instruments. ✉ *Cooke's La., Ennis* ☎ *065/682–1727* 🌐 *custysmusic.com.*

Ennis Bookshop

BOOKS | This long-established bookstore carries a wide range of local history and Irish-interest titles along with new publications. ✉ *13 Abbey St., Ennis* ☎ *065/682–9000* 🌐 *ennisbookshop.ie.*

Honan Antiques

ANTIQUES & COLLECTIBLES | Established in 1966 and specializing in antique clocks as well as Irish and internationally sourced antiques, this old gem of a shop is handily located in the town center. ✉ *14 Abbey St., Ennis* ☎ *065/682–8137* 🌐 *honanantiquesennis.ie.*

★ **Scéal Eile Books**

BOOKS | This little find in the heart of the town's market square is proof that there is hope for the traditional, independent bookstore. Every copy from the vast collection of rare, new, and used books is hand-chosen by a member of staff or requested by a customer, with a selection of new, out-of-print, or secondhand books available on-site. Scéal Eile (translated as "another story") doubles as a performance theater, and is popular as a book-signing venue. ✉ *16 Lower Market St., Ennis* ☎ *065/684–8648* 🌐 *scealeilebooks.ie.*

Seoidín

JEWELRY & WATCHES | Stop here for a good selection of gold and silver jewelry as well as some lovely Irish-made gifts. ✉ *52 O'Connell St., Ennis* ☎ *065/682–3510* 🌐 *seoidin.com.*

The Woollen Market

MIXED CLOTHING | Branded garments including throws, coats, capes, scarves, men's sweaters, and other woolly products sourced from select mills help stave off chilly weather while still looking chic. ✉ *36 Abbey St., Ennis* ☎ *065/686–7891* 🌐 *thewoollenmarket.com.*

Activities

BICYCLING

Tierney Cycles

BIKING | Follow the scenic Burren Cycleway (69 km [43 miles]) to the famous Cliffs of Moher, or join the Clare 250 Mile Cycle charity event in May, on a bike rented from family-run Tierney Cycles & Fishing. ✉ *17 Abbey St., Ennis* ☎ *065/682–9433* 🌐 *www.clarebikehire.com* 🎫 *From €20.*

Killaloe

50 km (31 miles) east of Ennis.

Killaloe, a gorgeous hillside little town on the southerly rim of Lough Derg, is separated from its sister town Ballina by an impressive 13-arch bridge across the River Shannon. It's also separated by a county border between Clare and Tipperary and a trek across the bridge is worthwhile for superior dining options. Killaloe—once the hometown of Ireland's greatest king, Brian Boru—is a good southern base from which to begin navigating the Shannon by boat.

TOURS

★ **Killaloe River Cruises**

BOAT TOURS | **FAMILY** | For an overview of the lake's significance from the birth of Brian Boru to the harnessing of its waters to create a canal system for transportation and the greatest edifice of modern Ireland, the Ardnacrusha Power Station, take "the Spirit of Killaoe" tour out onto Lough Derg. It's an hour of fresh lake air and sweeping views. ✉ *Killaloe* ✣ *On Ballina side of Killaloe Bridge* ☎ *086/814–0559* 🌐 *killaloerivercruises.com* 🎫 *€15.*

Sights

St. Flannan's Cathedral

CHURCH | Built by the O'Brien clan in the early 13th century, Killaloe Cathedral is the most prominent landmark in the town's streetscape. With a large-scale renovation to facilitate the arts and local community, the inside the cathedral showcases rare carvings including a Kilfenora Cross and the Thorgrim Stone, which has unique runic and ogham inscriptions.

TIP→ Capture the cathedral's beauty from across the lake in Ballina. ✉ *Royal Parade, Killaloe* 🌐 *cathedral.killaloe.anglican.org.*

Restaurants

Flanagan's on the Lake

$ | INTERNATIONAL | FAMILY | This lakeside restaurant, convenient for a bite before or after a River Shannon cruise, serves international fare with a breezy service. Locally produced standard fare like beef-and-Guinness pie as well as its reputable hamburgers, are favorites, but the restaurant also offers a good selection of vegetarian and gluten-free options. **Known for:** occasionally hosts whiskey-tasting tours; summer barbecues; lakeside setting. 💲 *Average main: €17* ✉ *Ballina Quay, Killaloe* ☎ *061/622–790* 🌐 *flanagansonthelake.com.*

Goosers

$ | IRISH | One of the most famous landmarks in town, complete with thatched roof, turf fire, and stone flooring, this classic Irish pub is a cozy retreat from the lake in winter and a popular spot for alfresco dining in summer. Goosers is directly across the lake from St. Flannan's Cathedral and close to the town bridge that links County Tipperary to County Clare (Goosers is technically on the Tipperary side, but just barely), and serves traditional fare like Irish stew, seafood chowder, and bacon and cabbage. **Known for:** lakeside setting; traditional Irish fare; lively weekend trade. 💲 *Average main: €16* ✉ *Ballina Rd., Killaloe* ☎ *061/376–791* 🌐 *goosers.ie* 🕓 *Closed Tues. and Wed.*

Hotels

Lakeside Hotel and Leisure Centre

$ | HOTEL | FAMILY | The trip across the Shannon on the one-way lane bridge is worth it for this stunningly appointed property with full-on lake views back over the town's historic 13-arch bridge. **Pros:** warm and attentive staff; spacious rooms; plenty of space for kids to play outside. **Cons:** architecturally bland; some rooms need an upgrade; popular with weddings. 💲 *Rooms from: €110* ✉ *Ballina, Killaloe* ☎ *061/376–122* 🌐 *lakesidehotel.ie* 🕓 *Closed Dec. 21–27* 🛏 *43 rooms* 🍽 *No Meals.*

Kilkee

56 km (35 miles) southwest of Ennis.

Kilkee is the access point to Loop Head and it is the only major town on the peninsula. Its faded Victorian allure is still recognizable behind the shabby facades along its promenade. Back in its 19th-century heyday the town was connected to Limerick City by steamboat, horse and carriage, or train service, which facilitated its growth and reputation as a bathing spot across Britain and Ireland. It attracted the literati like Charlotte Brontë, who honeymooned there, along with other notables including Alfred Tennyson, and Aubrey de Vere along with tragic Empress Sissi of Austria. In more recent decades, ocean explorer Jacques

Cousteau and Cuban revolutionary figure Che Guervara dropped by to marvel at its setting.

The transport between Limerick City and Kilkee is confined to the annals of history, but there's still a strong presence of Shannonsiders visiting the town, and with good reason. It has a pristine, horseshoe-shape beach and an epic cliff-side walk from Diamond Rock, passing the Pollock holes, natural swimming pools encased in stone.

Kilkee's main attraction is its convenient location on the eastern ridge of the Loop Head Peninsula. Loop Head is County Clare's most southwesterly point and an extension of the Wild Atlantic Way driving route. This wild and rugged coastline enjoyed relative obscurity for more than a century until the Star Wars film crew arrived to capture its end-of-world coastline in *The Last Jedi*.

Further into Loop Head Peninsula there's a hair-raising coastal drive with stopovers that include the Bridges of Ross, a coastal rock formation with blowholes, dolphin-watching tours, and deep-sea fishing.

Sights

The Little Ark

CHURCH | In a small annex at the Church of the Little Ark, just outside the tiny village of Kilbaha, is a wonderfully quirky slice of local history. During penal times Roman Catholic parishioners were restricted access to church, so Father Michael Meehan came up with the idea of holding mass in "no man's land" or rather, no man's *sea*, much to the frustration of local landlords. The little ark was the size of a carriage and fully assembled by 1852, when it was pulled into the shallow waters of a local cove, where locals could worship uninterrupted. ✉ *Church of the Little Ark, Kilbaha* ✣ *20 km (12 miles) southwest of Kilkee on R487* 🎟 *Free; doors to church remain open throughout the day.*

Loop Head Lighthouse

LIGHTHOUSE | Loop Head Lighthouse has kept navigators on the right watery path since its construction in 1670. The current, pint-size white tower house was built in 1854 and is open for tours. On a fine day, views from the balcony encompass the Blaskets in the south to the Twelve Pins Mountains in Connemara. There's a lighthouse exhibition in the lightkeeper's cottage. ✉ *Kilbaha South* 🌐 *loopheadlighthouse.ie* 🎟 *€7* 🕒 *Closed Oct.–mid-Apr.*

Scattery Island

ISLAND | Once a community, this remote island where the mouth of the Shannon River touches the Wild Atlantic Way is a time capsule of days gone by. St. Senan set up a monastery here in the 6th century believing that the remoteness of the island brought him closer to God. The six churches on the island today date from the 14th century, and its Round Tower at 120 feet is one of the tallest in Ireland. Drop by Kilrush Marina for a frequent ferry service to the island. ✉ *Kilrush Marina, Merchants Quay, Kilrush* ☎ *085/250–5514* 🌐 *scatteryislandtours.com* 🎟 *€26* 🕒 *Closed Oct.–Apr.*

Beaches

Kilkee Beach

BEACH | FAMILY | This wide, sweeping, crescent-shape, sandy beach is cradled by the town's rocky contours and slopes down gently to the ocean. It was a favorite of author Charlotte Brontë. The absence of a strong current means that it's one of the safest swimming spots on the west coast. **Amenities**: none. **Best for**: swimming, walking. ✉ *Kilkee Bay.*

Restaurants

★ The Long Dock

$ | **SEAFOOD** | Carrigaholt Village, with its crumbling medieval tower house perched on the coast, is home to this 200-year-old pub and restaurant, one of County Clare's great culinary finds. Seafood is sourced from the local pier as ingredients for the famous chowder, as are oysters, mussels, and lobsters—all served in the warm glow of an open-hearth fireplace and Liscannor stone flooring. **Known for:** ice cream in courtyard out back; historical paraphernalia; helpful and informative staff. *Average main: €17 ✉ West St., Carrigaholt ☎ 065/905–8106 🌐 thelongdock.com ⏲ Closed Jan. and Mon.–Wed off season.*

Morrissey's Seafood Bar and Grill

$ | **IRISH** | Set on a bend in the river a short drive north of Loop Head Peninsula, this unpretentious town house has gained a national reputation. The key to its success is simplicity, with a menu that keeps in season whether it's a heartwarming casserole in winter or fruit crumbles in late summer. **Known for:** homemade scampi and chips; crab claws with garlic and herb butter; simple, seasonal dishes. *Average main: €17 ✉ Main St., Doonbeg ✣ 9½ km (6 miles) north of Kilkee on N67 🌐 www.morrisseysdoonbeg.ie ⏲ Closed Mon. and Jan.–Mar.*

Hotels

Loop Head Lightkeeper's House

$$$$ | **HOUSE** | With 300 degrees of coastal views and little else but ocean between this retreat and New York, Loop Head Lighthouse is the place to rewind and charge batteries. **Pros:** wood-burning stove in the living room; incredibly romantic location; privacy. **Cons:** no water-main supply, so guests should bring bottled water for drinking; cliff-side location requires supervision for kids; two-night minimum stay. *Rooms from: €240 ✣ The tip of Loop Head Peninsula ☎ 01/670–4733 🌐 irishlandmark.com/property/loop-head-lightkeepers-house ⏲ Closed Jan. 3 rooms No Meals.*

Stella Maris Hotel

$$$ | **B&B/INN** | If a town the size and scale of Kilkee can have a grande dame property, then the Stella Maris is the place; it's a handsome, charming little hotel close to the sea, with a contemporary country style. **Pros:** friendly and accommodating staff; tasty breakfast options; excellent on-site restaurant. **Cons:** lack of street parking; furnishings dated; few leisure facilities on-site. *Rooms from: €190 ✉ O'Connell St., Kilkee ☎ 065/905–6455 🌐 stellamarishotel.com 12 rooms Free Breakfast.*

Lahinch

6 km (4 miles) south of the Cliffs of Moher, 29 km (18 miles) northwest of Ennis.

Lahinch's promenade is milling with a mix of locals and visitors out to inhale the fresh Atlantic air at all times of year. Its golf course consistently ranks in the world's top 100 links, but it's the surfers in search of the big one that have put this busy beach resort on the global map. Aileen's Wave is the product of the ocean pitted against the Cliffs of Moher, resulting in the perfect aquatic colossus.

The sandy beach backed by dunes brings a tenfold increase in population during summer months when pay parking is a challenge and lines spill out the doors of its restaurants. Arrive early on a sunny day.

GETTING HERE AND AROUND

Lahinch (also spelled Lehinch, on maps and GPS) is a seaside resort 29 km (18 miles) northwest of Ennis on the N85. Pay for parking on the seafront. It can be reached by the 350 bus that links Galway to Ennis (½ hour away) by coast.

Buy a Leap Card (🌐 *leapcard.ie*) ahead of travel to make stop-offs and to avail of discounts.

Beaches

★ Lahinch Beach

BEACH | **FAMILY** | At the first hint of sunshine, locals drop everything and flock to Lahinch's Blue Flag beach, a wide, sandy crescent about 2½ km (1½ miles) long, facing southwest onto the Atlantic Ocean. The most popular beach in County Clare, it has a good selection of facilities (even off-season), but it can get crowded—the trick is to arrive early. The beach has long been a family favorite, offering safe bathing and ideal conditions for beginner surfers. **Amenities**: food and drink, parking (fee), toilets, water sports. **Best for**: sunset, surfing, swimming, walking. ✉ *Lahinch Beach, Lahinch* ✣ *Arriving from Ennistymon on N85, ignore right-hand turn at village entrance for Cliffs of Moher (R478), and continue straight for about 50 meters to reach promenade and car park* 🎫 *Parking fee €2 for 3 hrs.*

Restaurants

Barrtrá Seafood Restaurant

$$ | **SEAFOOD** | Sweeping Atlantic views from this whitewashed cottage set the stage for a delightful meal of fresh catch from the waters lapping the Wild Atlantic Way. Mains from €26. **Known for:** offers gluten-free options; exceptional service; incredible desserts. [$] *Average main: €26* ✉ *Barrtrá, Lahinch* ✣ *4 km (2½ miles) south of Lahinch on N67* ☎ *65/708–1280* 🌐 *barrtra.com* ⏲ *Closed Jan. and Feb.; weekdays Mar.–Apr.; Sun. Oct.–Dec.; and Tues. May–Sept.*

Vaughan's on the Prom

$ | **MODERN IRISH** | Travelers come here to get up close and personal with the surf from behind a bowl of steaming Atlantic seafood chowder. Floor-to-ceiling windows capture the breath of the bay from a cozy distance, except in storm season when it can be a little too close for comfort. **Known for:** top-notch fish-and-chips; warm and friendly staff; delicious local oysters. [$] *Average main: €15* ✉ *Promenade, Lahinch* ☎ *065/708–1548* 🌐 *vaughans.ie* ⏲ *Closed Nov.–May.*

Nightlife

Cornerstone Bar

BARS | On the corner of the main street, this sandstone cottage, with its low roof, is the place to cozy up for a post-surf pint. Traditional food is served until 9 pm—specials are on a chalkboard, and there's live Irish music on weekends. ✉ *Main St., Lahinch* ☎ *065/708–1277* 🌐 *facebook.com/Cornerstone-Bar-Lahinch.*

Shopping

Lahinch Surf Shop

SPORTING GOODS | Rosemary Buckley's surf shop, the first in Ireland, dates from 1989 and is a landmark on Lahinch's Promenade. You'll find top-quality boards, wet suits, and accessories, as well as lots of local tips and advice. Check their website for daily surf reports and a live webcam. ✉ *The Promenade, Lahinch* ☎ *065/708–1543* 🌐 *lahinchsurfshop.com.*

Activities

GOLF

★ Lahinch Golf Club

GOLF | It's known as "the St. Andrews of Ireland," and with good reason: Lahinch links architect Old Tom Morris also worked on the St. Andrew's course design and hailed from the town. The busy R478 (main road to the Cliffs of Moher) splits Lahinch's two 18-hole courses. The old course is littered with blind spots (particularly the 5th) and large bunkers. The more recent Castle Course, named after the castle ruin at hole 7, is flatter. Goats have lifelong membership of the course, and are free to wander at will. They have even infiltrated the club's emblem. ✉ *The Seafront, Lahinch* ☎ *065/708–1003* 🌐 *lahinchgolf.com* 🎫 *May–Sept., Old Course, €275, Castle Course €60. Mid-Mar.–late Apr. and Oct. 1–26, Old Course €225, Castle Course €50* ⛳ *Old Lahinch: 18 holes, 6950 yards, par 72; Castle Course: 18 holes, 5700 yards, par 69* ☞ *Lahinch is a walking-only course.*

SURFING

Lahinch Surf School

SURFING | FAMILY | Surfing champion John McCarthy was one of the first to harness the west of Ireland's Atlantic waves; his unmissable kiosk near the promenade houses a surf school for budding surfers of all stages and ages. ✉ *Promenade, Lahinch* ☎ *087/960–9667* 🌐 *lahinchsurfschool.com* 🎫 *€40 (2-hr lesson)* ⏲ *Closed Dec. and Jan.*

The Cliffs of Moher

10 km (6 miles) northwest of Lahinch.

One of Ireland's most breathtaking natural sights, the magnificent Cliffs of Moher rise vertically out of the sea in a giant mass of sandstone and shale that stretches over an 8-km (5-mile) swathe of County Clare's coastline, reaching a height of 710 feet at their apex. On a clear day you can see the Aran Islands and the mountains of Connemara to the north, as well as the lighthouse on Loop Head and the mountains of Kerry to the south as far as Dingle. Get up close and you can study the stratified deposits of five different rock layers visible in the cliff face. But most visitors prefer to take in the grand distant vistas, especially as they open up every turn of the trail along the famous Burren Way that runs from Doolin to the cliffs.

GETTING HERE AND AROUND

Head north and west from Lahinch through Liscannor on the R478 for 19 km (12 miles)—or west from Lisdoonvarna for about the same distance on the R478—and you will come to the visitor center, a lone feature dominating the otherwise empty landscape, and its huge car park (fee), which is the only parking option. The parking fee includes entrance to the visitor center.

There is a bus service to the Cliffs of Moher Visitor Centre from both Ennis and Galway City. A bus from Ennis to the cliffs takes about 50 minutes. The bus trip from Galway City takes about one hour and 50 minutes.

CONTACTS Doolin Ferry Company. ✉ *Doolin Pier, Doolin* ☎ *065/707–5555* 🌐 *obrienline.com.* **Doolin 2 Aran Ferries.** ☎ *065/707–5949* 🌐 *doolin2aranferries.com.* **Ennis Bus Station.** ✉ *Station Rd., Ennis* ☎ *065/682–4177.*

TOURS

One of the most popular ways of viewing these natural wonders is by heading to Doolin (alternative port of departure: Liscannor) to sail on a Cliffs of Moher cruise. Take either of the two operators from Doolin Pier. Doolin2Aran Ferries and O'Brien Line offer one-hour cruises (€28) departing every day from noon, weather permitting, from "the first fine day in March" to early November. A new service from Galway City is available from Aran Island Ferries.

Sights

★ Cliffs of Moher

VIEWPOINT | FAMILY | Though not the tallest cliffs in Ireland, these giant bastions of Irish tourism feature high on the bucket list of visitors to Ireland because of one undeniable fact; they're magnificent. Reaching a colossal height of over 700 feet and looming over 8 km (5 miles) of County Clare's jagged coastline,

Did You Know?

Almost as much a knockout as the Cliffs of Moher themselves, their grass-roof, subterranean visitor center showcases the Atlantic Edge exhibition, whose highlight is the Ledge, a vertiginous virtual-reality tour of the cliffs seen from a bird's-eye view.

they offer panoramic views across the seaboard from County Kerry to County Galway. Numerous colonies of seabirds, including puffins and guillemots, make their homes in the shelves of rock on the cliffs.

The Cliffs of Moher Visitor Experience—a grass-roof, subterranean visitor center built into the cliff face—is a good refuge from passing rain squalls. The interior imitates the limestone caves of County Clare and contains a gift shop, public toilets, and a tearoom. The *Atlantic Edge* exhibition features information panels and interactive consoles for children; the highlight is the Ledge, a vertiginous virtual reality tour of the cliffs from a bird's-eye view. Outside the center, extensive hiking paths (some with elevated viewing platforms) give access to the real thing, including O'Brien's Tower, a 19th-century folly built on the cliffs' highest point (€2 extra for access to upper levels and O'Brien exhibit) at the northern extremity. Parking is on the opposite side of the R478; access is by a pedestrian crossing. Pedestrians may be asked to pay admission for the use of the visitor facilities. The addition of two "Lifts of Moher" provides transport for those with mobility issues.

■ **TIP→ Take the Cliffs of Moher cruise from Doolin or Liscannor for a different perspective of the cliffs below the giant stacks.** ✉ *Cliffs of Moher Visitor Centre (signposted on R478 north from Liscannor), Lahinch* ✣ *6½ km (4 miles) north of Liscannor on R478* ☎ *065/708–6141* 🌐 *cliffsofmoher.ie* 🎫 *From €7* ☞ *Arrive before 11 am or after 4 pm for lower rates and smaller crowds.*

Doolin

6 km (4 miles) north of the Cliffs of Moher.

Once an enchanting backwater with a row of colorful fishermen cottages, this tiny village—set at the point where the Cliffs of Moher flatten out and disappear into the sea as limestone plateaus—now seems to consist almost entirely of B&Bs, hostels, hotels, holiday homes, pubs, and restaurants. Built on a flat, low-lying plain that follows the River Aille a short walk from the pier, it's hard to identify where the village begins and ends. The frenzy of bank lending during Ireland's Celtic Tiger economic boom years is responsible for the explosion in development, making the little bridge that leads into Fisher Street almost impassible during peak-season travel. Doolin's frequent trad sessions and its seasonal ferry service to the Aran Islands draw the crowds from February when the village hosts the Micho Russell Festival.

GETTING HERE AND AROUND

Doolin is on the R479 about 6 km (4 miles) north of the Cliffs of Moher visitor center. Bus Éireann offers a bus service from Ennis or Galway.

At the pier, the two local ferry services with a plethora of online presence vie loudly for passing trade in front of their cabins. Both offer similar services, which include tours beneath the Cliffs of Moher. In the village, visitors flock to O'Connor's, McDermott's, and McGann's pubs to catch a trad session, the Doolin regains some of its old essence as a fisherman's hamlet in the quieter months.

■ **TIP→ Car parking fees are now payable at Doolin harbor. Expect to pay €1 for up to two hours; €5 for up to 30 hours; and €15 for a week.**

TOURS

Doolin2Aran Ferries

BOAT TOURS | Doolin2Aran Ferries offers transport to all the Aran Islands, with the option to cruise beneath the Cliffs of Moher. ✉ *Doolin Pier* ☎ *065/707–5949* 🌐 *doolin2aranferries.com* 🎟 *From €15.*

O'Brien Line

BOAT TOURS | O'Brien offers daily sailing from March to November to the three Aran Islands and an optional cruise beneath the Cliffs of Moher. The newest ship in the fleet, the *Doolin Express,* gets you from Doolin to the closest island in 15 minutes. ✉ *O'Brien Line Ferries, Doolin Pier, Doolin* ☎ *065/707–5618* 🌐 *obrienline.com* 🎟 *From €15.*

Sights

★ **Cliffs of Moher Walking Trail**

TRAIL | Avoid the tourist buses and take the lesser-seen view of the Cliffs of Moher by following the trail from Doolin to Liscannor. From Fisher Street in Doolin, climb up the steep, narrow road by the village's low stone wall and follow the trail through a meadow, which leads to a cliff-hugging pathway with Ireland's most dramatic seascape as its constant companion. Between Doolin and the Cliffs of Moher the terrain is hilly, with views over a giant slab of rock that creates a surf swell called Aill na Searrach. Stop and enjoy the staggering panorama of Galway Bay and the Aran Islands from the highest point of the Cliffs of Moher. The final leg of the trail brings Hag's Head into view before descending into Liscannor Village, the home of submarine inventor John P. Holland. The trail is 14 km (8½ miles) and it takes on average 3½ hours to complete. The trail is challenging, with features that include road walking on uneven surface; exposed, rail-free clifftop paths; and steep flagstone steps. Organized walks from Doolin leave from O'Connor's pub at 10 am daily.

⚠ **Parts of the northerly section of the route are under maintenance.** ✉ *Doolin.*

Doolin Cave

CAVE | Formed from a drop of water thousands of years ago, Doolin Cave's Great Stalactite hangs from the ceiling like a giant rocky sword. The 24-foot feature is one of the world's longest known free-hanging stalactites and the cave's star attraction. Tours of the cave run on the hour, and outside there's a walking trail around a working farm. ✉ *Doolin Cave, Craggycoradon E, Doolin* ✣ *4 km (2½ miles) from Doolin on R479* ☎ *65/707–5761* 🌐 *doolincave.ie* 🎟 *€9.*

Hotels

Ballinalacken Castle Hotel

$$$$ | **B&B/INN** | Not actually a castle, Ballinalacken is rather a mustard-color Victorian lodge in the shadow of medieval tower-house ruins, a few miles from Doolin Village. **Pros:** beautiful grounds for walking; peaceful setting; warm, old-fashioned welcome from the O'Callaghan family. **Cons:** not in fact a castle; remote; limited amenities. 💲 *Rooms from: €225* ✉ *Coast Rd., Doolin* ✣ *5 km (3 miles) outside Doolin on Lisdoonvarna Rd.* ☎ *065/707–4025* 🌐 *ballinalackencastle.com* ⏲ *Closed Nov.–mid-Apr. No dinner Tues.* 🛏 *10 rooms, 2 suites* 🍽 *Free Breakfast.*

Nightlife

Famous for their traditional-music sessions, Doolin's three traditional pubs can squeeze in big crowds, which means compromising comfort on busy nights. All pubs are furnished without pretension (or "notions" as locals coin it) with timber benches and well-worn bar stools, and they serve simple bar food from midday until 9 pm. As you might imagine, the word is out about Doolin's trad scene—the pubs regularly overflow with crowds (and the video cams can get really

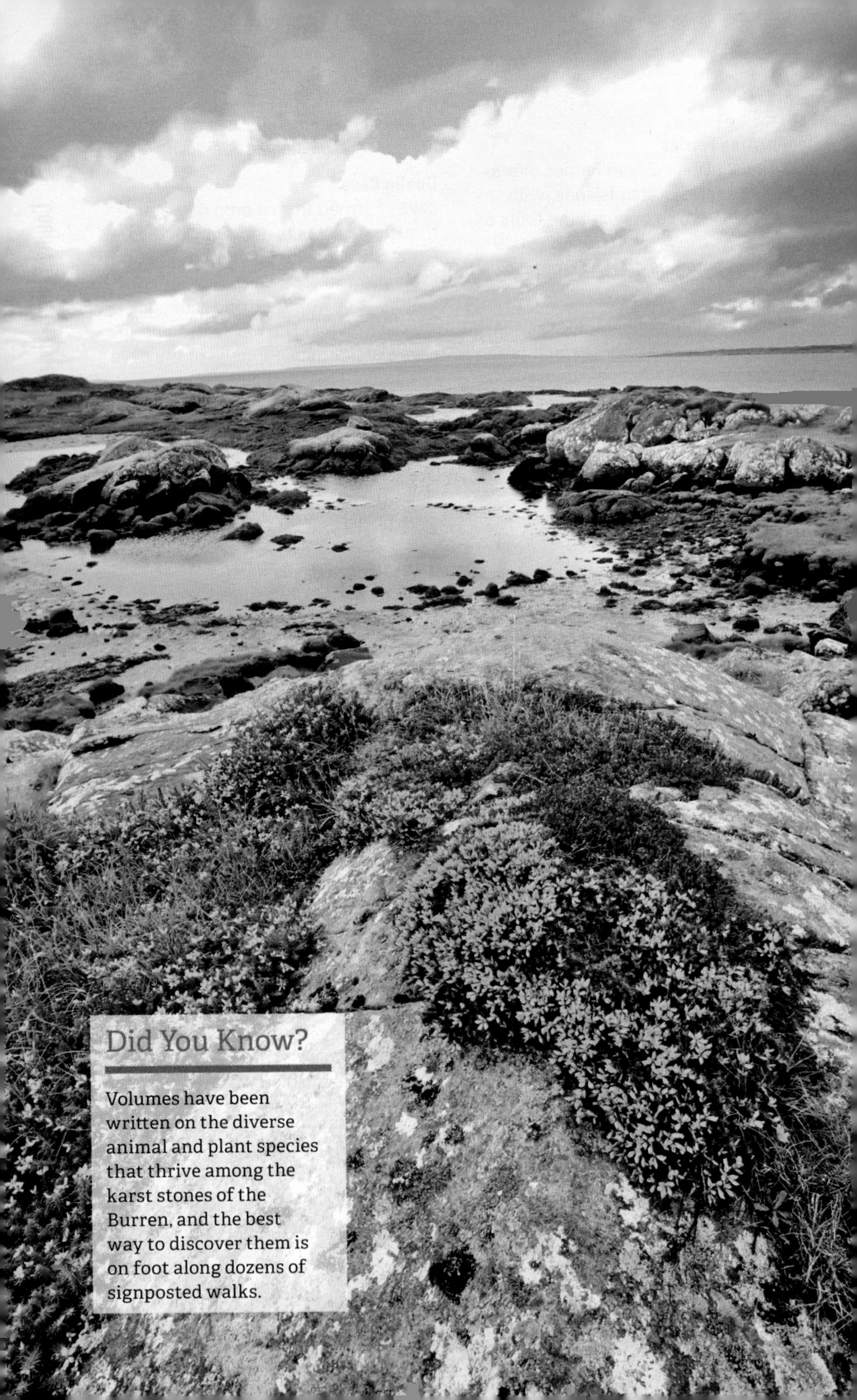

Did You Know?

Volumes have been written on the diverse animal and plant species that thrive among the karst stones of the Burren, and the best way to discover them is on foot along dozens of signposted walks.

annoying). Purists often hightail it to East Clare for serious trad sessions, except at the end of February when the **Micho Russell Festival** (🌐 *michorussellweekend.ie*) draws the best talent to Doolin.

★ Gus O'Connor's

PUBS | Set in the village's main (and only) street, popular Gus O'Connor's has tables outside near a stream and live music every night after 9:30 in the summertime. ✉ *Fisher St., Doolin* ☎ *065/707–4168* 🌐 *gusoconnorsdoolin.com.*

McDermott's

LIVE MUSIC | Popular with locals, McDermott's is a great spot for soul-warming live music and traditional fare. They have live music nightly early spring to late autumn, and weekends in winter. Note: it's sometimes closed during the day in low season. ✉ *R479, Doolin* ☎ *065/707–4328* 🌐 *mcdermottspub.com.*

McGann's Pub & Restaurant

PUBS | Across the road from McDermott's, McGann's is the smallest of Doolin's three famous pubs and has been run by the same family for 70 years. Breakfast is a highlight, so luckily, McGann's offers B&B, too (must book ahead). ✉ *R479, Doolin* ☎ *065/707–4133* 🌐 *mcgannspubdoolin.com.*

The Burren

Covering a vast land mass in northern County Clare, from the Cliffs of Moher in the south to Black Head in the north, and as far southeast as Corofin, The Burren's contrasting landscape, history and culture is one of the most remarkable in Europe. As you travel north toward Ballyvaughan, the landscape becomes rockier and stranger. Instead of the seemingly ubiquitous Irish green, gray becomes the prevailing color. You're now in the heart of the Burren, a 300-square-km (116-square-mile) expanse that has Ireland's most unusual terrain. With dramatic ocean-edge frontier land, *turloughs* (disappearing lakes), underground rivers, and a smooth lunar landscape that's scarred with ancient portal tombs, the Burren and the Cliffs of Moher are collectively designated a UNESCO Global Geopark site. Locals speculate that *Lord of the Rings* author J.R.R. Tolkien drew inspiration from the park's ruggedness when he imagined Middle Earth while working as an external examiner at nearby University College Galway.

The Burren is aptly named: it's an Anglicization of the Irish word *bhoireann* (a rocky place). Stretching off in all directions, as far as the eye can see, are vast, irregular slabs of fissured limestone, known as karst, with deep cracks harboring plant life that's as alien as the setting. Corkscrew Hill on the N67, a winding road carved into the landscape, offers the best overview of the Burren. Pull over onto one of its viewing areas to capture the rocky pavements and silver limestone hills framed by the cerulean Atlantic to the north.

Late spring is when plant life is most vibrant and it heralds the Burren in Bloom festival, with organized walks from mid-May to early June.

Human life on the barren landscape is equally fascinating, though almost paradoxical, because on first inspection it appears as though its terrain is too harsh to sustain life. However, locals harnessed the land and sea, and thrived. Their habits and customs stretching back thousands of years can be seen at the Burren Centre in Kilfenora.

Burial sites like the iconic Poulnabrone Dolmen or Roughan Hill's extensive network of homes, walls, and wedge tombs dating back more than 5,000 years identify a lifestyle that changed very slowly in the millennia that followed, up until the 17th century.

⚠ **Burren Park is fragile. Do not pick rare flowers, enter portal tombs, or toss cigarette butts on the roadside, as this leaves an indelible mark on this incredible landscape.**

GETTING HERE AND AROUND

Take the R476 from Ennis (look for road signs for Corofin) when approaching the Burren from the south, or N67 from Galway when coming from the north. The Burren has roads and lanes that weave through the landscape like a spider's web, so mapping a route is the best way to explore this rich tapestry of natural beauty, fascinating wildlife, and archaeological sites. Park only in designated car parks (free), which have been built adjacent to the major sites, and proceed by foot to avoid damage to the delicate ecology. The main bus stop for travelers to the Burren area is Ballyvaughan or Lisdoonvarna.

Sights

Burren Centre

VISITOR CENTER | Along with a café and a crafts shop with good maps and locally published guides, the tiny Burren Centre has a modest audiovisual display and other exhibits that explain the Burren's geology, flora, and archaeology. ✉ *8 km (5 miles) southeast of Lisdoonvarna on R476, Kilfenora* ☎ *065/708–8030* 🌐 *theburrencentre.ie* 🎫 *€6* 🕑 *Closed Nov.–mid-Mar.*

★ **The Burren Way**

TRAIL | You can explore the Burren area by car, from a bike, or from the back of a bus, but the very best way to soak in the raw beauty of this craggy landscape is on foot. The Burren Way is a 123-km (82-mile) way-marked hiking trail, its highlight being the stretch from Lahinch to Ballyvaughan on the shores of Galway Bay, a distance of 35 km (22 miles). If you're short on time/breath, you may want to focus on the most spectacular and popular section, which runs along the top of the Cliffs of Moher from Doolin to the coast near Lisdoonvarna, a distance of about 5 km (3 miles). The trail continues through the heart of the Burren's gray, rocky limestone landscape, with ever-changing views offshore of the Aran Islands and Galway Bay. Buy a map locally. 🌐 *burrengeopark.ie.*

Caherconnell Stone Fort

RUINS | There are several stone forts in the Burren thought to have been in use between AD 400 and 1200, but Caherconnell—1 km (½ mile) south of Poulnabrone—is the best preserved, and the only one excavated and easily accessible to visitors. The interpretive center has an audiovisual display on the chief archaeological features of the area, including burial places marked by dolmens or cairns. Ongoing excavations continue to fill in the blanks of this impressive structure's history. Be sure to check out the sheepdog demonstrations and café. ✉ *Caherconnell, Kilfenora* ☎ *065/708–9999* 🌐 *caherconnell.com* 🎫 *From €8* 🕑 *Closed Nov.–mid-Mar.*

★ **Cathedral of St. Fachtna**

CHURCH | Beside the Burren Centre in Kilfenora, the ruins of a small 12th-century church, once the Cathedral of St. Fachtna, have been partially restored as a parish church. Over the transept, a glass ceiling protects High Crosses and effigies from the harsh elements. Note the impressive Doorty Cross in the Lady's Chapel. There are some interesting carvings in the roofless choir, including an unusual, life-size human skeleton. In the chancel, there is an impressive east-facing window with ancient carvings. In a field, about 165 feet west of the ruins is an elaborately sculpted High Cross that is worth examining, though parts of it are badly weathered. Visit early evening when the High Crosses are illuminated to get a clearer view of their intricacies and scale. ✉ *Maryville, Kilfenora.*

Burren Driving Tour

Even locals find the Burren's labyrinthine network of narrow lanes and famine roads a challenge to navigate. With flaky phone signals, setting out with a plan (and map!) is best.

- From Ballyvaughan to Fanore Beach (16 km [10 miles]): Heading south along the R477 is always a good idea for taking advantage of County Clare's dramatic coastline, rather than catching a glimpse of it in the rearview mirror. Fanore is a blink-and-miss-it village that ribbons along the road with unimposing architecture. Fanore means "ring of gold," an effective description of the curving, sandy contour of its beach, which is located south of the village. It's an intimate beach, with a decked pathway down to the fine sand, which has ocean views that are interrupted only by the Aran Islands. Photo op: midway to Fanore Beach, and park the car near Black Head Lighthouse for panoramic views of Galway Bay.

- From Fanore Beach to Kilfenora (18 km [11 miles]): The small village of Kilfenora is also known as the "city of the crosses," due to the multitude of intricately inscribed High Crosses housed under the glass roof of **St. Fachtna's Cathedral.** This small village also has the **Burren Center,** a modest museum dedicated to Ireland's most fascinating landscape. Photo op: slip off onto the R478 via Lisdoonvarna and head for Doonagore for panoramic Aran Islands views over Doolin Village.

- From Kilfenora to Ailwee Caves (18 km [11 miles]): Head north via the R478, N67, and R480 to discover underground passages at **Ailwees Cave.** River stalactites and waterfalls lead to the core of the mountain that was once occupied by bears. Their remains are still visible today in the cave. There is also a birds-of-prey center on-site. Photo op: Corkscrew Hill, a series of steep, winding bends accurately described by its name provides staggering contrasting views of the Atlantic's deep blue water against the stark, gray contours of the Burren.

- From Ailwee Cave to the Burren Perfumery (16 km [10 miles]): Heading south on the R480, the **Caherconnell Stone Fort** has a visitor center and café. The ring fort dates back to the 11th century, and remained inhabited for more than 500 years. The **Burren Perfumery** on the L1014 captures fragrances from the Burren's unique foliage. Photo op: the most iconic landmark in the Burren is the Poulnabrone megalithic tomb, 8 km (5 miles) south of Ailwee Cave on the R480.

- From Burren Perfumery to Corcomroe Abbey (14 km [9 miles]): Heading north on the L1014, **Corcomroe Abbey** was coined St. Mary of the Fertile Rock by the Cistercian community who lived there centuries ago. Inside, an effigy of an O'Brien chieftain reclines in peace by a retaining wall. For a sweet diversion, head over to the **Hazel Mountain Chocolate Factory** five minutes away by car. Photo op: head off the radar to the remote Oughtmama, with abandoned churches and cairns that lie in the shadow of a bald limestone hill. It's a mesmerizing 9½-km (6-mile) coastal drive back to Ballyvaughan.

★ **Poulnabrone Megalithic Tomb**
HISTORIC SIGHT | The biggest and most famous of the Burren's megalithic tombs, Poulnabrone ("the hole of sorrows") is a portal grave/dolmen with a massive capstone and a majestic presence amid the craggy limestone fields shouldering the moody gray Burren skies. The monument was built around 4,500 years ago. Stand downwind and you might hear ancient whispers. There is a designated car park nearby with a historical timeline and a short gravel walkway to the dolmen (freely accessible). It's open and windy here, so grab an extra layer. ✉ *On R480, 8 km (5 miles) south of Ballyvaughan, Kilfenora.*

Restaurants

Hazel Mountain Cafe
$ | **CAFÉ** | This surprising find in a cottage on the northern ridge of the Burren is not only a refreshing place for a soup-and-sandwich break, it's also home to the boutique Hazel Mountain Chocolate Factory, which produces chocolate using the same techniques employed by the monks who once occupied nearby Corcomroe Abbey. Vegetables are grown on-site and the cakes baked star in their own cookbook. **Known for:** offers chocolate tours and tastings; hearty soup with homegrown vegetables; cottage farmhouse setting. ($) *Average main: €10* ✉ *Oughtmama* ☎ *065/707–8847* 🌐 *hazelmountainchocolate.com* ☞ *Factory tours available Mar.–Sept.*

★ **Wild Honey Inn**
$$ | **MODERN IRISH** | Owner-chef Aidan McGrath and Kate Sweeney's modest Victorian premises on the outskirts of Lisdoonvarna have become something of a culinary landmark by becoming Ireland's first pub to be awarded a Michelin star. A brief, well-thought-out menu showcases the best of local produce, which includes hake, lamb, rib-eye steak, and pork. **Known for:** perfectly presented and executed dishes; friendly and attentive staff; inn is a good base for Burren. ($) *Average main: €24* ✉ *Kincora Rd., Lisdoonvarna* ☎ *065/707–4300* 🌐 *wildhoneyinn.com* ⏲ *Closed Nov.–Feb.*

Nightlife

Roadside Tavern
PUBS | Husband-and-wife team Birgitta and Peter Curtain offer their own craft beer and innovative food sourced from their neighboring Burren Smokehouse store in the quirky Roadside Tavern just off the main street of Ireland's matchmaking capital, Lisdoonvarna. The pub, owned by generations of Curtains, has regular trad sessions and guaranteed banter from Peter. Hobbit enthusiasts are particularly welcome, as the premises is home to the Burren Tolkien Society. ✉ *Kincora Rd., Lisdoonvarna* ☎ *065/707–4084* 🌐 *burrenexperiences.ie.*

Vaughan's Pub
LIVE MUSIC | In the heart of Kilfenora Village this pub is known for its traditional-music sessions in a village famed for its céilí band, Vaughan's has been a local favorite for years. Its claim to fame is a cameo appearance in the television series *Father Ted*. Set-dancing sessions are held in the barn every Sunday at 9:30 pm.

TIP→ Renovated guest rooms with modern furnishings available on-site. ✉ *Main St., Kilfenora* ☎ *065/708–8004* 🌐 *vaughanspub.ie.*

Shopping

★ **Burren Perfumery**
PERFUME | Shopping opportunities are not abundant in this rocky terrain, so don't miss the chance to buy Burren-inspired organic perfumery products at this delightful spot. The Burren is known for its wildflowers, and the perfumery is committed to its conservation: all the products on sale are sourced from ethical

specialist growers and made on-site, in small batches. As well as perfume there are soaps, creams, and balms, and you can visit the workshops to see them being made (April–September). There is also an organic herb garden and a flower-bedecked tearoom (April–September) selling delicious organic home baking and light lunches. ✉ *The Burren Perfumery, Fahee North, Carron, Ballyvaughan* ☎ *065/708–9102* 🌐 *burrenperfumery.com.*

Activities

BICYCLING

West Ireland Cycling

BIKING | FAMILY | Take an organized or self-guided Burren tour or hire a top-of-the-range bike from this Galway-based outfit. They can also deliver up to 80 bikes by trailer for groups and offer a range of equipment including child seats and trailers for hauling your kids. ✉ *Earl's Island, Galway City* ✣ *Beside Monroe's Pub* ☎ *087/176–8480* 🌐 *westirelandcycling.com* 🎫 *Rentals from €20 per day, e-bikes €50. Tours for single start at €925 (€625 if sharing) and include accommodations.*

Ballyvaughan

37 km (23 miles) north of Ennis on R476 and R480.

A pretty little waterside village and a good base for exploring the Burren, Ballyvaughan attracts walkers and artists who enjoy the views of Galway Bay.

Sights

Aillwee Cave

CAVE | FAMILY | A vast 2-million-year-old cave, Aillwee is the biggest and most impressive chamber in the region accessible to those who aren't spelunkers. Illuminated for about 3,300 feet, the cave contains an underground river and waterfall. Aboveground, there are a big crafts shop, cheese-making demonstrations, a café, and the Burren Birds of Prey Centre, which puts on flying displays from eagles, falcons, hawks, and owls daily at noon and 3 pm (weather permitting). Discounts available if you book online. ✉ *5 km (3 miles) south of Ballyvaughan on R480, Ballyvaughan* ☎ *065/707–7036* 🌐 *aillweecave.ie* 🎫 *From €15.*

Restaurants

★ Linnane's Lobster Bar

$$ | IRISH | It doesn't get much better than this 300-year-old, slated, whitewashed cottage with a turf fire and full-length windows that open out onto a terrace overlooking Galway Bay. The specialty is seafood; clams, scallops, salmon, crab claws, and lobster—the restaurant's cornerstone dish. **Known for:** crab claws with butter sauce; great wine list; live music in the evenings. 💲 *Average main: €25* ✉ *Cartron, New Quay, Oughtmama* ✣ *12 km (7 miles) northeast on N67 of Ballyvaughan* ☎ *65/707–8120* 🌐 *linnanesbar.com* ⏲ *Closed Mon.–Thurs. Nov.–Mar.*

★ Monk's Pub

$ | MODERN IRISH | FAMILY | This landmark dining pub a stone's throw from Ballyvaughan Pier has changed hands and fortunes over the past few years, but all you need to know is that it is back on its game with a freshly renovated interior and menu. The welcoming fire and friendly service remain, as does the signature seafood chowder that lures locals and visitors from miles around. **Known for:** live music during the summer months; decadent desserts; fireside dining and drinks. 💲 *Average main: €15* ✉ *Ballyvaughan* ✣ *Near pier* ☎ *065/707–7059* 🌐 *monks.ie* ⏲ *Closed Oct.–May. No food Mon.–Thurs.*

Coffee and Quick Bites

Café Linnalla

$ | **CAFÉ** | **FAMILY** | Set in a peninsula on Galway Bay's Flaggy Shore, the enterprising Brid Fahy opened this farm-to-café experience back in 2006, thus establishing Europe's most westerly ice-cream parlor. Made with milk from the Friesian and Shorthorn herd from her five-generation farm, the ice cream here is fantastic, and for good reason: the cows cross between the mainland and a small island to graze and this gives the cow's milk a unique and varied flavor. **Known for:** decadent sundaes with homemade brownies; lovely Galway Bay views; fruit smoothies. *Average main: €3 The Burren, New Quay, Oughtmama 87/785–7569 linnallaicecream.ie Closed weekdays Nov.–Mar.*

Drumcreehy Country House

$ | **B&B/INN** | **FAMILY** | The pretty gabled facade with dormer windows is traditional in style, but, in fact, Bernadette Moloney and her German husband, Armin Grefkes, designed and built this house specifically as a B&B. **Pros:** big bedrooms for a B&B; nice waterfront location; peaceful nights. **Cons:** a long (1-mile-plus) walk down a narrow busy road to village; some communal spaces are small; standard design. *Rooms from: €100 Bishop's Quarter, Ballyvaughan 065/707–7377 drumcreehyhouse.com 12 rooms Free Breakfast.*

Gregans Castle Hotel

$$$$ | **HOTEL** | Miles from the nearest town, this handsome ivy-clad Georgian retreat lies in the heart of the Burren, its turf fires and antique furnishings a draw back to a simpler time. **Pros:** tea and fresh-baked scones available all day; beautiful gardens to wander; warm and attentive staff. **Cons:** TV-free zone, only one in-house; often minimum two-night stay; very remote, car essential. *Rooms from: €275 Base of Corkscrew Hill, Ballyvaughan 065/707–7005 gregans.ie Closed Dec. 2–mid-Feb. 15 rooms, 6 suites Free Breakfast.*

Hyland's Burren Hotel

$$ | **HOTEL** | A turf fire greets you in the lobby of this unpretentious coaching inn in the heart of the Burren, which dates from the early 18th century and has become a cheerful, welcoming spot with a reputation for friendliness and good entertainment. **Pros:** central location; spacious lounge on the first floor, with an outdoor deck; special midweek rates. **Cons:** won't win any style contests; no leisure facilities; bar and restaurant very busy July and August. *Rooms from: €120 Main St., Ballyvaughan 065/707–7037 hylandsburren.com Closed Jan. 32 rooms Free Breakfast.*

O'Lochlainns Bar

PUBS | No Ballyvaughan trip would be complete without this old-timer's pub, with its epic collection of whiskey brands. Set in a tidy building near the village square, with one eye on Galway Bay, O'Lochlainn's is a family business that opens every night from 8 pm (when the farming day is over) until late. Its intimate dark-wood interior is a throwback to the 1930s, when it was a store and local tea blender. *Ballyvaughan 065/707–7006.*

Kinvara

18 km (11 miles) north east of Ballyvaughan, 29 km (17½ miles) south of Galway City.

Kinvara, with its pretty harbor and iconic ocean-edge tower house that played a role in Ireland's literary revival, makes for a leisurely break along the busy tourist trek between the Cliffs of Moher and Galway City. Its quayside cafés and brightly painted pubs entice visitors to linger and toss aside the itinerary. Kinvara is home to the annual Fleadh na gCuach (Cuckoo Fleadh), a traditional music festival held the first weekend of May, as well as the long-standing early-August sailing event, Cruinniú na mBád (Festival of the Gathering of the Boats), in which traditional brown-sail Galway hookers laden with turf race across the bay.

GETTING HERE AND AROUND

The N67 coast road, a narrow but scenic route, follows the shore of Galway Bay from Ballyvaughan to Kinvara. From Kinvara, N67 joins the busy national route, the M18, at Clarenbridge and continues into Galway City (29 km [17 miles]). There is free but limited parking in Kinvara. Bus Éireann runs buses between Kinvara and Galway City; the journey takes about 30 minutes. The same bus continues to the Cliffs of Moher, Lisdoonvarna, and Doolin.

Sights

★ Dungaire Castle

CASTLE/PALACE | Like a chess piece flung onto a windswept rock a short stroll from the village of Kinvara, Dunguaire Castle has braced the Atlantic for 400 years, replacing the king of Connaught's 6th-century palace upon its construction. Built in 1520 by the O'Hynes clan, the tiny storybook castle takes its name from the fabled king of Connaught, Guaire. In 1924 it was purchased by Oliver St. John Gogarty, the noted surgeon, man of letters, and model for Buck Mulligan, a character in James Joyce's *Ulysses.* Many of the leading figures of the 19th-century Celtic revival in Irish literature came to visit his west coast outpost. Today Dunguaire is used for a medieval banquet that honors local writers and others with ties to the West, including Lady Gregory, W.B. Yeats, Seán O'Casey, and Pádraic Ó Conaire. **TIP→ Book in advance for the medieval banquet.** ✉ *Dungory West, Kinvara* ☎ *061/711–222* 🌐 *dunguairecastle.com* 🎟 *€8* ⏲ *Closed Oct.–Mar.*

Restaurants

★ Moran's Oyster Cottage

$$$ | **SEAFOOD** | This small thatched cottage is just upstream from where the Dunkellin River flows into Dunbulcaun Bay, the epicenter of Ireland's fresh oyster trade. The local oysters make a regular appearance, straight from bay to plate, though smoked salmon, crab claws fried in garlic butter, seafood cocktail, lobster with boiled potatoes and garlic butter, and fresh crab salad are also on offer. **Known for:** excellent fish-and-chips; seafood chowder from a recipe passed down seven generations; landmark restaurant for generations. $ *Average main: €33* ✉ *The Weir, Kilcolgan* ✣ *Signposted off main road on south side of Clarinbridge* ☎ *091/796–113* 🌐 *moransoystercottage.com* ⏲ *Closed Mon.*

Coole Park

24 km (15 miles) northeast of Corofin on M18.

This nature reserve attracts William Butler Yeats fans to see the famous autograph tree and others who just seek pleasant and easy walking trails.

Sights

Coole-Garryland Nature Reserve

NATURE PRESERVE | Coole Park was once the home of Lady Augusta Gregory (1859–1932), patron of W. B. Yeats and cofounder with the poet of Dublin's Abbey Theatre. Yeats visited here often, as did almost all the other writers who contributed to the Irish literary revival in the first half of the 20th century. The house became derelict after Lady Gregory's death and was demolished in

1941; the grounds are now a wildlife park with a herd of deer and 6 km (4 miles) of nature trails. Picnic tables make this a lovely alfresco lunch spot. There's also a visitor center with displays on Lady Gregory and W.B. Yeats. Don't miss the park's only reminder of its literary past, the Autograph Tree, a giant copper beech, on which many of Lady Gregory's famous guests carved their initials. ✉ *R458 (well signposted), Gort* ☎ *091/631–804* 🌐 *coolepark.ie* 🎫 *Free* 🕑 *Visitor center and tearooms closed Oct.–Easter.*

★ Kilmacduagh Monastery

RUINS | Kilmacduagh's 110-foot-high Round Tower, reputedly the tallest in the world, tilts 3 feet from the vertical over the monastery below. Arguably more impressive than the famous tower at Glendalough and without the backdrop of tour buses, Kilmacduagh is peaceful apart from the mournful lowing of cattle. The monastery was founded in the 7th century, but the tower, cathedral, churches, and abbot's home were built more than three centuries later. St. Colman, who founded the monastery, is buried behind the cathedral. Lying on his grave is believed to relieve back pain. The key to the site can be obtained across the street at the Tower View Guesthouse with a €5 deposit. ✉ *Kilmacduagh, Gort* ✥ *6 km (4 miles) southwest on R460 from Gort* 🎫 *Free.*

Thoor Ballylee (Yeats's Tower)

CASTLE/PALACE | W.B. Yeats wrote some of his finest poetry, including "The Tower" and "The Winding Stair" in Thoor Ballylee, a small castle just an eight-minute drive from Gort. You can take the winding staircase that led the famous poet up to his writer's garret. A tablet with the words "I, the poet William Yeats, With old mill boards and sea-green slates, And smithy work from the Gort forge, Restored this tower for my wife George. And may these characters remain, When all is ruin once again" is mounted outside as a testament to the time he spent in his summer retreat. Fans of Hollywood's golden age will remember Maureen O'Hara's character, Mary Kate Danagher from John Ford's movie *The Quiet Man* (1952), rambling by the river at the foot of the tower house.

■ TIP→ The tower house is susceptible to flooding so call ahead. ✉ *Gort* ✥ *1½ km (1 mile) off R458* 🌐 *yeatsthoorballylee.org* 🎫 *€7* 🕑 *Closed Nov.–Apr.*

Restaurants

Gallery Cafe

$ | **MODERN IRISH** | A chilled-out café in the middle of town, Gallery Cafe has heaps of character with local artist exhibitions and the occasional live performance providing an ever-changing setting. The seasonal menu often features local catch, stews, and braised venison as well as pizza and sandwiches. **Known for:** hearty and healthy breakfast menu; fantastic coffee; town-square setting. $ *Average main: €15* ✉ *The Square, Gort* ☎ *091/630–630* 🌐 *thegallerycafegort.com* 🕑 *Closed Mon. and Tues.*

Galway City

The harbor city of Galway is the unofficial capital of the west of Ireland and a stronghold of traditional Irish ways, from its rapturous music scene to its artisanal restaurants that reap the local seafood harvest.

Its streets, with their famed boho bars and cafés that spill out onto its cobbled medieval lanes, are a magnet for visitors. Despite being Ireland's fourth-largest city, it has retained the essence of a much smaller town, particularly in its compact and very walkable nucleus. The city's beating heart lies within this short thoroughfare and the twisting labyrinth of alleys that flow into it.

It's most alive later in the evening when streetlights come on and the sound of

City of the Tribes

Galway's urban elite was confined to 14 families who controlled the city for the greater part of the second millennium, until the arrival of Oliver Cromwell's troops in the 17th century.

The families lived within Galway's city walls and built up their wealth through international trade, while others lived in the hinterlands.

Their names are still common in Galway and elsewhere in Ireland: Athy, Blake, Bodkin, Browne, D'Arcy, Dean, Font, French, Kirwan, Joyce, Lynch, Morris, Martin, and Skerret.

The city's medieval heritage, a fusion of Gaelic and Norman influences, is apparent in the intimate two- and three-story stone buildings, winding streets, narrow passageways, and cobblestones underfoot.

uilleann pipes, harps, and bodhráns filters through the air. It's a vibrancy that's fueled both by the fact it's a university town and the epicenter of western Ireland, which ensures that it glows until the early hours.

While Galway has more than its fair share of Michelin stars, the foodie experience predictably balances the finest organic, locally sourced food with a chilled-out service in most restaurants.

However Galway is more than just pubs and restaurants. The Druid Lane Theatre, just off Quay Street, is the place where Hollywood darling and screenwriter Martin McDonagh launched his career and it hosts traveling and homegrown productions, while Macnas, a troupe of avant-garde performers and puppeteers, adds drama and color to city highlights from St. Patrick's Day to the Galway Halloween Parade.

Although you're not conscious of it when you're in the center of town, Galway is spectacularly situated on the north shore of Galway Bay, where the River Corrib flows from Lough Corrib to the sea. The seaside suburb of Salthill, on the south-facing shore of Galway Bay, has stunning vistas across the vividly blue bay to Black Head and the Burren on the opposite shore.

Galway's growth and popularity mean that at its busiest moments, its narrow, one-way streets are jam-packed with pedestrians, while cars are gridlocked on its ring road system.

TOURS

Lally Tours

BUS TOURS | While Galway's historic center is compact and can be explored on foot, many visitors enjoy a quick orientation. Hop aboard Lally Tours' vintage double-decker bus for an hour-long Old Galway City Tour. Every 90 minutes (every 45 minutes from June to August) buses leave from the tourist office in Forster Place on the corner of Eyre Square. ✉ *4 Forster St., Galway City* ☎ *091/562–905* 🌐 *lallytours.com* 🎫 *From €15.*

Sights

Most of the city's sights, aside from the cathedral and the university campus, can be found in a narrow slice of the medieval town center that runs in a southwesterly direction from Eyre Square to the River Corrib. Not only is the city center compact, but it's also largely pedestrian-friendly, so the best way to explore it is on foot. It takes only five minutes to

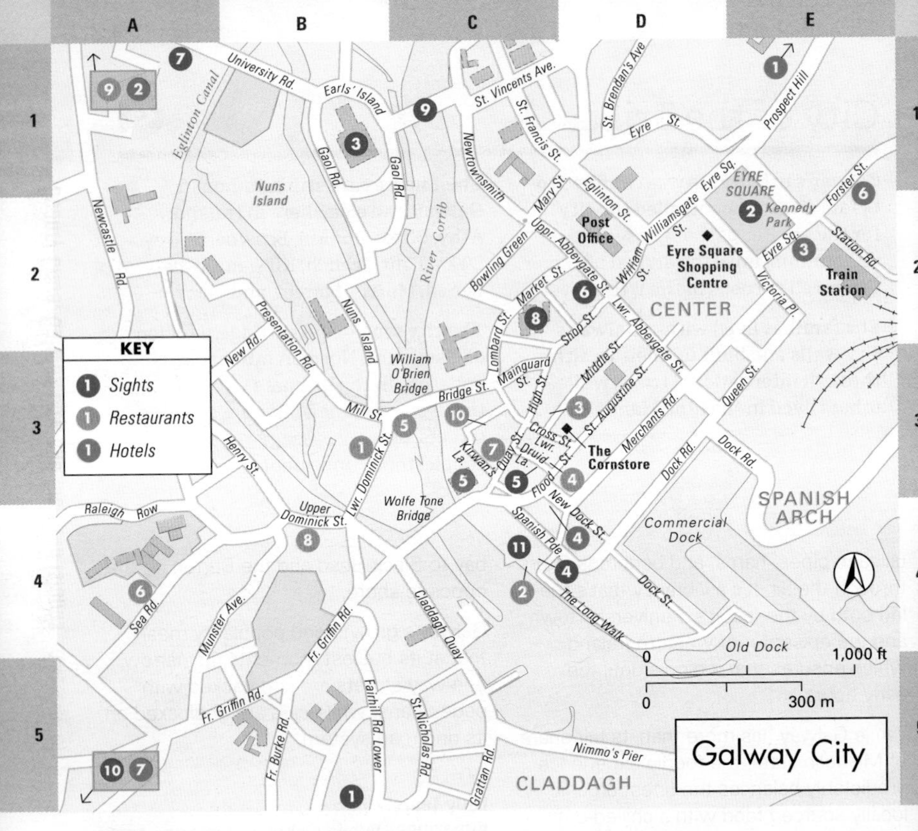

Sights

1 The Claddagh and Katie's Cottage and Arts Centre **B5**
2 Eyre Square **E2**
3 Galway Cathedral....... **B1**
4 Galway City Museum.... **C4**
5 The Hall of the Red Earl.................... **C3**
6 Lynch's Castle........... **D2**
7 NUI Galway.............. **A1**
8 St. Nicholas' Collegiate Church Galway........... **C2**
9 Salmon Weir Bridge..... **C1**
10 Salthill.................... **A5**
11 Spanish Arch............. **C4**

Restaurants

1 Aniar Restaurant **B3**
2 Ard Bia at Nimmo's...... **C4**
3 Cava Bodega............ **C3**
4 Éan **C3**
5 Il Vicola **C3**
6 Kai Restaurant.......... **A4**
7 McDonagh's Fish and Chips.............. **C3**
8 Oscar's Seafood Bistro.......... **B4**
9 The Pullman Restaurant.............. **A1**
10 The Seafood Bar at Kirwan's **C3**

Hotels

1 The Dean Hotel.......... **E1**
2 Glenlo Abbey Hotel...... **A1**
3 The Hardiman............ **E2**
4 The House Hotel......... **C4**
5 Jurys Inn Galway........ **C3**
6 Park House Hotel........ **E2**
7 Sea Breeze Lodge Bed and Breakfast **A5**

walk straight down Galway's main shopping street, the continuation of the north side of Eyre Square, to the River Corrib, where it ends (note that the name of this street changes several times).

The Claddagh and Katie's Cottage and Arts Centre

HISTORIC DISTRICT | On the west bank of the Corrib Estuary, this district was once an Irish-speaking fishing village outside the walls of the old town. The name is an Anglicization of the Irish *cladach,* which means "marshy ground." It retained a strong, separate identity until the 1930s, when its traditional thatched cottages were replaced by a conventional housing plan and its unique character and traditions were largely lost. One thing has survived: the claddagh ring, composed of two hands clasped around a heart with a crown above it (symbolizing love, friendship, and loyalty), was designed some 400 years ago by a goldsmith in this village and is still used by the Irish diaspora, sometimes as a wedding ring. Reproductions in gold or silver are favorite Galway souvenirs. Across the Corrib is the "Long Walk"—Galway's famous waterfront streetscape, for some Insta magic—or continue walking west for a magnificent coastal walk or run to Salthill. In the center of The Claddagh, in a residential area, is Katie's Cottage, a replica of a typical Claddagh home, which is open as a café and exhibition center. ✉ *Upper Fairhill Rd., The Claddagh, Galway City* 🌐 *wildatlanticworkshop.ie* 🎫 *From €3.*

Eyre Square

PLAZA/SQUARE | **FAMILY** | The largest open space in central Galway and the arrival and departure point by train and bus, this is a favorite chill-out spot on a sunny day for students, visitors, families and lunching locals. Eyre Square on the east side of the River Corrib incorporates a sculpture garden and children's play area, while its west side is bound by a heavily traveled road. In the center is Kennedy Park, a patch of lawn named in honor of John F. Kennedy, who spoke here when he visited the city in June 1963. At the north end of the park, a 20-foot-high steel sculpture standing in the pool of a fountain represents the brown sails seen on Galway hookers, the area's traditional sailing boats. Now a feature of Kennedy Park, the Browne Doorway was taken in 1905 from the Browne family's town house on Upper Abbeygate Street; it has the 17th-century coats of arms of both the Browne and Lynch families (two of Galway's 14 founding families). ✉ *Galway City.*

Galway Cathedral

CHURCH | Dominating Galway City's skyline for more than half a century with its massive, green, copper dome, Galway Cathedral's hulking brick exterior has had a mixed reception from critics since its construction. Inside, the limestone walls draw the eye up, while the stained-glass windows and the dome's light-filled contour add a heavenly perspective. ✉ *Gaol Rd., Nun's Island* ☎ *091/563–577* 🌐 *galwaycathedral.ie* 🎫 *Free.*

Galway City Museum

HISTORY MUSEUM | **FAMILY** | The city's civic museum, housed in a modern building behind the Spanish Arch, contains materials relating to local history: old photographs, antiquities (the oldest is a stone ax head carbon-dated to 3500 BC), and a full-scale Galway hooker (turf-carrying boat) in the stairwell, as well as information on the city's involvement in Ireland's 1916 Rising. On the top floor, there's a child-friendly ocean-life museum with panoramic Corrib River views. Its café, the Kitchen, is a lively lunch and coffee spot. ✉ *Spanish Parade, Spanish Arch* ☎ *091/532-460* 🌐 *galwaycitymuseum.ie* 🎫 *Free (donations accepted)* ⏲ *Closed Sun. and Mon.*

The Hall of the Red Earl

HISTORIC HOME | Galway's Custom's House discovered a hoard of artifacts in its foundation, which revealed the site's significant past as the palace of Ricard de Burgo, an earl who was the grandson of the city's founding father. It was the nerve center of Galway—its tax office, courthouse, and town hall all under one roof. Today, the floodlit foundation of the building can be explored from a gangway through a glass partition that surrounds the dig, unveiling city life in Galway in the 13th century, before the 14 tribes ruled the city. ✉ *Druid La., Center* 🎫 *Free.*

Lynch's Castle

CASTLE/PALACE | Lynch's Castle, once the stronghold of Galway's ruling family, dates back to 1600. These days it's occupied by a branch of a local bank, making its stone fireplace accessible to the public. Check out the gargoyles peering from its facade before heading around the corner to find Lynch's window. According to legend, magistrate and mayor James Lynch FitzStephen hanged his son from its sturdy Gothic frame as punishment for the murder of a Spanish sailor. ✉ *Shop St., Center.*

NUI Galway

COLLEGE | Thanks in part to its central location, NUI Galway has become an inextricable part of Galway life since its construction in 1845, as only a handful of other universities, such as Oxford, have done. In fact its Tudor Gothic–style quadrangle was modeled on Christ Church in Oxford. It houses Galway's "hidden museum," the **James Mitchell Geology Museum,** which has a collection of 15,000 rocks, gemstones, and fossils. ✉ *Newcastle Rd., University* ☎ *091/524–411* 🌐 *nuigalway.ie* 🎫 *Free.*

Salmon Weir Bridge

BRIDGE | The bridge itself is nothing special, but in season—from mid-April to early July—shoals of salmon are visible from its deck as they lie in the clear river water before making their way upstream to the spawning grounds of Lough Corrib. ✉ *West end of St. Vincent's Ave., Center.*

Salthill

PROMENADE | **FAMILY** | A lively, hugely popular seaside resort and peripheral Galway City neighborhood, Salthill is beloved for its old-fashioned seaside promenade—the traditional place "to sit and watch the moon rise over Claddagh, and see the sun go down on Galway Bay," as Bing Crosby used to croon in the most famous song about the city. Today locals use it for a routine run from the city center or weekend leap into the ocean from its diving boards. The main attraction of the village, set 3 km (2 miles) west of Galway, is the long sandy beach along the edge of Galway Bay and the promenade above it. New hotels, trendy restaurants, and craft beer pubs along the seafront have nevertheless left plenty of room for the traditional amusement arcades (full of slot machines), seasonal cafés, and a fairground.

Spanish Arch

HISTORIC SIGHT | Built in 1584 to protect Spanish ships that were unloading cargoes of wines and brandies at the quays, this impressive stone arch is now the central feature of the newly restored Spanish Parade, a riverside piazza that draws a gathering of buskers and leisure seekers. ✉ *Spanish Parade, Spanish Arch.*

St. Nicholas' Collegiate Church Galway

CHURCH | Built by the Anglo-Normans in 1320 and enlarged by members of the 14 tribes when they were at their most powerful during the 16th century, the church contains many fine carvings of lions, mermaids, and gargoyles dating from the late Middle Ages, and it's one of the best-preserved medieval churches in Ireland. Explorer Christopher Columbus prayed here on a visit to Galway in 1477. On Saturday morning a street market, held in the pedestrian way beside the church, attracts dozens of vendors and hundreds of shoppers. ✉ *Mainguard St. and Lombard St., Center* ☎ *091/564–648* 🌐 *stnicholas.ie* 🎫 *Free.*

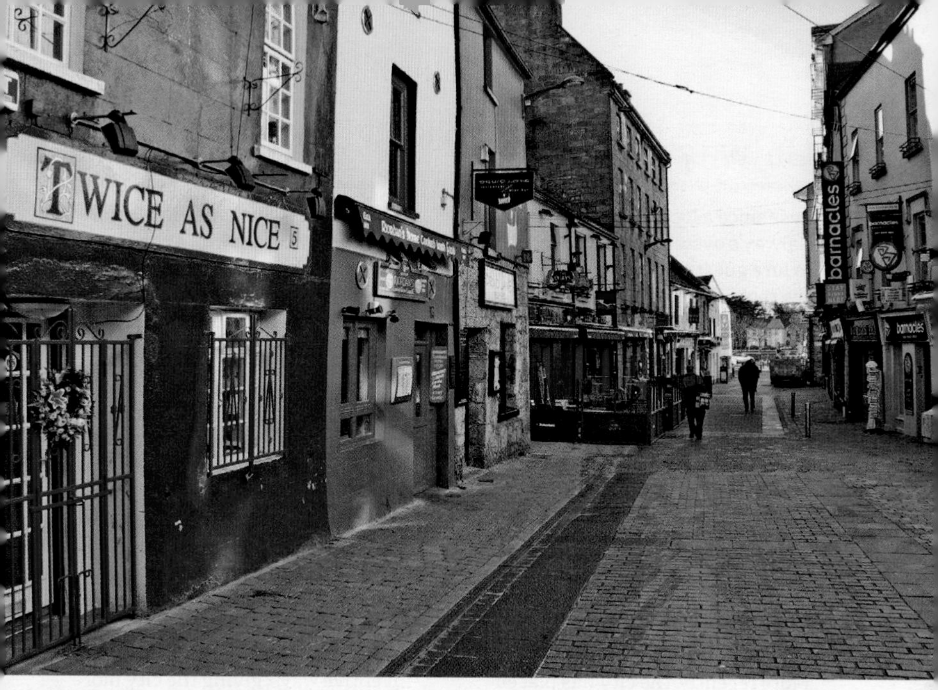

Pedestrian alleys and high-style boutiques help make Galway into a stroller's paradise—keep your eye out for the many 19th-century footscrapers.

Restaurants

★ Aniar Restaurant

$$$$ | IRISH | JP McMahon has caused quite a stir in the Galway dining scene with his tapas at Cava Bodega and the recently opened casual spot Tartare, but award-winning Aniar (meaning "from the west") is his flagship restaurant. A minimalist Nordic decor provides an unfussy backdrop for the chef's equally unfussy approach to food. **Known for:** seaweed ice cream; minimalist furnishings; locally sourced food. *Average main: €135* *53 Lower Dominick St., Center* *091/533–947* *aniarrestaurant.ie* *Closed Sun. and Mon.*

Ard Bia at Nimmo's

$$ | EUROPEAN | Expect to wait in line at this city-center restaurant set in an old stone house, with tables overlooking the Corrib. Ard Bia serves budget-conscious, freshly baked and sourced food, with a menu that changes according to what is in season. Jumbled furnishings from dressers to crockery in a casual setting contrasts the more spacious, timber-floored restaurant upstairs. **Known for:** all-day brunch; river views; seasonal menu. *Average main: €29* *The Long Walk, Spanish Arch* *Head for Spanish Arch and restaurant is right behind it* *091/561–114* *ardbia.com.*

Cava Bodega

$ | TAPAS | FAMILY | Tapping into Galway's past as a major trading post for Spain, chef-owners JP McMahon and Drigin Gaffey bring all the favorite aspects of authentic Spanish cuisine and wine while also serving excellent local produce in this vibrant and warm Galway hot spot. The more than 50 regional tapas served family-style on large, wooden communal tables are at the heart of this restaurant filled with Spanish flavors and Irish produce. **Known for:** offers tasty traditional and vegetarian paellas; superb desserts; carefully sourced Spanish wines and sherries. *Average main: €12* *Middle Street Mews, Unit 1, Galway City* *91/539–884* *cavarestaurant.ie* *No lunch weekdays.*

Galway's Emerging Food Scene

Ever since a local hotelier created Galway's oyster festival decades ago to lure guests off-season to sample the region's world-famous delicacy, the city has become one of Ireland's leading food hubs. Major annual food events have helped to create a citywide culinary environment that connects to the wider region. Each year Galway kicks off the season with its Food Festival at Easter, followed by the Oyster Festival in September and the Food On the Edge Festival a month later. By the end of the year, Eyre Square turns into a maze of timber kiosks selling artisanal food at Galway's Christmas market.

More recently, the city has placed itself firmly on the international culinary map with top-notch restaurants like Ard Bia, Aniar, and Kai, and by becoming a European Region of Gastronomy for 2018, an award that recognizes the region's integration of gastronomy into tourism, culture, and economy.

Good food has also become part of everyday Galway life. The Saturday food market (🌐 *galwaymarket.com*) brings in the best of local food producers into the city center to set up their stalls behind the Collegiate Church of St. Nicholas as far as Sheridan's Cheesemongers. It attracts locals into the city in the early morning. New restaurants look to local food producers using age-old cooking methods to draw out indigenous flavors in inventive ways, giving the city more than its fair share of Michelin-starred restaurants.

★ Éan
$ | **MODERN IRISH** | Tucked down a narrow lane, next door to the Druid Theatre, this exquisite little daytime artisan eatery serves freshly baked produce before it metamorphosizes into a sophisticated candlelit wine bar and restaurant in the evening. Operated by the same team from groundbreaking Loam Restaurant, expect the focus on sustainable and organic produce right down to the wine list. *Ⓢ Average main: €15 ✉ Druid La., Center ☎ 91/374–154 🌐 eangalway.com ⏲ Closed Mon. and Tues.*

★ Il Vicola
$$ | **ITALIAN** | Il Vicola (or alley in English), has a distinctly Venetian flavor, which complements the ample supply of fresh seafood that arrives into the city's docks daily. The River Corrib sweeps below the restaurant and the original mill wheel creates an atmospheric focal point. *Ⓢ Average main: €20 ✉ The Bridge Mills, O'Brien's Bridge, Center ☎ 91/530–515 🌐 www.ilvicolo.ie ⏲ Closed Tues.*

Kai Restaurant
$$ | **CONTEMPORARY** | Tucked inside a renovated cottage in the shadow of St. Ignatius's limestone belfry is one of Galway's best restaurants. The bare stone walls and floors are brightened by a pop of color from thrifted chairs and a skylight that draws in natural light, but what really shines is the reasonably priced and locally sourced organic food. **Known for:** amazing desserts; excellent wine list; reservations in demand. *Ⓢ Average main: €23 ✉ 20 Sea Rd., Center ☎ 091/526–003 🌐 kairestaurant.ie ⏲ Closed Sun. and Mon.*

McDonagh's Fish and Chips
$ | **SEAFOOD** | **FAMILY** | The humble fish-and-chip is king at this stalwart restaurant, serving deep-fried cod, whiting, haddock, and hake for decades. The reasonably

priced fish is served with a heap of fabulous, freshly cooked chips (which have won a nationwide competition for the best in Ireland) and eaten at communal tables—a great way to meet the locals. **Known for:** fast and friendly service; amazing fish soup; local oysters. $ *Average main: €10 ✉ 22 Quay St., Spanish Arch ☎ 091/565–001 🌐 mcdonaghs.net.*

Oscar's Seafood Bistro

$$ | **MODERN IRISH** | Taking full advantage of Galway's fish-rich waters, Oscar's offers a daily changing menu based on the availability of the straight-from-the-trawler catch at the local market. Its warm interior with a ruby red backdrop, billowing fabric, and pine furnishings in close quarters has the essence of a seafaring vessel, with mackerel from the Aran Islands, and monkfish and scallops. **Known for:** tasty local oysters; great-value early-bird meals; amazing desserts. $ *Average main: €20 ✉ Clan House, 22 Dominick St. Lower, Center ☎ 91/582–180 🌐 facebook.com/oscars.bistro ⏲ Closed Sun.*

The Pullman Restaurant

$$$$ | **MODERN IRISH** | Stationed on the grounds of Glenlo Abbey Hotel, overlooking Lough Corrib in the outskirts of Galway, is Ireland's most unique restaurant: two intricately restored train carriages that starred in Sidney Lumet's 1974 film, *Murder on the Orient Express*, starring Ingrid Bergman. Fully equipped with brass luggage racks and mahogany paneling, the carriages are as impressive as the menu, which highlights wild game, fish, and beef. **Known for:** great venue for a romantic dinner; lake views; excellent levels of service. $ *Average main: €63 ✉ Glenlo Abbey Hotel, Kentfield Bushy Park, Galway City ☎ 091/519–600 🌐 www.glenloabbeyhotel.ie/en/pullman-restaurant-galway ⏲ Closed weekdays Nov.–Feb.*

The Seafood Bar at Kirwan's

$$ | **SEAFOOD** | Nestled into a lamp-lit corner of Kirwan's Lane near the Quays, this slim, two-story oasis has served quality local seafood for more than 20 years. Its selection reads like a travel guide from the highlights of the Wild Atlantic Way: Burren smoked salmon, Dingle prawns, and Connemara mussels. **Known for:** decadent desserts; friendly staff and warm atmosphere; solid vegetarian options. $ *Average main: €25 ✉ Kirwan's La., Spanish Arch ☎ 091/568–266 🌐 kirwanslane.ie ⏲ No lunch Sun. Nov.–Apr.*

Hotels

The Dean Hotel

$$$ | **HOTEL** | Following its cool and cutting-edge brothers in Dublin and Cork, the Dean has added a splash of design to drab Prospect Hill, offering state-of-the-art facilities and trendy dining to the West. **Pros:** excellent facilities, including a gym; close to Eyre Square; outdoor heated pool. **Cons:** food options are all modern dining; no on-site parking; little of Galway is reflected in the design. $ *Rooms from: €209 ✉ 80 Prospect Hill, Galway City ☎ 01/223–4517 🌐 thedean.ie/galway 100 rooms No Meals.*

★ **Glenlo Abbey Hotel**

$$$$ | **HOTEL** | Just 5 km (3 miles) from the center of Galway City, Glenlo Abbey is aglow from a recent multimillion-euro makeover under its new MHL group affiliation. **Pros:** exceptionally pleasant and friendly staff; lovely views of distant lake; bargain off-season rates on the webite. **Cons:** out of town; no gym; often hosts large weddings. $ *Rooms from: €290 ✉ Bushy Park, Galway City ☎ 091/519–600 🌐 www.glenlo.com 47 rooms, 3 suites Free Breakfast.*

The Hardiman

$$ | **HOTEL** | Galway's grande-dame hotel (formerly Hotel Meyrick) was built to accommodate train passengers to the heart of Galway in the middle of the 19th century, but even after an expensive makeover, the hotel has managed to retain its Victorian character and restrained opulence with

black-and-white-checkered tiles, sash windows, solid oak fixtures, and crystal chandeliers. **Pros:** location on Eyre Square; fantastic on-site dining; rooftop hot tub. **Cons:** not all bedrooms have a/c; architecturally lacking and reflects little of the city; limited parking. *Rooms from: €155 Eyre Sq., Center 091/564–041 thehardiman.ie 103 rooms Free Breakfast.*

The House Hotel

$$$ | HOTEL | Sheltered from noise on a one-way street with views overlooking the River Corrib, the House Hotel is arguably Galway's best-appointed property, just a stone's throw from the city's vibrant restaurant and pub scene and a two-minute walk from the Quays. **Pros:** excellent city-center location; river views; serves a decadent afternoon tea. **Cons:** no fitness facilities; remote car parking; hotel location open to the elements. *Rooms from: €179 Spanish Parade, Spanish Arch 091/538–900 thehousehotel.ie 40 rooms Free Breakfast.*

Jurys Inn Galway

$$ | HOTEL | Expect good-quality budget accommodations at this four-story hotel set beside the historic Spanish Arch and the river. **Pros:** public car park adjacent to hotel offers discounted rates of €10 per 24 hours; reliable Irish budget hotel chain; great location for pubs, clubs, and river views. **Cons:** rates subject to demand, so book early; pared-back comfort; favorite for large bachelor/bachelorette parties. *Rooms from: €160 Quay St., Spanish Arch 091/566–444 jurysinn.com/hotels/galway 130 rooms Free Breakfast.*

Park House Hotel

$$$$ | HOTEL | Even though this is a large, luxury hotel in central Galway, snazzily converted from a 200-year-old warehouse, it feels like a home away from home, thanks to attentive owner-managers. **Pros:** friendly, professional staff; on-site parking; a haven of quiet. **Cons:** tricky to find vehicle entrance first time; limited parking spaces; no leisure facilities. *Rooms from: €230 Forster St., Center 091/564–924 parkhousehotel.ie 84 rooms Free Breakfast.*

Sea Breeze Lodge Bed and Breakfast

$$$$ | B&B/INN | Not your typical West of Ireland bolt-hole, this B&B has the elegance of a luxurious, small, boutique hotel with the charm and warm welcome of a B&B. **Pros:** great attention to detail from staff; truly wonderful breakfasts; walking distance to downtown. **Cons:** not in the city center; walk to pubs and restaurants; no typical hotel facilities. *Rooms from: €240 9 Cashelmara, Salthill 091/529–581 www.seabreezelodge.org Closed Nov.–mid-Mar. 6 rooms Free Breakfast.*

Nightlife

CLUBS

Hyde Bar and Gin Parlour

BARS | Gin is having a moment in Ireland right now and nowhere is that more evident or celebrated than Hyde Bar and Gin Parlour, where you will find more than 500 brands of gin, featuring flavors from potato to rhubarb to "Unicorn Tears." The bold interior, with electric-blue and shocking-pink furnishings and larger-than-life wall murals, comes as a surprise after entering the classic ivy-clad doorway. There's also a good selection of craft beer and the old reliable beverages. By day, this is a hugely popular brunch spot. *The Forster Court Hotel, Forster St., Center 91/564–111 hydebargalway.ie.*

PUBS

Áras na nGael

PUBS | Cross O'Brien Bridge and take the first left to find this Irish-speaking social club–pub, which is a great place to hear traditional music, watch (or join) dancing and language classes, and hear the Irish language in use. Non–Irish speakers are very welcome. Open weekdays

Galway's Craft Beer Scene

There's a quiet taste revolution taking place in Galway City, with a growing amount of taps dedicated to craft beer. To discover the city's earliest craft beer pub, head out by the ocean to Salthill Promenade and the **Oslo Microbrewery and Gastro Bar** (🌐 *galwaybaybrewery.com/oslo*). It's home to the Galway Bay Brewery, which has spawned a plethora of new pubs in Galway City and beyond. With 21 craft beers on tap, including six on rotation, **The Salt House** (🌐 *galwaybaybrewery.com/salthouse*) in Raven Terrace, across the Corrib from the Quays, offers an impressive range of 120 bottled brands. Other bars have moved in for a slice of the action, pairing food with their beers. For somewhere intimate with a rotating selection of beers and bespoke burgers, try **Caribou** (🌐 *facebook.com/caribougalway*) in Woodquay (near McSwiggan's). **Bierhaus** (🌐 *facebook.com/BierhausGalway*), at the bottom of Henry Street, has more than 60 craft beers available (20 on tap) with a new sandwich bar on-site.

only. ✉ *45 Dominick St., Galway City* ☎ *091/567–824* 🌐 *arasnangael.ie.*

The Crane Bar

PUBS | Arrive early to get a seat at this tiny bar to the west of Claddagh. Its two floors can get crammed during nightly trad sessions. ✉ *2 Sea Rd., Galway City* ☎ *091/587–419* 🌐 *thecranebar.com.*

★ **King's Head**

PUBS | With the most eye-catching facade on High Street, if not Galway City, the King's Head is dripping with 800 years of history. Its landlord, a henchman for Oliver Cromwell, seized the mayoral office and property (now the King's Head) and became Galway's first nonlocal mayor—a prize, some say, for his part in the execution King Charles I in 1649. Staff are charming and a *cúpla focal* (a few words in the Irish language) will put you in good favor. There are trad-music sessions nightly. ✉ *15 High St., Center* ☎ *091/566–630* 🌐 *thekingshead.ie.*

McSwiggan's

PUBS | A popular Galway City pub for students and locals with a restaurant upstairs, McSwiggan's has everything from church pews to ancient carriage lamps contributing to its eclectic character. ✉ *3 Eyre St., Wood Quay, Center* ☎ *091/568–917* 🌐 *mcswiggans.ie.*

Monroe's

LIVE MUSIC | A large and handsome street-corner pub, Monroe's has free music nightly from 9 pm and regularly hosts impressive rock acts. Quality bar food and a friendly service add to the appeal. ✉ *20 Dominick St., just across bridge from Claddagh, Center* ☎ *091/583–397* 🌐 *monroes.ie.*

Nova Bar

BARS | Cocktails, beer, and wine are served in this tiny bar on a quiet street just beyond the city center. It has a DJ and live entertainment, theme nights and discounted cocktails—and a very loyal student and LGBTQ+ customer base. ✉ *1 William St. W, Center* ☎ *091/725–693* 🌐 *facebook.com/novabargalway.*

★ **O'Connor's Pub**

PUBS | Fans of musician Ed Sheeran will instantly recognize the interior of this landmark pub as the location of his "Galway Girl" music video with actress Saoirse Ronan. Trading since 1942, this generous-size tavern in Salthill is a firm favorite with visitors who browse through the pub's vast collection of paraphernalia, from farmyard tools and grandma's garters (hanging over a hearth) to a life-size statue of the "Quiet Man," John Wayne. Its impressive collection of whiskey is showcased on an imposing shelf behind the bar counter. ⊠ *Salthill House, Upper Salthill Rd., Salthill* ☎ *091/523–468* ⊕ *oconnorsbar.com.*

The Quays

LIVE MUSIC | Behind the simple facade, this Gothic bar is a surprising labyrinth of rooms across three stories, kitted out with furnishings from a medieval church, including pews, a giant organ, and altar. There are regular rock and country sessions. ⊠ *Quay St., Center* ☎ *091/568–347* ⊕ *quaysgalway.ie.*

The Róisín Dubh

LIVE MUSIC | A legend in its own right and a serious venue for stand-up comics, silent discos, and emerging rock and traditional bands, the Róisín Dubh often showcases big, if still-struggling, talents. ⊠ *Dominick St., Spanish Arch* ☎ *091/586–540* ⊕ *roisindubh.net.*

Taaffe's Bar

PUBS | Open for 150 years, Taaffe's is bang in the city center and hosts regular trad-music sessions that start from 5:30 pm. ⊠ *19 Shop St., Center* ☎ *091/564–066* ⊕ *facebook.com/TaaffesBarGalway.*

★ Tigh Neachtain

PUBS | This bright-blue, mural-scarred pub is in the hub of Galway's medieval center and the core of its beating heart. For more than 120 years its mahogany snugs and alcoves have given patrons refuge from the city's infamous mist and rain while its stock of more than 130 brands of whiskey has fueled heat through their veins. Predictably, it's buzzing on the weekends. ⊠ *17 Cross St., Spanish Arch* ☎ *091/568–820* ⊕ *tighneachtain.com.*

Performing Arts

THEATER

An Taibhdhearc Theatre

THEATER | Founders of the Gate Theatre in Dublin, partners Hilton Edwards and Micheál Mac Liammóir created the national Irish-language theater, An Taibhdhearc (pronounced "*on tie*-vark"), to produce first-class Irish works in both English and Irish languages. Watch out for pop-up performances. ⊠ *Middle St., Center* ☎ *091/562–024* ⊕ *antaibhdhearc.com.*

★ Druid Theatre Company

THEATER | Ireland's theatrical hub outside the capital, the Druid has pioneered Galway's identity as a center for the arts. Playwright Martin McDonagh debuted here along with many other performers and producers. The Druid showcases 20th-century Irish and European plays and is considered a pioneer in the development of Irish theater. Its players have toured extensively and performed at Lincoln Center in New York, and several London venues. The Druid regularly presents a production at Galway Arts Festival in late July. ⊠ *Druid La., Center* ☎ *091/568–660* ⊕ *druid.ie.*

★ Macnas

PUPPET SHOWS | An internationally renowned, roving Galway-based troupe of performance artists, Macnas has raised street theater in Ireland to new levels. While their participation in the July Arts Festival's parade is always much anticipated, it's their broody, giant-scale procession at the Galway Aboo Halloween parade that's the annual highlight. ⊠ *Fisheries Field, Salmon Weir Bridge, Center* ☎ *091/561–462* ⊕ *macnas.com.*

Shopping

BOOKS

★ Charlie Byrne's Bookshop

BOOKS | Take extra time to leaf through this treasure trove of literature. Heaving with 10,000 publications, the flagship store has new, discounted, and out-of-print titles, and an unrivaled range of Irish-interest books. Check in on Saturday for good old children's storytelling sessions. ✉ *The Cornstore, Middle St., Center* ☎ *091/561–766* 🌐 *charliebyrne.ie.*

CLOTHING

O'Máille's

MIXED CLOTHING | O'Máille's is popular for its selection of Aran sweaters and handwoven tweeds. ✉ *16 High St., Center* ☎ *091/562–696* 🌐 *omaille.com.*

CRAFTS AND GIFTS

Cloon Keen Atelier

PERFUME | The candles, body-care products, and perfumes stocked here are produced in nearby Spiddal by dedicated artisans. ✉ *21a High St., Center* ☎ *091/565–736* 🌐 *cloonkeen.com.*

Galway Irish Crystal

GLASSWARE | A factory outlet on the city's ring road, Galway Irish Crystal sells handcut Irish glass, Belleek pottery, and other fine porcelain. ✉ *Dublin Rd., Merlin Park* ☎ *091/757–311* 🌐 *galwaycrystal.ie.*

★ Judy Greene Pottery

CERAMICS | Ceramics by Judy Greene—a local potter specializing in hand-thrown ceramics depicting landscapes and Irish flora—as well as handmade jewelry and knitwear can be found in this two-story store in atmospheric Kirwan's Lane. ✉ *Kirwan's La., Center* ☎ *091/561–753* 🌐 *judygreene.wixsite.com/galway.*

Kilkenny Shop

CRAFTS | Synonymous with good modern design in Ireland, the Kilkenny Shop stocks the best ceramics, crystal, leatherware, clothing, and other craft items from around the country. ✉ *6–7 High St., Center* ☎ *091/566–110* 🌐 *kilkennyshop.com.*

Mishnóc

LEATHER GOODS | Mishnóc guarantee that their material come directly from food producers, making their leather outlet in the center of Galway as environmentally friendly as possible. The design of their handcrafted belts, wallets, and bags is quintessentially Irish, with Celtic swirls and *Book of Kells* motifs. ✉ *Unit 3 Cathedral Bldgs., Abbeygate St. Lower, Center* ☎ *91/563–859* 🌐 *mishnoc.com.*

FOOD

McCambridge's

FOOD | This large, long-established deli on Galway's main street has a large selection of Irish and international specialist foods including home baking, wine, local confectionery, charcuterie, homemade jams and preserves, and farmhouse cheeses. Light snacks are served in the second-floor café. ✉ *38–39 Shop St., Center* ☎ *091/582–259* 🌐 *mccambridges.com* ⊙ *Closed Sun.*

★ Sheridan's Cheesemongers

FOOD | Together, Seamus and Kevin Sheridan know all of Ireland's artisanal-cheese makers personally and stock the widest possible range of delectable cheeses in their aromatic store to the rear of St. Nicholas' Collegiate Church. Italian charcuterie and home-branded chutneys along with the fine selection from the wineshop upstairs will complete your picnic. ✉ *16 Churchyard St., Center* ☎ *091/564–829* 🌐 *sheridanscheesemongers.com.*

JEWELRY

Cobwebs

JEWELRY & WATCHES | Phyllis MacNamara's cute two-story boutique is filled with an irresistible selection of antique jewelry (real and costume) and collectibles for men and women. A selection of jewelry from local goldsmiths is also available. ✉ *7 Quay La., Spanish Arch* ☎ *091/564–388* 🌐 *cobwebs.ie.*

Thomas Dillon's Claddagh Gold

JEWELRY & WATCHES | Dating from 1750, Thomas Dillon's claims to be the original maker of Galway's famous claddagh ring. In the back of the crimson shop the Claddagh Ring Museum has a small but interesting display of antique claddagh rings and old Galway memorabilia. ✉ *1 Quay St., Spanish Arch* ☎ *091/566–365* 🌐 *claddaghring.ie.*

MUSIC

Kieran Moloney

MUSIC | A display case of the craft of Irish luthiers, this lovely old-world shop stocks acoustic stringed instruments and some wind instruments, including Irish handmade uilleann pipes, Irish bouzoukis and, more tempting for the traveler, pocket-size tin whistles. ✉ *Olde Malt Arcade, 17 High St., Center* ☎ *091/566–488* 🌐 *moloneymusic.com.*

Activities

BICYCLING

Bike Hire Ireland

BIKING | Prebook your bike of choice from a wide range of brands if you have strong preferences, and just hit the road. Or opt for a self-guided tour: the company has handy drop-off points in Connemara, the Burren, and Kerry. ✉ *Westside Business Centre, Unit 1, Galway City* ☎ *091/525–007* 🌐 *bikehireireland.com* 💳 *Rentals from €13* ⏲ *Closed Sun.*

GOLF

Galway Bay Golf Resort

GOLF | An 18-hole parkland course near the village of Renville, 16 km (10 miles) from the city, Galway Bay Golf Resort is on the shores of Galway Bay, opposite the city, and was designed by former Ryder Cup and World Cup golfer, Christy O'Connor Jr. The Atlantic Ocean forms a dramatic backdrop to a course featuring mature trees, concealed bunkers, and highly praised putting surfaces. ✉ *Renville, Oranmore* ☎ *091/790–711* 🌐 *galwaybaygolfresort.com* 💳 *Oct.–Mar. €95; Apr.–Sept. €150* 🏌 *18 holes, 7308 yards, par 72.*

Galway Golf Club

GOLF | Galway Golf Club was established in 1895, and moved to its present location in suburban Salthill in 1925. At that point it was redesigned by course architect Alister McKenzie, who was also responsible for Augusta, home of the U.S. Masters. It has been the home base of two famous Irish pros, Christy O'Connor Sr., and his nephew, Christy O'Connor Jr. In spite of its proximity to the city, there are excellent views of Galway Bay, the Burren, and the Aran Islands. It has an abundance of trees, prickly gorse bushes in the rough, and some tricky fairways that run close to the ocean. ✉ *Blackrock, Salthill* ☎ *091/522–033* 🌐 *galwaygolf.com* 💳 *May–Sept. €125; Oct.–Apr. €90* 🏌 *18 holes, 2995 yards, par 70.*

RIVER CRUISING

Corrib Princess

BOATING | A lovely way to spend a fine afternoon is to take a Corrib Cruise from Wood Quay, behind the Town Hall Theatre, at the Rowing Club; it lasts 1½ hours and travels 8 km (5 miles) up the River Corrib and about 6 km (4 miles) around Lough Corrib. There's a bar on board, tea and coffee, and a commentary. The trip costs €17, and boats depart daily at 12:30 and 2:30 pm from May through September, with an additional departure at 4:30 pm July through August (except Saturday). You can also rent the boat for an evening. ✉ *Wood Quay, Galway City* ☎ *091/563–846* 🌐 *corribprincess.ie.*

The Oileáin Árainn (Aran Islands)

No one knows for certain when the Aran Islands—Inis Mór (Inishmore), Inis Meáin (Inishmaan), and Inis Oírr (Inisheer)—were first inhabited, but judging from the number of Bronze Age and Iron Age forts found here (especially on Inis Mór), 3000 BC is a safe guess.

Each island has a hotel, and there's no shortage of guesthouses, campsites, hostels, and B&Bs, many in simple family homes. There is also at least one

Aran Rediscovered

During the 1800s, the islands, wracked by famine and mass emigration, were virtually forgotten by mainland Ireland. At the turn of the 20th century, however, the books of J.M. Synge (1871–1909)—who learned Irish on Inis Meáin and wrote about its people in his famous play *Riders to the Sea*—prompted Gaelic revivalists to study and document this isolated bastion of Irish culture. To this day, Synge's travel book *The Aran Islands*, first published in 1907, and reissued by Penguin with a brilliant introduction by artist and mapmaker Tim Robinson in 1992, remains the best book ever written about the islands. Liam O'Flaherty became one of the most famous sons of Inis Mór through his novels, such as *Famine*. And in 1934, American director Robert Flaherty filmed his classic documentary *Man of Aran* on Inis Mór, recording the islanders' dramatic battles with sea and storm, and bringing the islands into the world spotlight. The film is still highly esteemed by the islanders, and there are frequent showings on Inis Mór during the summer months. Flaherty, incidentally, continues to be a common surname on the islands; it is hard to visit the islands *without* meeting a Flaherty. Playwright Martin McDonagh brings the islands to a fresh, modern audience with *The Cripple of Inishmaan* and *The Banshees of Inisherin*.

wine-licensed restaurant serving plain home cooking on the three islands. Most B&Bs will provide a packed lunch and an evening meal on request. Once the day-trippers leave, the islands regain a mellowness that's lost in the flurry to see everything. From spring to autumn the days are long, so the islands can be enjoyed at a leisurely pace while locals hit the pubs later in the evening and place drink orders in a mishmash of the English and Irish language.

GETTING HERE AND AROUND

The two main transport arteries to the Aran Islands are via Doolin in County Clare or Connemara in County Galway and a new seasonal service from Galway City.

Aer Arann Islands offers 10-minute flights to the Aran Islands. The nonislander fare is €55 round-trip, leaving from Connemara Airport near Inverin, 30 km (19 miles) west of Galway.

In Connemara, regular ferries service all three islands. Park at Rossaveal (Ros an Mhíl), 37 km (23 miles) west of Galway City, or book a shuttle bus from the city when buying your ticket. There are at least two sailings a day, and four or more in high season, timed to facilitate day trips. Ask when boarding about interisland ferries if you intend to visit more than one island. Inis Mór, the biggest island, is the only one with organized transport. Book a tour or taxi in advance (through the TIO in Galway), or hire a bicycle (including electric bikes) or pony and trap on landing.

The Doolin ferry crossing is seasonal from March to early November. The pier has recently increased in size, facilitating larger vessels such as the Doolin Express, which offers a quick and even sailing to the islands. Note there is a parking fee in Doolin.

CONTACTS Aer Arann Islands. ☎ *091/593–034* 🌐 *aerarannislands.ie.* **Galway Tourism.** ✉ *Forster St., Eyre Sq., Galway City* ☎ *091/537–700* 🌐 *galwaytourism.ie.*

As you arrive by plane over the Aran Islands, their famous stone-wall fences—built by medieval farmers to clear lands for farms—come into view.

Inis Mór (Inishmore)

20 km (12 miles) southwest of Rossaveal Ferry Port, 24 km (15 miles) north of Doolin Pier.

Dún Aengus Hillfort is the main draw to Inis Mór, the largest and most populated of Aran's three islands. Stretching more than 16 km (10 miles) long and about 2 km (1 mile) wide at most points, with an area of 7,640 acres, it's too large to fully explore on foot on a day trip, so hire a bicycle near the pier to navigate its lanes.

If time permits, head for the less frequented west of the island, visiting Dún Dúchathair, a dramatically sited, freely accessible promontory fort.

VISITOR INFORMATION
CONTACTS Oileáin Árainn (Aran Islands)–Inis Mór (Inishmore) Tourist Office. ✉ *Beside Inis Mór Bicycle Hire, Cill Ronáin [Kilronan]* ☎ *099/61263* 🌐 *www.discoverireland.ie.*

Sights

★ **Dún Aengus** (*Dún Aonghasa*)
RUINS | Even if you have only a few hours to explore Inis Mór, rent a bike (next to the pier) and head straight for Dún Aengus (or Dún Aonghasa). Set at the edge of a 300-foot precipice towering over the ocean, this semicircular fortress is one of the finest prehistoric monuments in Europe and the main draw to Inis Mór. Aengus was, according to lore, a God of summer, youth, and beauty. The purpose of its construction more than 3,000 years ago is a matter of conjecture, and also irrelevant to the legions of seabirds who occupy its scenic Atlantic perch looking out on Connemara and the 12 Pin Mountains. Beware: there is no barrier to the 300-foot drop at the edge. Allow 1–1½ hours for a visit.

⚠ **In order to protect this fragile monument from erosion, you should approach it only through the visitor center, which gives access to a 1-km (½-mile) uphill walk over uneven terrain—wear sturdy footwear.** ✉ *8* km (5 miles) east of Cill Ronáin (Kilronan), Kilmurvy ☎ 099/61008 ⊕ heritageireland.ie/places-to-visit/dun-aonghasa 🎟 €5 ☞ Free admission if staying overnight on the island.

Hotels

★ Aran Camping and Glamping
$$ | **APARTMENT** | Aran's glamping units, or *clocháns*, are igloo-shape (inspired by monks' medieval beehive huts) and fully heated, with en suite and cooking facilities. **Pros:** unique units; atmospheric setting on beach; heated, with cooking facilities. **Cons:** no Wi-Fi; groups discouraged; no TV. $ *Rooms from: €150* ✉ *Inis Mor, Frenchman's Beach, Aran Islands* ☎ *086/189–5823* ⊕ *irelandglamping.ie* *9 units* *No Meals.*

Ard Einne Guesthouse
$$ | **B&B/INN** | The rambling 80-year-old house on Inishmore, with its distinctive dormer windows, is close to both the beach and the town; many guests base themselves here for two or three nights, to make a thorough exploration of the island. **Pros:** excellent breakfast included; near the airport; warm, friendly hosts. **Cons:** one of the island's biggest guesthouses; no elevator; a walk from the island's main hub. $ *Rooms from: €120* ✉ *Cill Ronáin [Kilronan]* ☎ *099/61126* ⊕ *ardeinne.com* ⊙ *Closed Nov.–Jan.* *8 rooms* *Free Breakfast.*

Ostán Oileáin Árainn (Aran Island Hotel)
$$ | **MOTEL** | **FAMILY** | The addition of comfortable units (or chalets) make this a private, well-equipped refuge—set into a hilly backdrop with private decking, television (a luxury in island accommodation), Wi-Fi, and decent shower. **Pros:** private; modern facilities including Wi-Fi; views. **Cons:** lively pub on-site; not a conventional operation; lack of gym. $ *Rooms from: €130* ✉ *Cill Ronáin [Kilronan], Aran Islands* ☎ *099/61104* ⊕ *aranislandshotel.com.*

Nightlife

Joe Mac's
PUBS | Located right off the pier, Joe Mac's is a good place for a fireside pint while waiting for the ferry home. ✉ *Cill Ronáin [Kilronan]* ☎ *099/61248.*

Joe Watty's
PUBS | Located on the hill outside the village, Joe Watty's is the hub of Inis Mór's entertainment, with regular music sessions and reliable cooking—seafood is, predictably, a specialty. ✉ *Main Rd., Cill Ronáin [Kilronan]* ☎ *086/049–4509* ⊕ *joewattys.ie.*

Inis Meáin (Inishmaan)

3 km (2 miles) east of Inis Mór (Inishmore).

The middle island in both size and location, Inis Meáin has a population of about 300 and its empty beaches and breathtaking scenery can be explored on foot or bicycle with relative ease.

Sights

You have no alternative to walking if you want to reach the island's major antiquities: **Dún Conor (Conor Fort),** a smaller version of Dún Aengus; the ruins of two **early Christian churches**; and a chamber tomb known as the **Bed of Diarmuid and Grainne,** dating from about 2000 BC. You can also take wonderful cliff walks above secluded coves.

Traces of the author of *The Playboy of the Western World,* John Millington Synge, who stayed here more than a hundred years ago, dot the island—from his thatched residence to Synge's Chair, a collection of rocks on the isolated westerly side of the island where the writer honed his craft on a limestone cliff edge high above the ocean.

It's on Inis Meáin that the traditional Aran lifestyle is most evident. Most islanders

Who Was Father Ted?

Although the last episode of Channel 4's sitcom series *Father Ted* aired many years ago, the program, which features the unorthodox antics of three priests, has left its mark on County Clare and the Aran Islands, which doubled up as the infamous Craggy Island throughout three years of filming. Today this cult classic has resulted in a series of festivals, the most notable being TedFest (🌐 *tedfest.org*), which occurs in February on Inis Mór. It's a weekend of mayhem, with a hefty price tag of €150, which doesn't include transport, food, or accommodation. Independent Ted Heads can go to Inis Oírr to see the rusty shipwreck of the MV*Plassy* used in the series' opening credits or head back to the mainland for a photo op at Ted's old Parochial House (it's a private house on narrow road frontage) in the Burren. For a little context, and to understand the phenomenon of *Father Ted*, the series can be found on Amazon Prime.

still don hand-knitted Aran sweaters, though nowadays they wear them with jeans and sneakers.

Hotels

An Dún

$ | **B&B/INN** | The most comfortable accommodation on the island with breakfast (supplement) and evening meal available on-site. **Pros:** close to shop, John Millington Synge museum, and fort Dún Chonchuir; ocean views; food sources directly from the An Dun's garden or the island. **Cons:** dinner often only available if booked in advance; only five bedrooms; lengthy walk from the pier. *Rooms from: €105* ✉ *Aran Islands* ☎ *99/73047* 🌐 *inismeainaccommodation.ie/* ⏲ *Closed Nov.–Mar. 1* *5 rooms* ☞ *€2 fee for all credit card transactions.*

Shopping

Inis Meáin Knitting

OUTLET | Inis Meáin Knitting is a young company producing quality knitwear in luxury fibers (a slick twist on the standard Aran sweater) for the international market, including Barneys New York and Bergdorf Goodman. The factory showroom has an extensive selection of garments at discount prices. ✉ *Carrown Lisheen, Aran Islands* ✣ *From pier, walk 5 mins due west* ☎ *099/73009* 🌐 *inis-meain.ie* ⏲ *Closed weekends* ☞ *Opens 2 pm–4 pm.*

Inis Oírr (Inisheer)

4 km (2½ miles) east of Inis Meáin (Inishmaan), 8 km (5 miles) northwest of Doolin Docks.

Inis Oírr, the smallest island, can be explored on foot in an afternoon, though if the weather is fine you may be tempted to linger on the long sandy beach between the quay and the airfield. Only one stretch of road, about 500 yards long, links the airfield and the sole village; after that it's hilly pathways with panoramic views back to the mainland and the Cliffs of Moher. A cycle to the island's lighthouse offers rich views across the island's maze of stone walls, framed by the ocean.

To the east of the village, there is a holy well and seal colony.

For guests that linger for the night, Tigh Neds (Ned's House) near the pier is the

Aran Island Woolens

Made of plain, undyed wool and knit with distinctive crisscross patterns, sometimes referred to as *báinín* sweaters or "ganseys," the Aran sweater is a combination of folklore and fashion.

Since harsh weather made warmth and protection vital out in the Atlantic Ocean, the women of Aran long ago discovered the solution to this problem in this strong, comfortable, hand-knit sweater. Indeed, these Arans can hold 30% of their weight in water before they even start to feel wet. The reason? Traditionally, the wool used was unwashed and retained its water-repellent quality from natural sheep's lanolin.

Look for the Pattern

Not so long ago, these pullovers were worn by every County Donegal fisherman, usually made to a design belonging exclusively to his own family. It's said that a native can tell which family the knitter belongs to from the patterns used in a genuine Aran sweater. Often the patterns used religious symbols and folk motifs, such as the Tree of Life, the Honeycomb (standing for thrift and thought to be lucky), the SeaHorse, the Blackberry—all are patterns in the almost sculptured, deeply knitted work that characterizes the Aran method. Their famous basket stitch represents the fisherman's basket, a hope for a *curragh* (fishing boat) heavy with catch. A colorful belt called a *crios* (pronounced "criss") is handcrafted in many traditional designs as a useful accessory.

Making Your Purchase

Most of the Aran sweaters you'll see throughout Ireland are made far north of the islands themselves, in County Donegal, an area most associated with high-quality, handwoven textiles. The best are painstakingly knitted by hand, a process that can take weeks. As a result, prices are not cheap, and if you think you've found a bargain, check the label before buying—it's more likely a factory copy. Still, the less expensive, lighter-weight, hand-loomed sweaters (knitted on a mechanical loom, not with needles) are less than half the price and more practical for most lifestyles. But the real McCoy is still coveted: some of the finest examples woven by Inis Meáin are sold at luxury stores like Bergdorf Goodman and Wilkes Bashford. And young Irish designers like Liadain De Buitlear are giving the traditional Aran a newer-than-now spin, highly popular in Dublin boutiques.

place for an aperitif accompanied by the sound of the ocean, while Tigh Ruairi in the village offers hearty fare. The island has a campsite, hostel, self-catering, and a selection of guesthouses.

Sights

Church of Kevin

CHURCH | Signposted to the southeast of the quay, the Church of Kevin is a small, early Christian church that gets buried in sand by storms every winter. Each year the islanders dig it out of the sand for the celebration of St. Kevin's Day on June 14. ✉ *Inis Oirr.*

MV *Plassy* Shipwreck

NAUTICAL SIGHT | The hulking, rusty wreck lying on the island's west coast has gained a cult following ever since it appeared in the opening credits of the acclaimed Irish television show *Father*

Ted. Horses and traps stop by to explain its fleeting fame and cyclists stop here to take a selfie break. ✉ *Aran Islands* 🎫 *Free.*

O'Brien's Castle
CASTLE/PALACE | This ruined 15th-century tower house (also referred to as *An Tur Faire* or "the tower ruin") dominates the island from the top of a steep rocky hill; a Martello tower keeps it company. ✉ *Inis Oirr* 🎫 *Free.*

Restaurants

Teach an Tae (*Cafe Aran Tea Rooms*)
$ | **IRISH** | Michael and Alissa Donoghue do not have to travel far to get the ingredients for their little cottage café that overlooks the pier. Their flock of chickens provide eggs, and the vegetable and herb garden—nurtured with seaweed throughout the year—furnishes their salads. **Known for:** lemon poppy-seed cake; pretty cottage setting; free Wi-Fi. $ *Average main: €5* ✉ *Lurgan Village, Aran Islands* ☎ *099/75092* 🌐 *cafearan.ie.*

Hotels

Hotel Inisheer (*Óstán Inis Oírr*)
$$ | **HOTEL** | A basic low-rise in the middle of the island's only village, a few minutes' walk from the quay and the airstrip, this simple whitewashed building with a slate roof and tile flooring has bright, simply furnished rooms, with pine-frame beds, pine floors, and white bed linen. **Pros:** very clean; good location between pier and airstrip; friendly staff and attentive owners. **Cons:** building is uninspiring; restaurant can get very busy with day visitors; noise from the pub. $ *Rooms from: €120* ✉ *Inis Oirr* ☎ *099/75020* 🌐 *hotelinisoirr.com* ⏱ *Closed Oct.–Mar.* 🛏 *14 rooms* 🍽 *Free Breakfast.*

Island Nights

To appreciate the solitude of the Aran Islands you must spend the night on one. Because all the islands, especially Inishmore, crawl with day-trippers, it's difficult to let their rugged beauty sink into your soul until 10 pm, when the sky is dark and the pubs fill with the acrid smell of peat smoke and Guinness. Once the day-trippers clear out, the islands' stunningly fierce and brooding beauty is disturbed only by the bleating of the sheep and the incessant rush of the wind.

Activities

BICYCLING

Rothaí Inis Oírr (*Inisheer Bike Hire*)
BIKING | Just up from the pier, this small stone cabin rents bicycles and e-bikes and is a good place to stop for general advice. While horse and carriage rides offer an easier tour of the island, there is no more rewarding way to discover this little windswept corner of the Atlantic Ocean than by bike. If the owners aren't at the cabin, just knock at the door of their home, which is located directly behind.

■ **TIP→ If it's your first time here and you only have the day, manage your time: only explore the west of the island, saving time for the beach near the pier.** ✉ *Aran Islands* ☎ *099/75049* 🌐 *rothai-inisoirr.com* 🎫 *Rentals from €10.*

Chapter 10

CONNEMARA AND COUNTY MAYO

Updated by
Alexandra Pereira

Sights	Restaurants	Hotels	Shopping	Nightlife
★★★★★	★★☆☆☆	★★★★★	★★☆☆☆	★☆☆☆☆

WELCOME TO CONNEMARA AND COUNTY MAYO

TOP REASONS TO GO

★ **Captivating Connemara:** An almost uninhabited landscape of misty bogland, studded with deep blue lakes under huge Atlantic skies: painters have strived for generations to capture the ever-changing light.

★ **The Great Western Greenway:** Cycle this historical railway line from the alluring market town of Westport, past Newport's handsome, high-arched bridge to Achill Island with Clew Bay's islands as a constant companion.

★ **The Erris Peninsula:** Sheltering the western seaboard from the full brunt of the Atlantic's force, this forlorn and off-radar Gaeltacht (Irish-speaking region) is speckled with secret coves, enormous cliff edges, and breathtaking views.

★ **Clifden and the Sky Road:** Walk the Sky Road to take in its breathtaking scenery—sea views on one side, the Twelve Bens Mountains on the other—from the compact town of Clifden, the liveliest spot for miles around.

With the most westerly seaboard in Europe, this region is one of the wildest stretches of the Wild Atlantic Way. While just to the west and north of hip Galway City, this area is famed for its remoteness and rural character. Connemara sits in the northwest corner of County Galway. County Mayo is Ireland's third-largest county, with coast on three of its four sides, and the River Moy and the huge expanse of Lough Conn and Lough Cullin on the fourth. Bright lights are to be found in Clifden and Westport, both lively small towns of great charm.

1 Roundstone. This charming Connemara fishing village has an especially scenic setting, which makes it popular with artists and photographers.

2 Clifden. With the Twelve Bens Mountains backdrop and the Atlantic Ocean in the foreground, Clifden is a beautiful base for exploring the Connemara region.

3 Letterfrack. The gateway village to Connemara National Park and a convenient base for local hiking and spending time at Kylemore Abbey.

4 Kylemore Valley. A beautiful stretch of Connemara that contains the lakeside Kylemore Abbey.

5 Leenane. A tiny, idyllic village that is home to Killary Harbour and a cool food truck.

6 Cong. Hugging Ashford Castle, this small village is known as the setting for 1950s movie, *The Quiet Man*.

7 Westport. On an inlet of Clew Bay, this attractive town is a great base for exploring Achill Island and Croagh Patrick.

8 Castlebar. Not as pretty as Westport but Mayo's capital town is a lively town and home to the Museum of Country Life.

9 Foxford. A pretty village and home to Foxford Woollen Mills and showroom and its heirloom woolen blankets and throws.

10 Belmullet. This under-the-radar town is the perfect access point to the rugged and unspoiled Mullet Peninsula.

11 Killala. A pretty bay-side village and the gateway to Mayo's rugged northern coast.

Downpatrick Head
Belderrig
NORTH MAYO COAST
Ballycastle
MULLET PENINSULA
10
Belmullet
R314
R314
Killala
11
R313
Bangor
MAYO
N59
N59
Ballina
N59
Castlehill
Achill Head
Keel
Achill Island
R319
Achill Sound
Mulrany
N59
Newport
Lough Conn
Lough Cullin
N26
9
Foxford
N26
N58
N5
Castlebar
8
Bellavary
7
Clare Island
Westport
N5
Louisburgh
R335
N60
N84
Inishturk
N59
R335
Claremorris
Inishbofin
Delphi
Inishshark
Kylemore Valley
Kylemore Lough
5
Leenane
Lough Mask
Ballinrobe
Letterfrack
3
4
CONNEMARA
R336
6
Cong
N59
Maum
R345
Ashford Castle
The Sky Road
2
Twelve Bens
Lough Corrib
Clifden
Cashel
Ballynahinch
Recess
N59
Maam Cross
Oughterard
R341
1
Roundstone
GALWAY
N59
N84
R340
R336
Claregalway
Casla
Gorumna Island
Ros an Mhíl
Galway
R336
Ballynahown
North Sound
Galway Bay
ARAN ISLANDS
R477
N67
R478
N67
R476
Lahinch
Nags Head
Corrofin
Crusheen
Gort
M18
R380
Loughrea
R446
M18
N67
M6
Athenry
M6
M17
R354
N83
N63
N17
N60
N17
N5
Charlestown
N17
N4
Toberscanavan
Collooney
Ballysadare
N4
Skreen
N59
Sligo Town
Drumcliff
Sligo Bay
Cashelgarran
N15
Cliffony

0 20 mi
0 20 km

HIKING THE WEST

Eco-hiking in spectacular Connemara National Park.

More and more, travelers are discovering that Ireland's western regions are hiking heaven. In fact, hikes or guided walks through Connemara or County Mayo are the best ways to explore these territories at first hand, or rather, foot.

Why hike the West? It has some of the finest rugged scenery and dramatic indented coastline in all Ireland. In Connemara serried ranks of heather-clad mountains, interspersed with bright blue lakes, beckon to the walker as dramatic cloud formations scud across huge Atlantic skies. In County Mayo, the huge conical bulk of Croagh Patrick spectacularly looms above Clew Bay. Or what about earning some blisters among the free-range sheep of the Doolough Valley, set in the shadow of Mweelrea Mountain? The attraction lies in the terrific views nearly everywhere you look. Coastal views alternate with mountain vistas, often topped by a perfect rainbow. A daily highlight is the spectacular sunset over the Atlantic, at its biggest and best in late August.

PACK TO HIKE

You can't hike Connemara and Mayo in sneakers, due to the combination of bog, rocky terrain, and frequent showers. Wear waterproof hiking boots, quick-drying trousers rather than denim, and carry lightweight, waterproof rainwear (preferably breathable). Because of the wind, most Irish walkers wear knitted or fleece hats, so pack accordingly.

Hiking buffs are glad to know that the last decade has seen the completion of various "waymarked" (signposted) walking routes, which can be sampled in easy one- or two-hour "loops," or, for more serious walkers, made the focus of a visit.

Stop and smell the heather.

KNOW WHERE YOU'RE GOING

Walkers on waymarked trails are advised to buy an Ordnance Survey map of the area, which is sold locally. Most tourist offices also have free maps of less ambitious walks on roads and local footpaths.

TOP HIKING DESTINATIONS

The Western Way's County Galway section extends from Oughterard on Lough Corrib through the mountains of Connemara to Leenane on Killary Harbour, a distance of 50 km (30 miles). Its 177-km (110-mile) County Mayo section, known as the Western Way (Mayo), continues past Killary Harbour to Westport on Clew Bay to the Ox Mountains east of Ballina. This trail should be the first choice of serious walkers, as it includes some of the finest mountain and coastal scenery in Ireland. The Great Western Greenway is a traffic-free 42-km (26-mile) cycling and walking trail that follows the line of Mayo's Westport–Mulranny Railway (closed since 1937) along the northern shore of Clew Bay and has scenic walking and cycling with very few inclines, suitable for moderately fit people. Another perfect hiking destination is Connemara National Park, which consists of some 5,000 acres of untamed mountain wilderness in and around the Twelve Bens peaks. Allow an hour or two to hike the Diamond Hill Loop, along 7 km (4 miles) of gravel tracks and paved mountain paths to a 1,493-foot peak with a 360-degree vista taking in the distant sea, the turrets of Kylemore Abbey, and the higher peaks in the south. The nearby visitor center (March–October, free) has displays on the flora, fauna, and geology of Connemara.

Many waymarked hikes go past beautiful lakes like Lough Corrib.

WALKING IN COMPANY

Walking festivals are highly popular. Achill Island in County Mayo hosts the **Achill Walks Festival** in early April, to tempt people out again after the long dark winter, while the **Four Seasons Walking Festival** features excursions from Clifden guided by an archaeologist four times a year. 🌐 *visitachill.com/en/walks*

A landscape where the thundering Atlantic forms the pounding backbeat to the most westerly seaboards in Europe, this most distinct area of Ireland has been an escape from urban stress since its vast empty landscapes and rocky indented coast were "discovered" by writers and artists in the 19th century. While Mayo's bustling town of Westport has assumed the identity of popular destination to a younger, more confident Ireland, the surrounding countryside still attracts the traditional anglers, golfers, and seekers of rural solitude, along with savvy hikers, cyclists, and birders.

It is a landscape richly endowed with magnificent views: Connemara's combination of rugged coastline, mountains, moorland, and lakes; the distinctive cone-like shape of Croagh Patrick, towering over the 365 islands of Clew Bay, and the rippling waters of Lough Corrib, Lough Conn, and many smaller lakes. The Irish people are well aware of what a jewel they have in the largely unspoiled wilderness, grazed by sheep and herds of wild ponies, that is the 5,000-acre Connemara National Park, the result of a successful lobby for landscape preservation. Peatlands—or bogs, as they are called around here—are at last being valued for their unique botanical character.

Unlike most of Ireland where the marks of Viking, Norman, and English invaders blotted out much of the rich heritage of the ancient Irish kingdoms, these western counties retained, by virtue of their remoteness, those essential Celtic characteristics of rebellion and individuality, and the accompanying graces of unstinting hospitality and courtly good manners. These traits survive, despite the purges of Cromwell's English armies and the all-pervasive trauma of the Great Famine (1845–49). That era started a tradition of emigration that continued to deprive the area of the majority of its youth well into the 1960s. The growth of tourism since the 1970s, the building of fine new hotels, and the upgrading of traditional ones has helped to provide jobs for the local population. Another boost has come from the development of fish farming, and the fostering of local artisanal food producers, whose farmhouse cheese and smoked salmon enhance the menus of the West.

These unspoiled regions possess a spirit that has always spoken to the hidden poet within all who travel here. Images of spectacular red sunsets lingering over the Atlantic, that shocking lapis-lazuli blue of your first Connemara lough, and the fleeting moments when the way ahead was framed by a completely semicircular rainbow will likely haunt your memory long after you leave, as will the ancient whispers, cries, and melodies carried on the Connemara breeze. Here is where the magic lies.

MAJOR REGIONS

Connemara. Bordered by the long expanse of Lough Corrib on the east and the jagged coast of the Atlantic on the west is the rugged, desolate region of western County Galway known as Connemara. Like the American West, it's an area of spectacular, almost myth-making geography—of glacial lakes; gorgeous, silent mountains; lonely roads; and hushed, uninhabited boglands. Roundstone, a pretty harbor village that lies in the shadows of the glacially carved Twelve Bens mountain range, lures artists and visitors all year, while Connemara's "capital" town, Clifden, is the gateway to the panoramic Sky Road. Beyond the small towns and villages there are few people, since Connemara's population is sparse even by Irish standards. Especially in the off-season, you're far more likely to come across sheep strolling its roads than another car.

Two main routes—one inland, the other coastal—lead through Connemara. To take the inland route described below, leave Galway City on the well-signposted outer-ring road and follow signs for N59, the road that goes west through Moycullen, Oughterard, and Clifden (names that are also prominently signposted if you head out from Galway). If you choose to take the coastal route, travel due west from Galway City to Ros an Mhíl (Rossaveal) on R336 through Salthill, Bearna, and An Spidéal—all in the heart of the West's strong Gaeltacht, home to roughly 40,000 Irish speakers (note that most place signage hereabouts is in Irish, so a map with both English and Irish names proves handy). You can continue north on R336 from Ros an Mhil (Rossaveal) to Maam Cross and then head for coastal points west, or pick up R340 and putter along the coast.

South County Mayo. County Mayo has long empty roads that stretch for miles. Castlebar, the county town, has been overshadowed by its neighbor Westport, an elegantly laid-out 18th-century town with quays on the shore of island-studded Clew Bay, under the towering conical peak of St. Patrick's holy mountain, Croagh Patrick. Not only does Westport have scenery, it also has some excellent hotels and bars, some a legacy of the boom years that brought metropolitan chic to the heart of the West.

North County Mayo. Belmullet is a small fishing village on the edge of Ballycroy National Park, an area of sparse population that leads to one of the most dramatic coastlines in Ireland. Lough Conn and Lough Cullin are two great fishing lakes divided by a land bridge, Pontoon, under which their waters meet. The slopes of Mt. Nephin tower over untilled acres, teeming with otters, geese, snipe, and woodcock. Mayo's wild North Mayo coastline, with rebellious Killala at its ridge, has a plethora of historic landmarks woven into its untamed shoreline.

Planning

Getting Here and Around

A car is almost essential in Connemara and Mayo. Trains arrive from Dublin to Westport and Ballina, with Manulla Junction connecting these towns. The bus network is more flexible, but there are not many services each day, and the entire bus system goes into semi-hibernation during the winter months, so plan accordingly. If a rental car is out of the question, one option is to make Westport your base, and take a day trip to Connemara and Kylemore Abbey. Then get an Expressway bus to Ballina, and explore the north coast on local buses. The hardy can always consider making a biking trip through the region, even though it does get periods of strong rain.

AIR

Ryanair flies to Ireland West Airport Knock daily from London's Stansted Airport and Luton Airport; flying time is 80 minutes. Aer Lingus flies to Knock from Gatwick daily. Flybe and Ryanair have regular services to Knock from other major U.K. cities.

CONTACTS Aer Lingus. ☎ *1890/800–600* 🌐 *www.aerlingus.com.* **Ryanair.** ☎ *1520/444–004* 🌐 *www.ryanair.com.*

AIRPORTS

The West's only airport with a transatlantic service is Shannon, 25 km (16 miles) south of Ennis.

Ireland West Airport Knock, at Charlestown—near Knock, in County Mayo—has direct services to London's Stansted, Luton, and Gatwick, and to Manchester and East Midlands.

CONTACTS Ireland West Airport Knock. ☎ *094/936–8100* 🌐 *www.irelandwestairport.com.* **Shannon Airport.** ☎ *061/712–000* 🌐 *www.shannonairport.ie.*

BOAT AND FERRY

Corrib Cruises runs daily trips on Lough Corrib at 11:15 am year-round from the public pier at Cong, with clear views of Ashford Castle and the Connemara mountains, and an optional visit to the monastic ruins on Inchagoill Island. The boat has indoor and outdoor seating and a licensed bar. From April to October, you can board either at Cong or at Oughterard, on the opposite side of the lake. You can use the cruise as a ferry service from one village to the other, or opt for a historic cruise with guide (€30 from Cong, €25 from Oughterard in July and August).

The Inisbofin Ferry Company offers a twice-daily year-round, 30-minute service from Cleggan to Inisbofin for €25 round-trip.

Clare Island in Clew Bay and its smaller neighbor, Inishturk Island, are increasingly popular day-trip destinations with hikers and natural historians. Clare Island Ferry Company sails to Clare Island and Inishturk between May and September, leaving the mainland at 9:30 am (10:45 Monday and weekends) with last ferry returning at 6:15 pm (€17 round-trip). There is a scaled-down service from February to April and October; check the website for details. O'Malley Ferries is a year-round operator serving Inishturk. Both leave from Roonagh Pier at Louisburgh, a 35-minute drive west of Westport. Tickets can be bought at the Westport Tourist Office.

From April through October, Killary Cruises runs 90-minute trips around Killary Harbour (€25.50), Ireland's only fjord, in an enclosed catamaran launch with seating for 150 passengers, plus a bar and restaurant.

CONTACTS Inisbofin Ferry. ✉ *Inishbofin Island Discovery Ltd., Cloonamore, Inishbofin Island, Connemara* ☎ *095/37228* 🌐 *inishbofinislanddiscovery.com.* **O'Malley Ferries.** ✉ *O'Malley Ferries (Clare Island)*

Ltd., Prospect, Westport ☎ *098/25045* 🌐 *www.omalleyferries.com*.

BUS

Bus Éireann runs several Expressway buses into the region from Dublin, Cork City, and Limerick City to Galway City (change for Connemara) and Westport, the principal depots in the region. Bus Éireann also has two services an hour from Shannon Airport to Galway City. A one-way trip costs €12.40.

Citylink operates frequent buses, with up to 17 departures daily, between Clifden, Galway City, Dublin, and Dublin Airport. The trip costs €18 one-way if you book online, €22 on board.

Within Connemara and Mayo, bus routes are often slow and circuitous, and service can be erratic. The national transport website has an integrated journey planner that is useful for long cross-country trips, for example, Westport to Ballina. To plan local journeys, use the Bus Éireann website or phone the bus station (they are always very helpful).

Bus Éireann local buses travel from Galway City to Cong, Clifden, and Westport. There are no buses linking Cong, Clifden, and Westport: you must return to Galway City and take a different bus line out again to visit each place.

BUS CONTACTS Bus Éireann. ☎ *01/836–6111 in Dublin* 🌐 *www.buseireann.ie*. **Citylink.** ✉ *Unit 1, Forster Ct., 17 Forster St., Galway City* ☎ *091/564–164* 🌐 *www.citylink.ie*. **National Travel Website.** 🌐 *www.transportforireland.ie*.

BUS DEPOTS Ballina Bus Station. ☎ *096/71800* 🌐 *www.buseireann.ie*. **Galway City Bus Station.** (*Ceannt Station*) ☎ *091/562–000* 🌐 *www.buseireann.ie*.

CAR

The 207-km (129-mile) Dublin–Galway City trip is on a motorway (four-lane expressway) and takes about two hours, 20 minutes. The 196-km (122-mile) drive from Cork to Galway City (opt for the toll tunnel under Limerick) takes about three hours, and another 45 minutes to Oughterard, where the Connemara scenery begins. From Killarney, the shortest route to cover the 193 km (120 miles) to Galway (three hours) is to take N22 to Tralee, then N69 through Listowel to Tarbert and ferry across the Shannon Estuary to Killimer (⇨ *see Chapter 9: County Clare, Galway City, and the Aran Islands*). From here, join N68 in Kilrush, and then pick up the M18.

ROAD CONDITIONS

Connemara and Mayo have good, wide main roads (National Primary Routes) and better-than-average local roads (National Secondary Routes), both known as *N* routes. If you stray off the beaten track on the smaller Regional (*R*) or Local (*L*) routes, you may encounter some hazardous mountain roads. Narrow, steep, and twisty, they are also frequented by untended sheep, cows, and ponies grazing "the long acre" (as the strip of grass beside the road is called) or straying in search of greener pastures. If you find a sheep in your path, just sound the horn, and it should scramble away. A good maxim for these roads is: "You never know what's around the next corner." Bear this in mind, and adjust your speed accordingly. Hikers and cyclists constitute an additional hazard on narrow roads. Within the Connemara Irish-speaking area, signs are in Irish only. The main signs to recognize are Gaillimh (Galway), Ros an Mhíl (Rossaveal), An Teach Dóite (Maam Cross), and Sraith Salach (Recess).

TAXI

Within Westport, taxis operate on the meter. Outside the town, agree on the fare in advance.

TRAIN

The region's main rail stations are in Galway City, Westport, and Ballina. Trains leave from Dublin's Heuston Station. The journey time to Galway is three hours; to Westport and Ballina, 3½ hours. Rail service within the region is limited. The major destinations of Galway City and Westport/Ballina are on different branch lines. Connections can be made only between Galway and the other two cities by traveling inland for about an hour to Athlone.

CONTACTS Ballina Station. ✉ *Station Rd.* ☎ *096/71820* 🌐 *www.irishrail.ie/station/ballina.* **Dublin Heuston Station.** ✉ *St. Johns Rd. W* ☎ *01/836–6222* 🌐 *www.irishrail.ie/station/dublin-heuston.* **Galway Station.** ✉ *Iarnród Éireann, Céannt Station* ☎ *091/537–576* 🌐 *www.irishrail.ie/station/galway-ceannt.* **Westport Station.** ✉ *Altamont St.* ☎ *098/25253* 🌐 *www.irishrail.ie/station/westport.*

Hotels

Accommodations in the area tend to be traditional; outside Westport there are few with indoor pools and gyms. Instead there are informal, friendly places where you will probably end up comparing notes with other travelers over a huge cooked breakfast. Add variety by alternating rural isolation with the lively towns. Both Clifden in Connemara and Westport in Mayo have lively pub scenes. Clifden attracts a younger, mainly single, crowd, especially in July and August, so be prepared: the music might be rock rather than Irish.

Restaurants

Pubs and informal hotel restaurants are the main places to eat in this sparsely populated rural area, though there are also some fine-dining options. The only places with a choice of stand-alone restaurants are Clifden, the "capital" of Connemara (in fact a small village), and Westport, the chief resort in County Mayo. From Easter into the summer months, many menus feature Connemara lamb: the sheep graze on wild herbs on the mountain slopes, which gives the meat a distinctive flavor. The other star is local seafood, including crab and lobster in summer, and superb Atlantic salmon all year round, fresh or smoked. For seafood try the Tavern Bar and Restaurant near Westport, or Mitchell's in Clifden; for country house–style elegance go to Rosleague Manor in Letterfrack, or Mount Falcon near Ballina.

RESTAURANT AND HOTEL PRICES

⇨ *Restaurant prices are the average cost of a main course at dinner or, if dinner is not served, at lunch. Hotel prices are the lowest cost of a standard double room in high season. Restaurant and hotel reviews have been shortened. For full information, visit Fodors.com.*

What It Costs in Euros

$	$$	$$$	$$$$
RESTAURANTS			
under €19	€19–€24	€25–€32	over €32
HOTELS			
under €120	€120–€170	€171–€210	over €210

Tours

All TIOs (tourist information offices) in the West provide lists of suggested cycling tours. The only guided bus tours in the region, which take in the main sights of Connemara (€20), start from Galway and Westport and run between June and September only. Book at the bus station or tourist office.

Clew Bay Bike Hire and Outdoor Adventures
GUIDED TOURS | Cycling breaks and guided daylong cycle tours in the Westport area are available, as well as sea kayaking, and the opportunity to finish the day with a mini cruise across Clew Bay. The most popular product, however, is day hire of electric bicycles that take the hard work out of cycling. The company also has a free drop-off and pickup service via

minibus and cycle trailer—invaluable if the weather takes a turn. ✉ *Distillery Rd., Westport* ☎ *098/24818* 🌐 *www.clewbay-bikehire.ie* 🎫 *From €25.*

Connemara Adventure Tours

SELF-GUIDED TOURS | Self-guided or customized tours for walkers, cyclists, golfers, and horseback riders are available from this company. Groups of 8 to 16 people participate in three-, four-, or seven-day programs, staying in a comfortable B&B near Westport, or traveling to a new destination each night with luggage transfer. Walk Clare Island, climb Diamond Hill, or gallop along a sandy beach on Clew Bay. ✉ *Killary Adventure Centre, Leenane* ☎ *095/43411* 🌐 *www.connemaraadventuretours.com* 🎫 *From €855 for 7-day walking tour.*

Galway Tour Company

GUIDED TOURS | This Galway-based company runs a Connemara tour that takes in Clifden, Kylemore Abbey, and Cong, the famed location of the classic movie *The Quiet Man*. Tickets can be purchased from the Galway Tourist Information Office or on the tour bus. ☎ *091/566–566* 🌐 *www.galwaytourcompany.com* 🎫 *From €35.*

Lally Tours

GUIDED TOURS | Galway City–based Lally Tours runs a €35 day tour through Connemara and County Mayo. ✉ *4 Forster St., Galway City* ☎ *091/562–905* 🌐 *www.lallytours.com* 🎫 *From €20.*

Michael Gibbons Walking Ireland

GUIDED TOURS | This Clifden-based company organizes everything from daylong mountain treks to weeklong holidays, with an emphasis on archaeology. ✉ *Island House, Market St., Clifden* ☎ *095/21379* 🌐 *www.walkingireland.com.*

When to Go

There is a local saying in the Westport area: if you can't see the summit of Croagh Patrick, then it is raining; if you can see it, it is about to rain. While visiting between November and February has its own charms with cozy open fire settings and wild Atlantic winds, many places close for the season, and the days are short and often overcast. In fact, you could have your umbrellas out constantly during all times but the warmest months, July and August, when the average temperatures are around 15°C (60°F).

Festivals

Clifden Arts Festival

CULTURAL FESTIVALS | Held annually in mid-September since 1977, the Clifden Arts Festival has a great selection of music, arts, and poetry in a friendly, informal atmosphere and scenic environment, making it an excellent time to tune in to local culture. 🌐 *www.clifdenartsfestival.ie.*

Croagh Patrick Heritage Trail Walking Festival

CULTURAL FESTIVALS | This is a three-day guided walking festival in mid-March along 61 km (38 miles) of one of the most beautiful trails in the country. The accredited route takes you through lush farmland, forest paths, and remote boglands, past historic houses and archaeological remains, en route to Croagh Patrick, Ireland's most famous pilgrimage site. The trail includes moderate to hard walking and is held on the second weekend of March. ☎ *094/903–0687* 🌐 *www.cpht.ie* 🎫 *From €20.*

Planning Your Time

Visitors are often geared to a faster pace, but they should allow at least two days for exploring the region, four to six days if you intend to do some serious hiking or cycling, take a boat trip on Lough Corrib, visit an island, and enjoy the village (and pub) life of Clifden, Roundstone, and Westport. Although distances between sights are not great, you may want to take scenic—meaning slower—national secondary routes. Covering 130 to 160 km (80 to 100 miles) per day on these roads is a comfortable target.

If you love the outdoors, dramatic scenery, empty roads, and deserted coves, then you'll be in heaven in Connemara and Mayo. If you're a city lover, and tend to fade without daily doses of caffeine and retail therapy, then base yourself in Clifden for the first night, where there is coffee aplenty and surprisingly good shopping for a very small town (Irish designer wear, locally made tweed, traditional hand-knits, and wackier handcrafted knitwear).

IF YOU HAVE THREE DAYS

Allow a full day to meander slowly from Galway City to Clifden, perhaps stopping by Roundstone, a charming fishing village, to hike heather-clad Errisbeg Mountain or idle on the white sandy dunes of Dog's Bay. Next morning, take a stroll along the Sky Road before heading to the lovely Kylemore Abbey and its gardens. Drive the scenic Doolough Valley to Westport for your second night. Next day, hire a bike to cycle on the traffic-free coastal path, the Great Western Greenway, or drive across the bridge to Achill Island for some magnificent coastal scenery. If the weather grounds you, head up to Turlough and the nostalgic Museum of Country Life (allow two hours), but if it is fine, push on to the North Mayo coast, where you can walk in the footsteps of Stone Age farmers, and test your nerve on rugged Downpatrick Head.

Visitor Information

Discover Ireland provides free information service, tourist literature, and an accommodations booking service at its TIOs (tourist information offices). Oughterard, Castlebar, Ballina, Belmullet, and Westport TIOs are open all year, generally weekdays 9 am–6 pm during the high season. Other TIOs that operate seasonally, generally weekdays 9–6 and Saturday 9–1, include Clifden (March–October) and Cong (May–mid-September). In addition to this main website, we sometimes also list a town website in individual town sections; this is occasionally an ad-supported site that is unofficial, but still helpful. Generally speaking, tourism has been carefully nurtured in this region. Ferry services to the islands and on Lough Corrib have been upgraded, while walking and cycling holidays are a big growth area.

Roundstone

18 km (10 miles) south of Clifden.

The vibrantly colored vernacular facades that follow the hilly terrain of this ocean-harbor village, nestled in the shadows of the Twelve Bens Mountains, make for the most photogenic streetscape in the West of Ireland. Art, crafts, and custom-made musical instruments workshops line the street along with inviting restaurants and pubs. The village's terraced buildings overlook a deep blue bay, which is peppered with red and green fishing trawlers, traditional currachs (large, tar-lacquered canoes), and rowboats. Roundstone featured as the main setting for the 1997 romantic comedy movie *The Matchmaker,* starring Janeane Garofalo and Milo O'Shea.

GETTING HERE AND AROUND

Roundstone is located 18 km (10 miles) south of Clifden on the coastal road R341 and 76 km (47 miles) northwest from Galway City. Bus Éireann offers an irregular service from Galway and Clifden on bus No. 419.

Sights

Dog's Bay Beach

BEACH | Dog's Bay Beach lies back-to-back with Gurteen Beach, forming a tombolo that juts out into the ocean. Unlike other local limestone beaches, Dog's Bay's brilliant white sand was formed from seashells, and its horseshoe shape stretches for a mile along the Connemara coast. Its clear blue water is sheltered from currents, making it popular with swimmers and kitesurfers. **Amenities**: none. **Best for**: swimming; walking. ✉ *Ervallagh, Roundstone.*

Inis Ní Loop

ISLAND | Just when you think you've discovered Connemara's final Atlantic frontier, Inis Ní (or Inishnee) Island lures you miles farther into its ocean-fringed wilderness. This is one of the most northerly outposts of the south Connemara Gaeltacht. The trailhead is by a car park close to Roundstone, and from there it's an easy mile of country road to a small causeway. Discarded fishermen boats bob along a marshy inlet, at the start of the loop walk. The island's color palette varies with the season's blossoms as you meander past deserted, forlorn graveyards, granite walls caked in lichen and moss, and a pier where fishermen sort their stock from brightly painted boats. ✉ *Connemara* ✣ *Off R341, 2 km (1 mile) northeast of Roundstone. Cross bridge and trailhead is on your left.*

Restaurants

★ O'Dowds Seafood Bar and Restaurant

$ | **MODERN IRISH** | This fourth-generation establishment sits in the heart of Roundstone overlooking the harbor. It attracts year-round guests with its fresh-from-the-boats lobster, mussels, prawns, and crab, or other local produce such as Connemara lamb, and homey, open-fire setting. **Known for:** seafood chowder; harbor views; dillisk rice. [$] *Average main: €16* ✉ *Main St., Roundstone* ☎ *095/35809* 🌐 *www.odowdsseafoodbar.com.*

Hotels

★ Ballynahinch Castle Hotel

$$$$ | **HOTEL** | More like a rambling country house than a castle, this magnificent crenellated mansion sits beside a river amid 700 wooded acres with a rugged mountain backdrop and has arguably the finest hotel setting in Ireland. **Pros:** genuine Irish country-house experience; one of the best breakfasts in Ireland; stunning surroundings. **Cons:** authentic doesn't come cheap; car needed to explore the greater area; some rooms do not have river views. [$] *Rooms from: €320* ✉ *Ballynahinch Castle, Connemara* ✣ *After Recess, take R341 turn to your left, signposted Roundstone. The hotel is 5 km (3 miles) up this road on right* ☎ *095/31006* 🌐 *www.ballynahinch-castle.com* *45 rooms* *Free Breakfast.*

Island View House Guesthouse

$ | **B&B/INN** | In the heart of the picturesque village of Roundstone, this slim town house offers large, well-appointed rooms, with Bertraghboy Bay, Inis Rí island, and the Twelve Bens views, a full Irish breakfast, and a guest-only lounge for an edge on other local offerings. **Pros:** residents' lounge with fireplace; lovely rooms, some with bay views; fresh scones on arrival. **Cons:** parking across the street; set on the main street; not all rooms have views. [$] *Rooms from: €85* ✉ *Roundstone, Connemara* ☎ *95/35701* 🌐 *www.islandview.ie* *5 rooms, 1 self-catering cottage* *Free Breakfast.*

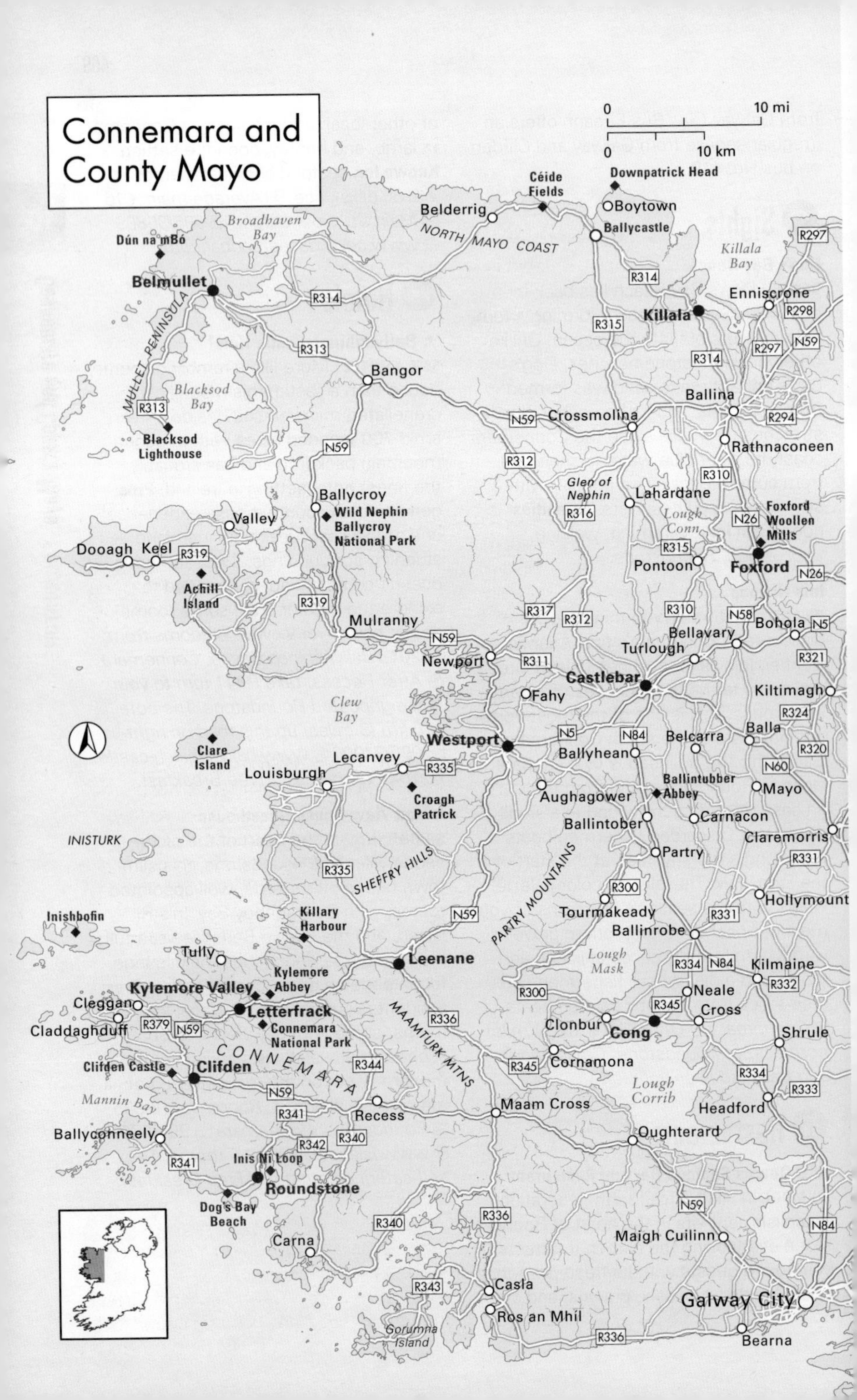

Connemara and County Mayo
0
10 mi
0
10 km
Downpatrick Head
Céide Fields
Belderrig
Boytown
Ballycastle
NORTH MAYO COAST
Broadhaven Bay
Dún na mBó
Belmullet
MULLET PENINSULA
R314
R297
Killala Bay
Enniscrone
R298
Killala
R315
R297
N59
R313
Bangor
Blacksod Bay
R313
Blacksod Lighthouse
R314
Ballina
N59
Crossmolina
R294
Rathnaconeen
N59
R312
R310
Glen of Nephin
Lahardane
R316
Ballycroy
Wild Nephin Ballycroy National Park
Valley
Lough Conn
N26
Foxford Woollen Mills
Dooagh
Keel
R319
Achill Island
R315
Pontoon
Foxford
N26
R319
R317
R312
R310
N58
Mulranny
Bohola
N5
N59
Bellavary
Newport
R311
Turlough
R321
Castlebar
Fahy
Kiltimagh
Clew Bay
R324
Clare Island
N5
N84
Westport
Belcarra
Balla
R320
Lecanvey
Ballyhean
R335
Louisburgh
N60
Croagh Patrick
Aughagower
Ballintubber Abbey
Mayo
Ballintober
Carnacon
INISTURK
Claremorris
SHEFFRY HILLS
PARTRY MOUNTAINS
Partry
R335
R331
R300
Hollymount
Tourmakeady
Inishbofin
Killary Harbour
N59
R331
Ballinrobe
Tully
Leenane
Lough Mask
R334
N84
Kilmaine
Kylemore Abbey
Kylemore Valley
R300
Neale
R332
Cleggan
Letterfrack
MAAMTURK MTNS
R345
Cross
Claddaghduff
R379
N59
Connemara National Park
R336
Clonbur
Cong
Shrule
CONNEMARA
Cornamona
Clifden Castle
Clifden
R344
R345
R334
Mannin Bay
N59
Lough Corrib
R333
Recess
Maam Cross
Headford
R341
Ballyconneely
R342
R340
Oughterard
R341
Inis Ní Loop
Roundstone
Dog's Bay Beach
N59
R340
R336
N84
Maigh Cuilinn
Carna
R343
Casla
Galway City
Ros an Mhíl
Gorumna Island
R336
Bearna

Clifden

66 km (41 miles) southwest of Cong, 79 km (49 miles) northwest of Galway.

With less than 2,000 residents, Clifden would be called a village by most, but in these parts it's looked on as something of a metropolis. Clifden's first attraction is its location—perched high above Clifden Bay on a forested plateau, its back to the spectacular Twelve Bens mountains. The tapering spires of the town's two churches add to its alpine look.

Clifden is a popular base thanks to its selection of small restaurants, lively bars with music most summer nights, pleasant accommodations, and excellent walks. It's quiet out of season, but in July and August crowds flock here, especially for August's world-famous Connemara Pony Show. Year-round, unfortunately, Clifden's popularity necessitates a chaotic one-way traffic system, and on summer Sunday afternoons loud techno music blasts out of certain bars. So if you're looking for a sleepy country town that time forgot, this may not be the place for you.

GETTING HERE AND AROUND

Clifden is 66 km (41 miles) southwest of Cong: travel via Maam Cross and take the N59 westward. The town is 79 km (49 miles) northwest of Galway City on the N59 and takes about 1½ hours to reach. It is a busy main road with only one lane in each direction, and delays can occur. Follow signs to find the car parks (and free parking).

Bus Éireann and Citylink have daily bus service from Galway Bus Station. Bus Éireann's route takes two hours (at least half of that through great scenery), while Citylink's service takes 1½ hours and continues from Galway to Dublin and Dublin Airport. Some of these services continue to Letterfrack (about 20 minutes) and Leenane (about an hour). Check with Galway Bus Station on day of travel.

VISITOR INFORMATION

CONTACTS Clifden Tourist Office. ✉ *Galway Rd., Clifden* ☎ *095/21163* 🌐 *www.discoverireland.ie/Activities-Adventure/clifden-tourist-information-centre/48273.*

Sights

Clifden Castle

CASTLE/PALACE | Clifden Castle—a Gothic Revival masterpiece—was built above the town in 1815 by John D'Arcy, the town's founder and high sheriff of Galway, who wished to establish a center of law and order in what he saw as the lawless wilderness of Connemara. Before the founding of Clifden, the interior of Connemara was largely uninhabited, with most of its population clinging to the seashore. Today there is just the shell of this former seat of power—but its setting off Sky Road is epic. Wear appropriate footwear as there is a lovely, 15-minute winding walk from the nearest car park. ✉ *Sky Rd., Clifden.*

The Derrigimlagh Walking Loop

TRAIL | In June 1919, pilot John Alcock and navigator Arthur Whitten Brown entered the annals of navigation history by taking the first transatlantic flight from Newfoundland to a bumpy crash-landing in the heart of Derrigimlagh Bog, close to Guglielmo Marconi's groundbreaking wireless station. Both the bog and the wireless station are noted in the staggeringly beautiful 5-km (3-mile) Derrigimlagh trail that passes miniature lakes, peat bogs, and rare flora and fauna. ✉ *Ballyconneely, Clifden* 🌐 *www.discoverireland.ie/Arts-Culture-Heritage/derrigimlagh/91306.*

Restaurants

Mitchell's Seafood

$ | **SEAFOOD** | A town-center shop has been cleverly converted into a stylish, two-story eatery. Beyond the plate-glass windows, there's a welcoming open fire, and you can eat at the bar or at one of the polished wood tables. **Known for:** cozy ambience with an open fire; fresh seafood; braised whole sea bass with fennel butter. *Average main: €18 Market St., Clifden 095/21867 mitchellsrestaurantclifden.com Closed Nov.–Feb.*

Coffee and Quick Bites

Connemara Hamper

$ | **IRISH** | Whether you're stocking up on local supplies for your Airbnb, stocking up on snacks for a Wild Atlantic Way drive, looking for picnic supplies or hamper gifts, or just stopping for a decent coffee and quick bite, this cute little artisanal food shop offers a wide variety of Irish farmhouse cheeses, meats, Connemara salmon, jams, pâtés, wines, and coffees, as well as a small nook to sit awhile. **Known for:** excellent cheese counter; freshly baked goods; smoked local meats and salmon. *Average main: €5 Market St., Clifden 095/21054 www.connemarahamper.com.*

Walsh's Bakery

$ | **BAKERY** | Coffee slices, cheesecake, apple pie, lemon drizzle, and a host of other delectable sweetness have greeted visitors for more than 65 years at this charming, second-generation bakery in the heart of Clifden. For those up early, a fine Irish breakfast will set the pace for a good day's sightseeing or hiking. **Known for:** fresh pastry and scones; good coffee; hearty breakfast. *Average main: €8 Market St., Clifden 95/21283 www.walshsbakery.ie.*

Hotels

★ Abbeyglen Castle Hotel

$$ | **HOTEL** | Creeper-covered, as if under a Sleeping Beauty spell, the gorgeous Victorian castle-manor of Abbeyglen sits framed by towering trees on a height above Clifden town—if time hasn't completely stopped here, it has certainly slowed down, but that's just the way the relaxed guests want it. **Pros:** complimentary tea and scones; pleasantly homey rather than luxurious; nice old-fashioned touches, like real room keys. **Cons:** uphill walk back from Clifden; more of a manor house than a castle; not a romantic hideaway: guests are expected to mingle. *Rooms from: €166 Sky Rd., Clifden 095/21201 www.abbeyglen.ie Closed Jan. and Feb. 42 rooms Free Breakfast.*

Dún Rí

$ | **B&B/INN** | An old town house in the lower, quieter part of Clifden has been extended and converted into a comfortable guesthouse with private parking. **Pros:** hotel-grade rooms at B&B prices; quiet yet central location; homemade breads and jams at breakfast. **Cons:** old furnishings; bland design; parking lot is effectively on-street, not secured. *Rooms from: €100 Hulk St., Clifden 095/21625 www.dunri.ie 13 rooms Free Breakfast.*

The Quay House

$$$ | **B&B/INN** | Nineteenth-century time travelers would feel right at home in this three-story, town-center Georgian house, Clifden's oldest building (1820) that once housed the harbormaster. **Pros:** fetching decor; quiet location; harbor views. **Cons:** uphill walk into town; rooms in new wing less attractive than those in the main house; you'll need to book well in advance. *Rooms from: €175 The Quay, Clifden 095/21369 www.thequayhouse.com Closed Nov.–mid-Mar. 14 rooms Free Breakfast.*

Nightlife

J Conneely's Bar

BARS | Irish music is played every night in the summer from 6:30 pm at this popular town-center bar. It gets livelier after 9 pm, when it stops serving food. *Market St., Clifden 095/22733.*

Lowry's Bar Lounge

PUBS | This central pub is famed for its traditional Irish music, played from 10 pm until late on weekdays, and on Sunday from 6 to 8:30 pm. Lowry's also has a wide range of whiskeys and decent pub grub. ✉ *Market St., Clifden* ☎ *095/21347* 🌐 *www.lowrysbar.ie.*

Shopping

All Things Connemara
CRAFTS | This friendly boutique is a showcase for crafts and artisanal products made in Connemara, from marble jewelry and seaweed-based cosmetics to Irish whiskey, knitwear, and handmade pottery. Electric bikes are also available for hire, and there's information about outdoor activities and guided tours. ✉ *Market St., Clifden* ☎ *095/22630* 🌐 *https://connemara.net/things-connemara.*

The Clifden Bookshop
BOOKS | As well as selling books of local interest, the bookshop also stocks artists' supplies and is an informal meeting point for visiting poets, writers, artists, and photographers. ✉ *Main St., Clifden* ☎ *095/22020* 🌐 *www.clifdenbookshop.com.*

Millar's Connemara Tweeds
CRAFTS | This long-established emporium sells a good selection of traditional tweeds, hand-knitted items, housewares, and gifts. ✉ *Main St., Clifden* ☎ *095/21038* 🌐 *www.millarsconnemara.ie.*

Activities

BICYCLING

Mannion Bike Hire
BIKING | Explore Connemara by renting a bike from this handy outfitter. ✉ *Bridge St., Clifden* ☎ *095/21160* 🌐 *www.clifdenbikes.com.*

GOLF

Connemara Golf Links
GOLF | On a dramatic stretch of Atlantic coastline, the links course masterminded by Eddie Hackett, Ireland's finest course designer, is situated between the Twelve Bens and the rugged coast, with unforgettable views of the sea, hills, and huge western sky. The opening hole has a challenging dogleg, while the back 9 make for a memorable golfing experience, considered equal to any in the world. ✉ *9 km (5½ miles) south of Clifden on R341, Ballyconneely* ☎ *095/23502* 🌐 *www.connemaragolflinks.com* 🎫 *Nov.–Mar. €110, Apr.–Oct. €150* 🏌 *18 holes, 7055 yards, par 72.*

Letterfrack

14 km (9 miles) north of Clifden.

This is the gateway village to the famous Connemara National Park. It also makes a handy base for those visiting spectacular Kylemore Abbey, one of Ireland's grandest ancestral estates.

GETTING HERE AND AROUND

Letterfrack is 14 km (9 miles) north of Clifden on the N59. The journey takes about 15 minutes. There is plenty of free parking in the village center. Bus Éireann has daily routes linking Letterfrack and Clifden, a 20-minute journey. There is another Bus Éireann service that originates in Galway and takes about two hours, 30 minutes to reach Letterfrack. Citylink also operates between Letterfrack and Clifden (continuing to Galway).

TOURS

★ **DK Connemara Oyster Farm Tours**
SPECIAL-INTEREST TOURS | Discover the three-year life cycle of an oyster from seed to plate, and the life skill of shucking and draining them correctly, in one of the oldest working oyster farms in Ireland. Reared right in the undiluted coastal water, with the wild and craggy Connemara landscape as a backdrop, it's hard to leave without gaining an insight into the hard work that goes into this delicacy. The guides, which include the owner David, take great pride in their work and pass on their knowledge during the one-hour tour (longer in springtime

Few landscapes are as quintessentially Irish as the ravishing ones found in Connemara National Park.

during high tide) with good humor, patience, and a real depth of knowledge. There is a shop on the premises for visitors to take home a sample of this unique experience. ✉ *Ballinakill Bay, Dawros, Letterfrack* ☎ *87/918–6997* 🌐 *www.dkconnemaraoysters.com* 🎫 *€30.*

Sights

★ Connemara National Park

NATIONAL PARK | The Irish people are well aware of what a jewel they have in the largely unspoiled wilderness, grazed by sheep and herds of wild ponies, that is the 5,000-acre Connemara National Park, the result of a successful lobby for landscape preservation. Like the American West, Connemara is an area of spectacular, almost myth-making geography—of glacial lakes; gorgeous, silent mountains; lonely roads; and hushed, uninhabited boglands. Letterfrack is the gateway village to the park and it makes a good base for exploring the park and nearby attractions, including Kylemore Abbey. Its visitor center covers the area's history and ecology, particularly the origins and growth of peat. You can also get advice and details on the many excellent walks and beaches in the area. One trail includes part of the famous Twelve Bens mountain range, which is best suited for experienced hill walkers. An easier hike is the Lower Diamond Hill Walk, at about 3 km (less than 2 miles). ✉ *Park and Visitor Centre, on N59 near Letterfrack, Letterfrack* ☎ *095/41054* 🌐 *www.connemaranationalpark.ie* 🎫 *Free* ⏲ *Visitor center closed Nov.–mid-Mar.*

★ Inishbofin

BEACH | Cleggan is the ferry port for this stark and unsettlingly beautiful outpost of Connemara. The island is a hiker's paradise, with loop routes that lead to a plethora of fine sandy beaches by the Atlantic's pristine water. Just 5 km (3 miles) by 3 km (2 miles), it was once a stronghold of the pirate queen Grainne O'Malley, and the crumbling ruin of a Cromwellian barracks is a stark reminder for visitors of the clergy held captive by troops before they were shipped afar.

The island is now a holiday retreat dotted with small pubs and inns for those who want quiet time. The ferry costs €25 round-trip for an adult. ✣ *14 km (8 miles) west of Letterfrack is Cleggan, the ferry port with 3 daily sailings to Inisbofin* ☎ *95/45819.*

Restaurants

★ Iniswallah

$ | MODERN IRISH | If the sight of a red double-decker bus parked outside a cottage in the desolately beautiful small island of Inisbofin comes as a surprise, then the delicious offerings at Austin and Kartika's gourmet outpost will floor you completely, in a good way. The bus has retired and functions as the couple's kitchen, dining area, and food counter, serving up pollock, crab, and mackerel sourced from local islander fishermen. **Known for:** gourmet street food; organic produce; quirky setting. $ *Average main: €10* ✉ *Island of Inisbofin, Letterfrack* ☎ *87/287–4139* ⏲ *Closed early Oct.–Easter.*

Veldon's Seafarer

$ | IRISH | Ship's wheels, fishing nets, and sculpted stone sharks leave little doubt that the Atlantic's catch takes center stage in this small, whitewashed cottage inn right in the heart of Letterfrack. Stuffed with timber nooks and crannies, and with an open fire, it's the place to warm up after a Connemara coastline hike. **Known for:** seafood chowder; local catch; posthike spot. $ *Average main: €15* ✉ *Letterfrack* ☎ *095/41046* 🌐 *www.veldons.ie.*

Hotels

★ Renvyle House Hotel

$$ | HOTEL | A lake at its front door, the Atlantic Ocean at the back, and the mountains of Connemara as a backdrop form the enthralling setting for this hotel 8 km (5 miles) north of Letterfrack, home to the Long Room, one of the most eminently civilized salons in Ireland—Arts and Crafts–style polished wood, original art, and red geraniums. **Pros:** secluded end-of-the-world location; history, character, and charm; excellent restaurant. **Cons:** driving neccessary; bar and restaurant very busy at peak times; rooms are well maintained but a little dated. $ *Rooms from: €160* ✉ *Renvyle* ☎ *095/46100* 🌐 *www.renvyle.com* ⏲ *Closed Jan. 6–mid-Feb.* *65 rooms, 3 apartments* 🍽 *Free Breakfast.*

Rosleague Manor

$$$ | HOTEL | This pink, creeper-clad, two-story Georgian house occupies 30 lovely acres and has a jaw-dropping view: a gorgeous lawn backdropped by Ballinakill Bay and the dreamy mountains of Connemara. **Pros:** quiet and elegant; mesmerizing views; excellent restaurant. **Cons:** can be very quiet off-season; usually fully booked from mid-July to end of August; closed to the public when hosting a wedding. $ *Rooms from: €210* ✉ *Rosleague Bay, Letterfrack* ☎ *095/41101* 🌐 *www.rosleague.com* ⏲ *Closed Nov.–mid-Mar.* *20 rooms* 🍽 *Free Breakfast.*

Nightlife

The Clover Fox

LIVE MUSIC | For traditional music, the best option in this region is the Clover Fox, formerly the Bards Den. The cottage also houses informal dining, an arts and crafts shop, and hostel. ✉ *Main St., Letterfrack* ☎ *095/41042* 🌐 *www.cloverfox.com.*

Kylemore Valley

Runs for 6½ km (4 miles) between Letterfrack and intersection of N59 and R344.

One of the more conventionally beautiful stretches of road in Connemara passes through Kylemore Valley, which is between the Twelve Bens to the south and the naturally forested Dorruagh

Mountains to the north. Kylemore (the name is derived from *Coill Mór,* Irish for "big wood") looks "as though some colossal giant had slashed it out with a couple of strokes from his mammoth sword," as artist and author John Fitz-Maurice Mills once wrote.

★ **Kylemore Abbey**

CASTLE/PALACE | One of the most magical "castles" in all of Europe, much-photographed Kylemore Abbey is set on a reedy lake with a backdrop of wooded hillside. The storybook Gothic Revival, gray-stone mansion was built as a private home between 1861 and 1868 by Mitchell Henry, a member of Parliament for County Galway, and his wife, Margaret, who had fallen in love with the spot during a carriage ride while on their honeymoon. The Henrys spared no expense—the final bill for their house is said to have come to £1.5 million—and they employed mostly local laborers, thereby abetting recovery from the famine (this area was among the worst hit in all of Ireland). Adjacent to the house (a short walk from the abbey) is a spectacular neo-Gothic chapel, which, sadly, became the burial place for Margaret, who died after contracting "Nile fever" on a trip to Egypt. In 1920, nuns from the Benedictine order, who fled their abbey in Belgium during World War I, sought refuge in Kylemore and ran a girls' boarding school here until 2010. Three reception rooms and the main hall are open to the public, as are a crafts center and cafeteria. You can prebook a guided hike and nature walk (€3) uphill to the life-size statue of Jesus for an unforgettable view of the tranquil abbey and lake from above. There's also a 6-acre walled Victorian garden; a shuttle bus (free with admission) from the abbey to the garden departs every 15 minutes during opening hours. An exhibition and video explaining the history of the house can be viewed year-round at the abbey, and the grounds are freely accessible most of the year.

TIP→ Be sure to visit the "Ironing Stone," a short walk from the chapel. Legend has it that this massive stone was tossed here by Irish mythical warrior Cú Chulainn. If you stand with your back to the rock and throw a pebble over the stone three times, your wish will be granted. ✉ *Entrance off N59 about 8 km (5 miles) east of Letterfrack, Letterfrack* ☎ *095/52001* 🌐 *www.kylemoreabbey.com* *€15* *Closed Nov.–Feb.*

Leenane and the Arts

Martin McDonagh's *Leenane Trilogy,* featuring a cast of tragicomic grotesques, presents an unflattering view of rural Irish life. An international hit, the plays brought a renown Leenane presumably could have done without. The plot thickened with Kevin Barry's "Fjord of Killary," a hilariously black short story set in a hotel in Leenane and published in *The New Yorker* in February 2010, and in Barry's collection *Dark Lies the Island* (2012).

Leenane

18 km (11 miles) east of Letterfrack.

Nestled idyllically at the foot of the Maamturk Mountains and overlooking the tranquil waters of Killary Harbour, Leenane is a tiny village noted for its role as the setting for the film *The Field,* which starred Richard Harris.

GETTING HERE AND AROUND

Leenane is 18 km (11 miles) east of Letterfrack on the N59. The journey takes just over 15 minutes. There is free parking in the village, on the streets, and in designated car parks. Leenane has at least one Bus Éireann schedule a day, traveling to Galway via Clifden, taking about one hour, 15 minutes to Clifden. In summer, there is also a bus to Westport, a 45-minute journey.

TOURS

Killary Cruises
BOAT TOURS | FAMILY | Take a 90-minute trip (€23.50) around Killary Harbour in an enclosed Killary Cruises catamaran launch with seating for 150 passengers, bar, and restaurant. ✉ *Nancy's Point, Leenane* ☎ *091/566–736* 🌐 *www.killary-fjord.com* ☞ *Closed Nov.–Mar.*

Sights

★ Killary Harbour
NATURE SIGHT | Beyond Kylemore, N59 travels for some miles along Killary Harbour, a narrow fjord that runs for 16 km (10 miles) between County Mayo's Mweelrea Mountain to the north and County Galway's Maamturk Mountains to the south. The dark, deep water of the fjord reflects the magnificent steep-sided hills that border it, creating a haunting scene of natural grandeur. The harbor has an extremely safe anchorage, 78 feet deep for almost its entire length, and is sheltered from storms by mountain walls. The rafts floating in Killary Harbour belong to fish-farming consortia that raise salmon and trout in cages beneath the water. This is a matter of some controversy all over the West. Although some people welcome the employment opportunities, others bemoan the visual blight of the rafts. ✉ *Killary, Leenane.*

The Sheep and Wool Centre
FACTORY | The Sheep and Wool Centre, in the center of Leenane, focuses on the traditional industry of North Connemara and West Mayo. Several breeds of sheep graze around the house, and there are demonstrations of carding, spinning, weaving, and the dyeing of wool with natural plant dyes. ✉ *Leenane* ☎ *095/42323* 🌐 *www.sheepandwoolcentre.com* 🎫 *Museum and wool craft demo €9* ⏲ *Closed Nov.–mid-Mar.*

Restaurants

★ Misunderstood Heron
$ | MODERN IRISH | Gaining a steady following from locals and visitors, Misunderstood Heron is serving some of the finest local produce from unlikely quarters—from the back of a food truck. It's usually parked in Killary Loop Trail—and offers guests far more than the standard truck fare like a humble kebab or burger. **Known for:** fresh produce; Killary Fjord views; cult following. Ⓢ *Average main: €12* ✉ *Killary Loop Trail, Leenane* ☎ *087/991–5179* 🌐 *www.misunderstoodheron.com* 💳 *No credit cards* ⏲ *Closed Nov.–Mar. Hrs vary seasonally, so call ahead to confirm.*

Hotels

★ Delphi Lodge
$$$$ | B&B/INN | In the heart of what is arguably Connemara's most spectacular mountain and lake scenery, 13 km (8 miles) north of Leenane off R335, this historic Georgian sporting lodge heavily stocked with fishing paraphernalia has a lovely lakeside setting. **Pros:** beautiful secluded location; abundant peace and quiet; good base for touring west Connemara and south Mayo. **Cons:** you've got to like fishing or walking; communal dining table seating up to 40 people; no in-room TVs, only one communal set. Ⓢ *Rooms from: €280* ✉ *Leenane* ☎ *095/42222* 🌐 *www.delphilodge.ie* ⏲ *Closed mid-Oct.–mid-Mar.* 🛏 *13 rooms, 5 cottages* 🍽 *Free Breakfast.*

Leenane Hotel
$$ | HOTEL | Built in the 1790s at the entrance to Leenane village as a coaching inn, this hotel is only separated from Killary Fjord by the main road. **Pros:** comfortable and atmospheric one-stop base; beautiful views; therapeutic seaweed baths. **Cons:** some of the older

Did You Know?

To best savor spectacular Kylemore Abbey, book a guided hike up the hill to the life-size statue of Jesus, usually surrounded by grazing sheep. The resident nuns will tell you that the view over the lake is well worth the effort.

En Route

Doolough Valley. You have two options for traveling onward from Leenane to Westport. The first is to take the direct route on the N59. The second is to detour through the Doolough Valley between Mweelrea Mountain (to the west) and the Sheeffry Hills (to the east) and on to Westport via Louisburgh (on the southern shore of Clew Bay), passing through the hauntingly beautiful Doolough Valley. A stark stone cross commemorates a particularly shameful chapter in Ireland's potato famine when people perished by the roadside when forced by poor relief officials to walk for an inspection in brutal weather conditions. The latter route adds about 24 km (15 miles) to the trip, but devotees of this part of the West claim that it takes you through the region's most impressive, unspoiled stretch of scenery. If you opt for the longer route, turn left onto R335 1½ km (1 mile) beyond Leenane. Just after this turn, you can hear the powerful rush of the Aasleagh Falls. You can park over the bridge, stroll along the river's shore, and soak in the splendor of the surrounding mountains. ✉ *Doolough Valley (R335).*

bedrooms very small; cars from road can get noisy; lighting rather dim in bar and lounge. $ *Rooms from: €120* ✉ *Leenane* ☎ *095/42249* 🌐 *www.leenanehotel.com* ⏲ *Closed mid-Nov.–mid-Mar.* 🛏 *66 rooms* 🍽 *Free Breakfast.*

Cong

23 km (14 miles) northeast of Maam Cross.

Set on a narrow isthmus between Lough Corrib and Lough Mask on the County Mayo border near Maam Cross, the pretty, old-fashioned village of Cong is still as camera-ready as it was when John Ford filmed *The Quiet Man* here in 1951. Dotted with ivy-covered thatched cottages with a cookie-cutter cuteness that may appear somewhat contrived, this tiny village still provides a wonderful photo backdrop.

Just two blocks long, and bisected by the chocolate-brown River Cong, the village is surrounded on all sides by thickly forested hills. Besides the much-vaunted *Quiet Man* connections, which may be puzzling to those who are not fans of the classic movie, you can walk among the riverside remains of the 12th-century abbey, and discover its Monks' Fishing House. Information boards in the village will guide you to a stone circle and the richly carved Market Cross. Apart from that, there's not a whole lot to do in Cong. Almost larger than the village itself is the celebrated luxury hotel found here, Ashford Castle, much beloved by its well-heeled patrons from around the world. A footpath runs from Cong Abbey to Ashford Castle, and out its gates is a pleasant walk of about 3 km (2 miles). There is now a €10 admission fee to the grounds of Ashford Castle, or a romantic way to see the castle is on a boat trip run by the local Corrib Cruises from the public pier in Cong.

GETTING HERE AND AROUND

Cong is 23 km (14 miles) northeast of Maam Cross on the N59, a scenic drive skirting the shores of Lough Corrib. The main car-parking area is on the edge of the village, a three-minute walk, and is clearly signposted. There is very limited parking in the village itself.

There is a limited Bus Éireann service from Galway Bus Station to Cong—be

President Reagan, Brad Pitt, Rory McIlroy ... and now you? Lucky travelers call Ashford Castle their Cong home-away-from-home.

sure to get a bus that goes to Ryan's, the bus stop in the village center. The journey takes just over an hour. You can also take a delightful day trip to Cong by Corrib Cruises boat from Oughterard between April and October.

VISITOR INFORMATION

CONTACTS Cong Tourist Office. ✉ *Abbey St., Cong* ☎ *094/954–6542* 🌐 *www.discoverireland.ie/Activities-Adventure/cong-tourist-office/48280.*

Sights

Augustine Abbey

RUINS | Cong is surrounded by many stone circles and burial mounds, but its most notable ruins are those of the Augustine Abbey, overlooking a river. Dating from the early 12th century when it was founded by Turlough O'Connor, the High King of Ireland, this abbey is an impressive example of ancient Irish architecture and still retains some finely carved details and a cloister; it served as a hospital and college in its day. Don't miss the fishing hut, an ingenious invention to keep fishermen dry. ✉ *Abbey St., Cong.*

Quiet Man Museum and Gift Shop

OTHER MUSEUM | Cong's 15 minutes of fame came in 1952, when John Ford's *The Quiet Man,* one of his most popular films, was released to a global audience. John Wayne plays a prizefighter who goes home to Ireland and courts the fiery Maureen O'Hara. The *Quiet Man* Museum, in the village center, is an exact replica of the cottage used in the film, with reproductions of the furniture and costumes, a few original artifacts, and pictures of actors Barry Fitzgerald and Maureen O'Hara on location. Margaret and Gerry Collins host *Quiet Man* walking tours, leaving the cottage at 11 am daily and exploring such Cong village sites as the river fight scene, the "hats in the air" scene, and Pat Cohan's Bar. There is also a chauffeur-driven tour option. ✉ *Circular Rd., Cong Village Center, Cong* ☎ *094/954–6089* 🌐 *www.*

quietmanmuseum.com 🎫 *€5, walking tour €15* ⏲ *By appointment only Nov.–Mar.*

Hotels

★ **Ashford Castle**

$$$$ | HOTEL | FAMILY | Flamboyantly turreted, this famed mock-Gothic baronial showpiece, dating from the 13th century, and rebuilt in 1870 for the Guinness family, has been wowing presidents and celebrities ever since. **Pros:** epitome of a romantic Irish castle; excellent facilities and activities; regal grounds. **Cons:** so luxurious you are cut off from the normal hubbub of Irish life; activities and dining options book up quickly at peak times; does not come cheap. $ *Rooms from: €675* ✉ *Ashford Castle Dr., Cong* ☎ *094/954–6003* 🌐 *www.ashfordcastle.com* 🛏 *82 rooms, 1 cottage* 🍽 *Free Breakfast.*

Ryan's Hotel

$ | B&B/INN | With framed fishing ties and specimen fish given pride of place on the lobby wall, you know you are in a hostelry favored by anglers. **Pros:** affordable alternative to Ashford Castle; central to village; good area for walkers and anglers. **Cons:** uninspiring views from most rooms; rooms on the main road can be noisy; decor needs updating. $ *Rooms from: €120* ✉ *Main St., Cong* ☎ *094/954–6243* 🌐 *www.ryanshotelcong.ie* 🛏 *12 rooms* 🍽 *Free Breakfast.*

Westport

32 km (20 miles) north of Leenane.

By far the most attractive town in County Mayo, Westport is on an inlet of Clew Bay, a wide expanse of sea dotted with islands and framed by mountain ranges. Its Georgian origins are clearly defined by the broad streets skirting the gentle Carrowbeg River and its lime-fringed Malls, avenues that hint of loftier expectations from the town's modest origins—but thankfully it retained its diminutive scale. Built as an O'Malley stronghold, the entire town received a face-lift when the Brownes arrived from Sussex in England during the Plantation of Ireland and constructed Westport House and much of the modern town, from funds generated from the tobacco and slave trade. The town was laid out by architect James Wyatt when he was employed to finish the grand estate of Westport House.

GETTING HERE AND AROUND

Westport is 32 km (20 miles) north of Leenane on the R335, and 78 km (48 miles) north of Clifden, a journey of about an hour. It is 80 km (50 miles) northwest of Galway on the N84 and R334 via Headford, picking up the N84 again before taking the R330 at Partry. The journey takes about one hour, 18 minutes. There is ample parking in the town center, on the streets, and in designated lots, with a nominal charge during business hours. There is more parking down on the quays.

There are Bus Éireann schedules daily from Westport (the Octagon monument) to Galway City, traveling on the nonscenic N17 via Claremorris. The express takes one hour, 50 minutes, while the nonexpress bus takes more than two hours. There are also direct buses from Westport to Ballina, a journey of about an hour. There is no bus station in Westport. Irish Rail trains travel from Dublin's Heuston Station to Westport, a journey of 3½ hours.

VISITOR INFORMATION

CONTACTS Westport Tourist Office. ✉ *Fáilte Ireland, Discover Ireland Centre, Bridge St., Westport* ☎ *098/25711* 🌐 *www.discoverireland.ie/places-to-go/westport.*

Sights

★ **Achill Island**

BEACH | Achill Island is only 20 feet from the mainland and has been connected

The village of Cong is world-famous as the setting for John Ford's Oscar-winning *The Quiet Man,* and the *Quiet Man* Museum takes you behind the scenes.

by a bridge since 1887, the latest (2008) being a €5 million swing bridge, known locally as "our Calatrava-style bridge." At 147 square km (57 square miles), Achill is Ireland's largest offshore island, with a population of 2,700. In summer, it attracts camper vans and families from the mainland who enjoy the wild open spaces of its unspoiled bogs with miles and miles of long empty beaches. The island is abundant with flora, especially wild heather and, in May and June, rhododendrons, while fuchsia blooms later in the summer.

The best introduction to Achill is to follow signs for the 20-km (12-mile) Atlantic Drive. The road runs through Keel, which has a 3-km-long (2-mile-long) beach with spectacular rock formations in the eastern cliffs. Dugort, on the north shore, is a small village with a beautiful golden strand. Above it is the 2,204-foot Slievemore, the island's highest summit. At its base is the Deserted Village, a settlement of 80 ruined one-room stone houses, abandoned since the 1845 famine. At the far westerly corner of the island are the 2,257-foot-high Croaghan Sea Cliffs, the third highest in Europe—and Keem Beach, a magnificent bone-white sandy bay beneath the shoulders of two enormous lush mountains. ✉ *Achill Island.*

Clare Island

ISLAND | Clew Bay is said to have 365 islands, one for every day of the year. The biggest and most interesting one to visit is Clare Island, at the mouth of the bay. In fine weather the rocky, hilly island, which is 8 km (5 miles) long and 5 km (3 miles) wide, has beautiful views south toward Connemara, east across Clew Bay, and north to Achill Island. About 150 people live on the island today, but before the 1845–47 famine it had a population of about 1,700. A 15th-century tower overlooking the harbor was once the stronghold of Granuaile, the pirate queen, who ruled the area until her death in 1603. She is buried on the island, in its 12th-century Cistercian abbey. Today most visitors seek out the island for its unusual peace and quiet, golden beaches, and unspoiled landscape. There are two ferry services to the island, one year-round, the other seasonal; both depart from Roonagh Pier, near Louisburgh, a scenic 19-km (12-mile) drive from Westport on the R335 past several long sandy beaches. ✉ *Clew Bay* ☎ *098/25045 for ferry info, 098/23737* 🌐 *www.clareisland.ie* 🎫 *Ferry €17 round-trip (discounted online)* ☞ *2 ferry companies serve Clare Island. Your return ticket will only be valid on a ferry belonging to the company you came out with.*

★ Croagh Patrick

MOUNTAIN | Look out as you travel north for the great bulk of 2,500-foot-high Croagh Patrick; its size and conical shape make it one of the West's most distinctive landmarks. On clear days a small white oratory is visible at its summit (it stands on a ½-acre plateau), as is the wide path that ascends to it. The latter is the Pilgrim's Path. Each year about 25,000 people, many of them barefoot, follow the path to pray to St. Patrick in the oratory on its peak. St. Patrick, who converted Ireland to Christianity, spent the 40 days and nights of Lent here in 441. The traditional date for the pilgrimage is the last Sunday in July. In the past, the walk was made at night, with pilgrims carrying burning torches, but that practice has been discontinued. The climb involves a gentle uphill slope, but you need to be fit and agile to complete the last half hour, over scree (small loose rocks with no trail). This is why most climbers carry a stick or staff (traditionally made of ash, and called an ash plant), which helps you to stop sliding backward. These can sometimes be bought in the parking area. The hike can be made in about three hours (round-trip) on any fine day and is well worth the effort for the magnificent views of the islands of Clew Bay, the Sheeffry Hills to the south (with the Bens visible behind them), and the peaks of Mayo to the north. The climb starts at Murrisk, a village about 8 km (5 miles) before Westport on the R335 Louisburgh Road. ✉ *Westport.*

Westport House

HISTORIC HOME | **FAMILY** | Westport House and Country Park, a stately home built on the site of an earlier castle (believed to have been the home of the 16th-century warrior queen, Grace O'Malley) is the town's most famous landmark. Set right on the shores of a lake, the house remained the property of the Browne family from the 17th century until recent years, when a local businessman purchased it. Architect Richard Cassels (who also designed Powerscourt in County Wicklow and the Irish government's nerve center, Leinster House) masterminded the design of the house, which was constructed in 1730 and added to in 1778, and then finally completed in 1788 by architect James Wyatt with a lavish budget from the Browne's slave trading history with Jamaica. The rectangular, three-story house is furnished with late-Georgian and Victorian pieces. Family portraits by Opie and Reynolds, a huge collection of old Irish silver and old Waterford glass, plus an opulent group of paintings—including *The Holy Family* by Rubens—are on display. A word of caution: Westport isn't your usual staid country house. The old dungeons now house interactive games, and the grounds have given way to an amusement park for children and an adventure center offering zip rides, laser combat games, and archery. In fact, the lake is now littered with swan-shape "pedaloes," boats that may be fun for families but help destroy the perfect Georgian grace of the setting. If these elements don't sound like a draw, arrive early, when it's less likely to be busy. There is also a 1½-km (1-mile) riverside walk, a tree trail, a gift shop, and a coffee shop.

A massive investment has been poured into the nature reserve that includes rewilding, more marked climbing trails, marked sunset spots, looped trails, and more. Explore the Destination Westport site for more. ✉ *Off N59, south of Westport, clearly signposted from Octagon, Westport* ☎ *098/27766* 🌐 *www.westporthouse.ie* 🎫 *House and gardens from €14.*

Restaurants

★ An Port Mór Restaurant

$$$ | **IRISH** | Nestled down a narrow laneway just off Bridge Street, this charming and intimate restaurant harbors the finest of local produce, exquisitely crafted into one of the best menus in Mayo by owner-chef Frankie Mallon. Daily specials include anything from pan-seared Clew Bay scallops to warm pork-cheek salad and black pudding served with apple and vanilla. **Known for:** reservations recommended; vibrant dishes made from local produce; gluten-free and vegetarian options. $ *Average main: €28* ✉ *1 Brewery Pl., Westport* ☎ *098/26730* 🌐 *www.anportmor.com.*

Cronin's Sheebeen

$ | **MODERN IRISH** | **FAMILY** | Overlooking Clew Bay on the outskirts of Westport, this whitewashed, thatched cottage–pub is the stuff of dreams, and so is the food offered by the father-and-son team who own it. The fresh salmon, hake, turbot, or mussels from nearby Rossaveal or the Corrib give the menu a sea-hopping freshness, providing balance to the bolder, more colorful choices, like prawn Laksa. **Known for:** warm ginger and banana cake; fresh Newport langoustine with wild garlic and lovage butter; Clew Bay seafood chowder. $ *Average main: €15* ✉ *Rosbeg, Westport, Westport* ✣ *4 km (2½ miles) west on L5840 from Westport* ☎ *98/26528* 🌐 *www.croninssheebeen.com* ⏲ *Closed Mon. and Tues.*

Hotels

Clew Bay Hotel

$ | **HOTEL** | In Westport's town center, this hotel welcomes guests with a traditional wooden facade but inside, a contemporary glass-roofed lobby becomes the centerpiece of a stylish modern interior decorated with original artwork. **Pros:** central location, adjacent to bars and shops; bespoke walking and cycling activity breaks; good value. **Cons:** risk of late-night noise in front rooms; no private parking; bathrooms a bit old-fashioned; popular with bachelor and bachelorette parties. $ *Rooms from: €100* ✉ *James St., Westport* ☎ *098/28088* 🌐 *www.clewbayhotel.com* 🛏 *40 rooms* 🍽 *Free Breakfast.*

Mulranny Park Hotel

$$ | **HOTEL** | **FAMILY** | Perched on a cliff overlooking a vast, sandy beach on the northern side of Clew Bay, 25 minutes' drive from Westport, this is one of Ireland's best-loved "bucket and spade" hotels, built in 1897 for holidaymakers arriving by train. **Pros:** that huge beach on your doorstep and panoramic sea views; indoor pool and leisure center; great Western Greenway walking/cycling route on-site. **Cons:** very popular with groups and extended families; must reserve evening meal in advance to ensure a place; village of Mulranny does not have much else to offer. $ *Rooms from: €150* ✉ *Mulranny, Westport* ☎ *098/36000* 🌐 *www.mulrannyparkhotel.ie* ⏲ *Closed Jan. 7–31* 🛏 *41 rooms, 20 apartments* 🍽 *Free Breakfast.*

Westport Plaza Hotel

$$ | **HOTEL** | **FAMILY** | With all the hallmarks of Ireland's Celtic Tiger boom time, this swish and stylish boutique hotel has a vast marble lobby with a double-sided gas fire and huge guest rooms with oversized, veneered, Art Deco–style furniture and bathrooms with Jacuzzi tubs and modern showers. **Pros:** some rooms have balconies overlooking roof garden; great amenities; quiet but central. **Cons:** avoid the few bedrooms with street views; you might forget you're in Ireland; guests have to walk outside to the pool. $ *Rooms from: €158* ✉ *Castlebar St.,*

Westport ☎ *098/51166* 🌐 *www.westportplazahotel.ie* 🛏 *85 rooms, 3 suites* 🍽 *Free Breakfast.*

Nightlife

★ Matt Molloy's

LIVE MUSIC | Matt Molloy of famed musical group the Chieftains curates this lively spot in Westport's town center. Traditional music is, naturally, the main attraction. Seven days a week, it serves nothing but drinks and a whole lot of fun. ✉ *Bridge St., Westport* ☎ *098/26655* 🌐 *www.mattmolloy.com.*

The Towers Bar & Restaurant

PUBS | A good spot for traditional music from 9 pm, the Towers is also known for its tasty homemade pub grub, which includes chowder, poached pears, seafood pie and gluten-free options. In summer, there are outdoor tables set up beside the bay. Children are welcome up to 7 pm. ✉ *The Quay, Westport* ☎ *098/24844* 🌐 *www.thetowersbar.com.*

Shopping

Thomas Moran's

SOUVENIRS | It's worth a visit to Thomas Moran's just to see the cluttered, quirky facade that has welcomed customers through its doors for well over a century. Inside, take some time to rummage through the irresistibly unique gifts: locally made blackthorn sticks, bargain umbrellas, and high-kitsch souvenirs. ✉ *Bridge St., Westport* ☎ *098/25562* ✉ *joemoran777@gmail.com.*

Activities

BICYCLING

Clew Bay Bike Hire

BIKING | Explore the scenic bike trails of Clew Bay, including the Great Western Greenway, on a top-of-the-range bike, available by the hour, day, or multiday. The minibus and bike trailer provide a free drop-off and collection service for an extra fee. In addition, kayak hire and escorted trips are available. ✉ *Distillery Rd., Westport* ☎ *098/24818* 🌐 *www.clewbaybikehire.ie.*

★ Great Western Greenway

BIKING | FAMILY | This 42-km (26-mile) off-road cycling and walking trail follows the route of the railway line that ran along the edge of Clew Bay through Newport and Mulranny from 1895 until 1937, connecting Westport to Achill Island. It passes through some of the most spectacular scenery in the West of Ireland, and has given a major boost to tourism in the area. The birdsong and the sound of the wind are praised as highly as the great coastal scenery. It is just as enjoyable to drive out along the N59 and walk a short section as it is to walk or cycle the whole path. ✉ *Great Western Greenway (N59)* 🌐 *www.greenway.ie.*

Castlebar

18 km (11 miles) east of Westport on N5.

The capital of Mayo, situated on its central limestone plain and once the biggest town for miles around, Castlebar is now a commercial and shopping hub for the region, overshadowed by its more scenic neighbor, Westport. Park in one of the many pay-and-display car parks, and proceed on foot.

GETTING HERE AND AROUND

Castlebar is 18 km (11 miles) east of Westport on the N5 and 40 km (25 miles) west of Knock Airport. The journey takes about 15 minutes by car. There are plenty of pay-and-display parking lots in the town center, which has a one-way traffic system and is compact and walkable. Bus Éireann has regional links from here to Galway City in the South (three hours, 30 minutes via Westport) and Ballina in the North (one hour). Dublin Airport is a meandering five-hour ride by bus; rail is a better option. The rail connection to Westport in the West takes 18 minutes, and it is three hours to Dublin Heuston in the East; change at Manulla Junction for the one-hour trip to Ballina.

VISITOR INFORMATION

CONTACTS Castlebar Tourist Information Office. ✉ *Linenhall St., Castlebar* ☎ *094/902–1207* 🌐 *www.mayo-ireland.ie.*

Sights

Ballintubber Abbey

NOTABLE BUILDING | This is the only church in Ireland founded by an Irish king and still in daily use. Ballintubber has greeted its faithful flock since 1216, when Cathal O'Connor built it on the site of St. Patrick's church, which was built some 800 years earlier, a replica of which can be found on the grounds. In the 1960s, the 15th-century cloister was unearthed by excavators in surprisingly good condition, given Cromwell had left his mark on the structure, and it now creates a serene space alongside the abbey. Scan the gardens for Seán na Sagart's (Sean the Priest Hunter's) Tree. He escaped the gallows indebted to local Sheriff Bingham—to be repaid by bringing him one head of a priest yearly. After Sean's death, the story goes, a blossomless tree grew from his grave and splintered in half when it was hit by lightning, creating a fitting epitaph for a black soul. In more recent times, 007 actor Pierce Brosnan's marriage to Keely Shaye Smith occurred in the abbey. ✉ *Castlebar* ✢ *14 km (9 miles) south of Castlebar on N84* ☎ *094/903–0934* 🌐 *www.ballintubber-abbey.ie* 🎟 *Free* ☞ *Abbey: daily, 9 am–midnight. Guided tours available 9:30–5 by arrangement.*

The Linenhall Arts Centre

ARTS CENTER | The town's arts center has a calendar of exhibitions, concerts and performances, a crafts shop, and a handy coffee shop with home baking. It occupies an imposing gray limestone building dating from 1790, when the town had a thriving linen industry. ✉ *Linenhall St., Castlebar* ☎ *094/902–3733* 🌐 *www.thelinenhall.com* 🎟 *Free; event ticket prices vary.*

The Mall

CITY PARK | At the center of Castlebar is the pleasant tree-lined Mall, with some good 18th-century houses. A memorial honors the French soldiers who died during the 1798 uprising when Castlebar was briefly the capital of "the Provisional Republic of Connaught." The Mall was once a cricket pitch belonging to the local landlord, Lord Lucan, and is now a town park. ✉ *Castlebar.*

Museum of Country Life

OTHER MUSEUM | FAMILY | At this highly acclaimed museum, the only branch of the National Museum of Ireland outside Dublin, you're invited to revisit rural life in Ireland between 1860 and 1960—before electrification and in-house running water. Among the displayed items are authentic furniture and utensils; hunting, fishing, and agricultural implements; clothing; and objects relating to games, pastimes, religion, and education.

The museum experience starts in Turlough Park House, built in the High Victorian Gothic style in 1865 and set in pretty lakeside gardens. Just three rooms have been restored to illustrate the way the landowners lived. A sensational modern four-story, curved building houses the main exhibit. Cleverly placed windows afford panoramic views of the surrounding park and the distant Round Tower, allowing you to reflect on the reality beyond the museum's walls. The shop sells museum-branded and handcrafted gift items and a café with indoor and outdoor tables is located in the stable yard, and you can take scenic lakeside walks in the park. ✉ *Museum of Country Life, Turlough Park House, Castlebar* ✢ *7 km (4 miles) south of Castlebar on N5* ☎ *094/903–1755* 🌐 *www.museum.ie/Country-Life* 🎟 *Free* ⏲ *Closed Sun. and Mon.*

Restaurants

Café Rua

$ | **MODERN IRISH** | **FAMILY** | This friendly, boho-chic café with its traditional red shop front (*rua* is Irish for red) is a showcase for fresh, locally produced foods, simply served. There's an imaginative children's menu, and at lunch there are three daily specials—roast meat, fish, and vegetarian—while many opt for the homemade soup and sandwich (served in a traditional soft roll known as a *blaa*), or a salad. **Known for:** fresh, simply prepared dishes; local produce; home baking. *Average main: €10* *New Antrim St., Castlebar* *094/928–6072* *www.caferua.com* *No credit cards* *Closed Sun. No dinner Mon.–Wed.*

Dining Room

$ | **MODERN IRISH** | A modern intimate dining room with rustic brickwork makes a fitting setting for chef Kevin Stirzaker's seasonal menu that offers the best of local produce, simply prepared to let the quality produce speak for itself. Menu highlights include Killary Fjord mussels and duck breast with beetroot and red onion jam. **Known for:** local produce; early-bird special; excellent service. *Average main: €18* *Main St., Castlebar* *094/902–1861* *www.diningroomcastlebar.com* *Closed Mon. and Tues.*

John McHale's Pub

PUBS | This classic Irish pub is one of the oldest in town and the best place for a bit of traditional local banter. It's known as the home of the "meejum" (or medium—a glass that measures somewhere between a half pint and pint) of Guinness and for the high quality of its stout. Open daily from 4 pm til 11:30 pm. *Newline, Chapel St. Lower, Castlebar* *094/902–1849.*

Foxford

As you travel from Turlough northeast to Ballina, you have a choice of two routes. The longer and more scenic is via the tiny, wooded village of Pontoon, skirting the western shore of Lough Conn and passing through the rough bogland of the Glen of Nephin, beneath the dramatic heather-clad slopes of Nephin Mountain (2,653 feet) to Crossmolina and Ballina. The shorter route follows the N5 and N58 to Foxford, a pretty village with several crafts and antiques shops.

GETTING HERE AND AROUND

Take the N5 and N58 from Turlough.

★ **Foxford Woolen Mills**

VISITOR CENTER | This site is just a 20-minute drive from Castlebar through the pretty village of Foxford which has several crafts and antiques shops. Woolen Mills Visitor Centre is a good stop heading north on the N5 where you can explore the crafts shop and grab a bite at the restaurant. Few first-time visitors leave without buying an heirloom-quality Foxford blanket. The *Foxford Experience* tells the story of the wool mill, famous for its tweeds and blankets, from the time of the famine in the mid-19th century—when it was founded by the Sisters of Charity to combat poverty—to the present day. Visitors can take the longer and more scenic route from Castlebar via the tiny, wooded village of Pontoon, skirting the western shore of Lough Conn and passing through the rough bogland of the Glen of Nephin, beneath the dramatic heather-clad slopes of Nephin Mountain to Crossmolina and Ballina. *Lower Main St., Foxford* *094/925–6104* *foxford.com.*

Belmullet

80 km (50 miles) northwest of Westport.

Belmullet's unconventional streetscape skirts its waterfront, and the town harbors a friendly, unpretentious attitude that harks back to an earlier time. Nestled in a quiet, northwest corner of the Irish coast, it's the place to go off-radar from the convoy of rental cars that blast their way along the Wild Atlantic Way, the popular trail that connects Ireland's western seaboard. Belmullet's real lure is its location as the capital and access point to the Mullet (or Erris) Peninsula, a windswept playground crammed with abandoned islands, ocean-carved blowholes, endless miles of beaches, rugged coastal trails, and an enormous skyline that lights up the night when the clouds retreat.

GETTING HERE AND AROUND

A car or hiking boots are the best methods of transport in this area. Bus Éireann bus No. 446 offers a twice-daily service between the larger town of Ballina and Belmullet as far as Blacksod.

TOURS

Geraghty Charters

BOAT TOURS | FAMILY | Geraghty Charters offers sightseeing trips to the deserted Inishkea Islands (Inis Gé) and nearby Achill Island, where you can witness the full scale of the Croaghan Sea Cliffs—the third highest in Europe. The Inishkea Islands have a rich history of tragedy and survival from ancient times to the 19th century—having escaped much of the potato famine due to their blustery location and rich fish harvest. A stormy night wiped out much of the young fishermen population in the 1920s, so they are now virtually deserted. They shimmer in shades of silver and green when the sun shines due to their composition of schist and gneiss, and they are fringed with powder-white sands which gives them almost a magical appearance—similar to neighboring Inishglora Island, which is said to be the final resting place of the mythical Children of Lir. Geraghty Charters also offer private trips and evening angling expeditions. ✉ *Blacksod Harbor, Belmullet* ☎ *086/269–5851* 🌐 *www.geraghtycharters.com* 🎫 *€35 per person (rates vary).*

Sights

Blacksod Lighthouse

LIGHTHOUSE | Few would believe that the modest, sandstone lighthouse on the southeast tip of the Mullet Peninsula could have had a pivotal role in history, but a weather report issued by the lighthouse keeper on June 3, 1944, convinced General Dwight D. Eisenhower to delay the D-Day invasion of Normandy by 24 hours. This delay saved the Allies from a catastrophic fate. Blacksod Lighthouse dates from 1864 and embraces the full brunt of the Atlantic Ocean's extreme weather. ✉ *Blacksod, Erris, Belmullet* ✣ *21 km (13 miles) south of Belmullet on R313* 🌐 *visitblacksodlighthouse.ie* ⏲ *Closed fall–spring. Contact ahead.*

Dún na mBó

NATURE SIGHT | Past the windswept townland of Gladree and seemingly at the very edge of the world is this magnificent blowhole, drilled vertically through solid rock by the elements to create an epic, natural fountain when the weather is wild and waves pound the shoreline below. Encased in wire and accessed through a triangular stone sculpture, the site has spectacular views across to Eagle Island Lighthouse and the Atlantic Ocean. ✉ *Erris Peninsula.*

The Tidal Pool

NATURE SIGHT | FAMILY | Head onto Bellmullet's Shore Road to discover the Tidal Pool, a feat of engineering and imagination from the 1980s that facilitates an ocean swim without the incumbent risk to life that the Atlantic's strong currents usually pose. Two large concrete basins fill and ebb with the ocean's water at high tide—one deep, the other shallow—offering hardy sorts an opportunity to swim or just soak in the waters of Blacksod Bay, depending on the tide, and within the confined space of a 20-meter pool. Of course, the ocean still can be hazardous with waves or sudden storms, so take precautions at all times. ✉ *Shore Rd., Belmullet.*

★ **Wild Nephin Ballycroy National Park**

NATIONAL PARK | Located in the southern territory of the Mullet Peninsula and covering 110 square km (42½ square miles) of Atlantic bogland and mountainous wilderness, Ballycroy is one of only six national parks in Ireland and utopia for the outdoor adventurer. Marked looped trails offer staggering views across Blacksod Bay and the Achill Islands. Once the sun sets, the area becomes a "dark-sky park," where visitors arrive with flashlights to witness the uninterrupted view of the heavens. The park is equipped with a visitor center and café. To camp, contact the park manager. ✉ *Ballycroy Village, Belmullet* ☎ *098/49888* 🌐 *www.ballycroynationalpark.ie* *Free* *Closed Nov.–mid-Mar.*

Erris Coast Hotel

$ | **HOTEL** | Close to the coast on the edge of Ballycroy National Park, this brand-new low-rise hotel has surprisingly luxurious rooms and furnishings despite its modest architecture and location in the cusp of Mayo's wilderness. **Pros:** good value; unexpectedly well-furnished rooms; strategic location for touring Ballycroy Park or the Wild Atlantic Way. **Cons:** architecturally unimpressive; can be weekend weddings; very remote—little else to do in the area or hotel. 💲 *Rooms from: €89* ✉ *Geesala* ✣ *16 Km (10 miles) south of Belmullet* ☎ *097/30010* 🌐 *erriscoasthotel.ie* *31 rooms* *No Meals.*

Talbot Hotel

$ | **HOTEL** | The quirky, modern-boutique-hotel hallmarks and Baroque color scheme are a little at odds with the town's otherwise plain offerings, but the focus on idiosyncratic style here does not in any way divert attention from comfort. **Pros:** town-center location; reliable pub food every night; large suites with spacious bathrooms. **Cons:** street parking; main restaurant closed Monday–Thursday; modern decor may not suit those seeking more traditional Irish country style. 💲 *Rooms from: €100* ✉ *Barrack St., Belmullet* ☎ *097/20484* 🌐 *www.thetalbothotel.ie* *21 rooms* *Free Breakfast.*

McDonnells

PUBS | The perfect antidote to a day hiking the peninsula, this cozy, open-fire pub is known locally as the "lobster pot," because once you're there, there's no getting out. It's the heart of the community where guests linger longer than planned, and where tourists only stand out if they don't join in with the conversation, dancing, or trad music session. Owned by the McDonnell family since 1942, the pub, in true rural Irish fashion, is adjacent to the family's other business—an undertakers—and so it has been the location of an occasional wake. ✉ *Lower Barrack St., Belmullet* ☎ *097/81194.*

Carne Golf Links

GOLF | Overlooking Blacksod Bay, with breathtaking views of Inis Géidhe and Inis Glóire, the final island home to the legendary "Children of Lir," Carne is in the sandy heartland of the peninsula and features in the top 50 courses in both Britain and Ireland. Currently in the process of expanding an extra 9 holes to bring the course to 27, it was the last course designed by Eddie Hackett, and many critics believe that it was his finest design. ✉ *Carne, Belmullet* ✣ *4 km (2½ miles) west of Belmullet on R313* ☎ *97/82292* 🌐 *www.carnegolflinks.com* 🎫 *Nov.–Mar., €60, Apr.–Oct. €130* 🏌 *18 holes, 6706 yards, par 72.*

Cross Loop Walk

HIKING & WALKING | With a dramatic trailhead at Cross Abbey and its hilltop Termoncarragh graveyard that has defied the force of the Atlantic for centuries, this trail weaves it way past sand dunes and the crystal-blue setting of the Iniskea Islands, where the Atlantic air swirls through the eerily deserted houses of an abandoned village. Start your hike at low tide to take advantage of the trail's 2½ km (1½ miles) of strand. Note that the beach has strong undercurrents and is not safe for swimming. A black post leads hikers across sandy dunes, then turns to curve around a lakeshore filled with wild swans. Cast an eye back to the Atlantic coast to see Inishglora (Inis Glóire), the tiny island where the fabled Children of Lir spent the last three centuries of their lives as swans. Stop by Ionad Deirbhile, a nearby visitor center and café in Blacksod, to get your bearings. ✉ *Belmullet* ✣ *Follow R313 west as far as Binghamstown, indicated by small church. Veer right to coastal road. Parking available at trailhead* ☎ *97/85727* 🌐 *www.ionaddeirbhile.ie.*

Killala

64 km (40 miles) northeast of Westport, 64 km (40 miles) east of Belmullet.

When a modest fleet of French military ships landed in this pretty bay-side village to aid the Irish in their quest for freedom back in 1798, Killala would forever mark its place in history as the point of the first failed Irish Rebellion, with countless heartfelt ballads like "Minstrel Boy" or "The Wind that Shakes the Barley" inspired by the bloodshed spilled by the conquerors. Dominating the village's narrow, twisting lanes is an impressive 12th-century limestone Round Tower. The 84-foot-high structure is visible from the surrounding countryside, and it's one of the finest examples of its kind in the country. Killala is also the gateway to Mayo's magnificent northern coast, a dramatic, windswept stretch of cliffs, where the wind howls in from the Atlantic directly from Iceland, the nearest westerly landmass. The cliffs at Downpatrick have spectacular blowholes and have weathered dramatically since Stone Age farmers built Céide Fields, now a unique visitor center showcasing one of the oldest known field systems in the world.

GETTING HERE AND AROUND

A car is the best way to explore this area. There is a commuter bus twice a day from Ballina, Route 445, as far as Ballycastle. Between May and mid-September, there is a private bus service visiting Killala, Ballycastle, and the Céide Fields; get details from Ballina Tourist Information Office.

Sights

Ballycastle

TOWN | Anywhere else in Ireland this tiny one-street village would be unremarkable, but out on this wild windswept coast, its brightly painted houses in the relatively sheltered valley of the Ballinglen River are a welcome sign of normal life and coziness. The Kiosk Cafe gives a warm welcome, while within shouting distance, Ballinglen Arts Foundation puts on art exhibitions between May and September. ✉ *Ballycastle* 🌐 *www.ballinglenartsfoundation.org.*

Céide Fields

RUINS | Buried below North Mayo's wild boglands is the most extensive Stone Age monument on Earth. The Céide Fields' megalithic tombs, dwelling sites, field system, and vast, stone-walled meadows stretch back 6,000 years and were unearthed in the 1930s when a local teacher noticed the stone formation when cutting turf. The visitor center is housed under a glass-and-steel pyramid and has a magnificent 4,300-year-old Scotch pine that looms alongside the staircase, which alone makes the visit worthwhile. Meander along the ancient pathways at leisure, and stop by the viewing platform to see the ocean over a 110-meter-high cliff. Guided tours are also worthwhile; check ahead for times. Admission includes an optional guided walk through an excavated section of the stones; wet-weather gear is provided when necessary. The Céide Fields are on the R314, 5 km (3 miles) west of Ballycastle. *Ballycastle* *096/43325* *heritageireland.ie/places-to-visit/ceide-fields* *€5* *Closed Nov.–Mar.*

Downpatrick Head

BEACH | On a clear day you can see the dramatic sea stack at Downpatrick Head in the distance from the Céide Fields Visitor Centre. It is worth getting closer. Wild Atlantic Way signposts lead you to a gravel car park a short walk across rough grass from the cliffs. Keep a tight hold on your kids: the unfenced cliffs rise 126 feet above the sea, and the wind can be strong. The sea stack, known in Irish as Dun Briste (the Broken Fort) is 262 feet offshore and rises to a height of about 164 feet. The sea has undermined the headland and spouts up to great heights through impressive blowholes, which are fenced off for safety. The sea stack was inhabited until the 14th century when nature rendered it an island. In May and June, the cliffs are covered in sea pinks and nesting seabirds.

Hotels

Mount Falcon Estate

$$$$ | **HOTEL** | **FAMILY** | About 19 km (12 miles) south of Killala and set in a 100-acre estate between Ballina and Foxford, this baronial 1876 cut-stone house is the centerpiece of a family-owned property with 45 luxury self-catering houses, a lake and river fishery, indoor pool, and spa. **Pros:** spacious, restful surroundings; high standard of comfort; excellent restaurants. **Cons:** busy with families during Irish school holiday; rooms in the new wing are a little plain; two-night minimum stay in summer. *Rooms from: €270* *Foxford Rd. (N26), Ballina* *20 mins south of Killala via N26 and R314* *096/74472* *www.mountfalcon.com* *45 rooms* *Free Breakfast.*

Stella Maris Country House Hotel

$$$ | **HOTEL** | Constructed in 1853, this former coast guard station and convent has a stunning waterside location looking across a wide bay to local landmark Downpatrick Head. **Pros:** high standard of comfort; talented owner-chef; unforgettable sea views. **Cons:** 3 km (2 miles) from nearest village; no leisure facilities; visited by some spectacular sea storms. *Rooms from: €175* *Ballycastle* *Drive west through Ballycastle village on R314 and after about 2 km (1¼ miles) look for fingerpost pointing to right* *096/43322* *www.stellamarisireland.com* *Closed mid-Oct.–mid-Apr.* *12 rooms* *Free Breakfast.*

Chapter 11

THE NORTHWEST

Updated by
Alexandra Pereira

Sights ★★★★★ | Restaurants ★★★☆☆ | Hotels ★★★☆☆ | Shopping ★★★☆☆ | Nightlife ★★★☆☆

WELCOME TO THE NORTHWEST

TOP REASONS TO GO

★ **Gaeltacht Country:** Venture to the seaside village of Ard an Rátha to listen to the seductive rhythms of locals conversing in full Irish (Gaelic) flight. Don't worry: everyone has English at the ready for lost visitors.

★ **Follow in the Yeatses' Footsteps:** From Sligo Town's museums, head out to the majestic Ben Bulben peak to seek out places special to the famous brother duo, W.B. Yeats, the great poet, and Jack B. Yeats, one of Ireland's finest 20th-century painters.

★ **Garbo's Castle:** The legendary screen actress was just one of the many notables who enjoyed a stay at Glenveagh Castle.

★ **Hiking the Slieve League Cliffs:** To truly humble yourself before ocean, cliff, and sky, hike these fabled headlands, among the highest sea cliffs in Europe.

★ **Lissadell House:** A magnificently restored ancestral home on the shores of Drumcliff Bay, not far from the grave of W.B. Yeats.

The Northwest region covers the most northerly part of Ireland's Atlantic shore, running from Sligo in the south up to Donegal's remote, windswept peninsulas.

1 **Sligo.** What William Butler Yeats would say about his old haunt Sligo Town—now a busy spot with a college and modern shopping malls—can only be imagined, but it makes a great jumping-off point for exploring Yeats Country.

2 **Lough Gill.** A freshwater lake shared between Sligo and Leitrim and a place of serene beauty.

3 **Lake Isle of Inisfree.** Famed in the poetry of W.B. Yeats, this island is on most visitors' itineraries.

4 **Carrick-on-Shannon.** A bustling town filled with shops and pubs, and a launching place to see the River Shannon.

5 **Rosses Point.** Small village at the entrance to Sligo Harbour, which features in the paintings of Jack B. Yeats.

6 **Drumcliff.** At the foot of Ben Bulben mountain, the church graveyard is a place of pilgrimage as the burial place of W.B. Yeats.

7 **Mullaghmore.** A long-established holiday village with a superb beach and ocean views.

8 **Bundoran.** One of Ireland's most popular seaside resorts, and a favorite haunt of holidaymakers from both sides of the border.

9 **Ballyshannon.** One of Ireland's oldest towns on the banks of the River Erne and a good base for exploration.

10 **Donegal Town.** A vibrant town noted for its historic 15th-century castle and excellent shopping.

11 **Killybegs.** This fishing town is one of Ireland's busiest ports and a regular stop for cruise liners.

12 **Gleann Cholm Cille (Glencolumbkille).** Wild and remote, Glencolumbkille is a serene destination by the ocean.

13 **Ard an Rátha (Ardara).** A laid-back, old-fashioned town noted for its weaving shops and time-burnished pubs.

14 **Letterkenny.** A large modern town with many historic buildings, well-suited for exploring the Wild Atlantic Way.

15 **Glenveagh National Park.** The wildest part of Donegal is home to a fairytale castle and nature trails.

16 **Gartan Lough.** Home to Glebe House and Gallery.

Malin Head
Toraigh (Tory Island)
ROSGUILL PENINSULA
Lough Swilly
FANAD PENINSULA
INISHOWEN PENINSULA
Tory Sound
Sheephaven Bay
Carrigart
R245
Creeslough
Rathmullan
R257
Glenveagh National Park
15
DERRYVEAGH MOUNTAINS
N56
Glenveagh Castle
Ramelton
Arіann Mhor (Aranmore Island)
Glebe House and Gallery
16
R245
N13
Gartan Lough
A2
Derry
THE ROSSES (NA ROSA)
Letterkenny
Pluck
A5
A6
14
DONEGAL
Gweebarra Bay
N14
N13
Loughros More Bay
N56
13
N15
Ard an Rátha (Ardara)
TYRONE
12
A5
Gleann Cholm Cille (Glencolumbkille)
N15
Newtownstewart
10
R263
N56
Slieve League Mountains
Killybegs
Bruckless
Donegal Town
NORTHERN IRELAND
11
Omagh
A505
Donegal Bay
N15
Clanabogan
0 10 mi
0 10 km
9
A5
Ballyshannon
Lower Lough Erne
Dromore
7 Bundoran
Mullaghmore
8
Irvinestown
Lough Melvin
N15
A32
Ben Bulben
Lissadell House
Trory
6
FERMANAGH
Enniskillen
5
Drumcliff
Sligo Bay
Rosses Point
Manorhamilton
A4
Sligo
A4
N16
Culkey
1
Knocknarea
2
Lake Isle of Innisfree
Mackan
Lisnaskea
N59
Lough Gill
3
Upper Lough Erne
Ballysadare
A34
LEITRIM
Derrylin
A509
SLIGO
CAVAN
N17
N4
N54
4
Kilconny
N3
Cloverhill

With its towering cliffs, secluded expanses of golden beaches, and sun-tinted waters, the Northwest is an untamed and wild part of Ireland—shaped, influenced, and tormented by the sea. Wide skies make it the perfect place to appreciate the shape-shifting light, slowly moving cloud formations, and crimson sunsets. As you drive around counties Sligo, Leitrim, and Donegal, you will discover roads curve this way and that, following the course of the indented coastline, a mountain valley, glen, or stream. But the only traffic jam you're likely to encounter will be a herd of heifers, reducing you to cow speed.

A place of nature on a grand scale, the Northwest should be appreciated in a leisurely way. Catch a cloudless evening and you may be enchanted by a night sky display of the aurora borealis, the northern lights; and amid this celestial light show, or even an astonishing star-filled sky, you will find a silence that kindles the imagination.

Like nowhere else, this region influenced the writer William Butler Yeats and his brother Jack Butler Yeats, a painter. Both immortalized this splendidly lush and rugged countryside in their work, and "Yeats Country" still attracts fans. Twenty-first-century Sligo pulses not only in the present but also with the charge of history, for it was the Yeatses' childhood home, the place that, more than any other, gave rise to their particular geniuses—or, as Jack B. put it: "Sligo was my school and the sky above it."

Northwest Ireland is overwhelmingly rural and underpopulated. That's not to say there isn't a bit of action here, with plenty to experience. Sligo Town, with its winding streets and Italian Quarter, is as busy as Galway—an amazing feat for a town of only 19,200.

After you've drunk in the best views in Europe, washed by the Atlantic Ocean at Slieve League, you can pick up unique tweeds in Donegal, look out for golden eagles at fairy-tale Glenveagh Castle, delve into the past at Glencolumbcille Folk Village, or sample burstingly fresh local seafood. Savor the boating town of Carrick-on-Shannon in Leitrim, a place full of architectural delights, or stroll through the county's glens and hillsides—a completely undiscovered part of the country.

MAJOR REGIONS

Donegal Bay. As you drive north to Donegal Town, the glens of the Dartry Mountains (to which Ben Bulben belongs) gloriously roll by to the east. Look across coastal fields for views of the waters of Donegal Bay to the west. In the distant horizon the Donegal hills beckon. This stretch, dotted with numerous prehistoric sites, is among Northwest Ireland's most popular vacation areas. There are a few small and unremarkable seashore resorts, and in some places you may find examples of haphazard and fairly tasteless construction that detracts from the scenery. In between these minor resort developments, wide-open spaces are free of traffic. The most intriguing area lies on the north side of the bay—all that rocky, indented coastline due west of Donegal Town. Here you enter the heart of away-from-it-all: County Donegal.

Northern Donegal. Traveling on northern County Donegal's country roads, you've escaped at last from the world's hurry and hassle. There's almost nothing up here but scenery, and plenty of it: broad, island-studded loughs of deep, dark tranquillity; unkempt, windswept, sheep-grazed grasses on mountain slopes; ribbons of luminous greenery following sparkling streams; and the mellow hues of wide boglands, all under shifting and changing cloudscapes. This trip begins in Letterkenny, the largest town in the county (population 19,300), and makes a beeline to the Irish Xanadu of Henry P. McIlhenny's Glenveagh Castle. Just one word of warning: don't be surprised if you find a sheep standing in the middle of a mountain road looking as though you, rather than it, are in the wrong place.

Sligo and Nearby. Just as James Joyce made Dublin his own through his novels and stories, Sligo and its environs, known locally as Yeats Country, are bound to the work of W.B. Yeats (1865–1939), Ireland's first of four Nobel laureates, and to the work of his brother Jack B. Yeats (1871–1957), one of Ireland's most important 20th-century painters, whose Expressionistic landscapes and portraits are as emotionally fraught as his brother's poems are lyrical and plangent. The brothers intimately knew and eloquently celebrated in their art not only Sligo Town itself, but also the surrounding countryside, with its lakes, farms, woodland, and dramatic mountains that rise up not far from the center of town. On the Sligo-to-Drumcliff route, you will often see glimpses of Ben Bulben mountain, which looms over the western end of the Dartry range. The areas covered here are the most accessible parts of Northwest Ireland, easily reached from Galway.

Planning

Getting Here and Around

AIR

The principal international air-arrival point to Northwest Ireland is Ireland West Airport Knock, 55 km (34 miles) southwest of Sligo Town. City of Derry Airport, a few miles over the border, receives flights from London Stansted, Liverpool, Edinburgh, and Glasgow. City of Derry (also called Eglinton) is a particularly convenient airport for reaching northern County Donegal. Donegal Airport, in Carrickfinn, typically receives flights from Dublin. Ryanair has daily flights to Ireland West Airport Knock from London Stansted and London Gatwick, while Loganair serves City of Derry Airport daily from London.

AIRPORTS City of Derry Airport. ☎ *028/7181–0784* 🌐 *www.cityofderryairport.com.* **Donegal Airport.** ✉ *Carrickfinn, Kincasslagh* ☎ *074/954–8232* 🌐 *www.donegalairport.ie.* **Ireland West Airport Knock.** ✉ *Knock* ☎ *094/936–8100* 🌐 *www.irelandwestairport.com.*

AIRLINES Aer Lingus. ☎ *01/761–7834* 🌐 *www.aerlingus.com.* **British Airways City Express.** ☎ *0344/493–0787* 🌐 *www.britishairways.com.* **Ryanair.** ☎ *0871/246–0000* 🌐 *www.ryanair.com.* **Loganair.** ☎ *0344/800–2855* 🌐 *www.loganair.co.uk.*

AIRPORT TRANSFERS

If you aren't driving, Ireland West Airport Knock becomes less attractive; there are no easy public transport links, except the once-a-day (in season) local bus to Charlestown, 11 km (7 miles) away. You can get taxis—both cars and minibuses—right outside Ireland West Airport Knock. The average rate is around €1.25 per kilometer. If you're not flying into Knock, you may have to phone a taxi company. Phone numbers of taxi companies are available from airport information desks and are also displayed beside pay phones.

BUS

Getting around by bus is easy enough if you plan to visit only the larger towns. Bus Éireann's routes are regular and reliable and there are also several privately run local bus companies, including McGeehan Coaches.

Bus Éireann accepts the Leap Card, which allows discounted fares on some bus services and can be purchased at 🌐 *www.leapcard.ie.* It is advisable to book intercity or expressway tickets online for reduced fares at 🌐 *www.expressway.ie.*

For arrival and departure information with Bus Éireann, log on to 🌐 *www.buseireann.ie.*

CONTACTS Bus Éireann. ☎ *01/836–6111 in Dublin, 071/916–0066 in Sligo, 074/912–1309 in Letterkenny* 🌐 *www.buseireann.ie.* **Bus Feda.** ☎ *074/954–8114* 🌐 *www.feda.ie.* **McGeehan Coaches.** ✉ *Fintown, Donegal Town* ☎ *074/954–6150* 🌐 *www.mcgeehancoaches.com.* **North West Busways.** ☎ *074/938–2116* 🌐 *www.northwestbusways.ie.*

CAR

There is only one way to fully explore the rural Northwest of Ireland and that's by car. Once here, you can always rent a car at Ireland West Airport Knock or Sligo Town. But if coming from Dublin, many opt to rent from one of the bigger companies at the larger airports. If arriving from Northern Ireland, there are rental agencies aplenty in Derry or Belfast, but be sure to tell your agency if you are planning to cross the border.

The roads between the larger towns are fairly well maintained and signposted, but go slightly off the beaten track and conditions can vary from bad to dirt track. As long as you're not in a mad rush, this can add to the delight of your journey. This is rural Ireland, and if the scenery doesn't make this blissfully clear, then the suspension on your rented car certainly will!

In the Irish-speaking areas, signposts are written only in the Irish (Gaelic) language, which can be confusing. Make sure that your map gives both English and Irish place-names.

TRAIN

Sligo Town is the northernmost direct rail link to Dublin. If you want to get to Sligo Town by rail from other provincial towns, you must make some inconvenient connections and take roundabout routes. The rest of the region has no railway service.

CONTACTS Irish Rail. ☎ *01/836–6222, 071/916–9888 for Sligo train station* 🌐 *www.irishrail.ie.*

The Wild Atlantic Way

The Wild Atlantic Way, Ireland's first long-distance driving route, runs from northern Donegal down to West Cork, traversing isolated headlands, inlets, and little-visited peninsulas. The route follows the tortuous twists of roads that hug this indented coastline for more than 2,500 km (1,500 miles), but is arguably at its most dramatic in the Northwest. Donegal, with nearly 30% of all Ireland's sandy beaches, has the lion's share of golden strands. Malinbeg beach or Rossnowlagh are places to get out of the car, listen to the booming breakers, and absorb the tingling fresh air that has crossed 4,828 km (3,000 miles) of sea.

All along the coast "Discovery Points" showcase areas of interest (including bars and restaurants), provide information on heritage and culture, and suggest viewpoints at which to breathe in the dramatic scenery and watch the interplay of light. Secret places to visit along the way are said to be "where the locals go," and generally speaking, local knowledge is the best advice to go on. The driving route, which is well signposted with new information boards pointing you in the right direction, has created a wave of regeneration throughout the area. Information is also available from tourist offices in Sligo, Donegal, and Letterkenny where you can pick up copies of the Fáilte Ireland Visitor Maps, including detailed suggestions for locations along the route. In the Northwest, highlights include the following favorite stopping points:

■ Start your journey at **Malin Head,** the most northerly point of the route and at the headland known as Banba's Crown, named after a mythical queen. Call into the Seaview Tavern where the owner Michael Doherty will direct you to local beauty spots. The spectacular stretch of coastline from **Bunbeg to Carrigart** includes Horn Head where squabbling seabirds converge, while across Sheephaven Bay, the rugged splendor of the Rosguill peninsula is ideal for a short looped walk or bike ride.

■ Famed for its musical connection and walls filled with memorabilia, Leo's Tavern at **Meenaleck** in western Donegal is the home of musicians Enya, Clannad, and Moya Brennan. It is the place to see dancers kick their heels in the air.(facebook.com/leostavern).

■ A narrow strip of Atlantic coastline at **Streedagh Beach** in northern County Sligo provides unique access to rocks encrusted with fossils as well as the site of three Spanish Armada shipwrecks.

■ Fancy a hearty gallop on a young horse along a deserted beach? Then canter along on your own private island that crosses an Atlantic channel to O'Connor's and Dernish Islands at **Grange** near Sligo.

■ One of Ireland's original coastal thatched pubs, the Beach Bar at **Aughris** in County Sligo is the place for a warming bowl of chowder surrounded by 300 years of maritime history. It's a pub where locals will happily spin you a yarn in exchange for a pint.

Hotels

True, it's the farthest-flung corner of Ireland, but thanks to the area's popularity, good bed-and-breakfasts and small hotels are abundant. In the two major towns—Sligo Town and Donegal Town—and the small coastal resorts in between, many traditional provincial hotels have been modernized (albeit not always elegantly). Yet most manage to retain some of the charm that comes with older buildings and personalized service. Away from these areas, your best overnight choice is usually a modest guesthouse that includes bed, breakfast, and an evening meal, though you can also find first-class country-house hotels with that gracious professionalism found elsewhere in Ireland. Consider staying in an Irish-speaking home to get to know some of the area's Gaeltacht population. Glencolumbkille's excellent Oideas Gael cultural center specializes in this; the local tourist information office (TIO) can be helpful in making a booking with an Irish-speaking family. There are also many options for self-catering cottages and houses.

Restaurants

Donegal mountain spring lamb, Glen Bay crab, Donegal Bay oysters and mussels, Lough Swilly wild salmon, Enniscrone lobster, freshly baked scones, crusty homemade brown bread, and Guinness cake are just some of the delicious reasons why you will not go hungry traveling through the Northwest. Sligo Town has established itself as a sort of last stop for food lovers, with a number of tempting shops promoting local produce that are well worth a visit. In recent years the emergence of inexpensive, high-quality cafés offering satisfying grub in smaller towns—including Cooloney's Nook, Strandhill's Shells Café, and Drumshanbo's Jinny's Bakery and Tearoom—has elevated dining even in more rural areas. You're likely to find the finest food at the higher-quality country houses, where chefs elegantly prepare local meat, fish, and produce in a hybrid Irish–French haute cuisine.

RESTAURANT AND HOTEL PRICES

⇨ *Restaurant prices are the average cost of a main course at dinner or, if dinner is not served, at lunch. Hotel prices are the lowest cost of a standard double room in high season. Restaurant and hotel reviews have been shortened. For full information, visit Fodors.com.*

What It Costs in Euros

	$	$$	$$$	$$$$
RESTAURANTS				
	under €19	€19–€24	€25–€32	over €32
HOTELS				
	under €120	€120–€170	€171–€210	over €210

Tours

Bus Éireann

BUS TOURS | Bus Éireann has budget-price, guided, one-day bus tours of the Donegal Highlands and to Glenveagh National Park; they start from Bundoran, Sligo Town, Ballyshannon, and Donegal Town. ☎ *01/836–6111* 🌐 *www.buseireann.ie.*

When to Go

When it rains, it really pours. Forget about the winter months, when inclement weather and a heavy fog swing in from the Atlantic and settle in until spring, masking much of the beautiful scenery. But in all seasons remember to pack a warm and waterproof coat (especially if you're headed to the coast) and bring a good pair of walking shoes. It's not all doom and gloom: the weather can be glorious in the summer months—just don't bet your house on it.

Festivals and Events

Sligo Live Music and Arts Festival

FESTIVALS | If you're visiting in the fall, don't miss the Sligo Live Music and Arts Festival, held at various venues around town with an impressive lineup of performers. Established in 2005, the festival runs during the last week of October, including both weekends, and has links with North America, particularly with WGBH in Boston. It's elbow-room only, as hotels, pubs, and cafés are crammed with scores of Irish and international acts, involving roots, folk, traditional, and country music, as well as comedy. For dates and details of gigs, visit the website, where you can buy tickets. ✉ *Sligo* 🌐 *www.sligolive.ie.*

Yeats Festivals

FESTIVALS | There's no getting away from events linked to the illustrious Yeats family. The Yeats International Summer School, which marked its 60th anniversary in 2019, is a permanent fixture involving readings, lectures, and writing workshops. It runs for 10 days from the end of July. The Yeats Winter School is held over a weekend in January and includes lectures and tours. W.B.'s brother, Jack B., the painter, is now in the limelight, with his work fetching high prices in auction houses. Tread Softly, a mix of theater, music, film, art, and readings, takes place at the same time as the summer school and explores the link between the brothers. June 13 has been designated Yeats Day, when costumed actors take to the streets for poetry readings and a host of other events. ✉ *Sligo* 🌐 *www.yeatssociety.com, www.treadsoftly.ie.*

Planning Your Time

The Northwest is one of Ireland's most compact regions, and beautifully designed so that you can see the best of it with a three- or five-day trip. The best starting place is the gateway town where all the trains deposit you: Sligo, an excellent base thanks to its first-class hotels and facilities.

Try to plan your visit around one of the many festivals held in the Northwest. Each village tends to have its own *féile* (festival) during the summer months, and it's often worth the money and effort to attend. Music festivals abound, from the traditional Irish Sligo Feis Ceoil in mid-April, to the chamber music festival in May and Music in Drumcliff. Bundoran hosts a country-and-western festival in March, and Sea Sessions Surf Music Festival in June. In the far north of Donegal, the Dunfanaghy Jazz & Blues Festival typically takes place in September. Every summer weekend you are guaranteed a bit of *craic* (fun) with lively sessions in most pubs. Sligo Town, Ard an Rátha (Ardara), Ballyshannon, and Letterkenny are all hot spots. There are village festivals dedicated to hill walking, fishing, poetry, art, and food—but with the disruption caused by the COVID-19 pandemic in recent years it is best to check websites or social media in advance.

IF YOU HAVE THREE DAYS

Start your tour with Sligo's walking trail, a signposted trail of the town with a free tourist board booklet to help you identify the important buildings and architectural surprises. Whatever else you do, don't forget to call into Hargadons time-burnished bar—unchanged since 1868—for some fresh mussels and a glass of stout. You can drive or take an organized tour in the afternoon to the Lake Isle of Innisfree, south of Sligo Town. Start early on Day 2 for a short trip out to catch the sea breezes at Strandhill, Rosses Point,

Donegal's Gaeltacht

County Donegal was part of the ancient kingdom of Ulster, not conquered by the English until the 17th century. By the time the British withdrew in the 1920s, they had still not eradicated rural Donegal's Celtic inheritance. It thus shouldn't come as a surprise that it contains Ireland's largest Gaeltacht (Irish-speaking) area. Driving in this part of the country, you may either be frustrated or amused when you come to a cross-roads whose signposts show only the Irish place-names, often so unlike the English versions as to be completely incomprehensible. To make things more confusing, some shop and hotel owners have opted to go with the English, not Irish, variant for their establishment's name. All is not lost, however, as maps generally give both the Irish and English names.

And locals are usually more than happy to help out with directions (in English)—often with a colorful yarn thrown in.

or Mullaghmore, followed by an onward drive north to Donegal. Stop en route at Drumcliff churchyard to pay your respects at W.B. Yeats's grave. West of Drumcliff, just off the Wild Atlantic Way driving route, take a short detour to the restored Lissadell House and gardens; but check the website first to ensure that this historic estate is open again to visitors. Donegal Town, with its Irish tweed stores, is good for a spot of shopping followed by a tour of the 15th-century Donegal Castle. After an hour's drive west over twisting roads and amid glorious mountain scenery via the fishing port of Killybegs, you will come to the "back of the beyonds," aka Glencolumbkille, where you can happily putter around the Folk Village Museum. You can overnight here or drive north to Letterkenny, a modest-size town with decent hotels, cafés, and restaurants. After a morning exploring Letterkenny's streets, you should devote the entire afternoon to Glenveagh: tour the castle and rhododendron-filled gardens, follow one of the short nature trails in search of the golden eagles that are found here, or join a ranger-guided hill walk and take a picnic with you.

Visitor Information

The tourist information office (TIO) in Sligo Town provides a 51-page Sligo Walking Guide, detailing urban, coastal, lake, river, forest, and long-distance walks around Sligo. The TIO also has extensive information on activities and places to stay in Sligo and is the main visitor information center for Northwest Ireland. Open hours are 9–5 for most of the year, but it is advisable to check the website at 🌐 *www.sligotourism.ie*. If you're traveling in County Donegal in the north, try the TIO at Letterkenny, about 1½ km (1 mile) south of town. It's open from June to August, weekdays 9–5. Check more at 🌐 *www.letterkennytidytowns.com/tourist-office.*The office at Bundoran is open all year, weekdays 11–3 and weekends 11:30–4. For more, visit 🌐 *www.discoverbundoran.com.*

Sligo

60 km (37 miles) northeast of Ballina, 138 km (86 miles) northeast of Galway, 209 km (130 miles) northwest of Dublin.

Sligo is the best place to begin a tour of Yeats Country. Squeezed on to a patch of land between Sligo Bay and Lough Gill, the heart of Sligo Town is clustered on the south shore of the River Garavogue, just east of where the river opens into the bay. Thanks to the pedestrian zone along the south shore of the river you can enjoy vistas of the swift-moving river while right in the center of town.

Sligo sits today on the ancient ford of the route between Ulster and Connacht. This strategic location was seized during the invasion of the Anglo-Normans, who built a castle there in 1242, captured in turn by the Irish O'Connells in 1315. The violent campaigns of the 17th century transformed Sligo with an influx of English and Scottish settlers, and in the 1840s the Great Famine saw thousands fleeing starvation on ships to the United States through Sligo port.

The Sligo of the 21st century is as lively and crowded as its considerably larger neighbor to the southwest, Galway, with locals, students from the town's college, and tourists bustling past its historic buildings and along its narrow sidewalks and winding streets.

They certainly enjoy their music in Sligo. Organized by the umbrella group Con Brio, event highlights encompass chamber music in Drumcliff in May, the Baroque Festival of Music at the end of September, the weeklong Sligo Live Music Festival at the end of October, and the annual Choral Festival in November. Informal musical offerings include the Rosses Point Wild Atlantic Sea Shanty Festival held in mid-June. If you want some social lubricant, try traditional music in local pubs such as Hargadons.

GETTING HERE AND AROUND

Sligo has several pay car parks, including Wine Street, Quayside Shopping Centre, and Connaughton Road. Prices are between €1 and €1.20 per hour. In other parts of the town, such as Temple Street (by the cathedral), you pay €3 for the day if you park before 11 am. In the morning, school runs and store deliveries can cause congestion, but the town is mostly free of any serious traffic problems. Sligo is two hours north of Galway on the N17 and three hours' driving time from Dublin on the N4.

Trains are in short supply in the Northwest region, but buses are plentiful. From Sligo Town, buses spider out frequently in all directions, serving rural towns and villages in counties Sligo, Leitrim, and much farther afield. The main service is operated by Bus Éireann, which has 51 departures daily from its McDiarmada Station at Lord Edward Street to many points of the Irish geographical compass. Six daily express services link Sligo with Dublin Airport and Dublin city center's Busáras Station. There are daily services south to Ballina in County Mayo. Galway City is a 2½-hour journey. Main bus corridors north of Sligo run to Bundoran, Donegal Town, Letterkenny, and Derry. There are also four daily services between Sligo and Belfast, a trip that takes about three hours, although you will have to change buses in Enniskillen.

Iarnród Éireann, the Irish Rail company, operates efficient intercity train connections from Sligo to Dublin. However, other towns in County Donegal are not served by trains, nor are other nearby cities in Ireland: even if you're traveling to Galway or Belfast, you must transfer in Dublin first. Eight services run on weekdays to and from Dublin's Connolly Station, taking three hours and five minutes to reach Sligo, with reduced service on weekends.

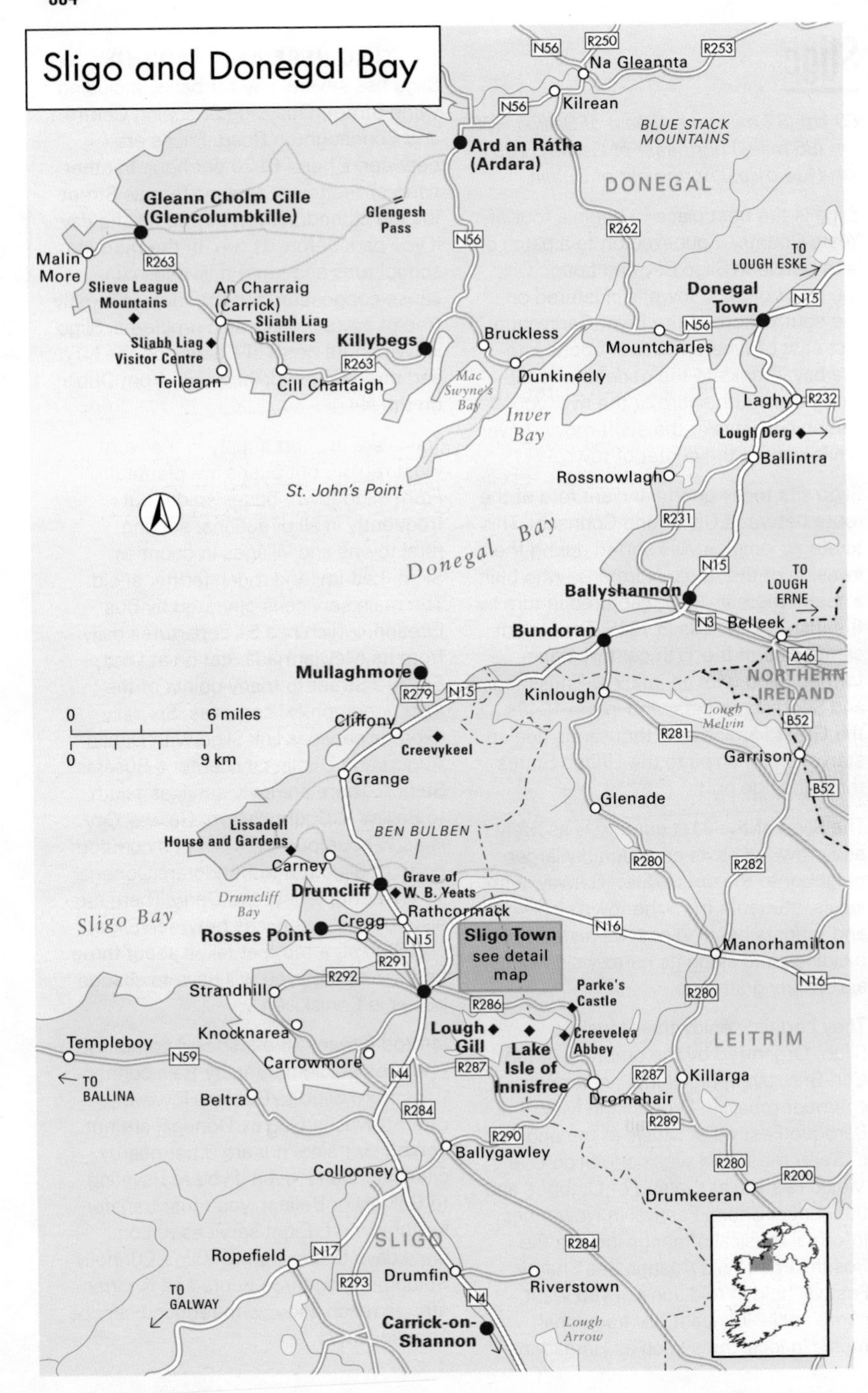

Sligo and Donegal Bay
Na Gleannta
Kilrean
BLUE STACK MOUNTAINS
DONEGAL
Ard an Rátha (Ardara)
Gleann Cholm Cille (Glencolumbkille)
Glengesh Pass
Malin More
Slieve League Mountains
An Charraig (Carrick)
Sliabh Liag Distillers
Sliabh Liag Visitor Centre
Teileann
Cill Chaitaigh
Killybegs
Bruckless
Dunkineely
Mac Swyne's Bay
Inver Bay
Donegal Town
TO LOUGH ESKE
Mountcharles
Laghy
Lough Derg
Ballintra
Rossnowlagh
St. John's Point
Donegal Bay
Ballyshannon
TO LOUGH ERNE
Belleek
Bundoran
NORTHERN IRELAND
Mullaghmore
Kinlough
Lough Melvin
Cliffony
Creevykeel
Garrison
0 6 miles
0 9 km
Grange
Glenade
BEN BULBEN
Lissadell House and Gardens
Carney
Drumcliff
Grave of W. B. Yeats
Drumcliff Bay
Sligo Bay
Rathcormack
Rosses Point
Cregg
Sligo Town see detail map
Manorhamilton
Strandhill
Parke's Castle
Knocknarea
Lough Gill
Lake Isle of Innisfree
Creevelea Abbey
LEITRIM
Templeboy
Carrowmore
Killarga
TO BALLINA
Beltra
Dromahair
Ballygawley
Collooney
Drumkeeran
SLIGO
Ropefield
Drumfin
Riverstown
TO GALWAY
Carrick-on-Shannon
Lough Arrow

■ TIP→ Standard-class round-trip fares are considerably cheaper if booked online.

Sligo's McDiarmada Station is a 10-minute walk to the city center (walk downhill and turn left).

CONTACTS Sligo Railway Station. ✉ *Lord Edward St., Sligo* ☎ *071/916–9888* 🌐 *www.irishrail.ie/en-ie/Station/sligo-macdiarmada.*

TOURS

SLIGO TOURS

In the summer a good way to get your bearings is to join one of the guided walking tours of Sligo that leave from the tourist office on O'Connell Street. From June–September these free two-hour tours (Monday–Saturday 11 am–1 pm, and 2:30 pm in August) are led by a knowledgeable guide and cover cultural history as well as stopping at many architectural highlights. These now also include a Sligo Dark Tales Tour, replete with stories of *Dracula* author Bram Stoker's Sligo connection and stories of crime in the 19th century.

★ Seatrails Walks and Horse Treks

GUIDED TOURS | Auriel Robinson is a maritime archaeologist with a wealth of knowledge about the coastal heritage and history of Sligo. She leads fascinating tours visiting such sites as Carrowmore megalithic cemetery, the majestic landscape surrounding Carrowkeel tombs, and Knocknarea Mountain, where you will hear stories of the fiery Queen Maeve. Other tours, lasting up to two hours, focus on the Spanish Armada shipwrecks at Streedagh Beach in 1588. Bespoke tours from a half day up to two or three days combining a mixture of these walks linking culture and history can also be organized. Check the website for pricing details. ✉ *Sligo* ☎ *087/240–5071* 🌐 *www.seatrails.ie* 🎫 *From €25 per guided tour* ⏲ *Closed for winter season; call in Mar./Apr.*

Sligo Food Trail

SELF-GUIDED TOURS | A wide range of restaurants, cafés, street markets, and bars make up this culinary trail, which extends through both the town and county. One of the highlights is the Oyster Experience, run through WB's Coffee House in Stephen Street, where you can learn the correct way to shuck and eat oysters. Pick up a detailed booklet on the trail at the tourist office and devise your own route, whether it's walking through town, driving, or cycling in the lush countryside. You will find everything from crepes, seafood, and frittatas bursting with flavor to Mammy Johnston's delectable ice-cream parlor at Strandhill. ✉ *Sligo town and county, Sligo* ☎ *185/023–0330* 🌐 *www.sligofoodtrail.ie.*

Taste of Sligo Food Tour

GUIDED TOURS | Led by a Sligonian, Anthony Gray, who helped evolve the food revolution in his native town, this fact-filled and fun gastronomic tour is held Wednesday–Saturday year-round. It leaves at noon and 3 pm from Hooked Restaurant on Rockwood Parade and lasts 2½ hours; advance booking is essential. Bookings can be made for groups of one to seven people, or eight or more. The tour stops off at five to seven venues where fresh local produce such as oysters, desserts, and craft beer is sampled. ✉ *3–4 Rockwood Pde, Sligo* ☎ *071/913–8591* 🌐 *www.hookedsligo.ie* 🎫 *€55.*

WALKING IN COUNTY SLIGO

Sligo's environs, made up of coast, mountains, forest, and lakes, offer some of the best walking anywhere in the Northwest. A detailed website featuring a series of suggested local walks covers everything from the long-distance Sligo Way to the magical and mysterious limestone caves at Keshcorran (25 minutes south of Sligo Town by car) or the Miners' Way & Historical Trail. It includes information on Sligo's flowers and fauna, and what to look out for when you pull

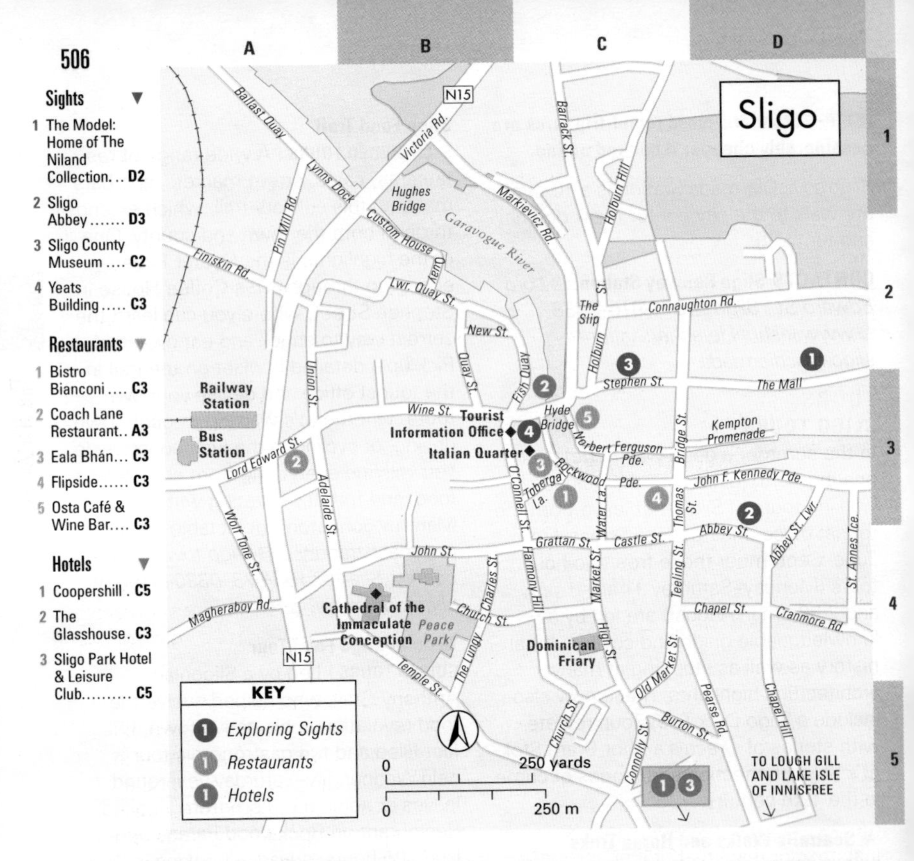

on your walking boots. View a PDF of the color brochure online at *www.sligowalks.ie*.

VISITOR INFORMATION

CONTACTS County Sligo Tourism. *Old Bank Bldg., O'Connell St., Sligo* *071/917–1905* *www.sligotourism.ie.*

Sights

★ The Model: Home of the Niland Collection

GARDEN | The main attraction at the Model, housed in a school built in 1862, is one of Ireland's largest collections of works by 20th-century artists from home and abroad, as well as a stunning new collection of artwork acquired by the gallery in 2018. Periodically, the Model displays works by famed Irish painter Jack B. Yeats, who once said, "I never did a painting without putting a thought of Sligo in it." At the heart of the collection is the work amassed by the woman whose name the gallery now bears, Nora Niland, who was the Sligo librarian from 1945 until the late 1970s, and who recognized the importance of Jack B.'s work. Only a small selection of this work is on display at any time, but you can view the whole collection on the Model's website. Free informal curators' tours are held along with talks by the artist-in-residence. The Model also has a 180-seat cinema with a program run in conjunction with the Sligo Film Society, and a good café. *The Mall, Sligo* *071/914–1405* *www.themodel.ie* *Free* *Closed Mon.*

Sligo Abbey

RUINS | A massive stone complex famed for its medieval tomb sculptures, Sligo Abbey is the town's only existing relic of the Middle Ages. Maurice FitzGerald erected the structure for the Dominicans in 1253. After a fire in 1414, it was extensively rebuilt, only to be destroyed again by Cromwell's Puritans under the command of Sir Frederick Hamilton, in 1642. Today the abbey consists of a ruined nave, aisle, transept, and tower. Some fine stonework remains, especially in the 15th-century cloisters. In the cloister east ambulatory, you'll find a love knot, which is said to represent the bond between earthly and spiritual love. Local custom holds that it is a wishing stone, so be sure to touch it and make a wish as you pass. The visitor center is the base for 30-minute guided tours, which are included with admission. ✉ *Abbey St., Sligo* ☎ *071/914–6406* 🌐 *www.heritageireland.ie* 🎫 *€5* 🕑 *Closed Nov.–Mar.*

Sligo County Museum

OTHER MUSEUM | The showpiece of this museum is its Yeats Room, which houses a collection of W. B. Yeats's writings from 1889 to 1936, various editions of his plays and prose (make an appointment in advance to view these), and the Irish tricolor (flag) that draped his coffin when he was buried at nearby Drumcliff. Letters from his muse, the writer Ethel Manning, and from his brother Jack B. to his mother are on display. Three framed pieces of needlework by his sister Lily Yeats, who was an embroiderer associated with the Celtic Revival, can also be viewed. After Sligo Borough Council was dissolved in 2014, two solid silver maces, which were used to accompany the mayor during public ceremonies, were presented to the museum. Now on display in a glass cabinet, they bear the Irish hallmark for the years 1702–03 and depict the emblems of Ireland (harp), England (rose), Scotland (thistle), and France (fleur-de-lis). ✉ *3 Stephen St., Sligo* ☎ *071/911–1679* 🌐 *www.sligoarts.ie/venuesprofile/sligocountymuseum* 🎫 *Free* 🕑 *Closed Sun. and Mon.*

Yeats Building

HISTORIC SIGHT | The Yeats Society made major updates to its imposing building on Hyde Bridge in 2018, reinventing the displays for a fresh new experience all carried out in time for the 60th-anniversary celebrations the following year. A stylish permanent exhibition, *Yeats and the Western World,* honors the poet, providing an insight into the influence that both the Irish West and North America played in W.B. Yeats's life and work. The poet visited Canada and the United States on five occasions, lunching with President Theodore Roosevelt in Washington and speaking to members of the Press Club, Authors' Club, and the Arts Club. The exhibition also features a mock-up of an Edwardian drawing room, including the desk owned by the Yeatses' sister Lily.

In 2019, the Society was gifted a significant acquisition of a previously unseen color film of Yeats's funeral in Sligo in 1948. Although the poet died in France in January 1939, his remains were repatriated nearly a decade later to their final resting place in Drumcliff churchyard. The amateur footage, filmed by musician Jimmy Garvey, who never published it, was discovered in a box and passed to his nephew who donated it to the Society. The three-minute film shows local dignitaries, clergymen, and members of the Yeats family (including W.B.'s brother Jack) at Drumcliff and is now a permanent and treasured part of the exhibition.

The society appointed Dan Mulhall, Irish ambassador to the United States, as its new honorary president in 2019. He has had a lifelong love of Yeats's poetry and has spoken at the summer school on several occasions. The building remains an active hub for lectures, poetry readings, discussion, and literary events, and is home to the Yeats International Summer School conducted here every August since 1959. On the first floor,

The stunning riverfront Sligo Town is clustered on the south shore of River Garavogue.

a gallery hosts a rotating exhibition of contemporary art. Research scholars can explore the Yeats Reference Library, which has more than 3,000 titles. While the ground floor café is currently shut, the Yeats Building is within walking distance of cafés, pubs, and restaurants. ✉ *Hyde Bridge, Sligo* ☎ *071/914–2693* 🌐 *www.yeatssociety.com* 🎫 *€3* 🕙 *Closed Sun. and Mon.*

Restaurants

★ Bistro Bianconi

$ | **ITALIAN** | In the heart of Sligo's busy Italian Quarter, Bistro Bianconi has built on its long-established reputation for top-class pizzas baked in a wood-burning oven. Inventive gourmet pizzas include the Michelangelo (goat cheese, caramelized onions, pepperoni, and a sprinkling of Parmesan), the Vegetariano, and the perennial favorite, Quatro Formaggi. **Known for:** irresistible pizzas; affordable prices; chicken bocconcini (with glazed ham and cheese). $ *Average main: €12* ✉ *Tobergal La., Sligo* ☎ *071/914–1744.*

★ Coach Lane Restaurant

$$$ | **MODERN IRISH** | This bustling eatery—deservedly one of Sligo's most popular and established since 1994—divides itself into two culinary halves: a relaxed downstairs bar (from 2 pm daily) with red-checkered tablecloths, serving fish pie and steaming bowls of beef-and-Guinness stew; and a more formal (and expensive) upstairs dining room (5:30–9 pm), where lamb, salmon, and steak, including fillet, strip loin, and tomahawk (all the restaurant's beef is air-dried for 45 days), share space on the menu with pasta, trout, scallops, seafood platters, or fine herb gnocchi with wild earth mushrooms. Reservations are required for both bar food and the dining room. **Known for:** fresh fish; monster tomahawk steaks; relaxed bar. $ *Average main: €27* ✉ *1–2 Lord Edward St., opposite bus and train station and across busy main road, Sligo* ☎ *071/916–2417* 🌐 *www.coachlanesligo.com.*

Eala Bhán

$$$ | MODERN IRISH | Preening swans (the name means "White Swan") are visible from the dining room window of this modern, comfortable restaurant, serving Irish food starring local produce. Steak and seafood are prominent on the evening dinner menu, as well as vegetarian dishes. **Known for:** seafood and meats; luxurious riverside dining; afternoon tea. *$ Average main: €29 ✉ Rockwood Parade, Sligo ☎ 071/914–5823 🌐 www.ealabhan.ie.*

Flipside

$ | IRISH | Opened in 2018, Flipside burger joint has quickly become a triumph across Sligo with its "Serious Burgers," served with flamin' fries or garlic butter and Parmesan fries. The modern corner building, heavy with glass, steel, and dark wood tables, hums with happy diners. **Known for:** best burgers in town; local produce and brews; river views. *$ Average main: €13 ✉ Unit 2, Embankment, Rockwood Parade, Sligo ☎ 071/932–6928 🌐 www.flipside.ie ⏲ No lunch weekdays.*

Osta Café & Wine Bar

$ | IRISH | Osta Café's philosophy is straightforward: serve locally sourced food, preferably organic, simply prepared. Come for light bites, lunch, or Sunday brunch; the "30-km breakfast" is named for the proud fact that all ingredients are from within that distance—with the exception of the fair-trade, organic Mexican and Peruvian arabica coffee (ethically sourced). **Known for:** local produce; crowd-pleasing brunches; natural, organic wines. *$ Average main: €10 ✉ Garavogue Weir, Stephen St., Sligo ☎ 071/914–4639 🌐 www.osta.ie.*

Hotels

★ Coopershill

$$$$ | HOTEL | Step beyond the elegant, symmetrical stone facade with its central Palladian window, and wander through an appealing mix of antique bureaus, marble busts, mounted deer heads, and 19th-century paintings that fill the large reception rooms of this three-story Georgian farmhouse. **Pros:** peaceful, luxurious, historied; free papers and mineral water; eco-friendly. **Cons:** rooms can be chilly on cold days; quite a trek to the nearest pub or shops; prices higher than in Sligo. *$ Rooms from: €275 ✉ Off N4, 20 km (12 miles) southeast of Sligo, Riverstown ☎ 071/916–5108 🌐 www.coopershill.com ⏲ Closed Nov.–Mar. 8 rooms Free Breakfast.*

★ The Glasshouse

$ | HOTEL | Cosmopolitan modernists will love this funky, six-story riverside hotel. **Pros:** excellent location—Sligo's bustling heart is around the corner; minigym; stylish restaurant. **Cons:** decor may be too vibrant for some; inconsistent service; charge for car parking. *$ Rooms from: €89 ✉ Swan Point, Sligo ☎ 071/919–4300 🌐 www.theglasshouse.ie 116 rooms Free Breakfast.*

Sligo Park Hotel & Leisure Club

$$$ | HOTEL | A three-year, top-to-bottom renovation of bedrooms and all public areas has been carried out at the Sligo Park, which is ideally located for those touring Yeats Country. **Pros:** fresh rooms with a view; good facilities include a fitness center, swimming pool, and ample parking; evening entertainment. **Cons:** it's a 30-minute walk into town; the dining focus is on pub grub rather than restaurant meals; pricey for the area. *$ Rooms from: €199 ✉ Pearse Rd. off N4, Sligo ☎ 071/919–0400 🌐 www.sligoparkhotel.com 136 rooms Free Breakfast.*

Nightlife

★ Hargadons Bar

PUBS | Part of the social fabric of Sligo since 1868, Hargadons Bar preserves its unique historic character and maintains high standards in a much-loved institution. Wood paneling, cozy snugs (small booths) for private powwows, marble-top counters, and little glass doors on hinges make this place especially conducive to that intangible Irish element, the craic. Check out the walls, covered with historical black-and-white photos as well as fading invoices from the bar's early days. Hearty food at great prices is served at lunchtime (12:30–3:30 pm) and the evening dinner menu (4–9 pm), featuring oysters, mussels, salmon, steak sandwiches, or chicken wings, lists local suppliers. The bar specializes in Irish craft beers with Andersons from Sligo and the White Hag from Ballymote among a wide selection. On Friday night, Irish traditional musicians often hold center stage, followed by a bluegrass group. On Saturday night you may hear country-rock, pop, or folk music. Walk through the bar and in separate premises at the back you will find the well-stocked Hargadons Wine Shop in Johnston Court. ✉ *4–5 O'Connell St., Sligo* ☎ *071/915–3709* 🌐 *www.hargadons.com.*

Performing Arts

THEATER

Hawk's Well Theatre

THEATER | With a jam-packed calendar year-round, Hawk's Well Theatre hosts amateur and professional companies from all over Ireland (and occasionally from Britain) in an eclectic mix of shows. Tickets run free–€50; the box office is currently open limited hours weekdays 10–2 (Thursday 10–5), but should have expanded opening hours postpandemic. ✉ *Temple St., Sligo* ☎ *071/916–1518* 🌐 *www.hawkswell.com.*

Shopping

Sligo Town has Northwest Ireland's most thriving shopping scene, with lots of food-related, crafts, and hand-knits shops. A useful website is 🌐 *www.sligotourism.ie*; leaflets can also be picked up from the tourist office.

The Cat & the Moon

CRAFTS | The Cat & the Moon specializes in eclectic and stylish Irish-made crafts, jewelry, pottery, skin care, and scarves; it's named after the play by W.B. Yeats. Upstairs is the Hamilton Gallery, featuring work by contemporary Irish artists. ✉ *4 Castle St., Sligo* ☎ *071/914–3686* 🌐 *www.thecatandthemoon.ie.*

Cosgrove and Son

FOOD | The upscale deli Cosgrove and Son, now in the fourth generation, sells everything from duck foie gras to carrageen dried seaweed (a local cure for coughs and colds). Stock up here for a picnic with excellent muesli, roast ham, local cheeses, salads, and peanut rayu sauce. ✉ *32 Market St., Sligo* ☎ *071/914–2809* 🌐 *cosgroveandson.ie.*

Lough Gill

1½ km (1 mile) east of Sligo Town.

Lough Gill means "lake of brightness." In fine weather, the beautiful river-fed lough and its surroundings are serenity itself: sunlight on the meadows, lough-side cottages, the gentle sound of water, salmon leaping, a boat sailing by.

GETTING HERE AND AROUND

To get to the lake from Sligo Town, head east on the N16 (signposted to Manorhamilton and Enniskillen) and turn right onto R286 toward Hazelwood Forest. Within minutes you can see gorgeous views of the lake so adored by the young W.B. Yeats.

Sights

Creevelea Abbey

RELIGIOUS BUILDING | Founded by the Franciscans in 1508, Creevelea was the last community to be established before the suppression of the monasteries by England's King Henry VIII, and the abbey now lies in handsome ruins. Like many other

Strandhill Detour

A short 8-km (5-mile) detour west of Sligo Town is Strandhill, a bustling little gem of a village, sitting on the Coolera peninsula and the official wellness capital of Ireland. The skyline is dominated by the bulk of the majestic Knocknarea mountain, and this spot has become seriously fashionable with good reason, including excellent surfing and surfing schools (with a new National Surf Centre planned), great pubs, and local seaweed baths. The Queen Maeve Trail is a two-hour walk leaving from the village which you can undertake yourself or with a guide. Try North West Adventure Tours, which organizes hikes, cycling, rewilding trips, and many other activities (🌐 *www.northwestadventuretours.ie*). Locals will tell you to be sure to take in the tame jet-black crows along the beachfront who follow visitors around, posing for photo ops. The charming Shells Café, on the shorefront, bears all the hallmarks of a Cape Cod café and is a bit of a destination-dining sensation. Above the Strand Bar, the newly opened Stoked restaurant taps into the produce on its doorstep with sharing plates and an array of fish dishes such as crab, vegan sushi, oysters, scallops, squid, and Spanish-style prawns (🌐 *www.stoked-strandhill.ie*). A 10-minute drive from Strandhill Village lies the townland of Carrowmore, which has become famous as one of Ireland's most extensive prehistoric megalithic cemeteries (🌐 *www.carrowmore.com*).

decrepit abbeys, the place still holds religious significance for the locals, who revere it. One curiosity here is the especially large south transept; notice, too, its cloisters, with well-executed carvings on the pillars of St. Francis of Assisi. The abbey is located a 10-minute walk from Dromahair by following a flower-filled path alongside the Bonet River. ✉ *R288, Dromahair* ✣ *On outskirts of Dromahair, 16 km (10 miles) southeast of Sligo.*

Parke's Castle

CASTLE/PALACE | This fortified house was built on the eastern shore of Lough Gill in the 17th century by an English Planter (a Protestant colonist settling on Irish lands confiscated from Catholic owners) who needed the strong fortifications to defend himself against a hostile populace. His relations with the people were made worse by the fact that he obtained his building materials mainly by dismantling a historic fortress on the site that had belonged to the clan leaders, the O'Rourkes of Breifne (once the name of the district). Don't miss the blacksmith's forge, which has been rebuilt, and the nearby tiny circular sweathouse (an early traditional sauna). New steel battlements have replaced wooden ones along the walkways of the Bawn area of the castle, improving visitor access. The entrance fee includes a short video on the castle and local history; guided tours are available on the hour and last 45 minutes. In summer, boat tours of the lough leave from here.

TIP→ For a breathtaking view of the nearby Lough Colgagh, drive west from Parke's Castle keeping the lake on your left. You will find a small car park from where you can drink in the spectacular views. ✉ *R288, Fivemilebourne* ☎ *071/916–4149* 🌐 *heritageireland.ie/places-to-visit/parkes-castle* 🎫 *€5* ⏲ *Closed Oct.–Mar.*

Hotels

Stanford Village Inn
$ | **B&B/INN** | With a 200-year-old pedigree, a recent refresh, and a legacy that spans six generations of the same family, this former mill, a rustic stone-front inn, is one of the few stops for sustenance near Lough Gill. **Pros:** blissful, pastoral location; log fires and slate floors add to the sense of history; traditional music on weekends. **Cons:** limited choice of food; not much activity locally; long way to Sligo's bright lights. *Rooms from: €90* *7 km (5 miles) from Parke's Castle, 19 km (12 miles) from Sligo Town, off R288, Dromahair* *071/916–4140* *www.discoverireland.ie/leitrim/stanford-s-inn* *5 rooms* *Free Breakfast.*

Lake Isle of Innisfree

19 km (12 miles) south of Sligo Town.

In 1888, W.B. Yeats was walking through the West End of London when, seeing in a shop window a ball dancing on a jet of water, he was suddenly overcome with nostalgia for the lakes of his Sligo home. It was the moment—and the feeling—that shaped itself into his most famous poem, "The Lake Isle of Innisfree":

I will arise and go now, and go to Innisfree,

And a small cabin build there, of clay and wattles made:

Nine bean-rows will I have there, a hive for the honey-bee,

And live alone in the bee-loud glade.

And I shall have some peace there, for peace comes dropping slow.

Although there's nothing visually exceptional about Innisfree (pronounced "*in-nish*-free"), the "Lake Isle" is a must-see if you're a W.B. fan. To reach Innisfree from Dromahair, take the R287, the minor road that heads back along the south side of Lough Gill, toward Sligo Town. Turn right at a small crossroads, after 4 or 5 km (2 or 3 miles), where signposts point to Innisfree. A little road leads another couple of miles down to the lakeside, where you can see the island just offshore.

Carrick-on-Shannon

55 km (34 miles) south of Sligo Town.

Carrick-on-Shannon grew up around the river that still plays an important role in the town's confidence. Its original Irish name, Cora Droma Rúisc, means "the stony ford of the ridge in the marsh." Today's prosperous town, with a population of 4,100, takes pride in its past and is full of architectural surprises. In the first decade of the 21st century, many old buildings were given life again, in some cases being turned into cultural or arts centers, offices, or restaurants. Bistro bars, stylish hotels, delis, and boutiques sit cheek by jowl with old-world pubs and family-run shops. In 1613, King James I granted the town a Royal Charter by which it became a Royal Borough with a corporation made up of a provost, burgesses, and commonalty. It had the right to send two members to the Irish Parliament and continued to do so up to the Act of Union in 1800 when the Parliament voted itself out of existence.

GETTING HERE AND AROUND

The main N4 Sligo–Dublin road that skirts Carrick-on-Shannon carries heavy traffic throughout the day, but the town avoids serious congestion. There is ample free parking in the Townspark area, between the Bush and Landmark hotels. An hourly metered charge applies for parking on the main street where a one-way traffic system operates. Sligo is an hour's drive west while Dublin is just about two hours, 20 minutes southeast on the N4.

Six daily Bus Éireann departures leave Carrick-on-Shannon for Dublin (airport and city center); journey time is 2½–3 hours, and the fare is €30.95 round-trip to the city center. Sligo is an hour's bus journey with six departures in each direction Monday–Saturday (five on Sunday) and costs €16.40 one-way. Regular daily services from Carrick also run to Boyle, Longford, Mullingar, and Athlone. There is no bus station in Carrick, so the pickup point is at the waterfront near the Landmark Hotel.

Carrick-on-Shannon is well served by Irish Rail. The town is on the main Dublin–Sligo intercity rail line and eight trains run weekdays with a restricted service on weekends. From Dublin, trains take just over two hours to reach Carrick (€14-€20 round-trip). From Sligo, the journey takes 55 minutes. The small station is on the outskirts of town, so if you're laden with luggage, you'll need a cab for the final leg into town. You can also catch a train from Carrick to neighboring towns such as Ballymote, Collooney, Boyle, Longford, and Mullingar. Fares are cheaper if booked online one week in advance at 🌐 *www.irishrail.ie.*

VISITOR INFORMATION

CONTACTS Fáilte Ireland Tourist Information Office. ✉ *Old Barrel Store, The Quays* ☎ *071/962–0170* 🌐 *www.leitrimtourism.com.*

Sights

Attic Memorial at Carrick Workhouse

CEMETERY | Follow the stylized footprints of a mother and child from St. George's Heritage Centre to the Attic Memorial at Carrick Workhouse to step back into tragic Leitrim. This workhouse opened in 1842 to accommodate hundreds who sought refuge here from the Great Famine. With bare floorboards and whitewashed walls, it looks pretty much as it did in the 1840s. Wexford artist Alanna O'Kelly's multimedia installation, *No colouring can deepen the darkness of truth,* brings a fresh dimension to this thought-provoking place, which also houses a reading room. You can also listen to audio transcripts of witness testimonies from the Famine period. Nearby is a Great Famine Commemoration Graveyard. To arrange a tour, contact the Heritage Centre directly. ✉ *Summerhill* ☎ *071/962–1757* 🌐 *www.leitrimtourism.com* 🎫 *€5.*

Costello Memorial Chapel

RELIGIOUS BUILDING | Ask at the tourist office for a copy of the signposted historical walking-town-trail booklet and accompanying map (€2). A top sight is one of Ireland's tiniest: the Costello Memorial Chapel, built in 1879, is the smallest church in Ireland and a testament to a man's love for his wife. Built by local businessman Edward Costello in memory of Mary Josephine, its tiny dimensions are a mere 16 feet long, 12 feet wide, and 30 feet high. The church is open during daytime hours and admission is free. ✉ *Bridge St.*

Shannon Blueway

TRAIL | **FAMILY** | Developed by Waterways Ireland, the Shannon Blueway—the first recreational trails of its kind in Ireland—runs along the Lough Allen Canal and follows the river from Drumshanbo to Leitrim village and on to Carrick-on-Shannon. Cycle along the 16½ km (10 miles) of leafy trails, kayak on the lake, or walk along the newly opened boardwalk, known locally as the "snake in the lake" for the way it twists along the lakeside for 525 feet. Maps and details of the trails are available at the Sliabh an Iarainn visitor center in Drumshanbo (open seasonally, contact for opening hours). Electric bikes are available from Electric Bike Trails in Leitrim village (🌐 *www.electricbiketrails.ie*). ☎ *086/828–8747, 071/964–1522 for visitor center* 🌐 *www.bluewaysireland.org.*

★ St. George's Heritage & Visitor Centre

OTHER MUSEUM | Restored by a local heritage group, St. George's Heritage & Visitor Centre occupies St. George's (Church of

Ireland), built in 1827. The bright interior houses the Telford Organ (built in 1846), the magnificent altarpiece entitled *The Adoration of the Shepherds* (painted in 1831 by the Swedish artist Carl Gustave Plagemann), and dazzling displays of ecclesiastical silver. But many eyes will be focused on the array of motorized banners choreographed to rise and fall to classical organ music, as they unfurl the names of more than 270 Leitrim men killed during World War I. A central theme is "Twin Traditions," the mingling of Gaelic and Planter cultures entwined for the past 400 years. Next door, the story of Leitrim is told in a lyrical 10-minute film, *Leitrim: Enduring and Enchanting,* in the visitor center. ✉ *St. Mary's Close* ☎ *071/962–1757* 🌐 *www.leitrimtourism.com* 🎫 *€5* ⏲ *Closed weekends Oct.–Apr.*

Restaurants

★ The Cottage Restaurant

$ | ASIAN | A refreshing blend of European and Asian-influenced food with a friendly Leitrim flourish makes this whitewashed restaurant in the tiny village of Jamestown, just 4 km (2½ miles) from Carrick-on-Shannon, an extremely popular evening venue. Situated across from the river, some diners arrive straight from the quayside to sample dishes such as Thai-style beef carpaccio, spiced monkfish with lemongrass, or Tandoori-style quail with plum and onion chutney. **Known for:** Irish twist to Malaysian flavors; chef's spices and sauces; delightful riverside location. 💲 *Average main: €17* ✉ *Jamestown* ☎ *071/962–5933,* 🌐 *www.cottagerestaurant.ie* ⏲ *Closed Mon.–Wed.*

The Oarsman Bar & Restaurant

$$ | IRISH | A Carrick institution, this gastropub is very popular, so advance reservations for dinner are usually needed. Main-course dishes may include glazed pork belly, Hereford beef burger, 12-hour slow-cooked beef daube, or sustainable fish such as ling. **Known for:** mussels; superb range of craft beers; live music. 💲 *Average main: €21* ✉ *Bridge St.* ☎ *071/962–1733* 🌐 *www.theoarsman.com.*

Hotels

Bush Hotel

$ | HOTEL | With roots stretching back to 1794, this historic and convivial hotel enjoys a central location in the heart of Carrick. **Pros:** superb breakfast; relaxing place to appreciate the layers of Irish history; comfortable rooms. **Cons:** room lights slow to warm up but all in all an eco-friendly cause; noisy revelers on main street; not many amenities. 💲 *Rooms from: €119* ✉ *Main St.* ☎ *071/967–1000* 🌐 *www.bushhotel.com* 🛏 *60 rooms* 🍽 *Free Breakfast.*

★ The Landmark Hotel

$ | HOTEL | If you want to watch the River Shannon cast its calming spell as you sip the best cocktails in Leitrim, head to this waterfront landmark where guest rooms are sleek, spacious, spotlessly well-appointed, and most have riverside views. **Pros:** top location; riverside views; resident mixologist. **Cons:** service tested at peak times; traffic noise from busy bypass road; frequent bachelor and bachelorette parties. 💲 *Rooms from: €110* ✉ *The Waterfront* ☎ *071/962–2222* 🌐 *www.thelandmarkhotel.com* 🛏 *49 rooms* 🍽 *Free Breakfast.*

Performing Arts

Dock Arts Centre

ARTS CENTERS | Carrick's impressive Dock Arts Centre is a former courthouse and now a happening place to take in a concert, play, or arts event. Sympathetically restored as Leitrim's first integrated arts center, it houses a chic theater with seating for more than 100 and the Jury Room café-bar. Shows run €12–€25. ✉ *St. George's Terr.* ☎ *071/965–0828* 🌐 *www.thedock.ie.*

Shopping

Leitrim Design House

CRAFTS | In the same building as the Dock Arts Centre you'll find the Leitrim Design House, which promotes modern Irish craftsmanship. It sells bespoke fine art, original prints, jewelry, ceramics, glass, textiles, and natural cosmetics as well as stationery and greetings cards, all helping to conserve the rich cultural identity of Leitrim. ✉ *St. George's Terr.* ☎ *071/965–0550* 🌐 *www.leitrimdesignhouse.ie.*

Market Yard Centre

MARKET | Carrick's architectural gem, the Market Yard Centre is in the heart of the town; known in 1839 as the Shambles, it is now home to a popular weekly farmers' market (Thursday 10–2) where you can buy everything from freshly picked vegetables and French breads to succulent cuts of organic meats. ✉ *Main St.* ☎ *071/965–0816* 🌐 *www.themarket-yardcentre.com.*

Trinity Rare Books

BOOKS | Hidden-away Trinity Rare Books is run by a garrulous Canadian with a depth of knowledge of both the Irish and international book market. Five hundred of the owner's rare books are available here. The shop is also helping revive the vinyl record market and stocks many 1970s and '80s pop classics. More than 1,000 of the shop's records for sale can be viewed on-site. ✉ *Bridge St.* ☎ *071/962–2144* 🌐 *trinityrarebooks.wordpress.com.*

Rosses Point

8 km (5 miles) northwest of Sligo Town.

It's obvious why W.B. and Jack B. Yeats often stayed at Rosses Point during their summer vacations: glorious pink-and-gold summer sunsets over a seemingly endless stretch of sandy beach. Coney Island lies just off Rosses Point. Local lore has it that the captain of the ship *Arathusa* christened Brooklyn's Coney Island after this one, but there's probably more legend than truth to this, as it's widely agreed that New York's Coney Island was named after the Dutch word *konijn* (wild rabbits, which abounded there during the 17th century).

GETTING HERE AND AROUND

Rosses Point is an 8-km (5-mile) drive west of Sligo Town on the R291 around the northern arm of Sligo Harbour. There's a free car park with dramatic views overlooking Drumcliff Bay. Bus Éireann operates a service from Sligo bus station to Rosses Point and drops you off at the Catholic church. The bus serves Rosses Point beach only in July and August.

Activities

GOLF

★ **County Sligo Golf Club**

GOLF | Founded in 1894 on land leased from an uncle of W.B. Yeats, and one of Ireland's grand old venues, the popular County Sligo coastal links course is situated in the heart of Yeats Country at Rosses Point, a seaside village 8 km (5 miles) north of Sligo Town. Ominous Ben Bulben mountain (best viewed from the par-5 3rd hole) dominates the northern views on this infamously windy course, which will test any player's ability to keep the ball low off the tee. In recent years, many improvements have been made which has led to the strategic repositioning of eight bunkers on the championship course. The signature 17th hole—a long par-4 with a steeply uphill green—was extended to make it more player-friendly. Coastal erosion and three separate storms in early 2020 caused damage to the dunes; the Atlantic is edging ever closer to the course, with the 16th green just eight paces from the sea at high tide—a fence to the right of the par-three 16th was washed into the sea and another section close to the 17th has lost in the region of 8 meters. Climate crisis aside, a remarkable feature of the course is the array of wildlife; it teems with flora and fauna, a wonderful distraction for visitors. Big-hitting names in the golfing world, including Sir Nick Faldo, Padraig Harrington, Rory McIlroy, and the 2019 British Open winner Shane Lowry are honorary members. On Saturday, the course is open to members only until noon, after which time visitors may play. ✉ *Rosses Point, Sligo* ☎ *071/917–7134* 🌐 *www.countysligogolfclub.ie* *Apr.–Oct., Sun.–Fri. 18 holes €205, Sat. €220* *18 holes, 7095 yards, par 71.*

Drumcliff

9 km (6 miles) northeast of Rosses Point, 7 km (4½ miles) north of Sligo Town.

W.B. Yeats lies buried with his wife, Georgie, in an unpretentious grave in the cemetery of Drumcliff's simple Protestant church, where his grandfather was rector for many years. W.B. died on the French Riviera in 1939; it took almost a decade for his body to be brought back to the place that more than any other might be called his soul-land. It is easy to see why the majestic Ben Bulben (1,730 feet), with its sawed-off peak (not unlike Yosemite's Half Dome), made such an impression on the poet: the mountain gazes calmly down upon the small church, as it does on all of the surrounding landscape—and at the same time stands as a sentinel facing the mighty Atlantic.

Drumcliff is where St. Columba, a recluse and missionary who established Christian churches and religious communities in Northwest Ireland, is thought to have founded a monastic settlement around AD 574. The monastery that he founded before sailing off to the Scottish isle of Iona flourished for many centuries, but all that is left of it now is a carved High Cross and the base of a Round Tower (across the N15 from the church) dating from around AD 1000, with scenes from the Old and New Testaments, including Adam and Eve with the serpent and Cain slaying Abel.

Hilltop Doings 

The massive flat-dome plateau of Ben Bulben dominates the surrounding bogland. The 1,730-foot climb has superb views, but it is a challenging hike. Remember: it is always windy on top and frequently soggy underfoot. Scientists recently used DNA analysis of the fringed sandworth flower that grows on Ben Bulben to prove that this rare plant survived the last Ice Age, unlike most other plants and animals that colonized the country after the retreat of the ice 15,000 years ago.

GETTING HERE AND AROUND

Follow the main N15 north of Sligo Town, taking the signposts for Donegal, and you will come to Drumcliff. There is ample parking at the church. It's a 15-minute drive from Sligo to Drumcliff. The Sligo–Donegal Town bus stops at Drumcliff and sets down passengers around a five-minute walk to the grave of W.B. Yeats. Journey time is 15 minutes and a round-trip costs €7.30.

Sights

★ Lissadell House and Gardens

GARDEN | Standing beside the Atlantic waters of Drumcliff Bay, on the peninsula that juts out between Donegal and Sligo bays, Lissadell is an austere but classical residence built in the 1830s by Sir Robert Gore-Booth. Lavishly restored to the tune of €9 million, the house, designed by the London architect Francis Goodwin, is regarded as the leading attraction in the Northwest and highlight of the Wild Atlantic Way coastal driving route. Two of its most notable features are a dramatic 65-foot-long gallery, with 24-foot-tall

Doric columns, clerestory windows, and skylights. Lissadell was the ancestral home of the Gore-Booth family, whose members Eva and Constance were close friends of W.B. Yeats. The house became a holiday retreat for the poet, and a copy of his poem "In Memory of Eva Gore-Booth and Con Markievicz" is on display. Constance Gore-Booth, who later became Countess Markievicz, fought in the 1916 Easter Rising in Dublin. She was the first woman to be elected to the House of Commons (although she did not take her seat) and later became the first female member of the Dáil (Irish Parliament). A fascinating exhibition features her paintings and letters. The Yeats Gallery contains first editions, letters, paintings, drawings, and photographs relating to the work of W.B., his brother Jack, father John, and sisters Lily and Lolly. Among the recent acquisitions is a table from Coole Park in County Galway where W.B. dined with Lady Gregory. The "March of a Nation" exhibition features artifacts from the Lissadell Collection from 1798 up to the formation of the Irish Free State in 1922. Dating from 1740, the Alpine Garden, which had been neglected for 60 years, has been restored with thousands of bulbs planted to add to the natural beauty of the woodland walk and the 18th-century ponds. The walled Victorian kitchen garden, created in 1840, now showcases heritage vegetables and fruit similar to those grown in its heyday. A staggering 180 varieties of potatoes—one was first grown here in the 19th century—are lovingly tended, and the garden is a work in progress.

The Tea Rooms serve wholesome fare including Lissadell's own apple and mint jelly, other produce from the kitchen garden, and oysters from their own beds.

Lissadell was closed to visitors during the COVID-19 pandemic, instead hosting a drive-in movie theater on the grounds. Be sure to phone or view the website prior to organizing a visit to check that the house and gardens are open. ✉ *Lissadell, Ballinfull, 8 km (5 miles) north of Sligo Town, Sligo ✣ Take N15 north for 7 km (4 miles), then turn left after Drumcliff and follow road through Carney for 7 km (4 miles). The Lissadell entrance is 3rd road on left after Carney ☎ 085/278–1767 🌐 www.lissadellhouse.com 🎫 €14 includes guided tour of house.*

Coffee and Quick Bites

Pink Clover

$ | **CAFÉ** | The friendly café formerly known as Drumcliff Tea Rooms has resurrected in the same spot, just next to the church and the grave of Yeats. A magenta wall and a portrait of the poet feature alongside sleek and comfy armchairs where you can feast on lemon drizzle or blueberry scones and coffee. **Known for:** exotic-flavored home-fermented kombucha and kefir; pink clover club sandwich; homemade soda bread and pink clover jam. [$] *Average main: €3* ✉ *Drumcliff Church ☞ Check church opening times especially in off-season.*

Mullaghmore

37 km (24 miles) north of Sligo Town.

In July and August, the sleepy fishing village of Mullaghmore becomes congested with tourists. Its main attractions: a 3-km-long (2-mile-long) sandy beach, and the turreted, fairy-tale Classie Bawn—the late Lord Louis Mountbatten's home. (He, his grandson, and a local boy were killed when the IRA blew up his boat in the bay in 1979; the castle is still privately owned and not open to the public.) A short drive along the headland is punctuated by unobstructed views beyond the rocky coastline out over Donegal Bay. When the weather is fair, you can see all the way across to St. John's Point and Drumanoo Head in Donegal.

GETTING HERE AND AROUND

Mullaghmore is a 30-minute drive from Sligo along the N15 main road to Donegal. Look for the turnoff signpost at the village of Cliffony; from there it's a five-minute drive along a narrow country road to reach Mullaghmore. There is a large free car park.

Sights

Creevykeel

RUINS | One of Ireland's best megalithic court-tombs, dating 4–2,500 BC, Creevykeel contains a burial area and an enclosed open-air court. Bronze artifacts found here are now in the National Museum in Dublin. The site (signposted from the N15) lies off the road, just beyond the edge of the village of Cliffony. ✉ *3 km (2 miles) southeast of Mullaghmore off N15, Mullaghmore.*

Hotels

Beach Hotel

$$ | **HOTEL** | If there's a chill in the air, you can warm up at the roaring fires in the restaurant and residents' lounge of this large harborside Victorian hotel. **Pros:** sea views; acclaimed seafood restaurant; packages include excursions with local fishermen. **Cons:** the single beds are pretty tight; extra charge of €10 per night for a sea view room; no elevator. *Rooms from: €165* ✉ *The Harbour, Mullaghmore* ☎ *071/251–2262* 🌐 *www.beachhotelmullaghmore.com* ⏲ *Closed Nov.–Mar.* *28 rooms* *Free Breakfast.*

Bundoran

15 km (9 miles) northeast of Mullaghmore, 35 km (22 miles) northeast of Sligo Town.

Resting on the south coast of County Donegal, Bundoran is one of Ireland's most popular seaside resorts, a favorite haunt of holidaymakers from both sides of the border. Somewhat ambitiously, the tourist board labels Bundoran "Ireland's Capital of Fun." The place has worked hard to sell its big draw, the quality of its surfing waves, and in recent years it has attracted water warriors from Hawaii, South Africa, Brazil, Australia, and Germany—they can't all be wrong about this surf hot spot.

GETTING HERE AND AROUND

The coastal town of Bundoran is on the main N15 Sligo–Donegal route. From April to September, you pay at a meter for hourly parking on the main street. It's €3 to park all day at Waterworld or €2 for parking at the main supermarkets. Over in the west end of town, opposite the Allingham Arms Hotel, parking is free. Driving time south to Sligo is 35 minutes and it's 30 minutes north to Donegal Town.

Bundoran is on a main bus route linking Sligo and Donegal Town. Seven Bus Éireann services come through the town Monday through Saturday year-round with three stops: one at the west end of town on the Sligo Road, one in the center of the town opposite Foam Café, and the other at the east on Finner Road. You can catch an express bus onward from here to Donegal Town for connections to places in the west of the county or north on the N15 to towns up to Derry City. The fare from Bundoran to Letterkenny is €16 one-way, €26 round-trip.

VISITOR INFORMATION

CONTACTS Bundoran Tourist Office. ✉ *Main St., Bundoran* ☎ *071/984–1350* 🌐 *www.discoverbundoran.com.*

Sights

To escape Bundoran's souvenir shops and amusement arcades, head north of the center to the handsome beach at Tullan Strand, washed by giant surfing waves. Between the main beach and Tullan, the Atlantic has sculpted cliff-side rock formations that the locals have christened with whimsical names such as the Fairy Bridges, the Wishing Chair, and the Puffing Hole (which blows wind and water from the waves pounding below). The surf here is regarded as not just the best in Ireland, but on a par with the best in the world. Storms produce huge and highly dangerous swells—perfect surfing conditions for extreme wave chasers.

Bundoran Waterworld

WATER PARK | FAMILY | When the weather closes in, retreat indoors with the kids to Bundoran's Waterworld, with waterslides such as the 65-meter Whizzer, as well as the Tornado, Gravity, and Twister slides, and a pirate ship overlooking a wave pool. In July and August, a café serves hot and cold drinks, sandwiches, snacks, and ice cream.

Next to Waterworld, from March to October adults can visit Bundoran Seaweed Baths, with individual and dual bathing rooms. Individual seaweed baths, including face mask and seaweed serum, are €25 (*www.bundoranseaweedbaths.com*). *The Promenade, Bundoran* *071/984–1172* *www.waterworld-bundoran.com* *€15* *Closed early Sept.–early Apr.*

Holyrood Hotel

$ | HOTEL | With the mountains on one side and the sea on the other, the Holyrood, part of the fabric of Bundoran for more than 60 years, is delightfully hemmed in and conveniently placed along Main Street. **Pros:** central location with sea views; leisure center and spa; free car parking. **Cons:** few frills; can be noisy in summer with families; not much to do in the area unless you're a surfer. *Rooms from: €99* *Main St., Bundoran* *071/984–1232* *www.holyroodhotel.com* *91 rooms* *Free Breakfast.*

Ballyshannon

23 km (15 miles) north of Mullaghmore, 42 km (26 miles) northeast of Sligo Town.

The former garrison town of Ballyshannon rises gently from the banks of the River Erne and has good views of Donegal Bay and the surrounding mountains. Come early August, this quiet village springs to life with a grand fest of traditional music, the Ballyshannon Folk Festival (*086/252–7400* *www.ballyshannonfolkfestival.com*), Ireland's longest-running music gathering. The town is a hodgepodge of shops, arcades, and hotels. Its triangular central area has several bars and places to grab a snack. The town was also the birthplace of the prolific poet William Allingham. Another son of Ballyshannon, the legendary rock guitarist Rory Gallagher, who died in 1995, is also honored with an annual summer musical tribute. More than 10,000 visitors pour into the town to ensure his spirit lives on in the hearts of many fans years after his death. The Rory Gallagher International Tribute Festival (*www.rorygallagherfestival.com*) is held over the June bank holiday week.

GETTING HERE AND AROUND

Ballyshannon is on the main N15 Sligo–Donegal route, about 20 minutes south of Donegal Town. There are several free car parks around the town, but parking on the main street is metered.

Belleek Pottery Ltd.

FACTORY | For generations the name Belleek has been synonymous with much of Ireland's delicate ivory porcelain figurines and woven china baskets (sometimes painted with shamrocks). In 2017, Belleek celebrated its 160th anniversary, producing a limited range of products from each decade since it was established in 1857. The main factories are in Northern Ireland (which is why their prices are

Some of Ireland's most delicate woven porcelain baskets are made by Belleek, just across the border from Ballyshannon in Northern Ireland.

quoted in pounds sterling, not euros) just down the road from Ballyshannon. Watch the introductory film, take the 30-minute tour, stop by for refreshment in the tearoom, or just head to the on-site shop. The factory-museum-store is near the border with Northern Ireland. Company products can also be found in the shops of Donegal and Sligo. ✉ *9 km (6 miles) east of Ballyshannon, 3 Main St.* ☎ *028/6865–8501 in Northern Ireland* 🌐 *www.belleek.com* 🎫 *£5* ⏱ *Closed Sun.; closed Sat. Oct.–Dec.*

Lough Derg

ISLAND | From Whitsunday to the Feast of the Assumption (June to mid-August), tens of thousands beat a path to the shores of Lough Derg, ringed by heather-clad slopes. In the center of the lake, Station Island—known as St. Patrick's Purgatory (the saint is said to have fasted here for 40 days and nights)—is one of Ireland's most popular pilgrimage sites and a haven for those seeking spiritual renewal. It's also the most rigorous and austere of such sites in the country. Pilgrims stay on the island for three days with restricted sleeping, and ingest only black tea and dry toast. They pay €75 to walk barefoot around the island, on its flinty stones, and pray at a succession of shrines. Nonpilgrims may not visit the island from June to mid-August. Outside this period you can also visit the island for a "Quiet Day" trip (9:30 am–4:30 pm) that costs €45 including the boat journey and lunch. In the Basilica of St. Patrick's Purgatory look out for the astonishing work of the Irish stained-glass artist Harry Clarke, whose 14 windows feature the apostles, St. Paul, and the Virgin Mary. To find out how to become a pilgrim, phone or visit the website for more details. To reach the shores of Lough Derg, turn off the main N15 Sligo–Donegal road in the village of Laghy on to the minor R232 Pettigo road, which hauls itself over the Black Gap and descends sharply into the border village of Pettigo, about 21 km (13 miles) from the N15. From here, take the Lough Derg access road for 8 km

Traditional Irish Crafts

While the entire country is blooming with craftsworkers, the Northwest region offers some quality shopping, thanks to hand-knit Aran sweaters, fine Parian china, and handwoven tweeds. Those who want to make browsing—and buying—easy will find the famous multidealer town cooperatives (such as Midleton's Courtyard Crafts or Doolin's Celtic Waves) tempting. But, in general, the more interesting craftspeople are found outside the main cities, and intrepid consumers should head for smaller towns where overheads are lower (and the scenery is better). Don't buy the first blackthorn walking stick you see. Take a good look around and visit any number of crafts shops—you'll probably end up with a bogwood paperweight and basketweave china tureen as well!

Belleek China

China has been made in Belleek, a village just on the border with County Fermanagh, Northern Ireland, since 1857. This local product is a lustrous fine-bone china with a delicate green or yellow-on-white design and often incorporates weave-effect pottery. Americans love it. Old Belleek is an expensive collector's item, but modern Belleek is more reasonably priced and very likely to appreciate in value over the years (according to some experts).

Claddagh Rings

Born in the Claddagh area of Galway during the 17th century, the claddagh ring incorporates three symbols: a heart (for love), a pair of hands (for friendship), and a crown (for loyalty). Worn on the right hand, with crown and heart facing out, it symbolizes the wearer is still "free"; worn on the left, with symbols tucked under, indicates marriage.

Irish Lace

Traditional Irish crochet and lace-making use a fine cotton and date back to 1820 when they originated in the cottage homes and lace schools of Carrickmacross.

Spongeware Pottery

One of Ireland's most beautiful collectibles, Irish spongeware first appeared in 18th-century potteries. With the use of a cut sponge, patterns, and images—often "rural" in flavor, like plants and sheep—are applied to the lovely cream-color surface.

Waterford Crystal

Founded in 1783, Waterford crystal is noted for its sparkle, clarity, and heft. Thicker glass means that each piece can be wedge-cut on a diamond wheel to dramatic effect (as you can see during the famous factory tour held at the Waterford factory in Southeast Ireland). Waterford artisans apprentice for eight years.

(5 miles). During pilgrim season, buses connect to Pettigo, but it is best to phone or check the website before the new season starts in May, as details can vary from year to year. ✉ *Pettigoe* ☎ *071/986–1518* 🌐 *www.loughderg.org.*

Nightlife

Dicey Reilly's

BREWPUBS | "Dicey's," as the locals call it, has been selling beer in a variety of forms since 1856. Also noted for its selection of quality wines from around the world, the company has branched into handcrafted beers and opened a microbrewery beside the bar. It's no surprise that Donegal Blonde, with the merest hints of biscuit and malt, and a fine balance of hop flavors, is one of its most popular beers. Other favorites are the Donegal Brewing Amber ale with fruity hops and the West Coast Pale Ale. If these aren't to your liking, there are a staggering 350 craft beers and 600 wines from which to choose. Food is served in the bar at lunchtime and in the early evenings or you could try the pop-up burger bar in the beer garden which operates on weekends from March to December. Glass cabinets hold a veritable social and cultural history of Ballyshannon, with old bus timetables and drama and music festival programs from the 1960s, while tins of Old Holborn Blended Virginia, Campbell's Tea, and Grate Polish sit side by side on shelves. Guided tours of the brewery lasting 40 minutes are held by appointment. ✉ *Market St., Ballyshannon* ☎ *071/985–1371* 🌐 *www.diceys.com.*

Seán Óg's

PUBS | One of the largest and most popular pubs in Ballyshannon, Seán Óg's, has a DJ playing hits on Saturday evenings. On occasion, Irish traditional musicians come out to perform at this local pub. ✉ *6 Castle St., Ballyshannon* ☎ *071/985–8964.*

Donegal Town

21 km (13 miles) north of Ballyshannon, 66 km (41 miles) northeast of Sligo Town.

With a population of about 2,600, Donegal is the fourth-largest town in the county—marking the entry into the back-of-the-beyond of the wilds of County Donegal. The town is centered on the triangular Diamond, where three roads converge (N56 to the west, N15 to the south and the northeast) and the mouth of the River Eske pours gently into Donegal Bay. You should have your bearings in five minutes, and seeing the historical sights takes less than an hour; if you stick around any longer, it'll probably be to do some shopping—arguably Donegal Town's top attraction.

The town of Donegal was previously known in Irish as Dún na nGall, or "fort of the foreigners." The foreigners were Vikings, who set up camp here in the 9th century to facilitate their pillaging and looting. Later Donegal became dominated by the powerful O'Donnell clan (originally Cinel Conail), who made it the capital of Tyrconnell, their extensive Ulster territories. Donegal was rebuilt in the early 17th century, during the Plantation period, when Protestant colonists were planted on Irish property confiscated from its Catholic owners.

The Diamond, like that of many other Irish villages, dates from this period. Once a marketplace, it has a 20-foot-tall obelisk monument (1937), which honors the town monks who, before being

A Taste of Donegal

If you happen to be in town over the last weekend in August, you will inevitably come across the huge food festival, Taste of Donegal. Chefs flaunt their skills in cooking demonstrations and host master classes in beer and cocktail making, while more than 120 exhibitors showcase their products. Music and street entertainment is guaranteed, and the weekend ends in a thrilling fireworks display over Donegal Bay. Suspended during the COVID-19 pandemic, the festiva (at time of print) went ahead in 2023. 🌐 ***www.atasteofdonegal.com***

driven out by the English in the 17th century, took the time to copy down a series of old Irish legends in what they called *The Annals of the Four Masters.*

GETTING HERE AND AROUND

Donegal is a 60-minute drive from Sligo north along the N15. The main pay car park is at the quay beside the tourist information office on the approach road from the south. Catch the wrong day in the height of summer and Donegal Town is a bottleneck. Fortunately, that doesn't occur very often—the reason may be a local wedding, a festival, a funeral, or a Gaelic football match. The main delays focus on the one-way system operating around the Diamond. Try to avoid this area around 5 pm.

Public transport throughout Donegal is limited to buses. Bus Éireann operates direct daily services from Donegal Town to Dublin Airport and the city center, which also stop in the nearby towns of Ballyshannon and Belleek. It runs regular services between the bigger towns linking Donegal Town with Bundoran, Letterkenny, and west to Killybegs, Glencolumbkille, Glenties, and Dungloe. There is no bus station, but buses stop outside the Abbey Hotel in the Diamond. A raft of smaller independently run buses crisscrosses Donegal's roads—including McGeehan Coaches, Patrick Gallagher Coaches, Feda O'Donnell Coaches, John McGinley Coach Travel, and Donegal Coaches—and these companies pick up and drop off in Quay Street.

VISITOR INFORMATION

CONTACTS Tourist Information Centre, Donegal Town. ✉ *The Quay, Donegal Town* ☎ *01/605–7700* 🌐 *www.govisitdonegal.com.*

Sights

Donegal Castle

CASTLE/PALACE | Donegal Castle was built by clan leader Hugh O'Donnell in the 1470s. More than a century later, this structure was the home of his descendant, Hugh Roe O'Donnell, who faced the might of the invading English and was the last clan chief of Tyrconnell. In 1602, he died on a trip to Spain while trying to rally reinforcements from his allies. Its new English owner, Sir Basil Brooke, modified the little castle after taking over in the 1610s, fitting Jacobean towers and turrets to the main fort and adding a Jacobean mansion (which is now a ruin). Inside, you can peer into the garderobe (the restroom) and the storeroom, and survey a great banquet hall with an exceptional vaulted wood-beam roof. Also of note is the gargantuan sandstone fireplace nicely wrought with minute details. Mind your head on the low doorways and be careful on the narrow trip stairwell. The small, enclosed grounds are pleasant. Guided tours are available, but not at set times. ✉ *Tirchonaill St., near north corner of Diamond, Donegal Town* ☎ *074/972–2405* 🌐 *www.heritageireland.ie* 🎫 *€5* ⏲ *Closed Tues. and Wed. Oct.–Mar.*

Franciscan Abbey

RELIGIOUS BUILDING | The ruins of the Franciscan Abbey, founded in 1474 by Hugh O'Donnell, are a five-minute walk south of town at a spectacular site perched at the end of the quay above the Eske River, where it begins to open up into Donegal Bay. The complex was plundered by the English in 1588, and much of the abbey was destroyed in a gunpowder explosion during the siege of 1601; the ruins include the choir, south transept, and two sides of the cloisters, between which lie hundreds of graves dating to the 18th century. The abbey was probably where *The Annals of the Four Masters,* which chronicles the whole of Celtic history and mythology of Ireland from earliest times up to the year 1616, was written from 1632 to 1636. The Four Masters were monks who believed (correctly, as it turned out) that Celtic culture was doomed by the English conquest, and they wanted to preserve as much of it as they could. At the National Library in Dublin, you can see copies of the monks' work; the original is kept under lock and key. ✉ *Off N15, at end of quay, Donegal Town* 🎟 *Free.*

Restaurants

Blueberry Tea Room and Restaurant

$ | CAFÉ | Proprietors Brian and Ruperta Gallagher serve breakfast, lunch, afternoon tea, and a light early evening meal—always using homegrown herbs in this congenial but unassuming tearoom. Daily specials—Irish lamb stew, pasta dishes, and turkey or corn-fed chicken—are served from 9 am to 7 pm. **Known for:** pasta specials; fresh sandwiches; chocolate steam pudding. *$ Average main: €12* ✉ *Castle St., Donegal Town* ☎ *074/972–2933* 🌐 *theblueberrytearooms.ie* 🕓 *Closed Sun.*

Quay West

$$ | IRISH | Take a seat upstairs overlooking the serene waters of Donegal Bay and feast on some of the area's best produce. The menu is vast and plentiful, where you'll find steak, chicken, Guinness-braised shank of Donegal mountain lamb, or fisherman's pie made up of a robust combination of cod, hake, shellfish, and smokies (smoked haddock) straight from the boats. **Known for:** local fresh fish; Donegal mountain lamb; pier-side views. *$ Average main: €19* ✉ *Quay St., Donegal Town* ☎ *074/972–1590* 🌐 *www.quaywestdonegal.ie* 🕓 *Closed Mon. and Tues. Oct.–Mar.*

Hotels

★ **The Central Hotel**

$$$ | HOTEL | With its bright white shutters and boldly red facade, this family-run pretty-as-an-Irish-picture inn sits smack on Donegal's central square, the Diamond. **Pros:** convenient location; views of Donegal Bay and the River Eske; suites with spacious lounge areas. **Cons:** no frills; relentless surge of taxis and motorbikes circling the Diamond; street-facing rooms can be noisy. *$ Rooms from: €174* ✉ *The Diamond, Donegal Town* ☎ *074/972–1027* 🌐 *www.centralhoteldonegal.com* *117 rooms* *Free Breakfast.*

★ **Harvey's Point Country Hotel**

$$$$ | HOTEL | Set in a remote and breathtaking location in landscaped gardens on the shores of Lough Eske at the foot of the Blue Stack Mountains, Harvey's Point has, since 1989, been a spirit-lifting escape. **Pros:** timeless grandeur; peaceful surroundings; Sunday lunch buffet. **Cons:** older rooms lack the opulence of new ones; long walk to ATM; books up quickly in summer. *$ Rooms from: €270* ✉ *6 km (4 miles) northwest of Donegal Town, off N15, Lough Eske* ☎ *074/972–2208* 🌐 *www.harveyspoint.com* *64 rooms* *Free Breakfast.*

★ **Lough Eske Castle**

$$$$ | HOTEL | Most guests gasp as they come down the sweeping drive through ancient woodland and arrive at this magnificent Tudor-style baronial castle—complete with tower and crenellations and a suitably regal backdrop of Lough Eske and the Blue Stack Mountains. **Pros:** stunning location; gracefully furnished bedrooms; despite size, still feels intimate. **Cons:** lines form at busy breakfast times; limited choice on the dinner menu; pricey afternoon tea. *$ Rooms from: €215* ✉ *6 km (4 miles) north of Donegal Town, Lough Eske* ☎ *074/972–5100* 🌐 *www.lougheskecastlehotel.com* *97 rooms* *Free Breakfast.*

Nightlife

The Abbey Hotel

LIVE MUSIC | Visit for music every night in July and August and live bands every Saturday night throughout the year, mostly Irish traditional, but not always. Also a decent hotel. ✉ *The Diamond, Donegal Town* ☎ *074/972–1014* 🌐 *www.abbeyhoteldonegal.com.*

Shopping

Long the principal marketplace for the region's wool products, Donegal Town has several smaller shops with local hand weaving, knits, and crafts.

Donegal Craft Village

CRAFTS | Explore this small cluster of workshops where you can buy hand-woven goods, jewelry, and glass from young, local craftspeople. You can even watch the items being made Monday to Saturday 10–5. The Aroma Café in the Craft Village is a top-class spot for home-made cakes and breads, and also serves dishes with a Mexican twist. The Village is closed on Sunday in the spring and summer and during the winter months it closes on Sunday and Monday. ✉ *R267, 2 km (1 mile) south of town, Donegal Town* ☎ *074/972–5928* 🌐 *www.donegalcraftvillage.com.*

Four Masters Bookshop

BOOKS | For the best selection of local history books on Donegal and Ireland in general, Ordnance Survey maps, and travel guides, as well as music and Celtic jewelry, the Four Masters Bookshop is a great place to browse. ✉ *The Diamond, Donegal Town* ☎ *074/972–1526.*

Magee's

CRAFTS | The main hand-weaving store in town, trading for more than 150 years, Magee's carries renowned private-label tweeds for both men and women (jackets, hats, scarves, suits, and more), as well as pottery, linen, crystal, and Irish-made jams, preserves, and chocolates. An upstairs café, the Weaver's Loft, serves hot food at lunchtime as well as snacks, teas, and coffees. ✉ *The Diamond, Donegal Town* ☎ *074/972–4811* 🌐 *www.magee1866.com.*

Simple Simon's

FOOD | The only health-food shop hereabouts, Simple Simon's sells whole food, essential oils, and other whole-earth items, as well as breads and cakes from the kitchen on the premises. A small café serves herbal teas and coffee. ✉ *The Diamond, Donegal Town* ☎ *074/972–3690* 🌐 *www.simplesimons.ie.*

En Route

As you travel west on N56, which runs slightly inland from a magnificent shoreline of rocky inlets with great sea views, it's worthwhile to turn off the road from time to time to catch a better view of the coast. About 6 km (4 miles) out of Donegal Town, N56 skirts Mountcharles, a bleak hillside village that looks back across the bay. And while you're there, stop for a cup of tea in the delightfully quaint Olde Village Tea Room in Lower Main Street.

Activities

GOLF

Donegal Golf Club

GOLF | Highly rated by both local and visiting golfers, this course, on the Murvagh peninsula on the shores of Donegal Bay, is approached through a forest. The windswept links are shadowed by the Blue Stack Mountains, with the Atlantic as a dramatic backdrop. The greens are large, but the rough is deep and penal, and there's a constant battle against erosion by the sea. The par-3 5th, fittingly called the "Valley of Tears," begins a run of four of the course's biggest challenges, which could have you discreetly hiding your scorecard by the time you reach the 18th. Between 2016 and 2019, the course was enhanced with extra bunkers added at the 16th while the 17th was extended by more than 150 meters, along with several other small changes. Keep an eye out for rare flora on the course including pyramidal orchids as wells as bog pimpernel and dog violet. ✉ *Murvagh, Laghy* ☎ *074/973–4054* 🌐 *www.*

donegalgolfclub.ie 🎫 *May–Sept. €170; Apr. and Oct. €120; Nov.–Mar. €50* 🏌 *18 holes, 7400 yards, par 73.*

Killybegs

28 km (17 miles) west of Donegal Town.

Trawlers from Spain, Portugal, and Norway are moored in the harbor at Killybegs, one of Ireland's busiest fishing ports. Though it's one of the most industrialized places along this coast, it's not without some charm thanks to its waterfront location. Killybegs once served as a center for the manufacture of Donegal hand-tufted carpets, examples of which are in the White House and the Vatican.

GETTING HERE AND AROUND

Killybegs is a 30-minute drive west of Donegal Town along the N56. It's a busy fishing and tourist port in the summer months, but there are plenty of parking spaces at the harbor front or along the side roads off the main street, which is a one-way system. Regular daily bus connections link Killybegs with Donegal Town or north to Ardara. Services west to Glencolumbkille along the narrow and twisty R263 are much less frequent.

Sights

Sliabh Liag Distillers

DISTILLERY | The Sliabh Liag Distillers (pronounced "Slieve league") began producing rich, smoky, and peaty whiskeys in 2014, tapping into a renaissance of interest in a long-forgotten Donegal heritage. Illicit distilling of *poitín* (pronounced "potcheen") in this area goes back hundreds of years; its capital was in nearby Glen Lough. More than 170 years after the last official production in the county, the company now produces the Silkie, a smooth whiskey said to have a gentle butteriness and flavor inspired by the folktales of the Donegal Gaeltacht's legendary shape-shifters, called "selkies." It also produces An Dúlamán, a maritime gin made from carrageen moss and dulse harvested from the sea. ✉ *Ardara* ☎ *074/973–9875* 🌐 *www.sliabhliagdistillers.com* 🎫 *€15 without tasting, €25 with.*

Sliabh Liag Visitor Centre

MOUNTAIN | As part of the drive to attract more visitors to sample this spectacular section of the Wild Atlantic Way, a €5 million visitor center opened just 3 km (2 miles) from the cliffs at Sliabh Liag (Slieve League in the English spelling) in 2019. Roads were also improved and a new 2½-km (1½-mile) stretch of upland path was put in place to allow walkers better access. Large stones for the path were taken from the scree slopes on the hillside and dropped into place by airlifts. Interpretative panels in the center called "On the Edge" reflect the area's folklore, spotlighting its rich tapestry of flora, fauna, archaeology, and geology. There are maps of the routes, safety advice, a café, and tourist information point. After your strenuous uphill trek you will have earned a visit to the Rusty Mackerel bar in nearby Teelin where you can enjoy hearty food and drink, including locally caught fish, craft beers, and Silkie Irish whiskey beside the warmth of a glowing turf fire. ✉ *Teelin, Bunglas Rd., Teelin* ✣ *20 km (12 miles) from Killybegs and 3 km (2 miles) from Carrick village. Turn right at Rusty Mackerel bar* ☎ *074/973–9620* 🌐 *www.sliabhliag.com.*

★ **Slieve League Mountains**

MOUNTAIN | The dramatic Slieve League cliffs and mountains have become the starting point for the Irish leg of the International Applachian Trail, an extension to the original route stretching from Georgia to Maine and then on to Newfoundland. And what more spectacular setting could you have for such a renowned trail linking two pieces of land separated by thousands of kilometers of ocean?

Make no mistake, the landscape hereabouts is awe-inspiring. The narrows and

To make the Slieve League mountains—Ireland's highest—more accessible, a viewing station allows access to one of Europe's grandest sea vistas.

twists of the R263 afford terrific views of Donegal Bay before descending into pretty Cill Chartaigh (Kilcar), a traditional center of tweed making. Signposted by its Irish name, the next village, An Charraig (Carrick), clings to the foot of the Slieve League Mountains, whose color-streaked ocean cliffs are, at 2,000 feet, among the highest in Ireland. Slieve League (Sliabh Liag in Irish) is a ragged, razor-back rise bordered by the River Glen. To see the cliffs, follow the little road to the Irish-speaking village of Teileann, 1½ km (1 mile) south from Carrick. Then take the narrow lane (signposted "Bunglass Cliffs") and park your car at the newly opened Sliabh Liag Visitor Centre where you will find route details and safety advice. The mountain looks deceptively easy from the back (the inaccessible point borders the Atlantic), but once the fog rolls in, the footing can be perilous. A viewing point over the sea cliffs ensures visitors can appreciate one of the finest panoramas in Europe in safety. The designation of the Slieve League Cliffs as one of the leading Signature Discovery Points on the Wild Atlantic Way means you may have to share the stunning views.

If you've a mind for a hike, then follow the Appalachian Trail through County Donegal, head eastward along the Bluestacks Way, cross the Irish border on to the Ulster Way and end up on the Causeway Coast Way, finishing your trek at Ballycastle in the far north of County Antrim. Now, that's a walk that'll require a certain amount of advance training—never mind a little stamina and some planning. And, if you feel like an even grander challenge, then Scotland—just a few miles across the sea—has also signed up for the trail. ✉ *Teelin* ✣ *20 km (12½ miles) from Killybegs.*

Restaurants

Ahoy Café

$ | **IRISH** | Catch a sunny day and it's hard to beat an outside table at this small family-run whitewashed café on the waterfront overlooking the busy harbor. The breakfast menu runs until midday while lunchtime sandwiches with soup and salad are served all afternoon. **Known for:** nourishing soups; local mussels; scenic setting. *Average main: €13 ✉ Shore Rd., Killybegs ✣ Across road from harbor ☎ 074/913–1952 🌐 www.instagram.com/ahoycafekillybegs.*

Mellys Café

$ | **IRISH** | With more than 65 years in business—it opened in 1956 and you get the impression that very little has changed since then—Mellys is a family-run Killybegs institution with a focus on consistently superb fish. Haddock, plaice, hake, and calamari are all staples served with generous portions of tasty chips (fries). **Known for:** simple, well-done seafood; local banter; enduring warmth. *Average main: €12 ✉ Main St., Killybegs ☎ 074/973–1093 🌐 www.instagram.com/mellyscafekillybegs.*

★ Bay View Hotel

$ | **HOTEL** | One of Ireland's most historic hotels, Bay View is well placed for seeing Donegal Bay and the nearby Slieve League Cliffs; its shiny guest rooms and lively bar and restaurant are all part of the scenic package. **Pros:** excellent rooms; ideal base for exploring southern Donegal; free car parking. **Cons:** sea-view rooms cost extra; smells from the harbor can be strong; sports TV can get rowdy crowds. *Rooms from: €93 ✉ Main St., Carrick ☎ 074/973–1950 🌐 www.bayviewhotel.ie ➪ 40 rooms 🍽 Free Breakfast.*

Tara Hotel

$$ | **HOTEL** | This modern, bright, and airy harborside hotel—an ideal base to explore this alluring corner of southern Donegal—has 31 well-equipped guest rooms tastefully decorated in warm colors with dark-red carpets and teakwood; most have expansive harbor vistas, and some come with small balconies. **Pros:** rooms with harbor views; excellent seafood restaurant; convenient location. **Cons:** no pool; noisy during big sporting events; no fancy frills. *Rooms from: €120 ✉ Harbor front, Killybegs ☎ 074/974–1700 🌐 www.tarahotel.ie ➪ 31 rooms 🍽 Free Breakfast.*

Gleann Cholm Cille (Glencolumbkille)

27 km (17 miles) west of Killybegs on R263, 54 km (27 miles) west of Donegal Town.

"The back of beyond" at the far end of a stretch of barren moorland, the tiny hamlet of Gleann Cholm Cille clings dramatically to the rockbound harbor of Glen Bay. Known alternatively as Glencolumbkille (pronounced "glen-colm- *kill*"), it remains the heart of County Donegal's shrinking Gaeltacht region and retains a strong rural Irish flavor, as do its pubs and brightly painted row houses. The name means St. Columba's Glen; the legend goes that St. Columba, the Christian missionary, lived here during the 6th century with a group of followers before many of them moved on to find greater glory by settling Scotland's Isle of Iona. Prehistoric cairns, scattered around the village, have become connected locally with the St. Columba myths. There are no hotels in town, but walking lodges, village B&Bs, and friendly inns that cater to hikers are worth checking out.

Cliffs surrounding Gleann Cholm Cille rise up to more than 700 feet, including Glen Head; many cliffs are studded with ancient hermit cells. Also of note is a squat Martello tower, built by the British in 1805 to protect against an anticipated French invasion that never happened. Another good walk is the 8-km (5-mile) trek to Malinbeg, reached by the coast road running past Doon Point. Look for the ruins of no less than five burial cairns, a ring fort, a second Martello tower, and one of the best beaches in Ireland, renowned for its calm waters, dramatic scenery, and lovely golden sand.

GETTING HERE AND AROUND

It's a roller-coaster mountain road to Glencolumbkille, and you need your wits about you on the R263 from Killybegs. The journey time is 30 minutes (at a top speed of 65 kph [40 mph]). Once you get to Glencolumbkille, car parking is not a problem. Ardara, to the northeast along the R230, is a 45-minute drive (but it'll take much longer if you stop to drink in the stunning scenery).

The main Donegal Town–Dungloe Bus Éireann service does not go to Glencolumbkille, but there is twice-daily Bus Éireann service (at 9:30 am and 6:15 pm, Monday–Saturday) that leaves Donegal Town for Glencolumbkille year-round. There is also a Monday–Saturday bus from Glencolumbkille to Donegal Town at 7:05 am. There are three buses each day from Donegal Town to Dungloe; the service goes via Killybegs, Ardara, and Glenties.

For buses to Teelin or Glenveagh National Park it is best to check online or directly with the bus station in Stranorlar as there are frequent changes to the service.

CONTACTS Stranorlar Bus Station. ☎ *074/913–1008.*

Sights

Glencolmcille Folk Village Museum

OTHER MUSEUM | Walk through the beachfront Folk Village Museum to explore rural life. This *clachan,* or tiny village, comprises eight cottages, all of which are whitewashed, thatch-roofed, and extremely modest in appearance. Three showcase particular years in Irish culture: 1720, 1820, and 1920; pride of place goes to the 1881 schoolhouse and the re-created *shebeen* (pub). You'll also find an interpretive center, tea shop, regular demonstrations of hand weaving (there is a newly installed working loom), and crafts shop selling local handmade products. Three small cottages, with bare-earth floors, represent the basic living conditions over three centuries. The signposted circular nature and history trail is a tranquil and reflective place that includes a sweathouse (early Irish sauna), replica lime kilns, and mass rocks. Standing in the car park at 15 feet tall is a unique stone map of Ireland, Clocha na hEireann, which is made up of a stone from all 32 counties. It was erected in 2016 to commemorate the 100th anniversary of the Easter Rising in 1916. ✉ *Near beach, Glencolumbkille* ☎ *074/973–0017* 🌐 *www.glenfolkvillage.com* 🎟 *€7* ⏲ *Closed Nov.–Easter.*

Oideas Gael: Sport & Culture

COLLEGE | If you fancy expanding your mind and horizons, both from a sporting and cultural point of view, then Oideas Gael has an excellent selection of courses—both weekend and weeklong—for the culturally curious holidaymaker. Since it was formed in 1984, Oideas Gael has run acclaimed Irish-language classes as well as programs on hill walking, archaeology, landscape, and the environment. Other activities include painting, traditional music, playing the harp—and even tapestry hand weaving—one of Donegal's renowned crafts. The courses, which attract thousands of participants from all over the world, run from March to October. Accommodations are based in self-catering hostels or with local families. For a rundown on the schedule and prices, check the website. ✉ *Glencolumbkille* ☎ *074/973–0248* 🌐 *www.oideasgael.ie.*

Silver Strand Beach

BEACH | An Trá Bhán lives up to its name: it's a beautifully enclosed small silvery-white sandy beach, quiet and hidden from view and visitor traffic. Peaceful solitude is the name of the game here, but if your hair is standing on end it's

To step back in time, just head to Gleann Cholm Cille—if you're lucky you'll catch the locals rethatching their roofs.

because you're being watched; there are a few peeping sheep on the surrounding hillsides. **Amenities**: parking (no fee). **Best for**: swimming; walking.

■ TIP→ When you've had your fill of sand and serenity, explore the ruined promontory fort, Dun Allt, directly above the beach. It was built around 300 BC, and archaeologists believe it was used as a defensive fortification when the community was in danger of attack. ✉ *Gleann Cholm Cille, Glencolumbkille.*

Turas Cholmcille

HISTORIC SIGHT | Atop the cliff rising north of the village, the Turas Cholmcille pilgrimage takes place at midnight on June 9 each year, traditionally in bare feet. The three-hour route consists of stone cross pillars, natural features, and megalithic tombs, associated with St. Columba. Details on the mysterious stone cairns and pillars are available in the Glencolmcille Folk Village museum. ✉ *Glencolumbkille* 🌐 *www.glencolmcille.ie/turas.htm.*

 Hotels

Ionad Siúl Walking Lodge

$ | B&B/INN | Not a hotel per se—there isn't a bar, pool, or meal plan—Ionad Siúl has clean, comfortable, and spacious rooms, all en suite (bathroom included), with a handy kitchen for those who can whip up their own breakfasts. **Pros:** set in spectacular countryside; place to meet fellow travelers; good value. **Cons:** rooms are basic; limited facilities; little dining choice nearby. Ⓢ *Rooms from: €45* ✉ *Glencolumbkille* ☎ *074/973–0302* 🛏 *12 rooms* 🍽 *No Meals.*

Ard an Rátha (Ardara)

28 km (17 miles) northeast of Gleann Cholm Cille, 30 km (19 miles) northwest of Donegal Town.

At the head of a lovely ocean inlet, the unpretentious, old-fashioned hamlet of Ard an Rátha (Ardara) is built around the L-shape intersection of its two main

Donegal Tweed

When it comes to Donegal tweed, weavers—inspired by the soft greens, red rusts, and dove grays of the famed Donegal landscape—have had centuries of experience. In long-gone days, crofters' wives concocted the dyes to give Donegal tweed its distinctive flecks, and their husbands wove the cloth into tweed. Traditional Donegal tweed was a salt-and-pepper mix, but gradually weavers began adding dyes distilled from yellow gorse, purple blackberries, orange lichen, and green moss. Today most tweed comes from factories. However, there are still about 25 local craftsmen working from their cottages. Chic fashion designers such as Armani, Ralph Lauren, and Burberry all use handwoven Donegal tweed—obviously, more fashionable than ever. As with Aran sweaters, Donegal tweed is today regarded as a badge of iconic chic—a 21st-century symbol of Irish folk art.

streets. (If you come from Glencolumbkille, expect a scenic drive full of hairpin curves and steep hills as you cross over Glengesh Pass.) For centuries, great cloth fairs were held on the first of every month; cottage workers in the surrounding countryside still provide Ard an Rátha (and County Donegal) with high-quality, handwoven cloths and hand knits. The village was thrust into the spotlight on St. Patrick's Day 2012 when it set a record for the most St. Patricks gathered in one place. A total of 229 such saints turned up with their crosiers, including visiting saint clones from Europe.

GETTING HERE AND AROUND

Three main roads from the north, east, and south converge on Ardara, which really only gets busy in the summer months. There is ample, free street parking in the town. It's 25 minutes from Killybegs and 30 minutes from Donegal Town to the south and east. Letterkenny is a 60-minute drive north along the N56 to Glenties, followed by the narrower R250.

Restaurants

Ramblers Bar & Restaurant

$$ | **IRISH** | Huge steaks and fresh, locally sourced fish dominate the dinner menu in the renovated upstairs restaurant in the Nesbitt Arms Hotel. Decor still harks back to the days when Ardara was Donegal's foremost weaving and wool center; tweed throws and blankets will keep you warm on a night of wild Atlantic weather. **Known for:** great steaks; quality lunch on the go; local whiskeys. *$ Average main: €23 ✉ Main St., Ardara ☎ 074/954–1103 🌐 www.nesbittarms.com.*

Hotels

★ Woodhill House

$ | **B&B/INN** | High ceilings, marble fireplaces, and stained glass adorn the interior of this spacious Victorian manor house; bedrooms have superb views of the Donegal mountains, and some guest rooms overlook the garden. **Pros:** quiet location; beautifully maintained house and gardens; in-house bar. **Cons:** complaints about poor TV reception; long, dark walk from town at night; few extra frills. *$ Rooms from: €110 ✉ Wood Rd., Ardara ☎ 074/954–1112 🌐 www.woodhill-house.com ⏲ Closed Christmas 13 rooms Free Breakfast.*

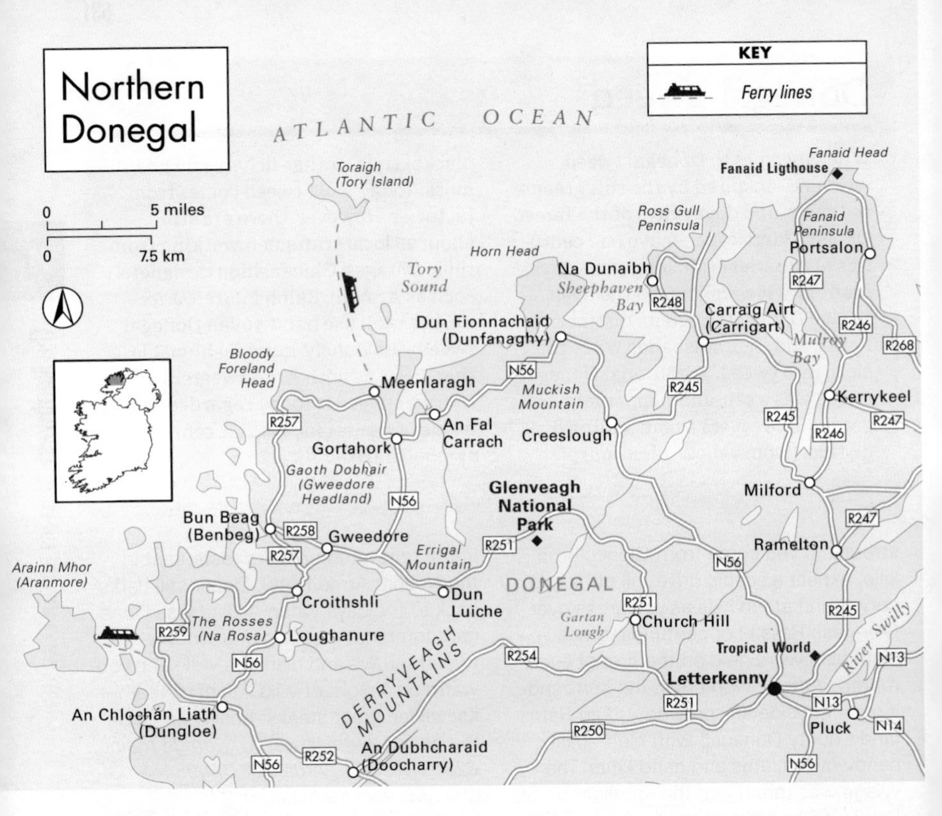

Nightlife

For a small, old-fashioned village, Ard an Rátha has a surprising number of pubs, many of which have traditional music in the evening.

The Corner House

PIANO BARS | You'll likely find this place packed, as it features music almost every night from May to September and on weekends the rest of the year. It's a great place to mix with locals as well. ✉ *Main St., Ardara* ☎ *074/954–1736* 🌐 *ardara.ie/?ait-item=the-corner-house.*

Nancy's Pub

PUBS | With its glowing fire, Nancy's, now in its eighth generation of the same family, makes you wonder if you've wandered into the owner's sitting room. The walls are filled with framed black-and-white photographs of the family and of old Ardara. Seafood, in the form of chowder, oysters, prawns, and mussels, dominates the menu served noon to 9 year-round. Ask for the house special, the Louis Armstrong sandwich, which consists of "jazzed-up" smoked salmon with grilled cheese on wheat bread. To accompany your food, try the old-fashioned, naturally fermented farmyard cider—a big hit with summer visitors. There's also live music on Friday and Saturday nights during the summer months. ✉ *Front St., Ardara* ☎ *074/954–1187* 🌐 *www.nancysbarardara.com.*

Shopping

Many handwoven and locally made knitwear items are on sale in Ard an Rátha. Some stores commission goods directly from knitters, and prices are about as low as anywhere. Handsome, chunky Aran hand-knit sweaters (€80–€130), cardigans (similar prices), and scarves (€25) are all widely available.

C. Bonner and Son
MIXED CLOTHING | Factory knitwear from €100 to €320 is for sale here, as well as pottery, tweeds, jewelry, and gifts. There's also a good selection of hand-knit Aran sweaters and cardigans available. ✉ *Front St., Ardara* ☎ *074/954–1196* 🌐 *bonnerofireland.com.*

Campbells Tweed Shop
MIXED CLOTHING | Stores such as Campbells are treasure troves of ready-to-wear tweeds—with sweaters from around €100. ✉ *Front St., Ardara* ☎ *87/720–6971* 🌐 *campbellsofardara.com.*

Eddie Doherty Handwoven Tweed
MIXED CLOTHING | Through the work of one of the last weavers in Donegal this store showcases handwoven tweeds, from scarves for €25 to capes for €245, from Ard an Rátha and other parts of the country. ✉ *Front St., Ardara* ☎ *087/699–6360* 🌐 *www.handwoventweed.com.*

John Molloy Woollen Mills
MIXED CLOTHING | High-quality handwoven Donegal tweed and hand-knit Aran sweaters are on sale at this factory shop, on the Killybegs Road, on the outskirts of town. After a 10-minute factory tour during which you can watch the hand-weaving and knitting processes, the Weavers coffee shop is an ideal place for a break. ✉ *Killybegs Rd., Ardara* ☎ *074/954–1133* 🌐 *www.johnmolloy.com.*

Letterkenny

55 km (34 miles) northeast of Ard an Rátha, 51 km (32 miles) northeast of Donegal Town, 35 km (21 miles) west of Derry.

Letterkenny, like Donegal to the south, is at the gateway to the far Northwest; you're likely to come through here if you're driving west out of Northern Ireland. Letterkenny's claim to fame has been that it has the longest main street in the whole country, but it's also a bustling, modest-size Irish town with family-run shops, and a good place to get a sense of the warm local identity.

GETTING HERE AND AROUND

Standing at the intersection of the main roads linking Derry and Donegal Town, Letterkenny is at the southern end of Lough Swilly and serves as a handy refueling stop for many drivers. Parking along the main street is free for the first 30 minutes only; use the pay-and-display ticketing system at €1 per hour when your free time is up. There are three main car parks that also have a metered charge, but you can park free in the grounds of the cathedral.

Derry is just 30 minutes away along the N13 on a wide fast road, while Donegal is 60 minutes south. The area's major tourist attraction, Glenveagh National Park, is a 30-minute drive northwest along the N56 and then R255.

Bus Éireann runs nine daily services to and from Dublin city center (via Dublin Airport) and Letterkenny with a journey time of four hours. This part of Donegal is served well by independent operators, with many routes connecting with Derry and the Inishowen Peninsula. Most buses leave Derry city's bus station in Foyle Street.

Fields of Gold

In 2018, farmers digging in a wet corner of a field in Tullydonnell near Convoy, 15 km (9 miles) south of Letterkenny, made an astonishing find of historical significance. After removing a stone boulder, they saw flashes of light and uncovered four overlapping rings of gold in perfect condition. The rings have been described as gold bullion, intended for manufacturing finer gold goods. Dating to the Bronze Age, they are the heaviest prehistoric gold objects ever found in Ireland. Known as the Tullydonnell Hoard, they are now on permanent display at the National Museum in Dublin. For now, these fields are indeed just fields to the naked eye, but they are worth stopping to admire if only to ponder the recent yield and perhaps other yet-to-be-discovered treasures of Ireland's ancient past.

VISITOR INFORMATION

CONTACTS Tourist Information Office.
✉ *Neil T. Blaney Rd., Letterkenny*
☎ *850/230–330* 🌐 *www.discoverireland.ie/northwest.*

Sights

An Grianán Theatre

MUSIC | The 383-seat An Grianán Theatre hosts a wide variety of cultural and artistic events. The program includes drama, comedy, music, and dance, while changing exhibitions feature the work of local artists and photographers. An Grianán also hosts, along with several other venues, the Letterkenny trad week held in January, which features traditional groups and singers as well as bluegrass bands from the United States. The Eatery Café serves light meals and drinks from 9:30 am to 3:30 pm. ✉ *Port Rd., Letterkenny* ☎ *074/912–0777* 🌐 *www.angrianan.com.*

St. Eunan's Cathedral

RELIGIOUS BUILDING | With its 212-foot-high spire St. Eunan's Cathedral is the most outstanding building in Letterkenny, dominating the town, especially when illuminated at night. This striking, ornate Gothic Revival structure was finally finished in 1901, and is the only cathedral in the county. Designed by William Hague of Dublin and built of white Donegal sandstone, the exterior of the building is said to be in perfect classical-rule proportion. Inside, the intricate decorative ceilings and ceramic floor mosaics are the work of Italian artist Signor Amici of Rome. The main and side altars are carved from the finest Italian marble, while the great nave arch depicts, in a series of panels in bas-relief, the lives of St. Eunan and St. Columba in meticulous detail. ✉ *Ard Choluim, Letterkenny* ☎ *074/912–1021* 🌐 *www.steunanscathedral.ie.*

Tropical World

ZOO | **FAMILY** | Drama from the world of nature, in the form of an amazing butterfly house, is on display at Alcorn's Tropical World and minizoo, near Letterkenny. You will also find an eclectic collection of lizards, lemurs, geckos, squirrel monkeys, bearded dragons, and even snakes—who said St. Patrick banished them all from Ireland's fair shores? The addition of a Jurassic Land and a Bug World, as well as toucans, rainbow lorikeets, and a pair of cockatiels has brought added dimensions of color. There's a covered play area for children as well as a café and garden center. ✉ *Loughnagin, Letterkenny* ☎ *074/912–1541* 🌐 *www.tropicalworld.ie* 🎫 *€9* 🕐 *Closed Oct.–Mar.*

Restaurants

The Quiet Moment Tea Rooms
$ | IRISH | This delightful, old-fashioned tearoom with granite tables and mahogany paneling serves light bites and more substantial fare for breakfast and lunch. Breakfasts may be the full Irish (€8.95, served until noon), waffles, or pancakes with a multiplicity of fillings. **Known for:** awesome breakfasts; sweet chili deluxe triple sandwich; flavored lattes. *Average main: €9 94–96 Upper Main St., Letterkenny 074/912–8382 www.quietmoment.ie.*

Clanree Hotel
$ | HOTEL | Formerly a Holiday Inn, this hotel has reinvented itself with flair, and the spacious entrance hall—with framed tweed pieces hung on walls, reflecting the area's connection to the industry—strikes a distinctive and welcoming note. **Pros:** fully equipped health and fitness center; excellent value bar food; superb location for touring countryside. **Cons:** room service can be slow; queues for the breakfast buffet; not many extra frills. *Rooms from: €89 Derry Rd., Letterkenny 074/912–4369 www.clanreehotel.com 120 rooms Free Breakfast.*

Frewin House
$$ | B&B/INN | An elegant creeper-clad manor house with many period features on the outskirts of Ramelton, Frewin's history stretches back to the 1880s when it was a rectory. **Pros:** well-appointed rooms; delicious breakfasts; great location for exploring the area. **Cons:** few extra facilities; no bar but try Conway's thatched pub for music; limited rooms. *Rooms from: €170 Rectory Rd., Ramelton 074/915–1246 www.frewinhouse.com Closed Nov.–Mar. 3 rooms, 1 self-catering cottage Free Breakfast.*

Glenveagh National Park

21 km (13 miles) northwest of Letterkenny.

GETTING HERE AND AROUND

Glenveagh National Park is 30 minutes northwest of Letterkenny along the N56 through Kilmacrenan and then left on to the R255, a road that leads on to Gweedore on the western Donegal coastline. There is a free car park at the visitor center.

★ Glenveagh National Park
TRAIL | Bordered by the Derryveagh Mountains (Derryveagh means "forest of oak and birch"), Glenveagh National Park encompasses 40,000 acres of wilderness—mountain, moorland, lakes, and woods—that has been called the largest and most dramatic tract in the wildest part of Donegal. Within its borders, a thick carpet of russet-color heath and dense woodland rolls down the Derryveagh slopes into the broad open valley of the River Veagh (or Owenbeagh), which opens out into Glenveagh's spine: the long and narrow, dark and clear Lough Beagh.

Between 1857 and 1859, John George Adair, a ruthless gentleman farmer, assembled the estate that now makes up the park. In 1861 he evicted the estate's hundreds of poor tenants without compensation and destroyed their cottages. Nine years later Adair began to build Glenveagh Castle on the eastern shore of Lough Veagh, but he soon departed for Texas. He died in 1885 without returning to Ireland, but his widow, Cornelia, moved back to make Glenveagh her home. She created four gardens, covering 27 acres; planted luxuriant rhododendrons; and began the job of making this turret-and-battlement-laden 19th-century folly livable.

The castle gardens in particular— known as "Genius Loci Glenveaghensis"—are regarded as one of Ireland's outstanding horticultural masterpieces. At the end of a dramatic 3-km-long (2-mile-long) entryway, perched over the lake waters, this is a true fairy-tale castle. Beyond the castle, footpaths lead into more remote sections of the park, including the Derrylahan Nature Trail, a 1½-km (1-mile) signposted trail where you may suddenly catch sight of a soaring golden eagle or chance upon a shy red deer. ✉ *R251, Church Hill* ☎ *01/539–3232* 🌐 *www.glenveaghnationalpark.ie* 🎫 *Castle tour €7, shuttle bus €3, weekend bus €3.*

Hotels

Fanad Lighthouse
$$$$ | **HOUSE** | One of the brand-new attractions along the Wild Atlantic Way, Fanad Lighthouse offers accommodations in a remote and spectacular area, as well as a unique tour for visitors. **Pros:** outstanding views; unique accommodation; the waters are famed for cetaceans. **Cons:** long way from nearby towns; make your own meals; two-night minimum stay. $ *Rooms from: €280* ✉ *Fanad Head Lighthouse, Fanad Head, Kincasslagh* ✣ *Fanad Head is at northern tip of Fanad peninsula, about 42 km (26 miles) north of Letterkenny at mouth of Lough Swilly* ☎ *083/809–1199* 🌐 *www.fanadlighthouse.com* ⇨ *3 houses* 🍽 *No Meals.*

Rathmullan House
$$$$ | **HOTEL** | There is an otherworldliness to Lough Swilly, which is mirrored in the classic country-house comfort of Rathmullan where log fires roar in antiques-filled surroundings in a place that drips with character. **Pros:** dream location at the water's edge; good on-site restaurants; ideal for exploring the Wild Atlantic Way route to Fanad Head. **Cons:** popular for lively family gatherings; restaurant very busy at peak times; pricey rooms. $ *Rooms from: €250* ✉ *Coast Rd., Rathmullan* ✣ *34 km (21 miles) from Glenveagh* ☎ *074/915–8188* 🌐 *www.rathmullanhouse.com* ⏲ *Closed Jan., and weekdays in Dec., Feb., and Mar.* ⇨ *34 rooms* 🍽 *Free Breakfast.*

Chapter 12

THE NORTHEAST

Updated by
Vic O'Sullivan

Sights ★★★★★ | Restaurants ★★★☆☆ | Hotels ★★★☆☆ | Shopping ★★☆☆☆ | Nightlife ★☆☆☆☆

WELCOME TO THE NORTHEAST

TOP REASONS TO GO

★ **Walk through history.** Explore Carlingford's magnificent medieval streetscape.

★ **Scenic Trim.** Visit Trim Castle, Ireland's largest Norman castle, and other sights along the River Boyne.

★ **Unique souvenirs.** Take home the gift of Irish lace from Carrickmacross.

★ **The Lake Country.** Enjoy fine dining, luxury retreats, and waterfront activities in County Cavan.

★ **Sliabh na Calliagh.** Discover atmospheric Loughcrew and its ancient tombs.

Despite this region's location, within an hour or two from the capital, it's often missed by visitors who speed through it on their way to more popular destinations. Yet, veer off the motorway onto the narrow roads that weave their way through the lush countryside to discover a different, authentic Ireland that marches to a slower beat. Fine dining, lakelands, fishing and historical buildings are aplenty, but without the crowds and jaded service.

1 Trim. County Meath's medieval heart, this town has Ireland's largest Norman fortress, which was used to dramatic effect in the movie *Braveheart*.

2 Loughcrew. The spirit of ancient Ireland lives on in this network of Neolithic tombs whose chambers illuminate with the dawn sunlight every equinox.

3 Carlingford and Cooley Peninsula. This sliver of land is where the sea meets the mountains and curving around the bay is Carlingford, one of Ireland's most atmospheric towns.

4 Monaghan Town. Decidedly untouristy Monaghan Town is the epicenter of the farming community where locals are refreshingly friendly.

5 Inniskeen. The home village of one of Ireland's most famous poets, Patrick Kavanagh.

6 Cavan Town. A broad market town in tumbling, lush countryside with a surprising trump card—excellent luxury hotels and restaurants.

7 Virginia. Little lakeside Virginia lies in an unspoiled corner of County Cavan's rich countryside.

Armagh
NORTHERN IRELAND
ARMAGH
Monaghan Town
FERMANAGH
MONAGHAN
Keady
Clones
Annayalla
Castleblayney
Newry
DOWN
Warrenpoint
Crossmaglen
Kilkeel
Carlingford
Carlingford Lough
COOLEY PENINSULA
Cootehill
Inniskeen
Dundalk
Carrickmacross
CAVAN
Cavan Town
Dundalk Bay
Kingscourt
LOUTH
Ardee
Ballyjamesduff
Virginia
Dunleer
Irish Sea
Oldcastle
Loughcrew
Mellifont Abbey
Kells
BOYNE VALLEY
Slane
Drogheda
Newgrange
Castlepollard
Navan
WESTMEATH
MEATH
Hill of Tara
Trim
Skerries
Mullingar
DUBLIN
Kinnegad
Swords
Lambay Island
Enfield
Tyrrellspass
Maynooth
DUBLIN
Dublin Bay
OFFALY
Straffan
KILDARE
Castletown House
Russborough House
Naas
Punchestown Racecourse
Bray
The Curragh
Blessington
0 10 mi
0 10 km
A27
A1
A3
N54
N2
N53
N52
N3
M1
N51
M3
N4
M7
M11
1
2
3
4
5
6
7

Counties Cavan and Monaghan to the north of this region are a tapestry of untamed, remote lakelands peppered with small fishing villages and hilly trials where hikers can enjoy a lonely expanse of wilderness in the shadow of the Cuilcagh Mountains. Shrouded in myth, this rich watery heartland is the source of the greatest river in both Ireland and Great Britain at Shannon Pot, and so it has also spawned the origins of many great Irish legends, most notably the tale of the Salmon of Knowledge.

Farther east, the lush landscapes of Meath and Louth offer a time travel opportunity through millennia of history from the mysterious Neolithic burial grounds at Loughcrew or Carlingford, a paragon of an Irish medieval settlement. Trim, where satirist Jonathan Swift served as vicar in the hinterlands, has a myriad of winding lanes and an epic castle that caught the attention of Hollywood and the world when it became a prime filming location for the movie *Braveheart* in 1995.

Yet, dig a little deeper and you'll discover a surprising range of quality hospitality for a seemingly off-grid location. In Cavan, McNean House is one of the finest restaurants in Ireland while luxury hotels like Cabra Castle, Farnham Estate, and The Slieve Russell Hotel offer comfortable weekend retreats an hour from the capital. Intricate crafts like lace, glass blowing, and weaving are high on the list for gift seekers. However, the region's greatest draws are its friendly locals, authentic charm, and unhurried pace of life.

MAJOR REGIONS

Medieval Ireland is still evident in this lesser-seen region. **Carlingford**, with its swirling streetscape that leads down to its harbor front, looks like it was peeled straight out from a period movie set, while across the border in **Trim**, its charm has, in fact, appeared in Hollywood movies.

Off-radar county market towns like **Virginia**, **Cavan Town**, and **Monaghan Town** haven't moved at the same pace as the rest of the county, so expect old manners and friendly banter with some fine local hospitality. **Loughcrew** in Meath is the place to discover ancient Ireland, while literary types can venture to **Inniskeen** to discover the birthplace of poet Patrick Kavanagh.

Foodies can get the best of local cooking at **Blacklion** in northern County Cavan.

Planning

Getting Here and Around

BOAT

While mostly landlocked, apart from the easterly shoreline of County Louth and Carlingford Lough, this area has rich lakelands where visitors can idle away full afternoons exploring the parks on a boat or fishing the waters for fresh catch.

Carlingford Lough Car Ferry Service links the Cooley Peninsula to County Down in Northern Ireland. The same company operates evening lake cruises with spectacular water settings.

CONTACT Carlingford Lough Ferry. ✉ *Greenore Port, The Harbour, Greenore, Louth* ☎ *1800/938–004* 🌐 *carlingfordferry.com.*

BUS

As there is no rail route through this area, bus travel is the only method of public transportation available. Bus Éireann offers an impressive bus network with low fares for Leap Card (🌐 *www.leapcard.ie*) holders. Expressway services 30 and 32 from Dublin Airport pass through Cavan and Monaghan throughout the day from early morning. Bus Éireann's commuter, rural, and local services offer a spiderweb service with a plethora of services that connect Cavan and Monaghan. Carlingford is linked to other locations like Trim, Cavan, and Monaghan through Dundalk on Route 161.

CONTACT Bus Éireann. ☎ *01/836–6111* 🌐 *buseireann.ie.*

CAR

Like everywhere else—or perhaps more than everywhere else—the cost of car rental has rocketed in Ireland. Coupled with an appetite for sustainable travel, travel-savvy visitors to Ireland are making use of the extensive network of public transportation. Car rental still brings a certain element of independence, with an extensive rental base at Dublin Airport and in regional offices around the area.

CONTACT Cavan Car and Van Hire. ✉ *Cockhill Rd., Cavan* ☎ *49/433–0856* 🌐 *enterprise.ie.*

TAXI

Carlingford, Trim, Cavan Town, and Monaghan Town offer a good range of private taxi and local tour services.

CONTACTS Cavan Cabs. ✉ *48/49 Main St., Cavan* ☎ *49/437–1155.*

Hotels

For a mostly rural location where tourism has developed at a slower pace than other parts of the country, this region has a surprisingly impressive range of hotels and other accommodation. In the more popular towns, Carlingford has charming guesthouses while Trim has modern properties.

The wild card is County Cavan. It has the best selection of luxury hotels, with top-class golfing resorts like The Slieve Russell Hotel or Farnham Estate, along with high-quality self-catering. Monaghan is replete with county hotels with standard-quality facilities.

Restaurants

Each subregion has its own set of culinary highlights. While Trim in County Meath has a dearth of fine-dining venues its family-friendly selection offers international food at good value. Carlingford's sea setting has put it at the helm of oyster dining. With its vast lakelands and good agricultural heartlands expect glorious local produce and cooking in County Cavan's excellent hotel restaurants and nationally renowned MacNean Restaurant in Blacklion.

RESTAURANT AND HOTEL PRICES

⇨ *Hotel prices in the reviews are the lowest cost of a standard double room in high season. Restaurant prices in the reviews are the average cost of a main course at dinner, or if dinner is not served, at lunch. Restaurant and hotel reviews have been shortened. For full information, visit Fodors.com.*

What It Costs In Euros

$	$$	$$$	$$$$
RESTAURANTS			
under €18	€18–€25	€26–€35	over €35
HOTELS			
under €120	€120–€180	€181–€220	over €220

Trim

50 km (31 miles) northwest of Dublin City on the M3 and R154.

There are few towns in Ireland that have the scale and volume of medieval buildings that lie within Trim's perimeter. Its origin dates to the 5th century, but it was in the 12th century that it came to prominence as an early stronghold of Norman power. Today, this handsome town is home to Ireland's largest castle and one of its oldest complete and unaltered working bridges.

That medieval legacy is marked by the hulking, ruined edifices that tower over Trim's low-rise, hilly streetscape lined with cafés, shops, and restaurants. Notable past residents include war strategist Arthur Wellesley (first duke of Wellington) and satirist and author of *Gulliver's Travels*, Jonathan Swift, who was a vicar in nearby Laracor.

GETTING HERE AND AROUND

Trim is small and best discovered on foot. There are car parks, including one on Castle Street (close to the castle) and pay parking on the streets is in operation between the hours of 9 and 6 Monday to Saturday. Expect to pay €1 per hour.

There is no train service through Trim, but bus services are aplenty. Bus Éireann's 109B service departs daily at 7:15 am and thereafter every two hours from Dublin City Center to Trim, while Route 111 offers a similar service. Bus 190 links Trim to larger regional towns like Drogheda and Navan.

TOURS

The Holy Trail of Knights and Monks
GUIDED TOURS | This is a guided walking tour by a local guide through the medieval Porch Fields to the Newtown ruins. A shorter Medieval Mile Tour is also available. ✉ *Trim* ☎ *46/943–7227* 🌐 *discoverboynevalley.ie* 🎫 *€5* ☞ *1 hr 15 mins.*

VISITOR INFORMATION

CONTACT Trim Tourist Office. ✉ *Castle St., Trim* ☎ *46/943–7227* 🌐 *discoverboynevalley.ie.*

Sights

Laracor
TOWN | In the village of Laracor, a wall to the left of the rectory marks the now-destroyed building where Jonathan Swift (1667–1745), the satirical writer, poet, and author of *Gulliver's Travels*, was rector from 1699 until 1713, when he was made dean of St. Patrick's Cathedral in Dublin. Nearby are the walls of the cottage where Esther Johnson, the "Stella" who inspired much of Swift's writings, once lived. ✉ *Laracor* ✥ *3 km (2 miles) south of Trim on R158.*

Newtown Abbey
RUINS | East of Trim on the banks of the River Boyne, Newtown contains the ruins

Trim Castle is one of the best-preserved Anglo-Norman castles in Ireland.

of what was once the largest cathedral in Ireland, built beginning in 1210 by Simon de Rochfort, the first Anglo-Norman bishop of Meath. ✉ *Trim* ✣ *1¼ km (¾ mile) east of Trim.*

The Old Bridge

BRIDGE | One of Ireland's oldest bridges, which has remained unaltered and fully operation since the Boyne River banks burst and floods destroyed a wooded erection back in 1330. This sturdy, handsome four-arched stone structure (also known as St Pater's Bridge or Newtown Bridge) is also unique because it's one of the few known instances of rent being imposed on people crossing an Irish bridge. The archbishops of Armagh leased Trim Castle from 1258 until 1443, and records highlight a crossing fee levied regularly on those who used the bridge. ✉ *Newtown Bridge.*

Royal Mint

RUINS | Part of Trim Castle and facing the river is the Royal Mint, a ruin that illustrates Trim's political importance in the Middle Ages. It produced coins with colorful names like "Irelands" and "Patricks" right up into the 15th century. ✉ *Trim Castle, Castle St., Trim* ⏲ *Closed weekdays Nov.–mid-Mar.*

St. Patrick's Cathedral

CHURCH | This church dates from early in the 19th century, but the square tower is from an earlier structure built in 1449. Bishops were enthroned here as early as 1536. The stained-glass window on the western side was the first commission of Edward Burne-Jones, the leading British Pre-Raphaelite. ✉ *Loman St., Trim.*

Summerhill

TOWN | One of the most pleasant villages of southern County Meath, Summerhill has a large square and a village green with a 15th-century cross. ✉ *Summerhill* ✣ *8 km (5 miles) southeast of Laracor along R158.*

★ **Trim Castle**

CASTLE/PALACE | This castle ruin, sometimes referred to as King John's Castle, is the largest Anglo-Norman fortification in Ireland. It took 30 years to complete its construction in 1172 by Hugh de Lacy and his descendants. Bearing all the hallmarks of a fortress, it had a water-filled moat, 20 herculean retaining tower walls in cruciform shape, and was essentially impenetrable in its day. A walkway offers an overview of its enormous scale. Movie buffs will recognize its role in *Braveheart* (1995). England's Henry V, formerly known as Prince Hal, was held captive here. ✉ *Béal na mBlath, Hill Rd., Trim* ☎ *85/887–0240* 🌐 *heritageireland.ie* 🎫 *€5* 🕐 *Closed Christmas wk* ☞ *Guided tour of the keep.*

The Wellington Column

MONUMENT | A statue of local man Arthur Wellesley, better known as The Duke of Wellington, stands atop a 23-meter-high Corinthian column. It was erected by Dublin Council in 1817 to commemorate Wellesley's astute military strategies that hastened the end of the Napoleonic Wars and, consequently, the construction of watchtowers around the Irish coastline. Wellesley spent much of his childhood in Dangan Castle on the Trim Road. ✉ *Trim.*

The Yellow Steeple & Sheep Gate

RUINS | All that remains of St. Mary's Augustinian Abbey is a jagged 40-meter-high, seven-story tower, and in the evening its masonry ignites in a yellow glow shortly before sunset. Locals refer to these 14th-century abbey ruins as the yellow steeple, and it is believed by local historians that it was constructed on the site of the first great church founded by St. Patrick. It was used as a garrison over the years, and one theory is that the final death blow to its structure was dealt by the Irish to prevent the building falling into the hands of Cromwell. The Sheep Gate near the Yellow Steeple is the only surviving medieval gateway to the walled town of Trim. ✉ *Trim.*

Restaurants

Despite its historical significance and steady stream of visitors, Trim dining options are confined mostly to cafés and family-friendly dining.

Franzinis

$ | **INTERNATIONAL** | **FAMILY** | Informal but friendly, its menu leans toward pizzeria but has enough options to throw a curveball at that definition. It's a hop and jump from Trim Castle, and the chef and team are experienced enough to guarantee dining satisfaction for the whole family. **Known for:** close to Trim Castle; value for money; family-friendly. $ *Average main: €15* ✉ *5–6 French's La.* ☎ *46/943–1002* 🌐 *franzinis.com.*

Hotels

Tigh Catháin

$ | **B&B/INN** | The "House of O'Catháin" is a Tudor-style country cottage with artfully decorated guest rooms and lovely gardens out back and in front that are perfect for lounging around in the sun. **Pros:** family-owned lodging; hearty breakfasts; glorious gardens. **Cons:** often books up far in advance; half a mile to nearest town; few facilities. $ *Rooms from: €76* ✉ *Longwood Rd., Trim* ✥ *About 1 km (½ mile) south of Trim on road toward Longwood* ☎ *086/257–7313* 🌐 *www.tighcathain-bnb.com* 💳 *No credit cards* 🛏 *4 rooms* 🍽 *Free Breakfast.*

Trim Castle Hotel

$$$ | **HOTEL** | If the ambition is to stay close to Trim Castle, then you've struck gold here. **Pros:** directly across from Trim Castle; modern facilities; car parking. **Cons:** impersonal design; popular with weddings; poor leisure facilities. $ *Rooms from: €185* ✉ *Castle St., Trim* ☎ *46/948–3000* 🌐 *trimcastlehotel.com* 🛏 *68 rooms* 🍽 *No Meals.*

Loughcrew

43 km (26 miles) northwest of Trim on M3.

There is something primitive and starkly real about this Neolithic network of graves that lies on a lonely, hilly terrain a world and millennia away from the more tourist-friendly site at Newgrange. Despite its relative obscurity, Loughcrew is one of Ireland's most significant archaeological sites, yet it's located in the heart of County Meath, 90 minutes from Dublin.

The passage tombs are scattered over three hilltops known as Carnbane West, Patrickstown, and Carnbane East and it's on the latter that Cairn T, the most impressive tomb, lies. Druids believed that a colossal enchantress, while passing over the area, dropped boulders from the cradle of her apron. Legend has it that these rocks formed the series of monuments that scar today's windswept terrain, which is why the name in pure Irish form is Sliabh na Caillí, which means Witch Mountain.

The cemetery dates back to 3,300 BC and it's spread over a vast area 3 km (2 miles) east of Oldcastle. The underground chambers, mostly sealed by mounds, are carved from soft green gritstone, which made them easy to chisel but prone to vandalism. Unique megalithic texts are etched onto the surface with swirling contours and radiating strokes.

GETTING HERE AND AROUND

Public transport via Bus Éireann's 187 service takes passengers as far as Oakcastle, and from there it's a 7-km (4-mile) hike or cycle to Cairn T. The climb to Cairn T is a steep incline on hilly terrain, so visitors should wear appropriate footwear and take the usual precautions. There is no access for visitors in wheelchairs as the approach road is very narrow and extreme caution is required.

There is a 10-car parking facility right at the start of the Loughcrew walk. The trailhead is visible from the car park and from the top of the hill there is a sweeping view across several counties.

TOURS

Loughcrew Guided Tour

GUIDED TOURS | This hike continues on to the visitor car park and uphill to cairns, starting at the Megalithic Centre. Stopping at vantage points along the way, guides tell the history and archaeological background. Passing the remains of seven cairns, the tour will give details of the sun's alignment and art forms. ✉ *Loughcrew, Corstown, Oldcastle* ☎ *86/736–1948 Niall, 87/211–3624 Sarah* 🌐 *loughcrewmegalithiccentre.com.*

Sights

★ Cairn T

TOMB | Cairn T is the largest and most convenient of the tombs in the Loughcrew complex. Its interior has a cruciform chamber with corbeled ceiling roof and a collection of fine Neolithic art. The cairn takes on new-age frenzy during the spring and autumn equinox dawn as the rays piece the chamber to illustrate the etchings. Guided tours from late May explore the history and mythology of Cairn T. ✉ *Corstown Oldcastle* ✣ *3 km (about 2 miles) east of Oldcastle, off R163* ☎ *87/052–4975* 🌐 *heritageireland.ie* 🎫 *Free.*

Loughcrew Megalithic Centre

VISITOR CENTER | This one-stop shop is the place to go to discover everything you need to know about Loughcrew, housed in stone cottages around the ridges of the site. Visitors can glamp, camp, park a caravan, or stay in yurts, join a walking tour, or have a slice of drizzle cake and a cup of Bewley's at the facility. ✉ *Summerbank Oldcastle* ☎ *86/736–1948* 🌐 *loughcrewmegalithiccentre.com.*

The cairns at Loughcrew were once covered with white quartz. A piece can still be found near the gate at Cairn T.

Carlingford and Cooley Peninsula

92 km (57 miles) north of Trim on M1.

Set on the edge of a vast lake at the base of the Cooley Mountains, with narrow streets that curve around historic buildings, Carlingford is one of the most striking towns in Ireland. Much of the 16th-century architecture and infrastructure is still preserved within the perimeter of the old walls.

A fine selection of bars in the historic center offer the local specialty, oysters, which is best enjoyed with a pint of Guinness by a fireplace as the wind swirls up from the lake.

GETTING HERE AND AROUND

The Dublin to Belfast train route stops at Dundalk and from there Bus Éireann's 161 is a regular service to Carlingford. Remember to buy a Leap Ticket for flexible and cheap fares. It's a direct 90-minute drive north on M1 from the capital.

Discard the car at the first opportunity to explore the winding streets on foot.

TOURS

Carlingford Medieval Town Tours

SPECIAL-INTEREST TOURS | An experienced local guide escorts visitors to the Dominican Priory, the Mint, the Tholsel, Taaffe's Castle, and King John's Castle in an informal stroll through the Medieval streets of this pretty harbor town. Graveyard and castle tours are also available. ✉ *Carlingford Tourist Office, Station House, Carlingford* ☎ *42/937–3650* 🎫 *€10* 🕐 *Closed in fall and winter.*

VISITOR INFORMATION

CONTACT Carlingford Tourist Office. ✉ *Station House, Fair Green* ☎ *42/937–3650* 🌐 *carlingford.ie.*

Sights

Carlingford Castle

CASTLE/PALACE | This late-12th-century harbor-front castle was seized in 1210 by King John of England, who had forced its owner into rebellion so that he could dominate him and curtail his growing power. From its vantage point it was always a critical point of defense for the region. It has often been at the crossroads of civil war. The Jacobite supporters of Catholic James II bombed the castle in the 17th century while William of Orange had a base there during the Battle of the Boyne. Carlingford Lough Heritage Trust provides guided tours of the castle from March to October. ☎ *42/937–3454* 🌐 *heritageireland.ie* 🎫 *Castle tour €8* 🕓 *Closed Nov.–Feb.*

Carlingford Heritage Centre

CHURCH | Base camp for all things Carlingford, drop by to explore triptych display cabinets, which give a chronological history of the town though maps, illustrations, and manuscripts of Carlingford from early settlement and the development of the medieval to modern community we see today, which was started by the Normans. The museum is in a restored 13th-century church and it's a trailhead for walking tours of the town. Organized walks can be arranged on-site. ✉ *Church Rd., Carlingford* ☎ *42/937–3454* 🌐 *carlingfordheritagecentre.com.*

Restaurants

Kingfisher Bistro

$ | CONTEMPORARY | The Kingfisher Bistro has all the usual suspects that you'd expect to find in a small contemporary restaurant, like herb-roasted chicken, fish of the day (sea-hopping fresh), and Thai pork. It opens for lunch on Sunday and fills a more interesting space with Carlingford mussels and prawns on the menu, with specials on offer. **Known for:** excellent service; lovely town center setting; Carlingford prawns. $ *Average main: €16* ✉ *Dundalk St.* ☎ *42/937–3716* 🌐 *kingfisherbistro.ie* 🕓 *Closed Tues. and Wed.*

Hotels

Carlingford House

$$ | B&B/INN | This 19th-century house in the center of Carlingford was once the local doctor's residence, but for the last few decades it's been the home of the Finegan family, who offer exceptional hospitality. **Pros:** clean lines; convenient to town; mountain view. **Cons:** sometimes a minimum two-night stay; street parking; shower only. $ *Rooms from: €180* ✉ *Dundalk St.* ☎ *42/937–3118* 🌐 *carlingfordhouse.com* 🛏 *5 rooms* 🍽 *No Meals.*

★ Ghan House

$$$ | B&B/INN | This is an elegant 18th-century house, set in its own walled grounds on the edge of Carlingford village. **Pros:** excellent food; very private; lake and mountain views. **Cons:** no elevator; most rooms not in main house; on the edge of town. $ *Rooms from: €190* ✉ *Old Quay La.* ☎ *42/937–3682* 🌐 *ghanhouse.com* 🕓 *Closed Christmas and New Year* 🛏 *12 rooms* 🍽 *Free Breakfast.*

Nightlife

★ PJ O'Hares

BARS | Hands down, this is the best place in town to eat and drink simple well-prepared food. You step back in time the minute you pass through the doorway. It has a grocery at the front and a pub with an open fire at the back where locals enjoy oysters with their Guinness. Outside spaces beckon, and it's busy on weekends. ✉ *Tholsel St.* ☎ *42/937–3106* 🌐 *pjoharescarlingford.ie.*

Activities

Carlingford Brewing Company Tour
FOOD AND DRINK TOURS | Owner Des Goldrick guides visitors through Carlingford's origins and the brewing process that makes his beer unique, followed by a sample tasting. Glodrick explores the legend of Donn Cúailnge, the Brown Bull of Cooley, and Carlingford's landmarks that have inspired the brew along the way. Stone-fired pizza is available in this exquisite mill setting, and tours and tastings last 1½ hours, which are on Saturday only unless by appointment. The premises are open for food Thursday–Sunday. *Old Mill, Riverstown 42/939–7519 carlingfordbrewing.ie €20 Closed Mon.–Wed.*

Carlingford Lough Cruise
CRUISES | Carlingford Ferry Company lets its hair down and dons a flower necklace in the summertime, harboring some fun time aboard its vessels to take passengers on a cruise that passes by the peninsula's southern shoreline and the medieval center of Carlingford with the Cooley Mountains as a backdrop. Across the bay are views of Greencastle Royal Castle and the Mourne Mountain Range. There are sunset options with dancing and drinks available on board. Ahoy! *Greenore Port, The Harbour, Greenore 1800/938–004 carlingfordloughcruises.com €22 Picnic tables available for groups.*

Monaghan Town

80 km (50 miles) northwest from Carlingford on N2.

A bustling market town in the heart of one of Ireland's major farming counties, Monaghan Town has an unexpected collection of architecturally pleasing buildings like its 17th-century Market House and its cathedral. It's refreshingly nontouristy, so expect the friendly locals to know your name at the local pub within an hour of arriving—and your business if you stay a little longer.

GETTING HERE AND AROUND

While off the rail grid, there is an excellent bus that links to Monaghan Town directly from Dublin City and airport on Bus Éireann's 32 service. Other direct routes from Dundalk, Cavan, Galway, Athlone, and Belfast ensure that Monaghan remains well-connected by public transport. Buy a Leap Card for hefty discounts.

Monaghan has an e-Parking system where visitors and locals can pay for street parking on an app or use one of the many car parks in town. It's small enough to navigate on foot.

TOURS

Monaghan Town Heritage Trail
GUIDED TOURS | A self-guided map through the town's local landmarks like Old Cross Square, the disused train station, the County Museum, and Rossmore Monument can be downloaded from Monaghan Town's website. *monaghantourism.com.*

VISITOR INFORMATION

CONTACT Monaghan Tourist Office. *Market House, Monaghan 47/81122 monaghantourism.com.*

Sights

Monaghan County Museum
HISTORY MUSEUM | A rapid countdown of the 25,000 years of Irish history, recalled through 50,000 objects, including early Stone Age tools, Bronze Age weapons, a funerary bowl, Lisdrumturk cauldron, and clothing. Murals and other collections help to bring the past to life. *1–2 Hill St. 47/82928 monaghan.ie/museum Free Closed Sun.*

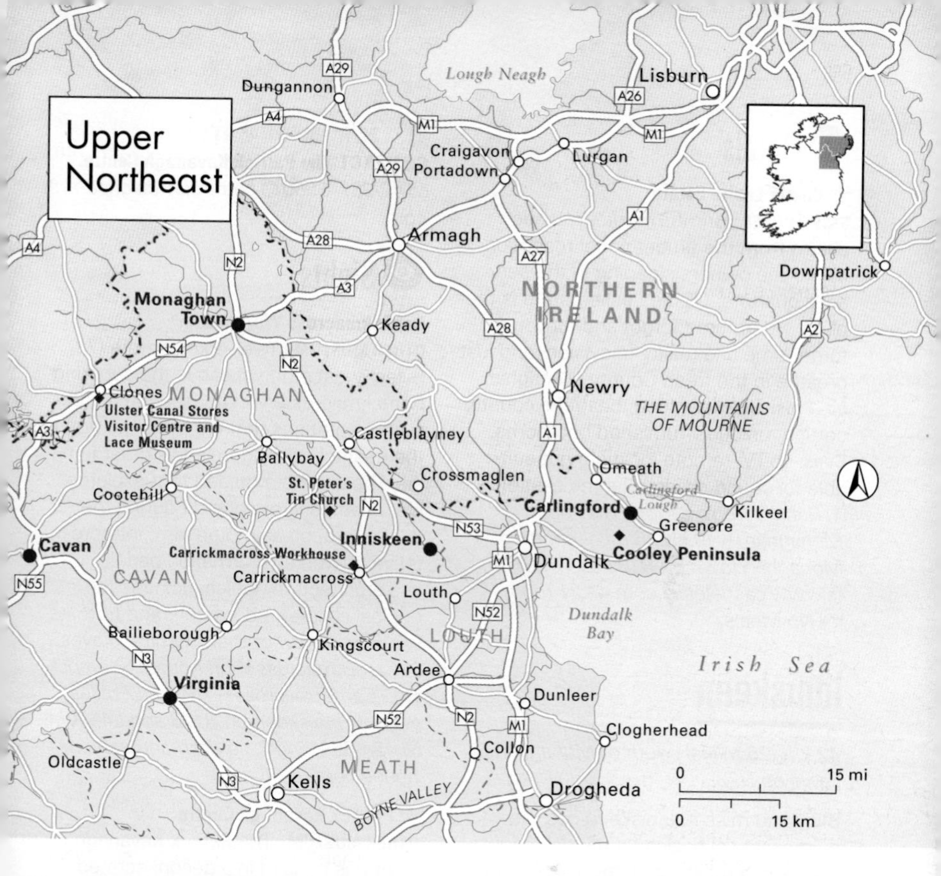

Ulster Canal Stores Visitor Centre and Lace Museum

OTHER MUSEUM | It's located in the pretty village of Clones, 21 km (13 miles) southwest of Monaghan, in a recently refurbished limestone canal storehouse built in the late 1800s. It houses the only museum in Ireland dedicated entirely to the crochet lace. It coined the "Linked by a Thread" exhibition, which follows the story of crochet lace from its beginnings in the post-famine period to its revival by dedicated locals in the 1980s. There's a collection dating from the Victorian era, right through to more modern designs like highly ornamental wedding dresses. The on-site café has tea and coffee with flavorsome local confectionery. ✉ *Cara St., Clones* ✣ *21 km (13 miles) southwest from Monaghan Town on N54* ☎ *47/52125* 🌐 *ulstercanalstoresvisitorcentre.ie* 🎫 *Free* 🕒 *Closed Sun. and Mon.*

Restaurants

Andy's Bar and Restaurant

$$ | **STEAKHOUSE** | **FAMILY** | Bringing unexpected quality to the center of Monaghan Town, this long-established family-owned bar and restaurant is a find. It offers generous and tasty local food, from its steak-house menu sourced from the the county's rich farmland to an impressive selection of fresh fish. **Known for:** craft beer range; good seafood; unexpected fine dining in a country town. $ *Average main: €18* ✉ *12 Market St.* ☎ *47/82277* 🌐 *andysrestaurant.ie* 🕒 *Closed Mon.*

Hotels

★ Castle Leslie Estate

$$$$ | **HOTEL** | Brimful of idiosyncratic charm from the timber panel reception hall to the owners sleeping in the servant's quarters, Castle Leslie Estate is the place where time forgot and for you to forget time and reality television, and just breathe in the fresh County Monaghan air. **Pros:** excellent food; beautiful country setting; uniquely furnished bedrooms. **Cons:** no TV; remote location; not suitable for young children (in the castle). *Rooms from: €300 ✉ Glaslough, Monaghan ✣ 10 km (6 miles) north of Monaghan Town on R185 ☎ 47/88100 ⊕ www.castleleslie.com 21 rooms No Meals.*

Inniskeen

42 km (26 miles) south of Monaghan Town on N2.

Blink and miss it. Inniskeen has the quintessential basics for an Irish country village: the mossy churchyard, primary school, a ribbon of bungalows and faux Georgian mansions on the peripheral, and, of course, a good local pub.

However, this seemingly innocuous residential crossroads stoked pent-up frustration with country living in one of Ireland's great poets, Patrick Kavanagh, who wrote of the area "you burgled my bank of youth." All has been forgiven by locals; there is a museum dedicated to his memory in the village.

GETTING HERE AND AROUND

Bus Éireann's 166 service toddles through Inniskeen a few times a day as it trundles on country roads between Dundalk and Cavan. A car or taxi gives greater flexibility in these parts. Street parking is free.

VISITOR INFORMATION

CONTACT The Patrick Kavanagh Centre. *☎ 42/937–8560 ⊕ patrickkavanaghcentre.com.*

Sights

Carrickmacross Workhouse

OTHER MUSEUM | Twelve kilometers (7 miles) west of Inniskeen is the sobering Carrickmacross Workhouse, one of 130 such institutions that were built to house the destitute during Ireland's great famine. The one-hour guided tour explores life, death, and emigration during the 1840s through animated film, interpretative artworks, information panels, and architecture, which includes the original children's dormitory and from its window, a view of mass famine graves. *✉ Carrickmacross Workhouse, Shercock Rd., Carrickmacross ✣ 12 km (7 miles) west of Inniskeen on R178 and L4620 ☎ 42/966–4540 ⊕ carrickmacrossworkhouse.com €6.*

★ Patrick Kavanagh Centre

OTHER MUSEUM | The Patrick Kavanagh Centre is housed in a deconsecrated Roman Catholic church that dates from 1820. Local lad Patrick Kavanagh, who rose to the very apex of Irish literary life with his lonesome prose, was baptized here in 1904. He attended regular Mass here and served as an altar boy. This church, St. Mary's, features in his novel *Tarry Flynn* and also in his semi-autobiographical book *The Green Fool.* Kavanagh is buried with his family in the adjoining churchyard.

The exhibition on-site follows the different stages of Patrick Kavanagh's life and the development of his literary craft. Touchscreens, memory boxes, letters, early-20th-century ephemera, and a short film help to reawaken the thoughts, soul, and memories of this isolated man of words. *☎ 42/937–8560 ⊕ patrickkavanaghcentre.com €10 Closed Fri.–Sun. ☞ Guided tour €15.*

St. Peter's Tin Church

CHURCH | One of Ireland's oddest sights is nestled into a forest by the old mill village of Laragh. Built in a Swiss Gothic hybrid style in 1890 by mill owner James McKean as a post-honeymoon gift to his bride, the Tin Church is something of an oddity in its woodland setting in County Mayo. It's a listed building and certainly unique to Ireland, and like its namesake St. Peter, a rock is the foundation of this exquisite little building.

The setting is almost as impressive as the corrugated iron–clad church, rising over a boulder by a rushing river with lush green ferns and leafy foliage in the background. It was deconsecrated in the 1950s. ✉ *Laragh Dooraa, Laragh* ✣ *17 km (10 miles) west of Inniskeen on L8100* ☎ *87/895–7680* 🌐 *tinchurch.ie* 🎫 *Free.*

Restaurants

★ **Courthouse Restaurant**

$$ | **IRISH** | Moody decor, pared-back sandstone walls, mahogany furnishing, white linen, and atmospheric lighting help to create this intimate upstairs dining space in busy Carrickmacross on the westerly side of County Monaghan. The reasonably priced menu offers daily specials, à la carte or a tasting tapas selection, and is anchored in local produce like fish, crab, pork, and duck. **Known for:** historical building in town center; good value for food quality; elegant, pared-back decor. $ *Average main: €23* ✉ *1 Monaghan St., Carrickmacross* ✣ *11 km (7 miles) west of Inniskeen on R178 and L4620* ☎ *42/969–2848* 🌐 *courthouserestaurant.ie* ⏲ *Closed Mon.–Wed.*

Nightlife

Daniel McNello's Bar

BARS | Established in 1710, this famous red-painted stone pub has a nickname, The Kavanagh Hideout, as the famous poet was known to idle away time here. The interior is full-on traditional old-world charm and is almost a shrine to Patrick Kavanagh, with several paintings and images dedicated to him. ✉ *Candlefort, Inniskeen* ☎ *42/937–8355.*

Shopping

★ **Carrickmacross Lace**

FABRICS | Based in a stone building on the market square of this busy County Monaghan hamlet 11 km (7 miles) west of Inniskeen, the legacy of this fine craft outlet stretches back to 1820. It's operated by the Carrickmacross Lace Co-op and is designed with unique motifs and exquisite detail. In fact, the soft intricate material was the fabric of choice for England's Queen Victoria. However, it was when fashion designers the Emmanuelles used Carrickmacross lace on the late Princess Diana's wedding dress that it gained an international audience. Demonstrations are available on request in the light airy showroom with a history of the lace on display along with retail. ✉ *Market Sq., Carrickmacross* ☎ *42/966–4176* 🌐 *carrickmacrosslace.ie* ⏲ *Closed Sun.*

Cavan

36 km (22 miles) north of Fore, 114 km (71 miles) northwest of Dublin.

Like all the larger towns of the region, Cavan is growing and prosperous. It is perhaps best known for its crystal factory. But as one of the main transportation hubs of the Midlands, Cavan has also attracted an impressive array of restaurants and hotels, so this is a fine base for exploring this region, which lies near the border to Northern Ireland. There are two central streets: Main Street is like many other streets in similar Irish towns, with its pubs and shops; Farnham Street has Georgian houses, churches, a courthouse, and a bus station.

GETTING HERE AND AROUND

Cavan is a thriving market town on the main N3 from Navan to Enniskillen in Northern Ireland. There is metered pay-parking in the town center. The town and surrounding south Ulster area, including neighboring Monaghan, relies on an extensive bus network for public transport. Cavan is equidistant from Belfast and Galway with a three-hour travel time to both cities by bus. Bus Éireann serves Cavan on Galway–Belfast, Athlone–Belfast, and Dublin–Donegal Expressway routes, and there is weekday service to small towns throughout Cavan and Monaghan.

CONTACTS Cavan Bus Office. ✉ *Farnham St., Cavan* ☎ *049/433–1709.*

VISITOR INFORMATION

CONTACTS Cavan Tourist Office. ✉ *Farnham St., Cavan* ☎ *049/433–1942* 🌐 *www.thisiscavan.ie.*

★ MacNean's House & Restaurant

$$$$ | **IRISH** | Run by Neven Maguire, one of Ireland's top chefs, MacNean's is one of the best restaurants in the country; in fact, there's a waiting list of up to two years for weekends. The Menu Prestige, at €110 (€170, including wine), delivers a staggering selection of courses. **Known for:** delicious local duck; eight-course dinner menu; very difficult to get a table. 💲 *Average main: €89* ✉ *Main St., Blacklion* ☎ *071/985–3022* 🌐 *www.nevenmaguire.com* ⏲ *Closed Mon. and Tues. No lunch Wed.–Sat.* *Jacket required.*

Murph's Gastro Pub

$$ | **MODERN IRISH** | The open fire and rustic finishes in this riverside bar make it a warm and inviting location for a drink or a casual meal. The restaurant adds more of an occasion and in the summer the riverside terrace can be quite special. **Known for:** stunning interior sometimes used as a reception venue; great place to stop on road trips; reasonable pricing. 💲 *Average main: €20* ✉ *The Derragarra Inn, Derragarra Lower, Butlersbridge, Cavan* ✣ *7 km (4 miles) north of Cavan Town on the R198* ☎ *49/433–1033* 🌐 *murphsgastropub.ie* ⏲ *Closed Mon. and Tues.*

Oak Room Restaurant

$$$$ | **MODERN IRISH** | Paired-back elegance with exposed timber flooring, dimmed lighting, and bare tables, this restaurant is operated by an experienced and well-recognized chef in Ireland's culinary scene. Given the abundance of in-season ingredients and skill, the sensible price tag comes as a welcome bonus. **Known for:** top table restaurant; reasonable price; sophisticated menu. 💲 *Average main: €36* ✉ *24 Bridge St., Cavan* ☎ *49/437–1414* 🌐 *theoakroom.ie* ⏲ *Closed Mon. and Tues.*

★ The Olde Post Inn

$$$$ | **IRISH** | A restored, stone former post office in an elegantly landscaped garden, the Olde Post Inn has won a clutch of awards and, as a result, is often booked solid. Sea bass, steak, game, and bacon and cabbage terrine are main-course favorites and highlight local and seasonal ingredients. **Known for:** outstanding venison; impressive wine selection; dreamy rural location. 💲 *Average main: €69* ✉ *Cloverhill, N54, Cavan* ✣ *11 km (8 miles) north of Cavan* ☎ *047/55555* 🌐 *www.theoldepostinn.com* ⏲ *Closed Mon. and Tues. Closed Wed. off-season. No lunch Wed.–Sat.* ☞ *Early dinner menu available, €49.*

Cabra Castle

$$$$ | **HOTEL** | With its collection of mock-Gothic towers, turrets, and crenellations, along with rumors of paranormal activity, Cabra Castle has been deemed one of the world's scariest hotels; the Irish Ghosthunters Association has confirmed that it was indeed a place visited by spirits. **Pros:** stunning views of the countryside; superb range of rooms;

Victorian Gothic charm. **Cons:** emphasis on weddings; not for the easily spooked; some rooms in castle are small. *Rooms from: €230 Carrickmacross Rd., Kingscourt 45 km (27 miles) south of Cavan, on R179 042/966–7030 www.cabracastle.com 105 rooms Free Breakfast.*

Cavan Crystal Hotel
$ | **HOTEL** | **FAMILY** | Very much a modern hotel in its heyday just before the big crash in 2006, when money from parks flowed irresponsibly and properties of this scale cropped up or were extended with grand designs in unlikely places. **Pros:** Value; Pool and gym and free parking; Striking glass foyer entrance. **Cons:** No grounds; Contemporary design relects little of the area; A miles outside town center. *Rooms from: €85 Dublin Road, Cavan 49/436 0600 cavancrystalhotel.com 85 rooms No Meals.*

★ **Farnham Estate Spa and Golf Resort**
$$ | **HOTEL** | A blend of stone, wood, and glass, the Farnham Estate—one of the top spots in the Midlands to detox and purify—exudes the promise of contentment over its 1,300 acres, as well as offering a superb choice of dining options. **Pros:** revitalizing spa; cathedral-like silence of the grounds; nature trails. **Cons:** slow service at peak times; spa gets very busy; weddings and conferences can take over. *Rooms from: €179 Farnham Estate, Killashandra Rd., Farnham 049/437–7700 www.farnhamestate.ie 158 rooms Free Breakfast.*

Slieve Russell Hotel Golf and Country Club
$$ | **HOTEL** | Outdoors types, especially golfers, prick up their ears when they hear of the facilities on offer at this modern country hotel set on 300 acres—apart from two golf courses, it also has an excellent health club. **Pros:** opulent rooms, all with large beds; excellent dining options; convenient place to break up a journey between Dublin and Sligo. **Cons:** busy with families during school breaks; unimpressive exterior; late-night noise in some areas. *Rooms from: €178 Off N87, 26 km (16 miles) west of Cavan, Cranaghan Take N3 to Belturbet, then take left turn for Ballyconnell and hotel is 8 km (5 miles) along this road 049/952–6444 www.slieverussell.ie 222 rooms Free Breakfast.*

Activities

GOLF

County Cavan Golf Club
GOLF | Visitors are welcome at this beautifully manicured 18-hole course, set amid parkland in the heart of the southern Ulster lakelands. The Cavan Club has a long pedigree stretching back to 1894; it moved to its present location in 1920.

The visual reshaping included work on the fairways lined with mature trees and present a challenge, especially on holes 14–18. The 197-yard 10th is difficult from a tee-box in front of the clubhouse to a new green under an old chestnut tree. Golfers can sharpen their pitching, chipping, bunker, and putting techniques in a top-notch practice area. *Arnmore House, Drumelis 049/433–1541 www.cavangolf.ie Mon. and Tues. €20, Wed.–Sun. €25 18 holes, 6164 yards, par 70.*

Virginia

30 km (190 miles) southeast of Cavan Town on N3.

Sweet little Virginia on the shores of Lough Ramor has a spiderweb of trails through its streets and into the forested surroundings.

GETTING HERE AND AROUND

Directly accessible from Dublin on Bus Éireann's 109 service, the village also has Route 187 to connect it to Kells and Oakcastle (near Loughcrew Cairns).

The village is a 90-minute drive from Dublin on M3.

Cavan County Museum

NOTABLE BUILDING | Constructed in 1872 as a convent for the Poor Clare Sisters, this building retains many of its Victorian architectural features which exemplify its austere past. Outside, a permanent World War I Trench Experience replicates the life of an Irish guard according to the manual produced by the Royal Irish Fusiliers at the Somme. Other exhibits recall the 1916 Rising. Internal galleries have unique collections dating from the Stone Age to the 20th century and they depict life in penal times and the devastating effects of a dominant, unenlightened, and unfair landlord class system. ✉ *Virginia Rd., Ballyjamesduff, Virginia* ☎ *49/854–4070* 🌐 *cavanmuseum.ie* 🎫 *€6* ⏲ *Closed Sun. and Mon.*

The Ramor Theatre

THEATER | The Ramor Theatre is the only professional performance space in County Cavan. It has regular theater, comedy, and performance from local amateurs to nationally acclaimed artists. It also exhibits paintings and sculpture. ✉ *Main St., Virginia* ☎ *49/854–7074* 🌐 *ramortheatre.com* ⏲ *Closed Sat.–Mon.*

Chapter 13

BELFAST

Updated by
Robin Gauldie

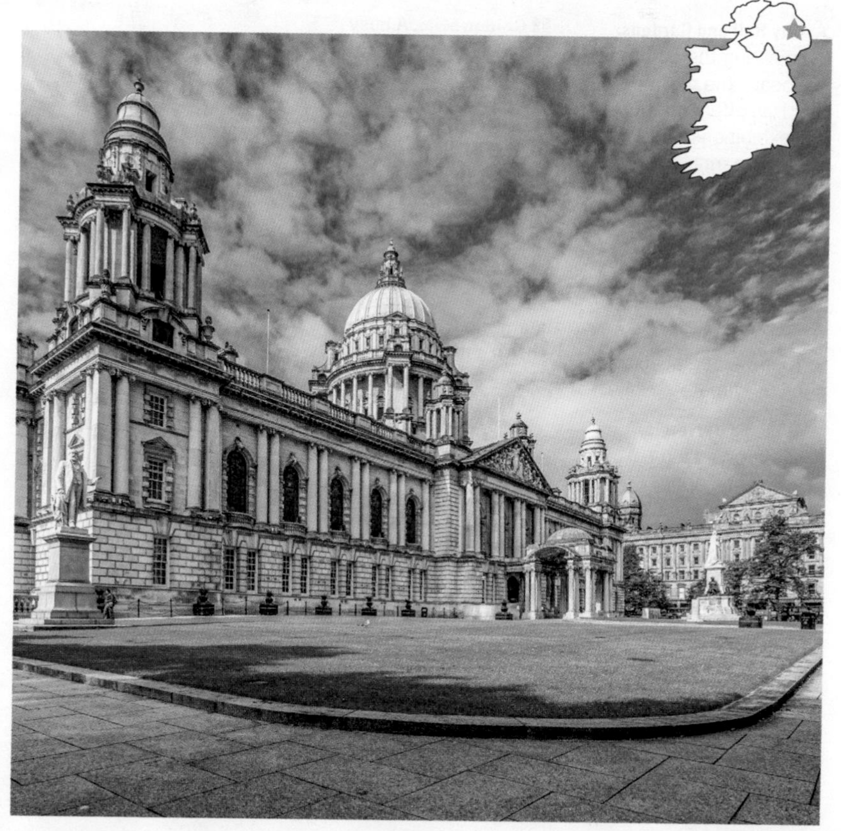

Sights ★★★★☆ Restaurants ★★★★★ Hotels ★★★★☆ Shopping ★★★★☆ Nightlife ★★★☆☆

WELCOME TO BELFAST

TOP REASONS TO GO

★ ***Titanic* Belfast:** Opened in memory of the tragic liner built in the city, the hugely successful *Titanic* Belfast exhibition center is a dazzling mix of reconstructions and special effects.

★ **City Hall and Gardens:** Dominating the commercial heart, the restored City Hall offers interactive exhibitions, a dome and whispering gallery, stunning gardens, and a serene courtyard.

★ **Murals:** Colorful political wall murals are a compelling reminder of the Troubles, while newer art forms reflect global issues such as climate change.

★ **Queen's University Area:** A rewarding oasis of mellow redbrick Victorian architecture and a place to be wowed by the treasures of Ulster Museum and the delightful Botanic Gardens.

★ **Cathedral Quarter:** The Merchant Hotel and Metropolitan Arts Centre are just two attractions of the hip Cathedral Quarter, a network of cobbled streets and 19th-century alleyways overflowing with traditional pubs.

Standing on the banks of the River Lagan on the east coast of Northern Ireland, Belfast is the capital and largest city of Northern Ireland. A relatively small city, Belfast is divided into several quarters and districts, each known for its own distinct character.

1 Golden Mile. A busy strip with historic redbrick buildings, but now noted for its high-spirited nightlife as it is filled with bars, restaurants, and hotels. Highlights here include the Crumlin Road Gaol and the Grand Opera House.

2 Central District. The main shopping heart of the city, made up of pedestrianized streets and atmospheric old alleyways with traditional music bars and contemporary cafés. Within this district, you'll find the Cathedral Quarter with its art galleries and lively bistros, and Titanic Quarter, with its world-class museum, tours, Titanic Hotel, and busy waterfront.

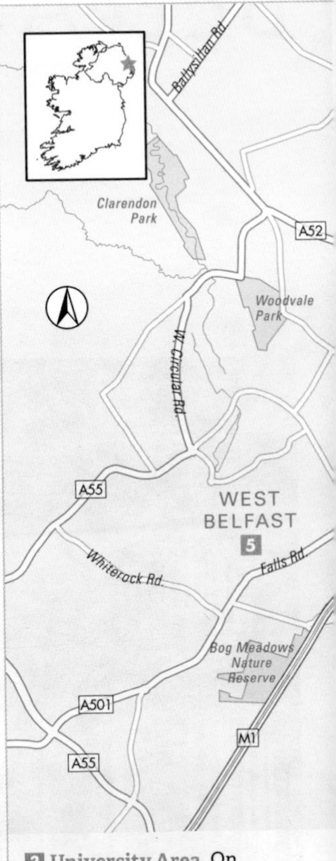

3 University Area. On the southern side of Belfast, this area is ideal for strolling through public parks and the wonderful Botanic Gardens, as well as admiring the university buildings and museum treasures. Another highlight is the Ulster Museum.

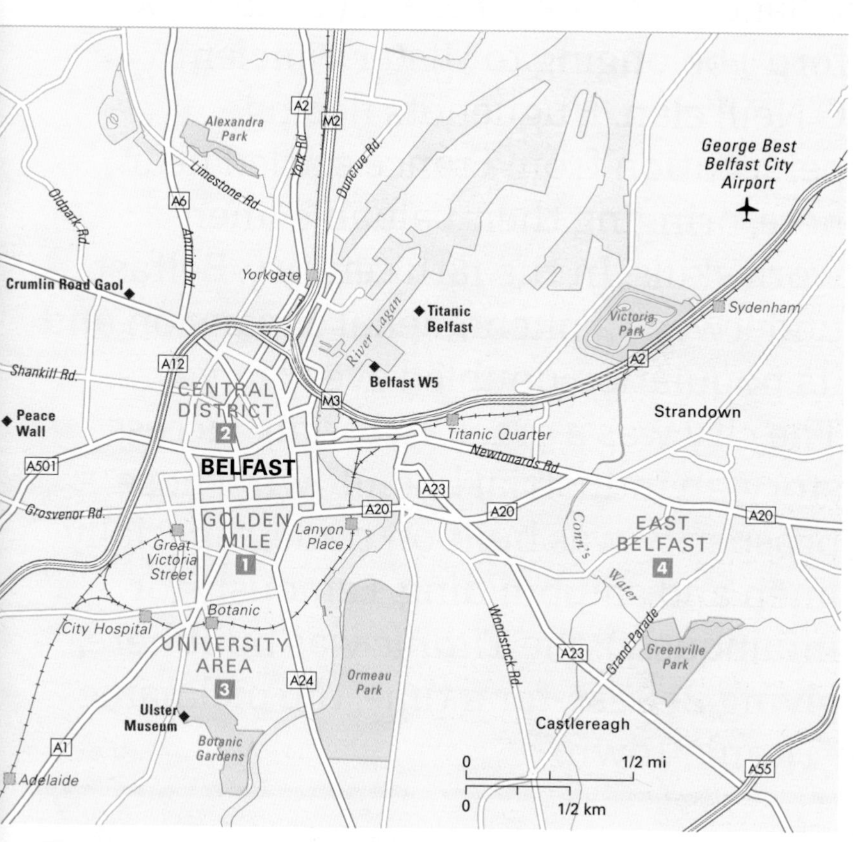

4 East Belfast. Home to an ever-growing number of buzzy restaurants, cafés, and designer shops, the east side is also the location of the Stormont Parliament, which runs public tours.

5 West Belfast. Visitors come here for the famed political wall murals, but you can also stop off at Culturlann, an Irish language café, and shop or look around the James Connolly center on Falls Road.

Before English and Scottish settlers arrived in the 1600s, Belfast was a tiny village called Béal Feirste ("sandbank ford") belonging to Ulster's ancient O'Neill clan. Huguenots fleeing persecution from France settled near here, bringing their valuable linen-work skills. In the 18th century, Belfast underwent a phenomenal expansion and its population doubled every 10 years. The city was a great Victorian success story, an industrial boomtown whose prosperity was built on trade, especially linen and shipbuilding. Famously (or infamously), the *Titanic* was built here, giving Belfast, for a time, the nickname "Titanic Town."

Civil unrest in the city in the late 1960s over the allocation of houses and jobs for Catholics led to the "Troubles," a 30-year conflict that resulted in old animosities flaring up between Catholics and Protestants. Peace was eventually restored in 1998 after the signing of the Belfast Good Friday Agreement, and although some sectarian divisions still exist, the two communities now live in relative harmony. Today the city's population is nearly 300,000, tourist numbers have increased, and this dramatically transformed city is enjoying an unparalleled renaissance.

This is all a welcome change from the period when news about Belfast meant reports about the Troubles. Since the 1994 ceasefire, Northern Ireland's capital city has benefited from major hotel investment, gentrified quaysides (or strands), a sophisticated new performing arts center, and major initiatives to boost tourism such as the opening of *Titanic* Belfast.

As part of this embattled city's rediscovered identity, it has in recent years restored most of its major public buildings such as museums, churches, theaters, City Hall, Ulster Hall—and even the glorious Crown Bar—spending millions of pounds on its built heritage. A jail that at the height of the Troubles held some of the most notorious murderers involved in paramilitary violence is now a major visitor attraction. Even more than 20 years after the peace agreement of 1998, the political wall murals continue to attract visitors, although parts of the city center have also seen a surge of new nonsectarian street art.

Belfast's city center is made up of three roughly contiguous areas that are easy to navigate on foot. From the south end to the north, it's about an hour's leisurely walk. The three main areas cover the Queen's University district, the central shopping area, and the Cathedral Quarter. The university area takes in the bohemian Botanic Avenue, Dublin Road, and Great Victoria Street; radiating out from City Hall are mostly pedestrianized streets making up the central zone with some attractive covered arcades and the Victoria Square shopping center; the Cathedral Quarter is the trendy part of the city close to St. Anne's Cathedral beside the stunning Metropolitan Arts Centre. This area consists of trendy restaurants, cafés, and whiskey bars hidden along cobbled streets or in narrow passageways called "entries," and is buzzing with activity by night. Many tourists also gravitate to other sections of the city such as the Titanic Quarter, a 20-minute walk from the city center or short bus ride across the River Lagan, while the new Gaeltacht Quarter, straddling the Falls Road, nurtures the city's Irish Gaelic–speaking culture and heritage.

Planning

Getting Here and Around

AIR

Belfast International Airport at Aldergrove is the North's principal airport, 30½ km (19 miles) north of town. George Best Belfast City Airport is the secondary airport, 6½ km (4 miles) east of the city. It receives flights from U.K. provincial airports, from London's Gatwick and Heathrow, and from Stansted and Luton (both near London). Few airlines serve Northern Ireland from beyond the UK; there are plentiful international connections via Glasgow and Edinburgh (both less than one hour's flying time) and London Heathrow.

Belfast International Airport at Aldergrove is the North's principal airport, 30½ km (19 miles) north of town. George Best Belfast City Airport is the secondary airport, 6½ km (4 miles) east of the city. It receives flights from U.K. provincial airports, from London's Gatwick and Heathrow, and from Stansted and Luton (both near London). United Airlines and several Europe-based airlines are the major carriers serving Northern Ireland's airports.

AIRPORT CONTACTS Belfast International Airport at Aldergove. ☎ *028/9448–4848* 🌐 *www.belfastairport.com.* **City of Derry Airport.** ☎ *028/7181–0784* 🌐 *www.cityofderryairport.com.* **George Best Belfast City Airport.** ☎ *028/9093–9093* 🌐 *www.belfastcityairport.com.*

FLIGHTS

Scheduled services from the United States and Canada are mostly routed through Dublin, Glasgow, London, or Manchester. Frequent services to Belfast's two airports are scheduled throughout the day from London Heathrow, London Gatwick, and Luton (all of which have fast coordinated subway or

The Troubles

Northern Ireland's historic conflict between Catholic and Protestant, Irish and English, had its roots in the first Norman incursions in the 12th century, when the English endeavored to subdue the potential enemy they saw in Ireland. The northern province of Ulster proved the hardest to conquer, but in 1607, its Irish nobility fled, their lands then given by the English to "the Planters," Protestants from England and Scotland.

Fast-forward through three centuries of smoldering tensions and religious strife to the 1918 nationalist vote across Ireland for Sinn Féin ("Ourselves Alone"), the party that believed in independence for all of Ireland. In Ulster, however, 22 (out of 29) seats went to the Unionists, who believed in maintaining British rule. After 50 years of living with a Unionist majority, students in Belfast's Queen's University launched a civil rights protest in 1968, claiming equal rights in jobs, housing, and opportunity. They were met by brutal British suppression, which awoke the Irish Republican Army (IRA), dormant for decades. Britain then imposed Direct Rule. This struggle tragically came to a head on Bloody Sunday, January 30, 1972, when British paratroopers opened fire on people participating in a nonviolent protest in Derry against the British policy of internment without trial. When the smoke cleared, 13 people—all Catholic and unarmed—had been killed.

Decades of guerrilla conflict ensued between the IRA, the UDA/UVF (Protestant/Loyalist paramilitaries), and the British government and continued until 1998's Good Friday Agreement, which finally gave the province its own parliament. But two months later, a massive car bomb exploded in the quiet market town of Omagh on August 15. A minority of dissident Republicans had succeeded in killing 31 people. Despite this, the peace process continued, and Unionists eventually entered government proceedings with Sinn Féin at the end of 1999.

In September 2005, the IRA decommissioned its weapons. In 2009, the Loyalist paramilitaries—the Ulster Volunteer Force and the Red Hand Commando destroyed their weapons. By 2010, the biggest Loyalist paramilitary group, the Ulster Defense Association, decommissioned all weapons and was closely followed by two Irish Republican paramilitary groups—the extreme Irish National Liberation Army and the Official IRA—who also announced they had put weapons beyond use. The endorsement of what was hoped to be a "final political deal" culminated in the Hillsborough Castle Agreement (2010), securing the stability of the Northern Ireland Assembly.

For many nationalists, the icing on the political cake came in June 2010 from the British government: an apology for Bloody Sunday saying it was "unjustified and unjustifiable."

However, the government's attempt in 2021 to halt the prosecution of the only British soldier to be charged with homicide on Bloody Sunday—which was overruled by the Belfast High Court in 2022—and renewed allegations of collusion in the 1990s between the Royal Ulster Constabulary and "loyalist" terrorists have highlighted the nationalist community's ongoing grievances.

rail connections to central London) and from 17 other U.K. airports.

CONTACTS Aer Arann Islands. ☎ *091/593–034* 🌐 *www.aerarannislands.ie.* **Aer Lingus.** ☎ *0333/004–5000* 🌐 *www.aerlingus.com.* **British Airways.** ☎ *0844/493–0787* 🌐 *www.ba.com.* **EasyJet.** ☎ *033/3055–1515* 🌐 *www.easyjet.com.* **Jet2.** ☎ *0333/300–0042* 🌐 *www.jet2.com.* **Ryanair.** ☎ *01279/58395* 🌐 *www.ryanair.com.* **United.** ☎ *0845/607–6760* 🌐 *www.united.com.*

AIRPORT TRANSFERS

Ulsterbus, a branch of Translink, operates Airport Express 300 buses (one-way £8, round-trip £11.50) several times an hour between Belfast International Airport and Belfast city center (6:50 am–6:15 pm), and Airport Express 600 buses between George Best Belfast City Airport and the city center (one-way £2.60; every 20 minutes, weekdays 6 am–9:30 pm). From the City Airport, you can also travel into Belfast by train from Sydenham Halt to Lanyon Place Station or catch a taxi from the airport to your hotel. Value Cabs serves both Belfast airports. The fare from Belfast International to Belfast city center is around £32; from Belfast City Airport to the city center is around £8.

CONTACTS Airporter. ✉ *Belfast* ☎ *028/7126–9996* 🌐 *www.airporter.co.uk.* **Translink Airport Services.** ✉ *Belfast* ☎ *028/9066–6630* 🌐 *www.translink.co.uk/usingourservicesandproducts/airportservices.* **Value Cabs.** ✉ *Belfast* ☎ *028/9080–9080* 🌐 *www.valuecabs.co.uk.*

BUS

Pink-and-white Metro buses are the best way to get around. Fares range from £1.40 to £2, depending on the zone. A Metro day ticket costs £4 and takes you anywhere on the network. Most bus routes start from Donegal Square or adjoining streets. The new Glider is a rapid-bus cross-city transit system that links west and east Belfast and takes in the Titanic Quarter via the city center. The service, which has two routes, G1 and G2, is operated by Translink and connects with the wider bus and rail network. The G1 runs from the Twinbrook area in the west of the city, via the center, to the east as far as Dundonald. The G2 operates from Wellington Place in the city center to Titanic Quarter. You can buy a ticket for the Glider at the Metro Kiosk at Donegall Square West or in the Visit Belfast Tourist Office, Donegall Square North, both of which are just a few yards from where the bus starts at Wellington Place (or they can be bought at main bus stations). A single journey is £2. You must have a ticket before you board. One-day unlimited travel on all Glider and Metro services costs £4.

CAR

Belfast is 167 km (104 miles) north of Dublin. Motorways, or dual carriageways, lead into Belfast's city center from the main airports and seaports, and the fast N1/A1 motorway links the city with Dublin. The trip takes about two hours. The drive from Derry takes 90 minutes. The main arterial routes into central Belfast are busy only at peak commuter times, between 8 and 9 am and 5 and 6 pm.

Street parking costs £1.30 per hour for a pay-and-display ticket from a meter. The maximum parking time is two hours for such street spaces. Be careful not to overstay, as zealous clamping wardens operate. Multistory parking garages are at the Victoria Square and Castle Court shopping centers. Some, but not all, hotels have parking. If you need it, ask a hotel or inn prior to booking.

TRAIN

As the capital city of Northern Ireland, Belfast is well served by an efficient train network. Most trains arrive and leave from Lanyon Place Station, a 15-minute walk from the city center.

CONTACTS Belfast Metro Service. ✉ *Donegall Sq. W, Belfast* ☎ *028/9066–6630*

🌐 *www.translink.co.uk/metro.* **Lanyon Place Rail Station.** ✉ *E. Bridge St., Belfast* ☎ *028/9066–6630.*

Restaurants and Hotels

Belfast has experienced an influx of au courant and internationally influenced restaurants, bistros, wine bars, and—as in Dublin—European-style café-bars where you can get good food most of the day and linger over a drink. By the standards of the United States, or even the rest of the United Kingdom, restaurant prices can be surprisingly moderate. In Belfast's surrounding area, you can also choose from the humblest terraced town houses or farm cottages to the grandest country houses. Dining rooms of country-house lodgings frequently match the standard of top-quality restaurants. A service charge of 10% may be added to the check; it's customary to pay this, unless the service was bad.

With the lifting of COVID restrictions in 2022, demand for accommodations has rebounded. So have hotel rates, which increased by an average 10% and in some cases almost doubled in 2022. At least three new hotels, with a total of 350 rooms, were set to open in the city center in 2023, so increased competition may help to bring prices down.

PRICES

⇨ *Restaurant prices are the average cost of a main course at dinner or, if dinner is not served, at lunch. Hotel prices are the lowest cost of a standard double room in high season. Restaurant and hotel reviews have been shortened. For full information, visit Fodors.com.*

What It Costs in Pounds Sterling

$	$$	$$$	$$$$
RESTAURANTS			
under £21	£21–£25	£26–£30	over £30
HOTELS			
under £82	£82–£115	£116–£160	over £160

Tours

BICYCLE TOURS

Belfast City Bike Tours

BICYCLE TOURS | Join guided bike rides of many areas with Belfast City Bike Tours. Cycle lanes are provided on most main roads and excellent paths link up all sections of the towpath and riverbank with signposted trails. ✉ *Belfast* ☎ *077/8049–6969* 🌐 *www.belfastcitybiketours.com* 🎫 *From £35.*

BUS TOURS

★ **Belfast City Sightseeing**

BUS TOURS | Belfast City Sightseeing runs the most comprehensive open-top tour through Belfast. The Belfast City Tour covers the City Hall, University Quarter, Shipyard, Titanic Quarter, Stormont, Shankill and Falls Roads, peace lines, Crumlin Road Gaol, and the Grand Opera House on Great Victoria Street. You can hop off and hop on as you please at any of the 23 stops. The entire route, without stops, takes about an hour and a half. The combo ticket allows discounted entry prices to some visitor attractions. The full-day *Game of Thrones* Tour takes in locations in North Antrim and runs daily throughout the year. ✉ *City Tour departs from Castle Place; Game of Thrones Tour departs daily from Glengall St., Central District* ☎ *028/9024–7797* 🌐 *www.belfastcitysightseeing.com* 🎫 *City Tour from £18; Game of Thrones Tour £35, includes Giant's Causeway.*

Belfast Music Tour

BUS TOURS | To delve into Belfast's rock-music history, book a ride with the Belfast Music Tour, a musical bus journey on which you'll learn about the places where internationally acclaimed performers like Van Morrison and flautist James Galway grew up. You'll also learn the stories of such bands as the Undertones, Stiff Little Fingers, and Snow Patrol. The tours—tickets £17, available at the Visit Belfast Centre—last two hours and leave the Ulster Hall, Bedford Street, at 2 pm mostly on the last Saturday of each month, but check the website for details. The final stop is the Oh Yeah Music Centre (✉ *15–21 Gordon St.*), which exhibits costumes, equipment, and rock memorabilia, all part of the Belfast Music Exhibition. Admission to the center is free whether you're on the tour or not. ✉ *15–21 Gordon St., Cathedral Quarter* ☎ *028/9031–0845* 🌐 *www.ohyeahbelfast.com.*

Giants Causeway Coastal Tours

DRIVING TOURS | Historical walking and driving tours that come with tales of myths and legends are the specialty of Giants Causeway Coastal Tours. The company also runs excursions outside Belfast to some of Northern Ireland's major tourist attractions. The owner tailors his tours to suit individual interests and requirements and picks up visitors from Dublin Airport, Belfast International Airport, and cruise ships. ✉ *Central District* ☎ *079/1229–0935* 🌐 *www.giantscausewaycoastaltours.com* 🎫 *Full-day tour for 6 people £300.*

McComb's Coach Travel

BUS TOURS | McComb's specializes in a *Game of Thrones* tour costing £30 per person. As part of the tour, optional tickets can also be purchased for visiting the Giant's Causeway and cost an extra £15. Parts of the *Game of Thrones* series were filmed in Belfast, County Antrim, and other areas of Northern Ireland. ✉ *22 Donegall Rd., Central District* ✣ *Beside the Belfast International Youth Hostel* ☎ *028/9031–5333* 🌐 *www.mccombscoaches.com/tours* 🎫 *£30.*

TAXI TOURS

The Official Black Taxi Tours

DRIVING TOURS | All the main political highlights and trouble spots of the 1970s and '80s, such as the Falls and Shankill Roads, are covered by the comprehensive Official Black Taxi Tours. They also run day tours to the Giant's Causeway and Antrim coast. Pickups are available from your hotel or bed-and-breakfast, or from bus and train stations. ✉ *Belfast* ☎ *028/9064–2264* 🌐 *www.belfasttours.com* 🎫 *From £55.*

TaxiTrax Tours

DRIVING TOURS | The itinerary of the popular TaxiTrax Tours provides a balanced history lesson covering the Troubles and includes the peace wall and the city's famed murals. ✉ *King St., Belfast* ☎ *028/9031–5777* 🌐 *www.taxitrax.com* 🎫 *From £50.*

Titanic Tours Belfast

SPECIAL-INTEREST TOURS | For an in-depth *Titanic* tour—one that also takes in the *Nomadic,* the *Titanic*'s dock and pump house, as well as several other locations—consider Titanic Tours Belfast, a tour by taxi, run by Susie Millar, the great-granddaughter of an assistant deck engineer who sailed on the ill-fated liner. Tours are by appointment and can accommodate up to four people. They last nearly three hours. Pickup is arranged from your accommodations. ✉ *Belfast* ☎ *078/5271–6655* 🌐 *www.titanictours-belfast.co.uk* 🎫 *From £30.*

WALKING TOURS

Experience Belfast

WALKING TOURS | Focusing on the Troubles as well as hidden buildings and history, Experience Belfast operates two walking tours, which meet at the front gates of Belfast City Hall; look for the Experience Belfast umbrella. The Troubles Tour: Walls & Bridges leaves at 10 am from

Monday to Saturday and Sunday at noon, and lasts 2½ hours. In the summer, it is held twice daily. The Hidden Belfast Tour leaves at 11 am in July and August. Check website for departure times and phone in advance to confirm. ✉ *Donegall Sq. N, Central District* ✣ *Meet outside front gates of City Hall* ☎ *077/7164–0746* 🌐 *www.experiencebelfast.com* 🎫 *£18.*

Parliament Buildings Tour

PRIVATE GUIDES | Free tours of Parliament Buildings are held twice every weekday at 11 am and 2 pm. Take a stroll around the home of the Northern Ireland Assembly to see one of the city's most striking pieces of architecture. The Members' Dining Room is open to the public for lunch (£21 for three courses) or afternoon tea (£16), from where you can enjoy a view overlooking the Stormont estate and the rolling Castlereagh hills of east Belfast. It is open 10–4 weekdays, and booking is mandatory via its website or by phone (☎ *028/9052–1695*). ✉ *Upper Newtownards Rd., Stormont, East Belfast* ☎ *028/9052–1802* 🌐 *www.niassembly.gov.uk.*

Titanic Walking Tours

WALKING TOURS | Colin Cobb holds fascinating guided tours of Queen's Island, which explores all things *Titanic*. Tours last 90 minutes and visitors are taken through the highlights of the main buildings associated with the liner. The meeting point is outside the main entrance of *Titanic* Belfast on Queen's Road in the Titanic Quarter. From the city center you can take the Glider bus, G2, which leaves from Wellington Place close to the City Hall. ✉ *Titanic Quarter* ☎ *079/0435–0339* 🌐 *www.titanicwalk.com* 🎫 *£10.*

Festivals and Events

The Belfast International Arts Festival, held in October, is one of the biggest, with a packed program of arts, music, and literature. Belfast's Cathedral Arts Quarter Festival, held late April to early May, uses established, new, and unusual venues throughout the oldest part of the city center for two weeks of music, theater, and visual arts. In early April, the Titanic Festival commemorates the anniversary of the sinking in 1912 of RMS *Titanic,* built in Belfast. Féile an Phobail, the West Belfast Festival (🌐 *www.feilebelfast.com*), held in early August, is a 10-day schedule of events with an avowedly republican, nationalist, and internationalist tinge.

Arts Council of Northern Ireland

ARTS FESTIVALS | The country's main arts agency supports a range of cultural events, including many Belfast festivals, and has information about them. ✉ *The Sidings, Lisburn* ☎ *028/9262–3555* 🌐 *www.artscouncil-ni.org.*

Belfast International Arts Festival

FESTIVALS | This long-established Belfast festival lasts for three weeks in October and is the city's major arts festival. ☎ *028/9033–2261* 🌐 *www.belfastinternationalartsfestival.com.*

Cathedral Quarter Arts Festival

FESTIVALS | This early-May festival, always buzzing with energy, attracts local, national, and international visual and performing artists. Its base of operations is the Black Box on Hill Street, at the heart of the Cathedral Quarter, where a café serves snacks during the day and light lunches. The same organization runs the very successful Out to Lunch festival in January. ☎ *028/9023–2403* 🌐 *www.cqaf.com.*

Festival of Fools

FESTIVALS | This vibrant three-day street-theater event coinciding with the Cathedral Quarter Arts Festival spills into public spaces across Belfast the first weekend in May. The popular event has been running since 2003 and features world-class entertainers in the form of acrobats and visiting artistes. ✉ *Cathedral Quarter* ☎ *028/9023–6007* 🌐 *www.foolsfestival.com.*

Visitor Information

Visit Belfast Welcome Centre

VISITOR INFORMATION | Directly opposite City Hall, this is the first stop to find out what's on, to buy tickets for events and tours, or to book accommodations and travel. Multimedia information touch screens and self-service kiosks provide a signposting service for more than 400 attractions throughout Northern Ireland. A Translink desk helps plan and organize travel within Northern Ireland and farther afield. There's also free Wi-Fi access, a currency exchange, and left-luggage facilities. It costs £4 to leave your luggage for four hours, and £6 for more than four hours. Ask about the Belfast Visitor Pass, which allows discounts of between 10% and 40% at some restaurants, visitor attractions, and tours as well as savings offering unlimited travel on bus and train routes. An adult day pass costs £6, two days £11, and three days £14.50. ✉ *8–9 Donegall Sq. N, Central District* ☎ *028/9024–6609* 🌐 *www.visitbelfast.com.*

Golden Mile

Although it doesn't glow in quite the way the name suggests, the bustling Golden Mile and its immediate environs harbor noteworthy historic buildings. In addition, the area is filled with hotels and major civic and office buildings, as well as some restaurants, cafés, and shops. Even if you don't end up staying here, you're likely to pass through it often.

Sights

★ Crown Liquor Saloon

OTHER ATTRACTION | Belfast is blessed with some exceptional pubs, but the Crown is one of the city's glories. Owned by the National Trust (the U.K.'s official conservation organization), it's an ostentatious box of delights and immaculately preserved. Opposite the Europa Hotel, it began life in 1826 as the Railway Tavern and is still lighted by gas; in 1885 the owner asked Italian craftsmen working on churches in Ireland to moonlight on rebuilding it, and its place in Irish architectural pub history was assured. Richly carved woodwork around cozy snugs (cubicles—known to regulars as "confessional boxes"), leather seats, color tile work, and an abundance of mirrors make up the decor. But the pièce de résistance is the embossed ceiling with its swirling arabesques and rosettes of burnished primrose, amber, and gold, as dazzling now as the day it was installed. The Crown claims to serve the perfect pint of Guinness—so no need to ask what anyone's drinking. When you settle down with your glass, note the little gunmetal plates used by the Victorians for lighting their matches as well as the antique push-button bells for ordering another round. Ageless, timeless, and classless—some would say the Crown is even priceless. If you wish to eat, choose the upstairs dining room, which has a much wider and better selection of food. ✉ *46 Great Victoria St., Golden Mile* ☎ *028/9024–3187* 🌐 *www.nicholsons-pubs.co.uk.*

★ Crumlin Road Gaol

JAIL/PRISON | **FAMILY** | Designed by Charles Lanyon, and opened in 1846, this jail held more than 500 prisoners at its peak; today it is one of Belfast's hottest tourist tickets. Throughout its 150-year lifetime, around 25,000 convicts passed through its doors. During the worst years of the Troubles, between 1969 and 1996 (when the prison closed), it held some of the North's most notorious prisoners, including many involved in paramilitary violence. The building has undergone a £10 million restoration, and, with its cream-walled corridors and black railings, has been transformed to reflect the way it looked in Victorian days. The engrossing 75-minute tour takes in the holding, punishment, and condemned cells—the latter where the prisoners were held

What's Next for the North?

Since the peace process and the Good Friday Agreement of 1998, considerable change has come about in Northern Ireland. Another political accord, the Stormont House Agreement, was endorsed in 2014 and facilitated with a £2 billion financial package from the British government. This brought a newfound business confidence, driven by tourism, that generated millions for the economy. But divisions still remained and after three years of deadlock without a local government (2016–19), the main political parties finally broke the polarization in 2020. They began a fresh round of talks, putting aside their differences and retaking their seats at the Stormont Parliament. Almost 100 years on from the partitioning of Ireland in 1921 this marked the start of a new era of compromise in power-sharing across the North and was seen as another staging post on the long road to peace. A new joint British and Irish government blueprint called "New Decade, New Approach" provided the framework for the return of devolved government to Northern Ireland.

It is also important to remember that the cycle of commemoration is strong. Ritual historic practices survive, which are significant to many on both sides of the community. These include bonfires, burning effigies, defiant graffiti, flying flags, and marching commemorations with band parades and drum beating, most of which occur without incident. At the start of the third decade of the 21st century, Northern Ireland is enjoying the greatest prosperity and longest period of stability in its 100-year history and few commentators forecast a return to the Troubles. Talk to anyone on the streets of Belfast or Derry and they're likely to tell you that while the situation may not be perfect, it is infinitely better than the dark days of the Troubles.

However, the United Kingdom's exit from the European Community—a move that was opposed by a large majority of the people of Northern Ireland—has brought new uncertainty, with the risk of a "hard border in the Irish Sea" between Northern Ireland and the rest of the United Kingdom, new obstacles to trade and travel between the North and the Republic of Ireland, and a significant negative impact on the North's fragile economy.

before being taken to the gallows for execution. The tour's climax is the execution chamber, hidden behind a moving bookcase where the guide explains the gory details of how the long-drop method was used to break the prisoner's neck. Exhibits in the museum include handcuffs, a flogging rack with the birch used for punishment, photographs, and maps. The jail is said to be one of the most haunted buildings in Belfast, and paranormal tours, ghost, and historical evening tours are held occasionally. A British army Wessex helicopter that patrolled the skies during the Troubles has been added to the display. The helicopter was retired from service in 2002 and has been restored. It was given to the museum by the Royal Air Force in 2019. The Crum Café sells daytime snacks, while Cuffs Bar and Grill is open for evening dining. ✉ *53–55 Crumlin Rd., North Belfast* ☎ *028/9074–1500* 🌐 *www.crumlinroadgaol.com* 🎫 *£12.*

The Grand Opera House is Northern Ireland's only remaining Victorian theater.

Europa Hotel

HOTEL | A landmark in Belfast, the Europa is seen as a monument to the resilience of the city in the face of the Troubles. The most bombed hotel in Western Europe, the hotel was targeted 11 times by the IRA starting in the early 1970s and refurbished every time; today it shows no signs of its explosive history after a £1 million renovation. President Bill Clinton and First Lady Hillary Clinton chose the hotel for an overnight visit during their 1995 visit—for 24 hours the phones were answered with "White House Belfast, can I help you?" The former president's room is now called the Clinton Suite and contains memorabilia from the presidential stay. ✉ *38 Great Victoria St., at Glengall St., Golden Mile* ☎ *028/9027–1066* 🌐 *www.hastingshotels.com.*

★ **Grand Opera House**

HISTORIC SIGHT | Fresh from a dazzling £12 million face-lift, Belfast's opera house, which regularly hosts musicals, plays, and concerts, has been restored to its original 1890s glamour with a new auditorium and ornate boxes. Visitors can now appreciate the beauty of the plasterwork alongside repairs and repainting of decorative features such as elephant heads and the glorious ceilings devised by the renowned theater architect Frank Matcham in 1894. New purpose-designed seats have replaced the old cinema-style ones in use since the 1960s and stalls, circle crush bars, sound, lighting, sets, and scenery were all upgraded. An impressive new permanent display reflects many of the famous names who have taken to this stage over its more-than-125-year history, including Laurel and Hardy and Luciano Pavarotti. The building, which had already achieved listed status for its architectural merit and is Northern Ireland's only remaining Victorian theater, now takes its place among the city's premier attractions. ✉ *2 Great Victoria St., Golden Mile* ☎ *028/9024–1919* 🌐 *www.goh.co.uk.*

Tracing your Roots

A staggering 3 million documents are stored in the archives of the **Public Record Office of Northern Ireland** (PRONI), with 900,000 official government files and 300,000 maps—a wonderful place to stir the imagination of researchers and visitors. Most records date from around 1600 to the present. For those interested in roots tourism, or anyone with ancestors from the northern third of Ireland, it is an amateur genealogist's dream; those precious transcripts could provide a vivid piece of the family jigsaw. The Record Office is open by appointment only. (✉ *Titanic Blvd., Queen's Island, Titanic Quarter, Belfast* ☎ *028/9053–4800* 🌐 *www.nidirect.gov.uk/proni*)

The **Ulster Historical Foundation** has a skilled team to help with genealogical research. In recent years, with many more records available online, there is greater access to them, and the staff are adept at unearthing information about those elusive Irish or Scots-Irish ancestors. The UHF offers personal consultation, assessment, and research, as well as document retrieval. Its research offices are in Belfast's Cathedral Quarter. (✉ *Corn Exchange, 31 Gordon St., Belfast* ☎ *028/9066–1988* 🌐 *ancestryireland.com*)

For a different take on Ulster-Scots history and language, it's worth calling into the **Ulster-Scots Visitor Centre**. This government-funded agency promotes the study of Ulster-Scots as a living language as well as its culture and history. You can tour the Discover Ulster-Scots Centre and view exhibition panels on dialect and heritage. (✉ *Ulster-Scots Agency, Corn Exchange, 31 Gordon St., Belfast* ☎ *028/9023–1113* 🌐 *ulsterscotsagency.com*)

Restaurants

★ The Ginger Bistro

$ | **MODERN IRISH** | Modern Irish classics with an international twist attract the foodie crowd to this cheerful bistro just off Great Victoria Street. A short but perfectly balanced menu emphasizes locally sourced seafood and lean meats. **Known for:** best-selling squid and dips; sublime fish pie; outstanding wine and beer menu. $ *Average main: £20* ✉ *68–72 Great Victoria St., Golden Mile* ☎ *028/9024–4421* 🌐 *www.gingerbistro.com* ⏲ *Closed Sun.–Tues.*

John Long's

$ | **IRISH** | Hearty eaters adore this long-standing institution, which has served fish-and-chips for more than 100 years, and now serves wine and local beers with food. The completely basic Athol Street premises, close to the city center, welcomes garbage collectors, business execs, schoolboys from the nearby Royal Belfast Academical Institution, and patrons from every sector, who flock here for the secret-batter-recipe fish. **Known for:** classic fish-and-chips; local favorite; best value in town. $ *Average main: £7* ✉ *39 Athol St., Golden Mile* ☎ *028/9032–1848* 🌐 *www.johnlongs.com* ⏲ *Closed Sun. and Mon.*

Nu Delhi

$ | **INDIAN** | Decorated with candlelit tables, redbrick walls, and vibrant artwork featuring Bollywood actresses, the loft-like 100-seat Indian restaurant is an energetic space filled with glamour and buzz and a menu that fuses traditional with the unexpected. Chicken and lamb dishes—ranging from mild to vindaloo hot—dominate, but the fusion grill also serves up kebabs, tender chops, and monkfish or sea bass and more conventional bhajis and *pakoras* (battered and deep-fried meat or vegetable). **Known for:** squid masala; daal makani; house cocktail. $ *Average main: £15* ✉ *68–72 Great Victoria St., Golden Mile* ✣ *Above Ginger Bistro* ☎ *028/9024–4747* 🌐 *www.nu-delhilounge.com* ⏲ *No lunch Sun.*

Red Panda

$ | CHINESE | The £9.90 two-course lunch on Thursday and Friday is an exceptional value at this long-established central eatery. It includes a starter of fresh fruit or salad, along with a main-course dish of your choice with rice. **Known for:** stuffed chitterlings with salt; honey chili chicken; super seafood selection. $ *Average main: £17* ✉ *Andras House, 60 Great Victoria St., Golden Mile* ☎ *028/9080–8700* 🌐 *www.theredpanda.co.uk* ⏲ *No lunch Sat.*

Nightlife

The glorious Crown Liquor Saloon is far from being the only old pub in the Golden Mile area—some, but by no means all, of Belfast's evening life takes place in bars and restaurants here. At several replicated Victorian bars, more locals and fewer visitors gather.

Brennan's Bar

PUBS | A noisy, modern pub, this bar jams on up-to-the-minute music. It can get a bit boisterous, so some may prefer a quiet snug (booth) across the road in the more serene Crown Liquor Saloon. Food is served from noon daily (Monday through Thursday until 8:30, weekends until 7). ✉ *48 Great Victoria St., Golden Mile* ☎ *028/9024–2986.*

Robinsons

PUBS | A popular pub encompassing five venues under one roof, Robinsons draws a young crowd with folk music in its Fibber Magees bar on Sunday; pop in the redesigned Robinson's Lounge on weekends. Food is served daily from 12:30 to 4 pm and from 6 to 9 pm. ✉ *38–42 Great Victoria St., Golden Mile* ☎ *028/9024–7447* 🌐 *www.robinsonsbar.co.uk.*

Performing Arts

★ Grand Opera House

THEATER | Shows from all over Ireland and Britain—and sometimes farther afield—play at this beautifully restored Victorian theater that reopened at the end of 2020 following a major refurbishment. Though it has no resident company of its own, major West End musicals and plays pass through, plus the occasional opera or ballet. It's worth attending a show just to enjoy the gigantic and splendid opera house itself. The Baby Grand—a theater-within-a-theater—hosts comedy, live music, and educational workshops, as well as film and special events. Guided backstage tours are available, mostly on alternate Saturday mornings (10:30–11:30) and cost £8.50; check the website for details. ✉ *2 Great Victoria St., Golden Mile* ☎ *028/9024–1919* 🌐 *www.goh.co.uk.*

Central District

Belfast's Central District, immediately north of the Golden Mile, is not geographically the center of the city, but it's the old heart of Belfast. It's a frenetic place, where both locals and visitors shop. Cafés, pubs, offices, and shops of all kinds occupy the redbrick, white Portland stone, and modern buildings that line its narrow streets. Many streets are pedestrian-only, so it's a good place to take a leisurely stroll, browse the windows, and see some sights to boot. It's easy to get waylaid shopping and investigating sights along the river when taking this walk, so give yourself at least two hours to cover the area comfortably.

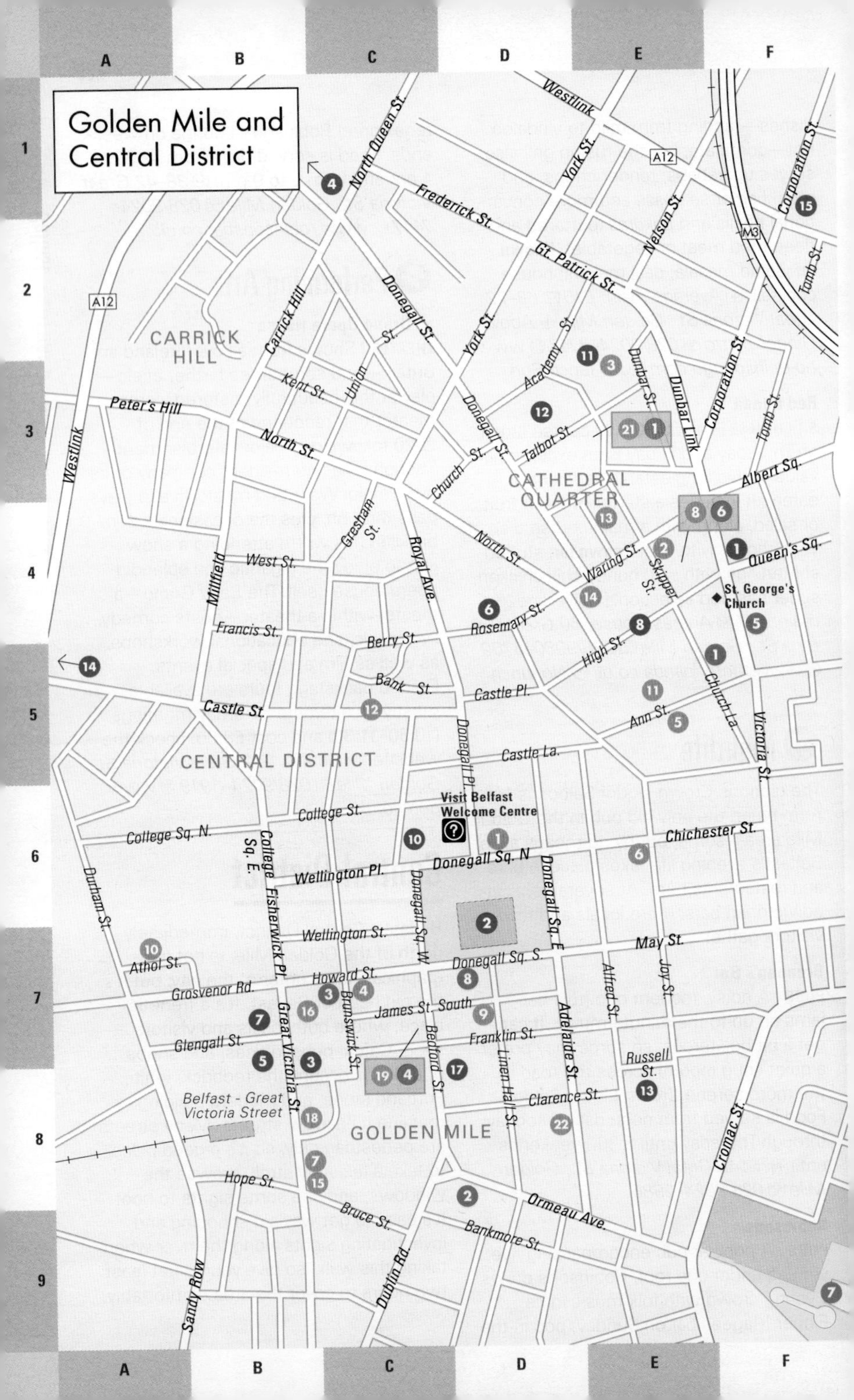
Golden Mile and Central District
A B C D E F
1 2 3 4 5 6 7 8 9
Westlink
North Queen St.
Frederick St.
York St.
Nelson St.
Corporation St.
Tomb St.
Gt. Patrick St.
A12
M3
Donegall St.
Carrick Hill
CARRICK HILL
Union St.
Kent St.
Academy St.
Dunbar St.
Dunbar Link
Peter's Hill
North St.
Talbot St.
Church St.
CATHEDRAL QUARTER
Albert Sq.
Queen's Sq.
St. George's Church
Gresham St.
Royal Ave.
Millfield
West St.
Waring St.
Skipper St.
Francis St.
Berry St.
Rosemary St.
High St.
Bank St.
Castle Pl.
Castle St.
Church La.
Ann St.
Victoria St.
CENTRAL DISTRICT
Donegall Pl.
Castle La.
Visit Belfast Welcome Centre
College St.
College Sq. N.
College Sq. E.
Chichester St.
Fisherwick Pl.
Wellington Pl.
Donegall Sq. N
Donegall Sq. W
Donegall Sq. E
Durham St.
Wellington St.
May St.
Athol St.
Donegall Sq. S.
Howard St.
Alfred St.
Joy St.
Grosvenor Rd.
Great Victoria St.
Brunswick St.
James St. South
Adelaide St.
Glengall St.
Bedford St.
Franklin St.
Linen Hall St.
Russell St.
Belfast - Great Victoria Street
Clarence St.
GOLDEN MILE
Cromac St.
Hope St.
Bruce St.
Ormeau Ave.
Bankmore St.
Dublin Rd.
Sandy Row

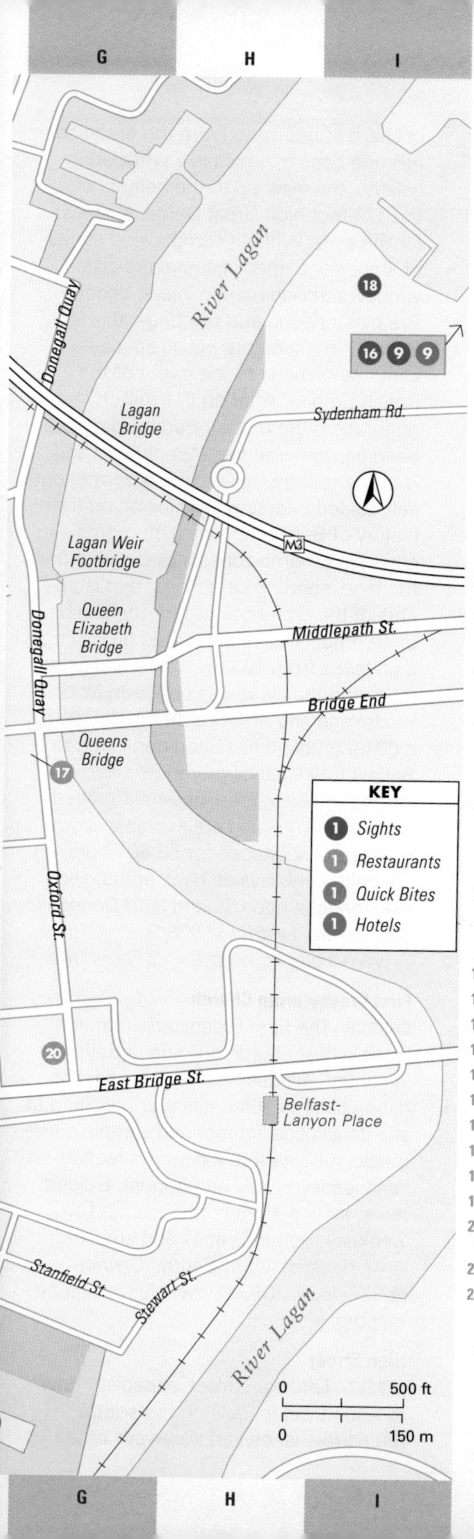

Sights

1 Albert Memorial Clock Tower F4
2 City Hall D7
3 Crown Liquor Saloon.................... B7
4 Crumlin Road Gaol.......C1
5 Europa Hotel B7
6 First Presbyterian Church D4
7 Grand Opera House B7
8 High Street E4
9 HMS *Caroline* I2
10 Linen Hall Library C6
11 Metropolitan Arts Centre (MAC)............. E3
12 St. Anne's Cathedral D3
13 St. Malachy's Church ... E8
14 St. Peter's Cathedral.... A5
15 Sinclair Seamen's Church F1
16 Titanic Belfast.............I2
17 Ulster Hall D8
18 W5 Belfast.................I2

Restaurants

1 Café Parisien............ D6
2 The Cloth Ear............. E4
3 Coppi E3
4 Deanes Restaurant...... C7
5 Fish City................... E5
6 The Garrick Bar.......... E6
7 The Ginger Bistro....... B8
8 The Great Room.......... E4
9 James Street & Co...... D7
10 John Long's............. A7
11 The Morning Star........ E5
12 Mourne Seafood Bar.... C5
13 The Muddlers Club E4
14 The Northern Whig...... E4
15 Nu Delhi.................. B8
16 Ora Wine and Tapas.... B7
17 Ox Restaurant........... G5
18 Red Panda............... B8
19 Seahorse C7
20 Stock Kitchen and Bar G7
21 Yard Bird.................. E3
22 Zen D8

Quick Bites

1 Established Coffee E3

Hotels

1 Bullitt Hotel............... F5
2 Clayton Hotel Belfast... D8
3 The Flint................... C7
4 Grand Central Hotel C7
5 Malmaison................ F4
6 The Merchant Hotel..... E4
7 Radisson Blu Belfast.... F9
8 Ten Square D7
9 Titanic Hotel............... I2

The Central District contains what locals call the Cathedral Quarter: radiating out from the new, mock neo-Palladian development of St. Anne's Square. Small privately owned art galleries, alongside the Black Box—a major performance venue—line the side streets and are crammed in alongside a new wave of bars and lively bistros, making it the new restaurant central. Crowning it all is the dramatic Metropolitan Arts Centre, Northern Ireland's flagship location for the arts.

Sights

Albert Memorial Clock Tower

CLOCK | Tilting a little to one side—not unlike Pisa's more notorious leaning landmark—this clock tower was named for Queen Victoria's husband, Prince Albert. The once-dilapidated Queen's Square on which it stands has undergone a face-lift, and a restoration has brought the clock back to its original glory. The tower itself is not open to the public. ✉ *Queen's Sq., Central District.*

★ City Hall

GOVERNMENT BUILDING | Built of Portland stone between 1898 and 1906 and modeled on St. Paul's Cathedral in London, this Renaissance revival–style edifice—the cynosure of central Belfast—was designed by Brumwell Thomas (who was knighted but had to sue to get his fee). Before you enter, take a stroll around Donegall Square to see statues of Queen Victoria and a column honoring the U.S. Expeditionary Force, which landed in the city on January 26, 1942—the first contingent of the U.S. Army to arrive in Europe during World War II. A monument commemorating the *Titanic* stands in the grounds, and in 2012, a granite memorial was unveiled in a *Titanic* memorial garden opened for the 100th anniversary of the ship's sinking. The memorial, on the east side of the grounds, lists the names of everyone who died in the tragedy. Enter the building under the porte cochere at the front. From the entrance hall (the base of which is a whispering gallery), the view up to the heights of the 173-foot-high Great Dome is a feast for the eyes. With its complicated series of arches and openings, stained-glass windows, Italian-marble inlays, decorative plasterwork, and paintings, this is Belfast's most ornate public space—a veritable homage to the might of the British Empire. After an £11 million restoration, the modernized building has been brought into the 21st century and is home to the Bobbin café. A permanent self-guided interactive exhibition on the history of Belfast spanning 16 rooms covers six theme zones including cultural heritage, sporting celebrities, and laureates of the arts. Look out for the exhibit of ceremonial keys presented by visiting dignitaries from 10 U.S. towns and cities, reflecting the close ties between Northern Ireland and America. In the courtyard a 60-jet fountain has been dedicated to Belfast City Council members killed during the Troubles. Free, one-hour guided tours of the building are available or you can rent headphones for £3.50. Tours are held weekdays at 11, 2, and 3, and weekends at noon, 2, and 3. ✉ *Donegall Sq., Central District* ☎ *028/9027–0456* 🌐 *www.belfastcity.gov.uk* 🎫 *Tours free.*

First Presbyterian Church

CHURCH | The First Presbyterian Church is the oldest church building in Belfast in continuous use, with a congregation dating back to 1644. It is worth visiting to see its elliptical interior and sample some music. It hosts free lunchtime recitals on Wednesday in July and August. Guided tours, lasting 45 minutes, are held on weekday mornings at 11 and are free. ✉ *41 Rosemary St., Central District* ☎ *077/4036–2093* 🌐 *www.firstchurchbelfast.org.*

High Street

STREET | Off High Street, especially down to Ann Street (parallel to the south), run narrow lanes and alleyways called entries. Though mostly cleaned up and turned into chic shopping lanes, they still hang on to something of their raffish character, and have distinctive pubs with little-altered Victorian interiors. Among the most notable are the Morning Star (Pottinger's Entry off High Street), with its large windows and fine curving bar; White's Tavern (entry off High Street), Belfast's oldest pub, founded in 1630, with plush seats and a big, open fire; and the delectable Muriel's Café Bar in Church Lane, with its damask drapes and velvet seats, themed on a 1920s hat shop. Look into St. George's Church, at one end of High Street, a beautiful building with a magnificent portico transported by canal from the house of the eccentric Earl Bishop of Derry.

TIP→ Don't miss Kelly's Cellars, a 200-year-old pub in Bank Street, not far from High Street.

The bar was the meeting place of the militant nationalist group, the Society of United Irishmen, whose leader Wolfe Tone is remembered as the founder of Irish Republicanism. A colorful wall mural erected in the upstairs bar in 2018 features the poet Seamus Heaney, writers such as Oscar Wilde, Brendan Behan, and Samuel Beckett, and musicians including Phil Lynott and Sinéad O'Connor. At lunchtime they serve tasty bowls of filling beef stew, but get there early as stocks are limited (☎ *028/9024–6058*). ✉ *High St., Central District.*

HMS *Caroline*

NAUTICAL SIGHT | **FAMILY** | The last survivor of the Battle of Jutland (1916) and the only accessible World War I ship, HMS *Caroline* is a unique vessel, which has been sensitively restored alongside an absorbing visitor center. An immersive 11-minute film tells the graphic story of the largest naval battle in history over the fight for control of the North Sea. By the end, 25 ships had been sunk and more than 8,500 men lost their lives. Displays recount personal testimonies of those who served on the ship (they called themselves "Carries"), which a torpedo missed by a whisker. They also reflect the imaginative restoration process now featuring interactive exhibits, touch screens, cybercode games, and a naval-theme playpark creating an action-packed family atmosphere. Special care should be taken during your visit since there are steep stairs, uneven floors, trip hazards, and low ceilings, and the decks can be slippery when wet. Refreshments and snack lunches are served in the Mess Deck Café on the lower deck (10–5 daily) where you can also sample the West Indies Porter or Titanic Quarter Pale Ale.

TIP→ There's a 20% reduction on the admission price if you book tickets online.
✉ *Queen's Island, Queen's Rd, Alexandra Dock, Titanic Quarter* ✣ *Glider bus service from the city hall stops nearby* ☎ *028/9045–4484* 🌐 *www.nmrn.org.uk/exhibitions-projects/hms-caroline/hms-caroline-experience* 🎫 *£11* 🕙 *Closed Mon. and Tues. Apr.–May and Oct.–Mar.*

★ Linen Hall Library

LIBRARY | With its distinctive grayish-yellow brick, this library—the oldest subscription library in Ireland—is a comfortable place to escape the bustle of the city streets. The library, which has been awarded museum status, has an unparalleled collection of tens of thousands of documents and books relating to the Troubles, regarded as the definitive archive and attracting scholars from all over the world. A digital archive launched in 2018, *Divided Society,* features a wide range of material relating to the peace process of the 1990s resulting in the Belfast Agreement on Good Friday in 1998. One early librarian, Thomas Russell, was hanged in 1803 for supporting an Irish uprising; another early user, Henry Joy McCracken, a founding member of the United Irishmen, went to the scaffold owing the library £1.30 in subscriptions arrears, a debt that was eventually paid by a descendant in 2001.

American visitors in particular like to see one extremely rare item: the original document recording the first-ever acts passed by the American Congress in New York on March 4, 1789. On the walls are paintings and prints depicting Belfast views and landmarks. Much of this artwork is for sale. Look out for the beautiful stained-glass windows on the first floor featuring portraits of men eminent in literature and science. It's an ideal hideaway for relaxing with a newspaper, enjoying the library's café, and falling into conversation. Guided 45-minute tours are held at 10:30 am weekdays. ✉ *17 Donegall Sq. N, Central District* ☎ *028/9032–1707* 🌐 *www.linenhall.com* 🎫 *Free, suggested donation £3.* ⏲ *Closed weekends.*

Metropolitan Arts Centre (MAC)

ART GALLERY | Eye-catchingly beautiful, and flooded with light, the Metropolitan Arts Centre (MAC) is Northern Ireland's flagship home for the arts and energizer of the Cathedral Quarter's flourishing creative scene. Six stories tall, and with two theaters, three art galleries, and artists' studios—along with a café, bar, and restaurant—the MAC is the centerpiece of the neo-Palladian St. Anne's Square development. The MAC makes an astonishing statement with redbrick and dark basalt, oak furnishings, Danish fabric panels, steel balustrades, bronze window frames, and dark-gray terrazzo flooring. Downstairs is a 350-seat auditorium, while upstairs is a 120-seat studio. The galleries present up-and-coming Northern Irish artists as well as attention-grabbing temporary exhibitions incorporating the works of world-renowned artists. The only permanent display is a sculptural artwork by Mark Garry, commissioned by the MAC and the Thomas Devlin Fund, created in memory of a 15-year-old boy killed in an unprovoked attack in North Belfast. Made up of 400 metal wires in the main foyer, it creates a color spectrum through the space with the aim of highlighting the futility of violence. Ushers, known as "MACtivists," are on hand to help point you in the right direction. ✉ *St. Anne's Sq., Exchange St., Cathedral Quarter* ☎ *028/9023–5053* 🌐 *www.themaclive.com* 🎫 *Galleries free* ⏲ *Closed Mon. and Tues.*

St. Anne's Cathedral

CHURCH | At the center of the eponymous Cathedral Quarter, St. Anne's is a turn-of-the-20th century edifice in the Irish neo-Romanesque style. Lord Carson (1854–1935), who was largely responsible for keeping the six counties inside the United Kingdom, is buried here by virtue of a special Act of Parliament. His is the only tomb. The 175-foot stainless-steel Spire of Hope atop the cathedral's roof adds to the city's skyline and shines brightly as a beacon of newfound optimism for the future. A multilingual audio guide or guided tour allow visitors to immerse themselves in the history of the cathedral. The German Luftwaffe bombed this section of Belfast during World War II; on the cathedral's Talbot Street side, at No. 21, the Northern Ireland War Memorial has an interactive exhibit about the war. ✉ *Donegall St., Cathedral Quarter* ☎ *028/9032–8332* 🌐 *www.belfastcathedral.org* 🎫 *£5, includes tour, guidebook, and audio guide.*

St. Malachy's Church

CHURCH | Opened in 1844, this is one of the most impressive redbrick Tudor revival churches in Ireland. One of the interior highlights is the densely patterned fan-vaulted ceiling, a delightfully swirling masterpiece of plasterwork—whose inspiration was taken from the chapel of Henry VII at Westminster Abbey in London—that's been tastefully repainted in cream. The painting over the high altarpiece, *Journey to Calvary,* was carried out by portraitist Felix Piccioni, whose family were refugees from the Austrian region of Italy. In 1868, the largest bell in Belfast was added to the church, but after complaints that its deafening noise was interfering with the maturing of whiskey in the nearby Dunville distillery, it was wrapped in felt to soften its peal and vibration. Along the southeast wall of the church gazing out in contemplative mood with his brown eyes and torn chocolate-brown coat is the delicate statue of the Ragged Saint. St. Benedict Joseph Labre, the patron saint of the unemployed, welcomes visitors into the ethereal elegance of one of Belfast's most architecturally romantic buildings. ✉ *Alfred St., Central District* ☎ *028/9032–1713* 🌐 *www.saintmalachysparish.com* 🎫 *Free.*

St. Peter's Cathedral

CHURCH | The elegant neo-Gothic "twin spires" of St. Peter's Cathedral dominate the skyline of West Belfast. Finding this Roman Catholic cathedral is difficult, but worth the effort. Built in 1866, when the Catholic population was rapidly increasing, St. Peter's acted as a focal point for the community. ✉ *St. Peter's Sq., West Belfast* ✢ *Located in the Divis area off the Lower Falls Rd. in West Belfast* ☎ *028/9032–7573.*

Sinclair Seamen's Church

CHURCH | By the riverfront is one of the most appealing churches, Presbyterian Sinclair Seamen's Church. Designed by Charles Lanyon, the architect of Queen's University, it has served the seafaring community since 1857. The pulpit is shaped like a ship's prow; the bell is from HMS *Hood,* a Royal Navy battleship sunk in Portland Harbor on the south coast of England in 1914; and even the collection plates are shaped like lifeboats. Tours are offered between March and December on Wednesday from 2 to 4:30 pm. ✉ *Corporation Sq., off Donegall Quay, Central District* ☎ *028/9031–9931* 🌐 *www.sinclairschurch.co.uk* ⏲ *Closed Jan. and Feb.*

★ ***Titanic* Belfast**

OTHER MUSEUM | **FAMILY** | This world-class attraction headlines a "Titanic Experience" exhibition along with showcasing nine linked interpretative galleries that outline the *Titanic*'s dramatic story as well as the wider theme of Belfast's seafaring and industrial heritage. The stunning bow-shape facade of the six-story building reflects the lines of the great ship, the shardlike appearance created from 3,000 different-shape panels each folded from silver anodized aluminum sheets into asymmetrical geometries. The ultimate, startling effect is of light caught by a cut diamond. As you wander through *Titanic* Belfast, you learn about the thriving boomtown at the turn of the 20th century; the ride through the reconstruction of the shipyards echoes with the sounds and sensations of more than 100 years ago. In one of the galleries, the ship's saga is brought up to the present with the discovery of the wreck and into the future with live links to contemporary undersea exploration. Also on-site is a movie theater designed by the *Titanic* explorer Robert Ballard (he discovered the wreck in 1985), which shows films about the ship. From time to time new exhibits are added; one of these is the original plan used during the British Titanic Inquiry held one month after the sinking. The historic plan was a vital reference tool and contains markings indicating where the liner struck the iceberg. The inquiry concluded that the loss of the liner had been brought about by "excessive speed." Tours are self-guided; audio guides are available in seven languages and cost £4. The one-hour Discovery Tour (£13) explores the symbolism of the Titanic building and incorporates the new Titanic Hotel, the converted former drawing offices of Harland & Wolff shipyard. The admission price to *Titanic* Belfast includes access to the nearby SS *Nomadic, Titanic's* original tender ship and the last remaining White Star Line vessel. Following a stint as a Parisian restaurant and nightclub, *Nomadic* was restored and visitors can experience a permanent and tangible piece of maritime heritage at Hamilton Dock. You can separately book a visit to the *Nomadic* on its own. Tickets are £7. You can also buy a White Star Premium Pass (£51.50) for daylong benefits such as discounts in the bistro and in the Titanic Store, as well as access to SS *Nomadic* and a commemorative coin. Tickets for *Titanic* Belfast are based on a timed ticketing, with slots available every 15 minutes throughout opening times; last admission is one hour, 45 minutes before closing time.

■ TIP→ **On selected Sundays, afternoon tea is hosted by the grand staircase in the *Titanic* Suite but must be booked in advance. The cost is £35, £41 with a glass of prosecco, or £46 with a glass of Heidsieck Monopole Champagne, the official champagne of the RMS *Titanic*.** ✉ *Olympic Way, 6 Queen's Rd., Titanic Quarter* ☎ *028/9076–6386* 🌐 *www.titanicbelfast.com* 🎫 *£20 includes Titanic Experience tour at Titanic Belfast and entrance to SS Nomadic; discovery tour £10.*

Ulster Hall

PERFORMANCE VENUE | It has hosted Charles Dickens, the Rolling Stones, and Rachmaninov as well as a diverse range of Irish politicians from Charles Stewart Parnell to Ian Paisley. Built in 1862 as a ballroom, the Ulster Hall, affectionately known as the Grand Dame of Bedford Street, is still thriving. Much of W.J. Barre's original decor has been restored and 13 historic oil paintings reflecting the history and mythology of Belfast by local artist Joseph Carey are on display in their original magnificence in the Carey Gallery. Another highlight is an interpretative display featuring poetry, pictures, and sound telling the history of the hall through personal reminiscences. During World War II, the building was used as a dance hall by U.S. troops based in Northern Ireland. The hall is also the permanent home of the Ulster Orchestra. Drink in some of Belfast's colorful history, and reflect on the fact that it was here in March 1971 that Led Zeppelin debuted "Stairway to Heaven" on stage. At the box office you can buy tickets for all upcoming events at both Ulster Hall and Waterfront Hall. ✉ *Bedford St., Central District* ☎ *028/9033–4455* 🌐 *www.ulsterhall.co.uk.*

W5 Belfast

CHILDREN'S MUSEUM | **FAMILY** | Part of the Odyssey complex in Belfast's docks, the W5 center underwent a £4.5 million revamp during 2020, and it takes a high-tech approach to interpreting science and creativity for adults and children. It offers scores of brand-new exhibits for kids to explore through games. Video displays and flashing lights enhance the futuristic feel, and you can do everything from exploring the weather to building houses, bridges, and robots. The Discovery exhibits for children under eight cover subjects such as spying, forensics, and nature. A huge multistory climbing structure called Climbit, a cross between a maze and a jungle gym, is a fun feature in the atrium for kids three and up.

■ TIP→ **Make your way to the upper floors for spectacular views over the city and beyond.** ✉ *2 Queen's Quay, Titanic Quarter* ☎ *028/9046–7700* 🌐 *www.w5online.co.uk* 🎫 *£10.*

Restaurants

Café Parisien

$ | **FRENCH** | Taking its name from the eponymous first-class café on RMS *Titanic*, Café Parisien divides itself into a downstairs crêperie and a stylish upstairs restaurant in a landmark six-story sandstone building opposite City Hall. Choose from an array of savory or sweet crêpes and galettes or head upstairs for main courses at lunch or dinner, which may include beef bourguignon or bouillabaisse, the celebrated stew of Provence. **Known for:** cod fillet, mussels, and white bean cassoulet; hot smoked salmon omelet; vegan beetroot rosti with tofu and pickled vegetables. 💲 *Average main: £16* ✉ *Cleaver House, 1–3 Donegall Sq. N, Central District* ☎ *028/9590–4338*

The *Titanic* Belfast is a modern, world-class museum and experience center that takes a deep dive into the ship and its tragic maiden voyage.

🌐 *www.cafeparisienbelfast.com* 🕑 *Closed Mon.–Wed.*

The Cloth Ear

$ | **IRISH** | The Merchant Hotel's lively gastropub combines all the decorative charms of a traditional Belfast watering hole with a great choice of ales, wines, and whiskeys, and a menu that blends old-school favorites with imaginative modern fusion twists. **Known for:** smoked cod chowder; slow-braised lamb shoulder; signature chicken curry. 💲 *Average main: £15* ✉ *16 Skipper St., Cathedral Quarter* ☎ *028/9026–2719* 🌐 *www.themerchanthotel.com/the-cloth-ear.*

Coppi

$ | **ITALIAN** | The small dishes known as *cicchetti,* beloved of Venetian bars and the Italian counterpart to Spanish tapas, draw the crowds to Coppi in the ever-popular Cathedral Quarter. Named after a world-champion Italian racing cyclist, Angelo Fausto Coppi, it serves flavorful Mediterranean cuisine amid modern industrial decor. **Known for:** huge T-bone steaks; Venetian-style pizzetta (mini-pizzas); best tiramisu in town. 💲 *Average main: £16* ✉ *St. Anne's Sq., Cathedral Quarter* ☎ *028/9031–1959* 🌐 *www.coppi.co.uk* 🕑 *Closed Mon. and Tues.*

★ **Deanes Restaurant**

$$ | **EUROPEAN** | For 25 years, Michael Deane has been the leader of the Belfast culinary pack, and his flagship operation has three distinct restaurants in one building: The Meat Locker, Eipic, and Love Fish. The Meat Locker is a beef-driven grill room and steak house; Eipic is an upscale, one–Michelin star restaurant and opulent champagne bar serving a variety of multicourse menus; and Love Fish is a less formal seafood restaurant with a Hamptons vibe. **Known for:** locally sourced beef at the Meat Locker; elegant food at Eipic; great value seafood at Love Fish. 💲 *Average main: £25* ✉ *28–40 Howard St., Central District* ☎ *028/9033–1134* 🌐 *www.michaeldeane.co.uk* 🕑 *Eipic closed Sun.–Tues.; Meat Locker and Love Fish closed Sun. and Mon.*

★ Fish City

$ | **SEAFOOD** | A cut above the average fish-and-chips restaurant, award-winning Fish City serves sustainably sourced seafood including Carlingford oysters, cod, scampi, and other treats. For nonpescatarians there are vegan and vegetarian options, too. **Known for:** Fish City Kiev; fisherman's curry; gourmet burgers. *Average main: £19 ✉ 33 Ann St., Central District ☎ 028/9023–1000 🌐 www.fish-city.com.*

★ The Garrick Bar

$ | **IRISH** | This popular (and historic) gastropub offers all-day and Sunday menus, meal deals, and value-for-money buffet lunches. The menu is meaty, but vegetarians will find options like chickpea and corn falafel with tzatziki or butternut squash, sweet potato, and coconut soup. **Known for:** pork and leek sauces with champ, gravy, and sautéed leeks; pulled pork burger with spiced apple and whiskey sauce; massive rib-eye steaks. *Average main: £17 ✉ 29 Chichester St., Central District ☎ 028/9032–1984 🌐 www.thegarrickbar.com.*

★ The Great Room

$$$$ | **EUROPEAN** | Inside the lavish Merchant Hotel, beneath the grand dome of this former bank's great hall and Ireland's biggest chandelier, find the perfect setting for a memorable dinner of adventurous European fare. Exceptional dishes include wild Irish venison loin, lamb saddle, or, for vegetarians, pappardelle pasta with black truffles and olive oil. **Known for:** halibut with lobster mousee; Thornhill duck breast; Kilkeel crab with green apple, celeriac, and imperial caviar. *Average main: £32 ✉ 35 Waring St., Cathedral Quarter ☎ 028/9023–4888 🌐 www.themerchanthotel.com.*

James Street & Co.

$$$ | **MODERN IRISH** | The mainstay of this classy city-center big hitter with an epic reputation is County Tyrone sirloin, rib eye, or beef fillet steaks as well as prime cuts including enormous Tomahawk steaks (for two) cooked to your liking on a charcoal grill. Based in a former linen mill, exposed brick walls and leather banquettes set the scene for a terrific meal. **Known for:** charcoal grill chateaubriand and tomahawk steaks; seared scallops and Irish pork belly with cauliflower and apple; Irish cod with shaved fennel and pea puree. *Average main: £26 ✉ 21 James St. S, Central District ☎ 028/9560–0700 🌐 www.jamesstandco.com ⏲ Closed Tues. and Wed.*

★ The Morning Star

$ | **IRISH** | Halfway down a narrow lane is the 19th-century Morning Star, one of the city's most historic pubs, first built as a coaching stop for the Belfast-to-Dublin post. There's a traditional bar downstairs and a cozy velvet and wood-panel restaurant upstairs serving locally sourced food. **Known for:** grass-fed beef from family farm; local mussels; artisanal breads. *Average main: £14 ✉ 17–19 Pottinger's Entry, Central District ☎ 028/9023–5986 🌐 www.themorningstarbar.co.uk.*

Mourne Seafood Bar

$ | **SEAFOOD** | Hidden down a side street, connoisseurs of fresh fish and shellfish love Mourne Seafood, whose offerings come from the local ports of Annalong and Kilkeel and depend on the day's catch. Mussels are from Strangford Lough while oysters are sourced from shellfish beds in Carlingford Lough. **Known for:** crack-and-eat crab claws; seafood casserole; well-aged sirloin steaks. *Average main: £18 ✉ 34–36 Bank St., Central District ☎ 028/9024–8544 🌐 www.mourneseafood.com.*

The Muddlers Club

$$$$ | **IRISH** | Though its name is derived from a revolutionary secret society that met here 200 years ago, there is nothing exactly covert about it beyond the fact that it is hidden away in a historic back alley and kind of hard to find. Fashionably unfussy, the succinct menu showcases blackened Mourne lamb, sea trout with Caesar salad, turbot, crab bisque, and

pasta all artfully arranged. **Known for:** multicourse tasting menu; venison loin with red cabbage; inventive vegetarian menu options. *Average main: £85 1 Warehouse La., Cathedral Quarter In a laneway off Waring St. or Exchange Pl. 028/9031–3199 www.themuddlersclubbelfast.com Closed Sun.–Tues. No lunch Wed. and Thurs.*

The Northern Whig

$ | **BRASSERIE** | Housed in an elegant former newspaper building in Belfast's historic Cathedral Quarter, the Northern Whig is spacious and stylish. From Thursday to Sunday evening, one wall slides away so you can watch a jazz band or a DJ playing funk and pop. **Known for:** brasserie-style food; traditional wooden bar; cocktails. *Average main: £15 2–10 Bridge St., Central District 028/9050–9888 www.thenorthernwhig.com.*

Ora Wine and Tapas

$ | **TAPAS** | Living up to its Maori name—Ora means "life"—this airy tapas restaurant specializes in hot and cold small plates such as crab claws, Manchego Caesar tacos, or chicken, chorizo, and buffalo mozzarella fritters. More substantial dishes are spiced glazed pork, braised shiitake, and barbecue mushroom, or a cumin roasted cauliflower curry. **Known for:** pickled chilli crab; jaumbo tempura scampi; baby back hoisin-glazed ribs. *Average main: £19 12 Great Victoria St., Central District About 100 meters from the Crown Bar 028/9031–5565 orabelfast.com Closed Sun.–Tues.*

★ **Ox Restaurant**

$$$$ | **MODERN IRISH** | You'd be hard-pressed to eat this well from lunch and dinner tasting menus in such relaxed surroundings anywhere else in Northern Ireland or indeed the whole island. Lunches are either two courses (£40) or three (£45) with choices such as smoked Armagh goose, wild wood pigeon with figs and salisfy, or halibut and lemongrass, and to cap it all, views through the large windows stretch over the River Lagan to the glowing 56-foot-tall Ring of Thanksgiving beacon by the Scottish artist Andy Scott. **Known for:** venison tartare; salt-aged lamb; grilled hispi, black garlic and smoked potato. *Average main: £80 1 Oxford St., Central District 028/9031–4121 www.oxbelfast.com Closed Sun., Mon., and Tues.*

★ **Seahorse**

$$$$ | **ECLECTIC** | The Grand Central Hotel's first-floor brasserie is a bright, stylish space and a favorite rendezvous for well-heeled locals, especially on weekends. Entrées lean toward modern Irish treatments of local surf-and-turf dishes, but there are tasty vegetarian options, too. **Known for:** rack of Mourne lamb; roast monkfish; tender sirloin steaks. *Average main: £34 Grand Central Hotel, 9–15 Bedford St., Central District 028/9023–1066 www.grandcentralhotelbelfast.com/seahorse.*

★ **Stock Kitchen and Bar**

$ | **IRISH** | Overlooking the bustle of the St. George's Market hall, this glass-roofed bar and restaurant offers imaginative cocktails like Jameson stout with lime peel and ginger ale, excellent pints and a locally-inspired menu. Treats include Wagyu beef and lamb from Country Down, oysters from Carlingford Lough, crabs and scallops from east coast fishing harbors and fresh vegetables from St. George's Market. **Known for:** seared Strangford scallops; deviled lamb kidneys on sourdough toast; cote de boeuf with fresh market vegetables. *Average main: £18 St. George's Market, 1st fl., Central District 028/9024–0014 www.stockbelfast.com Closed Mon.–Wed.*

Yard Bird

$ | **BRITISH** | The humble chicken is the raison d'être of Yard Bird, on the site of a linen warehouse built in the 1750s. Start your visit with an aperitif in the Dirty Onion bar downstairs (ask the bartender about the pub's name), which retains the original, evocative tree-trunk-size beams, bare floors, and walls of the 18th century. **Known for:** tender rotisserie chicken; fast service; authentic pub with live music. *Average main: £16 3 Hill St., Cathedral Quarter 028/9024–3712 www.thedirtyonion.com.*

Zen

$ | **JAPANESE** | Offering a blend of Asian fusion, the standout dishes at Belfast's finest Japanese restaurant are the sea bass and sole, or the Zen monkfish. Among the discerning diners who frequent this lively spot, the delicious assorted mushroom teppanyaki is also a big hit, as well as the sushi and sashimi. **Known for:** sea bass and sole; Carlingford oysters; sushi and sashimi. *Average main: £16 55–59 Adelaide St., behind City Hall, Central District 028/9023–2244 www.zenbelfast.co.uk No lunch weekends.*

Coffee and Quick Bites

Established Coffee

$ | **CAFÉ** | In a world of behemoth coffee chains it is heartwarming to find an independent store with a funky vibe serving freshly ground beans from plantations in Kenya, Ethiopia, and Guatemala. Right in the heart of the Cathedral Quarter, this unpretentious café with its minimalist surroundings, communal wooden tables, and cement floor attracts a crowd of MacBook and smartphone lovers, as well as those looking for a caffeine hit. **Known for:** espresso filter coffee; luxurious cinnamon swirls; cool place to hang out. *Average main: £10 54 Hill St., Cathedral Quarter A short walk from St. Anne's Cathedral 028/9031–9416 www.established.coffee No dinner.*

Hotels

Bullitt Hotel

$$$ | **HOTEL** | This centrally located hotel takes its trendy vibes (and name) from the "King of Cool," Steve McQueen, and delivers a no-frills experience with compact rooms. **Pros:** stylish with a sense of humor; central location; free cancellation policy. **Cons:** rooms are small; not many facilities; traffic noise from busy street. *Rooms from: £119 40A Church La., Central District 028/9590–0600 www.bullitthotel.com 74 rooms No Meals.*

Clayton Hotel Belfast

$$$$ | **B&B/INN** | A 10-minute stroll from the city center, the Clayton has a lively bar and restaurant, Avenue 22, but if you wish to venture out, there's a great choice of restaurants, bars, and cafés nearby. **Pros:** value deals; health club and facilities are top-notch; excellent breakfasts. **Cons:** lacks character; lack of car parking; surrounding streets can be noisy at night. *Rooms from: £170 22 Ormeau Ave., Central District 028/9032–8511 www.claytonhotelbelfast.com 170 rooms Free Breakfast.*

The Flint

$$$$ | **APARTMENT** | Centrally located in a dignified historic building, The Flint offers guests compact studio-suites with self-catering facilities (including microwave ovens and dishwashers) along with perks such as fluffy bathrobes and luxurious rain showers. **Pros:** stylish suites with kitchenettes; free baggage storage; free laundry facilities. **Cons:** not all suites have views; no bar or restaurant; no on-site parking. *Rooms from: £200 48 Howard St., Central District 028/9066–6400 www.theflintbelfast.com 55 rooms No Meals.*

Grand Central Hotel

$$$$ | **HOTEL** | Beyond a doubt the coolest place to stay, dine, and hang out in Belfast, this swish 23-floor venue is part of the Hastings portfolio and boasts the highest bar in Ireland. **Pros:** top location; valet parking; panoramic views from top-floor bar. **Cons:** no on-site parking; no pool; frustrating waits for elevators. *Rooms from: £220 Bedford St., Central District City center, 5-min walk*

from City Hall ☎ 028/9023–1066 ⊕ www.grandcentralhotelbelfast.com ⇆ 300 rooms ꟾ◯ꟾ Free Breakfast.

★ Malmaison

$$$ | **HOTEL** | Living up to its claim to be "a hotel that dares to be different," this transformed 19th-century grain warehouse incorporates trendy decor choices, modern facilities, and elegant finishes, all the while retaining original details like cast-iron pillars, wood beams, and giant portholes (inside) and gargoyles (outside). **Pros:** trendy decor; sometimes offers very good value for money; lively bar and good restaurant. **Cons:** tries a little too hard to be cool; bar can be crowded and noisy; popular with rugby fans during international fixtures. *$ Rooms from: £160 ✉ 34–38 Victoria St., Central District ☎ 028/9600–1405 ⊕ www.malmaison.com ⇆ 62 rooms ꟾ◯ꟾ No Meals.*

★ The Merchant Hotel

$$$$ | **HOTEL** | A mix of glorious Victorian grandeur and Art Deco–inspired modernity, this hotel—regarded by some as Ireland's most spectacular—was built as the headquarters of Ulster Bank in the mid-19th century and still leads the way in style and sophistication. **Pros:** superhelpful staff; fabulous gym and spa; discounted off-street parking available just steps away. **Cons:** elevator occasionally unreliable; Wi-Fi access intermittent in some rooms; labyrinthine corridors. *$ Rooms from: £289 ✉ 16 Skipper St., Cathedral Quarter ☎ 028/9023–4888 ⊕ www.themerchanthotel.com ⇆ 67 rooms ꟾ◯ꟾ Free Breakfast.*

Radisson Blu Belfast

$ | **HOTEL** | A little way from the city center (around a 25-minute walk from Donegall Square), this businesslike modern hotel has a corporate feel but offers in-room frills such as fluffy robes and room service, plus amenities including restaurant and bar. **Pros:** big rooms with city or river views; off-street parking; full-service hotel at rates that compete with nearby no-frills rivals. **Cons:** no alternative dining options nearby; no easy access to public transportation; disappointing, overpriced restaurant menu. *$ Rooms from: £76 ✉ The Gasworks, 3 Cromac Pl., Central District ☎ 028/9043–4065 ⊕ www.radissonhotels.com ⇆ 120 rooms ꟾ◯ꟾ Free Breakfast.*

Ten Square

$$$$ | **HOTEL** | You don't get much more downtown or contemporary than this fashionable boutique hotel (a former post office) right behind City Hall. **Pros:** luxurious surroundings; bargain package offers; good choice of bars and restaurants. **Cons:** favored by hen night and wedding parties; outside seating gets traffic fumes; no car parking. *$ Rooms from: £190 ✉ 10 Donegall Sq. S, Central District ☎ 028/9024–1001 ⊕ www.tensquare.co.uk ⇆ 130 rooms ꟾ◯ꟾ Free Breakfast.*

★ Titanic Hotel

$$$$ | **HOTEL** | The former drawing office headquarters of Harland & Wolff shipyard where the RMS *Titanic* plans were created has been repurposed with panache and is now a stylish hotel that honors its nautical heritage. **Pros:** award-winning restaurant; very good value two-night packages and midweek rates; museum-worthy artifacts on display. **Cons:** slightly inconvenient location; bleak postindustrial surroundings; hallways are a little dark. *$ Rooms from: £161 ✉ 8 Queens Rd., Titanic Quarter ✣ Next door to Titanic Belfast ☎ 028/9508–2000 ⊕ www.titanichotelbelfast.com ⇆ 119 rooms ꟾ◯ꟾ Free Breakfast.*

Nightlife

Bert's Jazz Bar

LIVE MUSIC | Belfast's only dedicated jazz bar offers live music seven nights a week and excellent cocktails in surroundings calculated to evoke New York at the height of the golden age of jazz. *✉ The Merchant Hotel, 16 Skipper St., Cathedral*

Quarter ☎ *028/9026–2713* 🌐 *www.themerchanthotel.com/berts-jazz-bar.*

Bittles Bar

PUBS | Colorful drawings of political, cultural, and social life hang on the walls of this triangular Victorian pub on the fringes of the Cathedral Quarter, which claims to sell more pints of Guinness per square foot of floor space than any other pub in Ireland. The drawings are by talented local artist Joe O'Kane, a pub patron. From a selection of rotating taps, Bittles serves local craft brews such as Farmageddon cider, Hilden ales, and Beavertown IPA (a company founded by Logan Plant, the son of Led Zeppelin's Robert Plant). As well as premium Irish whiskeys, the bar also stocks a large range of craft gins, including Gunpowder from Drumshanbo in Leitrim, and two local ones, Shortcross, distilled at Crossgar in County Down and Echlinville Pot Still from the Ards Peninsula. ✉ *70 Upper Church La., Cathedral Quarter* 🌐 *www.bittlesbar.com.*

Hell Cat Maggies

PUBS | This first-floor New York–inspired bar beside City Hall is named after a formidable character who was born in Ireland and raised hell with the Dead Rabbit street gang, one of the infamous gangs of New York in the 1800s. Drinks, such as Mulberry Street, Paradise Square, and Gentleman Jasper reflect the connection. The food, served from noon, includes mussels with Guinness and garlic, falafel burgers, chicken stack, waffle fries, or shrimp cocktail. ✉ *2 Donegall Sq. W, Central District* ☎ *028/9099–4120* 🌐 *www.hellcat-maggies.com.*

The John Hewitt Bar

BARS | A must for every traveler, this bar named after one of Ulster's most famous poets (who ironically wasn't a big drinker) is traditional in style with a marble counter, waist-high wooden paneling, high ceilings, and open fire. It channels Hewitt's socialist sensibility, as it's owned by the Belfast Unemployed Centre (which it helps fund with its profits). Top pub grub is served from noon to 4 pm and live music is featured most nights. Irish artisanal cider and bottled craft beers are the most popular. ✉ *51 Donegall St., Cathedral Quarter* ☎ *028/9023–3768* 🌐 *www.thejohnhewitt.com.*

Kremlin

BARS | A massive statue of Lenin above the front door greets patrons of the undisputed center of the Belfast gay scene. The over-the-top Soviet theme continues inside. Superstar DJs regularly fly in to perform. ✉ *96 Donegall St., Cathedral Quarter* ☎ *028/9031–6060* 🌐 *www.kremlin-belfast.com.*

McHugh's

BARS | In Belfast's oldest building (1711), McHugh's has three floors of bars and restaurants, and live music Thursday to Sunday. Food is served from lunchtime in the downstairs bar, while dinner—including special "on the hot rock" steaks, cooked to your liking—is available 6 pm–9 pm in the upstairs restaurant. McHugh's retains the character of an early-18th-century dockside inn and exudes a homey feel with open fires. ✉ *29–31 Queen's Sq., Central District* ☎ *028/9050–9999* 🌐 *www.mchughsbar.com.*

★ The National Grande Café

CAFÉS | Named after its former bank occupant, the National is proud of its green credentials, with energy-efficient heating in its popular beer garden, and a closed-loop system enabling all parts of the fruit to be used in cocktails without waste. Ingredients in the food are sourced within 64 km (40 miles) of Belfast and, to cut down the amount of glass or plastic, the bar filters and carbonates its own tap water. Quality deluxe sandwiches with beef brisket, chicken, or pulled pork, along with tapas, croques, and salads span the menu throughout the day; to wash your food down choose from hangover cures, low-alcohol gin, or bracing cocktails such as the National Spritz, Nitro Espresso martini, or Irish

Get your perfect pint of Guinness at the Crown Liquor Saloon, a Victorian extravaganza of embossed ceilings, gilded arabesques, and carved woodwork.

coffee made with Powers whiskey. The upstairs nightclub has also been rebranded as Sixty-6. In the beer garden, look for the quirky art installation "Living Barrels." It was created by French artist Sylvain Ristori, who collaborated with Jameson whiskey brand to produce a sculpture using recycled materials from the barrel staves of Midleton Distillery. ✉ *62–68 High St., Central District* ☎ *028/9031–1130* 🌐 *www.thenationalbelfast.com.*

Observatory

COCKTAIL LOUNGES | Spectacular sunsets and nighttime views over the city are the key selling points of the Grand Central Hotel's posh penthouse lounge. It's the highest bar in Ireland, with an imaginative cocktail list and a swank clientele. Reserve a table ahead of time and dress to impress. ✉ *Grand Central Hotel, 9–15 Bedford St., Central District* ☎ *028/9023–1066* 🌐 *www.grandcentralhotelbelfast.com/observatory.*

Union Street Pub

PUBS | A gay-friendly bar near the Cathedral Quarter, Union Street is housed in a converted 19th-century shoe factory. The three-story redbrick Victorian is one of the city's few gastropubs, with a more formal upstairs evening restaurant that's popular with local foodies. ✉ *8–14 Union St., Central District* ☎ *028/9031–6060* 🌐 *www.unionstreetbar.com.*

White's Tavern and the Oyster Rooms

PUBS | White's Tavern rather trades on its reputation as "Belfast's oldest public house." It serves decent pub grub and there's live music in the downstairs bar on weekends, but for young locals the big attraction is the alfresco White's Garden, a covered alley where patrons can drink, socialize, smoke, and vape while kept warm by patio heaters even in winter.

A roaring fire greets you as soon as you enter White's Tavern. Friendly staff serve pub grub until 8 pm, although a better bet is to head upstairs, which has been redesigned as the elegant Oyster Rooms restaurant. Its bare, thick-walled brick and high ceiling remain the same, but the culinary options step up a gear and include fresh and firm Carlingford Lough oysters, served on the half shell and dressed in vinaigrette (six for £12), steak tartare, beef and Guinness stew, pork belly, or sole. Live-music sessions are held in the downstairs bar on weekend evenings. ✉ *2–4 Winecellar Entry, Central District* ☎ *028/9031–2582* 🌐 *www.whitestavernbelfast.com.*

Performing Arts

Belfast Waterfront

CONCERTS | This world-class performance venue houses a 2,200-seat concert hall (for ballet and classical, rock, and Irish music) and a 500-seat studio space (for modern dance, jazz, and experimental theater). From the Waterfront bar you can have a pint and enjoy the river views before or after your culture fix. The main box office for booking events here is based at the Ulster Hall in Bedford Street. ✉ *2 Lanyon Pl., Central District* ☎ *028/9033–4455* 🌐 *www.waterfront.co.uk.*

The Black Box

CONCERTS | This nonprofit performance space, housed in a historic 19th-century building, opened in 2006 and is a vibrant venue for live music, theater, comedy, and cabaret, with a special interest in developing new local creative talent. ✉ *18–22 Hill St., Cathedral Quarter* ☎ *028/9031–6060* 🌐 *www.blackboxbelfast.com.*

Ulster Hall

CONCERTS | The historic Ulster Hall (it once hosted Rachmaninov) is the permanent home of the Ulster Orchestra. The classical music season runs here from September through April. Concerts are mostly held on Fridays, but you can call or check online (🌐 *www.ulsterorchestra.org.uk*) to learn about other dates, free open rehearsals, and 50-minute lunchtime concerts. Apart from classical, the hall presents rock, folk, traditional Irish, blues, jazz, and other forms, along with comedy and cabaret acts. With its superb acoustics, Ulster Hall provides the perfect listening and foot-tapping experience. ✉ *34 Bedford St., Central District* ☎ *028/9033–4455* 🌐 *www.ulsterhall.co.uk.*

Shopping

FOOD

★ Sawers Deli

FOOD | From feta cheese to foie gras, there's a dazzling selection of artisanal foods from local and international suppliers at this deli, founded in 1897. Among the most popular is Irish Black Butter, which is not actually a dairy product but a delicious spread made from cider, brandy, spices, and treacle for toast or local soda bread. Browse the shelves for a trip through some of the finest Northern Irish produce. Find Robert Ditty's Irish oatcakes rolled with County Armagh oats; Ballylisk, a white mold cream cheese known as the "Triple Rose of Armagh"; and a raft of jams and spiced apple chutney from Erin Grove Preserves in Fermanagh—all set alongside a selection of wheat and focaccia breads. Sawers's own acclaimed coffee, roasted on Belfast's Falls Road, comes in four different blends, and don't forget the Suki tea made by the Belfast Brew company, which specializes in loose-leaf teas and old-fashioned teapots. All these treats and drinks can be sampled in a small café at the back of the premises. ✉ *Fountain Centre, 5–6 College St., Central District* ☎ *028/9032–2021* 🌐 *www.sawersbelfast.com.*

GALLERIES

Belfast Exposed

ART GALLERIES | A photography gallery, Belfast Exposed also has a large digital archive of images. Book launches and talks by local artists and exhibitions are held regularly. There's an excellent range of large-format photographic books for sale, including many featuring the Troubles. ✉ *23 Donegall St., Cathedral*

Brexit and Its Aftermath

On January 31, 2020, the United Kingdom, including Northern Ireland, left the European Union after 47 years of membership. The Brexit debate over Britain's departure lasted 3½ years. For most of that time the political leaders in Northern Ireland had not taken their seats at the Stormont Parliament in Belfast because of their own political wrangling, although they resolved their differences and took up their seats again early in 2020. On June 23, 2016, against all predictions, a majority of people in the United Kingdom (51.9%) voted to leave the EU. In the same referendum, along with Scotland, the majority of people (55.8%) in Northern Ireland voted to remain in the EU, which left many people aggrieved to be stripped of a European identity that they had cherished. The leader of the Social Democratic and Labour Party (one of the North's main political parties), Colum Eastwood, described Brexit as: "An act of constitutional violence inflicted on the people of Northern Ireland and Scotland by an English electorate."

One of the most complex issues with which the governments had to deal was the question of the Irish border separating Northern Ireland from the Republic of Ireland. The new Free State—later called the Republic—was formed for 26 counties while the six counties of Northern Ireland chose to remain within the United Kingdom. The Republic remains firmly in the EU, and in currency terms, in the euro zone, and although Northern Ireland is in the sterling region, many businesses in the North, especially along the border, accept euros. Leaving the EU presents a major regime change with political, economic, and social consequences, primarily the creation of either a "hard border" between Northern Ireland and the Republic or between the North and the rest of the United Kingdom. Either solution creates major problems for businesses, haulers, and cross-border workers. The wavering by the U.K. government on its commitment to "no border in the Irish Sea" has given the Unionist community another grievance to add to its treasury of grudges; the "Northern Ireland protocol," under which the province remains within the U.K.'s customs territory and internal market, burdens companies trading with the mainland with new and onerous customs processes and is naturally widely disliked by business. The protocol remains a bone of contention between the U.K. and the EU.

As a result of Brexit, the prospect of Irish unity has taken on a new dynamic. Brexit is being seen as a game changer, which will reshape the political and economic conversation across the island of Ireland. Long-term demographic change—with the North's Catholic community set to become the majority population within a matter of years—and Sinn Féin's success in the Republic's elections in February 2020 mean that the prospect of a United Ireland is a less remote possibility than ever before. The practicalities and economic realities of this would be subject to lengthy discussion and negotiation, while obstacles and uncertainties remain.

Quarter ☎ *028/9023–0965* 🌐 *www.belfastexposed.org.*

Craft NI Gallery

ART GALLERIES | Unique gifts are for sale in this shop that is the retail branch of Craft Northern Ireland, a collective of local artists and designers. Here you will find traditional-frame-weaving baskets made from willow, terra-cotta plates, ceramic figurines, pewter jewelry, hand-carved papier mâché dolls, machine-stitched maps, bespoke furniture, and much more. The shop hosts exhibitions as well as the Arts Council craft collection each year and in August holds a craft month encouraging people to make, see, learn about, and buy craft products. ✉ *115–119, Royal Ave., 1st fl., Central District* ☎ *028/9032–9342* 🌐 *www.craftni.org.*

Golden Thread Gallery

ART GALLERIES | One of Belfast's best arts venues, the Golden Thread has exhibited at the internationally acclaimed Venice Biennale. The gallery presents visual art from paintings on canvas to the latest digital arts. Their two key objectives are to increase public access to the contemporary visual arts and generate support for Northern Irish art and artists. ✉ *84–94 Great Patrick St., Cathedral Quarter* ☎ *028/9033–0920* 🌐 *www.goldenthreadgallery.co.uk.*

JEWELRY

Queen's Arcade

MALL | Running between Donegall Place and Fountain Street, this historic mall is home to upscale brands such as Gucci, TAG Heuer, Rolex, and Mont Blanc, and to the cozy Queen's Café Bar (closed Sunday and Monday), which serves massive cooked breakfasts, sandwiches, and burgers from 11:30 am–5 pm. ✉ *Queen's Arcade, 29–33 Donegall Pl., Central District* ✣ *Runs between Donegall Pl. and Fountain St.* ☎ *028/9032–7954* 🌐 *www.queensarcadebelfast.com.*

The Steensons

JEWELRY & WATCHES | A major draw (for fans) of the superb handcrafted and locally designed jewelry in this goldsmiths is a range of products created for the *Game of Thrones* TV series. Display cabinets showcase sterling silver cuff links, necklaces, earrings, and a range of pins and pendants connected to the series. Pieces include crowns, Margaery's "Purple Wedding," Cersei's lion pendant, and Littlefinger's mockingbird pin. The shop also stocks the work of more than 50 European and local designers. ✉ *Bedford House, Bedford St., Central District* ☎ *028/9024–8269* 🌐 *www.thesteensons.com.*

MARKETS AND MALLS

★ **St. George's Market**

MARKET | For an authentic blast of Belfast life, make your way to the enormous indoor St. George's Market on Friday, Saturday, and Sunday. When it opened in the 1890s, this historic market sold butter, eggs, poultry, and fruit. Today it is a vibrant place with as many as 200 traders selling everything from oysters and live lobsters to organically grown produce, antiques, local art, and curios. The Friday Variety Market starts at 8 am and runs until 2 pm; the Saturday City Food and Craft Market, 9–3; and the Sunday Market, Craft, and Antique market, 10–3. There's an international culinary flavor with Cuban sandwiches, savory crepes, paella, tapas, pizzas, and Thai dishes. Foodies love the treats at Aunt Sandra's Candy Factory stall, with its fudge and flavored sweets, terrific breads from Riley's Home Bakery, and Tom and Ollie's for mouthwatering cheeses, pickles, and charcuterie. An excellent place to pick up picnic ingredients or stock your kitchen if you're using self-catering accommodations. ✉ *12–20 E. Bridge St., Central District* ☎ *028/9043–5704* 🌐 *www.belfastcity.gov.uk/stgeorgesmarket.*

Fern Madness

One of the highlights of a visit to Belfast's Botanic Gardens is the Tropical Ravine House, a lush cathedral of greenery, restored during 2018 at a cost of £3.8 million, and an internationally significant building. Victorians brought many specimens back to Ireland from their travels in the mid–19th century that natural history experts labeled pteridomania, or "fern madness." Through pictorial signboards, information panels, microscopes, audio, and hands-on displays, visitors can explore close-up the life cycle of these exotic plants against a background of birdsong. Old features such as the waterfall, cascade, and pool have been reinstated and are home to the giant lily Victoria amazonica. Walk around the upper canopy and cast-iron columns and you will be astounded at the smells and the scale of the ferns and trees. Some, such as the firewheel tree, are native to the Australian rain forest, while the custard tree, which blends the taste of banana, pineapple, papaya, peach, and strawberry, is from Central and South America. Hour-long guided tours are held at 11 am on Tuesday and Thursday morning and at 2 pm on Wednesday afternoon. Closed Monday. Advance booking is essential. *www.belfastcity.gov.uk/tropicalravine*

★ **Victoria Square**

MALL | Occupying an eight-block site in central Belfast, this shopping center dominates the city skyline. The eight-story, 800,000-square-foot mall, all glittering steel, is topped by a vast geodesic glass dome with a viewing gallery that offers amazing panoramic views of the city. Sadly, that's the only thing that makes Victoria Square worth visiting: the on-site retail and fast-food and beverage outlets are the same run-of-the-mill brands found in similar malls all over the United Kingdom, so there are many better places in which to spend your time in Belfast.

TIP→ Make your way up to the viewing gallery for great views of Belfast; admission is free and a guide can show you the sights. *1 Victoria Sq., at Chichester, Montgomery, Ann, and Victoria Sts., Central District* *028/9032–2277* *www.victoriasquare.com.*

University Area

At Belfast's southern end, the part of the city around Queen's University is dotted with parks, botanical gardens, and leafy streets with fine, intact two- and three-story 19th-century buildings. The area evokes an older, more leisurely pace of life. The many pubs and restaurants make this area a nightlife hub for younger residents, but for most venues the core clientele is drawn from the university's 25,000-strong student body—which means cheap drinks and loud music are standard, especially on weekends, and anyone over 25 may feel a little out of place.

Sights

Botanic Gardens

GARDEN | In the Victorian heyday it was not unusual to find 10,000 of Belfast's citizens strolling about here on a Saturday afternoon. These gardens are a glorious haven of grass, trees, flowers, curving walks, and wrought-iron benches, all laid

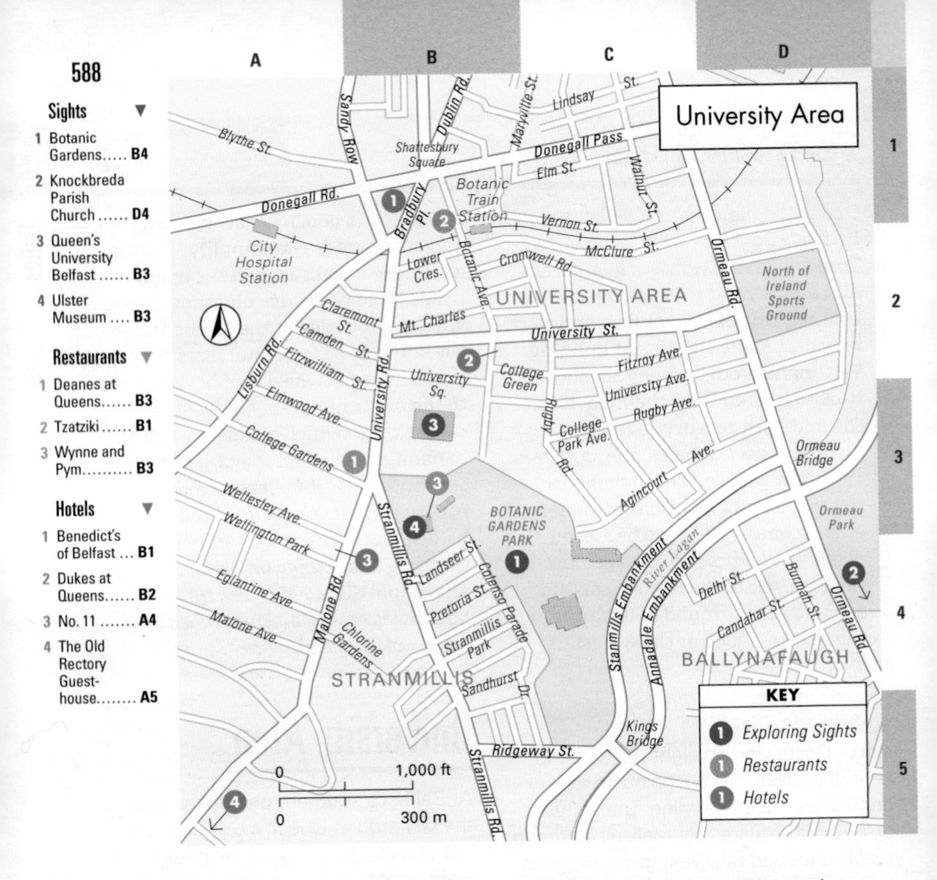

out in 1827 on land that slopes down to the River Lagan.

■ TIP→ The curved-iron and glass Palm House is a conservatory marvel designed in 1839 by Charles Lanyon.

Inside, the hot "stove wing" is a minijungle of exotic plants such as the bird-of-paradise flower and heavily scented frangipani. In the main grounds you can wander around the arboretum and the 100-year-old rockery, or in summer savor the colors and scents of the herbaceous borders. On the last Sunday of August each year more than 30,000 people converge on the grounds for the Belfast Mela, a program of music, dance, food, and arts. Stalls and stands are laid out, and street theater, drummers, and choirs from many countries take part in the festivities alongside global cuisine in a world-food market, while tastings and tea-leaf readings are held in a tea emporium.

■ TIP→ A fun challenge is to follow the Tree Trail, which leads you around 20 trees, many planted in the 19th century, with specimens such as the tree of heaven, Japanese red cedar, and the wonderful ginkgo biloba from China. ✉ *Stranmillis Rd., University Area* ☎ *028/9032–0202* 🌐 *www.belfastcity.gov.uk* 🎟 *Free.*

Knockbreda Parish Church

CHURCH | Belfast has so many churches you could visit a different one nearly every day of the year and still not make it to them all. The oldest house of worship is the Church of Ireland Knockbreda Parish Church. This dark structure was built in 1737 by Richard Cassels, who designed many of Ireland's finest mansions. It quickly became *the* place to be buried—witness the vast 18th-century tombs in the churchyard. ✉ *Church Rd., off A24, Belfast* ☎ *028/9064–5372* 🌐 *www.knockbredaparish.org.*

Queen's University Belfast

COLLEGE | Dominating University Road is Queen's University. The main buildings, modeled on Oxford's Magdalen College and designed by Charles Lanyon, were built in 1849 in the Tudor Revival style. The long, handsome, redbrick-and-sandstone facade of the main building features large lead-glass windows, and is topped with three square towers and crenellations galore. University Square, really a terrace, is from the same era. The Seamus Heaney Library is named after the Ulster-born, 1997 Nobel Prize–winning poet who died in 2013. The McClay Library in College Park features a multistory open atrium, 1.5 million volumes, and the Brian Friel Theatre, named in honor of one of Ireland's most illustrious playwrights. The C.S. Lewis reading room on the first floor has a replica of the wardrobe door used in the film *The Lion, the Witch, and the Wardrobe.* The Queen's Welcome Centre hosts a program of exhibitions and serves as a visitor information point. Guided tours are available but must be booked in advance.

With a student population of 25,000, the university has been making waves internationally for its research in many fields. In 2020 Queen's appointed Hillary Clinton as its new chancellor to serve for a five-year term. It is the first time that a woman has taken on what is a largely ceremonial role and has boosted the university's prestige. The Clintons first came to Northern Ireland in November 1995 when Bill, as U.S. president, was a key player involved in talks leading to the Northern Ireland peace process. In 2018 Hillary received an honorary degree from Queen's and a scholarship was set up in her name for postgraduate study in politics, human rights, and peace-building. ✉ *University Rd., University Area* ☎ *028/9024–5133* 🌐 *www.qub.ac.uk* 🎫 *Free.*

★ Ulster Museum

HISTORY MUSEUM | FAMILY | Next door to the Botanic Gardens, the rejuvenated Ulster Museum is a big hit with visitors for its spacious light-filled atrium and polished steel. The museum's forte is the history and prehistory of Ireland, using exhibitions to colorfully trace the rise of Belfast's crafts, trade, and industry. In addition, the museum has a large natural history section, with a famed skeleton of the extinct Irish giant deer and a trove of jewelry and gold ornaments recovered from the Spanish Armada vessel *Girona,* which sank off the Antrim Coast in 1588. Take time to seek out the *Girona*'s stunning gold salamander studded with rubies and still dazzling after 400 years in the Atlantic. The museum includes a first-rate collection of 19th- and 20th-century art from Europe, Britain, and America. The Modern History gallery tells the story of Ulster from 1500 to 1968 and shows a remarkable range of objects from the history collection, many on display for the first time. A permanent exhibition installed in 2018 presents a somber look at the history of the civil and political conflict in Northern Ireland. "The Troubles and Beyond" recounts in a graphic way the story of three decades of communal violence covering the 1970s, '80s, and '90s. Through a wide variety of images, including reproduction of wall murals, maps, photographs, and propaganda ephemera, as well as videos, listening posts, and screens, the harrowing story of the conflict, which claimed more than 3,000 lives, is told in an engaging way. Look out for two poignant wall exhibits: the Peace Quilt, a red fabric with white birds representing the dove of peace and a teddy bear as a reminder of the children who suffered the loss of loved ones; and a powerful oil painting by the artist Jack Pakenham, *Peace Talks,* completed

At a conservative estimate, there are more than 70 wall murals throughout the city.

in 1992 as Northern Ireland moved slowly toward a resolution of the Troubles. In 2020, the museum received six etchings by the Dutch master Rembrandt, which were gifted as a major acquisition by the Arts Council of England. The delicate etchings, which are on permanent display, date from 1630 to the 1650s. They include Dutch landscapes such as *Six's Bridge*, which Rembrandt made in 1645 while visiting the country estate of Jan Six, a wealthy Amsterdam merchant who was his friend and patron.

TIP→ The art, history, and nature discovery zones are packed with hands-on activities for children. Kids enjoy the Peter the Polar Bear exhibit and the famed Egyptian mummy, Takabuti.

TIP→ Sunday morning is the quietest time to visit, but go early before the crowds. Afterward, lay out a picnic in the Belfast Botanical Gardens next door. ✉ *Stranmillis Rd., University Area* ☎ *028/9044–0000* 🌐 *www.nmni.com/um* 🎫 *Free* 🕑 *Closed Mon., except for Northern Irish holidays.*

Restaurants

★ Deanes at Queens

$$ | INTERNATIONAL | FAMILY | The only upscale eatery in the University area, this classy outpost of Michael Deane's Belfast empire has an attractive outdoor terrace for summer lunching and a menu that emphasizes meat and seafood but caters adequately to vegetarians, too. **Known for:** vegetarian Parmesan risotto; confit of duck with potato fondant; pan-roasted sea bass on cracked potato. $ *Average main: £22* ✉ *1 College Gardens, University Area* ☎ *028/9038–2111* 🌐 *www.michaeldeane.co.uk/deanes-at-queens* 🕑 *Closed Mon. and Tues.* M *Botanics.*

Tzatziki

$ | GREEK | This newcomer to the Botanic Avenue dining scene (where eateries mainly aim to satisfy hungry, cost-conscious students) stands out with authentic Hellenic offerings including meat skewers, savory pastries and crisp salads. **Known for:** cheese and spinach

Belfast's Wall Murals

More than two decades after the Good Friday Peace Agreement in 1998, the city's symbolic and political wall murals still continue to attract attention and visitors. Often bold, graphic, and eye-catching, Belfast's murals increasingly reflect a wider nonsectarian view of global themes such as human rights, climate change, public health concerns, and other hot-topic issues.

Styles differ between the murals of the Catholic (Republican) and the Protestant (Loyalist) communities. Along Lower Newtownards Road, in east Belfast, a wall known as Freedom Corner portrays armed Loyalist balaclava-wearing paramilitaries. In most Republican areas—but not all—murals no longer glorify gunmen and are inspired by local and international events.

While commentators feel the contentious militaristic murals should be consigned to history and that they do not represent the vibrant and largely peaceful face of 21st-century Belfast, as with other aspects of city life, opinion is divided. Some Loyalist artwork has been reimagined in the Shankill district to reflect contemporary issues like equality and women's and children's rights. Loyalist murals also showcase history and war, including the part played by the 36th Ulster Division at the Battle of the Somme in 1916, while industrial, sporting, and musical heritage is depicted.

On the Republican side, many murals recall the dark days of the Troubles. A gable wall at Sevastopol Street on the Falls Road in West Belfast commemorates Bobby Sands, the first IRA prisoner to die in the 1981 hunger strike protest. Farther along the road, the muralists have been active on what is dubbed "The International Wall," now a major tourist attraction. A tapestry of political events concentrates on themes as diverse as Basque independence, the Cuban Revolution, and Picasso's *Guernica*. Elsewhere in West Belfast, subjects are far-reaching, with murals drawing on themes inspired by Celtic mythology featuring, for example, the Tuatha Dé Danann, the people of the goddess Danu.

Two startling murals in the Cathedral Quarter (in the Central District) are particularly worth seeking out. "The Duel of Belfast, Dance by Candlelight" by the Cork-born graffiti artist Conor Harrington, is on the gable wall of the Black Box performance center on Hill Street, and has become a signature piece about decay, the end of empires, and the colonial west. "Son of Protagoras" by the French artist known as MTO (real name Mateo) on Talbot Street by St. Anne's Cathedral, features the Greek philosopher, Protagoras, and shows a dove pierced by arrows bearing the cross of the Knights of Malta and the Latin cross.

The best way to see the political murals is on an organized tour, which will provide context. Join a guided tour with Belfast City Sightseeing or one of the many other bus or taxi tour companies. Two-hour walking tours of the street artwork in the Cathedral Quarter are held each Sunday at noon and cost £10; the meeting point is outside the Duke of York pub, an entryway off Hill Street. 🌐 *www.seedheadarts.com*

pastries; chicken and lamb souvlaki; generous meze platters. *Average main: £14* *35 Botanic Ave., University Area* *028/9508–2272* *Closed Mon.* *Botanics.*

Wynne and Pym

$ | **CAFÉ** | **FAMILY** | This bright modern adjunct to the Ulster Museum is the perfect place to pause after a stroll through the Botanic Gardens and the Museum. It offers plenty of tea and coffee choices, cakes, and more substantial hot and cold sandwiches. **Known for:** hot croques monsieur; choice of teas, tisanes, and coffees; fresh-baked scones and pastries. *Average main: £7* *Ulster Museum, Stranmillis Rd., University Area* *Botanic Gardens* *028/9044–0000* *www.ulstermuseum.org/food-drink* *Botanics.*

Hotels

Benedict's of Belfast

$$$ | **HOTEL** | Friendly, lively, and convenient, Benedict's looms large on Bradbury Place in the heart of the action beside the bright lights of Shaftesbury Square. **Pros:** complimentary welcome drink; great inexpensive dining; 10-minute walk from the city center. **Cons:** bar attracts a youthful local clientele so can get rowdy; not many extras; service can be inconsistent. *Rooms from: £125* *7–21 Bradbury Pl., University Area* *028/9059–1999* *www.benedictshotel.co.uk* *32 rooms* *Free Breakfast.*

Dukes at Queens

$$$ | **HOTEL** | Although it retains its distinguished redbrick Victorian facade, the inside of this handsome hotel on bohemian Botanic Avenue has been revamped in a cool contemporary style with chic, modern guest rooms. **Pros:** stylish; good value for the price; five-minute walk from Queen's University and the Botanic Gardens. **Cons:** noisy, busy area; bar can get very crowded; on-street parking difficult. *Rooms from: £121* *65–67 University St., University Area* *028/9023–6666* *www.dukesatqueens.com* *32 rooms* *Free Breakfast.*

No. 11

$ | **B&B/INN** | More like an upscale B&B than a full-service hotel, No. 11, in the heart of the university quarter, is part of a dignified terrace of red sandstone town houses and offers comfortable, quiet rooms. **Pros:** excellent value for money; free baggage storage; free parking. **Cons:** no check-in before 3 pm; some distance from city center attractions; no bar or restaurant. *Rooms from: £55* *11 Malone Rd., University Area* *028/9099–5121* *www.warrencollection.com/number11* *12 rooms* *No Meals.*

The Old Rectory Guesthouse

$$ | **B&B/INN** | Upscale breakfasts are the big draw at Mary and Jerry Callan's well-appointed South Belfast house built in 1896 as a Church of Ireland rectory. **Pros:** beautifully prepared, hearty breakfasts; suite-size rooms; free off-street parking. **Cons:** two-night minimum stay at some times of year; no bar; not all rooms are en suite. *Rooms from: £98* *148 Malone Rd., University Area* *028/9066–7882* *www.anoldrectory.co.uk* *7 rooms* *Free Breakfast.*

Nightlife

Alibi

DANCE CLUBS | On Friday and Saturday night, Alibi comes alive upstairs for clubbers and local nighthawks. Downstairs, from 5 to 10 pm, the bar serves pizzas or chips while the prosecco flows on Friday. *23–31 Bradbury Pl., University Area* *028/9023–3131* *www.alibibelfast.com.*

★ **Belfast Empire Music Hall**

LIVE MUSIC | Inside a deconsecrated church, the Music Hall has been one of the city's leading music venues for more than 30 years. Most nights are devoted to concerts from local groups and tribute acts, while stand-up comedy shows are usually on Tuesday—TV personality

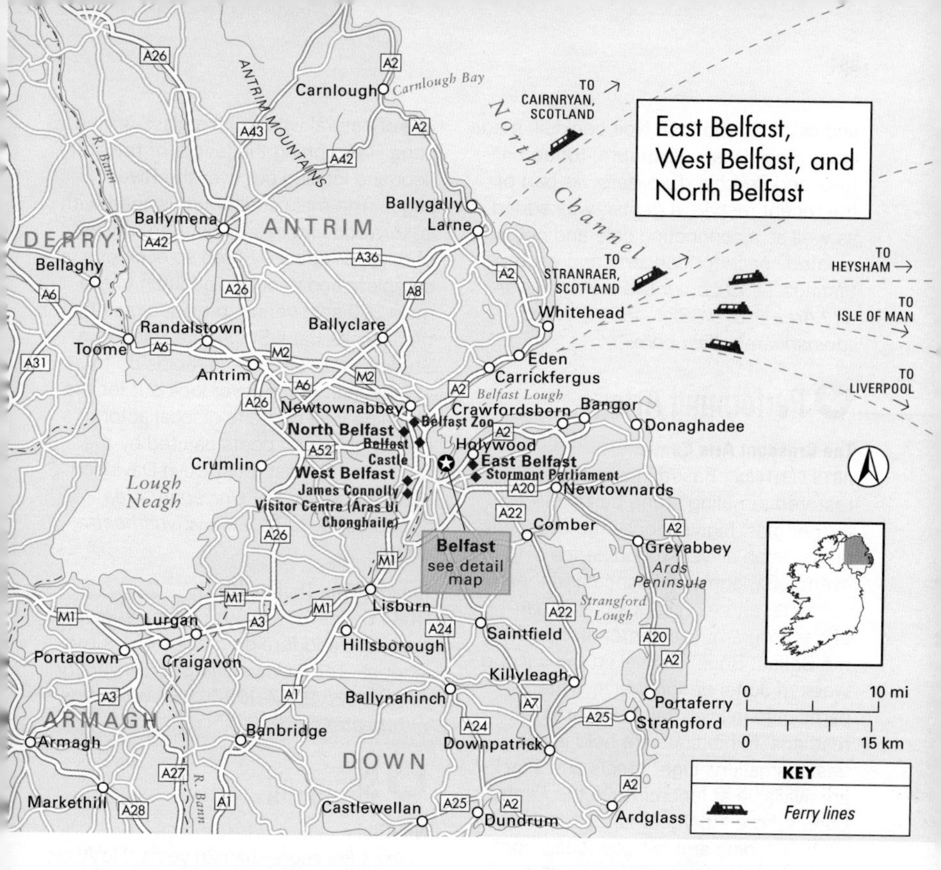

Patrick Kielty was a regular until he hit the big time in London. ✉ *42 Botanic Ave., University Area* ☎ *028/9024–9276* 🌐 *www.thebelfastempire.com.*

Cutters Wharf

BARS | Down by the river south of the university, this bar and upstairs restaurant is at its best on summer evenings and during live music performances featuring acoustic guitar and classic rock on Friday or Saturday after 6 pm. Food is served until 9 pm. Spacious and light inside, it rarely gets too packed; if seating is limited, try the picnic tables and chairs on the wooden deck outside. ✉ *4 Lockview Rd., University Area* ☎ *028/9080–5100* 🌐 *www.cutterswharf.co.uk.*

The Playwright

BARS | Moody black-and-white framed portraits of famous Irish novelists, poets, and playwrights such as Oscar Wilde and George Bernard Shaw adorn the walls of this liquor lounge and taphouse, popular with students and visitors. Sip a glass of wine or beer and reflect on the words of Wilde, who said, "Alcohol, taken in sufficient quantities, may produce all the effects of drunkenness." Live bar entertainment features acoustic acts from Thursday to Sunday, while the huge Time nightclub on the first and second floors is open Friday and Saturday nights with music from local DJs. ✉ *5–6 Lower Crescent, University Area* ☎ *028/9031–2742.*

Town Square Bar

BARS | Gin is top of the bill at Town Square, which offers a sparkling collection of cocktails. The local Jawbox gin is paired with ginger ale, lime, and coriander, while the Aviation cocktail comes with star anise, berries, and tonic—all alongside a range of rotating taps of beer and cider. Try the Irish Noir cocktail, made up of Black Bush, vermouth, toffee tincture, and Peychaud's bitters. As part of the recent restyle, a gin bar was added, as well as a connecting café and newly created space for concerts and wine tastings. ✉ *13 Lower Crescent, University Area* ☎ *079/3824–4851* 🌐 *www.townsquarebelfast.com.*

Performing Arts

The Crescent Arts Centre

ARTS CENTERS | Based in a beautifully restored rambling stone building—a former girls' high school—the Crescent presents an all-year-round series of events. Experimental dance and theater, concerts, and workshops are all part of the program. The center also hosts the Belfast Book Festival (in the second week of June) during which writers participate in lively talks, lectures, and readings. Exhibitions are held in the upstairs gallery. Light meals and snacks are available at lunchtime in the Pantry Café, where storyboards tell the history of the building and famous locals connected to it.

TIP→ Nature note: between May and July, common swifts fly in from southern Africa to nest above the center's stone walls. Special "swift bricks" have been installed to provide nesting sites. ✉ *2 University Rd., University Area* ☎ *028/9024–2338* 🌐 *www.crescentarts.org.*

★ Lyric Theatre

THEATER | One of Northern Ireland's most prized cultural organizations, the Lyric presents a diverse repertory of classical, popular, and contemporary drama, frequently showcasing the work of local playwrights. With its angular brick bulk topped by three distinctive sloping roofs, the theater is an impressive modernist achievement. The Lyric's famed patron Liam Neeson made his 1976 stage debut here in Brian Friel's *Philadelphia, Here I Come!* Strong emphasis is placed on the use of natural light, with a glass-walled Long Hall running the length of the first floor and looking out over the River Lagan. The main auditorium is lined with iroko wood and has 33 different styles of brick, all specially fired so each one is complete and uncut. In addition to the main 390-seat venue, presided over by the Danske Bank Stage, the Naughton Studios, a theater space, holds up to 125 people. In the foyer look out for the stunning wall portraits of local actors, playwrights, and poets painted by the renowned Belfast artist Colin Davidson. ✉ *55 Ridgeway St., University Area* ☎ *028/9038–1081* 🌐 *www.lyrictheatre.co.uk.*

Queen's Film Theatre (QFT)

FILM | Belfast's main art cinema shows domestic and foreign movies on its two screens. ✉ *20 University Sq., University Area* ☎ *028/9097–1097* 🌐 *www.queens-filmtheatre.com.*

Shopping

No Alibis

BOOKS | For more than 20 years, No Alibis has been specializing in Irish, British, and American crime thrillers, as well as general fiction and nonfiction, plus a smattering of work by local novelists and poets. All in all, it's a bibliophile's delight with knowledgeable staff and regular book launches and literary readings, some of which are held in the nearby Ulster Museum. ✉ *83 Botanic Ave., University Area* ☎ *028/9031–9601* 🌐 *www.noalibis.com.*

East Belfast

A number of excellent restaurants and cafés have sprung up in East Belfast. These are a handy stopping-off point, especially if you are visiting Parliament Buildings at Stormont for a tour or a walk around the grounds, or are exploring sights along the coast leading

In the early 20th century, the marchioness of Londonderry remade her Mount Stewart estate into the horticultural showplace of Northern Ireland.

down to Strangford Lough. The main suburban area to focus on is Ballyhackamore, on the Upper Newtownards Road, and because of a proliferation of new restaurants, cafés, and bars, the area has become known to locals as "Bally-snack-amore."

If you are driving, you can park in some of the area's side streets or hop on the Glider bus (G1), a rapid-transit service connecting the east and west of the city, which leaves from close to City Hall and takes about 20 minutes to reach the area.

Sights

Stormont Parliament

GOVERNMENT BUILDING | The Northern Ireland Assembly, the province's elected legislature, sits (when not suspended due to the intransigence of some political parties) within this grand edifice with its six-column portico on the Stormont Estate. Built in 1921 to house the new Government of Northern Ireland, created following the partition of the island, it sits in a wooded, 235-acre estate, dotted with statues and memorials, including a larger-than-life effigy of Lord Carson, leader of the Ulster Unionist Party at the time of Irish independence.

Other buildings on the estate include the 19th-century mock-baronial Stormont Castle, built for the wealthy Cleland family (unfortunately, the castle is not normally open to the public). Home to the Office of the First Minister headquarters of the Northern Ireland Executive, the government's administrative branch, it is now Belfast's answer to the White House. You can get here via Metro Bus 3g, 3h, 7h, or Ulsterbus 4. Tours are available at 11 am and 2 pm weekdays, with advance tickets. ✉ *Stormont Estate, Upper Newtownards Rd., Ballymiscaw, East Belfast* ✥ *8 km (5 miles) east of city center* ☎ *028/9052–1900, 028/9052–1802 for tours* 🌐 *www.niassembly.gov.uk* 🎫 *Free* ⏲ *Closed weekends.*

Restaurants

Neill's Hill Cafe & Brasserie

$ | **EUROPEAN** | Named after a long-forgotten railway station in East Belfast, this casual brasserie has established itself as a calming spot in buzzy Ballyhackamore, where lunchtimes can get crowded. Dishes change monthly, but typical main courses for dinner are burgers, steaks, pork fillet, prawns, lemon sole, and sea bass from Walter Ewing, Belfast's top fish supplier. **Known for:** local Portavogie prawns; awesome weekend brunches; Sunday roast carvery dinner. *Average main: £17* *229 Upper Newtownards Rd., East Belfast* *028/9065–0079* *www.neillshill.com* *Closed Mon.*

Performing Arts

SSE Arena

CONCERTS | The Belfast Giants hockey team is the main tenant of the 10,000-seat SSE Arena, but Northern Ireland's biggest indoor venue also hosts rock, pop, and classical concerts. The box office for tickets opens one hour before each event or you can book tickets online. The adjacent SSE Pavilion complex has bars, restaurants, shops, and nightclubs. *2 Queen's Quay, Titanic Quarter* *www.ssearenabelfast.com.*

West Belfast

The self-contained, village-y feel of Andersonstown (known to locals as Andy-town) bustles with shops, restaurants, bars, and takeaways. If you are on a tour of the murals of the area, the Falls Road is a 20-minute walk away. You can reach the area on the Glider G1 bus service or Metro bus, or simply hail one of the many taxis that operate around the roads. During the height of the Troubles in the 1970s and '80s, this area experienced some of the worst violence, but is now a safe place to visit.

Sights

★ James Connolly Visitor Centre (Áras Uí Chonghaile)

VISITOR CENTER | The fascinating story of James Connolly, from his birth in 1868 to his execution in Dublin for his part in the Easter Rising in 1916, is told in this £1 million interactive visitor center, opened in 2019 by the Irish President Michael D. Higgins and funded largely by American labor unions. The bilingual exhibition—in Irish and English—explores Connolly's crucial role as a pioneer of the early trade union movement, his travels throughout America, and his work closer to home. A laborer, docker, engineer, and salesman, Connolly was also a soldier, political activist, and writer. In 1902, he went on a five-month tour of America, later emigrating to the States. A huge map charts his journey, which involved traveling by train to Colorado and New Mexico to address workers. In the ground-floor exhibition, excerpts from Connolly's letters and his quotations are brought to life through an audio library of poetry, music, and an interview with his daughter. Visitors hear stories of the citizen army he founded to protect workers, his influence on the text of the Easter Proclamation, his leadership in the Rising, and his subsequent court-martial and death sentence. A display cabinet contains his pistol and the knocker from the GPO in Dublin, the headquarters of the uprising's leader. *374–76 Falls Rd., West Belfast* *About 50 meters from Glider bus stop* *028/9099–1005* *www.arasuichonghaile.com* *£10* *Closed weekends* *Metro Bus No. 10; board the Glider service from city center to Beechview Park.*

Restaurants

Wolf and Whistle Restaurant

$ | **IRISH** | Beside Casement Park—home ground of the Antrim Gaelic Athletic Club—this popular restaurant is just the place to catch your breath after taking a Black Taxi tour of the nearby political murals. The menu focuses on steaks and burgers, but you can also enjoy a wide selection of salads. **Known for:** seafood chowder; Malaysian chicken curry; cauliflower wings with buffalo sauce. *$ Average main: £15 ✉ 67–71 Andersonstown Rd., West Belfast ☎ 028/9060–2210 🌐 www.wolfandwhistlebar.co.uk.*

Performing Arts

Cultúrlann McAdam Ó Fiaich

ARTS CENTERS | During 2021, this cosmopolitan arts center celebrated 30 years since it opened its doors in an area of the city that was seriously lacking visitor attractions. Promoting *Gaeilge* (Irish language) and culture, the center hosts exhibitions, book launches, concerts, theater, and poetry readings. Two choirs—one from a children's drama school and the other from resident theater company Aisling Ghéar—are based here. For travelers interested in the Gaeltacht experience, this is a great place to start. On the ground floor, the Dillon Gallery, named after the Falls Road artist Gerard Dillon, who spent much time painting in Connemara in the West of Ireland, mounts shows by top local and international artists. A shop, An Ceathrú Póilí (The Fourth Policeman), sells Irish-language and English books as well as crafts and the all-important West Belfast Mural Map. Also here are a tourist information point, Wi-Fi access, and Restaurant Bia. Ask for information about the Gaeltacht Way, a 4-km (2½-mile) walking route that takes in the major Irish language-related sites of the area. *✉ 216 Falls Rd., West Belfast ☎ 028/9096–4180 🌐 www.culturlann.ie.*

North Belfast

The sights along the Ards Peninsula, mid-County Down, and the North Coast are a short drive from Belfast—an hour or less, perfect for day trips.

Sights

★ Belfast Castle

CASTLE/PALACE | In 1934, this spectacularly baronial castle, built for the marquess of Donegall in 1865, was passed to the Belfast Corporation. Although the castle functions primarily as a restaurant, it also houses, in the cellar, the visitor center, which provides information about the castle's history and its natural surroundings in Cave Hill Country Park. Tours are self-guided and take in the reception rooms built by the Earls of Shaftesbury. For a fine introduction to the castle and park, check out the excellent eight-minute video *Watching over Belfast.* In fact, the best reason to visit the castle is to stroll the ornamental gardens and then make the ascent to McArt's Fort. This promontory, at the top of sheer cliffs 1,200 feet above the city, affords an excellent view across Belfast. Take the path uphill from the parking lot, turn right at the next intersection of pathways, and then keep left as you journey up the steep-in-places hill to the fort. *✉ Antrim Rd., North Belfast ☎ 028/9077–6925 🌐 www.belfastcastle.co.uk 🎫 Free.*

Belfast Zoo

ZOO | **FAMILY** | From the superstar Chilean flamingos and a gorilla troop reigned over by silverback alpha male Gugas—whose latest offspring, Kofi, celebrated his first birthday in October 2022—to spot-necked otters, West African chimps, and Goodfellow's tree kangaroos, you can enjoy the spectacle of more than 150 types of the world's most exotic creatures on a visit to Belfast Zoo. Note that it's on the steep side of Cave Hill and getting around the zoo involves a strenuous uphill walk for even the most energetic (not ideal for anyone with mobility problems)—a stroller would be advisable for small children. A popular attraction at the Rainforest House, a walk-through exhibition with dense tropical landscaping, is the toco toucan, with its huge, bright yellow-orange bill. The zoo is also noted for its children's farm and underwater views of the resident penguins and sea lions.

TIP→ The Treetops Tearoom (at the top of the Cave Hill site) affords the perfect view over Belfast Lough and is surrounded by the Malayan sun bear and cheetah enclosures. ✉ *Antrim Rd., North Belfast* ☎ *028/9077–6277* 🌐 *www.belfastcity.gov.uk/zoo* 🎫 *£14.*

Hotels

Maldron Hotel Belfast International Airport
$$ | **HOTEL** | Belfast International Airport is a considerable distance from the city center, so this modern hotel opposite the terminal is a good option for travelers arriving late at night or catching an early-morning flight. **Pros:** close to car-rental desks; next to airport terminal; free parking on night of stay. **Cons:** no alternative eating and drinking options nearby; out of town; bland decor. $ *Rooms from: £109* ✉ *200 Airport Rd.* ☎ *028/9445–7000* 🌐 *www.maldronhotelbelfastinternational.com* *104 rooms* *Free Breakfast.*

Chapter 14

NORTHERN IRELAND

Updated by
Robin Gauldie

Sights	Restaurants	Hotels	Shopping	Nightlife
★★★★★	★★★★★	★★★★☆	★★★☆☆	★★★★☆

WELCOME TO NORTHERN IRELAND

TOP REASONS TO GO

★ **The Giant's Causeway:** This spectacular remnant of Ireland's volcanic period steals you away from the 21st century and transports you to a time when the giant Finn MacCool roamed the land.

★ **Nine Glens of Antrim:** Fabled haunt of "the wee folk," the glacier-carved valleys have a beauty that has become synonymous with Irishness. Don't miss Glenariff, dubbed "Little Switzerland" by Thackeray.

★ **The Dark Hedges:** An atmospheric road tunnel of 250-year-old beech trees near Ballymoney in North Antrim that has attracted thousands of fans of the TV series *Game of Thrones*.

★ **Ulster-American Folk Park:** A tale of two countries joined by a common people is told at this museum, which re-creates a 19th-century Tyrone village and boasts the Mellon Centre for Migration Studies.

North of the vibrant Victorian city of Belfast, ageless wonders of the Causeway Coast step from the sea, while south of the inspiring skyline of Derry lie the border counties, where tiny "Ulster" towns dot the scenic landscapes around the Lakes of Fermanagh and Mountains of Mourne.

1 **Carrickfergus and Larne.** Home to Carrickfergus Castle.

2 **Glens of Antrim.** Lush and scenic coastline.

3 **Ballycastle.** Popular seaside town.

4 **Giant's Causeway.** One of Ireland's top attractions.

5 **Bushmills.** Home to the world-famous distillery.

6 **Dunluce Castle.** The north's most evocative ruins.

7 **Limavady.** The inspiration for "Danny Boy."

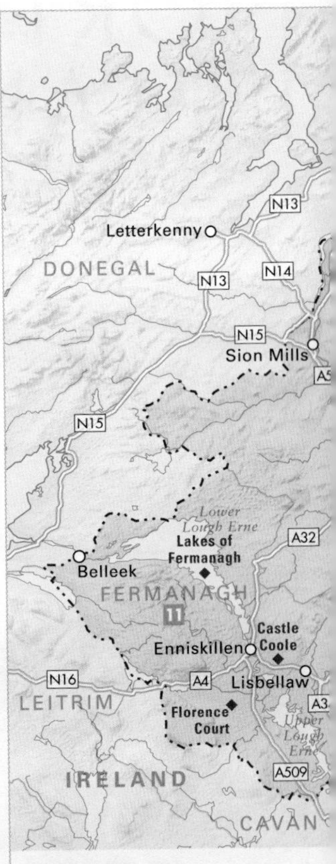

8 **Bellaghy.** Nobel laureate Seamus Heaney put this rural village on the map.

9 **Derry.** A vibrant and storied walled city.

10 **Tyrone.** Home to the county town of Omagh.

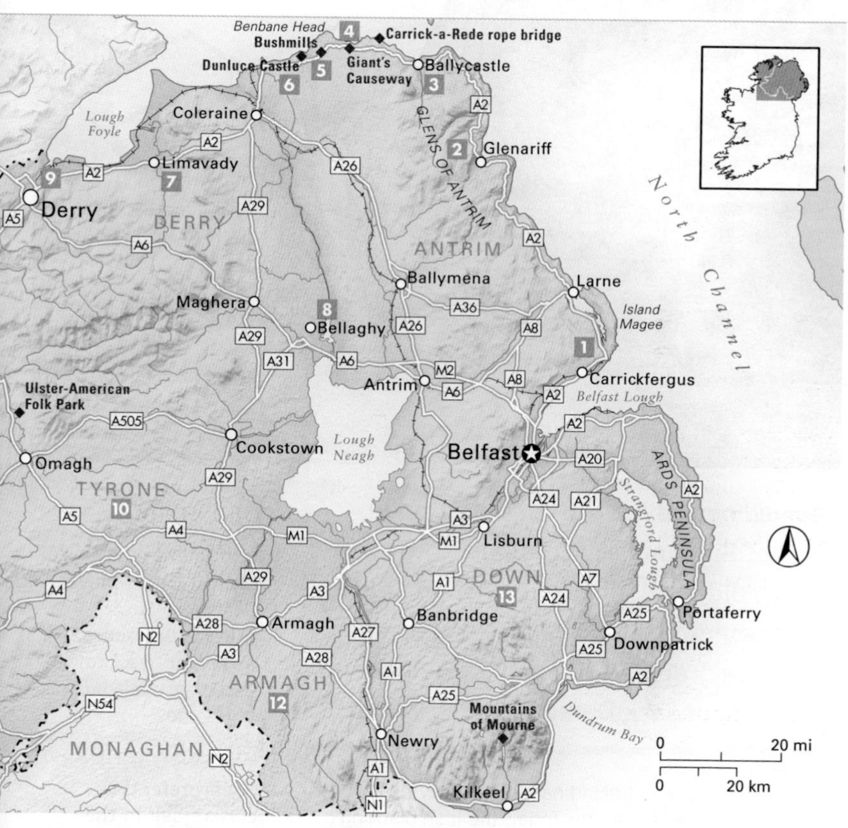

11 Fermanagh. Highlights of this county town include Belleek pottery, Florence Court, and Castle Coole.

12 Armagh. Ireland's spiritual capital just one hour from Belfast.

13 Down. Famous for its ancient High Cross, Castleward (aka Winterfell), Hillsborough Castle and Gardens, Montalto Estate, and the gorgeous countryside of the Mountains of Mourne.

ALL ABOUT IRISH WHISKEYS

Liquid history on view at Bushmills Distillery

Located on the Antrim coast, the small town of Bushmills lays claim to the world's oldest distillery. Today, its name is synonymous with the best in whiskey. Taste one drop and you may never drink Jim Beam or Jack Daniels again.

Some 135 years ago, Ireland had 28 whiskey distilleries in what was a great industry. Today, the Irish distilling industry is undergoing a revival with a rapid growth in new distilleries. A young generation of whiskey makers are operating, and there are now more than 40 new or proposed distilleries throughout Ireland. Four of the newest are on the Powerscourt estate in County Wicklow, on the Slane Castle estate in County Meath, the Liberties distillery in Dublin, and Echlinville in County Down—the first new distillery in the North in more than 125 years. The Irish boxer Conor McGregor has even launched his own celebrity brand whiskey label, Proper No. Twelve, a triple-distilled premium spirit. For some, Bushmills is the best, literally, and has the titles to prove it. It is also the only distillery in Ireland to make triple-distilled single malt whiskey.

OLD BUSHMILLS

☎ 028/2073–3218
£8 *Tours Apr.–Oct., Mon.–Sat. 9:15–5, Sun. noon–5; Nov.–Mar., weekdays 9:30–3:30, weekends 12:30–3:30*

WHAT TO DRINK?

Some prefer the classic melt-in-the-mouth Black Bush (drunk neat) to the more expensive malt. Other delights include the limited-edition 1608, the Original, and four single malts: aged 10 years, 12 years, 16 years, and 21 years.

THE "WATER OF LIFE"

Whiskey is a word that comes from the Irish *uisce beatha,* meaning "water of life." Water is a major factor influencing the flavor of any whiskey. For Bushmills, it flows from the crystal clear St. Columb's Rill, taking its character from the basalt and turf bed of the River Bush. Another key ingredient is malted barley, which is here ground into grist in the mash house and added to boiling water in vats to become wort. Yeast is then added to the mix, and the fermentation turns the sugars to alcohol. The wash goes into a copper pot and is distilled three times, each distillation making the alcohol purer. By comparison, American whiskey is distilled only once. The spirit is diluted, then matured in oak casks, and seasoned by sherry, bourbon, or port. A small portion, about 2% of the distillate, evaporates and is affectionately known as the "angels' share." Remember to first try Bushmills neat and then add water in teaspoonful increments, as a soupçon of water unlocks the flavor while knocking a little fire out of the whiskey—there's a crucial tipping point, so don't dilute too much!

WHAT'S IRISH ABOUT WHISKEY?

First off, it is spelled with an "e," to distinguish it from Scotch whisky. "Irish" has a characteristic flavor that distinguishes it from Scotch, bourbon, or rye; try it straight or with water, as it is best without a mixer. And don't go chasing after *poitín* (pronounced pot-cheen), the famed Irish moonshine. Any attempts by a "stranger" to procure it results either in meeting a brick wall or a wild goose chase. Just as well: it produces one of the worst hangovers known to man or woman.

Learn how malted barley and yeasts are alchemized into whiskey.

Drink Bushmills neat.

TOURING THE DISTILLERY

Set in an area of natural beauty a short distance from the Giant's Causeway, Bushmills was granted its first license in 1608, although records refer as far back as 1276. Visitors to the distillery are shown around a jumbled collection of redbrick and whitewashed buildings that include 20 warehouses brimming with 350,000 barrels of whiskey. Look out for the long rows of Oloroso sherry casks, where the drink is aged in some instances for more than 25 years (they favor a generous gestation here). A one-hour tours costs £15 and the £40 premium tour and tasting offers tastings of six whiskies, including drawing your own dram.

Once a region torn apart by civil strife and sectarian violence, Northern Ireland has changed beyond recognition since the beginning of the 21st century. Regeneration has led to the rebirth of its two major cities, Belfast and Derry. A creative and cultural renaissance has brought a surge of interest from many parts of the world, and new luxury hotels, trendy bars, and chic restaurants have created a huge number of opportunities for holidaymakers.

The six counties that make up Northern Ireland cover less than 14,245 square km (5,500 square miles)—the country is less than one-fifth the size of the Republic of Ireland, its neighbor to the south. But within Northern Ireland's boundaries is some of the most unspoiled scenery you could ever hope to find on this earth: the granite Mountains of Mourne; the Giant's Causeway, made of extraordinary volcanic rock; more than 320 km (200 miles) of coastline beaches and hidden coves; and rivers and leaf-sheltered lakes, including the U.K.'s largest freshwater lake, Lough Neagh, that provide fabled fishing grounds. Ancient castles and Palladian-perfect 18th-century houses are as numerous here as almost anywhere else in Europe, and each has its own tale of heroic feats, dastardly deeds, and lovelorn ghosts.

Northern Ireland not only houses this heritage within its native stone, but has also given the world perhaps an even greater legacy: its roster of celebrated descendants. Nearly one in six of the millions of Irish who journeyed across the Atlantic in search of fortune in the New World came from Ulster (the historic name for this part of Ireland that geographically—although not politically—includes Donegal, Cavan, and Monaghan, which are part of the republic) and of this group (and from their family stock), more than a few left their mark in America: Davy Crockett, President Andrew Jackson, General Ulysses S. Grant, President Woodrow Wilson, General Stonewall Jackson, financier Thomas Mellon, merchant J. Paul Getty, writers Edgar Allan Poe and Mark Twain, and astronaut Neil Armstrong.

In the 1970s, '80s, and early '90s, Northern Ireland was synonymous with conflict; sectarian killings and car bomb explosions were an almost daily occurrence from 1969 to 1994, amounting to the deaths of more than 3,500 people.

The "peace process," begun with the help of President Clinton, has been a long journey but the two communities now live in relative harmony as a younger generation embraces life without violence.

Present-day Northern Ireland, a province of just 1.8 million people that along with Great Britain composes the political entity of the United Kingdom, retains its sense of separation, both in the vernacular of the landscape and, some would say, in the character of the people. For all that, the border between north and south is of little consequence if you're just here to see the country, and though political divisions still exist, peace reigns in Northern Ireland today. There are no border checkpoints, no one is stopped or questioned, no passports are checked, and there isn't even a sign announcing you are passing from the north into the south. The long political debate over Brexit—the United Kingdom, including Northern Ireland's departure from the European Union—resulted in the establishment of a new trade border in the Irish Sea. To the cautious relief of many, it has not yet not led to a "hard border" of customs, trade, or security being reintroduced between the north and south of Ireland, though the recalcitrance of the Unionist faction in Ulster politics, and the U.K. government, means this is an ongoing issue.

It's also a golfing powerhouse, with some of the world's best golfers and a staggering total of 95 courses from which to choose; its young bands are renowned; its writers and poets have been internationally acclaimed; and Belfast is home to the *Titanic* Belfast, one of Europe's leading visitor attractions.

MAJOR REGIONS

Starting in Belfast and stretching 80 km (50 miles) along Northern Ireland's Atlantic shore, **the Giant's Causeway Coast** holds many of the province's don't-miss attractions. The man-made brilliance of the castle at Dunluce, the endless string of whitewashed fishing villages along the sea, and the world-famous natural wonder that is the Giant's Causeway are just some of the delights to be discovered here. Once your car or mountain bike (ideal for the Causeway's flat terrain) makes it past some fair-size towns, you'll enter the splendid Glens area—one of the more "gentle" (an Irish turn of phrase for supernatural) places in all Ireland. Here, ageless villages, still inhabited by descendants of the ancient Irish and the Hebridean Scots who hailed from across the narrow Sea of Moyle, are set in peaceful, old-growth forests that have become synonymous with Irishness. Nearer the Giant's Causeway more cosmopolitan pleasures are to be found, including Bushmills—the oldest licensed distillery in the world—and the old walled city of Derry. The hot new attractions along the Causeway Coast are the locations used for the *Game of Thrones* TV series, in particular the Dark Hedges, a road tunnel of ancient beech trees.

While blissfully off the beaten track, the **Border Counties** major regions covering the counties of Antrim, Derry, Fermanagh, Tyrone, Armagh, and Down contain some dazzling sights: Derry city and its walls, worth a full day; the Ulster American Folk Park; the great stately houses of Castle Coole and Florence Court; the pottery town of Belleek; the breathtaking Mountains of Mourne; and the blessed St. Patrick sites in Armagh and Down. During the worst of the Troubles, the counties of Armagh and Down, which border the republic, were known as "bandit country," but now you can enjoy a worry-free trip through the calm countryside and stop in at some very "Ulster" towns—delightfully distinct from the rest of Ireland.

Planning

Getting Here and Around

Because Northern Ireland is so small, one option is to base yourself in the two main cities, Belfast or Derry, and make day trips out. However, one of the real glories is the endless supply of spectacular rural scenery. The good news is that bus travel is both quick and fairly priced, with express buses operating on all the high-traffic routes. The bad news is that rail options are somewhat limited: there are just three main routes out of Belfast. That said, you can easily access much of the country by bus or train, though in some areas, including the wildly popular Causeway Coast, you may end up on smaller bus routes such as the Causeway Coast Express if you don't drive a car.

AIR

Belfast International Airport at Aldergrove is the North's principal airport, 30½ km (19 miles) north of town. George Best Belfast City Airport is the secondary airport, 6½ km (4 miles) east of the city. It receives flights from U.K. provincial airports, from London's Gatwick and Heathrow, and from Stansted and Luton (both near London). City of Derry Airport is 8 km (5 miles) from Derry and receives flights from Glasgow, Edinburgh, Liverpool, and London. United Airlines and several Europe-based airlines are the major carriers serving Northern Ireland's airports.

AIRPORT TRANSFERS

If you arrive at the City of Derry Airport, you may need to call a taxi to get to your destination. The fare for Foyle cabs is about £12 to the city center. A direct bus service, the Airporter, links Derry with both Belfast International and George Best Belfast City airports (one-way £20, round-trip £30).

CONTACTS City Cabs. ✉ *Derry* ☎ *028/7126–2626* 🌐 *www.citycabsderry.com.* **Foyle Taxis.** ✉ *Newmarket St., Derry* ☎ *028/7127–9999* 🌐 *www.foyletaxis.com.*

BOAT AND FERRY

P&O Ferries has a one-hour sailing from Cairnryan, Scotland, to Larne, and a two-hour ferry, both with train (more convenient) or bus connections to Belfast, 35½ km (22 miles) to the south. Stena Line has eight-hour daytime or overnight car ferries that connect Belfast with the English west-coast port of Liverpool every day. Stena Line also operates a fast catamaran (2¼ hours) between Belfast and Cairnryan, Scotland.

CONTACTS P&O Ferries. ☎ *013/0444–8888* 🌐 *www.poferries.com.* **Stena Line.** ✉ *Victoria Terminal 4, W. Bank Rd., Belfast* ☎ *03447/707–070* 🌐 *www.stenaline.co.uk.*

BUS

Northern Ireland's main bus company, Ulsterbus, operates direct Goldline service—superior express buses with modern, comfortable seats—between Dublin and Belfast. Bus Éireann runs direct service to Belfast from Dublin, calling at Dublin Airport. The ride takes three hours; both company's buses arrive at Belfast's Europa Buscentre, just behind the Europa Hotel. The Aircoach operates a direct service every hour from Belfast to Dublin airport and takes two hours. If you are planning a trip to the Giant's Causeway from Belfast by bus then Translink operates a special daily Goldline coach service (No. 221) on this route from April to October for £12.50.

You can take advantage of frequent and inexpensive Ulsterbus links between all Northern Ireland towns. If you want to tour the North by bus and train, contact Translink: an iLink ticket allows unlimited travel on bus or train (£16.50 per day, or £58 per week; it costs £1 to buy the card). Best buy: the Sunday Rambler

Ticket, from 9:30 am for £9.50 for unlimited travel on all scheduled Ulsterbus services.

CONTACTS Bus Éireann. ✉ *Dublin* ☎ *01/836–6111 in Dublin* 🌐 *www.buseireann.ie.* **Europa Buscentre.** ✉ *Great Victoria St., Golden Mile* ✣ *Entry to bus center is via shopping mall to left-hand side of Europa hotel* ☎ *028/9066–6630* 🌐 *www.translink.co.uk.* **Translink Ulsterbus.** ✉ *Glengall St., Belfast* ☎ *028/9066–6630* 🌐 *www.translink.co.uk/ulsterbus.*

TAXI

Most taxis operate on the meter; ask for a price for longer journeys. You can order in advance. The minimum daytime fare (6 am–8 pm) on weekdays is £2.50 to £2.90 (£3.80 at weekends), then £1.70 per mile. Uber is also available in Northern Ireland, but taxis are much more abundant.

CONTACTS FonaCAB. ✉ *Belfast* ☎ *028/9033–3333* 🌐 *www.fonacab.com.* **Foyle Taxis.** ✉ *10a Market St., Derry* ☎ *028/7126–2626* 🌐 *www.foyletaxis.com.* **Value Cabs.** ✉ *Belfast* ☎ *028/9080–9080* 🌐 *www.valuecabs.co.uk.*

TRAIN

The Dublin-to-Belfast Enterprise Service, run jointly by Northern Ireland Railways (a company operated by Translink) and Irish Rail–Iarnród Éireann (which only services the Republic of Ireland), operates trains, the fastest of which take about two hours, between Dublin and Belfast's Central Station. A single journey from Dublin costs €30.40; a same-day return is €32. You can change trains at Lanyon Place Station for the city-center Great Victoria Street Station, which is adjacent the Europa Buscentre.

Northern Ireland Railways (NIR) runs four rail routes from Belfast's Lanyon Place Station: northwest to Derry via Coleraine; east to Bangor along the shore of Belfast Lough; northeast to Larne (for the P&O European ferry to Scotland); and south to Portadown, Newry, and Dublin. Nine daily weekday trains operate between Belfast and Derry, with seven trains on Saturday and five on Sunday. The journey time is about two hours, and a round-trip ticket costs £19. If you travel after 9:30 am, you'll get a third off the standard fare, reducing it to £12.70. Best buy: the £7.50 Sunday Day Tracker gives you unlimited travel on all scheduled train services within Northern Ireland.

There are frequent connections to Lanyon Place Station from the city-center Great Victoria Street Station and from Botanic Station in the university area. If you want to tour the North by train, contact Northern Ireland Railways–Translink: an iLink ticket allows unlimited travel on bus or train (£16.50 per day, or £58 per week; it costs £1 to buy the card).

CONTACTS Enterprise Service. ✉ *Lanyon Place Station, E. Bridge St., Belfast* ☎ *028/9066–6630* 🌐 *www.translink.co.uk/enterprise.* **Iarnród Éireann.** ✉ *Dublin* ☎ *00353/836–6222 timetables* 🌐 *www.irishrail.ie.* **Northern Ireland Railways.** ✉ *Lanyon Place Station, East Bridge St.* ☎ *028/9066–6630* 🌐 *www.translink.co.uk/services/ni-railways.*

TRAIN STATIONS Botanic Station. ✉ *Botanic Ave., Belfast* ☎ *028/9089–9400.* **Lanyon Place Station.** ✉ *E. Bridge St., Belfast* ☎ *028/9089–9400* 🌐 *www.translink.co.uk.*

Hotels

Major hotel chains have invested in Northern Ireland's cities. Many accommodations in the province volunteer for inspection and grading by Tourism Northern Ireland, while Discover Northern Ireland publishes hostelry information, contact details, and links to individual lodgings booking sites online. Hundreds of excellent-value specials—single nights to weekend deals, the most intimate bed-and-breakfasts to Belfast's finest hotels—become available in the low season, from October to March.

Restaurants

Local produce and seasonal creativity are the order of the day here with top-quality fresh local meat and experimental chefs constantly trying out new ideas. Traditional dishes still dominate some menus and include Guinness-and-beef pie; steak, chicken, and pork; champ (creamy, buttery mashed potatoes with scallions); oysters from Strangford Lough; Ardglass herring; mussels from Dundrum; and smoked salmon from Glenarm. By the standards of the United States, or even the rest of the United Kingdom, restaurant prices can be surprisingly moderate. A service charge of 10% may be added to the bill; it's customary to pay this unless the service was bad.

RESTAURANT AND HOTEL PRICES

⇨ *Restaurant prices are the average cost of a main course at dinner or, if dinner is not served, at lunch. Hotel prices are the lowest cost of a standard double room in high season. Restaurant and hotel reviews have been shortened. For full information, visit Fodors.com.*

What It Costs in Pounds Sterling

$	$$	$$$	$$$$
RESTAURANTS			
under £20	£20–£30	£31–£35	over £35
HOTELS			
under £82	£82–£115	£116–£160	over £160

Money

Unlike Ireland, Northern Ireland uses British currency (the pound sterling). Euros are accepted in some shops along the border areas. You may sometimes be given sterling banknotes issued by Ulster Bank, Northern Bank, and Bank of Ireland. These are rarely accepted or exchangeable outside of Northern Ireland, so change them for Bank of England sterling notes, euros, or dollars before you leave.

Tours

BICYCLE TOURS

Iron Donkey Bicycle Touring

BICYCLE TOURS | Some of the most scenic parts of Northern Ireland are opened up by Iron Donkey Bicycle Touring, which organizes multiday tours. Itineraries include the Mourne Mountains, Glens of Antrim, Causeway Coast, the Sperrin Mountains, and other destinations. ☎ *077/8049–6969* 🌐 *www.irondonkey.com.*

BUS TOURS

Allens Tours

BUS TOURS | Allens Tours operates day tours from Belfast to the Giant's Causeway and Carrick-a-Rede rope bridge with stops at Carrickfergus Castle and the Dark Hedges in County Antrim, the scene of some of the filming for *Game of Thrones*. Check the website where the price is reduced by £5 for online booking. ✉ *Belfast* ☎ *028/9091–5613* 🌐 *www.allensbelfastbustours.com* 🎫 *£30 for a 1-day tour.*

BOAT TOURS

Carnlough Bay Boat Tours

BOAT TOURS | FAMILY | Carnlough Bay Boat Tours offers 30-minute cruises on the bay aboard its 13-passenger vessel *Curiosity*, with the chance of seeing dolphins and seals as well as picturesque coastal scenery. Binoculars are provided for passengers. ✉ *Carnlough* ☎ *077/2046–4044* 🌐 *carnloughboattours.weebly.com* 🎫 *£6.*

When to Go

If the weather is good—and most of the year it isn't—touring Northern Ireland can be a real pleasure. But the place is so green for a reason: lots of rain, which means you should certainly pack your

Game of Thrones

From the Dark Hedges, an eerie road tunnel of enormous 18th-century beech trees near Ballymoney (known in the series as Kingsroad), through which Arya Stark made her escape from King's Landing, to the nearby Slemish Mountain—the setting of Shillanavogy Valley—to the dramatic headland, Fair Head in County Antrim, where Davos Seaworth was shipwrecked after the battle of King's Landing, it is no wonder the Northern Irish landscape is immediately recognizable to fans as a backdrop for the Seven Kingdoms in the hit series, *Game of Thrones*.

These age-old trees are threatened by climate change, and when several of the Dark Hedges beech trees came down in a fierce storm in 2016, the wood from two of them was salvaged and transformed into 10 ornately carved wooden doors, each depicting moments inspired by the show. These "Doors of Thrones" hang in pubs, restaurants, and other venues across Northern Ireland, near filming locations, giving visitors a *Game of Thrones* trail to follow.

TIP→ The Kingsroad can get very busy, so avoid the crowds by going at first light or later in the day.

In County Down, the farmyard of the historic mansion Castle Ward doubles as the castle of Winterfell, home of the Stark family. Another major film location in south Down is Tollymore Forest Park, in the Mourne Mountains, where you can sign up for an immersive guided tour, with Stark cloaks provided at no extra cost. This tour, the Belfast Winterfell Day Tour, costs £49 (🌐 *www.gameofthronestours.com*). All told, there are more than 45 sites throughout Northern Ireland with some form of connection to the blockbuster series and, consequently, there are a large number of tour companies vying for your business. One of the best theme tours is a McComb's Coaches day tour, which takes in key geographical locations along the Antrim coast and costs £30.

As the series finally drew to a close in 2019 after 10 years of filming in Northern Ireland, six beautifully crafted freestanding stained-glass windows were created in Belfast to ensure its legacy. Using fan search data, the "Glass of Thrones" windows trail depicts the most talked about moments of the entire series. The fascinating process of making the windows started with identifying and categorizing scenes, themes, and characters from the storyline. Illustrators visualized these findings, first by hand, then digitally before they were brought to life using computer-aided design and manufacturing technology, which was then meticulously hand-stained by artists. Each of the six windows has been given a name: Stark, Lannister, Baratheon, Targaryen, White Walkers, and The Iron Throne. This is a fun trail to follow so grab a map leaflet outlining the locations—they run from City Hall to the Titanic Quarter—at the Visit Belfast Welcome Centre and set off on your own windows odyssey. 🌐 *www.discovernorthernireland.com*

raincoat. Because you're on the coast, even on bright summer days you can feel the chill from the sea, so it's best to wear layers. The weather from May to September is a little friendlier to tourists.

Planning Your Time

Though Northern Ireland may not look that big on paper, tackling a fair share of its many attractions in less than a week is a challenge. If your time is limited, choose the eastern half (Belfast, the Antrim Coast, and the Mountains of Mourne) or the western half (Derry and the Border Counties). The cities are small enough to tour in a day or two. But remember that the rural wonders—the Antrim Coast, the Fermanagh lakes, the Mountains of Mourne—cast their spell easily. You may head out to enjoy them for a day trip and find yourself wishing that you'd factored in more time to explore postcard-worthy villages, misty glens, and rugged mountains. Distances are not great, but neither are the roads—you'll spend most of your time traveling smaller roads, not major express highways. If you have three days, spend an extra night and day in Derry. A half-day side trip should also be made to the top-class Ulster American Folk Park at Omagh, where the contribution of Northern Irish people to American history is traced.

FESTIVALS AND EVENTS

When planning your visit, remember that Northern Ireland is a great place for festivals: almost every town has its own theme festival of some sort. Early in May, tens of thousands of revelers flock to Derry for an annual five-day extravaganza, the City of Derry Jazz and Big Band Festival (🌐 *www.cityofderryjazzfestival.com*), held at various venues.

⇨ *See the Belfast chapter for festivals and events within the city.*

The Ould Lammas Fair

CULTURAL FESTIVALS | Every year since 1606, on the last Monday and Tuesday in August, Ballycastle has hosted the Ould Lammas Fair, a modern version of the ancient Celtic harvest festival of Lughnasa (Irish for "August"). Ireland's oldest fair, this is a very popular two-day event with entertainers, several hundred shopping stalls, and even a pony show. Treat yourself to the fair's traditional snacks, dulse (sun-dried seaweed; also known as dillisk) and yellowman (rock-hard yellow toffee). ✉ *Ballycastle* 🌐 *www.discovernorthernireland.com.*

Visitor Information

Tourism Northern Ireland provides information about attractions, accommodations, and activities online and at its central and regional tourist information offices (TIOs). The offices in Belfast and Derry are open year-round; other useful TIOs are in Enniskillen, Armagh, Newcastle, Carrickfergus, and at the Giant's Causeway on the North Antrim coast.

CONTACTS Tourism Northern Ireland. ✉ *Linum Chambers, Bedford Sq., Bedford St., 10th fl.–12th fl., Belfast* ☎ *028/9023–1221* 🌐 *www.discovernorthernireland.com.*

Carrickfergus and Larne

16 km (10 miles) northeast of Belfast.

Carrickfergus, on the shore of Belfast Lough, grew up around its ancient castle. When the town was enclosed by ramparts at the start of the 17th century, it was the only English-speaking town in Ulster. Not surprisingly, this was the loyal port where William of Orange chose to land on his way to fight the Catholic forces at the Battle of the Boyne in 1690. However, the English did have one or two small setbacks, including the improbable victory in 1778 of John Paul

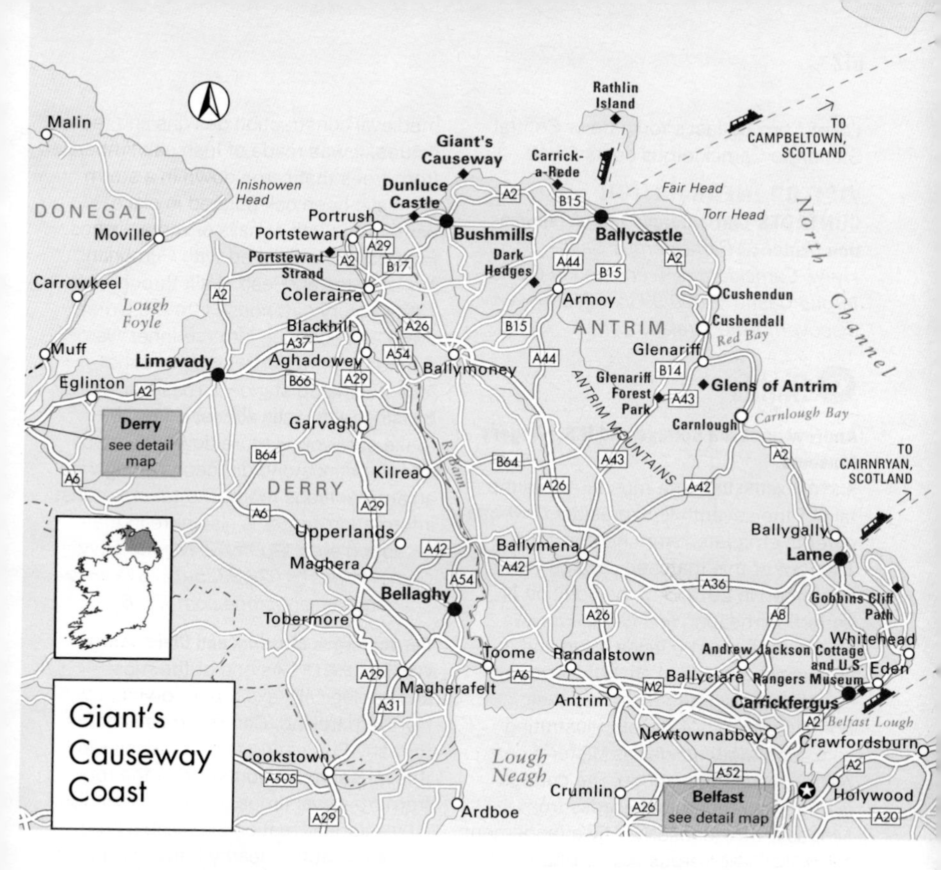

Jones, the American naval hero, over the British warship HMS *Drake*. Although a long way from home, this stands as the first naval victory of America's fledgling fleet. After this battle, which was waged in Belfast Lough, the inhabitants of Carrickfergus stood on the waterfront and cheered Jones when his ship passed the town castle, demonstrating their support for the American Revolution. Carrickfergus's past can still be seen in some of its old buildings. St. Nicholas's Church, built by John de Courcy in 1205 (remodeled in 1614), and the North Gate in the town's medieval walls are worth checking out. Dobbins Inn on High Street has been a hotel for more than three centuries and is a popular local watering hole. Since 2019, several buildings that are steeped in history, including Dobbins, have benefited from the Carrickfergus Townscape Heritage Initiative, a program that helps to refurbish and preserve old properties in the town's conservation area. Its aim is to engage both locals and visitors with the built heritage, creating a greater understanding of the town's quality architecture.

GETTING HERE AND AROUND

A 15-minute drive northeast of Belfast on A2, Carrickfergus is an easy town to negotiate. There's a huge free parking lot beside the castle, and parking on the main streets is free, though limited to one hour. Pay-and-display lots, costing £0.40 per hour, operate at Joymount, Bride, and Lancastrian Streets.

Trains run by Northern Ireland Railways from Belfast on this section of the Antrim Coast go only as far as the 40 km (25 miles) to Larne. Daily service stops at a number of towns, including Carrickfergus, Whitehead, and Glynn. A round-trip ticket from Belfast's Yorkgate or Central Station to Carrickfergus costs £9.40.

VISITOR INFORMATION

CONTACTS Carrickfergus Tourist Information Center. ✉ *Carrickfergus Castle, Marine Hwy., Carrickfergus* ⊕ *Located in Carrickfergus Castle* ☎ *028/9335–8262* 🌐 *www.discovernorthernireland.com.*

Andrew Jackson Cottage and U.S. Rangers Museum

HISTORY MUSEUM | The museum tells the tale of the seventh U.S. president, whose parents emigrated from here in 1765. The roof of this thatched cottage was reinforced in 2019 with the addition of underfloor heating and its facade was restored. It is just outside town and is a reconstruction of an 18th-century structure thought to resemble their home. Interpretive panels, illustrating Jackson's story as well as Ulster–Scots history, have been added. The cottage is open year-round, but access from Monday to Wednesday is by arrangement through Carrickfergus tourist office. ✉ *Larne Rd., 1½ km (1 mile) northeast of Carrickfergus, 2 Boneybefore, Carrickfergus* ☎ *028/9335–8222* 🌐 *www.midandeastantrim.gov.uk* 🎫 *Free.*

★ Carrickfergus Castle

CASTLE/PALACE | Built atop a rock ledge in 1180 by John de Courcy, provincial Ulster's first Anglo-Norman invader, Carrickfergus Castle is still in good shape and has sparked renewed visitor appeal with the opening of its dungeons. Apart from being captured briefly by the French in 1760, the castle—one of Ireland's largest—stood as a bastion of British rule until 1928, at which time it still functioned as an English garrison. It is the longest continually used castle of its type. During 2020 work was completed on a huge £1 million conservation project replacing the roof of the Great Tower with a new double-pitched roof. Built using medieval construction designs and techniques, it was made of Irish oak timber from trees that came down in a storm and have been oak-pegged in place without the use of nails or metal fixings. Externally it is finished with Cumbrian stone slates and lead. Walk through the 13th-century gatehouse into the Outer Ward and continue into the Inner Ward, the heart of the fortress, where the four-story keep stands, a massive, sturdy building with walls almost 8 feet thick. Make sure you venture down the steps into the dark stone dungeons along with an ammunitions room. The town's tourist information center is also here in the reception area. ✉ *Off A2, Marine Hwy., Carrickfergus* ☎ *028/9335–1273* 🌐 *www.shapedbyseaandstone.com* 🎫 *£6.*

Carrickfergus Museum and Civic Centre

VISITOR CENTER | As one of the most archaeologically excavated towns in Northern Ireland, Carrickfergus is home to many fascinating finds on display in this museum, exploring life in the town from medieval times to the present. Tourist visitor information is available here as well as at the nearby Carrickfergus Castle. A guided walk that starts from outside the castle, "Lead the Way Tour," showcases the role of the town during World War II. It costs £10; see 🌐 *www.leadthewaytour.com* for timings. ✉ *11 Antrim St., Carrickfergus* ☎ *300/124–5000* 🌐 *www.midandeastantrim.gov.uk.*

Gobbins Cliff Path

TRAIL | Thrill seekers love this revived dramatic cliff walk in east County Antrim. Cut into the towering rock on the eastern side of Islandmagee Peninsula, the path is linked with a new metal staircase and is one of Northern Ireland's best-kept secrets. Originally built in 1902 by the railway magnate Berkeley Deane Wise, in its heyday it was as popular as the Giant's Causeway but fell into disrepair and closed to the public after World War II. Today it merits a government-approved acronym, ASSI, for Area of Special

Scientific Interest, and is noted for its noisy colonies of puffins, razorbills, fulmars, peregrine falcons, and guillemots. On a clear day, panoramic views across the North Channel stretch from the Scottish Outer Hebrides in the north to the English Lake District in the south. Legends associated with the Gobbins include mythical figures such as Gobbin Saor, a giant who lived in the cliffs. An exhibition room with interpretation, a café and crafts shop, and a tourist information point are located at the site.

⚠ **On occasion, due to stormy weather, the path is closed to visitors. Call in advance to make sure it is fully operational.** ✉ *68 Middle Rd., Islandmagee, Larne* ☎ *028/9337–2318* 🌐 *www.thegobbinscliffpath.com* 🎫 *£20.*

Whiteford Railway Museum

OTHER MUSEUM | FAMILY | Home to the Railway Preservation Society of Ireland, this working museum run by volunteers preserves veteran Irish steam locomotives (from both sides of the border) and keeps some of them in running order. There are steam train trips of varying duration several times a year, so if you're a steam enthusiast check the website for details and bookings. A collection of steam locos and rolling stock is on display, and you can also visit workshops, and a restored signal box. Pride of place goes to the venerable engine No. 171, *Slieve Gullion* (currently under restoration). There is a cozy café in the old station building. ✉ *Whiteford Station, Castleview Rd., Carrickfergus* ☎ *028/9538–6200* 🌐 *www.steamtrainsireland.com* 🎫 *£7* ⏲ *Closed Sun.–Wed.* ✍ *Booking strongly advised.*

Glens of Antrim

Beginning 24 km (15 miles) north of Carrickfergus at Larne.

North of Carrickfergus after Larne, the coast of County Antrim becomes spectacular—wave upon wave of bare hills, dotted with wooded glens, curve down to a patchwork of fields among valleys carved out by glaciers at the end of the last Ice Age. Before you tackle the Glens, though, it's worth considering a short detour from Larne to the nearby peninsula of Islandmagee where the Gobbins path is a dramatic cliff-face walk cut into the towering rock. Nine wooded river valleys occupy the 86 km (54 miles) between Larne and Ballycastle, the two largest towns in the Glens of Antrim. Until the building of the narrow coastal road in 1834, the Glens were home to isolated farming communities, whose residents adhered to the romantic, mystical Celtic legends and the everyday use of the Irish language. Steeped in Irish mythology, the Glens were first inhabited by small bands of Irish monks as early as AD 700. Some claim that the quasi-mythical Celtic bard Ossian is buried near Glenaan. Though the Glens were made famous as local beauty spots by 19th-century Romantic poets, some visitors may feel that their scenery—scarred as it is by commercial forestry—does not compare well with the landscapes of the English Lake District, the Scottish Highlands, or upland Wales.

The Causeway Coast and Glens website, 🌐 *www.visitcausewaycoastandglens.com*, provides practical advice for visitors.

GETTING HERE AND AROUND

The scenic Antrim Coaster Goldline buses from Larne to Ballycastle traverse part of the coastline—a 110-km (68-mile), three-hour journey. It is best to buy a Rambler ticket at £9. The service operates Monday through Sunday, from early July to mid-September. Because reservations are not accepted, arrive early in summer to be assured a window seat. To start the journey from Belfast you must first take a bus or train to Larne.

Oft lauded as one of Ireland's most scenic drives—on a clear day you can see Scotland—the A2 Antrim coastal route is a delightful, narrow, winding, two-lane road that hugs the slim strip of land between the hills and sea, bringing you to the magnificent Glens of Antrim. In most towns, cars park free of charge on the main street or in lots overlooking the harbor. The road is busy in summer, so allow extra travel time.

VISITOR INFORMATION

CONTACTS Ballymena Visitor Information Centre. ✉ *The Braid, Ballymena Town Hall Museum and Arts Centre, 1–29 Bridge St., Ballymena* ☎ *028/2563–5010* 🌐 *www.discovernorthernireland.com.* **Larne Tourist Information.** ✉ *96B Main St., Larne* ☎ *028/2826–2450.*

Sights

The Glens merit several days of serious exploration. Super-narrow B-roads curl west off the A2, up each of the beautiful glens, where trails await hikers. You need a full week and a rainproof tent to complete the nine-glen circuit (from south to north: Glenarm, Glencloy, Glenariff, Glenballyeamon, Glenaan, Glencorp, Glendun, Glenshesk, and Glentaisie); or you could just head for Glenariff Park, the most accessible glen.

Carnlough

TOWN | A little resort made of white limestone, Carnlough overlooks a small harbor surrounded by stone walls. The harbor can be reached by crossing over the limestone bridge from Main Street, built especially for the Marquess of Londonderry. The small harbor, once a port of call for fishermen, now shelters pleasure yachts and is a base for wildlife-watching boat trips. Carnlough is surrounded on three sides by hills that rise 1,000 feet from the sea. ✉ *Carnlough.*

Cushendall

TOWN | Turnley's Tower—a curious, fortified square tower of red stone, built in 1820 as a curfew tower and jail for "idlers and rioters"—stands at a crossroads in the middle of Cushendall, called the capital of the Glens because it has a few more streets than the other villages nearby. The road from Waterfoot to Cushendall is barely a mile long and worth the stroll or cycle out to see the coastal caves (one of which had a resident for many years, a local woman named Anne Murray) that line the route. ✉ *3 km (2 miles) north of Glenariff on A2, Cushendall* ☎ *028/2177–1180* 🌐 *www.visitcausewaycoastandglens.com.*

★ Cushendun

TOWN | Off the main A2 route, the road between Cushendall and Cushendun turns into one of a Tour-de-France hilliness, so cyclists beware. Your reward, however, is the tiny jewel of a village, Cushendun, which was designed in 1912 by Clough Williams-Ellis (who also designed the famous Italianate village of Portmeirion in Wales) at the request of Ronald John McNeill, Baron Cushendun. Up sprang a series of cottages and a village square of seven houses, all done up in the Cornish taste courtesy of the Penzance-born wife of the baron. To top it all off, the baron had Glenmona House built in the regal neo-Georgian style. From this part of the coast you can see the Mull of Kintyre on the Scottish mainland. Hikes along the beachy strand have inspired poets and artists, including John Masefield. Glenmona House is now used for community and social events and next door to it in Church Lane—barely visible through the trees—the former Church of Ireland, built in 1840 and deconsecrated in 2003, reopened to the public as an arts, heritage, and information center in 2019. They hold concerts, talks, and stage exhibitions and it is worth calling in to see how the former place of worship has been transformed by the Cushendun Building Preservation Trust. The Ulster History Circle has also erected a blue plaque on the building to Moira O'Neill, a poet and novelist from Cushendun famed for her book *Songs of the Glens of Antrim.* The Old Church Centre is run by volunteers and is open mostly from noon to 4 pm, Friday–Sunday. ✉ *2 km (1½ miles) north of Cushendall on Coast Rd., Old Church Centre, Church La. off Bay Rd., Cushendun* ☎ *028/2176–1522* 🌐 *www.theoldchurchcentre.com.*

★ **Dark Hedges**

TRAIL | A narrow single-track road lined by twisted beech trees whose numbers are steadily being diminished by gales and climate change, the Dark Hedges is a bit anticlimactic even for fanatical *Game of Thrones*–location tourists hoping for a classic selfie. The avenue of trees was originally planted in the early 1770s by the Stuart family, wealthy local landowners.

Since its role as Kingsroad in *Game of Thrones*, the Dark Hedges has become the most visited of the Irish sights linked to the TV series, attracting tens of thousands of visitors annually. With its foreboding atmosphere, the road—more an unprepossessing single-track lane with a few twisted beech trees—has become a backdrop for Instagram antics. It has also been filmed for scenes in *Transformers: The Last Knight* (2017), which has added to its movie-buff status. In the early 1770s when the Stuart family built their house called Gracehill, they lined the avenue with two rows of 150 beeches to impress visitors. The road now comes with a preservation order in a place that is so crowded with "location tourists" that it is closed to all but local traffic; few would have guessed some years ago that their narrow country lane would be so popular with film and TV directors that it would become a victim of overtourism. Parking on either the Bregagh Road (the Dark Hedges road itself), which is off Ballinlea Road, is prohibited. The surrounding fields are privately owned and not open to the public; visitors are asked to respect the trees and not to deface or mark the bark. The road is prone to flooding in the winter so the best time to visit is in spring when, if you catch the right day, the area is alive with birdsong and the melodic warbles of finches, tits, robins, and blackcaps.

■ TIP→ Get there early in the morning or leave your visit until later in the day when it is quieter.

There is parking (£2 per car) at the Dark Hedges Experience visitor center, open 10 am–3 pm, weekdays and 10 am–4 pm on weekends; parking is free if you are a customer of the hotel. You can find information in the center on the history of the site, alongside merchandise from the *Game of Thrones* series such as T-shirts, hoodies, candles, and fridge magnets. Tours are held, but times vary and it is best to check with the center or with the Causeway Coast and Glens tourist office in the main street of the village of Armoy, a 10-minute drive. The center and car park is a 5- to 10-minute walk from the Dark Hedges road. ✉ *Bregagh Rd., Ballymena* ✢ *Off Ballinlea Rd., Stranocum* 🎫 *Free.*

★ **Glenariff Forest Park**

FOREST | The best-known and most accessible of Antrim's glens opens on to Red Bay at the village of Glenariff (also known as Waterfoot). Inside the park are picnic facilities and some easy hikes. Bisecting the park are two lovely rivers, the Inver and the Glenariff, which help sculpt the rocky gorges here and culminate in the famous 5½-km (3½-mile) Waterfall Trail, marked with red arrows, which passes outstanding views of the Glenariff and its three small waterfalls. Its higher expanses are a less charming mix of bare moorland, scarred by the remnants of commercial conifer forestry. There's an abrupt transition back to a patchwork of trim fields as you head back toward the coast.

Escape from the summer crowds by taking one of the longest trails, such as the Scenic Hike (9 km [5½ miles]) or the shorter Viewpoint Trail and the Rainbow Trail, both half a mile. Pick up a detailed trail map at the park visitor center, which also has a small cafeteria. ✉ *98 Glenariff Rd., 7 km (4½ miles) north of Carnlough, off A2, Glenariff* ☎ *028/7034–0870* 🌐 *www.nidirect.gov.uk/forests* 🎫 *Vehicles £5.*

Hotels

Ballygally Castle

$$$ | **HOTEL** | Connoisseurs of sea views love this little mock-baronial castle, originally built by a Scottish lord in 1625. **Pros:** deluxe rooms have coastal views; afternoon tea packages; free parking. **Cons:** popular with wedding parties; somewhat bland, if comfortable, furnishings; service can be hit or miss. $ *Rooms from: £130* ✉ *274 Coast Rd., Ballygally* ☎ *028/2858–1066* 🌐 *www.hastingshotels.com* *54 rooms* 🍽 *Free Breakfast.*

★ **Galgorm Spa and Golf Resort**

$$$$ | **RESORT** | The original Italianate house dates from the 1850s, but the completion of a £10 million renovation pushed this manor house resort into the premier league. **Pros:** an elegant mix of cozy and luxurious; access to sports, fishing, and golf; relaxing spa. **Cons:** if not a golfer, swimmer, or spa fan, there's not a lot to do in the immediate area; somewhat remote and a long walk to shops; pricey food and beverages. $ *Rooms from: £200* ✉ *136 Fenaghy Rd., 40 km (25 miles) east of Larne on A36, Ballymena* ☎ *028/2588–1001* 🌐 *www.galgorm.com* *123 rooms, 6 riverside cottages, 6 fishermen's cottages, 6 log cabins* 🍽 *Free Breakfast.*

★ **The Londonderry Arms Hotel**

$$$ | **HOTEL** | What awaits at this lovely traditional inn are ivy-clad walls, gorgeous antiques, regional paintings, prints and maps, rare whiskeys, and lots of fresh flowers—all time-burnished accents well befitting an estate once inhabited by Sir Winston Churchill. **Pros:** fine historic vibe; good in-house dining and drinking options; spacious rooms. **Cons:** no good local alternative spots to eat and drink; old-fashioned hotels (and creaky floorboards) aren't to everyone's taste; service sometimes moves at a slow pace. $ *Rooms from: £120* ✉ *20 Harbor Rd., Carnlough* ☎ *028/2888–5255* 🌐 *www.londonderryarmshotel.com* *35 rooms* 🍽 *Free Breakfast.*

Ballycastle

86 km (54 miles) northwest of Larne.

Ballycastle is the main resort at the northern end of the Glens of Antrim. People flock here in summer, but apart from peak season, this is a quiet town although brimming with community spirit. Ballycastle is shaped like an hourglass, with its strand and dock on one end, its pubs and chippers on the other, and the 1-km (½-mile) Quay Road in between. Shops and pubs line its Castle, Diamond, and Main Streets. On specific dates during spring and summer a lively artisan market is held when stallholders take over the seafront. Organized by Naturally North Coast and Glens Artisan traders, they sell handmade crafts and local food such as free-range rose veal, ethical goat meat, organically farmed salmon with fresh red dulce edible seaweed, and pollan, a delicious freshwater whitefish from Lough Neagh. The market is held on a rotating schedule in various coastal towns so it's best to check the website for dates: 🌐 *www.naturallynorthcoastandglens.co.uk.* While this market is extremely popular, the big annual event that attracts thousands to the town is the Ould Lammas Fair held on a fixed date over the bank holiday weekend at the end of August. The seaside town is taken over by hundreds of street traders, horse dealers, musicians, and a fireworks display in what is Ireland's oldest traditional fair.

GETTING HERE AND AROUND

Regular bus services link Ballycastle with the main towns of Bushmills, Coleraine, Ballymoney, and Ballymena. Translink buses run daily between the towns. The Antrim Coaster 252 also stops in Ballycastle.

Ballycastle is an hour's drive north of Belfast on the M2, which leads on to A26 before branching off to the narrower A44. You can park free along the seafront and at the marina. Other car parks are on Quay Road and Ann Street.

VISITOR INFORMATION

CONTACTS Ballycastle Visitor Information Centre. ✉ *Portnagree House, 14 Bayview Rd., Ballycastle* ☎ *028/2076–2024* 🌐 *www.visitcausewaycoastandglens.com.*

Sights

★ Carrick-a-Rede

BRIDGE | Adrenaline junkies love the rope bridge—off the coast at Ballintoy in Larrybane—which spans a 60-foot gap between the mainland and tiny Carrick-a-Rede Island. The island's name means "rock in the road" and refers to how it stands in the path of the salmon that follow the coast as they migrate to their home rivers to spawn. The bridge is open to the public daily, weather permitting. More than 480,000 visitors cross it (or at least take a look at it) each year, looking down on heart-stopping views of the crashing waves 100 feet below. For an exhilarating clifftop experience, the rope bridge walk is hard to beat. The island's small two-roomed Fishermen's Cottage, where they mended nets and kept materials, has been restored and opened to the public on selected dates on weekends once a month. The whole area is designated a Site of Special Scientific Interest because of its unique geology, flowers, and fauna. The area has also been identified as a dark-sky discovery site and with the absence of any light pollution is the ideal place to view the stars. If you need warming up after your walk, the Weighbridge tearoom serves snacks and hot drinks. From May until August the rope bridge increases its evening opening hours—check the website for details.

■ **TIP→ It is strongly advised to book in advance online; there may be up to a three-hour wait at peak times.** ✉ *119a White Park Rd., 8 km (5 miles) west of Ballycastle on B15, Ballintoy* ☎ *028/2073–1855* 🌐 *www.nationaltrust.org.uk/carrick-a-rede* 🎫 *£13.*

Rathlin Island

ISLAND | There's a sense of dreamy loneliness about this spot, rising 8 km (5 miles) offshore beyond the tide rip of Sloch na Marra (Valley of the Sea). One hundred people still live on Northern Ireland's only offshore island, amid the twin delights of history and wildlife. In 1306, the Scottish king Robert the Bruce took shelter in a cave (under the east lighthouse) and, according to the popular legend, was inspired to continue his armed struggle against the English by watching a spider patiently spinning its web. It was on Rathlin in 1898 that Guglielmo Marconi set up the world's first cross-water radio link, from the island's lighthouse to Ballycastle. Hiking and bird-watching—look out for the Atlantic nomads: choughs, puffins, guillemots, and razorbills nesting on the cliffs and sea stacks in the summer—as well as visiting the Rathlin West Light Seabird Centre and Lighthouse are the island's main activities. A high-speed passenger-only catamaran, the M.V. *Rathlin Express,* cuts the 10-km (6-mile) journey time crossing over the Sea of Moyle to 25 minutes; from July to September it runs six round-trips daily (£12; reservations 24 hours ahead essential). ✉ *Rathlin Island, 9½ km (6 miles) from Ballycastle, Ballycastle* ☎ *028/2076–9299* 🌐 *www.rathlinballycastleferry.com* 🎫 *Lighthouse £5; Boathouse Visitor Centre free.*

Hotels

Marine Hotel

$$ | **HOTEL** | Overlooking the harbor, this comfortable hotel is an ideal overnight stop en route to or from Rathlin Island. **Pros:** comfortable modern rooms; some rooms with sea-view balconies; close to Rathlin Island ferry terminal. **Cons:** gets very busy in summer; a little bland; some street noise. *Rooms from: £110* *Ballycastle* *028/2076–2222* *www.marinehotelballycastle.com* *41 rooms* *Free Breakfast.*

Activities

GOLF

Ballycastle Golf Club

GOLF | Pleasure comes first here, with challenge as an afterthought. It's beautiful (five holes wind around the remains of a 13th-century friary), short (less than 6,000 yards), and has an unusual mix of links, parkland, and heathland holes. Views stretch across the north Antrim coastline to the hills of Donegal and on a clear day, north to the coast of Scotland. It's also just a few miles from Bushmills, the world's oldest distillery. *2 Cushendall Rd., Ballycastle* *028/2076–2536* *www.ballycastlegolfclub.com* *£90* *18 holes, 5876 yards, par 71.*

Giant's Causeway

19½ km (12 miles) west of Ballycastle.

Northern Ireland's most scenic seascape is a natural wonder that no visitor to the area should miss.

GETTING HERE AND AROUND

BUS

The Translink Causeway Rambler high-frequency service (from June to mid-September) hits all the main visitor attractions, including Bushmills Distillery, Giant's Causeway, and the Carrick-a-Rede rope bridge. An all-day Rambler ticket allows you to hop on and off as many times as you like. It costs £9.50 per adult and £5.25 for a child and is valid only the day of purchase, available at the Europa Buscentre in Belfast or at any Translink station.

CAR

The causeway is just off the A2 coast road. The nearest towns are Coleraine (a 20-minute drive), Ballycastle (10 minutes), and Ballymoney (35 minutes). In summer, the roads are congested, particularly on bank holidays and festival weekends. You can park your car at the center itself, which has 400 spaces (the parking fee is included in the admission price), or leave it in nearby Bushmills, where a park-and-ride service operates. The National Trust, which runs this site, has introduced a Green Travel Admission Ticket for visitors arriving by park and ride or public transportation, knocking £1.50 off the standard adult admission price.

TRAIN

No regular public trains serve the Giant's Causeway, but a fun passenger link is provided on a narrow-gauge train running from Bushmills. The Giant's Causeway and Bushmills Railway leaves Runkerry Road, Bushmills, for the 3-km (2-mile) journey along the track bed of the former causeway tram. The train operates every weekend from Easter until the end of June, and daily in July and August. The nearest Translink train stations are 21 km (14 miles) away in Portrush or 18 km (11 miles) west in Coleraine, where the main Belfast–Derry train stops (£19 round-trip, after 9:30 am £12.70). If you buy a one-day iLink ticket, you can ride buses and trains to get to and from the Giant's Causeway.

CONTACTS Giant's Causeway and Bushmills Railway. *028/2073–2844* *www.freewebs.com/giantscausewayrailway.*

If you summon up the nerve to cross the famous 60-foot-long Carrick-a-Rede rope bridge, which sways over a rocky outcrop and the turbulent sea, be mindful that you have to do it again to get back to the mainland.

TOURS

Two bus tours from Belfast (among many) are the Giant's Causeway Tour by Allen's Tours and a same-named offering from McComb's.

Allen's Giant's Causeway Tour
BUS TOURS | Allen's Tours operates day tours to the Giant's Causeway as well as to the nearby Carrick-a-Rede rope bridge (£30). ☎ *028/9091–5613* 🌐 *www.allens-belfastbustours.com.*

McComb's Giant's Causeway Tour
BUS TOURS | McComb's/MiniCoach operates day tours of Belfast to the Giant's Causeway (£30) and *Game of Thrones* tours (£30). ✉ *Belfast* ☎ *028/9031–5333* 🌐 *www.mccombscoaches.com.*

VISITOR INFORMATION

CONTACTS Giant's Causeway Tourist Office. ✉ *Visitor Centre, Giant's Causeway Centre, 44 Causeway Rd., Bushmills* ☎ *028/2073–1855* 🌐 *nationaltrust.org.uk/giants-causeway.*

Sights

★ **Giant's Causeway**
NATURE SIGHT | **FAMILY** | Northern Ireland's only UNESCO World Heritage site, the Giant's Causeway is a mass of almost 40,000 mostly hexagonal pillars of volcanic basalt, clustered like a giant honeycomb and extending hundreds of yards into the sea. This "causeway" was created 60 million years ago, when boiling lava, erupting from an underground fissure that stretched from the north of Ireland to the Scottish coast, crystallized as it burst into the sea. As all Ulster folk know, though, the truth is that the giant Finn MacCool, in a bid to reach a giantess he'd fallen in love with on the Scottish island of Staffa (where the causeway resurfaces), created the columns as stepping-stones. Unfortunately, the giantess's boyfriend found out, and in the ensuing battle, Finn pulled out a huge chunk of earth and flung it toward Scotland. The resulting hole became Lough

Did You Know?

Geologists say the 40,000 basalt columns of the Giant's Causeway were formed by cooling lava 60 million years ago, but locals swear they were stepping-stones created by Finn McCool to wage battle with Benandonner, Scotland's legendary Übermensch.

Neagh, and the sod landed to create the Isle of Man. In the peak summer months it can be very busy—get here early or leave your visit until late afternoon, when it's generally quieter.

To reach the causeway, you can either walk 1½ km (1 mile) down a long, scenic hill or take the Causeway Coaster minibus. A popular option with many visitors is to take the 20-minute walk downhill to the main causeway and catch the shuttle bus back uphill (£2 return).

Be sure to allow time for the Giant's Causeway Visitor Experience, made of locally quarried basalt from the very same lava flows that formed the causeway. The glass front ensures spectacular coastal views, and the building is sunken into the ground, blending so effectively into the landscape that the indigenous grasses on the roof restore the natural ridgeline and provide a habitat for wildlife.

Inside the building, a stunning exhibition, complete with the 21st-century commercialization of Finn MacCool, is made up of five parts: coastal map, geological history, people and their stories, natural life, and the power of the landscape. Guided one-hour tours of the stones are included in the admission price, and visitors are issued a handheld device with recorded snippets of oral history. ✉ *44 Causeway Rd., Bushmills* ☎ *028/2073–1582* 🌐 *www.nationaltrust.org.uk/giantscauseway* 🎫 *£15, includes on-site parking* ☞ *Causeway Coast Way Car Park £10.*

Bushmills

3 km (2 miles) southwest of Giant's Causeway.

The pleasant town of Bushmills is world-famous for its centuries-old distillery.

GETTING HERE AND AROUND

Bushmills is on the A2 coastal route and an ideal stopping place for refueling. It has the best parking facilities for exploring the Giant's Causeway. A park-and-ride service operates from the town to the visitor center and saves you the trouble of finding a space. If visiting Bushmills Distillery, there's a large free car park out front. Parking is free in the town along main streets and in the large public car park opposite the Bushmills Inn.

Sights

★ Bushmills

DISTILLERY | Reputedly the oldest licensed distillery in the world, Bushmills was first granted a charter by King James I in 1608, though historical records refer to a distillery here as early as 1276. Bushmills produces the most famous of Irish whiskeys—its namesake—and a rarer black-label version, Black Bush, widely regarded as the best of the best. On the guided tour, discover the secrets of the special water from St. Columb's Rill, the story behind malted Irish barley, and learn about triple distillation in copper stills and aging (which happens for long years in oak casks). ✉ *2 Distillery Rd., off A2, Bushmills* ☎ *028/2073–3218* 🌐 *www.bushmills.eu* 🎫 *Tours from £15; children under 8 not permitted on tour.*

Giant's Causeway and Bushmills Railway

TRAIN TOURS | This minitrain with three neat little maroon-trimmed white wooden carriages runs on a 3-km (2-mile) stretch of narrow-gauge track between Bushmills Platform (a five-minute walk from the distillery) and its other terminus below the Giant's Causeway Information Centre (a stiff uphill hike). Timetables vary, so call for information. ✉ *Bushmills Platform, Bushmills* ☎ *028/2073–2844* 🌐 *giantscausewayrailway.webs.com* 🎫 *£7 (one-way or round-trip).*

Hotels

The Bushmills Inn

$$$$ | **B&B/INN** | This comfortable old coach inn dating from the 1600s welcomes with peat fires and cozy rooms; the master distiller's suite even comes with fluffy slippers and bathrobes. **Pros:** close to distillery and the Giant's Causeway; easy to find in central location; secure off-street parking. **Cons:** if you're tall, look out for the low timber beams; very expensive for what you get; overrated menu. *Rooms from: £230* *9 Dunluce Rd., Bushmills* *028/2073–3000* *www.bushmillsinn.com* *41 rooms* *Free Breakfast.*

Causeway Hotel

$$$ | **HOTEL** | Owned by the U.K.'s National Trust and flaunting a stunning location overlooking the Atlantic Ocean, this 1840s hotel is less than a half mile from the celebrated Giant's Causeway. Older rooms have been fully refurbished and freshened with a calming shade of duck-egg blue. **Pros:** free parking; old-world charm with modern comforts; as close as it gets to the Giant's Causeway. **Cons:** too many family parties; service can be a tad churlish; isolated with nowhere to eat or drink nearby. *Rooms from: £140* *40 Causeway Rd., Bushmills* *028/2073–1210* *www.thecausewayhotel.com* *28 rooms* *Free Breakfast.*

Carbing Up

When it comes to food, Northern Ireland is most famed (or notorious) for its Ulster fry, a fried-up carbohydrate blowout of a breakfast that is a cardiologist's nightmare. Sausage, bacon, eggs, black pudding, fried soda bread, and potato bread (and perhaps a grilled tomato or fried mushrooms) all make a meal that sounds as dangerous to your health as bungee jumping without a harness. After a night on the Guinness, however, you'll understand why this breakfast is so popular: it makes a great cure for a hangover.

Dunluce Castle

3 km (2 miles) west of Bushmills.

Dunluce is midway between Bushmills and Portrush, and its photogenic castle makes it a worthy stop.

GETTING HERE AND AROUND

There is a small, free car park at the castle, but it isn't big enough to accommodate large numbers at busy times.

TIP→ Park free in Bushmills or Portrush, both a 10-minute drive away, and hop on the Causeway Rambler bus, which operates in summer along the A2 coastal route and drops you at the castle.

Coleraine is the nearest big town. Derry is an hour's drive west.

Sights

Dunluce Castle

CASTLE/PALACE | **FAMILY** | Dramatically perched on a 100-foot-high basalt-rock cliff, halfway between Portrush and the Giant's Causeway, Dunluce Castle is one of the north's most evocative ruins. Even roofless, this shattered hulk conjures up a strength and aura that is quintessentially Antrim. Originally a 13th-century Norman fortress, Dunluce was captured in the 16th century by the local MacDonnell clan chiefs. They enlarged it, in part using profits from salvaging the Spanish galleon *Girona,* and made it an important base for ruling northeastern Ulster. Perhaps the MacDonnells expanded the castle a bit too much, for in 1639 faulty construction caused the kitchens (with all the cooks) to plummet into the sea during a storm. Between 2009 and 2012, archaeologists uncovered belt buckles, thimbles, dress fastenings, jewelry, clay pipes, animal bones, and shards of pottery that are now on display in the Discovery Room. An eight-minute introductory film explores the castle's history. Colorful leaflets are available on-site dealing with the castle's checkered history. Guided tours are held every day at 11 am and 2 pm in the summer months and last 45 minutes. *87 Dunluce Rd.* *028/2073–1938* *www.discovernorthernireland.com* *£6.*

Portstewart Strand

BEACH | **FAMILY** | Signposted as "The Strand" at all major junctions in town, this magnificent 3-km (2-mile) stretch of golden sand is one of the north coast's finest beaches, suitable for all ages. Owned by the National Trust, well maintained, and clean, it's the ideal spot for picnics, swimming (though the water can be quite chilly), or long walks among sand dunes that are a haven for wildflowers such as bird's foot trefoil, wild pansy, and thyme, and butterflies including common blue, meadow brown, and dark green fritillary. Lifeguards are on duty at Easter, during weekends in May and September, and full-time from June to August. The beach has an undertow at certain points and small sections have seaweed, but it's not a big nuisance. Two-hour guided butterfly safaris aimed at families are held on occasional weekends during the summer as well as orchid walks and nature strolls through the dunes. On warm days the beach fills with cars, but its size ensures that it is never completely crowded. **Amenities**: food and drink; parking; showers; toilets. **Best for**: surfing; swimming; walking. *118 Strand Rd., Portstewart* *028/7083–6396* *www.nationaltrust.org.uk/portstewartstrand* *£8 per car.*

Restaurants

★ Harry's Shack

$ | **IRISH** | With its raw wooden tables, wood-burning stove, sand on the floor, and outdoor terrace, this beachside restaurant in Portstewart, about 20 minutes from Dunluce, is *the* destination restaurant par excellence of the north coast. Brunches might consist of pancakes with maple syrup, smoked salmon and scrambled eggs, or pasta. **Known for:** fresh, tasty lobster; local pale ale; on-the-beach dining with outdoor bar. *Average main: £15* *118 Strand Rd., Portstewart* *028/7083–1783* *No dinner Sun.–Wed.*

Ramore Restaurants

$ | **ECLECTIC** | **FAMILY** | Creative, moderately priced fare, alongside panoramic views in an elegant setting, attract locals and tourists to this popular restaurant and wine bar complex with multiple venues. The light-filled Mermaid Kitchen and Bar, serving seafood, conjures up a beachside feel evocative of coastal Maine, except you're looking out on Portrush's West Strand (although admittedly Belfast is only 100 km [60 miles] south); the more informal Harbour Bistro serves wood-fired steaks and burgers; Neptune and Prawn, on the other side of the harbor, serves Asian-inspired fare; and the Tourist Restaurant has a Mexican theme with burritos, nachos, and tacos and specializes in pizzas and burgers. **Known for:** multiple venues; wood-fired burgers and grilled fish; sea and sunset views. *Average main: £13* *Landsdown Harbour, Portrush* *07506/990–345* *www.ramorerestaurant.com.*

Activities

GOLF

Castlerock Golf Club

GOLF | The Mussenden Course underwent major reconstruction during 2018 and 2019, which resulted in nine holes being

While cliff erosion has played havoc with what's left of its battlements, Dunluce Castle still remains one of Northern Ireland's most intensely beautiful sights.

altered, although there was no change to one of its most unusual, "Leg o' Mutton," a 200-yard par-3 with railway tracks to the right and a burn to the left. The course has bedded well and is regarded as having the best greens in Ireland. The finish is spectacular: from the elevated 17th tee, where you can see the shores of Scotland, to the majestic 18th, which plays uphill to a plateau green. The club also boasts the equally scenic 9-hole Bann Course. ✉ *65 Circular Rd., Derry* ☎ *028/7084–8314* 🌐 *www.castlerockgc.co.uk* 🎫 *Mussenden: £135; Bann: weekdays £30* ⛳ *Mussenden: 18 holes, 6747 yards, par 73; Bann: 9 holes, 4892 yards, par 68.*

Portstewart Golf Club

GOLF | More than 120 years old, Portstewart may scare you with its opening hole, known as "Tubber Patrick," generally regarded as the toughest starter in Ireland. Picture a 425-yard par-4 that descends from an elevated tee to a small green tucked between the dunes. The Strand Course is affectionately called "The Sleeping Giant," and the manicured greens are known for uniformity and speed. Eight of the holes have been redesigned to toughen the course and two have been lengthened. From its rolling fairways and undulating dunes the views stretch across the Atlantic Ocean to north Donegal. ✉ *117 Strand Rd., Portstewart* ☎ *028/7083–2015* 🌐 *www.portstewartgc.co.uk* 🎫 *The Strand: Apr. £165; May–Oct. daily £215; Nov.–Mar. £70; Old Course: summer weekdays £15, winter £10, weekends £15 all year; Riverside: weekdays £25, weekends £30* ⛳ *The Strand: 18 holes, 7118 yards, par 72; Old Course: 18 holes, 4730 yards, par 64; Riverside: 18 holes, 5725 yards, par 68.*

★ **Royal Portrush Golf Club**

GOLF | Hosting the British Open in 2019 resulted in a radical reshaping of the Dunluce course at Royal Portrush to ensure the perfect stage for the game's oldest major, and at the same time seriously raising the club's profile. It was the first time that the championship had been held at the club for almost 70 years and it was a memorable occasion—made even more so by the fact that Irish golfer Shane Lowry from the Esker Hills club in County Offaly lifted the coveted Claret Jug, six shots clear of his nearest challenger. Subtle alterations were made to almost every hole to stretch the course length, and it was reconfigured to create space for an amphitheater, freeing up land for spectators and a sprawling tented village for tens of thousands of fans. One of the main adjustments involved major changes to the 17th and 18th holes, which were too weak for the tournament. With the skillful eye of leading architect Martin Ebert, the course was revised by exploiting the second-string Valley Course that runs alongside, instigating what became known as a "land grab." The Valley's 5th and 6th holes were sacrificed to create the Dunluce's new 7th and 8th. The loss of the old 17th meant the disappearance of its notorious "Big Nellie" bunker, but the architecture incorporated a replica "Wee Nellie" into the new 7th, while a new bunker was created on the left-hand side of the 17th. The Open left a considerable legacy that boosted the reputation, not only of the club, but of the north Irish coast as a premier destination for international events, and has left a satisfying afterglow. In a poll of Irish golf legends, Dunluce was voted the best in Ireland—among those who have graced the greens here are Gary Player, Arnold Palmer, Jack Nicklaus, and Ernie Els. Darren Clarke plays his golf here when he's home, and it's where Graeme McDowell, former U.S. Open champion, learned his golf at an early age. ✉ *Dunluce Rd., Portrush* ☎ *028/7082–2311* 🌐 *www.royalportrushgolfclub.com* 🎫 *Dunluce: May–Sept. £295. Valley: Apr.–Oct., £80; Nov.–Mar., weekdays only £40* 🏌 *Dunluce: 18 holes, 7317 yards, par 72; Valley: 18 holes, 6346 yards, par 75.*

Limavady

27 km (17 miles) east of Derry.

In 1851, at No. 51 on Limavady's Georgian main street, Jane Ross wrote down the tune played by a traveling fiddler and called it "Londonderry Air," better known now as "Danny Boy." While staying at an inn on Ballyclose Street, William Thackeray (1811–63) wrote his rather lustful poem "Peg of Limavady" about a barmaid. Among the many Americans descended from Ulster emigrants was President James Monroe, whose relatives came from the Limavady area.

GETTING HERE AND AROUND

Translink buses leave Limavady every hour during the day for Derry; journey time is 35 minutes. There is no train station, but you can connect with the train to Belfast by taking a bus to Coleraine or Ballymena.

On the main route between Derry and Coleraine, Limavady is well served with car parking. Motorists park free on the main street with a one-hour time limit. Pay-and-display parking, costing £0.40 per hour, is available at Newtown Square (off Linenhall Street) and on Connell Street.

VISITOR INFORMATION

CONTACTS Limavady Tourist Office. ✉ *Roe Valley Arts Centre, 24 Main St., Limavady* ☎ *028/7776–0650* 🌐 *www.visitcausewaycoastandglens.com.*

Hotels

Roe Park Resort

$$$$ | **RESORT** | A country estate serves as the model for this modern deluxe resort on 155 acres straddling the banks of the River Roe—the place is relatively large and impersonal, although the lobby is welcoming and guest rooms have simple, clean-line beds in woods and rich earth tones. **Pros:** ideal location for golfers and spa lovers; lively bars;

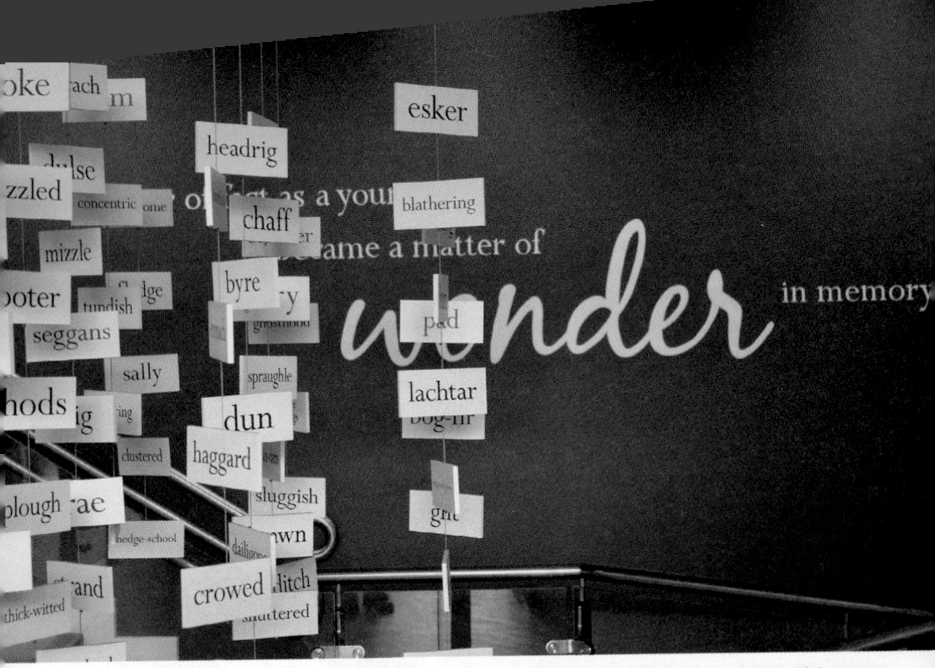

Dangling mobiles of words from Seamus Heaney's poems invite visitors to HomePlace to play with language.

family-friendly. **Cons:** can be noisy with evening wedding parties; new suites are expensive; limited public transport, you need a car. $ *Rooms from: £175* ✉ *Roe Park, Limavady* ☎ *028/7772–2222* 🌐 *www.roeparkresort.com* 118 *rooms* 🍽 *Free Breakfast.*

Bellaghy

32 miles (51 km) south of Dunluce Castle, 20 miles (32 km) north of Belfast International Airport.

In the rural heartland of South Derry, close to the River Bann that divides Counties Derry and Antrim, lies the small town of Bellaghy (pop. 1,100). Halfway between Belfast and Derry (making it an easy stop on a drive between both), Bellaghy is on the fringe of Lough Neagh—Ireland's biggest inland lake and a place memorialized in the poetry of Seamus Heaney.

Sights

★ **Seamus Heaney HomePlace**

VISITOR CENTER | Dedicated to the memory of the prize-winning poet and Nobel laureate Seamus Heaney, this £4.25 million arts center in his home village of Bellaghy explores his life and work, arranged over two floors with displays, touch screens, and interactive exhibits. Heaney, whose lyrical poetry is rooted in the land of his birth but speaks to people around the world, won the Nobel Prize for Literature in 1995. Everyone from Bill Clinton to local schoolchildren have expressed their high esteem for Heaney; Robert Lowell called him the greatest Irish poet since Yeats. Through words, images, artifacts, and powerful voice recordings, his distinctive accent and rhythm come alive. Highlights include the Poetry Wall, where visitors can engage with the building blocks, tools, and methods he employed, and an Attic Study, where you can see how his original manuscripts were revised and rewritten. A substantial library houses his poetry and translations of his work in more than 20 languages. There's a 190-seat theater with a regular series of readings, music, and talks. You can also pick up local literature from a newly established tourist information point. Guided bus tours of Heaney Country are organized by Eugene Kielt (🌐 *laurel-villa.com/product/seamus-heaney-tours*), who also runs Laurel Villa, a superb Victorian B&B in nearby Magherafelt with a strong poetry slant. ✉ *45 Main St.* ✢ *Equidistant between Belfast and Derry, a 45-min drive from both cities* ☎ *028/7938–7444* 🌐 *www.seamusheaneyhome.com* 🎟 *£10* ⏲ *Closed Sun. morning.*

Derry

Wrapped in historic walls and hilly cobbled streets, Derry (or Londonderry, as it's also known) oozes character. With a population of just over 100,000, it's a relatively small city on the rise, with the imprint of the past around every corner, proud of its 400-year-old walls and architectural heritage as well as the multimillion-pound beautification project that has seen landmark buildings emerge in recent years. Derry's remarkable history is told in expressive visual terms: walls and stained glass, a compelling open-air gallery of 21st-century political murals, the rejuvenated Guildhall, and a spectacular Peace Bridge across the River Foyle. The bridge links the city center with Ebrington Square, a redeveloped military parade ground now turned into a spacious playground filled with concerts and tai chi practitioners. The base figured in World War II's Battle of the Atlantic, and its developers are slowly building a gallery, art center, studios, a brewery and bar, shops, and a maritime museum.

GETTING HERE AND AROUND

BUS

Translink runs double-decker Goldline express coaches on its fast route between Belfast and Derry over the Glenshane Pass. At peak times services operate every 15 minutes and include nine direct daily services between the two cities (£13 single, £19.50 same-day return, £23 open return, valid for one month). Journey time is one hour and 40 minutes. Weekend service, especially on Sunday, is less frequent. An alternative, slightly longer route, operated by Translink Goldline between Belfast and Derry, travels along the M1 motorway and through County Tyrone—it takes about two hours. Translink buses run from Derry to neighboring towns, with fares averaging about £16.50 round-trip. You can also catch a bus from City of Derry Airport into the Foyle Street bus station in the city center (£6.50 round-trip). The Airporter Coach, which leaves from the Foyleside shopping center coachpark, operates between Derry and Belfast International Airport and George Best Belfast City Airport. Tickets to both airports cost £30 round-trip. If you're traveling across the border from Derry into Donegal, then you have a choice of using Bus Éireann or North West Busways. 🌐 *www.northwestbusways.ie*

CAR

The city's two main shopping centers, Foyleside and Quayside, have multistory car parking garages. Collect a ticket on entry and pay at a machine on departure. Other main car parks, which are mostly pay-by-the-hour via metered ticket machines, are located at Foyle Street, Carlisle Road, William Street, Society Street, Queens Quay, Alfred Street, and Victoria Market. Derry is a 75-minute drive from Belfast; the A6 takes you over the mountainous Glenshane Pass. Roads lead south to Strabane and Omagh on the A5 and on to Dublin (about four hours away, depending on road conditions and traffic). Derry is also the jumping-off point for exploring the Inishowen Peninsula by car and the beautifully remote northern Donegal region.

An annual bluegrass music festival at the Ulster American Folk Park reaffirms the strong links between Northern Ireland and the United States.

TRAIN

One of the most relaxing ways to arrive in Derry is by train. Frequent daily services on Northern Ireland Railways link it with Coleraine, Ballymena, Antrim, and Belfast. For the final 20-minute section of the journey—along the County Derry coastline—the track runs parallel to the sea and is one of Ireland's most stunning routes. The journey time from Belfast to Derry is about two hours (£19.50 round-trip, £13 after 9:30 am; trains run at 20 minutes past the hour from 6 am until 9 pm). The main station is in the Waterside area of the city; catch a free 10-minute shuttle bus across Craigavon Bridge to get to the West Bank, where most attractions are concentrated.

CONTACTS Airporter Coach. ☎ *028/7126–9996* 🌐 *www.airporter.co.uk.*

TOURS

Bogside History Tours

WALKING TOURS | Paul Doherty's Bogside tours come with personal knowledge since his father, Patrick, was one of a group of civilians killed by British soldiers during a civil rights march on January 30, 1972. His 75-minute tour provides an educational, and at times emotional, insight into the era and retraces parts of the original march stopping at places where the dead and injured fell. The company also offers a city walls tour. Tours are held all year at 11 am and 1 pm, with an additional tour at 3 pm from June through August. The meeting point is at the Guildhall in the city center. ✉ *Guildhall St., Bogside* ☎ *077/3145–0088* 🌐 *www.bogsidehistorytours.com* 💷 *£10.*

Martin McCrossan City Walking Tours

WALKING TOURS | These walks leave daily at 10 am, noon, 2, and 4 pm year-round. The departure point is 11 Carlisle Road (just show up and look for the yellow-jacketed guides; reservations not necessary). Tours last one hour and incorporate not only history and centuries-old stories but also architecture and engaging bits of local lore and humor. All tours also end with a free cup of tea or coffee. The operator also offers *Derry Girls* tours leaving from the mural Saturdays at noon

Northern Irish Food: Baking Crazy

The sweet aroma of freshly baked cakes will distract you during a visit to Northern Ireland. It is famed for its bakeries, producing calorie-laden handmade fancies and traditional breads using age-old recipes. In family-run shops, shelves heave with fresh cream cakes, pastries, scones, and local specialties such as chocolate caramel squares or "fifteens"—made of 15 digestive biscuits, 15 marshmallows, and 15 glacé cherries—once tasted never forgotten. Local breads to try include the floury "Belfast Bap," often turned into a sandwich with fillings of Irish bacon, cheese, and sausage, and the soda "farl," cooked on the griddle rather than in the oven and most often found at breakfast time on either side of an Ulster fry.

for £10 and hitting the various filming locations. ✉ *11 Carlisle Rd., West Bank* ☎ *028/7127–1996* 🌐 *www.derrycitytours.com* 🎫 *£6.*

VISITOR INFORMATION

CONTACTS Visit Derry. ✉ *1–3 Waterloo Pl., West Bank* ☎ *028/7126–7284* 🌐 *www.visitderry.com.*

Sights

Derry's name shadows its history. Those in favor of British rule call the city Londonderry, its old Plantation-period name: the "London" part was tacked on in 1613 after the Flight of the Earls, when the city and county were handed over to the Corporation of London, which represented London's merchants. The corporation brought in a large population of English and Scottish Protestant settlers, built towns for them, and reconstructed Derry within the city walls (which survive almost unchanged to this day). Derry's sturdy ramparts have withstood many fierce attacks—they have never been breached, which explains the city's coy sobriquet, "The Maiden City." The most famous attack was the siege of 1688–89, begun after 13 apprentice boys slammed the city gates in the face of the Catholic king, James II. Inhabitants, who held out for 105 days and were reduced to eating dogs, cats, and laundry starch, nevertheless helped to secure the British throne for the Protestant king, William III. Whatever you choose to call it—and the latest name is Derry/Londonderry—the city is no longer an underrated place.

Centre for Contemporary Art (CCA)
ART GALLERY | Contemporary Irish and international artistic collaborations are part of the credo of this cutting-edge gallery. It has featured shows by emerging Irish artists and enjoys connections with galleries in India and France, as well as London and Dublin. There's a free public library where you can browse books on art. ✉ *10–12 Artillery St., West Bank* ☎ *028/7137–3538* 🌐 *www.ccadld.org.*

★ **Derry City Walls**
PROMENADE | Established under a charter by James I in 1613, Derry is among a small but distinctive coterie of places throughout Europe that have preserved their ancient ramparts, which are Northern Ireland's largest state monument and an enduring backdrop to daily lives. Built between 1614 and 1618, the walls today allow you to get a feel for Derry's deep history by strolling along the parapet walkway and pausing on a platform at Grand Parade where the cannons date from 1642 and are inscribed with the name of the London company that commissioned them. Pierced by eight

gates (originally four) and as much as 30 feet thick, the gray-stone ramparts are only 1½ km (1 mile) all around. In 2019 the Royal Bastion (a projecting section) and Plinth were redesigned and adapted for educational purposes. This area is accessible to visitors but may be entered only by using the key available from the Siege Museum, just a few meters away in Society Street. On your walk, take a break at a strategically placed café or simply drink in the local atmosphere. In summer when the walls are awash with tourists, "ambassadors" are on hand to point you the right way. ✉ *West Bank* 🌐 *www.visitderry.com.*

Derry Girls Mural

PUBLIC ART | Since it was erected in 2019, the *Derry Girls* mural has become the talk of the town and a must-see sight for tourists. The extensive 3-meter-high artwork, based on the cast of a hit British comedy TV series, *Derry Girls,* has been spray-painted on to the gable wall of Badgers bar in Orchard Street. The eye-catching wall of fame in the city center can be clearly seen from a walk on the walls and is a contrast to some politicized murals elsewhere. The sitcom, which has earned critical acclaim—the *Hollywood Reporter*'s reviewer declared it her favorite comedy of the year—features the adventures of five Derry teenagers navigating their way around the late-Troubles era of the early 1990s. It has been picked up by Netflix and turned into a second series, which ends with the re-creation of Bill Clinton's visit to Derry in 1995. You can also sample drinks made in the name of several of the characters from the series, including "Sister Michael" coconut stout and the "Wee English Fella," a strawberry pale ale, available from the Walled City Brewery on the city's Waterside. ✉ *18 Orchard St., Central District* ☎ *028/7136–3306.*

Derry Wall Murals

PUBLIC ART | Dramatic wall murals throughout Derry testify to the power of art as historical document, while also serving as a reminder of painful pasts. Symbolic of the different communities, the murals attract considerable curiosity from tourists. The Bogside Gallery of Murals, painted by William Kelly, Kevin Hasson, and Tom Kelly, are made up of 12 wall paintings known collectively as "The People's Gallery." They include the *Bloody Sunday Commemoration, The Death of Innocence, Civil Rights, The Hunger Strikes,* and a poignant one featuring the Nobel peace prize–winning Derry politician John Hume along with Martin Luther King Jr., Nelson Mandela, and Mother Teresa—all beside the Brooklyn Bridge. In 2015, a mural featuring John Hume and Ivan Cooper, founding members of the civil rights movement, was restored. The paintings span the length of Rossville Street in the heart of the Bogside. Some of the guided walking tours that leave from the tourist information center include the story of the murals. On the other side of the political divide, close to the city walls, the Protestant Fountain estate is home to one of the oldest King Billy murals along with other colorful ones linked to the siege of Derry. ✉ *Rossville St., Bogside* ☎ *028/7126–7284* 🌐 *www.extramuralactivity.com.*

Ebrington Square

PLAZA/SQUARE | Since its reincarnation as a venue for open-air concerts and other outdoor events, Ebrington Square, a former military barracks on the River Foyle's east bank, has become an established cultural hub. It was named for Lord Ebrington, the Lord Lieutenant of Ireland during the years 1839–41 when many of the military buildings here were erected, including the Star Fort, one of the architectural highlights. During World War II, the barracks became part of a naval base that later functioned as an antisubmarine training school for the Allied navies operating from the city. Derry's contribution to the Battle of the Atlantic was acknowledged with the unveiling in

2013 of the *International Sailor,* a bronze statue in the square, which pays tribute to seamen from the 12 Allied nations who protected shipping convoys. It is a replica of the *Mariner* statue in Halifax, Nova Scotia. There are two restaurants, the Walled City Brewery (WCB) and The Stables Inn. The WCB (🌐 *www.walledcitybrewery.com*), on the former parade ground next to the landmark clock tower building, does not hold official tours but instead offers a masterclass (one hour, 30 minutes) during which you can hear the brewers' stories and sample up to 10 craft beers with artisanal local snacks. It costs £25 and must be prebooked via the website. The restaurant has a tapas menu and offers delights such as a WCB burger or Malaysian laksa coconut lemongrass curry with rice noodles and bok choy chargrilled chicken. ✉ *Ebrington Sq., East Bank* 🌐 *www.yourebrington.com* 🎫 *Free.*

Garden of Reflection

GARDEN | An imaginative *rus in urbe,* this small city-center oasis of calm features a courtyard, amphitheater, and gallery space where travelers can escape the bustle of traffic and noise. A paved "river" runs through the garden, symbolic of life's journey, while artistic features include a crystal healing wall and specially commissioned artworks. In the words of the new era, it is "a shared space" that can be enjoyed by all sections of the community in a historic part of the walled city. Lunchtime events are sometimes held. ✉ *16 Bishop St., Derry* ☎ *028/7126–1941* 🎫 *Free.*

★ **Guildhall**

HISTORY MUSEUM | **FAMILY** | The rejuvenated Victorian Guildhall is an outstanding example of the city's ornate architecture. It has been refashioned as a visitor center with interactive exhibits telling the story of the Plantation of Ulster and the construction of the walled city, and how these events shaped present-day Derry. Touch-screen displays explain the building's special features, like the elaborate ceilings, baronial wood paneling, and a magnificent organ. For children, hands-on displays include a puzzle of a 1598 map of Ulster, and a wheel they can spin to find out about the different London companies and how land was divided. Kids can also build a *bawn,* stone house, or castle using wooden blocks, or dress up in the clothes of Planters or Irish people of the period. Look out, too, for the delightful scale model of the city in 1738 showing just a few thatched cabins outside the perimeter wall. A conserved page (a folio) from the Great Parchment Book of 1639 detailing the account of the Plantation is also on display. Other highlights include the 23 superb stained-glass windows in the reception area, up the stairs, and in the first floor main hall reflecting the siege of 1689 and other aspects of the city's history. With the gleaming restoration, one of the most famous of all Derry's local sayings, "You've more faces than the Guildhall clock"—not a compliment—has renewed resonance.

TIP→ Enjoy an alfresco coffee in the Guild Café at the harbor square entrance overlooking the Foyle, an ideal spot to catch the riverine light and reflect on 400 turbulent years of history. ✉ *Guildhall Sq., West Bank* ☎ *028/7137–6510* 🌐 *www.derrystrabane.com/guildhall* 🎫 *Free.*

★ **Museum of Free Derry** (*The Bloody Sunday Center*)

HISTORY MUSEUM | At Free Derry Corner stands the white gable wall where in 1969 Catholics defiantly painted the slogan "You are now entering Free Derry" as a declaration of a zone from which police and the British Army were banned until 1972, when the army broke down the barricades. The black lettering became instantly recognizable as a symbol of resistance, and more than 50 years later the words are still there but have taken on much wider significance. They also now represent

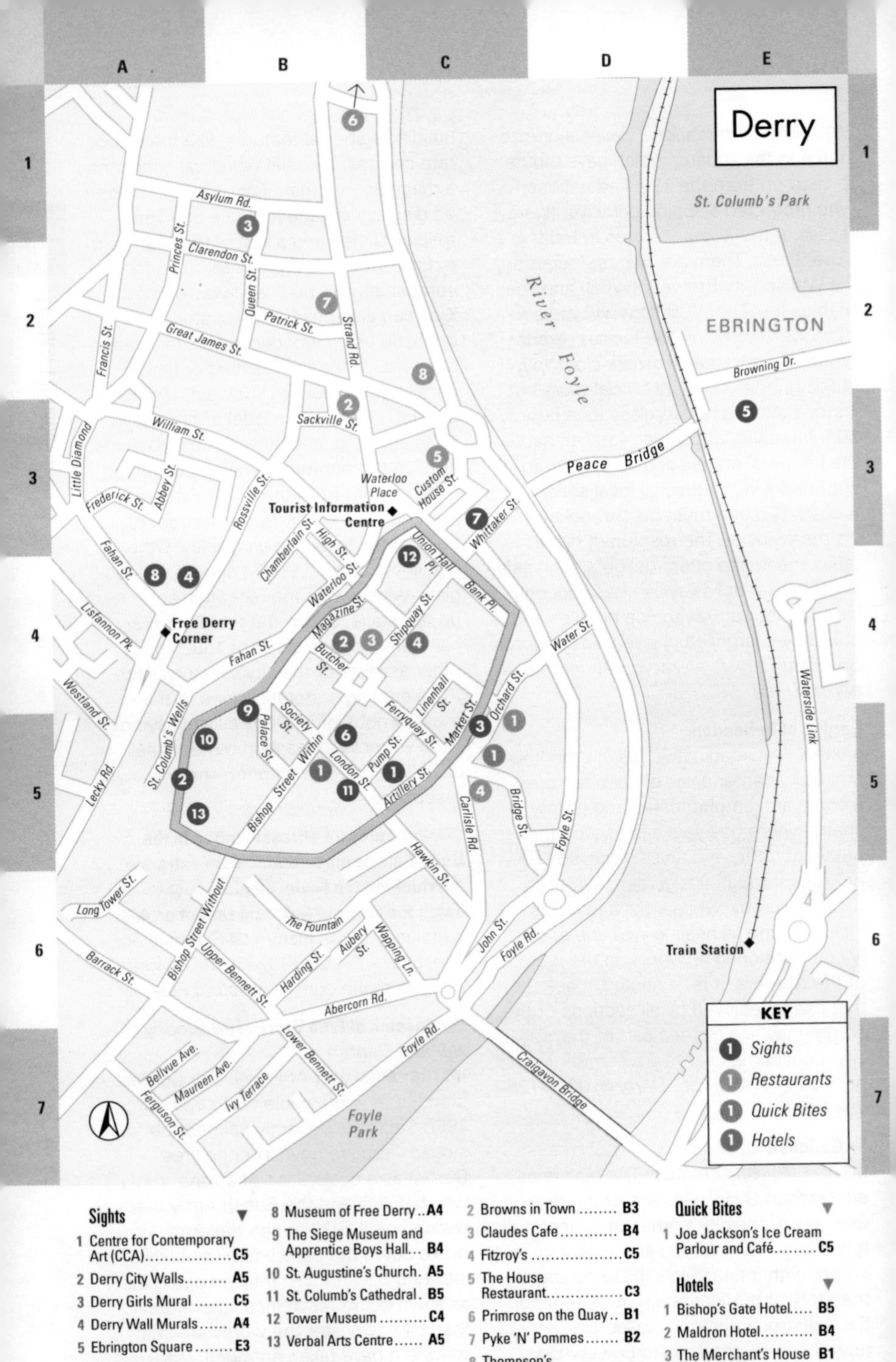

Sights

1 Centre for Contemporary Art (CCA) **C5**
2 Derry City Walls **A5**
3 Derry Girls Mural **C5**
4 Derry Wall Murals **A4**
5 Ebrington Square **E3**
6 Garden of Reflection **B5**
7 Guildhall **C3**
8 Museum of Free Derry **A4**
9 The Siege Museum and Apprentice Boys Hall **B4**
10 St. Augustine's Church **A5**
11 St. Columb's Cathedral **B5**
12 Tower Museum **C4**
13 Verbal Arts Centre **A5**

Restaurants

1 Badger's **C5**
2 Browns in Town **B3**
3 Claudes Cafe **B4**
4 Fitzroy's **C5**
5 The House Restaurant **C3**
6 Primrose on the Quay **B1**
7 Pyke 'N' Pommes **B2**
8 Thompson's Restaurant **C2**

Quick Bites

1 Joe Jackson's Ice Cream Parlour and Café **C5**

Hotels

1 Bishop's Gate Hotel **B5**
2 Maldron Hotel **B4**
3 The Merchant's House **B1**
4 Shipquay Boutique Hotel **C4**

Walking Derry

It's easy to find your own way around Derry's streets and riverside. Walkers and cyclists can explore the new traffic-free Waterside Greenway, an extended 6½-km (4-mile) route through parkland over the Peace Bridge to the Foyle Bridge, running parallel with the railway line and affording spectacular views across Lough Foyle to the hills of Donegal on the Inishowen peninsula. This route will take you through Ebrington Barracks and into St. Columb's Park, a public space of 70 acres with serene glades and woodland seating, which has been rejuvenated in a £6 million transformation. Stop off to see the historic restored walled garden redeveloped in 2019 with newly planted apple and pear trees, a separate herb garden, greenhouses, and a Celtic knot paving pattern. There's a café in St. Columb's Park House, a reconciliation center for visiting groups. You can also follow the Pathway to Peace, a youth-led initiative that emerged after the unveiling of Ireland's first peace flame in Derry by Martin Luther King III in 2013. At one end of Ebrington Square visitors can view more than 400 peace pledges, which have been engraved on illuminated metal trees, part of the Pathway to Peace. Details are available at the tourist office.

social and international themes, including marriage equality, gay pride, or medical issues such as cancer, when for several weeks the wall is painted a different color. On January 30, 1972, 13 civil rights marchers were shot and killed by British soldiers and a 14th man died later from his wounds. Thirty-eight years later, the British government released its official report on the shootings, which resulted in a hugely significant official apology from Prime Minister David Cameron, saying that he was "deeply sorry" for what happened on Bloody Sunday and that it "had been unjustified and unjustifiable." His speech to the House of Commons is played in its entirety on a loop in one room. The £2.2 million, two-story museum built on the same site and opened by the civil rights activist Reverend Jesse Jackson in 2017 tells the complete story of that day and the many years of campaigning for an apology. Saved sections of the front face of the old building retain the bullet scars from that fateful day and glass cabinets display clothes worn by some of the victims. Eyewitness talks are also held in the museum and take place every Wednesday and Friday at noon.

■ TIP→ **One-hour Free Derry Walking Tours (£5) leave from the museum at 10, noon, and 2 each day.** ✉ *The Museum of Free Derry (locally known as the Bloody Sunday Centre), 55 Glenfada Park, off Rossville St., West Bank* ☎ *02871/136–0880* 🌐 *www.museumoffreederry.org* 🎫 *£8 (last admission 30 mins before closing).*

The Siege Museum and Apprentice Boys Hall

HISTORY MUSEUM | Imposing in its Scottish Baronial fortified grandeur, this is a meeting place for the exclusively Protestant organization set up in 1714 to honor 13 Apprentice Boys who slammed the city gate in the face of the Catholic King James in 1688, sparking the Siege of Derry. The Memorial Hall has been renovated, and next door to it stands a £2 million center that tells the fascinating story of the 105-day siege and chronicles the history of the Apprentice Boys. A lookalike sandstone scale model of Walker's

Pillar—blown up by the IRA in 1973—has been re-created. During excavation work in 2014, before the new museum was built, archaeologists unearthed Derry's oldest building, believed to date to at least 1602. The brick-and-wood structure perished during the O'Doherty Rebellion of 1608—predating the historic city walls by several years. Excited archaeologists also uncovered musket balls, a cannonball, pottery shards, clay pipes, and even some intact centuries-old wine bottles—although their drinking maturity has yet to be established. Combined guided tours of the museum, Memorial Hall, and city walls with access to the Royal Bastion and Plinth of Walker's Pillar cost £7 and last two hours. ✉ *13 Society St., West Bank* ☎ *028/7126–1219* 🌐 *www.thesiegemuseum.org* 🎫 *£5.*

St. Augustine's Church

CHURCH | This small jewel of a church is wedged just inside the ramparts of the walls. In the ancient graveyard a large board map registers the location of 163 gravestones in alphabetical order. The site was known as "God's Little Acre," indicating a much larger graveyard, but now sits in an area of a quarter of an acre. It has been a sacred spot since St. Columba founded his first abbey here in AD 546. The oldest gravestone—in the church porch—is that of Richard Carrec, an Elizabethan soldier, dating from circa 1609. Immerse yourself in the serenity of the graveyard under the shadow of the cherry trees, tune into the birdsong, a world away from the tour groups being corralled around the walls. Visitors can tour the church and adjoining graveyard from May to October and are welcome at worship on Sunday or at morning communion on Tuesday at 10:30 am. ✉ *Palace St., West Bank* ☎ *028/7136–6041* 🌐 *www.saintaugustines.co.uk.*

★ **St. Columb's Cathedral**

RELIGIOUS BUILDING | The first Protestant cathedral built in the United Kingdom after the Reformation, this houses the oldest and largest bells in Ireland (dating from the 1620s). It's a treasure house of Derry Protestant emblems, memorials, and relics from the siege of 1688–89; most visitors come to see the keys that locked the four main gates of the city during the siege. The church was built in 1633 in simple Planter's Gothic style, with an intricate corbelled roof and austere spire. In the vestibule is the 270-pound mortar ball that was fired over the wall during the Siege of Derry, with an invitation to surrender sent by King James. Legend has it that when it was read, every man, woman, and child in the city rushed to the walls and shouted, "No surrender!"—a Protestant battle cry to this day. The attached Chapter House Museum has the oldest surviving copy of a map of Derry (from 1600) and the Bible owned by Governor George Walker during the siege. View the information panels and artifacts in display cases that include the original keys to the city and other relics. In recent years the tower and spire have been restored and the stonework and stained-glass windows repaired. A new LED lighting system reveals the beauty of the elegant Canadian pine ceiling. Knowledgeable tour guides are on hand. ✉ *London St., off Bishop St., 17 London St., West Bank* ☎ *07794/666–754* 🌐 *www.stcolumbscathedral.org* 🎫 *£2 suggested donation.*

Tower Museum

HISTORY MUSEUM | The history of Derry is chronicled in this tall, medieval, and magical granite tower that houses the Tower Museum. The original building was constructed in 1615 by the O'Dohertys for their overlords, the O'Donnells, in lieu of tax payments. The museum has excellent information celebrating the life and legacy of St. Columba, with a Discovery Zone on the first floor. The vivid *Story of Derry*, which includes a 15-minute film, covers the city's history, from its origins as a monastic settlement in an oak grove up to the Troubles, which began in 1969 after years of institutionalized discrimination in jobs and public housing. There's also an exhibition—spread over four floors—on the Spanish Armada, thanks to the fact that its fourth-largest ship, *La Trinidad Valencera*, foundered in Kinnagoe Bay, in County Donegal, in 1588.

■ TIP→ **If you have already been on an official guided walking tour of the city walls, then you are eligible for a reduced admission fee of £1 to visit the museum.** ✉ *Union Hall Pl., West Bank* ☎ *028/7137–2411* 🌐 *www.derrystrabane.com/towermuseum* 🎫 *£4.*

Verbal Arts Centre

ARTS CENTER | You might expect to see it in Dublin, but the complete manuscript of James Joyce's *Ulysses* has been handwritten on the walls of the Verbal Arts Centre by Colin Dark. You don't, of course, have time to read all of it, but while you're here, admire the marble floor designed by celebrated Irish artist Louis le Brocquy. The center is a hotbed of literary activity promoting the spoken and written word, and presents storytelling re-created in the old Irish tradition of fireside tales. ✉ *Stable La. and Mall Wall, Bishop St., West Bank* ☎ *028/7126–6946* 🌐 *theverbal.co.*

Restaurants

Badger's

$ | IRISH | The famous *Derry Girls* mural adorns one outside wall of this old-school tavern. Inside, wood-paneled walls are covered with photos of local sporting legends. **Known for:** traditional Irish pub decorations; Sunday roast dinners; Guinness pints. 💲 *Average main: £13* ✉ *18 Orchard St., Central District* ☎ *028/7136–3306.*

Browns in Town

$ | IRISH | The owner, Ian Orr, a former maestro chef who has handed over the cooking to others, has put Derry on the culinary map. Candles on tables and leather-upholstered horseshoe booths with calming cream and brown timber shades set a stylish scene, where the three-course dinner menu at £35 is a hit. **Known for:** Greencastle seafood chowder; pressed beef with buttered greens and celeriac remoulade; sugar pit pork. 💲 *Average main: £18* ✉ *23 Strand Rd., Central District* ☎ *028/7136–2889* 🌐 *www.brownsintown.com.*

Claudes Cafe

$ | CAFÉ | "Say nothin' till ye see Claude," was a famous old Derry saying in the days when Claude Wilton, a solicitor and civil rights campaigner represented all classes and creeds. Although he died in 2008, his name lives on on T-shirts and in this central, bike-theme café. **Known for:** full Irish breakfast; freshly roasted Segafredo coffee; homemade Irish stew. 💲 *Average main: £7* ✉ *4 Shipquay St., Central District* ☎ *028/7127–9379* 🌐 *www.claudescafe.com* 🕑 *Closed Sun. No dinner.*

Fitzroy's

$ | EUROPEAN | FAMILY | Great-value portions of burgers, steaks, lamb shank, fish, and Caesar salads are dinner favorites at this popular city-center brasserie that has chalked up over a quarter century satisfying the Derry palate—it's rumored that the first cappuccino in the city was served here. The lunch dishes may include seafood chowder or the delectable chicken melter, made up of cheese, tobacco onions, and bacon with Mexican spices. **Known for:** firecracker burgers; king prawn linguine; thyme and mushroom risotto. 💲 *Average main: £13* ✉ *2–4 Bridge St., Central District* ☎ *028/7126–6211* 🌐 *www.fitzroysrestaurant.com.*

The House Restaurant

$ | EUROPEAN | A duo of dining experiences is reflected in different rooms at this refashioned old waterfront building, which was once Derry's Custom House where taxes were collected from ships arriving at the port. Beef, chicken, and fish dominate the main restaurant, Entrada, where you can also enjoy snacks such as meatballs, salted cod fritters, or cured meats and cheeses. **Known for:** variety of options; sirloin steaks; classic cocktails. *Average main: £17* *Custom House St., Queen's Quay, Central District* *028/7137–3366* *www.thehousederry.com* *Closed Mon.*

★ Primrose on the Quay

$ | **MODERN IRISH** | Part restaurant and café, part cocktail bar, part French-style patisserie, Primrose overlooks the Quay and is all raves from Derry foodies. Main courses may include roasted cod loin with parsnips and butter sauce, bacon loin with choucroute, pulled pork, or haddock with buttermilk batter, best washed down with local craft beers such as Northbound's Oak Smoked Beer from their Campsie brewery near Derry. **Known for:** roasted cod loin; lemon meringue pie; sensational pastries and tarts made from scratch. *Average main: £14* *2 Atlantic Quay, Beech Hill* *028/7136–5511.*

★ Pyke 'N' Pommes

$ | **IRISH** | Starting life as a street food truck, PNP is now a full-service restaurant (with a liquor license) but is still serving up its authentic street-food dishes such as Legenderry, Veganderry, and jalapeño burgers. Long bare bulbs hang over rough-hewn tables made with thick wooden scaffold planks and 1960s reclaimed school chairs. **Known for:** classic street-style burgers; squid tacos; charcoal-grilled whole fish. *Average main: £7* *57 Strand Rd., West Bank* *028/7167–2691* *www.pykenpommes.ie* *Closed Mon. and Tues.*

Thompson's Restaurant

$ | **IRISH** | On the banks of the River Foyle, this airy and cool main restaurant of the City Hotel, taking its name from the old Thompson's Mill that once occupied this site, is a fine place to chill while taking in some great river views. The menu might include pork belly, oven-baked salmon, or chicken supreme with an herb stuffing. **Known for:** delicious chicken supreme; impressive, inexpensive wine list; river views. *Average main: £15* *City Hotel on Queen's Quay, Central District* *028/7136–5800* *www.cityhotelderry.com* *No lunch Mon.–Sat.*

Coffee and Quick Bites

Joe Jackson's Ice Cream Parlour and Café

$ | **ICE CREAM** | **FAMILY** | If you feel like a treat, several dozen colorful flavors of ice cream including chocolate, honeycomb, mint, and Ferrero Rocher are available at Joe Jackon's bustling city center café. Belgian waffles, crepes, muffins, apple tart, and other snacks are served during the day along with shakes, smoothies, or sundaes such as the Shoeless Joe or MoJoe. **Known for:** delicious ice-cream range; waffles and crepes; novel vegan and vegetarian offerings. *Average main: £5* *15 Ferryquay St., West Bank* *100 meters from the Diamond* *028/7135–7135.*

Hotels

★ Bishop's Gate Hotel

$$$ | **HOTEL** | Restored from a historic city-center building that was once a gentleman's club, Bishop's Gate Hotel has kept its Edwardian craftsmanship and original architectural details but the plush rooms with velvet furnishings are all fit for the 21st century; just for fun, the guest rooms have retained their antique telephones with rotary dials—and yes, they do work. **Pros:** elegant restoration; central location; valet parking available. **Cons:** surrounding streets can be noisy at night; short on amenities; popular with wedding parties. *Rooms from: £129* *24 Bishop St., Central District* *028/7114–0300* *www.bishopsgatehotelderry.com* *31 rooms* *Free Breakfast.*

Maldron Hotel

$$ | **HOTEL** | A long-established hotel within the historic walls, the Maldron is ideally suited for exploration of the city center and for guided walking tours. **Pros:** top-notch location for exploring Derry's

walls, sights, and shops; tastefully decorated rooms with modern facilities; lively bar. **Cons:** limited parking available; standard rooms adequate but small; few amenities. *Rooms from: £105* *Butcher St., Central District* *028/7137–1000* *www.maldronhotelderry.com* *93 rooms* *Free Breakfast.*

★ The Merchant's House

$ | **B&B/INN** | Originally a Victorian merchant's family home built to Georgian proportions, No. 16 Queen Street was then a rectory and bank, before Joan Pyne turned it into one of the city's grandest B&Bs—garnet-color walls, elaborate plasterwork, and a fireplace make the parlor warm and cheerful. **Pros:** graceful and elegant; great value; owners are knowledgeable about local sights. **Cons:** rooms next to kitchen noisy in morning; small bathrooms; no amenities. *Rooms from: £75* *16 Queen St., West Bank* *028/7126–9691* *www.thesaddlershouse.com* *8 rooms in Merchant's House; 7 rooms with shared bath in Saddler's House* *Free Breakfast.*

Shipquay Boutique Hotel

$$ | **HOTEL** | This elegant Italianate building, built in 1895 for the Provincial Bank of Ireland, has contemporary bedrooms over five floors. **Pros:** each room is unique; great value bottomless brunch; central location in Derry. **Cons:** some rooms are outdated; restaurant may feel overpriced; can get busy. *Rooms from: £105* *15–17 Shipquay St., Central District* *028/7126–7266* *www.shipquayhotel.com* *21 rooms* *Free Breakfast.*

Nightlife

Peadar O'Donnell's Bar

BARS | Traditional Irish and folk music sessions are held most nights in the main downstairs bar. There's a different musical personality in the nightclub Gweedore Upstairs, where you're likely to hear everything from indie and house music to rock and chart disco. *59–63 Waterloo St., West Bank* *028/7126–7295.*

Tinney's Bar

BARS | A quintessential slice of city life, Tinney's is one of Derry's oldest bars and a family-owned business that can trace its pedigree back to 1847. Drop in to hear some Derry-speak (the "barrs" is a local term for gossip) where conviviality is the theme. Warm yourself at the glowing open fire with a pint of stout, sometimes humorously referred to as "soup of the day." An upstairs room focuses on the city's shirt factory heritage with a display of mounted photographs and Singer sewing machines repurposed as pub tables. Each Tuesday the venue hosts Irish traditional musicians, including gigs by the renowned Foyle Folk Club and popular storytelling sessions. *4 Patrick St., Central District* *Just off Strand Rd.* *028/7136–2091.*

Trinity

LIVE MUSIC | Derry's newest nightspot is over-the-top decadent, with thronelike gilt mock Louis Quinze chairs, ornate stucco ceilings, chandeliers, and a lengthy cocktail list. It's favored by a young and flashily dressed clientele on Friday and Saturday nights; "jazz, booze and blues" on Saturday afternoons appeals to a slightly more mature audience. *24 Strand St., Central District* *028/7127–6610.*

Performing Arts

If there's one thing about Derry, it certainly knows how to throw a good party. A maelstrom of creative energy was released by the city's role in 2013 as the U.K. City of Culture, and through that cultural transformation the city strengthened its musical mojo. Long celebrated as a place of music, Derry has always expressed its soul in words and songs. Phil Coulter, its most famous musical son, wrote "Ireland's Call," the politically neutral anthem played at Irish rugby, cricket, and hockey internationals, and composed a new song, "Bright, Brand New Day," to celebrate the cultural year. Other famed musical offspring of the city include Feargal Sharkey and his band the Undertones, and Nadine Coyle from Girls Aloud.

Music festivals take pride of place in the annual calendar of events. During the City of Derry Big Band Jazz Festival in May, it's a case of boogie all over town: R&B, swing, jive, soul, and blues singers, as well as tribute acts, take over bars, cafés, hotels, restaurants, and community centers. Music also tops the bill at the Foyle Folk Festival, the Walled City Music Festival, and the Maiden City Festival. Literature, drama, and film are all given prominence throughout the year. During the last week of July the Foyle Maritime Festival features keynote events, live performances, food trails, and visiting ships (🌐 *www.foylemaritime.com*). For one week in mid-August the Foyle Pride Festival celebrates diversity and equality hosting a wide range of cultural activities including films, plays, storytelling, and lectures. Organizers create a Pink Mile of bars and cafés recommended as fun spaces for Pride regulars and visitors. On October 31, the Banks of the Foyle Halloween Carnival morphs into what the tourism bureau calls "the largest street party in Ireland." As part of the Halloween season, the Legenderry Food Trail has been embraced in cafés, restaurants, and bars on both sides of the River Foyle with chefs inviting visitors to sample a range of bespoke dishes (🌐 *www.legenderry-food.com*). The city has also reinvented itself with cultural centers and new galleries sprouting up—excellent places for visual snacking.

Millennium Forum

CONCERTS | This catchall venue hosts everything from boy bands and comedians to plays, musicals, tattoo conventions, and even weddings (invitations required). The Arbutus at the Forum restaurant on the ground floor offers discounts on show nights and snacks during the day from noon. ✉ *Newmarket St., West Bank* ☎ *028/7126–4455* 🌐 *www.millenniumforum.co.uk.*

Playhouse

THEATER | With its impressive auditorium and workshop spaces, the Playhouse stages traditional and contemporary plays and holds concerts. ✉ *5–7 Artillery St., West Bank* ☎ *028/7126–8027* 🌐 *www.derryplayhouse.co.uk.*

Shopping

Although the major retail department stores are here, shopping is generally low-key. There are some upscale examples of Irish craftsmanship to be found, however. Stroll up Shipquay Street to discover small arts-and-crafts stores and an indoor shopping center. Walk through the Craft Village (just off Shipquay Street or via Magazine Street) to see the way the city used to look. The Village, with its glass canopy, re-creates life between the 16th and 19th centuries and sells Derry crystal, handwoven cloth, ceramics, jewelry, and books. The Cottage, a beautiful thatched and whitewashed building in the heart of the Village, serves delectable sweet and savory crepes while the new Soda and Starch pantry and grill specializes in local and seasonal produce all from within a 40-mile radius. More details of the Village can be found at 🌐 *www.derrycraftvillage.com.* At the Shipquay Street entrance to the Village look out for two huge comic book–style murals, *Factory Girls,* on the walls. These paintings celebrate the legacy of the women who worked in the once-thriving shirt-making factories that developed in the late 19th century. At one time more than 40 factories, almost exclusively employing women, were found all over the city—one of the few remaining ones closed in 2019. Not to be outdone by Belfast, Derry has set up its own Cathedral Quarter. In the heart of the old city, streets leading from the cathedral—Pump Street,

Artillery Street, and Bishop Street—are busy with craft workers, goldsmiths, and jewelers; art galleries sit cheek by jowl with nail bars, solariums, and treatment spas. Bedlam, a maze of rooms on Bishop Street, is a humming nest of traders under one roof. Vintage clothes, antiques, retro furnishings, and New Age products are on sale.

To appreciate the beauty and scale of the area's Georgian architecture, walk slowly along Pump Street, with a copy of *City of Derry,* an excellent historical gazetteer to the built heritage—it has a wealth of information and color about each individual building. As you wander around the streets, look out for the Golden Teapot—a 19th-century trade sign in the shape of a gilded copper teapot—restored and hanging outside Faller's jewelers on Strand Road; catch the right moment and a plume of environmentally friendly smoke is discharged from its spout. The only other one in the world is in Boston.

BOOKS

Foyle Books

BOOKS | Derry's largest selection of secondhand and antiquarian titles can be found here. The specialties include English lit, Irish-language books, criticism, poetry, biography, local history, heritage and culture, travel, music, and sports. For further browsing check the website, where it is known as Walled City Books accessible through the Abe Books site. ✉ *12 Magazine St., West Bank* ☎ *028/7137–2530* 🌐 *walledcitybooks.com.*

CRAFTS, GIFTS, AND JEWELRY

Faller The Jeweller

JEWELRY & WATCHES | It's worth calling in to hear the history of the restored Victorian golden teapot hanging outside this long-established family-run shop. Faller's specializes in brooches and icons, reflecting local landmarks in its Drop of Derry range; you can even buy a small replica of the famed teapot. The city's cultural history, music, and sporting life are featured in designs as well as Roaring Meg cannon, the Peace Bridge, Guildhall, Heart of Derry, and city walls. Even more popular are the High Crosses of Inishowen in nearby Donegal; ancient Celtic crosses such as St. Mura, Donagh, and Cooley are all available as pendants or rings. ✉ *12 Strand Rd., West Bank* ☎ *028/7136–2710* 🌐 *www.faller.com.*

Smart Swag

SOUVENIRS | As you walk through the front door of this gift shop and studio—hidden halfway down a narrow street—a rich aroma of soy candles and sacred tree incense envelops you. Bespoke jewelry made from vintage elements, lovingly handcrafted gifts, and screen-printed T-shirts sit alongside *Derry Girls* mugs (£10) and digitally designed fun postcards of the city with artwork by local illustrator Domnáll Starkie. The downstairs room is crammed with retro furniture and upcycled antiques. ✉ *12 London St., Central District* ✥ *Shop is along the side of Bishop's Gate Hotel* ☎ *077/5154–0703* ⏲ *Closed Sun. and Mon.*

Thomas the Goldsmith

JEWELRY & WATCHES | Head here for exquisite work by Irish and U.K. jewelry designers. Ask about their Peace Bridge Collection, handcrafted and individually designed in the workshop, which includes pendants, brooches, bracelets, and cuff links. ✉ *7 Pump St., West Bank* ☎ *028/7137–4549* 🌐 *www.thomasgoldsmiths.com.*

Tyrone

55 km (34 miles) south of Derry.

Omagh, the county town of Tyrone, lies close to the Sperrin Mountains, with the River Strule to the north. Aside from Omagh, County Tyrone, which is the biggest in Northern Ireland, takes in the towns of Strabane, Dungannon, and Cookstown, and pretty Clogher Valley towns in the south of the county. The playwright Brian Friel was born in Omagh and the novelist and short story writer Ben Kiely was brought up in the town. Sadly, it's better known as the scene of the worst atrocity of the Troubles, when an IRA bomb killed 31 people in 1998. On the 10th anniversary of the bombing, the **Garden of Light,** a touching memorial by artist Sean Hillen and landscape architect Desmond Fitzgerald, was opened. A heliostatic mirror in the memorial park tracks the sun and directs a beam of light onto 31 small mirrors, each etched with the name of a victim. They in turn bounce the light via another hidden mirror onto a heart-shape crystal in an obelisk at the bomb site in Market Street. An entire room in Omagh Library, housing more than 800 books of condolence and reflecting worldwide media coverage, is dedicated to the memory of the attack. Ask about access to this archive at the tourist office, which is in the Strule Arts Centre, a good place for a relaxing snack or meal, and where you may also find out about any events or shows being held. Pick up a voucher booklet, Explore Omagh, which offers discounts in many shops and restaurants, as well as two-for-one entrance deals to the Ulster American Folk Park (🌐 *www.exploreomaghsperrins.com*). Midway between Omagh and Cookstown, at the other end of the Sperrins, is the new OM Dark Sky Observatory. The center, in Davagh Forest, is also linked to an ancient stone circle in the mountainy bog northwest of Cookstown.

GETTING HERE

The Translink Goldline service operates buses between Derry and Belfast and traverses delightfully mellifluous-sounding Tyrone towns, from Strabane to Ballygawley, and thence along the M1 into Belfast. Journey time is just under two hours (£19.50 round-trip, or £13 after 9:30 am). Services in both directions stop on request at the popular Ulster American Folk Park.

Omagh, 55 km (34 miles) south of Derry on A5, is a busy hub. Free parking on the town's two main central streets, High and Market, is available for one hour. Pay-and-display ticket machines, costing £0.40 per hour, operate in car parks at Mountjoy Road (beside the bus station) and Kevlin Avenue. You can also park free for two hours in the retail park at the Showgrounds, on Sedan Avenue.

Sights

OM Dark Sky Observatory

OBSERVATORY | Deep in the wild Sperrin Mountains of Tyrone, a lack of light pollution allows for astonishing views of the night sky and creates an ideal location for seeing crystal-clear star constellations. Northern Ireland's first dark-sky observatory opened in Davagh Forest in the foothills of the mountains in 2020. The new center houses a retractable roof, observatory, and telescope showcasing the dark-sky site, combining technology from holographic installations to virtual reality headsets and interpretation panels so you can explore the solar system. On a cloud-free night, you may be lucky enough to see the Milky Way, the Perseid meteor shower (if here in August), or deep-sky objects such as the Pleiades, the Orion Nebula, and depending on conditions, the northern lights.

TIP→ Without your own transport, a taxi from Cookstown is the only way to reach the site and costs around £20. ✉ *Davagh Forest, Omagh* ✣ *Located 24 km (15 miles) northwest of Cookstown signposted off the main A505 Cookstown to Omagh Rd.* ☎ *028/8876–0681* 🌐 *www.omdarksky.com* 🎫 *£5.*

★ Ulster American Folk Park

HISTORIC SIGHT | The excellent Ulster American Folk Park re-creates a Tyrone village of two centuries ago, a log-built American settlement of the same period, and the docks and ships that the emigrants to America would have used. The centerpiece is an old whitewashed cottage, now a museum, which is the ancestral home of Thomas Mellon (1813–1908), the U.S. banker and philanthropist. Another thatch cottage is a reconstruction of the boyhood home of Archbishop John Hughes, founder of New York's St. Patrick's Cathedral. There are full-scale replicas of Irish peasant cottages, a New York tenement room, immigrant transport ship holders, and a 19th-century Ulster village, complete with staff dressed in period costumes. It's a good idea to prebook a slot for your visit (online or by phone).

Within the Ulster American Folk Park, the Mellon Centre for Migration Studies contains 16,000 books and periodicals, an Irish emigration database including passenger lists from 1800 to 1860, emigrant letters, and maps of geographical regions of both Ireland and America. Other notable exhibits include William Murray's drapery store and W.G. O'Doherty's original candy store on the bustling Ulster Street, where visitors can explore the world of retail therapy in the early 1900s. ✉ *Mellon Rd., Castletown, 10 km (6 miles) north of Omagh on A5, Omagh* ☎ *028/8225–6315* 🌐 *www.ulsteramericanfolkpark.org; www.mellonmigrationcentre.com* 🎟 *£10* 🕒 *Closed Mon. Sept.–June; Mellon Centre closed Sun. and Mon.*

Fermanagh

42 km (25 miles) southwest of Omagh.

Enniskillen is the pleasant, smart-looking capital of County Fermanagh and the only place of any size in it. The town center is, strikingly, on an island in the River Erne between Lower and Upper Lough Erne. The principal thoroughfares, Townhall and High Streets, are crowded with old-style pubs, family-run shops, and rows of red-brick Georgian flats. The tall, dark spires of the 19th-century St. Michael's and St. Macartin's Cathedrals, both on Church Street, tower over the leafy town center. World-famous Belleek Pottery is made in the old town of Belleek, on the northwestern edge of Lower Lough Erne, at the border with Northwest Ireland. Other porcelain-ware makers are a couple of miles across the border.

GETTING HERE AND AROUND

Translink's Goldline express buses connect Enniskillen with Belfast, 145 km (90 miles) east. Buses run from early morning to late evening, with a two-hour journey time (£19.50 round-trip, £13 after 9:30 am). Enniskillen also has a slew of cross-border services in many directions. Bus Éireann operates expressway routes west to Sligo.

Enniskillen is 85 km (52 miles) south of Derry on the A32 and A5. The town has many car parks, including ones at East Bridge, Eden, Market, and Townhall Streets. Be warned: parking attendants clamp down on all drivers lacking a ticket for the required duration of their stay. On the street there are few free spaces, so be careful where you park.

Belleek is on the A46, a scenic route running along the southern shore of Lower Lough Erne between Enniskillen (a 30-minute drive), in County Fermanagh, and Ballyshannon (15 minutes), in County Donegal. There is ample car parking at the pottery factory—the reason most people come here—with no time restrictions. You can also park free along main or side streets.

VISITOR INFORMATION

Enniskillen Castle Visitor Information and Museum

VISITOR INFORMATION | Your first stop should be the tourist information office on Wellington Road—based at Castlebarracks—for an excellent array of leaflets, maps, and guidebooks. Pick up brochures on History and Heritage Trails, Natural Heritage Trails, and shopping

Beautiful Belleek

The origins of Belleek china are every bit as romantic as the Belleek blessing plates traditionally given to brides and grooms on their wedding day—that is, if you believe the legends. The story goes that in the mid-1800s, John Caldwell Bloomfield, the man behind the world-famous porcelain, accidentally discovered the raw ingredients necessary to produce china. After inheriting his father's estate in the Fermanagh Lakelands on the shore of the Erne River, he whitewashed his cottage using a flaky white powder dug up in his backyard. A passerby, struck by the luminescent sheen of the freshly painted cottage, commented on the unusual brightness of the walls to Bloomfield, who promptly ordered a survey of the land, which duly uncovered all the minerals needed to make porcelain. The venture was complete when Bloomfield met his business partners, London architect Robert Armstrong and wealthy Dublin merchant David McBirney. They decided to first produce earthenware, and then porcelain. The rest, as they say, is history. The delicate, flawless porcelain (Bloomfield declared that any piece with even the slightest blemish should be destroyed) soon attracted the attention of Queen Victoria and other aristocrats. Other companies tried to mimic the china's delicate beauty, but genuine Belleek porcelain is recognizable by its seashell designs, basket weaves, and marine themes. It has become a favored tradition in Ireland to give a piece of Belleek china at weddings, giving rise to a saying: "If a newly married couple receives a piece of Belleek, their marriage will be blessed with lasting happiness."

and arts and crafts throughout County Fermanagh.

The Fermanagh Genealogy Centre is also based in this building and assists visitors in finding their family history connections in Fermanagh by providing a free 30-minute consultation. The center is open for appointments on Monday, Wednesday, and Thursday afternoon 2–5. ✉ *Castlebarracks, Wellington Rd., Enniskillen* ☎ *028/6632–5000* 🌐 *www.enniskillencastle.co.uk.*

TOURS

Erne Tours

BOAT TOURS | Fancy a dreamy boat tour on Lough Erne? This company operates tours, about 100 minutes long on the lower lough, aboard the *Kestrel,* a 56-seat water bus. The boat leaves from Round O Pier at Enniskillen. Each day it stops for 45 minutes at Devenish Island. From early July to the end of August, the company also has an Island Town Dinner and Cruise (£27) departing at 4 pm and combining a two-hour cruise with dinner at The Firehouse tapas restaurant, Grove's Nest gastropub, or the Westville Hotel. ✉ *Round O Pier, Enniskillen* ☎ *028/6632–2882* 🌐 *www.ernetours.com* 🎫 *100-min tour £10; private cruises from £100 for group of 8.*

Erne Water Taxi

BOAT TOURS | Barry Flanagan's boat tours are one of the most popular ways of exploring Devenish Island, which boasts Ireland's best example of a Round Tower dating from the 12th century. His new Islander Pass tour, running from April to September, takes one hour, 45 minutes and operates four times a day in the spring and summer: 11 am, 1 pm, 3 pm, and 5 pm. The boat departs from Enniskillen jetty and the price of £20 includes the tour and free entry to Enniskillen Castle followed by tea or coffee and a scone. The company also runs private tours of Lough Erne with prices starting from £100 for a group of eight. In 2021, the company added an environmentally friendly all-electric boat, *Island Discover*, to its fleet, along with themed tours such as a "whiskey and blues" cruise. Check the website for details of these tours, which must be booked in advance. ✉ *Enniskillen jetty, Enniskillen* ☎ *077/1977–0588* 🌐 *www.ernewatertaxi.com.*

Sights

★ Belleek Pottery

FACTORY | On the riverbank stands the visitor center of Belleek Pottery Ltd., producers of Parian china; a fine, eggshell-thin, ivory porcelain shaped into dishes, figurines, vases, and baskets. There's a factory, showroom, exhibition, museum, and café. You can watch a 20-minute audiovisual presentation or join a 30-minute tour of the factory, where you can get up close and talk to craftspeople—there's hardly any noise coming from machinery in the workshops. Everything here is made by hand just as workers did back in 1857. The showroom is filled with beautiful but pricey gifts. ✉ *3 Main St., Belleek* ☎ *028/6865–8501* 🌐 *www.belleek.ie* 🎟 *£6 for tour.*

Blakes of the Hollow

RESTAURANT | Among the several relaxed and welcoming old pubs in Enniskillen's town center, the one with the most appeal is Blakes, a place hardly altered since it opened in 1887. Its name derives from the fact that the heart of the town lies in a slight hollow and the pub's landlord is named William Blake. Traditional music sessions are held on Friday night in the front bar, which is also the best place for local gossip and stories. If the *druth*—a local word for thirst—is on you, then it's worth trying the craft beer, Inishmacsaint, from an island in Lough Erne that reflects an ancient tradition established by monks 900 years ago; or you could try the exclusive Midleton Single Cask Irish Whiskey, 26 years in the making. Bottled exclusively for Blake's, it went on sale in 2019, although you can't buy it by the glass—only by the bottle—and for a cool £795. A cheaper option is the Midleton Very Rare 2018 produced with specially selected malt and grain whiskey and costing £15.50 a glass. The bar displays one of the doors from the *Game of Thrones* TV series filmed in parts of Northern Ireland. The door was salvaged from beech trees that came down in a storm in 2016 and were transformed into unique works of art. This one, Door 4, depicts House Targaryen's return to power. Lunch and dinner are served in the adjoining Café Merlot. ✉ *6 Church St., Enniskillen* ☎ *028/6632–0918 Cafe Merlot reservations, 028/6632–2143* 🌐 *www.blakesofthehollow.com.*

Buttermarket

STORE/MALL | More than 20 wonderful arts-and-crafts shops selling Fermanagh pottery, jewelry, and paintings are gathered at the Buttermarket, a restored dairy market built in 1835. The organically run skin-care shop, The Natural Beauty Pot, sells biodegradable products, free of artificial coloring or fragrances and not tested on animals. You can relax in the courtyard of Rebecca's coffee shop, which sells terrific tray bakes and freshly prepared lunches including homemade cottage pie and salads. ✉ *Down St., Enniskillen* ☎ *028/6632–3117* 🌐 *www.enniskillen.com.*

Castle Coole

CASTLE/PALACE | Although the Irish architect Richard Johnston made the original drawings in the 1790s, and was responsible for the foundation, the castle was, for all intents and purposes, the work of James Wyatt, commissioned by the first earl of Belmore. One of the best-known architects of his time, Wyatt was based in London but visited Ireland only once,

Off The Beaten Path

Marble Arch Caves Global Geopark. This geopark—one of Europe's finest show caves—has an interpretative center and trail walking routes in the surrounding mountainous uplands, including Cuilcagh, the highest point shared between counties Fermanagh and Cavan. The only UNESCO geopark in Northern Ireland, it's an ideal half-day underground activity, especially if it's a wet day in Fermanagh. Stalactites glisten above streams as you admire fragile mineral veils and cascades of calcite-coated walls and waterfalls. Guided boat tours, run by knowledgeable tour guides, last 75 minutes but may not be available after heavy rain. The show cave requires climbing 150 steps so it is not accessible for wheelchairs or strollers. For more information on the geological timescale of the caves and geopark ask for a free copy of the excellent color booklet *Rockin' Around the Marble Arch Caves.*

TIP→ Bring walking shoes and a warm sweater. Tours begin at Marlbank Scenic Loop Centre, Florencecourt. There are frequent events that are suitable for children, such as fossil fun days and wildlife walks—check the website for details. There's also a restaurant and souvenir shop. ✉ *43 Marlbank Rd., Legnabrocky, Florencecourt, Enniskillen* ✣ *The geopark is in south Fermanagh, 19 km (12 miles) south of Enniskillen and about 3 km (2 miles) from village of Florencecourt. It also lies 8 km (5 miles) on northern side of Irish border separating Cavan from Fermanagh* ☎ *028/6632–1815* 🌐 *www.marblearchcaves.co.uk* 🎫 *£10* ⏲ *Closed Nov.–early Mar.*

so Alexander Stewart was drafted as the resident builder–architect. The designer wasn't the only imported element; in fact, much of Castle Coole came from England, including the main facade, which is clad in Portland stone and was hauled here by bullock carts. And what a facade it is—in perfect symmetry, white colonnaded wings extend from either side of the mansion's three-story, nine-bay center block, with a Palladian central portico and pediment. It is perhaps the apotheosis of the 18th century's reverence for the Greeks.

Inside, the house is remarkably preserved; most of the lavish plasterwork and original furnishings are in place. The saloon is one of the finest rooms in the house, with a vast expanse of oak flooring, gilded Regency furniture, and gray scagliola pilasters with Corinthian capitals. One-hour tours are held daily, with the last one at 4:15 pm, and include Life Below Stairs, which explores the servants' rooms and service quarters; above stairs is the home of the present earl of Belmore, who still lives on the estate. During the day the Tallow House tearoom serves lunches and snacks.

TIP→ In the summer months, you can indulge in the Queen Anne Afternoon Tea Experience. This includes a guided tour looking deeper into the history behind the original Queen Anne site on the estate followed by afternoon tea served in the lavish Breakfast Room. It costs £20; check the website for dates and availability. ✉ *Dublin Rd., A4, Enniskillen* ☎ *028/6632–2690* 🌐 *www.nationaltrust.org.uk/castle-coole* 🎫 *House and grounds £12; grounds only £5.*

Enniskillen Castle

CASTLE/PALACE | Strategically sited overlooking the River Erne, Enniskillen's 600-year-old waterfront castle is one of the best-preserved monuments in the north, and has undergone a multimillion-pound redevelopment, which has seen the tourist office merging with the castle complex, creating a new gateway to the region. Built in the early 15th century by the Gaelic Maguires to command the waterway, the castle was of tremendous importance in guarding one of the few passes into Ulster and the crossing point between Upper and Lower Lough Erne. After a yearlong program of work costing £3.3 million, four new galleries spread over two floors are now in place in the restored barrack coach house. A new building, in the shape of the original armory, links the visitor center with the coach house, allowing tourists a glimpse of the original castle wall. The center, styling itself as a "history hub," combines tourism, genealogy, archive, and heritage services alongside a café and shop. ✉ *Castlebarracks, Wellington Rd., Enniskillen* ☎ *028/6632–5000* 🌐 *www.enniskillencastle.co.uk* 🎫 *£5.*

Enniskillen Royal Grammar School

COLLEGE | Beyond the West Bridge is Enniskillen Royal Grammar School, formerly Portora Royal School (it became co-ed in 2017), established in 1608 by King James I. On the grounds are some ruins of Portora Castle. Writers educated here included Samuel Beckett and Oscar Wilde, the pride of the school (until his trial for homosexuality). The life and writings of Beckett, the droll existentialist and arch-modernizer born near Dublin in 1906, is celebrated at the Happy Days International Beckett Festival; some festival events are held at the school, as well as other locations around Fermanagh over the bank holiday weekend at the end of August. The multidisciplinary festival incorporates literature, theater, visual arts, film, and comedy, and offers a chance to savor some of Beckett's killer lines, such as this one from *Waiting for Godot*: "Let us not then speak ill of our generation, it is not any unhappier than its predecessors." ✉ *Derrygonnelly Rd., Enniskillen* ☎ *028/6632–2658* 🌐 *www.artsoverborders.com.*

★ Florence Court

HISTORIC HOME | FAMILY | Less known than some showier estates, this three-story Anglo-Irish mansion was built around 1730 for John Cole, father of the first earl of Enniskillen. Topped off about 1760 with its distinctive two flanking colonnaded wings, the central house contains a surfeit of Palladian windows, keystones, and balustrades—thanks to, as one architectural historian put it, "the vaingloriousness of a provincial hand." Even more impressive is its bucolic, baroque setting, as the Cuilcagh Mountains form a wonderful contrast to the shimmering white-stone facade. Showstoppers in terms of design are the rococo plasterwork ceilings in the dining room; the Venetian Room; and the famous staircase—all ascribed to Robert West, one of Dublin's most famous *stuccadores* (plasterworkers). For a peek at the "downstairs" world, check out the restored kitchen and other service quarters. You can browse a gift shop and secondhand bookstore; holiday accommodations are available at the Butler's Apartment. Two greenhouses have been renovated and produce from them is available to buy in the shop and the historic 2-acre Kitchen Garden, which has been undergoing a £375,000 face-lift, is due for completion in 2022–23 when it will be returned to full horticultural production. A visitor center, opposite the walled garden, with an outdoor shop sells takeaway snacks. ✉ *11 km (7 miles) south of Enniskillen on A4 and A32, Enniskillen* ☎ *028/6634–5440* 🌐 *www.nationaltrust.org.uk/florence-court* 🎫 *£13 for house, park, and grounds.*

Water Gate

MILITARY SIGHT | At the Erne riverside, the 16th-century Water Gate, between two handsome turrets, protected the town from invading armies. The flag of St. George flies over the building, a tradition

Fabled haunt of "the little people," the stately abode of Florence Court sits in a vale reputedly populated by leprechauns and fairies.

that dates back to the 17th century, when local soldiers of the Inniskilling Regiments fought for the Protestant William of Orange against the Catholic James II. ✉ *Enniskillen.*

Restaurants

The Thatch

$ | **CAFÉ** | Housed in a lovely building dating to the 18th century, this simple café is worth a visit—not just for the excellent soups, sandwiches, baked potatoes, and similarly light fare—but also because it's the only thatch-roof establishment in the entire county. Full of locals and the sounds of easy banter, it's the perfect place to glean insider knowledge and gossip about the surrounding area. **Known for:** excellent hot and iced coffees; rustic cottage feel; homemade scones. *Average main: £10* ✉ *22 Main St., Belleek* ☎ *028/6865–8181* *No credit cards* *Closed Sun.*

Hotels

★ Lough Erne Resort

$$$ | **RESORT** | Set between two serene lakes on the small island of Ely, the manicured lawns of the Lough Erne Resort, with its backdrop of shimmering Castle Hume Lough, is a special property with a country-house feel in a mix of reconstituted sandstone and Danish timber. **Pros:** handsome rooms with great amenities; Thai spa and pool; two championship golf courses. **Cons:** luxury comes at a steep price; no loungers for swimming pool users; service slow at busy times. *Rooms from: £149* ✉ *Belleek Rd., 5 km (3 miles) north of Enniskillen, Enniskillen* ☎ *028/6632–3230* *www.lougherneresort.com* *120 rooms* *Free Breakfast.*

Activities

The Castle Basin

HIKING & WALKING | A newly opened 2-km-long (1-mile-long) walkway on the banks of the River Erne in Enniskillen is also accessible to cyclists. The Castle Basin path stretches from the back of Enniskillen Castle around the water's edge and is an ideal place for bird-watching and relaxation. Concerts and other events are held here in the summer. If you want something more energetic, then drive south of the town for approximately 30 km (19 miles) and bring your walking boots and waterproof clothing to tackle Cuilcagh (pronounced *quil*-ka) mountain, the highest point in Fermanagh. A wooden handrail and boardwalk, known as the "Stairway to Heaven," takes you right to the summit viewing platform where the scarce habitat of montane heath spreads out before you. A special area of conservation, it is home to rare mosses, lichens, and plants such as crowberry and dwarf willow. A reasonable level of fitness is required for this latter walk, which should take approximately four hours round-trip. ✉ *River Erne, Enniskillen* ✣ *Behind Enniskillen Castle* ☎ *028/6632–5000* 🌐 *www.walkni.com.*

Armagh

Armagh is 64½ km (40 miles) east of Belfast.

The spiritual capital of Ireland for 5,000 years, and the seat of both Protestant and Catholic archbishops, Armagh is the most venerated of Irish cities. St. Patrick called it "my sweet hill" and built his stone church on the hill where the Anglican cathedral now stands. On the opposite hill, the twin-spire Catholic cathedral is flanked by two large marble statues of archbishops, who look across the land. Despite the pleasing Georgian terraces around the elegant mall east of the town center, Armagh can seem drab. It suffered as a trouble spot in the sectarian conflict, though it's now the scene of some spirited and sympathetic renovation.

GETTING HERE AND AROUND

Buses link Armagh with neighboring towns as well as Belfast, an 80-minute journey. You can catch a Translink Goldline express from the Buscentre on the Lonsdale Road in Armagh (£18 round-trip, one-third discount after 9:30 am, £12). Cross-border buses also operate out of Armagh—you can hop aboard the Belfast–Galway Bus Éireann bus that runs via Athlone. Round-trip to Galway is £45.50. The Armagh–Dublin bus journey (three times each day at 8 am, noon, and 8 pm) takes 2¾ hours and costs £22.50 round-trip.

Armagh is a one-hour drive from Belfast along the A3 before joining the M1 at Portadown. Dublin is just over two hours south via Newry on the A28 and A1, before crossing the Irish border to join the motorway for the rest of your journey. There are several pay-and-display parking lots in Armagh city center. The main one is next to the tourist office, on English Street. You can also park at the mall, and there is free parking on side streets.

VISITOR INFORMATION

CONTACTS Armagh Visitor Information Centre. ✉ *40 Upper English St., Armagh* ☎ *028/3752–1800* 🌐 *www.visitarmagh.com.*

Sights

Armagh Observatory and Planetarium

OBSERVATORY | FAMILY | Displayed here in all its nickel-iron glory is Ireland's largest meteorite, an astonishing 4.5 billion years old and weighing 336 pounds. Elsewhere, find a spaceship, satellite models, a moon map on which you can walk, and the Digital Theater with Digistar 5—sit back and navigate the night sky in the company of experts. Weekend children's activities include building and launching rockets. Outside, stroll through the solar system and the Milky Way at the huge scale model of the universe.

Thackeray admired the Church of Ireland's St. Patrick's Cathedral, which, with St. Patrick's Roman Catholic Cathedral, jointly presides over Armagh.

■ **TIP→ Reduction on admission price if tickets are booked online.** ✉ *College Hill, Armagh* ☎ *028/3752–3689* 🌐 *www.armagh.space* 🎫 *£9.*

Navan Centre and Fort

HISTORIC SIGHT | FAMILY | Just outside Armagh is Ulster's Camelot—the region's ancient capital. Excavations date activity to 700 BC. Legend has it that thousands of years ago this was the site of the palace of Queen Macha; subsequent tales call it the barracks of the legendary Ulster warrior Cuchulainn and his Red Branch Knights. Remains dating from 94 BC are particularly intriguing: a great conical structure, 120 feet in diameter, was formed from five concentric circles made of 275 wooden posts, with a 276th, about 12 yards high, situated in the center. In 2020 the center underwent a modern-day rebranding making it a more immersive Iron Age Celtic experience for visitors. On arrival you are welcomed into the clan with a cleansing ceremony and purification involving smoke and fire. Traditional herb bread and mead is offered as stories of Ulster's heroes and warriors are recounted; those who feel the need may connect with the land and energy through some calming Celtic Mindfulness, all served up with music and mythology. ✉ *81 Killyleagh Rd., 3 km (2 miles) west of Armagh on A28, Armagh* ☎ *028/3752–9644* 🌐 *www.visitarmagh.com/places-to-explore/navan-centre-fort* 🎫 *Apr.–Sept. £13; Oct.–Mar. £7* ⏲ *Closed Mon.*

No. 5 Vicars' Hill

OTHER MUSEUM | In Armagh you can enjoy what they like to call a "Moth" morning, which has nothing to do with entomology but is an acronym for "Morning on the Hill." It incorporates a visit to No. 5 Vicars' Hill, now a museum with touch screens and displays of ancient coins and prints. You can see early Christian and pre-Christian artifacts and the 5th-century ogham stone (an early medieval alphabet in Irish inscription) known as the Drumconwell Stone donated to the library in 1879. There's a scale model of the old town, maps of Armagh, and records from the

Beresford Collection. For the remainder of the morning your visit may include the nearby Robinson Library (✉ *43 Abbey St.*), which contains 8,000 antiquarian books on theology, philosophy, voyages, and travel, as well as history, medicine, and law. Complete your morning by calling into St. Patrick's Church of Ireland (Anglican) Cathedral. ✉ *5 Vicars' Hill, Armagh* ✣ *Vicars' Hill is right beside St. Patrick's Church of Ireland Cathedral and close to the Robinson Library on Abbey St.* ☎ *028/3751–1420* 🌐 *www.armagh-robinsonlibrary.co.uk* 🎫 *Free, tours £3 per venue* ☞ *No. 5 is open by appointment only.*

St. Patrick's Anglican Cathedral

CHURCH | Near the city center, a squat battlement tower identifies the cathedral, in simple, early-19th-century low-Gothic style. On the site of much older churches, it contains relics of Armagh's long history. Brian Boru, the High King (King of All Ireland) is buried here. In 1014, he drove the Vikings out of Ireland but was killed after the battle was won. Some memorials and tombs here are by important 18th-century sculptors such as Roubiliac and Rysbrack. The cathedral's atmospheric crypt is also open to visitors by prior arrangement. Dating from the Middle Ages, this sanctuary was where law-abiding citizens safely stored their valuable goods. A few archbishops are buried here, too. And because of its position on a hilltop there are superb views of Armagh city and the surrounding countryside. ✉ *43 Abbey St., Cathedral Close* ☎ *028/3752–3142* 🌐 *www.stpatricks-cathedral.org* 🎫 *£4.*

St. Patrick's Roman Catholic Cathedral

CHURCH | The pale limestone St. Patrick's, the seat of a Roman Catholic archdiocese, rises above a hill to dominate the north end of Armagh. The cathedral's rather gloomy interior is enlivened by a magnificent organ, the potential of which is fully realized at services. Construction of the twin-spire structure started in 1840 in the neo-Gothic style, but the Great Famine brought work to a halt until 1854, and it wasn't completed until 1873. An arcade of statues over the main doorway on the exterior is one of the cathedral's most interesting features. The altar is solid Irish granite, and the woodwork is Austrian oak. ✉ *Cathedral Rd., Armagh* ☎ *028/3752–2813* 🌐 *www.armagharchdiocese.org/st-patricks-cathedral* 🎫 *Self-guided tours £2.*

County Down

52½ km (32½ miles) southeast of Armagh on A28, 51 km (32 miles) south of Belfast.

County Down has a connection to the patron saint in Downpatrick, one of his disputed burial places. It is a landscape of drumlins (little hills), interspersed with farms and quiet boreens or *loanen* (laneways) as they're known here, stretching from the Mourne Mountains in the southern region, north to the serenity of the winding shores of Strangford Lough and the Ards peninsula sheltered by bays and creeks. The county boasts several historic houses open to the public such as the stately Mount Stewart and the Neoclassical Castle Ward (both run by the National Trust conservation group), the elegant Montalto Estate and grounds, and Ireland's only royal residence, the exquisite Georgian Hillsborough Castle. The Ulster Folk and Transport Museum at Cultra, near Holywood, showcases the social history of Northern Irish life.

Downpatrick once was called plain and simple "Down" but had its name changed by John de Courcy, a Norman knight who moved here in 1176. De Courcy set about promoting St. Patrick, the 5th-century Briton who was captured by the Irish and served as a slave in the Down area before escaping to France, where he learned about Christianity and bravely returned to try to convert the

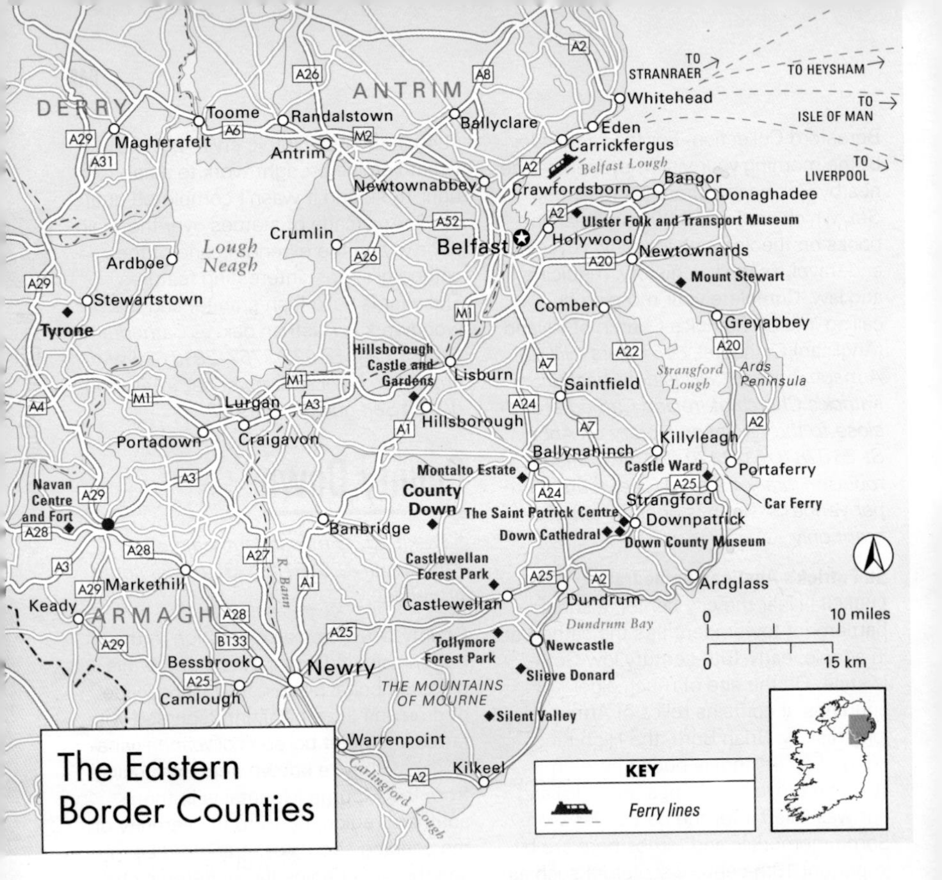

local chiefs. Although it's not true that Patrick brought a new faith to Ireland—there was already a bishop of Ireland before Patrick got here—he must have been a better missionary than most because he did indeed win influential converts. The clan chief of the Down area gave him land at the village of Saul, near Downpatrick, to build a monastery. You could happily spend a morning here visiting a trio of top-class sites: Down Cathedral, Down County Museum (now housing the ancient High Cross of Down), and the Saint Patrick Centre are all clustered within a few minutes' walk of each other.

GETTING HERE AND AROUND

Buses arrive at the main station in Downpatrick from many points of County Down and beyond. Frequent Translink Goldline express services 515 and 215 run to and from Belfast. The journey time is one hour (£13.20 round-trip). Some services link up with the Belfast Metro network of suburban routes. To visit Strangford, there are daily services from Downpatrick (£13.50 round-trip); to visit Castle Ward, ask the driver to stop by the roadside.

Downpatrick is 21 km (14 miles) east of Newcastle on the A2 and A25 and 30 km (22 miles) south of Belfast on the A24. On-street parking is free but restricted to either 30 or 60 minutes. The car park at the Grove shopping center is pay-and-display and costs £0.40 per hour. There is free parking on English and Market Streets and beside the bus station.

VISITOR INFORMATION

CONTACTS Downpatrick Visitor Information Centre. ✉ *53A Market St., Downpatrick* ☎ *028/4461–9000* 🌐 *www.visitmournemountains.co.uk.*

★ Castle Ward

CASTLE/PALACE | With a 500-acre park, an artificial lake, a Neoclassical temple, and a vast house in Bath stone magically set on the slopes running down to the Narrows of the southern shore of Strangford Lough, Castle Ward must have been some place to call home. About 3 km (2 miles) from the village of Strangford, off the road to Downpatrick, this regal stately home was designed around 1760 in, rather famously, two differing styles. Bernard Ward, first Viscount Bangor, could rarely see eye to eye (gossip had it) with his wife, Lady Anne, and the result was that he decided to make the entrance and salons elegant exercises in Palladian Neoclassicism, while milady transformed the garden facade and her own rooms using the most fashionable style of the day, Strawberry Hill Gothic. His white-and-beige Music Room is picked out in exquisite plasterwork, while her Boudoir has an undulating fan-vaulted ceiling that conjures up the "gothick" medievalisms of King Henry VII's chapel at Westminster. Tours are held every hour.

■ TIP→ There are walking and cycling trails of the grounds from where you can look out over the lough shore and see the location of Winterfell used for the TV series *Game of Thrones*.

In the spring and summer months sea safaris, as well as high tea and sea voyages around Strangford Lough, are organized at Castle Ward and leave from the pier at Strangford; these should be booked directly through Clear Sky Adventures (🌐 *www.clearsky-adventure.com*). ✉ *3 km (2 miles) west of Strangford on Downpatrick Rd. (A25), Downpatrick* ☎ *028/4488–1204* 🌐 *www.nationaltrust.org.uk/castle-ward* 🎫 *£11.*

Castlewellan Forest Park

FOREST | A huge maze, grown to symbolize Northern Ireland's convoluted path to peace, comprises 1,150 acres of forested hills running between the Mourne Mountains and Slieve Croob. There are also signposted mountain-biking trails, ranging from short routes of 4 km (2½ miles) up to 19 km (12 miles), and 7½ km (5 miles) of walking trails. Look out for the multi-stemmed sequoia, a giant redwood in the walled garden dating from the 1850s, which, in 2018, was named as Northern Ireland's Tree of the Year by the Woodland Trust, a conservation charity. With the maze, lake, secluded arbors, and arboretum, the park makes an excellent introduction to the area. Bike and canoe rental is available at the center starting from £29 for three hours. ✉ *Castlewellan* ☎ *033/0137–4046* 🌐 *www.thegreatadventure.com* 🎫 *Free, vehicles £5.*

Down Cathedral

CHURCH | The Cathedral of the Holy Trinity, or Down Cathedral as it's commonly known, is one of the disputed burial places of St. Patrick. In the churchyard, a somber flat stone slab inscribed "Patric" is supposedly the saint's tomb. It might be here, at Saul, or, some scholars argue, more likely at Armagh. The stone was quarried in 1990 at Slieve-na-Largie near Castlewellan and took 12 men 14 days to cut from the quarry. The church, which lay ruined from 1538 to 1790 (it reopened in 1818), preserves parts of some of the earlier churches and monasteries that have stood on this site, the oldest of which dates to the 6th century. Even by then, the cathedral site had long been an important fortified settlement: Down takes its name from the Celtic word *dun*, or fort. Information panels tell the history of the building through a timeline, showing the connection with St. Patrick, and give details on the war memorials. In the summer of 2018 a replica of St. Patrick's Cross was installed in the grounds of the cathedral, just yards from where he is said to be buried. The reproduction, sculpted from Mourne granite, is on the Hill of Down where the original cross once stood. There's also a shop selling souvenirs. Entry is free but if you would like a guided 30-minute tour (which must be booked in advance) it costs £2. ✉ *35 English St., Downpatrick* ☎ *028/4461–4922* 🌐 *www.downcathedral.org* 🎫 *Free entry, £2 for guided tour.*

★ **Down County Museum**

OTHER MUSEUM | With the transfer of the 1,100-year-old Mourne granite High Cross as the centerpiece of an elaborate extension, this museum, housed in an 18th-century jail, has gained serious cachet. The Downpatrick High Cross had stood in front of nearby Down Cathedral since the late 19th century, but had suffered deterioration through weather damage—never mind the Viking pillagers—and has been moved permanently indoors. The original location of the intricately patterned cross, carved around AD 900 as a "prayer in stone," is believed to have been the early medieval monastery on the Hill of Down. The extension houses a display, *Raising the Cross in Down,* alongside two new galleries reflecting the maritime and agricultural history of the area. Elsewhere, look into the small cells in the jail along a narrow whitewashed corridor. The other main exhibition is *Down through Time,* while frequent photographic exhibitions and artwork are on display in other rooms. Behind the building, a short signposted trail leads to an example of a Norman motte and bailey known as the Mound of Down or "Dundalethglas." A large egg-shape enclosure, this is one of Northern Ireland's most impressive earthen fortifications and may have been a royal stronghold of the Dál Fiatach, the dynasty that ruled this part of County Down in the first millennium AD. The Cathedral View Tearoom serves homemade lunches and snacks. ✉ *The Mall, English St., Downpatrick* ☎ *033/0137–4049* 🌐 *www.downcountymuseum.com* 🎫 *Free.*

★ **Hillsborough Castle and Gardens**

CASTLE/PALACE | This Georgian palace—the only royal residence in Ireland and for 50 years the official home of the governor of Northern Ireland—opened its doors to the public for the first time in 2015, and has since become a leading attraction involving a £24 million investment. It was built in the 1770s by Wills Hill, the first marquess of Downshire, Ireland's largest landowner and secretary of the American colonies. Benjamin Franklin's five-day stay here is said to have contributed directly to the American War of Independence, such was the animosity between Franklin and Hill. Other visits included that of President George W. Bush and the historic meeting in 2005 between the Queen and Mary McAleese, then president of Ireland. The building was the location for talks during the 1985 Anglo-Irish Agreement and the more recent Northern Ireland peace process and is the current home of the secretary of state for Northern Ireland. On busy days up to four guided 45-minute castle tours are held hourly from 10 am to 4 pm. Visitors are brought through eight elegant state rooms, still used by the royal family, including the throne room, which comes with three magnificent Dublin teardrop crystal chandeliers and graceful drawing room where paintings from Irish artists including Derek Hill, James Dixon, David Crone, and Gareth Reid are on display. A highlight of the red room is 40 Henry Bone miniature portraits of sovereigns and their consorts; these small, exquisite, enamel-on-copper paintings were commissioned by Prince Albert in 1843. Look out, too, for impressive royal portraits and paintings by old masters such as Gainsborough and Van Dyck. Separate guided tours focusing on art, politics, royalty, and gender identity are also held on selected dates. The Hillsborough Castle café opened in 2019, which means that for the first time in the castle's 250-year history the public can enjoy snacks, lunches, or afternoon tea (£29.95) in royal surroundings. From the visitor center to the main house, where the Stable Yard Tea Room opens in the spring and summer, it is a 15-minute walk, although a shuttle bus also operates.

TIP→ Explore the 100 acres of beautiful gardens, tended by 17 full-time gardeners, by following signposts through peaceful woods, waterways, and neatly manicured lawns. It is worth taking time to wander around the walled garden or Pinetum and take the yew tree walk to Lady Alice's Temple. Be aware that some of the paths have steps and steep slopes, which are slippery in wet weather.

If time permits after your castle visit, you can stroll around or join a guided walking tour of the town. An attractive place with Georgian architecture, Hillsborough boasts a fort dating from 1630, and an 18th-century church all cheek by jowl with boutiques, gift shops, and a selection of genteel cafés and gastropubs such as the Hillside, the Plough, and the Parson's Nose, all serving food at lunchtime and early evening. Details and times of the walking tours with qualified guides are available at Hillsborough Visitor Information Centre in the former courthouse in the Square right beside the entrance/exit to the castle from the town (☎ 028/9628–9717). ✉ *The Square, Hillsborough* ✣ *By car along main A1 Belfast-Dublin dual carriageway turn off for castle, which is clearly signposted and park at visitor center* ☎ *028/9268–1308* 🌐 *www.hrp.org.uk/hillsborough-castle* 🎫 *£16 (castle and gardens), £10 (gardens only)* ☞ *Castle open only for group visits, minimum 15 people, £14 each. Castle normally closed Jan. and Feb.*

★ Montalto Estate

HISTORIC HOME | The elegant beauty of this centuries-old estate transports visitors into a different realm to explore a historic demesne, which opened to the public in 2018. The Montalto Estate, near Ballynahinch in mid County Down, was built in the 1750s and inherited by the Earl of Moira, who made the Georgian mansion his permanent home, bringing exotic plants from all over the world. The estate played a leading role in the Battle of Ballynahinch, fought during the Irish Rebellion in June 1798, when it suffered severe damage. The army, which lost 40 troopers, was victorious, but during the battle up to 100 insurgents were killed. After falling into neglect, the estate has now been revitalized with a visitor center, gift shop, and café, as well as several wonderful walking trails: the lake walk, the garden walk, and the woodland walk. A huge amount of attention has been lavished on the landscape with the planting of thousands of trees and the creation of six new gardens, an orchard, and wildflower meadow, alongside dazzling additions including a summer house, witch's cottage, tree house, and boathouse. There's also a signposted history trail recounting the Battle of Ballynahinch and leading uphill to a rath, a circular earthen enclosure or dwelling.

TIP→ Montalto house and grounds are in private ownership, and the house is not open to the public except for prearranged private tours. Call or check website before visiting. ✉ *Montalto Estate, Spa Rd., Ballynahinch, Belfast* ✣ *The entrance is on Spa Rd., about 2 km (1 mile) south of Ballynahinch town, which is 24 km (15 miles) south of Belfast* ☎ *028/9756–6100* 🌐 *www.montaltoestate.com* 🎫 *£8 for grounds only.*

★ Mount Stewart

HISTORIC HOME | Now in the care of the National Trust, and completely renovated in 2015, this stately Neoclassical home near Belfast was formerly the country estate of the marquesses of Londonderry. Mount Stewart was constructed in two stages where an earlier house had stood: George Dance designed the west facade (1804–05), and William Vitruvius

Morrison designed the Neoclassical main part of the building (1845–49), complete with an awe-inspiring Grecian portico facade. The seventh marchioness, Edith, managed to wave her wand over the interior—after a fashion: Chinese vases, Louis-Philippe tables, and Spanish oak chairs do their worst to clutter up the rooms here. Still, the house does have some noted 18th-century interiors, including the central hall and the grand staircase hung with one of George Stubbs's most famous portraits, that of the celebrated racehorse Hambletonian—this is perhaps the greatest in situ setting for a painting in Ireland. There are no fewer than 18 named garden walks to choose between. ✉ *Portaferry Rd., Newtownards* ✥ *Ulsterbus 10 on Belfast to Portaferry route stops near front entrance* ☎ *028/4278–8387* 🌐 *www.nationaltrust.org.uk/mount-stewart* 🎫 *£11.*

Newcastle

RESORT | A disarmingly subtle resort, Newcastle offers cool restaurants, art galleries, independent shops, antiques emporia, chic cafés, and ice-cream boutiques on its 3-km-long (2-mile-long) energizing stretch of waterfront. But you will still find old-fashioned amusement arcades, fun fairs, and children's play areas to serve up a little seaside resort nostalgia. Sculptures, named by local schoolchildren, are arranged close to the beach and reflect the town's maritime connection. The visitor information center, at 10–14 Central Promenade, is well stocked with details on local attractions, and books and maps of walking and biking trails in the Mourne Mountains and forest parks. A range of cycle route maps are also available on the website. ✉ *10–14 Central Promenade, Newcastle* ☎ *0330/137–4046* 🌐 *www.visitmournemountains.co.uk.*

The Saint Patrick Centre

HISTORY MUSEUM | **FAMILY** | The interactive exhibits here bring the ancient myths and stories of early Christian Ireland to life. You can explore how St. Patrick's legacy developed in early Christian times, examine the art and metalwork that were produced during this golden age, and listen to modern debates about Ireland's patron saint. Interpretative boards outline local sites connected with the saint. Self-guided tours of sites linked with St. Patrick last about 70 minutes and take you across a bridge over the River of Words. ✉ *St. Patrick's Sq., 53A Lower Market St., Downpatrick* ☎ *028/4461–9000* 🌐 *www.saintpatrickcentre.com* 🎫 *£6* 🕒 *Closed Sun. Nov.–Feb.*

Silent Valley

TRAIL | The road to Silent Valley Reservoir Park leads to mountain views and excellent photo ops. Also here is a visitor center with an informative exhibition explaining the history of Silent Valley. Look into the Locals Room, which celebrates the men who worked on the building of the reservoir as well as the Mourne Wall. You can also pick up information on a walking and heritage trail of 1.8 km (just over 1 mile) or the more strenuous Ben Crom Dam Walk, which is 10 km (6 miles). ✉ *Kilkeel* ✥ *6 km (4 miles) north of Kilkeel off B27, right turn* ☎ *028/9035–4716* 🌐 *www.niwater.com/silent-valley* 🎫 *£2, vehicles £5.*

Slieve Donard

MOUNTAIN | Looming above Newcastle is Slieve Donard, its panoramic, 2,796-foot-high summit grandly claiming views into England, Wales, and Scotland "when it's clear enough"—in other words, "rarely," say the pessimists. It's not possible to drive up the mountain, so leave your car in the Donard parking lot and follow signs for the Slieve Donard Trail. It should take roughly three hours to climb to the summit and no longer than two hours to descend. Experienced hikers should not find it difficult, but if you prefer an easier trek, follow the trails signposted in Tollymore Forest Park or follow the Mourne Coastal Footpath. Hiking boots are essential and, as the weather can be unpredictable, it's advisable to take an extra layer of clothing, even in summer. The Mourne Wall, at 35 km (22 miles), which runs up and down Slieve Donard, was completed in 1922 by the Belfast Water Commissioners and had fallen into a poor condition. During 2019, it was restored in a £1.6 million community-led project and protects the water catchment that feeds the Silent Valley and Ben Crom Reservoirs. It was given a listed status in 1996 and is owned by Northern Ireland Water. ✉ *Mourne Mountains, Newcastle.*

St. Patrick's Trail

TRAIL | After returning to Ireland in the year AD 432, Ireland's patron saint seems to have popped up everywhere on his peregrinations. You can explore places associated with him along St. Patrick's Trail, a 148-km (92-mile) signposted driving route linking 15 historic and ecclesiastical sites across the beautiful drumlin hills of Counties Down and Armagh. Pick up a trail map at the tourist office in Armagh or Downpatrick, and at major attractions on the route you qualify for two-for-one entry. ✉ *Downpatrick* ☎ *028/3752–1800* 🌐 *www.discovernorthernireland.com.*

Tollymore Forest Park

TRAIL | Covering 1,300 acres and entered through Gothic gateways, Tollymore Forest Park has been thrust into the spotlight because of its starring role in the TV series *Game of Thrones,* standing in for the Haunted Forest, the Wolfswood near Winterfell, and the Kings Road near Castle Black. The arboretum at Tollymore has the widest range of tree species of any park in Ireland. Apart from the better-known oak, birch, beech, and Sitka spruce, the eucalyptus from Australia and Tasmania stand out and bring a cheerful note. *Game of Thrones* fans can book a Tollymore guided locations trek held at 10 and 3 each day for £8 (this does not include the entrance fee to the forest park). The tour, lasting an hour and 45 minutes, is an immersive experience; Stark cloaks are provided at no extra cost. Alternatively, you can do the trek yourself without an official guide. ✉ *Tullybrannigan Rd., Mourne Mountains* ☎ *028/4372–2428* 🌐 *www.nidirect.gov.uk* 🎫 *Vehicles £5.*

★ **Ulster Folk and Transport Museum**

HISTORY MUSEUM | Devoted to the province's social history, the excellent Ulster Folk and Transport Museum vividly brings the past to life and is a 20-minute drive east of Belfast. The museum first invites you to visit Ballycultra—a typical Ulster town of the early 1900s—which comes alive thanks to costumed guides who practice such regional skills as lace making, sampler making, spinning, weaving, wood turning, forgework, printing, open-hearth cooking, carpentry, basket making, and needlework. The setting is evocative: a score of reconstructed buildings moved here from around the region, including a traditional weaver's dwelling, terraces of Victorian town houses, an 18th-century country church, a village flax mill, a farmhouse, and a rural school. The museum also houses special collections and archives of interest to researchers on topics such as folklife, Ulster dialect, an oral history of linen, and radio and television archives of BBC Northern Ireland. Across the main road (by the footbridge) is the beautifully designed Transport Museum, where exhibits include locally built airplanes and motorcycles, as well as the iconoclastic car produced by former General Motors whiz kid John DeLorean in his Belfast factory in 1982. The Transport Museum also houses the *TITANICa* exhibition, which tells the story of the liner's construction in Belfast and what life was like on board. The museum is on the 70 acres of Cultra Manor, encircled by a larger park and recreation area. ✉ *153 Bangor Rd., 11 km (7 miles) east of Belfast on A2, Cultra* ☎ *028/9042–8428* 🌐 *www.ulstertransportmuseum.org* 🎫 *From £10* 🕒 *Closed Mon.*

A four-hour ascent of the Slieve Donard peak—queen of the magnificent Mountains of Mourne—offers vistas that reach as far as Scotland and the Isle of Man.

Restaurants

Brunel's

$ | **MODERN IRISH** | A huge mural on brick walls features a top-hatted Isambard Kingdom Brunel, this relaxed seafood restaurant's namesake and a famous figure in engineering history with connections to the area. The food philosophy here means using seasonal and local produce, and the menu features wild ingredients freshly foraged from nearby Dundrum Bay or Strangford Lough. **Known for:** grilled scallops with roast cauliflower puree, cured salmon and golden raisins; New York strip; wild mushroom and blue cheese rigatoni. *Average main: £16* *32 Downs Rd., Mourne Mountains* *The restaurant overlooks seafront a few mins' walk from Slieve Donard Hotel* *028/4372–3951* *www.brunelsrestaurant.co.uk.*

★ **Carrick Cottage Café**

$ | **IRISH** | Venture a few miles south of Newcastle and a 10-minute drive toward Annalong to Head Road where hedgerows are replaced by stone walls to find a 100-year-old traditional whitewashed building that has been refashioned as a cozy café against the backdrop of Slieve Bingian mountain. Set amid the timeless wide-angle landscape of undulating countryside and green fields unspooling to the distant horizon of coast and sea, this is the place for those hungry for scenery as much as tray bakes, sandwiches, and salads. **Known for:** delicious homemade snacks and cakes; Illy coffee adds perfection; jaw-dropping vistas of mountains and sea. *Average main: £10* *204 Head Rd., Mourne Mountains* *Drive south from Newcastle along A2 road to Annalong and turn right to signpost for Carrick Little where you can park and walk to café a few mins away* *075/9592–9307* *www.carrickcottagecafe.co.uk* *Closed Thurs. Oct.–Mar.*

Denvir's Coaching Inn Restaurant

$ | **IRISH** | In this atmospheric, whitewashed coaching inn dating to 1642, noted for its architectural merit, exposed oak beams, stone floors, and a large open fireplace testify to the antiquity; the Snug bar top was crafted from timbers of ships wrecked in Lough Foyle. On the menu, solid traditional dishes dominate—fish from Ardglass, chargrilled steaks, burgers, chicken, and spring lamb. **Known for:** seafood chowder; prime beef burgers; veggie cauliflower and quinoa burgers. *$ Average main: £13 ✉ 14–16 English St., Downpatrick ☎ 028/4461–2012 🌐 www.denvirs.com.*

Hotels

Briers Country House
$$ | **B&B/INN** | An elegant 18th-century country house with mature gardens, this is the ideal place to feel the fresh sea breezes and sample the delights of Newcastle and the surrounding mountainous countryside. **Pros:** scenic location; unlimited tea and coffee; free parking. **Cons:** some rooms slightly cramped; gets very busy in high season; few facilities. *$ Rooms from: £100 ✉ 39 Middle Tollymore Rd., Newcastle ✣ 400 yards from front entrance to Tollymore Forest Park ☎ 028/4372–4347 🌐 www.thebriers.co.uk ➡ 9 rooms, 1 3-bedroom cottage 🍴 Free Breakfast.*

★ **Culloden Estate & Spa**
$$$$ | **HOTEL** | This imposing, grand vision in Belfast stone presides over the forested slopes of the Holywood hills and the busy waters of Belfast Lough. **Pros:** mansion is rich in character; comfy Egyptian-cotton bedding; fairy-tale setting with great views. **Cons:** restaurant can get busy; massages, manicures, and vintage champagne don't come cheap; 10-minute drive from city center. *$ Rooms from: £261 ✉ 142 Bangor Rd., 8 km (5 miles) east of Belfast on A2, Holywood ☎ 028/9042–1066 🌐 www.hastingshotels.com/culloden-estate-and-spa ➡ 98 rooms 🍴 Free Breakfast.*

★ **Dufferin Coaching Inn**
$$ | **B&B/INN** | An elegant Georgian inn dating from 1803, this historic building sits next to picture-perfect, grandly gracious Killyleagh Castle—reputedly the longest-inhabited castle in Ireland and arguably the country's prettiest. **Pros:** ideal for exploring Strangford Lough attractions; good value for the money; graceful period house. **Cons:** far from the bright city lights; no elevator; lacks amenities. *$ Rooms from: £110 ✉ 33 High St., 10 km (6 miles) north of Downpatrick, Killyleagh ☎ 028/4482–1134 🌐 www.dufferincoachinginn.com ➡ 7 rooms 🍴 Free Breakfast.*

★ **The Old Inn**
$$$ | **B&B/INN** | Set in the village of Crawfordsburn, this 1614 coach inn—reputedly Ireland's oldest—certainly looks the part: it's pure 17th century, with a sculpted thatch roof, half doors, and leaded-glass windows. **Pros:** a proverbial step back in time; lots of 17th-century character; comfortable rooms. **Cons:** slow service; breakfasts not always up to snuff; public transport limited so a car is necessary. *$ Rooms from: £145 ✉ 15 Main St., 16 km (10 miles) east of Belfast on A2, Crawfordsburn ✣ The Old Inn is in center of Crawfordsburn, just off main A2 road to Bangor County Down ☎ 028/9185–3255 🌐 www.theoldinn.com ➡ 33 rooms 🍴 Free Breakfast.*

Rayanne House
$$$ | **B&B/INN** | Since the 100th anniversary of the sinking of the RMS *Titanic* in 2012, this country house has enjoyed unparalleled success by re-creating the liner's "last meal," a highlight of any stay here. **Pros:** bright, airy rooms with garden views; handsome furnishings; sumptuous nine-course menu. **Cons:** Holywood nightlife is limited to a few bars; bit of a trek to city center; few amenities. *$ Rooms from: £145 ✉ 60 Demesne Rd., Holywood ✣ Follow A2 east of Belfast to town of Holywood, approx 8 km (5 miles) by car on main road to Bangor,*

County Down ☎ *028/9042–5859* 🌐 *www.rayannehouse.com* 🛏 *11 rooms* 🍽 *Free Breakfast.*

★ **Slieve Donard Resort & Spa**

$$$$ | RESORT | A lavish redbrick monument to Victoriana, this turreted hotel, built in 1898, stands like a palace on green lawns at one end of Newcastle's 6½-km (4-mile) sandy beach; the traditional furnishings help make it feel like stepping back in time to the town's turn-of-the-20th-century heyday as an elegant seaside resort, though the bright guest rooms have modern comforts. **Pros:** appealing mix of luxury, history, and style; King Koil "cloud beds" in all rooms; breakfasts are top-notch. **Cons:** slightly corporate feel despite elegant architecture; occasional noise from wedding receptions; sea-view rooms are pricey. *$ Rooms from: £233* ✉ *Downs Rd., Newcastle* ☎ *028/4372–1066* 🌐 *www.slievedonardhotel.com* 🛏 *180 rooms* 🍽 *Free Breakfast.*

Activities

BICYCLING

Bicycling

BIKING | The Mournes and surrounding area are renowned for spectacular walking countryside, but increasingly have also become noted for top-class bike trails, seaside rides alongside beaches, tracks through sylvan forests, and cross-country cycle routes. Nine magnificent cycling tours through the region have been created and range from gentle cycling mainly on quiet, flat roads to longer routes with steep ascents. For details of these trails pick up the free leaflet from the tourist board office, "Make Your Day Cycle Routes," which includes a map and information on distance, grade, and points of interest. The tourist office can also supply details on bike rental. ✉ *Central Promenade, Newcastle, Mourne Mountains* ☎ *0330/137–4046* 🌐 *visitmournemountains.co.uk.*

GOLF

★ **Royal County Down**

GOLF | With a stunning backdrop of mountains and sea, Royal County Down is a links course with craterlike bunkers and small dunes; catch it on the right day at the right time, and you may think you're on the moon. For better players, every day is the right one. Back in his day, Harry Vardon labeled it the toughest course in the Emerald Isle, and if you can't hit your drive long and straight, you may find it so. No visitors are allowed on Wednesday or Saturday. ✉ *36 Golf Links Rd., Newcastle* ☎ *028/4372–3314* 🌐 *www.royalcountydown.org* 🎫 *Championship: weekdays and Sat. £300, Sun. £290; Annesley: £50* ⛳ *Championship: 18 holes, 7186 yards, par 71; Annesley: 18 holes, 4594 yards, par 66.*

HIKING

Tollymore National Outdoor Centre

HIKING & WALKING | If you need advice on mountain climbing, canoeing, and hiking trails, this impressive center is the place to head. ✉ *Bryansford, Newcastle* ☎ *028/4372–2158* 🌐 *www.tollymore.com.*

Index

A

B

C

D

E

F

G

H

I

N

Photo Credits

Front Cover: Maurizio Rellini / Sime / eStock Photo [Description: Ireland, Donegal, Fanad Head lighthouse at night]. **Back cover, from left to right:** Gianliguori/iStockPhoto. RafalStachura/iStockPhoto. Semolina Marianna/Shutterstock. **Spine:** Nhtg/Shutterstock. **Interior, from left to right:** Elementals/ istockphoto (1). Mustang_79/ istockphoto (2-3). Shutterupeire/Shutterstock (5). **Chapter 1: Experience Ireland:** Bart_Kowski/ istockphoto (8-9). Aervisions (10-11). Nataliya Hora / Shutterstock (11). Ruth Medjber (11). Chris Hill/Tourism Ireland (12). Jamegaw/Shutterstock (12). Sue Burton PhotographyLtd/Shutterstock (12). Victoriasky1/Dreamstime (12). Macmillan Media/ Tourism Ireland (13). Zhu_zhu/Dreamstime (13). Gardiner Mitchell/Ireland Tourism (14). Tourism Ireland (14). Stefano_Valeri/Shutterstock (15). Stefan Missing/ shutterstock (16). Chris Bellew/Fennell Photography (16). Lukasz Warzecha (16). Asford Castle (16). Tourism Ireland (17). Rihardzz/Dreamstime (17). Jerpoint Glass (17). 4kclips/shutterstock (17). Nhtg/Dreamstime (18). Douglas Gray/shutterstock (18). Christopher Hill/Tourism Ireland (19). MNStudio/Shutterstock (24). Michael Prior Photography (25). Alison Crummy/Fáilte Ireland (26). Tourism Ireland (26). James Brittain/Historic Royal Palaces (26). Brian Morrison/Tourism Ireland (26). Chris Hill Photographic (27). Tourism Ireland (28). Chris Hill/Courtesy of Tourism Ireland (28). Chris Hill/Courtesy of Tourism Ireland (28). Lukassek/Shutterstock (29). Failte Ireland/Courtesy of Tourism Ireland (29). Courtesy of Adare Manor (30). Courtesy of Hayfield manor (30). Courtesy of Ashford Castle (30). Shutterupeire/Shutterstock (30). Courtesy of Lough Eske Castle (31). Barry Murphy (31). Courtesy of Ballynachin Castle (31). Courtesy of Bellingham Castle (31). Natalia Ruedisueli/shutterstock (32). Ireland Tourism (33). Courtesy of MourneTextiles (34). Courtesy of Celtic Whiskey Shop (35). Jed Niezgoda/Cork Opera House Concert Orchestra (36). Fáilte Ireland/Courtesy of Tourism Ireland (36). Don MacMonagle (36). Clare Keogh (37). David Ribeiro/Dreamstime (37). **Chapter 3: Dublin:** Trabantos/Shutterstock (69). Kit Leong/Shutterstock (72). Iacob Cupcea/Shutterstock (73). Rasulov/Shutterstock (73). Rob Wilson/Shutterstock (90). Hochgeladen von Tormod/wikipedia.org (104). STLJB/Shutterstock (106). Beinecke Rare Book and Manuscript Library, Yale University (106). Travel-Fr/Shutterstock (107). GulliversTravels [CC BY-SA 2.0]/Wikimedia Commons (107). Arrow Books (107). Macmillan (107). Kitleong/ Dreamstime (108). Whpics/Dreamstime (108). Janetmck, [CC BY 2.0]/Flickr (109). Georgios Kollidas/iStockphoto (110). Library of Congress Prints and Photographs Division (110). National Portrait Gallery, London [CC BY-SA 2.0]/Wikimedia Commons (110). [CC BY-SA 2.0]/Wikimedia Commons (111). Zuma Press, Inc. / Alamy Stock Photo (111). Ida Kar Collection/Mary Evans Picture Library (111). Alex Ehrenzweig, [CC BY-SA 2.0]/Wikimedia Commons (112). William Murphy/ Flickr (112). Abd/Shutterstock (112). Razvan Stroie/Shutterstock (114). Daniel M. Cisilino (Danielc1998)/Dreamstime (123). 4H4 Photography/ Shutterstock (125). Lucian Milasan/Shutterstock (131). Jacinta O'Halloran (138). **Chapter 4: Dublin Environs:** MNStudio/Dreamstime (161). MNStudio/Dreamstime (164). Amanda Bullock (165). Pyma/Shutterstock (165). Unaphoto/ Dreamstime (174). Gail Johnson/Shutterstock (179). Eireann/Shutterstock (186). Warrenfish/wikipedia.org (188). Al Kelly/Shutterstock (192-193). Department of the Environment, Heritage and Local Government, Ireland (194). Joe Cornish/Dorling Kindersley (194). Joe Cornish/ Dorling Kindersley (195). Joe Cornish/Dorling Kindersley (195). Joe Cornish/Dorling Kindersley (195). Joe Cornish/Dorling Kindersley (195). Russborough (196). Russborough (196). Russborough (196). Russborough (197). Web Gallery of Art (197). Lokono/Dreamstime (198). **Chapter 5: The Midlands:** Daniel M. Cisilino (Danielc1998)/Dreamstime (203). Jan Miko/Shutterstock (206). Andreybl/ Dreamstime (207). FotoParaTi/ Dreamstime (207). Daniel M. Cisilino (Danielc1998) /Dreamstime (219). Phbcz/Dreamstime (226). William Murphy/Flickr (236). **Chapter 6: The Southeast:** LittlenyStock/Shutterstock (243). Littleny/Dreamstime (253). Andresconema/Dreamstime (256). Philippa Reid/Shutterstock (263). Terry Murphy/Tourism Ireland (274). Irimaxim/Dreamstime (280). Walshphotos/Shutterstock (282). Thomas Bresenhuber/Shutterstock (285). Patryk Kosmider/Shutterstock (286). Irish Typepad, [CC BY-SA 2.0]/Flickr (286). Patryk Kosmider/ Shutterstock (287). Patryk Kosmider/ Shutterstock (288). Warren LeMay/Flickr (288). Marc C. Johnson/Shutterstock (288-289). Abbey/David Ribeiro/Dcr1979\Dreamstime (289). DavePrimov/Shutterstock (290). Marc C. Johnson/Shutterstock (291). **Chapter 7: County Cork:** Madrugada Verde/Shutterstock (295). Gubbeen Farmhouse Products (298). Jaroslaw Grudzinski/Shutterstock (299). D.Ribeiro/Shutterstock (299). Gabriel12/Shutterstock (311). Kanuman/ Shutterstock (313). Walshphotos/Shutterstock (314-315). Gabriel12/Shutterstock (318). Geoffrey B. Johnson_Media/Shutterstock (329). Fabiano's_Photo/Shutterstock (338). **Chapter 8: The Southwest:** Ramon Mascaró/ istockphoto (343). Walshphotos/Shutterstock (356). Magann/ Dreamstime (365). MNStudio/Dreamstime (367). Mikemike10/Shutterstock (374-375). Jonathan Hession/Tourism Ireland (375). Gabriel12/ Shutterstock (375). Shutterupeire/ Shutterstock (376). Teddiviscious/Shutterstock (377). Cork Kerry Tourism (378). Gabriel12/Shutterstock (378). Insuratelu Gabriela Gianina/Shutterstock (378). Jonathan Hession/Tourism Ireland (379). MNStudio/Shutterstock (379). Stephan Hoerold/ iStockphoto (380). ingmar wesemann/iStockphoto (380). Ariel Cione/iStockphoto (380). Michelle Nadal (382). Justin James Wilson/Shutterstock (388). David Mason/iStockphoto (392). Mustang79/ Dreamstime (394). **Chapter 9: County Clare, Galway City, and the Aran Islands:** PiotrMachowczyk/Shutterstock (401). Patryk Kosmider/Shutterstock (426-427). Laurentiu Iordache/Dreamstime (430). Rejflinger, [CC BY 2.0]/ Flickr (443). Chris Hill/Tourism Ireland (452). **Chapter 10: Connemara and County Mayo:** Shawn Williams/ istockphoto (457). Ivica Drusany/ Shutterstock (460). Holger Leue/Tourism Ireland (461). Greg Fellmann/Shutterstock (461). Roger Kinkead/Tourism Ireland (474). Wiltilroeotte/ Dreamstime (478-479). Lukasz Pajor/Shutterstock (481). Steve Cukrov/Shutterstock (483). **Chapter 11: The Northwest:** Holger Leue/Tourism Ireland (493). Milosz Maslanka/Shutterstock (508). Red/Dreamstime (520). Holger Leue/Tourism Ireland (527). Thomas Lukassek/Dreamstime (530). **Chapter 12: The Northeast:** Remizov/Shutterstock (537). Danielc1998/Dreamstime (543). Sirtravelalot/ Shutterstock (546). **Chapter 13: Belfast:** Alex Cimbal/ Shuttterstock (555). Yuriy Chertok/ Shutterstock (567). Nataliya Hora/Shutterstock (577). Brian Logan Photography/ Shutterstock (583). Federico Zovadelli/Shutterstock (590). Brian Morrison/Tourism Ireland (595). **Chapter 14: Northern Ireland:** Brian Morrison/Northern Ireland Tourist Board (599). Francesco Ricciardi Exp/Shutterstock (602). Yvescosentino,[CC BY 2.0]/Flickr (603). David Cordner/ Northern Ireland Tourist Board (603). S-F/Shutterstock (619). Josemaria Toscano/Shutterstock (620). Krzysztof Nahlik/Dreamstime (624). Keith Ewing/Flickr (626). Geray Sweeney/Tourism Ireland (628). Brian Morrison/Northern Ireland Tourist Board (646). Tony Pleavin/Northern Ireland Tourist Board (648). Tony Pleavin/Northern Ireland Tourist Board (656). **About Our Writers:** All photos are courtesy of the writers except for the following: Anto Howard, courtesy of William Hederman.

*Every effort has been made to trace the copyright holders, and we apologize in advance for any accidental errors. We would be happy to apply the corrections in the following edition of this publication.

Notes

Fodor's ESSENTIAL IRELAND 2024

Publisher: Stephen Horowitz, *General Manager*

Editorial: Douglas Stallings, *Editorial Director*, Jill Fergus, Amanda Sadlowski, *Senior Editors*; Brian Eschrich, Alexis Kelly, *Editors;* Angelique Kennedy-Chavannes, *Assistant Editor;* Yoojin Shin, *Associate Editor*

Design: Tina Malaney, *Director of Design and Production*; Jessica Gonzalez, *Senior Designer*

Production: Jennifer DePrima, *Editorial Production Manager*; Elyse Rozelle, *Senior Production Editor;* Monica White, *Production Editor*

Maps: Rebecca Baer, *Senior Map Editor*, David Lindroth, Mark Stroud (Moon Street Cartography), *Cartographers*

Photography: Viviane Teles, *Senior Photo Editor;* Namrata Aggarwal, Neha Gupta, Payal Gupta, Ashok Kumar, *Photo Editors;* Eddie Aldrete, *Photo Production Intern;* Kadeem McPherson, *Photo Production Associate Intern*

Business and Operations: Chuck Hoover, *Chief Marketing Officer;* Robert Ames, *Group General Manager*

Public Relations and Marketing: Joe Ewaskiw, *Senior Director of Communications and Public Relations*

Fodors.com: Jeremy Tarr, *Editorial Director;* Rachael Levitt, *Managing Editor*

Technology: Jon Atkinson, *Director of Technology;* Rudresh Teotia, *Associate Director of Technology;* Alison Lieu, *Project Manager*

Writers: Robin Gauldie, Anto Howard, Vic O'Sullivan, Alexandra Pereira

Editor: Angelique Kennedy-Chavannes

Production Editor: Elyse Rozelle

6th Edition

ISBN 978–1–64097–628–3

ISSN 2471-9188

PRINTED IN THE UNITED STATES OF AMERICA

10 9 8 7 6 5 4 3 2 1

About Our Writers

Robin Gauldie graduated from Edinburgh University with an MA degree in history before becoming a journalist specializing in travel and the travel industry. He has traveled widely in Europe, Asia, Africa, and the Americas and has written and contributed to more than 30 travel guidebooks to destinations including Ireland, his native Scotland, France (where he has a second home), and Greece, where he spends up to three months each summer. He also contributes to numerous British and international print and online travel publications and reviews hotels for The Hotel Guru, an online review site. He lives in Leith, Edinburgh's increasingly trendy docklands neighborhood, with his partner Zoe Ross, an editor and book indexer.

For our coverage of Dublin, **Anto Howard** has checked every fact, burnished every metaphor to the fine gleam of ancient brogues, and has so lovingly described the towns and villages found in the Dublin Environs and Southeast chapters that even their natives will leave for the pleasure of coming back. Six postgraduate years of living in New York City recently convinced Anto of the charms of his native Ireland, and he duly returned to take up residence in Dublin. He has written and edited books and articles about such far-flung places as Costa Rica, Las Vegas, and Russia, and has contributed to such publications as *National Geographic Traveler* and *Budget Travel.* Anto (christened Anthony—Dubliners have a habit of abbreviating perfectly good names) is also a playwright, and his shows have been produced in Dublin and in New York. He has also written the book *Slow Dublin,* a manual for living life to the full in his home city.

Vic O'Sullivan spent his early years in Toronto before moving to County Clare in Ireland. He graduated as a chartered certified accountant and worked in aircraft finance and the hospitality sector before returning to the University of Limerick to study journalism. He has written on travel for the *Los Angeles Times, Chicago Tribune, Guardian, Daily Mail, Irish Examiner, Lonely Planet,* and *Sunday Business Post,* and contributes regularly to the *Sunday Times* and the *Irish Times.* He has traveled extensively, is a fair-weather runner and avid reader, and lives with his family and a cocker spaniel called Anakin Skywalker in Bunratty Village, County Clare. Find Vic on Twitter @VicBunratty.

Alexandra Pereira is a Scandinavia-based writer originally from Worcester, England. She worked in film and television and has written about travel and the arts for *Condé Nast Traveler, Vanity Fair, Suitcase, Playboy,*the *Paris Review,* and a host of international in-flight magazines.